Handbook of Heterogeneous Networking 1999

Raj Rajagopal, *Editor*

AUERBACH

Boca Raton London New York Washington, D.C.

Acquiring Editor:	Theron Shreve
Project Editor:	Sylvia Wood
Marketing Manager:	Rod Bell
Manufacturing Manager:	Carol Slatter
Compositor:	Constance Grigutis
Production Manager:	Claire Miller

Library of Congress Cataloging-in-Publication Data

Handbook of heterogeneous networking: / Raj Rajagopal, consulting editor.

p. cm.

Includes bibliographical references and index.

ISBN 0-8493-9989-0 (alk. paper)

1. Internetworking (Telecommunication) I. Rajagopal, Raj.

TK5105.5H363 1998

004.6—dc21 98-42548

CIP

International Standard Book Number 0-8493-9989-0
Library of Congress Card Number 98-42548
Printed in the United States of America 1 2 3 4 5 6 7 8 9 0
Printed on acid-free paper

Contributors

AL BERG, *Director of Strategic Technologies, NETLAN, Inc., New York, NY*

CHARLES BREAKFIELD, *Senior Network Architect, Andersen Consulting, Dallas, TX*

GLENN R. BROWN, *Consulting Network Analyst, Atlanta, GA*

ROXANNE BURKEY, *Independent Consultant, Dallas, TX*

GARY CANNON, *Senior Consultant, North American Sales Department, GE Information Service, New York, NY*

MICHAEL CAREY, *Research Staff Member, Almaden Research Laboratory, IBM, San Jose, CA*

JEFFREY CARR, *Managing Director, CKS, Pittsburgh, PA*

JOHN L. CONNOR, *Director, Automation Products Marketing, Boole & Babbage, Inc., Dallas, TX*

WILLIAM R. CONSTABLE, JR., *Independent Consultant, Philadelphia, PA*

STEVEN P. CRAIG, *Managing Partner, Venture Resources Management Systems, Lake Forest, CA*

PAUL CULLEN, *EDP Audit Specialist, Norwest Audit Services, Inc., Minneapolis, MN*

MARY ANN DAVIDSON, *Product Manager, Oracle Secure Systems, Redwood Shores, CA*

LINDA DEMICHIEL, *Research Staff Member, Almaden Research Laboratory, IBM, San Jose, CA*

STEFAN DESSLOCH, *Senior Software Engineer, Database Technology Institute, IBM, San Jose, CA*

WAYNE O. EVANS, *Independent Security Consultant, Tucson, AZ*

ADAM FALDALLA, PH.D., *Assistant Professor, Computer and Information Science, Cleveland State University, Cleveland, OH*

JOHN FISKE, *Director, Johns & Noble Communication Partners, Prides Crossing, MA*

THOMAS FLEISHMAN, *Vice President and Director, Information Services, Kaiser Permanente, Pasadena, CA*

NARASIMHAIAH GORLA, *Associate Professor, Business Administration, Cleveland State University, Cleveland, OH*

ANURA GURUGE, *Strategic Independent Analyst, New Ipswich, NH*

JEFF C. HAFER, *Telecommunications Manager, GPU Service Inc., Reading, PA*

Gilbert Held, *Director, 4-Degree Consulting, Macon, GA*

Ira Hertzoff, *President, Datagram, Columbus, OH*

Paul J. Jalics, Ph.D., *Professor, Computer and Information Science, Cleveland State University, Cleveland, OH*

Yemm anur Jayachandra, *Senior Consultant, Bank of America, San Francisco, CA*

Gita Jayachandra, *Graduate Student, San Jose State University, San Jose, CA*

Brian Jeffery, *Managing Director and Cofounder, International Technology Group, Mountain View, CA*

Ray Kaplan, *Independent Consultant, Issaquah, WA*

Randy Keck, *Technology Manager, Operations Control Systems, Palo Alto, CA*

Keith G. Knightson, *Associate Director, Telecom Architect Program, Canadian Government Telecommunications Agency, Kanata, Ontario, Canada*

David Koehler, *Director, Network Technology, The NetPlex Group, Somerville, NJ*

Kenneth W. Kousky, *President, Wave Technologies, St. Louis, MO*

Joe Kovara, *Product Development Manager, CyberSafe, Inc., Redmond, WA*

Michael D. Krasowski, *Senior Principal Consultant, McDonnell Douglas Corp.,*

Steve Krehbiel, *Doctoral Student, Business Administration, Cleveland State University, Cleveland, OH*

Carol L. Larson, *Technical Writer and Desktop Publisher, Hillsboro, OR*

James A. Larson, *Senior Software Engineer, Intel Architecture Laboratory, Hillsboro, OR*

Allen B. Lum, *Senior Manager, Information Systems Audit and Security Group, Ernst & Young, New York, NY*

Victor Matos, Ph.D., *Associate Professor, Computer and Information Science, Cleveland State University, Cleveland, OH*

Nelson Mattos, *Chief Architect, Object-Relational Technology, IBM, San Jose, CA*

Noelle Mesick, *Graduate Student, College of Information Studies, Drexel University, Philadelphia, PA*

C. Kenneth Miller, *Founder and Chairman/Chief Technology Officer, StarBurst Communications, Concord, MA*

Nathan J. Muller, *Independent Consultant, Huntsville, AL*

William Hugh Murray, *Executive Consultant, Information Systems Security, Deloitte & Touche, New Canaan, CT*

Randall A. Nagy, *President, Network Data Processing Systems, KS*

Jeffrey L. Ott, *Partner, Available and Secured Knowledge (ASK) Consulting, Berthoud, CO*

James A. Papola, *Director, Facilities Management, Windon Capital Management, Reading, PA*

John Parodi, *Consulting Technical Writer, Enterprise Software Group, Digital Equipment Corp., Nashua, NH*

Raymond J. Posch, *Manager, Education Services, Covia Technologies, Englewood, CO*

JOE PRUSKOWSKI, *Vice President and Chief Technical Officer, InterConnections, Inc., Bellevue, WA*
STEVEN RABIN, *Director, Application Development Technologies, American Software, Inc., Atlanta, GA*
RAJ RAJAGOPAL, *Senior Computer Scientist, Illinois Institute of Technology Research Institute, Potomac, MD*
RICHARD ROSS, *Managing Director, Decision Strategies Group, Greenwich, CT*
HAL SANDERS, *Chief Executive Officer, Nusan Corp., Watsonville, CA*
RAVI S. SANDHU, *Professor, Software and Systems Engineering, George Mason University, Fairfax, VA*
DAN SCHULTES, *Audit Specialist, Phillips Petroleum Company, Bartlesville, OK*
ROSHAN L. SHARMA, *Principal, Telecom Network Science, Dallas, TX*
ANTONIO SI, *Assistant Professor, Department of Computing, Hong-Kong Polytechnic University, Hong Kong, China*
CAROL A. SIEGEL, *Vice President, Internet Security & Architecture Group, J.P. Morgan, Inc., New York, NY*
STEPHEN E. SMAHA, *President, Haystack Laboratories Inc., Austin, TX*
MARTIN D. SOLOMON, *Associate, C.W. Costello, Inc., Middletown, CT*
IL-YEOL SONG, *Associate Professor, College of Information Studies, Drexel University, Philadelphia, PA*
WILLIAM STALLINGS, *President, Comp-Comm Consulting, Brewster, MA*
DICK THUNEN, *Marketing Representative, Sync Research, Inc., Irvine, CA*
BHAVANI THURAISINGHAM, *Lead Engineer, Center for Integrated Intelligence Systems, The MITRE Corporation, Bedford, MA*
ROB WALTON, *Manager, Rob Walton Associates, Redmond, WA*
JESSICA WINSLOW, *Vice President, Support, Haystack Laboratories Inc., Austin, TX*
JAMES WOODS, *Independent Consultant, Lewisville, TX*
COLIN WYND, *Business Development Manager, NetMetrix Division, Hewlett-Packard Co., Colorado Springs, CO*
BILL YAMAN, *Vice President, Solutions Management, Candle Corp., Santa Monica, CA*
ROBIN L. ZAK, *Technical Marketing Manager, Timeplex, Glastonbury, CT*
GLEN ZORN, *Senior Scientist, CyberSafe, Inc., Redmond, WA*

Contents

SECTION I	**INTRODUCTION**	I-1
1	A Brief History of LAN Operating Systems *Rob Walton and Kenneth W. Kousky*	1-1
2	Assessing Desktop Operating Systems *Randall A. Nagy*	2-1
3	Evaluating Client/Server Operating Systems: Focus on Windows NT *Gilbert Held*	3-1
4	Transitioning to Windows NT *Nathan J. Muller*	4-1
SECTION II	**PORTING AND DEVELOPING APPLICATIONS IN A HETEROGENEOUS ENVIRONMENT**	II-1
5	Porting Issues Due to Operating System Differences *Raj Rajagopal*	5-1
6	Porting Applications between Heterogeneous Environments/Rewriting Applications *Raj Rajagopal*	6-1
7	Porting GUI Programs *Adam Faldalla, Victor Matos, and Paul J. Jalics*	7-1
8	Visual Basic and Object-Oriented Development *William R. Constable, Jr. and Il-Yeol Song*	8-1
9	Developing New Applications in a Heterogeneous Environment *Raj Rajagopal*	9-1
10	Accessing Windows Applications from UNIX and Vice Versa *Raj Rajagopal*	10-1
11	Developing Workstation–Based Client/Server Applications *Steven Rabin*	11-1
12	Using Middleware for Interoperable Systems *Raymond J. Posch*	12-1

13	Implementing OLE on Non.Windows Platforms Using ObjectBroker *Jeff Tancill and John Parodi*	13-1
14	Comparing Object.Oriented Development and Component-Based Development Using Visual Basic, Powerbuilder, and Visual C++ *Steve Krehbiel and Narasimhaiah Gorla*	14-1
15	Java Application Development Including Database and Network Integration *Nathan J. Muller*	15-1
16	Using Java for Application Development and Comparison with CGI/PERL *Nathan J. Muller*	16-1
SECTION III	**DESKTOPS IN A HETEROGENEOUS ENVIRONMENT**	III-1
17	Enterprise Desktops and Emulators *Raj Rajagopal*	17-1
18	Desktop Evolution Driving Connectivity Technologies *Robin L. Zak*	18-1
19	Considerations for Implementing Corporate Intranets *Nathan J. Muller*	19-1
20	The Mainframe as Enterprise Server *Brian Jeffery*	20-1
21	Managing Applications on the Network *Bill Yaman and John Fiske*	21-1
SECTION IV	**DATA ACCESS IN A HETEROGENEOUS ENVIRONMENT**	IV-1
22	Equivalent Features of DB2, Oracle, Sybase, and Ingres *Noelle Mesick and Il-Yeol Song*	22-1
23	Distributed Databases *James A. Larson and Carol L. Larson*	23-1
24	Publishing Database Information on the World Wide Web *James A. Larson and Carol L. Larson*	24-1
25	Heterogeneous Network File and Print Access *Raj Rajagopal*	25-1
26	Using CORBA to Integrate Database Systems *Bhavani Thuraisingham*	26-1
27	Accessing Multiple Databases Using Federated Databases *James A. Larson and Carol L. Larson*	27-1

28 Database Interoperability: From Federated Database to a Mobile Federation 28-1
Antonio Si

29 Database Gateways and Interoperability 29-1
Martin D. Solomon

30 Managing Multiple Databases Across Heterogeneous Hardware and Software Systems 30-1
James Woods

31 Object-Relational DB2 31-1
Nelson Mattos, Stefan Dessloch, Linda DeMichiel, and Michael Carey

32 Legacy Data Conversion 32-1
James A. Larson and Carol L. Larson

SECTION V SYSTEMS ADMINISTRATION IN A HETEROGENEOUS ENVIRONMENT V-1

33 NetWare Considerations 33-1
Raj Rajagopal

34 Configuring Windows NT clients in a NetWare Environment 34-1
Gilbert Held

35 Comparing Windows NT and UNIX System Administration 35-1
Raj Rajagopal

36 Managing Distributed Network Systems Using Single Sign-on, Password Synchronization, and the Authentication Server 36-1
Jeffrey Carr

37 Managing Heterogeneous Environments 37-1
Raj Rajagopal

38 Business Continuity in the Distributed Environment 38-1
Steven P. Craig

39 Controlling a Multivendor Environment 39-1
Thomas Fleishman
Thomas Fleishman

40 The Help Desk in a Distributed Environment 40-1
John L. Connor

41 Job Scheduling in the Open Systems Environment 41-1
Randy Keck

42 Multiple Protocols: The Network Manager's Headache 42-1
Joe Pruskowski

43 Managing Multivendor Networks Using DEC's Polycenter Framework 43-1
Nathan J. Muller

44 Managing Multivendor Networks Using Hewlett-Packard's OpenView 44-1
Nathan J. Muller

SECTION VI COMMUNICATIONS IN A HETEROGENEOUS ENVIRONMENT VI-1

45 The Essentials of Enterprise Networking 45-1
Keith G. Knightson

46 High-Speed Services for LAN Interconnection 46-1
Nathan J. Muller

47 Enterprise Network Monitoring and Analysis 47-1
Colin Wynd

48 Multicast Network Infrastructures 48-1
C. Kenneth Miller

49 Internetworking at the Physical and Data Link Layers 49-1
David Koehler

50 Planning, Designing, and Optimization of Enterprise Networks 50-1
Roshan L. Sharma

51 Distributed Network Support and Control 51-1
Ira Hertzoff

52 Comparing Popular E-mail Systems 52-1
Gary Cannon

53 E.Mail and Internet in Heterogeneous Environments 53-1
Raj Rajagopal

54 Managing Coexisting SNA and LAN Internetworks 54-1
Anura Guruge

55 SNA-LAN Integration Strategies 55-1
Nathan J. Muller

56 SNA Over Frame Relay 56-1
Dick Thunen

57 Operating a Network Manager's Help Desk in a Heterogeneous Environment 57-1
Jeff C. Hafer

58 An Expert Operating System That Manages Multi-Network Communications 58-1
Yemm anur Jayachandra, Hal Sanders, Gita Jayachandra

SECTION VII SECURITY IN A HETEROGENEOUS ENVIRONMENT VII-1

59 Windows NT Server Security Features 59-1
Carol A. Siegel

60 UNIX Security Features 60-1
Allen B. Lum

61 Software Tools for Detecting Misuse on UNIX Systems 61-1
Stephen E. Smaha and Jessica Winslow

62 Novell NetWare 4.X Security 62-1
Jeffrey L. Ott

63 AS/400 Security Controls 63-1
Wayne O. Evans

64 Implementing Kerberos in Distributed Systems 64-1
Ray Kaplan, Joe Kovara, and Glen Zorn

65 E-Mail Security Using Pretty Good Privacy 65-1
William Stallings

66 An Introduction to Internet Security and Firewall Policies 66-1
William Hugh Murray

67 Applets and Network Security 67-1
Al Berg

68 Oracle Database Security 68-1
Mary Ann Davidson

69 Relational Database Access Controls Using SQL 69-1
Ravi S. Sandhu

SECTION VIII DISTRIBUTED HETEROGENEOUS SYSTEMS VIII-1

70 Developments and Challenges in Distributed Data Communications Management Systems 70-1
Bhavani Thuraisingham

71 Distributed Processing for Distributed Databases 71-1
Michael D. Krasowski

72 Securing Distributed Data Networks 72-1
Nathan J. Muller

73 Managing Distributed Computing 73-1
Richard Ross

SECTION IX IMPLEMENTING HETEROGENEOUS SYSTEMS IX-1

74 Solution Selection Factors and Guidelines 74-1
Raj Rajagopal

75 Acquiring Systems for Multivendor Environments 75-1
Thomas Fleishman

76 Evaluating Vendor Support Policies 76-1
James A. Papola

77 WAN Network Integration: A Case Study 77-1
Charles Breakfield

78 Remote LAN/WAN Connections: A Case Study 78-1
Charles Breakfield and Roxanne Burkey

79 Frame Relay in an IBM Environment 79-1
Glenn R. Brown

80 Turning Host Developers into Object Technicians 80-1
Steven Rabin

SECTION X AUDITING SYSTEMS X-1

81 Auditing Windows NT LANs 81-1
Paul Cullen

82 Auditing UNIX: General, Log-in, and Superuser Security 82-1
Dan Schultes

83 Auditing UNIX: Security Issues, Change Control, and Disaster Recovery 83-1
Dan Schultes

APPENDIXES

A Additional Information A-1

B Glossary B-1

INDEX In-1

Introduction

Although the computer industry is known for rapid changes, the one factor that users have had to deal with since the very beginning is living in a heterogeneous computing environment, with hardware, software, and network equipment from a number of different vendors. This is because the natural evolution of data processing in many organizations is toward heterogeneous environments. From time to time, departments and organizational units develop or buy data processing environments and systems. It is virtually impossible and probably not cost-effective to attempt to coordinate all computer-related purchases across an entire organization in trying to standardize the use of selected vendors and/or products.

This was true even in the days when IBM was the predominant computer supplier. And, with the increased number of players and the advent of client/server and the Internet/intranet, this trend toward heterogeneity is even more pronounced. It is true today even with significant market shares being held by Microsoft, Intel, and IBM in different segments of the computer market.

The heterogeneity in computing is unlikely to change, because computer users, like other consumers, will buy hardware, software, and network primarily based on whether their requirements are met and cost, and, secondarily, on the actual vendor providing the solution. Exhibit 1 shows a typical heterogeneous computing environment such as is found in many organizations.

Nevertheless, many organizations have internal debates on the advantages and disadvantages of a homogenous environment vs. a heterogeneous environment. For example, one aspect of the debate centers around whether organizations should standardize on the Windows environment for both production applications and office applications. Another debate centers on adopting Windows NT workstation as a standard desktop and using Windows NT as the network operating system. There are pros and cons for both approaches and these are summarized in Exhibit 2.

In almost all aspects of computing there are competing technologies and products from multiple vendors. Although Windows 95 is the *de facto*

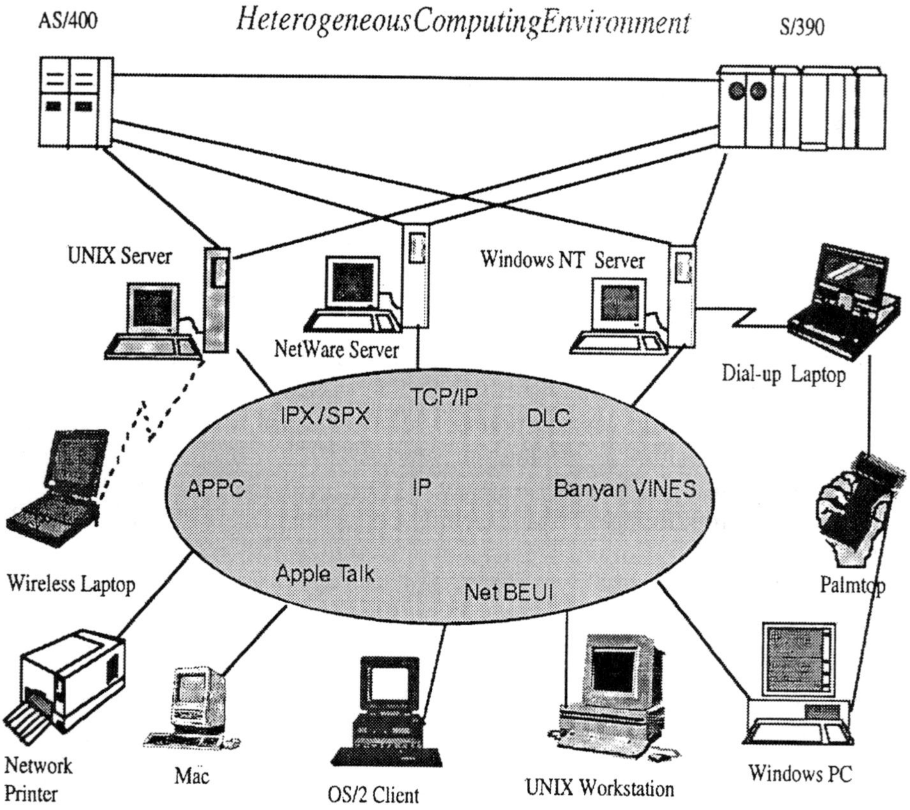

Exhibit 1. Heterogeneous computing environment.

standard for Operating systems in PCs used in homes, very few segments in the computing market are as homogeneous. One of the hotly contested areas is the desktop and server operating system market, as illustrated below.

According to International Data Corporation, Windows NT accounted for 36 percent of unit volume sales, while UNIXs (including Linux) accounted for 27.5 percent, and NetWare 26.4 percent out of a total unit sales volume of 3.5 million units in 1997. OS/2 finished fourth with 6.3 percent. However, since Windows NT is typically priced less than UNIX, the different UNIXes shared 45.8 percent of the total revenue, while Windows NT had 34.2 percent, and NetWare had 19 percent out of a total of $5.6 billion in server OS sales. A year ago, Windows NT was still gaining marketshare from NetWare. Microsoft shipped 732,000 NT licenses (for versions 4.0 and 3.51) in 1996, an 86 percent increase over 1995.

Exhibit 2. Comparing homogeneous and heterogeneous environments.

Homogeneous Environments	Heterogeneous Environments
Advantages	**Disadvantages**
• Improved productivity through interface consistency • Reduced system administration costs • Reduced network administration costs • Exchange of documents and data within the organization is easier	• Interface inconsistency problems • Need to perform system administration for multiple environments • Need to connect and bridge different types of networks • Exchange of documents and data is difficult and often requires format translations and loss of data fidelity
Disadvantages	**Advantages**
• Costs of moving to a homogeneous environment • Cost of maintaining a homogeneous environment • Possibility of lock-in to one or more vendors • Extensive Retraining of users using different systems	• Organization can pick the most cost effective solution at any given point • The natural evolution is towards heterogeneous environments, no additional costs involved in trying to move to another environment • Possibility of lock-in to one or more vendors reduced

Such competition is not restricted to the OS market segment. Exhibit 3 illustrates the different segments of computing and the popular technologies and products addressing that segment.

Given that heterogeneous environments are here to stay, vendors will of course attempt to market their products, regardless of how well the products interface with products from other vendors. End-users must figure out how the competing products best fit into their environments. This book will help end-users do just that.

Exhibit 3. Technologies addressing problems of specific computing segments.

Computing Segment	Popular technologies and Products
Server and Desktop Operating Systems	Windows NT, Windows 95, NetWare, UNIX, Macintosh, OS/2, OS/400
Application Development Languages	C++, Java, COBOL
4GL/Component-based Development	PowerBuilder, Visual Basic
Web Related Development	CGI, ActiveX, PERL
Databases	Oracle, Sybase, Informix, DB2, SQL Server
Web Browsers	Netscape Communicator, Internet Explorer
Office Suites	Microsoft Office, Corel WordPerfect
Transaction Processing Monitors	Tuxedo, Encina

Even if an organization decides to standardize on a homogeneous environment, it must undergo a transition period in which multiple environments will be supported. Applications written to one API must be migrated to the other, or interfaces must be provided across different heterogeneous systems. The problems that arise in these heterogeneous environments require special tools and techniques for solution.

This book classifies the different aspects of heterogeneous computing and is organized into multiple sections, with each section addressing one major aspect of heterogeneous computing where guidance is required for end-users. The sections are:

- Introduction
- Porting and Developing Applications in a Heterogeneous Environment
- Desktops in a Heterogeneous Environment
- Data Access in a Heterogeneous Environment
- Systems Administration in a Heterogeneous Environment
- Communications in a Heterogeneous Environment
- Security in a Heterogeneous Environment
- Distributed Heterogeneous Systems
- Implementing heterogeneous systems
- Auditing Systems

We will look at each of the sections in great detail throughout this handbook. Each comprises multiple papers from different well-known authors that address salient topics pertaining to that section.

The handbook has a practical, hands-on approach. Almost all papers selected provide product-level hands-on information required by professionals implementing heterogeneous systems on a day-to-day basis. The professionals include managers and architects who must understand the different choices offered by technologies and products and the developers and administrators who need to make system-design and system-engineering decisions in the course of implementing their systems and solutions.

Section I
Introduction

In any undertaking, it is worthwhile to quickly review salient topics before launching into different facets. The topics we review in this section are the basic building blocks of any heterogeneous environment. These basic building blocks are operating systems and databases. We will briefly cover operating systems in this section and databases in later sections.

Operating systems can be classified as desktop operating systems, network operating systems, server operating systems, and mainframe operating systems. At times, there is some overlap among these systems. For example, Windows NT provides both network and server operating system functions. We start with a brief history of LAN operating system in the first chapter. This chapter also covers DOS, which is the forerunner of all desktop and many server operating systems today.

Chapter I-2 provides a quick overview of the strengths and weaknesses of several of the more popular desktop and server operating systems. The criteria used for comparing these systems include networking and multiuser capabilities, security features, third-party software support, GUI support, and software development support. IT and network managers can use these criteria to do their own assessment of how well an OS fits with their organization's needs. The OSs covered include DOS, Windows (all flavors), OS/2, and UNIX. If you are familiar with one operating system and not another this chapter will help you develop a common understanding of the capabilities of other operating systems.

Chapter I-3 focuses on Windows NT — with good reason. According to International Data Corporation, Windows NT accounted for 36 percent of unit volume sales. This chapter addresses the different features of Windows NT such as network support, user interface, scalability, etc. of both versions of Windows NT — Windows NT Server and Windows.

Chapter I-4 provides a quick overview of the various topics involved when users want to utilize Windows NT either as a replacement or in addition to UNIX and NetWare. Many of the topics in this chapter are expanded in later sections. Thus, this chapter sets the stage for getting into greater detail in the following sections.

Chapter 1
A Brief History of LAN Operating Systems

Rob Walton
Kenneth W. Kousky

Networking systems have been available from the earliest days of the microcomputer, the first being proprietary file or disk servers manufactured to control network operations. Novell's NetWare S-Net was one of the pioneers. A clunky-looking white box powered by a Motorola, Inc., 68000 chip, it was designed as a star topology with a relatively low number of users. From the beginning, S-Net needed an operating system to provide services to the workstations that used CP/M and then DOS. Novell hired a development team to build its first network operating system, which existed as software independent of Novell's proprietary server. NetWare was the result. Other organizations followed similar routes.

These first systems sold well enough to keep companies in business, but they did not really flourish until the release of the IBM XT and its clones. The inclusion of a hard disk and the enhancement of RAM capabilities in a microcomputer supplied sufficient storage and memory space for the machine to be used as a file or disk server. Quite a number of companies realized this opportunity and rushed products to the market.

Some of the earliest contenders were Orchid Technology, Inc.'s PCnet; Corvus Systems, Inc.'s OMNInet; Gateway Communications, Inc.'s G-Net; and Proteon, Inc.'s ProNet. Although each provided basic levels of services, each posed a real problem for those deciding which to adopt because they all had proprietary operating systems and the amount of software available that ran in a shared mode was minimal. In addition, most of the LAN vendors had built their *network operating systems* on top of *DOS*, which was inherently a single-user, single-tasking operating system.

0-8493-9989-0/99/$0.00+$.50

Novell laid the foundation for its overwhelming success in the LAN business by having Superset port its NetWare operating system from the S-Net box to the XT. This allowed freedom in computers but not in network tables and cards. Initially, NetWare was released for the Gateway G-Net card, but Novell decided that it should do ports for the other best-selling hardware, which included the 3Com Ethernet, Corvus OMNInet, and Proteon Token Ring *network interface cards*. Because NetWare was originally written for a non-DOS environment and was modeled to emulate mini and mainframe management operations, it was multithreaded and multitasking from the beginning. It was built to run circles around any *DOS*-based operating system software and proved it by outperforming each proprietary LAN operating system on its own card.

At Novell, product design set the stage, but marketing brought in the revenues. This was accomplished by convincing software developers that writing NetWare hooks into their products brought immediate support for a whole variety of cards and then convincing network card vendors that a large number of applications would run on their systems through a single NetWare port — and at significantly faster speeds. This marketing program was called DIO for do it once, and it pushed the development of shared application software from a few applications in 1984 to more than 2,000 18 months later. It also placed NetWare as the operating system of choice on every major LAN card.

This brought Novell a lot of attention from hardware companies, particularly those that did not like the idea of customizing their products for NetWare. This started early LAN battles among Novell, 3Com, and other network hardware manufacturers. While hardware vendors concentrated on the transfer rates of their *NIC* cards, software developers eventually prevailed when Novell proved that the key to performance on a LAN was an efficient software-based file server and not the hardware with a disk server alone. Novell was able to show that a 64K-bps S-Net card running NetWare could outperform a 10M-bps Ethernet card running EtherShare. One by one, companies realized the trend and put NetWare on their systems.

Microsoft viewed these early battles from the software point of view. It produced Microsoft MSnet primarily as a product to be used with other companies'network hardware solutions. It signed up third parties in an effort to thwart the growing NetWare threat, and some, like 3Com, built quite a business around it early on.

Next, Microsoft, in its role as the purveyor of industry standards, released version 3.1 of DOS, which, among other things, allowed local area network file locking. IBM developed its PCnet product around the Microsoft MSnet standard, and, for the first time, all three major vendors were in the market at the same time.

During development of its networking strategy, Microsoft was also working on a new operating environment to help users at the workstation and mask many of the inherent inefficiencies of DOS. This operating environment was called Windows, and was more or less based on the technology developed by Xerox Corp. and promulgated by Apple Computer, Inc. The first two versions of Windows were rudimentary, lacking speed and sophistication, but they were revolutionary to many users. Microsoft began to preach the importance of the graphical user interface (GUI).

However, users continued to buy NetWare in vast quantities, and they largely ignored Windows. GUIs were still seen as a weak interface used only in design and drawing applications. Microsoft changed some of that with the release of its Excel spreadsheet for the Apple Macintosh. For the first time, real business power was available in a graphical environment. It was the first realization for many that the Macintosh was a powerful business tool and its graphical interface was a large part of the reason. Microsoft's success with applications, however, did not translate into success with LAN operating systems.

Microsoft and IBM were left behind by Novell early in the LAN operating system battle. Although Microsoft saw the need for connectivity, it was too caught up in its own technology to see the solution. Microsoft was gathering the best and brightest developers in the country to prove that it could be preeminent through work from within. In addition, MSnet was DOS-based; Microsoft could add all the bells and whistles in the world, but the engine would remain flawed.

IBM, on the other hand, was left behind not out of misdirection but out of apathy. As local area networks became a valid alternative for businesses in the U.S., IBM was hesitant to jump right in. Even the most rudimentary local area network system was a potential threat to the very profitable IBM minicomputer business. Only when large IBM customers screamed loud enough did it come up with its own MSnet-based LAN solution, IBM PCnet. IBM's apathy was aided by ignorance as it misjudged the potential developments and the needs of its customers. Throughout the 1980s, IBM's belief was that a LAN would be peer-oriented, allowing printers and hard disks attached to various PCs to be shared. In this model, any node could be a server.

The idea that all nodes would be both clients and servers was supposed to drive the continued expansion of workstation capabilities. The reality has fallen well short of this goal because the functional requirements have now gone far beyond printer and file sharing. Without servers, there was no assumption of heavy loads at a single board; the transfer rates of IBM's Token-Ring boards are still a critical shortcoming of the Token-Ring product.

As a result of each of these situations, Novell NetWare was more or less assured acceptance everywhere, and that is just what happened. To fortify against the ongoing threat of NetWare market dominance, IBM and Microsoft teamed up again with the development of OS/2. It was introduced in April of 1987 along with a new line of IBM hardware, the PS/2. Arm in arm, these two companies foretold the future of personal computing, and that future was built around OS/2. It proclaimed high-powered machines running high-resolution graphics with high-speed buses and sophisticated peripherals. It highlighted Presentation Manager, the OS/2 graphical user interface designed for ease of use and productivity. OS/2 was a multithreaded, multitasking power device for workstations. It promised to deliver everything that NetWare had become and more.

When the IBM–Microsoft collaboration began, OS/2 was portrayed as providing all the core capabilities necessary for both client and server computing. The two organizations predicted it would gain acceptance among developers and users so rapidly it would relegate DOS to the back seat within two to three years and push it right out the door within five to six.

In this early frame of reference, Microsoft's Windows strategy was secondary to both organizations, with Windows being merely a stepping stone to higher-level computing with OS/2. This was an easy position for Microsoft to support because Windows had been a lackluster performer to that date. IBM, on the other hand, was building its personal computing future on OS/2 and LAN Server, and Windows was not in the plans.

The transition from DOS to OS/2 has never materialized. The promised functions of OS/2 were late in arriving, and the Microsoft-IBM relationship cooled as Microsoft began to develop its own strategy for OS/2 to include unique APIs, different client/server engines, and a wider participation for Windows-based workstations. It did not take long for either company to realize that NetWare was firmly entrenched and that neither strategy would easily unseat the market leader.

One of the other obvious market failures was the linking of LAN Manager and LAN Server to OS/2. The public failed to judge OS/2's feasibility as a server platform separately from its success at the workstation or node. If OS/2 did not go on the microcomputer, why should it go on the server? Although NetWare has never been judged on this basis, it was Microsoft and IBM that set the stage for this faulty analysis of the OS/2's feasibility.

Then version 3.0 of Windows finally hit a responsive chord. All the development efforts bore fruit, and the product was received with open arms. Literally millions of copies were sold in the first few months, exceeding even Microsoft's wildest expectations. The sudden success changed many things in the IBMlationship as well as perceptions in the LAN marketplace.

Many of the earlier justifications for DOS users to move to OS/2 were removed with Windows 3.0. This element of uncertainty relating to workstations caused a growth in the uncertainty surrounding the servers. With sales of OS/2 -based LAN systems languishing, Microsoft reorganized its networking group and assured the public and the press that everything was on schedule, pouring more dollars into the LAN Manager abyss. Although IBM tried to keep on a relatively close development schedule for OS/2 and LAN Server product deliveries, the harder it pushed, the more it fell behind.

As Windows sales continued to soar, the IBMapart. Microsoft set out on a new course using Windows workstations as the focal point, abandoning OS/2 development altogether. Microsoft stated that it would continue to provide code to those writing applications for OS/2 but that it would not actively promote its sales or use. Microsoft also announced that there would not be an OS/2 version 3.0 but that its next-generation operating system would be called NT, for new technology, and it would take advantage of 32-bit processor capabilities. Microsoft stated further that it would upgrade its workstation capabilities with Win/32, the code name for a 32-bit version of Windows.

IBM consolidated its position by signing an agreement with Novell to sell NetWare through its own sales force as an adjunct to its LAN Server strategy. IBM noted that this was in no way a denial of the OS/2 LAN Server platform but merely the recognition of NetWare's installed base and a response to the demands of its customers. Novell currently owns more than 60 percent of the LAN operating system market (estimates range from 60 percent to 80 percent) with IBM and Microsoft hovering at about 8 percent to 10 percent each.

The Turbulent Present and Likely Future

With IBM's release of OS/2 version 2.0 and the upgrade to LAN Server, the battles among the three companies continue. IBM has stated repeatedly that the time has arrived for the delivery of all the promises made since 1987. IBM is on its own with this platform now, and OS/2 will fly or fail depending on the performance of version 2.0 during the next year. IBM has stated that it will provide better DOS than DOS, better Windows than Windows, and better OS/2 than OS/2. If it does, Microsoft must equal OS/2 2.0 with NT.

Microsoft has moved so far away from OS/2 that it does not want to have third parties promote Windows on OS/2 in any platform and will not even guarantee that Windows 3.1 will work on OS/2. As a workstation product, 3.1 promises better speed and capabilities but is not a major upgrade from 3.0. Microsoft is promoting Windows 3.1 to distract potential buyers from

OS/2, create incompatibilities, and forestall market movement to OS/2 before the arrival of NT.

Novell has been rather tight-lipped about future development projects but is busy working to put NetWare on the few platforms that it is not already on. NetWare is still the technological and sales leader, and Novell plans it to continue that way in the future.

Although IBM can still sell NetWare, if the company is to finally be a major player in the LAN business, it will have to be so with OS/2 and LAN Server versions 2.0. If it can indeed deliver on its promises for better everything than everything, it has a reasonable chance of finding a long-term place in the LAN operating system marketplace. However, according to early beta testers, as well as those who have sampled the latest prerelease product, OS/2 version 2.0 is large and slow and demands a lot of RAM. Perhaps it can be fine-tuned. From an applications point of view, it had better be. The cadre of software legions writing for OS/2 has diminished, and many projects are on hold, pending the results of the latest release.

OS/2 differs strategically from NetWare in that all nodes can become servers. Although NT will also use this peer approach, it will require applications that actually use the approach to replace NetWare. It may be a more robust platform than NetWare's NLM (NetWare Loadable Modules) option, but without applications, IBM will lose ground. It is likely that the reviews for OS/2 2.0 will continue to be mixed, and ultimate success will depend on whether the marginal negatives and positives fall out in favor of more software development. Without a large amount of OS/2-based software, IBM will not be successful in this market. If the tide turns toward more development and the overhead problems are minimized, OS/2 could find a nice niche with large, established IBM customers and networks that use strong client/server environments. It could beat NT or even eventually steal back market share from NetWare. IBM's current 8 percent of the market could increase to as much as 15 percent over the next year with positive reviews for version 2.0. Chances are that it will not grow much past that, but 15 percent of the potential 10 million stations per year is a respectable amount.

If IBM is successful, it is not a foregone conclusion that its success will come at the expense of Novell or Microsoft — 20 percent of the market is controlled by companies outside of the big three. However, the high-end networking business is owned almost exclusively by these three companies. Banyan Systems, Inc., has held a strong foothold in the past, especially in the LAN to WAN environment, but it is on the wane; the additional 7 percent to 8 percent of market share will be carved out of Microsoft or Novell.

Microsoft missed the target with MSnet, and it is far afield with LAN Manager and OS/2. Now it is unveiling NT and Win/32. This has been a little confusing and disconcerting; continued confusion is likely to have a negative effect on Microsoft and its LAN operating system plans. Several major corporations have standardized on the Microsoft platform only to have Microsoft abandon them. These Microsoft loyalists, and those that have observed them, are more than a little reluctant to go back to Microsoft or sign on to their new offerings.

Developers of applications and LAN-related software are too shell-shocked right now to jump into another potential void. Most LAN administrators, IS executives, and EUC support professionals are looking for a stable product. Chances are that they do not see this in NT.

Microsoft is likely to be more successful by dominating the desktop with workstation environments and applications. Windows 3.1 is likely to continue to lead the masses to graphical interfaces. It is clearly the best environment ever for DOS-based machines, and it will have still greater potential with 32-bit capabilities.

Actually, over a longer enough period of time, Windows might lead Microsoft to LAN OS success. After the dust settles from the OS/2 wars and the corporate jitters of the Fortune 500 standards committees are soothed, NT might surface as a strong competitor. However, the aggregate percentage of Microsoft's LAN operating system market share is likely to decline in the near term.

Pundits say that when someone is at the top, there is no way to go but down. Novell remains at the top, and it is likely to continue to prove the doomsayers wrong. While IBM and Microsoft have feuded the last couple of years, Novell has entrenched itself in a majority of clients, markets, and countries.

With more than half of all LAN users in the fold, Novell guards every move. The lack of public knowledge of NetWare enhancements does not mean that there are no improvements in the pipeline. Waiting until these improvements are ready is a wise move for the company that promised to deliver SFT Level III NetWare at least five years ago.

As a result, Novell is not likely to see its market share drop below 60 percent for the next couple of years. If IBM finds success with OS/2 version 2, and if Microsoft's NT strategy bears fruit in a couple of years, Novell could see its market share percentage decrease. Even in this case, however, Novell's aggregate numbers will continue to increase because the market itself will continue to grow. A smaller percentage of a larger market still means an increasing amount of dollars.

Answers for EUC Support

So what does all this mean for the network administrator, end user, or end-user support professional? The answer depends on the customers' current situation and their needs. If an organization has already established networking standards, and if its current system is meeting its needs, this analysis could serve as the basis for evaluating the network's ability to meet future requirements.

Organizations that currently own a system based on OS/2 should carefully monitor the capabilities and acceptance of OS/2 version 2.0. If it lives up to its billing, the products and services most organizations need will probably be available into the foreseeable future. If 2.0 is a major disappointment, organizations should review alternative systems and standards.

Organizations that have established a network standard based on Microsoft's LAN Manager must perform two levels of monitoring. If the company intends to continue with OS/2 as the platform, the EUC support staff should evaluate version 2.0 and find a server product that is supported on it. If the company intends to opt for the NT alternative with future LAN Manager support, EUC support must evaluate the enhancements to the server products and to the NT environment.

Because many questions remain as to exact support and exact dates, this is a very fluid environment on which to base business. Microsoft will probably give a lot of dates and assurances; however, the individual company must decide how much confidence to put into them.

Organizations that have built their internal standard around NetWare have hooked up with the organization that has a strong support staff and the most promising future. The IBM vote of confidence was not needed for Novell's continued success, but it may have been the final vote cast for another decade's worth of market leadership for NetWare. As the number-one player, Novell will need to solve the changing problems of its users. Novell is well suited from an organization and development viewpoint to handle consumer demands and concerns and keep consumer confidence.

For organizations just getting ready to establish a standard, now is actually a good time. The sales forces at Novell and IBM are primed and ready to answer questions and will soon be able to provide hands-on support of their claims. Their promises can be rated against the company's computing needs to help make a decision. Certainly, the Microsoft sales force will have something to say as well, but its ability to deliver the full solution in the near future is still in question. Although it may certainly be worth the time to evaluate Microsoft's claims, the real test will come when the NT-Win/32 solution is available.

If OS/2 2.0 lives up to expectations, and if the organization's system intends to use client/server operations, moving to IBM should be considered. NetWare covers most of the bases quite well, and it is nice to have a choice.

What about organizations that are starting out with limited connectivity needs? Small or even medium-sized companies with limited connectivity needs might be well served with one of the peer-to-peer networks available in increasing numbers (e.g., Sitka 10net or Tops, Artisoft Lantastic, or NetWare Lite).These systems require little overhead for hard disk or RAM and are inexpensive and uncomplicated. They meet the basic data and device-sharing needs. In most polls of network users, even on the largest systems, most users are taking advantage of their network connections only for the most basic printing and file service operations. That being the case, the simpler networks have their place.

Will these simple systems work for anyone then? Software and systems are making great strides in providing the sophisticated computing environments that the industry leaders have been touting for years. Although electronic mail and scheduling, SQL client/server systems, groupware, and publish-and-subscribe facilities have been in place for quite some time, they are just gaining acceptance.

Systems requirements planning must match a company's needs against these full systems capabilities. Simple networks have their place but only as a portion of the total solution. Smaller companies that plan to remain that way might find them sufficient; however, companies that expect to grow past basic operations need to sketch out a competent upgrade path.

Are there any technologies that everyone will need? The world had better be ready for graphical workstations because they are likely to be the common thread of all systems by mid-decade. They allow microcomputers to be what they were originally designed to be — tools that extend the workers'capabilities— rather than to become an end unto themselves. Windows, the Macintosh interface, Presentation Manager, and others are the future today. Versions 3.0 and 3.1 of Windows guarantee the vision that Apple brought to the world. Although character-oriented environments still predominate on microcomputers, they are going the way of the vinyl record and the manual typewriter. End-user support departments should establish a graphical standard for the sake of productivity and profits as well as common sense. If they do, their clients will be able to use more tools, more often, and with greater ease.

When will peer-to-peer networks displace the client/server approach? When the majority of workstations run 32-bit operating systems, such as UNIX, NT, or OS/2 2.0, most stations will begin to periodically offer services to others on the network. This transition will occur gradually and will not require a yes-or-no decision regarding NetWare. Instead, coexistence of these operating systems will ensure a gradual transition process.

What does it all mean? That is up to the individual organization. However, there are a few final observations:

- NetWare will continue to lead the way.
- People are still confused about Microsoft and LANs.
- IBM's PC networking hopes rest with OS/2 version 2.0.
- Windows is here to stay and will dominate the desktop.
- Companies must set LAN standards today.
- There is a place for peer-to-peer networks, especially if they can allow for growth.

Chapter 2
Assessing Desktop Operating Systems

Randall A. Nagy

When viewing the operating system scene objectively, it becomes apparent that no single operating environment can fulfill all the needs of all organizations. Rather, deciding what is best for an organization typically has a great deal to do with how that organization works and grows, as well as with the more-technical operating system details.

Like just about everything else in the business world, a successful marriage between operating environment and user is more apt to occur when the needs and idiosyncrasies of both the system and its users are understood and blended together. For example, large interconnected organizations might require a great deal of password security and database journaling activity, whereas decentralized, task-oriented work groups might find both of these operating system features annoying and even counterproductive.

In selecting an operating environment that will continue to meet the needs of business users over time, information technology managers should be familiar with the key capabilities of the more popular operating environments, as well as with the needs of end users themselves. The process of matching high-tech capabilities to real-world user requirements becomes a greater challenge when IT management is wrestling a budget at the same time. However, spending the time, trouble, and money to acquire a best-fit solution can keep the IT staff, the IT budget, and the company's users on track the next time even newer operating systems are introduced into the company.

This article explains the key strengths and weaknesses of several popular operating environments with a large installed base in business today. Additional information that IT managers need for making their assessment lies within the time-tested testimonials of the user communities within their organizations.

0-8493-9989-0/99/$0.00+$.50

PROS AND CONS OF SPECIFIC DESKTOP OPERATING SYSTEMS

The operating systems discussed in this article are MS-DOS, Microsoft Windows, Windows for Workgroups 3.11, OS/2 and OS/2 Warp, Windows NT, and UNIX. Emphasis is given to explaining how well each operating system functions in networked, multiuser, and security-conscious environments.

MS-DOS

MS/PC-DOS (or DOS) was originally developed for text-based, single-user, and single-tasking environments. Evolving as it did from Digital Research's Control Program for Microcomputers (CP/M 80)operating system, DOS was originally designed to be a bootstrap program (i.e., a program that runs only for the amount of time that is required to load and run a single-user application).

DOS originally provided only the most basic terminal and disk input/output routines to application programs. Because of these limitations, many systemwide support facilities were (and are still) missing from DOS. Such features as memory management, DOS reentrancy, virtual storage, multitasking, user accounting, and system security are a few of the critical omissions from the DOS environment.

Because DOS does not manage the tasks previously mentioned, the microprocessor and the DOS program itself have more time to perform more-critical tasks. Real-time process monitoring, low-level device control, and catering to the requests of the end user in general are what DOS does best.

Perhaps the most important reason for businesses to use DOS is to take advantage of the abundance of available software. From state-of-the art computer programming tools to the latest in desktop publishing and multimedia, the DOS workstation user can choose from a variety of highly customizable tools that have become indispensable in most offices.

Problems Creating, Securing, and Administering DOS LANs

Given the single-user origins of DOS, problems invariably arise when these workstations are incorporated into multiuser local area networks (LANs). When constructing a LAN out of DOS workstations, not only are there many conflicting networking solutions available, but the user is often placed in the awkward position of having to add those features omitted by DOS.

Most LAN vendors do not provide secure, adequately administered operating environments for their DOS users, which is one of the reasons that computer virus threats continue to occur. Because DOS itself has no built-in mechanisms for computer security, most network vendors have developed their own DOS security programs. Unfortunately, there is no agreement among DOS LAN vendors concerning how much security, if any at all, should be provided. Consequently, few DOS LAN or hybrid DOS LAN systems are safe from widespread viral attacks and user abuse.

Because of their low cost and popularity with users, DOS workstations are widely procured to function as standalone platforms. As dozens of them show up at a particular site, it is almost impossible to keep users from networking these computers together. An unfortunate consequence of this uncontrolled proliferation of these machines is that if these DOS LANs become infected with a virus, production can be halted for several days. Furthermore, because DOS is missing several components — mail, group permissions, user accounting, and automatic backups, for example — the creation and administration of DOS LANs is difficult.

Although DOS has proven adept and highly successful at performing real-time and single-user applications, this single-tasking operating system is not suited for serious network and multiuser environments. Experience has shown that large DOS-based LANs should be avoided. For many organizations, user accounting and security are far too important to include in any network operating environment as an afterthought.

Microsoft Windows and Windows for Workgroups

As the inventor of DOS, Microsoft Corp. (Redmond WA) has had to contend with its problems and limitations. Not only have the missing memory management and poor multitasking features plagued DOS developers since the creation of the product, but DOS applications developers themselves have added to the problem by writing their own highly sophisticated virtual-memory-management routines and graphics drivers. With this variety of solutions, programs often clash when each attempts to manage a single resource in its own (often unique) manner.

To make matters worse, software vendors often have ignored vital portions of the DOS operating system entirely by building alternative systems into their applications programs. This situation led to the development of the Microsoft Windows product and the more team-oriented Microsoft Windows for Workgroups.

In general, Microsoft Windows is a DOS enhancement program that was developed to take control of the entire DOS workstation and share it with other programs. Although Microsoft Windows accomplishes this by adding such much-needed features as RAM overcommit and device sharing, Windows' nonpreemptive, nondeterministic nature prevents it from serving as a serious multitasking platform. In other words, Windows tasks that have been placed in the background are often "starved out" while waiting for another foreground application to surrender the computer. This occurs because, unlike OS/2, NT, and UNIX, no user-driven priority schemes are available that would, for example, allow a background Windows 3.1x task to run slower or faster than other Windows tasks.

Although Microsoft Windows for Workgroups has fine-tuned the kernel for a more smooth sharing of the computer in general, even Windows for Workgroups relies on applications' cooperating properly between themselves to perform the lion's share of the work that needs to be accomplished. For example, when performing time-critical operations(e.g., file downloading, printing, or sending a fax), the cooperative multitasking metaphor breaks down severely under Windows. It is not unusual for communications sessions to abort prematurely, for example, when files are being saved while communications activities are occurring under Windows or Windows for Workgroups.

DOS Compatibility and UAE Worries. Because the greatest of the strengths of DOS is the abundance of software written for it, DOS compatibility has become an important issue for all microcomputer systems. Although each operating system discussed in this article has some type of solution that allows it to run DOS software, the Windows/DOS solution is still the most comprehensive.

Because Windows itself is a DOS application, it can naturally run more DOS software than any other microcomputer operating systems. It is important to note, however, that DOS programs not written explicitly for Windows cannot fully take advantage of many of the advanced features that Windows has brought to DOS. Furthermore, because Microsoft Windows is DOS based (i.e., a nonreentrant, single-tasking, single-user operating system), errant programs frequently crash Windows much more often than is experienced under either OS/2, NT, or UNIX.

Although the need to restart an operating system can be acceptable in the world of "personal" computing, the need to help end users recover from a Windows unrecoverable application error (UAE) or an outright system crash can cost larger companies a great deal of money in terms of user productivity and redundant customer support.

Networking with Windows for Workgroups. As a network operating system, Windows adds little to the realm of accountable, secure, network operations, although new interprocess communications methodologies — for example, Networked Dynamic Data Exchange (DDE), Object Linking and Embedding (OLE2), and built-in NetBIOS support services — mark some milestones in the DOS world.

Windows for Workgroups adds interworkstation file and device sharing. When licensed or configured properly, a networkable clipboard, electronic mail application, and scheduler can add a refreshing team feeling to the standalone Windows experience. Software drivers for popular network operating systems (e.g., Novell and TCP/IP) are also included with Windows for Workgroups and are better supported than under Windows 3.1. However, because file system resources themselves are shared on a per-user basis (i.e., users can only use what others want them to use), file duplication and collisions can result. Third-party software management software tools or management paradigms are needed to resolve these problems.

The assessment of Windows is very much like the assessment of DOS. Windows is acceptable for the individual user, and Windows for Workgroups is fine for small work groups of three to eight users. Overall, however, Windows is a relatively poor choice for widespread enterprise use throughout a large company network.

OS/2 and OS/2 Warp

The introduction of OS/2 by IBM Corp. (Armonk NY) in 1987 left more people waiting for the success of the operating system than people wishing for it to succeed (which is perhaps the only thing that OS/2 has in common with Microsoft's Windows NT). Like Microsoft's Windows, OS/2 attempts to resolve many of DOS's limitations. Unlike Windows NT and UNIX, OS/2 is based on a good deal of Windows 3.1x technology. Indeed, from the point of view of the underlying technologies involved, it would be fair to say that far more software is available for Microsoft's "old technology" (e.g., Windows 3.1x and OS/2) than might ever be available to run in native mode under any Microsoft New Technology (NT) operating system.

OS/2 Virtues: Preemptive, Deterministic Multitasking. OS/2 makes advances in microcomputer operating systems that even the sophisticated UNIX and POSIX-compliant systems cannot claim. OS/supports national languages (by supporting double-byte characters), a very lavish interprocess communications network, and adequate network support (including recently added out-of-the box Internet support).OS/2 can serve as the basis for developing sophisticated, networked, multinational applications.

Like UNIX, OS/2 allows a single user to balance programs in relationship to one other through the use of internal process priority schemes. The resulting preemptive and deterministic multitasking rivals the capabilities of UNIX and mainframe-class computers.

Unfortunately, like Windows NT, OS/2 does little to correct DOS's omission of file-level security and protection (such as is available in POSIX's user group recommendations and UNIX's Network File System).

Software Support. After DOS and Windows, OS/2 has currently captured more of the third-party applications market (i.e., the sector responsible for the tremendous success of DOS) than either NT or UNIX. Furthermore, because OS/2 is based on the same technology used in Microsoft Windows, it is not surprising that OS/2 is more compatible with Windows and DOS applications than is Windows NT.

Unfortunately, even the Warp incarnation of OS/2 has yet to live up to the boast of providing "better DOS than DOS, and better Windows than Windows," which IBM had promised. Therefore, if running a large number of DOS and Windows 3.1 applications are a primary concern, IT managers should be cautious of being overzealous in their use of either OS/2, UNIX, and Windows NT.

Moving Away from Common User Access. A few years ago, OS/2 was being used mostly by large corporations with strong commitments to IBM. By enabling these companies to maintain their commitment to IBM's Systems Application Architecture (SAA) — in which OS/2 Extended Edition played an important role — OS/2 found a strong initial installed base, since DOS, Windows NT, AIX (IBM's version of UNIX), and Windows are not part of the SAA family.

Because IBM has seemingly abandoned its previously stated goal to have all of its products present the same look and feel to users, OS/2 has become, to some extent, just another pretty face in the GUI world. The movement from a rigidly dictated standard toward an interface that promotes artistic expression has not necessarily been a negative happenstance. However, as other IBM products continue to evolve in their own directions, it is doubtful that the IBM vision of maintaining a common user access among all IBM platforms will ever be realized.

Poor Multiuser Capabilities. It is important to note, however, that like DOS and Windows, OS/2 by itself fails to provide suitable user accounting and security, even in the LAN environment. Even add-on programs, such as LAN Manager, fail to adequately protect the LANs from abuse.

In the case of DOS and Windows, this omission might be understandable. In the case of OS/2, however, it could be argued that such multiuser capabilities should have been built into any operating system kernel designed for connectivity. With microcomputers now operating at speeds in the range of multiple millions of instructions per second, turnkey ways to share CPU power with other users should be more available than they are on OS/2.

In 1995, eight years after the introduction of OS/2, perhaps the most important characteristic of the OS/2 operating system is its successful deployment on PCs in Fortune 500 companies. The firm entrenchment of the operating system in Microsoft's old technologies (the ones that everyone is still writing to under DOS and Windows) make OS/2 the natural choice for those who need to upgrade from Windows to the power of a fully preemptive, deterministic processing environment with minimum compatibility problems.

Although OS/2 is criticized for providing multitasking without maintaining many multiuser capabilities, OS/2 Warp does allow OS/2 to look more like the logical successor to Windows than Windows NT in the standalone workstation environment. In general, people who select OS/2 over Windows NT or UNIX do so because they desire to keep a higher compatibility with DOS and Windows applications than is presently offered by these competing platforms.

Windows NT. Windows NT is a bold attempt at creating an object-oriented operating system from the ground up. Perceived by many as being spurred on more by legal necessity than technological need, the challenge of NT was to maintain some reasonable compatibility with Microsoft's old technology (which IBM has many licenses to), while still taking advantage of the multitasking and linear address capabilities of fully enabled 32-bit computing.

Making NT available to non-Intel processors (like the Alpha family of processors from Digital Equipment Corp.) was also an important objective while NT was being developed. NT was supposed to be a highly portable operating system like UNIX. It was Microsoft's stated objective while developing the NT kernel to eliminate dependencies on Intel technologies by writing the entire operating system in C.

While working toward these towering objectives, NT suffered through seemingly endless delays as time-critical operating system features(e.g., mouse I/O) were "de-objectized," compatibilities were triaged, and processor differences were accounted for in C. Today, although versions of Windows NT can be found running on non-Intel processors, the single major area where NT is found thriving is still overwhelmingly on native Intel processor architectures.

DOS Compatibility. Part of the reason that Intel is still the mainstay on NT certainly is because it is able to simply boot DOS when required. Like OS/2, NT can, at a moment's notice, be rebooted as a simple, responsive DOS workstation. Of course, when running as a pure DOS workstation, 100 percent DOS and Windows 3.x compatibility is completely assured.

When running as a pure NT workstation, however, NT does not fare quite as well as OS/2 in the area of DOS compatibility. OS/2 is, for better or worse, much more firmly entrenched in both Intel and Windows technologies. For this reason, getting a DOS or Windows session to run on several other processor architectures (e.g., the DEC Alpha, Motorola 68xxx, or NEC processors) has proven to be just as difficult as getting the same programs to run under, for example, several different processor variants of UNIX's System V.

TCP/IP Support. Like Windows for Workgroups, NT has a networkable clipboard and other built-in tools that make work group out-of-the box computing very attractive. Unlike Windows for Workgroups, however, very little third-party support is available for growing this capability into more than what comes stock with NT.

Some might argue that because NT runs many Windows applications, this is a moot point. However, users must realize that native-mode applications on any operating system will not only run faster, but DOS and Windows programs will share outboard devices (e.g., COM ports and network adapters) the same as DOS or Windows (not Windows NT) requires. This is exactly why even OS/2 Warp is presently being sold with its own fax software bundled in.

Like UNIX and OS/2, Windows NT has standardized on Transmission Control Protocol/Internet Protocol (TCP/IP) support at the networking layer. Although driver support for Novell's IPX/SPX — the *de facto* DOS and Windows standard in networking protocols — is available, delays in the provisioning of reliable drivers have made TCP/IP the protocol of choice for use under NT.

Multiuser Security and Administration. From the vantage point of the end user, it really does not matter what lines are being painted on the ramps they use to get on their local information highway. What is of paramount importance is how well their information is being protected and maintained. From this perspective, the issue of networking support simply boils down to just how well data is being protected by the file systems being used.

Both the OS/2 and NT dual-boot file systems, though adequate for work group usage, can be much less secure than an adequately administered enterprisewide network environment under UNIX's NFS/POSIX combination. Because they inherit these limitations and the requirement to be backward-compatible with DOS, both NT and OS/2 do poorly when it comes to securing corporatewide resources under their operating systems.

This means that, for example, when archiving data to tapes, CD-ROMs, or floppy disks, file-level protection can be much more easily circumvented than under an adequately administered UNIX scenario. Even the integrity of the preferred file systems for NT and OS/2 (NTFS and HPFS, respectively), though more secure than the DOS FAT file system support, could be "hacked" into from a DOS session by a savvy and determined programmer. Given the choice between OS/2 and NT, however, users may find that NT manages multiuser security far better than OS/2.

Finally, from the vantage point of a larger company's systems administrator, Windows NT work group, device sharing, and mail (i.e., post office) capabilities are far easier to administer than either the UNIX or OS/2 multiworkstation resource management paradigms.

UNIX

The history of UNIX (AT&T Technologies Inc., Berkeley Heights NJ) is exceptional in the world of computer operating systems, for several reasons. First, rather than being developed by a hardware vendor interested in supporting (i.e., selling) its own product line, UNIX was adapted during the early stages of its development to support the hardware of as many vendors as possible. Second, the thinking behind UNIX design was that smaller is better, which has allowed users to apply more of the computing power available to the service of end-user requests, rather than running the operating system itself. Third, as a result of the huge popularity of the C programming language, the UNIX operating system (which is written almost entirely in C) has been ported to every major vendor's hardware.

Finally, because UNIX has been designed from the ground up to be a truly multiuser system, it is the only popular, nonproprietary operating system that can run on the user's desktop at home as well as on the corporate mainframe. UNIX provides a completely scalable, unified, enterprisewide operating system architecture that no operating system can match.

Multiuser, Multitasking, with Built-in Security. Unlike DOS, OS/2, and Windows, UNIX is both a multiuser and a multitasking operating system. Unlike Windows NT, this multiuser capability permeates through and around every device and resource found throughout all modes of operation on the UNIX workstation.

For example, when archiving data to tapes, CD-ROMs, or floppy disks, file-level protection under an adequately administered UNIX scenario allows this data to exist outside the computer in such a manner as to maintain proper personal and user-group security levels. This is possible because all files and devices on UNIX are set up with built-in securities related to commonly maintained security files. Therefore, when files migrate, their relative permission levels migrate with them. This capability allows for a truly powerful set of security features to be deployed across enterprise boundaries.

It is worth noting, too, that because few users will actually have their own UNIX workstations at home, software piracy, virus, and license abuses are much less likely to become an issue when using UNIX workstations.

To share a UNIX system among many users, all that is required to start is a serial port, an asynchronous terminal, or a terminal emulation package. User accounting, file sharing, electronic mail, preemptive multitasking, and simple turnkey networking are all built into the basic UNIX operating system right out of the box. Although Windows NT also maintains a similar asynchronous networking capability, the entry-level hardware and software requirements for use of the operating platform tools, electronic mail, workplace sessions (termed "shell"), and security features are far smaller under UNIX.

Set-Up and Administration Difficulties. High-speed, packet networking is difficult to set up and administer on UNIX. Fortunately, many UNIX vendors have worked hard to make network configuration easier on their own brands of UNIX. In general, however, Windows NT, OS/2, and Windows for Workgroups fare far better than UNIX on all counts of user-friendliness when setting up and using the system.

Fortunately, too, the UNIX world has (like Windows NT and OS/2) adapted a *de facto* networking standard under TCP/IP. Furthermore, because UNIX also usually supports either the open Sun Network File System (NFS) or, less commonly, AT&T's Remote File System (RFS) — both of which are POSIX compliant — user data is more secure than when running on a OS/2 or NT-sponsored DOS file allocation table (FAT) system, whereby people can just boot DOS, or under NT's file system or OS/2's High-Performance File System(HPFS). Again, the reason is that, unlike any other operating system discussed in this article, the UNIX file system (and therefore all devices, since most are files under UNIX) maintains all of the built-in file-level features that make highly sophisticated wide-area networking more efficient.

Unfortunately, all of this power does come at the cost of a common ease of set up and administration. Many users are initially intimidated by the terse UNIX command set and are hesitant to administer multiuser resources. Like Windows NT (but unlike OS/2, DOS, and Windows), UNIX requires users to log on to the computing resource and governs how much access a user can have on the UNIX system (the term superuser reflects more than just a security class on UNIX; it is also often associated with a skill set).

DOS and Windows Compatibility. Both DOS and Windows 3.x compatibility have been achieved on UNIX. Unfortunately, UNIX support of sophisticated network devices and peripherals running under DOS often fare as poorly as DOS support does under Windows NT. Many DOS device-driver programs do not work as well on UNIX, NT, and OS/2 as they do on DOS alone.

Furthermore, recent attempts to get Windows running more responsively under UNIX by using more advanced emulation techniques — such as the Windows Application Binary Interface(WABI2) — are not going well. The main reason for their failure is that many Windows applications are still finding unique ways to circumvent the cooperative Windows APIs to (for example) use DOS interrupts to provide more-reasonable multitasking support for time-critical events.

If 100 percent DOS and Windows compatibility is important for an organization's UNIX workstations, then IT managers should select a UNIX system that is based on Intel technology, because most Intel-based UNIX operating systems allow users to just boot DOS as required. Keep in mind, however, that although the ability to reboot a workstation can be very attractive, this advantage can work against the user when servers are involved: For security, support, and network maintenance reasons, it might be better to deploy UNIX servers that are decidedly not Intel compatible.

In a similar vein, although a common object file format has been designed for UNIX, and there have been several attempts at providing a common executable format for the many binary flavors within the UNIX family of operating systems, complicated programs will never run as well on other processors as they can on native-code machines. In other words, programs written on Sun Microsystems Inc.'s (Mountain View CA) 68000-based UNIX will need to be recompiled to run as effectively as possible on, for example, IBM's RISC-based AIX or on SCO Inc.'s (Louisville CO) 386-based UNIX V. Microprocessor vendors have simply not been able to develop an effective cross-compatible computer instruction set.

Most Common Internet Platform. When considering applying UNIX to networked operations, an excellent example of how the organization might best be able to use the operating platform could be found by examining the use of that platform throughout the Internet. UNIX is the mainstay of the telecommunications industry. Although many OS/2, NT, and even DOS servers can be found serving as turnstiles on America's information highway, UNIX is today the server of choice for administering the majority of the time-critical, server-based, multiuser applications. To understand why, one only needs to imagine making an OS/2, DOS, Windows, or NT Workstation function as a host for 200 or so concurrent users. It just would not work.

Because many UNIX machines are capable of performing to these type of mainframe standards, it becomes obvious why UNIX is so widespread in large WAN operations, such as on the Internet. UNIX alone is capable of operating in all environments, from a single-user, standalone desktop application to the departmental LAN to the company's IS shop, and finally, across a corporatewide WAN.

In short, UNIX can be difficult to learn and to administer, although the connectivity, security, and user administrative solutions are available, robust, and enterprise-ready. UNIX, therefore, tends to be less frequently chosen as a workstation and more often found functioning as a backbone server network in most data processing organizations.

A BRIEF COMPARISON BY CATEGORY

As each of the operating environments discussed is examined in relationship to the others, it becomes clear that no single operating environment can be said to win in all categories. Which operating systems an individual or corporation chooses to standardize on continues to be a decision that must be based on existing operating system and networking requirements, as well as on individual user capabilities and preferences.

To assist readers in the process of gauging which operating environment is appropriate for business and home use, here is a summation of how well each operating system fares in several important categories:

- System requirements.
- Third-party software support
- Graphical user interface (GUI) support
- Networking capability
- Operating system software development
- Future outlook

System Requirements. In terms of system requirements, DOS can still operate in 640K of RAM with as little as 5 to 20MB of hard disk. Windows 3.1x functions with 4MB RAM and 80 to 100MB of disk, while OS/2 does best with 6 to 8MB of RAM and 120 to 200MB of disk space. By contrast, Windows NT easily gobbles up 16 to 20MB of RAM and, realistically, should have about 250MB disk space.

Text-based commercial flavors of UNIX can be found that operate in as little as 2MB of RAM, with as little as 30MB of disk (or less).Realistically, however, a modern, graphical, adequately provisioned UNIX workstation should have at its disposal about the same amount of RAM and disk as suggested for use under Windows NT.

Third-Party Software Support. DOS and Windows are the unquestioned champions of the third-party market. From artificial-intelligence programs to simple games, more individual software titles exist for DOS and Windows than for any other operating system combination. Because programs running under DOS can be much more responsive than when operating under any other operating system discussed in this article (including Windows 3.1x),there are few practical alternatives to DOS development for software developers who require the absolute best software performance possible.

Windows runs DOS programs more reliably than any other operating system discussed in this article, although DOS emulation under OS/2 is slightly more compatible under OS/2 than under Windows NT. Regardless, there will certainly be more software written for Windows than for either OS/2 or NT, in part because of Windows' smaller system requirements and processing overhead, as well as its formidable installed base.

In addition, the early positioning of Windows as the GUI for the masses, through both affordable pricing and economical systems requirements, has given Windows a much larger market share than either OS/2, NT, or UNIX. Of course, the ultra-affordable price tag presently associated with OS/2 Warp ($79 upgrade for Windows 3.x users) will prompt more individuals to experiment with OS/2 rather than with NT or UNIX. Because of OS/2's reasonable pricing and better DOS compatibility, OS/2 could be seen catching up to Windows in popularity within the next few years.

GUI Support. Graphical user interfaces are integral parts of each of the operating systems discussed. Although Windows is the most prevalent GUI for DOS, it is by no means the only (or necessarily the best) graphical user interface available for the DOS operating system. By contrast, the proprietary Presentation Managers (PMs) of OS/2 and NT are the only alternatives for graphical software development on these two platforms. Although versions of * Windows (a windowing system developed by MIT and running under UNIX) could be ported to all operating platforms, * Windows presently enjoys support only on DOS and UNIX workstations.

Although the PMs in Microsoft Windows, OS/2, and NT are more object-oriented environments, * Windows maintains a distinctly procedural environment for software development. This has produced serious performance problems for * Windows, as events tend to be chained, rather than posted, between scheduled applications. In general, the * Windows message-chaining paradigm does not work efficiently under the present UNIX preemption scheme, because a chained event will often have to work its way through several links in a chain before it arrives at its final destination. Therefore, much like security features must be retrofitted on DOS, GUI support on UNIX can be clearly seen as a retrofit.

As graphical interfaces go, OS/2 and NT Presentation Managers have gone to great lengths to attempt to enforce a common look and feel among programs developed for their systems; by contrast, * Windows allows for several different styles (or widget sets) to run under and cooperate within itself. In other words, it would be much easier to make an * Windows program look and feel like a common user access (CUA) application than to make an OS/2 or Windows program resemble an * Windows environment such as Motif, the standard user interface in the UNIX world.

Finally, on a positive note, much like the rest of UNIX, the * Windows GUI itself is entirely networkable (under the * client and * server paradigm), whereas the Presentation Managers of OS/2, NT, and Windows are decidedly anchored to their single-user workstations.

Networking Capability. Of the operating systems reviewed, only UNIX and NT provide truly group-oriented, turnkey, multiuser networking solutions that let any computer be effectively shared by several users. By contrast, OS/2,DOS, and even Windows for Workgroups depend on having total control of all sharable computing resources; thus they perform poorly in networks. Standalone DOS networking and multitasking solutions are primitive at best, although many networking options are available through third-party vendors.

Operating System Development Support. OS/2 and NT offer more interprocess communications mechanisms for developing robust, fault-tolerant, international networking solutions than any of the other operating systems. National language support and SAA make OS/2 a natural for larger corporations that want to develop their own software applications for standalone workstations.

UNIX's responsive virtual-memory management and rich subset of OS/2 interprocess communications capabilities make it the natural selection where multiple users (not just multiple programs) need to share a single computer at the same time. NT is an administrator's dream to install and operate, whereas the open UNIX system allows more vendors to compete on a level playing field, rather than guess at the working of undocumented system features that have given other products an unfair competitive edge by allowing their applications to use undocumented features.

When several applications need more than small bootstrap-type services for working together in an orderly manner, Windows provides not only the vehicle but the software availability to allow users to get the job done without much software development. Basic DOS is excellent for running programs that are highly specialized, requiring customized software, device drivers, or throughput requirements.

Future Outlook on 32-bit Computing. The OS/2 operating system is much more likely to be successful in the all-important third-party software development market than Windows NT or UNIX. Of course, DOS and Windows games and applications will continue to proliferate faster than applications show up for all of the other operating platforms discussed in this article, combined.

After approximately three years of public access to the system, there are fewer applications available for NT than there were for DOS after its first year of public availability. Although network support for the NT operating system is far superior to anything that DOS or Windows has to offer, UNIX alone is capable of adequately sharing its entire NFS/POSIX file system, GUI, and interprocess communications within a large networking community.

Because an operating system's success is often defined in terms of software availability, the future of NT looks rather dim. OS/2 is apt to be the first to be procured when thoughts turn to trailing preemptive, multitasking, 32-bit computing. With its reasonable entry-level price tag (expressed both in terms of system requirements and entry-level costs) and its DOS compatibility, OS/could be seen catching up to Windows in popularity within the next few years.

As a server, UNIX does not need to entice too many more software developers into its realm to guarantee continued success. Multiuser support, a host of database and middleware options, communications, open systems, infinite scalability, and connectivity — all of these are certainly the issues that will continue to make UNIX the operating system of choice for those interested in corporatewide, multivendor networking.

CONCLUSION

In the final analysis, DOS has in many ways been the hero of the 1980s and 1990s, escorting more computing power to a greater variety of users than any other operating system in history. The only system that runs more DOS programs than Microsoft's Windows is DOS itself, so Windows should remain the most popular system in the standalone, single-user environment. Windows for Workgroups is an excellent vehicle to interconnect groups of Windows enthusiasts, with far fewer compromises than when running DOS under OS/2, NT, or UNIX.

When searching for something to be more robust and reliable than Windows but more compatible with Microsoft's old technologies, buyers should feel confident in taking a long, hard look at OS/2. When larger work groups are more important than online, networked, DOS (or Windows) compatibility, then NT can be an appropriate choice. Finally, behind it all, UNIX makes an extremely capable, and infinitely more expandable, server.

Chapter 3
Evaluating Client/Server Operating Systems: Focus on Windows NT

Gilbert Held

Although the market penetration of Microsoft Corp.'s Windows NT at the client/server level only recently exceeded 10 percent, actual development of this client/server operating system began in 1988. Windows NT was primarily developed by a team of former Digital Equipment Corp. employees originally responsible for the development of DEC's VAX operating system, which explains why people familiar with VAX note many similarities between the two operating systems.

Windows NT version 4.0 represents the current version of the system and sports the Windows 95 interface. Both the client, known as Windows NT Workstation, and the server, known as Windows NT Server, are marketed by Microsoft. The key difference between the two versions of Windows NT concerns scalability and network and file support.

Windows NT Server, as its name implies, was developed as a network-based server. The operating system is optimized to support network requests to the server, which include the access and transfer of information in the form of files.

In addition, because the server is the focal point of a client/server network, Windows NT Server is scalable and able to operate on a computer containing up to four processors. An organization can therefore purchase a computer with a single processor that has a motherboard designed to support up to four processors, then add processors as computing requirements increase.

0-8493-9989-0/99/$0.00+$.50

In comparison, Windows NT Workstation was developed to favor workstation processing. This means that the workstation operating system does not have to be scalable to support additional network-related processing nor concerned with providing network services to users, which is a key function of Windows NT Server.

SYSTEM REQUIREMENTS

Both Windows NT Server and Windows NT Workstation currently operate on three hardware platforms: Intel X86-based processors, DEC AXP, and MIPS Reduced Instruction Set (RISC) computers. In addition, Apple Computer and IBM Corp. are considering porting both versions of NT to their PowerPC product line.

Windows NT Workstation requires 12MB of RAM when operating on Intel platforms and 16MB for use on DEC and MIPS RISC-based computers. Although Windows NT Server also operates with a similar amount of RAM, the amount is sufficient only when the server supports fewer than 50 workstations. As workstation support requirements increase, RAM requirements can increase; the applications supported by the server as well as the number of workstations supported govern the amount of RAM required. Although Microsoft publishes a guide to the minimum amount of memory that should be installed for use with Windows NT Server, networks with 50 or more workstations should use servers with a minimum of 32MB of RAM.

SYSTEM FEATURES

Both Windows NT Workstation and Windows NT Server include a core set of features that differentiate them from other client/server operating systems, such as Novell's NetWare and UNIX-based systems. Those features include the scalability of the server operating system as well as security, performance monitoring, and network support enhancements. Examining these features provides IS and network managers with a basis for comparing and selecting a client/server operating system.

Scalability

As discussed previously, Windows NT Server is scalable, capable of running on a four-processor computer. In addition, because Windows NT operates on Intel, DEC Alpha, and MIPS machines, users can migrate their server from a relatively low-cost Intel single-processor platform to a multiprocessor higher-performance DEC Alpha or MIPS platform while continuing to use NT.

NetWare is currently restricted to operating on Intel platforms and cannot provide the migration path associated with the use of Windows NT. Although UNIX operates on a variety of hardware platforms ranging from

PCs to Sun Microsystems, Hewlett-Packard, and IBM high-performance workstations that function as servers, differences among the versions of UNIX supported by each platform could inhibit organizations from migrating applications from one UNIX-based system to another. NT thus provides the only server-based operating system that is truly portable for applications migrated from one vendor platform to another.

Performance Monitoring

Both Windows NT Workstation and Windows NT Server include a performance-monitoring capability that is extremely valuable for determining when or if the current hardware platform should be changed. In addition to monitoring, for example, processor metrics, NT's Performance Monitor program also generate alarms and plots the performance of a large number of network-related metrics, such as session timeouts, retries, and number of open connections.

Under NetWare, performance monitoring is accomplished through the use of the MONITOR utility program, a passive tool that cannot be used to set alarms. Although several third-party products that perform in a manner similar to Windows NT in a NetWare environment are available, these products are not bundled with NetWare and require the expenditure of additional funds. Some versions of UNIX include a built-in performance-monitoring capability, but most versions of it also depend on the use of third-party products. Windows NT thus provides a built-in performance-monitoring capability that remains in place if the need to migrate to a different hardware platform arises.

Security

Users of Windows NT notice immediately that once the system is installed, unauthorized individuals cannot power the hardware off and back on and take control of the computer by inserting a disk into the A drive. Instead, NT has a User Manager that limits computer access to predefined users, such as the administrator and any guest or individual accounts that permit employees to use a workstation or a server.

Exhibit 1 illustrates the Windows NT User Manager screen common to both server and workstation versions of the operating system. To illustrate the utility of the User Manager, Exhibit 2 shows the user properties it supports. Note that an authorized person can assign and change user passwords as well as control the password's expiration and, if so desired, disable an account.

NetWare is similar to Windows NT in its support of predefined groups, such as guests and administrators (called supervisor under NetWare). The key differences between NetWare and Windows NT lies in the ability of

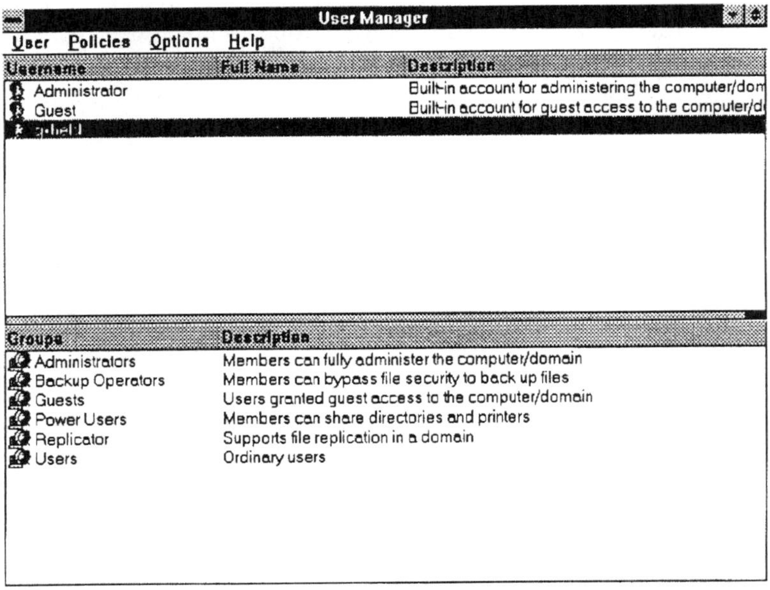

Exhibit 1. Windows NT User Manager screen.

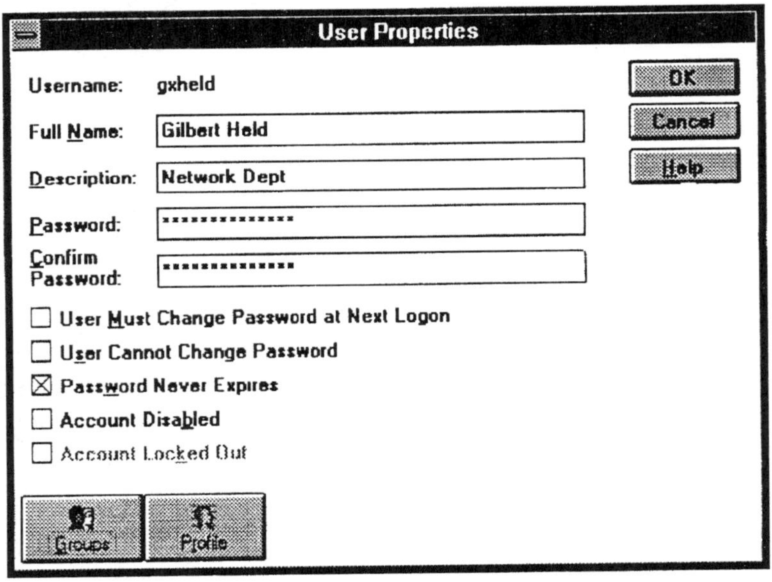

Exhibit 2. User properties supported by the Windows NT User Manager.

client workstations in the latter system to control access to the computer and in its ease of use.

In the Group Memberships dialog box, for example, simply clicking on a button after highlighting an entry changes a user's group membership. Although NetWare has a similar feature, it requires slightly more manual intervention, which becomes significant if a server supports a large number of users. In the case of UNIX, each version of the system differs in its security and network administration, so the administration training effort increases if computer platforms are switched.

Network Support

One of the most important features of any server is its ability to support organizational networking requirements. Windows NT truly excels in this area, because it supports a diverse and comprehensive range of network protocols ranging from NetBIOS to AppleTalk, IBM's Data Link Control (DLC), NetWare's NWLink IPX/SPX, and TCP/IP (Transmission Control Protocol/Internet Protocol).

In addition to supporting a large variety of networking protocols, Windows NT includes direct support for more than 20 network adapter cards and indirect support for more than 100 additional adapters. Direct adapter support is in the form of drivers included in the operating system, and indirect support is in the form of vendor-supplied drivers that typically accompany the hardware as a disk with files that must be loaded by the operating system.

Exhibit 3 illustrates the Windows NT Network Settings dialog box. This dialog box is invoked from the icon labeled Network in the Windows NT control panel, a method similar to the one employed by users of Windows and Windows 95 to control network settings. Thus, in addition to supporting a wide range of network protocols, use of Windows NT may significantly reduce training and administrative costs for many organizations.

Although NetWare supports several network protocols, its main built-in support is limited to IPX/SPX, the native method of communications used in a NetWare environment. The use of other network protocols commonly requires the acquisition of drivers from the Novell bulletin board or user forum and the loading of those drivers on workstations and servers. Similarly, most UNIX systems are limited to a built-in support of TCP/IP, requiring other network protocols to be acquired and loaded onto workstations and servers.

Another advantage of Windows NT is its capability to support multiple network bindings, or the association of a network protocol to a network adapter or a network service to a network protocol. It is important to note

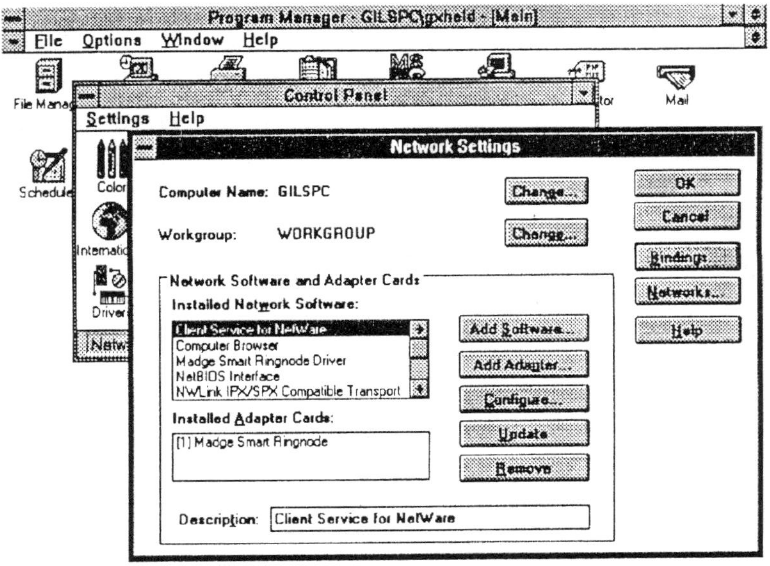

Exhibit 3. Windows NT network settings dialog box.

---

that Windows NT supports more than 10 simultaneous bindings, which makes a server most suitable for supporting NetWare, UNIX, AppleTalk, and other network protocols transported from different client or server platforms to a Windows NT server.

In addition, because Windows NT Workstation also supports the same bindings capability as Windows NT Server, a Windows NT Workstation can be used to obtain simultaneous access to NetWare servers and Windows NT servers. This is accomplished through use of the Frye Utilities for NetWare Management program, a NetWare-based utility program that provides NetWare server performance metrics, operating under Windows NT. In fact, owing to Windows NT's extensive support of different network protocols and network adapter cards, it is quite common for users of Windows NT Workstation to employ that operating system to connect to multiple server platforms.

Advantages of Other Operating Systems

Although Windows NT Server includes features that make it the server of choice for many organizations, Novell's NetWare continues to excel in two key areas:

1. The ability to support thousands of users
2. Suitability of the directory structure for an enterprise network

Unlike Windows NT, which can only keep pace with NetWare 4.1 when supporting up to 100 to 200 users, NetWare supports several times that number of users without significant performance degradation. This means that large organizations may require multiple Windows NT servers in place of one large NetWare 4.1 server.

As for directory services, under NetWare 4.X, a hierarchical enterprisewide structure can be set up that lets users on one network easily access resources on other segments. In comparison, Windows NT's Domain Services, although efficient in terms of setup and resource management, uses a replication scheme that becomes inefficient for large groups. For this reason, NetWare is probably the network of choice for large organizations with thousands of workstations.

IMPLEMENTATION CONSIDERATIONS

Although Windows NT is relatively easy to install, careful planning is required to ensure that its rich set of options are appropriately configured and implemented.

Before installing the operating system, it is prudent to review the bundled products distributed with Windows NT, such as the built-in FTP (file transfer protocol) server capability included in Windows NT Server. Before simply clicking on the appropriate button to install the FTP software module, IS staff must determine whether to set up the module to permit anonymous access or access only to persons with accounts on the NT server. Similarly, with the introduction of Windows NT 4.0 Server, Microsoft added a bundled Web site software module that turns an NT server into a World Wide Web server. Using the software, however, requires the correct configuration of several software settings, such as IP address and address mask, so the server can recognize requests directed to it.

Because of the number of variables that may require settings, an appropriate testing procedure is key to any implementation plan. A well-thought-out test plan should ensure that each service thought be operational works according to the desired configuration of the operating system. For example, installation of the FTP server software on a Windows NT server as an anonymous FTP server should be tested by accessing the server with an FTP client to verify the configuration of the FTP server module.

In addition, if the server will be connected to the Internet as well as the organization's private network, the connection should be verified through both the internal (i.e., private) network connection and the Internet. This dual verification ensures that access through the Internet resulting in data flowing through a router with filters set up as a firewall barrier or as a firewall allows access to the FTP server. If it does not, IS staff members then have time to request the necessary modifications to the router or firewall before moving to a production environment.

Another important consideration in an implementation plan involves global applications such as calendaring or e-mail. Although available products vary greatly in terms of requirements, they share many common elements, including the need for a predefined naming structure. Instead of simply naming e-mail post offices as PO1, PO2, and PO3, for example, it is more effective and efficient for users and staff, both in terms of meaningfulness and diagnostic testing, to use site names such as ATLANTA, BOSTON, or MACON.

CONCLUSION

Windows NT Server is a robust, scalable operating system with substantial built-in security, performance monitoring, and networking capabilities. IS managers in organizations whose future networking requirements are anticipated to grow should consider using the Windows NT Server operating system because it runs on different platforms and supports the use of multiple processors. This allows the organization to retain the use of the operating system as its networking requirements grow.

In addition, because Windows NT Server's security, performance-monitoring, and networking capabilities now exceed the features offered by NetWare and most UNIX systems, NT is a more robust operating system. Perhaps this explains why several trade journals predict that Windows NT will encompass more than 50 percent of the server market by 1998.

Although Windows NT offers several advantages over competitive network operating systems, it is important to remember that technology does not remain static. Novell's planned new version of NetWare may provide some of the key features now associated with Windows NT. In addition, NetWare continues to retain several advantages over Windows NT that make it more suitable for large networks.

Because most IS managers and network administrators must make decisions based on released technology, it is important to note that Window's NT Workstation provides access to NetWare servers, and Windows NT Server can be used in a NetWare IPX/SPX networking environment. This means that the use of both Windows NT platforms coexists with NetWare as well as with TCP/IP UNIX-based systems. Thus, another key reason to consider the use of Windows NT is to be able to use one or more of the new applications being developed to run on an NT server without having to change an existing network.

Chapter 4
Transitioning to Windows NT

Nathan J. Muller

Windows NT provides a secure, easy-to-manage, powerful foundation for a new generation of business applications using low-cost PC hardware. Microsoft's Windows NT 3.5 builds on the reliability and stability of Windows NT 3.1 (the first version of Windows NT) to greatly enhance speed and provide better connectivity to other systems, particularly Novell NetWare and UNIX environments.

NT 3.5 offers a high degree of protection for critical business applications and their data, and provides complete security for desktop systems. By supporting industry standards, Windows NT works with existing systems and networks. Windows NT delivers a networking architecture that fully optimizes the power of desktop and server operating systems and interoperates with other vendor's systems in the corporate computing environment.

As a 32-byte operating system with preemptive multitasking, strong networking support, no memory limits, and no dependency on DOS, Windows NT 3.5 surpasses Windows NT 3.1 and Windows 95 and matches the power of UNIX. Users can run both technical and business applications on a single desktop platform, which in most cases is far less expensive than a UNIX workstation.

UNIX INTEROPERABILITY

Because UNIX works well for large, networked organizations, most IS managers are hesitant to change hardware and software for anything less than very compelling reasons. Windows NT is interoperable with UNIX, allowing Windows-based products to be added as the need to add more users arises. Interoperability is achieved through:

- Common, standard networking protocols
- Character and graphical terminal support
- Standards-based distributed processing support

0-8493-9989-0/99/$0.00+$.50

- Standards-based file systems and data sharing
- Application portability

UNIX Variants

At the most basic level, Windows NT Server includes communications protocol support, network utilities, and application programming interfaces (APIs) that allow it to communicate with most UNIX variants, including Transmission Control Protocol and Internet Protocol (TCP/IP), TCP/IP utilities, and simple network management protocol (SNMP) support.

TCP/IP. Windows NT Server has TCP/IP support built in, which means the Windows NT Server can communicate right out of the box. The core TCP/IP protocols included with Windows NT include the User Datagram Protocol, address resolution protocol (ARP), and the Internet control message protocol (ICMP).

TCP/IP Utilities. More than a dozen basic network utilities are included with Windows NT that provide terminal access to, or file transfer capabilities to and from, most UNIX-based systems. The basic TCP/IP connectivity applications include finger, File Transfer Protocol, RCP, Telnet, Rexec, Rsh, and TFTP. TCP/IP diagnostic utilities include ARP, hostname, ipconfig, nbstate, netstap, ping, and route.

SNMP Support. Windows NT Server provides several facilities for integrating Windows NT-based systems into networks that use SNMP, a common TCP/IP-based network management facility. This component allows a Windows NT Server to be administered remotely using such enterprise-level management platforms as Hewlett-Packard's OpenView, IBM's NetView, and Sun's Solstice SunNet Manager.

Assigning IP Addresses

With regard to TCP/IP, Windows NT Server is the only server operating system that provides Dynamic Host Control Protocol (DHCP) management. DHCP is the facility that assigns TCP/IP addresses, eliminating the process of manual address allocation every time users request a connection.

The proliferation of TCP/IP-based networks, coupled with the growing demand for Internet addresses, makes it necessary to conserve IP addresses. Issuing IP addresses on a dynamic basis is a way to recycle this increasingly scarce resource. Even companies with private intranets are using dynamic IP addresses instead of issuing unique IP addresses to every machine.

With DHCP, which was developed by the Internet Engineering Task Force (IETF), IP addresses can be doled out from a pool of IP addresses as users need them to establish network connections. When they log off the net, the IP addresses are released and become available to other users. Assigning addresses can consume a majority of a network manager's time if done manually. With DHCP support, Windows NT automates this task.

A related feature provided by Windows NT is the Windows Internet Name Service(WINS), which maps computer names to IP addresses, allowing users to refer to their machines with an easy-to-remember plain-text name rather than by an IP address such as 123.456.789.22, for example.

Windows NT includes native support for NetBEUI and IPX/SPX as well as TCP/IP. Regardless of the protocol used, each system hides the details of the underlying network from the applications and the end user. The network administrator can choose the protocol that best addresses the company's network requirements.

Character and Graphical Terminal Support

Although designed to support business-strength client/server computing, Windows NT can also host a variety of terminal emulation capabilities for easy integration with UNIX-based hosts, including the ones described in the following sections.

Telnet and Third-Party Terminal Emulators. Basic character-oriented terminal access using Telnet is included with Windows NT and integrated with the Windows Terminal applet. A variety of terminal emulators with more advanced features are also available from third-party vendors.

X Servers. X servers are available from a variety of third-party vendors to allow users of Windows NT to access and run existing X-based application on their UNIX-variant hosts.

Standards-based Distributed Processing Support

Windows NT Server includes API to support computing in a distributed environment. The APIs provided are discussed in the following sections.

DCE-compatible RPC. Remote Procedure Calls (RPCs) are a critical component needed to build distributed applications. The RCP built into Windows NT Server is compatible with the Open Software Foundation's Distributed Computing Environment (DCE) RPC. Using this RPC, developers can build distributed applications that include other Windows NT-based systems, as well as any system that supports Data Circuit-terminating Equipment-compatible RPC — including those from Digital Equipment Corp., Hewlett-Packard, and other vendors.

Windows Sockets. Windows Sockets is an APIs that is compatible with Berkeley-style sockets, a popular distributed computing mechanism among UNIX variants. Windows Sockets enables developers to build applications that interoperate with any other system that supports this industry-standard APIs.

Windows Open Services Architecture (WOSA). WOSA is a set of Microsoft-developed open APIs for integrating Windows platforms with a broad range of back-end services from multiple vendors.

Standards-based File Systems and Data Sharing

Windows NT supports the following standards for file systems and data sharing.

LAN Manager for UNIX (LMU)

LMU is an implementation of Microsoft Windows networking for servers that run UNIX variants. LMU allows Microsoft network clients to access data stored on UNIX hosts, including data on remotely mountable UNIX file systems. LMU uses Server Message Blocks (SMBs), a set of protocols developed by Microsoft that are now an X/Open standard.

Network File System (NFS). Sun's Network File System is a popular tool for sharing files among different UNIX operating systems and is available for Windows NT Server from several third-party vendors, including Sun-Select.

File Transfer Protocol (FTP). Microsoft has also developed client and server versions of FTP for Windows NT Server. FTP is a popular TCP/IP-based utility that allows users to copy files among diverse systems, including UNIX and non-UNIX systems.

Application Portability

Native Application Ports. There are thousands of 32-byte applications for Windows NT, including many applications originally developed for UNIX variants, virtual memory system (VMS), or multiple virtual storage (MVS). In fact, approximately 25 percent of the applications being developed for Windows NT are ports from these other platforms. Many of these are high-end technical and business applications.

POSIX. The IEEE 1003.1-1990 standard — usually referred to as Portable Operating System Inferface for UNIX.1 — specifies a set of APIs that describe an interface between applications and an operating system. Windows NT Server includes a protected subsystem that provides full support for POSIX.1.

Windows Libraries for UNIX. Microsoft has licensed Windows source code and test suites to several companies that will develop products that allow Windows-based applications to run on all major implementations of the UNIX operating system, including Solaris SunOS, UNIXWare, SCO UNIX, Advanced Interactive Executive, and HP-UX. These agreements make the Windows APIs a universal standard for both the Intel and Reduced Instruction Set Computer-based UNIX platforms, and help ensure that users can take advantage of evolving 32-byte Windows technology in both their operating systems and applications development.

SERVICES FOR NETWARE

Microsoft's networking strategy is to ensure that any desktop computer can access any server. Therefore, Microsoft has equipped Windows NT Server (and NT Workstation) with several utilities that make it easier for NetWare users to make the transition to Windows NT.

File and Print Services for NetWare

File and Print Services for NetWare is a utility that makes Windows NT Server look like a NetWare 3.x-compatible file and print server. Without changing their NetWare client software, users can access file and print services, as well as their server applications, on the same multipurpose Windows NT Server-based machine from their desktops. The Windows NT directory service provides single network log-on, replication, and centralized management.

Client Service for NetWare

Client Service for NetWare provides NetWare client capabilities for the Windows NT Workstation. It allows the Windows NT Workstation to connect to file and print services provided by NetWare servers. Windows NT Workstations can store and print information on NetWare servers, and they can have access to many of the most commonly used NetWare-aware applications, such as NetWare SAA and Lotus Notes. Users who have supervisor rights are also able to run administrative utilities, such as Syscom and Pconsole, commonly used in managing NetWare servers.

Client Service for NetWare integrates into both the Windows NT and NetWare environments. It can be configured so that a single log-on provides access to the Windows NT Workstation, NetWare file and print servers, and Windows NT-based application servers.

Gateway Service for NetWare

Gateway Service for NetWare provides networked and remote users connected to a Windows NT Server access to the file storage and printer resources on NetWare servers. This gateway is a useful integration tool for companies that run both NetWare and Microsoft clients in a heterogeneous server environment. The network administrator controls access to the gateway so only those with permission can use file and print resources on designated NetWare servers.

Gateway Service for NetWare can be used to isolate IPX/SPX traffic and ease the transition to TCP/IP, as well as to run the remote access capability available with Windows NT Server. With remote access, clients can securely dial into the network from a remote location and access all services as if they were directly connected to the LAN.

NWLink

NetWare users can access server applications such as Microsoft SQL Server, SNA Server, and others running on Windows NT Server without changing their client software. This capability is accomplished by using NWLink, the IPX/SPX-compatible transport that comes standard with Windows NT Workstation and Windows NT Server. These applications appear to a NetWare user in the same way as a NetWare Loadable Module (NLM) does. During installation, Windows NT Server automatically checks the network to see which transport is running. If it finds IPX/SPX, the server automatically defaults to the NWLink (i.e., IPX/SPX) transport.

Migration Tool for NetWare

Migration Tool for NetWare in Windows NT Server aids network administrators by copying user accounts and files from NetWare servers to a Windows NT Server while maintaining security. It has the capabilities of both a migration and an integration tool.

For migration, the Windows NT Server Migration Tool for NetWare lets administrators transfer users and data to the Windows NT Server platform. They can migrate a single NetWare server to a single Windows NT Server, multiple NetWare servers to a single Windows NT Server, or many other configurations, allowing for the redistribution of information across the servers on a network.

Because there are some security differences between NetWare and Windows NT Server, the Migration Tool includes a trial migration process that generates detailed log files. These files assist the administrator in keeping track of any changes that may occur during the migration process.

When integrating new servers into the network, administrators are always looking for ways to avoid duplicating user accounts across a variety of servers. The Migration Tool for NetWare simply copies the users, groups, files, and directories to the Windows NT Server, leaving the NetWare server fully intact. For example, if an administrator is setting up an application server in a NetWare environment, user accounts can automatically be populated on the Windows NT Server running SQL Server, for example, by copying the NetWare binary information. These accounts would mirror the user accounts that already exist on the NetWare server, saving the administrator valuable time in the initial server setup.

To test the interoperability of Windows NT Server with NetWare, Microsoft recommends the following procedure:

- Set up Windows NT Server as an application server with Microsoft SQL Server using the NWLink protocol.
- Install the Client Services for NetWare on a Windows NT-based machine and test its functionality as a NetWare client.
- Install the IPX/SPX transport protocol on both a workstation and the server and test its functionality in a routed environment.
- Set up the Gateway Services for NetWare on Windows NT Server and test its effectiveness.

REMOTE ACCESS

Portable systems represent a large and growing share of personal computers. They are used by telecommuters, systems administrators, and mobile workers. Through Windows NT Server's Remote Access Server (RAS), network administrators can extend the local area network across a telephone line, allowing remote computers to appear as if they are directly attached to the network. Up to 256 sessions are supported. Remote users can participate fully in the network, sharing files and printers, accessing data bases, connecting to hosts, and communicating with colleagues over e-mail. Windows NT Server also supports Point-to-Point Protocol and serial-line IP (SLIP), making Internet access a routine task.

PPP is a set of industry-standard framing, authentication, and network configuration protocols that allows remote-access solutions to interoperate in a multivendor network. Point-to-Point Protocol support allows Windows NT Server to receive calls from and provide network access to other vendors' remote-access workstation software.

SLIP is similar to point-to-point protocol (PPP), except that it is an older standard that only addresses TCP/IP connections over serial lines. It does not provide automatic negotiation of network configuration without user intervention. It also does not support encrypted authentication. Although Serial Line Internet Protocol is not recommended, it is supported by Windows NT to accommodate users who already have Serial Line Internet Protocol servers installed.

RAS supports any combination of NetBEUI, TCP/IP, and Internetwork Packet eXchange protocols to access remote networks. Internetwork

Packet eXchange turns Windows NT Server into a remote-access server for NetWare networks. TCP/IP support makes Windows NT an Internet-ready operating system, allowing users to access the vast resources of the World Wide Web with any browsing tool.

Windows NT Server enhances the RAS architecture by adding an IP/IPX router capability. This allows clients to run TCP/IP and IPX locally and run Windows Sockets applications or NetBIOS applications over their local TCP/IP and IPX protocols. This feature enhances RAS's multiprotocol support and makes it a good solution for NetWare and UNIX networks.

DIRECTORY SERVICES

Windows NT implements a distributed directory model that tracks user accounts and resources across a network. Users, groups, and resources such as volumes, directories, files, and printers are divided into domains for distributed access. Each domain is an administrator-defined collection of workstations and servers where one sender is designated the primary domain controller (PDC). The PDC contains a directory of users' accounts and resources within its domain. The directory itself is replicated to Backup Domain Controllers for fault tolerance.

When a user logs on to the network, the directory authenticates the user's identity using the password stored in the directory. The directory also keeps track of the groups to which users have been assigned by administrators based on their workgroups or activities. Based on the user's ID and assigned group rights, the directory grants access to all appropriate resources across all the workstations and servers in the domain. Administrators as well as users can set access control privileges for resources as specific as individual files.

For very large networks where access to the domain controller cannot be guaranteed for the administrator or user, the NT Directory Server employs a "trusted" domain model. Administrators in one domain can certify other domains as "trusted," thereby granting full access to all users from the foreign domain. Using this domain model for directory services, users have the benefit of a single log-on to the entire network while preserving administrative control through trust certifications and access control lists.

In addition to primary and backup directory controllers, a member server can be set up. The member server can participate in directory security, although it does not have to. A server that participates in a directory gets the benefits of the directory's single log-on, but without having to spend resources authorizing log-on attempts or receiving replicated copies of the directory's user database. Instead, it can perform time-critical tasks or devote all of its resources to running applications.

PERFORMANCE

One of the goals of Microsoft has been to reduce memory use and improve system performance. Accordingly, the size of the working set needed by Windows NT Server has been reduced by 4MB to 6MB. This means that the operating system functions more efficiently with the same amount of system memory.

According to Microsoft's internal testing, Windows NT Server 3.5 performs better on typical server tasks, including file and print. Using the BAPCo network load benchmark, the performance of Windows NT Server 3.5 is more than double that of Windows NT. For example, running a 48-client BAPCo network load, the performance was 6,296 seconds with Windows NT 3.1 versus 2,641 seconds for Windows NT 3.5 — an improvement of 2.38 times that of Windows NT 3.1.

These improvements are most evident when using the preferred client, Windows for Workgroups 3.11, which supports the use of 32-byte protect mode networking components to communicate with Windows NT Server. These networking components include 32-byte protocols such as NetBEUI and an IPX/SPX compatible transport, as well as a 32-byte protect mode network redirector. The use of a 32-byte network card driver provides a 32-byte code path from the network card to the network redirector, resulting in improved performance over DOS-based solutions while consuming only 4KB of conventional memory.

Windows for Workgroups 3.11 supports the use of client-side cache with a feature called 32-byte File Access. This is a 32-byte protected mode replacement for the DOS-based SmartDrive disk cache program. The caching routines provided as part of 32-byte File Access differ from that offered by SmartDrive in the following ways:

- 32-byte File Access caching routines are implemented as 32-byte protected mode code, thus reducing the need to transition to real mode to cache disk information.
- 32-byte File Access read-ahead routines work on a per-file basis rather than on a per-sector basis, resulting in a higher probability that information read into the disk cache will be used.
- 32-byte File Access caching routines share cache memory with the protected mode network redirector, thus reducing the memory overhead for maintaining multiple cache buffers.

Windows NT Server provides thread scheduling that allows dynamic load balancing across multiple Central Processing Units. Microsoft has concentrated on providing smooth scalability for up to four processors, the maximum supported by Windows NT Server. Although OEMs can optimize Windows NT Server to support more processors, no operating system provides application performance that increases linearly by a factor of the number of CPUs installed. There are several reasons for this, including hardware designs, the application itself, performance limits caused by physical input and output, and the overhead associated with the operating system's management of multiple Central Processing Units.

With regard to Windows NT Workstation, performance tests using WinBench, a benchmark testing a range of graphics and disk access capabilities, revealed that performance tripled on the graphics portion — from 4.1 WinMarks on Windows NT 3.1 to 12.6 WinMarks on Windows NT Workstation 3.5. The tests used Microsoft's minimum memory configuration of 12MB. In other similar tests, the graphics performance of Windows NT 3.5 Workstation running on dual Pentium machines was as much as four times as high, demonstrating the scalability of performance.

SECURITY

One of the biggest advantages of Windows NT over UNIX is in the critical area of security. Hackers are attracted to UNIX because it offers many weak spots and back doors. Although NT does have some weak spots (for example, NT's built-in File Transfer Protocol server by default gives root access to the disk volume selected for sharing), it was built with a much tighter security model than UNIX, which makes it more difficult to hack. For example, pressing Ctrl+Alt+Del is a hacker's easy way into a DOS or Windows system, making it simple to cut through the password on a screen saver. If this is tried on NT, the computer's security module is invoked, which requests a user name and password.

Another important security feature is Account Lockout, which provides the ability to lock a user's account after a specified number of unsuccessful log-on attempts. This feature makes Windows NT Server more secure from intruders who try to log on by guessing the passwords of valid user accounts. The administrator can lock the account for a specified period of time or until the account is reset.

EASE OF USE

Another advantage Windows NT has over UNIX is ease of use. Configuring a UNIX server is so complicated that it can take days to get things running properly. On the other hand, it takes relatively few mouse clicks to get an off-the-shelf Pentium up and running with Windows NT Server. After installation, the NT system is far easier to administer and maintain than a UNIX system.

To complicate matters for UNIX, there is no single UNIX platform. This means users cannot run a UNIX program designed for one type of system on a UNIX platform from a different vendor — it is as if Compaq, Dell, IBM, and Gateway 2000 all sold slightly different versions of Windows and users had to buy special software for each of these variants. When Novell bought the main UNIX standard from AT&T a few years ago, it looked as if the competitors might finally unite around a common UNIX standard. But that did not happen, leaving Microsoft to successfully exploit the market with an easier-to-use platform than that of UNIX.

APPLICATIONS DEVELOPMENT

Windows NT attracts mainstream software developers because it has inherited many applications that run with Windows 95 and Windows 3.x. It has also netted a supply of native applications, especially those related to the Internet. One of the leading applications on the Internet is the Netscape server software, which was originally sold only for UNIX. Now a Windows NT version is available that offers all the functionality of the UNIX version. Making it even more of a lure is its price: the NT version costs about 75 percent less than the UNIX program.

Megabyte for megabyte, an NT Server system costs less to construct than a UNIX system. NT is also cheaper to configure with the critical software needed to run a World Wide Web server. Although UNIX servers currently maintain a slight performance edge, that will dissolve quickly because of parallel processing, the Pentium Pro, the Alpha, and the PowerPC.

RELIABILITY

Reliability is another benefit of Windows NT. Although a Windows NT machine crashes at roughly the same frequency as a UNIX machine, when a crash does occur under Windows NT, the system does not have to be rebooted—only the affected window is closed out and it is immediately restarted. When a UNIX workstation crashes, on the other hand, the user has to power down and reboot.

An administrator can specify how Windows NT Server behaves when a fatal system error occurs. This feature — Dump Facility with Automatic Reboot — writes an event to the system log, alerts the administrator, dumps system memory to a file that can be used for debugging, and then automatically reboots the server. Clients can take advantage of the Remoteboot Service, whereby their operating systems are rebooted using software on the server's hard disk instead of their own hard disk.

CONCLUSION

Much of the success of Windows NT Server is attributable to the substantial improvements in version 3.5 over version 3.1. Although a good application server, version 3.1 suffered in comparison with NetWare as a file and print server. In addition, version 3.1 required too much memory to compete against workstations with similar performance. The current version of Windows NT Server combines excellent file service with a wide variety of performance and management features needed for mission-critical applications. This enables Windows NT Server to play an important role in enabling members of an organization to make optimal use of information and processing power throughout the enterprise. Today, Windows NT Server 3.5 is a viable alternative to Novell's NetWare as an application server and file and print server, while Windows NT Workstation 3.5 is rapidly gaining against UNIX variants running on workstations.

Section II
Porting and Developing Applications in a Heterogeneous Environment

Starting with Section II, we cover each of the different facets of heterogeneous computing in detail. The focus of Section II is applications.

This section identifies and classifies the solutions and products available to support migration and coexistence of applications among UNIX, Windows, and NetWare. It discusses porting applications and developing new applications using cross-platform development techniques. Based on this guidance, users can determine which tools are best suited to help mitigate their problems in the migration/coexistence among UNIX, Windows, and NetWare. This section also covers the client/server evolution and its impact on applications and the effect of thin and fat clients on applications. The section will conclude with a look at interfacing with mainframe legacy applications and managing applications on a network.

PORTING/REWRITING APPLICATIONS

Whenever users introduce a new environment into an organization, they have an option of porting or rewriting their current applications for the new environment. Exhibit 1 summarizes the approaches available to address porting/rewriting applications.

Even an application written in C that is fully standards-compliant is unlikely to execute without change when the application is moved from one environment to another, such as from UNIX to Windows NT. One of the main causes is the fundamental differences between the operating

Exhibit 1. Porting/rewriting applications.

Issue	Approach	Products
Porting Applications		
Run UNIX applications on Windows NT servers.	Port UNIX application to Windows NT using porting products.	*Nu*TCRACKER Portage OpenNT eXcursion
Run Windows applications on UNIX servers.	Use products that support Win32 on UNIX	MainWin Wind/U
	Emulate Windows on UNIX	WABI SoftWindows
Porting Database Applications	Use multiplatform ODBC drivers	VisiODBC DataDirect
Distributed Applications with UNIX and Windows	Supplement NT DCE support with other DCE components.	DCE Services for Windows NT
	Port ONC RPC to DCE RPC	RhaPC-d
Rewriting Applications		
Capture the business logic in current applications	Use a tool that analyzes source and captures logic	Discover

systems. Porting applications among environments can be accomplished using tools or manually changing the code. In the case of the latter solution, the users must be familiar with the operating system differences and this is covered in Chapter II.1.

Alternatively, users can use a porting tool that lets them port applications from one environment to another. Porting and rewriting applications using tools is covered in Chapter II.2.

One of the most significant porting problem areas is the user interface. Chapter II.3 presents a case study of a genealogical family-tree application implemented in six different GUI systems, to illustrate the cross-GUI platform portability problems, and a proposal is presented for making such applications more portable across various GUI systems.

Developing new applications in heterogeneous environments

In the area of new application development, users are using a number of approaches. Some users use a component-based approach and use languages like Visual Basic and its built-in components. Others use C language applications along with support from the libraries/classes for the particular environment they are developing. For example, C programmers developing Windows applications use MFC. Yet others use 4GL tools such as PowerBuilder. Finally, some users use object-oriented frameworks to develop object-oriented applications.

Exhibit 2. Developing applications to work in more than one environment.

Issue	Approach	Products
Develop Applications that will run on both UNIX and Windows NT	Use proprietary APIs - common subset, layered, or emulated	AppWare
	Develop for Windows NT and port to UNIX or vice versa	See porting products above
	4GL tools	PowerBuilder
	Object frameworks	Allegris DSC++ zAPP
Develop distributed heterogeneous applications	Develop DCE based applications and supplement Distributed services support in Windows NT	DCE services for Windows NT PC-DCE
Access distributed databases	Transparent, seamless access of data across heterogeneous environments	Rdb distributed product suite
Interface with legacy mainframe applications and access mainframe data	Use emulation, gateways, and WWW	Microsoft BackOffice, SNA client for UNIX, Novell NetWare for SAA BEA Jolt

Exhibit 2 summarizes the issues and approaches available to address developing applications that can execute in different environments.

Some users prefer the object approach to application development and would like to do the application-development steps up to the design using object-oriented techniques, but would like to use a component-based approach for implementation. This is possible to some extent. Chapter II.4 presents an eight-step implementation of an object-oriented design in Visual Basic. Benefits include the ability to select and manipulate graphical objects on screen, an object-oriented interface to Windows objects libraries, and creating command buttons and objects with properties similar to object-oriented programming languages.

For users who want to use only an object-oriented approach, different choices are available. Chapter II.5 compares object-oriented development using SmallTalk, C++, Java, and Object-Oriented COBOL.

Some users want applications they develop in one environment to execute in other environments with very little change. In the common example where users want applications that can run in both Windows NT and UNIX, this can be accomplished in one of three ways:

1. Use APIs. There are three flavors of this approach.
   i. Layered APIs that reside on top of native APIs
   ii. Layered APIs plus extensions
   iii. Emulated APIs
2. Use Win32 and port to UNIX
3. Use POSIX and port to Win32

Chapter II.6 covers this topic in detail.

Users developing new applications often compare the different approaches mentioned above, in particular the comparison between a component-based approach and an object-based approach. Chapter II.11 compares two Windows-based, component-based software development (Visual Basic and PowerBuilder) languages with one Windows-based, object-oriented language (Visual C++). Although the product versions themselves are dated, the underlying concepts are still applicable.

One of the latest trends in application development is the use of Java. Java is used for creating applets and scripts for complex, distributed networks such as the Internet and intranets. Chapter II.12 covers the use of Java for application development and touches upon accessing databases from Java applications and performing networking functions using Java. Chapter II.13 also discusses using Java for application development and compares Java with CGI/PERL.

Coexistence of applications in heterogeneous environments. Sometimes users may not want to port their application to the new environment, but would like their applications in one environment to continue to execute in that environment, but be accessible from workstations in another environment. Exhibit 3 summarizes the issues and approaches available to address applications coexistence.

Chapter II.7 covers in detail the topic of accessing UNIX applications from Windows and vice versa.

Chapter II.8 discusses how to leverage existing assets, both code and people, when developing new applications. Leveraging existing assets is one of the keys to successfully developing new distributed applications and this chapter describes a strategy for creating distributed client/server applications by combining code that currently exists with new code.

The need for enterprise-level client/server applications to communicate with one another has engendered both the challenge of interoperability and its potential solution — middleware. Chapter II.9 discusses the business and technical issues associated with enterprise computing and how middleware is being used to resolve them.

Exhibit 3. Application coexistence in heterogeneous environments.

Issue	Approach	Products
Access character based UNIX applications from Windows desktop	Use Telnet	Many vendors and products
Access graphical UNIX applications from NT desktop.	Use PC X server software on the Windows NT desktops and access UNIX server	eXceed, XVision, OpenNT X11 server, PC-Xware, X OnNet, NuTCRACKER X server, eXalt-X, Reflection, Chameleon, eXpertise
Access Windows applications from existing UNIX desktops	Use a Windows NT multiuser server and add Windows to the X station	WinDD, WinTED, Ntrigue, HP 500 WinCenter, NTerprise
Access legacy IBM applications from the NT desktop	Use IBM TN3270 & TN5250 emulators on the NT desktop.	
Enterprise Desktops	Use a desktop designed to support heterogeneous environments	WinTerm, Explora, Network Computer, Personal Workstations, ViewPoint
Mac clients in Windows NT	Use built-in Mac client support in Windows NT	Windows NT

One of the technologies used heavily in programming for Windows environments is OLE — Object Embedding and Linking. While the required interfaces are well defined within the Windows environment, OLE poses a problem when Windows applications need to interface with non-Windows applications. One of the solutions to this problem is Digital's ObjectBroker. ObjectBroker's Object Linking and Embedding Network Portal provides Microsoft's OLE functions for data objects stored on non-Microsoft platforms. The portal enables OLE-supporting applications (e.g., current versions of Microsoft Word and Excel, Lotus 1-2-3, and AmiPro) to link and embed OLE data objects that reside on UNIX and OpenVMS servers. Chapter II.10 describes ObjectBroker in detail.

Finally, a transaction-processing environment invariably uses a transaction-processing monitor. While CICS is the undisputed leader of transaction-processing monitors in the mainframe world, there are more choices for such monitors for distributed and client/server environments. Chapter II.14 covers the topic of choosing a transaction-processing monitor.

Chapter 5

Porting Issues Caused by Operating System Differences

Raj Rajagopal

This chapter will look at some of the basic differences among the operating systems. These differences lead to the need for migration and coexistence solutions among the operating system environments. In particular, the differences among the operating systems lead to the need for porting applications from one environment to another. Here the focus will be on Windows NT and UNIX.

OPERATING SYSTEM FEATURES AND COMPARISONS

Windows NT and UNIX provide network operating system functions as well as application development and execution functions. NetWare has traditionally been well known for its network operating system functions. Although NetWare provides some facilities such as NetWare Loadable Modules (NLMs) for application support in NetWare environments, there are many more applications, particularly mission-critical applications in UNIX and Windows NT, than in NetWare. When the three operating systems are compared, it is worthwhile noting their history.

UNIX started out of a joint Bell Labs/MIT research project in the early 1970s. AT&T, which then owned Bell Labs, could not sell computer-related products due to an antitrust decree and gave UNIX source away to divisions within AT&T and to universities. University of California, Berkeley, in particular did a lot of work on UNIX. Different recipients of the source made their own additions to the operating system and thus the different flavors of UNIX came into existence. The incompatibilities among the flavors spawned standardization efforts, the most notable of which is the POSIX APIs.

0-8493-9989-0/99/$0.00+$.50

With the growing popularity of LANs and the need to share expensive peripherals like laser printers, plotters, etc., Novell came up with the NetWare network operating system to let computers on a network use one or more common file and print servers. Although Novell made some enhancements for supporting applications to NetWare (such as NLMs), there are many more applications in UNIX than in NetWare.

Windows NT is the most recent of the operating systems and has in many ways built on the strengths of prior operating systems while trying to avoid the drawbacks.

Windows NT is used as the base operating system for feature comparisons. If a feature is mentioned, it is available in Windows NT. The availability of the same or similar feature in other operating systems is mentioned where appropriate. Exhibit 1 shows an overview of the Windows NT operating system and its components.

One of the fundamental differences between Windows NT and UNIX is the design assumption about the end user. Some articles claim that UNIX is a true multiuser system and Windows NT is not. For the most part, UNIX presumes the user as a human accessing the UNIX operating system from a dumb terminal. There is list of authorized users in UNIX who can access the system. Windows NT server and Windows NT workstation maintain a list of authorized users, but these are typically users accessing the server

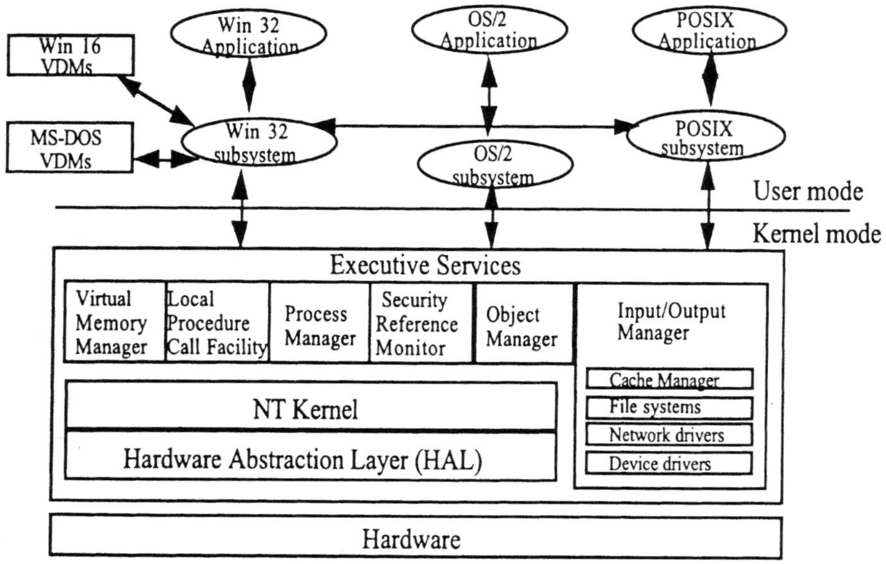

Exhibit 1. Windows NT operating system and components. Host-centric and Client/server computing.

on the same physical computer or a domain and are not as centralized as UNIX. Windows NT's concept of a user accessing the operating system is a client computer (which likely has a human interfacing with it). This difference affects many other aspects of the operating systems.

OPERATING SYSTEM COMPONENTS

Kernel

The kernel is the layer of operating system code that is just above the layer of code that shields the hardware. Operating Systems, including Windows NT, are designed to run on multiple hardware platforms and platform-specific details are masked to the rest of the operating system by a *hardware abstraction layer.* The kernel is the nucleus of the operating system. The kernel executes in a privileged mode called the *kernel mode*, where it has direct access to the hardware and other system software. The kernel is resident in memory and cannot be preempted (except by some interrupts). Applications, on the other hand, execute in non-privileged *user mode* and do not have the access that the kernel does. When an application needs to have access to the hardware, for example when an application wants to print or read data from a disk, it invokes the operating system services, usually through a set of well defined interfaces called *Application Programming Interfaces* (APIs). Some of the functions performed by the kernel are:

- Handle hardware exceptions and interrupts
- Schedule, Prioritize, and Dispatch threads (threads are the basic unit of execution)
- Synchronize execution across processors in a multiprocessor environment

Though UNIX and Windows NT are similar in many ways, one of the areas of difference is the kernel. Windows NT uses a *microkernel*-based approach, where the core kernel functions are kept as small as possible and the other functions of the operating system are performed in non-privileged portions of the operating system called *protected subsystems*. This is in contrast to UNIX where it is not uncommon for the kernel to be a lot bigger and encompass many more operating system functions. One consequence of the bigger kernel is that it needs to be changed more often than Windows NT. UNIX administrators recompile the operating system and reboot the system. Windows NT administrators do not have or modify the Windows NT source. The only significant change to the operating system itself is when patches are applied.

Executive

The *Executive*, in Windows NT, refers to the operating system code that runs in kernel mode. Besides the kernel and the *hardware abstraction layer,* the Executive includes modules that provide services for applications such as memory management, I/O handling, object handling, process management, security monitoring, and a local procedure call facility. These modules are not implemented as a layered hierarchy, one on top of the other.

Unlike UNIX, this portion of the operating system in Windows NT is not changed locally by a System Administrator and is updated only by upgrades issued by Microsoft.

Protected subsystems. The operating system functions not performed by the kernel are performed by a set of nonprivileged servers known as protected subsystems (Exhibit 1). When an application makes an NT API call, these calls are handled by the protected subsystems. One of the advantages of the protected subsystems approach is that it permits modular development of new protected subsystems without impacting either the base operating system or the other existing protected subsystems. The same is true for enhancements to protected subsystems as well.

For example, if Microsoft wants to drop support for OS/2 or POSIX applications then essentially all that needs to be done is to drop the code contained in those protected subsystems. Although Windows NT is designed to run POSIX and OS/2 applications, it is not possible to pass data or files back and forth between a Windows and POSIX (or OS/2) application. Nor can the graphical user interface Windows is famous for be seen — both POSIX and OS/2 support only character mode applications. This is because the *Win32 Subsystem* is the primary subsystem and supports the programming of text, graphics, networking, and all other functions available in Windows NT.

The *OS/2* and *POSIX Subsystems*, on the other hand, are "compatibility mode" subsystems with just text support and without graphics or network support. The lines between the OS/2 or POSIX subsystems and the Win32 subsystem in Exhibit 1 indicate that for many application calls, the OS/2 and POSIX subsystems actually call on the Win32 subsystem.

Process Management

A *process* is the execution instance of a program. Each process has its own memory-address space (4 GB in Windows NT and many UNIX systems) where the code that makes up the process resides. Each process also owns resources required for the process such as files, threads (see below), etc. The process manager portion of the Executive manages the creation and deletion of processes.

Unlike UNIX, processes in Windows NT are not executable by themselves. Also unlike UNIX, Windows NT does not automatically establish a parent/child relationship when one process creates another.

Even though a process is an execution instance, the process itself does not execute. A process is made up of one or more *threads*. Threads are the basic units of execution. A process has at least one thread. Multiple threads can be created. Each thread has its own memory. Threads are a convenient and efficient way to split functions that can be done in the background, while the main thread continues with other processing. In multiprocessor systems, two ore more threads of the same process can be executing in parallel, thereby allowing portions of the same program to execute in parallel.

However, the price to pay for the convenience and efficiency is the need to synchronize threads. If a thread is used to perform a big sort in the background, the main thread must ensure that the sort input data has not changed and the main thread must be notified when the sort is done. Both Windows NT handle scheduling a process or thread for execution, and also handle priority for execution.

Processor Support

Until recently, most computing at the desktop and server level used machines that had only one processor (CPU). Multiprocessing, where multiple processors exist on the same physical machine, have been used in the mainframes for some time. With the advent of cheaper processors and operating systems that support multiple processors, multiprocessing is becoming more commonplace in desktops and servers.

In *Asymmetric MultiProcessing* (ASMP), the operating system uses one or more processors for itself and schedules and runs the application programs in the remaining processors. Operating systems that support *Symmetric MultiProcessing* (SMP) do not impose such restrictions on processors.

The ability to run any program on any processor provides better load balancing (the processor that runs the operating system can be idle while applications are waiting to use the other processor[s]). Fault tolerance is also improved in SMP since the failure of a processor dedicated for the operating system in ASMP means the whole machine is not operational, even though other processor(s) may be operational. The price to pay for improved load-balancing and fault-tolerance is complexity. SMP operating systems are more complex to build and maintain.

Windows NT and many UNIX operating systems support SMP, which is usually transparent to applications.

Memory Management

As mentioned earlier, each process gets its own address space of 4 GB. Most desktops and servers do not have that amount of real memory. Considering that there will be multiple processes at the same time, it is obvious that there must be a mechanism that maps the process address space to real memory. This process is virtual-memory management. The 'virtual' is to indicate that most (or all) of a process memory is not real memory. Contents of the address space that are not held in real memory are held on the disk.

During the course of execution, programs may need additional memory. This might be because program control gets transferred to part of the code that is not resident in memory, or the program asks for more memory. In either case, since real memory is limited, some contents of real memory have to be swapped out. The process of swapping memory contents is called demand paging. A page is the minimum amount of memory that will be swapped in or out. The typical page size is 4K. Both the process-address space and the real memory are divided into pages. Each process thus has (4GB/4K) a million pages. If there is 32MB real memory, there are (32MB/4K) 8000 real-memory pages. The technique of selecting which pages will be moved out is called *first-in-first-out* or FIFO. The operating system keeps track of which pages came in first and selects those for swapping out. The idea behind this technique is that the more recent a page, the more the chances that it will be used and should be kept in real memory.

Virtual-memory management attempts to strike the proper balance. If too much memory is allocated to processes, fewer processes will run and real memory occupied by some processes are not being accessed fast enough and are being wasted. Allocating too little memory to processes may cause frequent swapping of pages, resulting in a situation where the operating system is taking up a lot of CPU time that could have otherwise been used by application processes. To compound this, the memory-access patterns will vary between processes and what is optimal for one will not be for another. The operating system monitors the number of pages allocated and used by each process (also called the working set) and automatically fine tunes memory allocation.

Both Windows NT and UNIX systems use 32 bit *linear memory addressing*. This means that the whole memory is considered one big layout and each memory address is one value between in the 32 bit address. Contrast this with the segmented memory model of Windows 3.1, where memory is considered to be composed of 64KB segments. The 4GB limit comes from the 32 bit address (2^{32}). Half of the process-address space (2GB) is used by the application process and the other half for system functions (for the application process).

Both Windows NT and UNIX also use *demand paging*. Both systems also support *memory mapped files*, which is a technique of speeding up file access by keeping files in memory rather on disk. In addition, both systems also use *heaps*, which are unstructured memory.

However, there are differences. Windows NT has a richer API set for virtual-memory management and for managing heaps. In addition, while UNIX requires that swap space be managed as a separate partition, Windows NT treats swap space as a file and uses the local file system to manage it.

Input/Output Management

This part of the NT executive deals with all input and output, including input from and output to displays, disks, CD-ROM drives, etc. The I/O manager uses what is called a uniform driver model. In this model, every I/O request to a device is through an *I/O request packet* (IRP) regardless of the specific type of I/O device. The device specifics are handled at a level below the I/O manager. The I/O manager performs the I/O task asynchronously. The process that issued the I/O request is preempted by the operating system and waits until it gets a *signal* that the I/O has been completed.

Both Windows NT and UNIX consider all forms of I/O data as a string of bytes or a file. Both systems also implement task preempting for I/O requests.

The I/O manager of Windows NT uses a number of subcomponents such as *Network Redirector/Server* (RAS), *cache manager, file systems, network drivers*, and *device drivers*.

The RAS is covered later in the Networking section. In both Windows NT and UNIX, cache is used to store frequently accessed data from disk (such as file data) to speed up future requests for data. Unlike some other fixed-cache-size systems, the cache size in Windows NT varies, depending on the amount of available memory.

Cache Manager. In both Windows NT and UNIX, cache is used to store frequently accessed data from disk (such as file data) to speed up future requests for data.

Device drivers. The need for device drivers is very simple. An operating system can support hundreds of printers, disk drives, CD-ROM drives, and other peripherals attached to it. The low-level code to drive each of these devices is unique to the device. For example, the line feed command for an HP printer would be different from an Epson. It could even be different for different printer models from the same manufacturer. If a word processing application wants to print, it would not be efficient for the operating system to format the output including the device-unique codes. The job of formatting output for the specific device is taken care of by device drivers.

All operating systems support the concept of device drivers.

Security

Both Windows NT, many UNIX systems, and NetWare provide security functions to ensure that only authorized users are given the appropriate access. Windows NT includes a Security Reference Monitor. Some UNIX systems support Kerberos, while NetWare has its own set of security functions.

Application Programming Interfaces

The application programming interfaces for Windows have evolved over the years starting with the Win16 API. The current one is Win32 API, a 32 bit version supported by Windows NT. The UNIX systems have supported POSIX, which is not compatible with Win32. POSIX has evolved over the years and some common subsets include POSIX.1 and POSIX.2. Recently the X/Open organization has come up with UNIX 95, which is the most recent version of the UNIX standard.

Login Scripts

Windows NT, UNIX, and NetWare support the concept of login scripts. Conceptually, the function provided to the log-on scripts is the same — to set up an environment tailored to the user when the user starts using the system. However, the similarity ends there. In UNIX, the script runs on the server and creates an environment at the server for the user. In Windows NT, the scripts run at the client and tailors the client to the user. This is an example of the user-setup fundamental difference mentioned earlier in this article. The scripting languages (and hence the scripts) are not compatible among the systems. However, there is a way to run NetWare login scripts when accessing a NetWare server from a Windows machine using a Windows client supplied by Microsoft.

Daemons and Services. Operating systems require programs that run in the background (even when no user or client is accessing the operating system) waiting to process requests such as open connections. These are the programs that are started when an operating system boots up. These programs also handle cleanup related to user or client requests, such as closing connections when the operating system is shut down. In UNIX, these programs are called *daemons*. In Windows NT these program functions are performed by Windows NT *services*.

Note: There are many vendor products covered throughout this handbook. The information about the products was gathered from different published sources, but primarily from vendor-published information including on-line Web pages. The Web addresses and other contact information is included in the description for each vendor and in Appendix. The products are being updated quickly and the product vendor should be contacted for the latest information. Most vendors also offer free evaluations that are downloadable from their Web sites.

The handbook is not intended to select one vendor over another. Migration/coexistence solutions that meet individual requirements should be chosen and an evaluation of vendor products should be performed. The inclusion of vendor information is provided to give an overview of the capabilities of the products and as a quick reference to obtain further information and software.

Following is a more detailed look at the differences between the operating systems and how those differences lead to porting problems. Coding tips that will help port applications from one environment to another or to develop applications that will execute in multiple environments are also examined.

PORTING ISSUES CAUSED BY OPERATING SYSTEM DIFFERENCES

Although NetWare has some application facilities, porting applications are a common issue when applications need to be ported between UNIX and Windows NT. The term "migration" is used instead of porting. It should also be noted that the most common form of porting between UNIX and Windows NT is from UNIX to Windows NT. This is also reflected in the number of tools available for porting from UNIX to Windows NT.

Both Windows NT and UNIX are preemptive, multitasking, demand-paged virtual-memory-supporting operating systems that have some common origins. Although they are similar at the upper levels, there are enough differences in the details to make porting applications from one to the other a challenge. One of the major differences is the APIs available for applications.

What is Porting?

Let us start with understanding "porting." Porting attempts to take current applications in one environment (e.g., UNIX) and make them run in another environment (e.g., Windows) without significant effort. There are three ways in which porting can be accomplished:

1. *Manual Porting* — One way would be to manually replace every language library call, every operating system call, and other functions such as database access or transaction processing calls with equivalent calls in the environment to be ported to.
2. *Porting Source Code using tools* — An alternative to manual porting would be to leave the calls for language libraries and operating system services etc. in the source and instead "field" the calls and convert them to equivalent calls that the ported to environment can process.
3. *Executing Object Code using Emulation Software* — This method bypasses the source altogether. The executable is run under an emulation layer that sits on top of the native (ported-to) environment

and emulates the environment in which the executable was meant to run.

Tip: *The term port (or migration) might give the impression that once porting (or migration) of an application is carried out, the source or the source environment is no longer necessary. This is true only if the application is ported manually and the calls made by the application are replaced into equivalent calls in the ported-to environment.*

Manual Porting between UNIX and Windows needs to take into account the differences between the UNIX and Windows operating environments. If the source code is ported using tools, the tools take care of most (but not all), of the environment differences.

If porting from UNIX to Windows, to make the same calls work in the Windows environment, a layer of *wrapper* code is required to field the calls. This wrapper code allows the application to continue to make the calls as it did before, fields the calls, and performs the intended function of the calls using the operating system being ported to. The reverse should happen when the results are sent from the operating system back to the calling application through the wrapper code. One way of providing the wrapper code is through a separate library that is link edited with the program, as shown in Exhibit 2.

Both methods have some advantages and disadvantages as summarized in Exhibit 3.

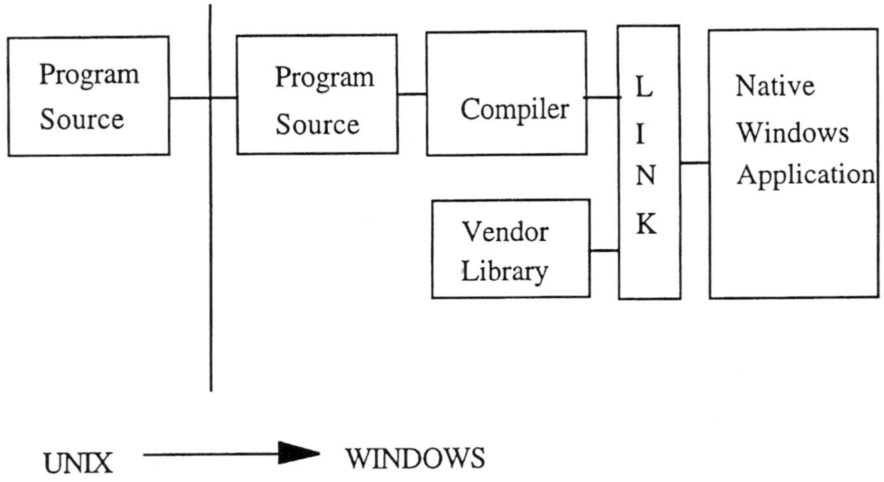

Exhibit 2. Porting from UNIX to Windows using source code porting tool.

Exhibit 3. Comparing manual porting and tool based porting.

Manual Porting	Tool based Porting
Can be costly and time consuming, particularly for porting large applications	Can be accomplished faster compared with manual porting
Once ported and tested, original source and development environments are not required	Original source is still in native environment and enhancements need to be made to it
Requires in-depth skills in both (porting from and ported to) environments	Skill requirements not as critical as in manual porting
Typically applicable to small applications	Larger applications can be ported than with manual porting since the source code is not being significantly altered

However, Windows NT, through its kernel and protected subsystems architecture, supports multiple Application Programming Interfaces (API) such as Win32, POSIX, and OS/2, while support for only one API set (POSIX) is normally found in UNIX systems. A natural question at this point is, "If Windows NT has native POSIX support, why should anyone port POSIX applications?" The answer is that the native POSIX support in Windows NT is not adequate for most applications.

Porting-tool vendors have filled in the gap for native POSIX support in Windows NT. If manual porting is chosen, the detail implementation differences between UNIX and Windows NT must be addressed. If the user has decided to port and has the skill base to do the porting, the differences can be addressed. There are also vendors to be hired to port such as Digital Equipment and Sector 7 Limited.

UNIX, WINDOWS NT DIFFERENCES

The detailed implementation level differences between UNIX and Windows NT are summarized below.

- Architectural differences
- Signal differences
- Handle differences
- Distributed computing differences
- Memory-management differences
- File system differences
- File input/output differences
- User interface differences
- Security model differences
- Network support differences
- Multiuser vs. single-user differences
- Style differences

Following is a look at each of these in some detail.

Architectural Differences

There are some basic differences between the architectures of UNIX and Windows NT in the areas of processes, threads, signals, handles, etc.

Process Differences. Both Windows NT and UNIX allow you to create new processes. In both Windows NT and UNIX, a process has its own protected memory, resources, and priority. The procedure is called *CreateProcess* in Windows NT and *fork* in UNIX (actually it is *fork* and *exec*, but it is very common in UNIX to exec immediately following a *fork*). However, there are differences in implementation:

- When UNIX process is forked, a parent-child relationship is automatically established, unlike CreateProcess in Windows NT.
- Unlike a UNIX process, a Windows NT process does not execute. Instead, a Windows NT process has one or more executables called threads. Windows NT kernel schedules threads for execution (not the process).
- You can pass arguments to CreateProcess to control environment, file handling, security, and other attributes, unlike UNIX where the forked process inherits all attributes by default. A process created in Win32 can inherit the handles of the process that created it by setting the *bInherit* flag.
- Win32 does not support terminal process groups, which were meant to support dumb terminals. However, the applications can be bunched into groups controlled by a parent process using *create_new_process_group* flag of the *CreateProcess* API
- While Windows NT and UNIX systems assume a linear memory space addressable by 32 bits, there are differences in how processes use memory. In UNIX, programmers normally make assumptions about the layout of data in memory, particularly the order and relative locations of data, code, and stack, and sometimes exploit this information by keeping the data around beyond the life of the process to gain performance at startup. In Windows, such assumptions usually cannot be made, although *OpenProcess* can be utilized to examine and modify memory, stacks, and threads.
- A running process can be cloned together with its memory contents in UNIX, while Win32 does not directly support cloning. But threads can be used and/or data can be passed using IPC, once CreateProcess has been carried out besides using inheritance options.
- In UNIX, the procedure is *pthread_create*, while in Windows NT it is *CreateThread*. However, the concept of threads is much stronger in Windows NT. A thread has its own stack, handle, local storage, and unique numerical ID, and there are APIs to use threads, as there are for processes. Threads can signal. One of the benefits of this approach is that it permits multiple threads to execute on different processors in a

multiprocessor machine, thus having more than one portion of a program executing simultaneously. A thread can be started in a suspended state. There are differences in the way threads are implemented across UNIX systems, and thread usage in UNIX applications is not as common as it is in Windows.

- In Windows NT, when a created process terminates, all data associated with it is erased from memory. This implies that there are no zombie processes (processes in UNIX that are no longer executing but which have open handles). If data is needed from the created process, for example the exit code, steps must be taken to capture that data before the created process terminates.
- UNIX uses *setuid* to associate a user ID to a process. There is no direct equivalent in Windows NT. However, named pipes, the *ImpersonateNamedPipeClient* API, and a server program that uses the named pipe to communicate to a client to associate the security context of the client can be used. If *setuid* was being used for a daemon, a Windows NT service could be used.

Inter Process Communication

UNIX has several mechanisms for IPC such as sockets, memory mapped files, different variations of pipes, etc. Windows NT supports the above and includes message-oriented pipes as well.

Bits and Bytes Differences

Windows NT is a 32 bit operating system, while UNIX has mostly 32 bit and some 64 bit versions. The order in which the bytes are packed in a word may be different between Windows NT and some UNIX versions. The byte order difference is also called *little-endian* vs. *big-endian*. Most UNIX systems (those that are RISC based), have the most significant byte first (within a word), while Intel-based PCs have the least significant byte first. Windows NT aligns data on boundaries and so do many UNIX operating systems, but there may still be differences.

Although applications are normally shielded from these bits-and-byte differences by the operating system as well as the language compilers, minor hardware -elated porting problems might still be experienced, particularly in the presence of old code and low-level codes that attempt to take advantage of the hardware capabilities.

Signal Differences

A signal can be raised by a thread in Windows NT and is processed by the same thread, unlike UNIX. As such, signaling cannot be used for IPC as is done, at times, in UNIX, which commonly uses signals to indicate completion of asynchronous I/O. Windows NT's preferred method to signal I/O completion would be to use an event object and the OVERLAPPED I/O structure parameter for *Readfile* or *Writefile* call. The C run-time libraries included with Windows NT SDK support the signals SIGINT, SIGFPE, SIGILL, SIGBREAK, SIGABRT, SIGSEGV, and SIGTERM.

Signals are also commonly used in UNIX to handle exceptions where a programmer writes code to handle exceptions and picks a signal to indicate when the exception occurs. Windows NT provides unlimited user-defined exceptions for the programmer to handle exceptions.

Handle Differences

The use of handles is very common in the Windows environment and just about all object that gets created, such as Processes, Events, Semaphores, etc. returns a handle. The returned handle is an index to a process-specific handle table, which, among other things, has the ACL for each handle. As discussed under security, the ACL governs access. Handles are obtained when explicitly creating an object or opening a named object, when they are inherited or duplicated and can be passed between processes to let processes access resources of other processes. Windows also uses handles while accessing files, while UNIX uses file descriptors. Handles do not have a direct equivalent in UNIX.

Distributed Computing Differences

Distributed computing is still evolving, although many aspects of it are already supported. Both Windows NT and UNIX have domains, although what they stand for is different. In UNIX, a domain is how a computer is named on a TCP/IP network (this is the same as in DNS). In Windows NT, a domain is a server group sharing common security policy and user account databases running on Windows NT Servers.

Name Resolution Differences

Typically, a computer on a network is identified with both a name and an address. In TCP/IP systems, computers are identified by unique IP addresses and computer names. The mechanism for converting computer names into their corresponding IP addresses is known as name resolution.

For dynamic name resolution, it is common in UNIX to use the Domain Name Services (DNS). Windows NT includes all the resolver functionality necessary for using DNS on the Internet.

Windows NT can use the following methods for name resolution in TCP/IP networks:

- **Windows Internet Name Service (WINS)** — Provides a dynamic database for registering and querying name-to-IP address mappings in a routed network environment. When a client moves from one subnet to another, the IP address change is updated automatically in the WINS database. WINS can be used in conjunction with Dynamic Host Configuration Protocol (DHCP).

- **Domain Name Services (DNS)** — DNS uses static configuration for computer name-to-IP address mapping and allows name resolution for any computer anywhere in the network. There is a major difference between WINS and DNS. DNS mapping is static, while WINS mapping is dynamic and requires less administration. WINS is practical only for relatively small network segments.
- **A HOSTS file** — A flat file used to specify the DNS computer name and IP address mapping, comparable to /etc/hosts on UNIX.
- **An LMHOSTS file** — A flat file used to specify the NetBIOS computer name and IP address mapping. PATHWORKS for Digital UNIX (Advanced Server) supports an LMHOSTS file for wide area domain support

Domain names are resolved (mapped to IP addresses) using WINS in the Windows NT environment, while DNS is used in the UNIX environment. DNS resolves names based on static configuration, while WINS supports dynamic configuration changes.

Memory-Management Differences

UNIX applications typically use the *malloc* and *free* C library functions to allocate and free memory. You can use the same C library functions in Windows NT. Both UNIX and Windows NT use the term *heap* for unstructured memory as well. Windows NT has a richer API set for virtual-memory management. Windows NT allows you to allocate and manage multiple heaps (unlike UNIX). In Windows NT, memory need not be allocated until actually required. This is accomplished using *VirtualAlloc*, *VirtualLock*, and other virtual-memory-management APIs. The heap APIs *HeapCreate* and *HeapAlloc* allow you to allocate separate memory structures and manage multiple heaps, which leads to better performance.

The UNIX functions *bzero* and *bcopy* are not available in Windows NT. You can use the equivalent routines *memset( )* and *memcpy( )*.

Memory-Mapped Files

Memory-mapped files are a fast way to access disk data by keeping files in memory, rather on disk. This technique avoids using expensive disk input and output. Most UNIX systems support memory-mapped files using *mmap* and so does Windows NT using *CreateFileMapping* and *MapViewOfFile*. A memory-mapped file can act as shared memory between processes.

File System Differences

Windows NT supports multiple file systems, such as File Allocation Table (FAT), NT File System (NTFS), and High Performance File System

(HPFS), common in OS/2 environments. HPFS was supported up to NT 3.51. The first area of difference to check is whether the specific file system the particular UNIX application uses is supported by Windows NT in a similar manner. NTFS is the closest to file systems used in UNIX systems, such as NFS, AFS, or Veritas. Windows NT also supports Compact Disc File Systems (CDFS). As such, it can read the CD-ROMs readable by UNIX systems supporting CDFS, like Digital UNIX.

Even within the same file system, there are differences. UNIX file hierarchy typically starts with the root (/) while Windows NT supports multiple drives (such as C:, D:, etc.) and each drive has its own root. Windows NT provides some file access structures, just for compatibility, without actual support. For example, the *stat* call will return *st* structure members that do not have valid values. In this case, if a program tests for these values and makes decisions, erroneous results would occur. Such a check may need to be rewritten using *GetFileInformationByHandle*.

Tests for symbolic linked files using i-node numbers will not work properly in the Windows environment since Windows NT does not use the i-node representation. A POSIX application using the POSIX subsystem can create hard linked file references (required for compliance with the POSIX specification) and this is supported by the NTFS file system. However, this can be done only by a POSIX application, not by a Win32 application.

File access is governed by ACLs in Windows NT, while they are governed by permissions in UNIX. The ACL for a file can be set using the *CreateFile* API. Valid file access can be verified using the *AccessCheck* API.

Some special characters that may be allowed in some UNIX file systems are not allowed in Windows NT. Windows NT doesn't allow any of the characters enclosed in the following parentheses: (/,\,<,>,",:,|), and ASCII characters from 0–31. The common hierarchical separator in UNIX is / (e.g., /pub/bin) while the same in Windows NT would be \ (\pub\bin). While Windows NT is not normally case-sensitive, Windows NT will list files with their original case (using the case in which they were first created on the system).

File Input/Output Differences

While Windows NT supports standard C file I/O calls such as *fopen*, these are meant more for compatibility. Windows NT character applications use these calls for console input and output and can be ported without difficulty. Programs that use UNIX system calls (as opposed to standard C calls) may be supported in some cases. However, to use advanced file functions such as asynchronous I/O it is necessary to use the Win32 APIs such as *CreateFile*.

Standard C and Win32 calls cannot be mixed and matched. For example, *ReadFile* cannot be used to read information from a file opened with *fopen*.

UNIX uses file descriptors 0, 1, and 2 to represent standard input, standard output, and standard error.

Windows NT implements the equivalent function through handles. The *GetStdHandle* API will return the handle for standard input, output, or error. The returned handle can be compared with the predefined constants *STD_INPUT_HANDLE*, *STD_OUTPUT_HANDLE*, and *STD_ERROR_HANDLE*. The UNIX *dupcall* function can be implemented in Windows NT by using the *SetStdHandle* API, or by filling in the *StdHandles* element of the *StartupInfo* structure in the *CreateProcess* API, which redirects one of the standard handles to an existing file.

Unlike UNIX, you cannot change the flag values associated with open files. For example, in UNIX you use the *oflag* in *fcntl* to determine if the file was opened for read only or read–write and set it if need be. In Windows NT, you can get similar information from the *fdwAttrsAndFlags* parameter of *CreateFile*, but you cannot change it.

UNIX supports long file names. If you are porting a file from UNIX to a Windows system that uses the FAT file system, you may have to come up with a name in the 8-dot-3 format.

UNIX names are case-sensitive and care must be taken not to overlay files when they are ported from UNIX to Windows. For example, "Filename" and "filename" are two different files in UNIX, but cannot be two different files in the FAT file system. Even Windows NT (with NTFS) is case-aware, but not fully case-sensitive. NTFS preserves the case of the filename as it was created and display it in filename lists such as Windows NT Explorer, but ignores the case for other purposes such as searching.

UNIX files use a linefeed (LF) character for line separation, while Windows NT files use carriage return and linefeed (CRLF). Whether this is a problem depends on the type of file being ported and how the file is used after the port. If a text file is ported from UNIX to Windows NT and an attempt is made to print it, this difference could cause a problem. On the other hand, if the file is a program source file and it is compiled, then it may not be a problem. Many porting tools, including N*u*TCRACKER, automatically take care of inserting a carriage return (CR) character when required.

User-Interface Differences

User interfaces can be classified as text based or graphical depending on content. A typical example of text-based interface is the command line. Both UNIX and Windows support the command line.

Command Lines, UNIX, and Windows NT

With the popularity of the Windows graphical interface including icons, drag-and-drop, and mouse clicks, Command Line and Text in Windows NT may seem out of place, but Windows NT does provide facilities to handle Command Lines and Text.

A terminal in UNIX is a console in Windows NT. Thanks to C Standards, C run-time libraries are fairly standard across operating systems, including Windows NT. Thus, if a text application does not use UNIX-specific extensions (such as *termio*), the application should work with just recompilation. There are other instances (such as *curses*) and dumb terminal support that may require third-party add-ons to get the application to work in Windows NT. Windows NT command line options start with a slash (/) while UNIX command line options start with a hyphen (-).

Another method of dealing with text requires more work, but will provide some benefits. The method would be to use Windows graphic functions to create a window and position and display characters, for example by using *Textout*. This gives the user the appearance of a text window, but Windows will treat the text window just the same as any other window on the desktop. This means that the user can interact with the text window and perform functions like cut and paste, scrolling, resizing, etc.

It is important to remember that the supported fonts between UNIX and Windows systems are normally different.

Graphical User Interface(GUI)

Unlike text, the situation is different when it comes to graphical user interfaces. Windows has GDI and other Win32 GUI APIs and UNIX have Motif, X Windows. While the interfaces may look similar from an end-user perspective, the two are very different from a programming perspective. This is mentioned for the end-user perspective, because there are differences that may be annoying to the user who has to switch back and forth between the systems frequently.

For example, the new Windows 95 and Windows NT 4.0 have three icons in the top right hand corner to indicate minimize, maximize, and close while Motif/X Window windows normally use only two icons. This is a problem for a user who has to switch back and forth between the two window types (end-user issues are covered in detail later). There are GUI functions that are present in one environment and not the other. For example, Windows supports notebook controls and Motif does not. Besides the font differences mentioned earlier, there are also color-palette differences between Windows NT and UNIX. From a programming perspective, there are differences between Windows and X11 and some of these are summarized below.

WS_CLIPSIBLING

When the *WS_CLIPSIBLING* style is not set at window creation, painting on the window should also paint on overlapping siblings windows. However, this behavior is not configurable and not easily duplicated under X11.

Transparent Windows. In Windows, windows that don't erase their background are visually transparent (the groupbox and combobox controls are good examples). If they respond correctly to the *WM_NCHITTEST* (with *HTTRANSPARENT*), they can also be transparent to mouse events. This is a problem area when using X11 child window management.

Window Scrolling. When *ScrollWindow* is used to scroll windows containing child windows, the code scrolls the bitmap representation of whatever appears on the screen, and then internally updates the position of the child windows. With X11, after scrolling the bitmap representation on the screen, the individual child windows must be moved one by one, and the display area exposed must be repainted.

Message dispatching. X11 event dispatching is based on a model simpler than Windows and does not take into account the *WM_NCHITTEST* result or the fact that windows can be disabled. MainWin, from MainSoft, overcomes the Windows and X11 differences using what it calls "X-Ray technology." MainWin uses Microsoft NT code (under license from Microsoft), imported directly, for child windows management, thereby more accurately reproducing Windows user-interface behavior. This approach also helps reduce network load by freeing the X11 server from performing child window management.

If it becomes necessary to port GUI code from UNIX to Windows, there are four approaches:

1. Rewrite the GUI code using a GUI utility and fill in ported non-GUI code. (Of course, it can be rewritten completely from scratch too.)
2. Run the application on a UNIX client and use an X server program to connect (this is one area where the UNIX client and server terminology is the exact opposite of the standard usage for client and server).
3. Use a third-party software that will provide run-time support for fielding the Motif calls on Windows NT the application will make.
4. Maintain a common source base for different environments and conditionally compile for the different environments.

Security model differences

There are fundamental differences in the way security is implemented between Windows NT and UNIX. To Windows NT, just about everything is objects. Each object — at least at the kernel level — and files have an Access Control List (ACL) that determines who is allowed to do what with the object or file. Each access to the object or file is evaluated for security by comparing the security ID of the access requester (such as processes and threads) with the ACL.

As mentioned earlier, one of the fundamental differences between Windows NT and UNIX is the definition of a user. A user in UNIX is typically the human who logs onto a terminal that communicates with the UNIX host, while the user for Windows NT could be a client machine. One of the consequences of this difference is that Windows NT doesn't have the equivalent of the */etc/passwd* file that UNIX systems use to store user information such as hashed passwords. Even when Windows NT recognizes multiple users (such as the users of one Windows NT machine), Windows NT, unlike UNIX, doesn't provide direct access to passwords in any format. The system administrator cannot find a lost or forgotten password. Passwords can only be reset.

UNIX has a User/Group/Permission model for security. To port an application, most of the security code is likely to be significantly modified. The concept of grouping users with similar needs and administering the group as an entity is similar between UNIX and Windows NT. However, Windows NT has some group features that do not exist in UNIX. For example, in Windows NT a group can own a file, a group can be a member of another group, and several different groups can be given different permissions on the same file.

Add-on security is available for many UNIX systems such as Kerberos, which is expected to be included in a future version of Windows NT.

Network support differences

As with security, there are some fundamental differences between UNIX and Windows NT for network support. Unlike many UNIX operating systems where network support is an add-on or where the number of network protocols supported is limited, Windows NT integrates network support within the operating system and supports multiple network protocols, such as TCP/IP, Novell's IPX/SPX, NBF (derivation of NetBEUI), AppleTalk, and DLC. Many STREAMS-based transport protocol drivers should work with Windows NT with little or no change. Winsock is compatible with BSD sockets API.

However, compatible does not mean that a UNIX code will work without change. This is because Windows-specific constructs such as *WSAStartup* need to be used to initialize Windows sockets and the API returns a handle (unlike an integer in UNIX). Redirector/server subsystems are implemented in Windows NT as file system drivers and are functionally equivalent to file systems in UNIX such as Network File Systems (NFS) and Andrew File Systems (AFS). Windows NT provides transparent access to other networks through provider/redirector pairs.

For example, the add-ons Client Service for NetWare for the Windows NT Workstation and the Gateway Service for NetWare for Windows NT Server enable a computer running Windows NT to connect as a client to a NetWare network. While the Named Pipes facility is similar and is supported by UNIX and Windows NT, the code is not directly compatible.

Windows NT RPC is compatible and interoperable with other OSF DCE based RPC systems. Again, that does not mean that the code will port without change. This is because the interface definition languages are not the same and each one supports some features not supported by the other and vice versa. The routine names are also different.

For example the UNIX routine *rpc_server_use_all_protseqs* has the Windows NT equivalent *RpcServerUseAllProtseqs*. Windows NT RPC does not include naming, security, and time DCE servers. If you are using Windows NT in your DCE environment, these services must be provided by products from other vendors, such as DCE services for Windows NT from Digital. Support for ONC RPC is not built in, but is supported by third parties such as the RhaPC-d developers' toolkit from Intergraph.

"Multiuser" vs. "Single-User" Differences

Windows NT is not a multiuser operating system in the way UNIX or mainframe operating systems are. But, there are functions within Windows NT that keep track of users. On the log-on screen of Windows NT, for example, different users can log on and Windows NT will validate their user ID and password. UNIX and mainframe operating systems evolved from the era of dumb terminals and multiple users logging on simultaneously. This multiuser concept is carried forward in the rest of the operating system components as well (such as security, file access, etc.). Windows NT is designed to be a client/server operating system and users access Windows NT (server) through clients, which are intelligent devices like PCs and not dumb terminals. So, typically, there would not be multiple users logging on simultaneously to Windows NT.

There are some areas in migration/coexistence where this difference must be noticed and dealt with. Citrix Systems has licensed Windows NT source code and added multiuser support. Many companies that offer different products in the migration/coexistence market have licensed the multiuser technology from Citrix. Microsoft has also licensed Citrix multiuser technology from Citrix.

Style Differences

Besides the technical differences listed above that must be taken care of to allow porting to work, there are also some style differences that should be taken into consideration:

- It probably would be possible to type a lot more (and faster too) when using UNIX than Windows NT, where the mouse rules.
- Unlike POSIX and other UNIX APIs, the Win32 APIs are normally longer. To make the API readable, Win32 normally mixes upper and lower cases in the API name with the upper case used to indicate start of significant words. Win32 APIs also normally support more parameters than the UNIX counterparts.
- Windows NT program file sizes typically are larger than UNIX equivalents, in part due to the longer names for variables, data types, and APIs (as mentioned above).

Checklist of likely changes for porting. The above list of differences should not deter any user from porting. It is meant to help know which areas must be attended to when porting. It will also help in estimating the amount of effort required for porting. The following list identifies the areas that should be looked for when porting is planned.

- Source code changes
- Makefiles —The line *include ntwin32.mak* must be included in the makefile to set up the proper library files, processor variables, etc. Windows NT SDK has a command-line *nmake* utility, which is tailored for command-line usage (like UNIX) and includes some common UNIX options such as *-f* or */F. nmake* is different from the Windows NT makefile. Within the makefile itself, it may be necessary to change macros defining source directory paths, header and include file paths, and convert command options from UNIX to equivalent NT command options. It may be necessary to change file extensions. If a macro in a UNIX makefile expands a string to a length longer than what Windows NT command-line interpreters handle, inline files can be used as a workaround. Refer to the *nmake* on-line documentation.
- *#include* statements — Statements dealing with file names in your program code as well as makefiles

POST PORTING

So far, this chapter has examined areas that are available under both Windows NT and UNIX, and focused on the differences in implementation. Windows also has programming constructs and styles that do not have a direct equivalent in UNIX. UNIX programmers learning Windows, or involved in porting from UNIX to Windows, who want to enhance programs after porting should examine the following areas:

- Windows low-level programming
  a. Windows message loops
  b. Inter Process communication features such as shared memory
  c. Function callbacks
  d. Using Handles
  e. Clipboard interface
  f. Windows Resources
- Windows high-level programming
  a. Microsoft Foundation Classes (MFC) programming
  b. Visual Programming Tools–Visual Basic, Visual C++
  c. Graphics Device Interface (GDI)
  d. Object Linking and Embedding (OLE) and Enterprise OLE
  e. Dynamic Data Exchange (DDE)
  f. C2 (Security)
  g. Messaging API (MAPI)
  h. Open Database Connectivity (ODBC) to access databases

WINDOWS NT NATIVE POSIX SUPPORT

So far, POSIX in general has been discussed, presuming that all the POSIX required services are supported by the Operating System, in this case, Windows NT. However, there are some serious limitations of the Windows NT-native POSIX support.

Windows NT POSIX support comes in the form of a protected subsystem. Windows NT implementation of POSIX is strictly what is required in the POSIX.1 standard. The subsystem starts automatically when a POSIX application loads and remains active until shutdown. The process name is *psxss*. This is run-time support.

Windows NT has built-in support for TCP/IP commands commonly used in the UNIX environment such as *ftp*, *ping*, and *rcp* and the Windows NT Resource kit also includes support for POSIX utilities such as *vi*, *sh*, *cat*, etc. The Resource kit also includes the source for the utilities, which can also be downloaded from Microsoft at no cost. Besides the run-time support and utilities, there is SDK support for developing POSIX applications. However, quoting from "Microsoft Windows NT from a UNIX Point of View," a white paper from Microsoft, "The POSIX and OS/2 subsystems provide 'compatibility-mode' environments for their respective applications and, by definition, are not as feature-rich as the Win32 subsystem."

A more technical quote from the Windows NT resource kit: "With this release of Windows NT, POSIX applications have no direct access to any of the facilities and features of the Win32 subsystem, such as memory mapped files, networking, graphics, or dynamic data exchange."

Translated, no graphics means that the popular Windows graphical user interface is not natively available for a POSIX application and users are restricted to Console text applications; no networking means no Winsock, PPP, etc. In providing POSIX support the way it did, Microsoft ensured that Windows NT could be bid on federal and state acquisitions that mandate POSIX compliance, while ensuring that there is enough incentive for users to switch and take advantage of the other Win32 features.

TIPS FOR WRITING PORTABLE SOURCE CODE

This section contains recommendations from Bristol Technology and MainSoft Corporation. Editors: Need to get permission.

Compiler Differences

UNIX C++ compilers are usually based on the AT&T CFront 3.0 implementation, and most Windows C++ compilers are CFront 3.0 compatible. The Microsoft Visual C++ compiler is very compatible with the C++ 3.0 compilers supplied by some of the UNIX vendors. This section lists some minor differences that could be encountered.

Semicolons in Class Definitions

Visual C++ allows an extra semicolon at the end of class definitions, as in the following example:

```
DECLARE_DYNAMIC(ClassName);
```

To make this statement portable to UNIX, leave off the trailing semicolon, as follows:

```
DECLARE_DYNAMIC(ClassName)
```

Access to Base Class Private Members

Visual C++ allows derived classes to access base class private members, as in the following example:

```
class  base
{
private:
    int  some_member
}...
```

To make this code portable to UNIX, allow access to the member by making it protected in the base class, as follows:

```
class  base
{
```

```
protected:
    int  some_member
}...
```

Type Casting

Visual C++ allows type casting using function call syntax, as in the following example:

```
date.d_Day=unsigned  char  (i)
```

UNIX C++ compilers only support the C syntax for type casting, as in the following example:

```
date.d_Day=(unsigned  char)i;
```

Interchanging Types

Visual C++ allows you to interchange int and BOOL types, as in the following example:

```
BOOL  WinCalApp::ExitInstance( )
```

With UNIX C++ compilers, these are different types and the return value must match the base class return value type, as follows:

```
int  WinCalApp::ExitInstance( )
```

Variable Declarations

Visual C++ allows variable declarations in switch statement cases without requiring a new scope, as in the following example:

```
default:
//  a  real  day
int   real_day=d_CellType[cell];
Doit(real_day)
```

To make this code portable, enclose the statements in a pair of braces to explicitly define the scope of the new variable, as follows:

```
default:
{
    //  a  real  day
    int   real_day=d_CellType[cell];
    Doit(real_day)
}
```

Pragmas

MFC uses Visual C++ compiler #pragma warning (disable:4xxx) directives to eliminate warning messages during compiles. These pragmas are not portable to UNIX C++ compilers. Therefore, warnings such as the following that reference MFC include files can be ignored:

```
"afxwin.h", line 1694: warning: CStatic::Create()
    hides virtual CWnd::Create()
```

Constructor Calls

Visual C++ allows complex statements in constructor calls, as in the following example:

```
//Constructor
CRecorderRecord(RecordID rid=NullRID,
    WORD monitorID=0, long counter=0,
    CProcess &process);
```

Inline Functions

Visual C++ allows complex inline functions with multiple return points. For UNIX C++ compilers, inline functions must be rewritten to remove multiple return points, or remove the inline keyword.

New and Delete Operators

As a general rule, if you use [] when you call new, you must use [] when you call delete to make your code more portable and safe. In MFC, if the delete object is not a derived class from CObject, cast the object to a void pointer and make sure a global delete operator is called. For example:

```
struct CRowColInfo {
.
.
.
} *m_pRowInfo;
::delete [] (char *)m_pRowInfo;
```

Anonymous Unions

Visual C++ allows anonymous, or unnamed, unions, as in the following example, which you would access as struct_name.fred:

```
struct{
        union{
                char  fred[10].
                struct{
                        }jim
        }
}
```

Many UNIX C and C++ compilers do not allow anonymous unions. Instead, you must name the union, as in the following example. You would then use struct_name.tony.jim.

```
struct{
        union{
                char  fred[10].
                struct{
                        }jim
        }tony
}
```

Compiler Warnings

Programmers sometimes ignore warning messages when they appear during a compilation. They have learned that the reported problems do not affect either the performance or reliability of their code and do not take the time to isolate them. However, warnings about nonportable code, signed/unsigned mismatches, or data type conversions must be heeded during a port to a new platform. A clean compile in a Windows environment will help to eliminate tedious debugging on the UNIX target.

Using Conditional Compilation

When modifying the source code, conditional compilation should be avoided if possible. If that is not feasible, the code modifications can be written in the following way:

```
#ifdef  unix   (or  #ifdef  MAINWIN)
        /* Modified code for UNIX compilation... */
        ...  /...
#else
```

```
        /*  Original  windows  code  ...  */
        .../...
    #end
```

Pointer Calculation

Any pointer arithmetic based on an assumption of a segmented memory architecture (segment:offset) must be reviewed. When computing offsets to arrays of structures, do not create pointers by combining a computed 16-bit offset with the high-order 16 bits of an address pointer, as this type of computation depends on segment:offset encoded addresses. RISC architectures all have large linear address spaces.

Also, code that uses 16-bit pointer address-wrapping will not work in a linear address architecture and must be rewritten.

C Data Types

Exhibit 4 lists common C data types for reference, illustrating how they change when going from 16-bit to 32-bit systems.

Special note should be taken of the following:

- Integer data types such as int and unsigned int may not be portable in the application. Special attention should be paid to this issue if the Windows compilation already generates signed/unsigned or conversion warnings that have been ignored in the past. Also, because the int data type grows to 32 bits, the sign extension bit moves to bit 31. (Note that Digital UNIX is a 64-bit platform.)
- Any assumptions about the 32768 or 65536 range for an int must be reviewed.
- Loops that depend on a 16-bit int may experience problems when the int grows to 32 bits. (Note that Digital UNIX is a 64-bit platform.)
- Both NEAR and FAR pointers will be 32 bits on UNIX (64 bits on Digital UNIX) and must be managed as such. When recompiling under MainWin, qualifiers such as NEAR and FAR are defined out by the C preprocessor.
- For instance, in Windows.h, #define NEAR. As a result, all pointers will be 32-bit pointers. A code must not make the assumption that they are 2 bytes long.
- Members of a bit field may not be stored in the same order by different compilers or architectures.
- Care must be taken with char. ANSI C does not impose a rule that it always be a signed char.

Exhibit 4. C data types.

C Data Type	16-bit Platform	32-bit Platform
char	8	8
int	16	32
short	16	16
long	32	32 (64 on Alpha)
enum	16	32
float	32	32
double	64	64
long double	64	64 (80 on some machines)
bit field	16	32

C Library Differences. In most cases, there are minimal or no differences between the UNIX implementation of the C library functions and their counterparts in Windows NT, but there are some.

Some of the Windows NT C library functions are preceded with an underscore; thus the UNIX C library function strdup() needs to be replaced by _strdup() on Windows NT. Exhibit 5 shows the original UNIX C library functions and their replacements in Windows NT.

Exhibit 5. C library differences between UNIX & Windows NT.

UNIX C Library Function	Windows NT Replacement
strdup()	_strdup()
strcasecmp()	_stricmp()
stricmp()	_stricmp()
iaascii()	_isascii()

When opening a binary file for either reading or writing, it is necessary to specify the file type in the *fopen*() call; thus, the UNIX function call:

```
fd = fopen(filename, "w");
```

needs to be replaced by:

```
fd = fopen(filename, "wb");
```

The *fopen*(directory_name, "r") call returns NULL whether directory_name exists or not. In general, Windows NT treats files and directories differently.

The function *bzero*( ) is not available in Windows NT; thus the UNIX function call:

```
bzero(NamedColors, sizeof(NamedColors);
```

needs to be replaced with:

```
memset(NamedColors, '\0', sizeof(NamedColors);
```

The function *bcopy*( ) is not available in Windows NT; thus the UNIX function call:

```
bcopy (ddata, sdata, ndata);
```

needs to be replaced with:

```
memcpy (ddata, sdata, ndata);
```

Windows Data Types. Exhibit 6 lists common Windows data types for reference, illustrating how they change when going from 16-bit to 32-bit systems and how they are used in one of the porting tools that let Windows applications run on UNIX, MainWin.

Exhibit 6. Windows data types.

Windows Data Type	Windows 3.1	Windows NT	MainWin
HANDLE	16	32	32
UINT	16	32	32
BOOL	16	32	32
WORD	16	16	16
BYTE	8	8	8
DWORD	32	32	32
WPARAM	16	32	32
LPARAM	32	32	32

Review the usage of those variables that change, especially WPARAM, because it is used so often.

PC-Specific Compiler Directives. To deactivate PC-specific directives, we suggest that you use the C preprocessor. In fact, the MainWin system already removes NEAR, FAR, PASCAL, and many other directives. It is not necessary to worry about these.

MainWin header files use an #ifdef to deactivate NEAR and FAR directives on UNIX. This method can be used to deactivate other undesirable directives:

```
#ifdef unix
        #define NEAR
        #define FAR
#endif
```

Using New TYPEDEFs to Improve Portability. A Windows source code can remain the same for both 16-bit and 32-bit versions if unique typedefs are used. Using specialized typedefs when defining or casting Windows objects as well as application-specific data types and structures will make them easier to modify when porting to different platforms, especially if they are managed by a

```
#ifdef unix..

#endif construct.
```

Microsoft recommends that two new data types be defined to improve portability to 32-bit platforms:

1. It is recommended that UINT be an unsigned int, which would be 16 bits on a 16-bit machine and 32 bits on a 32-bit machine. The UINT type would be used for objects that naturally widen to 32 bits on the 32-bit target machine. MainSoft also recommends that UINT be used as the type for bitfields.
2. The WORD typedef is defined as unsigned short, fixing it at 16 bits, independent of platform architectures. The WORD type is used to specify objects that must remain 16 bits in multiple architectures. You should also try to use the typedefs defined by the Windows API as much as possible.

Redefining Standard Functions. Be careful not to redefine standard UNIX functions (such as *toupper*) because MainWin may rely on them.

Byte Ordering. Byte ordering problems can arise when a nonportable construct is used to pack two shorts into a long or other similar operation. The Microsoft macros MAKELONG, HIWORD, and LOWORD, which have appropriate definitions provided by system include files, should be used.

For example, to save a short in a byte array (this form is nonportable):

```
short VarData;

unsigned char dlist[2];

*(short *)dlist=VarData;
```

This cast/assignment assumes a specific byte order, a nonportable assumption. The statement should be rewritten as follows (portable form):

```
short VarData;

unsigned char dlist[2];

*dlist = LOBYTE (VarData);

*(dlist+1)= HIBYTE (VarData);
```

This ensures that all byte ordering in byte streams are "little endian."

String Concatenation Differences. Be careful when assuming that methods used in string concatenation on PCs will work the same on 32-bit machines. The C language does not specify that strings will be placed consecutively in memory. Often, on the UNIX side, each string is placed on a word boundary (4 bytes usually).

For example, using the *GetOpenFileName* function, the *lpstrFilter* member should point to something like the following:

```
Text Files\0*.txt\0\0
```

On the PC with the Microsoft compiler, you could get the previous pattern by using the following:

```
char pFilter[] = {"Text Files", "*.txt", ""};
```

This will not work with the UNIX version because the strings do not concatenate seamlessly. A gap is introduced because the compiler starts each string on 4-byte boundaries.

The correct way to do it is as follows:

```
char *pFilter = "Text Files\0*.txt\0";
```

Using MAKEINTRESOURCE

On UNIX, the MAKEINTRESOURCE macro flags the high-order word with a unique bit pattern to distinguish between real strings and an integer resource name. A simple cast to LPSTR, as might be done in Windows, is not enough because it does not flag the high-order word.

Structure Member Alignment. Access to data that are not aligned to proper boundaries can cause problems on most RISC platforms. Arrays of structures can suffer from the same kind of problem.

In some cases, misaligned data elements are illegal in the target architecture and will generate bus error signals. These can introduce a significant performance penalty. Therefore, all data elements should be aligned to their natural boundaries, depending on their type.

When declaring structures and accessing them in a regular way, the compiler will manage the alignment requirements for the target machine, allocating extra space in front of structure items with alignment requirements. However, if it is desired to access memory directly, using (char*) pointers cast to another data type, then the alignment requirements of the target system must be taken into account.

The technical literature of the target system should be reviewed to ascertain the proper alignments for each data type and make appropriate changes to the source code.

Example 1:

```
char    szBuffer[10];
short    nIndex;
nIndex  =  *(short*)szBuffer[1];
```

This last line would cause a problem on RISC machines because a short has to be aligned on an even address boundary. Instead use:

```
nIndex  =  MAKEWORD(szBuffer[1],szBuffer[2]);
```

Example 2:

```
struct  {
             short  nX;
             short  nY;
         }  position;
         long  xy;
         xy  =  *(long*)&position.nX
```

This last statement may cause an alignment error. Instead use:

```
xy  =  MAKELONG  (position.nX,position.nY);
```

It is very important, for example, never to directly assign a Windows POINT structure to a LONG, or vice versa.

Casts. Casts should be scrutinized carefully, especially those dealing with pointers. A comment may be added if the purpose of the cast is not obvious. If there are many casts for the same purpose, use a preprocessor macro, activated

```
with  #ifdef  unix.
```

File I/O. If sizeof(var) is used in file I/O function calls, data written to a file on a 16-bit machine may not be read correctly by a 32-bit machine.

For example:

```
f/*  write  data  to  file,  16-bit  */
write(&buf,sizeof(var),1,fp);
/*  read  data  from  file,  32-bit  */
fread(&buf,sizeof(var),1,fp);
```

If the size of the variable is different on the two machines, the code will not be portable. The source code must be examined and file I/O operations evaluated for this kind of problem. In fact, all sizeof(var)-type operations, for file I/O or not, are suspect.

To keep a binary file in the Intel DOS format but still be able to read and write them transparently under UNIX, the DDR facility provided with MainWin can be used.

Buffer Allocations. Hard-coded buffer sizes, especially for path names and environment strings, should be avoided if supporting the long path and file names found in UNIX environments is desired.

Assembly Language Routines. All assembly language routines must be eliminated or rewritten using ANSI C and the run-time library calls available under UNIX. This includes any inline assembler code within C modules, using inline assembly extensions provided by some C compiler vendors.

To solve this problem, MainWin includes two source files that implement some functionalities of the MS-DOS 21h interrupt:

```
${MWHOME}/doc/InDosCW.c
${MWHOME}/doc/InDosCW.h
```

Eliminate References to DOS ROM-BIOS or the PC/AT Hardware. References to DOS (for instance, INT 21h), the ROM-BIOS (for instance, INT 13h), or motherboard I/O ports or memory addresses must be eliminated as they are intrinsically nonportable.

Keyboard Scan Codes. Raw keyboard scan codes should be avoided in programs. Virtual key codes only should be used.

Operating System Differences. In DOS and Windows, lines in text files are terminated by a combination of a Line Feed and Carriage Return. UNIX uses just a Line Feed to denote the end of a line. Many applications depend on the Line Feed/Carriage Return combination to work properly. Some applications may have to be changed to modify code to work the same in both environments.

Another example of Carriage Return/Line Feed incompatibilities is Edit Controls. The text retrieved from an edit control will not have the Line Feed/Carriage Return, only the UNIX style Line Feed.

Another major difference between Windows files and UNIX files is that UNIX uses the forward slash (/) as a directory separator, while Windows uses backslash (\) characters. UNIX file names are also case sensitive and much larger (256 characters) than Windows file names. Some applications handle these differences.

UNIX also does not have any concept of drive letters. Applications should not depend on a:\filename style file names.

To avoid differences between fonts, controls, and focus highlights between Windows and Motif dialog boxes, Wind/U uses the same ratios as Windows. To minimize problems when porting dialogs, follow these guidelines:

- Avoid using Layout->Size to Content. The control must always be created about 20 percent wider than produced by Size to Content, to ensure that the strings fit cleanly inside the controls with the X fonts, which are slightly different from Windows default fonts.
- Controls must always be kept about 12 dialog units from the dialog edges. Bristol Technology's App Studio (part of Wind/U) partially enforces this guideline, because it does not allow a control to be placed closer than 10 dialog units to the edge.
- Always leave about 10 dialog units between controls.

Architecture Differences

Certain architectural differences between UNIX and Windows warrant discussion, as they may impact certain types of applications.

Storage Order and Alignment. Wind/U runs on a variety of architectures, so it is important that a code be made as portable as possible.

As a general rule, the fields of a structure should always be used, instead of assumptions being made about their location or size in the structure.

Shared Memory Model. As with Windows NT, all instance data in UNIX is private to the application and cannot be accessed from other modules (for example, *GetInstanceData* is not supported).

Application Message Queues. Like Windows NT, each Wind/U application has its own message queue that is inaccessible to other applications. A module instance handle is unique only to the modules that compose the application. Other applications executing on the system may have the same instance handle. Likewise, each application contains its own handle table, so handles are not system unique. For these reasons, interapplication message passing is currently unsupported by Wind/U. However, Wind/U supports interapplication message passing via DDEML.

Preemptive Multitasking. In some instances, the UNIX preemptive multitasking scheduler may require files to be locked (for example, to prevent race conditions between different applications that access common files). An application ported by Wind/U must not assume that it has indefinite control of the CPU until it returns to the message loop (for example, *GetMessage*, *WaitMessage*, Yield). The application may be time-sliced at any time.

Debugging Tools. In addition to MainWin and Wind/U debugging tools, third-party tools can also be used to help in debugging a UNIX application. For example, a tool for identifying memory leaks in an application is Purify from Pure Software Corporation. Wind/U has been tested thoroughly with Purify, using many sample programs. Although Purify may still report some problems, Wind/U is relatively free of significant memory-access errors or memory leaks. If Purify is used with an application, the following should be kept in mind:

- Most C library implementations of malloc( ) under UNIX never return memory to the operating system. Thus, the amount of memory used by the program as shown by utilities such as *ps* will never shrink. An increasing amount of memory consumption as shown by *ps* does not in and of itself indicate a memory leak.
- Use Purify's Memory In Use (MIU) reporting with care.
- The X, Xt, and Motif libraries on some systems generate a number of Purify warnings. If some or all of these messages should be repressed; the Purify documentation should be consulted for details. Another third-party tool is XRunner from Mercury Interactive Corporation. Mercury Interactive's WinRunner and Xrunner products are automated testing tools that can be used without any changes to the application. WinRunner can be used to test the Windows version of the application and XRunner to test the UNIX version. To use XRunner, it must be included in the LD_LIBRARY_PATH, SHLIB_PATH, or LIBPATH environment variable.

Other Debugging Hints. Here are a few other hints that will help identify problems unique to the UNIX version of an application.

- Both the Windows and UNIX versions of an application must compile cleanly with the strictest warning level set.
- A small sample should be used to isolate problems quickly.
- Configuration should be varied. For example, if the OpenLook Window Manager is running, does the problem also occur with the Motif Window Manager? DISPLAY should be set to a different server to see if that server has the same problem (this is particularly helpful for X errors).

Error Handling

UNIX system functions relay errors in a global variable, *errno*. Applications usually test to see if a function has completed successfully. If not, they get the error from *errno*, and use the *strerror*( ) function to translate the number into a text message. The *errno* variable is unique for each process, but in a multithreaded environment like Windows NT, this solution is not adequate.

Win32 provides the *GetLastError*( ) API, which provides a reliable way for a thread in a multithreaded process to obtain per-thread error information. The *FormatMessage*( ) API should be used to turn this value into a character string, as shown in the following code example:

```
ErrMsgLen = FormatMessage
    (FORMAT_MESSAGE_ALLOCATE_BUFFER |
FORMAT_MESSAGE_FROM_SYSTEM, NULL, GetLastError( ),
    MAKELANGID
(LANG_ENGLISH, SUBLANG_ENGLISH_US),
    (LPTSTR)&lpvMessage, 0, NULL);
WriteFile(hStderr, lpvMessage, ErrMsgLen,
    &n_write, NULL);
```

Microsoft SDK online help is useful for the prototypes and more information.

Cross Compiler Support

If portable applications are being developed, cross-compilation support provided by some vendors may be useful. Digital has planned a number of tools that will allow applications to be developed on Windows NT and deployed on Digital UNIX. Digital's C and C++ compilers for UNIX and OpenVMS include a compiler option to enforce Microsoft's syntax (even though the resulting executable will run on Digital UNIX or OpenVMS). This facilitates future porting of these applications to Windows platforms as well as using the same source code to generate applications for different platforms. The Java Development Kit (JDK) for DIGITAL UNIX allows programmers to develop applications on UNIX that will run seamlessly on Windows NT.

Chapter 6
Porting Applications between Heterogeneous Environments/Rewriting Applications

Raj Rajagopal

An organization must examine its current portfolio of applications to determine whether each application should be left as is, ported to another environment, or rewritten. This decision depends on a variety of factors such as expected useful life of the current application, size of the application, existing skill base of developers and system administrators, familiarity of users with their user interface, etc. These factors are covered later in the handbook. This chapter will address porting applications to another operating environment and rewriting applications. Porting can be done either manually or using a tool. Manual porting was covered earlier in the handbook. We will discuss tool based porting in this chapter. To make an application from one environment work in another environment, either the source can be ported or the required environment can be emulated at run time. This chapter deals with porting using source code. Emulation is covered later in the handbook.

PORTING CONSIDERATIONS

To port or rewrite one or more applications to another environment, some business and technical considerations need to addressed. Porting considerations are addressed in this section. Rewriting applications is addressed later in this chapter.

0-8493-9989-0/99/$0.00+$.50

Business Porting Considerations

Some business benefits that can be derived by porting:

- The biggest benefit of porting is that it permits a stepping-stone approach to a potentially complex transition.
- Porting permits system administrators and their custom utilities to immediately transition and be productive in the new environment.
- Porting permits continued use of development and maintenance skills during transition to the new environment.
- Depending on which applications are available, it may be possible to get them working in the new environment with little effort.
- End users can start using existing applications in the new environment without having to relearn the applications.
- Unique features available in the new environment can be utilized as a post porting step, but this may introduce divergence in the source between the sources in the old and new environments.

The business application might have been developed from scratch, purchased as a package, or purchased as a package and modified to fit a specific environment. If the application package was purchased, its vendor should be contacted to see if a version that runs in the particular environment is available. The vendor may also offer porting assistance, in particular for the custom modifications desired. An in-house application would be an appropriate porting candidate under the following conditions:

- The application has a long expected life.
- The current development and maintenance programmer skill base dealing with the application would require a big learning curve for a new environment.
- The benefits of making the application work in the new environment outweigh leaving the application as is or rewriting it.
- The application size is large enough to gain some benefits when ported, but not so large as to make porting a long, error-prone, and risky process

If managers are wondering how serious a porting problem they might have, they should check their codes against the following list of things that makes it easy to port:

- Codes in which end-user interface handling and business logic handling are isolated.
- Codes in which vendor extensions to standards are isolated.
- Codes in which dependencies on a specific operating system are isolated (particularly true for UNIX with its many flavors).
- Overall program flow is separated into logical, modular blocks.

The more a code satisfies the above points, the better. However, regardless of how good a code is, some code changes are to be expected. Time and resources for making source code changes must be available when porting to another environment.

Sometimes it may be possible to port and make the application work in a limited fashion in the new environment, but to take full advantage of the new environment, the code may need to be modified. For example, in a situation such as a UNIX program performing file access that is being ported to Windows NT, if the program uses standard C functions such as *fopen*, the program will still work when ported to Windows NT, but it may be unable to take advantage of advanced features like asynchronous I/O unless the *fopen* is replaced by an equivalent Win32 API call.

Technical Porting Considerations

Besides the application code itself, a few other items need to be addressed when an application is ported:

- Any shell scripts used by the application either during development or execution need to be ported or rewritten.
- UNIX has built-in commands used in application development. If tools are used to port a code, tool vendors provide most of the commands on Windows NT. If the code is being manually ported, the equivalent tools must be written or obtained, the Windows NT equivalent of the tools' function must be found.
- UNIX uses a number of utilities for application development as well as System Administration. Equivalent utilities in the new environment must be used or the utilities need to be ported or rewritten. Many porting-tool vendors include UNIX utilities equivalents with their products. These are covered with the tools later in this chapter. There are also some public-domain utilities. Most of these are available from public FTP sites such as ftp.iastate.edu, ftp.cica.indiana.edu, sunsite.unc.edu, and ftp.uu.net. Such tools include *ci, ident, perl, rcsdiff, tic, co, lex, rcs, rcsmerge, yacc, cprge, rcsclean*, and *rlog*.
- Any available documentation such as help files and online manuals that may need to be ported.
- Testing scripts that may have been set up to perform automated and other testing will also need to be ported.
- Daemons and other standalone utilities that perform some applications functions in the background must be ported.
- UNIX shared libraries used by programs must be ported.
- Web-related unique application code using languages such as PERL must be ported.

Exhibit 1. Equivalent program types between Windows NT and UNIX.

UNIX Program Type	Windows NT Program Type
C and C++ programs	C and C++ programs
Shared Libraries	Dynamic Linked Libraries (DLLs)
Daemons	Windows NT services
Fortran programs	Fortran programs
Scripts – Shell, login, etc.	Scripts (scripting languages not compatible)
X Windows/Motif programs	Windows GUI programs
UNIX configuration files and programs	Windows NT Registry edit program and APIs
POSIX and other APIs	Win32 APIs

Exhibit 1 summarizes some common types of UNIX programs and the equivalent type in Windows NT.

Let us look at the steps involved in porting application source.

Porting Steps

The following steps are involved in porting an application:

- Copy the source code from the UNIX machine to the Windows NT machine (or in some cases Windows 95). There are a number of different ways to transfer the source and accessory files and these ways are covered later in this chapter.
- Copy compiling accessories to the source such as makefiles, resource files, and scripts.
- Make any changes required to the accessory files. Makefile changes may required. Porting Scripts is discussed later in this chapter.
- Windows-specific code, such as Win32 calls, can be added to take advantage of functions not available in UNIX.
- Compile the ported source into object modules using the appropriate language compiler in the new environment.
- Compile required accessories such as resource files.
- Link the object modules with appropriate Windows and tool libraries.
- Test the ported application and identify problem areas in the port, if any.
- Repeat steps 3 through 8 until the ported application works satisfactorily.

These steps are just a high-level overview. Many details must be addressed at each stage. While the major steps outlined above are applicable to any porting tool, the details will vary depending on the tool selected.

Transferring files from UNIX to Windows NT

Source and accessory files can be transferred from the UNIX machine to a Windows NT machine in a number of different ways. These are listed below.

- Use floppy disks to copy.
- Use the built-in File Transfer Protocol (FTP) function in Windows to transfer files between the UNIX server and the Windows machine.
- Use built-in tftp function in Windows NT.
- Use the built-in rcp function in Windows NT.
- Use a serial link.
- Use a network operating system with built-in support to access UNIX server files.
- Use third-party Network File System (NFS) packages.

Porting C Programs

In C programs without database or transaction processing calls, it may seem that if the C program follows C coding standards, it should compile and execute easily in the other environment. This is seldom the case. There are a number of reasons beyond standards for this:

- Path names are pretty standard in the UNIX world-header files are under */sys*, binary executables are under */bin*, etc. In Windows NT the user selects most path names.
- Path names are passed as string arguments in many instances. UNIX supports only the forward slash (/), while Windows NT supports both forward and reverse slashes (except for the command prompt).
- UNIX is case sensitive, while NT is, for the most part, not case sensitive (NTFS preserves case for directory listings. Examining files in File Manager for example, will reveal the case used when the file was created.
- It is not uncommon for UNIX applications to hard code directory paths. For example, the code may be looking for a file in */usr/local/bin* presuming a standard UNIX environment. The ported code will almost certainly not be able to find the file in that path and thus fail. These paths must be identified and taken care of before the ported application would work in the new environment.
- Vendor extension to standards. Where there is a rule, there is an exception. Where there is a standard, there is a vendor extension. In most cases, it is difficult not to use the vendor extension, since the functionality of the standard by itself is limited. The "wrapper code" may provide support for the standard, but may not provide for all vendor extensions of different vendors.

Porting Scripts

Scripts are utilities written in a scripting language that are part of an application in the same manner as programs written in a language like C. Programmers and system administrators typically use scripts to automate routine, repetitive tasks. UNIX Operating Systems include a shell that supports scripts and so does the Win 32 shell. Vendors providing support for porting code provide tools to create and/or port UNIX scripts to Windows NT. These scripts can run not only the ported UNIX programs but also native Win 32 programs.

Porting Applications from UNIX to Windows

This chapter first considers tool-based porting and takes a brief look at some vendor tools. Manual porting is addressed later in this chapter.

Common Porting Products

This section presents an overview of some common porting products available. The information was gathered from different published sources including vendors' online Web pages. The Web addresses and other contact information are included in the description for each vendor and in Appendix A. The tools are being updated quickly and the tool vendor should be contacted for the latest information. Most vendors also offer free evaluations that are downloadable from their Web sites.

Note: This book is not intended to help readers select one vendor over another. They should pick migration/coexistence solutions that meet individual requirements and perform an evaluation of vendor products. The inclusion of vendor information is provided to give readers an idea of the capabilities of the products and a quick reference to get further information and software.

Common products that help in porting applications from Windows to UNIX include N*u*TCRACKER from DataFocus Software and Portage from Consensys Computers.

N*u*TCRACKER

Information on N*u*TCRACKER is available online at http://www.datafocus.com.

N*u*TCRACKER is a product family for developers who want to port their character-based and X/Motif UNIX applications to Windows NT or Windows 95.

Using N*u*TCRACKER, developers can recompile UNIX C, C++, or FORTRAN source code and link it to N*u*TCRACKER DLLs resulting in native Win32 applications. A schematic of this process is illustrated in Exhibit 2.

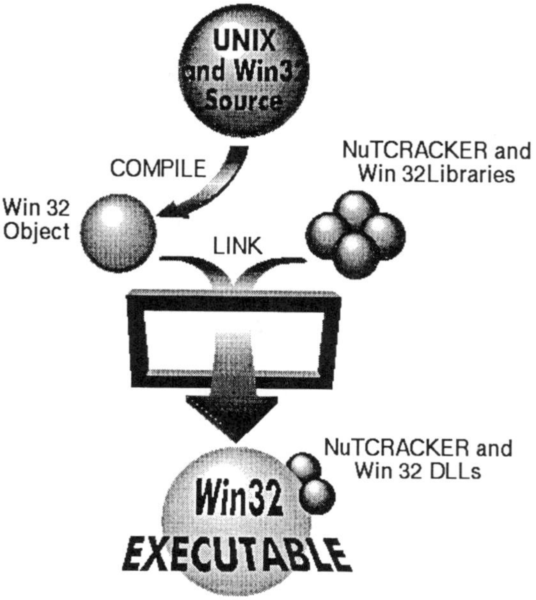

Exhibit 2. Porting an application from UNIX to Windows using N*u*TCRACKER.

N*u*TCRACKER supports Intel, Alpha, MIPS, and PowerPC platforms. So if source is available on any of those platforms, Windows NT can be obtained for that platform, along with the corresponding N*u*TCRACKER version, and the source can be ported. (IBM recently decided NOT to support Windows NT on the PowerPC.)

The N*u*TCRACKER Product Family

The N*u*TCRACKER Product Family currently consists of three products:

1. N*u*TCRACKER SDK: N*u*TCRACKER Software Development Kit (SDK) for porting character-based and daemon applications. It consists of the Application Program Interface (API) (which includes system calls and library routines) and a comprehensive set of development utilities. N*u*TCRACKER SDK contains the user-interface options, including curses and client-server-designed Win32 enhancements, for applications ported using the SDK.
2. N*u*TCRACKER: X/Software Development Kit (X/SDK) provides the porting environment needed if the application is question is designed with an X/Motif user interface. If porting with the X/SDK, N*u*TCRACKER X/Operating Environment (described below) may need to be purchased for distribution with the end-user applications. In addition to X11R5 and Motif API support to port X/Motif

applications to Win32, N*u*TCRACKER X/SDK also includes the following features for porting X Window applications to Windows NT:

- Windows NT versions of the X Window System and Motif libraries
- OSF/Motif Toolkit and widgets, including the Motif User Interface Language (UIL) compiler and Window Manager
- Motif extensions for Toolkit widget creation and manipulation routines, message routines, font routines, and convenience routines that have been added to supplement those provided by the OSF/Motif Toolkit
- Motif extensions to the Motif User Interface Language
- An X Server that allows the X application on a Windows NT computer to be tested
- A Motif replacement library, Wintif, that allows the Motif applications to be presented with a Windows "look and feel"
- The Remote Startup Service, which simulates the rexec daemon and allows X applications located on a Windows NT computer to be started from the N*u*TCRACKER X Server Control Panel

3. N*u*TCRACKER X/Operating Environment (X/OE)-provides a 32-bit X Server environment for end-user X/Motif applications and the N*u*TCRACKER DLLs necessary to run ported applications. It can also be used to run X applications performing on UNIX platforms.

UNIX functionality supported by N*u*TCRACKER

APIs. *Process Control.* N*u*TCRACKER provides a true UNIX fork with proper inheritance of resources such as handles. Processes and threads are slightly different between UNIX and Windows NT. This function lets UNIX programs with fork execute as they would in UNIX.

Shared Memory. Applications can use shared memory consistent with UNIX standards, which supports cross-platform interprocess communication and data access.

Security. N*u*TCRACKER preserves security permissions for User, Group, etc. as set up in the UNIX environment and applications.

Networking. N*u*TCRACKER provides BSD sockets to support networked applications. Sockets are handled as file descriptors, which allow the UNIX code to use other IPC mechanisms without modification. All of Windows NT's supported protocols are available to applications.

User Interfaces. The N*u*TCRACKER SDK API library includes integrated support for curses user interfaces, while the N*u*TCRACKER X/SDK provides integrated support for X/Motif APIs in the xlib, xt, and other libraries.

Windows NT and Motif end-user interfaces are similar. While the interfaces look similar from an end-user perspective, similar is not same and the differences may be annoying to the user who has to switch back and forth between the systems often. To overcome this problem, N*u*TCRACKER provides the Wintif technology, which lets Motif applications be displayed with a Windows look and feel. Note that Wintif is optional and the Motif interface is supported as well, for users who prefer it.

Environment and Utilities

User Environment. As in UNIX, the user environment is fully managed through environment variables that can be set on either a permanent or temporary basis.

Build Environment. The build environment is set up as it is in UNIX with UNIX *make* environment variables. With N*u*TCRACKER, it is also possible to convert to *nmake* and Windows NT's *make* if so desired.

Utilities. A comprehensive set of UNIX commands and utilities (over 140 in all) exists and this maintains productivity in the Windows NT environment. The commands and utilities provided address broad areas such as text manipulation, record keeping, the program execution environment, editing, and arithmetic operations.

An exhaustive list of the APIs and Utilities can be found in *NuTCRACKER Installation and Porting Guide*, a 200+ page document, available through the DataFocus Web page http://www.datafocus.com. The N*u*TCRACKER X/SDK includes X and Motif APIs in the xlib, xt, and other libraries.

N*u*TCRACKER includes utilities that are part of the MKS Toolkit, which is covered later in the handbook. Besides the MKS Toolkit utilities, N*u*TCRACKER includes other utilities such as *chmod, whoami, process, sdiff,* etc.

Portage

Information on Portage is available online at http://www.consensys.com.

Portage is an integration of UNIX SVR4 with Windows NT, including more than 125 standard UNIX utilities. It has a base and an SDK. There are four main functions provided by the Portage Base System, which allows users to:

1. Use Portage UNIX utilities from the NT Command Prompt.
2. Use one of the Portage UNIX shells (ksh or csh) instead of the NT command prompt.
3. Use the Portage Windows Interface to manage UNIX shells.
4. Access the Portage online manual pages as Windows Help.

The main components of the Portage SDK are:

- Thirty software development utilities, including *ar, cc, ld, yacc, lex, make* and *SCCS*
- More than 700 system calls and subroutines

Besides the Portage SDK, the Windows NT environment and C/C++ compilation tools are necessary to port applications.

Portage makes UNIX an integral part of Windows NT sharing the same hardware. Portage utilities can operate on files and directories created by Windows NT programs, and Windows NT programs can operate on files and directories created by Portage utilities. The Portage shells *ksh* and *csh* can run Windows NT programs, and the Windows NT Command Prompt can run UNIX programs.

Developers can use the Microsoft Windows NT compilers and debuggers directly to develop UNIX programs, or use the standard UNIX *ar, cc, ld* and *make* commands included in the Portage SDK. The Portage SDK also enables developers to create hybrid UNIX/Windows NT programs that combine the UNIX API with the Win32 API. Windows NT stores environment variables in the Registry. The Windows NT environment is read by the Portage Kernel when it starts up, and is imported into all Portage programs when they start up.

Portage Base

Portage Base supports the Windows command prompt and provides UNIX command prompt functions.

NT Command Prompt

All Portage utilities can be run from the NT Command Prompt or Console. Since the Command Prompt passes command line arguments unchanged to programs (unlike UNIX shells, which perform wild-card expansion and much more), Portage programs are able to provide an overlapping set of UNIX-like and DOS-like syntax. In particular, from the NT Command Prompt, path names can use either UNIX style / or Windows style \ notation. Supported functions include

- Pattern matching is UNIX style, including '*', '?', single quotes and double quotes.
- The Portage environment variables (UNIXROOT, UNIXTMP, SYMLINKS, and CASENAMES) are in effect.

Of course, shell-specific features like $X for environment variables and backquotes for sub-shells are not available from the Command Prompt.

An example of a valid Command Prompt command line is *ls -lrt /bin/b**.

There are several name conflicts between NT commands and Portage UNIX utilities. The echo command is built into the Command Prompt (as it is in UNIX shells), so it will always use the NT syntax. Other commands like *more* and *mkdir* are not built in, so whichever one is found first by following the PATH environment variable will appear.

When Portage is installed, the bin directory is added to the end of the PATH, so by default the NT version of these utilities will be accessed. The PATH environment variable can be changed, but that may break existing batch and other Windows NT functions using the Path. The simplest solution is to use one of the UNIX shells, where $PORTAGE/bin is added to the front of the PATH environment variable by default.

The UNIX Shells

Portage provides both the Korn Shell (*ksh*) and the C Shell (*csh*). Both of these shells run in the console. This means that a very large buffer size, say 200 lines or more, can be set, and that much interactive history can be kept available for browsing. A *ksh* or *csh* can be launched from icons in the Portage program group. *ksh* or *csh* can simply be typed at an NT command prompt. To run multiple shells, (maximum of 20 can be active at any one time), the preferred method is probably to use the Portage Windows Interface to start them.

Once *ksh* or *csh* is running, a UNIX environment has been entered. The shell window provides an emulation of a VT100 terminal (a VT100 subset), and the *term* environment variable will be set to VT100. The window also provides a limited tty line discipline, and *stty*(1) can be used to view the options in effect or to change a subset of them.

In general, it should be unable to tell the difference between the behavior under one of the Portage UNIX shells and a native SVR4 implementation. A list of the few known differences is provided in the Portage documentation.

If graphical user interfaces are preferred, Portage includes the Portage Windows Interface, which serves a number of important functions:

- It allows easy start up and management of multiple UNIX shells.
- It customization of the default settings of shell windows (e.g. size, colors, etc.).
- It provides a dialog box interface to all Portage UNIX commands.
- It provides easy access to online manual pages for every command.

The Portage Windows Interface can be started up by clicking on its icon in the Portage program group. The program's main feature is a set of 140 buttons providing dialog-box access to UNIX utilities. The Portage SDK has an even larger set of buttons (170) than the Base System. Screen shots are available at http://www.consensys.com.

Portage SDK

The Portage SDK includes utilities, system routines, etc.

Portage SDK Utilities. The Portage SDK provides all of the software development tools from standard SVR4 except the basic C/C++ compilation system (compiler, linker, archiver and debugger). In order to compile and link programs for Portage on Windows NT, Microsoft Visual C++ must be installed.

Portage does include SVR4-compatible versions of *ar*, *cc*, and *ld*, which call the relevant Microsoft utilities to perform the actual work. This means that existing UNIX makefiles can be used with only minor changes.

When compiling and linking existing UNIX SVR4 programs with the Portage SDK, either the Portage *make* command or the Microsoft *nmake* command can be used. Using *nmake* may require more effort than Portage *make*. Portage includes standard makefile templates for both *make* and *nmake* that can be included at the beginning of the new makefiles. Examples and sample programs are available online at http://www.consensys.com.

Terminal-oriented programs linked with the Portage SDK display their output in a console window within the Win32 subsystem (the same as the NT Command Prompt, and all Portage utilities). The Portage console window provides a (partial) emulation of a VT100 terminal to support full screen functionality, and the Portage SDK includes the complete curses library.

System Calls and Subroutines. The Portage SDK subroutines are supplied in a set of libraries that comes with the Portage product. Individual subroutines can be found in the same libraries as on native UNIX (for example, the math routines are in *libm.lib*). The standard SVR4 libraries provided are *libc.lib*, *libcmd.lib*, *libcurses.lib*, *libgen.lib*, *libgenIO.lib*, *libm.lib*, and *libw.lib*.

There are two cases where Portage does not implement UNIX features so that they are accessible by non-Portage programs — symbolic links and case-sensitive file names. Portage has implemented both of these features in a file system-independent manner, but non-Portage Windows NT programs cannot follow symbolic links, nor create two filenames that differ only in case (e.g. makefile and Makefile). In both instances, Portage provides environment variables (SYMLINKS and CASENAMES) that allow each user to decide whether to enable or disable the feature.

Sometimes, Windows NT has greater functionality than UNIX. In those cases, Portage has enhanced the UNIX subroutines and utilities to take advantage of the extended capabilities while maintaining complete backwards compatibility with UNIX SVR4. For example, Portage has extended the *chmod* and *ls* utilities and the related subroutine calls to allow users to view and modify a larger subset of the extended NT file permissions than the standard UNIX read, write, and execute.

There are some differences between Portage and native UNIX SVR4 and they are listed with the Portage documentation. The only significant UNIX SVR4 programs not provided in this release of Portage are the *uucp* family of utilities.

There are a handful of cases where Portage includes new subroutines to implement specific tasks that either must be done differently on Portage than on UNIX, or can be done more efficiently by a different method on Portage than on UNIX.

OpenNT

Information on OpenNT is available online at http://www.softway.com/OpenNT/.

A schematic of OpenNT Architecture is illustrated in Exhibit 3.

OpenNT is based on a virtual sub-system design allowing for the hosting of a true conforming UNIX environment. By using the POSIX.1 sub-system built into Windows NT, users are given a secure environment that supports many of the features required by POSIX and UNIX systems. Some of the supported features include:

- proper case sensitive file names within the NT file system (for example, files Report and report can coexist in the same directory)
- file links are supported (i.e. one file can have multiple names)
- background processing and job control via the OpenNT shell
- full control over file user ownership, group ownership and access modes
- ability to run both UNIX/POSIX and Windows applications from the OpenNT shell

Softway Systems is committed to providing complete user and developer products for Microsoft Windows NT that conform to IEEE POSIX and X/Open specifications. As a demonstration, Softway Systems products will maintain the appropriate National Institute of Standards (NIST) certifications for FIPS 151-2 (POSIX.1) and FIPS 189 (POSIX.2) and the appropriate X/Open brands in future releases.

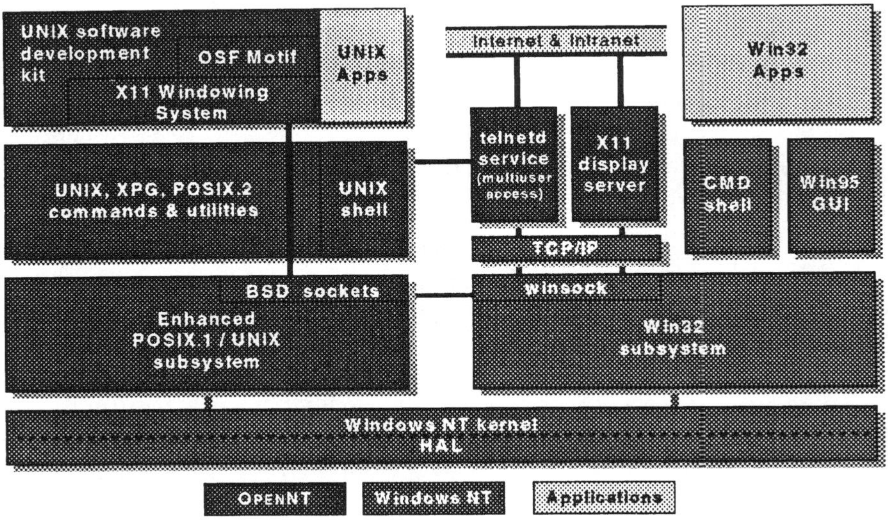

Exhibit 3. OpenNT architecture schematic.

The OpenNT Product Family

The OpenNT product family includes the following products:

- OpenNT Commands and Utilities
- OpenNT Software Development Kit
- OpenNT X11 Server
- OpenNT Telnet Server

OpenNT Commands and Utilities. OpenNT Commands and Utilities is a set of utilities that provide functions similar to the UNIX utilities, and a POSIX command shell for Windows NT. The product provides conformance to the IEEE POSIX.2 Execution Environment Utilities standard as defined in FIPS 189 (FIPS 189 is the Federal Information Processing Standard required by many federal government agencies and departments for operating system procurements).

OpenNT also adds a new POSIX.1 sub-system (which is meant as a replacement POSIX.1 sub-system for older Windows NT systems) with increased functionality to provide seamless integration of the POSIX environment with the other components of Windows NT. Additional UNIX utilities supported include *vi, more, uuencode*, etc.

OpenNT Software Development Kit. OpenNT Software Development Kit is a development system for porting and developing POSIX and UNIX applications on Windows NT. In combination with the OpenNT Command and

Utilities product mentioned above, this development environment includes the tools necessary for providing a development platform to develop and run UNIX applications. Applications built with the OpenNT environment run as native 32-bit Windows NT applications.

Third-party compilers and tools (for example, Microsoft Visual C/C++, GNU tools) can be used within the development system. Utilities such as *lex, yacc, make*, and *rcs* are included as standard components in the product.

OpenNT X11 Server. The OpenNT X11 server for Windows NT (and Windows 95) is a PC X Display Server. The OpenNT X11 server supports bi-directional copy-and-paste of text and graphics between X clients and Windows NT/Windows 95 applications. From the same desktop, users can run:

- Win16 (Windows 3.1) applications
- Win32 (Windows 95 and Windows NT) applications
- POSIX and UNIX text-based applications via the OpenNT shell
- X11/Motif applications running natively on Windows NT via the OpenNT X11
- Windowing System and OpenNT Motif (check with the vendor on the timing for the availability of Motif support)
- Remote network-based X Windows and Motif applications

UNIX window managers supported by the OpenNT server include Motif, OpenLook, VUE, and CDE. The OpenNT server also supports XDMCP security through X authority. A full set of X11R6 fonts is provided with automatic font substitution and a choice of full-screen single-window mode or multiple-window mode.

OpenNT Telnet Server. The OpenNT Telnet Server is a telnet daemon service for Windows NT. Telnet users get full access to the Windows NT Common Command Shell or the OpenNT POSIX/UNIX shell. Multiple users can access one Windows NT server and simultaneously run a variety of Win32, DOS, OS/2, and POSIX character-based applications.

OpenNT Telnet Server provides a set of configuration options to the Windows NT system administrator, allowing user access and permissions to be defined for individual users and groups of users. OpenNT Telnet Server allows the Windows NT administrator to specify that a user or group of users be dropped directly into a custom application rather than a command line. Windows NT's security features are maintained.

The telnet daemon allows access by telnet clients on any system connected to a TCP/IP network. Clients can be UNIX systems, Macintosh, Windows, DOS or network terminals connected to the local area network. Dumb terminals connected to a terminal server on the network can also log into the system. Clients can even access the shell from remote sites over the Internet.

The product allows telnet users to log on to the Windows NT server without interfering with the Windows NT console user or file server users.

OpenNT Telnet Server provides ANSI/VT100 terminal emulation to the network client that logs into the system. Certain keystroke sequences map to special PC function keys and can be passed through by terminal emulators and interpreted by applications. This feature allows users to make use of function keys, arrow keys and ALT key combinations in PC programs while logged into the system. Full screen applications can be run and support is provided for character attributes, color, and line drawing characters.

The product supports the connection of multiple dumb terminals when used with a network terminal server. With OpenNT Telnet Server users can access the server to perform text mode command-line operations and run any character-based application.

OpenNT Telnet Server can drop a user directly into a custom application or shell after logging in. This allows users on dedicated terminals to see only their application, shielding them from the computer system or a shell.

When the user exits the program, the telnet client is disconnected from OpenNT Telnet Server. A feature of OpenNT Telnet Server is its integration with the rest of the OpenNT environment. Users can select the OpenNT UNIX shell as their default shell and log in directly to an environment that is consistent with today's UNIX operating systems.

OpenNT Telnet Server uses the security features of Windows NT. OpenNT Telnet Server abides by access restrictions imposed by the server. Individual users run in their own appropriate security context, with all their own permissions in place, just as if they had logged in from the console. OpenNT Telnet Server preserves all of the C2 security features that come with Windows NT.

OpenNT Telnet Server features a graphical user interface application for administration and setup. The system administrator can control:

- User access and permissions
- Maintaining a log of all events and user activities
- Starting, stopping and pausing the telnet service
- Terminal emulation features and color control
- User shell options and default directory
- Time slice and priority administration
- Program licensing and registration

eXcursion

The following is a brief summary of eXcursion from Digital. Information on eXcursion is available online at http://www.digital.com.

The eXcursion Software Developer's Kit from Digital contains the libraries and headers necessary to port Motif and X applications from the UNIX operating system to Windows NT. The eXcursion SDK includes X Window System and Motif libraries for Windows NT, Motif Toolkit and widgets, the Motif User Interface Language (UIL) compiler and Motif Window Manager (MWM), DECwindows Motif extensions, example X and Motif applications for Windows NT, a platform-independent imake utility, and the eXcursion X server.

The eXcursion Software Developer's Kit supports Microsoft's Visual C++, and can operate with Microsoft's TCP/IP (included with Windows NT) and DECnet (included with PATHWORKS for Windows NT).

eXceed XDK

Hummingbird's X Development Kits incorporate all of the X Window System standard libraries and toolkits that are required to develop X applications on the PC, which include Xlib, Xt intrinsics, Xaw and Xmu.

Also available are the OSF/Motif and UIL compilers, in addition to sample source and sample applications.

PC X server software provides users with a full X Window System implementation typically found on workstations. Available for the Windows, Windows 95, Windows NT (Intel and Alpha), and OS/2 platforms, the Hummingbird eXceed X Development Kits (XDKs) give today's PCs powerful workstationlike functionality by transforming them into a client-host and server, all at the same time.

Local X support permits X clients to be started and displayed locally or remotely on other X servers in the network. Local X support also permits local X clients to run on stand-alone PCs with no network support.

Hummingbird's eXceed 3D for Windows NT includes additional libraries for developing OpenGL X applications on PCs.

PORTING APPLICATIONS FROM WINDOWS TO UNIX

The previous section examined porting applications from UNIX to Windows. This section looks at porting in the opposite direction. It will examine applications written for the Windows environment and look at tools that let the application execute in the UNIX environment.

Windows applications can be run on UNIX in three ways:

In one way (which is actually a rewrite and not a port), some vendors saw a market opportunity in providing Windows lookalike native UNIX applications for popular office products. The idea was that customers need not buy any Windows operating environments or software, but could still use office applications using the familiar Windows graphical interface on the same desktop with production UNIX applications. Applications ported in this manner have generally not been very successful, such as Quorum's ports of Microsoft Word and Excel.

A second way is to port the source manually. With this method, care must be taken of the operating system differences between Windows NT and UNIX. Programming language differences such as C language differences must also be seen to. In addition, if there are old Windows sources written for the 16-bit world, the following must be addressed:

- Direct hardware calls or access to memory space (that would not normally be allowed in 32-bit applications)
- Near and Far pointers
- Compiler options specific to 16 bits such as NEAR or PASCAL

A third way would be to provide tools that assume the role of Windows in UNIX systems. These tools would provide the function calls, messages, device contexts, and controls on top of the UNIX operating system that Windows provides for application programs executing in the Windows environment. Besides providing support for the Operating System functions, the tools also provide support in the UNIX environment for Windows-unique features such as OLE, MFC, etc.

Common Porting Products

Some of the tools that help in porting from Windows to UNIX include Wind\U from Bristol Technology, MainWin Studio from MainSoft, and the Willows Toolkit from Willows Software.

Wind/U

Information on Wind/U is available online at http://www.bristol.com.

Wind/U is an implementation of the Microsoft Windows API under UNIX. Wind/U leverages Microsoft Windows source code, licensed to Bristol Technology as part of the Microsoft WISE program. WISE is covered later in the handbook. Wind/U supports Win32 with Microsoft Foundation Classes (MFC). Exhibit 4 shows where Wind/U fits in when applications using Visual C++ and MFC are developed in the Microsoft environment and they are to be run in the UNIX environment. The Visual C++ and/or MFC application runs on Windows NT and Windows 95 by using the Win32 and MFC libraries. The same applications can also run on UNIX machines such as those from SUN, HP, and DEC using Wind/U libraries.

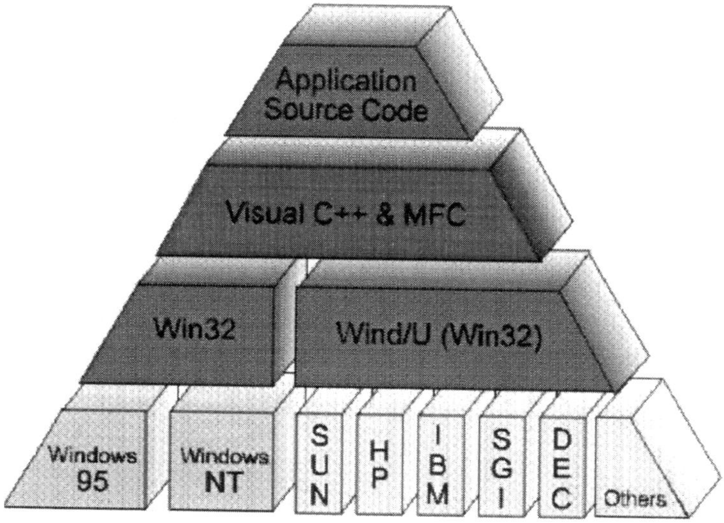

Exhibit 4. Using Wind/U to run Windows applications in UNIX.

The following advanced Windows features are supported to make Windows applications using them portable to UNIX:

- GUI features such as Multiple Document Interface (MDI), combo boxes, Common Dialogs, Common Controls, Palettes, and Graphical Device Interface (GDI) including logical coordinate mapping
- Architectural APIs for Dynamically Linked Libraries (DLLs)
- Dynamic Data Exchange Management Library (DDEML)
- Object Linking and Embedding (OLE)
- Windows Sockets
- Kernel Layer APIs for all non-GUI APIs in the Windows environment, including file I/O, memory management, memory-mapped files, etc.
- Advanced printing capabilities through Bristol's Xprinter
- PostScript and PCL Language Library. Together, Xprinter and the GDI layer provide transparent access to the display and PostScript and PCL printers.
- Online help through Bristol's Microsoft Windows-compatible help subsystem, HyperHelp. HyperHelp allows use of the same rich-text format (RTF) source files from a Windows version to create an equivalent help system in the UNIX or environment.

All of these features are provided as libraries that an application is linked to after recompilation in the native UNIX environment. The result is a truly native application that maintains identical functionality with the Windows version.

The toolkit also includes several tools for the programmer:

- Wind/U Wizard — automatically verifies installation, checks the environment setup, and contacts Bristol support via e-mail
- Wind/U Documentation Online — provides the complete content of Wind/U printed documentation in a cross-referenced, browsable format
- make_windumakefile — scans the original Windows source code to create an appropriate make file for the UNIX environment
- prepare_source — scans the original Windows source to automatically replace DOS format characters (end-of-line, etc.) with equivalent UNIX or OpenVMS characters
- resource compiler — a ported version of the Microsoft resource compiler that accepts Windows resources as input
- regedit — a ported version of the Microsoft Registry Editor that enables the setting in the system registry to be changed
- dllink — creates a dynamic link library from a set of objects and a definition file
- windu_clientd — a color management daemon that enables sharing of Wind/U color resources across Wind/U applications
- windu_registryd — manages communication between applications and the Wind/U registry
- windu_scmd — manages interaction between OLE processes and the Wind/U registry

Wind/U is currently available for the following platforms — HP 900 Series 700 and 800, Sun SPARC (SunOS and Solaris), IBM RS/6000, Silicon Graphics, Digital UNIX, and Digital OpenVMS.

MainWin Studio

Information on MainWin is available online from Mainsoft at http://www.mainsoft.com.

MainWin Studio is a complete set of development components that enable a software developer to port an application written to the Microsoft Windows API onto all major UNIX platforms. Exhibit 5 shows an overview of the MainWin XDE environment.

The components of MainWin Studio are:

- MainWin XDE (eXtended Development Environment), which includes MainWin Help (the Microsoft Help engine on UNIX)
- MainWin Test (testing tool to generate test cases and port test scripts across platforms, equivalent of Microsoft Test)

- Visual SourceSafe for UNIX (source code manager, equivalent of Microsoft Visual SourceSafe for Windows)

MainWin XDE. MainWin XDE provides a complete package of development tools for cross-developing Windows applications to run on multiple UNIX platforms. It includes support for MFC Libraries, Common Controls, resource compiler, help engine, automatic makefile generator, specialized source files to include with application programs and a set of tools that implement the cross-development environment on the target systems.

The MainWin XDE Dedicated Library is required to enable the Windows Application Programming Interface (API) on each individual UNIX workstation. MainWin supports both a Windows and Motif look, selected "on the fly" by the end-user.

The MainWin XDE Dedicated Library is based on Microsoft Windows source code and essentially replaces Motif. MainWin has source code license agreements with Microsoft for Windows, Windows 95, and NT, Microsoft Test, and Microsoft Visual SourceSafe. MainWin XDE Dedicated Library improves performance by directly interfacing to Xlib.

Mainsoft has ported the Microsoft Foundation Class (MFC) library to work on UNIX platforms. MFC is included as part of MainWin XDE. While MFC DLLs can be shared extension DLLs or statically linked USER DLLs, MainWin supports only the extension DLL model.

Extension DLLs are more resource efficient as they link to a single instance of the MFC library. MainWin does not support USER DLLs, as

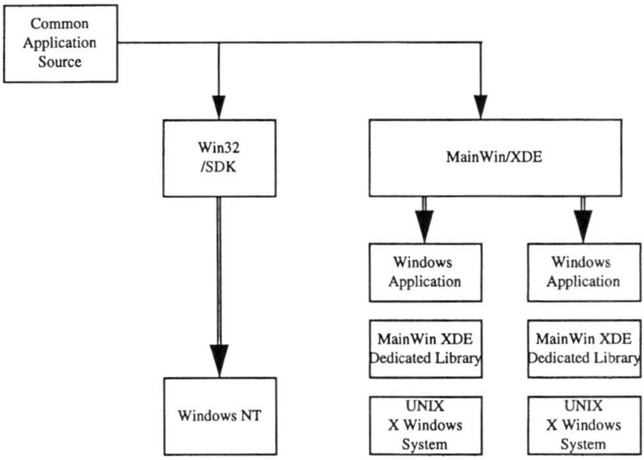

Exhibit 5. MainWin XDE environment.

many UNIX linkers do not discriminate among the symbols in multiple instances of MFC libraries. Support for MFC DLLs with "state" information (DLLs with AFX_MANAGE_STATE) is planned for a future release of MainWin XDE.

MainWin Test. MainWin Test is an automated testing tool that permits retesting of applications on multiple platforms. MainWin Test leverages the investment in test script development by letting the test scripts be used for different platforms. MainWin Test is compatible with test scripts developed using Microsoft Test on the PC.

MainWin Test has its own scripting language (TestBasic) and Bristol is a Microsoft Test source code licensee. Platforms supported by MainWin Test include DEC, HP, IBM, SCO, SGI, and Sun. An included syntax editor and debugger provides an interactive environment for test script development and a Trap error handler allows the unattended collection of test results.

Visual SourceSafe for UNIX. Visual SourceSafe for UNIX is a project-oriented version-control system that provides a graphical user interface. Mainsoft is a Microsoft SourceSafe source code licensee and Visual SourceSafe for UNIX is compatible with Microsoft SourceSafe (both can share a single repository). Visual SourceSafe for UNIX features drag-and-drop file sharing, user-configurable options, visual file difference displays, and a central code repository.

Visual SourceSafe for UNIX supports file sharing, which allows source code modules to be re-used across projects. Changes to shared code checked into one project are automatically propagated. Visual SourceSafe supports UNIX platforms from DEC, HP, IBM, SCO, SGI, and Sun.

Willows Toolkit from Willows Software

Willows Toolkit lets applications to the Win APIs run on UNIX and Macintosh. Additional information on the Willows toolkit is available online at http://www.willows.com.

The 16-bit version of the Willows Toolkit was known as TWIN APIW. Willows Toolkit Version 2.0 added Win32 Support. Willows Toolkit is royalty-free.

PORTING DATABASE APPLICATIONS

If applications that access a database are being ported, the C language calls, the POSIX or Win32 API calls, other operating system calls, and the calls to the database must be ported as well.

In the Windows environment, the common method of accessing databases is using Open Database Connectivity (ODBC). ODBC is an attempt to shield an application from variations in databases. If direct Structured Query Language (SQL) was used, the SQL may need to be changed and the application recompiled and relinked to change databases. ODBC has two main components — an ODBC driver manager and ODBC drivers.

ODBC lets an application make the same calls, and handles the variations of databases through ODBC drivers, typically one driver for each database. The application calls the ODBC driver manager, which interacts with the correct ODBC driver and returns the result to the program. ODBC drivers shield the database specifics in much the same way as device drivers (for example, printer drivers) shield the specifics of the device from the application.

Support for porting database calls depends on the porting vendor. For example, Wind/U provides a stubbed ODBC library that compiles and links successfully but returns failure codes at runtime. Bristol Technology is working with third-party vendors to provide the actual ODBC driver manager and database drivers in future versions of Wind/U.

Third-party vendors that provide ODBC on UNIX include:

- Visigenic Software, Inc.
- Q+E Software/Intersolv

Visigenic Database Connectivity Software

Information about Visigenic is available at http://www.visigenic.com.

Database Connectivity Software from Visigenic Software includes VisiChannel, VisiODBC DriverSets, and VisiODBC SDKs.

VisiODBC Channel. VisiChannel is the overall architecture (see Exhibit 6).

VisiChannel is based on the ODBC standard. VisiChannel is database-independent, and supports the JDBC API for Java applets and applications.

VisiODBC DriverSets

With the VisiODBC Drivers (formerly Visigenic ODBC Drivers), cross-platform access is available to the most popular SQL databases including CA-Ingres, IBM DB2, Informix, Microsoft SQL Server, Oracle, Sybase DBLib, and Sybase SQL Server from any ODBC-enabled application. The VisiODBC drivers are available for Windows, Windows NT, Windows 95, ATT GIS, IBM AIX, HP-UX, SCO, Solaris, Sun OS, Macintosh and Power Macintosh, and OS/2.

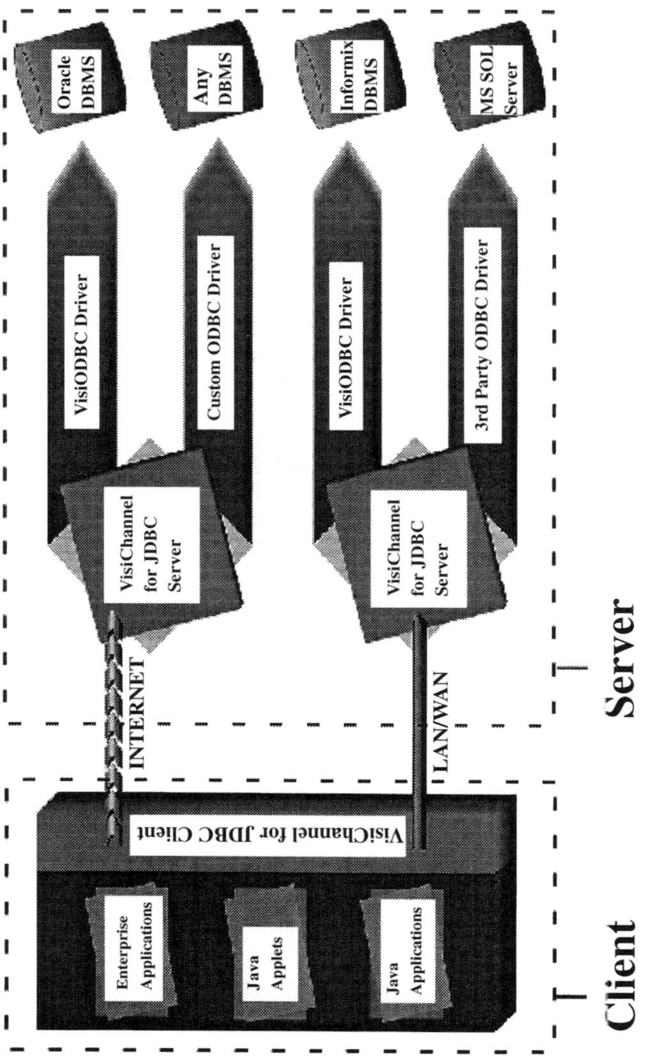

Exhibit 6. Visichannel architecture.

VisiODBC SDKs. VisiODBC SDKs (formerly Visigenic ODBC SDKs) are SDKs for developers to develop vendor-independent database applications and ODBC-compliant drivers. Microsoft has agreed to allow Visigenic to license and port the Microsoft ODBC Software Development Kit (SDK) to all non-Windows platforms. Visigenic has ported the Microsoft ODBC SDK to ATT GIS, IBM AIX, HP-UX, SCO, Solaris, Sun OS, Macintosh and Power Macintosh, and OS/2.

DataDirect

Information about DataDirect is available at http://www.intersolv.com.

INTERSOLV's DataDirect includes both client-based and server-based ODBC data access, connecting to most current databases, on most standard server platforms. See Exhibit 7.

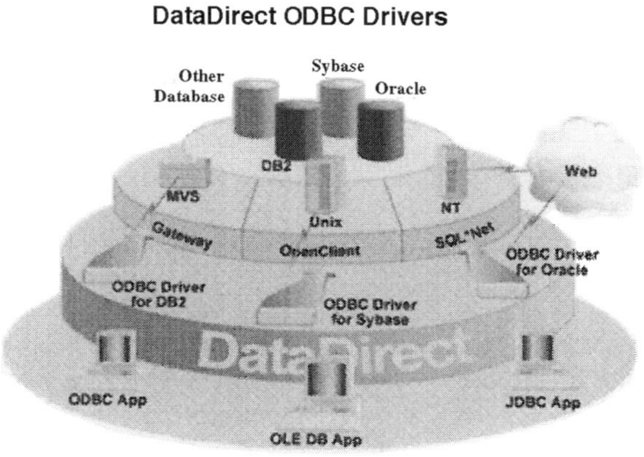

Exhibit 7. DataDirect data connectivity.

DataDirect's client-based connectivity implementation offers ODBC access from clients, including all Microsoft platforms, Mac, OS/2 and many flavors of UNIX through client-based drivers. DataDirect includes connectivity to 35 databases right out of the box.

Server-based Connectivity offers the same functionality as client-based ODBC, without the need for database-specific client middleware. DataDirect server-based connectivity includes direct point-to-point or multi-tier platform data access to different databases and networks and can be accessed concurrently through DataDirect SequeLink. Server-based Connectivity has a single ODBC Driver on the client and a thin server listening piece.

Exhibit 8 summarizes the criteria to choose between client-based and server-based connectivities.

Exhibit 8. Comparing client-based and server-based connectivity options.

DataDirect ODBC Drivers	DataDirect SequeLink
Access to one or two relational databases	Concurrent, heterogeneous access to multiple DBMSs
Database vendor's client software already installed on each workstation	Server-based data access for high performance, especially in WAN environments
Enables embedding drivers with application	Enables setting of a corporate standard for enterprisewide data access
Provides SQL access to flat files (for example-dBASE, Excel, Paradox)	Provides simplified installation, management and administration through a thin client
Provides the ability to use existing gateways for mainframe access	Supports direct non-gateway access to mainframe databases (e.g., DB2, AS/400)

If using databases, including some of the advanced versions such as the Oracle parallel server, from vendors such as Oracle, users should check with the vendor to see if the same version is available in the ported-to environment (such as Windows NT).

By the time this book is released, Oracle will have announced a parallel version of its database, Oracle Parallel Server, for Microsoft's Windows NT operating system. The Windows NT version makes it possible to divide database workload across multiple servers running Windows NT.

Oracle has already been selling Parallel Server versions for Unix platforms and Digital Equipment's VMS operating system for a few years. Compared with the UNIX version, which can run across a large number of UNIX servers, the first versions of the NT version of the parallel server would be able to use two to eight servers.

PORTING TRANSACTION-PROCESSING APPLICATIONS

Most transaction-processing applications are developed using programming interfaces such as X/OPEN organization's X Application to Transaction Manager Interface (XATMI) or the remote procedure call interface — X/Open's TxRPC interface.

Porting the transaction processing part of an application should be relatively straightforward if the following conditions are met:

- The transaction-processing monitor software used supports standards such as TxRPC and ATMI.
- The code used is fairly standards compliant.
- The TP vendor has a version that runs in both the current environment and the environment to be ported to and supports an (almost) identical programming interface in both.

Most of the major TP products such as Tuxedo, Top End, Encina, etc., come with versions supporting a fairly standard API for Windows and UNIX.

PORTING 3GL/4GL APPLICATIONS

So far, this book has covered programs written in programming languages with additional database- or transaction-processing calls embedded in them. For applications developed using application-development tools like PowerBuilder, the best bet is to check if the user's application-development tool vendor provides a version that runs in the target environment. The application source should be portable, but the vendor will know about platform-specific differences and whether they provide support in porting an application's source to the target environment.

PowerBuilder 5.0, for example, has a UNIX and a Mac version. If Tivoli for Application Management is being used, then Tivoli has a UNIX version as well.

PORTING WEB APPLICATIONS

Web applications are similar to other applications with some differences. The languages used to develop web applications include Hyper Text Markup Language (HTML), PERL, and Java. HTML standards exist although they are being updated with uncommon frequency.

There should be no major problem porting HTML source between UNIX and Windows NT environments. By design, Java is intended to be platform independent and there should be no problem porting Java code. Java, being relatively new, does not have many porting references in the industry. PERL has been used for a while in UNIX web applications, and porting-tool manufacturers, such as N*u*TCRACKER, support porting PERL applications.

PORTING DISTRIBUTED APPLICATIONS

If distributed applications are being ported, the area to be focused on is porting the Remote Procedure Calls (RPC) in the distributed applications. While DCE RPC is a very common flavor of RPC, there are some applications that use Sun Microsystems' Open Network Computing (ONC) RPC. Some UNIX systems support ONC RPC. Windows NT provides RPC support that is compatible with DCE RPC. Tools that let you port ONC RPC applications to DCE RPC include RhaPC-d from Intergraph.

RhaPC-d

Information on RhaPC-d is available online at http://www.intergraph.com.

RhaPC-d (pronounced "rhapsody"), Intergraph's Remote Procedure Call development toolkit, lets programmers transfer applications across a client–server network without learning network protocols or sockets programming. RhaPC-d operates over both TCP and UDP transport protocols.

On Windows NT, you can link with RhaPC-d's RPC library while compiling your applications. RhaPC-d supplies the protocols needed for exchanging data using ONC RPC and for encoding data using the eXternal Data Representation (xdr) standard.

RhaPC-d provides interoperability with existing RPC-based client–server applications and facilitates their porting to the Windows NT environment. RhaPC-d's port mapper and the Windows NT Service Control Manager combine to allow Windows NT to operate as both a client and a full-function server.

RhaPC-d provides a static library that eliminates the need to deliver additional libraries or DLLs with the application program. RhaPC-d also provides an API interface to create network RPC packets in xdr format. The RhaPC-d RPC protocol compiler generates C code from an RPC protocol description file.

Porting International Applications

If you have applications written for international use using different code pages, Multi Byte Character Sets (MBCS) or UNICODE (see box below), Windows NT and many UNIX systems support code pages and MBCS. Windows NT also supports UNICODE, although not all UNIX systems support UNICODE.

The Win32 API and Windows NT support UNICODE. Windows NT uses UNICODE extensively in its internal operations. For example, all text strings in Graphics Device Interface (GDI) APIs are in UNICODE, New Technology File System (NTFS) uses UNICODE for file, path, and directory names, object names, and all system information files are in UNICODE.

The Windows NT subsystems take care of many of the conversions. For example, the Win32 subsystem converts ASCII characters it receives into UNICODE strings and converts them back to ASCII, if necessary, for output. Microsoft Visual C++ and the Microsoft Foundation Class (MFC) library support the most common form of MBCS–DBCS (two bytes per character).

Digital UNIX supports XPG4-compliant internationalization and includes 22 multibyte versions, primarily for the Asian market.

UNICODE

Developed by the UNICODE Consortium, a non-profit consortium sponsored by a number of computer companies, UNICODE is a fixed-width encoding scheme where each character is represented by 16 bits. The number of characters that can be represented by UNICODE is thus 2^{16} or 65,536.

Using UNICODE, we can represent all the characters from character sets like ANSI, characters from the Cyrillic character set, special-purpose characters such as publishing characters and mathematical symbols — in short, everything we want to represent (as of now). For a complete description of the UNICODE standard, the characters represented, etc. refer to *The UNICODE Standard: Worldwide Character Encoding*, by Addison-Wesley Publishing Company: ISBN 0201567881.

Porting OS/2 applications to Windows NT

If OS/2 applications are to be ported to Windows NT, most of the porting considerations discussed here, such as source code issues and scripts, apply to OS/2 to Windows NT porting as well.

In manual porting, OS/2 to Windows NT porting may be a little easier than UNIX to Windows NT porting. Earlier versions of OS/2 and Windows were developed with collaboration between IBM and Microsoft and many concepts between OS/2 and Windows are similar. HPFS and NTFS have many similar features. In addition, unlike the UNIX world, there is only one flavor of OS/2 from one company.

Third-party assistance is also available in the OS/2 to Windows port. Tandem, for one, offers OS/2 to Windows NT porting services. Tandem uses a two-phase approach. The first phase scans OS/2 programs for code that is not compatible with Windows NT and has to be rewritten. The scanning phase gives an idea of the amount of code to be rewritten and also helps create project requirements.

The second phase ports OS/2 source code that can be ported to Windows NT. The second phase also tests and validates the system.

Other porting considerations

Object models are at the root of many programming technologies. The object model specifies the rules for object interaction. Examples of object models include the Component Object Model (COM) and Distributed Component Object Model (DCOM) from Microsoft, and System Object Model (SOM) and Distributed System Object Model (DSOM) from IBM. The object models become important because of the technologies the model supports. For example, COM is the basis for Microsoft's ActiveX and OLE technologies.

Microsoft recently announced that Digital Equipment and Hewlett-Packard will support Microsoft's component object model (COM) on their operating systems in a year. HP's support will be in HP-UX while Digital Equipment will provide COM support in Digital UNIX and OpenVMS.

Once the underlying model is supported in the operating system, it will be possible to develop or buy applications using the model-based technologies on these operating system. Porting OLE and ACTIVE X applications to UNIX will become easier.

Rewriting Applications

Managers might decide that rewriting an application is better than porting it. Applications that match the following criteria qualify for rewriting:

- The application is near the end of its life expectancy.
- The source code for some or all of the application is no longer available.
- The programmers who wrote or have knowledge about the application are no longer available.
- The application is a maintenance nightmare.
- The application uses obsolete technology (language, architecture, hardware, etc.) that should be replaced.

Without people who have knowledge of the application and lacking the source, a significant rewriting effort is inevitable. With the source, but without people knowledgeable in the application, there are some tools, such as Discover, that may help to capture the business knowledge in the application.

Discover

DISCOVER scans all C and C++ code and identifies every inter- and intradependency in the software, and then builds a complete Information Model of the entire software system. The Information Model is a highly associative repository that keeps track of every dependency, regardless of the size of the application, allowing all changes to the software to be immediately reflected.

The knowledge stored in the Information Model is leveraged by application sets designed for specific development tasks, providing overall improvements in software process and quality.

There are five major applications sets that make use of the DISCOVER Information Model. Each of these tool sets is a value-added application. The sets include:

1. DEVELOP/SET consisting of PROGRAM/sw, DESIGN/sw, DEBUG/sw, and DEBUG+/sw
2. REENGINEER/SET consisting of PACKAGE/sw, PARTITION/sw, EXTRACT/sw, and SIMPLIFY.H/sw
3. CM/SET consisting of CM/sw.ATRIA, CM/sw.CONTINUUS, CM/sw.CVS, CM/sw.RCS, and CM/sw.SCCS
4. ADMIN/SET consisting of ADMIN/sw
5. DOC/SET consisting of DOC/sw.FRAME and REPORT/sw

PROGRAM/sw provides software comprehension through its browsing, navigation, query, editing, and graphical views. In addition, PROGRAM/sw supplies automated risk-assessment and -management capabilities through Impact Analysis, which reports on the systemwide impact of any proposed change before the change is submitted. Impact Analysis gives organizations the information necessary for making accurate development decisions, improving software quality during development, not after a release.

Change Propagation, another PROGRAM/sw capability, automatically checks out all needed files from the existing configuration management system and implements the approved change. This unique capability automates a usually tedious and error-prone aspect of development, freeing up time for more creative work while also increasing the quality of the software produced.

DESIGN/sw provides the ability to create and modify graphical views — data charts, entity relation diagrams and class inheritance diagrams. Modifying any of these diagrams results in automatic modification (or incremental generation) of the associated code to reflect those changes, speeding development and ensuring accuracy.

DEBUG/sw is an integrated debugger interface to industry-standard debuggers such as GDB, DBX and DDE. The interface emulates the most popular debuggers and translates familiar commands and conventions to the installed debugger. DEBUG+/sw enhances the chosen debugger by the addition of mixed-mode debugging capability.

CM/SET provides seamless integration with many popular configuration-management systems, including Atria's ClearCase, Continuus' Continuus/CM, CVS, RCS, and SCCS.

REENGINEER/SET, used alone or in tandem, breaks large, monolithic applications into smaller, more manageable modules or components that incorporate a subset of the functionality of the original software.

EXTRACT/sw module allows users to create and extract subsystems from existing source code, either manually or automatically. This module also provides dormant code analysis, identifying those functions, variables, structures, and classes not utilized by the software system. Automatic elimination of dead code enables organizations to easily remove software that is no longer called upon.

PACKAGE/sw subdivides an application into logical components based on the dynamic relationships of the functions and data in the program.

PARTITION/sw performs application restructuring. Teams can physically rearrange software into a new structure that accurately reflects the logical structure. Using this approach, teams can reorganize existing software into more-manageable pieces, to delete unnecessary code, or to divide the software into two or more applications.

SIMPLIFY.H/sw uses the information contained in the Information Model to pare down header files to a necessary minimum, resulting in fewer compilations needed after a change. In addition, compilations that are done proceed more quickly since the compiler does not waste time reading and parsing nonessential information.

DOC/SET consists of *DOC/sw.FRAME and REPORT/sw. DOC/sw.FRAME* provides multiple methods for establishing direct links between source code and documents, while *REPORT/sw* generates systemwide "as-built" software documentation. Both applications enable organizations to keep software and documentation synchronized.

ADMIN/sw includes software administration utilities for set-up and usage of DISCOVER. These utilities include makefile readers, batch mode support, a Project Definition File generator and debugger.

Conclusion

This chapter has looked at porting applications from UNIX to Windows NT and vice versa and at some common porting products available. Porting is not limited to C or C++ programs. Porting applications that access database, web applications, transaction processing applications, etc., were also examined.

Chapter 7
Porting GUI Programs

Adam Faldalla
Victor Matos
Paul J. Jalics

The success of the ubiquitous personal computer (PC) as a multipurpose tool is largely due to the simplification of the graphical user interface (GUI). The new generation of interfaces is based on intuitive, self-explanatory graphics that invite the user to explore the application in a more natural way. Programming for GUI-based applications, however, is much more complex than writing non-GUI-based programs. This difference is especially apparent when object-oriented (OO) design, implementation methodologies, and OO programming languages are involved. The programmer can only hope that the additional complexity of writing such programs is counterbalanced by the quality of the human interface and the application's ease of use once running. Most important, the proliferation of GUI wizards, systems, and languages makes the portability of such applications across systems difficult indeed. This chapter presents a case study of a genealogical family-tree application implemented in six different GUI systems, which illustrates the cross-GUI platform portability problems. The authors also propose a solution for making such applications more portable across various GUI systems.

Higher-level programming languages, such as C and C++, have made great strides in program portability from platform to platform and across operating systems in the past 10 to 15 years. This portability is no longer so prevalent in GUI-based programs, because the GUI system calls are so different on the various GUI environments. Furthermore, even if the GUI calls are the same, class libraries that help simplify GUI access are generally incompatible across different compilers. Finally, even general-purpose libraries, such as container-class libraries, are significantly incompatible on different compilers. Some hope of alleviating the problems exists in this area: A number of GUI systems, such as PowerBuilder,

0-8493-9989-0/99/$0.00+$.50

are available on multiple platforms. Of even more significance, Java browsers and GUI class libraries are designed to be platform- and operating-system independent.

Today's programmer need only look at current PC and workstation applications to appreciate the quality of such applications as word processors, spreadsheets, and accounting packages. Not only do these programs provide an attractive graphical interface, but in many cases, they also can be used without any training, because they adhere to common conventions and are designed to be intuitive. Most of these programs can be categorized as GUI programs, because they use GUI and in addition are organized very differently from non-GUI programs.

Non-GUI programs tend to be deterministic: The program starts at the top, and then often goes into a loop, inputting data and waiting for the data to be ready. It then processes the data and outputs some results. The program executes operating system requests, which on a typical UNIX system could be any of about 64 services mostly related to input/output; with disk file reads and writes the most highly requested a vast majority of the time.

GUI programs, on the other hand, often consist of code to paint a screen or window and then put themselves in an endless loop, waiting for such events as mouse clicks, character inputs, the push of a button, or the selection of a menu item. When one of these events occurs, the appropriate event-handler procedure is executed. Most application code is placed either in the event-handling procedures themselves or in procedure calls made from the event-handling procedures. GUI programs typically call on system services that are more complex, consisting of more than 350 services on Microsoft windows and about 700 services on OS/2 Presentation Manager.

To illustrate the points covered in this chapter, a case study of the FamTree application will be discussed in some detail. It is a family tree application with three screens, each of which has menus:

- A People Screen — used to input, view, and modify data about individual persons in the family data base, including name, gender, and birth and death dates (see Exhibit 1)
- A Relationships Screen — used to input, edit, and view relationships between any two persons in the family database (see Exhibit 2)
- A FamTree Report Screen — used to produce ancestor trees and descendent trees of persons in the family database (see Exhibit 3)

In this case study, a student wrote the application as a research project on a Macintosh using Think C, an object-oriented language similar to C++. The application consists of 2,636 lines of Think C code. The program makes use of an object-oriented class library (Think) to interface to the GUI on the

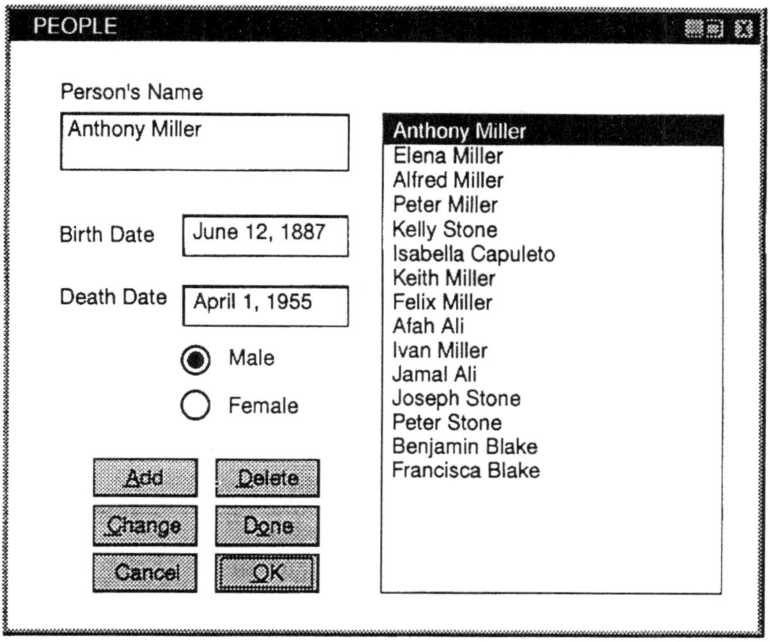

Exhibit 1. The FamTree people screen.

Macintosh. The authors of this chapter started with very little knowledge of any of the seven GUI systems involved but with a solid background in computer science and systems programming.

The project's goal was to learn about application portability by making this application work in the same way on seven different GUI systems:

1. Macintosh Think C
2. Microsoft Visual C++ on Microsoft Windows
3. Borland C++ on Microsoft Windows
4. X-Windows using the OSF/Motif GUI System
5. Tcl/Tk on X-Windows interfacing to the C++ application code
6. Microsoft Visual Basic interfacing to the C++ application code
7. Microsoft Access under Windows

PORTING TO MICROSOFT VISUAL C++: PORT 1

The first port (port 1) turned the Think C Application code into C++ with minimal difficulties. The GUI interface, however, was totally different and hard to understand. Replacing it with the Microsoft Foundation Classes (MFC) GUI Application Framework usage turned out to be a challenge.

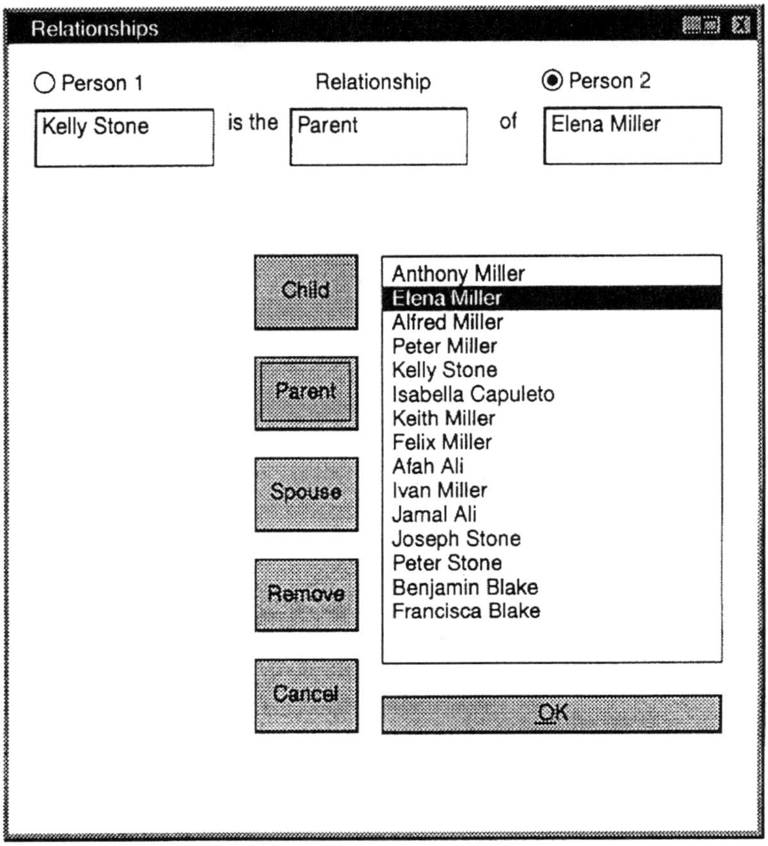

Exhibit 2. The FamTree relationship screen.

The menu, window, and screen (dialog box) creations were all in Think C calls and were replaced totally by design work in the interactive application studio. The studio allowed the menus and the three dialog boxes to be created in minutes in a totally visual manner, with no code written at all and thus, not a single GUI system call and none of the myriad of parameters usually required for such calls.

The rest of the application contained a few dozen GUI calls throughout the various implementation functions that were difficult to identify and replace with MFC calls. The C++ compiler proved very useful in pinpointing C++ classes that were in the Think C application framework but not in the Visual C++ environment. In fact, there is very little, if any, commonality of GUI interfaces at this time across different systems. As a first step, these calls were commented out and analogous calls were sought in the MFC application framework.

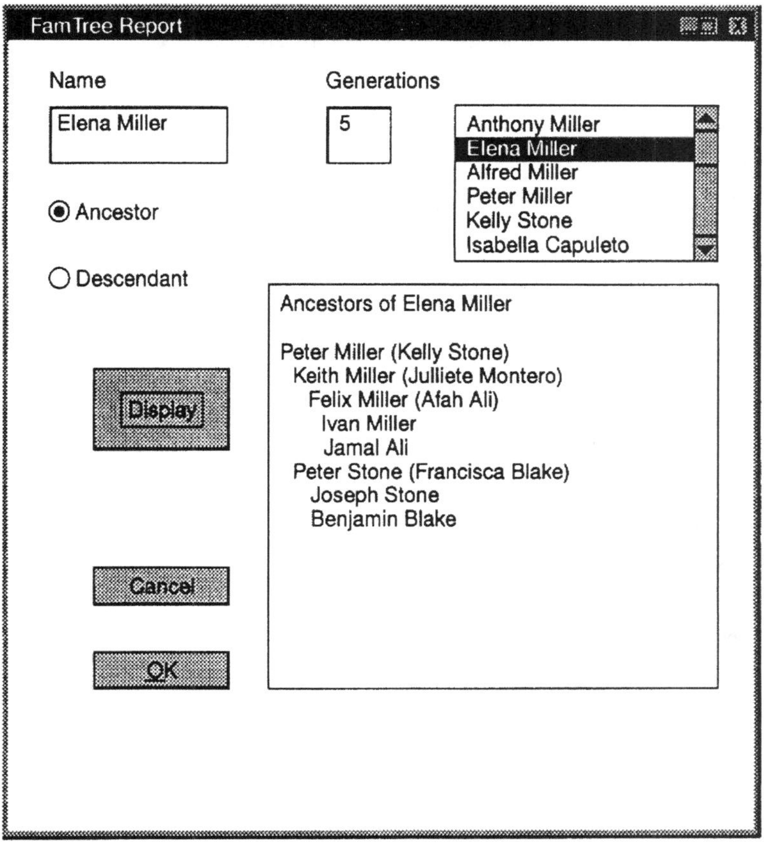

Exhibit 3. The FamTree report screen.

The use of a dynamically growing array to store the people data posed another problem. This was done on the Macintosh using a container-class library class, which did not exist in the other systems. The immediate solution was to substitute the MFC class for such arrays, but the same problem recurred on the next port to Borland C++. Finally, a new class was created and used throughout the application. The class was implemented as a wrapper class for the MFC class, so that the next port would simply involve changing the implementation of this class. The use of this array throughout the application reduces the effort at each porting.

PORTING TO BORLAND C++: PORT 2

This port is very similar to port 1; the developers, however, were more familiar with the application this time. The menus and the three dialog boxes were again created by time spent in the Resource Workshop, in which the facilities were similar to those in the Visual C++. The rest of the GUI calls were reinvented, but this process was much simpler because the functions that needed to be done, and in what places in the code, were very clear.

Investigation of the functionality of the Object Windows application framework was time-consuming, but the results most often were in the form of a line-for-line replacement of the MFC C++ code with Object Windows calling code.

Inconveniences included situations in which both of the systems have a facility for serializing or archiving the family database, but the code to do it was considerably different, and the disk files written by one could not be read by the other.

PORTING TO OSF/MOTIF AND X-WINDOWS: PORT 3

Another important GUI system is X-Windows on UNIX systems; the system is available in OSF/Motif and Xlib libraries of subroutines. The starting point was the Borland C++ code from port 2, although the Microsoft Visual C++ code (port 1) would have required just the same effort. There is nothing analogous to the Application Studio in this case, and the system does not have the polish of the previous two systems investigated, from the developer's point of view. The menu and dialog box creation was all done using Motif or Xlib calls from within the code, similar to what was done originally in the Macintosh program. The debugging tools were also inferior to the previous two systems, although easy printf and I/O stream debug outputs to the UNIX window were easier and very useful for debugging. The code worked in a relatively short time, although the original appearance of the dialog boxes from the Macintosh was hard to mimic, because of the power and flexibility of placement of controls in a window and because of all the dynamic resizing based on current data and window size.

PORTING TO TCL/TK UNDER X-WINDOWS: PORT 4

In search of a system more polished and automated than Motif and X-Windows on UNIX systems, the authors attempted an interesting scripting language called Tcl, from UC Berkeley, with an X-Windows add-on called Tk. The goal here was to keep as much of the C++ application intact but to do the GUI in Tcl/Tk. This necessitated isolation of the GUI portion from the family-tree application itself; the family-tree application manages the family database of persons and their relationships, and it is able to produce reports of those relationships. Because only the GUI aspects are to be done in Tk and the application itself did not need to be rewritten in Tcl, identification was necessary of all the GUI code. The developers had to remove it and replace it with procedure calls to a new C++ module, PortableGui.C,

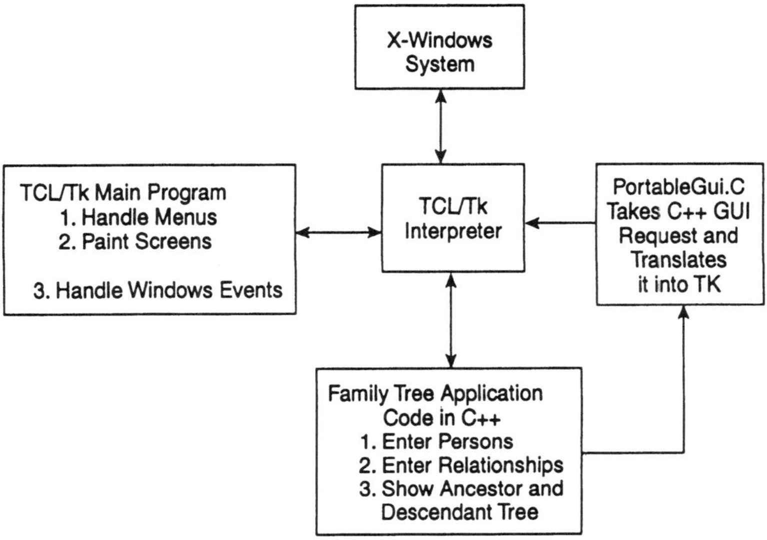

Exhibit 4. The TCL/Tk program structure.

---

which then made calls to Tk, which had access to all the GUI interfaces. Exhibit 4 depicts the organization of this Tk-based family-tree application.

THE TCL/TK PROGRAM STRUCTURE

Creating the menus and dialog boxes was ultimately much simpler than creating them in Motif, but the same difficulties showed up as did in Motif, in terms of recreating the screens to appear exactly like the originals in the Macintosh. Whereas this system is not at all like the Application Studio, it is easier than Motif calls from C++ and can be recommended for a host of applications under X-Windows.

PortableGui.C had 24 functions to replace the 24 different GUI calls found in the C++ application after the port to Borland C++. The functions included setting and getting the values of text boxes, radio buttons, adding to and deleting from list boxes, and finding the currently selected entry in list boxes. (Exhibit 5 contains a full list of the functions.)

This one part of the GUI interface was always called from the C++ family tree application code; it set some part of the screen or instructed the C++ application as to what data was in that part of the screen. The other part of the GUI interface was the event handler, which by this point in the project was coded in Tk; the event handler needed to call the C++ family-tree application whenever a menu choice was made or a button was pressed by the user, such as the one that caused a person to be added to

Exhibit 5. GUI access calls needed by the FamTree application.

```
SetFileName(char *newfilename);
GetFileName(char*filename, int maxlen);
SetRel(char *newrelname);
SetPerson1(char*newname);
SetPerson2(char *newname);
GetGens(char *newnumgens,int maxlen);
int GetAncestor();
AddFtree(char *newname,int position);
AddList1(char *newname,int position);
AddList2(char*newname,int position);
AddList3(char *newname,int position);
DeleteList1(int position);
GetRoot(char *newname,int maxlen);
SetRoot(char*newname);
GetName(char *newname,int maxlen);
GetBirth(char*newname,int maxlen);
GetDeath(char *newname,int maxlen);
int GetMale();
int GetPerson1B();
SetName(char *newname);
SetBirth(char*newname);
SetDeath(char *newname);
SetMale(int);
int GetListPos(int listboxid);
```

the family database in the People dialog box. In these cases, no data is passed to the C++ application. Instead, a C++ event-handler function is executed, and it can call PortableGui.C for getting the needed GUI data.

PORTING TO VISUAL BASIC: PORT 5

Perhaps the most interesting port was to Microsoft Visual Basic (VB). The GUI aspects of Visual Basic were very impressive. The developers wanted to experiment with linking a VB GUI with the C++ application as it existed after the Tcl/Tk port. All that was needed was to replace the implementation of PortableGui.C with an implementation that calls VB instead

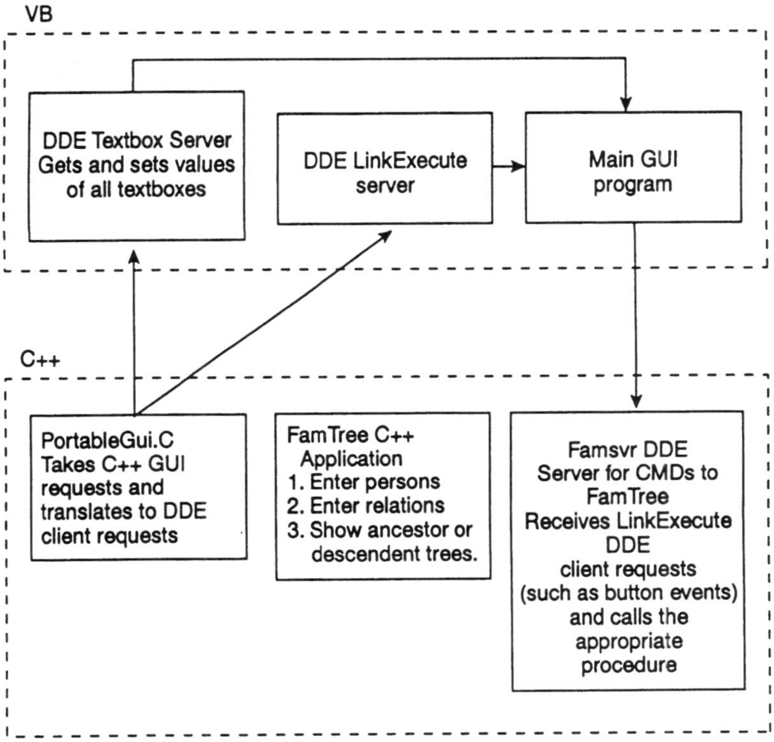

Exhibit 6. Structure of a VB application.

of Tk. After much experimentation, the developers used a Windows facility, called Dynamic Data Exchange (DDE), to link VB with the C++ application, as shown in Exhibit 6. DDE functionality is now provided as part of OLE. Each of the text boxes became a DDE server that would respond to DDE requests from the C++ application. In addition, the C++ application became a server to which command requests could be sent from VB, such as for a menu selection or a button's having been pressed. A DDE remote-execute facility was used to communicate with some other controls, such as list boxes and radio buttons.

STRUCTURE OF A VB APPLICATION

Porting to Microsoft Access under Windows: Port 6

The final port was attempted because a data base package might be seen as a natural choice for implementing the FamTree application. Interfacing to the C++ application was not considered; instead, however, the application was rewritten in Access Basic. The menu and dialog box design was done in an application studio similar to Borland C++ or Visual C++. The application code was rewritten in Access macros (80 lines) whenever possible and in Access Basic (941 lines) for the rest. Recoding the application code in Access Basic took less time and trouble than anticipated, and the language itself is much improved over the not-so-impressive ancestor, Basic.

The number of lines of code is only half as many as any of the other implementations. However, the GUI work of dialog boxes and menus is not easily measured in lines of code, because this design work is all done interactively. There is no printable output similar to the noninteractively written code to create menus and dialog boxes, as is the C++ code in the Macintosh and X-Windows implementations.

Effort Needed for Each Porting

Exhibit 7 shows the number of hours of work required for each of the portings of the family-tree application. The authors had much experience with C++, some experience with an older DOS-based Borland GUI class library called TurboVision, and very little GUI programming experience outside of small modifications to a small X-Windows program.

Exhibit 7. Hours required for each porting.

Environment	Conversion Hours	Code Size (Lines)
Macintosh Think C	0	2636
Microsoft Visual C++	79	2959
Borland C++	75	3550
OSF/Motif+X-Windows	92	2807
Tcl/Tk	82	2016
VB-DDE-C++	157	3223
Microsoft Access	102	949

The average time for porting the application is about 98 hours. Surprisingly, the very first port, Microsoft Visual C++ on Microsoft Windows, required one of the shortest times — 79 hours: The application was unknown to the authors when this began, and the Visual C++ environment was new to them as well.

Port 2, Borland C++, took the shortest time: 75 hours. The authors had no experience with Borland C++, but by this time the application was better known and the functionality and ways of Borland and Visual C++ were quite familiar. Furthermore, the authors had some experience with Borland's earlier C++ compiler and the TurboVision GUI for DOS, as well as with the Borland container-class library.

X-Windows, port 3, took 92 hours, much of which was spent learning to paint the screens, which had to be programmed. The scheme for programming screens is complicated: Multiple layers of window frames had to be created and positioned to place the controls on the screen as desired. The algorithm of recursively going through the layers of window frames, determining what each needs for its dimensions, and then sizing each accordingly is very powerful but also difficult to work with.

Tcl/Tk took 82 hours, most of which was spent on learning the Tcl/Tk scripting language and how it interfaces to C++ application code. Results for a subsequent GUI application would likely yield much better times.

Visual Basic took the longest time, 157 hours, most of which was spent trying to establish communication between the C++ application and Visual Basic. Learning to make clients and servers of both the application and the Visual Basic GUI is certainly in tune with current trends. The authors would, however, avoid this combination of C++ and Visual Basic if at all possible.

Finally, Microsoft Access took 102 hours, most of which was spent learning this fourth-generation tool, which is very different from the other third-generation language tools. If the authors were to choose a tool for implementing a similar GUI application, they might well choose Access in hopes of recovering their investment in time in the second application.

SEPARATING THE APPLICATION FROM THE GUI

The above ports of the FamTree application naturally emphasized the need for creating GUI application programs to be portable across widely varying GUI systems. This is especially true because there is little standardization of GUI systems across platforms, operating systems, and language systems. As one example, one company has built a large business application in Objective C on a Next but now may need to rewrite it all in a Windows 95 environment. The amount of work needed to make this conversion is staggering. The road to the portability of GUI applications begins by separating the code into three parts:

1. *The Application Code* — This is GUI system independent; it calls the interface to access GUI.
2. *The Interface Module* — This module is called from the Application module to access GUI services. It is completely different for each application and consists of 24 very short procedures for FamTree.
3. *The GUI Module* — This part handles menus, paints the screens, and responds to such events as button pushes and mouse movements by calling the Application module.

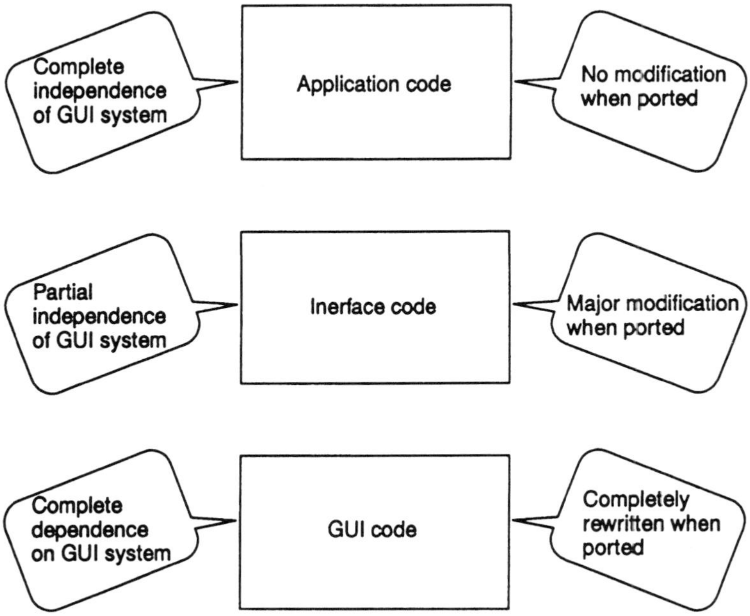

Exhibit 8. Overview of GUI programs portability framework.

This decomposition process is summarized in the GUI programs' portability framework, as illustrated in Exhibit 8. Such decomposition is imperative, because the GUI code would by default be intermixed all over the application. The first goal in a portable system is to design the application part of the code so that it needs only to be recompiled to move to another system. The interface module (i.e., as in PortableGui.C) must implement GUI calls of the given system and will be rewritten completely for each GUI system for which the application needs to be ported. Finally, the GUI part must be written from scratch for each system.

OVERVIEW OF GUI PROGRAMS PORTABILITY FRAMEWORK

For the FamTree application — the X-Windows Motif version — the application code is 1,506 lines of code, or 75% of the total; the interface is 166 lines, or 8%; and the GUI code is 344 lines, 17%. When porting this application, developers may find that 75% of the code can stay untouched, that the 8% Interface needs major modification, and that the 17% GUI needs to be rewritten from scratch. The GUI code is often automatically generated based on interactive design in an application studio or resource workshop. Therefore, in such environments, the code for the main program, the event handlers, and the screen and menu display is all written by the compiler system itself. In a more polished system, such as Microsoft Visual C++ or

Borland C++, porting an application involves some interactive work. This means using an application wizard to make the main program, using a resource workshop to design menus and screens, and a class wizard to create the event handlers required and then insert calls to the application code for each event. After that, the user must adapt the interface code to that GUI system. Thus the actual lines of code that need to be rewritten come to about 10% for the above application. In the judgment of the authors, this is a very satisfactory level of effort for porting a GUI application.

Finally, if an application is ported again to a third system, the porting work done on the first port is so similar that it can be done with very modest effort. The only challenge is to learn the GUI class library calls for the new target system, which is needed to modify the Interface.

INTERFACES BETWEEN THE APPLICATION AND THE GUI

The People screen (which is used to enter people and their data and to view and modify this data) is an example of the interface that the application code uses to access GUI data. The application needs the following functions, which are implemented in PortableGui.C, where they make up 10 of the 24 interface procedures:

```
[Tab]GetName(char * name, int maxlen)

SetName(char* newname)

GetBirth(char * bdate, int maxlen)

SetBirth(char* newname)

GetDeath(char * bdate, int maxlen)

SetDeath(char* newname)

int GetMale()

SetMale(int maleis1)

AddList1(char* newname, int position)

DeleteList1(char * int position)
```

Exhibit 1, the FamTree People screen, shows that all the application needs to retrieve data that the user has typed on the screen is to use the Get procedures, which typically return a character string whose maximum length is specified as the second parameter. At other times, when the user has selected a different person by clicking the appropriate entry in the list box on the right, the application code must find and put on the screen the data for that person, which is done by the Set procedures. Finally, the AddList1 procedure adds an entry to the list box on the right at the position specified, whereas DeleteList1 deletes an existing entry. The only functions supported are those the FamTree uses, so there might be a Set for some controls without a Get if the application does not require one.

As an example of the use of the above procedures, clicking Peter Miller in the list box causes the application to set the Name text box to Peter Miller using SetName("Peter Miller"). The application sets the birth-date text box to 08-18-45 by executing SetBirth("08-18-45"), then executes Set-Death(" "), and finally executes SetMale(1).

There is no need for Set or Get procedures for the four buttons ADD, CHANGE, DELETE, and CLEAR, because users can select these themselves, causing an event-handling procedure that is part of the GUI code to be executed. That GUI event-handling procedure, perhaps, for example, named OnAddButton will, in turn, call the application-code procedure

```
DoCommand(ADDBUTTON).
```

As an example of the implementation of this Interface, the implementations of GetName and SetMale for Visual C++ are shown as they occur in PortableGui.C:

```
GetName(XLPSTR  cptr,  int  smax)
  {  gpPeople->GetDlgItemText
        (IDC_PPL_EDIT_NAME,(LPSTR)  cptr,  smax);
  return  0;
  }
SetMale(int  ind)
  {  int  checked=ind  ?  IDC_PPL_RAD_MALE  :
     IDC_PPL_RAD_FEMALE;
  gpPeople->CheckRadioButton(IDC_PPL_RAD_MALE,
     IDC_PPL_RAD_FEMALE,
  checked);
  return  0;
}
```

The code is GUI system-dependent and changes with every port. Porting GUI applications requires substantial effort unless the program design clearly isolates the application code, the GUI code, and an interface module that allows the application code to talk to the GUI components. If the code is so organized, porting such an application is simpler, the code to be changed is well isolated and identified, and the amount of code that needs to be modified is as little as 10% of the total lines.

The beginner's efforts to port an application for the various GUI systems attempted are all close, with only about a 20% difference between all but one system. Also, the work is smallest for the two commercial GUI systems, in which most of the GUI work is done interactively in an application studio instead of writing code that calls GUI system calls to paint screens and menus. These produce larger code sizes, but most of the extra code is automatically generated. Surprisingly, the results for some of the latest 4GL tools, such as Access and Visual Basic, took more time than the traditional C++ programming environments.

One of the obstacles to portability is that the GUI Class libraries are completely different on every compiler, on every platform. Until more standardization is achieved in this area, the authors' proposition is to isolate GUI code in an interface module clearly identified and localized.

Similarly, general-purpose class libraries, such as container classes, are a stumbling block to portability. Users can avoid using these class libraries altogether to improve portability, or they can create wrapper classes of their own that make use of the local class libraries in implementing the wrapper class. Therefore, the application is unaware of their use, and porting to a new system consists of simply replacing the class implementation with the best facilities in the target environment.

A special case of the above relates to the highly useful facility in C++ class libraries called archiving or serializing data to files. Not only are these facilities totally incompatible in the various systems, but the data files they create are incompatible across compilers. So if the developer wants to make the data from an application also portable, these facilities should be avoided in favor of the traditional way of writing the data to normal files that are more easily portable.

Experimentation such as was done in this project is most useful in, even essential to, staying current in this rapidly changing field of applied computer science.

Chapter 8
Visual Basic and Object-Oriented Development

William R. Constable, Jr.
Il-Yeol Song

This chapter presents an eight-step implementation of an object-oriented design in Visual Basic. Benefits include the ability to select and manipulate graphical objects on screen, an object-oriented interface to Windows objects libraries, and creating command buttons and objects with properties similar to object-oriented programming languages. Although Visual Basic is described as an object-oriented environment for developing Windows applications, it is not an object-oriented programming language. This chapter takes the systems manager step by step through the implementation of the abstract objects in this non-object-oriented language.

INTRODUCTION

Mapping an object-oriented design to Microsoft Visual Basic presents unique problems, because even though Visual Basic has some object-oriented features, it is not an Object-Oriented Programming Language. It provides a visual, object-oriented environment for creating a graphical user interface GUI. Behind the visual objects of the GUI, however, the abstract objects, behavior, and constraints from the application domain are implemented in Visual Basic's non-object-oriented procedural language. This chapter presents both a method for implementing these arbitrary objects in Visual Basic using James Rumbaugh's Object Modeling Technique and the benefits to be derived.

DEFINING OBJECT-ORIENTED

Visual Basic is sometimes referred to as an object-oriented environment for developing Windows applications. So why is it necessary to be

0-8493-9989-0/99/$0.00+$.50

concerned with object-oriented implementation issues? The answer lies in the ambiguity that surrounds the term *object-oriented.* Visual Basic's program development environment is object oriented in that it is a GUI, allowing the programmer to select and manipulate application components as graphical objects directly on the screen. Also, Visual Basic has a tool bar consisting of common Windows controls, such as text box, command button, and label and frame, as well as common graphic tools that allow the programmer to draw lines, circles, and boxes. Each application window is painted by placing these controls on the window form. For example, a command button can be created by selecting the button icon on the toolbox and placing a button on a form. The button object has such properties as height and width, and such methods as drag, move, and refresh. It recognizes events (i.e., messages) such as click and lost focus. Clearly, the properties and methods of controls are concepts borrowed from Object-Oriented Programming Language.

Visual Basic is also object oriented in that it provides an object-oriented interface to its library of Windows objects. Each object (i.e., control) has encapsulated properties, methods, and events to which it can respond. Events can be fired by a user action on a control, other controls, or the application itself.

In terms of creating a GUI, Visual Basic could be referred to as object oriented in a general sense. However, once past the creation of the visual objects that make up the GUI, implementation of the application's behavior and data structures is necessary. Windows-based applications are event driven, so program code must be written behind each graphical control to cause it to behave as required. Further, applications have procedural aspects and abstract objects from the application domain that must be implemented in data structures (e.g., employees, departments, and projects). For this, Visual Basic provides the Beginner's All-Purpose Symbolic Instruction Code (BASIC) programming language, which is not an object-oriented programming language.

Given that Visual Basic's underlying programming language is not object oriented, it is clear that implementing an object-oriented system design in Visual Basic is not trivial and requires that object-oriented concepts be intentionally mapped to the language, just as they must be in other non-object-oriented languages, such as C, APL, and Formula Translation.

Rumbaugh's chapter 16, "Non-Object-Oriented Languages," (J. Rumbaugh, et al. *Object-Oriented Modeling and Design*. Englewood Cliffs, NJ, Prentice-Hall, 1991) is one guide to mapping object-oriented concepts to Visual Basic. The chapter discusses techniques for implementation in three non-object-oriented languages, C, Ada, and FORTRAN; this chapter extends this body of knowledge to include Visual Basic by offering techniques adapted to that language.

Rumbaugh lists eight steps to implementing an Object-Oriented Design. The programmer must:

1. Translate classes into data structures
2. Pass arguments to methods
3. Allocate storage for objects
4. Implement inheritance in data structures
5. Implement method resolution
6. Implement associations
7. Deal with concurrency
8. Encapsulate internal details of classes

To provide continuity with Rumbaugh's work, this chapter uses the same Graphics Editor application for programming examples. This is not the best application for these examples, because such an interactive graphics editor could easily be constructed using graphical objects already provided by Visual Basic; however, it does provide for direct comparison with examples in the other languages discussed by Rumbaugh. The object model for the Graphics Editor application is shown in Exhibit 1.

AN OVERVIEW OF LANGUAGE FEATURES

A brief description of Visual Basic language features is relevant to the following object-oriented programming techniques presented. Visual Basic's procedural programming language provides certain features that make mapping object-oriented concepts to the language possible. However, it is up to the programmer to use these features to manually create an object-oriented framework for the application. For example, user-defined data types allow the definition of record structures, which can consist of primitive data types, arrays, and other structures. Dynamic arrays of user-defined structures can be declared and, at run time, can be resized. The `ReDim Preserve` command allows the reallocation of an array without loss of its current contents. But other than dynamic arrays, Visual Basic lacks dynamic memory allocation and does not provide for pointers to data structures or functions. This makes instantiation more difficult in Visual Basic than in languages that provide these features.

Related procedures and functions can be grouped in separate program modules supporting encapsulation, although full implementation of abstract data types can be difficult. Variable scope can be global, module level, or local, but procedures are accessible from any module, blurring the distinction between public and private data and behavior. Visual Basic allows procedure arguments to be passed by value or by reference, which

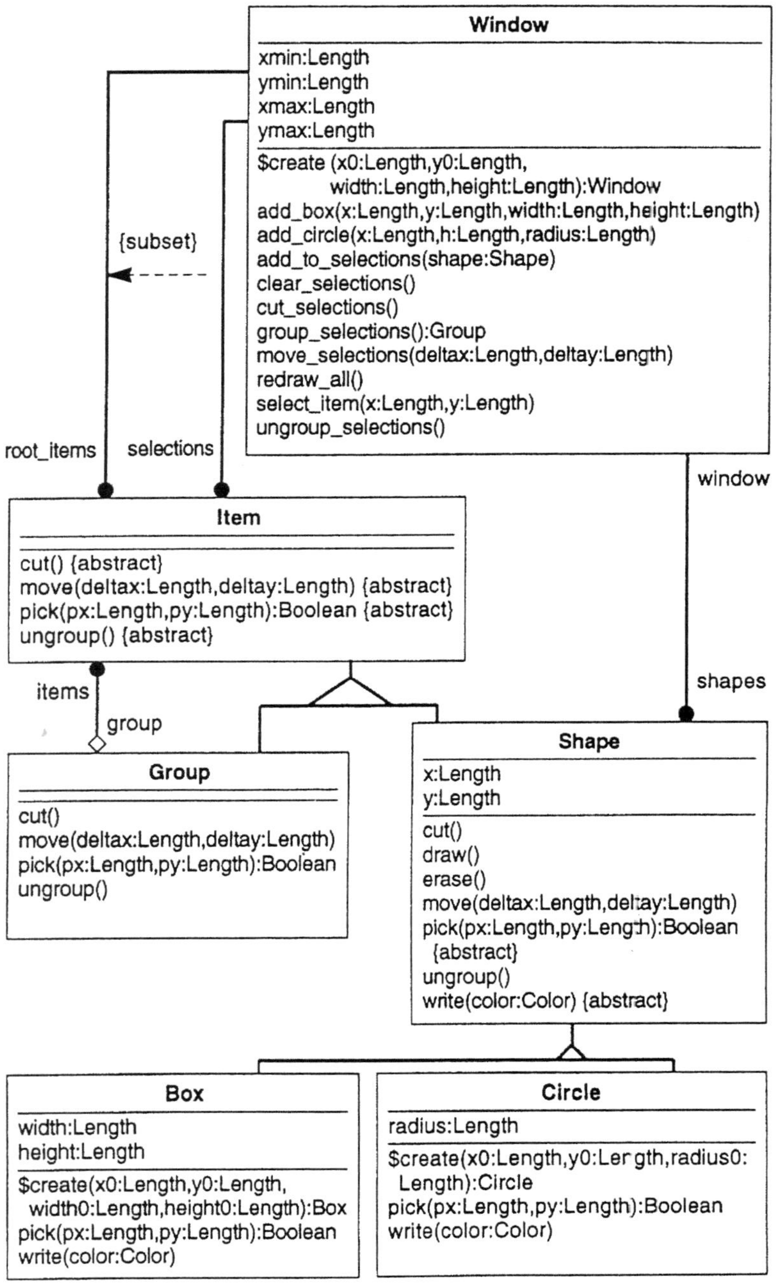

Exhibit 1. Object model for graphics editor.

becomes important when passing objects as arguments to methods and in implementing method resolution (i.e., polymorphism).

TRANSLATING CLASSES INTO DATA STRUCTURES

There are two parts to class translation. First, the class must be defined. Second, variables that identify objects must be implemented as shareable references, not simply as a copy of the object's attribute values. Each instance of the object has an implicit and unique identity. In programming terms, this means that an object should be implemented so it can be referenced by the same variable name throughout the program.

That is, each instance of a defined object has the same name and differs from the other instances of that object only in its memory location, such as an index value, in the case of arrays. The unique memory location, or index value, gives each instance its identity. Object-oriented languages have a constructor operation that allocates memory and assigns a unique object ID for each object instance of a class. Non-object-oriented languages do not provide this feature, so the program must allocate and deallocate memory and provide identity for object instances manually.

Defining a Class

Defining a class in Visual Basic can be accomplished by creating a user-defined data type for the class (known as a STRUCT in C and a record in Pascal). Unfortunately, unlike Pascal, BASIC does not provide for variant records. The type statement can be used only in the declarations section of a module, so the scope of the type definition is global to the entire application. However, variables declared as a user-defined type can be global, module level, or local in scope.

The use of a naming convention is helpful to identify the user-defined data type as an object class. A simple convention would be to prefix the type name with cls. The type definition for the Window class would be:

```
Type  clsWindow
xmin  as  single
ymin  as  single
xmax  as  single
ymax  as  single
End  Type
```

An object reference can be represented as a dynamic array of type clsWindow. A useful naming convention is to prefix an object definition with obj.

```
Dim objWindow( ) as clsWindow
```

At run time, each new instance of the objWindow object is created by adding another element to the objWindow array. This requires that the program track the number of currently allocated object instances (i.e., elements in the array). Here iNumWindows is a class attribute that contains the number of instances of the Window class. Visual Basic provides a UBound function, which returns the upper bound of an array. Because array elements are contiguous, this function can be used to determine the current size of a dynamic array:

```
Global iNumWindows as integer

iNumWindows = iNumWindows + 1

ReDim Preserve objWindow(iNumWindows)
```

or:

```
ReDim Preserve objWindow(UBound(objWindow) + 1)
```

Each instance of the Window class would be referenced by an integer subscript value pointing to an element in the objWindowarray:

```
Dim AWindow as integer

Dim x1 as single

AWindow = UBound(objWindow)

x1 = objWindow(AWindow).xmin
```

If the maximum number of object instances is known at design time, this class definition can be enhanced to include CurrentInstance and NumInstances class descriptors as well as the object array itself. The structure includes the array that contains all the object instances. BASIC allows the inclusion of arrays in user-defined types, but they must be of fixed size:

```
Type clsMetaWindow

CurrentInstance as integer 'self identifier

NumInstances as integer

Window(1000) as clsWindow

End Type
```

CurrentInstance is the ID of the current active instance of the object, which in this case would be a subscripts value to the Window object array. The object is then referenced by declaring a variable of type clsMetaWindow. Each instance of the object is an element in the Window object array:

GLOBAL OBJWINDOW AS CLSMETAWINDOW

Passing Arguments to Methods

There are several techniques for passing arguments to methods in Visual Basic. A method is the implementation of an operation for a specific object class. All objects in a class share the same operations. Methods are implemented as functions that have a target object. In object-oriented languages, this target object is an implicit argument to the function (referred to as "self").

This built-in reference to the current instance of an object is an important object-oriented concept, which must be emulated in a non-object-oriented language with an explicitly declared object ID. The "self" argument establishes object identity, and because the behavior of an operation depends on the class of its target, it provides the means for method resolution.

Pointers are useful in passing arguments to functions. Unfortunately, Visual Basic does not have pointers; it does, however, allow arguments to be passed to procedures by reference. The input arguments to a function could be passed by value, but passing them by reference is usually more efficient and "provides a uniform means of access for both queries and updates." (Rumbaugh et al, 1991) Visual Basic always passes arguments of user-defined types by reference.

In Visual Basic, either the object itself is passed by reference (i.e., the array element) or a subscript is passed, because the ID of an object instance is a subscripts to the object array for its class.

What is still lacking here is the ability to tightly couple an object instance with its class. The subscript identifies the object within the object array, but it is simply an integer value. It does not implicitly identify the class of the object, making automatic method resolution impossible.

In terms of programming technique, then, there are two ways to pass a target object to a function. If the class object has been declared globally, the subscripts of the object array element can be passed. Or, the array element itself can be passed by reference.

What is lost with this second technique is that element's subscripts value, unless it is also explicitly passed to the function. Both techniques are useful. If the method is just changing the value of an object's attribute, the array element can be passed as an argument. If the method isn't changing an attribute value but needs to refer to the identifier for that object instance (e.g., the Pick operation), the subscripts of the array element can be passed.

Defining the object class globally with class attributes (see clsMetaWindow) and referencing object instances by their subscripts gets closer to the object-oriented paradigm, even though it is then up to the method to know to which object array a subscripts argument belongs.

Rumbaugh recommends a naming convention for method function names that consists of the class name, followed by the method name, and separated by two underscores. Because in a non-object-oriented language, the programmer must manually associate methods with classes, this naming convention makes these associations easy to recognize. Rumbaugh's naming convention is as follows:

```
Sub Window__Add_to_selections( self as clsWindow,
        shape as clsShape)

    'method code goes here

End Sub
```

The method call would be:

```
Window__Add_to_selections objWindow(AWindow),
        objShape(AShape)
```

Here, the actual array elements are passed by reference. Self and shape are pointers to object instances (i.e., array elements), objWindow(AWindow) and objShape(AShape).Window__Add_to_selections is a method of class Window.Shape is being added to the set of object selections in self (the current instance of Window). Passing these variables by reference is equivalent to passing a pointer to a structure in C.

The same method implemented by passing array subscripts rather than array elements would be:

```
Sub Window__Add_to_selections( self as integer,
        shape as integer )

    'method code goes here

    'procedure must know that self as shape are

    'subscripts to the global arrays

    'objWindow and objShape

End Sub

Window__Add_to_selections AWindow, Ashape
```

ALLOCATING OBJECTS

This section presents techniques for static and dynamic allocation of objects in Visual Basic.

Static Allocation

Statically allocated objects can be implemented as global variables allocated by the compiler. In Visual Basic, a global object defined in the declarations section of a module is global to the entire application:

```
Global objOuterWindow as clsWindow
```

The attribute values can be assigned in any procedure:

```
objOuterWindow.xmin = 0.0

objOuterWindow.ymin = 0.0

objOuterWindow.xmax = 8.5

objOuterWindow.ymax = 11.0
```

Dynamic Allocation

Dynamic memory allocation provides run-time instantiation of objects by making memory available from the heap as required. In Visual Basic, such GUI objects as forms can be created at run time using the New command. For example, the NewForm method creates a new instance of a form object. But for arbitrary objects in the application domain (e.g., employee, department, and account), there is no built-in method of instantiation. Dynamic arrays do provide dynamic memory allocation capability because they can be resized at run time.

In object-oriented languages, a constructor method creates a new object instance and has the same name as the class to which it belongs. It is a special kind of method, because the object instance on which it operates does not exist when the method is invoked (the constructor creates the object instance). Again, the method's implicit argument is the object ID, a pointer to a new object of the class to which the method belongs. In Visual Basic, a constructor function could be written to input the values to be assigned to the new object, to create a new entry in the object array, and to return an integer subscript value of the element in the array containing the new object instance.

The object array could either be passed as an argument or, if globally defined, could simply be referenced in the function. Semantically, defining object arrays as global seems to fit the object-oriented paradigm better. By invoking the constructor function, the class (and therefore the object array that is acting as dynamic memory) is implied. On the other hand, having procedures modify global variables is considered poor programming practice. However, as long as it is done consistently, it is better to define the object array globally and not pass it as an argument.

This supports encapsulation, because keeping objects in an array is really an implementation issue, and as long as the object array is accessed only through its class s methods, it is acceptable to define it globally. The array is needed to act as dynamic memory and to provide a context for object identity (i.e., array name plus a subscripts equals an object instance). In contrast to C, in which pointers are available, the object instances would be declared as pointers to a structure, which defines the object class. In Visual Basic, the object array is just a memory structure used out of necessity. The focus of the program's semantics should be on the class (user-defined type) itself, not on the data structure used to implement it. Further, programmers should conceptualize an array element containing an object instance, for example objWindow(Window) as pointer to an object class, such as clsWindow(Window), rather than thinking of the object array itself as the class. This is a subtle difference but it maintains a distinction between the object-oriented concepts and their specific implementation in Visual Basic.

Method 1. This is defined as a function, when objWindow is defined as a global array.

```
Function Window__create%( xmin!, ymin!, wide!,
        high! )

Dim iSub%

iSub = UBound(objWindow) + 1

ReDim Preserve objWindow(iSub)

objWindow(iSub).xmin = xmin

objWindow(iSub).ymin = ymin

objWindow(iSub).xmax = xmin + wide

objWindow(iSub).ymax = ymin + high

Window_create = iSub

End Function
```

[For the remaining coding examples, BASIC type-declaration characters will be used rather than the var as type notation, as this shorthand method is widely used and understood. The percent sign character (%) declares an integer. The exclamation point (!) declares a single-precision floating-point number.]

Method 2. This is defined as a function, when theobjWindow array is not global but instead is explicitly passed to the constructor method.

```
Function Window__create%( window() as clsWindow,
        xmin!, ymin!, wide!, high! )
Dim iSub%
iSub = UBound(window) + 1
ReDim Preserve window(iSub)
window(iSub.xmin - xmin
window(iSub).ymin = ymin
window(iSub).xmax = xmin + wide
window(iSub).ymax = ymin + high
window(iSub).ymax = ymin + high
Window_crete = iSub
End Function
```

Because objects can be deleted as well as created, the preceding techniques do not provide for effective memory management. As objects are deleted, unused "holes" in the object array are created. An improvement is to maintain a linked list of available array elements. The systems manager should ReDim the array only if all existing elements are in use:

```
Function Window__create%( xmin!, ymin!, wide!,
        high! )
    Dim iSub%
    iSub = Window-GetAvailNode
    objWindow(iSub).xmin = xmin
    objWindow(iSub).ymin = ymin
    objWindow(iSub).xmax = xmin + wide
    objWindow(iSub).ymax = ymin + high
End Function
    if UBound(WindowAvailStack) = 0 then
        Window_GetAvailNode = UBound(objWindow) + 1
        ReDim Preserve objWindow(iSub)
    else Window-GetAvailNode = Pop-WindowAvailStack
    end if
End Function
```

Pop-WindowAvailStack and other stack-related details are omitted here; examples of implementing a stack structure abound in textbooks and literature.

```
Function  Window__GetAvailNode%( )
```

In Visual Basic, a function cannot be declared as a user-defined data type, so methods that return an object (pointer to an object) cannot be implemented directly. A function can, however, return the subscript to an array object. This further supports the notion of referencing an object by its subscripts rather than by the object array element itself.

The rest of this chapter outlines the step-by-step implementation of Visual Basic with James Rumbaugh's object modeling technique (OMT), including implementing inheritance in data structures, implementing method resolution, implementing associations, dealing with concurrency, and encapsulating internal details of classes.

James Rumbaugh's OMT is organized into eight steps that address the implementation of classes, methods, associations and parameter passing, and the concepts of identity, classification, inheritance, polymorphism, concurrency and encapsulation. Some concepts are easier than others to implement in Visual Basic: dynamic arrays provide for dynamic memory allocation, but the lack of pointers make inheritance and polymorphism difficult to accomplish. These problems, as well as concurrency, encapsulation and implementing method resolution and associations, are discussed in this chapter.

Naming conventions, as follow, are used throughout:

- cls, to identify the user-defined data type as an object class
- obj, to prefix an object definition
- BASIC-type declaration characters, rather than the var as type notation, because this shorthand method is widely used and understood
- The percent sign character (%), to declare an integer
- The exclamation point (!), to declare a single-precision floating-point number

IMPLEMENTING INHERITANCE

There are several methods for implementing inheritance in Visual Basic. This section defines the approaches to inheritance and contains an evaluation of three implementation methods in terms of practical application.

Three Approaches to Inheritance

Rumbaugh offers three approaches to inheritance in a non-object-oriented language:

1. *Avoiding it altogether.* Every class should be designed and implemented as a separate and complete data structure.
2. *Flattening the class hierarchy.* Inheritance should be modeled in the design, but each concrete subclass should be implemented as a separate data structure. Each object declaration includes its own declaration of the attributes and operations that the modeled subclasses share in inheritance from the superclass. This introduces duplication, but through consistent naming of the common attributes, the semantics of the inheritance hierarchy can be captured.
3. *Declaring a separate object class for the abstract superclass, with a reference to the superclass object within each subclass.* In this approach, there is a superclass instance for every instance of every subclass in the worst scenario and fewer instances in which some subclass object instances share a common superclass instance.

Only the second and third approaches warrant further consideration here. Single inheritance can be implemented in Visual Basic with some redundancy. Two features of the language lend themselves to implementing inheritance. User-defined data types enable the declaration of a record type containing attributes common to all subclasses (i.e., the attributes of their abstract superclass), which can then be included in the declaration of each subclass. The variant data type allows for the declaration of structures whose fields can be defined generically, with data types that may vary at run time.

Method One

The first method for implementing inheritance in Visual Basic is a mixture of the second and third approaches described. Inheritance is implemented explicitly at the declarative level, but only objects of concrete subclasses are actually created at run time, so data redundancy still exists. The systems manager declares a user-defined data type for each abstract superclass containing the shared attributes and a user-defined type for each concrete subclass. In each subclass-type definition, the manager includes the type defined for the higher-level (i.e., inherited) class (see Exhibit 1). Examples of each type definition follow.

Object Model for Graphics Editor Window

Abstract Classes. The systems manager declares user-defined data type:

```
Type  clsItem

'no attributes, but defined to reflect the hierarchy

End  Type

Type  clsShape
```

```
item as clsItem       'inherited from clsItem
x as single
y as single
End Type
```

Concrete Subclasses. The systems manager declares user-defined type, including the type for the higher-level class:

```
Type clsBox
point as clsShape     'inherited from clsShape
wide as single
high as single
End Type
Type clsCircle
point as clsShape     'inherited from clsShape
radius as single
End Type
```

In this method, only variables of type clsBox and clsCircle are defined. These are the concrete classes. In general, one instance of the hierarchy represents one concrete object. For example, a box is a shape, which is an item and is therefore one concrete object.

Method Two

This method is quite restrictive, but when it can be used, it gets much closer to true inheritance than the other methods. If the hierarchy is only one level deep, and the concrete subclasses have all atomic attributes, a variant record can be implemented. Visual Basic does not provide directly for variant record types, but with the variant data type, the application can implement its equivalent. To do so, a class object can be declared containing the shared attributes of the superclass, followed by enough variant fields to allow for the subclass with the most number of attributes. A discriminant attribute can also be defined to identify the subclass type of each object instance. Methods could then be defined to operate on the class as a whole, but each method would have to check the discriminant to see which subclass it was dealing with at any given instance:

```
    Shape class declaration
Type clsShape
    x as single
```

```
    y as single
    discriminant as integer '1 = box, 2 = circle
    a1 as variant
    a2 as variant
End Type
'Declare the array of Shape object instances
Global objShape() as clsShape
'Declare constants for the discriminant values
Const SHAPE_BOX = 1
Const SHAPE_CIRCLE = 2
'Draw method for Shape class
Function Shape_Draw%( self% )
'draw shape, depending on class of target object
    Select Case objShape(self).discriminant
        Case SHAPE_BOX
            'objShape(self).a1 contains wide
            'objShape(self).a2 contains high
            (code to draw the box)
        Case SHAPE_CIRCLE
            'objShape(self).a1 contains radius
            (code to draw the circle)
    End Select
    Shape_Draw = True
End Function
```

The method must explicitly declare a self-argument. It would be convenient if the shape_draw method could be qualified by the object name (i.e., objShape.Shape_Draw), but there is no such syntax in BASIC. The application logic must tie this function to the shape object:

```
Function Box_Create%(x!, y!, wide!, high!)
    dim iSub%
    'get the subscript of an available node in
```

```
        'the objShape global array
        iSub = Shape_GetAvailNode
        'Create the new object
        objShape(iSub).x = x
        objShape(iSub).y = y
        objShape(iSub).discriminant = SHAPE_BOX
        objShape(iSub).a1 = wide
        objShape(iSub).a2 = high
        Box_Create = iSub
    End Function
```

The box object constructor method would create an instance of the shape object and fill in the appropriate attributes to make it a box. Constructor methods are designated as a class operation in the object model, because the instance of the object being created does not exist initially; the method cannot exist before the object instance does. The constructor function cannot return the new instance of a box object, because functions cannot return user-defined data types in Visual Basic. Nor does Visual Basic have pointers, so it cannot return a pointer to a variable of that type; it returns the subscript that points to the element in the objShape array holding the new object instance. Following is an example using shape_draw to draw a box:

```
    iNewShape = Box_Create( 125, 100, 25, 100 )
    Success = Shape_Draw( iNewShape )
```

A problem with this method is that separation between program and data is lost. The program must decide what is in attributes a1 and a2 based on the discriminant.

In the example, box and circle are actually the subclasses of a two-level hierarchy, with item as the superclass. In this case, this two-level hierarchy could also be implemented with the previous method. However, this is a special situation, because only the shape path of the hierarchy has attributes (see Exhibit 1). In general, this method is less appealing for multilevel hierarchies, because variant data types can be resolved only to atomic types. Therefore, the higher-level record types would have to carry a definition for every lower-level type, and then only one would be used in any given instance. This is similar to Rumbaugh's technique of a universal record, which contains an attribute for every attribute in every descendant class. In any given instance, any attributes that do not apply are ignored, which can be very wasteful if there are many attributes. Universal records are discussed in following sections.

Method Three

This method follows Rumbaugh's third approach and is intended for multilevel hierarchies. A class is declared for each abstract class as well as for the descendant concrete classes, and an array is allocated for each of the classes. (In this example, the number of atomic attributes is small, so a universal record could be defined for both the box and circle concrete subclasses.) For the sake of example, a number_of_items attribute has been added to the group subclass, to demonstrate a multilevel hierarchy:

```
Type clsItem
    item Class as integer' 1 = group, 2 = shape
    childID as integer ' points to a group or shape
End type
Type clsGroup
    iNumItems as integer
    ParentID as integer ' points to item
End type
    Type clsShape
    shapeClass as integer    '1 = box, 2 = circle
    childID as integer ' points to a box or circle
    parentID as integer ' points to item
End Type
    Type cls Box
    wide as single
    high as single
    parentID as integer ' points to shape
End Type
    Type clsCircle
    radius as single
    parentID as integer ' points to shape
End Type
```

```
Global objItem( ) as clsItem     ' abstract class
Global objGroup( ) as clsGroup ' recursive
                               ' aggregate class
Global objShape( ) as clsShape ' abstract class
Global objBox( ) as clsBox     ' concrete class
Global objCircle( ) as clsCircle'concrete class
```

Here, whenever a box or circle is created, an entry in the objShape and objItem arrays must also be created. Whenever a group is created, an entry must be created in the objItem array. So an instance of a box object would consist of a node in the objItem array pointing to a node in the objShape array, which points to a node in the objBox array. ChildID in each node allows downward traversal through the hierarchy tree, whereas parentID allows upward traversal through the tree. Externally, the group, shape, box, and circle objects can typically be accessed through the item object, or the root, hiding the details of the hierarchy, but they can also be accessed directly.

This technique is possible, but the extra coding and program complexity may outweigh the benefits. The intent of implementing an Object-Oriented Design by mapping object-oriented concepts to this language is to improve the relationship between design and implementation by bringing the level of abstraction of the program closer to that of the design. Introducing program complexity works against the goal of better understanding. In general, it is better to flatten the hierarchy and to use one of the simpler methods for implementing inheritance. If generalization is needed, the programmer should keep it to one level and use method two.

Implementing Method Resolution

This section presents alternative methods for implementing polymorphism in Visual Basic and has recommendations based on their applicability.

Non-object-oriented programming languages do not support the concept of polymorphism, which allows an operation to be implemented by many objects, each as a method with its own distinct behavior. Rumbaugh offers three ways to handle method resolution in which run-time method resolution is not provided by the language.

Method One

The first way is to avoid it altogether, by defining operations only once in a class hierarchy, thus eliminating the need for polymorphism. The operation behaves the same for all subclasses. To avoid it, the

Object-Oriented Design must not define any subclasses that override an inherited operation.

Method Two

The second technique is to resolve methods at compile time. This technique simply uses the traditional programming approach of writing specific functions, or methods, to operate on each object class, or data structure, and in the program's procedures, calling the appropriate function based on the class of the object. It is significant only when one or more subclasses override inherited operations in a class hierarchy.

For example, to draw a box object, a box_draw routine is called. To draw a circle, a separate circle_draw routine is called. This is in contrast to true polymorphism, which would simply have a draw operation whose behavior would depend on the class of the target object. Here, the method inheritance can be made apparent in the program through careful naming of the method. In the graphics editor example, the draw operation is inherited from shape by box and circle. The behavior of the draw operation depends on the subclass's implementation. By naming these methods box_draw and circle_draw, it makes it clear that these methods are versions of the draw operation.

This technique can present problems, though. If the structure of the hierarchy or the behavior of one of the functions is changed, there can be a ripple effect on the rest of the program, requiring careful examination of any code that uses the function. If the inheritance hierarchy is changed, it may be necessary to rename the function to properly reflect the new hierarchy.

Method Three

The third technique is to resolve methods at run time. Again, this is necessary only when an abstract operation is shared by more than one class and its behavior differs, depending on the class of the object it is operating on. If the behavior of an operation is the same for all classes that use it, there is no need for polymorphism. In this case, the correct function calls are coded directly in the program, because there is never any question about which method applies to an object to perform a given operation. When polymorphism is necessary, an object-oriented language automatically tests to which class an object belongs and invokes the correct method to perform a given operation on that object. In a non-object-oriented language, dynamic method resolution must be implemented manually.

However, a fourth approach, a combination of the second and third, is preferable. The first technique avoids polymorphism altogether. The second technique alone is safe and traditional but does not lend much of an object-oriented feel to the program. Dynamic method resolution can be implemented in Visual Basic by creating a dispatch procedure for the abstract operation, which tests the class of the object to be operated on, and then calls the appropriate method. How this is done depends on how inheritance was implemented in the declaration of the object classes.

For example, the item generalization hierarchy contains only a few attributes, so it could be implemented using a universal record as follows. Here, separate routines still exist for each class, but they are not visible externally. All pick operations are done using the Pick function:

```
Type clsItem
    discriminant as integer    '1 = group, 2 = box,
                               '3 = circle
        x as single            'Shape attribute
        y as single            'Shape attribute
        wide as single         'Box attribute
        high as single         'Box attribute
        radius as single       'Circle attribute
End Type
Global objItem( ) as clsItem 'the object array
Function Pick%( self%, px!, py! )
    Select Case objItem(self).discriminant
    Case GROUP
        Pick = Group-Pick( self, px, py )
    Case SHAPE_BOX
        Pick = Box_Pick( self, px, py )
    Case SHAPE_CIRCLE
        Pick = Circle_Pick( self, px, py )
    Case Else
        Pick = False
    End Select
End Function
```

An example would be

```
rc = Pick( ItemToPick, 100, 200 ).
```

Implementing Associations

This section discusses issues surrounding the implementation of associations in Visual Basic and presents techniques for implementing binary associations between objects of each cardinality.

In implementing associations, some fundamental programming principles apply. Association traversal and update logic should not be coded directly in the main program but rather in separate traversal and update routines that can be called by the program. The advantage here is that the details of the implementation are hidden from the main program, making changes easier.

In the object model, bidirectional associations are assumed. However, in implementation, it may be that the association applies only in one direction. In general, if an association is implemented only on one direction, provisions should be made to add the other direction if necessary.

Translating Associations from the Object Model

Associations can be translated from the object model in a method similar to translating relationships in an entity-relationship model:

- A one-to-one association can be implemented by the programmer placing a pointer and link attributes in one of the participating classes.
- A one-to-many association can be implemented by the programmer placing pointer and link attributes in the many-sided class, if that class has total participation. If not, the programmer should create an association object, which will have only one instance for each pair of participating objects. This eliminates the wasted space created by burying pointer and link attributes in the many-sided class and by having non-participating instances contain an empty pointer and link attributes.
- A many-to-many association can be implemented by the programmer creating an association object with an instance for each association instance between the participating classes. Many-to-many associations can also be implemented by the programmer placing a list of pointers in each participating class, pointing to the associated instances of the other class. (This technique does not carry over from relational database design.) If the association has link attributes, a separate association object should be created, because the link attributes cannot be associated with either class individually.
- Higher-order (i.e., n-ary) associations must be implemented with association objects.

Implementing Associations in Visual Basic

In Visual Basic, associations can be implemented with either buried pointers or separate association objects, depending on the multiplicity and participation of the association and on whether there are link attributes.

Because Visual Basic's only dynamic memory allocation is through dynamic arrays, implementing associations is one of the more difficult tasks in mapping object-oriented concepts to this language:

- A bidirectional, one-to-one association is easily implemented as mutual pointers between the participating objects. A pointer attribute for the association is added to each class definition.
- A one-to-many association is implemented on the many-sided association in the same way as a bidirectional, one-to-one association. For example, in the one-to-many relationship between item and group, each item belongs to one group. Therefore, a group pointer that points to the corresponding group object instance could be added to the item class definition. Because object instances in Visual Basic have been implemented as array elements, pointers are subscript to the object arrays. A null pointer value should be established that is outside of the range of valid subscript for the array. For example, if the base of an object array is 1, a value of 0 could indicate a null pointer. The list looks like this:

```
Type clsItem
    group as integer subscript of related group
    (remainder of Group description)
End Type
Type cls Group
    items as integer   'subscript of first item
                       'related to this group
End Type
Type clsItem
    group as integer   'subscript of the related
                       'group
nextInGroup as integer 'subscript of next item
                       'in the related group
    (remainder of Item description)
End Type
```

To traverse the linked list, the first item subscripts from the group object must be obtained, then the list can be traversed using the nextInGroup subscripts until nextInGroup = 0 (i.e., a null pointer).

A bidirectional many-to-many association without link attributes could be implemented in a similar manner, with a linked lists established in both participating objects. For example, an item could be part of more than one group:

```
Type clsGroup
NextItem as integer      'subscript of next group
                         'instance (next item in
                         'same group)
(remainder of Group description)
End Type
Type clsItem
nextGroup as integer     'subscript of next item
                         'instance (next group for
                         'same item)
(remainder of Item description)
End Type
```

This approach, however, creates a redundancy. In effect, every link or ordered pair making up the association is represented by a separate instance of the group and item objects. Now, there must be an instance of a given group object for every item in that group. Likewise, there must be an instance of the same item for each group the item is in. This wastes memory if the objects have many attributes and creates possible update anomalies, because whenever an association instance is created or deleted, both linked lists must be kept in synch. These are similar to update anomalies created by a relational schema that has not been normalized:

- When a new link or instance of an association between item and group is created, a new instance of both the item and group objects must be created, duplicating the attribute values in each of these objects.
- An item object cannot be created without also creating a group object, because every item is part of exactly one group.
- If the last item of a group is deleted, the group object will remain unless it is explicitly deleted. In the graphics editor object model, clearly a group object should not really exist if it has no items.
- If a group or item object attribute value changes, every occurrence in the object array for the affected object instance must be found and updated.

A better approach in this case, and a mandatory one if there are link attributes, is to create an association object, which simply contains instances of the association that hold pointers to each participating object along with the link attributes:

```
Type ascItemGroup        'association object class
    item as integer      'subscript of item object
    group as integer     'subscript of group object
    (no link attributes in this case)
End Type
```

Dealing with Concurrency

Concurrency refers to the sharing of objects by concurrent tasks. This is not a possibility in Visual Basic because it does not provide for parallel tasks within an application, and the scope of even a global piece of data is the application itself and therefore not accessible by other applications. Therefore, any concurrency issues encountered in implementing an Object-Oriented Design in Visual Basic would be the result of objects residing elsewhere. For example, if the Visual Basic application is a multi-user client/server application accessing a database on a Remote Data Base server, concurrency must be dealt with in the context of the database management system and Network Operating System.

Encapsulating Internal Details of Classes

The basic premise of encapsulation is that objects are interacted with through their methods.

This encapsulates internal details of the object and provides a well-defined interface to the object. The idea is to address objects through methods using messages, rather than to manipulate their attributes directly. By maintaining an external (i.e., public) view of the object and its operations, which is separate from the internal structure (i.e., private), changes can be made to the implementation of the operations without affecting the applications using the object.

There are opportunities to implement encapsulation in a Visual Basic program, even though the language does not explicitly provide for this. User-defined data types are global by definition in Visual Basic and must be defined in the declarations section of a program module. It is good practice to create a separate program module for each object class that contains the type declaration as well as the methods for that class. Global variables should not be used for any object attributes. Objects should be operated on only through their methods, and input and output data should always be passed as arguments.

User-defined data types make encapsulation of the object's structure possible. Objects should be referenced by their subscript to the object array. Object attributes are accessed by means of qualified references [e.g., objItem(i).x]. Referencing object arrays themselves[e.g., ObjItem( )] should be avoided. Arrays are simply data structures used to implement dynamic memory allocation in Visual Basic and have no significance in the object model.

CONCLUSION

It is possible to implement an Object-Oriented Design in Visual Basic. The question, however, is whether these techniques provide significant advantages over traditional programming practices. Continued use and refinement over time will answer this question. From work out so far, there are limits to the practical value of some of the more complex techniques, but designing a Visual Basic program with object-oriented concepts in mind produces definite benefits. All the object-oriented concepts together provide a basis for effective programming practice, with specific object-oriented techniques being used when appropriate. In general, the simplest approach to implementing a specific technique is usually the best. Because of the lack of pointers, especially function pointers, some of the concepts, such as inheritance and polymorphism, can be emulated but not fully implemented without undue complexity.

One significant benefit that can be derived from this method is encapsulated, reusable code. The notion of isolating functionally related code into a subprogram with a well-defined interface is certainly not a new technique. But objects are more than this. A full abstraction of a real-world object consists of its behavior, attributes and constraints. Such encapsulation is possible to an extent in Visual Basic by placing all data declarations and procedures for each class in a separate program module. Each program module in Visual Basic is stored as a separate file, so class modules, once defined and tested, can be easily added to a project from a common library and shared by many applications.

The method for implementing an object-oriented design in Visual Basic using Rumbaugh's Object Modeling Technique is organized into steps that address the implementation of classes, methods, associations and parameter passing, and the concepts of identity, classification, inheritance, polymorphism, concurrency, and encapsulation. This chapter offers techniques that employ the available language features.

Some concepts are easier to implement than others. Dynamic arrays provide for dynamic memory allocation, but the lack of pointers make inheritance and polymorphism difficult to accomplish. It may not be possible to implement fully encapsulated objects, which provide a complete abstraction of the application domain, but an Object-Oriented Programming Language is not required to adopt object-oriented concepts.

Chapter 9
Developing New Applications in a Heterogeneous Environment

Raj Rajagopal

As mentioned earlier in the handbook, there are many organizations that have heterogeneous computing environments and will probably continue to have them for the foreseeable future. Developing new applications in these organizations invariably raises a number of environment related issues that need to be addressed.

In planning or developing new applications, the following few questions probably will be raised:

- Should a Windows application or a UNIX application be developed?
- If one environment is chosen for the long term, is there a way to easily make it work in another environment in the short term?
- Should the traditional languages and APIs be used or should new application development tools be chosen?
- Should object-oriented frameworks be used?
- How are legacy applications interfaced with and how is the data that resides in the corporate databases accessed?
- What language is best to develop the application?

This chapter is not intended to be a primer on new application development, but will look at developing new applications from a Windows, UNIX, NetWare coexistence and migration viewpoint. Applications can be developed that will execute across platforms in a number of ways:

- The application can be developed once using a proprietary API and run in different environments

0-8493-9989-0/99/$0.00+$.50

- APIs can be developed for one environment (such as Win32 for Windows NT) and executed in another (such as UNIX) using porting tools. Porting applications was covered earlier in the handbook.
- Distributed applications can be developed in a heterogeneous environment.
- Applications can be developed using 4GL products or object-oriented frameworks.
- Standard 3GL languages, such as C/C++, and compile switches to isolate environment-specific code can be used.

Besides executing in different environments, applications also must be able to:

- Interface with legacy applications
- Access the data that resides in the corporate databases
- Perform transaction processing across heterogeneous systems

CROSS-PLATFORM APPLICATION DEVELOPMENT

API-based applications that can run in both Windows NT and UNIX can be developed in one of three ways:

1. Proprietary APIs. This can be done in one of three ways.
   a) Layered APIs that reside on top of native APIs
   b) Layered APIs plus extensions
   c) Emulated APIs
2. Use Win32 and port to UNIX
3. Use POSIX and port to Win32

The API-based approach is covered later in this chapter.

The development can be moved a level higher than APIs and 4GL tools and other application generators can be used. Finally, Portable Object-Oriented Frameworks can be used. 4GL tools such as PowerBuilder are well known in the industry. 4GL products and Portable Object-Oriented Frameworks are covered later in this chapter.

If 4GL or other development tools that come with their own language(s) and script(s) are not being used, then the common development languages for which many cross-platform toolkits and porting tools are available are C and C++. Even when developing applications using C and C++, some constructs can be used to facilitate the generation of cross-platform applications. A detailed list of C and C++ differences was covered earlier in the handbook and compilations can be used conditionally to generate the executable for the chosen platform as shown below:

```
#ifdef  unix

    int  dfile;  /*  file  descriptor  */
```

```
#endif
#ifdef _MSC_VER HANDLE dfile; /* file handle */
#endif
.
.
.
#ifdef unix
   if ((dfile = open(DataFile, O_RDWR |
            O_CREAT))== -1)
#endif
#ifdef _MSC_VER /* using Visual C++ */
   if ((dfile = CreateFile(DataFile, GENERIC_READ |
   GENERIC_WRITE, FILE_SHARE_READ, NULL,
   OPEN_ALWAYS, FILE_ATTRIBUTE_NORMAL, NULL)) ==
   INVALID_HANDLE_VALUE) #endif
```

In developing web-based applications Java, HTML, etc. will most likely be used, which, for the most part, are portable across platforms. Mainframe-based applications must be interfaced with, or data must be accessed from mainframe-based databases.

Although COBOL is the language most commonly used in mainframe applications, mainframe applications can still be interfaced with using any language desired.

Cross-Platform Development using Proprietary APIs

There are three variations of proprietary APIs — Layered APIs supporting the least common subset, Layered APIs plus extensions, and Emulated APIs.

Here are a few advantages and disadvantages of using proprietary APIs.

The advantages are:

- Applications can be easily ported to different environments, in many cases transparently to the application. Thus operating systems can be switched with very little change to the applications themselves. This is one way to avoid standardizing on Windows or UNIX, but allowing the applications developed to run on either.

- It is easy to have a common source for developing applications that will eventually run on multiple hardware/software platforms, particularly if applications eventually need to run in multiple environments.

The disadvantages are:

- Proprietary APIs are tightly linked to the vendors that provide them. If all applications in an organization are written to a proprietary layer, the organization becomes dependent on that API and the API vendor.
- The number of environments the application will work on and the features the application can support depend on the number of environments and features supported by the API vendor.
- If the API vendor discontinues the API or goes out of business, it may be difficult to update an application to take advantage of enhancements to underlying OS and maintain the application.
- It is one more layer of software, which increases the chances of introducing bugs and interface problems.
- There may be a performance penalty (unlike a native application that does not use the APIs but uses OS calls directly) but the penalty may vary.
- Programming support usually comes from the software vendor and others using the software through newsgroups, etc. While vendor support depends on the vendor, support from others using the software depends on the popularity of the product.
- Proprietary APIs, as shown, avoid the differences among APIs of different platforms and operating systems by providing the least common subset of the underlying native APIs. The least common subset limitation can be overcome by providing additional proprietary APIs, as discussed below.
- If a proprietary API approach is chosen, managers may want to check availability and price of the API vendor's source code (either delivered outright, or at least held in escrow and deliverable in case the vendor goes out of business). While the source code may not be the best solution in case the API vendor goes out of business, it is at least one option to be exercised.

Layered APIs supporting least common subset. Proprietary APIs allow for the development of applications that are independent of target systems. As shown in Exhibit 1, proprietary APIs provide a layer of abstraction and map the APIs invoked by the applications to those provided in the native environment. Thus, the application always makes the same calls regardless of the target operating system.

"Layered APIs" is a reference to the fact that the APIs provide a cross-platform layer on top of a native OS layer. The main problem is that the

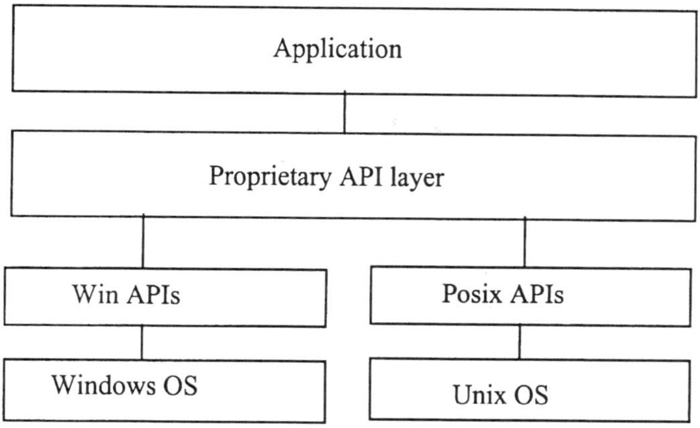

Exhibit 1. Layered APIs supporting the least common subset.

proprietary APIs, as shown above, support only functions that are common to the underlying environments, i.e. the APIs support the least common subset of the functions in the underlying environments.

Layered APIs plus extensions. The least common subset problem mentioned above can be overcome by the API vendor providing its own APIs for functions not supported in the native APIs. There are two ways in which this can be done. One way is use the native APIs wherever possible and provide extensions for unsupported functions.

Another method is to avoid using any native APIs, but instead provide a replacement API library for the native APIs. The second method is commonly called "emulated APIs" and is covered later in this chapter. The layered APIs plus extensions approach is shown in Exhibit 2.

Although the least common subset problem is solved, the proprietary extensions introduce diversity between the proprietary implementation and the operating system provider's native implementation. An application that uses the vendor's extension will not run natively.

Emulated APIs. Many operating environments include a set of low-level calls and a library of high-level calls that are built on top of the low-level calls. For example, Motif uses xlib calls for performing many user interface functions such as displaying a window.

When an application needs to display a window, it can call Motif or it can call xlib directly. If a third-party library, as a replacement for Motif, implements whatever Motif supports plus other functions available in other environments such as Windows, but not in Motif (example Notebook controls), such a library would be an emulated API library.

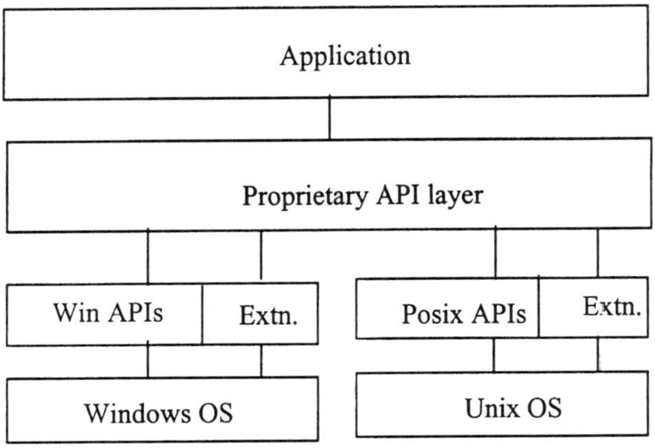

Exhibit 2. Layered APIs plus extensions.

There are advantages and disadvantages to the emulated API approach. The advantages are that porting applications across supported platforms tends to be relatively simple and an emulator can opt to provide a completely consistent look and feel across all platforms as it doesn't use the native functions.

However, since emulated APIs replace all the native high-level functions, the code size tends to be much higher than the layered APIs. And it may not be possible to use an enhancement to APIs made by the native OS vendor until an equivalent enhancement is made by the emulated API vendor. An example of Proprietary API would be AppWare from Novell, although Novell is de-emphasizing this product.

CROSS-PLATFORM GUI DEVELOPMENT

Many vendors provide cross-platform development tools that allow development of both GUI and non-GUI code. Regardless of which vendor is chosen, it is a good idea for to segment applications into GUI and non-GUI portions. Segmenting applications provides a number of benefits:

- It is easy to extend an application to another GUI environment as well as drop support for a GUI environment, if necessary.
- Developing, testing, and debugging applications is easier.
- Segmenting provides the option of implementing the GUI portion natively, particularly if performance is an issue.

While segmenting allows the source to be partitioned, when opting for native implementation of GUI, separate source libraries must be maintained for the different GUIs chosen. The cost of managing multiple sources for development and maintenance must be weighed against the performance benefits and potential cost benefits (of not using a porting toolkit). In addition, developers familiar with the environments chosen to go native will be needed, as well as developers familiar with the porting toolkit (if one is used).

DEVELOPING APPLICATIONS USING WIN32 API ON UNIX

Instead of proprietary APIs, there are tools that provide the Win32 API support on UNIX and thus enable Windows applications to run on UNIX. These tools assume the role of Windows in such systems, providing the function calls, messages, device contexts, and controls that Windows provides for application programs. Microsoft offers a licensing program called WISE to facilitate development using the Win32 API and subsequent porting to UNIX.

Examples of companies who have used WISE include MainSoft, Bristol Technology, Insignia Solutions, and Locus Computing. This approach offers cross-platform development capabilities starting with the WIN32 API, instead of a proprietary API. This approach also helps in porting current Windows applications (whose source is available) to UNIX, as covered earlier in the handbook.

Microsoft WISE. The Microsoft Windows Interface Source Environment (WISE) is a licensing program from Microsoft to enable customers to integrate Windows-based solutions with UNIX and Macintosh systems. WISE solutions come in two forms — WISE SDKs and WISE emulators.

WISE SDKs

WISE SDKs provide source code compatibility and the application source code must be recompiled for the different systems the application needs to run on. WISE SDKs are available on Macintosh and UNIX systems. A WISE SDK consists of tools to port code from a PC and libraries to compile Windows code on the Macintosh or UNIX systems.

An overview of WISE SDK is shown in Exhibit 3.

WISE SDKs typically include source code preprocessor, makefile generator, Windows libraries, resource compiler, MFC for UNIX, and online help.

- Source code preprocessor — The source code preprocessor changes PC source code to make it compatible with a UNIX system. For example, the source code preprocessor changes separators in a path name from \ to /. The preprocessor removes the carriage return character from each line to make the file compatible with a UNIX system.

- Makefile generator —automatically generates makefiles.
- Windows libraries — These libraries provide the same services to applications that Windows provides to Windows applications. Libraries can be built low level (using xlib functions) or at a higher level (using Motif functions).
- Resource compiler — The resource compiler is used to compile Windows resource script files (and associated files) that specify details of resources such as menus, dialog boxes, icons, cursors, strings, and bitmaps on the UNIX system and generate a UNIX version of the resource file.
- Microsoft Foundation Classes (MFC) for UNIX-WISE SDKs — include support for MFC on UNIX systems.
- Online help — Programmers can port rich text format files and help instructions from a PC and use the WISE SDK help compiler to compile and generate a UNIX system help file. The help engine displays the help file to a user.

Examples of WISE SDKs include MainWin from Mainsoft and Wind/U from Bristol.

WISE Emulators

WISE emulators provide object code compatibility and enable shrink-wrapped Windows-based applications to run unmodified on UNIX and Macintosh systems. A WISE emulator intercepts Windows calls from a Windows application and translates the calls into calls that can be satisfied by the host system's services. Examples of WISE emulators include SoftWindows from Insignia and Merge from Locus.

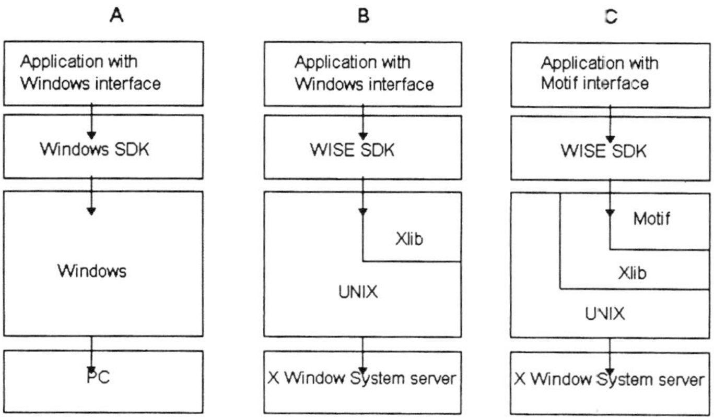

Exhibit 3. WISE SDK overview.

DEVELOPING APPLICATIONS USING 4GL TOOLS

Rather than adopting an API approach of writing to Win32 or POSIX or a proprietary API, applications can be developed using 4GL tools. 4GL tools come with versions that run on Windows as well as UNIX. Thus, if applications are developed using a 4GL tool in one environment, it should be possible to reuse the 4GL source for the other environments. The advantages and disadvantages mentioned for proprietary APIs apply to 4GL tools as well. One advantage that applies to 4GL tools that does not apply to proprietary APIs is that, in general, it is faster to develop applications using 4GL tools than with the more traditional programming language/APIs based approach.

As shown in Exhibit 4, there are several categories of 4GL application development tools. Ranging from GUI builders to CASE and Integrated CASE (ICASE), these categories can be differentiated by their support for application complexity and the scalability of users and transactions.

Exhibit 5 summarizes common products and vendors for each of the 4GL categories.

If a 4 GL product is being used for application development, the vendor should be consulted as to whether the resulting 4 GL application will execute in other environments that may be of interest.

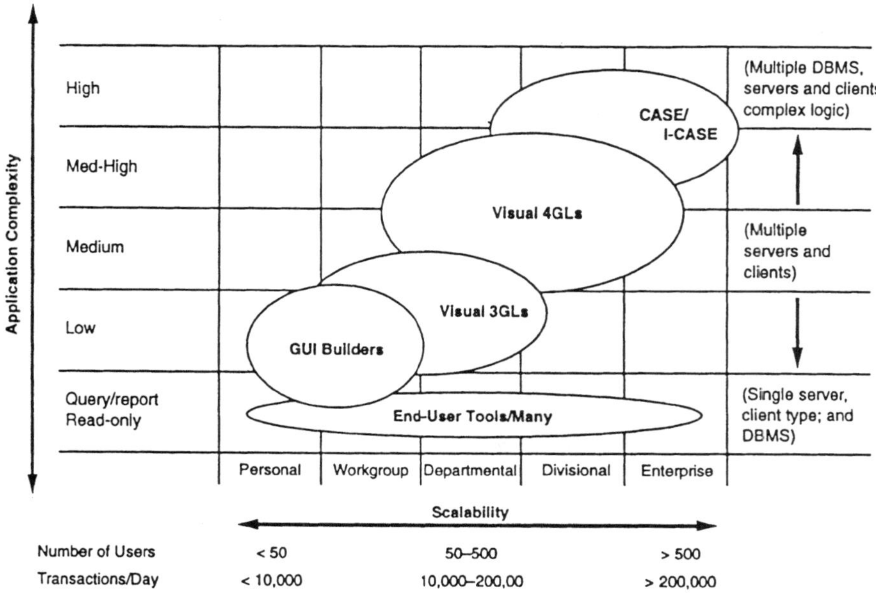

Exhibit 4. Categories of 4GL applications.

Exhibit 5. 4 GL products and vendors.

4GL Category	Products	Vendor
GUI Builders	Galaxy	Visix Software
	Elements Environment	Neuron Data
Visual 3 GLs	InterBase	Borland
	Visual Basic	Microsoft
	VisualWave	ParcPlace-Digitalk Systems
Visual 4 GLs	ApplixWare	Applix
	Sapphire/Web	Bluestone
	Axiant	Cognos
	UNIFACE SIX	Compuware
	DIGITAL Application Generator	Digital Equipment Corp.
	Forte Application Environment	Forte Software
	FOCUS	Information Builders
	APTuser	International Software Group
	Magic	Magic Software
	Elements environment	Neuron Data
	Oracle Designer/Developer	Oracle
	JAM 7	Prolifics
	PROGRESS	Progress Software
	Sapiens Ideo	Sapiens USA
	Unify Vision	Unify
	uniVerse	Vmark Software
CASE/ICASE	Foundation Design/I	Andersen Consulting
	Composer by IEF	Texas Instruments

PORTABLE OBJECT-ORIENTED FRAMEWORKS

Portable object-oriented application frameworks provide a set of C++ classes that can be reused to build portable applications and functions for print, file and other application services. Some application frameworks have the same least common subset problem as the proprietary APIs. To avoid this problem, some provide code that emulates the missing functions. Frameworks are attractive to customers interested in developing new application using object-oriented techniques and interested in portability. Some object-oriented frameworks are covered below.

DSC++

Information on DSC++ is available online at http://www.xvt.com.

XVT's Development Solution for C++ (DSC++) helps in cross-platform development by building applications in one platform, and then porting them easily to other platforms. DSC++ uses C++, which, after compilation, results in native applications.

The core of DSC++ is an application framework that contains a full set of functions common to all GUI-based applications, including documents, windows, scrolling views, visual interface objects, graphical primitives, geometry management, data managers, and inter-object communication. DSC++ also includes Rogue Wave Tools.h++ data structures.

The framework's visual tool allows users to design and interconnect reusable GUI components with clicks of the mouse. DSC++'s visual tool guides the user through the development process from defining architecture and laying out the interface to writing code and building the final application. Project files containing portable GUI application interface information be displayed and edited on any XVT-supported platform.

DSC++ generates C++ source code, application resources, and makefiles that can be used with a built-in development library to make an application natively.

Platforms supported by DSC++ include:

- Microsoft Windows including Windows NT
- Power Macintosh and Macintosh
- OS/2
- OSF/Motif (on many systems)

Allegris

Information on Allegris is available online at http://www.intersolv.com.

Allegris includes the following product series:

- Allegris Workshop
- Allegris Constructor
- Allegris Object Repository
- Allegris DataDesigner

The Allegris Series can be deployed on a product-by-product basis or as a complete integrated development environment as shown in Exhibit 6.

Allegris Workshop. Allegris Workshop is a complete OO development environment for building reusable components and client/server applications. Allegris Workshop combines a GUI developer offering full Windows 95 controls with Allegris Foundation, a class library of more than 170 cross-platform components.

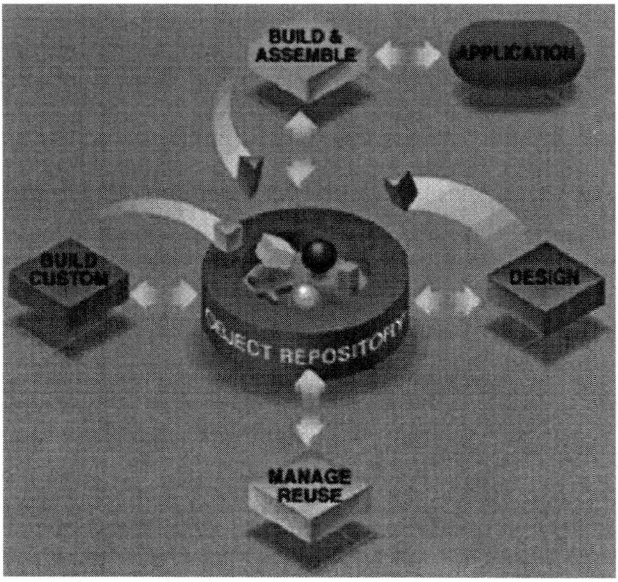

Exhibit 6. Allegris product series.

Windows 95 controls include notebooks; portable fonts and colors; enhanced status bar; and flexible, dockable toolbar; multilevel undo/redo; interactive property sheets; menu edito; and online help editor.

The class library includes classes for GUI design, event processing, data management, transparent internationalization, file handling and OLE 2 support. Allegris Workshop provides double-byte character support (DBCS) across all platforms using UNICODE as a basis. Allegris Workshop is built on a foundation of true object technology and offers the full object-orientation of the Smalltalk Model View Controller.

Allegris Workshop facilitates developing interoperable cross-platform applications using portable resource formats which support multiple languages from a single executable, without recompiling, and geometry management features. Allegris Workshop can be used in conjunction with the INTERSOLV DataDirect Developer's Toolkit for C++ to provide ODBC access to over 30 relational databases.

Allegris Workshop provides full ActiveX container support (linking, embedding, activation, and automation). Allegris Webshop, available as an add-on to Allegris Workshop, provides additional C++ classes for building Web-server applications and the Portable Resource Workshop can generate HTML forms.

Allegris Workshop is currently available for Windows 95, Windows NT, Windows 3.1, OS/2, SunSoft Solaris, IBM AIX, HP-UX and DEC UNIX.

Allegris Constructor. Allegris Constructor is a component-based development environment that enables developers to build and assemble scalable components from departmental applications to enterprise applications and Internet/intranet applications. Developers use point-and-click, drag-and-drop painters to build application components and control application behavior using scripts written in an object-oriented extension of standard Basic. For example, components are distributed across clients and servers through simple drag-and-drop.

Allegris Constructor delivers applications as compiled C++ applications. Allegris Constructor comes bundled with the command-line version of the Borland C++ compiler, linker and debugger. Applications created using Allegris Constructor can access data from Oracle, Sybase, Informix, SQL Server or any other ODBC-compliant data source. Mainframe databases are accessed through DataDirect SequeLink.

ActiveX insertables, controls and servers can be imported into the Allegris Object Repository for use in developing applications with Allegris Constructor. The capability to deploy components built with Allegris as ActiveX components is planned for the future.

Allegris Constructor can be hosted on either Windows 95 or Windows NT. The Allegris Object Repository (AOR) is supported by Oracle, Sybase System 10 or 11, SQL Server, Informix or Sybase SQL Anywhere databases. Upon installing Allegris Constructor, a stand-alone, single-user version of the Sybase SQL Anywhere repository is created.

Allegris Object Repository. The Allegris Object Repository (AOR) is a scalable repository that is tightly integrated with the other products in the Allegris Series and serves as the backbone for the Allegris development environment. It provides a workgroup-management framework to store, manage and reuse software components.

The AOR leverages INTERSOLV's DataDirect data connectivity technology and the BLOB (Binary Large Object) storage capability of major relational databases.

The Allegris Object Repository can be hosted on top of many popular databases such as FoxPro 3, Sybase SQL Anywhere, Sybase System 10 or 11, Oracle, SQL Server, Informix and DB2/2.

Components stored in the AOR, whether built with Allegris Constructor, designed with Allegris DataDesigner or imported as ActiveX components or DLLs, are assigned categories and given descriptions and these categories and descriptions, along with component types, can be used as search criteria when attempting to locate components for reuse.

Allegris DataDesigner. Allegris DataDesigner is the analysis and design component of Allegris that enables the design of static object models and relational databases for distributed object applications. Relational models are used in Allegris to automate access to data. Object models in DataDesigner are built using the Unified Modeling Language (UML) notation.

DataDesigner can import existing database definitions from SQL DDL or directly via ODBC.

zApp Developer's Suite 3

Information on zApp is available online at http://www.roguewave.com.

zApp Developer's Suite 3 includes the following components:

- zApp Application Framework
- zApp Interface Pack
- zHelp
- zApp Factory

The zApp Application Framework provides a hierarchy of more than 200 classes for standard application objects. The zApp Interface Pack adds components such as bitmap buttons and 3-D controls. The zApp Application Framework also includes a spreadsheet-like table object with a variety of cell types to display any kind of data in matrix format. zHelp is an online help system based on HTML.

zHelp includes a portable help viewer and supports popular features like hypertext links, inline images, and multiple fonts. zApp Factory is a visual development environment for zApp. zApp Factory features a WYSIWYG application generator that allows drag-and-drop construction of complete applications and generates the corresponding zApp source code. zApp factory features an integrated application development environment including the following:

- Project Manager — displays all application components in an organized, hierarchical fashion
- Modeless Object Manager — displays and edits an object's properties
- Window Designer — supports object alignment, sizing, spacing, and positioning, as well as drag-and-drop capability for adding controls, tool buttons, status items, icons, and bitmaps
- Code Generator — produces commented zApp source code, resources, make files, and project files for all supported environments.

Code Generator includes incremental and selective code generation and protects user code, so custom routines are preserved on code regeneration.

The zApp factory includes integrated and stand-alone test modes to let programmers run their prototype within the zApp Factory environment, or as a discrete application without compilation. It is possible to execute specific user written code either through a link to user source code that is triggered as a response to a particular event, or by embedding source code in blocks within the source file in constructs called protect blocks.

zApp is source-code portable across 12 operating environments, including X/Motif, OS/2, and 16- and 32-bit Windows. zApp provides a method of porting resource files across all supported platforms. zApp supports the current version of all major compilers for each platform and integrates with third-party development tools, such as editors, debuggers, and version control systems.

The zApp family of tools is built on Rogue Wave's Tools.h++. zApp's source code is included free of charge.

Systems Toolkit from ObjectSpace

Systems Toolkit is a C++ object library. More information on Systems toolkit is available online from ObjectSpace at http://www.objectspace.com.

Systems Toolkit is not a complete application development system as are the other frameworks. It provides operating system independence for many of the difficult-to-implement subsystems. One of the things it lacks to be a complete application development system is any functions for building the user interface.

CROSS-PLATFORM APPLICATION DEVELOPMENT USING JAVA

The most recent trend in business application development is to use Java and Intranets. Java provides a way to implement and script components that run on Web browsers. The Web server becomes the application engine, and the browser is the portable user interface.

For Java applications, portability is determined by the browser's ability to provide a Java run-time environment consistent with the Java specification. As with other computer standards, there are differences among Java implementations. Not all browsers implement Java while conforming strictly to the specification.

Besides the Web browsers such as Netscape and Internet Explorer, many operating systems have started providing Java support as well.

DEVELOPING DISTRIBUTED APPLICATIONS IN A HETEROGENEOUS ENVIRONMENT

Some of the application development tools, covered earlier in this chapter, support the development of distributed applications. These tools permit developing client/server applications where clients and servers are distributed. Developing distributed applications involves the development of an application where portions of the application could reside on heterogeneous systems at different nodes in a network, but work together to fulfill the functions of the application.

To accomplish this, the applications need an environment that will provide distributed services, a mechanism to pass messages between applications, functions to accomplish distributed transaction processing, ability to access data from different databases, and a mechanism to facilitate communication among objects in a distributed environment. This section covers the distributed application environment and services. The other topics are addressed later in this chapter.

Open Software Foundation (OSF)

Information about OSF is available online from its home page at http://www.osf.org.

The Open Software Foundation (OSF) is an industry consortium of hardware and software vendors that aims to advance the cause of distributed computing. The goal of distributed computing is to make the network and other supporting software running on different hardware as transparent as possible to an application. OSF's vision for distributed computing is its Distributed Computing Environment (DCE) specification, produced in 1990. The current DCE version is DCE 1.2.2.

OSF produced an Application Environment Specification (AES). AES consolidated DCE components from different vendors into one standard specification. AES is a reference implementation. AES includes source code and a Validation Test Suite (VTS). Vendors are expected to use AES to come up with their own DCE compliant product offering.

DCE

There are six core services that are part of a distributed application and these services are provided by DCE cells (A cell is a unit of one or more computers).

1. Remote Procedure Call (RPC) services to allow an application to access services provided by another computer on the network
2. Distributed directory services to locate any named object on the network using a single naming model
3. Threads service to be able to execute multiple threads

4. Distributed time services to maintain one time across all computers on the network by synchronizing the system clocks of different computers
5. Security services to authenticate users, authorize access to resources, and provide user and server account management on a distributed network
6. Distributed File Services to access files anywhere on a network

All the above services may not be available when developing distributed applications. The most important service from the above is the RPC service.

DCE, UNIX, and Windows NT

DCE services have been available on many UNIX environments for a while. Information on porting a UNIX DCE application to run on Windows NT, is to be found in the chapters on porting presented earlier in the handbook.

To develop distributed applications and Windows NT as part of a chosen environment, it should be noted that Windows NT, natively, includes only full RPC support. Microsoft is working on providing directory services. At this time, third-party software is necessary to provide the other services.

For example, Digital has a product known as Digital DCE Services for Windows NT that provides RPC services, Cell Directory Services, DCE Threads services, Distributed Time Services; and DCE Security Services and Gradient Technologies has DCE products that provide the core DCE services as well as distributed file services.

Digital DCE Services for Windows NT

Information on Digital DCE Services for Windows NT is available online at http://www.digital.com.

The Digital DCE for Windows NT is a product family that is an implementation of OSF DCE Release 1.0.3 adapted and enhanced for Windows NT with some additional capabilities from the OSF DCE R1.1 and R1.2 releases.

The Digital DCE for Windows NT product family consists of four separate products, each one of which is supported on both the Intel and Alpha platforms. The products are summarized below.

1. Digital DCE Runtime Services for Windows NT
2. Digital DCE Application Developer's Kit
3. Digital DCE Cell Directory Server for Windows NT
4. Digital DCE Security Server for Windows NT

Let us briefly look at these products.

Digital DCE Runtime Services for Windows NT. Every system within a DCE cell must run the DCE Runtime Services. The Digital DCE Runtime Services is a fully integrated set of services that provides applications with the essential capabilities required to use DCE's distributed services. The Digital DCE Runtime Services for Windows NT product makes the following DCE features available to distributed applications:

- OSF DCE RPC including:
  a) Transparent mapping to the Microsoft RPC API calls, so that applications that conform to the DCE RPC API can easily be ported to Windows NT
  b) Translation of the Microsoft RPC status codes to the standard DCE RPC status codes
  c) Use of the DCE Cell Directory Service for location-independent naming of application services
  d) Use of the DCE Security Service for authentication, authorization, and secure communication
- Distributed Time Services
- DCE Security Services
- DCE Name Services
- DCE Threads

The Runtime Services kit also includes new Windows-based DCE management tools:

- DCEsetup for configuring and managing the DCE services on a system
- DCE Director for managing DCE cells. It presents an object-oriented view of the DCE environment. The top-level object is the cell. Objects in the cell that a user can manage include users, groups, hosts, CDS directories, and servers. DCE Director makes it easy to perform management tasks such as creating, deleting, and modifying cell objects.
- In addition, the DCE Director allows access to the standard DCE control programs (rgy_edit, cdscp, acl_edit, and dtscp), while providing new functions, such as allowing authorized users to preconfigure host machines in a cell and manage user accounts.
- Visual ACL Editor for graphically managing DCE ACLs, which is integrated with the DCE Director or can also be used as a standalone tool

The Digital DCE for Windows NT product supports all the network transports that are supported in Windows NT. In addition, DECnet is supported if PATHWORKS for Windows NT is used. The Digital DCE Runtime Services for Windows NT kit must be installed first and is a prerequisite for installing and using the DCE Application Developer's Kit, the CDS Server kit, and the DCE Security Server kit.

The Digital DCE Application Developer's Kit for Windows NT. The Digital DCE Application Developer's Kit for Windows NT includes the tools and files required for the development of distributed applications. It includes:

- IDL compiler, which generates RPC interface stubs for C and C++ applications
- Standard DCE and additional Windows-based sample applications
- All public DCE application programming interfaces, including the DCE RPC API, DCE Threads API, DCE Security API, DCE name services API, and the DCE Time Services API

Digital DCE Cell Directory Server for Windows NT. Digital DCE Cell Directory Server for Windows NT, which provides the distributed repository supporting the DCE name services. The kit includes a Cell Directory Services (CDS) server and a Global Directory Agent (GDA) server. The CDS server provides naming services within a DCE cell.

A DCE cell must have one master CDS server and may add any number of read-only replica CDS servers to improve performance and reliability. The optional GDA server provides a means of linking multiple CDS namespaces via either X.500 or the Internet Domain Name Server (DNS BIND).

Digital DCE Security Server for Windows NT. Digital DCE Security Server for Windows NT provides the repository of security information in a cell used to protect resources from illegal access and allow secure communication within and between cells. The DCE Security Server accomplishes this through three services:

- DCE Authentication Service allows users and resources to prove their identity to each other. The DCE Authentication Service is based on Kerberos, which requires that all users and resources possess a secret key.
- DCE Authorization Service verifies operations that users may perform on resources. A DCE Registry Service contains a list of valid users. An Access Control List (ACL) associated with each resource identifies users allowed to access the resource and the types of operations they may perform.
- DCE Data Integrity Service protects network data from tampering. Cryptographic checksums automatically generated by RPC enable DCE to determine whether data has been corrupted in transmission.

There must be one master security server in every DCE cell. Additional read-only security servers, called replicas, can be installed in a cell to improve performance and reliability.

The core DCE functionality provided in the Digital DCE for Windows NT product family can be summarized as:

- DCE Remote Procedure Call (RPC): Provides the OSF DCE RPC API used to create and run client/server applications. It allows direct calls to application procedures running on remote systems as if they were local procedure calls. Authenticated (secure) RPC calls are supported through the use of the DCE Security facility provided in the Runtime Services. On Windows NT, the DCE RPC is layered on the native Microsoft Windows NT RPC. The Microsoft RPC is fully interoperable with DCE RPC running on all other DCE platforms.
- DCE Distributed Time Service (DTS): Synchronizes time on individual hosts in a distributed network environment.
- DCE Security Service Client: Provides access to DCE security services. It enables secure communications and access via authorization and authentication services. This access can be used by either the client or the server side of a DCE application.
- DCE Cell Directory Service (CDS) Client: Provides access to CDS name services allowing location-independent naming of resources. This access can be used by either the client or the server side of the user's application.
- The Interface Definition Language (IDL) Compiler: IDL is the language used to define remote procedure calls.
- DCE Threads Service: Provides user-context multiprocessing functionality. This provides a simple programming model for building applications that perform many operations simultaneously. The DCE Threads service has been integrated with the Windows NT kernel threads facility.

PC-DCE and DFS for Windows NT

Information on PC-DCE and DFS for Windows NT is available online at http://www.gradient.com.

Gradient Technologies produces DCE products for all Windows Operating Systems, many UNIX Operating Systems, Mac, etc. PC-DCE provides the core DCE services such as RPC, Security, etc. and DFS for Windows NT provides distributed file services. The PC-DCE architecture including DFS is shown in Exhibit 7.

PC-DCE for Windows NT and Windows 95 product family components are:

- PC-DCE Runtime for Windows NT and Windows 95
- PC-DCE Application Developers Kit (ADK) for Windows 95 and Windows NT
- PC-DCE Cell Directory Server (CDS) for Windows NT
- PC-DCE Security Server for Windows NT
- Regii Remote Configuration Tool for Windows 95 and Windows NT

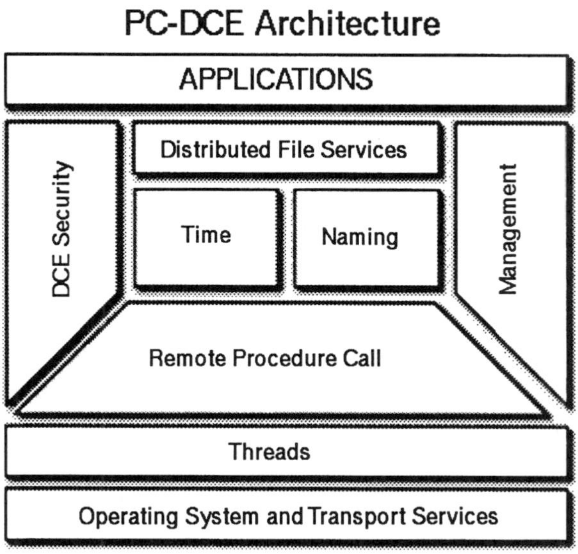

Exhibit 7. PC-DCE architecture.

Middleware Products for Distributed Applications

Middleware consists of both application programming interfaces (APIs) and protocols that support the mapping of applications to the resources they use in a distributed environment. Also, because middleware works across heterogeneous environments, it enables the integration of applications across those environments. See Exhibit 8.

Message-Oriented Middleware

Message-oriented middleware (MOM) provides reliable communications among the components of a distributed application. MOM allows applications to communicate asynchronously, meaning that the sender and receiver do not have to be available on the network at the same time, and that the sending program does not block while waiting for a response. MOM provides guaranteed message delivery even when a process, node, or network fails.

MOM may also provide queue-based semantics to provide other application benefits, such as having multiple writers and multiple readers of a queue. These features allow an application to prioritize messages, to perform publish/subscribe operations, and to do dynamic load balancing. If a queue is backlogged with messages, additional servers can be started up to pull messages off the queue.

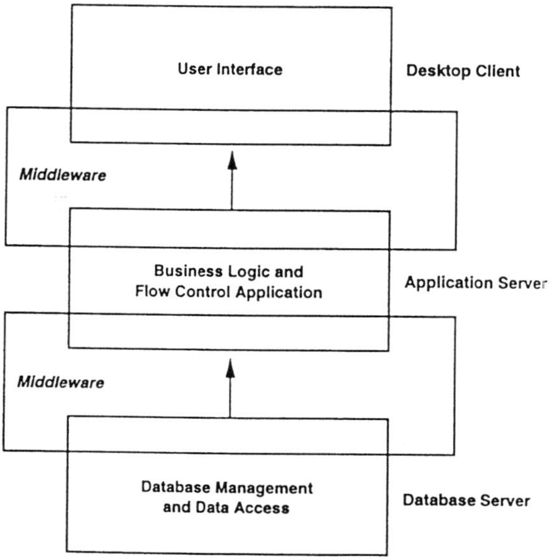

Exhibit 8. Middleware facilitates distributed client/server application development.

MOM has been used to integrate legacy applications with new applications, and is especially effective in dealing with distributed, heterogeneous environments. MOM has achieved great success in manufacturing, telecommunications, health care, and financial services environments.

DECmessageQ (DmQ) is the MOM product based on the message queuing paradigm. DmQ provides application developers with a simple, easy-to-use mechanism to integrate applications across multiple platforms — both DIGITAL and non-DIGITAL. It is primarily used when business solutions require asynchronous communications, high reliability and performance, quick development turnaround, and little to no training of expensive IT staff.

DECmessageQ provides a suite of distributed communication features such as publish and subscribe (message broadcasting), guaranteed delivery, priority selection, global naming, self-describing messages, and flexible configuration (failover and fail-back).

Accessing distributed databases

There are products that provide transparent access to distributed heterogeneous databases such as Oracle Rdb Distributed Product Suite from Oracle.

The Rdb Distributed Product Suite is data access and integration software that provides transparent, seamless integration of heterogeneous data for applications that run on OpenVMS, UNIX, Windows, and Windows/NT desktop systems. The Rdb Distributed Product Suite tool set includes:

- Rdb Distributed Option (formerly known as DEC DB Integrator or DBI, now included with Oracle Rdb)
- The Rdb Transparent Gateways to Oracle, DB2, Sybase, RMS, CODASYL DBMS, PC Data, and Custom Drivers (all purchased separately)
- Rdb Replication Option (formerly known as DEC Data Distributor, now included with Oracle Rdb).
- The DataBase Integrator (also formerly known as DEC DB Integrator, but purchased separately by customers who do not use Oracle Rdb)

With the Rdb Distributed Option, users transparently read/write data regardless of database management system, data formats, or the data's physical location. For example, legacy RMS files can be accessed on OpenVMS/VAX, an enterprise Rdb7 database on an OpenVMS Alpha, an Oracle7 on UNIX, and virtually any PC data on Windows or Windows NT like a single relational database. Multiple local and remote Rdb databases appear as a single Rdb database to the application.

The Rdb Distributed Option's unique query optimizes and analyzes both network costs and the capabilities of the source databases to enhance parallel query performance.

The read/write Rdb Transparent Gateways can be used separately or with the Rdb Distributed Option to integrate non-Rdb data sources. The Rdb Transparent Gateways can access Oracle and Sybase data on any platform supported by these database managers. The Rdb Transparent Gateway to PC data can read and write to all popular ODBC data sources, including Microsoft SQL Server, Microsoft Excel, Microsoft Access, dbase, Btrieve, FoxPro, Paradox, and ASCII files. The Rdb Transparent Gateway to Custom Drivers allows fast development of a Transparent Gateway to any custom data source on OpenVMS or DIGITAL UNIX.

The Rdb Replication Option can be used to provide scheduled and on-demand full or partial database replication on a single system or over the network. The Rdb Replication Option can transfer data among Rdb databases and, with the Rdb Distributed Option and Rdb Transparent Gateways, it can transfer distributed and heterogeneous data. For full replication or incremental transfers, the source database must be Rdb and the target database can be either Rdb, Oracle7, DB2, Sybase, or a relational PC data source. For data transfers (on-demand or scheduled), sources can be Rdb or any database accessible through the Rdb Transparent Gateways. Targets are Rdb, Oracle7, DB2, Sybase, or a relational PC data source.

Distributed Objects

Distributed applications that are object-oriented can be developed using distributed objects that interact with each other through an object request broker. Distributed objects is a very active topic and the technologies that are relevant here include:

- Common Object Request Broker Architecture (CORBA) from the Object Management Group (OMG)
- Active X and the Distributed Component Object Model from the Open Group (Microsoft has provided these technologies to the Open Group to standardize these technologies)
- Jav-based applets and applications

Some of the products that are available for developing distributed object-oriented applications in a heterogeneous environment include:

- ObjectBroker from Digital Equipment
- PowerBroker product family from Expersoft
- Orbix from Iona Technologies

There are still many mainframe applications in use today — by some estimates, over 80% of corporate data still resides on mainframe-based data storage. Following are some options that will allow users to interface with mainframe-based legacy applications and access legacy data.

MAINFRAME LEGACY APPLICATION INTERFACING AND DATA ACCESS

In developing new applications, a situation may arise where an application needs to interface with mainframe-based existing applications as well as retrieve data from mainframe-based databases. This section will look at some of the tools for Windows, UNIX, and NetWare environments that provide these functionalities. That is, the section will talk about applications access. When users on Windows or UNIX machines need to access mainframe applications, solutions like terminal emulation are available and these are covered later in Part II: Coexistence.

Microsoft BackOffice

Microsoft BackOffice is a suite of products based on Windows NT server for a number of server functions including interfacing with mainframes. The following is an extract of extensive data available at http://www.microsoft.com/backoffice. The products in the BackOffice family that pertain to mainframe interface include:

- Microsoft SNA Server — Integrates existing operational systems with the Internet and intranet for host connectivity.
- Microsoft SQL Server — A database server that supports large Internet and intranet Web databases

- Microsoft Transaction Server — formerly known by its code name, "Viper" — is a new product that combines the features of a TP monitor and an object request broker

Later, this chapter will examine these products briefly.

SNA Gateways

SNA gateways are used to for interfacing with mainframe applications including interactive access from a heterogeneous LAN attached workstation, program-to-program access, and file and data transfers. Exhibit 9 shows an SNA gateway. The gateway routes all client traffic to the mainframes and provides protocol and data translation where necessary.

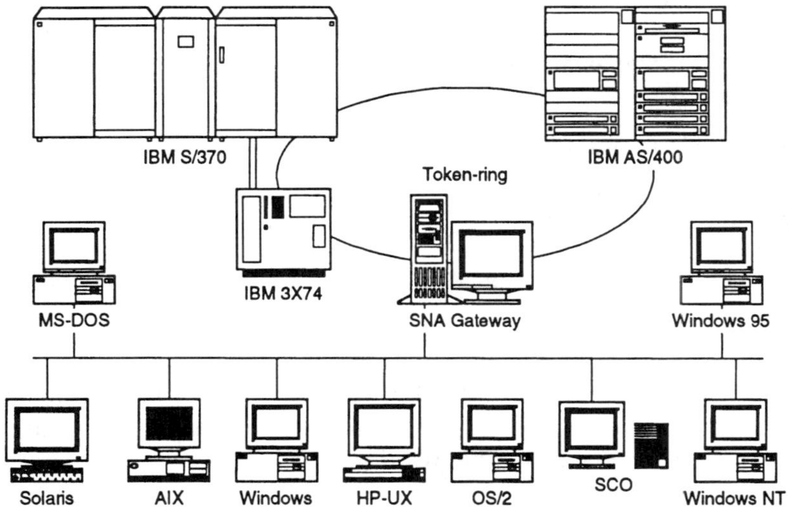

Exhibit 9. SNA Gateway to interface with mainframes.

The SNA TCP/IP gateways can be implemented in one of three ways:

- Branch-Based Deployment — The branch-based deployment is the traditional way to deploy SNA gateways. SNA servers are placed in the branch and communicate with the host using native SNA protocols either via dedicated SDLC lines or tunneled over DLC/802.2. Routers can be used to direct the traffic to the central site or MPR support of NT 4.0 can be used in lieu of a router.
- Centralized Deployment — Channel-attached or token-ring-attached SNA servers are placed at the data center and connect to the host using native SNA protocols. The centralized SNA servers provide

split-stack or TN3270 service for local and remote systems via TCP/IP. Additionally, client-based LU0 or LU6.2 applications can connect anywhere on the TCP/IP WAN.

- Distributed Deployment — Combines the two approaches. Branch-based SNA servers funnel TCP/IP-encapsulated traffic to centralized SNA servers. It is not required for each branch to have an SNA server; they may be distributed strategically throughout the network. The most significant advantages of distributed deployment over centralized deployment are improved host response times for users in the branch and reduced traffic load on the WAN.

Distributed deployment of SNA gateways is shown in Exhibit 10.

Microsoft SNA Server

SNA gateways are available from many vendors. Microsoft's SNA Server, which runs on top of Windows NT server, provides many built-in functions that let it perform as an SNA gateway to allow Windows and UNIX clients to access mainframe applications and data.

Exhibit 11 shows an overview of the Microsoft SNA Server.

Microsoft SNA Server includes a number of built-in or third party software for SNA gateway functions as shown in Exhibit 12.

The main features of the SNA Server are summarized below.

- Shared Folders Gateway — This feature allows PCs with no SNA client software installed to access "shared folders" files on the AS/400. Implemented as a native Windows NT Server file system, the Shared Folders Gateway (SFG) service makes AS/400 files appear to users as just another drive on the Windows NT Server.
- Single Signon — The single-sign-on feature of SNA Server 3.0 automatically provides SNA host account information when starting an SNA application on a client.
- TN5250 Service — This feature enables any TN5250 emulator to connect to the AS/400 via SNA Server without installing TCP/IP on the AS/400.
- SNA Server Manager — A graphical console used as the single point of control for configuring and managing all SNA Servers, host connections, sessions, users, security, auditing and other functions in a Windows NT domain. SNA Server Manager integrates the administration of SNA Server, TN3270 Service, TN5250 Service, SNA Print Service, Shared Folders Gateway, and Host Security into a single interface.
- SNA Print Service — This feature provides server-based 3270 and 5250 printer emulation, allowing mainframe and AS/400 applications to print to any LAN printer supported by Windows NT Server or NetWare.

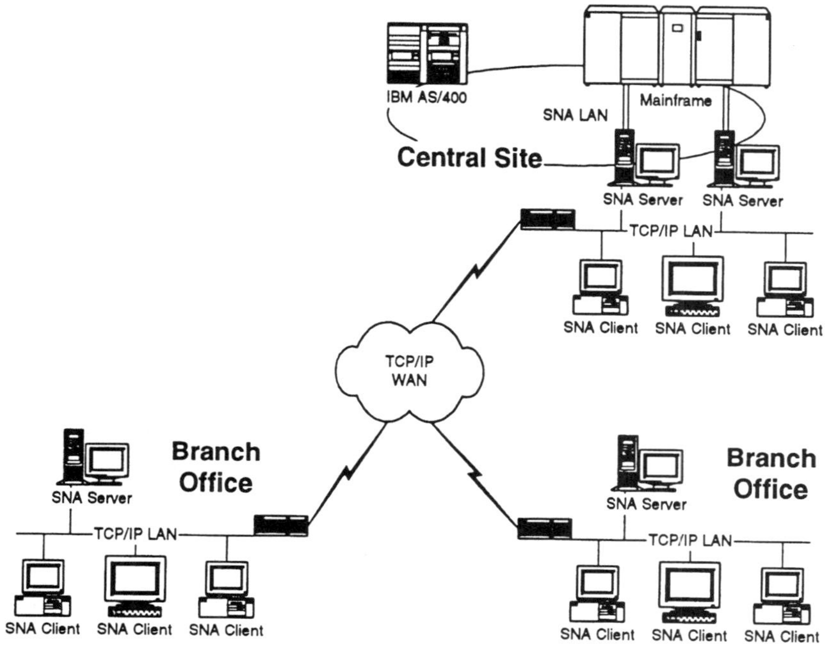

Exhibit 10. Distributed deployment of SNA gateways.

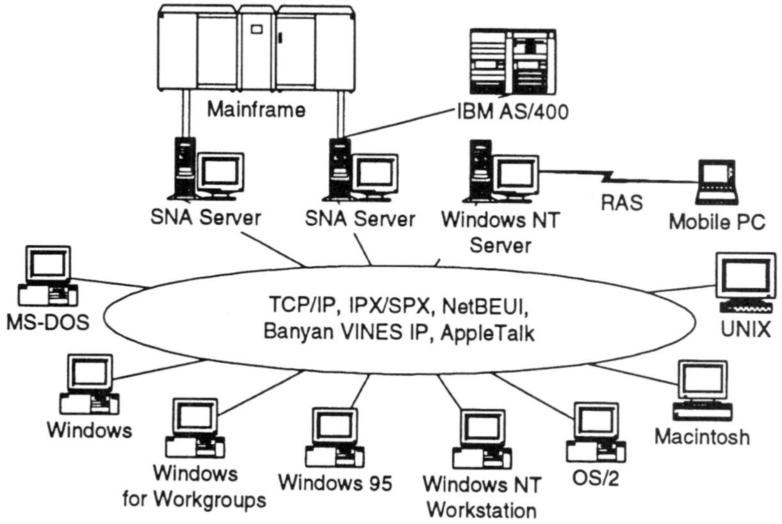

Exhibit 11. SNA gateway functions using Windows NT SNA server.

Exhibit 12. SNA Gateway functions in Microsoft SNA server.

Gateway function	SNA Server 3.0 solution
3270 emulation	tn3270-server, tn3270E
5250 emulation	tn5250-server
Printing	SNA Print Service
File Transfer (m/f)	IND$FILE (from tn3270 client)
	FTP-to-AFTP gateway
File Transfer (AS/400)	Shared Folders (i.e. FTP to a shared folder on the NT server)
	FTP-to-AFTP gateway
Remote Administration	SNA Remote Access Server (i.e., TCP-over-SNA), w/ MPR
Program-to-Program	Parker Software's SNA/APPC Client for UNIX

Mainframe printing supports both LU1 and LU3 data streams, including transparent print jobs sent by host-based print pre-processors. AS/400 printing supports standard SCS line printing as well as pass-thru support for host-based 3812 graphics printing emulation by using the IBM Host Print Transform function.

- SNA Client-Server Encryption — This feature provides encryption of all data between the SNA Server and the client using the RSA RC4 data encryption standard.
- Sync-Point Support for APPC — The SNA Server includes support for the APPC Syncpoint API, which is necessary to implement robust, cross-platform distributed transaction processing using host-based databases (such as DB2) and transaction resource managers (such as CICS).

A number of third-party add-ons to the SNA Server are available for 3270/5250 Emulation, Channel adapters, Channel Attached Gateways, Coax/Twinax Adapters, Database Replication/Gateways, File Transfer Products, Host Print Servers, SDLC/X.25 Adapters, Web to Host, and other products. More details including the names of vendors, products, and product descriptions are included on the Microsoft SNA Server Web page http://www.microsoft.com/products/backoffice/sna.

SNA Client for UNIX

SNA Client for UNIX is an implementation of Microsoft's SNA APIs for the UNIX environment by Parker Brothers. SNA Client supports the SNA interfaces APPC, CPI-C, LUA/LU0, and CSV for program-to-program communication to IBM mainframes and AS/400s. SNA Client utilizes an NT/SNA Server gateway to provide the underlying SNA transport

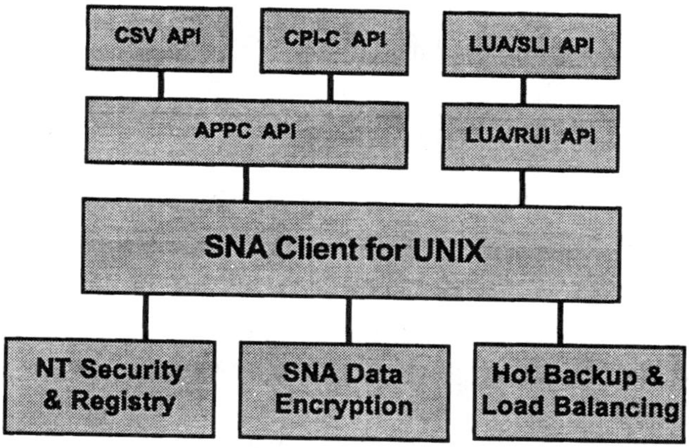

Exhibit 13. SNA Client for UNIX architecture.

mechanisms between UNIX and IBM systems. The architecture of SNA Client is shown in Exhibit 13.

APPC support includes syncpoint support. CPI-C level 1.2 is supported, with many level 2.0 extensions. LUA/LU0 support includes both the low-level RUI and high-level SLI interfaces. CSV includes character-set conversion tables, and an industry-standard programmatic interface to IBM's NetView. The SNA Client utilizes advanced SNA Server features such as load balancing and client/server encryption. Emulation support includes TN3270E, printing, HLLAPI, scripting and X/Motif.

Versions are available for Solaris, HP-UX, AIX and SCO. The SNA Client requires Microsoft SNA Server as a gateway (running on NT). SNA Client makes it possible to support Windows, DOS, OS/2 and UNIX clients from the same NT server.

As an alternative to using an SNA/APPC client, the IBM ANYNET product can be used. There are significant differences in the approaches between the two. See the white paper from Microsoft and Parker Brothers for more details.

Microsoft SQL Server

The Microsoft SQL Server is a database management system featuring support of standards such as ANSI SQL-92, SNMP, and ODBC.

The main features of the SQL server are summarized below.

- Distributed Transaction Coordinator to manage transactions that span two or more SQL Server systems

- Built-in heterogeneous data replication of text and image data types to enable distribution of data to non-SQL Server systems
- Dynamic Locking to reduce contention among users trying to insert rows on the same page simultaneously
- SQL Server systems can send and receive information via the Internet or intranets through tight integration with Microsoft Internet Information Server and other third-party Web servers. A Web Assistant generates HTML pages from SQL Server data on a scheduled or trigger-driven basis.
- SQL Server provides scalability through support for standard symmetric multiprocessing with automatic workload balancing across multiple processors.
- Integrated with C2/E3 security in Windows NT
- Distributed Data Warehousing
- Data warehousing functions including OLAP query support, CUBE, ROLLUP, and a new *Insert Exec* function that allows SQL Server to programmatically retrieve information from multiple sources and populate SQL Server tables with the results
- Mail Integration to send and receive electronic mail using Microsoft Exchange, or populate Exchange public folders with data from SQL Server. SQL Server can also send optional attachments automatically when the data changes or on a scheduled basis using the built-in scheduling capabilities of SQL Executive

Microsoft Transaction Server

The Microsoft Transaction Server is a recent addition to the Microsoft backoffice family. Some of the functions of the transaction server are:

- Developers can build Transaction Server applications as software components using tools that support ActiveX, including Microsoft Visual Basic, Visual C++, and Visual J++.
- Transaction Server includes a component packaging service to facilitate integration, installation, and deployment of many components as a single application.
- Transaction Server manages a pool of ODBC connections to a database.
- Transaction Server automatically provides transparent transaction support to applications running on the server. The application does not need to use low-level transaction control primitives to accomplish this.
- Transaction Server uses DCOM for component-to-component communications across a network. Microsoft is trying to license DCOM as an open-industry standard through the Open Group.
- Transaction Server works with many resource managers, including relational databases, file systems, and image stores, that support a transactional two-phase commit protocol. This enables businesses to leverage existing investments in UNIX and mainframe data stores.

- Win32 "fat" clients and HTML "thin" clients can access Transaction Server applications concurrently.
- Administrators can easily partition an application across multiple servers by deploying an application's components into several packages, with each package running on its own server.

Besides the BackOffice family products that are relevant to interfacing with mainframes, the BackOffice family includes many other products for Mail support (Microsoft Exchange), Internet/intranet support (Internet Information Server and Proxy Server), Systems Management support (Systems Management Server), etc. The BackOffice series runs as an integrated family on the Windows NT server platform. More details on Microsoft BackOffice is available online at http://www.microsoft.com/backoffice/.

Novell NetWare for SAA

Information about Novell NetWare for SAA is available from http://www.novell.com. The following is a brief extract.

NetWare for SAA is a result of a strategic alliance between Novell and IBM. It is a gateway for integrating NetWare and IntranetWare networks with IBM host systems (S/390s and AS/400s). It lets NetWare clients access applications and data on SNA-based IBM hosts via IPX/SPX, TCP/IP and AppleTalk. The clients could be DOS, Mac, Windows 3.1, Windows 95, Windows NT, and OS/2 clients.

NetWare for SAA includes TN3270E emulation support. It provides support for a variety of server-to-host link types and adapters including SDLC multipoint, Frame Relay and high-speed FDDI. It includes functions to administer desktops, gateways and host links from NetWare, remotely or from the host. It includes support for Lan-to-Host and Host-to-Lan printing. It comes in two flavors (NetWare for SAA 2.2 and NetWare for SAA: As/400 Edition). It uses Novell's directory services-NDS.

More than 100 third-party applications are available supporting NetWare-to-host integration with NetWare for SAA. Applications include host printing, software distribution, database access, centralized data backup, network management, and integrated security. Software development tools are also available for creating custom applications for 32-bit clients and NetWare platforms.

Some of the functions that can be performed using NetWare for SAA include:

- File Transfer — A networked client can download or upload files from and to MVS or AS/400 systems. The client can use IP on the network to communicate with the SAA gateway. The gateway then communicates with the MVS using APPC, thereby eliminating the requirement for TCP/IP on the mainframe.

- Self Defining Dependent Logical Unit (SDDLU) Support — SDDLU support allows a customer to activate a dependent LU without VTAM definitions on the host. By activating the LU only when it is needed, a big list of VTAM definitions need not be predefined and an LU can be added without requiring VTAM generations.

Besides some of the commercial products and add-ons mentioned above, there is public-domain software that performs some of the functions provided by the commercial products. Public-domain software is typically free and is not guaranteed. Support in many cases is by the author(s) and is on a best effort basis. Such an approach makes it difficult for public-domain software to be used for many business applications.

HETEROGENEOUS DATABASE ACCESS

There are database-access products that let an application access data from any type of PC databases, server databases, or even mainframe-based databases located anywhere on the network. Using these heterogeneous database servers, an organization can decide on the optimal data distribution strategy for the enterprise data and pick the optimal combination for the location of the data that satisfies data access and integrity requirements.

Empress

The Empress Heterogeneous Database Server from Empress is a fully distributed database management system that let users and applications running Empress and UNIX access data from any database. The database could be PC-based, workstation (server)-based or even mainframe-based. Details on Empress Heterogeneous Database Server are available online at http://www.empress.com

EDA

EDA, which stands for Electronic Data Access, is a family of client/server products from Information Builders that provide SQL based access to more than 60 relational and non-relational databases that reside on 35 different hardware platforms. More details on EDA/SQL are available online at http://www.ibi.com.

The EDA product family includes:

- EDA Client (EDA/Link communications, API/SQL, ODBC driver)
- EDA Server Engines (MVS, VM, Digital, Tandem, UNIX, AS/400, OS/2, and Windows NT) include the following components:
  - —EDA Hub Server
  - —EDA Transaction Server (CICS, IMS/DC)

  - EDA Relational Gateway (DB/2, Oracle, Informix, Sybase, Rdb, Ingres)
  - EDA Nonrelational Gateway (IMS, VSAM, IDMS, RMS, ISAM, etc.)
  - EDA Stored Procedure Gateway
- Oracle Transparent Gateway to EDA
- EDA Web Client Services
- EDA Open Database Gateway
- EDA Enterprise Copy Manager Overview and White Paper
- EDA Data Extenders (DB2, Oracle, Informix, Lotus DataLens, DDE)
- EDA Communication Gateways (OS/2, Windows NT, Novell NetWare)
- EDA Governing Services

Omni SQL Gateway

OMNI SQL Gateway from Sybase offers transparent read/write access to data across many heterogeneous data sources. OMNI SQL Gateway is part of Sybase's middleware product family called EnterpriseCONNECT.

Hyperstar

Hyperstar from Vmark Software provides a set of ODBC driver products that enable transparent read/write access to corporate databases on more than 30 different platforms that include popular database systems. Hyperstar works in conjunction with Vmark's relational database management system called UniVerse.

The HyperStar Fast Path Server for UniVerse is a middleware product designed specifically to provide fast, reliable, seamless access to data stored in UniVerse from 16- or 32-bit Windows-based third-party tools, programming languages, or an RDBMS running on a UNIX server, using ODBC.

This allows users of Excel, Lotus 1-2-3, Microsoft Word, and many more desktop productivity tools to access UniVerse data more conveniently and transparently, as well as to integrate the data into their applications. The HyperStar Fast Path Server is fully ODBC compliant, providing maximum flexibility in enterprise connectivity tasks. It also features built-in support for many TCP/IP stacks, allowing existing networks to be used without the need to purchase additional networking or TCP/IP products.

The combination of UniVerse and HyperStar supports the use of UniVerse tables, views, and files with D, S, and A dictionary types. This eliminates the need to make UniVerse data files appear more SQL-like to facilitate high-performance ODBC read-and-write access. The combination also takes full advantage of UniVerse multivalued data structures and extended features, such as select lists and I-types.

With HyperStar Fast Path server, UniVerse users can implement an ODBC solution today, and gradually migrate to using the full UniVerse SQL interface, with its security and declarative integrity features.

INTERFACING LEGACY APPLICATIONS WITH INTERNET

Legacy applications can from the Internet or Intranet using middleware such as BEA Jolt.

BEA Jolt

BEA Jolt, from BEA Systems, Inc., is software for enabling companies to make powerful, secure transaction systems running mission-critical or legacy applications immediately accessible from the Internet or an enterprise intranet, with no additional application programming.

Through BEA Jolt, mission-critical, legacy, or Internet applications can easily share business transactions in the Java environment, which is critical for Java to be used effectively across the enterprise.

BEA Jolt is based on the BEA TUXEDO middleware. BEA Jolt and BEA TUXEDO provide the infrastructure for ensuring that mission-critical and legacy applications can easily interoperate in an environment such as the Java Computing model.

CONCLUSION

This chapter looked at different ways to develop applications so that the applications will execute in different environments. Low-level API-based approaches or high-level 4GL or Object framework based approaches can be used. We also covered techniques to interface with legacy applications and data from the applications being developed.

Chapter 10
Accessing Windows Applications from UNIX and Vice Versa

Raj Rajagopal

Migrating from one environment to another takes planning, resources, and, most importantly, time (except in very trivial cases). This implies that even when eventually migrating to another environment, coexistence among environments must be dealt with in the interim. In many companies it would make good business sense not to migrate legacy systems at all. Instead, it may be better to develop new systems in the desired environment and let the legacy applications be phased out. The data created by the legacy applications is important and ways to ensure that data from the new environment can be accessed are important. Coexistence considerations are very important in this case.

Coexistence among Windows NT, UNIX, and NetWare has to deal with a number of related issues. It may be necessary to access Windows applications from a UNIX machine. It may be necessary to access UNIX applications from Windows desktops. Or, it may be preferable to have the same type of desktop ("an enterprise desktop") for all users and be able to access different environments. It could also be necessary to emulate one environment within another.

Access to services such as file and print services in heterogeneous environments may be called for. A set of interoperability products exist to enable clients attached to one type of server (e.g., UNIX, NetWare, and Windows NT) to have transparent access to services from other servers and mainframes as shown in Exhibit 1.

0-8493-9989-0/99/$0.00+$.50

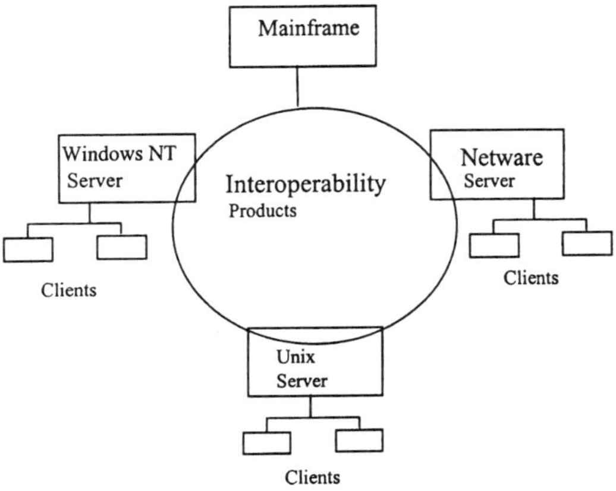

Exhibit 1. Heterogeneous client interconnectivity.

As mentioned earlier, access to the data available in another environment is very important and heterogeneous file access is imperative.

ACCESSING WINDOWS APPLICATIONS FROM AN X-STATION

Part I discussed the different options for porting or migrating applications among environments. There are situations where porting would make good business sense. There are other situations where the best business option would be to leave applications running in one environment as they are, and access these applications from other environments. There are many organizations that have existing UNIX applications that work fine. They are also using Windows desktops, primarily for office needs. An important requirement here is to access the Windows office applications from the same X-stations that are already accessing the UNIX applications. An X-station includes X-Terminals, UNIX workstations, and any device capable of performing a similar function.

Organizations can arrange access to different environments and applications by providing separate systems on users' desks or organize a shared pool of machines.

There are other options that provide access to applications executing in different environments from the same desktop. These are called coexistence options. Using coexistence options, different applications are accessed transparently to the user in multiple windows on the same desktop.

Coexistence options might avoid the necessity to port applications, but keep in mind that there are subtle end-user differences between the user interface used in UNIX and that used in Windows. These differences could become an annoying factor for a user to deal with, particularly if it is necessary to switch back and forth between Windows and UNIX applications often. Another potential problem is the lack of some Windows functionality such as OLE and Clipboard when these functions are not supported by the coexistence solution provider.

COEXISTENCE OPTIONS

There are different ways in which applications in different heterogeneous environments can coexist. These include:

- In an environment where X-stations or X-terminals are already connected to different applications, Windows applications can be added to the X-Station. Examples of this coexistence approach include WinDD from Tektronix, X Connection from ConnectSoft, and WinCenter from Network Computing Devices. Adding Windows applications to an X-station is covered in this article.
- Just as Windows can be added to an existing X-Station, an X-Server can be added to a PC that may already be running Windows applications to access non-Windows applications. Examples of this coexistence approach include DESQview/X from Quarterdeck, and eXceed from Hummingbird Communications. X-Server on Windows is covered later in this article.
- To cater to the needs of desktops capable of working in heterogeneous environments, some vendors have come up with machines with features useful for operating in heterogeneous environments. Such features include different connectivity options to connect to different networks. Examples of this coexistence approach include Personal Workstations from Digital. Multi-client desktops.
- There are emulation solutions that permit an executable developed in one environment to run on another through emulation. The emulation solutions interface between the application executable and the operating environment. Examples of emulation solutions include Windows Binary Application Interface (WABI), SoftWindows from Insignia, and MERGE from Locus Computing.
- In some instances, the applications and users' access are fine, but it may be desirable to access the data across environments. There are solutions that permit applications to have file access in heterogeneous networked environments. Examples of networked file access solutions include BW-Connect NFS, Chameleon 32 NFS, and PC-Interface and PC-NFS from Intergraph.

WINDOWS IN AN X-STATION

An overview of how a Windows application can be added to an existing X-station is shown in Exhibit 2.

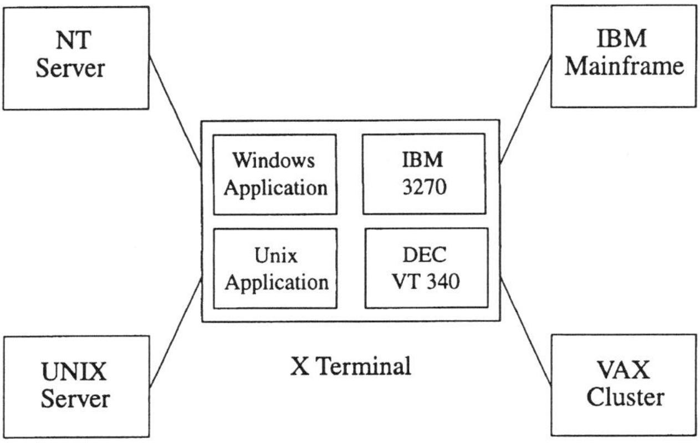

Exhibit 2. Windows in an X-station.

The X-station may already be attached to an IBM mainframe application using a 3270 emulation window, to a VAX application, and to a UNIX application as an X-Server. The Windows application is enabled as another window on the X-station and the new window is controlled by an application server running the Windows application.

How do X-Stations support Windows Applications?

A simplified conceptual view of how X-Stations support Windows Applications is shown in Exhibit 3.

The Windows application performs its application processing and invokes the operating system for end-user display services. Typically, the

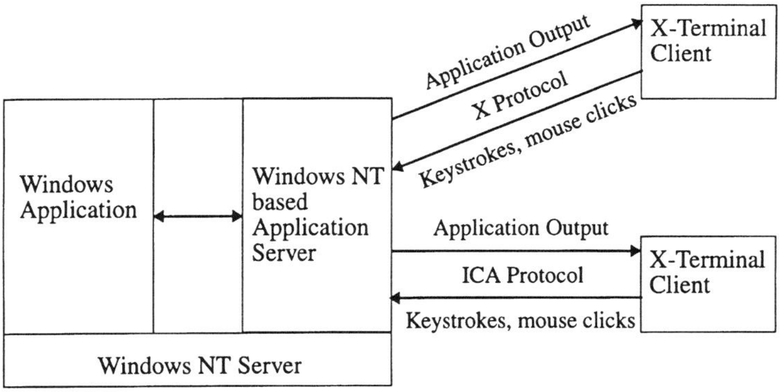

Exhibit 3. X-station support for Windows applications.

display is physically attached to the same machine the application runs on, but that need not always be the case.

The X-Station vendors provide a server piece and a client piece that come in between the Windows application and the display, and interface between the two. The client passes user responses such as keystrokes and mouse clicks to the server, which passes them to the Windows application. The Windows application responds to the user input just as it normally would.

The application server sends the output from the Windows application back to the client. The user sees the regular Windows application screens. The protocols used for the exchange between the application server and the client is the X-windows protocol or the Intelligent Console Architecture (ICA) protocol. The connection between the application server and the client could be LANs (if local), Intranets, or even the Internet.

The X-station approach should not be confused with keeping applications on a fileserver and loading them locally for execution. With X-stations, the windows applications run on an NT server that has been modified to add multi-user support and not locally.

Note on protocols: The X-windows protocol is the industry standard protocol for communication between a client and an X-server. Use of X protocol permits the use of any device that follows the protocol. The ICA is similar to the X-window protocol. ICA is a proprietary protocol developed by Citrix Systems. Citrix has licensed this protocol to some vendors such as Tektronix and Network Computing Devices.

Microsoft recently announced that it will include ICA support in future versions of Windows 95 and NT, and potentially in Internet Explorer as well. By using the ICA protocol, vendors have been able to provide more functionality and faster responses than the X-window protocol. The ICA protocol transmits less data. However, some graphics-rich and multimedia applications do not run well with ICA. ICA supports only 256 colors. X-station vendors typically offer a choice of protocols that the user can switch between.

Considerations in Using the X-Station Approach

Following are some some advantages and disadvantages of using an X-Station approach.

Advantages of the X-Station Approach

- By using an X-Station approach, it may be possible to provide access to Windows applications such as office applications and e-mail without having to buy a PC and Windows for every user.

- It is easier to administer Windows applications usage since the actual Windows application is installed on only one machine (the application server). It is also easier to control usage and availability of the Windows applications. For example, it can easily be enforced that users should get DOS sessions or Windows Sessions etc. and the Windows applications can be stopped and started, if needed.
- Productivity is improved over solutions like having shared PCs (which could be idle for long periods of time). Sharing PCs for occasional use is discussed later in the handbook.
- With an X-window machine that is PC-based, you can actually access Windows 95, Windows NT, and other 32-bit applications using a 486 or even 386 machine, which would not be possible natively.
- X-station approach also permits "roving" users to logon from any X-station. This makes it easier for users to retrieve their Windows-based e-mail from anywhere in the office building(s) or even remotely.
- User customization of how a Windows application works, which is a key design feature of Windows, goes with the user and the user interface behaves the same way, whichever station the user is logged on.
- Windows applications can be accessed remotely and, in some cases, even using the Internet.

Disadvantages of the X-Station Approach

- Since the application runs on only one machine, the machine must be capable of handling the load of a number of concurrent users. Typically, a certain amount of disk storage and memory is required on the server for each user and a processor or multiple processors capable of handling the load are necessary. There must be a central point of failure, although this can be mitigated by having multiple servers.
- Also, the products that support multiple users have licensed Microsoft source with added multi-user features. This implies that there could be a delay between when Microsoft introduces new features to Windows NT and when they are available to Windows applications since the X-station vendor must make corresponding changes to the vendor's extensions.
- Care must be taken when applying NT service packs from Microsoft. Since NT service packs are developed with the NT product (and without regard to how the NT source licensees may have changed the source), there is a chance that the service pack for NT may interfere with some vendor extension to the NT code. The X-station vendor must verify that any service pack, other than the vendor's own, can be applied.
- In addition, it is possible that when an application first becomes available, it may work with Windows NT, but not the Windows Application server of a particular X-station vendor due to conflicts with the

extension code provided by the vendor. Vendors normally fix these types of problems quickly.

Following are some common products that provide Windows in an X-Station support.

Common X-Station Products

The information about the products was gathered from different published sources, but primarily from vendors' published information, including online Web pages. The Web addresses and other contact information is included in the description for each vendor and in the appendix. The products are being updated quickly and the product vendor should be contacted for the latest information. Most vendors also offer free evaluations that are downloadable from their Web sites.

The book is not intended to aid in the selection of one vendor over another. Migration/coexistence solutions that meet particular requirements should be considered, and an evaluation of vendor products performed. The inclusion of vendor information is intended to give an idea of the capabilities of the products and as a quick reference to get further information and software.

WINDD PRODUCT FAMILY

More details about the WinDD product family is available at Tektronix home page http://www.tek.com.

WinDD (Windows Distributed Desktop) is a product family from Tektronix that delivers PC applications running in native mode to multiple users in a mixed desktop computing environment.

WinDD delivers Windows 3.1, Windows 95, and Windows NT applications including PC-based e-mail and schedulers in native mode to netstations, X-stations, UNIX workstations, and PCs over TCP/IP Ethernet or Token-Ring LANs. Under an agreement with Microsoft, Tektronix has added code to support multiple simultaneous users on Windows NT server. WinDD software can be housed on Intel Pentium or Pentium Pro-based servers with access to TCP/IP Ethernet LANs within the enterprise. The WinDD application server can be scaled using additional processors. WinDD automatically distributes the workload among all processors.

The WinDD Product family is shown in Exhibit 4.

The WinDD product family consists of:

- WinDD Server: Base server software package with the multi-user NT server software, and simultaneous user licenses.

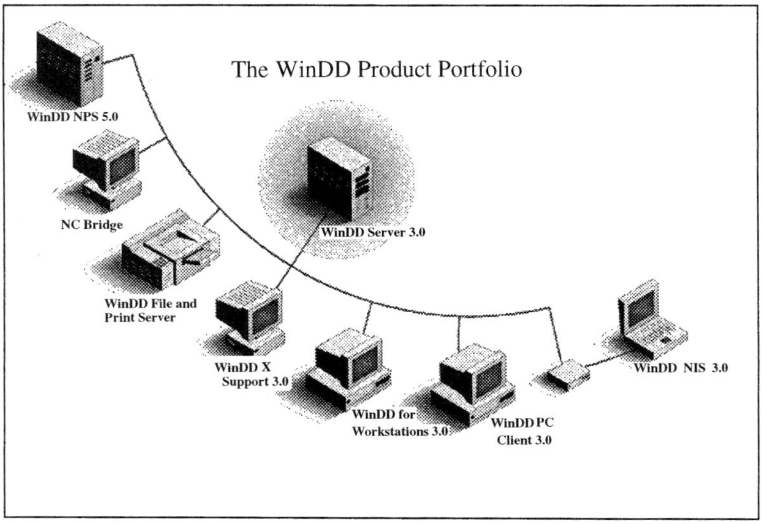

Exhibit 4. WinDD product family.

- WinDD File and Print Server: Optional extension to the base WinDD server, a full print server, file server, and domain controller and can add Macintosh services and remote access services.
- WinDD NFS: Allows bidirectional file sharing between PC and UNIX systems by providing NFS server and client functionality to the WinDD server. Files located on UNIX directories and mapped to Windows drive letters can be accessed, saved and recalled transparently from the standard file access menus in PC and Windows applications.
- WinDD NIS: Automates and synchronizes all passwords on all devices and coordinates with NFS dynamically. It allows system administrators to establish a single point of reference for information on user accounts.
- WinDD X-Support: Enables virtually any workstation, netstation or PC X-server to connect to the WinDD application server using the X-protocol.
- WinDD for Workstations: Provides ICA client support for major UNIX platforms including SunOS, Solaris, HP-UX, IBM AIX, SGI IRIX, Digital UNIX, and SCO UNIX. The benefits of ICA include low network traffic, shadowing, connect/disconnect, server broadcast/response, floppy-disk support, keyboard mapping functionality.
- WinDD Xpress for Netstations: Tektronix's first ICA client that runs on netstations.

- WinDD PC Client: Accepts the ICA datastream using a variety of network protocols including TCP/IP, NetBIOS, and IPX. The PC Client supports Windows 3.1, Windows 95, Windows NT Server, and MS-DOS.

ACCESSING WINDOWS APPLICATIONS

WinDD users can access their Windows applications via ICA clients or the X protocol. WinDD X Support provides Windows application-access based on the open system X-protocol to all X11-compliant displays, regardless of platform. The ICA approach provides lower network bandwidth and greater functionality, but does not support as many environments as the X-protocol.

ICA Clients. The features available through ICA clients include:

- Floppy disk support: Netstation users and Sun, HP, IBM, and SGI workstation users can read, write, and format floppy disks with Microsoft's File Manager. The floppy drive shows up as a "networked" A: drive icon in the File Manager.
- Cut-and-Paste of Text and Graphics: WinDD has a configurable clipboard that allows cut-and-paste of text to and from X, PC, and legacy applications. It is possible to specify which of several X buffers to copy to and paste from. The WinDD clipboard also allows cut-and-paste X graphics, windows, and screen captures into PC applications and Windows graphics into X/UNIX applications.
- Shadowing: Allows one ICA client user to see and interact with another user's session, whether that user is working on a Tektronix netstation, a UNIX workstation, or a PC. This feature is useful for support staff to debug user's problems and for educational purposes.
- If, as a WinDD user, the netstation is accidentally rebooted or disconnected, or if there is a power outage at the desktop, the WinDD session is suspended on the WinDD server. At reconnect, the screen is restored to the state it was in at disconnect time. Multiple disconnected WinStations are possible with WinDD and any one can be selected to return to at log-on.
- If there are multiple WinDD servers installed, any Winserver can be chosen to log on. The selection can be made from a list of available Winservers, which also shows the load factor indicating the load on each Winserver. It is also possible to choose to work with 16 or 256 colors by setting a configuration parameter before logging on to a Winserver. The user (or the administrator) can also custom-configure any keyboard

Windows X Support. As an alternative to the ICA client, WinDD X-Support provides Windows application access based on the open system

X-protocol to all X11-compliant displays, regardless of platform. WinDD X-Support includes features such as support for monochrome workstations and netstations, and connect/disconnect. Connect/disconnect functionality was discussed under ICA clients before.

For desktops that have an X11R5 or greater X-server, WinDD can utilize the desktop device's font server by loading the actual Microsoft Windows fonts directly onto the X-desktop. WinDD Server can simultaneously support X-11-compliant displays using Windows X-Support and ICA-connected displays.

WinDD Features. WinDD supports X, TCP/IP, ICA protocols. WinDD also provides NFS server and client support.

WinDD manages the PC Window on the display and passes only compressed, updated display information in a high-level GDI to the WinDD desktop client. The local client passes back keyboard and mouse events to the WinDD server for processing. Frequently used graphics such as buttons and menus are cached at the desktop.

Any WinDD desktop attached to the WinDD server can run WinDD's centralized administration tools. Helpdesk personnel can shadow a user's session to duplicate what is occurring at the user's station. Both the user and support staff can use the keyboard and the mouse simultaneously. The resulting display is transmitted to both desktops, even over a wide area network.

Even though the Windows application executes on the WinDD server, WinDD supports access to desktop peripherals such as floppy disks and local com ports at the client.

Planned enhancements for WinDD include better integration with UNIX environments using features such as automatic password updates between the Windows and UNIX interfaces and better support for World Wide Web-based environments.

Products that provide similar functionality include WinTerm from Wyse. Besides X-Station support, the WinTerm has a built-in browser, can run Java Applets, includes an e-mail client, and includes audio support.

NTRIGUE PRODUCT FAMILY

More details about the Ntrigue product family are available online from Insignia at http://www.insignia.com.

NTRIGUE is a family of products that delivers Windows 95, Windows 3.1, and Windows NT applications to enterprise desktops including X-stations, UNIX workstations, PCs, Macintosh, network computers, and Java desktops. Applications run natively on an Intel-based Windows NT server.

The Ntrigue product family is shown in Exhibit 5.

The family includes the following products:

- NTRIGUE for WinFrame: Application Server is an OEM version of Citrix' Systems WinFrame server. Citrix licensed NT source code from Microsoft and added multi-user extensions.
- WinFrame Clients for PCs: Thin clients that run under Windows 95, Windows 3.1 and Windows NT, and allow connection with NTRIGUE Application server from PCs. WinFrame Clients are optimized for performance over low bandwidth connections.
- NTRIGUE Mac Client: Provides full integration between PowerMac and Windows NT. NTRIGUE Mac Client is Insignia's enhanced version of White Pine Software's eXodus X server software, and is best suited for higher-end Power Macs.
- NTRIGUE Net Clients (for Mac and UNIX): A thin client that allows Mac and UNIX users to access Windows applications. NTRIGUE Net Client can also be configured as a helper application to an Internet browser to access Windows applications via a Web page. A simple click on a link to a Web page runs any application.
- NTRIGUE Web Kit
- NFS for NTRIGUE Server Option Pack: An option pack for NTRIGUE for X (NTRIGUE packaged for the UNIX, X-station and network computer environments). The option pack adds functionality to NTRIGUE for X for Remote Access Services, File and Print Services, Domain Services and Services for Macintosh.
- NTRIGUE Client for Java (In Beta development at the time of writing this book) : A thin client that allows Java-based desktops, such as Sun's JavaStation, to run Windows-based applications on an NTRIGUE server. Users can access Windows 95, Windows 3.x and Windows NT-based applications from these low-cost network-based computers. NTRIGUE X Client for Java is an applet based on the X-Windows system that is implemented in Java and optimized for Java-based desktops.

Ntrigue features. NTRIGUE supports both X and ICA protocols. It enables users to boot network computers, including computers using the Java OS such as Java station, and X-stations directly from an NTRIGUE server without requiring a UNIX host. NTRIGUE users can access local printers. NTRIGUE lets users access storage mediums on the local machine such as floppy disk, hard disk, and CD-ROM when using the ICA protocol.

Using NTRIGUE, system administrators can control users' access to disk drives. This can help an organization prevent unauthorized copying of data and programs. NTRIGUE includes NIS import features including directly importing user information. User information can be copied from a NetWare sever as well. NetWare users can access through NT's NetWare

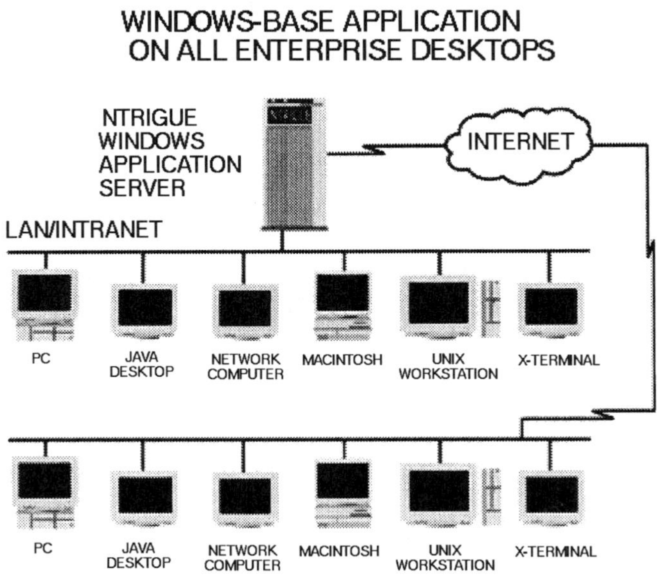

Exhibit 5. Ntrigue product family.

Gateway services. A disconnect/reconnect feature helps roving users, like system administrators, quit a session on one PC and resume it on any other desktop, including remote access.

An NTRIGUE server can be integrated into an existing network. The NTRIGUE server can be a backup controller, or it can be the primary domain for NTRIGUE /NT servers.

Web Access. One interesting variation NTRIGUE supports is web access of Windows applications. Net Client can be configured as a helper application within a Web browser, then connections to the NTRIGUE server can be established over the corporate intranet or the Internet. The server application could be Windows office application, but it could also be a Web browser. Thus, any client can access the Internet and the World Wide Web through the web browser running on the NTRIGUE server.

WINCENTER

More information about WinCenter is available online from National Computing Devices (NCD) at http://www.ncd.com.

WinCenter from NCD is a family of products from NCD for providing Windows applications over an intranet to heterogeneous desktops. WinCenter server software runs on Intel-compatible servers on a network. WinCenter supports any client capable of communicating with the X-Window protocol (including PCs, Macs, UNIX workstations, etc.) and the clients receive graphics and audio output of the Windows applications. WinCenter supports Windows 3.1, Windows 95, and Windows NT applications.

WinCenter Product Family

The WinCenter Product Family includes the following:

- WinCenter Pro
- WinCenter for Workgroups
- WinCenter Connect
- WinCenter Server Option Pack

Following is a brief look at these products.

WinCenter Pro

WinCenter Pro is a Windows application server consisting of the Microsoft Windows NT server plus added Microsoft-authorized multi-user support. The added multi-user support enables one server to provide graphical login sessions to many simultaneous users. On top of Windows NT is NCD's WinCenter Graphics Accelerator (WGA), which provides open systems graphics technology. WGA is covered later in this section.

Some of the key benefits of WinCenter Pro include:

- High-performance graphics from any enterprise desktop in an intranet. The desktop could be UNIX workstations, PCs, Macs, and Network Computers.
- Dial-up connectivity from remote PCs using Citrix Systems' ICA3 protocol
- Support for multimedia Windows applications, including audio
- Desktop floppy disk drives supported (as A: drive)
- Desktop printers appear as normal Windows printers
- Cut-and-paste of text and graphics between Windows, UNIX, and other application environments.
- Supports monochrome, grayscale, 256 color, and 16 million color desktops
- NT window is resizable to make organizing the desktop easier
- Native NT international keyboard support
- Existing files can be accessed using NFS client
- Less colormap "flashing" among Windows, UNIX, and other types of applications.
- Automatic connect from networked computers, PCs, and Macs, and automatic startup of Windows applications from remote systems
- Single UNIX wincenter command for starting a WinCenter session
- Graphical window for finding and selecting WinCenter hosts

WinCenter for Workgroups

WinCenter for Workgroups is a version of WinCenter Pro tailored to the needs of the smaller business or branch office.

WinCenter Connect

WinCenter Connect is a layered product that adds the WinCenter Graphics Accelerator and other NCD services to an existing multi-user NT system (such as WinFrame, NTRIGUE, or WinDD). With WinCenter Connect, the benefits of WinCenter Pro are available without having to reload a multi-user NT operating system or applications.

Server Option Pack

The WinCenter Server Option Pack adds the ability to use a WinCenter host as a network server for Windows PCs. With the WinCenter Server Option Pack, a WinCenter host can be a:

- PC file server, so this WinCenter host can share its files with desktop PCs, NT workstations, NT servers, or other WinCenter hosts
- PC printer server, so this WinCenter host can share its printers with desktop PCs, NT workstations, NT servers, or other WinCenter hosts
- NT domain management services, so this WinCenter host can be a Primary or Secondary Domain Controller for other NT machines

WinCenter Graphics Accelerator

WinCenter uses the WinCenter Graphics Accelerator (WGA) technology. WGA is not a hardware graphics accelerator card. WGA is a set of NT device drivers that intercept an application's graphics and audio calls to Windows NT. These graphics and audio calls are redirected to the client, for processing at the client, using the X-window protocol. This approach is in contrast to transmitting a graphics output (or a compressed graphics output) to the client after the output has been generated at the server.

WinCenter features. WinCenter also uses what it calls 'IntelliCache' technology, which can trade CPU and memory on the NT. WinCenter batches graphics calls together so they can be sent in a single packet. WinCenter supports different displays for client desktops including monochrome displays, 256 color displays, and even color displays capable of handling 16 million colors.

WinCenter uses the font server standard in X-11 to dynamically distribute font data over networks, when necessary. In addition, font glyph images are cached in the desktop so that text can be sent as strings of characters instead of as bitmaps. To ensure compatibility with all X-11 clients,

WinCenter uses an appropriate method of sending font data depending on the capabilities of the client. WinCenter uses the Network Audio System for audio support. Support for a variety of UNIX workstations is available in NCD's WinCenter Workstation+ product. NCD For those who wish to write their own drivers, NCD provides the source code for the Network Audio System. The source is available from its ftp site: ftp.ncd.com.

WinCenter supports cut-and-paste of text and graphics among Windows, UNIX, 3270, and other terminal environments. The standard UNIX rcp command copies files to and from Windows NT. The standard UNIX rsh command starts Windows applications over the network. This means, for example, that you can click on a spreadsheet attachment in your UNIX e-mail application and have Excel start up automatically (by issuing rcp from within the e-mail application to start Excel on the server).

NCD's Colormap Flash Protection makes it possible to switch among Windows applications in full 256-color mode to and from UNIX or other applications that do not support 256 colors. WinCenter Pro includes the NFS client from FTP Software to access UNIX files. WinCenter provides floppy disk drive access at the client machine. The floppy drive appears as the normal "A:" drive. File Manager and other Windows applications using the drive behave as expected.

WinCenter supports printing at a printer attached to the client, shared printers attached to the NT host, and network printers attached to other computers. Administration of printer attachments is handled centrally at the server. WinCenter incorporates services for booting the clients including Network Computers, X-stations, printers, and even network routers directly from the NT server using the TFTP standard.

WinCenter also provides the ability for clients to login directly to the NT server without requiring any UNIX (intermediary) host.

HP 500 WINDOWS APPLICATION SERVER

More details about the HP 500 Windows Application Server are available online from Insignia at http://www.hp.com.

The HP 500 Windows Application Server is an Intel processor server that resides on the UNIX network. The server runs Windows and Windows applications in native mode. The X-window system is used to display the applications over UNIX networks. The client could be any device that supports the X-window protocol and that includes X-stations and typical UNIX workstations. Users can cut and paste between Windows applications and UNIX applications. The HP 500 includes NFS and TCP/IP support. Users can print to network printers.

HP and Insignia Solutions recently announced a strategic alliance. NTRIGUE would run on HP-UX and complement the HP 500 application server by running Windows 95 and Windows NT applications.

NTERPRISE

NTerprise from Exodus Technologies lets you run Windows application programs from UNIX workstations and X-stations. More information about NTerprise is available from Exodus at http://www.exodustech.com (there is another company with the web address http://www.exodus.com).

Features of NTerprise include:

- Windows applications are run in an application server and are accessed by users
- Supports cut and paste of data between Windows and UNIX applications
- Supports execution of different applications in separate windows
- Windows applications share the X-station desktop as any other X-client
- Use the standard version of Windows NT
- Supports the X-protocols, including the XDM access protocol
- Supports Intel and Alpha platforms. Also includes SMP support
- Permits X-station users to boot their own stations from the Windows NT server without a UNIX host

Exodus includes a chart comparing NTRIGUE and competing products at its home page on the web (address mentioned at the beginning of this section).

WINTED

WinTED is an X-server from TriTeal. More information on WinTED is available online from TriTeal at http://www.triteal.com.

Some of the features of WinTED include:

- Provides auto-discovery of UNIX applications
- Offers an integrated ICA client
- File sharing is implemented on the server instead of the client. This saves the need to update clients

So far, solutions that let Windows applications be accessed from desktops that already have UNIX application access, such as X-Terminals, X stations, and UNIX workstations, have been examined. Following is a look at options that let a UNIX or another (non-Windows) host application be accessed from Windows desktops.

ACCESSING UNIX APPLICATIONS FROM WINDOWS DESKTOPS

The application could be a UNIX character-based (older) application or a more recent graphical application. There are two ways to access a UNIX application from Windows desktops. These are:

1. Use the Windows desktop as a remote terminal using software such as Telnet
2. Use X-server software to run X-Windows applications from Windows desktops

For the purposes of this discussion, the UNIX applications are not migrated or ported to the Windows environment.

Telnet

Telnet is commonly used in the UNIX environment for one UNIX computer to act as a terminal and get the command prompt of another UNIX computer. Windows NT includes Telnet client support, but not Telnet server support.

Tip: *Using Telnet in Windows NT, it is possible to get the UNIX command prompt of a UNIX computer. But Telnet cannot be used in a UNIX machine to get to the command prompt of a Windows machine. For one thing, Windows NT doesn't keep track of multiple users at different Windows NT machines and so it cannot verify someone as a valid user.*

Once the command prompt is up, all the command prompt commands, including system administration commands, program development commands, and so on, can be issued. The following sequence shows how to use Telnet to access a UNIX computer from a Windows NT computer. The Windows NT computer is running Windows NT 4.0. The UNIX computer is running Sun OS.

A Telnet session can be started by typing Telnet from **Start, MS_DOS Command Prompt** and the Windows NT command prompt is called up as shown in Exhibit 6.

Keying in Telnet brings up the Telnet application dialog shown in Exhibit 7.

The remote system is accessed by clicking on **Connect**, and selecting **Remote System**. This brings up the Connect Dialog box shown in Exhibit 8.

The name of the remote system must be entered in the host name. The port name and terminal type can usually be defaulted.

If Telnet has been used to access a remote host before, the computer names will be shown in the pull-down menu. A click on the host name will avoid rekeying the host name.

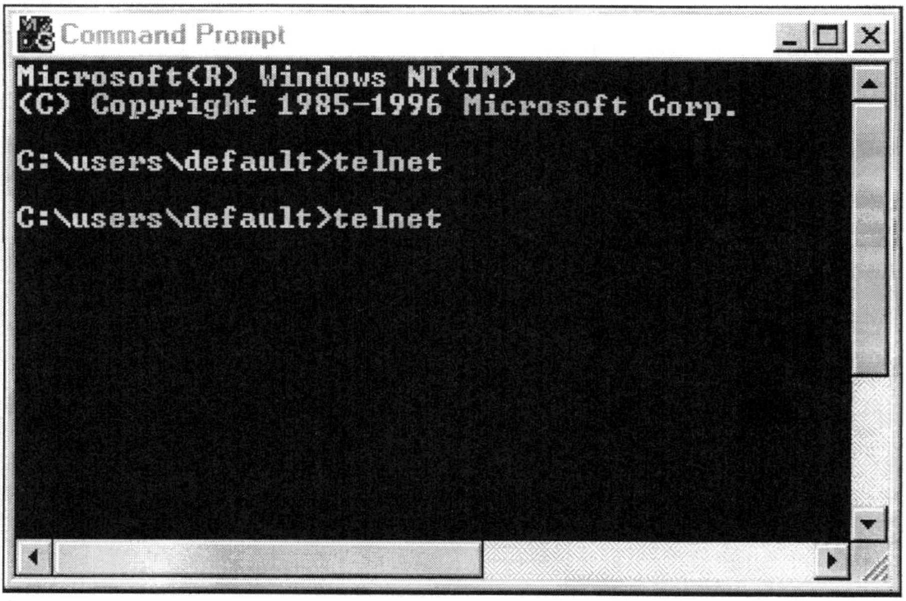

Exhibit 6. Starting a Telnet session using Windows NT command prompt.

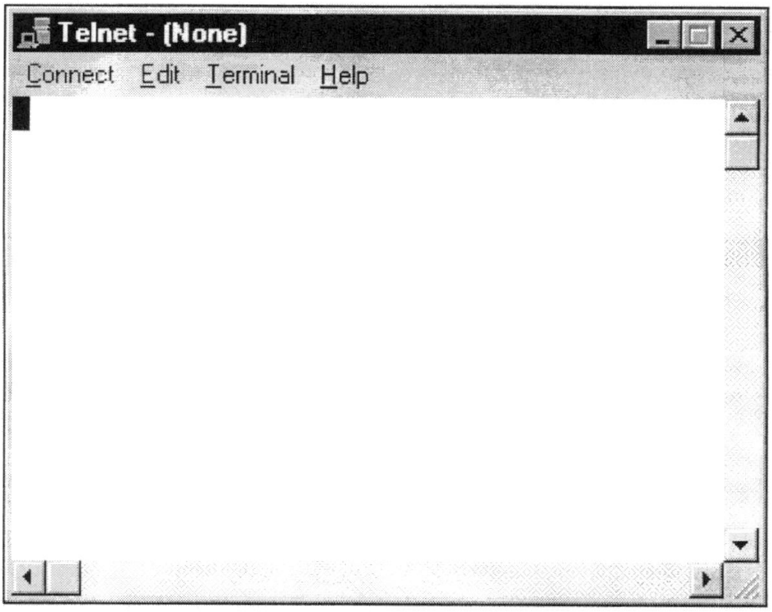

Exhibit 7. Telnet application dialog.

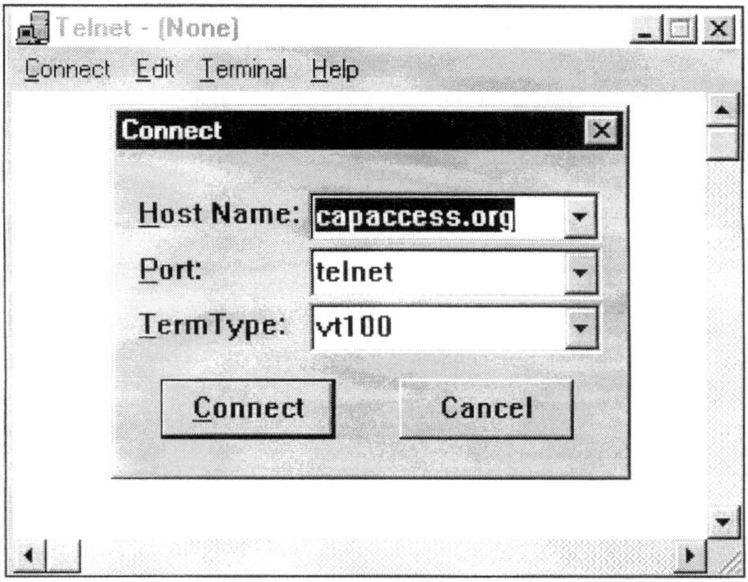

Exhibit 8. Connect dialog box of telnet.

Windows NT now tries to establish a Telnet session with the remote host and, if successful, will bring up the logon screen or the welcome screen of the remote computer as shown in Exhibit 9.

From now until logoff, the Telnet window is a terminal connected to the remote host and the contents and user interaction in the Telnet window are controlled by the remote host. But the Telnet window is just another window, and focus can be shifted to yet another window to perform other functions while the Telnet session remains connected to the remote host. (Of course, if the remote host normally logs off inactive terminals, it may log the user off if the telnet session is inactive for awhile).

Logon to the remote host may bring up a main menu as shown in Exhibit 10.

It is now possible to perform the same functions as on the remote computer. Exhibit 11 shows the read-mail function.

Telnet session settings such as the emulator type, fonts, terminal options, etc., can be changed by clicking from the menu. This brings up the Preferences dialog as shown in Exhibit 12. Using this dialog, the terminal type, such as VT52 or VT100, can be defined, whether a block or blinking cursor, etc., is desired.

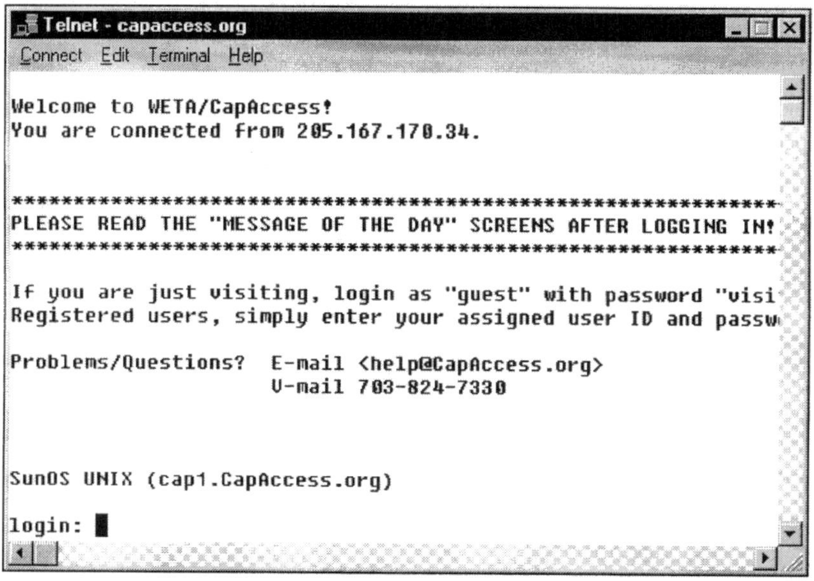

Exhibit 9. Logon screen of remote computer.

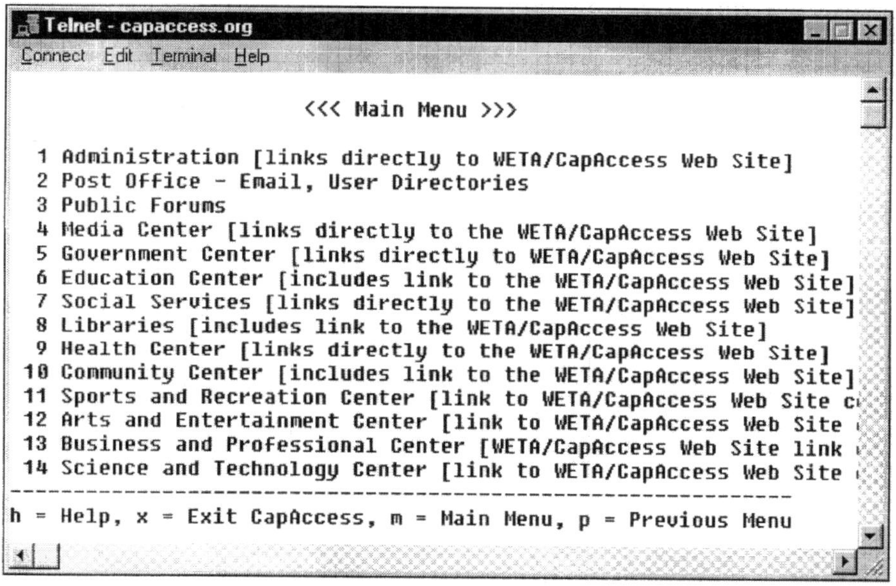

Exhibit 10. Main menu of the remote computer after logon.

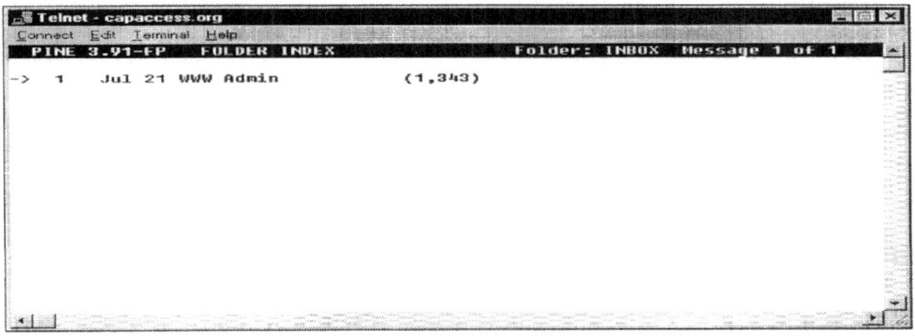

Exhibit 11. Reading mail at the remote host.

X-SERVER

A UNIX graphical application can be accessed from Windows machines using X-server software. The terms client/server are used in exactly the opposite way in the X-world as in others. In the X-world, the X-server is the code that runs in one machine and requests services from another machine, the X-client, on which the application that provides the services runs.

In a Windows environment, a machine running X-server software and having suitable connectivity can access a UNIX application running on another machine. The X-server application is another window on the Windows desktop.

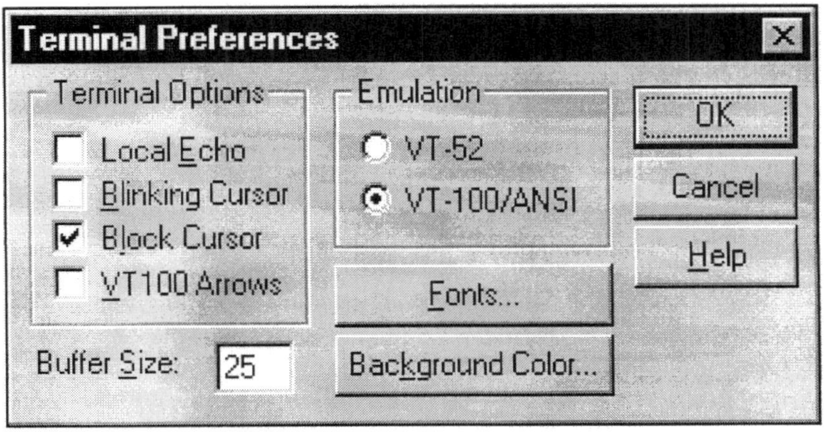

Exhibit 12. Setting preferences for Telnet sessions.

How Does X-Server Work?

Conceptually, the X-server works in exactly the same way as an X-terminal, discussed earlier in the article. An application running on one machine does the processing and displays the results on another machine's (X-server) window. The application's machine and the machine displaying the results could be connected by a telephone line with modems, LAN, or even the Internet/intranet. However, the more graphics that are present, the more time it is going to take for transmission. This could be a problem for modem connections, just as there are problems accessing graphics-rich web pages with slow modem connections. The protocol between an application and an X-server is typically the X-window protocol.

Considerations in Using the X-Server Approach

If a manager is trying to decide if an X-Server approach is right for his users, here are some advantages and disadvantages to consider.

Advantages of the X-Server Approach

- By using an X-server approach, access may be provided to non-Windows applications such as production UNIX applications from existing Windows desktops (without having to buy devices such as X-terminals or UNIX workstations). The alternatives are to provide two machines for each user (with associated footprint problems) or set up a pool of devices for accessing non-Windows applications. The latter approach could save some money, but has its own set of problems.
- As in the case of the X-terminal, the application still resides on a central server. All the advantages of having a central application server such as ease of upgrades, easier management and control, etc. are true for the X-server as well.
- Productivity can be improved over solutions like having two machines (one of which could be idle for extended periods of time). Having applications as windows on the same desktop provides for functions such as cut and paste between applications.
- With an X-server that runs on a PC, Windows 95 and other 32-bit applications can actually be run using a 486 or even 386 machine, which would not be possible natively.
- X-server approach also permits "roving" users to logon from any X-server. The state of the application on the server (for the user) could be preserved and the user could continue working.

DISADVANTAGES OF THE X-SERVER APPROACH

- Since the application runs on only one machine, it is necessary to ensure that the machine is capable of handling the load of a number

of concurrent users. Typically, a certain amount of disk storage and memory are required on the server for each user and a processor or multiple processors capable of handling the load must also be used.
- There is also a central point of failure, although this can be mitigated by having multiple severs.

COMMON X-SERVER PRODUCTS

This section presents an overview of some common X-Server products available. The information was gathered from different published sources including vendors' on-line Web pages. The Web addresses and other contact information is included in the description for each vendor and in Appendix. The tools are being updated quickly and the tool vendor should be contacted for the latest information. Most vendors also offer free evaluations that are downloadable from their Web sites.

This book is not intended to recommend one vendor over another. Migration/coexistence solutions that meet individual requirements should be chosen, and an evaluation of vendor products performed. The inclusion of vendor information is provided to offer an idea of the capabilities of the products and to supply a quick reference for further information and software.

Common X-Server products include:

- eXceed from Hummingbird Communications
- PC-Xware from NCD Software
- Reflection Suite for X from (WRQ)
- SCO Xvision from Santa Cruz Operation
- N*u*TCRACKER X-server from Datafocus
- eXalt-X from Intergraph
- Chameleon from NetManage
- OpenNT X11 server from Softway systems
- X OnNet from FTP Software

A brief overview of some of these products follows.

eXceed. More details on the eXceed product family is available online at http://www.hummingbird.com.

The eXceed family includes a line of X-servers that run on Windows NT, Windows 95, and Windows 3.1.

eXceed for Windows NT. eXceed is a native 32-bit Windows NT application that is X11R6-compliant. It runs in all environments Windows NT runs on. Local Windows and UNIX X applications run concurrently on the PC screen.

eXceed for Windows NT features. eXceed supports cut and paste of text and graphics among Windows applications and UNIX applications. eXceed is fully X11 Release 6 compliant and includes the X11R6.1 extensions Double Buffer, XTEST, SYNC, X input supporting mouse and keyboard, and X Image Extension (XIE) for high-performance image handling.

PC-XWARE

More information on PC-Xware is available online from NCD at http://www.ncd.com.

PC-Xware comes in two flavors. The PC-Xware Classic contains exclusively NCD's PC X-server. The PC-Xware Suite combines the PC X-server with NFS, terminal emulation, and network utilities.

Features of PC-Xware. PC-Xware is X/Open branded and Windows 95 logo compliant. It features an NFS Client and Server and its Xremote function allows remote access to X Windows applications over telephone lines. PC-Xware provides terminal emulation for IBM AS/400, VAX, Wyse, and HP in one program. It includes a graphical FTP client that features drag-and-drop file transfer between PCs and host computers over the network. It also includes a Graphical Keyboard Remapper that gives users a simple tool to customize their keyboards for any application.

N*u*TCRACKER X-Server. Information on N*u*TCRACKER products is available online at http://www.datafocus.com.

N*u*TCRACKER X-server is a 32-bit PC X-server that loads automatically with X-based applications, and is transparent to the user. It features seamless shutdown and restart of X sessions. It includes a virtual desktop manager and supports multiple profiles to run simultaneously.

REFLECTION SUITE FOR X FROM WRQ

Information on Reflection X product by Walker Richer and Quinn (WRQ) is available online at http://www.wrq.com.

Reflection X suite for X is more than just an X Server. It also includes terminal emulation and distributed files access (using NFS). To avoid duplication, this product is covered only here and not in terminal emulation or distributed file access. Besides Reflection Suite for X, WRQ also has other products such as Reflection Suite for the enterprise, Reflection Suite for TCP, etc. WRQ also lets you form your own suite by selecting a-la-carte from its products.

Features of Reflection Suite for X. Reflection Suite for X is a 32-bit Windows X server that is X11R6.1 compliant. It also includes specific X11R6 extensions, such as XTEST, Multi-Buffering Extension (MBX), and the X

Imaging Extension (XIE). It includes terminal emulation for a variety of terminals including VT420, VT320, VT220, VT102, VT54, SCO, ANSI, BBS ANSI; TN5250, and TN3270. The suite also supports TCP/IP and NFS for Windows 95.

Reflection Suite for X includes a set of administrative and diagnostic tools including ReadyX. ReadyX is designed to simplify PC X-connections for both users and system administrators. Reflection Suite for X provides remote X-connections via dial-up lines.

Reflection Suite for X provides a full range of Internet/Intranet functions including FTP, E-mail, Web client and Server, Newsreader, Finger client and Server, etc.

Reflection Suite Administration functions.

Reflection Suite for X includes management and administration functions. It includes a graphical interface that lets administrators control X-server settings by supplying default values or overriding user selections. Reflection Suite for X lets system administrators define the X-applications available on particular hosts, allowing PC X users to quickly create desktop icons from which to run those applications.

Reflection Suite for X includes a trace and replay utility that lets IS personnel evaluate the interaction between X-applications and the X-server by capturing the X-protocol for playback on any PC with Reflection X.

Reflection Suite for X support for Microsoft System Management Server (SMS) allows system administrators to perform unattended deployment of Reflection X to users' PCs from a network server.

User Interface features. Reflection Suite for X provides support for remote window managers such as Motif or OpenLook, as well as local window management with Microsoft Windows. Both can be used concurrently.

Reflection Suite for X comes with a full set of X11R5/X11R6 and host-specific fonts compiled into Microsoft Windows format. It also allows fonts to be stored locally or using a font server.

Reflection Suite for X can be configured to support displays up to a maximum of 32,000 x 32,000 pixels. Using configurable panning X-applications can be viewed that are too large to fit on the screen.

WRQ also sells Reflection for X, which includes the X-server, the terminal emulation functions, and FTP.

XVISION

More information on X Vision is available online from Santa Cruz Operation (SCO) at http://www.sco.com.

SCO XVision is part of the Windows-to-UNIX Integration product series from SCO.

The products in the series include:

- SCO SQL-Retriever: ODBC middleware
- SCO SuperVision: manage vision family desktops remotely
- SCO TermVision: extensible terminal emulator
- SCO VisionFS: UNIX file and print services for Windows
- SCO XVision: Transparent PC X-server
- SCO Wintif-Makes UNIX applications Windows friendly

XVision Eclipse. XVision Eclipse is a full 32-bit X-server that operates on Windows 95 and Windows NT. A version is available for Windows 3.1x as well. It provides access from a PC to character and graphical UNIX applications running on a UNIX Server. It is X11R6 compliant.

Features of Xvision Eclipse. Let us look at some of the Xvision features such as user interfaces, installation, and so on.

User Interface: Eclipse includes a virtual desktop manager, called "Zones." Each Zone is a different logical screen to the user. Eclipse lets different Windows managers be selected by configuration options. Support is provided for the Microsoft (local) window manager as well as a local Motif window manager. Eclipse features a UNIX Neighborhood Browser that has an identical interface to the Network Neighborhood on Windows 95 and Windows NT. This allows drag-and-drop file transfer between UNIX and Windows. X sessions can be suspended and resumed using another member of the Vision family, Vision Resume.

Installation: Eclipse includes a Windows 95-style setup wizard. Eclipse eases the task of iterative installations by providing functions to record a "script" detailing in which parts of the XVision Eclipse the software are to be installed. The recorded script can then be used for essentially unattended installs. An application wizard provides a list of UNIX servers the X-server can connect to as well as a list of applications on that server. Alternatively, the user can pick applications by browsing the UNIX file system. Once an application is selected, future access is made easy by using the Windows START or from a Program Group.

Administration: The Vision family includes SuperVision for the central management of Eclipse X-servers. SuperVision can display snapshots of the users' desktops so if users encounter problems, the system administrator can see what the user sees.

Graphics Optimizer: Eclipse includes a graphics optimizer. The graphics optimizer performs the most commonly used graphics operations using three different methods of drawing and timing each. The fastest method is remembered and is used to perform that specific operation in any future XVision Eclipse session.

Embed X Clients in Web Documents: Intranet users can start UNIX applications by clicking on embedded application information contained within Web pages.

Terminal Emulation Support: Eclipse includes terminal emulation support to access character-based legacy applications. Terminals supported include the vt420, vt320, vt200, vt100, vt52, wyse60, wyse50, and SCO ansi.

eXalt-X from Intergraph. eXalt is Intergraph's X11R6-compliant display server for X-based applications. More information on eXalt is available online from Intergraph at http://www.intergraph.com.

eXalt is designed to operate on Intel-based processors running Microsoft Windows 95 and Windows NT. eXalt integrates X Window applications over the network with desktop-based 32-bit Windows applications.

Features of eXalt include:

- Extensive font and digitizer support, including Intergraph's Font Server, supports .PCF, and .BDF formats, with network access of fonts through X11R6 Font Server
- Provides choice of window managers, startup modes, and installation levels for administrative flexibility and control
- Allows users to change keyboard language, set bell on/off, and adjust auto-repeat behavior with Keyboard Options
- Controls colors displayed by the eXalt server with the Color Database Options dialog
- Supports all four X Display Manager Control Protocol (XDMCP) startup modes (passive, query, broadcast, and indirect)

CHAMELEON XOFTWARE FROM NETMANAGE

NetManage has a number of products for migration and coexistence between UNIX and Windows NT. The product functionalities include heterogeneous e-mail, terminal emulation, distributed NFS file access, PC X-server, and web-enabled access to X-applications. More information is available online from NetManage at http://www.netmanage.com

The Chameleon product set includes a PC X-server that supports the latest release of X Windows (X11R6.3 or "Broadway"), Chameleon UNIXLink 97's PC X Server (XoftWare) provides seamless integration of X applications with web browsers. Users need only start their browsers, and click an HTML link to an X-application to get access to the X-application without needing to know X or UNIX connection commands.

OPENNT X SERVER

OpenNT X server is an X server from Softway systems. More information on the OpenNT X server is available online from Softway systems at http://www.softway.com.

OpenNT X server features include:

- X11R6 compliance
- 32-bit architecture
- Concurrent window managers — local Windows and host-based window manager
- Support for UNIX window managers — Motif, OpenLook, VUE, CDE
- Virtual screen-size support of 32,767 by 32,767 pixels
- Automatic window panning
- Copy and paste of text and graphics to and from Windows NT and Windows 95 clipboard to and from X Windows
- XDMCP security through X-authority
- Backing store and save unders
- Full set of X11R6 fonts are provided with automatic font substitution
- International keyboard support with a choice of 23 international layouts, 3-button mouse emulation for 2-button mouse
- Choice of full-screen single-window mode or multiple-window mode
- Full integration with Windows, providing familiar Windows GUI and ICCCM compatible operations for editing and window handling

eXpertise. eXpertise is a PC X-server from Quarterdeck. More information on eXpertise is available online from Quarterdeck at http://www.quarterdeck.com.

Features of eXpertise include:

- 32-bit or 16-bit PC X-Server with integrated Windows manager
- Choice of local or remote windows managers, with support for twm, mwm, and olwm
- 4-, 8-, 16-, and 24-bit display modes
- xdm support
- Font server
- Cut-and-paste capability between Windows applications and X applications
- Application Manager (users are able to launch the program from the Application Manager, from an icon, or from a menu item)
- Command-line FTP
- Line printer daemon (enables local printing)
- Automated installation
- Serial Xpress(TM) enhanced dial-up connectivity option

EMULATORS

A character-based UNIX application can be accessed using emulators that run on Windows. Emulators are also used for accessing non-UNIX and non-Windows host applications, the most common of which are the applications that run on IBM mainframes and IBM AS/400s. Emulators for accessing IBM host applications emulate devices such as the 3270 (for mainframes) and the 5250 (for the AS/400).

CONCLUSION

This chapter looked at different ways to can access UNIX applications from Windows desktops. The simplest way would be Telnet from Windows to the UNIX machine, but the capabilities of Telnet are limited. There are a number of vendors who provide X-server products that run in Windows and allow access to UNIX applications, including graphical applications. Some of the products were examined, and the advantages and disadvantages of X-servers were reviewed.

Chapter 11
Developing Workstation-Based Client/Server Applications

Steven Rabin

Leveraging existing assets, both code and people, is one of the keys to successfully developing new distributed applications. This article describes a strategy for creating distributed client/server applications by combining code that currently exists with new code.

INTRODUCTION

Advances in workstation technology have historically outpaced corresponding software improvements. Sophisticated computer processing chips were, in general, available years before the operating system software was able to exploit them (e.g., 32-bit processing technology was available on workstations well before any 32-bit software came out of the development laboratories). Application and corresponding systems support software has also lagged.

The introduction of stable operating systems and environments has changed this situation, providing database and network vendors with the opportunity to integrate their products with distributed platforms. In addition, a variety of software-development tools are available that allow developers to create new applications that effectively use distributed environments. These environments are usually open or network-oriented systems using a Graphical User Interface (GUI) and distributed Relational Database Management System.

To successfully shift development to these workstation-based environments, it is critical that an organization:

0-8493-9989-0/99/$0.00+$.50

- Understand what tasks must be performed.
- Have the right mix of people (and skills) to perform the given tasks.
- Agree on and stick to a common method of performing these tasks.
- Use effective, productive tools.
- Develop a distributed model.
- Implement a transformation strategy.
- Anticipate people, training, management, hardware, and software issues.

OBJECTIVE: EFFICIENT USE OF RESOURCES

Distributed applications need to be as portable as possible to maximize the long- and short-term investment being made to the application. This investment includes its technological underpinnings, the planned production environment, and future production environments.

Within the constraints of current business realities, for an organization to achieve competitive advantage with information technology, it must efficiently use available resources. Two key IS resources are current production applications and the employees who developed and are maintaining them.

Distributed applications (where applicable) can be created by combining code that currently exists (possibly from a host system or even simpler workstation application) with new code. This combination makes the best use of existing (and still valuable) application code while allowing new code and its underlying technology to be efficiently integrated. The resulting new application code should therefore meet the organization's design criteria in a most productive and cost-efficient way.

The blending together of old and new code involves the redevelopment of current application code. A determination must be made as to which portions of the code are still relevant and what, if anything, must be done to this code. This analysis process also lends itself to the creation of true platform-independent code—that is, a single set of source code that can be operated on a variety of platforms and environments with some recompilation.

This is a critical concept because no one can foresee all future production/development environments. As new users are introduced to the software, it is quite likely that the software will be required to operate on platforms that were not originally envisioned. All issues involving operating systems, diverse communications, databases, graphical (and nongraphical) interfaces, and client/server technologies need be examined in terms of portability.

INITIAL WORKSTATION DEVELOPMENT CONSIDERATIONS

Applications used to operate the business and provide competitiveness are a valuable resource. In addition, IS professionals have acquired a wealth of information about those systems and underlying business principles. Any distributed workstation development project must consider techniques and methodologies that use current application assets in a cost-effective way. This approach allows IS management to combat several existing development dilemmas, including backlog of work, containing or reducing IS costs, incorporating new technologies to increase competitiveness, and using the large amount of existing application code and the expert knowledge that was developed along with it.

Although this concept is not a new one, the idea of redeveloping older, outdated systems into new strategic systems is often overlooked. Because the concepts incorporate many of the best ideas of the past and present, this strategy can be successfully implemented in a wide variety of IS shops. It is not geared to any one particular methodology or environment and can be implemented in small, manageable, goal-oriented steps.

Initially, an application is selected that requires modernization, either technically or functionally. For the purposes of this discussion, this means an application that is being developed to operate in an environment that includes:

- Distributed cross-platform operating systems, most likely Disk Operating System, Windows, OS/2, or UNIX
- Client/server modeling to disperse application functions across the network
- GUI front ends, most likely Windows, Presentation Manager, or Motif
- Data modeling to distribute the data using a Relational Database Management System
- Communication facilities to handle multiple platform protocols (e.g., TCP/IP, APPC, or Internetwork Packet eXchange)

Although the goal may be to turn an existing application into a next-generation, state-of-the-art solution, this is not likely to happen all at once. It is better, especially for organizations new to distributed solutions, to phase the development of the system. This allows new tools and technologies to be assimilated into the organization while still providing ever-increasing benefits to the system's users.

For example, the base functions of an existing Canadian Independent Computing Services Association (CICSA) application may be redeveloped for a graphically based client/server environment. The first phase of this project might be to port the front end of the CICSA system to a graphical workstation environment. This benefits the user and starts the development of graphical code and expertise that can be used throughout the remainder of the project. Later phases would include converting to a distributed relational database, client/server functional modeling, and eventually incorporating support for all of the required communication interfaces (including host interfaces, proprietary systems, and currently popular platform protocols).

SCOPE AND GOALS OF DISTRIBUTED APPLICATIONS DEVELOPMENT

Once the application is selected and the business design issues are resolved, a variety of decisions must be made. The first of these concerns the target environment. It is always desirable to develop and execute the application in the most productive architecture possible. This may be a host, but distributed client/server or a combination of environments are the most likely architectures. Related user interface and communication issues must be examined. One decision will be whether a text-based or a GUI makes the most sense. Similarly, will the system be CICSA-based or will another communications protocol provide a better solution?

The distributed model also needs to be considered. This model is concerned with both the physical aspects of the application (and the enterprise it operates within) along with the conceptual aspects of how the business processes (and associated data) are to be split. Issues to be examined include whether key business processes will be performed on the client or server, or both, and where the data resides and how its integrity is to be ensured.

Although there are several standard distributed models in use, it is easier to build and manage an application that distributes data (and to a much lesser extent business processes) only when it is an absolute necessity. Building a distributed application must be done in stages, and the last stage is data distribution. This facility requires close coordination between the program, database, network, and associated middleware facilities.

In addition, plans need to be made for the testing and maintenance of these distributed and potentially platform-independent applications. Cataloged test scripts help, as does development that follows a single source code strategy. An automated method of delivering and possible implementing of the software may also be required. A method of delivering upgrades and fixes for distributed applications needs to be devised.

Testing is an area that requires careful attention when processes and possibly data are being distributed and the platforms/environments are not homogeneous. Distributed processes include business logic and the GUI presentation. The logic needs to be tested on both the client and server, although the presentation may reside on multiple desktops. Distributed client/server testing tools are becoming available to help execute testing procedures, but they are not a replacement for a sound testing methodology. A simple example illustrates this point. An error is found in the Windows program of a user data entry screen. This screen is also displayed to Presentation Manager and Motif users. Does the error also exist in these environments? Is the correction made to the Windows program the correct one for the other environments? Assuming that it is, is the correction made carefully so as not to introduce new errors? These are all critical issues in distributed testing that a tool can help with but not solve.

REDEVELOPMENT STRATEGY

Open environments offer a variety of benefits, but they require careful planning, a sound methodology, and a suite of integrated design, development, and maintenance tools. A single set of source code that can operate on multiple environments is the answer to many of these issues. It solves the problem of multiple sets of source code for specific environments and code integrity.

All of the distributed applications development work described in this article can be accomplished using Common Business Oriented Language (COBOL). This is true of all of the operating environments and all aspects of the code, including communications and GUI interfaces. This approach is recommended because many existing systems that are critical to the success of their businesses are mainframe- and COBOL-based. In addition, most of the systems people are trained in COBOL and its host environments (e.g., CICSA, Internet Multicasting Service, and database 2). IS organizations need to understand that their COBOL investment can fit in with strategic efforts for future systems.

This approach does not exclude other or mixed technology solutions; in fact, in certain instances they make sense. It does, however, emphasize that the mass of older application code can be profitably used across a variety of platforms and environments.

Because the changes implied throughout this chapter have an impact on many business disciplines, organizations must recruit the support required to complete what is usually a multiyear effort. IS can offer short-term deliverables within the longer-term strategic goals using certain fundamental principles and tools.

Fundamental Development Guidelines

Many questions come to mind when examining distributed development, usually pertaining to learning a new language, understanding multiple GUI APIs, data acquisition, and communicating between platforms. There is no reason to switch languages. Tools are available to handle the GUI environments, and distributed DBMSs are accessible with Structured

Query Language (SQL). Several high-level tools simplify even platform-to-platform communications issues.

When developing applications in and for a new platform, several basic development guidelines still apply. These include:

- Developing a conceptual development strategy
- Determining technical and functional development guidelines
- Determining technical and functional application guidelines
- Converting the conceptual development strategy into a logical transformation strategy

This analysis is usually performed by a combination of automated analysis and old-fashioned deskwork. People from the business and data processing sides of the application work together as a team. The organization, not IS, is creating a strategic system capable of taking the business through the end of the century.

Experience has repeatedly shown that certain fundamental practices must be in place before beginning a distributed development project (or any development project for that matter). First, a software development life cycle and methodology must exist. Second, policies and procedures for accepting and controlling deliverables must be implemented. This situation is equally true for a developer completing a program change or the project team completing the entire distributed system. Programs in the system will be expected to operate in different environments and must be tested accordingly. Finally, these points must be well defined and understood by all concerned. The organization must believe in and see the benefit of these methodologies and procedures if it is going to use them.

EXTENDING THE EXISTING DEVELOPMENT STRATEGY

Although training is going to be a requirement because developers need to understand the new platform and environment to be productive and design an application that makes significant use of its facilities, the bottom line is that a project can and should be implemented using a methodology and techniques that are similar to those currently in place.

In areas where the methodology needs to be revised—GUI design, for example—it is an extension to the existing development strategy. Similarly, a new tool is an extension to the tool set and not a new development workbench. The point is not to minimize potential changes being made to the code but to explain that these changes are evolutionary and must be integrated into the existing environment and organization design strategies. As shown in Exhibit 1, the time and tasks required to complete client/server projects are closely related to traditional applications development.

CLIENT/SERVER DEVELOPMENT

Transformation Methodologies

The heart of the distributed development process is the transformation methodology, which combines the business and technology visions into a coherent whole. This method is actually the coalescence of top-down (business vision) and bottom-up (technical vision) approaches. The result is the overall organization transformation policy, a strategical statement or contract defining what the system will be and what it will take to get there.

The top-down strategic input is required to understand the business vision. This input determines what the requirements of the new application are, or if it is an existing application, what needs to be revised. The prospective users of the new system and the environments in which the system is to be employed are also part of the business vision.

The bottom-up tactical input is required to understand the platform, environment, and technical issues of the new system, and to analyze the composition of the existing system, including data, program, process relationships, and associated software/hardware requirements. From this input, short-term deliverables can be identified under the long-term transformation strategy.

The last part of this phase is to determine feasibility and conformance to the vision. This takes participation from the business and IS sides, preferably in face-to-face meetings. It must be technically feasible and reasonable to develop and implement the business vision. If, for example, the business vision requires a palm-size, pen-based color computer with distributed networking capabilities, an evolutionary implementation may be required until the technology is both workable and available.

By no means should the business vision be cut short or revised by the IS organization, but it is the responsibility of IS to explain to corporate executives what it takes to meet the business vision. A technical compromise may be necessary so that the business functions can be properly implemented within a reasonable time frame and the design of the system meets the target audience's needs in a meaningful way.

CODE DEVELOPMENT

Functional Analysis

Once the plan is formalized and in place, the business of developing the system can begin in earnest. An analysis of the existing base of application code should be done to identify overlapping functions—that is, functions the target system and currently existing systems have in common.

There are many application-specific functions that can be used in the new system without change (e.g., date routines, calculations, and report formats). It is important to use this existing base of code because it is both proven and understood by the professionals developing the new application.

Because these functions may be used repeatedly during the development process, reusable code libraries or repositories should be developed. In addition to determining functional code that already exists, all other functions should be identified and cataloged. It may be that some of the target functions are excellent candidates for code generation (if that is available).

Once the functional analysis is complete, a wealth of information about existing code and new system processes (i.e., how the system is to accomplish its functions) should also be available. This information is critical when existing processes and underlying code are to be used as much as possible (in one form or another).

Data Requirements

Functions, processes, and the application code compose only half of the equation. Data relationships and requirements must also be defined. Distributed data models for the target system need to be analyzed and cataloged. A data repository is an excellent means of tracking the data requirements of the system and ensuring that the data is not duplicated. Equally important, data residence needs to be established if the data is to be truly distributed. The host, servers, and local workstations may each contain information critical to the application as a whole.

The analysis of data representations in the system often indicates where improvements can be made. Common problems include redundant data and inconsistent data use. It is not unusual to discover that some of the required data remains undocumented, a situation that must be corrected.

Modernizing data representations involves careful review of the design and (where applicable) the code. This involves identifying key data structures and where and how they are manipulated, as well as standardizing data names and definitions and propagating them throughout the system. Finally, data access methods should be reviewed to determine the means by which data will be acquired in the target environments.

Assembling Platform-Independent Code

Once the processes are isolated so that the platform-independent nature of the code can be formed, the application code can begin to be reassembled. To take advantage of specific environments, it may be necessary to symbolize the code.

Symbolization is simply a process of adding code that is assembled at compile time, most likely using a precompiler. Although this is not a requirement of distributed applications or platform independence, it provides certain advantages. A simple example is taking advantage of a monitor that displays 44 lines of data rather than the more traditional 25 lines.

The Problem of Diverse Interfaces

One of the major issues of coding for diverse environments is the many APIs that are encountered. This is especially true for data acquisition, GUI presentation, and communication protocols. Standardizing around SQL and databases that support distributed data access provides a solution to the data issue. GUI presentation is not as easily solved without the use of a tool. Several sophisticated tools are available that provide a common interface to many of the prevalent GUI.

A more detailed look at the communication issue helps explain how a single set of source code handles diverse interfaces. The use of tools that support a common communications interface (CCI) or application-to-application interface (AAI) allows the same code to execute across platforms, regardless of the protocol. APPC, Named Pipes, NetBIOS, and Internetwork Packet eXchange are several of the communication protocols that can be used to provide distributed services. An application can have access to both individual environments and distributed open environments in this manner. This allows the same source code to elegantly handle the complexities of distributed communications. Exhibit 2 illustrates this concept.

Communication Facilities for Distributed Services

In a distributed applications environment, each of the isolated functions must be tested as a coordinated whole under all target environments. The same code may be required to operate under DOS, OS/2 , Windows, or UNIX. Similarly, the integrity of the code must never be compromised. Regardless of the platform, the code operating on a single, secure version must be maintained.

Distributed Development Tools

There are many COBOL-oriented development and maintenance tools that allow developers of distributed workstation applications to take advantage of the techniques described in this chapter, including tools that provide cross-platform support and are compatible with code initially developed for other environments.

Workstation-based tools are available that support development for DOS, Windows, OS/2 Presentation Manager, UNIX, and UNIX Motif. These tools use a variety of platform-specific runtime environments so that the code need not be developed to that level of detail.

When the application code is developed at a higher level, it is possible for the same source to execute in diverse environments. For example, the Micro Focus Operating Systems Extensions (OSX) environment provides COBOL programs (and thus COBOL developers) with the same services and the same interfaces for all target operating environments. Applications developed on one system can be ported to another with minimal, if any, code modification. Other tools enable developers to prototype and create graphical and character-oriented user interfaces that can be ported across all target operating environments.

A set of communication and SQL database services tools support high-performance application interfaces to a variety of networks and databases. SQL services provide support for Gupta, Microsoft SQL Server, NetWare SQL, Oracle, OS/2 Database Manager, Informix, Sybase, XDB, and others. AAI and CCI provide network and client/server support. AAI allows program-to-program communication between platforms—that is, one program can call another program as if it were a localized routine. CCI supports network (and internetwork) application communications.

Distributed testing tools must operate on multiple platforms and have the ability to visually analyze the program logic and determine how much of the code is actually being executed during the test. A tool that provides the developer with a common interface across platforms is critical because developers may encounter a situation requiring them to test a function in an unfamiliar environment.

Because less-specific skills are needed for distributed applications development, selecting the definitive computing environment is a much smaller issue because applications can be moved to other platforms. Most important, scarce development resources can be used where they will have the greatest impact, developing business application code.

CONCLUSION

Distributed applications provide many benefits to the organization. They allow both business and systems professionals to solve problems while positioning their companies for the future. In many cases, code from existing systems can be salvaged and turned into high-quality, next-generation applications. Development staff members are already familiar with the code and, to a certain extent, the basic methodology and tools. It is not necessary to reinvent the wheel.

The key design criteria to be taken into account before moving applications development to a distributed client/server environment include:

- Process models
- Data models
- Object distribution
- Repositories
- Stored procedures
- Language
- Program modules
- Communications
- Desktop presentation (GUI)
- Distributed platform testing
- Application distribution

These criteria should be assimilated into the development process using the transformation strategies described in this chapter. In some respects, distributed applications development is different from other systems development efforts for mainframes, midranges, and standalone workstations, but there are similarities in the way the project should be approached. Data modeling, process design, function analysis, and prototype acceptance are examples of tasks that are performed in all structured applications development projects. It is not necessary or even advisable to get wrapped up in the technology. The ultimate tool, methodology, or environment is always going to be out there waiting to be discovered. A better approach is to take small, measurable steps with definable goals and allow the project to generate momentum with initial successes toward the organization's ultimate goals.

Chapter 12
Using Middleware for Interoperable Systems

Raymond J. Posch

The increasingly distributed nature of business locations and operations has led to a concomitant expansion of client/server computing from the department level to the enterprise level. Yet the successful implementation of client/server, or distributed, business applications depends on interoperability—the ability of applications to work together across a network to perform business functions. Systems integrators need to know exactly how a client application will talk with a server application before either can be designed or written. If they do not, unrealistic assumptions about applications-level connectivity can be project killers.

Because enterprises typically have many and diverse systems to meet their business needs, interoperability problems are almost always encountered as soon as applications on desktops, mainframes, midrange systems, and servers need to interact with each other. No products have emerged as clear-cut, widely supported standards, de facto or otherwise, for distributed enterprise applications. Systems integrators are tested to the utmost by the fact that these client/server applications must be developed with wide-ranging assortments of platforms, networks, databases, and tools.

The need for applications to be able to directly exchange information in real time in a distributed heterogeneous environment has led to the development of middleware—software that bridges the gap between business applications and systems-level services such as databases, network protocols, and operating systems. This chapter discusses the business issues in enterprise computing and the myriad interoperability problems associated with achieving distributed business applications. It then reviews how middleware is being used to solve these problems.

0-8493-9989-0/99/$0.00+$.50

DISTRIBUTED APPLICATIONS DEFINED

A distributed application is an automated business activity broken down into multiple processing functions running on different computers and performed in a coordinated fashion by sending information across a network. Depending on the relationship of the components, such applications are also referred to as client/server or peer-to-peer applications. Because the application components must work together across the network, the applications are more generally referred to as cooperative processing applications.

The so-called two-tier client/server model divides the processing into a client portion, which interfaces with the user, and a server portion, which interfaces with the database. Execution of business rules is divided among the client or server components.

The three-tier model divides the work into presentation on the client platform, business rules on one or more application platforms, and database access on one or more database platforms. This model attempts (at least conceptually) to isolate the business rules to the middle tier so that client applications and database server applications are less affected by the frequent changes that occur in business rules. It is believed that this approach can lead to applications that are easier to maintain and that scale better as the volume of business transactions grows.

BUSINESS ISSUES IN ENTERPRISE COMPUTING

IT Infrastructure, Legacy Systems, and Changing Technology

Organizations invest in the IT infrastructure necessary for conducting business. This IT infrastructure comprises computers, software, and networks. An organization that has been in business for any period of time is likely to have legacy systems (i.e., hardware, software, and networks) that may not be easily replaced as newer capabilities become available. Such an organization is also likely to replace its computers or networks to increase speed and capacity, for example.

Because technology, especially information technology, changes continuously, organizations face at least two major challenges to their ability to manage their investments in IT infrastructure:

1. Ensuring that business-critical applications can easily adapt and remain in operation when computers, operating systems, and networks are changed or replaced for reasons of capacity, price/performance, or functional fit. This is very much an issue of managing assets and operating costs.
2. Choosing infrastructure components that allow for the quick use of new technologies. This relates particularly to applications software,

because the cost efficiencies of operating the business are often directly related to the applications. New technologies often have steep learning curves and existing applications may not be easily adaptable. Although this is an issue of managing assets and costs, it is also one of business adaptability and responsiveness. It is especially important for a rapidly growing business.

Integration in a Distributed Business World

The challenges of managing an IT infrastructure are complicated further by the increasingly distributed nature of business organization and operations. Employees and business functions that were centralized in a single headquarters 10 years ago are now likely to be scattered in dozens or hundreds of locations around the globe. Departments that previously consisted of employees performing the same or similar functions are now often organized as distributed teams with team members in many different locations. This increasing physical distribution of people, functions, and supporting systems engenders at least three major challenges:

Integrating the business (internally) in a distributed environment. This issue actually breaks down into a series of related issues, such as:

- Ensuring that employees located in remote or branch offices have the information they need to do their work.
- Ensuring that employees across different locations can communicate effectively and work together as teams.
- Ensuring that employees across all locations understand critical objectives, are working together toward common goals, and receive the information feedback they need to evaluate and fine-tune their work. This is a huge problem and the reason that the concept of enterprisewide information systems is becoming more important.

Integrating externally with other entities. Companies that previously carried out business transactions with suppliers or customers primarily by phone or mail are now interacting through such electronic communications methods as *electronic data interchange (EDI)*, electronic mail (e-mail), and the World Wide Web. The question here is how to establish effective communication yet ensure that information is not shared inappropriately.

Providing a consistent—if not common or at least unified—supporting infrastructure. Such an infrastructure comprises voice communications, *fax*, networked computers, and information access and exchange across all locations.

INTEROPERABILITY: THE TECHNICAL CHALLENGE

Because organizations depend on the enabling tools of information technology, their business objectives for enterprise computing are accompanied by a host of technical issues. Interoperability, however, is most often the stumbling block to mission-critical client/server systems.

Large-scale client/server applications involve complex networks, usually with many local area networks (LANs) interconnected through a *wide area network (WAN)*. More often, such applications involve multiple *WANs* and multiple network protocols, such as IBM's *System Network Architecture (SNA)*, NetBIOS, *Transmission Control Protocol/Internet Protocol* (TCP/IP), and *frame relay*. They typically involve several different computing platforms, or different types of computers running different operating systems, such as PCs running Microsoft Corp.'s Windows; servers running Hewlett-Packard's HP-UX; and mainframes running IBM Corp.'s MVS and *CICS*. They often involve multiple databases, perhaps based on different database management system (DBMS) platforms, such as Oracle Corp.'s *ORACLE* and IBM's DB/2 and *IMS*. And, they will certainly involve business applications on distributed platforms tied together in a number of different ways, such as by transaction monitors, message-oriented middleware, data access middleware, and *remote procedure calls* (RPCs), or sometimes by clumsier mechanisms like file transfers or sequential batch processing jobs.

Systems integration at the enterprise level entails getting many different information systems components to work together across the enterprise network. Because these myriad components must interoperate effectively, interoperability is the first key to success. But, interoperability is not simply a problem of network protocol compatibility—it exists at many different levels, such as:

- Network interoperability
- Platform interoperability
- Database or data access interoperability
- Object or software component interoperability
- Presentation interoperability—graphical user interfaces (GUIs) and multimedia user interfaces (MUIs)
- Workgroup/workflow/e-mail interoperability
- Applications interoperability

Network Interoperability

Today, many companies running very large networks use multiple network protocols. If they are or were large IBM shops, they typically have 3270 terminal protocol, plus one or more *SNA* protocols on their *WAN*, NetBIOS on their LANs, *TCP/IP* on their Unix-based engineering networks, and perhaps even some Novell *IPX*. Multiple *network operating systems* may be a management issue, but at the application-to-application level (AAI), differing protocols and spanning across networks of varying types are usually the biggest problems. For example, on an *SNA LU* 6.2-only network, a client application can be written to invoke the APPC *application programming interface (API)* to establish a session and exchange information with a server application that also uses the APPC *API*. However, when one application is on an *SNA* network and the partner application is on a *TCP/IP* network, a major interoperability problem arises.

Platform Interoperability

Organizations striving to implement mission-critical distributed applications face the difficult challenge of interoperability among platforms of completely different types, such as *IMS* on IBM mainframes and Unix platforms. Much of what has been done to date under the client/server classification involves decision support applications. Most mission-critical functions are performed primarily with the assistance of mainframe applications; yet, getting *IMS* or *CICS* to talk to non-IBM platforms, and especially nonmainframe platforms, is proving to be difficult.

Database Interoperability

This category of interoperability has to do with applications accessing information in databases located on multiple systems, in databases on different platform types, or—the most difficult of all—in databases of completely different types (such as *ORACLE* and *IMS*). The interoperability problem is somewhat lessened if all databases are relational databases using *structured query language (SQL)*, although not all *SQLs* are the same. It is definitely easier if all databases use the same DBMS product, but even then there may be difficulties between certain platforms or with certain network protocols. In any of these cases, database interoperability is a major consideration, especially when legacy systems are involved and are expected to work with newer systems.

Object/Software Component Interoperability

The advent of object-oriented systems in which data is encapsulated in objects allows information to be exchanged among applications as objects. The exchange is handled by an *object request broker (ORB)*, originally defined by the *Object Management Group*. *ORBs* are now available from multiple software companies.

Issues are surfacing, however, with *ORB* dependence on *remote procedure calls* when operating across enterprise networks, and with *ORB*-to-ORB interoperability—that is, getting different *ORB* products from different vendors, usually also involving different platforms, to work together. Applications built using other types of component-based software are also becoming more commonplace—with Microsoft's VBX (Visual Basic Custom Controls) being the most frequently cited type. The major issues are how such reusable components exchange information with other components and how they can work consistently and compatibly on different platforms.

GUI/MUI Interoperability

Another issue concerns how applications using a *graphical user interface (GUI)* or *multimedia user interface (MUI)* can be written to work on different platforms. This is, in part, a portability problem rather than an interoperability problem.

The real interoperability problem with *MUI* applications, which are expected to proliferate in the future, is twofold. It concerns interoperation of *GUI* functions as part of client/server exchanges when different types of *GUIs* are involved, such as Windows, Presentation Manager, and Motif, and how to make *full-motion video* or interactive compound media information exchanges work across heterogeneous platforms and heterogeneous networks.

Workgroup/Workflow/E-Mail Interoperability

As *groupware* connectivity becomes more common, one workgroup using one *groupware* product will increasingly need to interoperate with other workgroups using different *groupware* products. This is especially true with intercompany connectivity. Workflow interoperability, therefore, is a problem of:

- Integrating different *groupware,* workflow, and e-mail products
- Supporting these types of applications across heterogeneous platforms and networks
- Integrating *groupware*, workflow, and e-mail applications with other types of applications
- Resolving differences in document formats so that, wherever possible, format conversion takes place automatically under the covers

Applications Interoperability

Distributed computing usually refers to distributing the processing among applications located on different systems. Enterprise computing extends distributed computing to a larger scale—across an enterprise network of LANs, *WANs*, and multiple kinds of platforms—but it may also go much further by integrating applications in different business disciplines, such as the employee skills database and corporate directory services. In both cases, at the level where things must happen based on business events, one application somewhere on the network must exchange data with another application somewhere else on the network. Interoperability in terms of client/server computing always comes down to AAI interoperability regardless of how many other kinds of interoperability issues are actually involved.

MIDDLEWARE SOLUTIONS

Nearly all cases of successful large-scale distributed computing applications involve the use of middleware to solve interoperability problems. Middleware, as the name is meant to imply, is software that sits between business applications and the systems-level services, or so-called platforms, that are the source of compatibility problems. Software layering, from which the middleware idea derives, is illustrated in Exhibit 1.

Exhibit 1. Layered software architecture.

Business Applications
Middleware
(Common Application Services)
System Services
(i.e., Database, Network, Operating System)

Because middleware is based on layering, with a new layer of software being inserted as a higher-level platform on which business applications will reside, it provides a degree of encapsulation or abstraction of the lower-level services. In fact, middleware typically introduces new *APIs* that are used to invoke the higher-level services. That is why it is common for applications designers and programmers to talk in terms of the new APIs—for example, Microsoft's *ODBC* or MAPI, or IBM's DRDA—when describing how applications will be interconnected and how one or more of the interoperability problems will be solved.

Because of the layering effect, middleware helps insulate business applications from changes in platforms, networks, or other systems services. IT executives can therefore change the underlying technologies, using more-effective and efficient ones, without changing the applications. The abstraction of services through the higher-level *APIs* also simplifies applications programming, enabling programmers to create or modify applications more quickly in response to business changes. By providing the means for linking applications together across a network, middleware provides a mechanism for applications interoperability and information access.

There are several types of middleware, including:

- X.400, MAPI, SMTP
- X.500, Streettalk

- ODBC, DRDA, distributed DBMS
- DCE, ONC
- CORBA/ORB, OLE2/COM, OpenDoc
- Gateways (such as SQL Server and OmniConnect)
- RPCs
- Message passing and queueing
- Transaction monitors

Most of these types of middleware are ultimately aimed at the AAI connectivity problem. Some are specific to e-mail interoperability (*X.400*, MAPI, *SMTP*); some are specific to database interoperability (*ODBC*, *DRDA*, distributed DBMS, database gateways); some are specific to object-oriented interoperability (ORB, OLE2, OpenDoc); and some are more generalized (*DCE*, *RPCs*, message passing and queueing).

All these types of middleware let one application exchange information with another. The exceptions are X.500 and Streettalk, which are directory services (i.e., middleware that addresses the problem of how applications are identified and actually found in large enterprise networks).

There are other interoperability solutions as well, such as protocol converters, bridges, gateways, data format translators, and other special-purpose hardware and software, but often these work at a system or network level and do not facilitate the AAI dialogues that are fundamental to client/server and other forms of distributed computing. The need for the direct exchange of information among applications in a heterogeneous environment has caused middleware to come into existence and to now play a dominant role in the IT architectures of progressive enterprises.

Message-Oriented Middleware

One particular type of middleware—message-oriented middleware—allows an application to send messages (i.e., data) to other applications and to receive messages in return. It encompasses message passing, message queueing, and transaction monitors. Messages in this context are any type of transaction or other exchange that might occur between distributed applications. The meaning and the format of the messages are defined by the structure and contents of the data to meet the requirements of each particular distributed application.

One example of commercial message-oriented middleware, and probably the earliest to be used in a mission-critical production environment, is the Communications Integrator (CI) of Covia Technologies (Englewood *CO*). The Communications Integrator, first used in the computerized airline reservations system industry, was initially developed by United Airlines for its Apollo reservations network. CI originated in the mid-1980s to allow applications to become independent of network protocols, which in turn would facilitate moving applications to new servers/hosts within the network, allow new hardware and software platforms to be added to the network more readily, and simplify the complexities of programming for AAI communication.

The Apollo network was already a very large network with database server applications running on mainframes, new services being added regularly, and transaction volumes growing rapidly. Because plans were being made for PCs and LANs at customer sites, LAN servers, and PC-based LAN-to-WAN gateways to be added to the reservations network, a much more dynamic and adaptable approach was needed for dealing with distributed applications in a changing network environment. It is also interesting to note that between 1985 and the early 1990s when commercial message-oriented middleware was not yet available, many other companies with large networks in industries other than airline reservations were going through similar transitions and developing their own in-house message middleware.

The approach used in the CI, which was sold for the first time in industries other than the airlines industry beginning in late 1991, was to architect an *API* having consistent functions, verb set, and options (i.e., parameters) across all platforms regardless of operating system, language used for the product implementation, or network protocols supported. The Communications Integrator *API* allows applications to register with the message service and then call a send routine to send messages or a receive routine to receive messages. Applications do not have to deal with the problems of network sessions because the Communications Integrator, running on each node, takes care of all session management under the covers.

When sending a message, applications take advantage of the CI's directory services to simply specify the name of the application to receive the message; select a message type (i.e., *asynchronous* or one-way, or synchronous or query with correlated reply); select other options such as priority, assurance level, and whether notification is requested; and then issue the send. When receiving a message, applications select the mode (i.e., blocking or nonblocking), select whether looking for a reply to a specific query or simply the next one available, and then issue the receive.

An Example of Middleware Use. Healthcare Data Exchange (HDX), headquartered in Malvern PA near Philadelphia, provides one example of how middleware is used in a large distributed application. Using the Communications Integrator, HDX has implemented a patient insurance eligibility and claims system for its multistate network of healthcare providers. Client applications resident in PCs at the admission desks of providers initiate requests for patient records, eligibility, and admissions based on information supplied by the patient. These requests are sent to appropriate server applications running on local servers or on mainframes at HDX data centers. Switching applications at intermediate servers may trigger multiple requests to systems both inside the HDX network (e.g., HDX claims processing on an IBM mainframe or HDX accounting systems on DEC mainframes) and outside (e.g., eligibility with Medicare or commercial insurance companies). Responses containing screen displays, printed patient records, admissions paperwork, or billing statements are sent back to the admission clerk's PC or to a print server application located nearby. Response times must, of course, be kept as short as possible.

The networked healthcare information business places great demands on client/server applications. In the HDX case, middleware provided flexibility and adaptability to deal with several different platforms, the possibility of future network changes such as from SNA to TCP/IP, and rapid growth, while at the same time simplifying programming through a higher-level message API.

Although the Communications Integrator is no longer being sold, other middleware products are now available. Some examples include MQSeries from IBM, DECmessageQ from Digital Equipment Corp., and Pipes from PeerLogic. In addition, distributed transaction monitors, such as Tuxedo from Novell and TopEnd from AT&T, are now also positioned as message-oriented middleware products.

TRENDS IN MIDDLEWARE DEVELOPMENT

Given the multiplatform, multiprotocol world in which most modern enterprises operate, middleware has come into existence in the last 10 years as a necessary means of providing applications with a degree of insulation from the differences across platforms and protocols. As such, middleware allows the applications to be less affected by changes in those platforms and protocols, while simultaneously providing interoperability across a heterogeneous IT environment.

There is a great explosion in products within each niche or type of middleware, and new types of middleware products are being developed to meet new needs and to solve new interoperability problems. The rapid growth of the Internet, for example, has generated new products for Internet-based applications, and middleware that allows applications on corporate desktops and servers to interact in real time with applications on Internet servers should be available soon. Middleware development is still in its growth stage, and the middleware marketplace has not yet seen much consolidation.

Ultimately, the market will determine which are the preferred middleware solutions. Such solutions will likely be strongly influenced by other IT trends, such as the development of object-oriented and multimedia technologies. In the end, the preferred middleware solutions must not only be embraced by end users, they must also be integrated by software vendors into the application and tool products that must interface with the end users' custom applications.

Critical issues to customers will be whether the middleware supports the customer's particular platforms and network protocols, is relatively easy to use, and to manage—that is, whether and how easily the middleware can be installed, configured, and tuned in a distributed manner. The market must also contend with issues relating to the degree of integration and compatibility with other middleware products and with common applications, especially those used by each customer to conduct day-to-day business.

Although applications developers would like it to be otherwise, evolution of middleware products, along with other client/server tools, will take time—maybe five to ten years. In the meantime, businesses must be able to solve their interoperability problems so that they can implement distributed computing solutions that meet business needs. In some cases, these systems might be characterized as enterprisewide information systems that are used throughout the enterprise and allow the enterprise to act in a more integrated way in serving customers. There may also be smaller enterprise client/server applications that improve some business process, such as customer support, by automating and facilitating customer interaction in a consistent way across many different functions of the enterprise.

In any case, distributed systems today, and for at least the next several years, will likely use point solutions—middleware tools selected according to the unique requirements of the particular system being implemented—rather than integrated solution sets that are suitable for use in all distributed applications of the enterprise.

Given time, however, client/server software and middleware tools will inevitably achieve greater maturity, and integrated solution sets will be offered by the major software companies. Many software vendors, just like end users, are struggling to deal with diverse platforms and protocols and the related interoperability problems. Some vendors specialize only in selected software markets and systems, such as PCs or Unix, but the most complete solutions will likely come from the software vendors who are now established players in enterprise networking, such as IBM or Computer Associates, or those who may be able to expand to that level, such as Microsoft.

RECOMMENDED COURSE OF ACTION

Because most situations in which organizations are striving to implement client/server applications are unique, IT staffs should research middleware options themselves or hire specialist consultants to find the best solutions to meet their specific requirements. In some cases, for example, a distributed DBMS such as ORACLE may fit the particular situation; in others, message-oriented middleware may provide the right interoperability solution.

Assessing and managing the risks involved in proposed solutions cannot be taken lightly, however. Proof of concept should be considered a necessary phase of any first-time undertaking or sizable project to ensure that the software and the hidden complexities that are part of large-scale and mission-critical client/server applications are fully understood. System requirements must address the adaptability and probable life of the middleware as part of the adaptability and probable life of the overall client/server application. These strategies can be used to manage middleware decisions and distributed application projects.

Many successful mission-critical applications have been implemented in recent years, and middleware tools supporting such applications should continue to evolve to meet the needs of the market. As the market matures, middleware products will have added functions and features, improve in performance, and become more proven in real business conditions. These are the attributes that enterprise-level client/server computing demands.

Chapter 13
Implementing OLE on Non-Windows Platforms Using ObjectBroker

Jeff Tancill
John Parodi

ObjectBroker's *OLE* Network Portal provides Microsoft's *Object Linking and Embedding (OLE)* functions for data objects stored on non-Microsoft platforms. The portal enables *OLE*-supporting applications (e.g., current versions of Microsoft Word and Excel, Lotus 1-2-3, and AmiPro) to link and embed *OLE* data objects that reside on Unix and OpenVMS servers. Additional platforms will be supported in the future.

The portal intercepts relevant OLE calls made on the personal computer (PC), translates them to CORBA messages, and passes them to ObjectBroker. ObjectBroker in turn forwards them to an appropriate server on the network for resolution. From the application user's perspective, the process is transparent; the object behaves as though it were stored locally on the PC. Within an OLE application, the ObjectBroker portal appears to be a local OLE V2 server application. In this way, information from sources across the network can be dynamically linked or embedded into desktop applications through ObjectBroker today.

The portal provides an intermediate step between OLE applications that interoperate on a single machine today and a true distributed object system based on OLE Integration, formerly the Common Object Model, which is being jointly developed by Digital and Microsoft. OLE Integration will be available in Microsoft's Cairo product and in a future release of ObjectBroker. ObjectBroker's Network Portal means that software developers

0-8493-9989-0/99/$0.00+$.50

can begin to network-enable OLE applications now, with assurance of an easy upgrade path. Further, because the Network Portal will manage and allow interoperation between both CORBA-style objects and OLE Integration objects, ObjectBroker will provide a most useful interconnectivity between the desktop and the distributed computing infrastructure.

Object Linking and Embedding (OLE) Version 2 is set of standard interfaces that support application integration and interoperation. OLE V1 was based on the compound document model. OLE V2 retains this model and introduces a common infrastructure for storage, manipulation, and programmability of objects. The ObjectBroker OLE Network Portal implements OLE V2 interfaces and also provides support for OLE V1 applications.

The data-centric model behind OLE is designed to support the task of combining information from numerous sources into what appears to be a single container, such as a document. In the past, the information objects OLE could handle had to be on a single machine running Microsoft Windows. ObjectBroker's Network Portal now allows data objects to be distributed across a network, with these data objects residing on remote CORBA servers.

OLE V1 supported the compound document approach described above. It allowed the end user to combine multiple information sources in a single container. OLE V2 improves on this approach with visual editing (i.e., in-place activation) and "drag and drop" functionality, which provide better integration and interoperability among information sources. OLE V2 also represents a shift away from handle-based application programming interfaces (APIs) to an object system where interfaces represent the contract between objects, and the objects themselves are fully described by the collection of interfaces they support. OLE V2 claims 100% compatibility with OLE V1. By implementing OLE V2 interfaces, ObjectBroker also supports OLE V1 and its style of displaying the server object in a separate window.

OLE Integration is the object technology that underlies OLE V2 and provides compatibility with OLE V2 applications. All OLE V2 objects are OLE Integration objects, although not all OLE Integration objects are OLE V2 objects. Thus OLE V2 uses the object model, which lays the evolutionary groundwork for distributed object computing in the years ahead. OLE Integration's Component Object Model specification describes how application objects expose their functions to the system as well as to other applications. OLE Integration allows an object's code to live anywhere (in another application and with distributed OLE Integration in Cairo, on another machine). In the meantime, OLE V2 provides a number of standard interfaces through which one can implement and manipulate OLE objects.

THE DIGITAL/MICROSOFT OLE INTEGRATION AGREEMENT

OLE Integration, announced in 1993 as the Common Object Model agreement, concerns the joint development of an object model and a wire protocol based on Microsoft's object extensions to DCE RPC. Digital is to provide OLE Integration and related services on the platforms where ObjectBroker runs. Digital is also to provide interoperability between OLE and CORBA-style objects to create a desktop-to-data center distributed object environment.

The OLE Network Portal supports Microsoft Windows clients communicating with non-Microsoft Windows servers. This approach provides initial, limited connectivity between the worlds of OLE and CORBA. The OLE Network Portal is an interim step to allow developers to create "OLE aware" servers for use by off-the-shelf OLE container applications to access remote data objects. In the future, these capabilities will be expanded by a full implementation of OLE Integration within ObjectBroker.

OBJECTBROKER'S OLE NETWORK PORTAL MODEL

The OLE Network Portal, running on a Microsoft Windows machine, provides simple embedding and linking of remote data objects by transforming certain OLE methods into requests to be serviced by a remote server.

The OLE Network Portal performs all the functions required by an OLE server application and acts as a surrogate server for the remote ObjectBroker server. Thus the OLE Network Portal provides a pass-through for data objects from the remote ObjectBroker server to the OLE container application. These objects are fully functional OLE objects that just happen to originate with an object server application on a remote node.

Exhibit 1 illustrates an OLE client/container application on MS-Windows bridging over the OLE Network Portal to an ObjectBroker server applications on a non-MS-Windows platform.

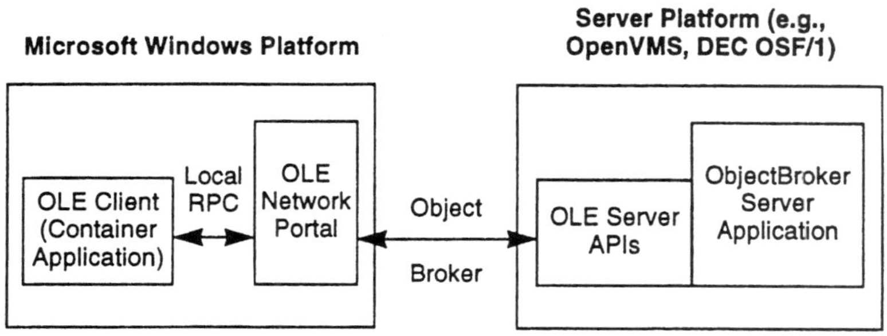

Exhibit 1. Bridging over object-broker.

The *OLE* Network Portal on Windows acts as the intermediary between a remote network service and a local *OLE* client application. The portal acts as a full-fledged *OLE* server application from the viewpoint of the container application; it maps *OLE* server application methods to *CORBA* requests, which are then forwarded to the actual server application on the network. The portal then provides the pass-through function for the data object, using a format and presentation understandable to the *OLE* container (i.e., client) application. At this time, only text format is supported.

SCENARIO: MS-WINDOWS CLIENT TO REMOTE SERVER FOR COMPOUND DOCUMENT COMPOSITION

In this scenario, a user of an *OLE*-aware compound document editor gathers information from other *OLE*-aware applications, combining the different types of information into a single compound document. This document-centered view provides a more intuitive environment in which the user can gather different types of information (i.e., objects) into a single container and work on each of them as part of a related task. The user can concentrate on the task at hand rather than the applications and tools that help accomplish the task.

The *OLE* Network Portal expands the source of information objects as well as the document-centered view from the local Windows machine to a network of remote data object servers. Users can access data objects from a multitude of applications that best suit their information-gathering needs—from any *OLE*-aware container application that can embed data from other applications.

SCENARIO: EXCEL FOR WINDOWS TO REMOTE STOCK DATA BASE

In this scenario, an Excel user wishes to monitor changing stock information on his or her desktop PC. The stock information is maintained and updated by a data base stock ticker service on a remote Unix (e.g., a Digital Unix) node. The Excel user initially establishes a link to the *OLE* Network Portal to find available, *OLE*-aware servers, one of which provides a remote stock object available on a data base server. Based on the user request to the link, an advisory connection is set up on the remote server on behalf of the *OLE* Network Portal, which acts as the surrogate server to the Excel container. When the stock data object changes in the *remote data base* server in response to a stock feed update, the remote server informs all advisory connections by calling the SendOnDataChange function. The *OLE* Network Portal informs the container and effects an update of the local data object within Excel.

SCENARIO: WORD FOR WINDOWS TO REMOTE DATA BASE

A Microsoft Word for Windows user wants to include the latest sales figures in his or her monthly report. The sales figures are maintained in a centralized relational data base on an OpenVMS cluster on the company network. An ObjectBroker server has been set up to service requests for particular data objects, and the Word user asks for the remote sales data object to be inserted into the report. Alternately, if the last month's sales figures were already present as an inserted object serviced by the remote ObjectBroker server, the user could double click on last month's figures to initiate an update process to retrieve this month's figures.

The result of either of these user-initiated actions is a GetData request sent to the registered server, which processes the request and sends the sales figure data object back to the OLE Network Portal that is acting as the surrogate server. Using the appropriate OLE V2 interfaces and format negotiation with the remote server, the data can be delivered by the OLE Network Portal in a format directly consumable by Word.

OLE V2 INTERFACES

To enable remote access from PC-based OLE container applications to ObjectBroker/CORBA servers on non-Microsoft-Windows platforms, ObjectBroker provides OLE-like interfaces on those platforms to allow the participation of CORBA servers. ObjectBroker provides those interfaces necessary to enable simple linking and embedding of data objects. ObjectBroker servers must support the creation of an OLE data object in response to a CreateInstance operation in the IClassFactory interface. Servers must also support the basic OLE V2 enumeration interfaces, IEnumFORMATETC and IEnumOLEVERB.

Servers must also implement portions of the IDataObjectinterface to support data object transfer, format negotiation, and advisory connection support. In addition, servers must support the DoVerb operation of the IOleObject interface as a way of providing support for various actions. Server-specific verbs can be enumerated and offered to the container application as actions to be taken, resulting in the subsequent transfer of one or more data objects.

As an *OLE* V2 server application, the *OLE* Network Portal implements the following *OLE* V2 general and server-related interfaces:

- IUnknown
- IClassFactory
- IOleObject
- IOleItemContainer
- IMessageFilter

- IPersistFile
- IPersistStorage
- IDataObject

Specific *OLE* interface member functions that are translated to *CORBA* messages and used between the *OLE* Network Portal and the remote ObjectBroker server include:

- IClassFactory_AddRef
- IClassFactory_CreateInstance
- IClassFactory_ Release
- IEnumFORMATETC_Next
- IEnumFORMATETC_Reset
- IAdviseSink_OnClose
- IAdviseSink_OnDataChange
- IDataObject_GetData
- IDataObject_QueryGetData
- IDataObject_DAdvise
- IDataObject_DUnadvise
- IEnumOLEVERB_Next
- IEnumOLEVERB_Reset
- IOleObject_Close
- IOleObject_DoVerb

As previously mentioned, the *OLE* Network Portal supports display in a separate window in the *OLE* V1 UI style, to allow participation by strictly *OLE* V1 client applications. The *OLE* Network Portal queries the client container application about its level of *OLE* support and provides a fall back for *OLE* V1 client application. The *OLE* Network Portal derives information about available remote servers from statically registered information contained in the \Classes subkey of the ADVERTISEMENT key in the ObjectBroker implementation registry.

OTHER NECESSARY FUNCTIONS

Other related functions are necessary to round out the API offerings for server support on non-Microsoft Windows platforms. Some of these involve registration of servers, and others are higher-level OLE helper functions.

To register as OLE aware, a server must first call OBB_OLE_Register. The \Classes subkey of the ADVERTISEMENT key in the implementation registry defines types or classes of objects provided by OLE server applications. OLE V2 information is stored under a class identifier (CLSID) subkey within a subkey of the corresponding unique identifier for that object class.

Using the ObjectBroker merge command, servers can place their object class information in the local advertisement registry (i.e., the ObjectBroker registry on the PC). The OLE Network Portal uses the registered information to present a list of available remote classes as well as to establish initial information about the servers that support those object classes. Thus the Windows registry knows about the Network Portal, and the portal keeps track of OLE-aware remote servers.

A good deal of OLE's user interface deals with the machine-local clipboard and the operations of Cut, Copy, Paste, and Paste Special. When formats allow, remote data objects are locally managed by the portal. The object is displayed in the OLE Network Portal's window and thus is available for clipboard operations from there.

CONCLUSION

The OLE Network Portal lets the systems manager network enable OLE applications. It provides OLE APIsand helper routines for distributing OLE data objects on non-Microsoft Windows platforms across a network.

The capabilities provided in ObjectBroker V2.5 are extremely attractive to users today and in addition provide the first steps—and a clear upgrade path—toward true distributed OLE Integration.

Chapter 14

Comparing Object-Oriented Development and Component-Based Development Using Visual Basic, PowerBuilder, and C++

Steve Krehbiel
Narasimhaiah Gorla

Object-oriented computing "failed to deliver on the promise of reuse," whereas reusable component-based software has provided for easy, rapid applications development. Based on the technology trend, only two types of programmers may very well prevail in the future: those who develop components using C, C++, and assembly language, and those who use component-based development systems to "glue" the components together into the applications.

This chapter compares the development features of component-based software and object-oriented software and evaluates the object-oriented features of component-based software and object-oriented software.

0-8493-9989-0/99/$0.00+$.50

Several concepts are usually associated with component-based languages. In general, components:

- Are discrete, distinguishable objects that encapsulate data and properties within the component.
- Respond to and initiate events and actions within the system.
- Are usually provided in the software development package or supplied by third-party suppliers, in binary form only with no opportunity for the software programmer to modify or extend the components' underlying source code.

As a means of comparison, objects in object-oriented languages can generally be defined as having four features:

- Identity. Objects are discrete, distinguishable entities.
- Encapsulation. Objects hide internal structure, functions, and operations from external objects.
- Inheritance. Objects share attributes and operations among classes based on hierarchical relationships.
- Polymorphism. Operations behave differently on different object classes.

In particular, this chapter examines two of the most popular component-based software, Visual Basic 3.0 and Powerbuilder 3.0, with the most popular object-oriented software, Visual C++ 1.0.

This chapter examines the object-oriented features of these two component-oriented development systems. As a base of comparison, Microsoft's Visual C++ was selected as the object-oriented systems development language.

SYSTEM DEVELOPMENT ENVIRONMENTS

Introduced in 1991 by Microsoft, Visual Basic simplified Windows-based software development for programmers, especially when compared with the original method of writing Windows programs using the C programming language and the Windows' Software Development Kit (SDK) libraries. This section details the development environment and discusses such relevant object-oriented features as class definition, objects, encapsulation, inheritance, and polymorphism.

Visual Basic 3.0

Visual Basic 3.0 is visually oriented, and its development environment allows the programmer to use the mouse to select and move components along with their properties. The developer points at icons on the screen and then, using drag-and-drop techniques, positions these pseudo-objects, or components, on the screen. To change the properties for the object on the screen, the user points at the object with the mouse, brings up the properties of the object using a function key, and changes the properties in a sub-window. Visual Basic's development environment consists of the following elements:

- **Projects.** A project consists of a definition file that contains all the names of the forms and controls used by the program.
- **Forms.** Forms are the windows upon which all controls are placed. A form has its own properties, events, and methods.
- **Standard and Custom Controls.** Controls are the "objects," or components, of Visual Basic's system development. The custom controls, like forms, have properties, events, and methods. Controls provide the prime functionality for the Visual Basic development system.
- **Toolbars.** The toolbar holds an icon for each of the controls available to the developer in the system.
- **Modules.** Modules are separate entities that consist of Visual Basic code to implement various functions using a highly structured form of BASIC.
- **Subroutines.** Subroutines, which consist of Visual Basic code modules, are attached to forms and controls.
- **Editor.** The Visual Basic editor supports most standard text editing features.

Powerbuilder 3.0

Powerbuilder is also visual in the development process. The developer usually selects the objects from menus and uses drag-and-drop techniques to position these pseudo-objects, or components, on the screen. As with Visual Basic, the system developer changes the properties for the object on the screen using point-and-click technology. Powerbuilder's development environment consists of the following elements:

- **Painters.** Work in Powerbuilder is done in one of several painters. A painter is the developers' environment for creating the higher-level objects in the system. For example, application painters are for creating the main application object, Window painters for creating forms and their controls, Menu painters for creating menus objects, Database painters for creating databases with their tables, and DataWindow painters to make DataWindows, which are Windows tied directly to the database in use.
- **Application.** This corresponds loosely to Visual Basic's projects. Application defines the global properties, the icon for the application, and the startup code.
- **Windows.** These correspond to Visual Basic forms and represent the windows that make up the application, along with the buttons, combo boxes, and other controls in the system. Six types of windows exist:

main, child, pop-up, response, MDI Frame, and MDI Frame with Microhelp. Child windows are always associated with the parent and exist completely within the parent.

- **Libraries.** These contain the code for objects and events in the system.
- **Controls.** The programmer creates controls by selecting an icon and then choosing menu options to define them.
- **PowerBar.** This feature shows icons of the various windows and controls available in the system. The user may not create new PowerBar icons without the use of C++.
- **Scripts.** PowerScript code modules (scripts) are attached to windows and controls to implement various functions in response to events and methods.
- **Editor.** Similar to Visual Basic's editor, Powerbuilder's editor has design-time editing and syntax checking, wrapping, and other word-processor features.

Visual C++ 1.0

Visual C++ 1.0 provides a visually oriented C++ systems development environment, which is focused around the "Visual Workbench." The system does not require predefined, binary-coded objects for system development, as do Visual Basic and Powerbuilder; however, the language provides for several functions to make the C++ development process easier. It provides "Wizards," which greatly reduce the effort required to make classes and let the developers make their own tools. These tools can be installed on the tools menu within its environment. Visual C++'s development environment consists of the following elements:

- **Visual Workbench**. The Workbench acts as the central point from which the developer makes the applications programs. It consists of a text editor, project manager, browser, and debugger in a single, integrated development environment.
- **Projects**. Projects are the main definition file for Visual C++'s Workbench. The project describes the source files and libraries that make up a program, as well as the compiler and linker commands to build the program. The project file consists of a make file and a status file.
- **Microsoft Foundation Class Library**. This is an extensive library that offers a wealth of functionality and features.
- **App Studio**. This feature provides the tools to create and edit applications resources, including the dialog boxes menus, icons, bitmaps, and cursors.
- **App Wizards**. These must be used first during the development of a Visual C++ application. Selecting options in AppWizard creates skeleton C++ source files with various levels of functionality.

- **Class Wizards**. These provide the tools to create new classes, map messages to class-member functions, and map controls to class-member variables.

Each of the three products offers a fully integrated Windows-based development environment. Visual Basic and Powerbuilder offer simpler, quicker development environments based on drag-and-drop and components than Visual C++, which requires much more code to develop the user interface and screen elements. Visual Basic and Powerbuilder offer less flexibility than Visual C++ in their ability to create new classes and to control the overall operating environment. General usage of Visual C++ requires more systems knowledge of memory usage, stacks, and "internal" system functions than general usage of Visual Basic and Powerbuilder. Visual C++ requires much more understanding of the Windows Application Program Interface (API) than the component languages require, though the component languages can use the Windows API through system calls.

CLASS DEFINITION

Visual Basic and Powerbuilder do not have class definitions available to the developer. The standard custom controls that each offers act as a type of class in that objects are the instantiation of these classes. To create new classes, or types of components, requires the use of a C compiler for these two languages. This is one of the primary weaknesses of these component-based systems.

The classes available to the Visual Basic and Powersoft programmer include such items as labels, text boxes, lines, and literally hundreds of other types of objects, which the user places on the screen for the development of the system. The underlying code for the components is not generally available to the developer, and thus no opportunity exists for having public and private functions. The components do offer the developer, however, some flexibility in how the component is presented to the user. For example, the developer can make the component invisible, change its color, or prevent the end user from having access to the object. No dynamic allocation or de-allocation of class objects from memory is provided.

Visual C++'s classes form the foundation for developing C++ applications. The classes truly are object-oriented in design, with inheritance, encapsulation, and polymorphism capabilities. Objects must be instantiated from classes within the Visual C++ code. Classes can be developed "from scratch," or the user can make use of the utility provided in the software called ClassWizard, which walks the user through the development of a new class.

ClassWizard's tools simplify the class creation process. ClassWizard steps the user through the class development process, maps messages to class-member functions, and maps controls to class-member variables. To make a new class with the ClassWizard, the user selects a base class from a listing of available base classes. The system creates the necessary source files, declarations, and implementation code to derive the new class.

OBJECTS

Visual Basic primary objects are forms, which are the window areas that hold the other Visual Basic objects, called controls. The primary form is opened automatically for the developer when he or she starts the Visual Basic development program. No Visual Basic program can be written without including this startup form. Some of the predefined objects include:

- **Forms**. Primary area on which other objects are positioned
- **Labels**. Display message labels on the screen
- **Text Boxes**. Display program text output/messages
- **List Boxes**. Display lists of items
- **Combo Boxes**. Display pop-up lists of items

Visual Basic objects include some system objects, such as Printer, Debug, Clipboard, Screen, and App, which are available in most cases to other Windows programs. New Visual Basic objects can be created only by using C++, which may be added to projects in the form of a VBX. In the marketplace, hundreds of VBX objects perform such tasks as barcode printing, full-featured word processing, database management, and spreadsheets, picture and video image manipulation, tab control, and elastic control.

Powerbuilder and Visual C++ Features

Some of the objects that Powerbuilder puts in the development package include:

- **Windows.** Primary area on which other objects are positioned
- **Command**. Pushed/clicked to begin, interrupt, or end process
- **Picture Box**. Similar to command button, yet displays picture on face
- **StaticLine Edit**. For entering label text
- **SingleLine Edit**. For entering single line of text
- **MultiLine Edit**. For entering large blocks of text
- **GroupBox.** Divides other controls into groups, like Visual Basic's frames
- **RadioButton**. Option buttons for individual options

The object types within the Powerbuilder development world must be developed outside the Powerbuilder environment. Objects are instantiated through menus and point-and-click methods. Placing the object on the window gives the system programmer full functionality of the object.

Visual C++ provides for complete object-derivation from its classes. This is a full C++ implementation of object instantiation, with provisions for such object-oriented techniques as base and derived classes, virtual functions and labels, abstract classes, encapsulation, multiple-inheritance, and polymorphism.

Visual C++ includes the Microsoft Foundation Class Library, which gives the developer classes that allow for printing, toolbars, scrolling, splitter windows, print preview, context-sensitive help, and many reusable components of the class library.

Comparison of Objects

Because the underlying code is not available to the developer in the component-based languages, their flexibility is minimal in comparison with Visual C++'s. However, the components often meet specific application uses and have been generally well-tested and well-debugged before reaching market. Good component manufacturers must provide solid, bug-free products to stay in business. Even shareware controls may offer solid, well-tested performance for very low costs. Thus, the tradeoff for flexibility and extensibility of Visual C++ objects is the quick and well-tested functionality of components that can be quickly added to the system under development.

ENCAPSULATION

Visual Basic objects include both the data and its behavior properties within the object itself. These data properties can be set at design time and changed by code. Example properties include the name of the control object, screen location coordinates, user visibility, foreground and background color, border style, fonts and size, and caption. Objects also respond to events and methods. Events are fairly standard for most objects: Click, Double Click, MouseMove, LostFocus, and GotFocus.

Similar to Visual Basic, each object has properties, which are called attributes, methods, and events. Attributes are set in the Window Style dialog box and include such characteristics as object position, visibility to user, control access (enabled or disabled), color of foreground and background, three-dimensional look, image (for picture boxes), border style, fonts and size, and caption. Methods are specific to an object and define how the system reacts to inputs.

Visual C++ provides for data and functions to be encapsulated within its classes and objects. The standard C++ functionality that Visual C++ offers enforces encapsulations so that data is "surrounded," or hidden, by its functions using public and private functions. The encapsulation is implemented through the class and object code.

Comparison of Encapsulation

The implementation of the concept of encapsulation in Visual Basic and Powerbuilder is much different from the Visual C++ approach. The Visual Basic and Powerbuilder approach is to enforce encapsulation through the use of components, their properties, and their methods and events. The component code is not available to the developer, and thus the manufacturers of the components build in the encapsulation when they develop the component. The Visual C++ requires the programmer to enforce the encapsulation through their code.

INHERITANCE

Visual Basic has some inheritance characteristics, but these are very limited in scope. Visual Basic has no child objects. Control arrays provide the most explicit example of inheritance characteristics, as they provide for code reuse among the objects. Specifically, a control array is an array of objects, in which each member of the array is instantiated in the program. All members of the control array share the same properties, events, and methods and therefore share data and code. For example, several text boxes respond to the same event when clicked, and each of the six objects inherits the code for the click event. The code reuse is a weak form of inheritance displayed by Visual Basic.

Powerbuilder. Powerbuilder supports inheritance to the extent that parent windows and objects can be used to define child objects. The child object inherits all properties, controls, and scripts of the parent. The child object can be modified by adding, modifying, or deleting controls or by modifying scripts and properties.

PowerBuilder inheritance functionality is only supported for windows, menus, and user objects. To create the child window, menu, or user object, select the inherit button on the painter screen. This launches another painter, which looks just like the painter of the parent, though the caption of the painter mentions that "[the painter is] inherited from [painter type name]." Once in the child, the programmer may change anything on the screen, for example, resizing windows and controls, moving controls, and changing properties of the controls and windows.

However, changes to the child prevent future parent changes from rippling down to the child for that specific item changed. The more that is changed, the less that is inherited from the parent during future parent changes. For example, the buttons on the child are moved, and no other changes are made. Then, one year later, the parents' controls and properties are changed significantly. The result is that the changes to the controls and properties are inherited by the child, with the exception of the changes to the button that had been changed. The tie to the parent has been lost for all changed properties of the child. Thus, the developer must be careful what is changed. PowerBuilder includes the reset attributes command to reset any inadvertent changes to child properties. The changes that are inherited by the child occur when the child is regenerated by the system.

Scripts must require explicit handling in the inherited child, as the developer may want to create an additional or use a modified script for the child's control in addition to the parent's inherited script. This is handled through extending, overriding, explicit calling, or cutting and pasting.

Visual C++. Visual C++ provides for class derivation, which provides inheritance directly and allows for code reuse. Base and derived classes (class hierarchy) for code sharing is widely used within the Visual C++ system development environment. Visual C++ provides support for multiple inheritance, where the sub-classes may be derived from more than one base super class.

Comparison of Inheritance

PowerBuilder includes inheritance functions to utilize script and property reuse, which simplifies and strengthens the development process greatly. Though the developer is bound by the inheritance techniques built into the package, the use of this object-oriented technique makes this much stronger object-orientation than Visual Basic. Powerbuilder's inheritance, though, is limited in comparison with the inheritance in Visual C++, which offers full base and derived class inheritance.

POLYMORPHISM

Neither Visual Basic nor Powerbuilder offers polymorphism for its component objects. The closest conceptual offering to polymorphism is Visual Basic's variant data type, which allows the program to let the requirement of knowing what the data type is (e.g., integer, string, or single precision) go until the program runs. Once the program is running and is presented with the data, Visual Basic can adapt to whatever type of data is presented for the variant type. This is a weak form of polymorphism. Visual C++ offers full object-oriented polymorphism features that allow the programmer to call member functions for an object without specifying its exact type through the use of virtual functions.

SUMMARY

This chapter reviewed two component-based languages, Power Builder and Visual Basic, and one object-oriented language, Visual C++. It compared their object-oriented features and other software engineering features, demonstrating that while component-based software is weak in object-oriented features, it is stronger, by virtue of its several other software engineering features, than object-oriented languages.

The three development systems reviewed offer well-integrated system development environment with plenty of tools and options to help the system developer. In the object-oriented evaluation, however, the only area where the component languages Visual Basic and Powerbuilder shine is in the encapsulation comparison, in that the data and functions are fully encapsulated in the object, or the component. Exhibit 1 lists the summary of object-oriented features included in the three packages.

Exhibit 1. Object-oriented features of three development systems.

	Visual Basic	Power Builder	Visual C++
Identity (Distinguishable/ Discrete Objects)	Yes	Yes	Yes
Encapsulation/ Information Hiding	Yes	Yes	Yes
Single Inheritance	Very Limited (arrays of objects respond to same events)	Yes (limited to four levels of inheritance)	Yes
Multiple Inheritance	No	No	Yes
Polymorphism	No	No	Yes

Each platform offers identity and encapsulation of the objects. Powerbuilder does offer some inheritance features similar to those found in Visual C++, though on a more modest scale, while Visual Basics inheritance is very limited. The component languages generally fall short of true object systems in class definition, class derivation, polymorphism, and other object-oriented techniques, such as operator overloading.

From a software engineering point of view, solid programming practices should result in high-quality software; software quality comprises reliability(i.e., the probability that the software performs its functions without failure, includes completeness, consistency, simplicity, and traceability), usability (i.e., the relative effort required for software training and operation), maintainability (i.e., the effort required to find and fix errors in software), and adaptability (i.e., the ease with which the system can be altered to meet different user needs and different system constraints; includes modifiability, expandability, and portability). (See Exhibit 2.)

Exhibit 2. Software quality assessment.

	Visual Basic	Power Builder	Visual C++
Reliability	High (uses well-tested components)	High (uses well-tested components)	Low
Usability	High (most code is predefined)	High (most code is predefined)	Low
Maintainability	High (easy-to-understand system)	High (easy-to-understand system)	Low
Adaptability	Low (impossible to change component code)	Low (impossible to change component code)	High

In general, the component-based software has better software quality attributes than object-oriented software. Recognizing some of the limitations that component software has in the object-oriented realm, Visual Basic has a new component model based on Microsoft's OLE (Object Linking and Embedding) model; OLE servers embed themselves in container documents and export their internal methods to callers by means of the OLE automation interface. In principle, the OLE controls are extendible through interface pointers rather than through inheritance. Similarly, Visual C++ developers can access Visual Basic's VBXs through code rather than drag-and-drop instantiation of the component languages.

Thus, in general, the object-oriented technology is lacking in software quality features; it needs demonstrable improvement to make the software more reusable. Similarly, component-oriented technology is lacking in such object-oriented features as inheritance and adaptability; thus, component-based software developers could create additional classes from scratch and provide modifiable components. This will improve the adaptability of component-based software. More software development efforts are needed that combine the benefits of both worlds, which will result in more effective software.

Chapter 15
Java Application Development Including Database and Network Integration

Nathan J. Muller

Developed by Sun Microsystems and introduced in 1995, Java is described by the company as "a simple, robust, object-oriented, platform-independent, multi-threaded, dynamic, general-purpose programming environment."

Simply put, Java is a scaled down version of the C++ programming language that omits many rarely used, poorly understood, and confusing features. It is used for creating applets for use on the Internet, intranets and any other complex, distributed network. Java provides the capability for distributing specific software functions to end-users in the form of applets, regardless of their location, hardware platform, hardware storage space, or processing power.

While Java is a compiled general purpose language that can be used to build a variety of business applications, JavaScript is a creation of Netscape Communications and is an interpreted scripting language that is focused on manipulating documents on the World Wide Web. JavaScript provides the means of adding interesting features to documents published on the Web, particularly those rendered by Netscape Navigator (version 2.0 or above).The scripts are embedded in the HTML document itself.

0-8493-9989-0/99/$0.00+$.50

The hypertext markup language (HTML) provides a set of tags that tell Web browsers how to render various elements of a document so it will be viewed as the author intended. A script placed between an HTML document's <HEAD>and </HEAD> tags can add such things as simple animations, a scrolling banner, digital clock, and other features to the Web page. It can also be used to open additional windows from within the browser's main window.

With browser software that is Java-enabled, the user has access to the functionality provided by Java applets and Java scripts. A browser that is "Java-enabled" is one that has a built-in Java interpreter. If the browser software is not Java-enabled, the applets and scripts are not available to the user and, in most cases, will be hidden from view. However, JavaScript offers limited functionality and it is not to be confused with Java.

JAVA APPLETS

Applets are distributed programs that are sent from Web servers to Web clients (i.e., PCs equipped with browsers) that have built-in Java interpreters. Applets can reduce hardware requirements at the desktop for many casual end users because both applications storage and processing take place at the server.

With the exception of the browser, software is maintained only at the server site, reducing the burden on IS staff. Applet technology can also help reduce the learning curve because casual users are given access to only the features they need for completing specific business transactions.

Applets provide World Wide Web users with ready access from their local system to additional Web page content that can be delivered in a more visually compelling way, such as through the use of animation. The user can view and interact with an applet—such as requesting that a product image rotate to provide a fuller view of its appearance—and then discard it when it is no longer needed. Applets reside on a Web server and are called from within a hypertext markup language (HTML) document. This allows the same applet to be used by many users. Applets also provide many other functions, such as access to corporate databases.

For example, through an electronic requisition applet, users can have easy access to central databases for online corporate and vendor catalogs. Users can also download an electronic form for requesting purchases. Once the user has completed a request, it is automatically routed for approval and processing through a workflow application. Casual users of the procurement system can access the applet via a browser without running a copy of the client application on their desktop.

DEVELOPING CORPORATE APPLICATIONS WITH JAVA

Whether Java is a good choice for corporate applications development depends on how well Java can contribute to improvements in the following key areas of IS:

- Speed of applications development
- Applications effectiveness and efficiency
- Program and programmer portability
- Development costs
- Maintenance and support
- Technical training

Speed of Applications Development

The Java language was designed as an object-oriented language from the ground up. The needs of distributed, client/server-based systems coincide with the packaged, message-passing paradigms of object-based software.

To function within increasingly complex, network-based environments, programming systems must adopt object-oriented concepts. The Java language provides a clean and efficient object-based development environment.

A key feature of object-oriented programming is code extensibility, a characteristic of objects that lets application developers reuse them to build, maintain, and enhance applications without having to access the program's source code. The ability to create new objects from existing objects, change them to suit specific needs, and otherwise reuse them across different applications offers an effective means of developing applications faster.

Applications Effectiveness and Efficiency

Large corporate applications development environments stress effectiveness over efficiency. Getting the work done is valued more than getting the work done efficiently. Being a simpler language than C++, Java allows programmers to concentrate on the application instead of the mechanics of building the application.

For example, programmers need not worry about managing memory-allocating memory, freeing memory, and keeping track of what memory can be freed because Java self-manages memory. Automatic garbage collection is an integral part of the Java language and runtime system. Once an object has been allocated, the runtime system keeps track of the object's status and automatically reclaims memory when objects are no longer in use, freeing memory for future use.

The Java's memory allocation model and automatic garbage collection make programming tasks easier and cut down on program bugs, crashes, and memory leaks that inhibit performance. In general, these Java features provide better performance than would be obtained through explicit memory management.

Freeing programmers of this and other tedious responsibilities allows work to be done efficiently as well as effectively.

Program and Programmer Portability

Most large corporations use a mix of computing platforms. Although a common application programming interface (*API*) can reduce the cost of corporate applications in heterogeneous computing environments, it is inadequate for the development of network-centric applications. Consequently, many programmers have given up on them, preferring instead to specialize in developing applications for one platform or another.

With a ported Java runtime environment for every platform architecture and a rich set of class libraries, programmers are finding it easier to develop applications that can run on multiple platforms. Applications written with Java are platform-independent because the code is entirely portable.

The Java *virtual machine* is based on a well-defined porting layer, primarily based on the Portable Operating System Interface for Unix (POSIX) interface standard, an industry standard definition of a portable system interface. Porting to new architectures is a relatively straightforward task.

Not only are the programs portable, the programmers are portable as well. This means the corporate applications group can develop programs for any architecture. Because the client and server parts of an application can both be written in the same language, there no longer need to be special groups scattered throughout the enterprise, such as the Sun Solaris C++ group in research, the PC Visual Basic programmers in document distribution, or the GNU developers working on special projects. Java requires only a corporate applications group.

Development Costs

Traditionally, the cost of developing applications on a workstation has been high. Although the overall hardware and long-term maintenance costs of a Sun Solaris workstation, for example, are very attractive to big businesses, the additional cost of software development with C++ is prohibitive to all but the largest companies.

The use of the corporate intranet and Java-based applications development tools can lower the cost of corporate computing considerably.

Java tools are priced at affordable PC levels. The success of the Internet has leveled the pricing of software to the point where software for high-powered Unix workstations costs nearly the same as versions that run on PCs. This is a pricing trend that should become more prevalent with Java-based software tools.

With the growing public-domain and shareware tools community that routinely include source code, corporate programmers have a rich selection of tools from which to choose. The introduction of Java has spawned a whole new market for tools that enable programmers and non-programmers to create, test, deploy, and document network-aware applications.

Program Support and Maintenance

An ongoing requirement with corporate software is the demand for program support. Although Java is not a panacea, it has several features that make certain tasks easier for programmers.

Javadoc is a component of the Java Development Kit (JDK). If programmers use certain commenting conventions in their Java source code, Javadoc will scan the code for these comments and create *HTML* pages that can be viewed with a browser. This eases the job of creating programmer documentation.

With regard to maintenance, Java applications can run on the server. If there are changes to the applications, they are made at the server. Programmers and network administrators do not have to worry about distributing changes to the PC. The next time users log in, they automatically get the most current applet. With Java, network administrators do not have to worry about runtime licenses or the distribution of dynamic-link libraries *(DLLs)* to all the PC clients.

Technical Training

A primary goal in the development of Java was to make it a simple language that could be programmed without extensive training and would be roughly attuned to current software practice. The fundamental concepts of the Java language can be grasped quickly, allowing programmers to be productive from the start.

Making the Java language a minimal subset of C++ while simultaneously retaining its look and feel means that programmers can migrate to the Java language easily and be productive quickly. The Java language learning curve can be as quick as a couple of days.

Programmers with knowledge of C++ who have some experience programming with a *graphical user interface (GUI)* library will be able to learn it quickly. If a programmer does not know C++ but knows another object-oriented programming language, it might take longer to learn the essentials of Java, but it is not necessary to learn C++ before learning Java.

If a programmer does not know any object-oriented language, the essentials of object-oriented technology must be learned before anything else. This knowledge can then be applied to Java.

New gateway software is designed to aid applications developers by translating C++ components into Java automatically. The gateway software operates during the build stage of an application, enabling a Java-based program to recognize C++ components and automatically generate a Java interface. Not only will this kind of software greatly reduce the Java learning curve, it will speed the migration of legacy applications to network-aware Java applications.

JAVA FOR NON-PROGRAMMERS

There are now Java development tools designed for Web authors instead of programmers. These tools provide a visual interface builder for Java that automatically generates Java code, allowing applications to be created simply by dragging and dropping typical controls such as buttons, list boxes, and menus. The generated source code can be used as provided or modified.

Other products allow users to build Java-based animations for Web pages. Users can build their own or customize animations selected from a library that comes with the development kit.

Visual authoring tools for creating Java applets allow users to create media-rich Java applets without the need for programming or scripting. Users work in a what-you-see-is-what-you-get (*WYSIWYG*) page-layout environment, visually specifying òliveó objects through a series of drag-and-drop actions.

INTEGRATING JAVA AND THE DATABASE

An important issue among Java developers is how to access corporate data necessary to support Java applications. Numerous solutions are becoming available to connect Web-based Java applications to the data on servers and hosts. That connection is critical if Java is to be more than just a technology for building small applets that can be downloaded to and run inside a Web browser. Until Java applets can make use of corporate data, their usefulness is limited.

To remedy this situation, Sun Microsystems' JavaSoft unit, which develops and markets Java tools, has come up with the Java Data Base Connectivity (JDBC) specification, which is intended to compete with Microsoft's *Open Data Base Connectivity (ODBC)* solution for allowing Java applets to connect to different vendors' SQL databases. The JDBC specification is expected to enable the building of large-scale Java-based application servers in corporate client/server networks. Without this type of interface, programmers would have to master a different interface for each database used by their company.

Bridges to ODBC and CORBA

JavaSoft unit even offers a bridging tool to link Java applications to databases that support Microsoft's *ODBC* interface. With the bridge, Java developers need only work with JDBC to build database applications that can also access existing *ODBC* data. The bridge is fully compatible with existing *ODBC* drivers.

In the future, as JDBC drivers are built for specific databases—such as those from Ingres, Oracle, and Sybase—developers can choose a pure JDBC link to databases or use the bridge to *ODBC*. JDBC will support interchangeable database drivers by means of a driver manager that would automatically load the proper JDBC driver for connecting to a specific database.

Third-party middleware solutions are emerging that link Java objects over the network using the Internet Inter-ORB Protocol (IIOP) specified in the *Common Object Request Broker Architecture (CORBA)*. Through this *CORBA* connection, developers can connect new Java applets to existing C or C++ programs. With the addition of an "object wrapper," this connection also links Java applets to host transactions and data.

At this writing, Sun's JavaSoft unit has announced plans to add new code that lets Java objects on different computers easily work with each other without additional middleware such as an object request broker (ORB). Javasoft is also developing the added capability of letting Java objects interact across a firewall. Firewalls control public Internet access to corporate backbones but also prevent client/server applications from working across broad portions of the Net.

INTEGRATING JAVA WITH AN OPERATING SYSTEM

Because Java is an interpreted language that relies on easily ported underlying code to talk to the operating system, it can easily run on Windows, Unix, and other common operating systems. Efforts are underway by the major operating system vendors to integrate Java into their systems, providing a way to make Java more accessible to developers and users. Developers will have easier access to Java programming on their platform of choice and users will be able to run Java applets and applications outside of their Web browsers.

Microsoft is embedding Java into future versions of Windows 95 and Windows NT. Apple will integrate Java into its Macintosh, Pippin, and Newton operating systems, as well as into its authoring technologies, Internet servers, client software, and CyberDog Internet suite. Silicon Graphics (SGI) plans to embed Java in its IRIX operating system, and Sun will embed it in Solaris. IBM Corp. is embedding Java in all its client and server product lines this year, including Lotus Notes and Merlin, its forthcoming new version of OS/2, as well as *AIX*, OS/400, and OS/390 (formerly MVS).

Other companies that plan to integrate Java into their operating systems include Hewlett-Packard, Hitachi Ltd., Novell, Santa Cruz Operation, and Tandem Computers.

Native Applications

Putting the Virtual Machine—Java's native operating environment—inside the operating system will give Java applications the speed of those written in a compiled language and still allow them to run cross-platform. In addition to speed, the benefits to users of a Java-embedded operating system include access to a greater number of applications that they can run natively, with or without a browser.

What remains to be seen is whether the operating system vendors will make extensions and additions in the form of *APIs* that could result in serious interoperability problems. If this happens, not only is the goal of Java's portability defeated, but the industry could see Java fragment into a multitude of flavors reminiscent of Unix.

JAVA SECURITY

The Java language was designed to operate in distributed environments. With security features designed into the language and runtime system, the Java language enables construction of tamper-free programs. In the networked environment, Java programs are secure from intrusion by unauthorized code attempting to get behind the scenes and create viruses or invade file systems.

Java's networking package provides the interfaces to handle the various wide area network protocols, including *hypertext transfer protocol (HTTP)*, *file transfer protocol (FTP)*, and *Telnet*, among others. The networking package can be set up to:

- Disallow all network accesses
- Allow network accesses to only the hosts from which the code was imported
- Allow network accesses only outside the firewall if the code came from outside
- Allow all network accesses

MAKING DUMB TERMINALS SMART

Several vendors, including IBM, offer *HTML* gateways that give users of 3270 and 5250 terminals easy access to the Web and corporate intranets. The gateway converts 3270 or 5250 datastreams into *HTTP* to call up Internet or intranet hosts.

SNA Integration

With *HTML* and other Web protocol support, 3270 and 5250 users will be able to participate in the Java environment as well. In essence, Java makes dumb terminals smart.

IBM estimates that more than 50% of its Systems Network Architecture (*SNA*) users will need Internet or intranet access. But with more than $20 trillion invested in *SNA* applications and about 40,000 *SNA* networks worldwide, users are not quite ready to throw away their *SNA* networks just yet.

Equipping 3270 and 5250 terminals to handle *HTML* and Java allows users to choose between Web browsers or terminal emulators when accessing host data. Browsers are appropriate for accessing host programs and data over intranets. Web browsers give users a structured, graphical view of data that facilitates intuitive point-and-click navigation through large databases.

In many cases, terminal emulation offers faster response time for data retrieval than graphically oriented Web browsers. For some applications, terminal emulators may be the preferred tools because familiar function keys provide a fast way to navigate files and initiate processes. Furthermore, certain types of legacy data are easier to import into desktop applications than Web-formatted data.

With access to *Transmission Control Protocol* and Internet Protocol (TCP/IP) and *SNA* networks, the huge investment in terminals and legacy applications can be extended while giving users access to the Web and Java-enabled applications.

CONCLUSION

The early success of the C++ programming language owes a great deal to its ability to access legacy code written in C. Likewise, Java preserves much of C++ and offers a number of compelling benefits: it is portable, high-level, secure, and easy to master. Together, these and other benefits of Java have the potential to free companies from the dependence of long applications-development cycles and let them adapt to changing business needs faster.

Once written, Java applications can be run unchanged on any operating system to which the Java interpreter has been ported. The code for an application written for Solaris-based SPARCstations, for example, can be copied to a Windows 95 Pentium workstation and will run with no recompilation. In contrast, programming in C with various cross-platform tools promises portability, but generally there is still some code to rework before the application can work on another platform.

Java does have some shortcomings. IS departments that are planning to deploy critical production systems built with Java must weigh its benefits against its shortcomings. For example:

- *There are differences in the way Java applications are displayed in different GUIs.* For example, a scroll bar works on Unix but not on Windows NT. These are the kinds of problems that can be expected in the first release of an applications-development tool and that will be ironed out in future releases of Java.
- *Security is still evolving.* Java's security does not let a downloaded Java application read or write to the local hard disk. This prevents a virus written in Java from being able to infect the computer's data and programs. The Netscape browser further restricts the application so that it can only communicate back to the server from which the data came, so a downloaded Java application cannot raid other servers. Yet these protections also limit what the application and end user can do. For example, spreadsheet users would not be able to update a local image of their spreadsheet from a central source because of the security restrictions in Java. Ultimately, Java will need to permit users to configure trusted applications.
- *Heavy-duty processing is limited.* Although Java's performance is adequate for the kinds of applications it is being used for now—interactive client applications—it must become faster at the server where heavy application processing is done. Java's code uses an interpreter as the application is being executed, so performance is slower than compiled third-generation code, such as C. The introduction of just-in-time (JIT) compilers for the Java clients and machine-code compilers for Java servers will make Java comparable in performance to raw C code.

Chapter 16
Using Java for Application Development and Comparison with CGI/PERL

Nathan J. Muller

Organizations are discovering the benefits of the Internet and development tools such as Java in such activities as electronic commerce, customer service, and collaborative business applications. Systems development managers will need to understand how to use Java to take advantage of performance, reliability, security, and portability improvements possible in the new development environment. This chapter compares Java with other interpretive languages and discusses other issues, such as platform independence, communication protocols, and network performance.

INTRODUCTION

Despite the initial promises held out for client/server solutions, today many are still dissatisfied with their implementation. Client/server solutions are too complex, desktops are too expensive to administer and upgrade, and the applications are not secure and reliable enough. Furthermore, client/server applications take too long to develop and deploy, and incompatible desktops prevent universal access. However, all this is about to change radically, as companies discover the benefits of the Internet and such new development tools as Java.

The Internet is fundamentally changing the way people in large organizations work and communicate with each other. Companies are

0-8493-9989-0/99/$0.00+$.50

looking to the TCP/IP-based Internet, as well as private intranets, for a variety of applications. In addition to electronic commerce, these networks are being used for interactive applications that involve customer access to corporate databases, collaborative business applications among corporate staff, and the distribution of multimedia training courses.

The Internet is a large, packet-based client/server network held together by links that run the industry-standard suite of TCP/IP protocols, which offer the advantages of stability, reliability, and openness. The servers and the clients can be located anywhere in the world. The Internet's appeal is its platform independence, which means that virtually any client can have instant access, whether it is based on Windows, OS/2, Macintosh, Unix, or any other type of operating environment. The same platform independence and ease of use makes this client/server network readily adaptable for use as a private intranet.

In fact, through the use of TCP/IP, client/server applications can be extended throughout the enterprise very economically. With tools such as Java, client/server applications can be developed faster, perform better, and even operate more reliably and securely than other enterprise computing solutions. With new protocols, such as the resource reservation protocol (RSVP), levels of bandwidth and delay can be assigned to bandwidth-intensive applications to improve their performance over packet-based intranets and the public Internet. New software development kits make it easy to integrate RSVP into multimedia applications.

THE INFLUENCE OF JAVA

Java is a relatively new language that originated with Sun Microsystems. Java is similar to C++, at least superficially, but it is really both a simplified version of C++ and an improvement on it. The language has been built to take full advantage of current software technologies. For example, it was designed to be completely object oriented. This is unlike C++, Object Pascal, and Visual Basic, which add object-oriented extensions to their languages but still retain the procedural orientation they had originally. Another way Java takes advantage of current technology is in its support for multiprocessing via threads. Threads make it easy to create background processes in Java.

Java's approach enforces a way of thinking about problems that helps the programmer to be consistent. To give programmers a head start, Java includes a standard set of objects for performing many tasks, such as socket-based network communication and graphical windowing.

All of these features make Java better suited to the development of distributed applications than other tools, especially the popular scripting languages. These languages, which include PERL and TCL, can also trace their lineage to the C language. The advantages Java brings to applications development include:

- **Performance.** Applications are fast because today's processors can provide efficient, virtual machine execution. The performance of graphical user interface (GUI) functions and graphical applications are enhanced through Java's integral multi-threading capability. Just-in-time (JIT) compilation and direct Java execution in silicon can deliver even higher performance.
- **Reliability.** Because the Java runtime system actively manages memory, management errors that plague traditional software development are eliminated.
- **Security.** Applications are more secure than those running native code because the Java runtime system (part of the Java Virtual Machine) checks all code for viruses and tampering before running it.
- **Portability.** Applications are able to run across computing platforms because the Java Virtual Machine is available on all systems.
- **Rapid Development.** Development is facilitated through code reuse, making it easier to test and faster to deploy applications via the Internet or corporate intranet.

JAVA ADVANTAGES

Java applications can run anywhere the Java Virtual Machine software is installed, including any Java-enabled browser, such as Microsoft's Internet Explorer and Netscape Communications' Netscape Navigator. The Virtual Machine functions exactly the same way on any "real" machine that hosts it. Java compilers generate code for the Java Virtual Machine, rather than for any specific computer or operating system. This automatically makes all Java programs into cross-platform applications. In being able to download and run any Java application, companies can free themselves of the complexity and client administration needs of traditional PCs.

COST SAVINGS

Sun estimates that the annual cost of operating Java-based "thin" clients in an enterprise environment is less than $2,500 per seat. In comparison, the typical expenses of managing heterogeneous desktop-centric clients or "fat" clients, such as Windows 95, Windows NT, Unix, OS/2, and Macintosh, are in the $10,000 to $15,000 range. According to The Gartner Group, located in Stamford CT, the annual cost of running fat clients is about $11,900 per seat. If only 10% of users needed to continue with a fat client for highly intense applications, tremendous savings could be realized for as many as 90% of an enterprise's clients. Thus, the savings from moving from a fat-client to a thin-client architecture could be as much as $84.6 million annually for a company with 10,000 clients.

(This is calculated as follows: $11,900 per fat client, minus $2,500 per thin client, multiplied by 10,000, equals $94 million. Because approximately 90% of desktops can be converted to thin clients, the total annual cost savings is $84.6 million.)

Aside from cost savings, Java can ensure that necessary features and functions are available to all enterprise users, with application front ends accessed through a common environment. This may be either a Java-enabled browser on an existing desktop platform or a more economical Java-based "network appliance." There is no need to discard current technology investments: Java applications can be enabled on currently installed computing platforms, followed by a phased migration to the most economic platforms. In the same way, Java-based client front ends can be added to existing legacy back ends in a phased, incremental approach.

SECURITY

Today's enterprise computing environments have a number of security vulnerabilities that are addressed by various Java features, including:

- **Strong Memory Protection.** Java eliminates the possibility that memory locations outside a program's boundaries can be maliciously or inadvertently read or corrupted, or both. This means Java applications, otherwise known as applets, cannot gain unauthorized memory access to read or change contents.
- **Encryption and Signatures.** Java supports the use of encryption technology to protect information from unauthorized users and verify through a signature that an applet came from an authorized source.
- **Rules Enforcement.** When Java objects and classes are used to represent corporate information entities, the rules governing the use of such objects can be explicitly stated. With these rules embedded within the objects themselves, the introduction of ad hoc access and manipulation methods can be closely controlled.

In addition, because Java devices get all of their programs and data over the network, they can be configured without local removable storage, thus enhancing security. This may be desirable to keep viruses out of the network or to keep data within the network, where it can be controlled.

RELIABILITY

The scale and complexity of enterprise computing today results in an inherent degradation of reliability. This is because a failure at any point in the network can cause a failure in the application. Java, on the other hand, provides a seamless environment spanning the network from server to client. The same Java applications run on all platforms and networks, and the simplicity of building the client and server software using the same Java programming platform significantly improves client/server reliability.

The Java language itself encourages the production of reliable, simple code. Because the language is object oriented, it promotes reuse, which, in turn, increases reliability. Once tested, objects can be used any number of times with the assurance of error-free code. Java also promotes sound software engineering practices with clear separation of interfaces and implementations and easy exception handling. Furthermore, Java's automatic memory management and lack of pointers remove one of the leading causes of programming errors.

PLATFORM INDEPENDENCE

Traditional enterprise environments require the porting of applications to each separate client environment. This raises the cost of implementation on all clients to an extent that cannot be justified for many applications. In addition, certain application features or functions may not be available on particular platforms because of inherent limitations of the platform. The result is the deployment of incompatible applications, often platform dependent, to meet specific needs in various parts of the enterprise. Java eliminates this situation through the deployment of consistent Virtual Machine platforms, which can run any Java-compliant application program across the enterprise. Consequently, the entire concept of porting an application to different client platforms becomes a thing of the past.

COMPARISON WITH INTERPRETIVE LANGUAGES

Before Java, many developers used PERL (Practical Extension and Report Language) and other interpretive languages, such as TCL, to create common gateway interfaces (CGI) between servers and clients on the Internet. A CGI defines how information, collected from a user by means of a form in a Web browser, is passed through the Web server to an executable program and how the results are passed back and displayed to the user by the Web browser. In most cases, the CGI script converts the results into a HyperText Markup Language (HTML) document, which is sent back to the client.

With interpretive languages, the script must be compiled and run each time it is called. Time and memory are required to start up and tear down the interpreter every time a script runs, which degrades performance. For complex tasks such as interactive multimedia and collaborative applications, performance bottlenecks can build up very quickly, especially when many users access the server at once.

When a CGI program is implemented in PERL, for example, two sources of bottlenecks exist. First, a process in which to run the PERL interpreter must be launched, which in turn runs the PERL program. Creating such a process once a minute is not a problem, but creating it several times a second is a major problem. Second, the PERL program takes time to send back the information it generates as output. Waiting for a small PERL script that does something simple like send the contents of an HTML form over e-mail is not a problem, but waiting for a large script that does something more complicated, such as allowing customers to access account information stored on a mainframe and execute financial transactions, definitely is a problem.

Netscape's Javascript is another interpretive language. Javascript is not really related to Java and is incapable of implementing true applications. Javascript is useful in adding items of interest to Web pages, such as scrolling text, digital clocks, prompts, windows, and other such features. To implement these and other features, Javascript code is embedded within the HTML page itself.

Java application code, in the form of applets, is dynamically downloaded from server to client, on demand. Java differs from the HTML and CGI approach in that the applets, once downloaded, can link directly with a database server on the Internet. The applets do not need a Web server as an intermediary and, consequently, do not degrade performance. In some cases, the applications are stored in cache on a hard disk at the client location and in others, they are stored in DRAM. Because applications are delivered to the client only as needed, administration is done at the server, ensuring that users have access to the latest application release level.

IMPROVING NETWORK PERFORMANCE

TCP/IP-based intranets and the Internet use packet technology to move information between source and destination computers. However, some types of data, such as digitized voice and video, which are key components of multimedia applications, are time-sensitive, and packet technology cannot guarantee that the traffic will get to its destination without the quality undergoing severe degradation. Building a dedicated net or making the jump to ATM to improve performance are not realistic options for most companies because of their high cost.

Several protocols from the Internet Engineering Task Force make it possible for packet networks to carry voice and video in addition to the burst traffic that is already coming off the LAN to the wide-area intranet. The protocols can be implemented in routers and host software.

The resource reservation protocol (RSVP), for instance, works by permitting an application transmitting data over a routed network to request and receive a given level of bandwidth. Two classes of reservation are defined: A controlled load reservation provides service approximating "best effort" service under unloaded conditions; a guaranteed service reservation provides service that guarantees both bandwidth and minimal delay. A key advantage of RSVP is that it works with any physical network architecture. In addition to Ethernet, it runs over other popular networks, such as Token Ring and FDDI, as long as IP is the underlying network protocol. This makes RSVP suitable for companywide intranets as well as the Internet, providing end-to-end service between them. RSVP is implemented by the routers on the network. Cisco Systems, for example, not only supports RSVP but also two other quality-of-service mechanisms as well: priority output queuing and weighted fair queuing. With priority output queuing, network managers can classify traffic into four priorities and provide the available bandwidth to the queues in the order of their priority. The highest priority queue gets as much bandwidth as it needs before lower priority queues get serviced.

A variation of these schemes—custom output queuing—enables multiple queues to be defined, with each assigned a portion of the total bandwidth. For example, custom queuing gives mission-critical network applications running over Novell's Internetwork Packet Exchange/Sequenced Packet Exchange (IPX/SPX) the ability to receive 40% of available bandwidth at all times; a video conference session on TCP/IP can be assigned 30% of capacity to ensure smooth reception, while other network applications can share the remaining 30%. When the video conference terminates, that amount of bandwidth goes back into the pool, ready to be reallocated to other network tasks.

Another technique used by Cisco routers is weighted fair queuing, which ensures that the queues do not starve for bandwidth and that the traffic gets guaranteed service. This is accomplished by classifying data into low-latency traffic and high-volume traffic and serving it fairly. This is similar in concept to the way supermarkets service customers with only a few items through express lanes and other customers through regular lanes. The request is passed on to an upstream router and then to the next router until eventually a path is established that meets the bandwidth and latency requirements of the application. However, if the bandwidth is not available, the request is returned to the application as undeliverable. The application is then responsible for the reissuing of the request at set intervals until the required bandwidth becomes available.

Several vendors, including Precept Software, Inc. and Microsoft Corp., offer various means to let programmers integrate RSVP into their applications. An RSVP Software Development Kit (SDK) from Precept is designed for creators of multimedia applications (e.g., videoconferencing, video broadcasting, Internet telephone) who want to ensure that these typically bandwidth-intensive applications are allocated sufficient network capacity for transmission over the public Internet or private IP-based networks. Precept's RSVP SDK runs on Windows 95 and Windows NT systems. It includes a 32-bit RSVP service application that runs on top of the Winsock 1.1 or 2.0 interface, an Application Programming Interface (API) library consisting of a set of C++ language functions that are linked into the end-user application and provide an interface to the RSVP application, and a sample application that illustrates the use of the APIs.

Precept's modular approach to RSVP implementation (i.e., a standalone RSVP application running over Winsock 1.1 or 2.0) contrasts with that of Microsoft, which has announced plans to integrate RSVP directly into the stack, but only for Winsock 2.0. Stack-integrated RSVP may be appropriate in several years, when Winsock 2.0 is ubiquitous. As yet, however, the specification for interfacing between RSVP and Winsock 2.0 is still evolving. More than 95% of users still have Winsock 1.1. Precept's approach can work for these users today; and later, as they upgrade to Winsock 2.0., Precept's API library will provide an easy migration path.

IP MULTICAST

The IETF has enhanced the basic IP communication protocol to support multicast delivery, a technique critical to conserving valuable network bandwidth as the Internet grows in use and as new data types such as audio and video multimedia transmissions proliferate. The deployment of these multicast enhancements will enable enterprise IP networks and the global Internet to dramatically increase the efficiency with which they use existing bandwidth.

One of these protocols, Protocol Independent Multicast, enables this multicast setup information to be communicated between the various routers so that only segments with clients wishing to receive the multimedia data stream actually get it. PIM allows data streams to be broadcast to multiple receivers using as little network bandwidth as possible. Instead of sending duplicate packets all over the network to reach the various receiving stations, PIM enables packet replication at the last possible router in the network (see Exhibit 1). PIM communicates multicast setup information between routers so that only segments with clients wishing to receive the multimedia data stream actually get it, thus consuming as little network bandwidth as possible. The result is substantial savings in bandwidth and less processing burden on the sending host.

Although several specifications and implementations of multicast for routers, switches, end-node adapters and protocol stacks already exist, movement to full deployment has been slow, primarily because the infrastructure vendors (i.e., product suppliers and Internet service providers) have waited for application demand before investing in the necessary software upgrades. Meanwhile, applications continue to overload the network

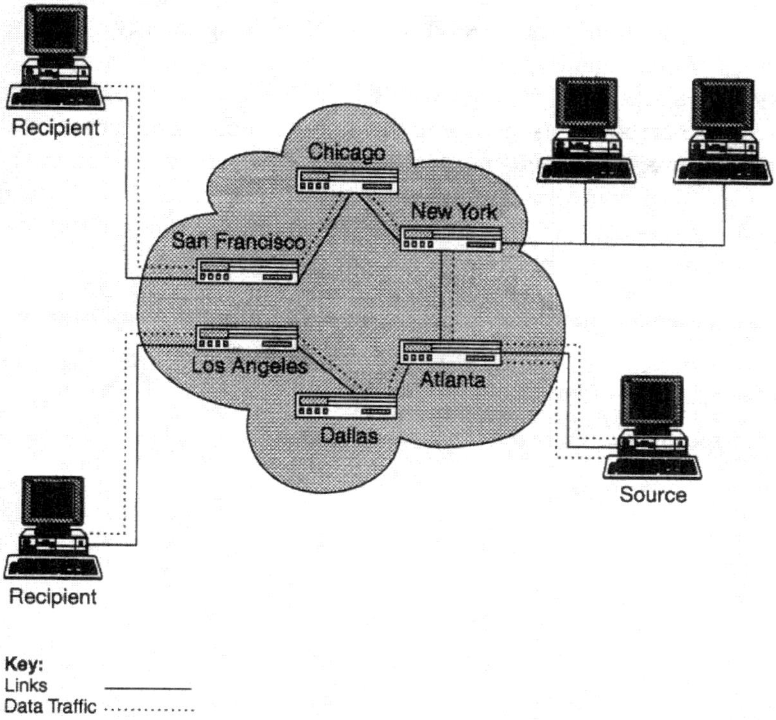

Exhibit 1. Protocol independent multicast schematic.

by saturating it with less efficient unicast (i.e., point-to-point) communication to multiple destinations because the infrastructure is not yet supporting multicast on a wide basis. The promising news is that several industry efforts currently are under way to address this situation.

CONCLUSION

Java and other Internet technologies can offer a major improvement in simplicity, expense, security and reliability vs. many of the enterprise computing environments in place today. Java reduces the time spent in application development, testing, and rollout, leaving more time and money for creating new added-value applications. Instant rollout of applications on an intranet Web site allows much shorter, more iterative application-development cycles and the ability to react quickly to bugs, which results in happier users. Java builder tools from a number of vendors enable programmers to improve productivity even more. Developers are seeing productivity increases of as much as five times over traditional languages such as C or C++.

Network performance can be improved by assigning a class of service to each application through RSVP and by deploying multicast enhancements that enable enterprise IP intranets and the global Internet to dramatically increase the efficiency with which they use existing bandwidth.

As more corporations migrate to the more economical net-centric model of client/server computing with most of the applications written in Java, there will be a corresponding need for developers to add in support for network protocols, such as RSVP and PIM, to ensure that their applications achieve optimal performance over the net.

Section III
Desktops in a Heterogeneous Environment

Section II examined two options for organizations that have one environment such as Unix, but want access to applications of another environment such as Windows. Starting with a typical Unix desktop such as an X-Terminal, Section II looked at methods that added Windows Applications access. Section II also considered solutions that add Unix applications access to a PC desktop. There is a yet another solution, however.

Realizing the requirements of the heterogeneous environments in many organizations, vendors are coming up with devices that are designed for performing as an "enterprise desktop" or a "multi-client desktop." Chapter 17 looks at Enterprise desktops and emulators that emulate one environment under another so that applications that execute in one environment can be made to run in another. Unlike porting or applications that are written to execute in multiple environments, emulators do not need the source code. Finally Chapter 17 covers Windows NT support for Macintosh clients.

Chapter 18 provides a brief history and covers the various connectivity options to connect desktops within a LAN and across LANs.

Intranets are currently the direction in which corporatewide connectivity is evolving. A corporate intranet entails the deployment and use of Internet technologies such as the Web, e-mail, and TCP/IP on a closed private network within one organization or within a group of organizations that share common relationships. Because intranets are based on TCP/IP networking standards, they can include anything that uses this protocol suite, including existing client/server technology and connectivity to legacy host systems. Assessing whether the corporate network has the capacity to support an intranet is a top priority for many network managers. Chapter 19 explains how to evaluate and improve network performance, accommodate intranet traffic demands, secure a new intranet, and, in general, create an intranet environment that is flexible and integrated.

While much of corporate computing has moved away from mainframes and toward client-server and intranet computing, mainframes have not disappeared. The mainframe continues to run core information systems, without which most businesses could not function, providing high levels of availability, data integrity, and security. Mainframe-based computing retains its embedded strengths of economy of scale, robustness, and business-critical computing. One of the common ways in which the mainframe has reinvented itself is as a corporate enterprise server. An upgraded mainframe system equipped with new database and application capabilities can function as an enterprise server. Chapter 20 explains techniques and proven solutions for making the transition from conventional mainframe computing to an enterprise server-based IS strategy.

The move toward client-server and intranet computing has resulted in more of the application processing being done at the client's desktop. Organizations have come to realize the need to have control over distributed applications and ensuring network/application availability has become a top business objective. Chapter 21 takes a look at managing applications on the network.

Chapter 17
Enterprise Desktops and Emulators

Raj Rajagopal

Under applications coexistence, so far, we have looked at two options. Starting with a typical UNIX desktop such as an X-terminal, we looked at solutions that added Windows applications access. We then looked at solutions that add UNIX applications access to a PC desktop. Realizing the requirements of the heterogeneous environments in many organizations, vendors are coming up with devices that are designed for performing as an "enterprise desktop" or a "multi-client desktop." We will take a look at enterprise desktops. We will also take a look at emulators that emulate one environment under another so that applications that execute in one environment can be made to run in another environment. Unlike porting or applications that are written to execute in multiple environments, emulators do not need the source code.

ENTERPRISE DESKTOP

Enterprise desktops are desktops capable of functioning in a heterogeneous computing environment with hardware and software from multiple vendors. If you are a business manager thinking about an enterprise desktop, look for one that is capable of meeting the following business and technical requirements:

Technical Requirements of Enterprise Desktops

- Provide one stop e-mail access capable of receiving e-mail from multiple e-mail servers.
- Provide legacy application access. Examples of legacy applications include applications that reside on IBM hosts such as a 390 mainframe or an AS/400. This support is primarily accomplished through an emulation function built into the desktop.
- Provjde access to file and printer servers attached to different servers across different networks.

0-8493-9989-0/99/$0.00+$.50

- Provide connectivity support, including support for different types of networks and protocols.
- Provide Internet access.
- Provide support for workgroup collaboration.

Business Requirements of Enterprise Desktops

- Provide functions that enable easy desktop management.
- Provide ease of use functions to minimize training and ongoing support costs.
- Minimize cost of upgrades.
- Provide robust security features.
- Provide functions to perform offline work, including word processing and offline e-mail functions. These offline functions permit users to be productive when the networks or servers (the desktop is attached to) are not available.
- Provide advanced (future) productivity functions such as multimedia support future functions such as desktop videoconferencing and collaboration, computer telephone integration, etc.

There are different types of desktops currently available in many enterprises. They include:

- Personal computers, including Macs
- Dumb terminals
- X-Stations
- Network PCs
- Laptops and other remote access devices

The desktops are capable of meeting the technical requirements with software that resides in the desktop itself or that resides on a server. Exhibit 1 illustrates how the different desktops compare in meeting business requirements.

Let us briefly look at some common enterprise desktops. ***Note:*** The information about the products was gathered from different published sources, but primarily from vendor-published information, including online Web pages. The Web addresses and other contact information are included in the description for each vendor and in the Appendix. The products are being updated quickly and you should check with the product vendor for the latest information. Most vendors also offer free evaluations that are downloadable from their Web sites.

This book is not intended to help you select one vendor over another. You should pick migration/coexistence solutions that meet your requirements and perform an evaluation of vendor products. The inclusion of vendor information is provided to give you an idea of the capabilities of the products and to give you a quick reference to get further information and software.

Exhibit 1. Enterprise desktops and features comparison.

	Desktop Management	Ease of Use	Upgrade Cost	Security	Advanced Function	Offline Working
PCs	L	M[2]	H	M	H	H
Dumb terminals	H	H	L	H	L	L
X-Stations	M[1]	M[2]	M[1]	M[1]	H	M[1]
Network PCs	H	M	L	H	H	M
Laptops	L	M	H	M	H	H

Note: H (high), M (medium), L (low) indicate level of support for a function by the desktop. For example, L for Desktop Management and PCs indicates that support for the desktop management function for PCs is low (L) compared to the other desktops.

[1] Functionality varies greatly as the capabilities of the X-Stations vary substantially. Low-end devices such as X-terminals offer lower functionality compared to high-end workstations.

[2] Depends on the type of usage. A stand-alone word processing usage may be easy compared to accessing multimedia applications across a network.

NETWORK COMPUTERS

There are many companies trying to come up with low-cost workstations that have virtually no software installed in them. For this reason, the network computer is sometimes also referred to as a thin-client. (Keep in mind though that the converse is not true. That is, a thin-client does not necessarily mean a network computer. Sometimes thin-clients are used as opposites of fat-clients, and thin vs. fat is more indicative of the amount of functionality in the client). Instead, the software resides on a server and is loaded on demand. Since there is virtually no software that is resident on the network computer, the network computer doesn't need a hard drive. There are many companies working on the network computer, including IBM, Oracle, Microsoft, Intel, etc. The IBM version is called NC (short for Network Computer), while the Microsoft, Intel version is called NetPC. The lack of software on the network computer provides its biggest advantage — lack of any maintenance or upgrade at the network computer level. This significantly reduces administrative costs associated with the network computer compared to a regular personal computer.

WinTerm from Wyse

WinTerm is a family of network computers (also called thin-clients) from Wyse. More information about the WinTerm family is available online from Wyse at http://www.wyse.com.

The features of WinTerm. include:

- Based on Java operating system from Javasoft
- Java Virtual Machine
- Embedded HTML 3.2-compliant browser
- Terminal emulation applettes (TNS27O, TN220)
- Citrix ICA3 client
- X-11 client (check with vendor on availability date)
- e-mail client for POPS, SMTP, IMAP4 hosts
- Audio support for .WAV and .AU sound file playback
- Graphics support for JPEG and GIF
- Multilevel security to minimize user access to setup, application, and Web sites
- Support for network printers
- Support for local printers (check with vendor on availability date)

Explora from NCD

More information about Explora is available online from NCD at http://www.ncd.com.

Explora is an enterprise desktop designed to provide seamless, simultaneous access to Windows, legacy, UNIX, applications (any networked applications) from the same desktop. Explora includes a 32-bit PowerPC RISC processor, graphics accelerator, and its own operating system called NCDware. Explora lets you customize your desktop and also supports a range of keyboards.

Heterogeneous application access: Explora provides access to Windows applications using the WinCenter Windows Application Server. WinCenter is covered in Chapter 5. Explora provides terminal emulation functions for a number of terminals, including 3270, VT320, etc. Terminal emulation provides access to IBM and other mainframe-based applications. UNIX graphical applications are supported by the built in X-Server, which is X11 compliant. It also includes Telnet and LAT to access other character-based applications supported by Telnet and LAT.

Heterogeneous network connectivity: Explora comes with built-in support for a number of network protocols, including TCP/IP as well as file server access using NFS.

NCD also has a high-end family of enterprise desktops called HMX. In addition to Explora's functions, HMX features better display resolution, better multimedia support, and support for Java applications (check with vendor for timing of availability).

Personal Workstations from DEC

More information on DEC workstations is available from DEC at http://www.digital.com.

DEC has a line of personal workstations designed to function as enterprise desktops. The personal workstation family includes three series of workstations:

- The i-series
- The a-series
- The au-series

The personal workstations are designed with Windows NT and UNIX migration coexistence features. The Digital Personal Workstation au-series is capable of supporting both Windows NT and Digital UNIX applications on a single workstation. Thus, you can continue using mission-critical technical (UNIX) applications today and seamlessly move to a Windows NT environment tomorrow using a single product family.

The Personal Workstation a-series ships with a Solution Pack CD-ROM containing a suite of enabling software tools designed to boost productivity and connectivity in a technical Windows NT workstation environment. Some of the Windows NT migration and coexistence tools included in the CD-ROM are eXceed and NFS Maestro. eXceed was covered in Chapter 6 and NFS Maestro will be covered in Chapter 8.

DEC also ships the binary emulator and translator software FX!32 free with many personal workstation systems to let Windows applications be run on UNIX. FX!32, the Alpha x86 binary translator, provides fast and transparent execution of x86 Win32 executables on Windows NT V4.0 Alpha. You can load a 32-bit x86 application on Alpha, double-click on its icon, and it runs as if it were running on a Pentium system. According to DEC, a Windows application "in most cases performance matches, and in some cases surpasses, Pentium Pro performance."

ViewPoint from Boundless Technologies

Information on the ViewPoint family of network computers is available at http://www.boundless.com. ViewPoint TC is a family of Intel-based, Windows-oriented network computers from Boundless Technologies. The ViewPoint TC family currently includes models that provide different capabilities but shares the same 133-MHz, x86-compatible hardware architecture. The models include:

- A text-based terminal
- A Windows NT workstation with added multi-user access
- An enhanced workstation that combines Windows and Java support with UNIX and legacy application integration

The multi-user access is based on Citrix System Inc.'s WinFrame, which adds multi-user capabilities to Windows NT. Microsoft recently licensed the multi-user technology from Citrix for use in future versions of the

Windows NT server. ViewPoint offerings are comparable to the product offerings from Wyse covered earlier in this chapter.

Network Computer from IBM

IBM is building the network computer, primarily as a replacement for the aging dumb terminals. By the time you read this book, IBM will have announced a version of OS/2 Warp Server to run on Network Computer, called Bluebird. Bluebird is optimized for network computing. Bluebird is a derivative of OS/2 Warp Server.

Bluebird will support up to six different desktop configurations on the server. These configurations are downloaded from the server to network computers when users boot up. The server also stores data files and the user's access to network services.

Bluebird's client systems include 3270 and 5250 mainframe terminal emulation, a WWW browser, and either DOS/Windows 3.x or a slimmed-down version of the Workplace Shell and Presentation Manager. The processing power to run these client systems is the equivalent of a 486-class processor. All client systems also include the Java Virtual Machine to run Java applications. Bluebird will support multiple network cards on a PC and automatically perform load balancing to maximize network throughput.

The first release of Bluebird will run on Intel-based PCs.

APPLICATION EMULATORS

Emulators can be broadly classified as:

- Application emulators
- Terminal emulators

Application emulators are covered here. Terminal emulators are covered in the next section.

Application emulators let the executable in one environment run in another environment by emulating the run-time environment required by the executable. For example, there are emulators that let a Windows application run on a UNIX machine. Application emulators are a layer of software that sit on top of the native environment.

As with other applications-related topics, the focus here will be on Windows NT and UNIX applications. At the time of writing, there are not any application emulators in widespread use that let a UNIX application run on Windows NT. This situation is likely to change soon. There are, however, a number of products that let a Windows application run on different environments. Let us take the instance of Mac clients that need to run Mac applications as well as Windows applications. There are emulator products that let a Mac run Windows applications.

These emulator products can be broadly classified as:

- Hardware-based emulators
- Software-based emulators

Hardware-based emulators essentially have a Mac and a PC in one box. Typically, an add-on board with an Intel processor and memory is added to a Mac, and Windows and Windows Applications use the add-on processor. Peripherals are shared. Since there is no emulation software to execute, hardware-based emulators can run applications at essentially the native speed of the add-on processor.

Software-based emulators do not require the addition of specialized boards or chips. Instead, software-based emulators provide all the emulation functions solely by software. Some of the common software-based emulators include WABI from Sun Microsystems, SoftWindows from Insignia Solutions, and Locus Merge from Locus Computing Corp. Please see the *Note* on vendor products earlier in the chapter.

For running Win32 applications, Insignia Solutions has SoftWindows 95 from Silicon Graphics, which allows users to run Windows 95 applications on UNIX workstations. No other platforms have been announced, but others will follow eventually. SoftWindows is discussed later in this chapter.

Emulation Choices

For 16-bit Windows applications, you have more emulation choices, including SoftWindows 2.0 for UNIX, Merge from Platinum Technology, and WABI from Sun Microsystems. These emulators provide somewhat complete Windows 3.1 and 3.11 environments. However, none of these products do anything for newer Windows 95 and Windows NT applications.

Emulation also has performance costs, and it presents a foreign look and feel to UNIX workstation users. Performance will vary with the hosting platform, but the need to emulate the Intel x86 instruction set hinders application performance when compared to native applications or to running the same application on an Intel platform.

SoftWindows

The following is a brief summary of SoftWindows from Insignia Web pages. Additional information about SoftWindows is available online from Insignia at http://www.insignia.com.

The latest version of SoftWindows lets you run your Windows 95 applications. It comes in two flavors: SoftWindows 95 and 3.0 for the Power Mac, the primary difference being which Microsoft operating system comes pre-installed. SoftWindows 95 includes Windows 95 pre-installed, and

SoftWindows 3.0 includes Windows 3.11 and MS-DOS 6.22 pre-installed. Features of SoftWindows include:

- Run Windows 95 applications on your Mac
- Support for local printer connected to your Mac
- Sound Blaster compatibility
- PC SCSI support that lets you access SCSI devices such as SyQuest/Zip drives and scanners

Applications Support. SoftWindows has a feature called "TurboStart" feature that enables the Power Mac to launch Windows 95 applications faster compared to the time it takes a typical PC to launch the same application.

Windows Programs that can run using SoftWindows 95 include Microsoft Office, Lotus SmartSuite, WordPerfect, Encarta, Lotus Notes, and CorelDRAW. Multimedia applications that use MIDI, QuickTime for Windows, or Video for Windows can play both video and audio. SoftWindows 95 includes a Windows driver that supports recording and playback of digital sound samples in .WAV format. You can copy and paste text and graphics between a Windows 95 application running under SoftWindows and a native Power Mac application. SoftWindows uses Apple Guide for online help, and you can create scripts to execute PC commands using AppleScript. Windows desktop size is configurable. SoftWindows emulates a 80486 processor.

Peripherals Support. Windows 95 is configured to print on any printer available through the Mac Chooser. Printing can include postscript and non-postscript output. The PC port (LPTI:) is emulated and is linked to the Mac Chooser. You can also print on a PC serial printer using the Mac modem and printer ports.

You can choose to store applications and data in Mac folders (which can be organized as drives E: through Z:) or within the SoftWindows 95 "hard disk" file. The Mac file system is accessible from Windows 95. SoftWindows supports up to two PC floppy drives (as A: and B:), and supports using 3.5-inch PC diskettes in SuperDrive, up to two PC hard disks (as C: and D:) up to 500 MB per hard disk, depending on available Macintosh disk space.

SoftWindows includes Microsoft CD-ROM extensions that enable PC CD-ROMs to be used in Macintosh CD drives. PC serial ports COM1: and COM2: can use Mac modem and printer ports.

Network Support. SoftWindows 95 is preconfigured to attach a SoftWindows-loaded Power Mac to PC networks through the Mac's built-in Ethernet or optional Token Ring connections. SoftWindows 95 also has Novell NetWare and LAN Manager clients pre-installed and connects to Novell NetWare, LAN Manager, TCP/IP, Windows NT Server, Banyan VINES, LAN

Server, Windows for Workgroups, and DEC PATHWORKS servers. SoftWindows 95 permits the simultaneous use of either the IPX protocol or the TCP/IP protocol in both Mac and PC environments.

Insignia includes information in its Web pages comparing SoftWindows with a hardware-based emulator.

WABI

More information on WABI is available online from Sun at http://www.sun.com.

Windows Application Binary Interface (WABI) is Sun's solution for Solaris users needing access to desktop Windows office applications. WABI is a software emulator that runs on Solaris and runs popular Windows 3.1x office applications.

Sun maintains a list of Windows applications that are certified to work the same under WABI as they do natively under Windows.

WABI Features. Key features of WABI include the following:

- Support for Windows ODBC applications
- Support for OLE and DDE between Windows applications
- Cut-and-paste between Windows and Solaris applications
- Access from Windows applications to network services such as printers and file servers

Besides the Sun Web pages, information about WABI is available through CompuServe and some Internet sites. Among other things, these sites provide a list of Windows applications known to run under WABI. (Keep in mind, though, that these applications are not certified.)

Windows NT Built-in 486 Emulator for RISC Systems

Starting with version 4.0, Windows NT versions that run on RISC (Reduced Instruction Set Computing) systems have a new software emulator. This emulator helps run DOS and Windows applications on the RISC systems without requiring other hardware or software. Applications requiring 386 enhanced mode or a 486 processor are supported. The performance problem common to emulators applies to this emulator as well.

WINDOWS NT AND MACINTOSH CLIENTS

Besides supporting clients that run different Windows operating systems, the Windows NT server also supports a Mac client in a Windows NT network. Windows NT includes Services for Macintosh (SfM) for this purpose. The Mac version should be 6.0.7 or above.

Setup for Macintosh Client on Windows NT Server

If you are adding services for Macintosh for the first time, follow the steps listed below. If you are not sure if services for Macintosh have already been installed, then select the services icon from the control panel that shows a list of services that have already been installed.

- From **Start** menu, select **Settings**, then select **Control Panel**, then double-click the Network icon from the Control Panel.
- From the Network property sheet that comes up, select the **Services** tab.
- From this screen, click the **Add** button, which brings up the Select Network Service dialog.
- Scroll down the list of services (if needed) and select ***Services for Macintosh*** **entry**.
- Windows NT may prompt you for the Windows NT 4.0 server install CD if necessary and copies the necessary files.
- Windows NT automatically starts the AppleTalk protocol and finds the Macintosh clients that may be connected to your network adapter. If you have multiple network adapters, you can enable routing using the Microsoft AppleTalk Protocol Properties dialog. After configuration completion, you are prompted to restart the system. When the system restarts, you can verify that the new file and print services for Macintosh clients have been installed and are active by checking the Services icon in Control Panel.

Setting Up the Mac Side of the Macintosh Client

The Mac client must run MacOS version 6.0.7 or above. You can check the version by clicking on the desktop and selecting *About this computer* under the Apple menu, as shown in Exhibit 2.

You can use the same built-in support in MacOS to access network files and printers to access the Windows NT network, and no add-on products are necessary. The typical sequence of accessing a file server is as follows:

Click on the *Apple menu* and Select *Chooser.* This brings up the screen shown in Exhibit 3. The AppleTalk zones are listed in the lower left comer. Each zone contains file servers, printers, mail servers, etc. Select the zone you are interested in (by clicking the zone entry) and then select AppleShare to select file servers in the selected zone. The right portion of the screen now shows the available file servers in the selected zone.

Accessing Windows NT Network Files from the Macintosh Client

Select the file server you want by double-clicking it. This brings up the logon screen shown in Exhibit 4.

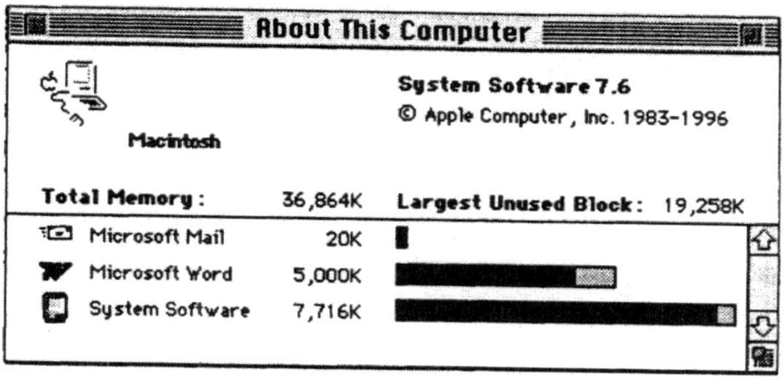

Exhibit 2. Checking the version level of MacOS.

Entry of a valid password logs you to the file server and shows a list of valid drives you can access. The drives also appear on your Mac desktop. Double-clicking the icon shows the list of folders and files. This list is the same as what you would see with another file server such as a NetWare file server.

Tip: *You may be familiar with* Associations *for a file in the Windows environment.* Associations *are what lets Windows invoke an associated program when you double-click on a file. For example, PowerPoint gets automatically*

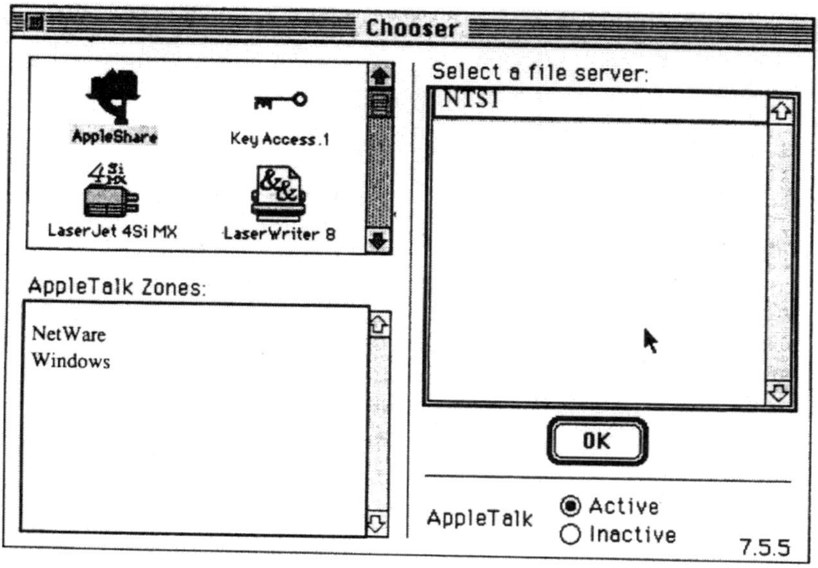

Exhibit 3. Selecting a file server.

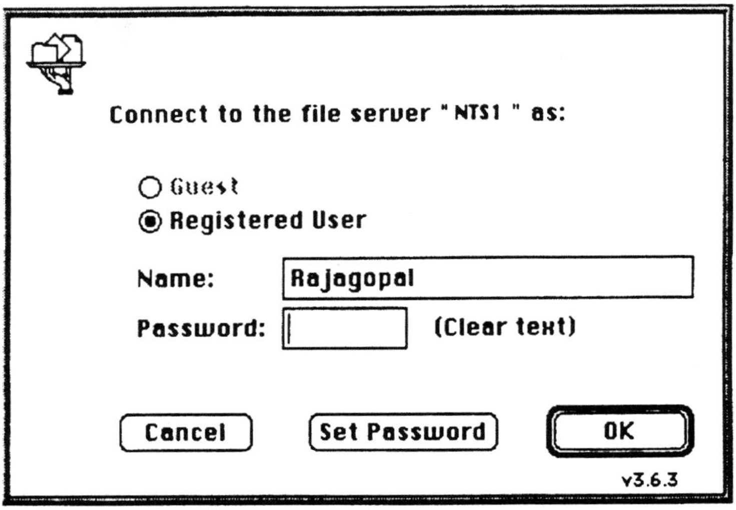

Exhibit 4. Logging to a Windows NT file server from a Mac client.

---

invoked when you double-click on a file with .ppt *extension. Similarly, you can associate a Macintosh program to be invoked when a Macintosh file stored on your Windows NT server is double-clicked.*

Accessing Windows NT Printers from the Macintosh Client

You can print to a printer on the Windows NT network from a Macintosh client in two ways:

- You can use a printer that is directly connected to the Windows NT server. This can be any printer that can be attached to the Windows NT server.
- You can use an AppleTalk-compatible printer that is directly connected to the network using a network adapter card.

You select the printer by following these steps in your Macintosh client.

Select *Chooser* from the *Apple menu* and the screen shown in Exhibit 5 will appear. From this screen, choose one of the printers (instead of choosing AppleShare for file server).

Tip: *As shown in Exhibit 5, Macintosh supports local print spooling at the client level using the Background Printing On/Off toggle switch. If you are using the Mac client to print to Windows NT network printers, disable spooling at the client by turning off Background Printing.*

Administering Macintosh Clients from Windows NT

When you install file and print services for Macintosh as described earlier, a MacFile icon gets added to the Control Panel. Double-clicking the

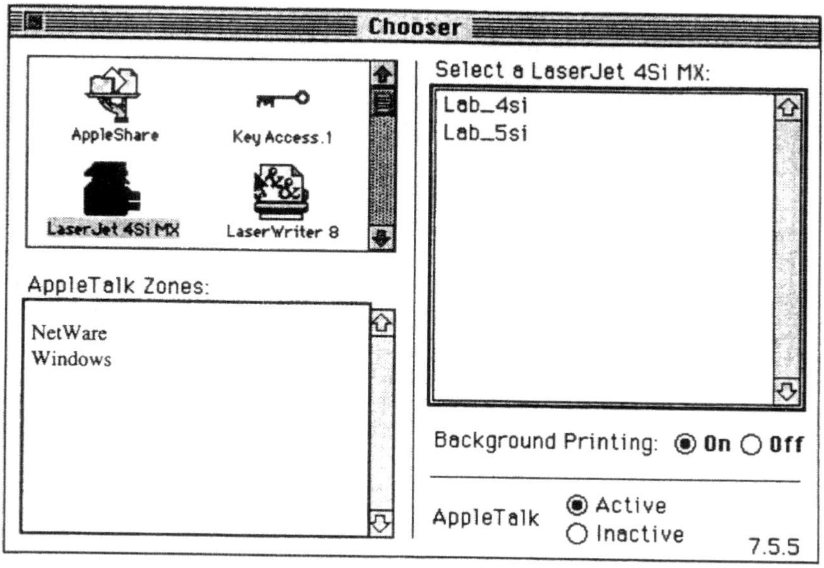

Exhibit 5. Selecting a printer from the Mac client.

MacFile icon brings up a dialog that lets you administer the Macintosh clients. The buttons on the MacFile Properties dialog and the functions are summarized in Exhibit 6.

While the volumes button showed you the list of Macintosh accessible volumes, you can create new Macintosh accessible volumes using the

Exhibit 6. MacFile Properties.

MacFile Properties Dialog Button	Function
Users	View, disconnect, and send messages to Macintosh client users.
Volumes	This Volumes dialog has two parts. The top part lists Macintosh-accessible volumes defined on the server. For each volume, the total number of users accessing the volume is also shown. You select a volume from the list by clicking on the volume entry in the list. The bottom part lists the users for the volume selected in the top part. Using this dialog, you can disconnect individual users or all users accessing a volume.
Files	Displays a dialog that lists the open files on the server, the users of the files, and if the files are locked.
Attributes	Displays a dialog that lets you control the attributes of services for Macintosh. You can control if guest logins are allowed, specify whether the clients have to use Microsoft Authentication, specify whether the number of sessions is unlimited, and so on.

Server manager dialog (which has a MacFile menu option when Services for Macintosh is installed).

Tip: *When you have Macintosh clients on a network with both NetWare servers and Windows NT servers, be consistent in the configuration setup between the servers for segments, zones, AppleTalk network numbers, etc.*

TERMINAL EMULATORS

Terminal emulators let mainframe applications be accessed from devices like PCs. To mainframe applications, PCs with terminal emulators appear like dumb terminals. Terminal emulators are commonly available to emulate the 3270 attached to an IBM mainframe, a 5250 attached to an IBM AS/400, or a VT 100/220 attached to Digital environments such as VAX.

There are a number of terminal emulators available on the market. Most of the migration and coexistence solution vendors mentioned in this book have the terminal emulation built into their products.

HARDWARE EMULATION SOLUTIONS

You can buy chips and motherboards with an Intel processor and install them in a machine running UNIX or MacOS. Thus, the machine has two CPUs. Using system software, Windows applications are executed using the Intel processor, while the native processor is used as it is normally used.

There are other possible chips and combinations to run a variety of applications on machines not normally supported, but the basic idea is the same. There are some advantages and disadvantages to this approach.

The primary advantage the hardware approach has over other alternatives (such as emulation) is the speed of execution. Since a dedicated processor designed for the application is used, no emulation or translation is necessary. This translates into faster execution speeds.

There are some disadvantages as well. The card is physically installed on one machine, which requires assistance in installing and it takes up a card slot on the machine. The card also typically requires its own physical memory, which may not be sharable with the existing memory on the machine where the card is installed. There may be some problems with Windows applications that require network access, since the application running using the special processor may not have access to network facilities.

PUBLIC DOMAIN EMULATORS

There are public domain emulators available to emulate one environment in another. For the purposes of this book, the one of interest is WINE.

WINE is both a program loader and an emulation library that will allow UNIX users to run MS Windows applications on an x86 hardware platform running under some UNIXes. The program loader will load and execute an MS Windows application binary, while the emulation library will take calls to MS Windows functions and translate these into calls to UNIX/X, so that equivalent functionality is achieved.

WINE is being developed specifically to run on the Intel x86 class of CPUs under certain UNIXes that run on the x86 platform. UNIXes currently being tested for WINE compatibility include Linux, NetBSD, FreeBSD, UnixWare, and SCO OpenServer 5.

Of course, the biggest problem with any public domain software is that, at best, the software is only voluntarily supported.

The newsgroup comp.emulators.ms-windows.wine discusses WINE and WINE-related Web sites include http://www.thepoint.com/unix/emulate/wine and http://www.linpro.no/wine/.

Chapter 18

Desktop Evolution Driving Connectivity Technologies

Robin L. Zak

Computing has made some profound changes over the past 20 years. In the early 1980s, computers took the space of an entire room and the I/O devices were the size of a small table and acted as the terminal and printer all in one. Response time was on the order of seconds to minutes for minor operations and everything was done in batch mode.

Then along came the personal computer, such as IBMs with one or two 5¼ diskette drives, 256K bytes of RAM, 4M bytes hard drive, and a 1,200 bps modem.

A few years later, while the engineers were still playing around with mainframes, a new movement began to arise. Colleges across the US started to provide a room at the library called a "PC Lab." IBM PC ATs and Macintosh Classics were lined up in rows, with a printer at the end of each row. Each PC would plug into some external device that would allow use of a printer. Only one PC could print at a time, so you had to keep an eye on this device to see when it was free before you sent your print job.

Around this time, file sharing evolved from the "sneaker net" to actual sharing of files over local area networks (LANs). Black cables lying across the floor connected everyone's PC and connected to a larger PC that was used as a file server. The black cables were a bit temperamental—one minor adjustment could wipe out everyone's connection to the server. This was an early Ethernet network. Most files would be stored locally on each PC, but shared files would be stored on the file server where anyone connected to this Ethernet could have access.

It did not take long before sharing files within a department was just not good enough. Users needed to share files between departments, and this is where the problems started. Not every department used the same type

0-8493-9989-0/99/$0.00+$.50

of LAN to connect their users to the file server. Not every department used the same word processing or spreadsheet programs either. Not only did files need to be shared, but now applications needed to be shared as well.

One version of application sharing involves the members of a workgroup actually running the applications from the server instead of locally from their PC. It makes more sense to load the application once and to allow 20 users access, than to load the same application 20 times on 20 different machines. While this frees quite a bit of disk space on the individual PC, the load on the network becomes tremendous. Each PC must "pull down" a subset of the application each time it is in use. This can be Mbytes worth of information for each user, which can cause network congestion and delays.

THE CHANGES IN DESKTOP APPLICATIONS

Let's focus on these applications for a moment. Why is it that the average life cycle of a PC is a year or less? Why is the PC purchased five years ago (a 386, 33Mhz, 80Mbyte hard disk and 8Mbyte memory) worthless today? One answer is that applications keep adding new features, thereby requiring more processing power, hard disk space, and memory. Five years ago, that PC could run the applications designed five years ago, but attempting to update the applications to the latest and greatest will most likely require an upgrade to the PC or worse, a new PC with a lot more horsepower.

The changes in applications such as word processing and spread sheet programs are obvious, but what about the new emerging applications that require hefty processors and lots of memory? Multimedia and video applications are beginning to emerge that also require quite a bit of processing, memory, and network resources. The latest craze is Web-based applications. These are not only being used for the Internet, but the Intranet and network management services as well.

All of these applications require some sort of network to share important information. It appears that the application designers automatically assume infinite bandwidth when it comes to networking, but networking professionals know better. Bandwidth is definitely finite and costly—especially on the wide area. The bulk of this chapter discusses the networking issues that arise when attempting to share these applications and files, not just within a department, but across departments and across buildings.

THE EFFECTS OF THE CHANGING DESKTOP ON THE NETWORK

Shared LANs

Remember that black cable? That was the local area network. It was, often, a 10M-bps Ethernet LAN that connected a limited number of users

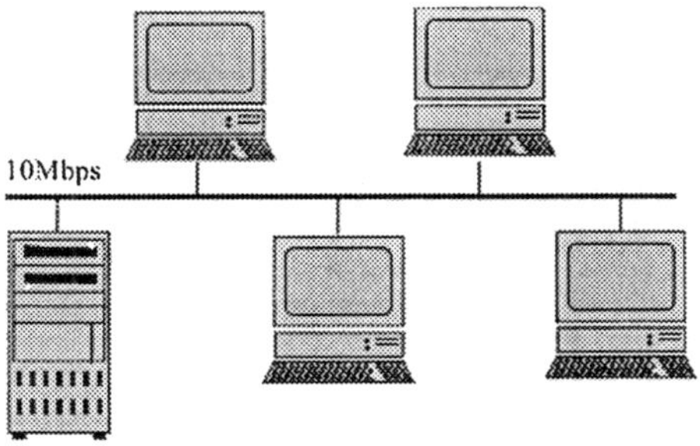

Exhibit 1. A Shared Ethernet LAN.

together to the file server. The 10M bps was shared so that each user had about 400K bps (10M bps/24 = 416K bps) on the average. 400Kbps is more than adequate when the files being transferred are on the order of 10–20Kbytes in size. Exhibit 1 shows a shared Ethernet LAN.

Most departments did not have a cable running across the floor, they had wall jacks where a cable from the PC would connect. The wiring from the wall jack would run back to a central closet to a wiring hub. This hub would act as a single Ethernet and would make troubleshooting of the Ethernet much easier. Exhibit 2 shows a shared Ethernet LAN using a central wiring hub.

Ethernet was not the only LAN technology to be used. Token ring was a common LAN technology among IBM customers. Also a shared LAN, Token Ring offers 4M-bps and 16M-bps versions. If network response time on a

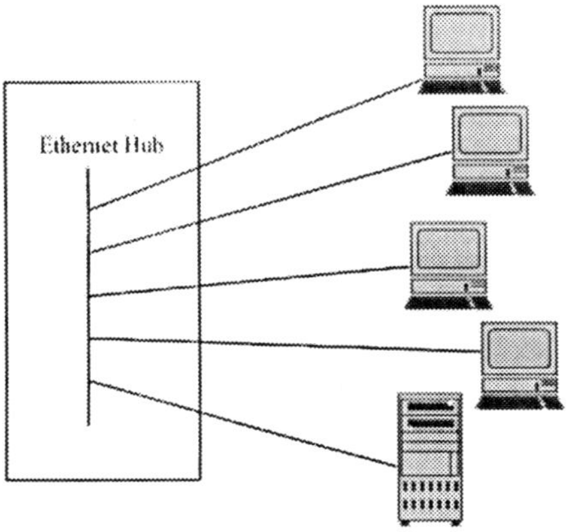

Exhibit 2. Shared Ethernet using Central Hub.

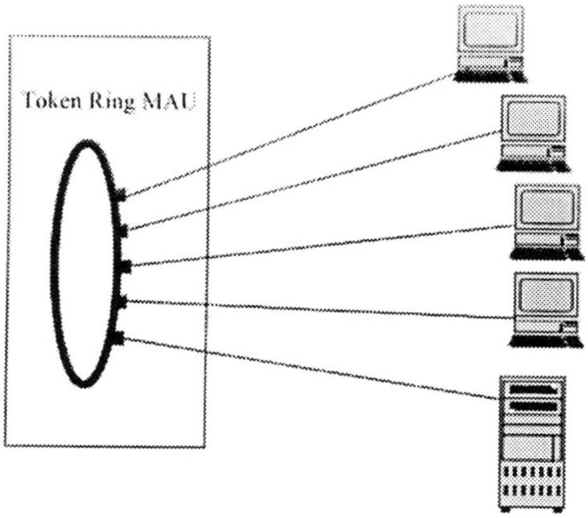

Exhibit 3. A Shared Token Ring LAN.

4M-bps Token Ring is slow, there is an option to upgrade the ring speed to 16M-bps by changing all the Network Interface Cards (NIC) on devices attached to the ring and upgrading the Multiport Access Unit (MAU). Exhibit 3 shows a shared Token Ring with a centralized MAU.

LAN Segmentation

As the files transiting the network become larger and larger, network response time grows longer. One way to alleviate this problem is to segment the LAN into two or more pieces. By splitting the users in half, there will be less contention for the Ethernet, therefore; response time should improve. Once the Ethernet is segmented, we open a can of worms on how to connect these segments. We call this can of worms bridging and routing.

Bridging

A bridge may connect two or more LANs and performs minor routing and filtering functions. The bridge receives data packets, scans the network address, and passes the packet to the appropriate network. A self-learning bridge can filter information by monitoring the traffic on the networks connected to it and learning the addresses that are associated with each network. By doing this, the bridge isolates the traffic destined to remain on the local segment of the network and broadcasts the rest to the other networks. Bridges are ideally suited for interconnecting similar networks in which protocol conversion is not required, security concerns are minimal, and where filtering is required.

The filtering capabilities enable the network manager to restrict the types of packets that go over the bridge, thereby alleviating traffic bottlenecks and limiting access to certain types of network resources. Exhibit 4 shows two bridging configurations for Ethernet LANs.

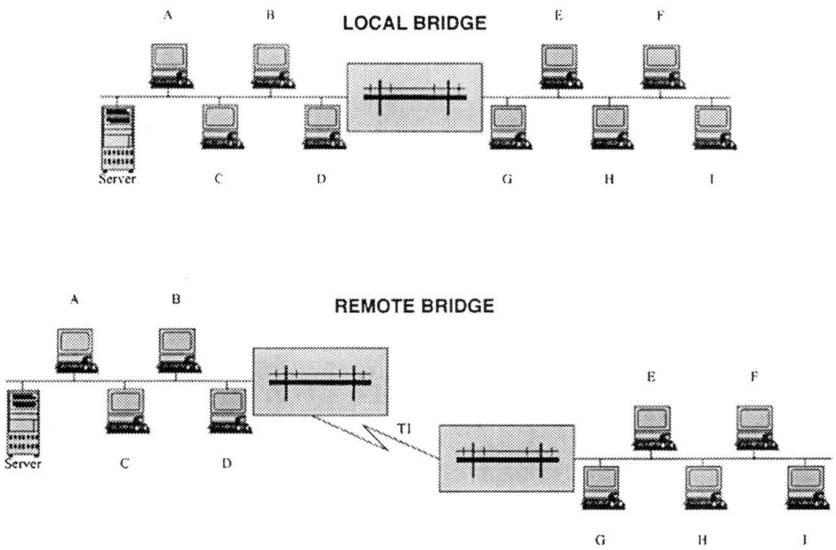

Exhibit 4. Bridging for Ethernet Lans.

In Exhibit 4, should workstation A need to communicate with the server, the traffic would stay local on the Ethernet segment. If workstation F wanted to access the server, the bridge would forward that traffic to the appropriate Ethernet segment. On the other hand, if F wanted to communicate with H, the traffic would not be forwarded to the other segment.

Routing

A router is similar to a bridge, but it offers a more sophisticated network management and functionality. It involves two basic activities: path determination and transport. Routing algorithms keep track of information like the desirability of a path, status of links, and next hop for a given destination. Once the router knows the best path for a given packet and finds that that path is available, the packet will be transported either to its destination or to the next hop on the way to its destination. Routing occurs at the Network Layer (Layer 3), thereby allowing devices connected to different types of LANs to communicate. Bridging occurs at the Data Link Layer (Layer 2).

Protocols like TCP/IP or IPX are commonly routed because they conform to the specifications of the Network Layer. These protocols have routing protocols built in. Some protocols like LAT must be bridged because they do not conform to Network Layer specifications. If a device at one IP address wants to communicate with a server at a different IP address, a router will look at the destination address, look up which port the address

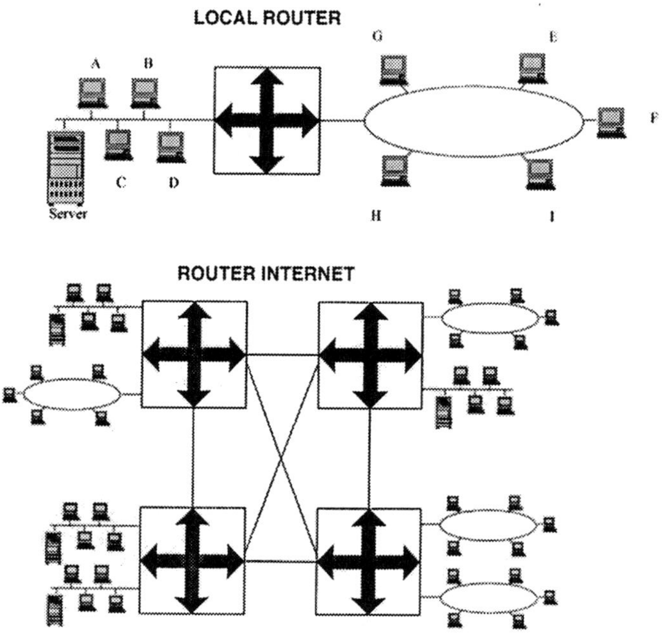

Exhibit 5. Routing configurations.

belongs to, and route the data packets to the appropriate port. Exhibit 5 shows some typical router configurations.

Both bridging and routing allow for extension of the LANs across the wide area. Routing not only allows for different protocols to traverse the same network, but also allows for devices on different LAN media (i.e., Ethernet and Token Ring) to communicate. Multiprotocol routers are the primary backbone data networking devices today.

LAN Switching

As router networks grow, performance issues begin to pop up. Protocols have hop count limitations, which may be exceeded in the case of a failure in the network. As the load on the network increases, it becomes impossible to predict delay end-to-end through multiple hops. Also, if there are many protocols being routed across the network, routing table updates can cause huge overhead (especially upon a failure and/or recovery) which can have serious effects on performance. New ways to internetwork are emerging that offload most of the local router traffic and let the routers route traffic across the WAN only. This is called LAN switching. Exhibit 6 shows shared LANs feeding into a LAN switch.

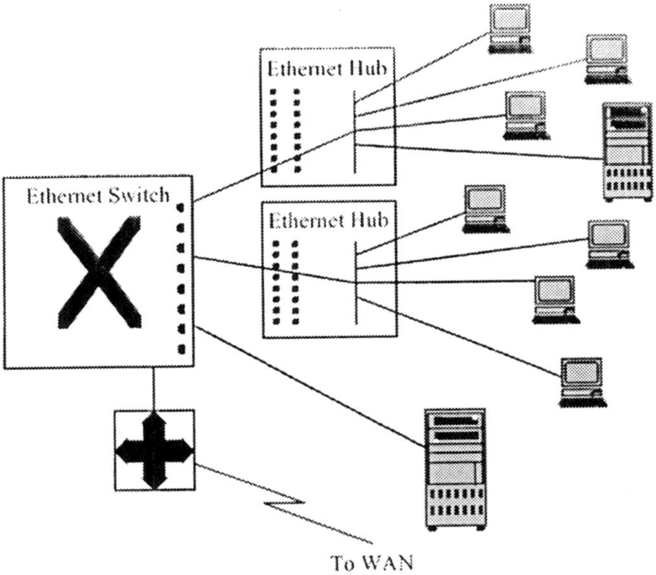

Exhibit 6. Switched Ethernet.

LAN switching handles most of the traffic within a building or campus. It allows traffic from each segment to be "switched" at Layer 2 (MAC address) to any other segment (provided the media is the same). Ethernet switching allows for each device to be on its own 10M-bps segment. Switches are connected together through an Ethernet port or through a high-speed uplink, like 155M-bps ATM or 100M-bps Ethernet. Exhibit 7 depicts this backbone.

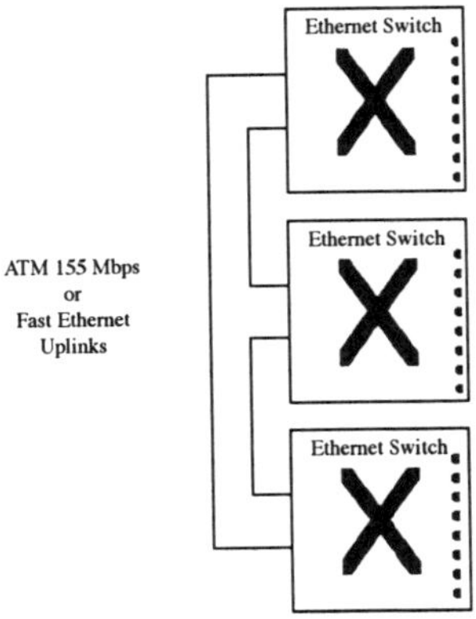

Exhibit 7. Switched Ethernet with ATM Backbone.

A routing table is built within the switch to map a MAC address with a physical port. The switch looks at the destination address within a frame, then "switches" the frame to the appropriate port. These ports may have shared or dedicated segments (i.e., each port may have only 1 MAC address, or several). There are many Ethernet segment switches on the market today from all of the major vendors. Some of these switches have "auto-learning" features that require minimal configuration. The switch learns which devices are attached upon start-up of the device and stores these addresses in its table. The switch may also group devices together in a virtual LAN (VLAN) based on which devices need to communicate with each other.

Should a device move from one port to another, there is no configuration of the switch. The switch will automatically update its table and maintain the same VLAN independent of the physical segment where the device resides. VLAN technology simplifies moves, adds, and changes for facilities people as well as network managers. Be careful, there are many different VLAN implementations today that are not compatible. Check each product thoroughly for the features and functions provided.

100M-bps Ethernet

If a dedicated 10M-bps connection to the desktop is not enough, consider 100M-bps. 100M-bps Ethernet has taken the market by storm during the mid-1990s mainly because it is relatively inexpensive. There are two 100M-bps Ethernet camps—the 100BaseT and the 100VG-AnyLAN. After quite a battle between the two camps, it appears that 100Base T has won the majority of the market. It operates in a similar manner as 10BaseT, so customers feel comfortable with the technology.

There are also NIC cards and hubs available from a variety of vendors that support both 10M bps and 100M bps. By using these NIC cards, a user can maintain their 10M-bps LANs, and upgrade portions as needed to 100M bps. Typically, the servers would be put on 100M bps connections while the users remained at 10M bps. This would reduce contention for the server, thereby improving performance and response time. Exhibit 8 shows a 10/100M-bps Ethernet switch.

ATM to the Desktop

In the mid-1990s, while Asynchronous Transfer Mode (ATM) was still quite a bit of hype, IBM introduced a way to get ATM to the desktop in a relatively inexpensive fashion. They developed a 25M-bps NIC and hub that allowed users to upgrade the speed to the desktop, while gaining the benefits of ATM. ATM was designed to support the integration of voice, video, and data traffic. Standard LAN technologies such as 10/100M-bps Ethernet, are data-only technologies, with no provision to support the services required by voice and video.

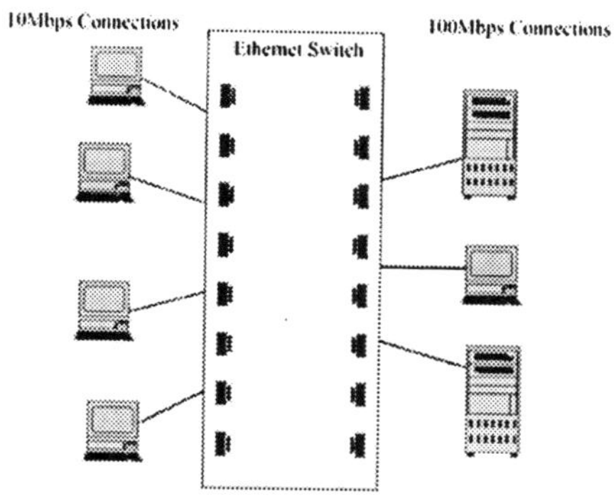

Exhibit 8. 10/100Mbps Ethernet Switch.

Of course, given enough bandwidth, you can put any kind of traffic down a pipe, and it will reach the other end with reasonable quality. The issue arises when there is congestion on the network—there is no way to guarantee service to voice or video with conventional LAN technologies. 25M bps allowed the entry into ATM technology as well as enabled new desktop applications to be deployed while guaranteeing some level of service to these new applications.

Most of the ATM to the desktop is either 25M bps or 155M bps. Needless to say, the market for ATM technology today is not at the desktop. As mentioned earlier, the desktop remains with the Ethernet technologies. The major demand for ATM is in the LAN backbone/campus backbone areas.

BACKBONE TECHNOLOGIES

LAN Backbone

Because there are many LAN segments connecting various users within an organization, these segments must be connected together to facilitate the sharing of departmental information. The hubs that create these segments are usually connected together through some kind of backbone.

Routers used to be the backbone device of choice for many organizations. LANs from different departments would feed into a central router, and the router would route traffic from one segment to another. Exhibit 9 shows a router-based collapsed backbone.

With the advent of LAN switching and VLANs, the routers were moved out of the LAN backbone to focus on WAN connectivity. The LAN switches provide a high speed uplink that allows for these switches to be cascaded together. Also, since switching is performed at Layer 2 (and not Layer 3 as in routers), the processing delay for each frame is much less than with a router. The backbone connecting these switches may be ATM-based, or

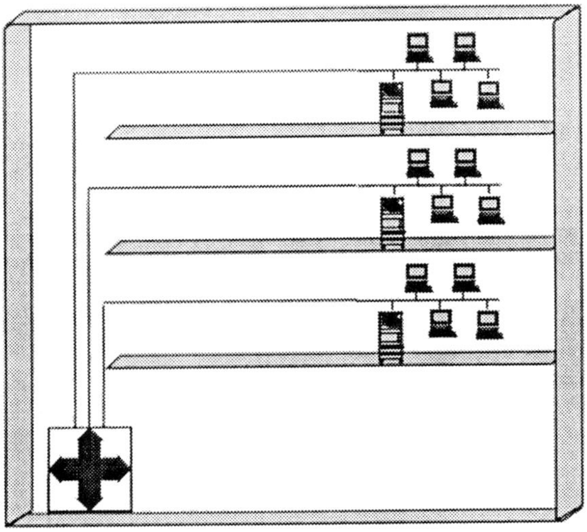

Exhibit 9. Router collapsed backbone.

100M-bps Ethernet. Work is currently being done on a standard for Gigabit Ethernet. 3Com, Bay Networks, Cisco, and Cabletron have all announced Gigabit Ethernet products ranging from NIC cards for high-end servers, to uplink modules for existing Ethernet switches, to gigabit Ethernet switches to tie all the gigabit uplink ports together. Most of these products will not ship until late 1997 or early 1998. Needless to say, Gigabit Ethernet will not be a desktop technology any time soon, but may be a competitive backbone technology.

Campus/Metropolitan Area Backbone

Looking toward the campus backbone, organizations with their own fiber have traditionally used Fiber Distributed Data Interface (FDDI) to connect these buildings together. Prior to the Ethernet craze, it was the fastest, most reliable technology available. The technology did not gain a huge following mainly because of the price of fiber and the price of the equipment. Most organizations treated the campus as a WAN, and used WAN connections like T1 or T3 to interconnect the buildings.

With the increase in speed to the desktop and LAN backbone, the campus backbone must be capable of supporting this additional traffic. Due to distance limitations with the fast Ethernet implementations, ATM is becoming the technology of choice for this area of the market (see Exhibit 10).

ATM allows for the integration of voice, video, and data traffic onto a common backbone. In a campus environment, chances are there will be many different kinds of traffic requiring different services from the network.

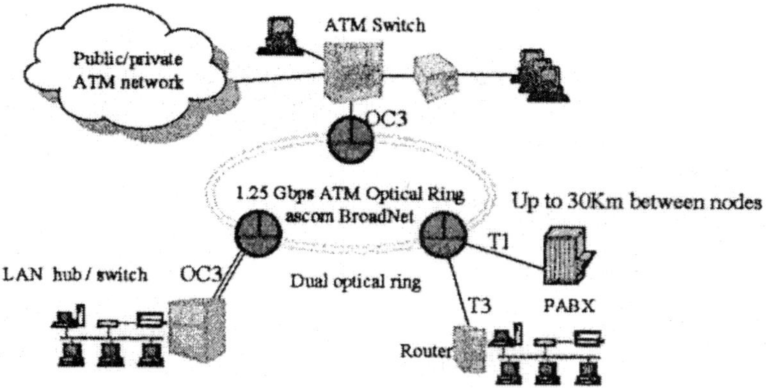

Exhibit 10. Gigabit ATM Campus/MAN Backbone.

ATM allows for different quality of service (QoS) parameters for the different traffic types.

There are many ATM vendors with products on the market today. Products can be divided into two classes: access multiplexers and switches. Access multiplexers take most kinds of native traffic and convert it into ATM cells for transport. These products will interface to native LAN (such as Ethernet, Token Ring, FDDI, and Fast Ethernet) and serial connections (such as RS232, V.35, T1) and convert everything to ATM cells for output onto a common high-speed link. Switches have multiple ATM ports (typically at OC3 rates, some go up to OC12) but also may support some native interfaces.

Most ATM transport today is done at the OC3 (155M bps) rate and below. While OC12 (622M bps) is available from some vendors (Fore Systems, Cisco), it is not widely deployed due to cost, performance, and standards issues.

There is a product available that will transport ATM cells at 1.25G bps across a private fiber backbone for distances up to 30Km. This product (from ascom Broadnet) can be used in a campus environment where the organization has their own dark fiber, or in a metropolitan area where service providers (who typically have a lot of fiber) can provision ATM services. This is the fastest ATM transport available today and the product could find a very nice niche within campus and metropolitan area environments.

Until recently, the metropolitan area network (MAN) was typically treated as a wide area network (WAN), using technologies such as T1, T3, and frame relay to transport traffic from one area to another. This works fine for relatively small amounts of traffic across these links, but when multiple 100M-bps LANs are connected together requiring some sort of MAN transport, 1.5M bps or even 45M bps does not even come close to handling the requirement. This area of the market is evolving from low-speed circuits to high speed optical circuits. Synchronous Optical Network (SONET) is not just for carriers anymore. Organizations are deploying SONET to handle the emerging bandwidth requirements either on a campus or within a metropolitan area. New service providers like Internet Service Providers (ISPs) and cable TV companies (CATV) are buying SONET equipment along with ATM switches to offer competitive solutions to the big carriers. SONET is defined for speeds up to OC192 (10G bps), but most SONET deployed is at OC3 to OC48 speeds.

SONET offers no switching capabilities whatsoever. An organization must build a switching infrastructure on top of the SONET physical layer. This is done by buying separate ATM switches and feeding them into the SONET multiplexers. This can be quite costly but it is the prevalent MAN and WAN architecture today.

Looking Toward the Future

The constant striving for improved productivity and doing more with less forces society to think of new ways to do things faster and cheaper. As long as there is competition in this world, we must continually improve our organizations and buying the best, most cost-effective technologies can enable just that.

LAN technologies will continue to offer increased speed to the desktop. New applications will use this newly gained bandwidth, requiring faster, more efficient technologies to the desktop. The any-to-any connectivity requirement is pushing this bandwidth usage across the campus and metropolitan area. Since these fast LAN technologies are not suited to campus and metropolitan areas, ATM will be the likely choice for this area of the market.

Chapter 19
Considerations for Implementing Corporate Intranets

Nathan J. Muller

Assessing whether the corporate network has the capacity to support an intranet is a top priority for many network managers. This article explains how to evaluate and improve network performance, accommodate intranet traffic demands, secure a new intranet, and, in general, create an intranet environment that is flexible and integrated.

INTRODUCTION

A corporate intranet entails the deployment and use of Internet technologies such as the Web, e-mail, and TCP/IP on a closed private network within one organization or within a group of organizations that share common relationships. Because intranets are based on TCP/IP networking standards, they can include anything that uses this protocol suite, including existing client/server technology and connectivity to legacy host systems. Companies can benefit from Internet technology and avoid its drawbacks—particularly its lethargic performance and lack of security.

Intranets support communication and collaboration; information retrieval, sharing, and management; and access to databases and applications. None of these functions is new, but the promise of an intranet is that it can use Internet and World Wide Web technologies to do things better than before.

For example, according to Microsoft Corp., Netscape Communications Corp.,Oracle Corp., and Sun Microsystems, Inc., a Web browser could become the standard interface used to access databases, legacy applications, and data warehouses throughout the enterprise. In this scenario, the thin client (i.e., the browser) can make applications easier to maintain, desktops easier to manage, and substantially trim the IT budget.

0-8493-9989-0/99/$0.00+$.50

A company's customers, suppliers, and strategic partners in turn can benefit from the improved communication, greater collaboration, and reduced IT expenditure associated with implementing an intranet. They can even access each other's intranet services directly, which would speed decision making as well as save time and money.

Achieving these benefits comes from properly implementing an intranet, which is far from straightforward. One of the more difficult issues to resolve is intranet content—determining what information will be presented, where it will come from, how its accuracy will be ensured, and how often it will be updated. The resources must be available to do this extra work.

Intranet content development is beyond the scope of this article, however. The focus here is on specific issues of network and server management. First, resources must be available to establish the service, to establish the Transmission Control Protocol/Internet Protocol (TCP/IP) network over which it runs, and to train users. Second, the impact on existing systems must be considered. This includes, for example, the capacity of the current network to support an intranet, the future usefulness of existing legacy systems, and the availability of hardware to run multimedia applications.

"FAT" VERSUS "THIN" CLIENTS

Corporate intranets provide an opportunity to ensure universal access to applications and databases while increasing the speed of applications development, improving the security and reliability of the applications, and reducing the cost of computing and ongoing administration.

"Fat" and "thin" refer primarily to the amount of processing being performed. Terminals are the ultimate thin clients because they rely exclusively on the server for applications and processing. Standalone PCs are the ultimate fat clients because they have the resources to run all applications locally and handle the processing themselves. Spanning the continuum from all-server processing to all-client processing is the client/server environment, where there is a distribution of work among the different processors.

Traditional Client/Server. A few years ago, client/server was thought to be the ideal computing solution. Despite the initial promises of client/server solutions, today there is much dissatisfaction with their implementation. Client/server solutions are too complex, desktops are too expensive to administer and upgrade, and the applications are still not secure and reliable enough. Furthermore, client/server applications take too long to develop and deploy, and incompatible desktops prevent universal access.

As companies discover the benefits of private intranets and new development tools such as Java and ActiveX, as well as various scripting languages such as JavaScript and VBScript, they can use these tools to redefine the traditional models of computing and reassess their IT infrastructure.

JAVA-ENABLED BROWSERS

Browsers that are used to navigate the World Wide Web are usually thin clients when they render documents sent by a server. The special tags used throughout these documents, known as the hypertext markup language (HTML), tell the browser how to render their contents on a computer screen.

However, browsers can get very fat when other components are sent from the server for execution within the browser. These components can be specialized files with audio or video that are interpreted by plug-ins registered with the browser. When the browser comes across an HTML tag that specifies a file type that is associated with one of these plug-ins, the application is automatically opened within the browser, permitting an audio or video stream to be played instantly without the user having to download the file to disk and open it with an external player.

Applets

Another way that the browser can become fat is by absorbing Java applets that are downloaded from the server with the HTML documents. Applets are small applications designed to be distributed over the network and are always hosted by another program such as Netscape's Navigator or Microsoft's Internet Explorer, both of which contain a "virtual machine" (VM) that runs the Java code. Because the Java code is written for the virtual machine rather than for a particular computer or operating system, by default all Java programs are cross-platform applications.

Java applications are fast because today's processors can provide efficient virtual machine execution. The performance of GUI functions and graphical applications are enhanced through Java's integral multithreading capability and just-in-time (JIT) compilation. The applications are also more secure than those running native code because the Java runtime system—part of the virtual machine—checks all code for viruses and tampering before running it.

Applications development is facilitated through code reuse, making it easier to deploy applications on the Internet or corporate intranet. Code reuse also makes the applications more reliable because many of the components have already been tested.

ActiveX and Java

Another way the browser can be fattened up is by bulking up on components written in ActiveX, Microsoft's answer to Sun's Java. Like Java, ActiveX is an object-oriented development tool that can be used to build such components as Excel spreadsheet interpreters and data entry programs. Functionally, the two development tools are headed for increasing levels of convergence.

For example, the Microsoft Java VM is an ActiveX control that allows Microsoft Internet Explorer 3.0 users to run Java applets. The control is installed as a component of Internet Explorer 3.0. The Java VM supports integration between other ActiveX controls and a Java applet. In addition, the Java VM understands the component object model (COM) and can load COM classes and expose COM interfaces. This means that developers can write ActiveX controls using Java.

Scripting Languages

Browsers can also fatten up by running functions written in scripting languages like Netscape's JavaScript and Microsoft's VBScript. VBScript is a Web-adapted subset of Visual Basic for Applications (VBA), Microsoft's standard Basic syntax. Both JavaScript and VBScript are used to manipulate HTML from objects like check boxes and radio buttons, as well as add pop-up windows, scroll bars, prompts, digital clocks, and simple animations to Web pages.

The important thing to remember about these tools is that the features they create rely on scripts that are embedded within the HTML document itself, initiating extensive local processing. Browsers are becoming "universal clients," so much so that Microsoft's next release of Windows 95 will even have the look and feel of a browser.

Most PCs today come bundled with a browser. Several vendors, including Microsoft, have endorsed the idea of offering a new breed of computer that relies on a browser as the GUI, Java or ActiveX as the operating system, and servers for the applications. With Java and ActiveX, a network-centric computing solution is emerging that can potentially offer major improvements in simplicity, expense, security, and reliability vs. many of the enterprise computing environments in place today.

FEEDING CLIENT APPLICATIONS

How fat the client is may be less important than how the code is delivered and executed on the client machine. Because Java applications originate at the server, clients only get the code when they need to run the application. If there are changes to the applications, they are made at the server. Programmers and network administrators do not have to worry about distributing all the changes to every client. The next time the client logs onto the server and accesses the application, it automatically gets the most current code. This method of delivering applications also reduces support costs.

"Fat" may be interpreted as how much the client application has to be fed to use it. For example, a locally installed emulator may have the same capabilities as a network-delivered, Java-based emulator, but there is more work to be done in installing and configuring the local emulator than the Java-based emulator that is delivered each time it is needed. The traditional emulator takes up local disk space whether it is being used or not. The Java-based emulator, in contrast, takes no local disk space.

ActiveX components are a cross between locally installed applications and network-delivered applications. They are not only sent to the client when initially needed, but are also installed on the local disk for future use. Local disk space is used even if the component was only used once and never again. Updates are easy to get because they can be sent over the network when required. With Java, the component is sent each time it is needed unless it is already in the browser's cache. This makes Java components instantly updatable.

Because Java is platform-independent, a Java-based T27 emulator for Unisys hosts or a 3270 emulator for IBM hosts, for example, can run on any hardware or software architecture that supports the Java virtual machine. This includes Windows, Macintosh, and Unix platforms as well as new network computers. Thus, any Java-enabled browser has access to legacy data and applications.

Cost Issues. As with most issues, "it depends." There is no right answer for all applications and all environments. Each has advantages and disadvantages, so it is necessary to do a cost/benefits analysis first. Even if a significant number of desktops must stay with the fat-client approach, there still may be enough incentive to move the others to the thin-client approach.

According to The Gartner Group (Stamford CT), the annual cost of supporting fat clients—Windows 95/NT, Unix, OS/2, and Macintosh—is about $11,900 per seat. Substantial savings could be realized for as many as 90% of an enterprise's clients, with only 10% of users needing to continue with a fat client for processing-intensive applications. Thus, the support costs for moving from a fat-client to a thin-client architecture could be as much as $84.6 million annually for a company with 10,000 clients.

IMPROVING NETWORK PERFORMANCE

Intranets are becoming pervasive because they allow network users to easily access information through standard Web browsers and other World Wide Web technologies and tools to provide a simple, reliable, universal, and low-cost way to exchange information among enterprise network users. However, the resulting changes in network traffic patterns require upgrading the network infrastructure to improve performance and prevent slow network response times.

- The corporate network may need to be upgraded to accommodate:
- The graphical nature of Web-based information, which significantly increases network traffic and demands greater network bandwidth
- The integration of the Internet Protocol (IP) throughout the network
- Easier access to data across the campus or across the globe, which leads to increased inter-subnetwork traffic that must be routed
- New, real-time multimedia feeds that require intelligent multicast control

LAN switches traditionally operate at layer 2 of the OSI model, or the data link layer, providing high-performance segmentation for workgroup-based client/server networks. Routing operates at layer 3, or the network layer, providing broadcast controls, WAN access, and bandwidth management vital to intranets. Most networks do not contain sufficient routing resources to handle the new inter-subnetwork traffic demands of enterprise intranets.

The optimal solution—intranet switching—is to add layer 3 switching, the portion of routing functionality required to forward intranet information among subnetworks to existing layer 2 switches. This solution allows network managers to cost-effectively upgrade the layer 3 performance in their networks. This is the approach being taken by new intranet switches and software upgrades to existing switches.

Intranet Switching

Intranets are increasingly being used to support real-time information, such as live audio and video feeds, over the network. These multimedia feeds are sent to all subscribers in a subnetwork, creating increased multicast traffic and impeding network performance by consuming ever-greater amounts of bandwidth.

Intelligent multicast control provided by intranet switches helps organizations conserve network bandwidth by eliminating the propagation of multicast traffic to all end stations in a subnetwork. The intranet switches monitor multicast requests and forward multicast frames only to the ports hosting members of a multicast group.

Most enterprise networks use multiple protocols. Intranets are IP-based, requiring IP on all intranet access systems throughout the network. To ease IP integration, intranet switching supports protocol-sensitive virtual local area networks (VLANs), which allows the addition of IP without changing the logical network structure for other protocols.

By combining IP and ATM routing through integrated private network-to-network interface (I-PNNI) signaling, network management is simplified because only one protocol is managed rather than two. Providing this unified view of the network by implementing a single protocol leads to better path selection and improved network performance.

To accommodate intranet traffic demands, increased switching capabilities must be added to both the edge of the network and to the backbone network. Many organizations are using intranets for mission-critical applications, so the backbone technology must deliver superior performance, scalability, and a high degree of resiliency. For these reasons, asynchronous transfer mode (ATM) may be the optimal choice for the core technology for intranet switches.

INTRANET OPERATING SYSTEM

As today's networks assimilate additional services originally developed for the global Internet, they are gaining new flexibility in the ways they provide access to computing resources and information. Network operating systems make this easier to accomplish greater information sharing by providing integral access to intranet resources such as Web servers, FTP(FTP) servers, and WAN connections to the Internet. Novell Inc.'s IntranetWare offering, which is built on the NetWare 4 network operating system, provides both IP and IPX access to intranet resources, for example.

IntranetWare

IntranetWare incorporates all of the networking services of NetWare 4.11, such as Novell Directory Services (NDS), symmetric multiprocessing (SMP),and core file and print services with new intranet and Internet capabilities. These solutions include a high-performance NetWare Web Server 2.5, FTP services (the Internet-standard method for allowing users to download files on remote servers via the Internet), Netscape Navigator, an IPX-to-IP gateway to provide IPX users with access to all IP resources (including World Wide Web pages), and integrated wide-area routing to connect geographically dispersed LANs to a corporate intranet or to the greater Internet.

At the heart of IntranetWare's management is NDS, which allows administrators to manage a network from any workstation and provides sophisticated access controls for all the resources on the intranet. With the centralized administration enabled by NDS, organizations can contain management and administration expenses, which are the primary costs of operating a network.

IntranetWare also qualifies for C2 network security certification, enabling the complete network—server, client, and connecting media—to be completely secure.

IntranetWare's routing capabilities let corporations extend their intranets to branch offices and to connect to the Internet via ISDN (ISDN), frame relay, ATM, or leased-line connections. Add-on software from Novell allows mainframe and midrange computers to become a part of the corporate intranet.

IntranetWare provides comprehensive client support for DOS, Windows, Windows 95, Windows NT, Macintosh, OS/2, and Unix workstations.

THE EVER-PRESENT FIREWALL

A firewall is server software that protects TCP/IP networks from unwanted external access to corporate resources. With a firewall, companies can connect their private TCP/IP networks to the global Internet or to other external TCP/IP networks and be assured that unauthorized users cannot obtain access to systems or files on their private network. Firewalls can also work in the opposite direction by controlling internal access to external services that are deemed inappropriate to accomplishing the company's business.

Firewalls come in three types: packet filters, circuit-level gateways, and application gateways. Some firewall products combine all three into one firewall server, offering organizations more flexibility in meeting their security needs.

Packet Filtering

With packet filtering, all IP packets traveling between the internal network and the external network must pass through the firewall. User-definable rules allow or disallow packets to be passed. The firewall's GUI allows systems administrators to implement packet filter rules easily and accurately.

Circuit-Level Gateway

All of the firewall's incoming and outgoing connections are circuit-level connections that are made automatically and transparently. The firewall can be configured to permit a variety of outgoing connections such as Telnet, FTP, WWW, Gopher, America Online, and user-defined applications such as mail and news. Incoming circuit-level connections include Telnet and FTP. Incoming connections are only permitted with authenticated inbound access using one-time password tokens.

Applications Servers

Some firewalls include support for several standard application servers, including mail, news, WWW, FTP, and DNS(DNS). Security is enhanced by compartmentalizing these applications from other firewall software, so that if an individual server is under attack, other servers/functions are not affected.

To aid security, firewalls offer logging capabilities as well as alarms that are activated when probing is detected. Log files are kept for all connection requests and server activity. The files can be viewed from the console displaying the most recent entries. The log scrolls in real time as new entries come in. The log files include:

- Connection requests
- Mail log files
- News log files
- Other servers
- Outbound FTP sessions
- Alarm conditions
- Administrative logs.
- Kernel messages

An alarm system watches for network probes. The alarm system can be configured to watch for TCP or user datagram protocol (UDP) probes from either the external or internal networks. Alarms can be configured to trigger e-mail, pop-up windows, and messages sent to a local printer, or halt the system upon detection of a security breach.

Another important function of firewalls is to remap and hide all internal IP addresses. The source IP addresses are written so that outgoing packets originate from the firewall. The result is that all of the organization's internal IP addresses are hidden from users on the greater Internet. This provides organizations with the important option of being able to use nonregistered IP addresses on their internal network. By not having to assign every computer a unique IP address and not having to register them for use over the greater Internet, which would result in conflicts, administrators can save hundreds of hours of work.

INTRANET SERVER MANAGEMENT

Intranets bring together yet another set of technologies that need to be managed. Instead of using different management systems, organizations should strive to monitor and administer intranet applications from the same console used to manage their underlying operating system software and server hardware. This is a distinct advantage when it comes to ensuring end-to-end availability of intranet resources to users.

For example, the hierarchical storage management capabilities of the Unicenter platform from Computer Associates can be extended to HTML pages on a Web server. HTML pages that are not accessed from the server for a given period of time can be migrated to less costly near-line storage.

If a user then tries to access such a page, storage management directs the query to the appropriate location.

Some enterprise management vendors are turning to partnerships to provide users of their management platforms with data on intranet server performance. For example, Hewlett-Packard Co. and Cabletron Systems, Inc. have joined with BMC Software Inc. to provide application management software that monitors Web-server performance and use. The software forwards the data it collects to management consoles, such as HP's OpenView and Cabletron's Spectrum, in the platforms' native format or as basic SNMP traps. Instead of looking at their internal Web sites in an isolated way, this integrated method allows full-fledged enterprisewide applications management.

IBM's Tivoli Systems unit provides Web server management through a combination of its internally developed applications and software from net.Genesis Corp. Tivoli is also working with IBM Corp. and SunSoft, Inc. to develop the Internet Management Specification (IMS) for submission to the Desktop Management Task Force. IMS would provide a standard interface for monitoring and controlling all types of Internet and intranet resources.

IP Administration

Managing Web servers is only one aspect of keeping an intranet up and running. IP administration can also become unwieldy as intranets lead to a proliferation of devices and addresses. Intranet-driven IP administration can be facilitated by dynamic host configuration protocol (DHCP) software, which streamlines the allocation and distribution of IP addresses and insulates network operators from the complexity of assigning addresses across multiple subnetworks and platforms. Because intranets depend on the accurate assignment of IP addresses throughout a company, such tools are invaluable to ensuring the availability of resources.

Managing Bandwidth

Intranets also have the potential to significantly increase traffic, causing bandwidth problems. For some technology managers, the obvious concern is that bandwidth for vital business applications is being consumed by less-than-vital intranet data. Users access files may contain large graphics files, and that alone has created a tremendous bandwidth issue. As Web servers across an enterprise entice users with new content, intranets also can alter the distribution patterns of network traffic as users hop from one business unit's intranet server to another's and as companies make it easier to access information and applications no matter where they may be located.

A Policy-Based Solution

More servers and bandwidth can be added and the network itself can be partitioned into more subnetworks to help confine bandwidth-intensive applications to various communities of interest. But these are expensive solutions. A policy-based solution can be just as effective, if not more economical.

To prevent these applications from wreaking too much havoc on the network infrastructure, companies can issue policies that establish limits to document size and the use of graphics so that bandwidth is not consumed unnecessarily. These policies can even be applied to e-mail servers, where the server can be instructed to reject messages that are too long or contain attachments that exceed a given file size.

CONCLUSION

Companies that have implemented intranets are gradually finding that they are able to use Internet technologies to communicate and link information—internally and externally—in ways that were not possible before. Many other companies may be tempted to jump on the intranet bandwagon using the fastest means possible. This tactic may meet basic requirements, but it often does not take into account future network growth, the advantages gained by leveraging existing data and resources, or how to add new intranet-enhancing products as they become available. These considerations demand that intranets be flexible, open, and integrated.

Any time a company makes information accessible to a wide group of people or extends an intranet to suppliers or vendors, it must establish appropriate security mechanisms, ranging from firewalls to access control to authentication and encryption. In addition, network managers upgrade the network infrastructure to support the increased traffic that will flow over the intranet and maintain acceptable network response times.

Despite the allure of corporate intranets and their benefits, companies will not be able to immediately move rapidly toward the kind of full-fledged intranet being predicted by some vendors, with a single browser-type interface and thin clients that download applications and data. For some considerable time to come, intranets, as defined by the browser suppliers, will be distinct from and complementary to existing systems.

Chapter 20
The Mainframe as Enterprise Server

Brian Jeffery

An upgraded mainframe system equipped with new database and application capabilities can function as an enterprise server. This article explains techniques and proven solutions for making the transition from conventional mainframe computing to an enterprise server-based IS strategy.

INTRODUCTION

The mainframe continues to run core information systems without which most businesses could not function, providing high levels of availability, data integrity, and security. Mainframe-based computing retains its embedded strengths of economy of scale, robustness, and business-critical computing.

These systems, however, must also acquire new client/server capabilities. Central databases play a new role in concentrating, protecting, and providing access to all corporate data resources. Users employ PCs, workstations, and portable computers to access this data and to communicate via organization-wide network infrastructures. New development tools deliver high-quality, flexible applications in a fraction of the time previously required. In most cases, legacy data, applications, and skills carry over to the new IS environment.

More important, there is no significant business disruption. In most companies, the transition from conventional mainframe computing to an enterprise server-based IS strategy can be realized within 12 to 18 months. Key applications can be brought online even more rapidly. In an organization that already uses mainframe systems efficiently and employs modern hardware and software technologies, much of the infrastructure is already in place.

Although costs will vary from company to company, such an IS strategy, if properly applied, can yield business gains and improvements in efficiency that more than justify the investments. Data center operating costs

0-8493-9989-0/99/$0.00+$.50

are frequently reduced by two to eight times. Applications development productivity can be increased up to eight times. PC/LAN costs can be lowered by 50% to 80%, and telecommunications costs by up to 50%.

ENTERPRISE SERVER-BASED STRATEGY IN PRACTICE

XYZ Company is a growing midsize retailer that has more than doubled its revenues during the last five years. Despite severe price-cutting and increased competition, gross margins have improved more than 30% over this period. John is an XYZ customer. On XYZ's mainframe is a file on John, as well as files on more than five million other XYZ customers. The file contains details on all John's purchases from the company over the past five years and more than 40 other categories of information. Because John is an XYZ preferred customer, he qualifies for discounts, special offers, and promotional rewards. This is why he buys from XYZ. Preferred customers are only 15% of XYZ's customer base, but account for more than 30% of sales and more than 40% of profits. XYZ's customer loyalty program is designed to keep existing preferred customers and find more of them.

When John makes a purchase, an hour later that purchase, along with hundreds of thousands of others, is being studied by XYZ's top managers. They view information displayed on a large-screen computer terminal showing precise sales patterns for every product line and department for each of the company's stores. If necessary, management can examine sales of any of the 12,000 inventory items the company carries, for each single checkout nationwide. They can examine not only the sale value, but also the profit contribution of each store, item, and customer.

Data is streamed upward from the point-of-sale systems in XYZ stores to a common customer database, where it is then analyzed automatically every hour for management by a highly sophisticated, custom-built command and control system. Exhibit 1 shows how a common customer database is the focal point of XYZ's entire IS infrastructure.

The XYZ Company profile is a composite of three of the fastest-growing retailers operating on three different continents. Similar examples can be found in a wide range of industries worldwide.

CONCENTRATING IS RESOURCES

In a large diversified company, it may make sense to decentralize IS resources within the organization and subdivide responsibilities among business units and divisions. By contrast, growing companies like XYZ target well-defined customer bases, are more focused in the products and services they supply, and usually operate within specific geographic markets. Management chains of command are relatively short, organizations are compact, and reporting structures are uncomplicated.

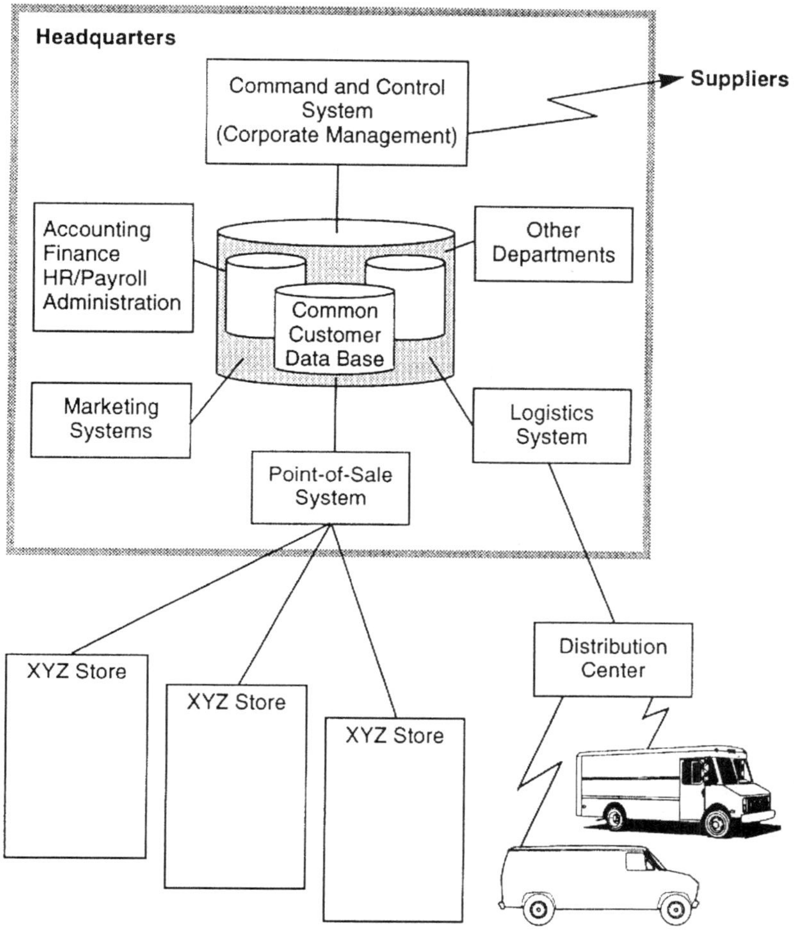

Exhibit 1. IS infrastructure built around a common customer database.

In this type of organization, there are major benefits in concentrating IS resources. This does not preclude the use of PCs, workstations, or distributed servers. However, for maximum business yield, all IS resources must work together with maximum effectiveness. The deployment of all IS resources needs to be driven by the goal of improving competitive performance. Specifically, IS resources are focused on three key variables: information, speed, and cost.

Information. Leadership companies employ information technology to learn precisely who their customers are and how they behave, when and why their buying patterns change, and when and why they buy from competitors. This knowledge is used to acquire more customers, sell them more products and services, and retain their loyalty over time. With a few modifications, the IS infrastructure also becomes the vehicle through which companies obtain valuable information about all the individuals, households, or businesses that should be their customers, as well as about market trends, the actions of competitors, and all the other factors that affect what management reports to company shareholders. It also generates information continuously about the company's internal operations. That information is used aggressively to maximize the efficiency with which all financial, material, and human resources within the business are used.

The primary IS structure is the company's core databases that are the repository of its information resources. Applications generate and interpret information. Networks distribute it. PCs, workstations, and mobile computers provide access to it.

Speed. In competitive markets, leadership companies are able to respond quickly and intelligently because they are supported by IS infrastructures designed to allow key business decisions and operations to occur in real time. The speed with which strategic decisions are made in the executive suite and with which tasks are performed by front-line employees provides a competitive edge.

There is not much point to having vast amounts of information if it takes too long to assimilate and act on it. In all companies, there is a path between the placing of a customer order and the final delivery of the product and service. That path should be as short and direct as possible. However, all too often that path goes astray; memos, forms, and printouts abound; one department after another checks, reviews, approves, signs off, and forwards reports to another department, where the process begins all over again.

The way in which IS is organized has a major impact on the business process. If applications and databases are fragmented because departments and workgroups work with separate, often incompatible computers, then data must be transferred among activities, functions, or operations through less than high-tech information-handling techniques. All of this slows the business. The enterprise server-based strategy tackles these problems by:

- **Using precision information systems** — These systems interpret large volumes of data and present information in a clear, easy-to-understand form that can be acted on not only by management, but also by front-line employees, sales personnel, and administrative staff. Exhibit 2 provides a blueprint for this type of system. These new systems are a quantum leap beyond 1980s-style query and decision support tools running on PCs or departmental servers. As large-scale systems that operate companywide, the impact on bottom-line business performance is greater.

- **Developing integrated product/service delivery systems using flexible, highly functional software technologies** — These systems eliminate administrative inefficiencies, consolidate fragmented applications and databases into single streamlined systems, and replace paper-based procedures with electronic information-handling. Such systems cut across traditional functional boundaries. Delivery of all products and services is accelerated, allowing the company to respond effectively and rapidly to changing market and competitive conditions.
- **Developing a command and control system** — Such a system assists the company's management team in determining market strategies, monitoring business performance, and initiating change. It is highly customized, using advanced technology to adapt to the planning needs, thinking processes, and work patterns of management.

Analyzing cost structures and projecting costs more effectively increases the company's control of its financial resources while improvements in

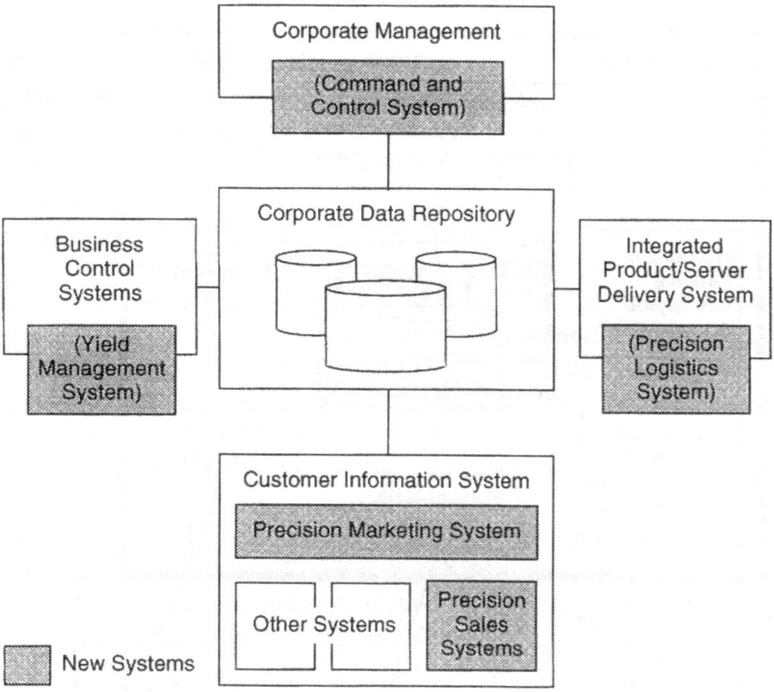

Exhibit 2. Blueprint for the IS strategy cost.

throughput, resulting from streamlined delivery processes, mean that staff can be reduced and overhead costs cut.

Cost reduction is not a byproduct of an IS strategy. It is one of its core mandates. Goals such as revenue generation or market share growth, or intangibles such as empowerment or flexibility, may be useful indicators of a company's vitality, but they are not business goals in themselves. In a leadership company, business goals are IS goals. Technology has no purpose other than to provide the necessary tools for realizing these goals.

New Types of Strategic Information Systems

Yield Management Systems. Yield management systems are being applied in a wide range of industries. Their goal is to maximize the efficiency with which all of the company's resources, including material, capital, and personnel assets, are used. Use of a yield management system starts with the proposition that any resource used at less than maximum efficiency is a cost. When efficiency improves, costs are reduced and profitability increases.

Precision Cost Analysis. Cost analysis in many organizations is handled in a piecemeal way. PC-based spreadsheets are usually employed in individual departments. A yield management system integrates and automates all procedures for cost accounting, analysis, and projection , while delivering radically higher levels of analytical power and statistical precision.

Cost analysis thus becomes a continuous, automatic process. Management can review cost patterns, identify emerging patterns, and exploit opportunities weekly, daily, or even hourly. Targeting improvements in efficiency becomes a normal part of business operations rather than an occasional event.

Functional Areas. A company's yield management system can be used within several different functional areas. It can, for example, act as an overlay to an integrated product or service delivery system, such as a precision logistics system. The system provides special value in cross-functional analyses.

For example, a retail company uses a yield management system to realize major savings in procurement. Mining data on companywide external purchases allows details (shown in Exhibit 3) to be collected and analyzed for all stores and departments.

The identification of cost anomalies in particular is targeted. The company had initially carried more than 12,000 items in inventory. After analyzing each category, quantifying costs, and determining the effect on sales

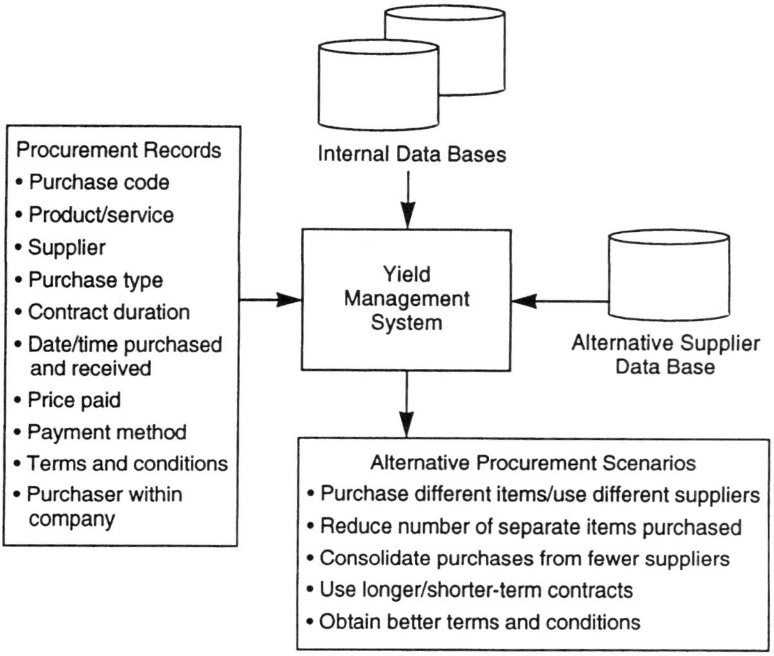

Exhibit 3. Yield management application.

of changing stocking mixes, the total was reduced to less than 8,000. Costs were reduced by more than 15% without any reduction in sales.

Command and Control Systems

In large companies, it may be logical for corporate executives to avoid the complexities of day-to-day operations and focus on questions of policy and strategy. In growth companies like retailer XYZ, decisions about inventory, pricing, and specific marketing programs are central to maintaining competitiveness. Corporate management is directly involved in these decisions.

Command and control systems are designed to enhance the value of the skills of management principals by supplying them with comprehensive, timely, accurate information. Management can monitor the overall picture, make strategic decisions, identify critical situations, and when necessary, intervene at the tactical level. If this type of system is properly designed and implemented, it maximizes the top managers' role while allowing line managers to continue to deal flexibly with local business conditions.

Technology Design. An effective command and control system does not require that managers operate the system. Usually, technical design, implementation, and operation are handled by IS professionals associated with either the executive staff or the IS organization. The system should learn the way management principles work, not vice versa. It can and should be heavily customized to the needs, work patterns, and thinking processes of these individuals. In terms of technology, an effective command and control system, illustrated in Exhibit 4, consists of three primary components:

- **Display interface.** Display mechanisms may include high-resolution color graphics, presentation of data in 3D form, moving images, and large-scale projection screens. The result is similar to a business presentation, except that precision is much greater and the recipient depends less on the presenter for the interpretation of information.
- **Database infrastructure.** In a company using consolidated databases, virtually all of the electronic data that exists within the company is immediately available to management. If high levels of computerization are employed in business operations, there will be few (if any) significant items of information that are not available.
- **Data interpretation tools.** To reduce the complexities that managers must deal with, mechanisms must be in place not only to mine large volumes of data, but also to render it into clear, easily understandable form. Conventional executive information systems (EISs) generally have not met expectations. PC-based tools may be appropriate for individual or departmental applications but they are underpowered when it comes to dealing with data volumes and interpretation tasks needed to support strategic decision making. Large-scale tools for identifying, querying, and interpreting data resources perform better.

Upgrading the Mainframe: Technical Implementation. The technical infrastructure for this IS strategy is based on upgrading a mainframe system with new capabilities that enable it to function as an enterprise server. The enterprise server is the cornerstone of this strategy. It concentrates key IS resources to better support distributed and remote users. It also increases the volume, quality, and accessibility of information for all users; improves availability of application, data, and network resources; and maximizes the cost-effectiveness with which all IS resources are used.

ENTERPRISE SERVER BASICS

An enterprise server combines the following distinct and, until recently, separate computing technology streams.

Mainframe Computing. The mainframe usually supports business control systems (i.e., accounting, finance, asset management, personnel administration, and payroll) and the core business-critical systems without which the company could not function. The mainframe's strengths are

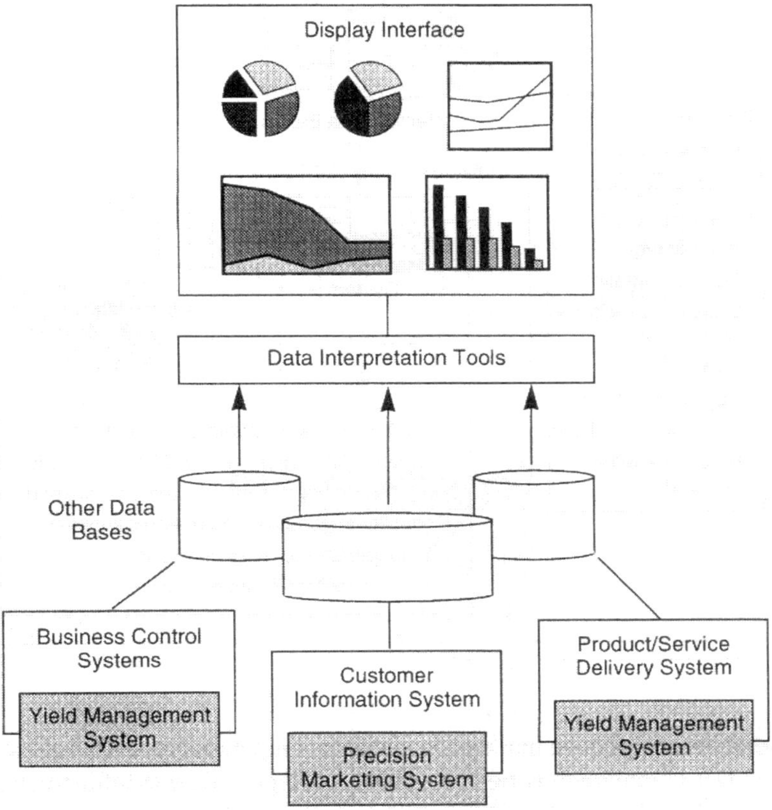

Exhibit 4. Technology components of command and control systems.

its robustness; its ability to handle large-scale, organizationwide workloads; its ability to provide high levels of availability and data integrity; and its capability to manage all system, data, and network resources effectively in performing these tasks.

Mainframes also leverage economies of scale, benefits of concentrated resources, and consistencies of architecture that are inherent to the central IS environment.

Client/Server Computing. In practice, client/server computing is not a single phenomenon; it involves several different types of applications, including text-processing, electronic mail, and personal productivity tools used on a PC or workstation. This category of applications is useful and fairly easy to implement in an end-user environment. From a business standpoint, the most valuable client/server applications are those that access, manipulate, and process data—for example, decision support,

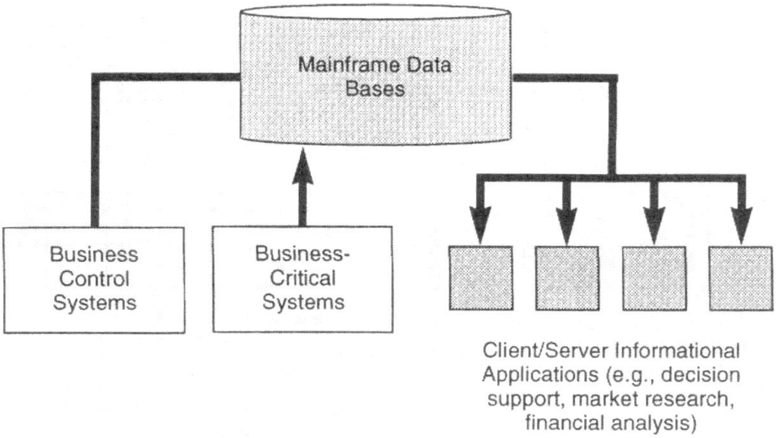

Exhibit 5. Mainframe and client/server synergy.

market research, financial analysis, human resources, and planning applications.

CONSOLIDATING MAINFRAME AND CLIENT/SERVER TECHNOLOGIES

In most organizations, mainframe databases are the primary source of data used by all such applications. The data is generated by the production business control and business-critical applications that run on mainframes. Thus, there is important synergy between mainframe and client/server computing (see Exhibit 5).

This synergy can be exploited to its full potential. By consolidating key databases and implementing reliable, organizationwide network infrastructures, all data can be made accessible at the workstation level.

In combining these technology streams, most growing companies are faced with the choice of upgrading a mainframe to act as a server or trying to equip a Unix server to act as a mainframe. Upgrading the mainframe is usually both less expensive and less disruptive.

Moreover, it is substantially less difficult to provide client/server capability to a mainframe than it is to provide mainframe-class robustness to a Unix server. The strengths of the mainframe environment have developed over more than 30 years. Few users have been prepared to entrust genuinely business-critical applications to Unix servers.

THE IMPLEMENTATION PLAN

- The steps for upgrading the mainframe to act as a server involve:
- The migration to a core database management system (DBMS)

- The selection of tools to deliver new applications
- The rebuilding of data center operations
- The integration of PC/LAN clusters
- The upgrade of the network infrastructure

Migrating to a Core DBMS. The DBMS must be capable of handling OnLine Transaction Processing and batch workloads required for business control and business-critical applications, as well as the new query-intensive workloads generated by organizationwide client/server computing.

Multiple databases, such as a common customer database and common operational database, are created within the core DBMS, which also ensures the accessibility, currency, integrity, security, and recoverability of all corporate data.

It may be necessary to replace older hierarchical database and file structures. This is, however, a relatively fast and easy process, especially if automated tools are used. Legacy data and applications can be converted to run on the new core DBMS. Existing applications written in Common Business Oriented Language (COBOL) and leading fourth-generation languages (4GLs) can be ported in this manner without the necessity for major rewrites. Exhibit 6 illustrates the migration from a legacy mainframe environment to a new core DBMS.

Selecting Tools for Building New Applications. Conventional COBOL- and 4GL-based techniques are often too slow for new applications and do

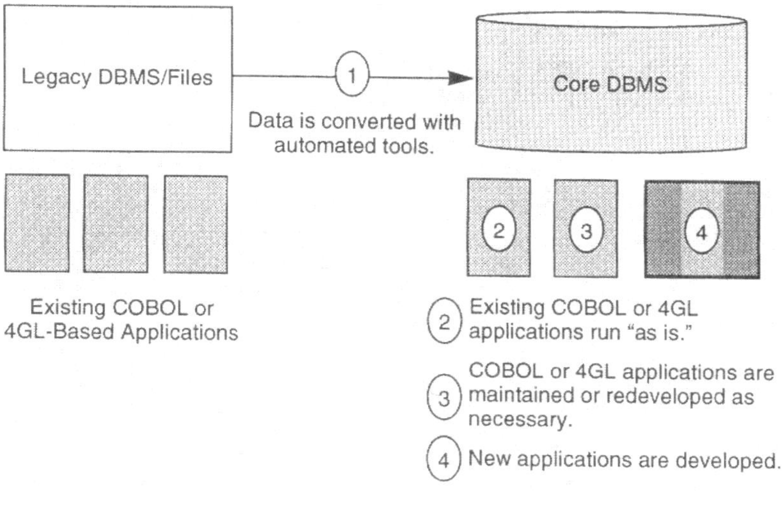

Exhibit 6. Migration from Legacy Mainframe Environment to New Core DBMS.

not provide adequate levels of integration and flexibility. Conversely, lightweight client/server development tools for PCs and small servers may not be able to handle the size and functional requirements of value-added solutions.

Packaged software can be used. However, most independent software vendor offerings address only standardized accounting or human resources requirements. They do not usually provide a direct competitive edge for companies that use them and are difficult to customize.

The tools to use to develop new high-value applications are latest-generation Computer-Aided Software Engineering, Rapid Application Development, and object-oriented development tools for the mainframe environment. Such tools deliver high-quality, large-scale applications that fully support client/server capabilities, including Graphical User Interface (GUIs). Moreover, they work in a fraction of the time required with conventional techniques.

Several techniques can be used to make existing applications more flexible and user-friendly. For example, PC-based graphical user interfaces can typically be added to legacy applications without making major changes in platforms or software architectures. Similarly, existing applications can be redeveloped and maintained using new PC-based COBOL visual programming tools.

Once the core DBMS is in place, considerable flexibility is possible. New systems can coexist with legacy applications, and light-duty database query, decision support, and related tools can also be employed (see Exhibit 7).

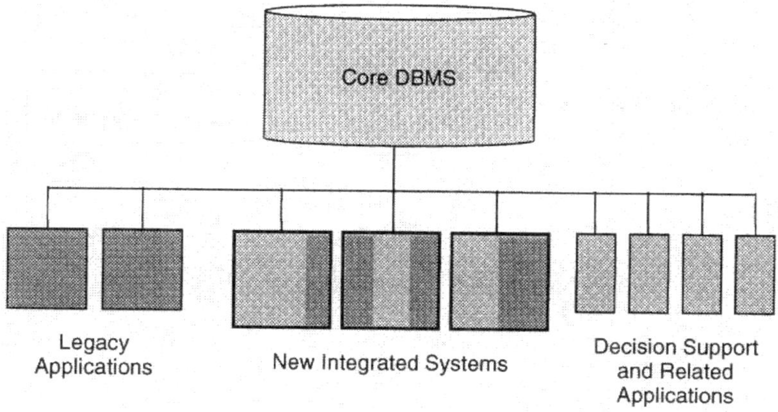

Exhibit 7. Coexistence of new and legacy applications.

Rebuilding Data Center Operations. Another part of the implementation plan involves rebuilding data center operations using modern, efficient hardware and software technologies, automation tools, and improved management practices. The result is high levels of capacity utilization, increased performance, reduced operating costs, and minimal outages or production job failures.

Integrating PC/LAN Clusters. To more effectively support distributed PC users within the organization, local area networks (LANs) are interconnected and managed from a central point. Tools are used to regularly backup data on LAN servers to data center storage, thus ensuring that departmental data is properly managed and protected and is accessible to other users within the organization. These initiatives, illustrated in Exhibit 8, significantly improve the quality and availability of LAN infrastructures and reduce support costs.

Upgrading the Network Infrastructure. The network infrastructure should be functional enough to allow information to flow freely throughout the organization. Increased use of client/server computing usually increases network loading, which may mean that more bandwidth is needed at both the local and Wide Area Network levels. In addition, wireless technologies can be used to support mobile sales, logistics and other applications. Networking for remote computing is typically simpler and less expensive to implement than for client/server solutions built around traditional PCs and LANs.

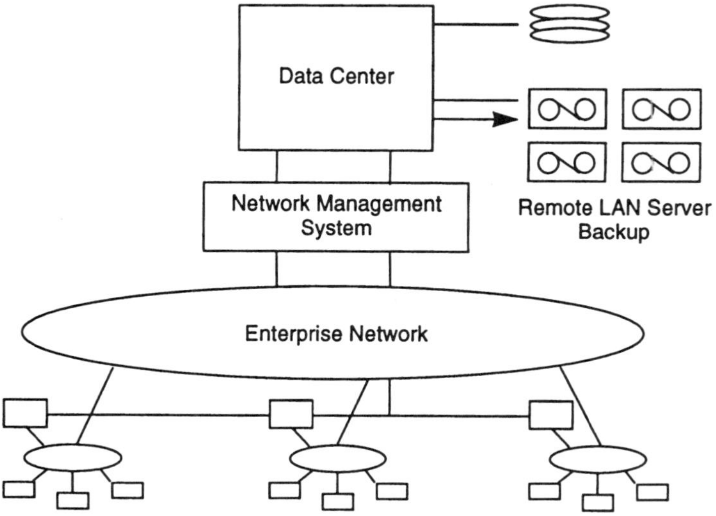

Exhibit 8. Enterprise server integration of PC/LAN clusters.

CONCLUSION

The initial investment to create a more efficient, functional IS infrastructure built around a mainframe-based enterprise server will yield major payoffs both in positive business benefits and in significantly higher yields from IS expenditures. The strategy means moving beyond using IS to automate business tasks and processes more effectively and instead using information technology to turn information itself into a dynamic new tool that can be employed throughout the organization, from the executive suite to the front-line worker.

More fundamentally, the IS strategy must also be about integration and coordination. A company does not succeed as a collection of individuals and departments. Similarly, the IS infrastructure must do more than empower individual users. It must provide a further level of value by creating a new cohesiveness in the way in which all of the company's resources are focused and deployed for success.

Chapter 21
Managing Applications on the Network

Bill Yaman
John Fiske

Businesses today depend on the availability of decentralized, multiplatform systems and network resources. Smooth-running, reliable networks are essential in today's business environment, but yesterday's systems management strategies are not sufficient nor effective in today's distributed client/server computing environments.

New, advanced management solutions now help you, the network manager, CIO, or IT architect, manage your company's large and complex systems. As your systems increase in size and complexity, you must find the optimal, and most time-, cost-, and resource-efficient way to manage your IT.

IT managers now realize that to make their client/server systems perform as intended, they need to have control over distributed applications. Usually the applications offer symptoms of a network malfunction; an improperly functioning application is the first indicator of a network problem. By using the application as access point into your network, you can look into your IT infrastructure to find out what is causing the application not to perform.

Until recently, most network systems and management strategies involved monitoring and managing the technology that supports applications, not the applications themselves. Network and systems problems were not viewed from the applications perspective. In a change, companies are finding that application management supports the business; in fact, ensuring network/application availability has become a top business objective.

0-8493-9989-0/99/$0.00+$.50

Application management was not addressed in centralized host environments because mainframes had embedded application monitoring facilities that could easily address issues involving application health, response time and administration. But now applications are deployed across multiple platforms nationally and internationally, and administrators are realizing that not being able to monitor or benchmark remote applications leaves them very vulnerable to problems that are hard to diagnose and even harder to solve.

Systems have become far too complex and heterogeneous to be managed with existing systems. In the "old days" when the entire enterprise ran off a single mainframe and attached dumb terminals, it was comparatively simple to look at the applications, and the network, such as it was. Systems management itself is not capable of providing a complete view of an application's journey through the enterprise. Nor do existing systems management devices allow the IT managers to look into the system from a single point.

DISTRIBUTED COMPUTING ENVIRONMENT

As managers gain control of their distributed computing environment, they have found application management produces multiple benefits. Well functioning networks with well functioning applications allow end users to be more productive by relieving them of the time-consuming headaches of managing desktops; it provides application consistency across the enterprise and helps ensure interoperability; and in addition, electronic software distribution yields cost savings.

Managing from business perspective means keeping your "eye on the prize," with the prize being your most critical applications. Since all systems are not equal, an effective method of application management is to isolate and monitor those things in your IT that are most important. It's a way to simplify a very complex environment.

Today, with distributed applications and client/server networks connected to the reliable old mainframes through middleware, the network has become a new kind of hybrid creature. And to complicate matters further, the distinction between application and network is no longer clear. Consider for a moment: is e-mail an application or a network? Or both?

THE PARADIGM

Application management should be focused on business value and must have end-user or customer perspective. This means the system and applications must be available when they are needed. So, applications management is about providing availability. What is availability? Availability is:

> Managing real-time behavior of applications and essential systems, subsystems, middleware and network resources to ensure their operational reliability, accessibility and performance in support of critical business processes.

The high cost of lost business means companies can't afford network slowdowns. If finding the one percent of faults means an x percent increase in market share, monitoring will be done. Yet problems in today's complex, distributed networks are harder to find and more costly then ever to fix. To ensure network problems don't threaten application availability you need to:

- Determine quickly and accurately the source of network problems
- View the health of your entire network from a single point
- Control IS costs by leveraging staff productivity and managing software distribution
- Protect applications from expensive threats to availability
- View only the information you need to manage users, groups, or specific areas of your network
- Simplify complexity by managing workloads, groups, and resources across multiple platforms
- Manage expansion as your systems and applications grow

As your company places more reliance on distributed mission-critical applications, your need for application management will intensify.

Application management is about providing and ensuring availability. The application management strategy requires a total application life cycle perspective that includes design, development, and operations of applications.

Managing applications is a new and huge challenge. The three main approaches to application management are measurement, modeling, and vendor management tools attached to enterprise applications. What follows is a discussion of each approach.

INSTRUMENTATION

The initial effort in applications management has been to instrument applications with fish tags and hooks located inside the application to give, for example, end-to-end response time. As an application is written, the instruments are written into the code.

While instrumentation intuitively is the approach you would want to use to monitor your applications and network, it requires a great amount of labor to construct. And often instrumentation looks at areas of your network that are not "mission critical."

Consider a hypothetical situation in which an insurance company buys a sales management tool which runs with an *Oracle* database on an AIX server. The sales management tool is expected to perform well and the company naturally wants to interface the database with the claims system on a mainframe. The mainframe is a legacy system. And a middleware pipe is built between the new sales tool and mainframe.

To instrument the new middleware and the new sales tool through to the mainframe would require people to rewrite the legacy. It might also require that the newly acquired application be "undone."

While it is technically simple to write and insert the code, it is a very laborious task, and then it needs to be maintained. And when the company adds more applications to the system, with more middleware and other supporting software and hardware, still more code would have to be written.

To monitor application and system health you need a sample of what is going on at all times. Ideally you would want to be able to instrument the entire system, but as we have seen, this is impractical.

IT people need an alternative. A good alternative is modeling.

MODELING

Modeling is a top down external method to monitor applications with the focus on the external view. The idea is to isolate mission critical packets of IT and create models of situations that can occur in other areas of the IT architecture. Viewing your IT from the "top," at the end-user application, you establish, through experience, those situations "down" in the IT system that affect the performance of the top, user-interface application. By its nature, because it uses predictions rather than actual measurements, modeling is not as precise as instrumentation. But by looking at specific packets in the network you get a business view of what is going on in the system. Modeling is about prioritizing to the things that are critical to your system. You organize around your critical business components, not around technology.

Modeling operates according to an 80/20 rule which predicts that if you can model 20 percent of the applications you get 80 percent impact, and subsequent operational improvement. Rather than looking at everything, which is impractical, modeling monitors for symptoms that show at the application level.

Modeling is a noise filter. It allows you to focus on the mission critical aspects of your IT, without your having to look at every last little bit of the system. It is simply a more efficient way of doing your business.

Although modeling is an efficient alternative to instrumentation, customizable, thoroughbred application management systems give systems operators even better control over their enterprise-wide IT. Several excellent applications management programs, provided by third party vendors, combine the techniques found in instrumentation and in modeling to give the best kind of applications management available.

OUT-OF-BOX VENDOR SUPPLIED MANAGEMENT SOFTWARE

Vendor supplied application monitoring products wrap monitoring around the application. The vendors provide the monitoring tools. In almost every case, the vendors partner with the system/application provider to develop the monitoring system. The partnership is advantageous to the application provider because the provider's expertise is more in developing the application, and not as much in command and control.

A Short Example

SAP R/3 is a large-scale client/server package to run a business. It runs order processing, general ledger, accounts payable, accounts receivable, inventory, manufacturing, production control, currency exchange, and other applications all integrated together. SAP was the first vendor to introduce this kind of system for the client/server environment. R/3 is built on a 3-tier architecture:

- Client (Win, MacOs, OS-2, UNIX).
- Network connection to application servers UNIX boxes HP 6000.
- Database server (*Oracle*). Application programs to run business on servers. Clients become terminals.

SAP created a Computer Center Management System (CCMS) to provide application and system management for R/3 at the same time it created R/3. At the time there were no third parties with monitoring equipment for R/3. CCMS was essentially a requirement for SAP to be able to sell R/3.

But as it has turned out, CCMS has not been a long-term adequate solution for companies with more than one SAP system, nor has it been able to keep up with R/3's advancing technology. Most companies have multiple SAP systems. Additionally, SAP has often been interfaced with a legacy mainframe. But CCMS only looks at SAP, but an open system command center can look into the whole network.

A third party vendor, such as Candle Corporation, Tivoli, and others can supply the open environment command system you need to manage the applications on your network.

In the above example, the key challenge to application management was to create an application-oriented view of the distributed computing environment. As it turns out this is the emerging challenge for all applications management systems.

APPLICATIONS ORIENTATION

The Hurwitz Group, a management consulting and software research firm in Massachusetts, says an applications orientation is the key to successful applications management. It sounds confusing, but it means that you use the user interface application to look inside your IT.

The Hurwitz Group identifies the criteria for effective applications management:

- The ability to relate logical application components to the underlying technology infrastructure, such as a key application service or a file system running on a specific server node, and
- The ability to monitor discrete application software components, such as application servers and database tables.

Systems management strategy should focus on system resources availability. Application management is the access port into the health of your systems. If, for example, a daily sales report application is blank, yielding no data, something, somewhere in the system, is wrong. Your applications are the first place you will find out that something is not right — unless you have a coordinated systems management strategy and the tools in place to support it.

The first criterion enables management systems to identify which logical application components are affected by the failure of specific infrastructure elements. To meet this criterion, all information about a particular application must be gathered, and all objects representing parts of the infrastructure must be logically mapped to the application components that use them.

System administrators must be able to monitor discrete application components in order to know what the actual impact of the component failure is on the application. For example, if an application accesses multiple databases and one of the database servers goes down, the failure may not prevent the application from continuing to provide other functions that do not require the failed database. To fully understand the health of the application, the administrator must be able to determine what happened to the application because of the failure. In many companies a typical application stack would look like Exhibit 1.

An application failure almost always indicates a failure somewhere in the stack. To meet the second criterion, a system must provide administrators with a full understanding of the application components and how they interrelate. An application can consist of many components that execute on different devices. These components, or processes, can be dependent or independent depending on how the application was written. If the processes are independent, a single failure of an infrastructure component

Exhibit 1. A typical applications stack.

• Application
• Application Services (SAP R/3, *Lotus Notes*)
• Middleware (MQSeries)
• Database (SQL, Com/Engine)
• Operating systems NT Server
• Network (Com/Middleware)

may not affect all the processes. Therefore, a management system that merely maps infrastructure components can give false readings of an application's true state of health; that system is not performing adequate, or thorough application management.

The management system also needs to be expandable and flexible in order to accommodate the constant changes in the stack. At any time new hardware may be added and old equipment may be taken off-line. These changes can and do alter the operation of your IT infrastructure, but they can be managed with the right equipment.

Applications Management requires:

- The ability to map logical application components to the underlying IT infrastructure
- The ability to monitor the discrete application components and their interdependencies
- Navigation capability to allow administrators to drill down through the stack for problem determination

To manage applications adequately, a management system must have the ability to correlate (map) logical application software components to each other and to the underlying technology infrastructure. It requires very advanced correlation capabilities that do not exist in all management systems. It also requires an understanding of the application architecture and the ability to view discrete logical components of the application as it executes in a distributed environment.

Navigation indicates the ability to "drill down" from application into the IT stack to identify the faulty components. A GUI interface can reduce problem determination time. As previously mentioned, system down-time can cost your company millions of dollars. Your objective is to prevent whole applications from crashing.

Vendor-supplied management systems provide the ability to monitor discrete things and the interdependencies. The system helps you probe into important areas of your stack to map it back to the higher level application. Discrete monitoring of application components and the components of the infrastructure enable you to know that when something is wrong at the high level, something else is wrong down below.

So, what do you do if you find out that you have only 15 minutes until a disk-full that brings down a mission critical Oracle database? With a good navigation tool, you would drill down to find out, as an example, it is on an NT server in the Boston office. You simply log-on from your remote location, and delete some data, to save the day.

Your job is to ensure system availability, and you want to prevent the system from going down, or you want to be able to find the trouble, correct it, and bring it back up quickly before (a) end users, irate, start calling you and, (b) before time elapses and business and dollars are lost.

To have this capability you need broad coverage either with your own product or other products with open interface to accept information from other sources. Legacy systems can't be changed easily; it's easier and simpler to configure the monitoring system to work with what is already in place. New client/server systems are designed to be monitored with user- or manager-interface management systems, but the legacy systems, which were not, must be somehow connected through in order to be "seen" through the client/server management system. A device sometimes called an "alert adapter" makes the technical links to accommodate the inevitable heterogeneity of today's complex client/server, mainframe and legacy systems. Alert adapters are must-have tools.

RULES AND THRESHOLDS

In out-of-box vendor supplied application management systems, rules and thresholds are customizable for each application and the underlying IT components in the stack. Typically, you develop sets of event/statistics values for specific functions, such as response time or other operating characteristics. Then you monitor for exceptions (if response time is greater than x...).

Rules are written within application products for each platform. Your sales management tool will have rules written to accommodate its location on the many different UNIX boxes, for example:

Rules are customized by platform by application:

Platform A/application X
Platform B/application X

Platform A/application Y
Platform B/application Y

Platform A/application Z
Platform B/application Z

And so on, with almost limitless variations.

Rules should be designed to say, if (a), and if (b), and if (c), then (result). This paradigm recognizes the interdependencies between hardware and software on all the layers within the stack. The rules are the critical operating elements in the management system, and must be embedded or captured into the system.

In a GUI control system, when the rules are triggered, an alert goes to a screen at a central location. The nature of the alert is indicated by color (green = OK; yellow = problem incipient; red = failure). Alerts can also be sent by beeper, pager, fax alert, or phone call.

COMMAND AND CONTROL

After finding the location of the failure, the next step, obviously, is to correct it. This is usually done manually, though in some cases automatic controls work.

In an example of manual control, with five applications on one mainframe or UNIX machine, during a period of high load, the control system warns of an incipient failure. The computer operator or manager, using the control system's tools locates the problem and issues commands to correct the problem. In this case, the IT manager makes a decision on which application shall be put temporarily down. The manager decides on a non-customer-interface application, and announces "for next hour payroll (or accounts) receivable will be down."

To translate manual procedures into automated task functions you need a history to predict what might happen. With the history you know that when a problem occurs, and you know it takes a-b-c-d to fix the problem, it becomes a simple matter to have the computer issue the commands. The advantage to automated control is much quicker response time. The challenge is defining all of the a-b-c-d operations to fix all the potential failures that can occur within a system.

E-MAIL

An example of the diffuse line between application and network is e-mail. Increasingly, e-mail is becoming a critical application. Companies simply run on e-mail.

E-mail is more than simply a communication device. In some companies, customer orders are entered by attaching the order to an e-mail message. Customer orders are attached to e-mail, and the orders get placed into an orders mailbox.

E-mail can also be fantastically complex. You rarely find a company with one e-mail system. A large corporation's e-mail systems may likely be a combination of Lotus Notes, CCMail, Eudora Pro, the Internet and other e-mail

mail applications. If internal e-mail is not complicated enough, it becomes more so when you have to talk with another company (a vendor, a partner, a contractor), and you do so on the Internet, and your message goes into another wholly different e-mail architecture. E-mail is sent across internal networks through routers at each location. Network with NetWare (OS) with post office.

How do you manage this? There are individual products that look at mail routers, post offices, *Lotus Notes*, *POP 3*, and other applications. You still need an umbrella that looks at all the infrastructure, the routers, the hubs, the underlying operating systems, NT, Netware, UNIX, in a bottom up approach.

Other products use a top-down approach. The control application sends an e-mail message through the network from point A to point B, and/or C, and/or D. If the test message gets through to the desired recipient location(s), the system is healthy, as far as it has been tested.

If not, something is not working correctly: for example, a message transfer agent's software is down. Or someone sent a 10MB CAD file and it was stored temporarily on a disk, but the disk was full and the disk crashed. Or perhaps someone changed an IP address and the network segment can't see the recipient server because the address changed.

E-mail should be treated as a mission critical application/system. With its own complexities, your e-mail system needs its own customizable management tools.

CONCLUSION

Application management provides, manages, and ensures availability through monitoring, using flexible, customizable rules and thresholds, manual and automated command and control in a heterogeneous network from a single command point.

Efforts to develop new systems on lower cost machines have led to the explosive growth of network-based computing. This has led to dramatic growth in the information that is processed and shared both across a corporation and among its trading partners. In some cases, distributed architectures have been appropriate, while in others, more traditional approaches may have been a better solution. The reality, however, is that technology infrastructures now consist of a vast array of new products and services that take advantage of network-oriented environments.

Two types of system and application monitors exist presently: GUI and scripted language. The GUI interface, as employed by Candle Corp.'s Command Center, is fast and easy to use. It requires, as do all GUI applications, a dense amount of code. The scripted language interface, as employed by

Tivoli's TME 10, is more flexible and is not as much work to write the front end. But it is somewhat slower to use than a GUI interface because the operator has to read the information on the screen.

The most important component of the your IT, from the business perspective, is the end-user application. It could be a complicated cross-platform application sitting on top of a stack. The top layer is the most important, but the problems occur down in the stack. The application may have a code problem, but it has presumably been tested. Within the stack, a hard drive could fill up and crash, or a server address could corrupt. These problems, however buried, cause the application at the top to malfunction.

The assortment of distributed solutions is likely to grow. Laptops, palmtops and other mobile-computing devices will serve as clients connect to the network through a variety of wireless communications media. The increasing need for greater bandwidth will continue to reshape the distributed computing infrastructure. Although the "network computer" promises to lower many costs, its simple existence adds to the complexity of enterprise computing and furthers the need for effective systems and application management.

REFERENCES

Wreden, Nick. "Mission: Control," *Communications Week*, Oct. 28, 1996.

Stafford, Jan. "Client-Server's Missing Link," *Var Business*, February 1997.

Grygo, Eugene M. "Find the Application (Then Manage It)," *Client/Server Computing*, December 1996.

Sobel, Ken. "Navigating the Application Hype," *Hurwitz Balanced View*. 1996.

Sobel, Ken. "Creating an Applications Management Strategy," *Hurwitz Balanced View Research Bulletin*, Oct. 24, 1996.

Dravis, Paul J. *The Systems Management Challenge*, Robertson Stephens & Co. Institutional Research, Dec. 10, 1996.

Interviews with Bill Yaman, Barry Ader, David Caddis and Carl Kotalik of Candle Corp., February–April, 1997.

Section IV
Data Access in a Heterogeneous Environment

Section IV covers one of the important facets of heterogeneous computing—accessing data from different environments. Most of the data resides in databases under the control of database-management systems and this section addresses the methods of accessing data from different DBMSs. This section also looks at accessing data that reside in files, and the conversion of data from files to a database.

Most of corporate data is stored and accessed by three database products—Oracle, Informix, and DB2. A key factor for the success of the database products is the availability of a standard language to access the data—SQL, although variations of SQL have been implemented by most commercial relational DBMS vendors. Chapter 22 evaluates four relational DBMSs (DB2.2, Ingres 6.3, Oracle 7.0 and Sybase 5.0) to examine SQL extensions for data integrity enforcement and SQL extensions and tools for data manipulation. Nine specific features are reviewed—data types, referential integrity constraints, triggers, rules, updates, views, outer joins, embedded SQL, and application tools. In addition, this chapter also compares all nine attributes using a multiattribute utility analysis (MAUA).

Chapter 23 provides an overview of the capabilities of various software components of distributed DBMSs that enable database administrators to choose a software architecture that supports the features they want. The key features of distributed database-management systems include location and replication transparency, DBMS transparency, and multisite update capability.

In today's business environment, users may be scattered across the globe and still need to access database information at their home enterprise or headquarters. To complicate matters, users access database information from a variety of computing platforms, including Windows, Macintosh, and Unix. It is important that users be able to access database information from their chosen platform in a consistent fashion. By publishing information on the Web, an organization can facilitate employees' access to enterprise databases from anywhere in the world. Chapter 24 explains how to publish databases on the Web and the methods by which users can query them.

Quite often there is a need in heterogeneous environments to access a file server or a networked printer in one environment from a client in another environment. Exhibit 1 summarizes the issues, approaches available to address heterogeneous file and print access, and the chapter reference in the book where you will find more information.

Exhibit 1. Issues, approaches, and products for network file and print access.

Network File and Print Access		
Issue	**Approach**	**Products**
Access Windows NT server files from Unix desktops	Use built-in file access support such as ftp or use network operating systems or NFS client software on the Windows NT desktop	Windows NT (ftp server), PC-NFS, PATHWORKS, Access NFS, Chameleon NFS, NFS Maestro, InterDrive, Reflection
Access Unix server files from NT desktops	Use built-in file access support such as ftp or use network operating systems or NFS client software on the Windows NT desktop	Windows NT (ftp, tftp, rcp) PATHWORKS PC-NFS, Access NFS, Chameleon NFS, NFS Maestro, InterDrive, Reflection
Print from Windows NT desktops to Unix controlled printers	Use built-in functions in Windows NT	Windows NT, Unix operating systems
Print from Unix desktops to Windows NT controlled printers	Use *lpr* in Unix clients and use *lpdsvc* in Windows NT	Windows NT, Unix operating systems

Networked file and print access between Windows and NetWare is relatively easy due to the software support provided by Microsoft and Novell and is covered later in the handbook. Chapter 25 covers the different ways in which file accesses can occur between Unix and Windows NT environments, including NFS, the method most common in the Unix world.

There are two aspects to the object-oriented approach to integrating heterogeneous database systems. In one, an object-oriented data model could be used as a generic representation scheme so that the schema transformations between the different database systems could be facilitated. In the other aspect, a distributed object-management system could be used to interconnect heterogeneous database systems. Chapter 26 explores the distributed object-management system approach to addressing interoperability and heterogeneity issues among different database systems by focusing on a specific distributed object-management system—the object management group's (OMG) Common Object Request Broker Architecture (CORBA).

Many organizations do not want to migrate data from one database to another. Instead, they want access to the data maintained by several databases. One approach to accessing data from many databases would be to install a federated database system, which is a special type of distributed database-management system (DDBMS) that does not have the overhead or all of the functions of a full-featured DDBMS. Chapters 27 and 28 cover all aspects of the federated database system approach including a mobile federation.

Another approach that helps in the heterogeneous database interoperability and data access problem is the use of database gateway software. Chapter 29 covers methods for choosing and implementing database gateway software.

It is very difficult not to duplicate data in some form when an organization has multiple databases. Consistency problems arise when data in one database is updated while the same data in another database is not. One method to solve this problem is through a functional bridge that brings transactions from one database to another so that there is a single update path for all data items. Chapter 30 covers, step by step, the planning and design decisions related to the communications infrastructure and the designation of the database master.

Finally, many organizations are looking at the capabilities and advantages of object-oriented databases and how to integrate an OODBMS with the relational databases they already have. Sensing this need, all of the top database-management-system (DBMS) vendors have introduced products that wed relational DBMS and object-oriented DBMS features, and these are typically termed object-relational databases. An object-relational DBMS not only manages diverse data but also allows users to perform integrated content searches. Chapter 31 covers the anatomy of IBM's object-relational database server.

Finally, almost all organizations go through the process of migrating their data from files to databases controlled by DBMSs for the many advantages they provide such as automatic backup and recovery, transaction processing, business rule enforcement, easy query formulation, and application generation. Chapter 32 provides guidelines to determine when and how to migrate files and associated applications to an RDBMS.

Chapter 22
Equivalent Features of DB2, Oracle, Sybase, and Ingres

Noelle Mesick
Il-Yeol Song

Relational database management systems (DBMSs) represent the core of modern information processing. Data processing services provided by relational DBMSs are essential to many daily routines now taken for granted in the modern world. Relational DBMSs' unique combination of power and flexibility has promoted their use in numerous applications in business, education, and industry. A key factor in the success of relational DBMSs is the implementation of a standard query language (SQL).

Variations of SQL have been implemented by most commercial relational DBMS vendors, and SQL has become the standard query language for relational DBMSs with standards supported by both theAmerican National Standards Institute (ANSI) and the International Standards Organization (ISO).

SQL extensions and application tools are explored in four different relational DBMSs that implement SQL as a query language—DB2 2.2, Ingres 6.3, Oracle 7.0, and Sybase 5.0. Another popular system, Informix, was not included in the study because adequate information about it was not obtained. Each of the four systems investigated possessed separately implemented extensions of SQL that add procedural language capabilities to the query language (e.g., loop structures). DB2 offers Dynamic SQL for applications programming. Ingres' extended SQL language is appropriately titled Ingres/SQL. Procedure Language/SQL (PL/SQL) adds procedural extensions to basic Oracle SQL. Sybase implements an enhanced version of SQL called Transact-SQL that increases the procedural programming power of SQL far more dramatically than any other system investigated. Transact-SQL practically eliminates the need for a procedural programming

0-8493-9989-0/99/$0.00+$.50

language. For this reason, Sybase is not a major implementor of embedded SQL. Currently, Transact-SQL can only be embedded in C, COBOL, and FORTRAN programming languages.

Two categories of SQL extension for relational DBMSs were analyzed—data integrity and data manipulation. The categories were further broken down into the nine investigated attributes: data types, referential integrity constraints, triggers, rules, updates, views, outer joins, application tools, and embedded SQL. The first six attributes are examined in this chapter.

DATA INTEGRITY

Three forms of integrity should be maintained in a relational DBMS—entity integrity, semantic integrity, and referential integrity. Entity integrity constraints must specify that primary key values cannot be null. The investigated relational DBMSs each support entity integrity by using a combination of UNIQUE and NOT NULL field specifiers for primary keys.

Semantic integrity is achieved when data has the proper form or range of values (e.g., a semantic integrity constraint would not allow a user to enter February 31 as a date; a semantic integrity constraint may specify that hours worked should never exceed 40). Standard SQL does not directly support semantic integrity constraints, however, these constraints are somewhat defined by data types and can be enforced with rules and triggers.

Referential integrity may perhaps be the most important integrity constraint for a relational database. Referential integrity constraints enforce consistency among tables by specifying constraints on relations between tables. For any set of related tables, the foreign key must exist as a primary key in a table in the related set. Referential integrity constraints are stored in the data dictionary. They can be defined with SQL statements, but they are often enforced with triggers.

Extended Data Types

Data types are evaluated as part of the semantic integrity category because they provide some basic semantic constraints. They do this by associating a fixed set of properties or constraints with a value. Data types also restrict the range of values that may be contained in a column or field. For this reason, certain extended data types can prove to be extremely valuable. Data type extensions include data types that represent money, date and time, as well as multimedia data types that hold images, bits, and large amounts of text. Exhibit 1 contains a comprehensive list of the data types offered by the relational DBMSs evaluated.

Exhibit 1. System data types.

Data Type	DB2	Ingres	Oracle	Sybase
BINARY	--	-	--	--
BOOLEAN	-	-	--	--
CHRACHER	--	--	--	--
DATE	--	--	--	--
DECIMAL	--	-	--	-
DOUBLE PRECISION	-	-	--	-
FLOAT	--	--	--	--
GRAPHIC	--	-	--	--
IMAGE	-	-	-	--
INTEGER	--	--	--	--
LONG	-	-	--	-
MONEY	-	--	-	--
NUMBER	-	-	--	-
REAL	-	-	--	-
ROWID	-	-	--	-
SMALLDATETIME	-	-	-	--
SMASLLINT	--	--	--	--
SMALLMONEY	-	-	-	--
SYSNAME	-	-	-	--
TEXT	-	--	--	--
TIME	--	-	-	--
TIMESTAMP	--	-	-	--
TINYINT	-	--	-	--
USER DEFINED	-	--	-	--
VARCHAR	--	--	--	--
VARGRAPHIC	--	-	--	--

Note: GRAPHIC and VARGRAPHIC data types are expressed in Sybase as BINARY and VARBINARY, respectively, and are represented in Oracle by RAW and LONG RAW respectively. Boolean is represented by BIT in Sybase.

User-Defined Data Types

DB2 and ORACLE do not offer user-defined data types. Sybase offers this feature through SQL Server's Transact-SQL, however, and Ingres supports user-defined data types through its object management extensions (OME). OME is a nonSQL extension, but it can be used by Ingres programmers to define data types that can be directly used in SQL commands.

In Sybase, user-defined data types are designed in terms of system data types. Rules and defaults can be associated with user-defined data types, giving them even more integrity and power. The system procedure sp-addtype is used to create user data types. Its parameters are the name of the user data type being created, the SQL server-supplied data type from which it is being built, a length (if one is required for SQL server data type), and an optional NULL or NOT NULLspecification (NOT NULL is the default). The syntax for sp-addtype is as follows: sp_addtype typename, phystype[(length)] [,nulltype]. To delete a user-defined data type, sp_droptype is executed as follows: sp-droptype typename.

REFERENTIAL INTEGRITY CONSTRAINTS

Referential integrity constraints are implicit and must be specified with the data definition language (DDL) during schema definition. To preserve referential integrity in a database system, primary and foreign key values in related tables must match exactly. The following sections evaluate the four relational DBMSs with respect to referential integrity constraints.

DB2

Referential integrity is maintained in DB2 by the declaration of primary keys and foreign keys. Foreign keys can be defined when the base table is created by using CREATE TABLE. They may also be added to an existing table by using ALTER TABLE. Indexes are not required for foreign keys, however, they enhance performance of a primary key-to-foreign key join as well as foreign key searches. The syntax of a DB2 foreign key definition is as follows:

```
FOREIGN KEY [ foreign-key ] ( column [, column ] ...)
    REFERENCES  base-table  [  ON  DELETE  effect  ]
```

When defined in the CREATE TABLE statement, enforcement of primary key and foreign key values is automatically performed by the DB2 database manager. The foreign key clause of a dependent table references the primary key of a parent table. Each specification in the FOREIGN KEY clause defines a referential constraint with an optionally specified constraint name.

In DB2, referential integrity possesses three rules: insert, update, and delete. The INSERT RULE is not explicitly specified on the foreign key. It states that if a row is inserted into a detail table, its foreign key value must be either NULL (if NULLS are permitted for the columns in the foreign key), or the foreign key value must be equal to a value of the corresponding primary key in its related master table.

The UPDATE RULE is not completely implemented in DB2. This rule is specified for each foreign key defined in a table. The UPDATE RULE implies the RESTRICT option, which states that the primary key value of a row of a parent table cannot be updated if rows of the dependent tables exist with a foreign key value equal to the primary key value in this row.

DB2's DELETE RULE is determined by theON DELETE clause. The delete rule specifies the constraints to be met when a row in a parent table is deleted. Three options are available for this constraint—the RESTRICT option, the CASCADE option, and the SET NULL option.

The RESTRICT options will not allow a row of a parent table to be deleted if rows exist in a dependent table with no foreign key values equal to the primary key value of this row. The CASCADE option specifies that if a row of a parent table is deleted, all rows in the dependent tables with a foreign key value equal to the primary key value of this row will also be deleted. If any of the deletes fail, the entire delete operation fails. The SET NULL option stipulates that if a row of a parent table is deleted, all rows in the dependent tables with a foreign key value equal to the primary key value of this row will have their foreign key changed to null.

An example of a DB2 primary key and foreign key definition in a CREATE TABLE statement is as follows:

```
CREATE TABLE SP
      ( S# CHAR (5) NOT NULL)
      ( P# CHAR (6) NOT NULL)
      QTY            INTEGER,
      PRIMARY KEY (S#, P#),
      FOREIGN KEY SFK (S#) REFERENCES S
                        ON DELETE CASCADE,
      FOREIGN KEY PFK (P#) REFERENCES P
                        ON DELETE RESTRICT
```

Ingres

Ingres uses the DDL command, CREATE INTEGRITY, to define integrity constraints for a table. Its syntax is as follows:

CREATE INTEGRITY on table IS search condition

where table is the name of the table for which the integrity constraint applies, and search condition is a condition that is true for each row existing in the table when the integrity constraint is issued. The search condition can contain any tables other than the one specified in the ON clause, and cannot contain a subselect or any set functions.

The DROP INTEGRITYcommand is used to delete a definition of an integrity constraint. Its syntax is as follows:

```
DROP INTEGRITY ON (table integer [, integer] ...)

        OR

DROP INTEGRITY ON table ALL
```

where integer identifies the constraint to be deleted. If all constraints should be deleted, ALL is used instead of integer.

Ingres also uses triggers to maintain referential integrity. Triggers can be created with the knowledge management extension (KME) of Ingres' intelligent DBMS. Triggers help to maintain referential integrity by monitoring update operations, and executing alternative actions when referential integrity is violated during an INSERT, DELETE, or UPDATE operation.

Oracle

The definition and enforcement of referential integrity constraints is supported by Oracle's latest version, Oracle 7.0. Oracle defines referential integrity in the same statement that defines a table or a view (i.e., CREATE TABLE and CREATE VIEW statements), and stores integrity constraints in the data dictionary. Referential integrity constraints are enforced directly by the data dictionary, wherever and whenever primary keys and foreign keys are defined.

The foreign key is the mechanism for supporting referential integrity. Oracle uses a constraint clause to restrict the range of acceptable values for a foreign key. All INSERT, UPDATE, and DELETE statements cause constraint clauses to be evaluated. For the statement to succeed, all relevant constraints must be satisfied.

Constraint clauses are defined in Oracle's column-element or the table-constraint of CREATE TABLE and ALTER TABLE statements. A column constraint is associated with a single column. A table constraint is associated with at least one column.

Oracle's constraints may take any of five forms. The NOT NULL constraint will not allow a column to contain a null value. This restriction can only be used in columns, not tables. The UNIQUE constraint specifies that a column or columns may not contain duplicate values. Indexes are used to enforce the UNIQUE constraint.

The PRIMARY KEY constraint stipulates that a column or columns compose the primary key and cannot contain duplicate values.PRIMARY KEY implies UNIQUE, but UNIQUE does not imply PRIMARY KEY.A table can only have one primary key, but it can have multiple UNIQUE columns. PRIMARY KEY also implies NOT NULL.

The FOREIGN KEY constraint labels a column or columns as composing a foreign key. Foreign key columns must have a matching primary key value in a corresponding table. Finally, the CHECK constraint stipulates that a row must satisfy the expression defined by the CHECKconstraint before a row is inserted or updated.

The syntax for referential integrity constraint clauses in Oracle is as follows:

Table Constraint

```
[{UNIQUE [Verbar] PRIMARY KEY} (column [, column] ...)
    [CONSTRAINT constraint] ]
[FOREIGN KEY (column [, column] ... )
    primary_key_name [user.]table [(column
              [,column]...)]
    [CONSTRAINT constraint] ]
[CHECK (condition) [CONSTRAINT constraint] ]
```

Column Constraint

```
Column [NULL] [Verbar] [NOT NULL [CONSTRAINT
              constraint] ]
[{UNIQUE [Verbar] PRIMARY KEY} [CONSTRAINT
              constraint] ]
[primary_key_name [user.] table (column [,column]
              ...)]
    [CONSTRAINT [constraint] ]
[CHECK (condition) [CONSTANT constraint] ]
```

Column specifies the name of the column to which the constraint should apply, and constraint specifies the name of the constraint. When Oracle's WITH CHECK OPTIONclause is used in the CREATE VIEW statement, additional forms of referential integrity are supported because the WITH CHECK OPTION prevents the insertion of a new row (with a new foreign key) into a view, unless the same value exists as a primary key value in the base table.

Sybase

In Sybase, referential integrity is coordinated through the use of primary and foreign key definition and triggers. The sp-primary key system procedure may be used to identify a primary key. This system procedure automatically enforces uniqueness (entity integrity). Sybase also provides standard SQL syntax for primary key definition by permitting primary keys to be defined in CREATE TABLE and ALTER TABLE statements. When primary keys are created using this standard SQL method, a UNIQUE index for the primary key is automatically created. NOT NULL must be declared explicitly for primary key columns. Beginning with release 5.0, Sybase provides support for uniqueness constraints, referential constraints, and check constraints.

Like primary keys, foreign keys may be specified with the sp-foreign key system procedure, and they may be specified using standard SQL foreign key definitions in CREATE TABLE and ALTER TABLE statements. Indexes are not required for foreign keys, but they are recommended.

ON DELETE and ON UPDATE restrictions are assumed for foreign keys. They are used to enforce referential integrity. The ON DELETE rule specifies that when a record in the referenced table with a certain primary key value is deleted, all rows in foreign key tables with a foreign key value equal to that primary key will automatically be deleted. The ON UPDATE rule specifies that a row in the referenced table with a given primary key value can only be updated to have a different primary key value if there are no rows with a foreign key value equal to the initial primary key value.

In addition to primary and foreign key definition, Sybase provides triggers to maintain referential integrity. When an INSERT, UPDATE, or DELETE statement affects a key column, triggers compare the new column values with related keys by using temporary work tables called trigger test tables. When triggers are written, comparisons are made based on the data temporarily stored in trigger test tables.

The deleted table and the inserted table are two trigger test tables used in trigger statements. These tables test the effects of data modification and set conditions for trigger actions. The data in the trigger test tables cannot be altered directly, but it can be used in SELECT statements to detect the effects of an INSERT, UPDATE, orDELETE.

Characteristics of the trigger test tables are as follows. The deleted table stores copies of the rows affected by DELETE and UPDATE statements. Usually, the deleted table and the resultant trigger table have no rows in common. The inserted table stores copies of the rows affected by INSERT and UPDATE statements. The rows inserted are copies of the new rows in the resultant trigger table. An UPDATE is essentially a DELETE followed by an INSERT. If a trigger is involved with an update operation, the deleted rows are copied to the deleted table, the inserted rows are placed in the resultant trigger table and are also copied to the inserted table.

When a new foreign key is inserted, the foreign key must match a primary key. A trigger checks integrity by establishing joins between the inserted rows in the primary key table, and rolls back any inserts of foreign keys that do not match a primary key value in the primary key table.

When a primary key is deleted, corresponding foreign key rows in related tables are deleted with a trigger that performs a cascading delete. This preserves referential integrity by ensuring that foreign key rows are removed when their primary key row is deleted. If this were not performed, foreign key rows could not be retrieved or identified and referential integrity would be lost.

TRIGGERS AND RULES

Triggers are stored procedures that are executed when an INSERT, DELETE, or UPDATE command is invoked. Triggers assist in the maintenance of referential integrity by preserving consistency among the logically related data located in different tables. Triggers possess this capacity because they are stored in one place—the data dictionary. They are automatically executed in specific response to at least one data manipulation language (DML) statement (e.g.,INSERT, UPDATE, or DELETE). Triggers are special because they not only detect integrity violations, but they also specify actions to be taken when violations are encountered.

Rules are integrity constraints that augment constraints suggested by a column's data type. They can be connected to one or more columns as well as to user-defined data types and are quite useful for enforcing semantic integrity. The following sections evaluate the four relational DBMSs with respect to triggers and rules.

DB2 (Rules)

DB2 applies rules to its tables by way of a nonSQL application development tool called application development facility (ADF). These rules direct the execution of the main application program and determine which modules are to be used and how they are to be executed.

Rules consist of static rules and dynamic rules. Static rules reference to the data dictionary and help to maintain the database definition as well as referential integrity constraints on related tables. Dynamic rules are used to specify things such as semantic integrity constraints on data types or specific attributes (columns).

Although these rules provide an enforcement mechanism for referential integrity and semantic integrity, this enforcement is not provided directly through SQL, and therefore cannot be considered an integral part of DB2. Unfortunately, not all DB2 programmers have access to the ADF.

Ingres (Triggers)

Ingres' intelligent DBMS includes KMEs that permit the creation of triggers. Triggers are created using Ingres's own OSL language rather than SQL. Ingres triggers are similar to those offered by Sybase, but Ingres permits multiple triggers for each data manipulation operation (e.g., INSERT, UPDATE, or DELETE) in each table, whereas Sybase permits only one trigger for each update operation per database.

Oracle (Triggers)

Triggers are available in Oracle by way of SQL*Forms. SQL*Forms is a nonprocedural tool for creating, maintaining, and executing forms-based, interactive applications for an Oracle database. Oracle's triggers not only fire when INSERT, UPDATE, and DELETE operations are invoked, they also fire for COMMIT, LOCK, ROLLBACK, VALIDATE, FETCH, and SELECT operations, as well as when entering or leaving a specified field or record, and before and after query execution.

Oracle's SQL*Forms triggers are like a combination of Sybase's rules and triggers because they can be stored in the data dictionary and can also be attached to an object in SQL*Forms. Although Oracle's triggers are somewhat more versatile than those implemented by Ingres and Sybase, they do not provide the same stability and integrity because they are attached at different object levels and executed in accordance with those levels. Ingres and Sybase triggers are always located at the same level—the data dictionary—and thus maintain consistent priority and ease of execution.

Sybase (Triggers and Rules)

In Sybase, both triggers and rules are considered to be database objects. Sybase's SQL Server verifies rule compliance with each INSERT or UPDATE statement. Rules can be created only for the current database. In addition, rule names must be unique for each database user. Syntax for rule creation is as follows:

```
CREATE RULE rule_name
as condition_expression
```

The AS clause defines the argument of the rule. A rule definition can include arithmetic operators and comparison operators, and it can contain any expression that is valid in a WHERE clause. Database objects cannot be directly referenced, however, in a rule definition.

The system procedure sp-bindrule binds a rule to a column or user-defined data type. Its syntax is as follows:

```
sp_bindrule rule_name, object_name [, futureonly]
```

Futureonly is used solely for user-defined data types. This specification prevents existing columns of the data type from inheriting the rule.

A rule cannot bind to columns of TEXT, IMAGE, or TIMESTAMP data types. Rules also cannot be directly bound to system data types. Rules bound to columns always take precedence over rules bound to data types. Unbinding a rule requires the use of the system procedure sp-unbindrule, or the replacement of the old rule by using the system procedure sp-bindrule to bind a new rule to the specific column or data type. To completely delete a rule from a database, the DROP RULEcommand is used. Its syntax is as follows: DROP RULE rule_name.

Sybase provides triggers for enforcing database-specific rules and referential integrity constraints. Triggers are associated with specific tables and cannot be manually invoked. Instead, triggers are automatically executed only once per SQL statement, after completion of a triggering statement (an INSERT, DELETE or UPDATE command). A trigger can compare the state of a table before and after data manipulation, and take actions based on the comparison.

Restrictions enforced by triggers are more complex than those stipulated with rules because triggers can be placed on both columns and database objects (e.g., tables or other triggers). A trigger is created by specifying the table and the data manipulation commands that cause the trigger to fire. CREATE TRIGGER syntax is as follows:

```
CREATE TRIGGER [owner.]trigger_name

on [owner.]table_name

{ FOR {INSERT, UPDATE, DELETE}

    AS

    SQL_statements [Verbar]

    FOR {INSERT, UPDATE}

    AS

    IF UPDATE (column_name)
```

```
    [{AND  [Verbar]  OR}  UPDATE  (column-name)]  ...
    SQL_statements  }
```

The CREATE clause creates and names the trigger. The ON clause identifies the table that activates the trigger, called the trigger table. Although a trigger is created in the current database, it also can reference objects in other databases. The FOR clause specifies which data manipulation statements activate the trigger.

SQL statements are usesd to specify trigger conditions and actions. Multiple trigger actions in an IF clause must be grouped withBEGINand END blocks. An IF UPDATEclause tests for an insert or update to a specified column. IF UPDATE cannot be used withDELETE. More than one column can be specified. The syntax is as follows:

```
CREATE  TRIGGER  trigger_name
FOR  {INSERT,  UPDATE}
AS  IF  UPDATE  (column  name)
[{AND  OR}  UPDATE  (column-name)]  ...
    SQL-statements
```

Because triggers are executed as part of a transaction, the following statements are not permitted when defining a trigger in Sybase:

- All CREATE commands (other thanCREATE TRIGGER)
- All DROP commands
- ALTER TABLE and ALTER DATABASE
- TRUNCATE TABLE
- GRANT and REVOKE
- UPDATE STATISTICS
- RECONFIGURE
- LOAD DATABASE and LOAD TRANsaction
- All DISK commands
- SELECT INTO (because it creates a table).

Further restrictions on Sybase's triggers are as follows:

- A table can have a maximum of three triggers—oneUPDATE, one INSERT, and one DELETE.
- Each trigger can apply to only one table. However, a single trigger may apply to all three user actions (i.e.,UPDATE, INSERT, or DELETE).
- Triggers cannot be created on views or temporary objects; however, they can reference views and temporary objects.
- An explicit NULL or a default assigns a value to a column, and thus activates the trigger, however, an implicit NULL does not.

- When triggers defined with ROLLBACK TRANsaction statements are executed from a batch or a user-defined transaction, the entire batch is aborted.
- Nested triggers are not recommended for an order-dependent sequence. Separate triggers should be used to cascade data manipulations.
- Although a trigger can call another trigger; it cannot call itself recursively.
- If the name of an object referenced by a trigger is changed, the trigger must be deleted and recreated, so its definition reflects the new name of the objects it references.

In Sybase, triggers can nest to a depth of 16 levels. If nested triggers are enabled, a trigger that fires on a table containing another trigger also fires the trigger associated with that table, which can in turn fire a third trigger. If a trigger activates an infinite loop, the maximum nesting level of 16 is exceeded, and the trigger aborts.

DATA MANIPULATION (UPDATES AND VIEWS)

Manipulating a database includes such functions as querying the database, updating the database, and generating views and reports. Typical manipulations are conducted with a DML such as SQL. More-extensive manipulations can be performed with embedded DMLs and application tools.

Updates. Update operations consist of three statements—INSERT, UPDATE, and DELETE. Update statements operate on both base tables and views, however, not all views are updatable. For instance, in standard SQL, a view cannot be updated if its definition involves an aggregate function or if the updated columns are not from the same base table.

Definitions for INSERT, UPDATE, andDELETE operations are standard for the four databases investigated, and their syntax is as follows:

The INSERT statement has the general form:

```
INSERT
INTO        table [ ( field [, field ] ...) ]
VALUES   (            constant [, constant ] ...);
          OR
INSERT
INTO  table  [  (  field  [,  field  ]  ...)  ]
subquery;
```

In the first format, a row that has the specified values for specified fields is inserted into the table, NULL is permissible as a constant. In the second format, the subquery is invoked, and a copy of the resulting set of rows is inserted into the table. In both formats, omitting the list of fields is the same as specifying a list of all fields in the table.

The UPDATE statement has the general form:

```
UPDATE  table
SET        field  =  expression
        [, field  =  expression  ]  ...
[ WHERE  predicate  ];
```

All records that satisfy the predicate condition are updated according to the expression in the SET clause.NULL is considered to be a legal expression, however, no other aggregate functions are permitted as expressions.

The DELETE statement has the general form:

```
DELETE
FROM          table
[ WHERE    predicate  ];
```

All records in the table that satisfy the predicate are deleted. If no predicate is specified, all records in the table are deleted.

Views. A view is an alternative way of looking at the data in one or more tables. It is derived from tables that are physically stored in the database, called base tables. A view can also be derived from another view. The definition of a view is stored in the data dictionary, however, no separate copies of data are associated with this stored definition. Viewed data remains stored in the base tables.

Views provide a security mechanism, and they provide partial logical data independence by shielding database users from changes in the underlying base tables. Logical independence is partial because not all data manipulation commands can be performed on views.

The syntax for view creation is standard for the four relational DBMSs surveyed. It is as follows:

```
CREATE VIEW view [ ( column [, column ] ...)]
    AS SELECT subquery
    [ WITH CHECK OPTION ];
```

The CREATE VIEW statement is often considered to be a part of SQL's DML rather than its DDL because views can only be completed using a SELECT command, which is a DML function. When a view is created, the subquery following the AS SELECT is not executed; instead, it is saved in the data dictionary under the specified view name. The clause WITH CHECK OPTION indicates that UPDATE and INSERT operations against the view are to be checked to ensure that the updated or inserted row satisfies the view-defining predicate.

The standard syntax to delete a view is:

```
DROP VIEW view ;
```

When a view is dropped, any views defined in terms of that view are dropped as well. If a base table is dropped, all views defined on that base table are automatically dropped.

When the data seen through a view is modified, the data in the base tables is actually changed. Conversely, changes to the data in the base tables tend not to be automatically reflected in the views derived from them. For this reason, there are typically many restrictions on updates to views. The following sections evaluate the four relational DBMSs with respect to updates and views.

DB2

There are a few update restrictions placed on DB2 tables: If the WHERE clause in UPDATE or DELETE includes a subquery, the FROM clause in that subquery must not refer to the table that is involved in that UPDATE or DELETE. In the subquery form of INSERT (INSERT ... SELECT), the FROM clause in that subquery cannot refer to the table that is involved in the INSERT. In addition, the subquery defining the view cannot include either UNION or ORDER BY, however, these statements can be used to retrieve a view. Aside from these restrictions, any SELECT that can appear as a standalone statement can also appear in a CREATE VIEW statement.

Retrieval operations on a DB2 view are converted into equivalent operations on the underlying base tables. Problems can arise when a field in a view is treated as a conventional field and that view field is derived from something other than a simple field of the underlying base table (e.g., if it is derived from a function). Predicates in a WHERE clause are not allowed to refer to aggregate functions. DB2 has always been weak in this area.

In DB2, only row-and-column-subset views can be updated. DB2's view updating mechanism does not operate in terms of key preservation (referential integrity). Instead it operates in terms of views that are derived from single base tables by simply eliminating certain rows and certain columns of that table. Other restrictions DB2 places on views are as follows:

If a field of the view is derived from a constant or an expression that involves a scaler operator, INSERT operations are not allowed, and UPDATE operations are not allowed on that column, but DELETE operations are allowed, and UPDATE operations are permitted on other columns.

- If a field of the view is derived from an aggregate function, the view cannot be updated.
- If the definition of the view includes a GROUP BY or HAVING clause, the view cannot be updated.
- If the definition of the view involves DISTINCT, the view cannot be updated.
- If the WHERE clause in the view definition includes a subquery and the FROM clause in that subquery refers to the view's base table, the view cannot be updated.
- If the FROM clause in the view definition involves multiple range variables, the view cannot be updated.
- If a view is defined with a nonupdatable view, it is not updatable.

Ingres

Ingres allows the use of any valid SQL query in a CREATE VIEW command, except the clauses ORDER BY, FOR UPDATE OF, and UNION. In Ingres, INSERT, UPDATE, and DELETE operations cannot be performed on a view if it was created from more than one table, if it was created from a non-updatable view, or if any columns in the view are derived from an aggregate function.

UPDATE and DELETE operations (but not INSERT operations) can be performed on a view if its definition contains a WHERE clause and specifies the WITH CHECK OPTION, or if any column in the base tables was declared as NOT NULL NOT DEFAULT and is not present in the view. Ingres also provides triggers that cascade updates in the same manner as Sybase's triggers. Triggers are placed on the primary and foreign key columns of a table, so if a key value is updated, the same updates are made to rows in logically related tables containing the key value.

Oracle

In Oracle, if a subquery refers to columns from the table being updated, Oracle will evaluate the subquery once for each row, rather than once for the entire update. This type of update is called a correlated update. The reference to columns from the table being updated is usually accomplished by means of a table alias. Each row evaluated by the UPDATE statement could potentially be updated with a different value as determined by the correlated subquery. Normal update statements will update each row with the same value. Oracle permits the defining query to be any valid SELECT statement without the use of ORDER BY and FOR UPDATE clauses.

Oracle permits a view to be used in a SQL statement anywhere a table may be used (e.g., INSERT, UPDATE, DELETE, or SELECT) with the restriction that views may be used in SELECT statements only if a join, a GROUP BY, CONNECT BY, or START WITH clause, or the DISTINCT clause, pseudo-columns or expressions are contained in the view query's column list. Oracle permits updates on views with pseudo-columns (columns that are not actually in the table, for example, ROWID) and expressions, as long as the update statement does not refer to any of the pseudo-columns or expressions of the view.

Sybase

In Sybase, triggers provide cascade updates. Triggers are placed on the key columns of a given table, so when a key value is modified with an INSERT, DELETE, or UPDATE command, the same modifications are made to rows in logically related tables containing that key value.

Transact-SQL has been enhanced so that there are no restrictions at all on querying through views, and fewer than usual on modifying them. It is possible to build indexes on views, build views on other views, and create procedures that reference views. It is also possible to define primary, foreign, and common keys on views. However, it is impossible to define rules, defaults, or triggers for a view. Temporary views cannot be created, nor can views be created on temporary tables.

There are a few restrictions on the SELECT statement in a view definition. ORDERBY and COMPUTE clauses, and DISTINCT and INTO keywords cannot be included, and temporary tables cannot be referenced in SELECT statements for view definition.

When data is retrieved through a view, Sybase's SQL Server verifies that all database objects referenced anywhere in the statement exist, and that they are valid in the context of the statement. If the checks are successful, SQL Server combines the statement with the stored definition of the view and translates the statement into a query on the view's base tables. This process is called view resolution. Sybase permits a view to be queried with joins, GROUP BY clauses, subqueries, and other techniques, in any combination. In other systems, special restrictions apply to retrieving data through views defined with built-in functions and GROUP BY clauses.

Although Sybase's SQL Server and Transact-SQL place fewer restrictions on views that most other SQL relational DBMSs, several DML commands are prohibited for views. Prohibited commands are as follows:

- If a column is computed or possesses an aggregate function, UPDATE, INSERT, and DELETE operations are not permitted.
- If a view includes built-in functions and a GROUP BY or COMPUTE BY clause, UPDATE, INSERT, and DELETE operations are not permissible.
- INSERT operations are not permitted on views unless all columns in the base table that have a NOT NULL restriction are included in the view.
- UPDATE and INSERT statements are only allowed if the columns being modified belong to the same base table. A view can contain columns from more than one base table, as long as the UPDATE and INSERT commands only apply to columns from the same table.

Obviously, the evaluated relational DBMSs possess some very different extensions of SQL, and the extensions they offer go beyond the scope of those discussed in this survey. Of the four systems, Sybase provides the most features—however, its overhead can be costly. Ingres's Knowledge and Object Management extensions give it technological superiority, but Ingres is relatively new to the SQL language, having implemented it only a few years ago, therefore most of its capabilities are not SQL extensions but application characteristics instead. Oracle is portable and contains useful applications support for those new to application development, but its new version—which significantly enhances the product—has not been around long enough to fully gain the same respect and confidence attributed to Sybase. DB2 represents an industry standard that maintains the stability of being an IBM product, while it too remains somewhat technologically backward.

OUTER JOINS

Joins are one of the most important concepts in relational databases. Relationships among tables become explicit when tables are joined. A number of joins exist including natural joins, self joins, and outer joins. Outer joins are the most complicated of the three joins, and are not effectively implemented on all SQL relational DBMSs. An outer join is a join between two or more tables that also returns rows from one table that has no direct match in the other table. Outer joins extend the result of a normal join because an outer join returns all the rows returned by the simple join as well as those rows from one table that do not match any rows in the other table. The following sections examine the four relational DBMSs with respect to outer joins.

DB2

DB2 currently offers no simple feature that provides the outer join function. The desired result may be achieved, however, with the UNION ALL statement. For example, two tables exist for a mail-order company. One contains mailing information (e.g., name, address, and custom number), and the other contains order information (e.g., order number, items, and customer number). A list is needed containing combined mailing and order information regardless of whether a person on the mailing has ever placed an order. This can be accomplished with an outer join, which in DB2, would be performed as follows:

```
SELECT  M.*,  O.ITEM.  O.SIZE,  O.PRICE
   FROM  MAIL_TABLE  M,  ORDER_TABLE  O
   WHERE  M.CUST#  =  O.CUST#
UNION  ALL
SELECT M.*, [lsquo ]bb[rsquo ], [lsquo ]bb[rsquo ],
              [lsquo  ]bb[rsquo  ]
   FROM  MAIL_TABLE  M
   WHERE  NOT  EXISTS
       (SELECT  *  FROM  ORDER_TABLE
          WHERE  CUST#  =  M.CUST#)
```

where [lsquo]bb[rsquo] represents blanks.

To retrieve all mailer records, a union is formed between the join and a select statement that selects all records in the employee table not matching any department table records.

To provide union compatibility, blank literal values are placed in the last three columns of the second select statement. These columns correspond to ITEM, SIZE, and PRICE in the result table of the first select statement. The results of this complicated query are the results expected for an outer join. The lack of a simple outer join command is a major weakness of DB2.

Ingres

Ingres uses a nonSQL concept, called JoinDef, to define outer joins. With a JoinDef, it is possible to append new data or update existing data, which will then be written into the common columns of the different tables that make up the JoinDef.

A JoinDef is a form based on a join between two or more tables. It is created by Ingres' Visual-Forms-Editor (VIFRED) and is invoked by query-by-forms (QBF). It forms a link between two or more tables that have at least one column with the same data type and one or more common values in those columns. The two join columns do not have to have the same name. In constructing a JoinDef, it is possible to join a maximum of 10 tables that together total more than 600 columns. A maximum of 50 join columns can be present in a JoinDef. A master-detail JoinDef corresponds to an outer join.

Oracle

Oracle provides outer join capabilities directly through SQL. The operation is accomplished as a SELECT statement clause that combines rows of two or more tables, using a plus sign (+) as the outer join operator. An outer join must contain a WHERE clause with a condition in one of these forms:

```
table 1.column = table2.column(+)

table 1.column (+) = table2.column
```

Extra null columns are temporarily created for the table with the(+) outer join operator. This table is then joined against all rows from the other table that would not have been returned in a normal join. The outer join symbol must follow a column reference within a join condition. Within a single SELECT statement, a table may be involved in an outer join with at most one other table. The syntax is as follows:

```
SELECT ...

    FROM table1, table2 ...

    WHERE table1.column = table2.column (+)
```

Sybase

In addition to Oracle, Sybase also supports the outer join operation by-way-of SQL statements. Its outer join operators are as follows:

```
*= is the operator for a left outer join.

=* is the operator for a right outer join.
```

A left outer join is an outer join that includes all the records from the first table to be specified in the join command. A right outer join is an outer join that includes all the records from the second table to be specified in the join command. Outer join syntax is as follows:

```
SELECT column ([, column] [, column] ...)

    FROM table1, table2

    WHERE table1.column *= table2.column
```

Sybase permits tables to participate in either an outer join clause or a regular join clause, but a table may not participate in both.

EMBEDDED SQL

One of the most important features of standard SQL is the facility to embed SQL statements in high-level programming languages. This provides the means to use well-established structured programming techniques to design applications and to extend flow-of-control features.

Standard SQL defines host language interfaces for COBOL, FORTRAN, Pascal, and PL/I. It also restricts the range of data types accessible from each of those languages. For example, INTEGER data is not accessible from PL/I in standard SQL.

DB2

The programming languages currently supported by DB2 are PL/I, COBOL, FORTRAN, C, APL, BASIC, and Assembler Language. The following characteristics apply:

- Any base tables or views used by the program should be declared by means of a DECLARE statement. This makes the program easy to follow, and helps the precompiler perform syntax checks.
- Embedded SQL statements must be preceded by EXEC SQL. They may be entered anywhere a host language executable statement can exist.
- Embedded SQL may involve data definition facilities(e.g., CREATE TABLE and DECLARE CURSOR), that are purely declarative.
- SQL statements may reference host language variables preceded by colons.
- Host variables that receive values from SQL must have data types compatible with the SQL field definitions. Compatibility is defined very loosely (e.g., character strings of varying length or numeric data of binary or decimal nature are considered compatible).DB2 performs appropriate conversions.
- SQL Communication Area (SQLCA) serves as the common feedback area between the application program and DB2. A status indicator SQLCODE contains a numeric value showing the result of a query.
- No cursor is required for a SQL retrieval query that returns a single tuple, or for UPDATE, DELETE, or INSERT statements.
- A special utility program called declarations generator (DCLGEN) may be used to construct DECLARE TABLE statements automatically in PL/I from the CREATE TABLE definitions in SQL. PL/I or COBOL structures that correspond to the table definitions are also automatically generated.

Ingres

The programming languages currently supported by Ingres are COBOL, Ada, Pascal, FORTRAN, PL/I, C, and Basic. Embedded SQL is precompiled with Ingres' precompiler, ESQLC. The following rules apply:

- The simplest statements to embed are INSERT, UPDATE, and DELETE.
- For the precompiler to recognize a variable, it must be included in an EXEC SQL DECLARE section.
- EXEC SQL INCLUDE statements must be used for files to be recognized by the precompiler.
- SQLCODE is an integer indicator that is positive if an embedded statement succeeds and negative if an embedded statement fails.

Ingres also allows SQL to be embedded in its own forms-runtime-system (FRS) to program forms.

Oracle

Oracle currently supports precompilers for Ada, C, COBOL, FORTRAN, Pascal, and PL/I. The precompilers accept all the standard interactive SQL commands in applications. The only special requirements for SQL statements in the host program is that they must begin with EXEC SQ Land end with the SQL statement terminator specific to the language.

Sybase

Sybase's Transact-SQL increases the power of SQL by reducing the number of occurrences where a procedural programming language must be used. For this reason, Sybase is not a major implementor of embedded SQL. Currently, Sybase's SQL Server supports embedded SQL for C, FORTRAN, and COBOL programming languages.

Embedded SQL statements must be prefixed by EXEC SQL, and must be terminated by a special termination symbol specific to the host language (e.g., a semicolon is used in C). An executable SQL statement can appear wherever an executable host language statement can be located.

Host variables can be used to represent the variable to be retrieved into, the value to be retrieved, compared, assigned, or inserted. References to host variables within the SQL statements must be prefixed by a colon, to distinguish them from column names because host variables and columns can have the same name.

APPLICATION TOOLS

Application tools are an extremely important factor in data manipulation because better applications are able to hide data manipulation from the end-user more easily. They also enable the application programmer to design complex data manipulations with simpler and user-friendly frontends. The following sections evaluate the four relational DBMSs with respect to application tools.

DB2

DB2 has application tools for the end user (e.g., QMF and AS) and application tools for the data processor (e.g., CSP and ADF). Query management facility (QMF) is a query tool for DB2 that allows end users to enter queries in SQL or in query-by-example. QMF also permits the generation of reports and graphs from the results of the queries. It includes an application support interface that allows application programs to use QMF functions.

Application system (AS) provides functions for query, decision support, and application development. Queries can be entered in either SQL or AS's own language. Query results can be formatted into reports or graphs. AS decision support and business functions include project management, statistical analysis, financial planning, and text processing functions. AS has more powerful capabilities than those found in QMF, but AS is less user-friendly.

Some applications may be too complex to be implemented with QMF or AS. Such applications can either be written in a third-generation language (e.g., COBOL, PL/I, or C), or they can be written with application development tools for the data processor—cross system product (CSP) and application development facility (ADF).

Cross system product (CSP) is a complete application development system that provides an integrated environment for screen development, application coding, and application testing and debugging. CSP applications can process data stored in DB2, SQL/DS, and IMS databases. An application can be developed in one environment for execution in another (hence, its name).

Application development facility (ADF) is an application generator that creates IMS and CICS applications using modules and rules defined by the application developer. The modules support screen formatting, data entry and validation, and data processing. The rules determine what modules to be used as well as the databases to be accessed and updated. ADF provides rules for DB2 to enforce integrity constraints.

Ingres

Ingres is a forms-based relational DBMS. Forms-runtime-system (FRS)is a built-in screen management system. It is an interface to all Ingres forms-based capabilities and custom applications using forms. FRS allows the definition of both function and control keys for use with any Ingres forms-based system. Ingres' main menu (RTIngres menu) has menu selections for all Ingres application tools—ABF,VIFRED, QBF, and RBF.

Applications-by-forms (ABF) is an Ingres tool used to create custom applications. An Ingres application uses query languages to access a database. An ABF application can use SQL or QUEL, however, only one language can be defined as the application default language. ABF provides:

- A code manager to keep track of the source code and compile only the source code that has changed.
- An interpreter for a faster test environment.
- An option for testing specific isolated frames and procedures.

By using a call statement, other Ingres subsystems can be invoked from within an application. The most frequently called subsystems are visual-forms-editor (to generate graphs and charts), query-by-forms (to query or maintain database tables), and report -by-forms and report writer (to create reports).

Visual-forms-editor (VIFRED) is a forms-based interface for editing Ingres forms. It creates and edits customized data entry forms through an interactive user interface. Forms can be created for single and joined tables.

Query-by-forms is an interactive, visually oriented, forms-based module used for adding, deleting, changing, and viewing data in a database. QBF has a JoinDef feature that offers the commands for a master-master join that corresponds to an equijoin, and a master-detail join that corresponds to an outer join.

Report-by-forms (RBF) is an interactive, visually oriented system used for creating, designing, modifying and producing reports from data in a database. RBF also offers access to a more advanced report writing system, Report Writer. Report Writer offers a set of tools and procedures that can be used to develop a customized report to meet very complex and sophisticated specifications.

Oracle

SQL*Forms, SQL*Menu and SQL*Report Writer all interface with the Oracle relational DBMS to create applications. They also interface with each other. SQL*Menu allows the programmer to use embedded PL/SQL for procedural logic within the menu system. It includes a library of standard routines that can be invoked from PL/SQL. It can request run-time parameters and pass them to called processes, and it relates closely with SQL*Forms, the two being able to share variables at run time. SQL*Menu has three menu styles: full-page, pull-down, and bar. The menu format is tightly controlled by Oracle. SQL*Menu offers the following:

- Choice of menu display styles (e.g., pull-down, bar style, and full-screen).
- Hierarchical and network menu linking.
- Functions as menu items.

- Run-time substitution of parameter values prompts the operator for information at runtime.
- Execution of user-entered operating system commands.
- Background menus provide excellerator keys for frequently used commands.
- Application security and dynamic menus.
- Integration with SQL*Forms.

SQL*Menu provides users with structured access to Oracle applications; it organizes functions into logical groupings and limits access to functions according to a user's authorization level. SQL*Menu has interfaces with SQL*Forms and SQL*Report Writer, which execute faster than invoking the products from the operating system prompt.

SQL*Forms is Oracle's transaction process generator. It is designed as the primary tool for maintaining database tables in an Oracle application system. SQL*Forms uses PL/SQL to program logic within its triggers. Like SQL*Menu, it comes with a library of packaged procedures invoked from PL/SQL to perform tasks specific to itself.

SQL*Forms can invoke SQL*Menu to present a user with a menu of alternatives within the framework of a form. Although its use is not restricted, SQL*Menu under SQL*Forms serves as a supplement to the function keys as a mechanism for initiating custom processes within a form. SQL*Report Writer can also be invoked through SQL*Forms.

SQL*Report Writer is a system of files and programs that combine report specifications with data from application database tables to produce a report. It is interpretive; a standard runtime module reads the report definition from one compiled table and a description of the printer from another table. It uses the two tables to format data it reads from the application tables. SQL*Report Writer consists of a report definition process, a printer definition process, and a runtime process supported by backup utilities. Reports can be invoked directly from either the menu or from SQL*Forms using a host command.

Sybase

Sybase provides two forms-based applications programming tools called Data Workbench and Applications Productivity Tools (APT) Workbench. Both use a windowed interface similar to that found in Macintosh software.

Data Workbench is a collection of menu-driven forms-based tools for entering and executing SQL statements, generating reports, data entry, and other database utilities. SQL commands can be entered directly through Data Workbench.

Although Data Workbench contains many facilities, the focus here is on its Report Workbench portion. Report Workbench is used to create, edit, and run reports. Reports are defined as a set of report objects and are stored in a database. Definitions are comprised of SQL batches, variables, layouts, breaks, and fields. In addition to SQL, Report Workbench also uses Report Processing Language (RPL) to print, specify page-breaks, repeat headings, and send SQL batch statements to SQL Server for processing.

APT Workbench offers forms-based application generation, editing and execution. It uses a special 4GL called APT-SQL. There are several components of APT Workbench, including APT-Editor, APT-Build, and APT-Execute.

APT-Edit is the primary component of APT Workbench. It provides form definition and editing facilities. Forms can call other forms; parameters can be passed between forms, and both APT-SQL and 3GL processing can occur. In addition, APT-Edit may be used to create reports. APT-Build automatically generates APT applications for the forms created by APT-Edit. APT-Execute runs applications created by APT-Build.

MULTIATTRIBUTE UTILITY ANALYSIS

Now that all attributes have been evaluated, a multiattribute utility analysis (MAUA) can be conducted. A MAUA is a subjective evaluation method described often in software and evaluation literature. It is used to determine the utility of alternatives having more than one valuable attribute. These alternatives must be evaluated on more than one attribute. A MAUA provides a method to combine the utility obtained from each attribute into a single measure of the alternative's overall utility. A MAUA is often used to select appropriate systems during or prior to the requirements analysis phase of system analysis and design, therefore, it represents a reliable measuring tool for relational DBMS evaluation.

This particular MAUA is slightly modified to analyze a feature-based criteria list for the two main investigated categories of DB2, Ingres, Oracle, and Sybase—data integrity and data manipulation. These categories have been broken-down into nine low-level attributes for final evaluation and analysis. This evaluation is relatively subjective and may change with the introduction of new software versions or if more or different features were evaluated.

Scoring

The second step in a MAUA (after attribute identification) is attribute measuring or scoring. Because of the literary rather than hands-on basis of all systems information evaluated, it seems the most appropriate measure for the attributes is a rank from best to worst (1to 4) for each

Exhibit 2. MAUA attribute scores.

Attribute	DB2	Ingres	Oracle	Sybase
Application	4	3	2	1
Tools				
Data Types	3	4	2	1
Embedded SQL	3	2	1	4
Outer Joins	4	3	1	2
Referential Integrity	4	3	2	1
Constraints				
Rules	2	0	0	1
Triggers	0	3	2	1
Updates	4	3	2	1
Views	3	4	2	1

attribute—with a rank of zero (0) meaning that an attribute is not implemented. Attribute rank was solely based on the information gathered in the previous pages. The attributes' scores are listed in Exhibit 2.

The rationale for the ranking format is as follows: Application tools were ranked according to their apparent ease-of-use. Sybase was ranked first for this attribute because of the apparent ease of its application tools' windows-based interface. DB2 ranked last because its application tools are not an integral part of DB2. Instead, they are separate products.

Data types were ranked according to the number of data types available on a system as well as their technological implications. Sybase ranked first because it not only possesses the most data types, but it also employs more multimedia data types, and it offers user-defined data types.

Embedded SQL capabilities were ranked primarily on the types of programming languages offered, secondarily on the restrictions placed on the different implementations of embedded SQL, and tertiarily on the number of programming languages offered. Oracle ranked first for this attribute because although it employs one less programming language than Ingres and DB2, it has few restrictions. Ingres ranked above DB2 because Pascal is a standard embedded SQL language while Assembler is not.

Outer joins were ranked according to SQL defined operators and ease of functional ability. DB2 came in an easy fourth because DB2 has no standard definition for outer joins. Ingres ranked third only because its outer joins are not defined using SQL language. Sybase and Oracle both have SQL outer join operators, however, Sybase appears to have more restriction on outer joins than does Oracle, so Oracle ranked first.

Referential integrity constraints were ranked according to their level of enforcement. DB2's referential integrity constraints are not fully implemented, so DB2 ranked fourth. Because Oracle is new at enforcing referential integrity constraints, they ranked second. Although Ingres is strong in referential integrity enforcement, its integrity constraints are not defined through SQL. Therefore, Ingres ranked third. Sybase ranked first because it provides numerous methods for referential integrity enforcement (both procedural and SQL definition).

Ingres and Oracle do not implement rules, so the contest was between DB2 and Sybase. Sybase ranked first because its rules are a part of its SQL extension (Transact-SQL), while DB2's rules are programmed with an application tool.

Sybase unquestionably ranked first for the triggers attribute because Sybase was the first system to define triggers through SQL extension and does so most reliably. Oracle ranked second because its triggers are not as strong as Sybase triggers, but they are defined with SQL extensions. Ingres triggers ranked third because they do not employ SQL. DB2 does not offer triggers.

Ranking for the updates and views attribute was based on apparent restrictions. Sybase ranked first for both updates and views. Of the four relational DBMSs evaluated, DB2 was the only one to never be ranked first. Sybase's SQL Server has the highest number of first-place ranks. Oracle and Ingres come in second and third respectively.

Utility Functions

The third step in a MAUA is to develop utility functions for each of the nine bottom-line attributes. The purpose of utility functions is to translate attribute scores into similar measurements. Because the attribute scores used in this MAUA are standard for all attributes, utility functions seem redundant. To place more quantitative emphasis on the scores, however, utility functions have been assigned. Utility functions for the nine attributes range from zero (0) to one hundred (100). Conversions from the scores to utility functions are listed in Exhibit 3. The converted attribute functions for each of the four relational DBMSs are listed in Exhibit 4.

Importance Weights

The fourth step in a MAUA is to obtain relative importance weights for both the criteria and the attributes evaluated. The weights determine relative value and permit the comparison of values for different attributes. Relative importance weights for the investigated relational DBMS criteria

Exhibit 3. Conversions from score to utility function.

Score	Utility Function
0	0
1	100
2	75
3	50
4	25

and attributes are listed in Exhibit 5. They were determined based on existing principles and preconceptions concerning relational DBMSs.

Overall Utility Scores

The fifth step in a MAUA is to obtain overall utility scores for criteria and attributes. The following equation is used to calculate utility scores for the attributes: U(a) = w1u(x1) + [hellip] wnu (x(n) where U(a) is the overall utility for a system a, there are n bottom level attributes, each w indicates the cumulative proportional weight on each attribute, and each u(x) is the utility scale value for the system's score on that bottom level attribute.

Overall utility scores placed the relational DBMSs in the following order (best to worst): Sybase, Oracle, Ingres, and DB2 (see Exhibit 6). The MAUA clearly indicates that Sybase provides the most utility among the four SQL relational DBMSs studied. Sybase gains its utility with robust enforcement of data integrity by way of data types, integrity constraints, rules, and triggers. No other system provides all four of the integrity attributes investigated. Sybase also came in second for data manipulation utility. Oracle's second place overall and first place for data manipulation definitely prove

Exhibit 4. Converted attribute functions.

	Utility Functions			
Attribute	**DB2**	**Ingres**	**Oracle**	**Sybase**
Application tools	25	50	75	100
Data types	50	25	75	100
Embedded SQL	50	75	100	25
Outer joins	25	50	100	75
Referential integrity constraints	25	50	75	100
Rules	75	0	0	100
Triggers	0	50	75	100
Updates	25	50	75	100
Views	50	25	75	100

Exhibit 5. Relative importance weights.

	Weight		Weight
Data integrity	0.60	Data Manipulation	0.40
Data types	0.30	Application Tools	0.25
Referential integrity constraints	0.50	Embedded SQL	0.15
		Outer Joins	0.25
Rules	0.05	Updates	0.20
Triggers	0.15	Views	0.15
Total:	1.00		1.00
Note: Weighting is subjective.			

that its latest version has boosted its utility in comparison to its competitors.

Clearly, this MAUA does not begin to explore all of the significant attributes of a relational DBMS. Perhaps results would be different if different attributes were investigated. In any case, it is important to conduct a MAUA or similar evaluation on attributes that are vital to an organization's information system when deciding what relational DBMS to use for system development.

Exhibit 6. Overall utility scores.

	MAUA Results			
Attribute	**DB2**	**Ingres**	**Oracle**	**Sybase**
Data Types	9.00	4.50	13.50	18.00
Referential Integrity Constraints	7.50	15.00	22.50	30.00
Rules	2.25	0.00	0.00	3.00
Triggers	0.00	4.50	6.75	9.00
Data Integrity	**18.75**	**24.00**	**42.75**	**60.00**
Application Tools	2.50	5.00	7.50	10.00
Embedded SQL	3.00	4.50	6.00	1.50
Outer Joins	2.50	5.00	10.00	7.50
Updates	2.00	4.00	6.00	8.00
Views	3.00	1.50	4.50	6.00
Data Manipulation	**13.00**	**20.00**	**34.00**	**33.00**
Overall Utility	31.75	44.00	76.75	93.00

CONCLUSION

Because advancing technology coupled with competition promotes the development of new versions of relational DBMSs at increasingly shorter intervals, it is important to pay careful attention to software versions. To be certain that the most effective DBMS is being used, it is also critical to conduct an evaluation (e.g., a MAUA) of competitive relational DBMS products before a new DBMS is purchased and before development and implementation of a DBMS-using system. For this DBMS MAUA to maintain its accuracy, modifications must be made to accommodate future versions of the investigated DBMSs. It would also be interesting to evaluate different DBMS attributes to see whether MAUA results are similar.

Chapter 23
Distributed Databases

James A. Larson
Carol L. Larson

A client/server architecture consists of several computers connected by a communications system. Some computers act as servers, and some act as clients. A user interacts with a client to formulate requests for information. The requests are transmitted to one or more servers through a communications system for processing. Each server accesses its local database or file system to respond to the request and transmits the results back to the client through the communications system.

Businesses are motivated to use a distributed client/server architecture because it allows them to:

- Save dollars by replacing expensive mainframe hardware with less expensive server hardware. A large cost savings may be realized if mainframe computers are phased out and replaced with servers and desktop computers.
- Leverage the existing investment in personal computers. Users want to be able to access and manipulate data from a mainframe database using the machines sitting on their desktops, as well as analyze and modify mainframe data using their PC applications.
- Replace terminals supporting command-line interfaces with Pcs supporting graphical user interfaces. Many users, especially novice users, can be more productive using graphical user interfaces available on the Pcs than the cryptic, keyboard-oriented user interfaces supported by computer terminals.

In addition, when installing software, systems administrators have the flexibility to upgrade existing clients and servers or to add additional clients and servers. The client/server architecture also allows multiple users to share data by accessing data on a data server through a client.

0-8493-9989-0/99/$0.00+$.50

A distributed database management system (DBMS) lets users access multiple servers and software. The remainder of this article discusses how to choose a distributed DBMS whose software architecture supports the features users need to perform their jobs.

DISTRIBUTED DBMS TECHNOLOGY

Database administrators are responsible for organizing the database so it is accessed efficiently. The database's collection of interrelated records is maintained by a data manager, such as a DBMS or a file system. If data managers exist on several computers, they are interconnected by a communications system. If several data managers share a computer, data is transmitted among them by facilities provided by the local operation system. Both cases are examples of distributed databases because different data managers maintain the data.

Access to Multiple Servers. With more and more essential data being collected and stored on desktop machines, users in many organizations are finding they need to access several microcomputers as well as their organization's mainframe system. Distributed DBMSs enable this accessibility.

A data server provides all of the advantages of centralized databases, allowing users to share up-to-date information managed by the server. Accessing data becomes more difficult for the user when there are multiple data servers. Users must perform the following tasks to access information stored in multiple servers:

- Determine which computers contain the data to be accessed.
- Formulate several queries, which will be executed on a different computer.
- Copy or transfer the results to a single computer for merging.
- Combine and merge the results.
- Extract the answer to the original request from the combined results.

The distributed DBMS assists users in performing these tasks.

FEATURES OF THE DISTRIBUTED DBMS

Three important features available in some distributed DBMSs are location and replication transparency, DBMS transparency, and multisite update capability. The availability of these features depends on the software architecture supported by the distributed DBMS. Database administrators choose the software to support the desired features.

Location and Replication Transparency. This feature supports a type of data independence, which enables the database administrator to change the physical location and replication of data without modifying existing application programs.

A distributed DBMS supports location transparency if the user is not aware of the location or site of the data being accessed. Replication transparency is supported if the user is not aware that more than one copy of the data exists. Although these features provide increased data independence, they may require the use of sophisticated and expensive software optimizers.

DBMS Transparency. DBMS transparency is the second important feature. A distributed DBMS needs DBMS transparency when it contains multiple types of local database managers. For example, a distributed DBMS that interconnects a file system located at one site, a relational DBMS at a second site, and an IMS DBMS at a third site contains three types of local data managers. When a distributed DBMS supports DBMS transparency, the user formulates requests in using structured query language (SQL). A translator, or gateway, transforms each SQL request to the language understood by a participating data manager.

Multisite Update Capability. The third important feature is the ability to update multiple local data abases with a single request. Some distributed DBMSs do not permit updates; users of those types of systems can retrieve data only.

Other distributed DBMSs allow users to update only a single database, disallowing updates that involve data at two or more sites. A few distributed DBMSs allow users to update data in several databases with a single request. These distributed DBMSs require sophisticated distributed concurrency control mechanisms that guarantee that two or more users do not attempt to update the same data simultaneously. They also require distributed commit protocols that allow distributed DBMSs to determine if and when updates to the database are completed. The distributed concurrency control and distributed commitment add to the complexity of the distributed DBMS and to the communications cost and response time of distributed requests.

DISTRIBUTED DBMS COMPONENTS

Exhibit 1 depicts the major software components of a distributed DBMS in a client/server environment. Distributed DBMS products differ in their components, and thus the availability of key features also differs.

Distributed DBMSs that contain a request optimizer support location and replication transparency, whereas distributed DBMSs containing gateways provide DBMS transparency. Distributed DBMSs containing a sophisticated distributed execution manager enable updates across multiple data mangers. The keyword here is sophistication—that is, all distributed DBMSs contain a distributed execution manager to retrieve data from

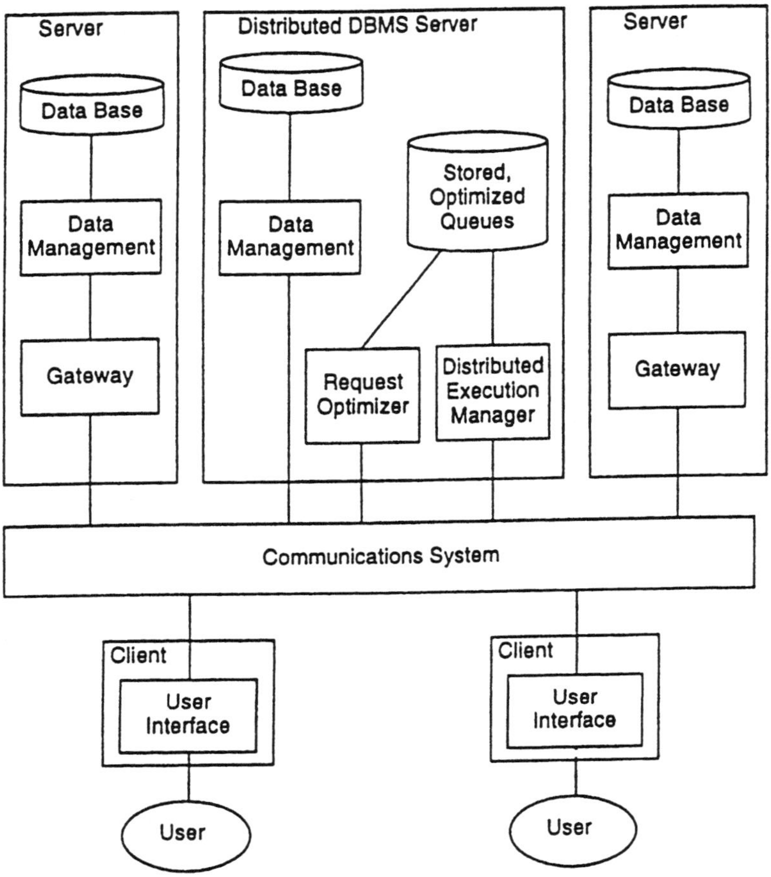

Exhibit 1. Major components of a distributed DBMS.

multiple data managers, but not all distributed execution managers are sufficiently powerful to support distributed updates.

Distributed Request Optimizer

The distributed request optimizer hides the existence of multiple databases from the user. The three relational database tables depicted in Exhibit 2 illustrate this point. Assuming the three tables are visible to a user who wants to retrieve employee Davis' salary, the user needs to retrieve the Davis information from the employee 1 table at site 1 and Davis information from the employee 2 table at either site 1 or site 2. The SQL request would be written as such (query 1):

```
select  Salary
   from  Employee  1  at  Site  1
```

```
where Name = "Davis"
UNION
select Salary
from Employee 2 at Site 2
where Name = "Davis";
```

Employee 1 — Site 1

Name	Salary	Department
Ackman	5000	Car
Baker	4500	Car

Employee 2 — Site 2

Name	Salary	Department
Carson	4800	Toy
Davis	5100	Toy

Employee 2 — Site 3

Name	Salary	Department
Carson	4800	Toy
Davis	5100	Toy

Exhibit 2. Employee database information replicated and distributed to three sites.

Alternatively, the user could formulate the request as if all of the data were in a centralized database. A simplified request is as follows (query 2):

```
select Salary
   from Employee
   where Name = "Davis";
```

The distributed request optimizer accesses data location and distribution information maintained by the distributed DBMS and converts query 2 to query 1.

Exhibit 3 illustrates a more compelling example. To change the department number of Smith from 3 to 15, the user or programmer would write query 3:

```
update Employee
   set Department=15
   where EmpId=100;
```

However, if the information in the table in Exhibit 3 is stored in four tables at four different sites (as shown in Exhibit 4), the distributed request optimizer modifies query 3 to the following complex program (query 4):

```
select Name, Sal, Tax, into $Name, $Sal,$Tax
   from Employee 1
   where EmpId=100;
select ManagerNumber into $ManagerNumber
   from Employee 2
   where EmpId = 100;
insert into Employee 3
   (EmpId, Name, Department)
   (100, $Name, 15);
insert into Employee 4
   (EmpId, Sal, Tax, ManagerNumber)
   (10, $Sal, $Tax, $ManagerNumber);
delete Employee 1
   where EmpId = 100;
delete Employee 2
   where EmpId = 100;
```

As this example illustrates, a distributed request optimizer greatly simplifies the task of the user or programmer because the request optimizer hides the four tables in Exhibit 4 from the user. The user or programmer can express the relatively simple request in query 3 terms rather than using query 4.

When the database administrator can move a table from one site to another, the users or programmers do not need to modify their request. Instead, the distributed request optimizer translates the user request with updated information about the table location.

Employee

EmpId	Name	Salary	Tax	ManagerNumber	Department
100	Smith	10000	1000	20	3
200	Jones	1333	122	40	14

Exhibit 3. Centralized employee information.

Employee 1 (Department <10)

EmpId	Name	Salary	Tax
100	Smith	10000	1000

Employee 2 (Department <10)

EmpId	ManagerNumber	Department
100	20	3

Employee 3 (Department ≥10)

Name	Name	Department
200	Jones	14

Employee 4 (Department ≥10)

EmpId	Salary	Tax	ManagerNumber
200	1333	122	40

Exhibit 4. Employee information distributed to four sites.

Distributed request optimizers have some disadvantages, but each disadvantage has a counter argument. For example:

- Distributed request optimizers are expensive to build or purchase. However, the expense should be offset by savings in the time necessary for users and programmers to formulate requests.
- Like any general optimizer, it may be possible to program a request that executes faster than the same request generated by the optimizer. However, optimizers take only seconds while human programmers may require hours to implement the optimizations.

Gateways

Some distributed DBMSs support multiple types of local data managers. When this occurs, each request or part of a request to be executed by the local data manager must be translated to a format that the local data manager can execute. Gateways perform this type of translation.

If the global request is expressed in SQL and a data manager supports SQL, the transformation may be trivial and only needs to consider different SQL dialects. However, if the global request is expressed in SQL and a data abase manager does not support SQL, then a much more sophisticated gateway is necessary.

Example 1. The translation problem can be illustrated with some examples. Suppose that a local data manager consists of two files—a Department file containing DepartmentName and Budget and an Employee file containing EmployeeName, Salary, and DepartmentName. The following SQL request must be translated to a program containing file I/O commands:

```
select  *
    from  employee
    where  DepartmentName  =  "Car";
```

Depending on the file structures used by the file system data manager, the resulting program may perform one of the following:

- Search linearly for all records in the Employee file with value Car in the DepartmentName field.
- Perform a binary search for records in the Employee file ordered by the Car field.
- Do an index lookup for records in the Employee file indexed by the Car field.

Example 2. The following SQL request requires that the generated program access and join together records from both theDepartment and Employeefiles that have the same value for theDepartmentName field:

```
select  *
    from  Department,  Employee
    where  Department.DepartmentName  =
               Employee.DepartmentName
```

Depending on the file structures used by the file system data manager, the resulting program may perform one of the following:

- Nested (inner-outer) loop. For each record in Employee, every record in Department is retrieved and tested to determine whether they match.
- Index. For each record in Employee, the index to DepartmentName is used to retrieve matching records in Department.
- Sort-merge join. If both Employee and Department are sorted physically by DepartmentName, then both files should be scanned at the same time to locate matching records.
- Hash join. The programmer hashes both Employee and Department files to the same hash file using the same hashing function applied to DepartmentName, then examines buckets for Employee and Department records that match.

Gateways have the same disadvantages and advantages as request optimizers:

- Gateways are expensive to build or purchase. However, the expense should be offset with savings in user and programmer programming effort.
- Like any general optimizer, it may be possible to manually translate a request that executes faster than the corresponding request generated by the gateway. However, gateways take only seconds to execute, whereas manual translation may require hours of programmer time.

Distributed Execution Manager

A distributed execution manager controls and coordinates the execution of requests or pieces of requests by one or more data managers. It also provides distributed concurrency control and commit protocols.

A transaction is a set of reads, writes, and ends with a commit (if all operations are successful) or with a rollback (if one or more of the operations is not successful). A distributed DBMS may execute several transactions concurrently as long as one transaction does not try to update data being accessed by another transaction. The execution of several concurrent transactions is said to be serializable if the results are the same as some serial execution of the transactions.

Several approaches are used to guarantee the serializability of concurrently executing transactions, including locking, timestamp ordering, and optimistic approaches. These approaches also are used in centralized databases, but their implementation is much more complicated in distributed systems.

Two-Phase Commit Protocol.

Distributed transactions that update data in several databases need a mechanism to determine whether to commit or rollback changes made in each database. Protocols have been developed to solve this problem; the most popular is the two-phase commit protocol. In the two-phase commit protocol, each local data manager reports its results to the distributed execution manager. When the distributed execution manager determines that all subrequests are completed, it performs the two-phase commit protocol:

- It sends a message asking each local data manager if it still can make local changes permanent.
- After receiving an OK to commit messages from each local data manager, it sends a final commit message to each local data manager. If anything goes wrong either before or during the two-phase commit protocol, the distributed execution manager sends rollback messages,

causing all local data managers to undo any changes made to their local databases.

The distributed concurrency control and commit protocol messages add expense and delay to the execution of requests that update data at multiple sites. To avoid these expenses and delays, some distributed database management systems do not permit updates at all, while others only permit updates to a single database. If updates to a single database are permitted, the local data manager performs the concurrency control and commit processing and avoids the overhead of the distributed concurrency control and commit protocol messages.

One of the biggest problems with implementing distributed DBMS using existing heterogeneous data managers is that existing data managers may use different forms of concurrency control and may not support the two-phase commit protocol. It is very difficult to modify the local managers to accommodate the distributed concurrency control and commit protocols. This is why distributed DBMSs that support multisite updates usually support only one type of data manager.

RECOMMENDED COURSE OF ACTION

Database administrators should assess the needs of users and decide if the client/server system is to support one or several data servers. If several data servers are needed, then the database administrator determines which of the following features are needed:

- Location and replication transparency. If this feature is needed, the database administrator should purchase or build a distributed DBMS that supports a request optimizer.
- DBMS transparency. A requirement for this feature means that the database administrator should build or buy gateways to hide the languages required by data managers.
- Multisite updates. If this feature is needed, it is best to build or buy a sophisticated distributed execution manager that supports concurrency control and commit protocols among the data managers.

BIBLIOGRAPHY

Ozsu, M.T. and Valduriez, P. *Principles of Distributed Database Systems* (Englewood Cliffs NJ: Prentice-Hall, 1991).

Chapter 24
Publishing Database Information on the World Wide Web

James A. Larson
Carol L. Larson

In today's business environment, users may be scattered across the globe and still need to access database information at their home enterprise or headquarters. How can users access database information from wherever they happen to be?

Typically, users access database information from a variety of computing platforms, including Windows, Macintosh, and Unix. It is important that users are able to access database information from their chosen platform in a consistent fashion. This chapter discusses how to publish database information on the World Wide Web and the methods by which users can access it.

THE WORLD WIDE WEB: AN EXPLOSION

The World Wide Web phenomenon has exploded onto the computing scene. In addition to e-mail and file transfer, the World Wide Web (or Web) supports document browsing. Users access a wide range of information available on the Web in the form of documents formatted using the hypertext markup language (HTML).

HTML Documents

HTML documents consist of three components:

- Content (the database information).
- Annotation (the format and layout of the document).
- Links (connections that chain documents together).

0-8493-9989-0/99/$0.00+$.50

Exhibit 1 illustrates a database table and its corresponding HTML document. HTML is used to annotate the document's content with tags (in Exhibit 1, tags are denoted by brackets). The tags specify how to format the content of the document when it is displayed to the user. Any platform can be used to display the document's contents because software on each platform interprets the tags in a manner appropriate for that computer. Thus, HTML provides "platform independence."

Once the publisher adds HTML tags to a document, the document can be presented to users. Not only does HTML describe the layout of text, it also integrates images, audio, and small applications (applets) for presentation to the user.

Uniform Resource Locators. A universal resource locator (URL) is a pointer to a document located in an HTML server connected to the Web. Documents can be linked explicitly by embedding a URL within an anchor tag of one document to provide the location on the Web of a related document. In Exhibit 1, URLs are used to link each employee with the home page of the employee's department and browse through sequences of related documents.

Common Gateway Interface Script. An HTML document is not limited to content containing static information; dynamic information can also be included within a document's content. The common gateway interface (CGI) gives programmers a language for specifying how to derive data for presentation to the user.

For example, a CGI script might invoke a hardware thermometer to measure the current temperature and record it in the document's content. CGI scripts can also be used to solicit a database query from the user and insert HTML tags into the query results. Programmers implement CGI scripts using Visual Basic, C, C++, TCL, Perl, or other languages executable on a Web server.

STATIC PUBLISHING: DISPLAYING DATABASE INFORMATION USING THE WEB

Exhibit 2 illustrates how database information is published on a Web server by extracting data and inserting HTML tags into the query results.

First, a database administrator (DBA) extracts the data to be published by submitting an SQL query to the database management system (DBMS). Programmers can insert HTML tags to control the appearance of the final HTML document. The resulting document is then placed on an HTML server that manages and accesses documents much like a DBMS manages database records. The HTML server responds to requests for documents

Name	Amount	Department
Able	400.00	*Toy*
Baker	350.00	*Car*
Carson	425.00	*Toy*

A

```
<TABLE BORDER=1>
     <TH>  Name    </TH>  <TH>  Amount  </TH>  <TH>  Department                                           </TH>
<TR> <TD>  Able    </TD>  <TD>  400.00  </TD>  <TD>  <A href=URL of Toy Department's Homepage>  Toy </A>  </TD>  </TR>
<TR> <TD>  Baker   </TD>  <TD>  350.00  </TD>  <TD>  <A href=URL of Car Department's Homepage>  Car </A>  </TD>  </TR>
<TR> <TD>  Carson  </TD>  <TD>  425.00  </TD>  <TD>  <A href=URL of Toy Department's Homepage>  Toy </A>  </TD>  </TR>
</TABLE>
```

B

<TABLE>, </TABLE>	Begin, End Table
<TH>, </TH>	Begin, End Table Heading
<TR>, </TR>	Begin, End Table Row
<TD>, </TD>	Begin, End Table Data Element
<A>, </A>	Begin, End Anchor

C

Exhibit 1. A database table and its HTML description.

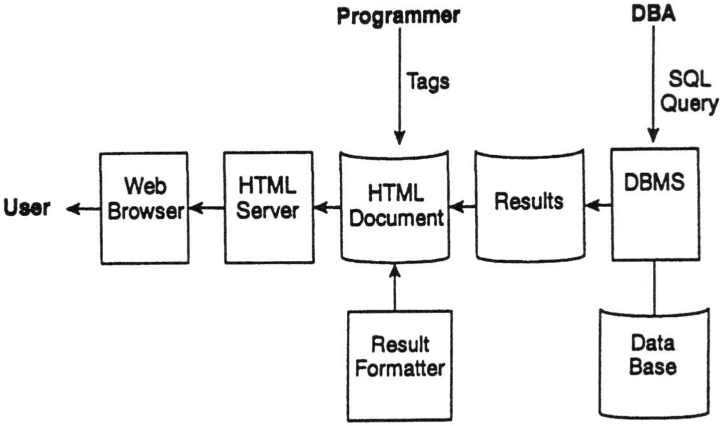

Exhibit 2. Static publishing.

by sending them to the requesting client browsers, which could be Netscape Navigator or Microsoft Internet Explorer.

Alternatively, software can automatically insert HTML tags to generate default layouts. For example, Corel's Web.Data uses a step-by-step process to create a database table to be inserted into an HTML document and guides the DBA through the required steps for formatting. The result is a "recipe file," which is a template describing how to process the results of a database query by inserting the appropriate HTML tags into the query's results. Corel's Web.Data can optimize the HTML document for Netscape Navigator or Microsoft Explorer.

BestWeb Pro Version 1.0 is another example of software that inserts HTML tags into ASCII files created by a database query. BestWeb allows the programmer to select specific properties and formatting options for each table field by indicating which fields should be indexed and customizing the HTML document with background images and corporate logos.

Static generation of HTML documents has its pros and cons. The primary advantage is that the process is straightforward because it is subject to automation. The resulting HTML documents are easy for users to browse, and no programming is required. However, the HTML documents are not linked to the source data in real time. The HTML document is not changed automatically when the user changes the source data in the DBMS. Users cannot change the data in the HTML document and can only change the underlying database directly by using traditional DBMS access facilities.

DYNAMIC PUBLISHING: INTERACTING WITH A DATABASE USING THE WEB

Although static publishing is sufficient for many applications—even desirable from a security point of view because users cannot change the underlying database when they access the corresponding HTML document—many applications require the user to submit a query to retrieve specific data.

Formulating a Query

To formulate a query, the user enters the query parameters into an HTML form consisting of input boxes or other user interface controls. A CGI script, which resides and executes on an HTML server, then takes the parameters and formulates an SQL query to the underlying DBMS, as illustrated in Exhibit 3. After the DBMS processes the query, it returns the extracted data to the CGI script, which reformats the response and inserts HTML tags. Finally, the reformatted response is sent to the user's browser and displayed.

Special controls and CGI scripts not only allow users to specify parameters for a database query, users may also specify a database update. Dynamic publishing enables users to obtain and modify up-to-the-minute database information.

Java Applets

CGI scripts reside and execute on HTML servers. Java applets reside on HTML servers, but are downloaded to and executed on the user's Web browser.

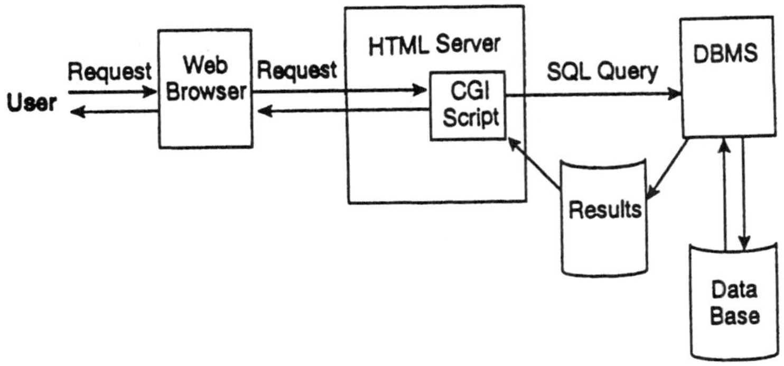

Exhibit 3. Dynamic publishing with a CGI Script.

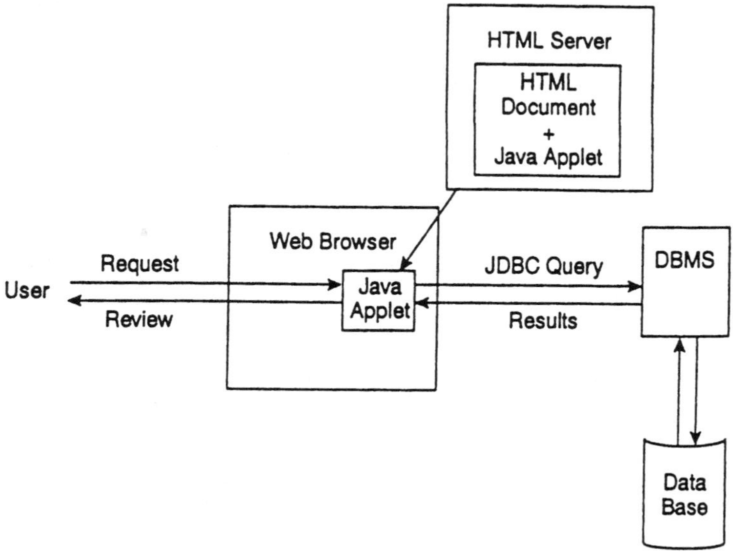

Exhibit 4. Dynamic publishing with a Java Applet.

Java applets are special types of applications written in the Java programming language. Applets cannot perform actions that may be harmful to the user's environment, such as accessing local disks and printers, accessing the user's identity, or accessing any server other than the one that provided the applet. These limits on what the applet can do ensure, to a degree, that it will not harm the user's computing environment.

Applets can be embedded within an HTML document as shown in Exhibit 4. When executed, a Java applet can produce animation, perform calculations, and dynamically determine the layout and format of information to be presented to the user.

The Java database connectivity (JDBC) standard describes the Java application programming interface (API) for accessing relational databases. Most DBMS vendors support JDBC. Java applets use JDBC to directly access a DBMS to perform database queries and modifications.

User Interface Controls. Java applets can present user interface controls, such as data boxes, pull-down menus, and other user interface widgets that allow users to enter database queries and update parameters. Applet Window Technology (AWT) is a series of Java classes that provide a collection of user interface controls. AWT is standard on all Java-enabled platforms, including Macintosh, Windows, and Unix, among others.

Alternatively, programmers also can create or reuse customized user interface controls. CGI scripts execute in the HTML server, whereas Java applets are downloaded from the HTML server and executed within the user's browser. This division of labor minimizes data transmissions between the HTML server and the user's platform.

Limiting Data Transmissions. Generally, database administrators prefer that data element translations and reformatting are done in the HTML server. Thus, a user's request can be satisfied by two data transmissions—one containing the request from the user's computing platform to the server and the second containing the translated, reformatted results from the server to the user's platform. DBAs write CGI scripts to perform the data element translations and data reformatting for execution on the HTML server.

User interface experts can write Java applets to accept data results from the HTML server and generate sophisticated user interfaces, which may involve graphics or animation. For example, Java applets can convert database data to graphs, bar charts, or even animated objects such as fluctuating temperature gauges, nodding heads, or moving clock hands. Java applets execute within the user's browser on the user's computing platform. By executing Java applets at the user's platform, no additional data transmissions are necessary between the user and the HTML server.

SECURITY MECHANISMS

HTML forms provide limited control over database access. Like a relational database view, a form restricts the database elements users may access. For example, the CGI script can provide additional security by requesting that the user supply passwords and by asking questions to authenticate identity. The hypertext transfer protocol (HTTP) can also be used to restrict access to users listed in a file or cause the browser to prompt the user for a password.

Researchers and practitioners have proposed other security mechanisms, such as encryption, watermarks, seals against modification, and certificates of authentication. Many of these advanced security techniques will soon be available, if they are not already.

CONCLUSION

Web publication allows users anywhere in the world with a Web browser to access specific databases subject to specified security constraints. Accessing database information over the Web requires an HTML server to manage documents.

Systems analysts determine whether users need to access static or dynamic data. If users can tolerate static data, software should be used to generate HTML documents automatically. If users require up-to-the-minute data, programmers must write CGI scripts or Java applets to allow them to request needed information. CGI scripts should be used to perform data transformation and formatting, and Java applets should be used for sophisticated user interfaces.

Chapter 25
Heterogeneous Network File and Print Access

Raj Rajagopal

In this chapter, we will look into a very common requirement within a heterogeneous environment — accessing a file server or a networked printer in one environment from a client in another environment. Networked file and print access between Windows and NetWare is relatively easy and is discussed in Chapter 33. We will consider file access between UNIX and Windows NT environments in this chapter.

ACCESSING UNIX SERVER FILES FROM WINDOWS NT CLIENTS

For occasional file transfers between a UNIX machine and a Windows NT machine, you can use floppy disks. UNIX systems normally include the ability to read and write DOS-compatible floppy disks (pcfs, for example). However, watch for problems when you transfer files. The problems you can encounter are listed under problems in file transfers section later in this chapter.

If you want to access Files and Printers that are on your UNIX server from your Windows machine without floppies, there are several ways in which you can do this:

- Use the built-in Telnet function, logon to the UNIX server and your Windows workstation becomes a terminal to the UNIX server. You can do file-related functions available for terminals such as viewing and editing files, executing program files, etc.
- Use the built-in File Transfer Protocol (FTP) function in Windows and exchange files between the UNIX server and the Windows machine. Windows NT also includes two other similar functions.
- Use the built-in rcp function in Windows NT.
- Use built-in tftp function in Windows NT.

0-8493-9989-0/99/$0.00+$.50

- Use a serial link between the UNIX machine and the Windows NT machine.
- Use a network operating system with built-in support to access UNIX server files.
- Use third-party Network File System (NFS) packages.

Let us look at these options in detail.

Telnet

Telnet is a communication protocol for terminal emulation. Windows has built-in Telnet client support. Besides the built-in support, there are a number of communication packages that include Telnet client support. All UNIX operating systems support Telnet. Typically, a Telnet daemon keeps running in background, awaiting requests from Telnet clients.

Once connectivity is established, the Telnet client can perform the same functions as a directly attached terminal. Functions for file and print access include browsing and editing files, executing programs, and submitting print requests.

Telnet is covered in detail in Chapter 11.

File Transfer Protocol (ftp)

If you have used the Internet, then you are likely to have downloaded (and maybe even uploaded) files using the ftp protocol. File transfers are typically accomplished using the File Transfer Protocol. Windows NT comes with built-in support for ftp and the Internet Information Server (IIS), an add-on product to Windows NT server for Internet functions, includes an advanced version of FTP.

Besides the built-in support, there are a number of third-party communication packages that include ftp support and many of the third-party ftp programs provide graphical user interfaces.

To run the ftp client in the Windows machine and access the UNIX server files, the UNIX server should be running the ftp daemon called *ftpd.*

Windows NT includes a command line version of ftp as well as a graphical version of ftp. The command line version is started by keying in ftp and the name of the remote host (ftp.microsoft.com in this example) at the command prompt as shown in Exhibit 1. The exhibit shows the connection from the ftp client to the server ftp.microsoft.com. The logon was an anonymous login (the userid was *anonymous* and the password was the e-mail address of the person requesting file access). Once connected, the exhibit shows a change directory command to change to a specific directory. You can use the *get* command to retrieve files and the *put* command to send files to the server.

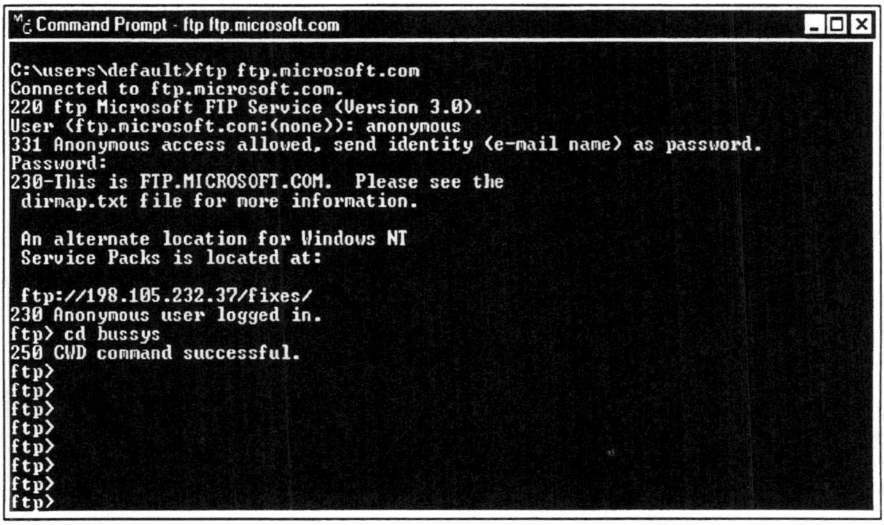

Exhibit 1. Nongraphical ftp using command line.

Windows NT also includes a graphical version of ftp; it is called WS_FTP32. You typically would find the ftp icon under network or you can search for "ftp" and double-click on the WS_FTP32 entry. The opening dialog of WS_FTP32 is shown in Exhibit 2.

You specify the remote host name, your userid, and your password, and WS_FTP32 attempts to establish an ftp connection. If successful, you get the dialog shown in Exhibit 3.

The dialog shows the highest level directory on the remote system and the subdirectories and files underneath the highest level directory. Clicking on a directory entry shows the list of directories and files underneath the directory. In this example, the directory *softlib* was chosen and the bottom half of the right pane shows the files and directories under *softlib*. The file README.TXT was selected. You can choose the destination on the left pane where a similar hierarchical file structure of the local system is shown. Once you have selected the source and the destination, clicking on the arrow that goes from remote to local (right to left) downloads the file. You can upload files using the other arrow. Exhibit 4 shows that the README.TXT file has been downloaded.

Remote Copy Program (rcp)

rcp is similar to ftp. To run the rcp client in the Windows machine and access the UNIX server files, the UNIX server should be running the rcp daemon called *rshd* (Remote Shell Daemon). *rshd* supports other

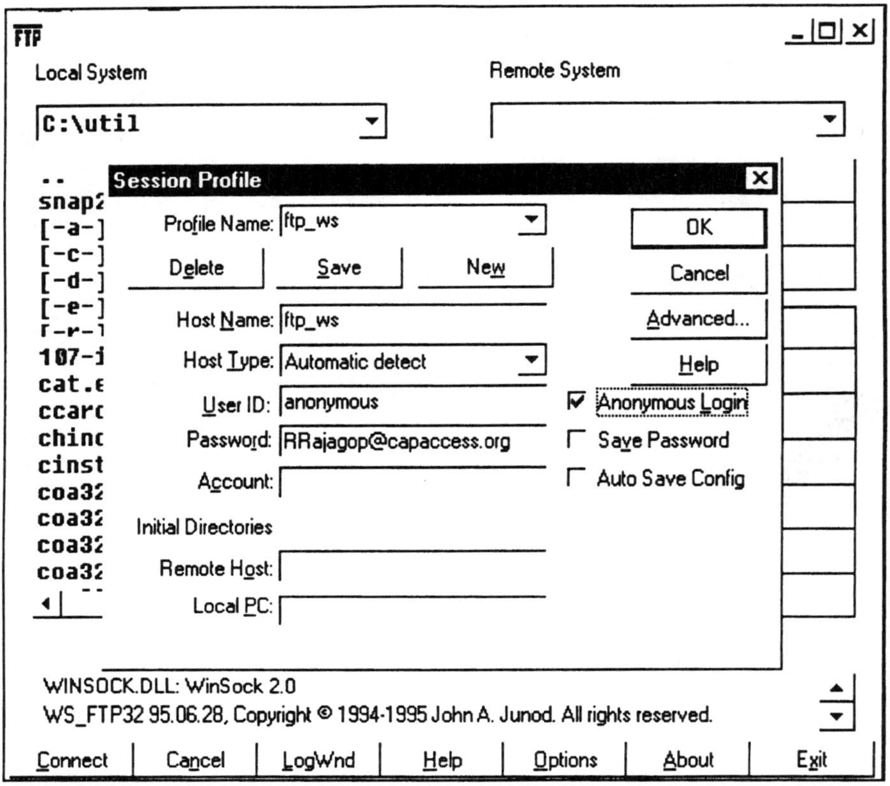

Exhibit 2. Graphical version of ftp.

commands besides rcp and hence has a more generic daemon name (other than rcpd). You can specify a source and a destination (which means your computer does not have to be either, and you can copy remotely from one computer to another from a third computer). rcp supports specifying security parameters as well as recursive copying of all files (including subdirectories) between source and destination. The name of the Windows computer should be present in the *.rmhosts* file in the UNIX machine.

You can invoke rcp by keying in rcp from the command prompt, and keying in rcp without parameters shows the help message shown in Exhibit 5.

Trivial File Transfer Protocol (tftp)

tftp, as the name implies, is a trivial (or less functional) version of ftp. One of the functions missing in tftp compared to ftp is security. You cannot specify user information and, hence, no user authentication takes place.

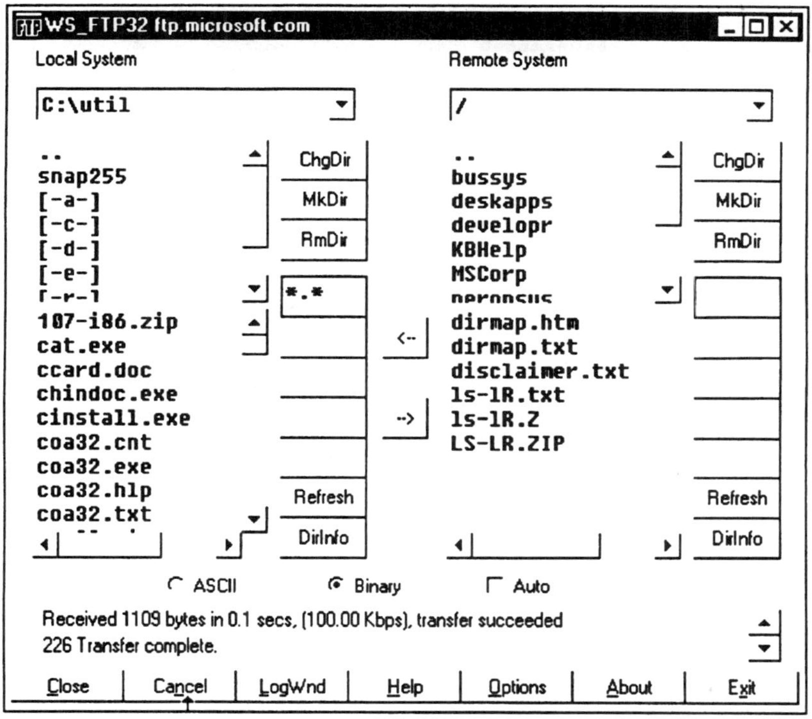

Exhibit 3. FTP connection with a remote host.

(In ftp, you may have come across hosts that do not support Anonymous ftp, and your access will be denied if you tried being an Anonymous user). Another function missing is file browsing capability. Windows NT comes only with a built-in tftp client and not a tftp server. This means that you can use tftp to transfer UNIX files from your Windows NT machine, but not vice versa.

You can invoke tftp by keying in **tftp** from the command prompt, and keying in tftp without parameters shows the help message shown in Exhibit 6.

Using a Serial Link

Files can also be transferred between UNIX and Windows machines using serial links between the computers. There are third-party tools available to facilitate this type of file transfer. You can also use the Terminal function contained within Accessories under Programs, under Start in conjunction with third-party tools to connect to a UNIX machine and download files.

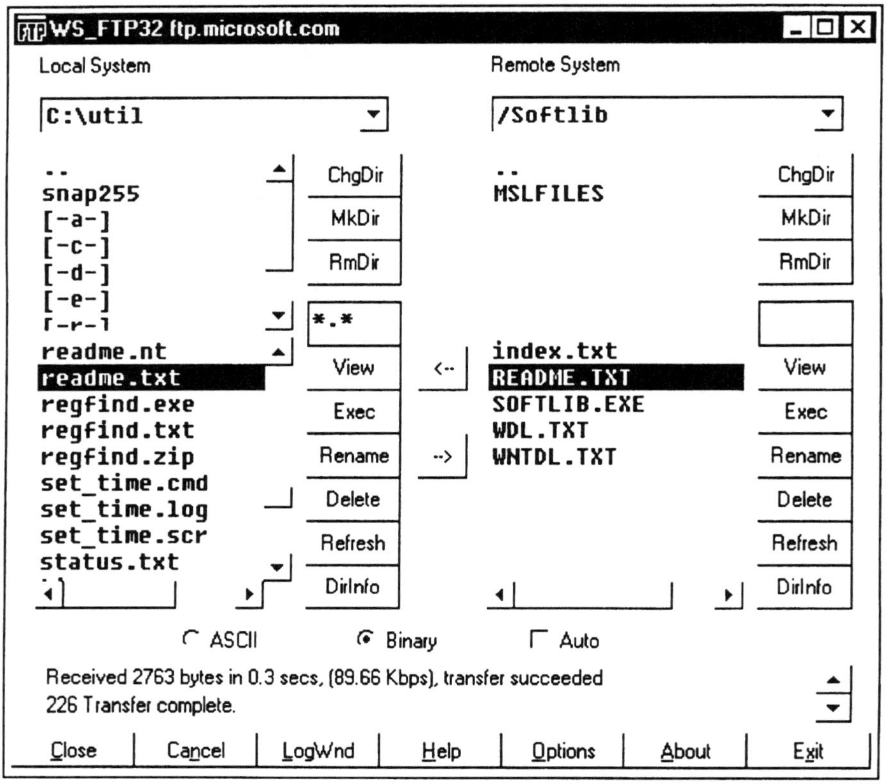

Exhibit 4. Downloading a file using ftp.

NETWORK OPERATING SYSTEMS WITH BUILT-IN FILE SERVER ACCESS

Network operating systems such as PATHWORKS from Digital and NetWare provide file and print services in heterogeneous environments.

Pathworks. The following is a brief summary of PATHWORKS from DEC Web pages. Additional information can be found at http://www.digital.com.

PATHWORKS from Digital provides built-in access to heterogeneous file servers. Using PATHWORKS, for example, a Windows NT client can access files from a Digital UNIX server. PATHWORKS makes NFS exported files automatically available to PCs, where the files can be accessed if the files are local to the PC. PATHWORKS is a family of network operating systems and includes PATHWORKS for Digital UNIX and PATHWORKS for Windows NT.

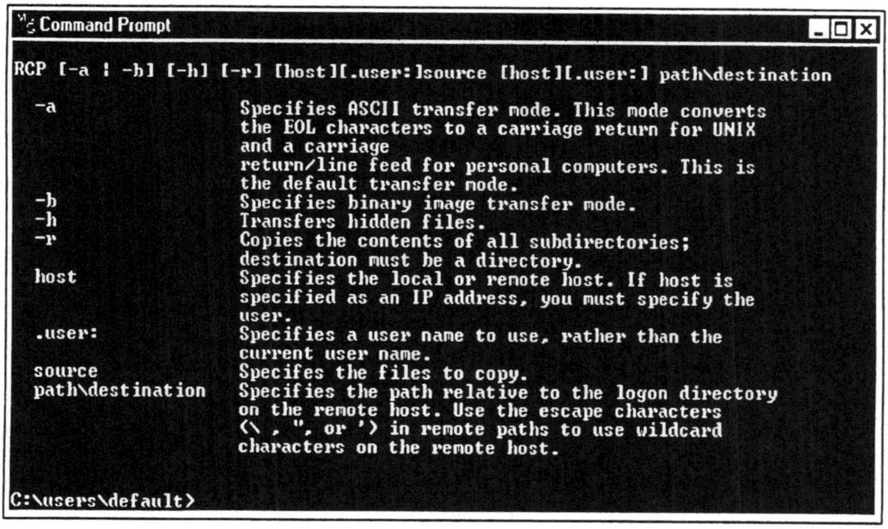

```
Command Prompt
RCP [-a | -b] [-h] [-r] [host][.user:]source [host][.user:] path\destination
  -a                    Specifies ASCII transfer mode. This mode converts
                        the EOL characters to a carriage return for UNIX
                        and a carriage
                        return/line feed for personal computers. This is
                        the default transfer mode.
  -b                    Specifies binary image transfer mode.
  -h                    Transfers hidden files.
  -r                    Copies the contents of all subdirectories;
                        destination must be a directory.
  host                  Specifies the local or remote host. If host is
                        specified as an IP address, you must specify the
                        user.
  .user:                Specifies a user name to use, rather than the
                        current user name.
  source                Specifes the files to copy.
  path\destination      Specifies the path relative to the logon directory
                        on the remote host. Use the escape characters
                        (\ , ", or ') in remote paths to use wildcard
                        characters on the remote host.

C:\users\default>
```

Exhibit 5. Invoking rcp from the command prompt.

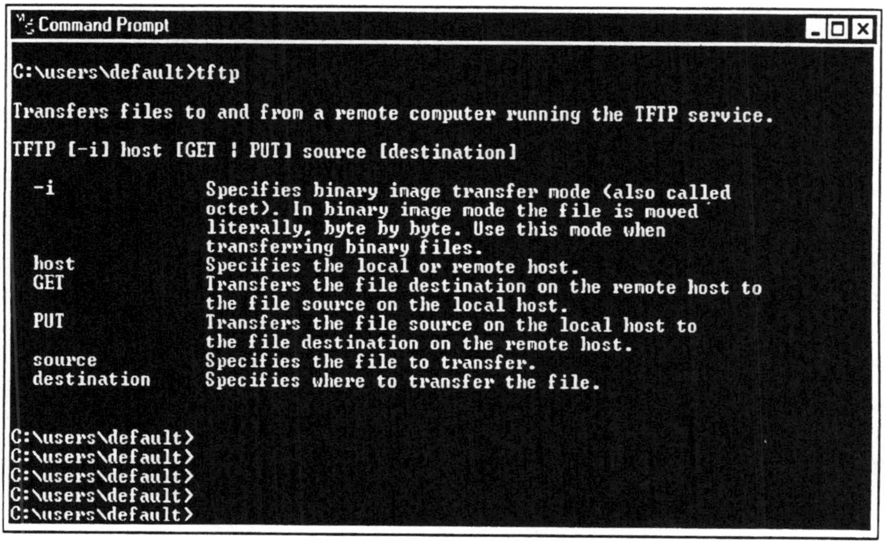

```
Command Prompt
C:\users\default>tftp

Transfers files to and from a remote computer running the TFTP service.

TFTP [-i] host [GET | PUT] source [destination]

  -i              Specifies binary image transfer mode (also called
                  octet). In binary image mode the file is moved
                  literally, byte by byte. Use this mode when
                  transferring binary files.
  host            Specifies the local or remote host.
  GET             Transfers the file destination on the remote host to
                  the file source on the local host.
  PUT             Transfers the file source on the local host to
                  the file destination on the remote host.
  source          Specifies the file to transfer.
  destination     Specifies where to transfer the file.

C:\users\default>
C:\users\default>
C:\users\default>
C:\users\default>
C:\users\default>
```

Exhibit 6. Invoking tftp from the command prompt.

PATHWORKS for Digital UNIX. PATHWORKS for Digital UNIX (Advanced Server) provides the following Windows NT-style enterprise services, allowing Digital UNIX to be a full peer in a Windows NT environment:

- Support for the Advanced Server (LAN Manager) 3.0 SMB protocol.
- Windows NT controller support: UNIX can act as both primary and backup domain controllers.
- Windows NT Trusted Domain support.
- Windows NT wide area domain support (through an LMHOSTS file and WINS client).
- Windows NT management APIs (provide the ability to manage and be managed by Windows NT system management applications).
- Windows NT user and file replication.
- Support for a TruCluster environment for highly available PC services under DIGITAL UNIX and the ability for PCs to browse UNIX NFS shares.

PATHWORKS for Digital UNIX (Advanced Server) provides Windows NT Server networking features for Digital UNIX platforms. In the past, this technology was known as LAN Manager for UNIX. Most recently, additional NT networking features have been added and the technology has evolved to be known as Advanced Server for UNIX.

PATHWORKS for Digital UNIX (Advanced Server) allows full participation of Digital UNIX in a Windows NT domain. The previous version allowed Digital UNIX to act as a backup controller only. PATHWORKS for Digital UNIX (Advanced Server) Version 6.1 ships "TruCluster ready," meaning that your Windows NT files have the high availability and reliability of clustering servers such as Digital UNIX clusters. High availability and reliability are key features for enterprise applications to be deployed on Windows NT.

PATHWORKS for Digital UNIX (NetWare) server software enables your Digital UNIX and native NetWare users — as well as PATHWORKS for DOS and Windows (NetWare) users — to share files, data, mail, applications, disks, printers, and other resources. Multiple NetWare-based or LAN Manager-based clients can concurrently access files stored on the server's disk through the file access modes and byte range locking that Digital UNIX provides.

PATHWORKS for Digital UNIX supports multiple file systems, including:

- UNIX File System (UFS)
- Network File System (NFS)
- Advanced File System (AdVFS)
- CD-ROM File System (CDFS), read-only

File and print services are based on NetWare Core Protocol (NCP) and are available directly from Digital UNIX over the NetWare transport. You can manage file and print services by using standard NetWare utilities such that your investment in NetWare management expertise is preserved.

PATHWORKS integrates the most popular network operating systems, NetWare, and LAN Manager, allowing users within different workgroups to share information and resources.

PATHWORKS supports all of the leading network protocols — TCP/IP, DECnet, IPX/SPX, NetBEUI, AppleTalk, and LAT. For enterprise backbones, Digital also offers a full range of "multilingual" networking solutions, including TCP/IP, DECnet, OSI, X.25, ISDN, and telephone (PSTN) protocols and connectivity to IBM SNA networks.

Through PATHWORKS, NetWare users can share information with UNIX and OpenVMS, as well as LAN Manager-based users, including Windows NT and OS/2 users.

PATHWORKS for Windows NT. PATHWORKS for Windows NT is a member of the PATHWORKS family for Windows NT. PATHWORKS for Windows NT, available for both Windows NT Workstations and Windows NT Server systems, extends the connectivity of Windows NT systems. PATHWORKS for Windows NT gives Windows NT clients additional connectivity to legacy Digital environments by enhancing the clients with LAT, DECnet, and VT terminal emulation access.

NetWare provides file and print server support for a wide range of clients and servers. NetWare is covered in more detail in Chapter 33. Another network operating system that provides heterogeneous file and print connectivity is Vines from Banyan.

Check with your network operating system vendor to ensure that the specific client(s) and the specific server(s) you are planning on using are supported.

NFS

NFS is a standard file-sharing and access protocol invented by Sun Microsystems. It is used widely in the UNIX world. A system running NFS-compliant software can access (open, close, read, and even write to) files on remote systems, and share all or part of its file system with other systems that are NFS compliant. For example, a UNIX network administrator can mount NFS file systems from remote hosts and make the file systems available as though they were local. The directories and files on the UNIX server to be shared with other machines on the network are set up as shared directories using the *exportfs* UNIX command. The *exportfs* command specifies the type of access allowed (read only, write, etc.).

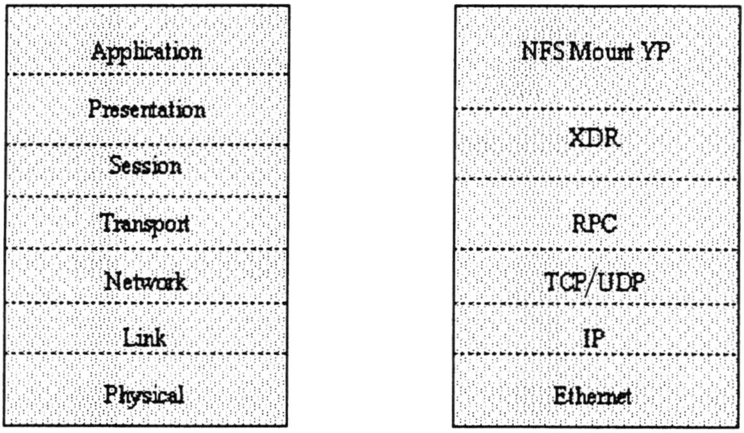

Exhibit 7. NFS Architecture mapped to the OSI model.

NFS Architecture

Exhibit 7 shows the architecture of NFS and how the different NFS functional layers map to the OSI 7 layer model.

As shown in Exhibit 7, NFS is an application layer built on top of external data representation (XDR), remote procedure call (RPC), and User Datagram Protocol (UDP).

NFS Components

Typical NFS components include:

- NFS client
- NFS server
- NFS daemons

The NFS client is the code that resides in a client, such as a PC, that handles the client portion of accessing remote drives and directories. To the user, the NFS client interface makes remote drives look the same as local drives. For example, if the client is a Windows machine, the remote drives appear as additional drive letters and the file listings of the remote drives appear in File Manager or Explorer (Windows Explorer not Internet Explorer), in the same way as local drives. Windows does not have a built-in NFS client. If you want to access UNIX NFS volumes from Windows machines, you need to get third-party NFS clients. Some NFS clients support multiple remote drives to be accessed simultaneously and some support peer-to-peer LAN networking as well.

NFS servers respond to NFS client requests. NFS servers provide read and write access to network drives, access network printers, and CD-ROM drives. NFS servers also allow file systems to be exported to other NFS servers on the network. Since NFS servers could be executing on computing environments from different vendors, heterogeneous file sharing is possible.

NFS daemons are meant for the same purpose as any other UNIX or other daemons. They wait and execute in the background, facilitating NFS client/server exchanges. The NFS daemons, their type (core vs. non-core), and the functions they perform are summarized in Exhibit 8.

Exhibit 8. NFS Daemons

Daemon	Type	Function
portmapd	Core	Direct NFS clients to appropriate servers
nfsd	Core	Start file system requests for NFS clients
mountd	Core	Enable NFS clients to mount the file system
pcnfsd	Non-core	Assign NFS client access rights and print request directives
timed	Non-core	Adjusts time between clients and servers
lockd	Non-core	Implements NFS file locking service
Note: pcnfsd and lockd are required when implementing NFS using PCs.		

Common NFS Products

There are a number of competing file systems to NFS. They include Remote File System (RFS), Andrew File System (AFS), and Windows NT's NTFS. Although Windows NT has built-in capability of supporting multiple file systems, NTFS is the one most suitable for heterogeneous system file access involving Windows NT. We will discuss NFS because the other file systems are either proprietary and/or do not have as good a market penetration as NFS.

NFS is usually supplied as an extension of the operating system by the UNIX system vendor, and is the standard for distributed file access in UNIX networks. In contrast, Macintosh, DOS, OS/2, Microsoft Windows, Windows NT, and Windows 95 NFS implementations have been developed independently by third-party TCP/IP software developers. Because NFS is built in as a feature of a specific vendor's TCP/IP, most NFS implementations will not run over different TCP/IP stacks, and are not compliant with Windows Sockets. NFS implementations for Windows NT and Windows 95, however, are compliant with Microsoft's TCP/IP kernel.

NFS products for the personal computer are normally offered as separate client and server applications, although there are some vendors that bundle client and server applications together in a single product. There are more than 100 different implementations of NFS for UNIX workstations, mainframes, and personal computers. The majority of NFS products support NFS Version 2 introduced in 1987, and many support the enhancements of NFS Version 3 (1989–1992).

Some of the third-party NFS products include InterDrive NT and InterDrive NT Server from FTP Software, NFS Maestro for Windows NT from Hummingbird Communications, PC NFS, DiskAccess (NFS clients for Windows NT), DiskShare (NFS server) from Intergraph, Chameleon from NetManage, Netpack NFS from Network Computing Devices, and PC NFS for Windows NT from SunSoft. NFS for Windows NT is also available from Beame and Whiteside and Process Software.

Let us take a brief look at the capabilities of some of these products.

NFS Maestro. More information on NFS Maestro is available online from Hummingbird at http://www.hummingbird.com.

NFS Maestro is a family of NFS products that includes:

- NFS Maestro Solo: The NFS client add-on to Hummingbird's eXceed PC X server (eXceed is covered in Chapter 11).
- NFS Maestro for Windows NT or Windows 95.
- NFS Maestro for Microsoft TCP/IP: TCP/IP stack and suite for DOS and Windows 3.x PCs.
- NFS Maestro for DOS and Windows: Client and Server.

Chameleon NFS/X. More details about Chameleon NFS/X are available online at http://www.netmanage.com.

NetManage provides products that enable access to NFS servers, X Window workstations, UNIX/VMS systems, IBM mainframes, and AS/400 systems from any Windows environment — Windows 3.1, 95, or NT. NetManage aims to provide the functions required of an enterprise desktop — host connectivity, e-mail, and messaging, file and printer sharing, Internet access, workgroup collaboration, and desktop management.

Chameleon NFS/X includes an NFS client and server software. Chameleon NFS also has NetManage's X-server, which is X11R6.1 compliant. The product also integrates terminal (TN3270/TN5250/Telnet) emulation. Chameleon NFS/X supports Windows NT 4.0. Cut-and-paste of text and graphics between UNIX and Windows desktop applications is supported.

Access NFS. More information on Access NFS is available online from Intergraph at http://www.intergraph.com.

Access NFS is part of the set of products to aid in the integration of Windows NT and UNIX from Intergraph. Access NFS includes:

- DiskAccess — NFS Client
- DiskShare — NFS Server

DiskAccess features: DiskAccess is an NFS client for Windows 95 and Windows NT based on NFS version 3. You can use your familiar Windows interface (Windows Explorer, Network Neighborhood, or File Manager) to browse and connect to file systems and printers located on UNIX or other NFS systems. DiskAccess replaces the PC-NFS product.

With DiskAccess, you can browse NFS file systems without committing a drive letter, accessing network resources as you need them. You also have the option of establishing a full-time link to your server. You can add frequently accessed NFS folders or files as a short-cut to the desktop. You can also use drag-and-drop or OLE-linked objects to establish connections.

DiskAccess supports UNIX-like symbolic links, and browsed connections are mounted and unmounted automatically, even if the desired file is located on an alternate server. You can manage file permissions using Windows property sheets. DiskAccess supports path-based (UNC) access to NFS files. DiskAccess is implemented as a multithreaded system service on Windows NT. On Windows 95, DiskAccess is implemented as a Virtual Device Driver (VxD). DiskAccess uses Microsoft's native TCP/IP stack.

Some of the other features of DiskAccess are:

- Terminal Emulation support for connecting to IBM mainframes, IBM AS/400, and DEC systems
- Network Time Protocol (NTP) supports NTP client to ensure time synchronization
- File Transfer Protocol (FTP) support
- Security functions through support for PCNFSD and NIS
- Utility to convert text files between DOS and UNIX

DiskShare features: DiskShare is an NFS server that runs on Windows NT and makes files on Windows NT available to UNIX and other non-Windows NFS clients. DiskShare provides NFS sharing directly from Windows' My Computer, File Manager, or Explorer interfaces.

DiskShare is implemented as a kernel-mode service, and runs at the most privileged CPU mode (ring 0). DiskShare uses Microsoft's native TCP/IP stack. DiskShare includes support for port mapper (portmap), extended data representation (xdr), mount protocol (mount), and network lock manager (nlm). DiskShare is available for Intel, PowerPC, MIPS, and Alpha processors. (Keep in mind that recently IBM and Microsoft announced that future Windows NT versions will not be supported on the PowerPC.)

DiskShare is integrated with Windows NT security. A system administrator can create or modify NFS user accounts and then associate them with local or domain-based Windows accounts. Once this is done, Windows takes care of the management and control of NFS access to Windows files. When the Windows NT account is modified or deleted, it is instantly reflected in NFS access to the system.

DiskShare supports PCNFSD version 2 to provide security and printing support for PC-based clients.

Intergraph also sells an NFS Solutions bundle that includes both DiskAccess and DiskShare.

InterDrive. InterDrive NT client (available for Windows NT and Windows 95) and InterDrive NT server are file access products from FTP Software. More details are available online at http://www.ftp.com.

InterDrive NT Client. The features of InterDrive client include:

- Installs on either Intel or DEC Alpha platforms
- Mount, Unmount, and Map File systems
- Displays Long, Uppercase, Lowercase, and NTFS, CDFS, and HPFS File Names
- Support for NT 4.0 Shell Extensions, plus maintains backward compatibility with NT 3.51
- Provides multiprocessor performance enhancements
- Support for UNC filenames
- Support for NFS printing
- Interoperates with other Network Operating Systems, such as LAN Manager, Banyan VINES, or Novell NetWare
- Take advantage of file locking
- Easily view and set file permissions from a command line utility
- Automatic alias support and (optional) server discovery
- Multi-user profile support

InterDrive NT Server. The features of InterDrive server include:

- 32-bit multi-threaded kernel-mode NFS server implementation
- Fully integrated LPD network print server
- Installs as a Windows NT service
- Installs/de-installs through network control panel
- Centralized server control application
- Event logging through Windows NT event logger
- Increased Security through advanced access control
- Case-sensitive file name support
- Long file name support
- Context-sensitive online help

Reflection. Reflection is a family of network products from WRQ. The Reflection family includes an NFS client for Windows 95. More details on the Reflection family of products from WRQ are available online at http://www.wrq.com.

Exceptional NFS (Windows 95 only) runs over the Windows 95 stack or WRQ's TCP/IP stack to facilitate integration with Microsoft desktops.

Features of the NFS support for Windows 95 include:

- Browse for NFS resources on the network
- Support for applications that use OLE file-locking, giving multiple users access to OLE
- Document files on NFS drives
- Full DOS session support
- APIs for developers that allow an application to log on to an NFS authentication server and establish connections to exported file systems and/or NFS printers, disconnect, and log off
- RPC (Remote Procedure Call) functions are also provided
- An NFS Administrator that lets you save time searching for server file systems, print queues, and daemons, and translates files from DOS format to UNIX format, and vice versa

ACCESSING WINDOWS NT SERVER FILES FROM UNIX CLIENTS

You can access Windows NT server files from UNIX clients in one of three ways:

- You can have an NFS server installed on Windows NT machines, and UNIX clients can access the Windows NT files just as they would access any other NFS files. NFS was discussed earlier in this chapter.
- You can use a network operating system such as PATHWORKS from Digital. PATHWORKS file functions were covered earlier in this chapter.
- You can let Windows NT provide ftp server functions and transfer files from UNIX clients using ftp.

File Transfer from Windows NT Server to UNIX Clients. Besides the ftp client function, Windows NT also includes the ftp server function. For simple file transfers, UNIX clients can use their ftp client and access the Windows NT ftp server. UNIX clients can also use third-party NFS products.

Windows NT must be running the ftp server (which is the equivalent of the UNIX ftpd daemon) before the UNIX clients can start transferring files. Windows NT versions prior to Version 4 included the ftp server as part of the TCP/IP service. Starting with Version 4, Windows NT includes the ftp server function with a different service, the Peer Web service.

ISSUES IN FILE TRANSFERS

There are issues involving file system differences that you may face when transferring files between UNIX and Windows.

- UNIX supports long file names and you may have to come up with a name in the 8-dot-3 format for DOS or Windows systems using the FAT file system.
- UNIX names are case sensitive and you have to be careful not to overlay files. For example, the files "SampFile" and "Sampfile" are two different files in UNIX, but cannot be two different files in the FAT file system used by DOS and Windows 3.x. Even Windows NT (with NTFS) is case-aware, but not fully case sensitive. Windows NT using NTFS preserves the case of file names when the name was generated and displays the case in file displays such as Windows NT explorer, but does not use the case information in other file functions such as file searches.
- UNIX files use a linefeed (LF) character for line separation, while Windows NT files use carriage return and linefeed (CRLF). Whether this is a problem depends on the type of file you are transferring and how you use the file after the transfer. If you transfer a text file from UNIX to Windows NT and attempt to print it, this difference could cause a problem. On the other hand, if the file is a program source file and you compile it, then it may not be a problem. Many porting tools, including N*u*TCRACKER, automatically take care of inserting a carriage return (CR) character when required.

PUBLIC DOMAIN PROGRAMS FOR HETEROGENEOUS FILE ACCESS

There are freeware and shareware tools that permit heterogeneous files access. The most popular one is probably Samba. Samba is a program suite that allows clients such as Windows to access files and printers on a server using the SMB (Server Message Block) protocol. Samba started with UNIX. Versions of Samba are now available for NetWare, OS/2, and VMS. A frequently asked question (FAQ) list on Samba is available online at http://samba.canberra.edu.au/pub/samba/docs/faq/sambafaq.html.

NETWORK DIRECTORIES

When you want to access directories in a Windows environment, you can do this in one of two ways. You can map network directories to drive letters. Alternately, you can have directory replication.

Mapping Network Drives

You can map a network directory to a drive letter. After this mapping, you can access directories and files using the drive letter, just as you would any local drive. Typically, the drive letters a: and b: are used for local floppy drives, and the drive letter c: for the local primary hard drive or partition. Additional partitions and CD-ROM drives are assigned drive letters starting with D:. When you assign drive letters for network drives, you are free to choose any unassigned letter. You can map a network directory using Windows NT explorer.

Directory Replication

Directory replication, as the name implies, is the mechanism by which copies of directories on a server are replicated on client workstations. If you or your users are frequently accessing files across the network, then directory replication will be of interest to you. Both Windows NT Server and Windows NT Workstation support directory replication.

How Does Replication Work? You create a set of exported directories on a file server. The exported directories are imported by the client workstations on the network. Changes to the contents of the exported directories on the server are automatically reflected on the imported directories at the workstations. This capability is useful in creating a standard directory setup for all the machines on a network.

Comparing Replication and Drive Mapping

The primary difference between replication and drive mapping is that the directories imported through replication reside on the local disk and behave the same way as other local mappings. This means that the performance of accessing the replicated directory is faster than accessing the same directory across a network. Probably, a more significant benefit of replication is that changes in server and network configurations may cause consequent changes to your drive mappings. This may cause setup and application problems where the mapped drive letters are used. Use of a local drive for replication shields many of these changes from your client workstation setup and applications.

Setting up and Monitoring Directory Replication

You can set up directory replication at a Windows NT workstation by following these steps:

- Set up a logon account at the server for the workstation replication service. Since this is a not a "real user" account, typical user account features such as expiring passwords should not apply to this account. In addition, ensure that the account has backup rights.
- Choose the **Replication** button from the Server Dialog box (Exhibit 9).
- In the Directory Replication dialog box, select the **Import Directories** option (Exhibit 10).
- Change the path name where the replicated directories will be created, if you do not want the default that Windows NT provides.
- Click the **Add** button to get a Select Domain dialog box as shown in Exhibit 11.
- Select a domain from the list provided, and click **OK**.

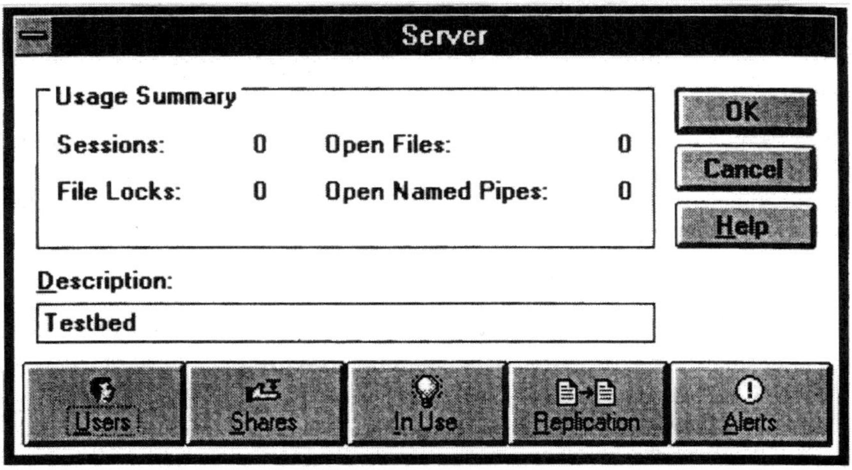

Exhibit 9. Selecting directory replication in the Server dialog.

You can monitor replication activity in your Windows NT server or Windows NT workstation using the Server applet in the Control Panel.

PRINTING FROM WINDOWS CLIENTS TO UNIX NETWORK PRINTERS

In a UNIX network, UNIX clients use software called Line Print Requester (LPR) to issue print requests to UNIX servers that control the printers. The UNIX servers run a daemon — the Line Printer Daemon, which receives

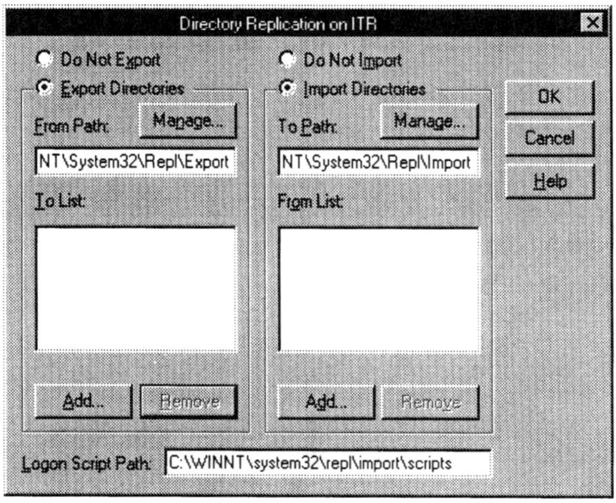

Exhibit 10. Main menu of server applet in control panel.

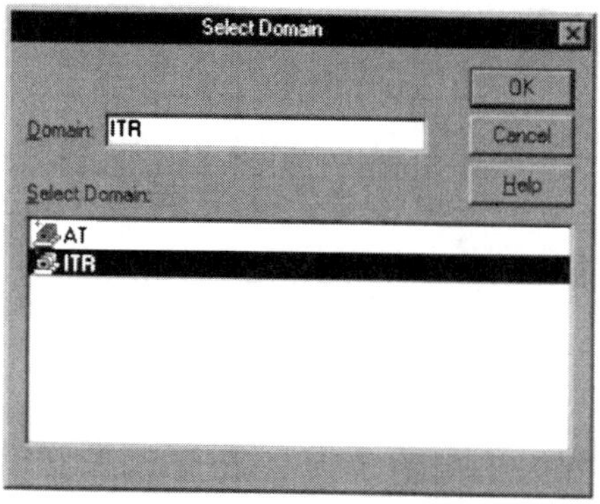

Exhibit 11. Directory replication status.

requests with the print output from the LPRs and transfers the print output to the print queue. The printers can be attached directly to the UNIX machine or directly to the network.

To access a UNIX network printer from a Windows client, you need to set up TCP/IP with the following set up information:

- The IP address (or the remote system alias)
- The name of the remote print queue
- TCP/IP printing option installation and configuration information

Once you collect the information, you can install TCP/IP printing service in Windows NT using the following steps.

1. Double-click the network icon from the **Control Panel,** under **Settings**, under **Start**.
2. Click the **Services** tab, and then click the **Add** button.
3. Click the Microsoft TCP/IP Printing Service from the list and click OK. This installs the TCP/IP printing service and the service is available to use when you restart your computer.

Once you have set up Microsoft TCP/IP printing services, you need to set up a printer port for the UNIX printer you want to print to. The following steps add a printer port.

1. Select **Printers**, under **Settings**, under **Start** (you can also use the control panel and double-click the printer icon). Note that the number and names of existing printers in your dialog will be different.
2. Double-click the **Add Printer** icon. Don't be concerned by the title "Add Printer." Add Printer not only adds printers, but it is also used to add printer ports.

3. Click the **My Computer** button (even though you want to print to a network printer).
4. Click **Add Port** and get to the Add LPR-compatible dialog.
5. Enter the IP address (or DNS name alias) and the printer (or printer queue) name.

Windows NT will try communicating with the printer and will give you an error message if it is not able to communicate with the printer. (If this happens, then it is most likely because your setup information is incorrect.)

Once you have added a port, you assign the UNIX network printer to the port by following these steps.

1. Click the box next to the port entry you just created for the network UNIX printer.
2. Select the manufacturer and model of your printer. Depending on your setup, Windows may prompt you to insert the Windows NT CD-ROM to copy the printer drivers for your printer from the CD-ROM.
3. Once the drivers are successfully copied, enter a name for the printer that makes it easy to identify the printer. This name will show up when you select Printer setup (or similarly named) function that lets you select the printer.
4. Optionally, you can share the printer with other computers. If you opt to share, you need to enter a share name and the computers that will be sharing the printer.

You may want to test your setup and access to the printer by printing a page.

Once you complete the setup, using the printer is just the same as using any shared printer attached to a Windows NT network.

PRINTING FROM UNIX CLIENTS TO WINDOWS NETWORK PRINTERS

In the prior section we looked at printing from a Windows client to a UNIX printer. You can go the other way too. You can print from a UNIX client to Windows NT-accessible network printers. The printer can be directly attached to a Windows NT server, or can be directly attached to the network, or can even be a NetWare printer that Windows NT can access.

Printing to a Windows network printer is transparent to a UNIX client. The UNIX client uses *lpr* just as it would for printing to a UNIX network printer. Windows NT server should be running the *lpdsvc* for the *lpr* to communicate to. You can start the *lpdsvc* if it is not already running, either by using the command line (key in *net start lpdsvc* at the command prompt) or using the GUI (Click Start, Settings, Control Panel, double-click Services, click TCP/IP Print Services, click Start). If you print regularly from UNIX clients to Windows network printers in your environment, then it may be more convenient to automatically start the TCP/IP Print Services whenever the system is booted. To designate that TCP/IP Print Services should be started automatically, select TCP/IP services as mentioned earlier, click the Startup button, and set the start-up type to Automatic and click OK.

You can check on the status of your print requests using the UNIX *lpq* command (just as you would for any UNIX network print request).

Accessing MS-DOS Files from UNIX

You can use Mtools to access diskettes and other media using the MS-DOS file system. Mtools is a public domain collection of programs that allow UNIX systems to read, write, and manipulate files in an MS-DOS file system, such as a diskette. Due to the differences in the environments, it is not possible to reproduce the command exactly as in MS-DOS. Each program attempts to emulate the MS-DOS equivalent command as closely as practical. There is a lot of information available on the Internet about Mtools, and the following is a brief extract. Information on Mtools is available at http://wauug.erols.com/pub/knaff/mtools.

Exhibit 12 summarizes the commands available as part of Mtools.

Exhibit 12. Mtools commands and descriptions.

Mtool Command	Description
mattrib	Change MS-DOS file attribute flags
mcopy	Copy MS-DOS files to/from UNIX
mcd	Change MS-DOS directory
mdel	Delete an MS-DOS file
mdir	Display an MS-DOS directory
mformat	Add an MS-DOS file system to a low-level formatted diskette
mlabel	Make an MS-DOS volume label
mmd	Make an MS-DOS subdirectory
mrd	Remove an MS-DOS subdirectory
mread	Low-level read (copy) an MS-DOS file to Unix
mren	Rename an existing MS-DOS file
mtype	Display contents of an MS-DOS file
mwrite	Low-level write (copy) a Unix file to MS-DOS

MS-DOS filenames are optionally composed of a drive letter followed by a colon, a subdirectory, and a filename. Subdirectory names can use either the '/' or '\' separator. The use of the '\' separator or wildcards will require the names to be enclosed in quotes to protect them from the shell.

The regular expression "pattern matching" routines follow the Unix-style rules. For example, '*' matches all MS-DOS files in lieu of '*.*'. The archive, hidden, read-only, and system attribute bits are ignored during pattern matching.

Not all UNIX filenames are appropriate in the MS-DOS world. The Mtools commands may have to alter Unix names to fit the MS-DOS filename restrictions. Most commands have a -v (verbose) option that will display the new names if they have been changed. The following exhibit (Exhibit 13) shows some examples of filename conversions.

Exhibit 13. UNIX and Windows file name conversion.

UNIX Name	MS-DOS Name	Reason for Change
Thisisatest	THISISAT	Filename too long
Emmet.gray	EMMET.GRA	Extension too long
prn.txt	XRN.TXT	PRN is a device name, not allowed in filename
.abc	X.ABC	Null filename
Hot+cold	HOTXCOLD	Illegal character

Unlike UNIX, MS-DOS filesystem is not case sensitive.

All options use the '–' (minus) flag, not '/' as you'd expect in MS-DOS.

The *mcd* command is used to establish the device and the current working directory (relative to the MS-DOS filesystem); otherwise, the default is assumed to be A:/.

All the Mtools commands return 0 on success, 1 on total failure, or 2 on partial failure.

Conclusion

In this chapter, we looked at how you can access a UNIX server from Windows clients for print and file services. We also looked at the reverse of accessing a Windows NT server from a UNIX client.

This concludes the coexistence part. In Part Three, we will take a look at system administration and other considerations such as e-mail and Internet access in heterogeneous environments.

Chapter 26
Using CORBA to Integrate Database Systems

Bhavani Thuraisingham

Information has become the most critical resource in many organizations, and the rapid growth of networking and database technologies has had a major impact on information processing requirements. Efficient access to information, and sharing it, have become urgent needs. As a result, an increasing number of databases in different sites are being interconnected. To reconcile the contrasting requirements of the different database management systems (DBMSs), tools that enable users of one system to data-use other systems are being developed. Efficient solutions for interconnecting and administering different database systems are also being investigated.

There are two aspects to the object-oriented approach to integrating heterogeneous database systems. In one approach, an object-oriented data model could be used as a generic representation scheme so the schema transformations among the different database systems could be facilitated. In the other approach, a distributed object management system could be used to interconnect heterogeneous database systems. This chapter explores the distributed object management system approach by focusing on a specific system, the object management group's (OMG) common object request broker architecture (CORBA).

INTEROPERABILITY ISSUES

Although research on interconnecting different DBMSs has been under way for over a decade, only recently have many of the difficult problems been addressed.

Schema Heterogeneity. Not all of the databases in a heterogeneous architecture are represented by the same schema (data model). Therefore, the

0-8493-9989-0/99/$0.00+$.50

different conceptual schemas have to be integrated. To do this, translators that transform the constructs of one schema into those of another are being developed.

Transaction Processing Heterogeneity. Different DBMSs may use different algorithms for transaction processing. Work is being directed toward integrating the various transaction processing mechanisms. Techniques that integrate locking, timestamping, and validation mechanisms are being developed. However, strict serializability may have to be sacrificed in order to create a heterogeneous environment.

Query Processing Heterogeneity. Different DBMSs may also use different query processing and optimization strategies. Research is being conducted to develop a global cost model for distributed query optimization.

Query Language Heterogeneity. Query language heterogeneity should also be addressed. Even if the DBMSs are based on the relational model, structured query language (SQL) and relational calculus could be used to achieve heterogeneity. Standardization efforts are under way to develop a uniform interface language.

Constraint Heterogeneity. Different DBMSs enforce different integrity constraints, which are often inconsistent. For example, one DBMS could enforce a constraint that all employees must work at least 40 hours, even though another DBMS may not enforce such a constraint.

Semantic Heterogeneity. Data may be interpreted differently by different components. For example, the entity address could represent just the country for one component, or it could represent the number, street, city, and country for another component.

COMMON OBJECT REQUEST BROKER ARCHITECTURE (CORBA)

The three major components of CORBA are the object model, the object request broker (ORB) and object adapters, and the interface definition language (CORBA-IDL).

The Object Model

The object model describes object semantics and object implementation. Object semantics describe the semantics of an object, type, requests, object creation and destruction, interfaces, operations, and attributes. Object implementation describes the execution model and the construction model. In general, the object model of CORBA has the essential constructs of most object models.

The Object Request Broker (ORB)

The ORB essentially enables communication between a client and a server object. A client invokes an operation on the object, and the object implementation provides the code and data needed to implement the object. The ORB provides the necessary mechanisms to find the object implementation for a particular request and enables it to receive the request. The communication mechanisms necessary to deliver the request are also provided by the ORB.

In addition, the ORB supports the activation and deactivation of objects and their implementations as well as generating and interpreting object references. Although the ORB provides the mechanisms to locate the object and communicate the client's request to the object, the exact location of the object, as well as the details of its implementation, are transparent to the client. Objects use object adapters to access the services provided by the ORB. Communication between a client and a server object using the ORB is illustrated in Exhibit 1.

Interface Definition Language (IDL)

IDL is the language used to describe the interfaces that are called by client objects and provided by object implementations. IDL is a declarative language; client and object implementations are not written in IDL. IDL grammar is a subset of ANSI C++ with additional constructs to support the operation invocation mechanism. An IDL binding to the C language has been specified, and other language bindings are being processed. Exhibit 2

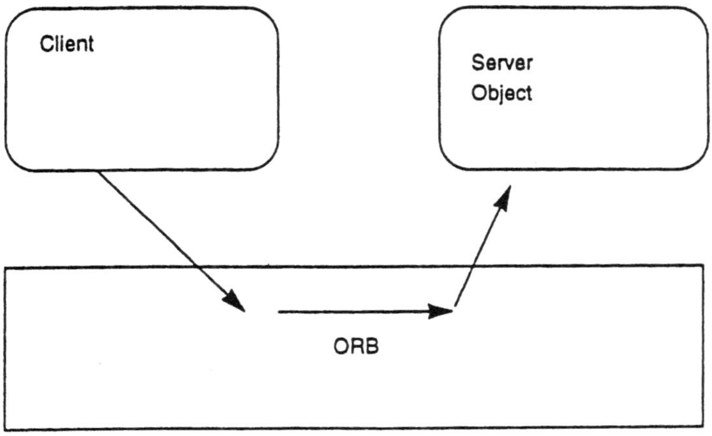

Exhibit 1. Communication through an Object Request Broker (ORB).

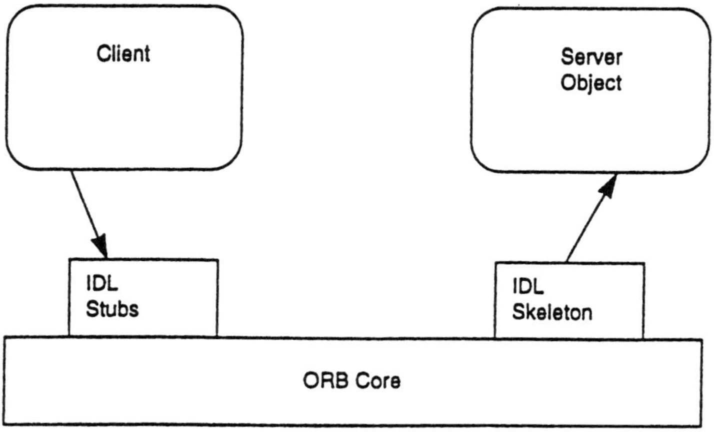

Exhibit 2. Interface Definition Language (IDL) interface to ORB.

illustrates how IDL is used for communication between a client and a server. The client's request is passed to the ORB using an IDL stub. An IDL skeleton delivers the request to the server object.

INTEGRATING HETEROGENEOUS DATABASE SYSTEMS

Migrating legacy databases to new generation architectures is difficult. Although it is desirable to migrate such databases and applications to client/server architectures, the costs involved in many cases are enormous. Therefore, the alternative approach is to keep the legacy databases and applications and develop mechanisms to integrate them with new systems. The distributed object management system approach in general, and the CORBA approach in particular, are examples of such mechanisms.

Although the major advantage of the CORBA approach is the ability to encapsulate legacy database systems and databases as objects without having to make any major modifications (see Exhibit 3), techniques for handling the various types of heterogeneity are still necessary. The CORBA approach does not handle problems such as transaction heterogeneity and semantic heterogeneity. However, the procedures used to handle the types of heterogeneity can be encapsulated in the CORBA environment and invoked appropriately.

Handling Client Communications with the Server

A client will need to communicate with the database servers, as shown in Exhibit 4. One method is to encapsulate the database servers as objects. The clients can issue appropriate requests and access the servers through an ORB. If the servers are SQL-based, then the entire SQL query/update request could be embedded in the message. When the method associated

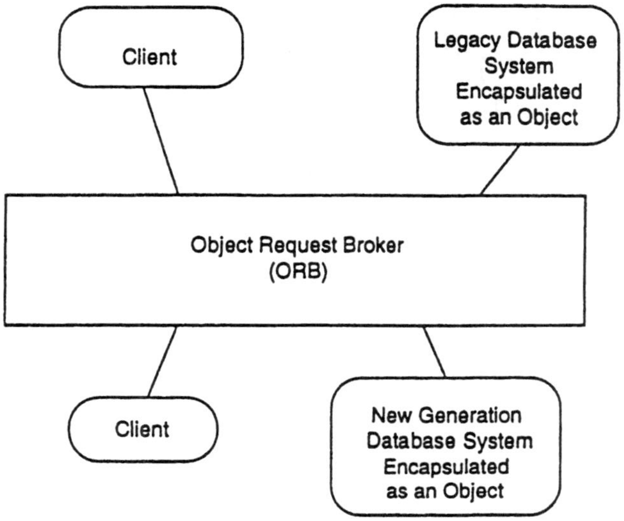

Exhibit 3. Encapsulating Legacy databases.

with the server object gets the message, it can extract the SQL request and pass it to the server. The results from the server objects are then encoded as a message and passed back to the client through the ORB. This approach is illustrated in Exhibit 5.

Handling Heterogeneity

Different types of heterogeneity must be handled in different ways. For example, if the client is SQL-based and the server is a legacy database

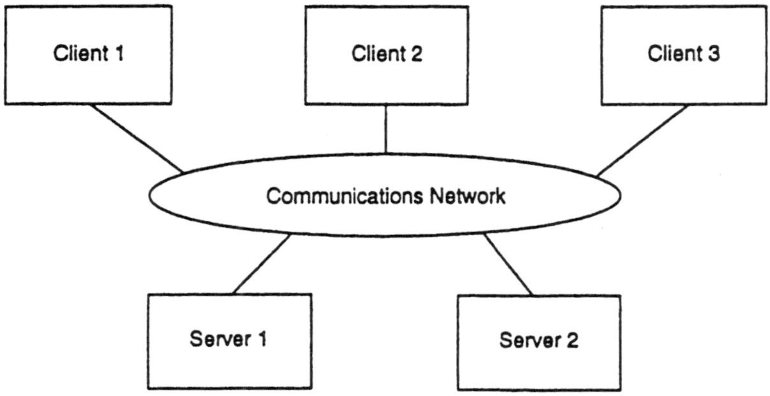

Exhibit 4. Client/server architecture.

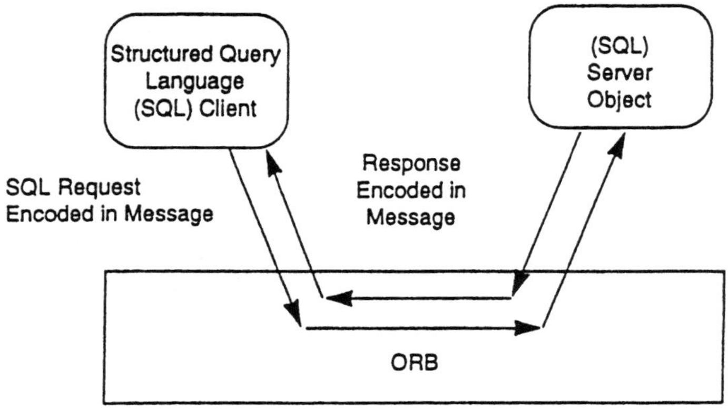

Exhibit 5. Common Object Request Broker Architecture (CORBA) for interoperability.

system based on the network model, then the SQL query by the client must be transformed into a language understood by the server. One representation scheme must be transformed into another. The client's request must first be sent to the module that is responsible for performing the transformations. In this module the transformer could be encapsulated as an object. As illustrated in Exhibit 6, the client's SQL request is sent to the transformer, which transforms the request into one understood by the server. The transformed request is then sent to the server object. The transformer could directly transform the SQL representation into a network representation, or it could use an intermediate representation to carry out the transformation.

The distributed processor could also be used to perform distributed data management functions. The distributed processor is responsible for handling functions such as global query optimization and global transaction management. This module is also encapsulated as an object and handles the global requests and responses. The response assembled by the server is also sent to the transformer to transform into a representation understood by the client. Response delivery is illustrated in Exhibit 7.

Semantic Heterogeneity. If semantic heterogeneity must be handled, then a repository should be maintained to store the different names given to a single object or the different objects represented by a single name. The repository could be encapsulated as an object that would resolve semantic heterogeneity. For example, a client could request that an object be retrieved from multiple servers. The request is first sent to the repository, which issues multiple requests to the appropriate servers depending on

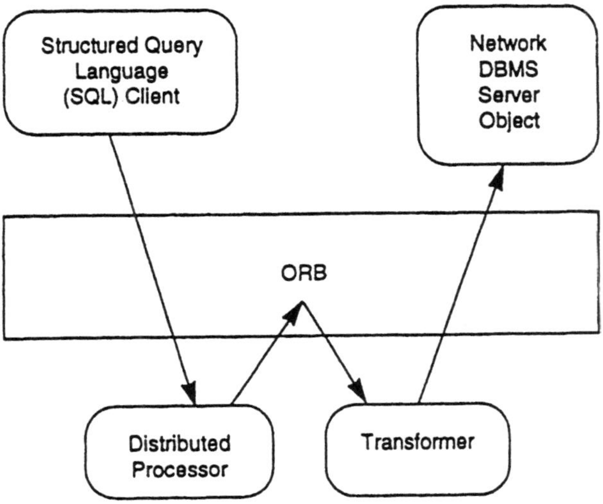

Exhibit 6. Handling transformations.

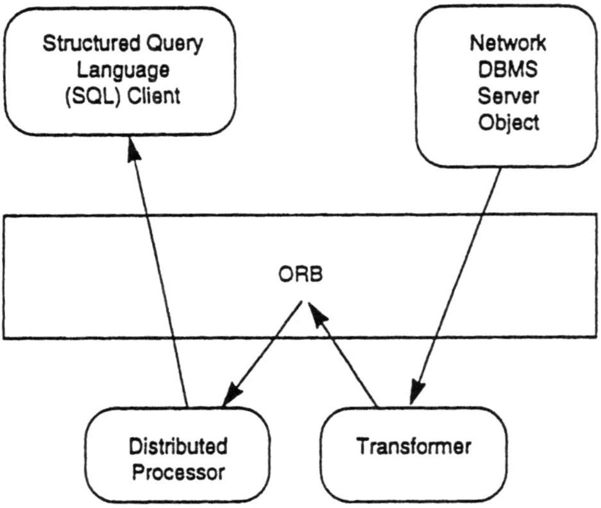

Exhibit 7. Delivering responses.

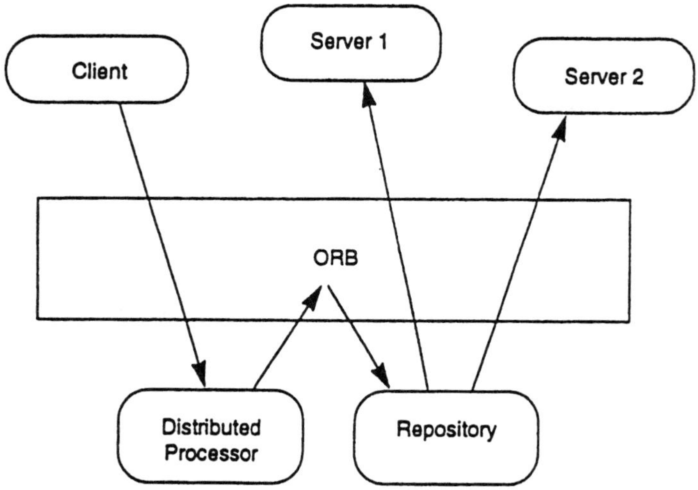

Exhibit 8. Handling semantic heterogeneity.

the names used to denote the object. This approach is illustrated in Exhibit 8. The response may also be sent to the repository so that it can be presented to the client in an appropriate manner. The repository could be an extension of the transformer illustrated in Exhibit 6. All the communications are carried out through the ORB.

CONCLUSION

The CORBA approach is an excellent means of addressing heterogeneity especially with respect to queries, languages, transactions, schemas, constraints, and semantics. However, although CORBA is useful for integrating heterogeneous database systems, there are still several issues that need further consideration. For example, should a server be encapsulated as an object? How can databases be encapsulated? Should an entire database be encapsulated as an object or should it consist of multiple objects? Should stored procedures be encapsulated also?

Although there is still much work to be done, the various approaches proposed to handle these issues show a lot of promise. Furthermore, until efficient approaches are developed to migrate the legacy databases and applications to client/server-based architectures, approaches like CORBA and other distributed object management systems for integrating heterogeneous databases and systems are needed.

Chapter 27
Federated Database Systems

James A. Larson
Carol L. Larson

Organizations requiring rapid and reliable access to data maintained by several databases should consider installing a federated database system. A federated database system is a special type of distributed database management system (DDBMS) that does not have the overhead nor all of the functions of a full-featured DDBMS. A variety of tools, including database drivers, driver managers, and World Wide Web (or Web) publishing tools, are available to construct federated databases. A full-featured DDBMS also can be used to construct a federated database system.

ACCESSING DISTRIBUTED DATABASES

Many operational databases are centralized with data stored on a single computer. Organizations often have several centralized databases and files located on different computers because:

- The organization is distributed geographically.
- The organization's information requirements are too vast to be met by a single centralized DBMS.
- Several databases were developed separately — for example, different suborganizations developed separate databases for different purposes.
- The introduction of PCs has resulted in several small, isolated databases.

Organizations often require rapid and reliable access to data in these separate databases. This is an arduous process requiring that a user:

- Determine which computers contain the data to be accessed.
- Formulate several queries, which may be executed on different computers.
- Copy or transfer the results to a single computer for merging results.
- Combine and merge the results.
- Extract the answer of the original query from the combined results.

0-8493-9989-0/99/$0.00+$.50

These tasks, which can be time-consuming, tedious, and error-prone, are candidates for automation in a special type of distributed database known as a *federated database system.*

FEATURES OF FEDERATED DATABASE SYSTEMS

A federated database system is a loosely coupled collection of databases and files that users access with a common interface. In federated database systems, there is no global schema to describe all of the data in all of the databases. Instead, there are several unified schemas, each describing portions of databases and files accessed by a class of users.

Exhibit 1 illustrates how users access databases at various sites within the federated database system. Each site, containing data to be shared with other sites, has one or more export schemas that describe the subset of the site's data, which may be accessed by specific users. Users may formulate a request against a unified schema, which describes a single database to a federated database user and is constructed logically from one or more export schemas. Federated database system components partition the request into multiple subrequests and route the subrequests to local databases, where they are transformed into a format required for processing by the local database management system or file system. Results derived from the local database or file are combined and routed to the user making the request.

Unified Schemas Support Location and Replication Transparency

Given a unified schema, users may access data subject to local security constraints without knowing the site at which the data are stored or whether the data is replicated. Apart from noticing reduced execution speeds, users are completely unaware that they are accessing data located in several separated databases.

Unified schemas support two important characteristics of a federated database system:

- *Location transparency.* The location of data is hidden from the user.
- *Replication transparency.* Data replication in more than one database is hidden from the user.

Export Schemas Support Database Autonomy and DBMS Transparency

Each site containing data to be shared with users of the federated database system has one or more export schemas. An export schema describes a subset of the site's data that may be accessed by specific users. Export

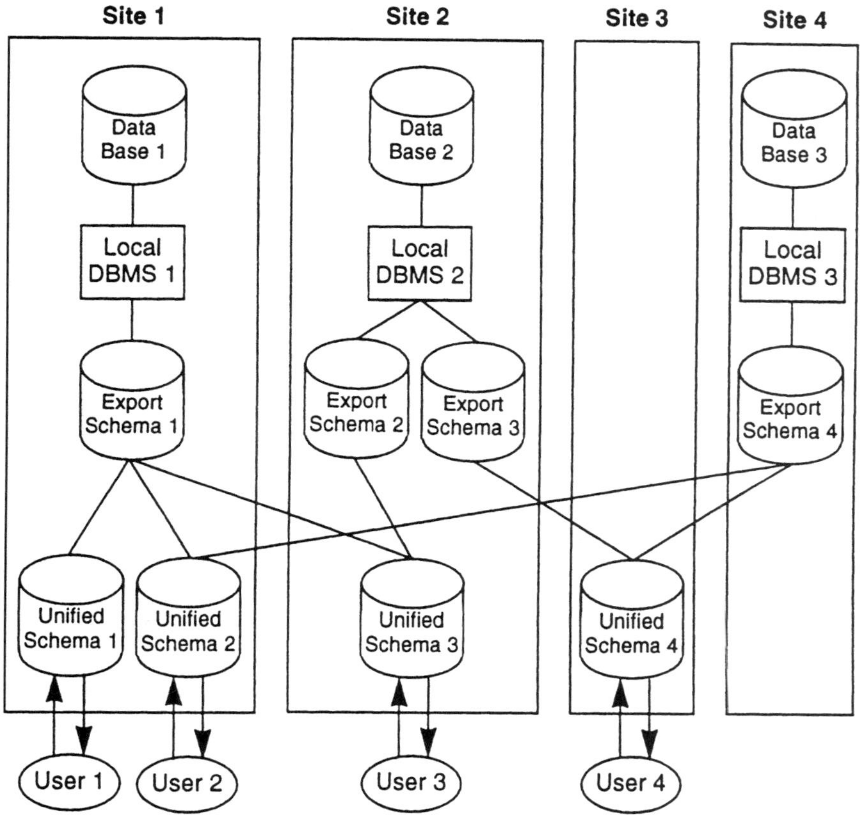

Exhibit 1. User access to a federated database system.

schemas support two additional characteristics of a federated database system:

- *DBMS transparency.* An export schema describes data exported for use by federated database system users in consistent format. The type of the local database management system or file system is hidden from the user.
- *DBMS autonomy.* The database administrator (DBA) of each database or file controls all access to the database or file. Administrators permit a class of federated users to access data by describing the data in the export schema for use by that particular class of users. DBAs may prohibit any federated database system user from accessing data by NOT including a description of the data in any export schema. Different subsets of the same data are described by various export schemas for use by various classes of federated users.

A federated database system is extremely flexible. It allows one class of users to access all of the data, or several classes of users to access different subsets of data. New unified and export schemas can be added for new classes of users, while existing schemas can be deleted at any time. A federated database system does not affect users who already have direct access to the database or file. Local users may continue to access the database or file system without using the federated database management system.

CONSTRUCTING A FEDERATED DATABASE SYSTEM

General approaches for constructing a federated database system include using ODBC drivers, Web publishing tools, and a distributed database. One approach, illustrated in Exhibit 2, uses drivers in place of export schemas, and applications with driver managers in place of unified schemas. Exhibit 3 illustrates the use of Web publishing tools to construct a federated database system, and the use of a distributed database management system is shown in Exhibit 4.

Using ODBC Drivers

ODBC drivers support database autonomy and DBMS transparency. Microsoft's Open Database Connectivity (ODBC) lets programmers write applications that access any ODBC-compliant database. ODBC describes an application program interface (API) that specifies functions for accessing a relational database. The ODBC driver implements these functions on top of each ODBC-compliant database management system or file system. An application written using an ODBC driver accesses the ODBC-compliant database or file. In effect, an ODBC driver hides the peculiarities of the local DBMS from the user by translating the user's request expressed in the standard ODBC format to the form required by the DBMS. ODBC drivers provide DBMS transparency.

ODBC also supports database autonomy. The database administrator determines what data to make available to federated users by making it available to the ODBC drivers. Exhibit 2 illustrates a federated database system implemented using ODBC drivers. Application 1 contains references conforming to the ODBC API. An ODBC driver associated with the database at Site 1 implements these functions, enabling User 1 to access Database 1 at Site 1.

Database driver managers support location and replication transparency. A database driver manager accepts commands from an application and routes the commands to the appropriate database drivers. In some cases, it also may replicate commands and route them to databases

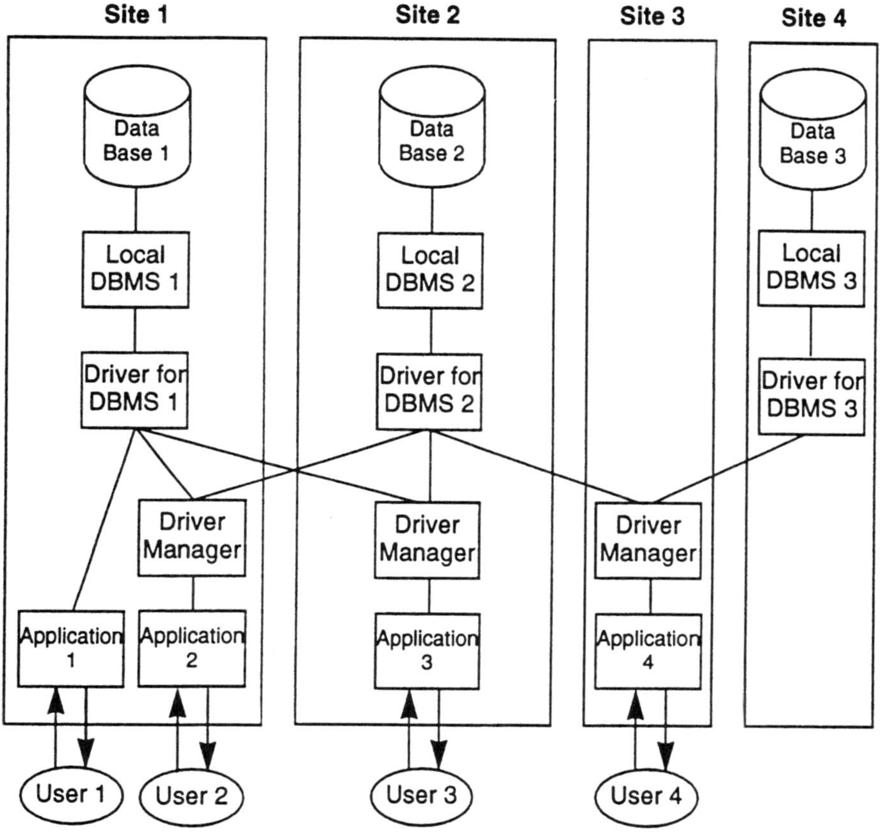

Exhibit 2. Federated database system using open database connectivity (ODBC) drivers.

containing replicated data. Driver managers support location and replication transparency.

In Exhibit 2, Users 2, 3, and 4 each have applications that access two databases. These applications contain a driver manager that routes database commands to the appropriate ODBC driver, which in turn performs the database access on behalf of the user.

Federated database systems work faster and are less expensive if no updates are permitted because updating involves overhead in the form of distributed concurrency control and distributed commit protocols. If updates are necessary, they should be restricted to one site at a time by using the local DBMS's concurrency control and commit protocols. Updates involving more than one site may not be possible in some federated databases.

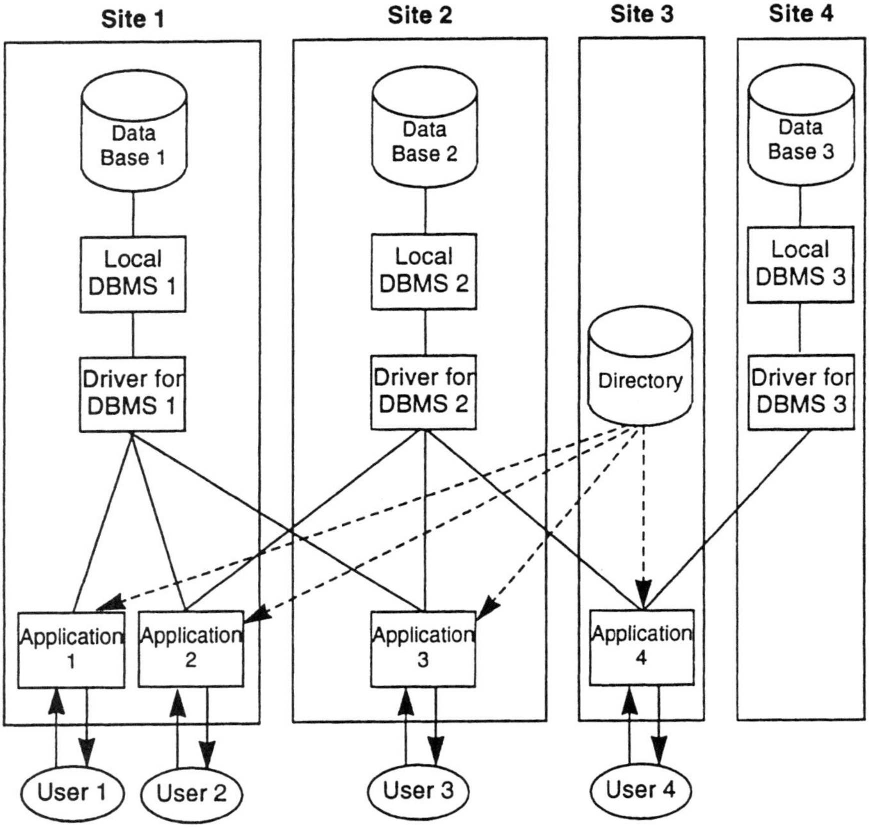

Exhibit 3. Federated database system using web publishing tools.

Using Web Publishing Tools

Enterprises may use the Web to enable users anywhere in the world to access the enterprise's data. By publishing a database in the hypertext markup language (HTML) format, users with various operating systems can access specific information using the connectivity provided by the Web.

One approach for transforming data to an HTML document is to extract the data from the database, export the data as ASCII files, and insert HTML tags into the files. Programmers may insert the HTML tags for fine control over the appearance of the final HTML document. Alternatively, software modules may insert HTML tags automatically. The HTML format acts as an export schema that prohibits users from updating the data.

Microsoft has introduced an Internet Server API (ISAPI) that is implemented by a special driver named http_odbc.dll. As shown in Exhibit 3,

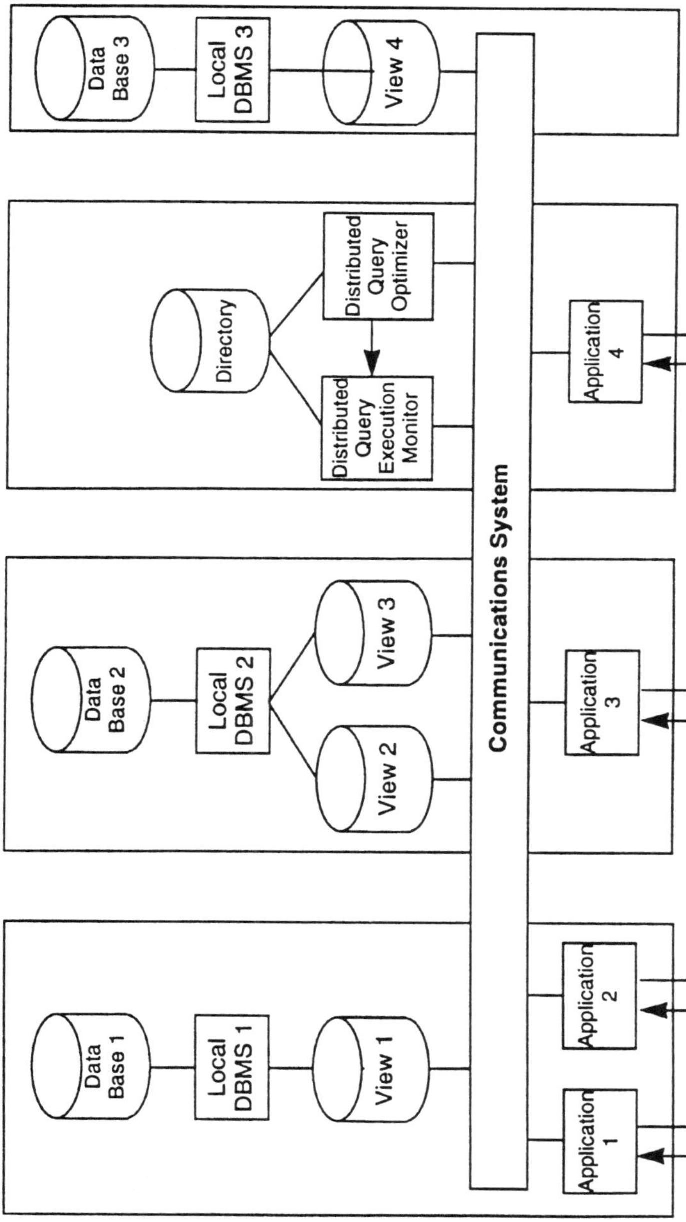

Exhibit 4. Federated database system using a distributed DBMS.

a user formulates a query by entering query parameters into input boxes or text areas and selecting options from pull-down menus embedded within an HTML form. This http_odbc.dll driver accepts query parameters entered by the user in an HTML form and converts them to ODBC commands according to instructions specified in an Internet Database Connectivity (IDC) file. An IDC file describes the data source, SQL statements, and other information needed to generate a valid ODBC request that can be processed by the local DBMS. In a sense, the IDC file acts as an export schema. Then, the result returned by ODBC is converted into an HTML format according to instructions specified in the HTML Extension Template (HTX) file. The HTX file also acts as an export schema. The http_odbc.ddl driver uses the IDC and HTX files to export the database to Web browsers.

Using a Distributed DBMS

Another approach for implementing a federated database is to use a distributed DBMS, as illustrated in Exhibit 4. A DDBMS is a collection of local DBMSs integrated together to give users the perception that they are accessing a centralized DBMS. A distributed DBMS uses the following mechanisms to support location and replication transparency:

- A directory maps each object name into one or more local databases or files. The directory provides location independence.
- The query optimizer transforms a query expressed in terms of a single, centralized database into multiple requests to be executed at local DBMSs. This enables the distributed DBMS to support DBMS transparency. The query optimizer also determines if multiple copies of the database exist and selects one copy for retrieval or all copies for updating. The DDBMS supports replication transparency.
- The distributed query execution monitor initiates and synchronizes local queries and integrates the results into a single result presented to the user.

A requesting application generates a database access request to be sent to a query optimizer. The query optimizer consults the directory to locate the appropriate databases for the request and creates subrequests that are executed by the query execution monitor. The query execution monitor transfers requests to one or more local DBMSs for execution and merges the results before sending them back to the requesting application.

Many distributed DBMSs also use ODBC drivers to provide DBMS transparency. Autonomy is supported by views (subsets of the local database) and passwords. However, DDBMSs are expensive to purchase, install, and operate. Their complexity requires skilled personnel, while their success requires that data be migrated to the local DBMSs supported by the distributed DBMS.

SUMMARY

Several tools are used to construct federated database systems. Drivers, such as ODBC, provide the minimal facilities to allow users to access data in multiple databases. Additional drivers, such as htt.odbc.dll, enable users to access data via Web browsers, such as the Netscape Navigator or Microsoft Internet Explorer. A distributed DBMS provides the most features for implementing a federated DBMS.

A federated DBMS enables the gradual migration from several centralized databases and file systems to a full-featured distributed DBMS. Initially, local DBAs construct export schemas so federated users can access some of the databases. Gradually, the DBAs enable additional federated users to access data by creating new export schemas and adding new data to existing export schemas. Eventually, all local databases and files are included in export schemas. One or more unified schemas enable federated database users to access precisely the data needed. Thus, the federated DBMS becomes equivalent to a distributed DBMS.

Chapter 28
Database Interoperability: From Federated Databases to a Mobile Federation

Antonio Si

One of the primary motivations for and successes of general-purpose database management systems has been the integration of separate collections of data files. Information sharing among applications subsystems is facilitated by combining and pooling data into a centralized conceptual database.

Developing a completely integrated database is often difficult. Many databases within and across organizations maintain overlapping or related information. Each individual database is autonomous and heterogeneous in nature as a consequence of its independent creation and evolution. A report by the telecommunication company U.S. West indicated that, generally, 5 terabytes of data are managed by 1000 separate systems, with customer information alone spread across 200 different databases.

Businesses are therefore motivated to implement mechanisms to support dynamic access to and sharing of related information among already existing database sources; this is sometimes referred to as the *database interoperability* problem.

It is possible, of course, to query each database individually and interrelate the results manually; however, this process is too time-consuming and error prone. GTE telephone, for example, reports that 27,000 data elements were recorded in just 40 of its applications; it also estimates that an

0-8493-9989-0/99/$0.00+$.50

average of 4 hours per data element is required to extract and document its semantics and information.

IMPACT OF WIRELESS NETWORKS AND MOBILE COMPUTING

Various techniques have been proposed to address the database interoperability problem in a network of heterogeneous and autonomous database systems. Such a collection of cooperating but autonomous database systems is termed a *federated database system*, or simply a *federation*. Each individual database system is called a *component*.

Wireless networks and mobile computing have opened up new possibilities for information access and sharing. The need to interoperate multiple heterogeneous, autonomous databases is no longer confined to a conventional federated environment.

Characteristics of a Mobile Federation

A mobile environment is usually composed of a collection of static servers and a collection of mobile clients. Each server is responsible for disseminating information over one or more wireless channels to a collection of mobile clients. The geographical area within which all mobile clients could be serviced by a particular server is called a *cell* of that server.

In this mobile environment, databases managed by database servers of different cells might be autonomous. Information maintained in a database will usually be most useful to clients within its geographical cell. In this respect, information maintained by databases of different cells might be disjoint or might be related. A mobile client, when migrating from one wireless cell to another, might want to access information maintained in the database server and relate it to the information maintained in its own database. Such an environment is termed a *mobile federation*, to distinguish it from a conventional federated environment. The database managed by a mobile client is termed a *mobile database*, while the database managed by the server is a *server database*. Using similar terminology, the database system managed by a mobile client is referred to as a *mobile component* and the database system managed by a server is referred to as a *server component*.

It is not clear if existing techniques can address interoperability in this newly evolved computing environment. This chapter presents a reference architecture for a conventional federated environment, proposes a set of functional requirements that a federated environment should support, and examines existing techniques for a federated environment with respect to each functional requirement in the context of the newly evolved mobile federation.

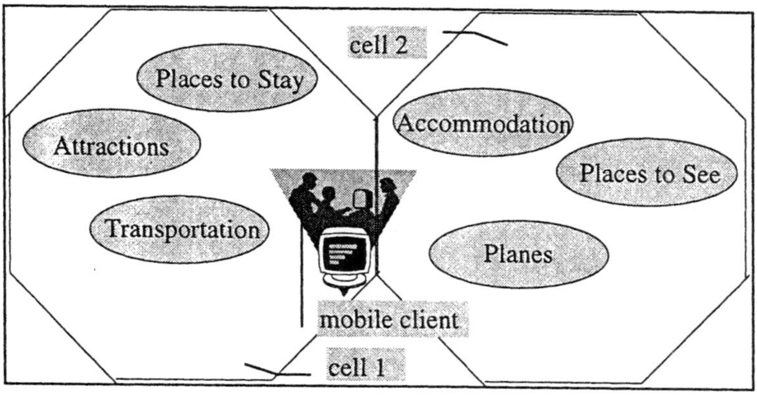

Exhibit 1. A working scenario: Snapshot of ATIS databases.

A Working Scenario

A tourist would like to discover information about attractions and accommodations within a certain area. With a portable computer equipped with a wireless communication interface, each mobile client (tourist) can receive travel information from the server over a wireless channel. Such an application might be called an Advanced Traveler Information System (ATIS).

In practice, each server database would maintain traveler information restricted to its own cell. For example, a server database serving the city of Los Angeles might provide vacancy information in all hotels within the Los Angeles area, such as the Holiday Inn near the Hollywood freeway. A user might query the server database to obtain all hotels that have vacancies. Information maintained by different server databases might, to a large extent, disjoint in this application domain, but there might still be some information overlap among different server databases.

For example, a Holiday Inn within the Los Angeles region might decide to maintain partial information on Holiday Inns in other regions, such as Pasadena. It is also important to note that different server databases will, in general, be autonomous, employing different database management tools and even different data models to manage its own information. Exhibit 1 illustrates a snapshot of the information maintained in different server databases and a mobile client who accesses information via a wireless channel.

It would be useful to have a high-level capability that allows structured units of information to be identified from a server database and incorporated into a local database managed by a mobile client. For example, a client might want to maintain information on all hotels in cell 1 and cell 2, since it travels to these two areas the most. A client visiting cell 1 (as shown in Exhibit 1) might issue a query to obtain all hotel information. When the client visits cell 2, the hotel information incorporated into his or her database will have to be interoperated with the existing information that the client previously incorporated from the server database in cell 1.This allows a mobile client to query the information using its own familiar database management tools. These various server databases, together with the local database of the mobile client, form a mobile federation. It is interesting to note that the local database maintained in a mobile client is, in effect, a *data warehouse* since its data is constructed by integrating data from various data sources.

The objective of a mobile federation is similar to a conventional federated database environment. Both environments are trying to share information among multiple autonomous databases. In a mobile federation, the sharing of information is implicit; the information is shared within the context of a mobile client. In a conventional federated system, the information is shared among the databases themselves. Obviously, the server databases of various cells could also share information among themselves, in which case the server databases form a conventional federated environment as well.

A REFERENCE ARCHITECTURE FOR A FEDERATED ENVIRONMENT

Exhibit 2 illustrates a typical federated environment. As the exhibit shows, a collection of independent database components is interconnected via a communication network. Each component consists of a database and a schema. A database is a repository of data structured or modeled according to the definition of the schema, which can be regarded as a collection of conceptual entity types. (The implementation of an entity type, of course, depends on the database model employed by the component; it may be a relation in a relational model, or it can be an object class, if an object-oriented model is employed.)

Information Sharing Techniques

Sharing of database information in this federated environment could be achieved at three different levels of granularity and abstraction:

- Entity types belonging to the schema of individual components could be shared such that modeled real-world concepts could be reused.
- Data instances stored in individual components' databases (the implementation of which also depends on the database model employed)

could be shared such that information of modeled real-world entities could be reused.

- Applications developed on a component's database could be shared among any other components. For example, if the server database in cell 1 in Exhibit 1 develops a pathfinder application that allows a mobile client to search for the shortest route to a destination, it could be reused by a mobile client in searching paths within cell 2 as well.

The simplest way to achieve information sharing in a database federation is for a component to simply browse through the content of a nonlocal (i.e., remote) component's database. In this respect, an *explorer* should be provided. Alternatively, a component could integrate remote information into its local database. The newly integrated information could be reused by the component in the future. To support such reuse of information, the database of a component, say X, is logically partitioned into three different subsets, as shown in Exhibit 2:

- *Local database.* The local database (LD) refers to the set of data instances originally created by X.
- *Import database.* The import database (ID) refers to the set of remote data instances that X retrieves from the export databases of remote components.
- *Export database.* The export database (ED) is a subset of the union of the local database and import database, which represents the set of data instances the component is willing to share with other components. In other words, a component should be able to export its imported data instances if the access privilege constraints specified on the imported instances are not violated.

Similarly, from the reference architecture in Exhibit 1, the schema of a component X is also partitioned into three different subsets. The local schema (LS) refers to the entity types originally created by X and is used to model the local database. The import schema (IS), which refers to the entity types X retrieves from the export schema of remote components, is used to model the import database. Finally, the export schema (ES), which is the subset of the union of LS and IS, is used to model the export database.

Integrating a remote application belonging to a remote component, say Y, into X's local system is difficult because X's local computer system might be different from that of Y. One possibility (proposed by D. Fang et al.) is to integrate the signature of the remote application into X's local system. To execute the application, X's local data is passed to component Y; the application is run on the remote component using X's data and the results are returned back to X. The Java virtual machine could make application sharing easier.

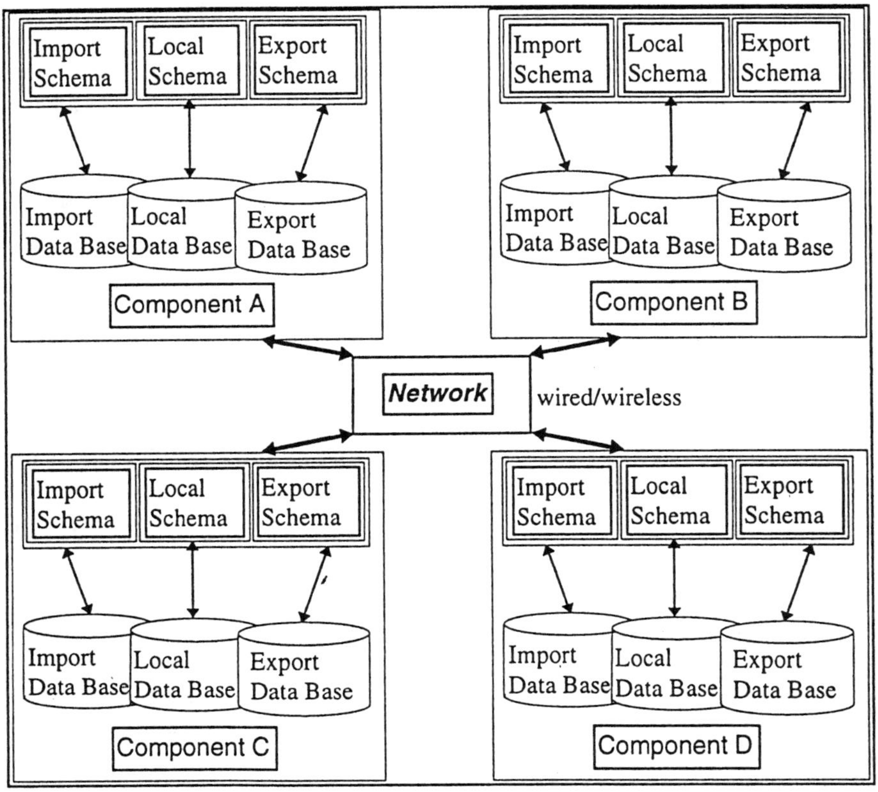

Exhibit 2. Reference architecture for a federated environment.

CHARACTERISTICS OF A FEDERATED DATABASE ENVIRONMENT

Each component within a federation is usually heterogeneous and autonomous in nature. Heterogeneity is a natural consequence of the independent creation and evolution of autonomous databases; it refers to the variations in which information is specified and structured in different components. Autonomy means each component is under separate and independent control.

Types of Heterogeneities

In general, a spectrum of heterogeneities of different levels of abstraction could be classified.

Database Model Heterogeneity. Each component may use different database models to describe the structure and constraints of its data.

Conceptual Schema Heterogeneity. Each component may model similar real-world concepts in different ways, such as the different schema used by the different database components of the multiple ATIS databases depicted in Exhibit 1. This is also referred to as *semantic heterogeneity.* This conceptual schema heterogeneity could be further divided into three discrepancies, each of which can be explained as follows:

- *Naming mismatch.* Two entity types from different components modeling the same real-world concept might use different naming conventions in representing the attributes. In the ATIS database in Exhibit 1, the ranking of a hotel might be modeled by an attribute called "rank" of Places to Stay in component A, while the same information might be modeled by an attribute called "number of stars" of Accommodation in component B.
- *Domain mismatch.* The same attribute of two entity types from different components might be represented in different domains. For example, both Attractions and Places to See of components A and B, respectively, in Exhibit 1 might have an attribute "zip code." However, component A might represent the attribute as an integer, while component B might represent it as a string.
- *Schematic discrepancy.* Data in one database might be represented as entity types in another database. In Exhibit 1, entity type Planes of component B might be represented as an attribute of Attractions in component A.
- *Data specification heterogeneity.* Each component may model similar real-world entities in different units of measure. One component might represent the distance of an attraction in meters, while another component might represent it in miles.
- *Update heterogeneity.* Since each component is under separate and independent control, data instances modeling the same real-world entity in different databases might be updated asynchronously. When the daily rate of a hotel is updated, databases A and B in Exhibit 26-1 might be updated at different times.
- *Database tools heterogeneity.* Each component may use different tools to manipulate its own database. For example, different components might use different query languages.

Types of Autonomy

Orthogonally, each component can exhibit several different types of autonomy.

Design Autonomy. This refers to the ability of a component to choose its own design on the data being managed, the representation of the data instances, the constraints of the data, and the implementation of the component's database system.

Association Autonomy. This refers to the ability of a component to decide to what extent the component would like to participate in the interoperability activity. A component is free to share its schema, data, or applications with other components; a component can even decide not to participate in the sharing activity at all.

Control Autonomy. This refers to the ability of a component to control the access privileges of any remote component on each of its exported information units (entity types or instances). In general, four types of access control privilege could be granted by a component to a remote component on each of its exported information units:

- Read access to the database instances (R)
- Read definition access to entity types (RD)
- Write access to database instances (W)
- Generate access for creating database instances (G)

These four access privileges form a partial order such that W > G > RD and W > R > RD. Neither G nor R dominates each other. For instance, if component X grants W access privilege to remote component Y on one of its exported entity types, component Y is allowed to read the instances of the entity type as well. By contrast, if X only grants R access privilege to Y on the entity type, Y is not allowed to modify any instances of the entity type.

If an exported unit of a component, say X, is imported from another component, Y, the capability of X to control the access privileges on the exported unit will depend on whether the unit is imported by copy or imported by reference from Y.

Execution Autonomy. This refers to the ability of a component to execute local operations without interference from external components. If, for example, component X might run an application on behalf of remote component Y. This autonomy implies that X can run the application as if it is a local execution (i.e., X can schedule, commit, or abort the application freely).

Functional Requirements of a Federated Database Environment

From the perspective of a component, X, several functional capabilities need to be supported in order to be able to participate in the interoperability activity with other components.

Information Exportation. Component X must be able to specify the information it is willing to share with other components. Such a facility should allow the component to specify the export schema, the export database, or any application that the component would like to be sharable.

Furthermore, X should be able to specify the access privileges of each remote component on each of its exported information units.

A mobile federation is comparatively more dynamic than a database federation, connecting and disconnecting from the wireless network frequently. A mobile component also enters and leaves a cell frequently. It is difficult for a server component to keep track of which mobile components are currently residing within the cell under its management. Furthermore, a cell can potentially have many components visiting at any moment. Therefore, it is not possible for a server component to indicate the access privileges of each mobile component. An access control mechanism that is scalable with respect to the number of mobile components is necessary. Due to the dynamic nature of a mobile component, it is not always possible to incorporate information from a mobile component.

Information Discovery. Before component X can access or use any remote information, X must be aware of the existence and availability of the information in which it is interested. A facility must be provided to allow X to discover any remote information of interest at various granularity or abstraction, including schema, data, or applications.

In general, there are two ways information could be discovered by component X. One possibility is that X can formulate a discovery request for its interested information, in which case a facility must be provided to identify the components containing information units that are relevant to the request. Another possibility is for component X to navigate or explore the exported information space of each remote component and look for the interested information. An explorer must then be provided for such a navigation purpose.

Information Importation. Once interested information units from remote components are discovered, component X can import the information units into its local database. Through importation, component X can reuse the discovered information in the future. In general, three importation capabilities are required: schema importation, data importation, and application importation.

Schema Importation. This refers to the process of importing remote export schema into X's local schema. This process is further composed of two activities — *heterogeneity resolution* and *schema integration*. Heterogeneity resolution is the process of resolving any conflict that exists between X's local schema and the remote schema.

Since different components might use different database models to specify the data, a facility must be provided to translate the remote schema from the remote database model to the one used in X's local system. Furthermore, since different components might model similar real-world concepts differently, another heterogeneity that must be resolved is to identify the relationship between X's local schema and the remote schema.

Referring back to the ATIS federation in Exhibit 1, two entity types belonging to two different schema might model the same real-world concept, such as the Attractions information of component A and the Places to See information of component B. Alternatively, two entity types might model related information, such as the Transportation information of component A and the Planes information of component B. Finally, two entity types might model different concepts, such as the Attractions information of component A and the Planes information of component B.

Data Importation. Similarly, data importation refers to the process of importing remote export database information into X's local database. This process is composed of two activities — *instance identification* and *data integration.*

Instance identification refers to the process of identifying the relationship between the remote database and the local database. Two data instances from different databases might model the same, related, or different real-world entities. This process is complicated because, on the one hand, instances from different databases cannot be expected to bear the same key attributes; on the other hand, merely matching non-key attributes may lead to unsatisfactory results because data instances modeling different entities may possess the same attribute values. This process is further complicated by possible update heterogeneity that might exist between the two instances.

Once the relationship between the remote database and X's local database is identified, the remote database can be integrated into the local database. Again, the remote database should be integrated such that its relationship with the local database is reflected.

There are two different data integration paradigms for integrating a remote data instance from a remote component, Y, into X's local database: *imported by copy* and *imported by reference.*

When a remote instance is imported by copy, the data instance is copied into the local database. The copied data instance becomes part of the local database. Any access to the imported instance is referred to its local copy.

When a remote instance is imported by reference, a reference to the remote instance is maintained in the local database. Any access to the imported data instance requires a network request to Y for up-to-date data value. When a remote data instance is imported by copy, the local component, X, has complete control on the local copy of the imported instance and is allowed to specify the access privileges of other remote components on the local copy of the imported instance. However, when a remote data instance is imported by reference from component Y, Y still maintains its control over the imported instance. Component X is still free to export the imported instance; however, X cannot modify the access privileges specified by Y on this imported data instance.

Application importation can only be achieved to a very limited extent due to the possible differences in the computer systems of the different components. However, with the advent of Java mobility code, this could soon become a reality.

In a mobile federation, communication between a mobile component and a server database is usually over an unreliable wireless channel. It is more efficient for a mobile federation to import an instance by copying since a component does not need to rely on the network to obtain the data value of the instance. A mobile component, in general, has less storage space than a federated component. A mobile component, therefore, might not be able to import all data instances and will have to maintain only those instances that it accesses most frequently.

Information Querying and Transaction Processing. Component X should be able to operate its imported information in its local system. The operation on the imported information should be transparent in the following manner:

- *Functional transparency.* All existing local tools of component X, such as its query language and DBMS software, should be operational on the imported information units in the same manner as they operate on the local information units.
- *Location transparency.* Users and tools operating on the imported information units should not be aware of their original locations and remote nature.

Very often, there is a conflict between supporting the described functional capabilities in a component and preserving the autonomy of the component. To preserve the autonomy of a component, modifying any component of the DBMS software is not recommended.

TECHNIQUES FOR DATABASE SHARING

To support database sharing functional capabilities, data model heterogeneity must be resolved. This is usually addressed by employing a common canonical model, which provides a communication forum among various components. Schema and instances represented in the local data model are required to convert to the canonical model. Most research

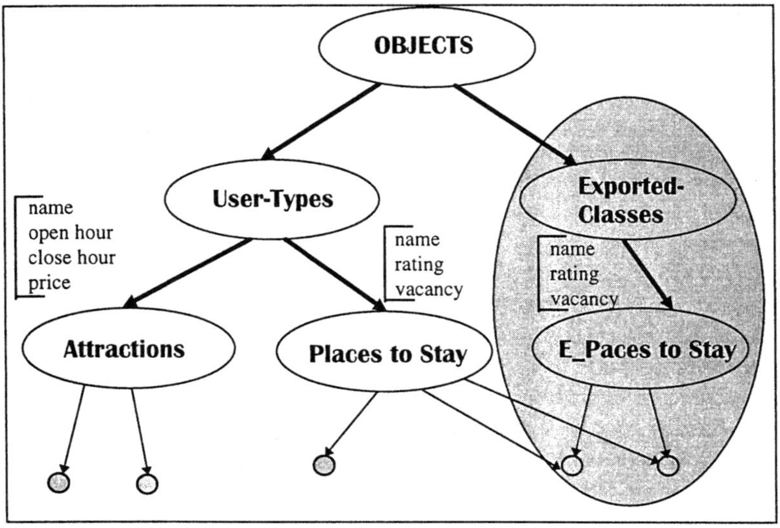

Exhibit 3. Information exportation via object view.

prototypes use an object model as the canonical model because of its expressive power. Most corporations, however, use relational models. ODBC from Microsoft and JDBC from Sun Microsystems are generally considered the industry standards.

Information Exportation

Information exportation can be easily achieved using database view mechanisms. Exhibit 3 illustrates the management of exported information. A sub-hierarchy rooted at class `Exported-Classes` is created under the root of the class hierarchy (i.e., `OBJECTS`). To export a class, `O`, a class name `E_O` is created as a subclass of `Exported-Classes`. To export an attribute of `O`, the same named attribute is created for `E_O`; this allows a component to specify exported information at the granularity of a single attribute.

Each exported instance is handled by a multiple-membership modeling construct of the object model, relating the original class to which the instance belongs to the `E_` counterpart. In effect, classes belonging to the sub-hierarchy rooted at `Exported-Classes` represent the export schema, and the instances belonging to the sub-hierarchy represent the export database (depicted by the shaded region in Exhibit 3).

In Exhibit 3, only class `Places to Stay` is exported because only `Places to Stay` has a corresponding `E_Places to Stay` class. All attributes of Places to Stay have the corresponding ones defined on E_Places to Stay. Furthermore, two instances of Places to Stay are exported, relating via a multiple membership construct to E_Places to Stay. A component employing a relational data model could use a similar technique to specify its exporting information units since the export schema and database are, in effect, a view of the database.

Access control mechanisms for exported information are limited and especially difficult to achieve in a mobile federation. It is difficult for a server component to keep track of which mobile components are within the cell under its management and specify their individual access privileges. A multilevel access control mechanism is more applicable in this domain.

In a multilevel system, database information units are classified into privilege levels. The privilege levels are arranged in an order such that possessing a privilege level implies possessing all its subordinate levels. For example, a typical multilevel system contains four privilege levels: top secret (TS), secret (S), confidential (C), and unclassified (U). A typical database system could have arbitrary number of privilege levels. To access an information unit, the user needs to obtain a clearance at least equal to the privilege level of the unit. In a mobile federation, a mobile component could join a privilege level that will inherit the database information units that it could access from the server database.

Information Discovery

Information discovery can be achieved by exploring the exported information of a database component. A typical device that explores the content of several databases is depicted in Exhibit 4. This explorer is implemented on the Netscape Navigator, providing a platform-independent browsing capability because of the availability of Netscape in UNIX workstations, Macintosh computers, and PCs.

The explorer in Exhibit 4 allows a component to explore multiple databases at the same time. It employs a relational model as the canonical model. Exported information units are viewed as relations. The explorer has windows to browse four separate databases of remote components and a window to the local database of a component.

An alternate approach to discovering remote information units that are interesting to a particular component is by specifying the requirements of the interested information units. Remote information units that are relevant to the discovery specification will be identified. Specification could be initiated in an ad hoc manner. Following are three different types of discovery requests:

- A component can request remote entity types (instances) that model the same real-world concept (entity) as a local entity type (instance).
- A component can request remote entity types (instances) that model a complementary view of a local entity type (instance).
- A component can request remote entity types (instances) that model an overlapping view of a local entity type (instance).

To support these three types of discovery requests, one approach is to use a probability model to determine the extent to which two entity types (instances) from different databases modeled the same real-world concept. The probability model is based on two heuristics derived from the common attributes of the two entity types: *intra-concept similarity indicator* and *inter-concept dissimilarity indicator.*

Intuitively, an intra-concept similarity indicator refers to the probability that the common attributes will be modeled in related entity types. Inter-concept dissimilarity indicator refers to the probability that the attributes

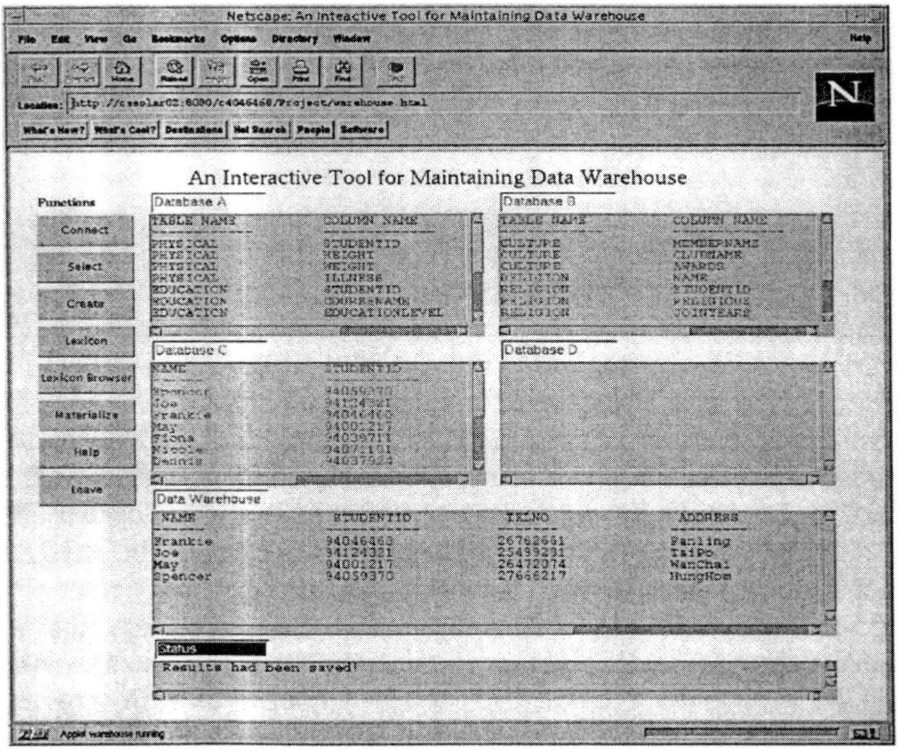

Exhibit 4. A sample information discovery explorer.

will be modeled in unrelated entity types. Two entity types from different databases will have a high probability of similarity if their overlapped attributes have a high intra-concept similarity indicator as well as a high inter-concept dissimilarity indicator. The use of these heuristics is based on the observation that different databases might model complementary or even disjointed views of the same concept; on the other hand, different databases might model different concepts similarly.

A more general specification could be achieved using first-order logic like language. Each component will thus require a mediator that understands the specification language and identifies information units relevant to the specification.

In a mobile federation, it is not important if a server database returns all information relevant to a discovery request; rather, it is much more important that the returned information units are indeed relevant because of the typically low bandwidth on a wireless channel. One approach to ensure this is to create a profile capturing the interests of each component.

Information Importation

Schema Importation. As mentioned previously, a component, X, can import (partial) remote schema from a remote component, Y, into its local schema by first resolving any heterogeneity between X's local schema and Y's schema.

One common approach to resolve schema heterogeneity between X's local schema and Y's remote schema is through a common knowledge base that contains various real-world concepts. Entity types from different databases are required to match with the concepts in the knowledge base. If both entity types map to the same concept in the knowledge base, they are regarded as modeling the same real-world concept. The knowledge base also provides instructions that define how a remote entity type could be integrated into the schema of a component's local database. The instructions could be specified in the form of rules or in a logic-like syntax. The former is easier to understand, but is less flexible. The latter is more flexible, but is less user-friendly.

In a mobile federation, it is difficult to specify a knowledge base that is applicable to all mobile components because there is a potentially unlimited number of mobile components visiting a wireless cell. It is perhaps more appropriate for a mobile component to provide its own knowledge or its personal profile, containing its own view for integrating remote schema into its own local schema.

Instance Importation. To identify the relationship between instances from two databases, one needs to address the data specification heterogeneity and the update heterogeneity problems. Data specification heterogeneity is usually resolved, again, via a knowledge base, indicating how the representation of a remote instance could be converted into the representation of the local database.

Exhibit 5 illustrates the importance of update heterogeneity in identifying the relationship between instances from various databases. In Exhibit 5, valid time denotes the time in which a fact was true in reality, while the transaction time denotes the time in which a fact was captured in a database.

One approach to addressing update heterogeneity is to use historical update information on the instances to determine their degree of similarity. The historical update patterns of each instance represent the changes of states of the instance since its creation, inherently capturing its behavioral properties. This allows the instance identification to be performed based on behavioral property in addition to their structural property, as is done traditionally. The historical update information of an instance could be easily obtained through a transaction log.

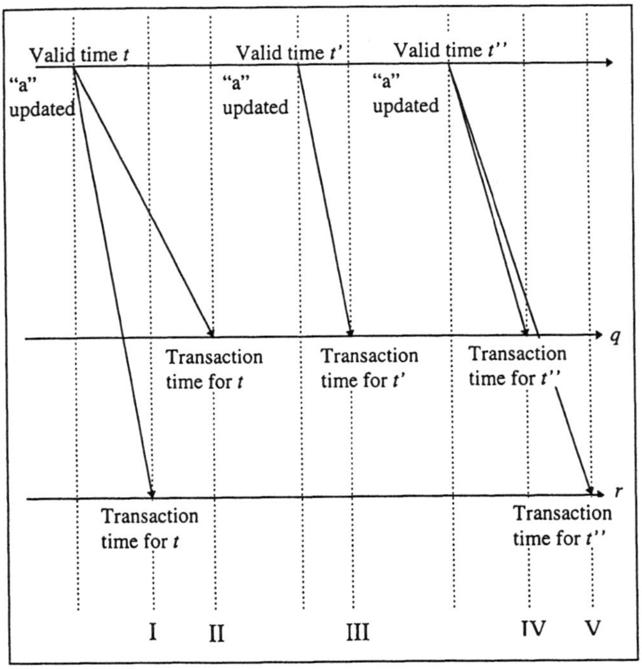

Exhibit 5. Update heterogeneity in a database federation.

As mentioned previously, instance integration could be performed via import by copy or import by reference. Using an object model as a canonical model, it is quite easy to support these two integration paradigms within one general framework. Exhibit 5 illustrates the partial conceptual schema of two components, A and B, of the ATIS databases from Exhibit 1. Instances x and y of component B are imported from class `Accommodation` of component A. The class `Remote-Classes` is created in component B to hold the oids (object instance of definitions) of the imported instances and the address of components from which the instances are imported (i.e., address of component A in the example). These two types of information are placed in the attributes `r_oid` and `r_host`, respectively. A class called `R_Accommodation` is created in component B as subclass of `Remote-Classes` to model the imported instances.

In effect, the sub-hierarchy rooted at `Remote-Classes` represents the import schema and the instances belonging to the sub-hierarchy represent the import database; this is depicted by the shaded region in Exhibit 6. Notice that the import sub-hierarchy has a mirror structure as the export sub-hierarchy mentioned previously.

Attributes of classes belonging to the Remote-Classes sub-hierarchy are user-defined methods. To obtain the attribute value for attribute "a" of an imported instance, x, the method "a" will obtain the "`r_oid`" of x and initiate a remote request to the remote component, whose address is specified in "`r_host`" of x, to obtain the attribute value for the instance. This achieves the effect of imported by reference. To support import by copy, the imported instances are added to a local class via multiple-membership construct. The additional inherited attributes could be used as placeholders for the copied attribute values of the imported instance. This is illustrated in Exhibit 6. The obtained value of an attribute of an instance returned from the corresponding method could be stored in the additional attributes inherited.

In a mobile federation, the connection between a mobile component and the server component could be disconnected at any moment, either due to the unreliability of a wireless channel or due to the movement of a mobile component to another cell. It is, thus, more appropriate for a component to import an instance by copy rather than by reference. This also has an effect of caching the instance into the local database of a mobile component. In this respect, one could regard the local database of a mobile component as a data warehouse since the local database is derived from multiple database sources.

Information discovery and importation could be provided within a uniform framework or interface. This allows discovered remote information units to be imported into the local database of a component. The explorer

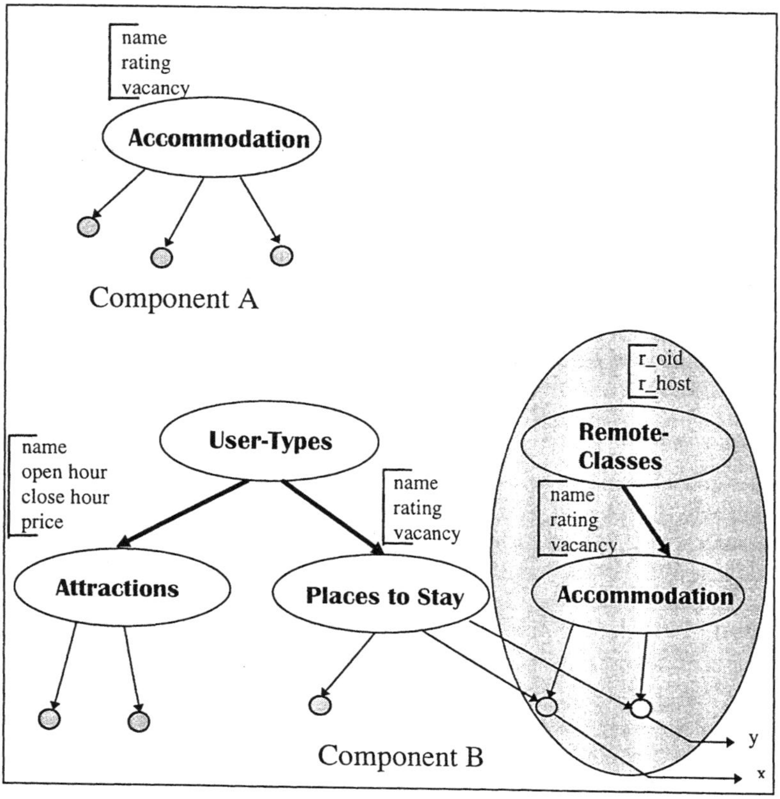

Exhibit 6. Data integration.

in Exhibit 4 also provides functions for information importation as well. In this particular system, a relational model is employed as a canonical model. The integration of information units from several databases is basically achieved via the "join" operation in this explorer. A component could also create a lexicon containing relationships among attributes of different databases. This resolves the conceptual heterogeneity. This lexicon acts as a localized profile of the component, capturing the perspectives of the component on the relationships among information units from different databases.

Information Querying and Transaction Processing

The notion of transaction is supported weakly in existing database federation prototypes. The reason stems from the fact that it is very difficult to support all the properties of transaction processing in a federated database system without seriously violating the autonomy of individual components and without rewriting the DBMS software of individual components.

Consider a situation in which a component X submits a transaction T to a remote component Y. The transaction T, when executed in component Y, is simply a local transaction of component Y. Component Y is free to abort the transaction without notifying component X. Component X, thus, might obtain inconsistent data.

SUMMARY

This chapter has presented a reference architecture and functional requirements for a federated database environment. Techniques for addressing each functional requirement have been presented. Limitations of existing techniques in the domain of a mobile federation have been discussed, and proposed solutions have also been briefly illustrated. Experiences with real applications in a mobile federation are necessary to further pinpoint additional problems that require research.

ACKNOWLEDGMENTS

This work is supported in part by the Hong Kong Polytechnic University Central Research Grant Number 351/217. Part of the materials in this chapter are the results of the Remote-Exchange project at the University of Southern California.

Chapter 29

Database Gateways and Interoperability

Martin D. Solomon

Whenever client/server systems are developed and introduced into existing large-size information systems environments, the need to have bidirectional access to legacy data is inevitable. Few developers have the luxury of building these systems without first having to inquire against or update to other databases or files somewhere else in the organization's infrastructure.

There are many software options for communicating with the various platforms. Primary choices include masking and screen scraping, advanced program-to-program communications (APPC), database gateway software, messaging software, and file transfer techniques.

This chapter is intended to help database managers understand how database gateways work, whether these products can provide effective solutions for their organizations' business issues, and how to choose and set up the gateway software and support infrastructure.

DATABASE GATEWAY SETUP

All database gateways provide a translation stop or box hop so that the data being shipped can be manipulated for arrival at the destination stop (see Exhibit 1). This stop takes the form of a gateway server and provides varying degrees of service including data translation, resource governing software, and load balancing or connection management tools. This server also manages the communications links and options between the data resources on the host and server platforms. This software is installed and coupled on its host and server counterparts in the enterprise at the location of the user's choice. Frequency and size of the requests coming through this stop determine performance and whether multiple gateway servers are required.

0-8493-9989-0/99/$0.00+$.50

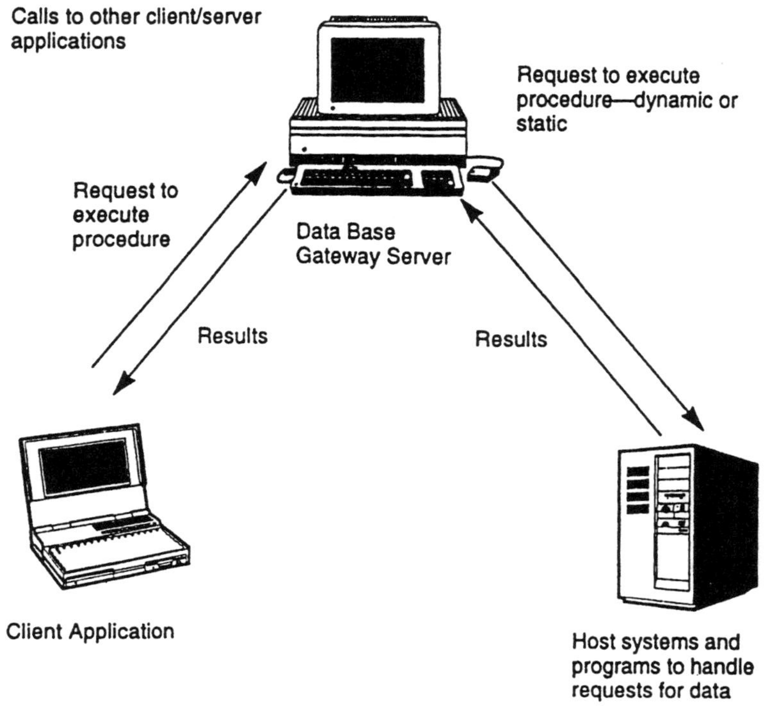

Exhibit 1. Client-Initiated Remote Procedure Call (RPC) to host.

DATABASE GATEWAY CAPACITY PLANNING

Several variables must be considered when choosing database gateway hardware and operating system software. Variables include maximum expected number of concurrent user connections to the gateway server, estimated daily and peak amounts of data to be passed through the gateway server, and the network protocols to be used in gateway access.

Concurrent User Connections

Concurrent user connections are a key determining factor in capacity planning because each user connected to the gateway hardware reserves memory on the server for address space, as much as 256K bytes per user, depending on the gateway software. To determine this parameter, it is important to know what types of applications are traversing the gateway and to gather information pertaining to performance expectations and the types of functions exploited on the gateway.

SQL Access.

Many database gateways also support dynamic SQL access for updates to the host data store. Depending on the type of front-end tool used to perform these accesses, data integrity in DB2, for example, may only be assured by carrying a conversational transaction into the transaction processing (TP) monitor (e.g., customer information control system [CICS]). This usually forces the client running the application to remain connected to the gateway and to the TP monitor for extended periods of time to ensure the integrity of the data. Therefore, a moderate-size departmental application performing data access in this manner could end up maintaining a relatively large number of gateway and TP monitor resources throughout the day if the gateway connections are allocated when the user opens the application.

Static Remote Procedure Calls.

In applications performing static remote procedure calls (RPCs) to the host, performance requirements become the key issue. Assuming that the application RPCs are constructed with stable single transaction units of work, the client application has no inherent need to maintain a continuous connection to the gateway server to preserve data integrity once the unit of work or transaction is completed. Each access, however, requires the establishment of a new address space on the gateway and a possible security-check exit routine. This can take anywhere from 50–500 milliseconds depending on the processing speed of the gateway server and network configuration. The additional time spent on reestablishing a connection should be carefully evaluated when designing the application.

Low- and High-Volume OLTP.

Low volume processing, which can be loosely defined as fewer than 2,500 online teleprocessing (OLTP) transactions per day, does not usually justify the tradeoff of using more memory and incurring the associated costs for the gain of about 200 milliseconds per transaction. High-volume OLTP-type systems with upwards of 15,000transactions per day generally require continuous connectivity to provide high-level response times for users.

In both cases—and especially if the expected use of the system cannot be clearly predicted as being at either end of the spectrum—it is worthwhile to invest the short amount of time it takes to code the system for either option. Any number of simple techniques can be used to develop a dynamic switch-type function to toggle the application between a continuous stay-connected mode and that of reestablishing a connection with each cross-platform request. This capability is even more valuable if several applications are expected to share a common database gateway server.

Amount of Data Passing Through the Server

The second determining factor in choosing the gateway hardware and operating system is the amount and frequency of data passed through the gateway server. The limits of technology still dictate that high-volume OLTP-type applications using the gateway should only send a relatively small amount of data for the average transaction, probably on the order of 1–2K bytes to ensure acceptable response time.

Frequently, however, database gateways are shared with other applications and ad hoc query users. With regard to multiple stable applications using static RPC calls, if the hardware requirements have been met for user connections, and the 1–2K bytes data-per-request maximum is adhered to, the amount of data being transported can also be managed adequately, provided the transaction workload is evenly distributed throughout the processing time periods.

Planning for ad hoc use and large data transfers (scheduled or otherwise) to and from the host and client/server DBMS poses a larger problem. Some database gateways can transfer large amounts of data across platforms (often to and from the host) using bulk copy functions. Nearly all gateways allow for ad hoc access to the host DBMS through user-friendly query tools. Either of these activities performed during peak processing times could severely impact response times for static applications or even affect host performance in unrelated applications.

For ad hoc query use, user education and tight control through the use of DBMS resource monitors and governors can go a long way in preventing gateway performance problems and maintaining an equally shared resource. If large queries and bulk copy functions must move an excess of about 100K bytes of data more than several times a day, then consideration must be given either to moving these functions to off-hours or acquiring a separate gateway server for those needs.

Network Protocols

Because most database gateway products are available for nearly all protocols, it is logical to remain consistent with the network architecture of the organization. A brief investigation into which protocols are supported by the vendor should be undertaken, but for the most part, performance of database gateway accesses are determined by the application design. If the database gateway applications or users request that large amounts of data be shipped across the network, a brief check should also be made with the network support area to ensure that the infrastructure is in place to support that requirement.

GATEWAY-TO-HOST SECURITY

Gateway security is often not considered until after the product is in-house and already being used for development. Ideally, the gateway security exits and processing should fit in with the existing security software infrastructure. However, this is almost never the case.

Most standard mainframe-based security packages can interrogate LU6.2-based transaction processing for valid logon IDs and passwords. Delivery of the resulting messages from the attempted logon back to the workstation executing the applications is a much more complicated issue. The application generally requires customized code to decipher the message received from the host security package and must know how to react to any number of situations, including a combination of incorrect or expired Ids or passwords. In addition, the application is likely to be accessing other systems and software on other platforms that have their own security logic.

For gateway-specific applications, the user may also be accessing other systems and products directly through an unrelated application or tool and traverse the same proprietary security system at the same time. As a result, users might on occasion log on to the gateway application with a given password, then at some point later, log on to another application system and be informed that their password has expired in the interim. If the system includes an E-mail system and an additional RDBMS on different platforms, for example, the potential for frustration is even greater.

Most security packages included with the gateway software are not robust enough to handle even the gateway-to-host security issues involved. A better method, and one that requires the most effort, is to standardize a custom-built front-end security application that automatically reviews and synchronizes user Ids and passwords across all products and platforms when users boot up their workstation. To minimize the inconvenience of this undertaking, the gateway security issues between client and host software could be the first to be addressed in a phased-in approach. Front-end security software could be developed or modified in concert with implementing the test gateway instances and continued through production.

Other alternatives include setting up unsecured gateway access to the host or having the individual application support personnel code routines. Both of these methods, however, can lead to much larger problems and security risks in the long run.

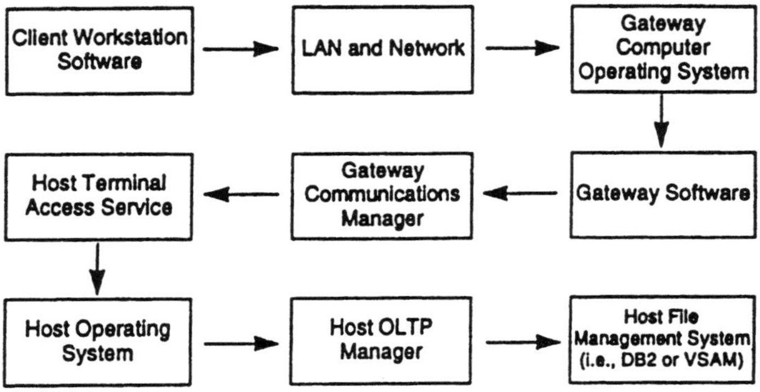

Exhibit 2. The path of Database Gateway access requests.

TECHNICAL SUPPORT

Because they are one of the most complex software products to support, database gateways require coordinated efforts from several system support groups (see Exhibit 2). Without the ability to quickly access experts from the database (e.g., mainframe and client/server), OLTP (e.g., CICS), network, workstation, and operating system support areas, resolving gateway problems can prove troublesome.

As with most distributed client/server systems, locating the problem is usually the most time-consuming and difficult part. If the application that uses the gateway solution is not functioning properly, the problem could be purely a workstation health issue or it could indicate network problems to the host processor and related software and hardware experiencing an outage. The potential for loss of valuable time is great if, for example, the problem is a particular mainframe database table being unavailable, yet the individuals who are working to locate the problem are not familiar with or are not in the notification chain for such issues.

The Help Desk. To streamline the process as much as possible, it is recommended that if an information systems help desk is available, the help desk staff should be trained to filter as many gateway-related problems as possible. This means giving help desk personnel documentation that relates how each database gateway instance is connected to each network address, OLTP system, and mainframe database subsystems. Therefore, if DB2 is unavailable, the support staff knows that any gateway traffic using that system is potentially impaired or may not be functioning at all. Because most database gateways rely on the proper functioning of other software products, the alternative to not having a help desk could be longer work interruptions and incorrect support personnel being notified to investigate problems.

Usage Considerations

Most database gateway software is relatively easy to use from a developer and end-user perspective. Nearly all of the complexities of cross-platform and heterogeneous data access are resolved during software installation and setup. Systems programmers handle maintenance and other access requirements behind the scenes. In most cases, the programmer only has to provide a few lines of source code plus minor modifications to a couple of client workstation files to provide access to the desired database or file. Once a few minor modifications are made and the proper drivers are installed, ad hoc users only need to start the desired front-end software program and host access to any number of host databases and files is possible.

The gateway solution may not provide the best fit for every situation, however. One example is an application that provides the client with all of the updates to a particular file unique to that user since the request was last made. Although coding this access using the gateway may be simple, the actual access is relatively time-consuming and resource intensive. A better choice may be a messaging solution where those updates are delivered at regular intervals in the background so that when the request is made, the results are essentially fully in place and quickly available. Similar examples can be found for other types of middleware connectivity choices.

DISASTER RECOVERY

The database gateway server should be placed in a restricted access area, just like any other critical LAN server in the IS shop. The only case to be made against this recommendation is if remote systems management of the gateway software is not possible and maintenance is scheduled frequently. Except for a departmental-type test gateway, this is usually not recommended.

Because the gateway server does not contain any client data, only the customized software to provide a conduit to it, maintaining a hot spare locally or off site is relatively easy. The cost of the hardware may be a limiting factor for an off-site unit, but local hot or warm spares can be set up on the test servers for emergency use. This can usually be accomplished by setting up and maintaining all of the production software, information, and the required customization on the designated test or development machine. If a major problem arises, the development server can be quickly switched to production mode until the problem is resolved. Depending on the stability of the test environment and the size of the machine, testing may have to be curtailed or discontinued during the outage.

ADD-ON SOFTWARE

Host as Client Processor. In most cases, the database gateway traffic consists of requests from the workstation or client/server database to the host, whether it be to query large mainframe data stores or to perform required updates to those files or databases. In some cases, however, it is necessary for a host-based process to initiate access to server-based data during the course of processing. Some gateway vendors offer additional software that can be installed for this process. Although this type of processing can also be accomplished with native-based code, it may be desirable to have these processes performed through this controlled software with built-in features similar to those used when processing client requests. In either case, it is something that should be considered.

Joins Across Engines and Files. Many database gateway vendors offer products in addition to the core gateway software that allows dynamic joins across platforms and data file systems. This could range from joining host and client/server relational data as well as host files (e.g., virtual storage access method [VSAM] or sequential). To have such capabilities, a careful watch must be kept on ad hoc queries to prevent CPU resource overuse.

For cases of reasonable ad hoc use where the business requires limited data multisource data access, however, this piece of add-on software could be quite beneficial. As with the core gateway software, these products require complex systems support and maintenance in the background. The relatively steep cost of these products may also play a role in evaluating the need for the additional capabilities provided.

CONCLUSION

With a small investment in research and analysis, database gateway software can be quickly implemented and provide relatively straightforward and efficient access to disparate data stores across the enterprise. It is, however, important to carefully consider usage and support requirements before acquisitions begin. Among the key issues to remember:

- The software is best suited for light to moderate OLTP-type processing to and from the host platforms, as well as for enabling controlled ad hoc access to mainframe RDBMSs.
- Although use of the software is simple, background support is complex and usually involves several areas of expertise within the organization. Building and orchestrating an efficient line of support for the gateway product is essential in providing continuous availability through the different platforms.

- Security requirements and routines should be provided concurrently with gateway deployment.
- Because the gateway provides easy access to many environments, it is crucial that the actual use of the tool for specific applications is carefully reviewed to ensure that it is the correct technology for the situation.

Chapter 30
Managing Multiple Databases Across Heterogeneous Hardware and Software Systems

James Woods

Corporate IS management is often challenged when it finds that it must control multiple databases that may reside on separate and disparate systems. However, the cost of not harnessing these multiple databases into a coherent whole is very high.

First, there is the problem of data redundancy. The data that designates a single fact is represented multiple times in the organization. Apart from the obvious storage requirement considerations, there is the problem of inconsistent information. Because the databases each have their own update paths, the data items are likely to have conflicting values. Even if the updates pass along the same value to each data item, it will most likely not be in the same time frame. This leads to information that is out of sync with the other data items. However, more than just one data item is involved in this problem; it is probably tens or hundreds of data items. Some of those items will be used for critical business decisions.

When the information is summarized and reported to top management, conflicts in the information will become obvious, though it will not be obvious which specific data items differ, only that the information from one department does not square with another. Confidence levels in the integrity of all the databases will drop.

0-8493-9989-0/99/$0.00+$.50

THE GOAL: A SINGLE FUNCTIONAL DATABASE

Multiple databases come into existence for any number of reasons:

- **Independent purchases.** A user department buys and uses a separate system because it believes that is the best answer to its needs or that IS cannot address its informational requirements within an acceptable time frame.
- **Legacy systems.** The system has been in place for some time while IS attended to more urgent matters. Eventually, the need for some form of technical management of the data becomes evident.
- **Acquisitions.** The company has just acquired a new division that has its own database system.

All the problems cited can be avoided if the databases, although physically separate (and possibly residing on different hardware and software platforms), are made to function as a single database. In other words, the update path for one database is the update path for the other. This eliminates all the problems except for data redundancy. Exhibit 1 illustrates, from a user's perspective, how multiple databases can be physically separated yet conceptually linked together.

The remainder of this chapter addresses how to build the bridge from one database to another so they function as one. Although the scenario described thus far considers two databases, more may be involved. The techniques suggested in this chapter will also work with multiple separate databases.

THE MANAGERIAL CHALLENGE

Although there are substantial technical considerations, the primary challenge is managerial. The reasons are threefold:

- Departmental and functional areas will cross in the formation of the solution. Without senior management involvement, turf lines may be drawn and the entire project risks becoming mired in political infighting.
- The lack of detailed data definitions frequently causes the cost of the project to go up and the effectiveness of the solution to go down. This activity is not primarily technical but rather managerial. The organization must decide who has what rights to the data and what, exactly, the data represents. As any database administrator can attest, this activity can be hampered by departmental disputes. Senior management support and involvement can help minimize these disputes. An attempt to harness two (or more) databases without a serious data definition effort will produce enough confusion to endanger the entire project.

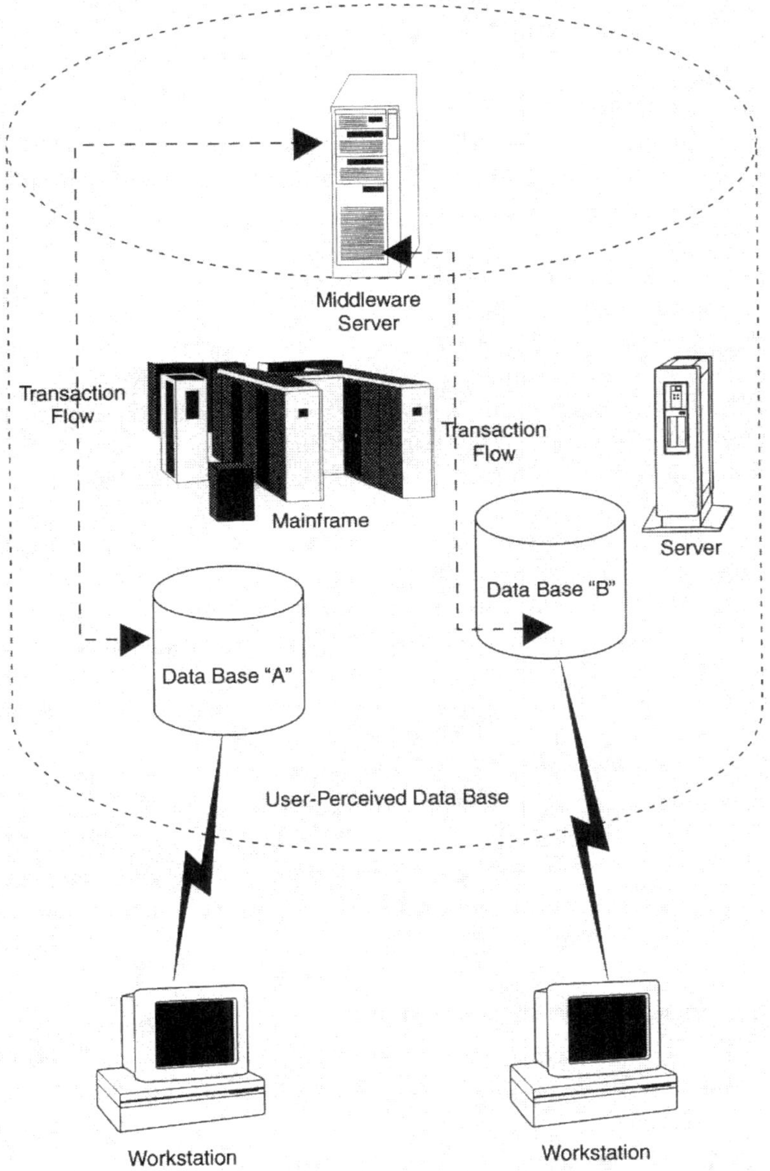

Exhibit 1. Physically separated but conceptually linked databases (user's perspective).

- Because the ramifications of project failure can materially affect the organization's bottom line, senior management must be involved. Management must recognize data as one of the most important assets of the organization.

EVALUATING ALTERNATIVES

Early in the project, alternatives to building a functional bridge might be evaluated. The alternatives fall into two main classes: incorporation versus consolidation of databases.

Incorporation. This technique involves expanding one database to cover the functions of the second. Data items that represent those not currently in the main database are added. New software must be created that provides the functional capabilities of the old system.

Although neither a small or simple project (depending on the complexity of the replaced system), incorporation of databases does have the advantage that it eliminates the data redundancy problem.

Consolidation of Databases. This alternative involves combining the two databases on the same platform. The databases remain separate but reside on the same hardware and under the same software. A functional bridge must still be built, but the communications aspect is completely eliminated and replaced by internal computer processes. However, as in the incorporation technique, the replaced system's functional capabilities must be replaced with new software.

In each of the alternatives, considerations should be given to the current system load, the number of added users to the primary database, among other factors. Incorporation is technically less ambitious than consolidation and is therefore the preferred of the two methods. However, both of the alternatives are generally more expensive to implement than the functional bridge.

THE FUNCTIONAL BRIDGE SOLUTION: STEP BY STEP

A functional bridge is a method to bring transactions from one database to the other so that there is a single update path for all data items.

Planning the Functional Bridge

The first step, of course, is to plan the bridge. There is a great deal more documentation and planning work required than technical implementation effort in building the bridge. If inadequate planning is performed, it is almost certain that no amount of technical prowess will compensate. There are two main initiatives in the planning phase of the functional database bridge:

- **Evaluations of the existing communications infrastructure, available expertise, and commercial middleware.** These evaluations are primarily technical in nature, although management will have some influence because new capabilities may be indicated. For example, if the current communications infrastructure is deemed inadequate, management must approve the building of the new abilities.
- **Designations of master databases, update frequency, and data ownership.** These designations, although influenced by technical considerations, are primarily management decisions and represent points that could materially alter business practices.

Evaluating the Communications Infrastructure. An evaluation of the existing communications infrastructure should establish the following information:

- **The available communications paths between the databases.** This may be a LAN, WAN, T1 line, batch tape, or any other way to move the information between systems.
- **The security of the communications paths.** Because there will now be transaction flow from one database to another, security considerations are important. For example, if the proposed communications channel is a T1 line from another city, it can be considered secure. If, however, the proposed channel is over a Unix system connected to the Internet (without a firewall), then steps should be taken to qualify all incoming transactions before an update (or any other action, for that matter) is applied.
- **The stability of the communications paths.** How reliable is the channel? How often does it go down?
- **The current load on the communications channel.** Is there enough bandwidth to accommodate the new transaction load? This evaluation necessitates an estimate of transactions per unit of time.
- **Failure analysis of the communications channel.** What are the ramifications if the communications carrier should fail? And how long can that failure continue before there are serious ramifications?
- **Protocols.** Some smaller (or older) systems do not natively possess modern communications protocols. The choices in this case are either to custom build an interface to the database, perhaps with vendor assistance (though adding a modern communications protocol to a system can be complicated) or to drop back to a less ambitious communications protocol—for example, batch tape transfer instead of TCP/IP transfer.

Designation of the Database Master. With multiple databases, one must be considered the master database. That is, the values of the data items in the master database are considered to be the final word. This designation as master, however, is on a data basis. For example, the database on the corporate mainframe may be considered the master for customer name and address, whereas the shipping database (which also contains the customer name and address) is considered the master for the shipping date for a customer's order.

In the determination of the master database, the following criteria should be considered:

- **Stability.** How stable is the database? How much maintenance is required?
- **Vendor support.** How effective is the vendor support for this system/database? How promptly does the vendor respond to support calls?
- **In-house expertise.** Who within the organization knows the system/database well enough to answer routine questions and solve performance problems?
- **Available consultant expertise.** If in-house expertise does not exist or should disappear, is there a pool of consultant expertise upon which to draw?
- **Volume of data.** What is the current volume of data on the database? If data fields are added, what are the ramifications?
- **User load on the host system.** How will the transactions affect system performance? Batch updates, for example, can almost negate online response while they are running. Again, an estimate of transaction volume should be made.

Making Critical Design Decisions

Overall Data Architecture. The design phase of the project should not be entirely end-user driven. The end user maintains a biased view of the data. A database administrator view, in this case, is required.

The DBA should obtain information about the data items in question from the end users because they know the data. However, the DBA should then take that information and put it into the context of the overall database structure.

For example, the users tell the DBA about a data item called Last_Contact. The DBA is required to find out the context of this field (i.e., contact by whom?). This may be different from the data item in the main database with a similar name.

Database Linkage. A determination should be made of how tightly linked the databases are—that is to say, how often should the cross communications occur? This factor is, of course, substantially affected by the communications infrastructure available.

Insofar as technically possible, this consideration should be made for business reasons. The update frequency of names and addresses will likely require no more than a batch update, whereas the update frequency of a medical chart location (in a hospital), for example, would require nothing less than a real-time update. The creation of additional communications ability may legitimately be driven by this design decision.

Data Item Map. The organizational aspects of generating the data definitions required for building the functional bridge were mentioned previously. The actual elements of that definition include:

- The name of the data field in both databases
- The form of the field in both databases
- The source of the data. It is not unusual for essentially different data to have the same or similar names across databases.
- The update path of the data. Where does the data originate? Is it original data (i.e., someone keys the data) or is it derived from other items in the database? Who audits the data, and who has the authority to change it?

Update Paths. The data definitions now become an essential ingredient to the design of the update paths. Without the documentation of the existing update paths for each data item involved, and the proposed new update paths, it will be impossible to create an effective transaction flow between the databases.

Changes in the update paths will undoubtedly change departmental procedures. This requires the full cooperation of that department's management and, of course, senior management support.

Communications Back-flow. In some cases, it will be necessary to send transactions in more than one direction. Communication in two or more directions is termed back-flow.

For example, names and addresses may originate in the corporate mainframe and it is considered the master. However, there could be a requirement that the data be updated from the satellite database at a customer service center, for example. Transactions must flow from the master to the satellite for a new customer, but also flow from the satellite to the master to ensure quality customer service. Again, these are not technical decisions (although they have technical ramifications). These decisions should be made for business reasons, not solely technical ones.

Ensuring Positive Feedback. No communications path is error free or fully functional 100% of the time. Good communications design requires a positive feedback. The receiving system must tell the sending system that the data it received was acceptable. This requirement is different from the standard acknowledgment/negative acknowledgment (ACK/NAK) code of a communications systems protocol. This feedback is done at the data application level. It must be known not only that all the bits of the address were received ACK/NAK, but also that the customer number pointed to a real existing customer.

Sometimes the positive feedback and the back-flow communications can be combined, thus reducing the network traffic. For example, a medical master database that is adding a new patient sends a transaction giving the demographic data. The satellite database reports back the local contract number assigned to the patient, which is added to the master as an alternative key. Thus, both functions are served with a single transaction.

Preventing Feedback Loops. Like a public address system, transaction systems can suffer from feedback. Transactions are usually triggered when a data field is updated. When this transaction arrives at the satellite database, the associated data field is updated as well. If the satellite database also reports changes in the data item, it would, of course, send a transaction to report the change just made. The result is a feedback loop that causes an endless chain of updates.

To avoid feedback loops, the triggering mechanisms must be aware of the source of the update. If the update came from the master database, the satellite database must recognize that fact and prohibit the change from being reported back to the master database.

Split Transactions. Occasionally, more than one satellite database must be updated with the same data from the master. It is good design to split the transaction rather than have the master send two transactions. Middleware software is usually used in this case. The transaction is received by the software and two (or more) transactions are forwarded to the satellite databases. The transactions may not have the same format (or even the same communications protocol), even though they convey the same information.

Recovery. What happens if the satellite system sends a transaction and the communications channel is down? An important feature of the network should be that it is not possible to lose a transaction. Therefore, if the communications channel is down, the software must wait and retry the transaction later.

This recovery feature is inherent in some middleware and some gateways. Regardless of where it exists or whether it was bought or built, it must be present in the functional bridge to have a reliable communications path.

Common Ground: Constructing the Bridge

Once the above design has been completed, the actual bridge can be constructed. The bridge consists of five parts: transactions, transaction carriers, gateways, middleware, and trigger events.

Transactions. At this stage of design, the data required and the associated update paths should be fully known and documented. Because multiple transaction systems are not unusual, the content of the transactions must be designed so that coherent sets of information are available during update.

Transaction Carriers. This is the protocol of the transactions. There are multiple levels of the communications protocol. The low level is usually handled by the software employed (multiple communications protocols could be involved, however, and ways of translating one protocol to another may be required). On another level, the transaction must have ways of identifying itself to the update software. This requires transaction identification within the transaction itself. Routing information may also be required for complex environments.

Gateways. The software that actually updates the database is typically known as a gateway. In some database systems, the gateway comes as an internal part of the database itself; with others, it must be added.

In extreme cases, it will be necessary to create the gateway. This kind of gateway is likely to be the most difficult to test and debug, since all combinations of data must be tested—a substantial task even for a moderate set of transactions.

Middleware. Early in the project, evaluations of existing commercial middleware should be undertaken. There are several products on the market with a range of capabilities, some better than others. This software can substantially reduce the technical aspect of the project and provide significantly better control than could (or would) be produced in-house.

Middleware is a generic name that refers to software that accepts and sends transactions, usually converting communications protocols along the way. Better commercial versions also offer transaction reformatting and splitting.

The control and statistical aspects of the software are also important because these features give the user the ability to shut down portions of the network and to keep track of the number, size, and status of the transactions.

Trigger Events. These are the events that cause a transaction to be sent or received. The trigger can be as simple as a command at the console (in the case of batch), the act of receiving a TCP/IP transaction, or a relational database stored procedure designed to act as a trigger.

In any case, the trigger event controls the flow of transactions over the bridge. Usually, these triggers must be coded in the database itself because it is at that point that the transaction originates.

RECOMMENDED COURSE OF ACTION

This chapter presents an overall view of the elements required for the successful management of multiple databases. The recommended approach is the construction of a functional bridge that allows the multiple databases to function as a single database.

The construction effort is largely one of management and definition, rather than technical implementation. Failure to implement an integration strategy, such as a functional bridge, for databases that contain related data will inevitably result in inaccurate information being supplied to the organization's management.

Chapter 31
Object-Relational DB2

Nelson Mattos
Stefan Dessloch
Linda DeMichiel
Michael Carey

Relational database systems manage data about enterprises. Most organizations have adopted relational database systems as the technology for new applications development.

Relational database systems are very good at what they do—provide concurrency control, crash recovery, and scalability for the data they manage. The most important feature of relational database systems, however, is not their ability to store and retrieve data, but their ability to search the data that they manage. It is primarily their flexible search capabilities that set relational database systems apart from first-generation database systems and file systems.

SQL AND RELATIONAL DATABASE SYSTEMS

Relational database systems provide a powerful, high-level query language—SQL, or structured query language—for use in searching. They also provide views and access control to meet the needs of different groups of users. Relational database systems serve as a central point of sharing for applications written in a variety of programming languages and developed using a variety of modern applications development tools. They provide mechanisms such as stored procedures, integrity constraints, and triggers that permit important business rules and procedures to be written once rather than being redundantly (and possibly erroneously) coded in every application program that updates the database.

Enterprises rely on all of these features and have become increasingly demanding of database technology for 24-hours-a-day, 7-days-a-week operations, and optimized online query access to data for decision support

0-8493-9989-0/99/$0.00+$.50

purposes. The SQL query capabilities of relational database systems support content-based specifications of the desired data and allow the data to be retrieved, joined, aggregated, and related in various ways. SQL queries are required for tables containing relatively simple numeric and character data.

Integrated Content Searches

Enterprises manage more than numbers and character strings, however. There are many non-traditional data objects, including textual documents, images, audio clips, video data, time series data, and spatial data. Moreover, business users need to access these objects and relate them to their existing numeric and character data through integrated content searches. The ability to issue SQL queries that can simultaneously filter and relate both traditional SQL data and non-traditional, more complex types of data objects is the hallmark of object-relational database systems.

BUSINESS APPLICATIONS OF OBJECT-RELATIONAL DATABASES

To clarify the challenges facing today's enterprises, and some of the ways in which support for integrated content searches can be invaluable, it is helpful to consider a few examples drawn from typical enterprises.

The Fashion Industry

Fashion is a multibillion-dollar industry in which it is critical to track the latest consumer trends and react to them quickly in tailoring advertising campaigns and product distribution. Integrated content searches can help enhance a fashion manufacturer or retailer's reaction time and predictive accuracy.

For example, a key element in fashion trends is color. Color is an extremely important variable in determining the popularity of, and thus the demand for, fashions from year to year and season to season. Color variations cannot be handled by simple (e.g., name-based) color encodings because such an approach cannot automatically find and rank similar but non-identical colors, especially when comparing related products across manufacturers or across segments of the fashion industry.

Product Distribution. Consider a large chain of fashion retail stores that maintains a sales-information warehouse using an object-relational database system that includes color images of all the merchandise sold in its stores. The retailer knows that certain geographic regions tend to be fashion leaders and that trends in those regions are good predictors of demands that are likely to spread throughout a region, or even throughout the country, within days, weeks, or months. An integrated content search makes it possible for the retailer to search the data in its sales warehouse with respect to color and sales trends, enabling the business to quickly spot the important emerging trends.

Once a trend is detected, the retailer can react by ordering additional stock of popular colors for regions where the sales volume is outstripping expectations, and by pre-shipping stock to stores in those regions to which the color trend is expected to spread. In addition, the color trends in one category, such as women's clothing, are often closely related to trends for other items, such as makeup. Integrated content searches allow the retailer to query the data pertaining to sales in multiple categories, providing an important tool for identifying products for which inventories should be reduced and products for which additional orders should be placed.

Interactive Shopping. Knowing that visual impact plays a key role in its customers' shopping interests, a fashion retailer can also use object-relational database technology to support interactive shopping. Again, integrated content searches play a key role, allowing customers to search online sales catalogs based on desirable combinations of properties such as color, item type, and price.

A customer begins by browsing or querying the catalog for a certain type of item, such as a sweater. When the customer finds a particularly appealing sweater, he or she then asks the online catalog to show shirts, pants, and other accessories that are color-coordinated with the original item. The customer can also ask for all items whose images are similar in color to particular colors in the selected sweater, and to have their images displayed together with information about fabrics, price, and available sizes. Online catalogs with support for such content-based searches of images will be very attractive to the retailer's customers, and can even entice the customer to make additional purchases.

Advertising. Another potentially important application of integrated content searches arises in the area of advertising. Integrated content searches can support a retailer in comparing the product success of items shown in magazine print advertisements with the success of items shown in video marketing campaigns. For this application, the retailer needs to query the information warehouse to relate images of items from magazine advertisements to images of items shown in videos, with video scene-detection techniques being used to identify scenes that contain images promoting certain items. The key here is the ability to perform an integrated content search involving both image and video data and sales data.

The Insurance Industry

Another strong candidate for exploiting integrated content searches, though often cited as an example of a traditional, bread-and-butter database application area, is the insurance industry.

An automobile insurance company can benefit from the ability to store multimedia data and perform integrated content searches over this data. In addition to keeping track of customer billing data, the company needs to manage information about all of its insurance claims. These claims can be rich in multimedia data, including both before and after images of damaged cars, sketches of the site of an accident, police reports and transcripts of conversations with the parties involved in an accident, and geographic information such as the location of the insured customer's home and the site of the accident.

All of these data types can be easily supported as extended data types in an object-relational database, and the relative cost trends for offline vs. online data storage, together with the advantages of having the data available in real time on an agent's desktop, make this an obvious direction for insurance companies that wish to be competitive in today's marketplace. A forward-thinking insurance company, in addition to simply storing and delivering data to agents' desktops, exploits the availability of this data in other ways as well.

Claims Processing and Rate Setting. Specifically, an insurance company can use integrated content searches to streamline the activities of claims processing and rate setting, thereby reducing the insurance company's average processing cost per claim. Given the availability of online images of the damaged car, together with the text of the police report and parametric data such as the type and age of the car, the claims processor's job can be simplified through queries that use content-based searches on text, images, and parametric data to locate comparable cars with similar damage. Given the cost data for comparable accidents, the claims adjuster can now perform write-offs without an on-site examination of the car.

As far as rate setting is concerned, analyses of image, text, and parametric data on the particular makes, models, and years of cars with regard to the damage sustained in collisions, taken together with online demographic data currently maintained by insurance companies, can provide more-effective methods for setting competitive automobile insurance rates.

Other Beneficiaries of Integrated Content Search Technology

Fashion retailers and insurance companies are just two examples of many enterprises that stand to reap almost immediate benefits from integrated content search technology. Almost every company has a significant investment in online document libraries, including spreadsheets, word-processing documents, foils for presentations containing images and product icons, marketing materials, and product manuals. When a company logo or icon is updated or replaced, it is necessary to find all active occurrences of images containing this logo or icon so that they can be updated. The benefits of image-based search capabilities here are clear.

Similarly, when new proposals need to be written, it would be extremely useful to be able to search the library of word-processing documents to find other proposals on the same topic, such as a marketing campaign. Assembling the materials for a marketing campaign would further entail a content-based search of online audio and video libraries, as well as text and image libraries, to find what has previously been shown and said about a particular product so that the new marketing campaign is able to effectively leverage off previous ones.

There are many other industries in which integrated content search technology is invaluable. In the health care industry, content searches can be used for patient-records management and HMO-wide or nationwide tracking of health and disease patterns. In the real estate industry, integrated content searches can be performed on geographic and pictorial data. Advertising agencies can use the technology for managing ad campaigns.

OBJECT-RELATIONAL DB2 INFRASTRUCTURE

The applications described in the previous sections demonstrate the clear business need for database systems that can effectively handle a variety of data types and integrate them with traditional data and with each other. These applications also demonstrate the capabilities of an integrated content search, which is a natural extension of the search capability for which relational database systems are well known. Object-Relational DB2, from IBM Corp., offers features that support integrated content searches. DB2 Version 2 implements SQL-92 with extensions from SQL3, including such features as user-defined types, user-defined functions, large objects, and triggers and constraints.

User-Defined Types

User-defined data types allow users to define new data types using SQL3's data definition syntax. User-defined types, like the built-in data types, can be used to define columns of tables and parameters of functions. Simple examples are user-defined types such as Text, Image, and Money.

The SQL3 draft standard provides strong typing, preventing values of disparate data types from being compared without first being converted into a correctly comparable form. Strong typing is an important object-oriented feature. It can prevent errors that would otherwise result when text in different languages or prices in different currencies are compared directly—errors that are easy to make in weakly typed systems.

User-Defined Functions

Hand in hand with user-defined type support is support for user-defined functions. User-defined functions assume the role of methods in the object-oriented world, as they can be used to implement the behavior of complex data types. They are key components of an object-relational system because they enable type definers to hide the representation of the type (i.e., to encapsulate their objects).

With encapsulation, applications see an object only through its behavior, as defined by its functions, not its representation. Because user-defined functions can be used in SQL queries, they are also the key to providing content-based search capabilities on user-defined types. User-defined functions in DB2 are integrated into query optimization, which takes into account their semantics and their expected execution cost.

Functions can be overloaded. This means that users can define similar functions with the same name to operate on different argument types, providing the object-oriented feature of polymorphism. For example, there can be multiple functions to compute the area of spatial objects based on their geometric form—one for circles, one for triangles, one for rectangles—all named "area." Overloading simplifies the development of applications. In this example, application writers only need to remember to invoke the function "area" when they need to compute the area of any kind of figure; the database automatically invokes the specific function that is appropriate for the given spatial object.

User-defined function capabilities can define arbitrarily complex operations to be executed on the server. Functions can be written in host languages (including 4GLs) following the SQL3 specification. What functions they can do is limited only by the capabilities of the language in which they are implemented. Users can exploit user-defined functions to create new function libraries, or they can buy third-party libraries (such as FORTRAN scientific libraries) and attach them.

Support for Large Objects

The object-relational DBMS permits the storage of very large (i.e., multimegabyte) binary or character objects (e.g., images, video clips, and audio clips) as built-in types. Large objects can also be used as the representation for new user-defined types. Any number of large object columns can be defined per table and manipulated by SQL queries. Storing large objects guarantees that they will participate in the application's transaction semantics, that they will be recovered after a machine failure, and that they will be backed up together with the rest of the database—all important features provided by relational databases today.

Triggers and Constraints

Triggers and constraints extend and enhance the other object-relational features. Triggers and constraints can be used to augment object-code-only libraries (whose methods cannot be modified) to support additional, application-specific attributes and constraint-checking. They can also be used to enforce interobject integrity rules and arbitrarily complex business rules on objects.

Sharing Is the Key

IBM's DB2 is an example of a database that supports many-to-many sharing of objects across many different programming languages and client platforms. A collection of DB2 clients may use different application languages, such as C/C++, COBOL, and FORTRAN, while sharing a set of object-relational features (i.e., user-defined types and functions, large objects, triggers and constraints) via SQL. This allows DB2 users to store objects that originate in environments such as C/C++, Java, Object Linking and Embedding (OLE), fourth-generation languages (4GLs), common object request broker architecture (CORBA), and System Object Model—or SOM, an implementation of CORBA by IBM—and to exploit them through powerful language libraries within SQL. This provides DB2 users with a single point of access and control for such objects, including integrated search capabilities and the ability to serve objects across the Web, DRDA, and open database connectivity (ODBC) connections.

By storing enterprise data in DB2, users can encapsulate data in a centralized repository where it can be shared by all client applications and queried in an integrated fashion. Such encapsulation ensures that business practices can be enforced by DB2's trigger and constraint mechanisms and applied to all application programs without having to be explicitly coded in each one. The result is a system that can manage not only enterprise data, but also the business rules and functions of the enterprise, making both the data and the associated business rules uniformly accessible throughout the enterprise.

DATABASE EXTENDERS

With object-relational features, the content-based search capabilities of the object-relational database can be extended to new data types such as images, video, and audio. Prepackaged collections of user-defined types, user-defined functions, triggers, constraints, and stored procedures can be plugged into the SQL engine to support integrated content searches. This allows users to quickly develop customized applications by using the functionality provided by the database and its relational extenders.

With the extenders, users can store text documents, images, and videos in tables, together with traditional enterprise data, by simply adding columns of the appropriate data types provided by relational extenders (e.g., Text or Image). No special requirements are imposed on the structure or the primary key columns of these tables.

In addition to the actual data content, these new data types also have internal attributes for their further description. For example, a text document has a language, a format, and a code page to further describe its individual characteristics. The user-defined functions that come with the Text Extender provide the means to initialize, update, and search on these document attributes.

INTEGRATED CONTENT SEARCHES IN DB2

Integrated content search is supported by the extenders via user-defined functions. The DB2 Image Extender, for example, offers a set of functions to support content-based searching over images. A user can use an Image Extender function in an SQL query to request images that are similar to an existing image. The user can also perform SQL-based searches for images using other criteria, such as average color, color distribution, and texture.

An important advantage of DB2's SQL-based approach to supporting integrated content searches is that a given query can search on multiple non-traditional data types as well as on traditional data. Users can formulate queries that combine content-based searches on images together with content-based searches on the text documents supported by the DB2 Text Extender. The Text Extender provides the power of a full-text search engine and, like the Image Extender, its functionality is made available to DB2 users as an extension of DB2's standard SQL interface. As a result, searches on text documents do not require additional application programming interfaces (APIs) or pre-processing steps; they can be directly specified with other search criteria, on other data, in the same SQL query.

Consider the example from the insurance industry. There is a table called "accidents" with a column called "report" that contains a detailed textual description of the accident, a column called "picture" that contains a photo of the damaged vehicle, and a column that contains information about the insured and his or her policy number. To find all of the accidents with major damage to the front door of a red car owned by a customer under 25 years old, a user of DB2's Text and Image Extenders would write a single SQL query:

```
SELECT name, policy no.

FROM accidents
```

```
WHERE contains(report, "damage" IN SAME SENTENCE AS
    "severe"  and  "front"AND  "door")=1
AND  score  (picture,  ôreddish')  .  0.5
AND  age  <  25
```

For each picture of a damaged car in this example, the database produces a score describing the quality of the color match; only pictures with scores over 0.5 will be selected. The database also searches through the structure of each report looking for documents with sentences describing accidents with severe damage to the front car doors, selecting only those documents. Finally, the database uses its traditional parametric search techniques to restrict the accidents considered to those involving young drivers. Only accident rows where all of these criteria are satisfied will be returned, and the query optimizer decides how best to order the actual evaluation of the query.

A Closer Look at the Text Extender

With the integration of the full-text search functions that it provides, DB2 becomes capable of understanding the structure of text documents in terms of words, sentences, and paragraphs. The user can search for documents containing specific words or phrases, or use a proximity search to retrieve all documents where some words appear in the same sentence or in the same paragraph as others, regardless of the word order. In the preceding insurance example, the result of the query would contain the names of insured people whose accident report contains sentences such as, "The accident caused severe damage of the left front door," or "The right door in the front of the car shows severe damage."

The DB2 Text Extender's linguistic search capabilities include language-specific processing and decomposition of words into their stemmed forms. The user, therefore, also finds documents that contain linguistic variations of the search terms, such as singular vs. plural forms or different verb inflections. For example, the search term "damage" would also match documents containing "damages," "damaging," and so on. Linguistic searches can be further enhanced with synonym expansion. The search term "severe" would then also match documents containing the words "major" or "serious." The DB2 Text Extender provides both linguistic and synonym search support for 17 different languages.

Additional capabilities of the DB2 Text Extender include wildcard search, Boolean combinations of search terms, support for various document and word-processor formats, and retrieval of ranking information. A rank value describes how well a given document matches a search pattern. Moreover, the Text Extender supports text search on legacy character data that was already contained in the database before the Text Extender was plugged in. This support requires no migration efforts or data definition language (DDL) changes and therefore does not disturb existing application programs. All of the search capabilities provided by the Text Extender are supported using efficient, state-of-the-art text retrieval indexing techniques.

Putting the Extenders to Work

DB2's Relational Extenders are already in use today. The CareerPath system illustrates how the DB2 Text Extender can be exploited in an actual production system. This application offers online access to job ads appearing in 14 major U.S. newspapers, including *The New York Times*, the *Chicago Tribune*, and the *San Jose Mercury News,* through a World Wide Web site (http://www.careerpath.com).The ads are stored in DB2, and the DB2 Text Extender is used to support keyword searches over them.

Another Text Extender application is available through an IBM Web page, http://www.software.ibm.com/data/db2 support/servinfo/index.html. This site provides DB2 product manuals and documentation in content-searchable form. For readers interested in further information about the Text Extender, the complete DB2 Text Extender Application and Programming Guide is available via this Web page.

In summary, DB2's Relational Extenders support integrated content search for a number of important non-traditional data types. Using the Extenders, DB2 users need not always build their own application parts for handling new data types; instead the data types can be the part assemblers by exploiting the Extenders' search capabilities.

Because these capabilities are provided in functional form, via the standard SQL interface, there is essentially no limit to the ways in which queries can combine non-traditional data predicates in their search requests. Finally, the Relational Extenders are based on an open architecture, so anyone can build a new extender for an additional data type by exploiting the object-relational capabilities of DB2.

CONCLUSION

Enterprises of all sizes are awash in a sea of new data types. In addition to numeric and character data, they must manage documents, images, audio, video, and many other complex data types. They require the same levels of robustness, performance, and scalability that they have come to rely on for yesterday's data, and they need to have integrated content search capabilities for all of this data. This chapter provides an overview of the benefits of an object-relational DBMS, and clearly they are substantial.

Chapter 32
Legacy Data Conversion

James A. Larson
Carol L. Larson

Relational database management system (RDBMS) features not generally found in file systems include automatic backup and recovery procedures, transaction processing, business rule enforcement, easy query formulation, and application generation facilities. However, to obtain these benefits, files must be migrated to a relational database. This chapter explains how, when, and why to migrate a file into a relational database, and how to modify an application to a relational database system.

THREE-PHASE MIGRATION STRATEGY

Exhibit 1 illustrates the three phases for migrating files and applications to an RDBMS:

- *Phase 1: Analysis and planning.* Before migrating files to a relational database, the costs and benefits should be analyzed, the files and applications should be partitioned into classes to be migrated independently, and a plan for the migration should be developed.
- *Phase 2: Migration.* This phase consists of several substeps, which are repeated for each class identified in Phase 1:
  - —A relational schema describing the data to be migrated should be designed.
  - —Business rules for enforcement by the RDBMS should be specified.
  - —The database should be populated by migrating data from files into the RDBMS.
  - —Applications should be modified to access the RDBMS.
  - —The applications and the populated RDBMS should be tested.
  - —Production should be switched from the file system to the RDBMS if the tests succeed.
- *Phase 3: Fine-tuning.* The database description should be revised to conform to changing application needs. Finally, performance statistics

0-8493-9989-0/99/$0.00+$.50

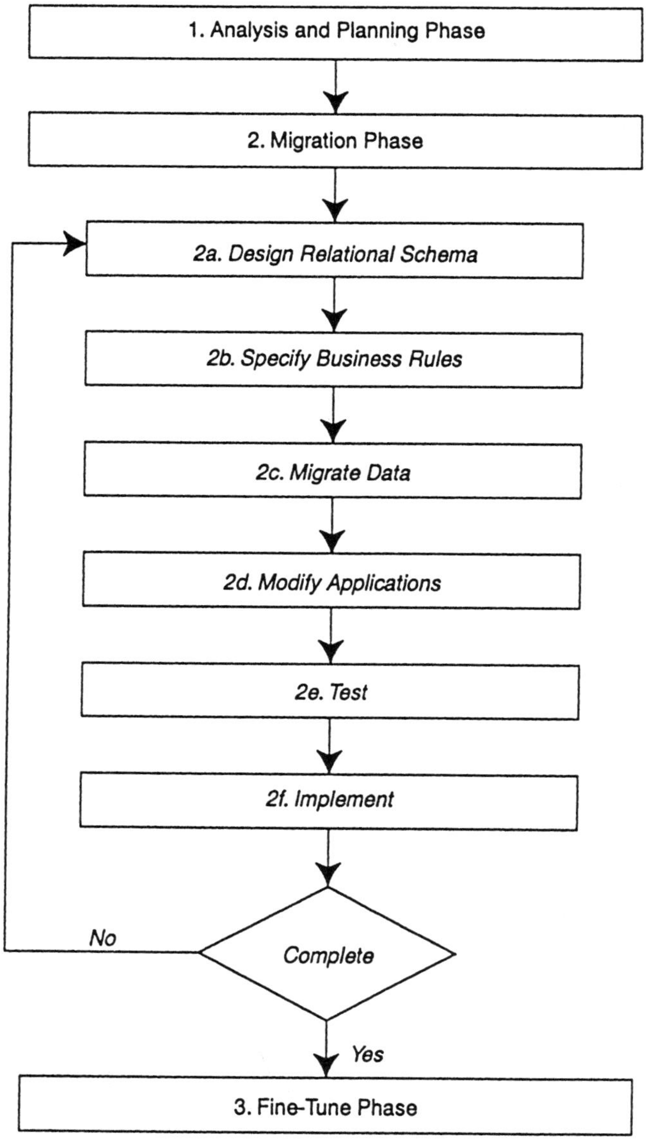

Exhibit 1. Three phases of migration strategy.

should be analyzed and physical structures, such as the indexes, should be reimplemented to improve the overall performance of the relational database.

Why Migrate a File into a Relational Database?

File systems are extremely popular among data processing practitioners. Files store data created by one application and enable other applications to access that data. Files also enable multiple applications to share the same data. As popular as they are, there are some fundamental problems with files.

The Data Dependency Problem. Each application must contain a description of the file's data elements. Whenever a database administrator changes the file's data elements, such as adding a new data element or changing the format of an existing data element, programmers must change the file's description in each application. After the file's description is changed in each application, the programmers must recompile and test the revised applications.

The Business Rule Maintenance Problem. Business rules describe the valid values of each data element and the conditions under which data element values may be changed. Each application that updates data in a file must enforce the business rules. Whenever a business rule changes, programmers must examine each application that updates data and modify those applications to enforce the revised business rule.

The Backup Problem. Data processing specialists create backup copies of files for use in the event that a file is corrupted or lost. Managing backup copies and file generations is a tedious task that is easy to forget or perform incorrectly.

The Application Queuing Problem. Many files can be accessed by only one application at a time, resulting in lengthy turnaround time and a lot of waiting by users, who need to access the files.

RDBMS BENEFITS

Database management systems and, more recently, relational database management systems, are software systems with facilities to help solve the previously mentioned problems.

Solving the Data Dependency Problem. Database management systems maintain a centralized description of all data elements managed by the DBMS. If a new data element is added to a file, the database administrator only needs to modify this centralized description and those applications affected directly by the change. It is not necessary to recompile and test all applications.

This feature, called *data independence,* makes it easy for database administrators to change the data structures. Another benefit of centralized data description in database management systems is that users can easily determine the contents of a database and whether it contains the data that will satisfy their needs.

Solving the Business Rule Maintenance Problem. Database management systems contain triggers and stored procedures that enforce business rules. If a business rule changes, the database administrator only needs to update the affected data and modify the associated triggers and stored procedures, without modifying applications that update the database.

Solving the Backup Problem. Database management systems automatically back up their data and provide utilities so the database administrator can restore the data if the database becomes damaged or lost.

Solving the Application Queuing Problem. Database management systems support concurrency control mechanisms that guarantee that two applications do not try to update the same data element at the same time, but enable multiple applications — and users — to access the same files at the same time.

PHASE 1: ANALYSIS AND PLANNING

In this phase, the database administrator analyzes the problem and develops plans to migrate files into a relational database system. The first step, designing the relational database, involves:

- Determining which files to include in the relational database
- Describing each of these files in terms of the relational data model
- Integrating the descriptions of common data from multiple files
- Extracting and integrating the business rules from file applications
- Integrating these business rules into the triggers and stored procedures of the relational database

Actually migrating data from the files to a relational database involves a separate series of tasks, including:

- Converting file data element formats to database formats
- Detecting and resolving inconsistencies in data values of common data from multiple files
- Detecting and resolving incorrect and missing file data

Migrating existing applications to the database may involve one of the following activities:

- Replacing data I/O commands in the application
- Restructuring significant portions of the application
- Rewriting the entire application

Also, data processing procedures must be changed to accommodate the database management system. This effort involves changing the way applications are processed. Many applications can be processed in parallel, so explicit backup procedures can be eliminated.

Cost-Benefit Analysis and Other Business Decisions

Several factors affect the decision to stop spending effort and time to maintain an existing file system and begin the conversion to a relational system. Database administrators should consider:

- How frequently data elements are changed and how much effort is necessary to implement the changes.
- How frequently business rules are changed and how much effort is necessary to implement the changes.
- How much effort is expended to create and manage backup file copies.
- The cost of waiting for the results of applications processed sequentially.

Database administrators should perform a cost-benefit analysis by calculating the annual cost of maintaining the existing file system, estimating the total cost of migration to a relational database system, and estimating the annual cost of maintaining a relational database system. From these figures, it is possible to estimate the time required to recoup the cost of migrating to a RDBMS and the expected return on the investment. Other factors that may influence the decision to migrate from a file system to a RDBMS include the availability of trained systems analysts, programmers, and database administrators to carry out the migration, as well as the risk of the project falling behind schedule.

Once these issues are resolved, the users are now ready to enter the second phase of migrating files to a relational database system.

PHASE 2: MIGRATING TO A RELATIONAL DATABASE SYSTEM

Files support three major concepts: record types, fields, and unique identifiers. Each of these three concepts corresponds to similar concepts in the relational data model — a record type corresponds to a relational table, a field corresponds to a relational column, and a unique identifier corresponds to a primary key.

Exhibit 2 illustrates an example file and the corresponding relational table. The four records in the employee file are translated to the four rows of the table with the same name. The three fields of the employee file are

Employee File

Chang	3000	Shoes
Lopez	2900	Shoes
Rossi	3200	Jewelry
Thomas	2700	Jewelry

→

Employee

Employee Name	Employee Salary	Department Name
Chang	3000	Shoes
Lopez	2900	Shoes
Rossi	3200	Jewelry
Thomas	2700	Jewelry

Exhibit 2. Mapping a file to a table.

mapped to the three columns of the Employee table. Finally, the unique identifier field of the file is mapped to the primary key, EmployeeName, in the relational table. The names of the primary keys are underlined in Exhibit 2. Although the file-to-relational data structure mapping is straightforward for this example, occasionally any one of four problems may arise:

- *Some files do not have records with unique identifiers.* Exhibit 3 illustrates a file with no unique identifier. One approach for solving this problem is to generate a new column that contains a unique identifier. In Exhibit 3, the ID column contains generated values that do not exist in the file.
- *The order of records in a file implies information not represented by field values.* For example, the order of records in the file implies a sequential waiting list or ranking. One approach for solving this problem is to generate a new field containing values that explicitly indicate the ranking among employees. In the corresponding relational table shown in Exhibit 4, this ranking is made explicit by the new column, Rank.
- *A single record of a file may contain a repeating group.* A repeating group is a set of fields that may occur several times within a record. Exhibit 5 illustrates an example of a file containing three records with some of the records having a group of fields that repeats. This problem could be solved by building a new table for the repeating group. In Exhibit 5, each row of the Child table contains values for fields of the repeating group. The Employee table also contains an Employee column whose values identify the Employee who is the parent or guardian of the child. The Employee column in the Child table is sometimes called a foreign key and is an example of a referential integrity business rule.
- *Some files contain more than one type of record.* For example, Exhibit 6 illustrates a file containing two types of records — Department records have a "D" in the first field, and Employee records have an "E" in the first field. Records of employees who work for a department follow the record of the department for which they work. The solution to this problem is to split the file into two tables, as shown in Exhibit 6.

Employee

Chang	34
Lopez	40
Rossi	35
Thomas	26
Chang	38
Rossi	19

→

Employee

Id	Name	Points
1001	Chang	34
1002	Lopez	40
1003	Rossi	35
1004	Thomas	26
1005	Chang	38
1006	Rossi	19

Exhibit 3. Mapping a file with no unique identifier to a table.

The Employee table contains the new column, Dept, which relates employees to departments.

Specifying Business Rules

Business rules describe valid data item values and the conditions where they may be changed. Much of the code of traditional file applications is devoted to describing business rules and their enforcement. Migrating to a RDBMS provides the database administrator with an opportunity to factor application business rules out of the application and centralize them in the database management system. The database administrator must have a good understanding of the data and how it is to be used to specify a complete set of business rules.

Database administrators can specify many business rules nonprocedurally. Nonprocedural business rules include:

- *Constraints on a single data item.* For example, the values of a person's age must fall into the range 0–119. This example illustrates a domain constraint because it restricts values of a data item to take on one of the values within its domain. Database administrators specify a

Employee File

Chang	3000	Shoes
Lopez	2900	Shoes
Rossi	3200	Jewelry
Thomas	2700	Jewelry

→

Employee

Rank	Employee Name	Employee Salary	Department Name
1	Chang	3000	Shoes
2	Lopez	2900	Shoes
3	Rossi	3200	Jewelry
4	Thomas	2700	Jewelry

Exhibit 4. Mapping a file with an implied ranking.

Employee File

Burns	51000	3	Michelle	87	David	89	Cari	92
Maves	52000	2	John	88	Jenny	88		
Quon	54000	1	Lee	85				

↓

Employee

Employee	Salary
Burns	51000
Maves	52000
Quon	54000

Employee

Employee	Child	Birthdate
Burns	Michelle	87
Burns	David	89
Burns	Cari	92
Maves	John	88
Maves	Jenny	88
Quon	Lee	85

Exhibit 5. Mapping a file with a repeating group to two tables.

Example File

D	Jewelry	46000000
E	Rossi	00003200
E	Thomas	00002700
D	Shoes	42000000
E	Chang	00003000
E	Lopez	00002900

↓

Department

DName	Budget
Jewelry	46000000
Shoes	42000000

Employee

Dept	EName	Salary
Jewelry	Rossi	3200
Jewelry	David	2700
Shoes	Chang	3000
Shoes	Lopez	2900

Exhibit 6. Mapping a file with multiple record types to two tables.

domain constraint for an RDBMS by defining a specific domain of values for a column.

- *Constraints among records within a file.* For example, no two employee records may have the same value for the employee identifier. This example illustrates an entity integrity constraint. Database administrators specify an entity integrity constraint by declaring that a table has a unique key.
- *Constraints between records in two different files.* For example, the department number of the department for which an employee works must exist as a value for the primary key of the department file. This example illustrates a referential integrity constraint. Database administrators specify a referential integrity constraint by declaring that a table have a foreign key.

Stored Procedures. Not all business rules can be specified nonprocedurally. Database administrators use stored procedures to specify nonprocedural business rules.

A stored procedure is a named, compiled procedure that is stored as part of the database. The RDBMS executes a stored procedure whenever a special condition, called a trigger, is executed.

The database administrator defines a trigger by specifying a command (i.e., update, insert, delete), a database object (i.e., a specific table, row, data item), and either a structured query language (SQL) statement or the name of a stored procedure. Whenever the command is executed against the specified object, the SQL statement or stored procedure is executed automatically by the database management system.

Populating the RDBMS

The utilities supplied by the vendor of the RDBMS can be used, or an application can be written to extract, convert, and load files into the RDBMS.

Modifying Applications to Access the RDBMS

Most existing applications are written using procedural file I/O commands where each command accesses a single record of the file. Most RDBMS also support commands that access a single record in the database management system.

Because of the many messages exchanged between the application and the database management system, it is not recommended that programmers replace procedural file I/O commands with procedural database commands. This may be especially troublesome if the database management system executes on a server and the application executes on a client.

A better approach is to modify the application so it accesses several database records with a single SQL command. An SQL cursor enables procedural application code to sequentially process multiple records returned by a single SQL request. The programmer replaces a loop containing procedural-file I/O commands by an SQL cursor and specifies the appropriate SQL nonprocedural command.

Several other modifications must be made to the application code, including commands to locate and open the database, lock and unlock the portions of the database to be used exclusively by the application, and write the code to examine the various completion codes returned by the RDBMS. Generally, programmers must make extensive changes to a file application and test it thoroughly.

When modifying a file application to access a relational database, it is also tempting to replace the application user interface with a graphical user interface (GUI). Although transitioning to a GUI adds more risk to the migration effort, it may improve user productivity. Several GUI generators are available to help the programmer and user interface designer specify and implement GUI interfaces.

AVOIDING MIGRATION OF MANY APPLICATIONS AT ONCE

Database administrators can use two approaches — postponing the application modification or postponing the file migration to relational databases — to avoid migrating many applications and files to a relational database system at the same time.

The choice between postponing application modification or file migration is a function of the availability of a gateway, which makes application modification postponement possible, and influences the length of the proposed postponement and the relative effort to carry out each type of postponement.

Postponing the Application Modification

Because of the work involved in migrating applications, it is sometimes necessary to postpone modifying some applications. For these applications, it may be possible to quickly generate a utility that extracts data from the database and creates the file structure required by the application. The application then executes against the file structure. Then, any data output by the application must be loaded back into the database. This approach is recommended only when time constraints do not permit immediate application modification.

Postponing the File Migration

Some database management systems support gateways that enable database applications to access non-database files. By using gateways, it is possible to modify some applications and keep the remaining applications in production. A file is then migrated to the RDBMS only after all of the applications that access the file have been migrated. This approach is recommended when time constraints do not permit immediate file migration.

Testing the Revised Applications and the Populated DBMS

Database administrators should develop test suites to validate the new relational database and its modified applications. It is recommended that the new database system be run in parallel with the old file system for at least one processing cycle. If something is wrong with the new system, the old system is still available.

Once the new system is in place, the final phase of fine-tuning the database description and the overall performance for efficiency can begin.

PHASE 3: FINE-TUNING

Modern businesses change constantly, and so must the database management systems that support the businesses. As requirements change, the RDBMS must incorporate changes to data items, business rules, and applications that access the relational database.

One of the major reasons for migrating to a relational database is data independence, which is the ability to change the data structure easily with minimal impact to the applications. Database administrators should also refine the physical data organization to provide efficient processing of the current set of applications.

Relational databases also lend themselves to future changes in data processing strategies. An organization may want to distribute enterprise data across multiple databases on different computers connected by a local area network, control access to a relational database with browsers from anywhere in the world via the Internet, or introduce new data types, especially images, audio, and video.

SUMMARY

Data should be migrated to an RDBMS only if the savings offered by the DBMS outweigh the expense of the migration. Schemas for the RDBMS should be designed using triggers, SQL statements, and stored procedures to implement business rules.

Finally, an incremental approach should be used to migrate the files and applications to the DBMS with file extractors and by using gateways to postpone file or application migration.

Section V
Systems Administration in a Heterogeneous Environment

Section V focuses on another facet of heterogeneous computing—Systems Administration aspects in heterogeneous environments.

One of the more common heterogeneous environment situations is when Windows NT is being introduced where NetWare is already being utilized. NetWare was and still is the predominant Network Operating System in terms of install base. However, recently Windows NT is gaining marketshare from NetWare. Windows NT had one advantage over Unix in its competition with NetWare. Unlike Unix with its many variants, NetWare was a well-defined target. NetWare was relatively easy to develop migration and coexistence solutions for. Just as it introduced WordPerfect-compatibility features (such as document translation filters for WordPerfect documents and user guides that provide comparable Word functions for WordPerfect functions) to appeal to the WordPerfect install base, Microsoft included NetWare compatibility features in Windows NT. Besides Windows NT, Windows 95 and Windows for Workgroups integrate with NetWare as well. Microsoft's provided functions include:

- File and Print Services for NetWare (FPNW)
- Client Services for NetWare (CSNW)
- Gateway Services for NetWare (GSNW)
- Migration tool to migrate NetWare information to Windows NT

Exhibit 1 summarizes the approaches available to address Windows NT- and NetWare-integration issues and the products that implement the specified approaches.

Chapter 33 covers Windows NT and NetWare migration and coexistence.

Chapter 33 provides more detail in configuring Windows NT client workstations and servers to connect to a NetWare-based local area network. When configuring a Windows NT platform to work on a Novell network,

Exhibit 1. Windows NT and NetWare: migration and coexistence issues, approaches, and products.

Windows NT and NetWare		
Issue	**Approach**	**Products**
Access NetWare server transparently from Windows clients for file and print services	Microsoft built in support for NetWare in Windows NT and Windows 95	Client Services for NetWare (CSNW)
	Novell NetWare client for Windows NT, Windows 95, Windows 3.x and DOS	Novell NetWare client
	Access through Gateway	Gateway Services for NetWare (GSNW)
Access Windows NT transparently from NetWare clients for file, print services	Microsoft built in support for NetWare in Windows NT	File and Print services for NetWare (FPNW)
Migrate System information in NetWare servers to Windows NT	Microsoft built in support for NetWare in Windows NT	Migration tool from Microsoft

there are several variables that govern the network manager's ability to connect the platform into a NetWare environment. Chapter 33 provides network managers and administrators the tips necessary to correctly configure their Windows NT platform to work in a NetWare environment.

First, this section looks at the different administration functions in managing heterogeneous environments. Next, it examines what Unix administrators use every day—Unix shell and utilities—and at some tools that allow the Unix shell and utilities to be available in Windows NT. Next, the section looks at some typical system administration functions and how equivalent functions are implemented in Windows and Unix. Microsoft has included a number of built-in functions in Windows NT to coexist in NetWare networks. Microsoft also provides tools to let NetWare users migrate to Windows NT without having to re-create valuable system administration data.

Exhibit 2 summarizes the approaches available to address system administration issues in heterogeneous environments.

One of the easiest ways to learn something new about an environment is to equate the functions in that new environment to equivalent familiar functions from the familiar environment being exited. With this idea in mind, chapter 35 covers various system administration functions and points out how equivalent functions are performed in Unix and Windows NT. In making the comparison, two things must be kept in mind:

Exhibit 2. System administration issues and approaches for heterogeneous systems.

Systems Administration in Heterogeneous Environments		
Issue	**Approach**	**Products**
Unix shell on Windows NT	Use shells that simulate Unix command environment in Windows NT	MKS toolkit Hamilton C shell Portage Base
System administration functions in heterogeneous environments	Use third party software for the different aspects of System administration as needed	POLYCENTER, TME 10, Unicenter, others

The primary difference between system administration in Unix and Windows NT is in the end-user interface. Windows NT uses the graphical user interface, while the command line (character-based interface) is heavily used in Unix. Some system administration functions in some Unix systems use the X-Windows based graphical interface, but the X-Windows is an add-on that may or may not be used, unlike Windows NT, where the primary means of user interface is the Windows GUI.

Windows NT is based on the client/server model. This changes the concept of users, user administration, and other system administration functions as well.

For most corporations worldwide, the move to distributed systems has been both beneficial and problematic. A distributed system's ability to provide data to end users on a timely basis has greatly improved service levels. However, when distributed data is to be channeled through complex and varied network configurations, industry has been hard-pressed to design and to manage these new systems. Moreover, as the bills are paid for these efforts, it is becoming increasingly clear that the costs associated with client/server technology are much higher than originally estimated. Chapter 36 discusses solutions for managing today's distributed network environment, focusing on the implementation of single sign-on, password synchronization, and the authentication server.

Chapter 37 covers system administration functions in a heterogeneous environment, which include:

- Enterprise systems management
- Disk and file backup and restore
- System performance management
- Security management
- Help desk software
- Background job scheduling
- Software distribution and asset management

- Output management
- Network management
- Application management

Enterprise Systems Management provides cohesive, integrated administration of the entire IT infrastructure of an organization, which could include systems, networks, applications, and databases, Internet access, desktops, processors, and PDAs. Disk and file backup provides these functions across heterogeneous environments. System performance management collects and displays performance data from heterogeneous systems in a consistent manner. Security management functions are typically provided by the operating system and the level of security provided is indicated in a scale whose ranges include D (least-secure level) to A (most-secure level) with intermediate classifications. Most operating system vendors aim for level C2, which is required in many federal computer procurements. Windows NT meets the requirements for the C2 security level and so do many Unix systems, including Digital Unix. With an optional product, DEC MLS+, Digital Unix can meet some security requirements at the B1 level. Digital Unix, starting with version 4.0, also includes support for Access Control Lists (ACLs). ACLs are standard in Windows NT. Unix includes some basic background job scheduling functions such as *cron* and *at*. Windows NT includes *at*. But many organizations need much more sophisticated job scheduling functions and typically use third-party software. Output management deals with printing, spooling, paging, and other output operations in a heterogeneous environment.

Chapter 38 provides a framework for managing distributed operations called MODE (Management of Distributed Environments) and includes a sample service-level agreement in the appendix.

Chapter 39 covers the process of business recovery planning for heterogeneous systems, specifically for local area networks (LANs) and the components that compose the LAN.

A help desk is a data center's contact point with its customers. If customers are dissatisfied with the help desk, they are probably also dissatisfied with the data center. Chapter 40 explains why many help desks have not been as successful as their customers would like and discusses ways data center managers can build successful help desks in a distributed client/server environment.

Multivendor computing environments pose significant administrative and operational challenges. IS management must develop clear policies and procedures within which the multivendor installation must function. Chapter 41 addresses some key management issues in multivendor installations.

Administering and supporting job scheduling has been complicated by the drive toward open systems, which often include client/server architectures. When evaluating job-scheduling software, the data center manager must examine such issues as centralized vs. decentralized computing, high-availability requirements, and mission-critical work loads. Only after the data center manager addresses these issues can an organization be positioned to perform the in-depth software evaluation needed to successfully implement job scheduling within an open systems environment. Chapter 41 elaborates on this concept.

Many corporations have a mix of both departmental and corporate LAN systems combined with legacy systems, all with disparate methods of communicating in a network. In this situation, network managers often face the need to manage multiple protocols. Chapter 42 covers different methods of connectivity that help manage multiple protocols, including multistacking and the use of software-based gateway technology.

The diversity of network devices and differences in media and protocols tends to complicate rather than simplify network management, prompting users to seek a unified management solution. Among the most prominent integrated network management solutions are IBM Corp's NetView, Digital Equipment Corp.'s (DEC) Polycenter Framework, and Hewlett-Packard's (HP) OpenView. All of these management systems underwent major shifts in market positioning in recent years. Chapter 43 covers PolyCenter. Chapter 44 looks at OpenView

DEC, now part of Compaq, has been working toward the objective of open systems and multivendor integration since 1988, when it articulated its Enterprise Management Architecture (EMA) strategy for managing multivendor environments. EMA is a blueprint for managing open, integrated, heterogeneous, and distributed systems.

EMA distinguishes between the resource being managed and the management software that performs the management function. EMA specifies application-programming interfaces that developers use to integrate system and network management in a modular framework. DECmcc used this approach in 1989, however, it addressed only the integration of various network-management applications. DECmcc is now known as the Polycenter Framework, and it incorporates components of the Distributed Management Environment (DME) of the Open Software Foundation, or Operations Systems Functions.

Polycenter is the cornerstone for Digital's implementation of EMA. The components of the Polycenter Framework and how they provide solutions to the most common types of management needs are described in Chapter 43.

Chapter 33
NetWare Considerations

Raj Rajagopal

In this chapter we will look at migration and coexistence options between Windows NT and NetWare. Novell NetWare was, and still is, the predominant Network Operating System. However, recently Windows NT is gaining market share from NetWare. Windows NT had one advantage in its competition with NetWare compared to UNIX. Unlike UNIX with its many variants, NetWare is a well-defined target. NetWare was relatively easy to develop migration and coexistence solutions for. Just as it introduced WordPerfect compatibility features (such as document translation filters for WordPerfect documents and user guides that provide comparable Word functions for WordPerfect functions) to appeal to the WordPerfect install base, Microsoft included NetWare compatibility features in Windows NT. Besides Windows NT, Windows 95 and Windows for Workgroups integrate with NetWare as well. These include:

- File and Print Services for NetWare (FPNW)
- Client Services for NetWare (CSNW)
- Gateway Services for NetWare (GSNW)
- Migration tool to migrate NetWare information to Windows NT

These compatibility features have been used by many customers, and you should find these very helpful if you are exploring migration and coexistence options between Windows NT and NetWare. We will cover these features in this chapter. We will also look at Novell server and client products that work in the Windows environment. Also in this chapter, we will look at system administration features that let you monitor and update the NetWare server using Windows NT functions.

WINDOWS NT AND NETWARE MIGRATION AND COEXISTENCE OPTIONS

You have a good set of migration and coexistence options when you want Windows NT and NetWare to coexist. For example, you can:

0-8493-9989-0/99/$0.00+$.50

- Access NetWare Servers using Microsoft Clients, access files on disks attached to the NetWare Server, and print to printers attached to the NetWare Server
- Access Windows NT Server using NetWare Clients, access files on disks attached to the Windows NT Server, and print to printers attached to the Windows NT Server
- Administer a NetWare server using built-in functions of Windows NT
- Migrate from NetWare to Windows NT; there are tools that permit you to copy the administration data (such as user data) from the NetWare server to the Windows NT server

Let us look at these options in detail.

Accessing Novell NetWare Servers Using Windows Clients

If you are using Microsoft Windows-based desktops and you want to access files and printers attached to Novell NetWare, you can do one of the following:

1. Get a Windows operating system with built-in NetWare client support. Windows operating systems that provide this support include Windows NT Workstation and Windows 95. The built-in client to access NetWare is also called Client Services for NetWare (CSNW). Using CSNW, you have full access to NetWare 3.1x (and below) servers. These clients also allow you to access NetWare 4.x servers in bindery emulation mode. Depending on the version of Windows 95 you have, you may not have built-in NDS support. Windows 95 started including full NDS support with Service Pack 1. Service Packs are available for download from **http://www.microsoft.com/windows/software/servpak1/enduser.htm**. You can also find Service Pack 1 in Microsoft's Software Library forum on CompuServe (GO CIS:MSL-30; Search for SNumber S15768). CSNW is covered in more detail later in this chapter.
2. Get a NetWare client from Novell. Novell provides NetWare clients that work in Windows 3.1, Windows 95, and DOS. Novell NetWare clients provide all the functionality for NetWare 3.1x and NetWare 4.x, including NDS access on NetWare 4.x. Novell NetWare client can coexist with the Microsoft client on the same machine (older versions of the NetWare client did not support this). You can download the 32-bit client for Windows 95 from **ftp.novell.com/pub/updates/nwos/nc32w952**, and for DOS/Windows 3.1x from **ftp.novell.com/pub/updates/nwos/cl32dw21**. Novell also provides support through its NetWire forum on CompuServe. You can also access NetWare information through the World Wide Web at http://www.novell.com.

3. Install Gateway Service for NetWare (GSNW) to let clients running only Microsoft Networking client software access NetWare server resources via gateway services provided by Windows NT Server.

These options are shown in Exhibit 1.

***Tip**: Both Microsoft and Novell provide products that have basically the same functions. If you are in an environment where both products coexist, try looking at the features in detail of both products, even though you may be very familiar with one. You may find that for some of your most commonly used functions, one of these products provides a simpler or faster way of accomplishing your functions.*

Your choice depends on the level of NetWare support you need, the types of client your users prefer, costs involved, and the administrative skill set you have. Let us look at each of the options in detail.

Using Windows Operating System with Built-in NetWare Client Support

Windows includes Client Services for NetWare (CSNW) in Windows 95 and Windows NT. CSNW supports NetWare access by using the Multiple Provider Router (MPR) API. Support for the MPR API is available in Windows 95 and Windows NT 4.0's Workstation and Server versions. MPR is not an acronym for the similar-sounding Multi-Protocol Routing Service. The multiple provider router ensures proper routing. For example, remote requests to Windows servers are sent to the proper server by the Windows redirector, while requests to NetWare servers are routed appropriately.

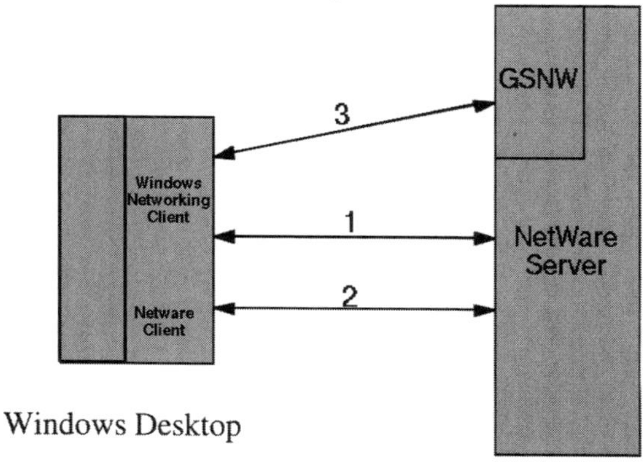

Exhibit 1. Accessing NetWare Server from Windows Desktop. (1) Windows built-in Networking Client accessing NetWare Server. (2) Novell's NetWare Client accessing NetWare Server. (3) Windows Networking Client accessing NetWare Server through Gateway.

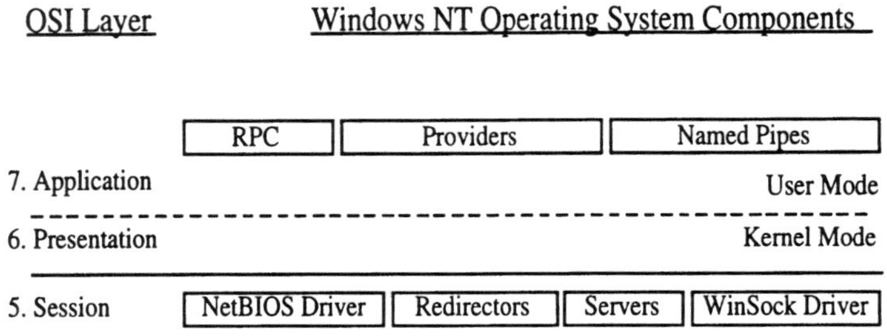

Exhibit 2. Upper layers of OSI model and Windows NT components.

MPR exports Win32 networking APIs and interacts with Network Providers and network DLLs. Exhibit 2 shows layers 5, 6, and 7 of International Standards Organization's Open System Interconnect (OSI) model and the components of the Windows NT operating system that implement these layers.

In Exhibit 2, for each redirector at the session level, there exists a provider at the application level. When there are multiple providers available, MPR handles the routing of a network service request to the appropriate provider. MPR facilitates user interfaces such as Windows Explorer to access the underlying networks. All network providers request network services such as connecting to servers, browsing servers, and disconnecting from servers through MPR. Besides NetWare Server access, the MPR API is also used as an application programming interface to the local file system and remote Windows network servers. In this scenario, there is no need for a NetWare-specific protocol stack.

Bindery: Access to file directories and printers on NetWare networks is on a per-user basis. When a NetWare server gets a request, it needs access to the list of authorized users to validate the request. In NetWare 3.x and earlier, access control information such as users, groups, passwords, and rights are stored in a database on the server called the *Bindery*. One of the problems with the bindery is that each server had its own bindery. If you wanted to let a user access multiple NetWare, then that user's information should be updated in the bindery of all the servers, one bindery at a time. NetWare fixed the bindery problems with the introduction of NetWare Directory Services (NDS). NDS uses an object-oriented approach to network management. For compatibility purposes, NDS emulates the presence of a bindery, by default. Windows 95 can use the bindery of one NetWare server.

Windows 95, NetWare, and Security. In NetWare environments, it is common for multiple departments to have a NetWare server of their own and provide access to selected users from other departments as required.

NetWare does this through the concept of NetWare domains and NetWare Name Service (NNS), an add-on service, that obtains user lists. Windows 95 can specify only one bindery and does not support the use of NetWare domains or NNS. This means that Windows 95 users can access the resources on one NetWare server, but cannot obtain pass-through validation on other NetWare servers. One suggestion to solve this problem, according to Microsoft documentation, is to list all NetWare users on one NetWare server. This server acts as the security clearing house for all Windows 95 users using File and Print Services for NetWare.

Using CSNW

You can access a NetWare server using the built-in client services of Windows; the following lists the sequence of activities that you need to follow:

- Install the necessary software and set up accounts
- Set up the NetWare connection configuration
- Set logon, printing, and other options

Let's look at these activities in detail:

Installing Software and Setting up Accounts. The following are the steps involved in installing the necessary software and setting up the required accounts. The steps presume that your client Windows operating system and the NetWare server operating system software have already been installed.

1. Install Networking support in your client workstation. This may have already been installed when the client operating system was installed. If it is not installed, then you (or your Network Administrator) need to install this first.
2. Set up a user account on the NetWare server, if one doesn't already exist. For NetWare 3.x and earlier, use the SYSCON, NETADMIN NetWare administration utility. For NetWare 4.x, use the NWADMIN utility that is part of NDS.
3. Install NWLink transport and related protocol support.

In following these steps, remember to check for the latest drivers from Microsoft and/or Novell. Successful installation of NetWare client support adds the CSNW applet to your control panel, as shown in Exhibit 3.

Configuring the NetWare connection. You use the CSNW applet that was added to your control panel to configure the NetWare connection. Double-clicking on the CSNW applet brings up the screen shown in Exhibit 4.

The three main parts of your configuration are the server specification (or tree/context specification if you are using NDS), your print options, and whether you want to use login scripts. If the NetWare server you specify runs NetWare 3.x or earlier, then bindery emulation is automatically used.

Exhibit 3. CSNW applet in the Control Panel.

For NetWare 4.x, then there is a choice between bindery emulation and NDS. If you choose to use NDS, then you should specify the name of a tree and context. Note that although NetWare natively includes support for both a preferred server and a default tree/context, Windows NT restricts you to choose one or the other.

Regardless of the version of the server, you must have an account in the NetWare server you want to access. You can specify *None* as a server name, in which case Windows NT will attempt to log you to the nearest available NetWare server, but this is not a good idea for two reasons. First, NetWare requires that a user account must be created before the user logs on. This means that an account must be set up for you in potentially all the NetWare servers that are near you. Second, this negates attempts by system administrators to distribute load on servers by assigning users to servers.

Follow these steps to configure NWLink:

1. In **Control Panel**, double-click **Network**
2. Click the **Protocols** tab
3. Click **NWLink IPX/SPX Compatible Transport** (See Exhibit 5)

4. Click **Properties**
5. Select either **Auto Frame Type Detection** or **Manual Frame Type Detection**
6. If you select Manual, click **Add**, and enter a Frame Type and Network Number for each type you want to add, and then click **Add**
7. Click **OK** to save your changes

Note: *Although NetBIOS is not very common in the NetWare world, NetWare supports its own version of NetBIOS that some users use. Besides NWLink IPX/SPX protocol support, Microsoft also includes an NWLink NetBIOS protocol for compatibility.*

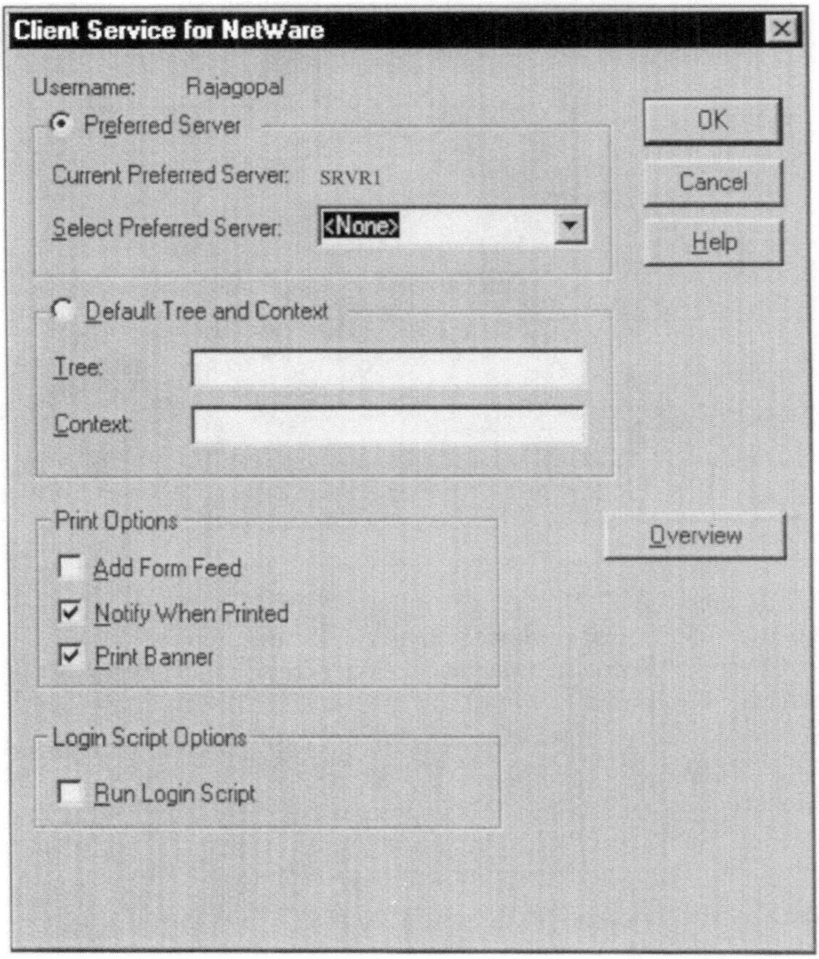

Exhibit 4. Configuring the NetWare connection using CSNW.

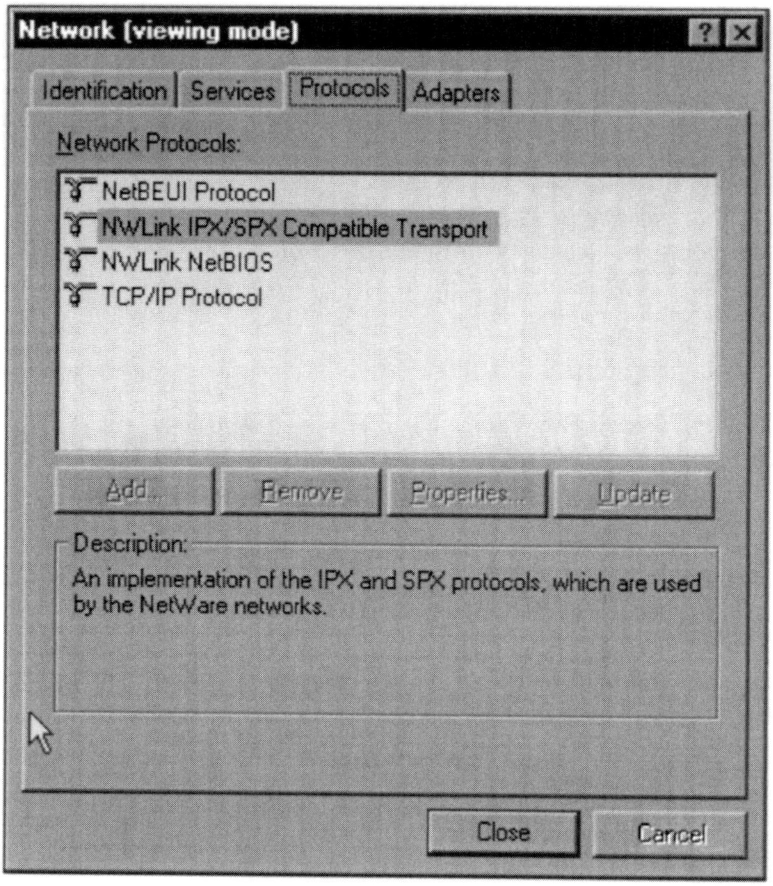

Exhibit 5. Selecting IPX/SPX compatible protocol for NWLink.

Setting Your Options. Your logon options depend on the NetWare server version, as mentioned earlier. Your print options available with CSNW include form feeds, completion notification, and printing a banner page, as shown in Exhibit 4.

Form feeds are required for compatibility with older applications that did not automatically include a form feed. If an older application just printed text for example and if this option is not selected, then the output of another application sent to the same printer will start after the output of the older application without any separation.

However, most new programs automatically include the form feed at the end of the print output, and selecting this box will add an additional form feed, resulting in waste of paper. Select this option only when you know you have older applications that do not include form feeds.

The print completion notification option informs you when the background printing is complete. If you have a printer attached to your computer and use it for printing or you do not want to be disturbed by the completion notification, then you can turn this option off.

Selecting the banner page option inserts a banner page with your user information along with your printed output to help separate print output of different users. Again, you don't need this if you have your own printer.

The other option you can specify when configuring CSNW is whether you want to use Login Scripts. This option is useful if you have login scripts that have already been created and are residing on the NetWare server. For example, you may have login scripts to handle security functions or for creating automatic search mapping. The system login script of a NetWare server (using bindery emulation) is in \PUBLIC\NET$LOG.DAT and individual user scripts are in the user's \MAIL directory. You can specify the location of your login script using the User Environmental Profile Dialog Box under User Manager. NDS login scripts can be edited using a GUI interface, while the older scripts are typically edited using simple DOS editors.

Tip: *You may be able to reduce the time taken to process your login script (and hence your logon time) by eliminating commands no longer needed or applicable in a Windows NT environment. One such command is the Greeting command.*

Locating and Logging to a NetWare Server

If you need to find the NetWare servers in your network, you can use the **Explorer** under **Start**, **Programs**. You can also use the Network Neighborhood or the **Computer** under **Start**, **Find**.

Exhibit 6 shows accessing a NetWare server using **Find** while Exhibit 7 shows how to access the same server using Network Neighborhood.

Once you have located the server icon or entry, double-clicking the icon or entry brings up the logon screen.

To logoff, select the server from the Network Neighborhood as you did for logon. Then choose **File**, **Log Out**. Confirm that you want to logoff from the confirmation dialog box, as shown in Exhibit 8.

You can logon to another server, if you choose. At any time, you can check the server you are logged on to and connection type by selecting **File**, **WhoAmI** when the server is selected in the Network Neighborhood window, as shown in Exhibit 9.

Accessing NetWare File Services. Once you have located your NetWare server and logged on to the server, you can access the directories and files on the NetWare server using the standard Windows functions.

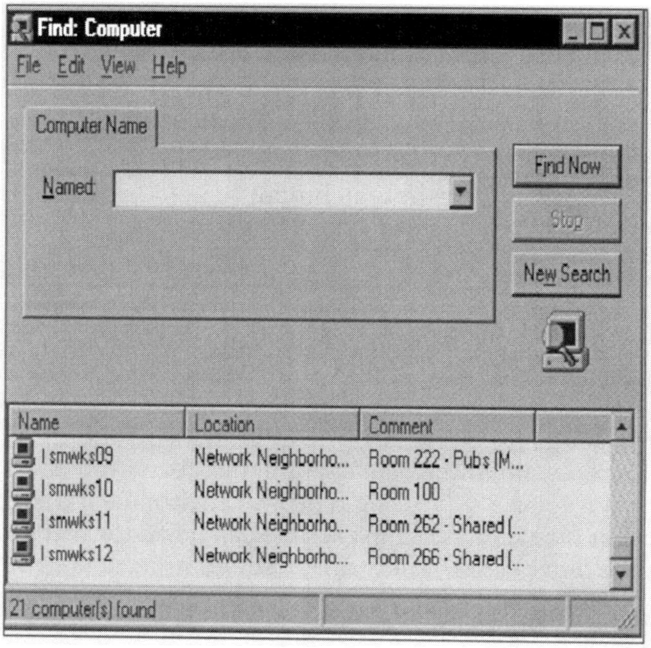

Exhibit 6. Locating a NetWare server using Find.

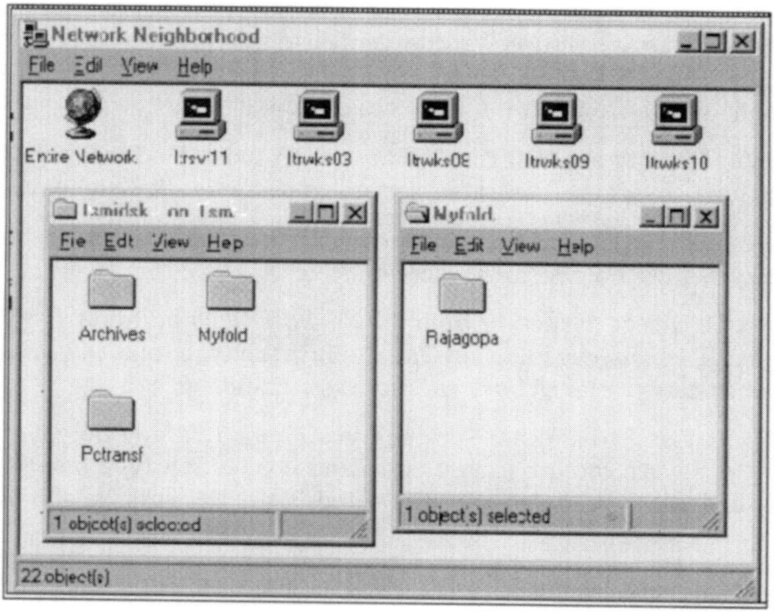

Exhibit 7. Locating a NetWare server using Network Neighborhood.

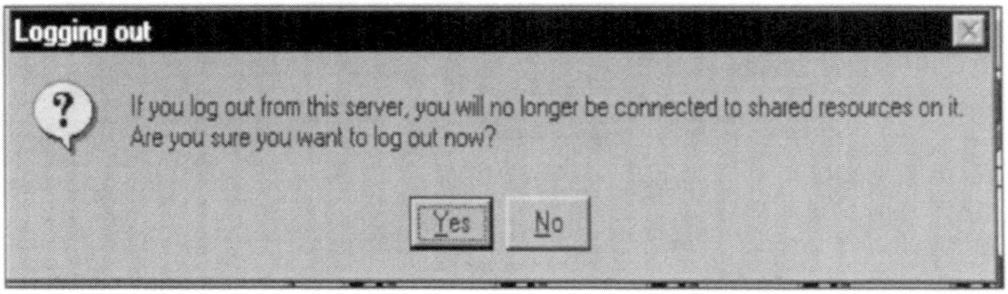

Exhibit 8. Logging out of a NetWare server.

You can access disks, directories, and files using Windows Explorer, Network neighborhood, and the File Manager. The File Manager is the standard interface for files in Windows NT 3.5x and Windows 3.x. Although the Explorer replaced the File Manager, you can still use the File Manager, if you prefer, by selecting **Start**, then **Run**, and keying in *WinFile*. An example of accessing a NetWare server using the Explorer is shown in Exhibit 10.

The use of the same interfaces for a NetWare server as a Windows NT server means that you do not have to learn anything new to use the directories and files on the NetWare server. Some functions that are available with a Windows NT server, such as sharing workstation directories, are not available when you access the NetWare server.

If you anticipate repeated access to specific directories and drives, you can set up drive mapping in Windows NT to make it easier and faster to access NetWare server and directories.

You can map a drive by selecting the Network Neighborhood and selecting the drive or server or folder you want to map to, as shown in Exhibit 11.

Alternatively, you can also use NetWare's MAP command to access drives, directories, and files.

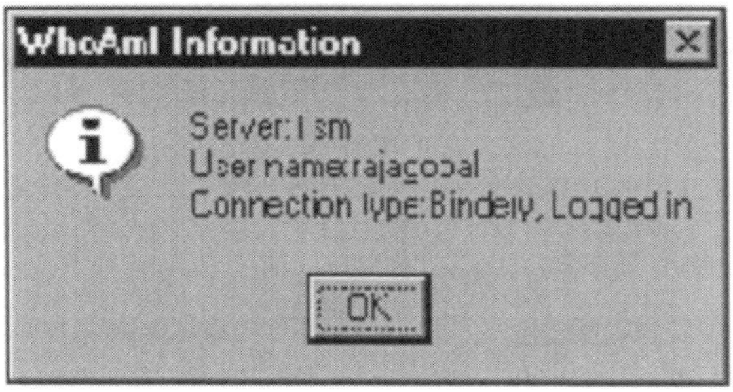

Exhibit 9. Determining the NetWare server logged on and the connection type.

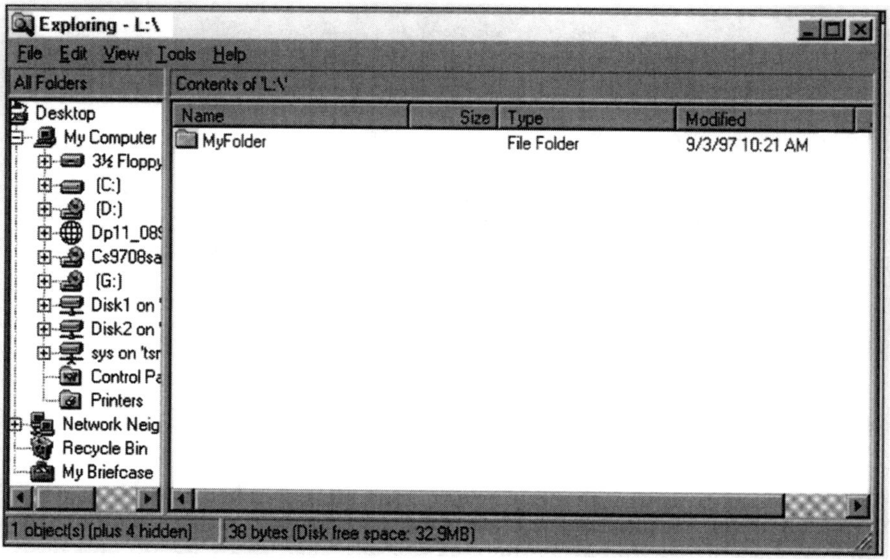

Exhibit 10. Accessing a NetWare server using Explorer.

Accessing NetWare Print Services. It is very common to share expensive laser printers in a NetWare network. Once a Windows client establishes connection, it can use the NetWare network printers. NetWare supports three ways to attach a printer to a NetWare network as follows:

- Attach the printer to a server machine running Novell NetWare. The NetWare server manages the print queues and other administration functions of the printer.
- Attach the printer directly to the network (with a network card in the printer), and manage the queues and administration of the printer from a NetWare server elsewhere on the network.
- Attach the printer to a PC as a simple print server using a spooler.

Regardless of how the printer is attached to the network, you can set up the printer for printing as follows.

Setting up a Novell NetWare Printer in Windows. You typically select printers the first time you log on or want to print. You can choose the printer in one of two ways. Before you select one of the ways and proceed with the steps that follow, make sure that you have a userid and password on the NetWare server and you are logged on to the Novell network.

From **Start**, select **Settings**, and then select **Printers**. Choose the option to **Add** printer and select Network printers. This will bring up the menu shown in Exhibit 12. Double-clicking on the NetWare Compatible Network

Exhibit 11. Mapping a network drive.

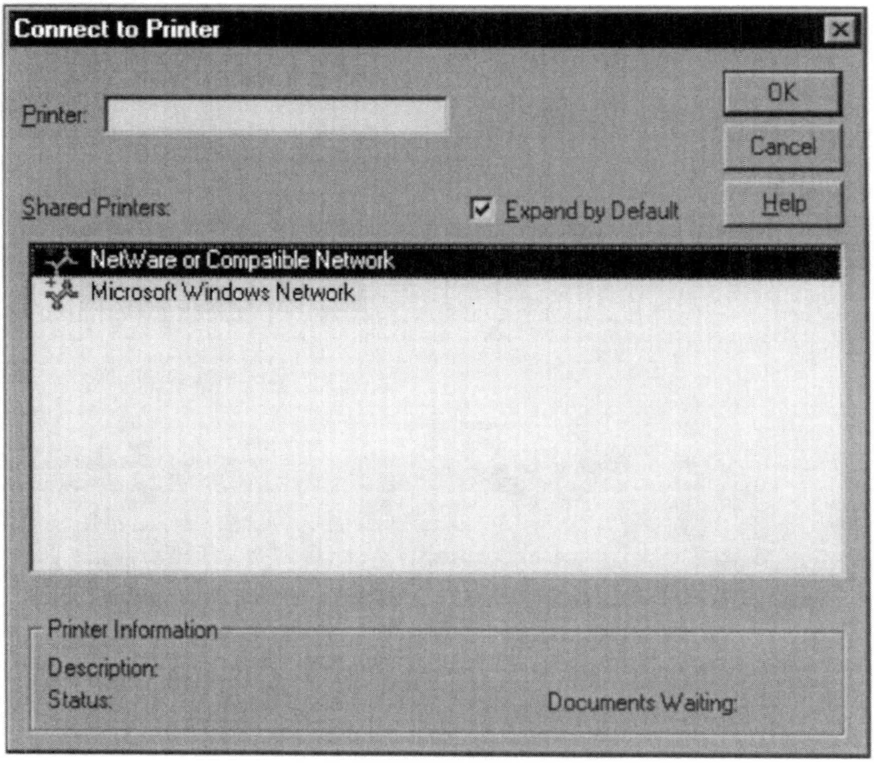

Exhibit 12. Locating NetWare printers.

entry will expand and eventually show all the NetWare printers you can use to print.

You can also use the following steps to set up a Novell NetWare printer.

- From the **Start** menu, choose the **Control Panel**.
- In **Control Panel**, choose **Printers** option.
- Select the option to add a printer. In the setup wizard, select a network printer instead of a local printer.
- Browse the network to find your printer; you will see the NetWare attached printers.

Select the one that you want (depending on the printer, you may need to use a driver diskette from the printer manufacturer) to complete the printer installation. When installation is complete, you can start using the printer. Repeat the above steps to add other network printers.

Managing Printers

Once you have set up a NetWare printer, you print from your application the same way as you would to any other printer. You can query and set any network printer as your default and you can change your default. You can also query about print jobs waiting at a printer and cancel outstanding print requests on a NetWare printer just as you would query or cancel any other print request as shown in Exhibit 13. To cancel a print request, select the entry from the print queue shown in Exhibit 13 and click on **Document** in the menu bar. From the pull-down menu, select **Cancel**.

Alternatively, you can also use the NetWare PCONSOLE command to manage print queues.

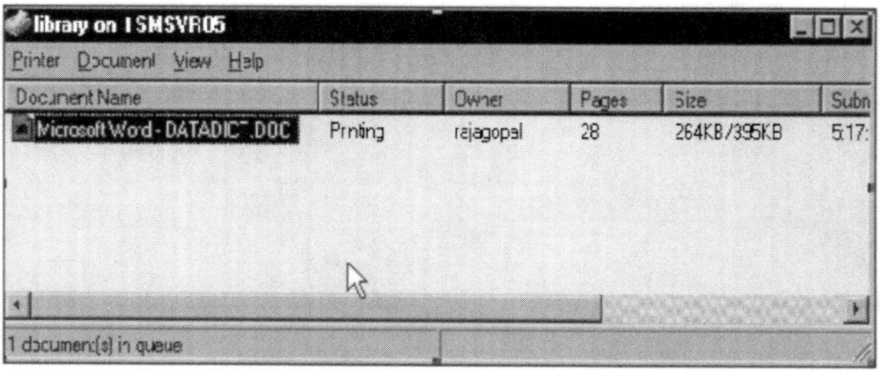

Exhibit 13. Print queue for a NetWare printer.

NOVELL'S NETWARE CLIENT

You can avoid some of the limitations, such as accessing only one bindery or having to define a NetWare server with all users for security, by using NetWare clients from Novell. Novell NetWare clients are available for DOS, Windows 3.x, Windows 95, Windows NT, OS/2, UNIX, and Macintosh. The advantages and disadvantages of this approach compared to using CSNW are summarized in Exhibit 14.

Exhibit 14. Comparing Novell Windows client and Microsoft built-in Netware client.

Advantages	Disadvantages
• Provides NetWare server access even when the native operating system doesn't provide built-in support • The NetWare client typically is a full function NetWare client without limitations • Has more features, particularly for the System Administrator. Some of these features include: • Support for 3270 emulators requiring DOS TSR capability • NetWare Internet Protocol support • NCP Packet Signature support • Custom component support	• Another piece of software that has to be installed and maintained • Additional resources such as memory (for a NetWare stack) and disk space required for the installation and operation of the NetWare client • The additional features seem to make the NetWare client a little slower for some functions compared to the Microsoft product

With NetWare 4.0, Novell included some significant enhancements to the client software. These include:

- The NETx shell used in prior NetWare versions clients was replaced by a Virtual Loadable Module (VLM) requester.
- The IPX driver (IPX.COM), which has some serious limitations, such as hardcoded network addresses and support for only one IPX protocol stack, has been replaced by Novell Open Datalink Interface (ODI).
- Drivers to facilitate interoperability between ODI and NDIS.

Regardless of whether you use NETx or VLM requester, you are better off using the newer ODI driver because it lets you run other protocols besides IPX, which is very important from a heterogeneous coexistence viewpoint.

GATEWAY SERVICE FOR NETWARE (GSNW)

GSNW allows clients running Microsoft client software to access shared files resident on a NetWare server. GSNW also allows Microsoft clients to print to NetWare printers.

Microsoft uses the Server Message Block (SMB) protocol for communication between an NT server and its clients running various Windows software. Novell uses the NetWare Core Protocol (NCP) for communication between NetWare server and NetWare clients. If Windows clients are to access a NetWare server transparently (thinking that they are still talking to Windows NT), translation is required between the SMB and NCP protocols. GSNW is the translator. GSNW translates the upper layer SMB calls to and from NetWare NCP calls. GSNW is part of the Windows NT Server 4.0 Directory Services Manager for NetWare (DSMN). The role of GSNW is shown in Exhibit 15.

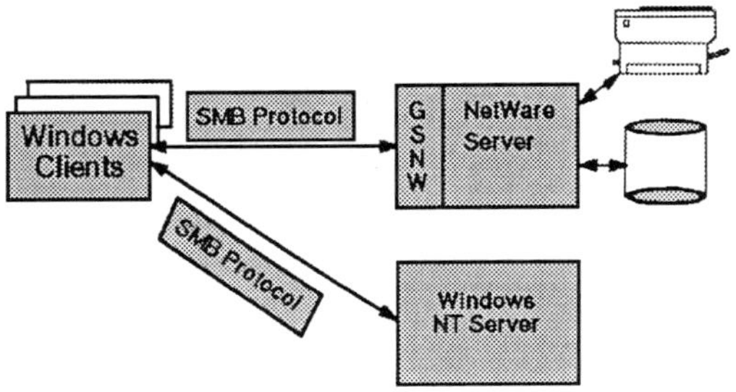

Exhibit 15. Gateway Services for NetWare (GSNW).

GSNW is included with Windows NT Server 4.0. GSNW is implemented as a Windows NT service.

To use GSNW, you need to install GSNW on your Windows NT server. This step is covered below. You also need to configure your NetWare server; this step is covered later in this chapter.

You install GSNW on a Windows NT server using the following steps:

1. From **Start**, click **Settings**, and click **Control Panel**, which brings up the Control Panel. Double-click the Network icon and select the Services tab in the Network Property sheet.
2. Click **Add** button, which displays the Select Network Service dialog. Choose Gateway client service for NetWare from the list of services and then click OK to bring up the Windows NT setup dialog.
3. Specify the complete path information where GSNW files are stored and click Continue.
4. When all files are copied, the Network Property sheet is displayed. The list of services now includes GSNW. Click **Close** and you will be prompted to restart the computer to activate the GSNW service.

5. The first time you use GSNW after installation, it will prompt you to enter a default NetWare server to which GSNW will connect (if more than one NetWare server exists on your network).

GSNW can be used along with Remote Access Service (RAS) built into Windows NT to allow remote Microsoft Networking clients to access NetWare file and print services transparently.

Some considerations in using GSNW:

1. If you use GSNW and want to print to a postscript printer, be sure to turn off the default option of including a banner page. Even though you are printing a postscript file, the banner page is non-postscript and the printer cannot handle the banner page.
2. NDS support — GSNW works fine in NetWare 2.x/3.x environments. GSNW doesn't support Novell NDS, and a GSNW client can access a NetWare 4.x server only in bindery emulation mode. If you do not want these limitations, then you can use the Novell NetWare client.
3. GSNW uses a single connection and a group account to the NetWare server that is used by all GSNW clients, including remote clients. This has many implications:
   a. All GSNW clients have identical trustee rights and permissions (those of the one group account).
   b. The number of clients as seen by NetWare is reduced; this has license and system administration implications.
   c. All requests from GSNW clients to the NetWare server are routed through GSNW. This has performance implications. This central routing also implies that if GSNW or the machine goes down, then all the GSNW clients are affected even though the NetWare server they are trying to access may be up and running.
   d. The GSNW clients cannot have individual login scripts since NetWare doesn't recognize them as individual clients.
   e. NetWare's built-in backup cannot be used to back up GSNW clients.

We have discussed different ways for a Windows desktop to access a NetWare server. Exhibit 16 compares the advantages and disadvantages of accessing a NetWare server directly vs. through a gateway.

There are multiple ways to attach a Windows client to access NetWare servers. Your choice depends on your environment, the types of NetWare services you need, and the skills you have for network administration.

ACCESSING WINDOWS NT SERVER USING NETWARE CLIENTS

Just as you can transparently access a NetWare server from a Windows client, you can transparently access a Windows NT server from a NetWare client using File and Print Services for NetWare.

Exhibit 16. Comparing direct and gateway connections.

Connecting through GSNW	Connecting Directly
Only one logon ID is required for the gateway at the NetWare server; clients accessing the gateway do not need their own NetWare logons	Each client workstation logging into the NetWare server needs a logon ID in the NetWare server
Easy to isolate the NT network and NetWare network and separate the traffic (e.g., by using different network cards for each network)	Difficult to separate the networks and traffic when multiple clients access both Windows NT server and NetWare server independently
Setup is more involved; setup is required at the NetWare server, gateway, and the clients	Setup is simpler; only the NetWare server and the clients need to be set up
The gateway becomes a central routing point for traffic, which could mean delays, downtime (a single point of failure)	Traffic is not centrally routed

File and Print Services for NetWare (FPNW)

FPNW allows the Windows NT Server to emulate a NetWare server. NetWare clients can access shared files and printers in the same way that they would access shared resources on any NetWare server. The Windows NT printers appear as print queues on a NetWare network. FPNW does not translate between SMB and NCP. It supports the NCP Protocol so that NetWare clients continue to use that protocol. The role of FPNW is shown in Exhibit 17.

NETWARE ADMINISTRATION FUNCTIONS FROM MICROSOFT

When you are administering NetWare servers and clients in a Windows environment, you have two choices. Microsoft includes network management functions as part of Windows NT. These functions are available in the Control Panel, Network Neighborhood, etc. We will look at some of these functions in this section.

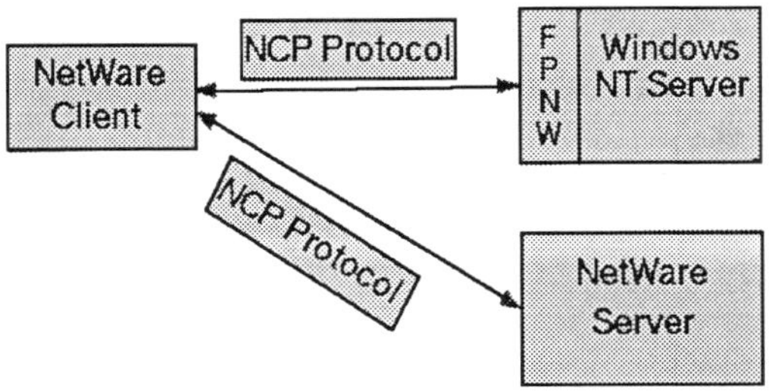

Exhibit 17. File and Print Services for NetWare (FPNW).

Your other choice is to administer NetWare servers and clients in a Windows environment using software from Novell. We will cover this approach in the next section.

Sometimes it is convenient to monitor and control a NetWare server using Windows NT functions rather than using NetWare administration functions. This may be the case, for example, if you are managing several servers using Windows NT facilities and a NetWare server happens to be one of them.

One of the Windows NT facilities to manage networks is the Server applet in the Control Panel. See Exhibit 18.

Exhibit 18. Server applet in Control Panel.

Double-clicking the server applet shows the Usage Summary area, which provides the following useful information:

- Sessions: shows the current number of open logons (the same user who logged in twice is counted as two logons)
- Open Files: shows the current number of open data and executable files

- File Locks: shows the current number of file locks (including locks on system, data, and executable files) active
- Open Named Pipes: shows the number of named pipes and mailslots that are open

User Administration Using the Server Applet

Besides the information about the server listed, you can perform user administration functions such as viewing and disconnecting one or more users logged onto a NetWare server. To do this, you click on the Users box from the server main menu.

In the user menu that comes up, each user with an active logon has an entry here. You can disconnect a single user by clicking on the user entry and clicking **Disconnect**, or sometimes you may want to disconnect all active users (for example when you want to perform maintenance on the server). Before disconnecting one or more users, ensure that the users are aware that they are going to be disconnected, because they might lose data otherwise. If you have the privileges, you can log the users out as well.

Shared Resources. You can see what server resources are being shared and by whom in one of two ways. The first way is by using the Shared Resources dialog box, which is accessed by clicking the **Shares** button in the server dialog box.

The top half of the Shared Resources dialog box shows the complete list of resources and a count of the number of users using each resource. If you are interested to see the actual list of users for a specific resource, select the resource by clicking it. The bottom half of the dialog box shows the list of users using that resource. You can disconnect a user or all users from this dialog box as well.

The second way you can see what server resources are being shared and by whom is by using the Open Resources dialog box. You invoke the Open Resources dialog box by clicking the In Use button in the server dialog box. The Open Resources dialog box gives a snapshot of the list of resources that any user has currently open and you can disconnect any resource a user has open. In contrast, if you disconnect a user using a shared resources dialog box, then all the resources that the user has open are disconnected. You can disconnect all resources (this comes in handy if you want to bring down the server, for example). You can also see the number of open file locks for a resource. You can update the snapshot at any time by clicking the **Refresh** button.

Alerts for a Windows NT Administrator about a NetWare Server. You can alert a Windows NT administrator about an event in a NetWare server, besides creating a log entry for the event. Windows NT provides this capability. You can set up alerts by clicking the **Alerts** button on the server applet that displays an Alerts dialog box.

You can send the alert to a computer or the administrator. In the Alerts dialog box, type the name of the administrator or a computer that the alert is to be sent to.

NETWARE ADMINISTRATION FUNCTIONS FROM NOVELL

The network management utility from Novell that runs in the Windows NT environment is called NWADMIN. NWADMIN provides a list of network objects, including users, servers, groups, printers, etc. You can add your own objects as well.

Older versions of NetWare used a number of DOS command-type utilities. The nature of these utilities was very similar to the DOS *.bat* files, except that these NetWare utilities had an *.ncf* extension. NWADMIN replaces all the old DOS utilities with a centralized management environment.

The major menu options provided by NWADMIN and their descriptions are summarized in Exhibit 19.

Older versions used a number of DOS utilities, and Exhibit 20 is a summary of these. Most of these utilities will run in the Windows NT command prompt.

Protocol Support and Administration

Another system administration function that you will be dealing with in heterogeneous environments is choosing the communications protocol.

Exhibit 19. NWADMIN menu options.

NWADMIN Menu Option	Description
Details	Displays user location and contact information. You can use this option to set up login scripts and security for a user
Rights	Displays the rights of the currently selected object for using/modifying other objects
Object trustees	Displays the users/groups that have the rights to access and manipulate an object; selecting a trustee entry displays the rights for that trustee
Browse	Displays the contents of a container object; container objects hold (or contain) other objects; an example of a container object is the organizational unit
Create	Displays a dialog box that has a list of the object types that can be contained by the container object
Delete	Removes the current object and all other objects contained within it

Exhibit 20. NetWare utilities.

NetWare Utility	Description
Fconsole	Console operations such as handling broadcast messages, console messages, file server status, etc.
Filer	Provides data about files such as Size, Owner, etc.
Rconsole	Provides file server console functions from a workstation
Salvage	Recovers deleted files
Session	Provides menu functions for network drives
Slist	Displays a list of NetWare servers
Syscon	Controls users, groups, servers, etc.

The vast majority of Novell NetWare networks use the IPX/SPX protocol for communication between NetWare clients and servers.

Windows NT supports multiple protocols, including IPX/SPX and NetBEUI (which are commonly used in Windows networks), and TCP/IP (which is commonly used in UNIX networks and the Internet). Novell has recently started including support for TCP/IP. Each of the protocols has strengths and weaknesses.

IPX/SPX is proven and is a routable protocol, but it is not an open protocol as TCP/IP is. NetBEUI is a simple protocol, but is not routable and does not handle well such complex tasks as database access. TCP/IP is open and is proven, but has complex setup and configuration. If you have played around with TCP/IP, Winsock, etc. to get connected to an Internet service provider, then you know the configuration work involved with TCP/IP.

You can have both Windows NT and NetWare servers and Windows clients accessing the servers in different ways, as discussed earlier. This may cause different protocols such as IPX/SPX and NetBEUI to coexist on the same network. For example, you can have workstations running Windows NT, and Windows 95, Windows for Workgroups on the same network with a NetWare server.

While the Windows NT workstation is communicating with the NetWare server, the other Windows workstations may be communicating with a Windows NT server using the NetBEUI protocol. In addition, the same workstation may be using TCP/IP to access the Internet in one window, for example, while browsing NetWare resources using IPX/SPX in another. Although Windows NT supports coexisting protocols, occasionally you may run into network problems due to protocol conflicts.

***Tip**: When you have different types of networks coexisting, try to get consistency in the way the networks are administered. For example, try to have* *a common response center and helpdesk, and try to get a single userid and password for different networks. If the same userid and password are not feasible, maintain consistency between different networks by using the same password lengths and duration for which passwords are valid, etc.*

Configuring Gateway Services for NetWare

If you plan to use GSNW, then you need to configure your NetWare server to use GSNW by following these steps (you will need supervisor access because you need to use the SYSCON utility):

- Run the SYSCON utility (SYSCON.EXE) and create a NetWare group calling it NTGATEWAY (this name must be used exactly as specified).
- Grant appropriate file, directory, and printer rights to this group. Remember that this is the group of all current and potential GSNW users.
- Create a NetWare user with supervisory rights in addition to file, directory, and printer rights. You can logon to a Windows NT server as the user you just created and perform maintenance functions and also run the migration tool provided by Microsoft (see Migration tool later in this chapter).
- Create other GSNW user accounts within the NTGATEWAY group.

Besides the setup at NetWare, you should also install GSNW on your Windows NT server before GSNW clients can access NetWare files and printers. This was addressed earlier in the chapter.

MIGRATION TOOL TO MIGRATE FROM NETWARE TO WINDOWS NT

Windows NT includes a migration tool to help customers migrate from NetWare to Windows NT. Besides migration, the tool can also assist in network reconfiguration.

The *migration tool* is useful to Network administrators. It automatically migrates NetWare user and group accounts, files and directories, and security and permissions from NetWare server(s) to a Windows NT server. The tool can also help network consolidation since administrators can use the tool to migrate different configurations such as a single NetWare server to a single Windows NT server, multiple NetWare servers to a single Windows NT server, etc. System administrators can use the migration tool to perform a trial migration. The migration tool generates detailed log files that provide an audit trail of changes that may occur during the migration process.

The migration tool just extracts the information from one or more NetWare servers and does not affect the data in the NetWare server. Once copied, the user information is available to other Windows NT server-based

BackOffice applications such as SQL Server, SNA Server, and Exchange Server since these applications share the same user account database as the Windows NT server.

NetWare and UNIX

Novell sold UnixWare to SCO. Prior to the sale, Novell had started enhanced compatibility between NetWare and UnixWare. UnixWare NetWare Services allows NetWare access for SCO UNIX clients. Additional information on UnixWare NetWare Services is available at http://www.sco.com/unixware.

SCO UnixWare NetWare Services (NWS). Starting with version 2.1, UnixWare provides standard NetWare 4.1 networking services in addition to the standard UNIX networking and application services. These services, called NetWare Services (NWS), provide NetWare 4.1 server capabilities that integrate seamlessly into existing Novell and UNIX environments.

With NWS, UnixWare can also act as the primary network server for businesses that need NetWare 4.1 file, print, and directory services, LAN security, and multiple client support.

NWS allows administrators to use native MS Windows-based NetWare tools like NWADMIN and PSERVER to administer the LAN environment.

NWS features include:

- Full NetWare File, Print, and Directory Services on a native SCO UnixWare environment
  - File services include:
    - Enables users to share files and information across the entire network
    - Supports DOS, Windows, Windows 95, UNIX, Mac NCP, and OS/2 clients
    - Works with standard SCO UnixWare 2.1 file systems (vxfs, ufs, sfs, s5) including NFS
    - Mounted file systems
    - Synchronized with host file system
    - Graphical volume manager
    - Combined security of NetWare and UNIX
  - Print services include:
    - Allows users to access any printer on the network by simply knowing the printer's name
    - Graphical printer setup utility
    - NDS based
    - Print Server v4.1
    - Remote printer print monitor for job status

- Full support for Novell Directory Services, NDS APIs, and Novell Cross Platform Services. NDS functions include:
  - Provides detailed map of available network users, resources, and services
  - Common source code with native NetWare, co-developers with Novell
  - Includes functionality for RSA authentication, schema, objects, partitions, replicas, and access
  - Controls, service controls, bindery emulation, and time synchronization
  - Multithreaded for scalable SMP performance
  - Administration using standard NetWare tools
- Supports up to 150 concurrent connections and can achieve performance close to native NetWare performance
- Graphical administration tools for installing and configuring all aspects of NWS operations:
  - NDS administration and repair
  - Administration of NetWare and UNIX System printers from a single tool
  - NWS volume administration
  - NWS networking configuration and tuning
- Supports DOS, Windows, Windows 95, UNIX, Mac, NCP, and OS/2 clients
- Works with standard SCO UnixWare file systems, including NFS-mounted file systems
- Transparent to clients, administrators, and network management system (like Novell ManageWise, etc.)
- Supports a range of protocols common in NetWare environment, including:
  - IPX, SPX2, IPX/SPX diagnostics protocols
  - SAP, RIP routing protocols
  - NCP and NCP Extensions (NCPx)
  - Novell Virtual Terminal (NVT2) terminal emulation over IPX/SPX
  - SNMP network management

Banyan VINES and Windows NT

Although NetWare is the predominant network operating system, there are other network operating systems that are being used as well. One of them is VINES from Banyan. If you have VINES and are interested in integrating with Windows NT or if you are interested in adding directory services to your Windows NT environment, then you may want to consider StreetTalk from Banyan. Banyan has a version of StreetTalk that runs natively on a Windows NT server. This product ties together the StreetTalk Access capabilities with a local copy of StreetTalk, STDA (StreetTalk Directory Assistance service), and Banyan's security and authentication service. Information on Banyan's products is available at http://www.banyan.com.

Basic features of StreetTalk include:

- StreetTalk, STDA, and Banyan's Security Service running as native Windows NT services, at the same level as VINES
- Full interoperability with StreetTalk in VINES
- Runs on Windows NT Server 3.51 and 4.0
- Integrated with Windows NT's Event Monitor and Performance Monitor, which can be SNMP-enabled
- Enhanced VINES protocol stack, enabling multiple sessions per server
- Support for Banyan's Sequenced Routing Transport Protocol
- Support for DOS, Windows 3.x, Windows 95, Windows NT, and OS/2 clients
- Support for both Windows NTFS and FAT file systems
- File and print services support (includes all of the capabilities of StreetTalk Access)
- Long file name support for Windows 95 and Windows NT clients
- Support for international file names, including double byte Kanji characters
- Support for OS/2 Extended Attributes
- TCP/IP support for Windows 95 and Windows NT clients
- A new 32-bit management tool ("StreetTalk Explorer" for Windows 95 or Windows NT) to manage all services

Banyan has issued two additional releases, adding such functionality as:

- Banyan's Intelligent Messaging Service
- Server-to-Server TCP/IP
- Enhanced StreetTalk Explorer functionality including modules for Users, Groups, Organizations, Lists, Nicknames, Security, StreetTalk, STDA, and Intelligent Messaging
- Optimize and Audit function to keep list, nickname, and user names current
- Remote restart and time synchronization services
- Enhanced backup and restore utilizing Legato's Networker for Windows NT
- Guaranteed login for DOS, Windows 3.1, Windows 95, and Windows NT clients
- Developers toolkit for integration of third-party services
- Support for Windows 95 System Policies

Conclusion

We looked at accessing Windows NT server from NetWare clients and vice versa for file and print services. Both Microsoft and Novell offer products for accomplishing these functions. We also looked at network administration functions from Microsoft and Novell, and briefly looked at the tool Microsoft provides to migrate from NetWare to Windows NT.

Chapter 34
Configuring Windows NT in a NetWare Environment

Gilbert Held

For companies that require Windows NT clients to work in a NetWare environment, getting the configuration setup right can save network administrators time and expense and boost productivity by facilitating the NetWare connection.

INTRODUCTION

Novell's NetWare is an excellent network operating system for facilitating shared file and print services. In comparison, some of the more robust features of Microsoft's Windows NT are its "crash proof" capability and its use as an application server.

A marriage of these two network operating systems can be accomplished through the use of Windows NT client workstations and servers connected to a NetWare-based local area network. However, when configuring a Windows NT platform to work on a Novell network, there are several variables that govern the network manager's ability to connect the platform into a NetWare environment.

Although Microsoft provides a reasonable level of documentation that describes the configuration process for making a Windows NT platform work on a NetWare network, certain hardware and software considerations are omitted. This chapter provides network managers and administrators with additional tips necessary to correctly configure their Windows NT platform to work in a NetWare environment and avoid countless hours of frustration.

NT NETWORK SUPPORT

Windows NT includes built-in support for a variety of network protocols. Protocols directly supported in Windows NT version 3.51 include

0-8493-9989-0/99/$0.00+$.50

AppleTalk, data link control (DLC), NetBEUI, NWLink IPX/SPX, and TCP/IP. Because the focus of this chapter is on using Windows NT in a NetWare environment, the selection and use of the Windows NT NWLink IPX/SPX protocol is described here.

The NWLink IPX/SPX protocol was developed by Microsoft to provide compatibility with Novell's proprietary communications protocol Internet Packet Exchange/Sequenced Packet Exchange (IPX/SPX). NWLink IPX/SPX turns a Windows NT platform into a NetWare client workstation. The installation of the network adapter card and certain parameters can considerably facilitate the operation of NWLink IPX/SPX.

Network Adapter Card Configurations

Many network adapter cards are preinstalled in personal computers purchased after 1994. Although the PC is usually shipped with DOS and a version of Windows, such as Windows 3.11 or Windows for Workgroups, most organizations add Windows NT at a later date.

This means that certain configuration setup data in the network adapter card that enables the computer to be connected to a LAN may be hidden from view when first attempting to install Windows NT. Even if the PC and LAN adapter cards are correctly configured to obtain a network connection, it is easy to overlook several other important adapter card settings needed to correctly install and configure NWLink IPX/SPX to work with the LAN adapter card. Thus, even before installing and configuring Windows NT, network administrators should examine and note the settings used with the network adapter card.

Many adapter card vendors provide a diagnostic program used to display and change configuration settings. Some of the configuration parameters worth checking are:

- Port (i.e., the I/O address used by an adapter card)
- IRQ (i.e., the interrupt request used by an adapter card)
- DMA (i.e., the Direct Memory Access channel, if direct memory access transfer is enabled)
- Slot (i.e., the expansion slot used by the adapter card)
- Frame type (i.e., the frame type bound to the adapter card)
- Node address (i.e., the locally or universally administered node address)

Different adapter cards require the use of different parameters, therefore only a subset of these parameters listed may be applicable for a particular network adapter card.

INSTALLING NWLINK IPX/SPX

The installation of Microsoft's NWLink IPX/SPX program requires the user to be logged on as a member of the administrator's group for the local computer. In other words, to install the IPX/SPX protocol, the user must first have an appropriate NT account.

Once this is accomplished, the addition of networking capabilities to a Windows NT workstation is obtained by the selection of the "Network" option from the operating system's Control Panel window, which is accessed through the Main window.

Exhibit 1 illustrates the network settings window, which is considerably different from the network window displayed under Windows 3.11 and Windows for Workgroups. Earlier versions of Windows did not allow users to directly add network software and adapter card support via a common window. Instead, the user had to use the File menu to run self-configuring programs that would operate as separate entities and provide little, if any, information on the network hardware and software already installed.

In Exhibit 2, the box labeled Installed Network Software provides a list of network software drivers that were previously installed or bundled with

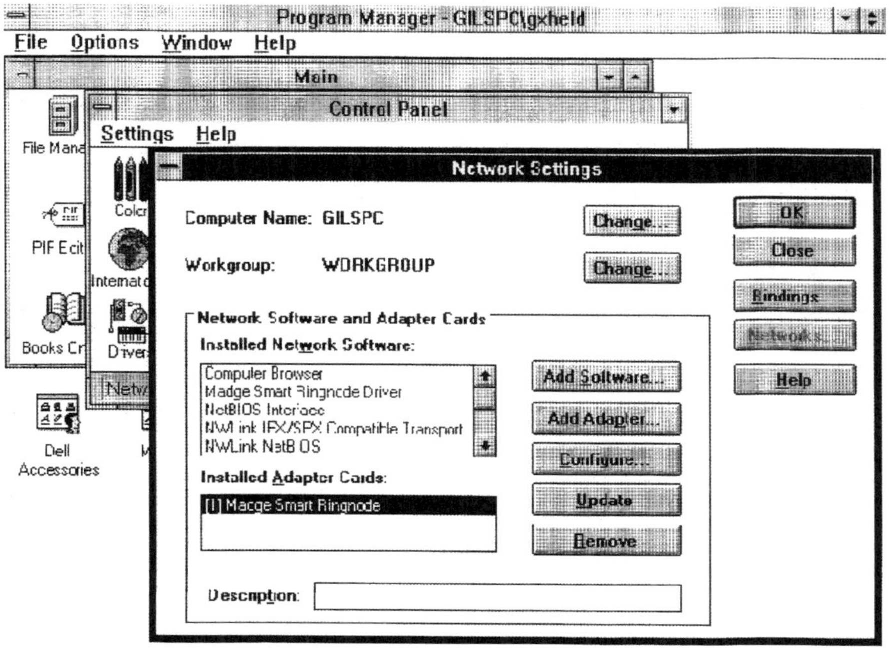

Exhibit 1. NT's network settings window.

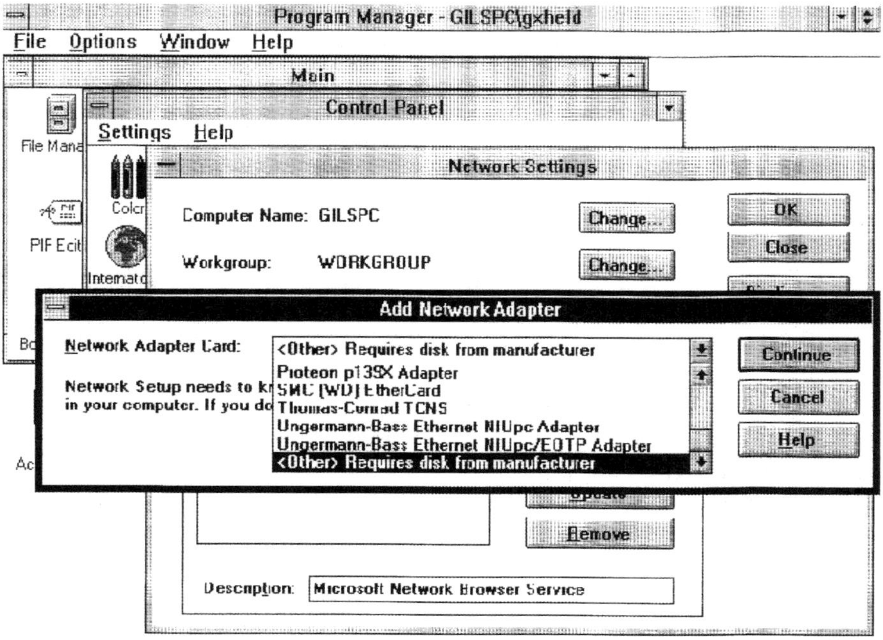

Exhibit 2. Adding a network adapter card.

Windows NT. Similarly, the box labeled Installed Adapter Cards lists those adapter cards previously configured under Windows NT—in this case, a Madge Smart Ringnode adapter card. When running the Windows NT setup, the program automatically installs a computer browser, NetBIOS, and a driver to support the adapter card installed in the computer.

Step-by-Step Adapter Card Setup

However, most people install Windows NT first to gain experience with its use, then later attempt to connect the NT platform to a Novell network, so the NWLink IPX/SPX software and the adapter card would not be configured at the outset. The steps necessary to install network software and a network adapter card are outlined next.

Most adapter cards are packaged with software drivers designed to support different operating systems, so first locate the diskettes distributed with the adapter card. To add network adapter card support, click on the Add Adapter button in the Network Settings window (see Exhibit 1). This action results in the display of another dialog box. Exhibit 2 shows this dialog box after the author scanned through the list of cards for which Microsoft includes built-in drivers in NT.

Tips for Using Adapter Cards Not Supported by NT. Because the Madge Networks Ringnode adapter card is not one of those on the list, the "Other" entry is selected from the pull-down list. Click on the Continue button after selecting "Other" as the network adapter card. Windows NT prompts the user to insert a diskette so the program can copy the appropriate files to the NT workstation's disk.

It is at this point that another common problem can occur that makes the installation of some network protocols a challenge. Several adapter card manufacturers distribute drivers for many operating systems on two diskettes. Those diskettes(which are typically labeled 1 and 2) also include a diagnostic program, text files, and other programs that are not applicable for use in a Windows NT environment.

The diskette labels do not, however, explain which disk to use with Windows NT. Only by reading through the manual included with the adapter card can the network administrator determine that the programs required to be used with Windows NT are located in the directory WINNT; however, the manual also fails to note which disk contains the WINNT directory and appropriate files in the directory.

If an adapter card falls into this category and two or more diskettes are packaged with the adapter, the diskette and the directory on the diskette containing the required Windows NT files must be determined. This step will save considerable time and frustration.

For example, if a network administrator were using the Madge Smart Ringnode adapter card and inserted disk 1 into drive A in response to the Windows NT prompt, not only are the required files not located there (they are on disk 2) but, in addition, the operating system software will not prompt the user to insert a second disk. Instead, it will prompt the user to insert three of the 22 diskettes included with Windows NT in an attempt to locate network adapter driver software on the Microsoft distribution diskettes. Since you an adapter in the "Other" category is being installed, the required drivers will not be located, and any attempt to correctly add the network adapter will fail.

A Walk Through a Vendor-Specific Setup. Once the user enters the correct diskette and specifies the appropriate directory for an adapter card that is not directly supported by Windows NT, it is more than likely that a vendor-specific setup menu will comes up next. Although a few vendors provide self-configuration modules; others require the Windows NT user to manually enter several key hardware configuration parameters.

Exhibit 3 illustrates the Madge Smart Ringnode Setup window that is displayed after the user has inserted the correct disk into the correct drive. The values displayed for the IRQ Level, I/O Loc/Slot, Direct Memory Access

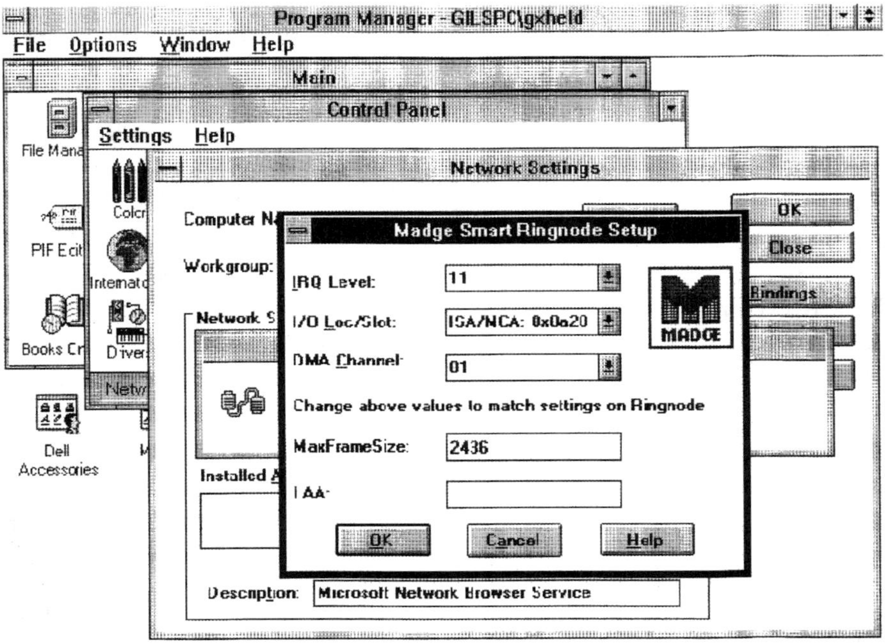

Exhibit 3. Madge Smart Ringnode Setup window with default parameters.

Channel, and MaxFrameSize represent default values that may or may not be appropriate.

Running a diagnostic program (if one is furnished by the adapter card manufacturer) before using the Windows NT Network Settings window should provide the correct settings that enable the adapter card's setup program to be correctly configured to match the settings used when the adapter card was originally installed under DOS or a different version of Windows. Otherwise, an inappropriate IRQ level or another incorrect parameter will prevent Windows NT from working in a network environment.

Unfortunately, an incorrect setup parameter that does not match the current adapter card configuration does not generate an appropriate and meaningful error message.

Adding Network Software

Once the adapter card parameter settings are adjusted, the appropriate software can be added through the Network Settings window. In comparison with the potential problems that can be encountered when adding an adapter card that is not directly supported by built-in Windows NT software, the selection of network software is a relatively simple process.

To install NWLink IPX/SPX, select the Add Software button from the Network Settings window. The resulting display is the Add Network Software window. From that window (see Exhibit 4), select the NWLink IPX/SPX Compatible Transport option, which is a built-in software module. Select the Continue button from the Add Network Software window, then the OK button from the Network Settings window.

Once the protocol software is installed, the next step is to configure NWLink IPX/SPX to associate a network adapter and frame type used on the network with the protocol. Because, for purposes of this example, a Madge Ringnode adapter was previously installed, that card would be selected to be bonded to the transport protocol.

To select the frame type, Windows NT supports an auto-detect feature that allows NWLink to check the frames being passed to the network adapter card the protocol is bound to. Alternately, the network administrator can select from IEEE 802.2, 802.3, and 802.5 frame types.

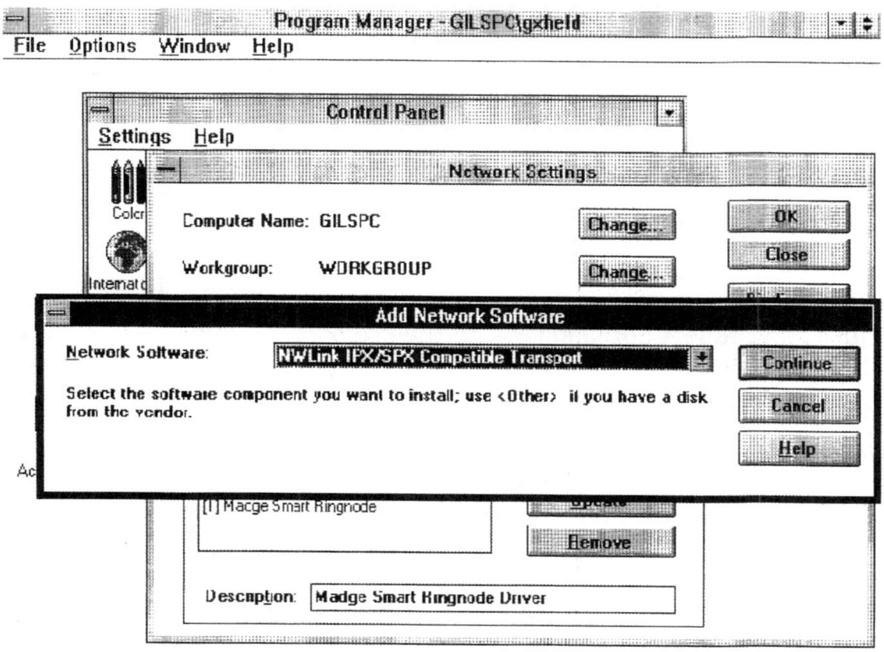

Exhibit 4. Installing NWLink IPX/SPX through the Add Network Software window.

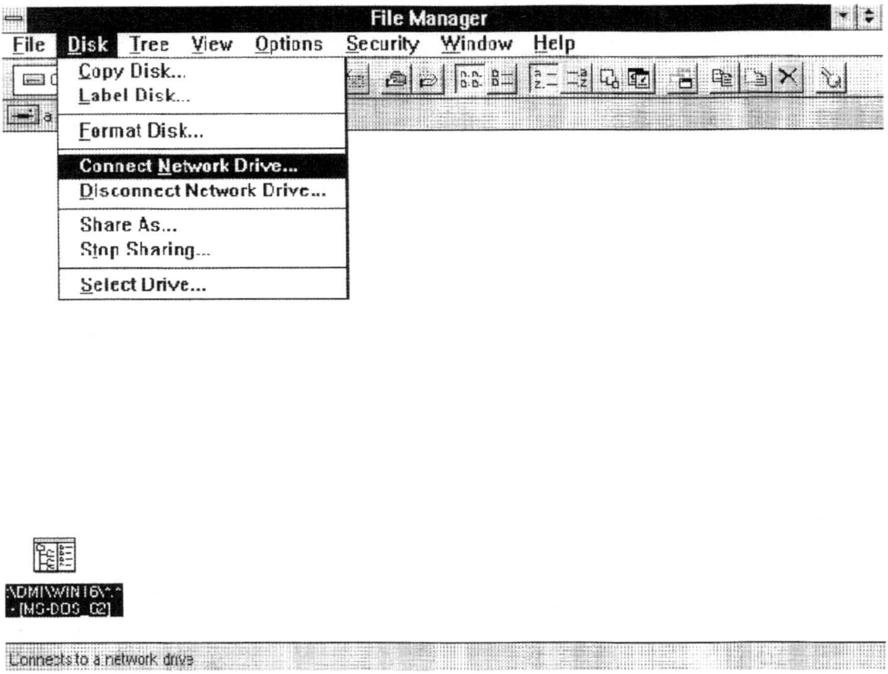

Exhibit 5. Network access through File Manager's disk menu.

After the adapter and frame type are selected, Windows NT prompts the user to restart the computer so that the network changes made can take effect.

CONNECTING TO A NETWARE SERVER

Upon restarting the computer, you are ready to initiate network operations. For readers not familiar with the use of Windows NT as a NetWare client, Exhibits 5 and 6 illustrate the connection of a computer using the Microsoft operating system to a NetWare server.

Access to a network drive is accomplished through the Disk menu from the File Manager window. Among the options in that menu is the Connect Network Drive option. When this option is highlighted (see Exhibit 5), the NWLink IPX/SPX client software displays a list of known servers. The network administrator can then select a preferred server as well as a drive letter for the first network drive, a path to a particular directory, and the user ID needed to establish a connection to the selected server.

Exhibit 6 illustrates the Connect Network Drive window after the selected server was double-clicked. This window is used to initiate a con-

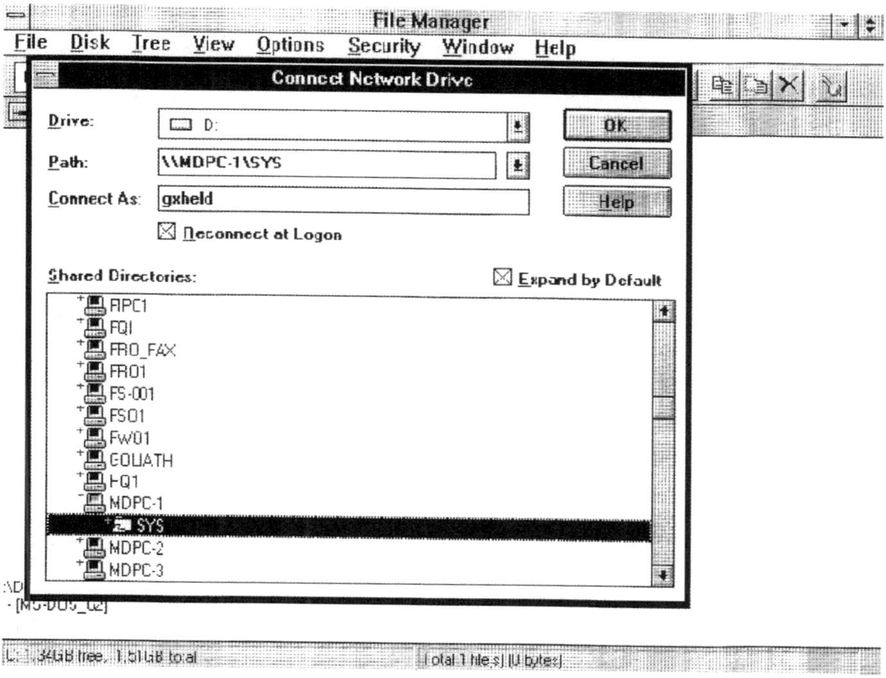

Exhibit 6. Connect Network Drive window initiates a connection to a NetWare server.

nection to a desired NetWare server. Here, the SYS directory is selected as the path on the server. Clicking the OK button enables the Windows NT computer to access a specific directory on a NetWare server, in effect converting the Windows NT computer into a client on a NetWare network.

CONCLUSION

Although the installation of NWLink IPX/SPX is relatively straightforward, the configuration and operation of many adapter cards under Windows NT can be time-consuming, especially if using adapter cards beyond the few Windows NT provides direct support for. Many vendors now charge for support, either requiring calls on a 900 telephone number or asking for a credit card, so the tips presented here can save network administrators time, frustration, and expense.

Chapter 35

Comparing Windows NT and UNIX System Administration

Raj Rajagopal

Continuing our focus on *system administration* aspects, this chapter will go into various system administration functions and point out how equivalent functions are performed in UNIX and Windows NT.

The primary difference between system administration in UNIX compared to Windows NT is in the end-user interface. Windows NT uses the graphical user interface, while the command line (character-based interface) is used heavily in UNIX. UNIX shells and Windows command prompts are discussed in Chapter 37. There are some system administration functions in some UNIX systems using the X-Windows-based graphical interface. However, the X-Windows is an add-on that may or may not be used, unlike Windows NT where the primary means of user interface is the Windows GUI.

The second important difference stems from the fact that Windows NT is based on the client/server model. This changes the concept of users, user administration, and other system administration functions as well.

EQUIVALENT WINDOWS NT, UNIX ADMINISTRATION FUNCTIONS

The primary menu for system administration functions in Windows NT is shown in Exhibit 1. You get to this menu by double-clicking **Windows NT Administration**, under **Programs**, under **Start**, in Windows NT 4.0.

In UNIX, you log on as the "root" to perform system administration functions.

0-8493-9989-0/99/$0.00+$.50

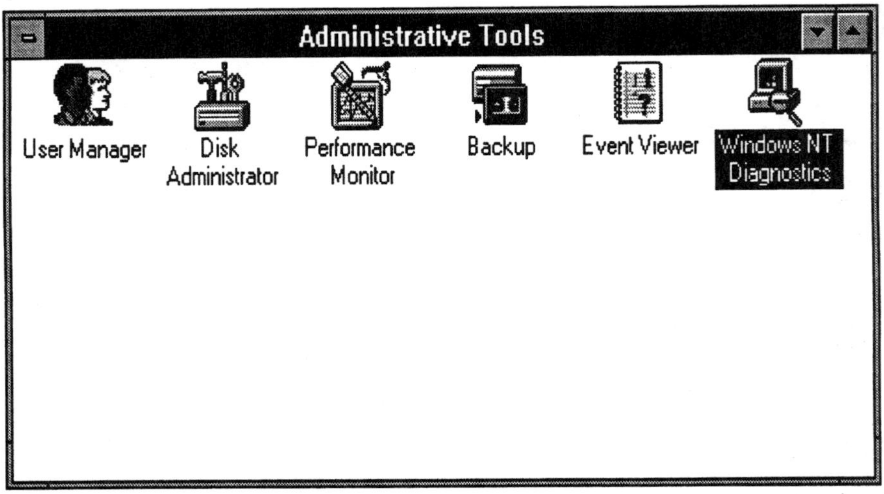

Exhibit 1. Main system administration menu in Windows NT.

Logon/Logoff

Administrator logon. *UNIX:* The administrator logs on as the "root." This automatically sets all the privileges required by the administrator to perform administration functions, as shown in Exhibit 2.

Windows NT: The administrator logs on as the "administrator" (Windows is not case sensitive, in general). You can get to the logon screen by

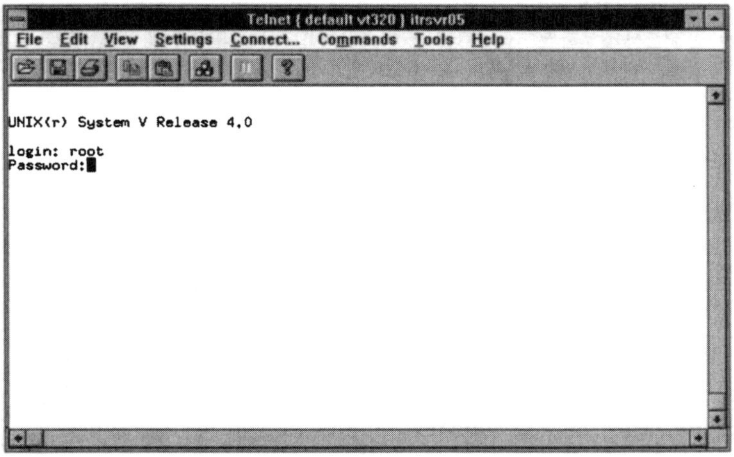

Exhibit 2. UNIX system administrator logs in as root.

pressing CTRL+ALT+DEL when no one is logged onto the system. This brings up a screen to enter userid and password. If some user is already logged onto the system, remember to log the user off because the user may not have the administrator privileges you need to perform system administration functions.

Changing Administrator Privileges. *UNIX:* You can change your ID and privileges using *su*. When you logon from a terminal other than the system console, your system may not allow you to logon as "root" as shown in Exhibit 3.

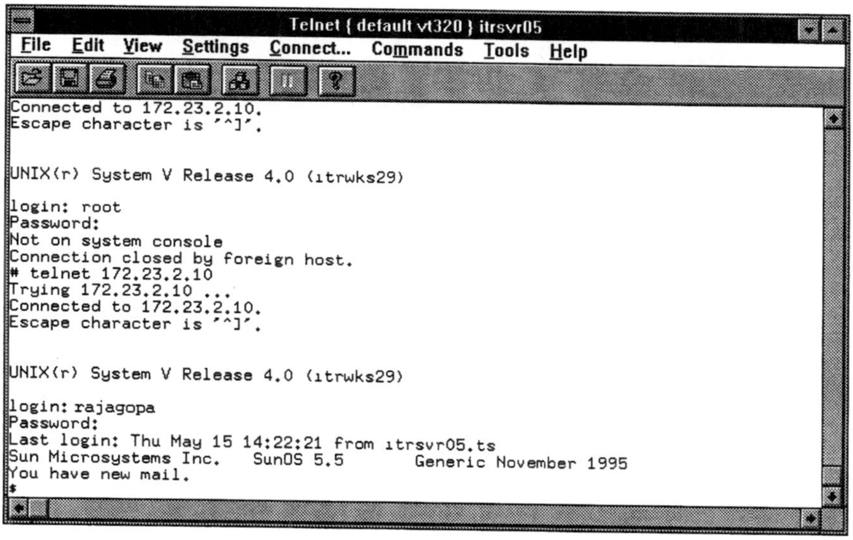

Exhibit 3. Prevent system administration login from non-system console.

If this is the case, logon as another user (this is one example where you should have your personal id, besides "root"). Then you can get the privileges of "root" by using the *su* command as shown in Exhibit 4.

Windows NT: An alternate way of performing administrative functions in Windows NT (other than logging in as administrator) is to grant administrator privileges to your personal (non-administrator) account via the User Manager. Of course, this privilege can be granted the first time only when you log on as the administrator. However, it is a good idea to keep the administrator privileges only with the administrator ID. From time to time, if you want to check if some functions are not available to non-administrator IDs, the simplest way is to use your personal ID (without special

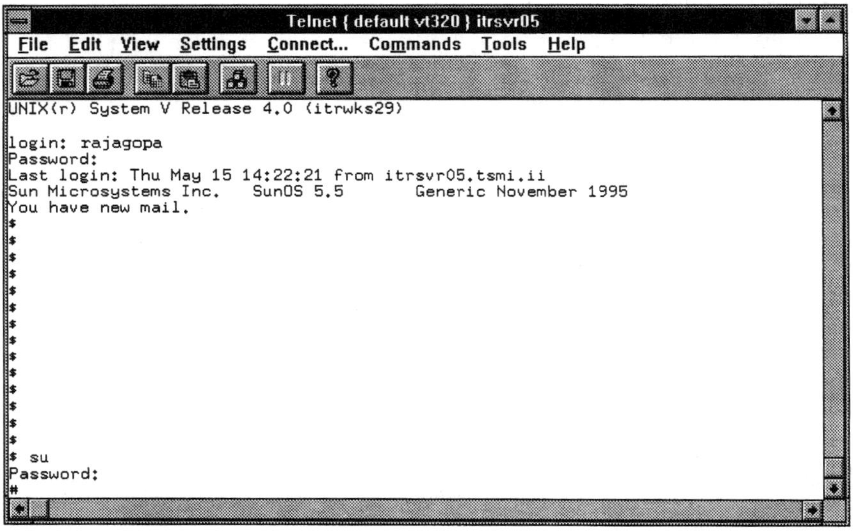

Exhibit 4. Using *su* to change privileges.

---

privileges).This is another reason for keeping your personal ID separate from your administrator ID.

There is no direct equivalent of *su* in Windows NT. If you want to change your ID, you need to log off and log on as another user.

Changing Administrator Password. *UNIX:* You can change passwords using the *passwd* command.

Windows NT: You can change your password in two ways:

- Use the User Manager
- Press Ctrl-Alt-Delete (Don't worry — unlike DOS, your machine is not going to reboot automatically). Click the **Change Password** button.

This is another thing you need to get used to in Windows. There are multiple ways to accomplish the same function. As another example, if you are looking for files, you can use **Find** in the **Start** menu, Use the My Computer icon, or use Windows **Explorer**. If users are asking for your help, you need to figure how they got there in the first place. Also, if you are writing instructions for users on how to access system resources, keep in mind that there may be more than one way of doing it.

Shutting Down the System

UNIX: You typically perform a UNIX shutdown using a script that you wrote or one supplied by the UNIX vendor. The script ensures that file system updates are complete by using a *sync* command. After all users have logged off and backup processes are done, *init* is soft killed.

Windows NT: You can shut down a Windows NT system in one of the following ways:

- Click on **Start** and choose **Shutdown** (Windows NT 4.0).
- Click on **File** in the **Program Manager** Menu and choose **Shutdown** from the pull-down menu (Windows NT 3.5x).
- Press Ctrl-Alt-Delete and choose **Shutdown.**

Disk Administration

Partition Disk. *UNIX:* Partitioning is many times already done by the UNIX system vendor or the disk manufacturer (when operating systems are preloaded). Some UNIX systems include *fdisk* for managing partitions.

Windows NT: Use the Disk Manager.

Creating Stripe/Volume Sets. *UNIX:* No direct equivalence, functions vary by UNIX implementation.

Windows NT: Use the Disk Manager.

Remote Disks. *UNIX:* Each machine has a single directory tree that includes all local and remote drives.

Windows NT: Each local and remote drive gets assigned a "drive letter." The drive letters are the alphabet letters A through Z. A file on drive A called **Myfile** shows up in Windows menus as **A:\Myfile**. Typically, the letters A and B are used for local floppy drives, and the letter C for the main (or only) local hard drive. Additional local hard drives are denoted starting with D. You are not constrained to assign the letters in alphabetical order, although you cannot assign a letter already assigned. You can access remote drives on the network using **Connect** in the **File Manager** or use the **Explorer**.

File Services

File Security. *UNIX:* File security is determined by permissions (rwxrwxrwx), as shown in Exhibit 5.

The left-most character is not permissions related. It is *d* for directories, *c* for special character files, - for regular files, etc. The remaining letters are composed of three user segments, each with three letters. The three user segments are owner, a group of users, and any other. For each segment, *r* indicates read permission, *w* indicates write permission, and *x* indicates execute. In Exhibit 5, for the file codeint.dat, the owner has read, write, and execute permissions while other users do not have write permissions.

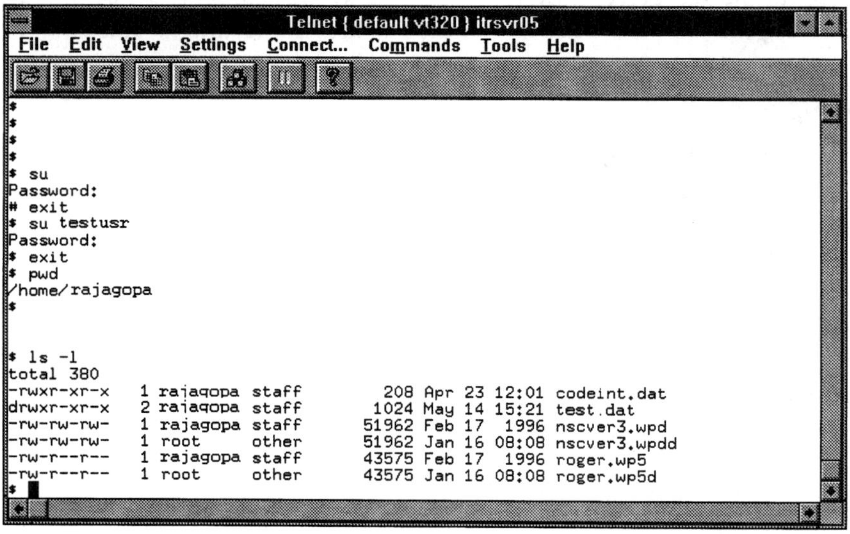

Exhibit 5. UNIX file permissions.

Windows NT: File security is controlled through Access Control Lists (ACLs). Use the Security tab in the Properties menu to administer file directory security. You can use the menu shown in Exhibit 6 to set security-related attributes.

You can also set up Directory permissions using the menu shown in Exhibit 7, which you get by clicking the Permission button in the dialog shown in Exhibit 6.

File Names. *UNIX:* File names are not restricted to the 8-dot-3 format and can contain almost any character.

Windows NT: Windows NT supports multiple file systems (FAT, NTFS, etc.) and the file name restrictions depend on the file system. FAT file names must follow the 8-dot-3 format. If a file with a long file name is copied into 8-dot-3 restricted file system, Windows NT changes the name and truncates it to fit in 8-dot-3 format.

Sharing Files. *UNIX:* The most common method to share disks, directories, and files in UNIX is to use NFS. NFS is covered in Chapter 25.

Windows NT: To share disks across Windows NT machines, use the **Share** option in **File Manager**. See Exhibit 8. To share disks, directories, and files in a heterogeneous environment with UNIX and Windows NT machines, use either the Network Operating System functions or a third-party NFS package. NFS is discussed in Chapter 25.

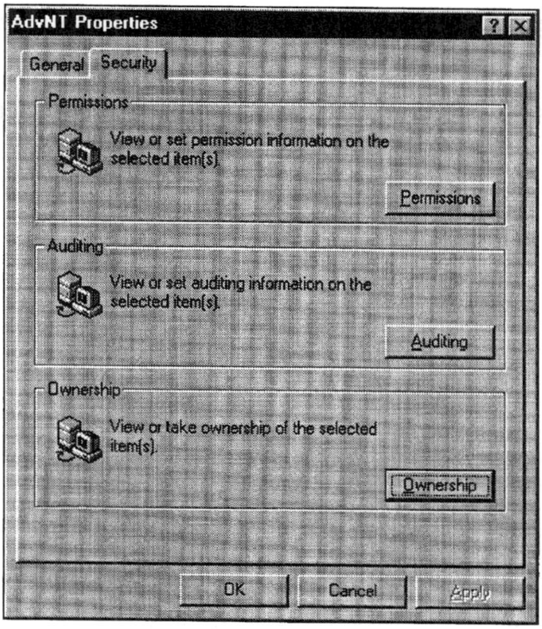

Exhibit 6. Setting security-related attributes.

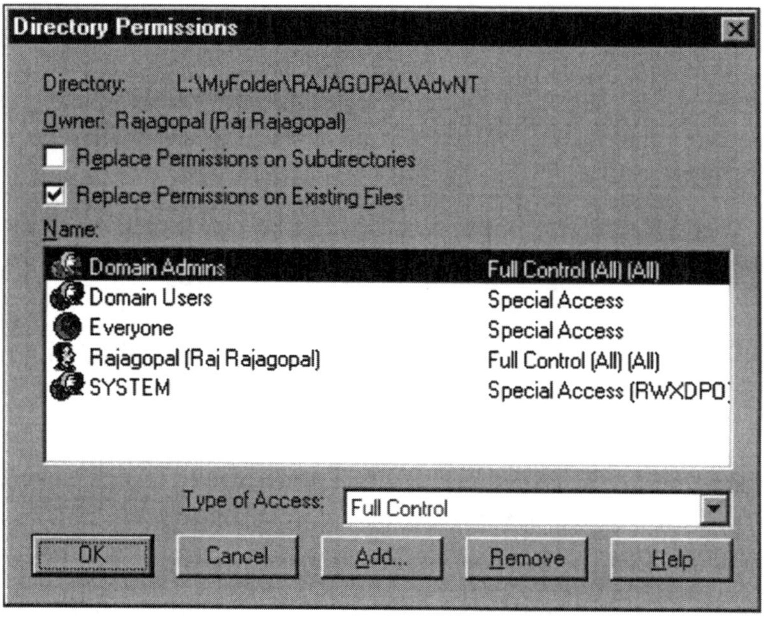

Exhibit 7. Directory permissions.

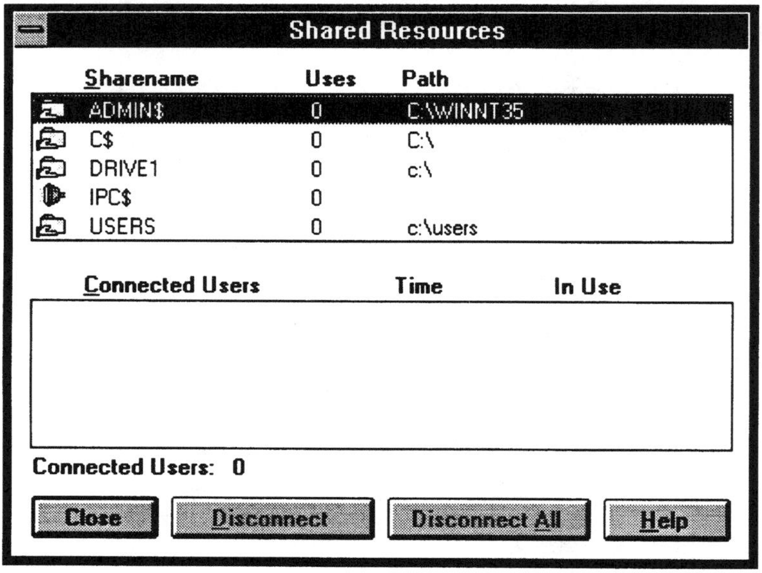

Exhibit 8. Shared resources in Windows NT.

Print Services

Printer Sharing. *UNIX:* Once set up, use *lpd* to spool print requests from all users (with *lpr*) to print.

Windows NT: Use the **Share** option in **Print Manager.**

Remote Printers. *UNIX:* Most NFS packages also provide remote printer support besides file access.

Windows NT: Use the **Connect** option in **Print Manager.** See Exhibit 9.

Adding/Changing Printers, Printer Drivers. *UNIX:* Printer drivers are in */etc/printcap.*

Windows NT: You add or change printer divers (when adding a new printer or updating an old copy of the printer driver) by using **Create Printer** in the **Print Manager.**

Communication Services

TCP/IP Setup/Change. *UNIX:* You can add and edit IP addresses in */etc/hosts.* You can *ping* to verify connection.

Windows NT: You can browse and update a machine's TCP/IP address using TCP/IP software module in the **Network** icon in the **Control Panel.** The TCP/IP Configuration menu is shown in Exhibit 10.

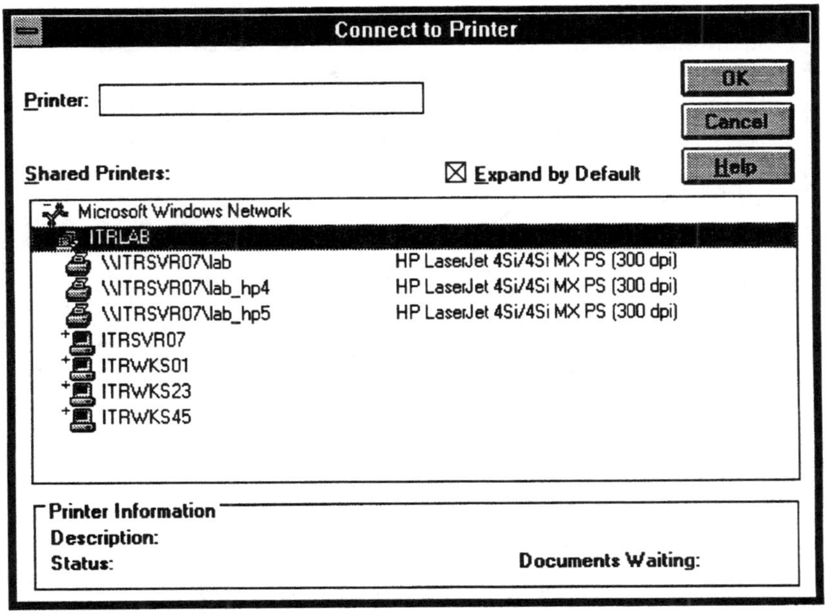

Exhibit 9. Connecting to a printer.

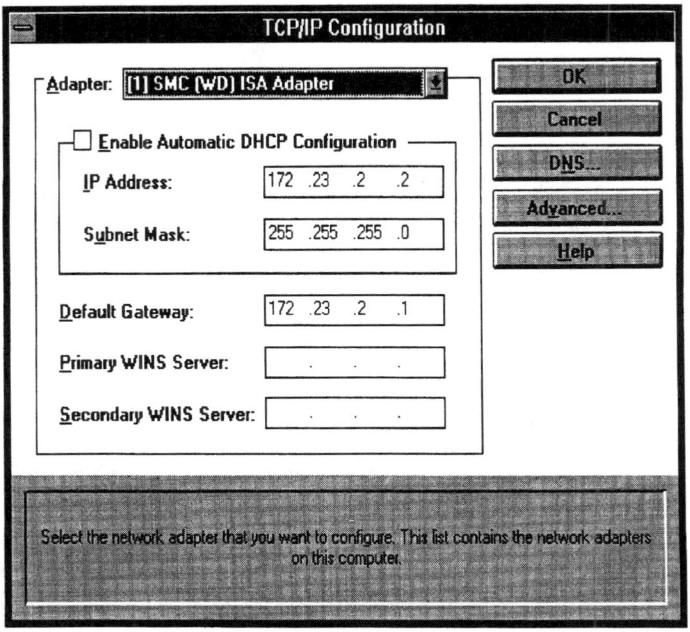

Exhibit 10. TCP/IP configuration in Windows NT.

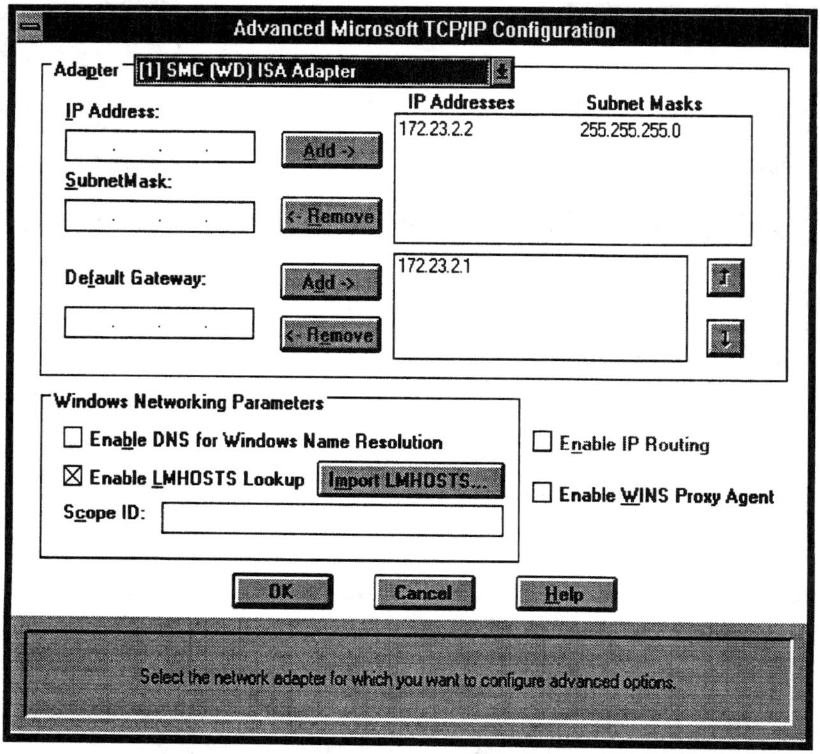

Exhibit 11. Advanced TCP/IP configuration.

Advanced TCP/IP Configurations are set using the menu shown in Exhibit 11. You get the menu shown in Exhibit 11 by clicking on the **Advanced** button in the menu shown in Exhibit 10.

FTP, TFTP, RCP, and Telnet. *UNIX:* FTP, TFTP, RCP, and Telnet are commands executed from the command line.

Windows NT: Windows NT includes command line versions of FTP, TFTP, RCP, and Telnet. Windows NT also includes a graphical version of FTP. A sample FTP session showing how to download a file using the graphical FTP is included in Chapter 25. A sample Telnet session showing how to log on to a remote host is included in Chapter 11.

e-mail. *UNIX:* e-mail is automatically enabled as a part of creating a user account.

Windows NT: e-mail has to be separately enabled. You create a post office and an associated administrative account. You then allow shared access to the post office. After this, either you can set up users to access the post office or the users can set up themselves.

Talk/Chat. *UNIX: Talk* is a standard command in UNIX, executed from the command line.

Windows NT: In Windows, the equivalent function to UNIX Talk is called Chat. Chat is built-in in Windows NT. You can access Chat by double-clicking on the Chat icon in the Accessories Group (or search for "chat" in Help, under **Start**). The Chat menu is shown in Exhibit 12. Clicking on conversation shows a list of computers you can chat with.

User Messages. *UNIX:* You **write** a message to a user or **wall** a message to all users.

Windows NT: You can either use the **net send** command (See Exhibit 13), or when using a domain controller, use the **Send Message** option.

Backup/Recovery

Tape Backup — tar/dump. *UNIX:* You use **tar** or **dump** to make tape backups.

Windows NT: Use **Tape backup** in the Administrative Tools group or (more likely) use third-party backup software.

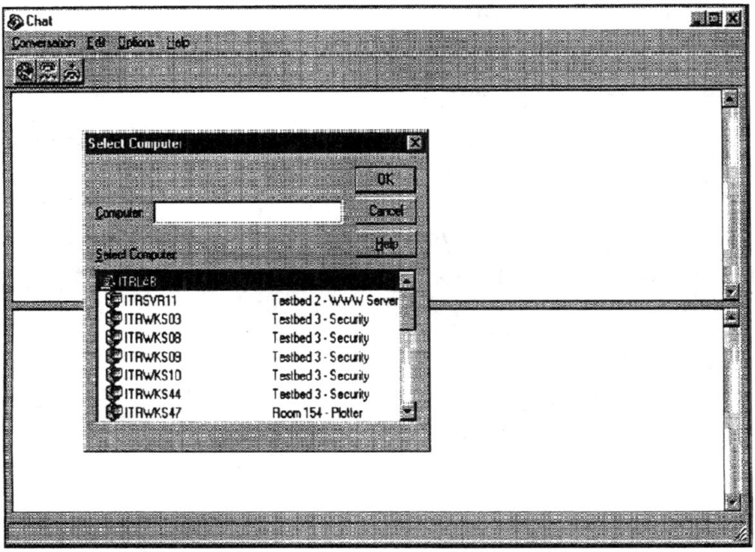

Exhibit 12. Chat menu in Windows NT.

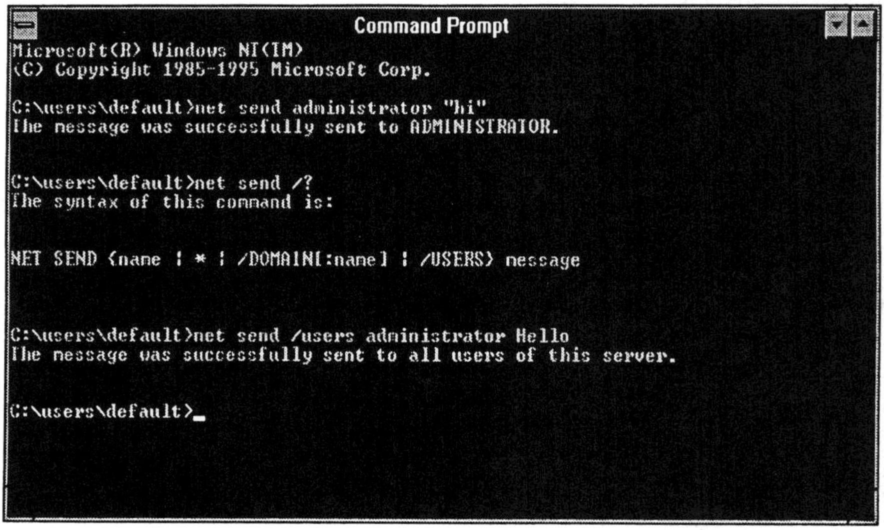

Exhibit 13. Sending a message to users in Windows NT.

---

pkzip/tar. *UNIX:* You can also use **tar** to save subdirectory trees into a single file.

Windows NT: You can use a shareware utility like *pkzip* or *Winzip* to compress and save all files within a subdirectory tree.

Compress/Uncompress/Expand

UNIX: You use **compress** and **uncompress** to reduce file sizes and later restore the file sizes.

Windows NT: The equivalent of **compress** is **compress.** The equivalent of **uncompress** is **expand.** The zip utilities mentioned earlier also compress while saving multiple files to a single zip file.

System Log Files

UNIX: The main log file is the syslog file. Most log files in UNIX contain plain text that can be read with a text editor.

Windows NT: Look for all log files under **Event Viewer** (see Exhibit 21) which is part of the **Administrative main menu** shown in Exhibit 1. The log files use an internal format and cannot be viewed with text editors.

Process/Task Management

Task Priority. *UNIX:* You can use the *jobs* command to view a list of executing and suspended shell's job. In many UNIX systems, particularly those based on BSD, you can use the *renice* command to alter the priority.

Windows NT: Use the **System** icon in the **Control Panel**.

Automatic Job Scheduling. *UNIX:* Use the **CRON** and **at** facilities to schedule job executions.

Windows NT: Use the **at** command in conjunction with the **Schedule** service. Windows NT Resource kit also includes **Command Scheduler**, a graphical utility.

If you are using third-party data center operations software such as POLYCENTER from DEC or CA-Unicenter from Computer Associates, check with the vendor to see if they have versions for your environment.

System Load Balancing. *UNIX:* Use the *w* or *uptime* commands to monitor system load.

Windows NT: Use the **Performance Monitor** in the **Administrative Tools** group.

Terminate Process/Task. *UNIX:* Use the *ps* to get a list of processes and *kill* to kill a process.

Windows NT: Use the *pview* application (it is available in the SDK). You can get a task list and select individual tasks and kill them.

Daemons. *UNIX:* Daemons are constantly running background processes which typically wait for and process messages.

Windows NT: The functionality of Daemons is implemented using *Services*. Use **Service Manager** in the **Control Panel**.

User Management

User Accounts, Groups, and Profiles. *UNIX:* Information about all users is stored in **/etc/passwd,** (user) group information is stored in **/etc/groups,** and user profile information in **/etc/profile files.** Updates are performed to the user data by editing these files using an editor like *vi*. Information about a specific user is contained in the *$home* environment variable and **.profile** and **.kshrc files**

Windows NT: The User Manager and User Profile editor are used to maintain user information. You can specify the path where user profile information should be stored and you can also change the path. The User Manager icon is normally found in the Windows NT Administrator main

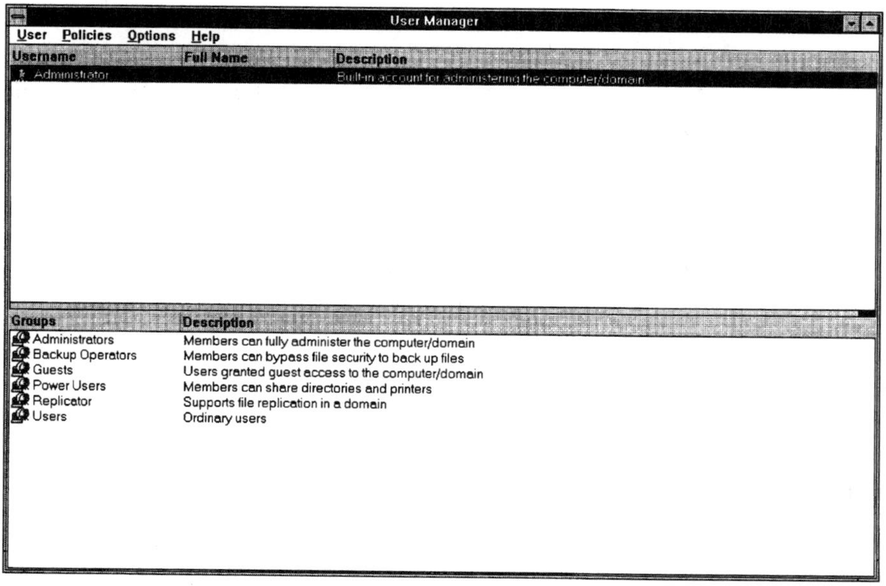

Exhibit 14. User Manager in Windows NT.

menu, as shown in Exhibit 1. Double-clicking on the User Manager icon brings up the menu shown in Exhibit 14. The menu is divided into two halves. The bottom half shows the list of valid user groups, and the top half shows the list of valid users within the group selected in the bottom half.

One of the administration functions you can perform for each user is to the audit policy for that user. You can set the audit policy using the menu shown in Exhibit 15 You can get this menu by clicking an individual user (click on one user entry in Exhibit 14) and selecting **Policies**, **Audit**, from the pull-down menu. You can audit user events such as logon and logoff, file and object access, etc.

Another user administration function is to set the User Rights Policy. Exhibit 16 shows the User Rights Policy menu that you can use to set user rights policy.

You can set the user account policy using the menu shown in Exhibit 17.

You can set the user properties using the menu shown in Exhibit 18.

You can set up the user environment, such as whether the user will have a login script and the name of the script, using the menu shown in Exhibit 19.

You can specify user group information using the menu shown in Exhibit 20.

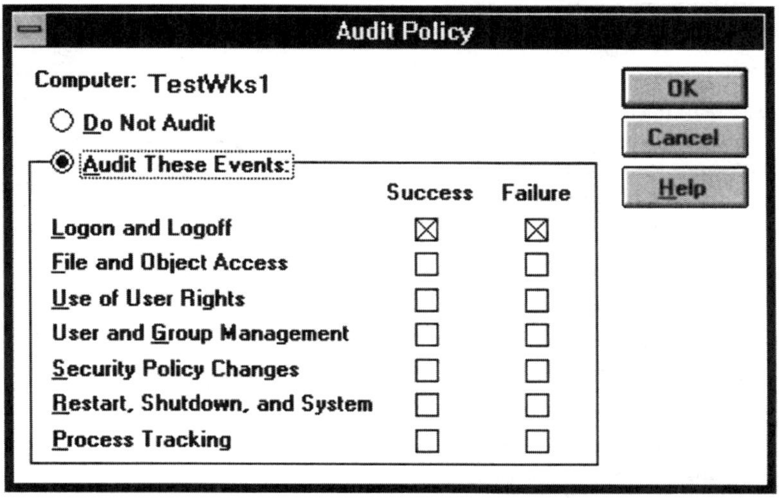

Exhibit 15. Setting Audit Policy for a user in Windows NT.

Migration Solution for Migrating NetWare Users

Windows NT includes a migration tool that lets system administration information such as user data be copied from one or more NetWare servers to a Windows NT server. The migration tool is discussed in Chapter 33 — *Windows NT and NetWare.*

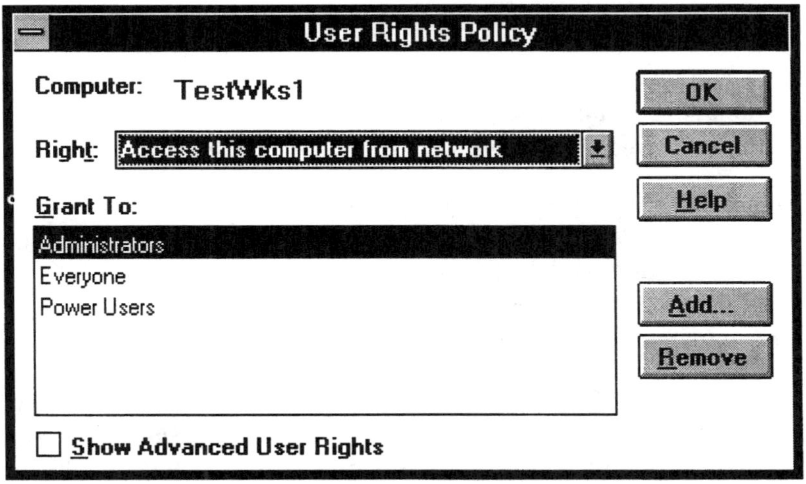

Exhibit 16. Setting User Rights Policy.

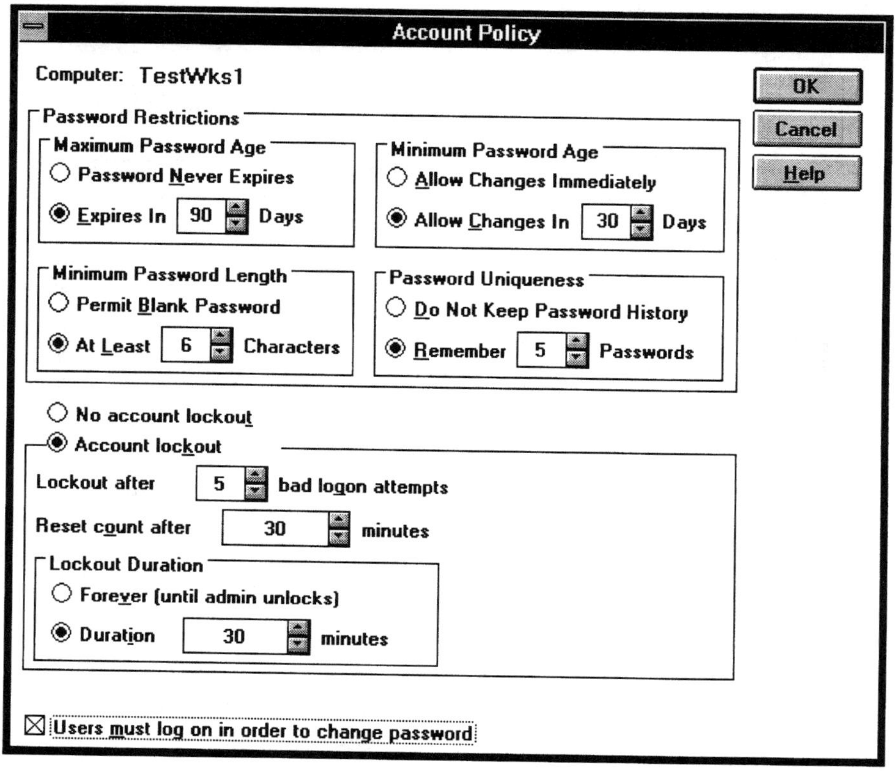

Exhibit 17. Setting user Account Policy.

LOGGING IN WINDOWS NT AND UNIX

Both Windows NT and UNIX support a number of logs that provide an audit trail of events about users, files, networks, etc. There are two primary differences between UNIX and Windows NT for logging:

- The logging administration and browsing utilities in UNIX for the most part are nongraphical, whereas Windows NT uses the GUI for logging administration and browsing.
- Many logs in UNIX store the log data in ASCII (plain text), whereas the log information in Windows NT is stored in a special format.

UNIX: The most important log is syslog, the system log, which logs various system-related information. Some logs that store user information are lastlog, UTMP, WTMP, sulog, etc. Logs that store file access information include LOGFILE (normally records UUCP activities). You use built-in UNIX functions or public domain tools to browse the logs.

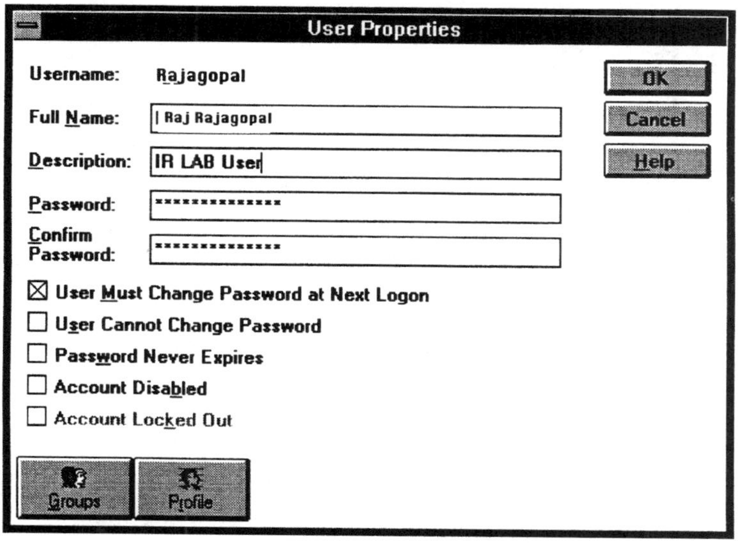

Exhibit 18. Setting user properties.

Windows NT: Windows NT uses three logs — the system log, the security log, and the application log. The security log has information about system accesses, illegal file accesses, invalid password entries, privileged objects accesses, user name and password changes, etc. The system log contains information about the system generated by system components. Application logs contain information generated by Windows NT applications.

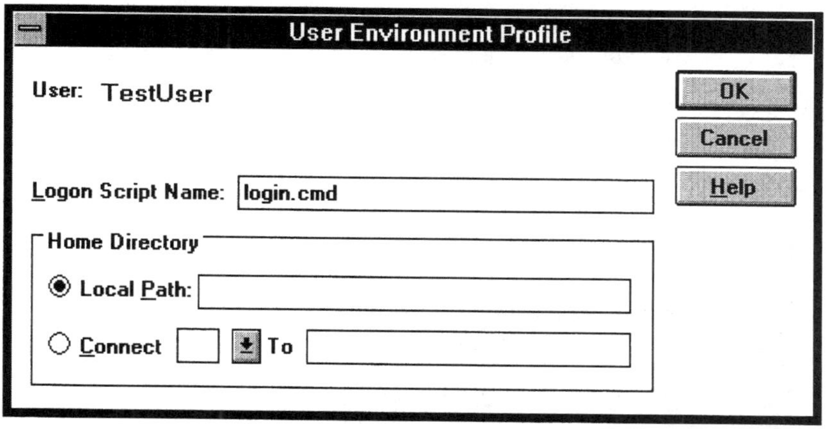

Exhibit 19. Setting the User Environment Profile.

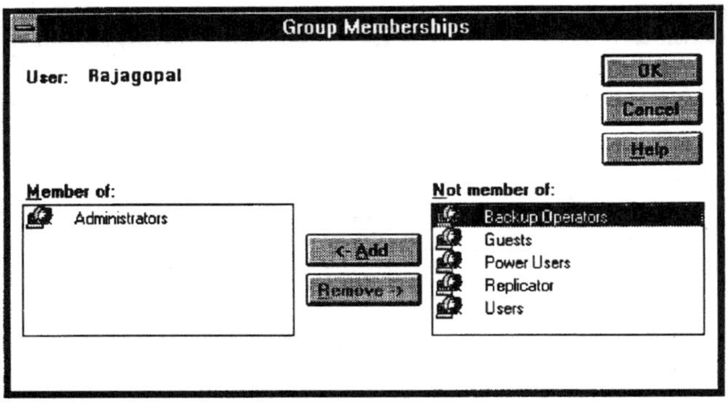

Exhibit 20. Setting User Group Memberships.

For example, an application that encounters a file access error logs the error in the application log. You use the Event Viewer shown in Exhibit 21 to view the Windows NT logs.

Logging Error Levels

UNIX: UNIX uses an eight level system to classify logging error levels. These levels and the associated descriptions are summarized in Exhibit 22.

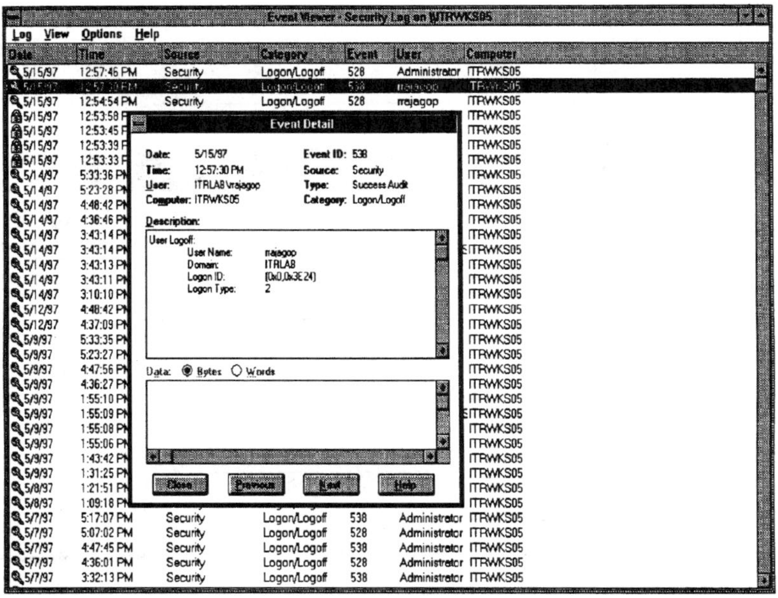

Exhibit 21. Using Event Viewer to view Windows NT logs.

Exhibit 22. UNIX logging message levels and descriptions.

Error Level	Description
emerg	Emergencies
alert	Alert conditions that require prompt administrator action
crit	Critical condition
err	Non-critical errors
warning	Warnings
Notice	Messages that need action, but are not errors
info	Informational messages
debug	Debugging messages

Windows NT: Windows NT uses a five-level system to classify logging error levels. In addition, Windows NT uses colored graphical symbols to indicate the error. The error symbols and the associated descriptions are summarized in Exhibit 23.

NETWORK COMMANDS

Windows NT also includes network commands that help you in your management of files and computers on your network. Exhibit 24

Exhibit 23. Windows logging message symbols and descriptions.

Error Symbol	Description
Red stop sign	Serious error (that needs attention) message
Yellow circle with an exclamation point	Warning message
Blue circle with the letter "I"	Informational message
Gray padlock	Invalid authorization message
Gold key	Authorization successful message

Exhibit 24. Windows NT network commands and descriptions.

Network Command	Description
net computer	Add/Delete computers to Windows NT server domains
net file	Displays all open shared file names on a server
net help	Displays network command names and descriptions. Optionally, you can include a command name for more description about the command
net helpmsg	Displays help information about a network error message
net print	Monitor and administer printers and printer queues
net start	Net start is actually a family of commands to start services and utilities such as the spooler, event log, etc. You specify the specific service or utility name after net start
net use	Displays current drive mapping information

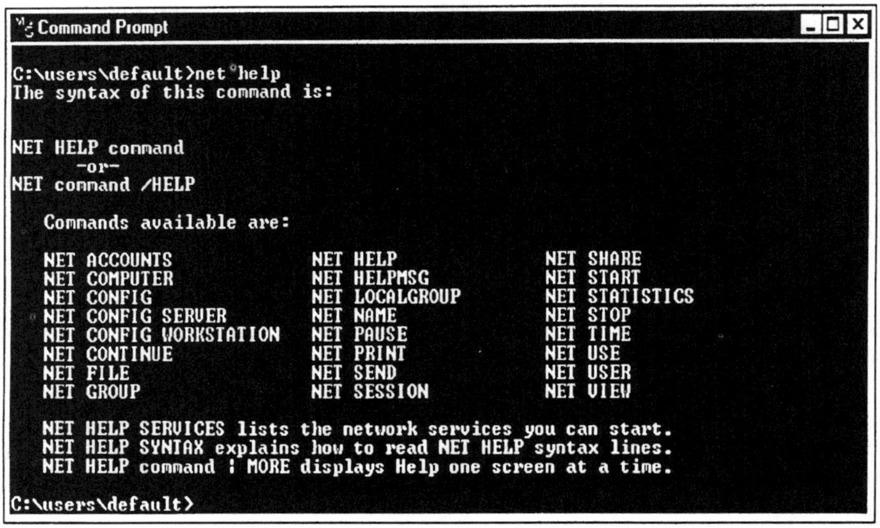

Exhibit 25. Net Help command.

summarizes the network commands. Keep in mind that there are more network commands and you can get a list of them with their descriptions by using the command *net help.* In addition, you can perform the functions performed by these commands by selecting from the graphical user interface instead of the command line.

The *net help* command is illustrated in Exhibit 25, and the *net use* command is illustrated in Exhibit 26.

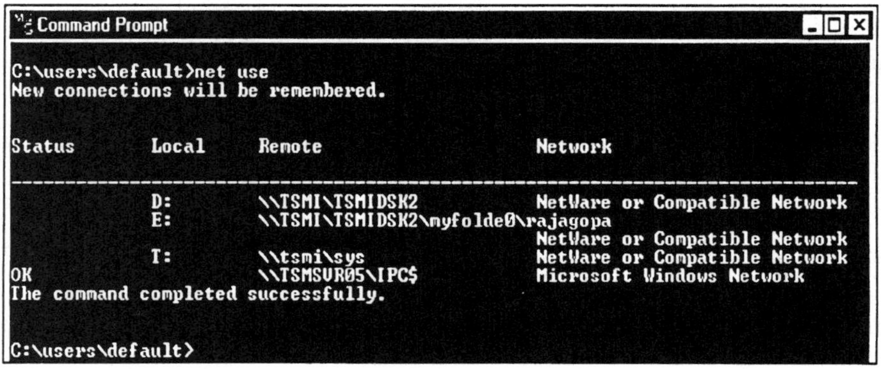

Exhibit 26. Net Use command.

Conclusion

We looked at some common system administration functions and reviewed the equivalent ways of executing the functions between UNIX and Windows NT. In the next chapter, we will look at some migration and coexistence topics between Windows NT and NetWare.

Chapter 36
Managing Distributed Network Systems Using Single Sign-On, Password Synchronization, and the Authentication Server

Jeffrey Carr

For most corporations worldwide, the move to distributed systems has been both beneficial and problematic. A distributed system's ability to provide data to end users on a timely basis has greatly improved service levels. However, when distributed data is to be channeled through complex and varied network configurations, industry has been hard-pressed both to design and to manage these new systems. Moreover, as the bills are paid for these efforts, it is becoming increasingly clear that the costs associated with client/server technology are much higher than originally estimated. This chapter discusses solutions for managing today's distributed network environment, focusing on the implementation of single sign-on, password synchronization, and the authentication server.

INTRODUCTION

Many recent studies have identified the high hidden costs associated with creating solutions for managing distributed networks. International

0-8493-9989-0/99/$0.00+$.50

Technology Group, in its study entitled Cost of Computing, compares the cost of mainframe computing with that of PCs and local area networks (LANs). The study demonstrated that, for high-transaction processing, PC/LANs could not compare in cost or efficiency with the venerable mainframe.

Barry Graham, a market researcher for the Mainframe Market Information, Xephon Group states, "The Mainframe is still the most cost-effective platform for organizations above a certain size, and will remain so for the foreseeable future. Downsizing, even partial downsizing, is in fact an expensive and potentially disastrous move for most mainframe users. Seventy percent of current attempts are reported in trouble and will no doubt cost others far more in the future."

Finally, another leading market researcher has declared what much of the industry has felt for some time about client/server technology: It is not delivering the cost benefits promised. Much of the blame, moreover, is aimed squarely at the lack of network management tools to support the new architectures.

In light of these facts, it is no coincidence that today's issues of network connectivity, security, maintenance, and administration are similar to those raised in past decades in terms of mainframe computing. Developing adequate solutions in these areas is essential for combating the inherent problems associated with managing distributed networks. Organizations are beginning to apply more-practical, cost-effective strategies to obtain the true benefits of client/server technology—strategies that grow from an understanding of the evolutionary process from centralized to distributed computing and that build on the strengths of both.

SINGLE SIGN-ON

Although PC/LANs have proliferated by the hundreds of thousands, the ability to control, secure, and administer them has been virtually nonexistent. Exhibit 1 illustrates examples of the problems once common with system network architecture (SNA)-based mainframes that are resurfacing today with distributed networks.

One of the most visible issues in information technology (IT) today is the single sign-on (SSO) requirement, or the ability to access data and applications on multiple heterogeneous systems via a single log-on with one user ID and password. In distributed environments, end-user access is difficult and time-consuming. Log-on procedures in particular are repetitive, complex, and error-prone, and multiple sign-on systems require too much time and technical infrastructure understanding from users.

Exhibit 1. Distributed network problems.

• Multiple End-User Passwords.
— Increased loss of productivity.
— High end-user frustration.
— Increased help desk intervention.
— Reduced security due to passwords being written down.
• No Central Point of Control.
— Difficulty of removing or changing all of a user's access rights.
— No single audit trail for network access.
— Difficulty in coordinating technology requirements and encouraging standards.
• Multiple Sign-On/Security Systems.
— Increased loss of productivity.
— High end-user frustration.
— Need to know where a system resides to know how to respond.
• No Central Point of Administration.
— Delays in delivering user services.
— High cost of staff and training.
— Difficulty of placing staff in remote sites for distributed systems.
• Cost Overruns.
— Cost of dealing with problems high in both man-time and dollars.
— Distracts business from real.

SCRIPTING TOOLS

The marketplace has begun to respond to the problems associated with sign-on in distributed environments. Technologies that address SSO access have become available. A variety of PC scripting products are now used to streamline access to LANs, mainframes, and Unix systems. Scripting is not a new technology; it has been used for a decade with mainframe access systems. Unlike their mainframe counterparts, however, scripts for distributed networks that include PC/LANs have several weaknesses.

Scripting tools for PC/LANs are complex and can be expensive to administer. They demand almost constant attention because passwords and application layouts frequently change. As often as a password changes or applications are added or deleted from a menu selection, scripts must be revised because PC scripts, by nature, are individualized to a particular PC or user ID. Knowledgeable end-users see scripts as a quick way to ease their own access to multiple systems; however, average end-users may not have the knowledge or the time to maintain the required changes to keep their script programs up to date.

Multiply the administration overhead a thousandfold for a well-populated organization and a large problem—lack of access—is displaced by an even larger one—lack of administration. Having to tailor and maintain thousands of scripts and track the necessary updates each time an application amendment is made is a monumental task for users and administrators.

Another issue that should be considered with respect to scripting tools is data security. Scripting tools do, in fact, weaken security. User IDs and passwords inserted in the scripts are generally transmitted across the network in clear text. Inexpensive line analyzers allow anyone to trace transmitted data. Without encryption, these user IDs and passwords can be detected and used to access networks. Scripting products also tend to hold the user ID and password themselves. A number of scripts then need to be tailored to allow passwords on other systems to be updated each time a user changes a password. Obviously, this heavy maintenance procedure is error-prone. An even worse scenario is created when users are forced to change their passwords by using the scripting product itself. If a user attempts to change a password directly in a system or when using a foreign terminal to access a system, the scripting product fails. Before it can be used again, the passwords on all the systems must be resynchronized manually. Thus, the functioning of the scripting product depends on password management. Removing this high-maintenance password management from the scripting system will make the system much more effective.

SYNCHRONIZATION: AN ENABLING TECHNOLOGY

A more robust and dynamic synchronization for password changes is required than that of current PC-based scripting products.

ONE PASSWORD

Password synchronization should be transparent to the user and work wherever and whenever a password is changed. This type of synchronization has been successfully demonstrated in recent years when events are synchronized in a distributed network environment. Facilities have been migrated across on-line, interconnected IBM enterprise host and LAN/WAN environments. Synchronization is a critical enabling or backbone technology for many data centers that will ultimately service event synchronization across a distributed network.

Password synchronization is a pressing need as organizations rush to implement SSO access. When passwords are synchronized between distributed LANs and the host security, the user maintains only one password. Once the password is validated on the host and LAN, SSO access for LAN users becomes less complex. To script to a host session requires only that the password used at log-in to the LAN be presented to the host. The password no longer needs to be held in the script or on the workstation. Complex password management need not be built into the SSO product. Simple emulator scripts can be used to implement SSO, because they often provide sophisticated scripting languages. Generic scripts can be created so that whenever users log on to the LAN, their user IDs and passwords are passed to their host applications.

Obtaining seamless synchronization of passwords is a real benefit, not only for users but for systems administrators and IS security staff as well. Maintaining only one password means a user is less likely to forget it, write it down, or request to have it reset. If a password does need resetting, administrators reset it once according to their usual procedure for doing so, and all other linked passwords are transparently reset at the same time.

REMOVING ACCOUNTS

Synchronization also encompasses the issue of removing or disabling user accounts. It is crucial to remove all access rights as employees depart a company. By synchronizing revoke and resume operations between hosts and LANs, a single administration action is all that is necessary to remove a user from every system to which the departed employee had access, with no possibility of oversight or omission.

AUTHENTICATION SERVER

As synchronization facilitates the management of distributed and decentralized IT settings, more structured networks that run centrally from an IT department are adapting the authentication server (AS) approach. As its name implies, an AS provides a central directory where all systems on a network can go to authenticate and validate users. Permission or refusal to enter the network is issued centrally by the AS based on a user's single-user ID/password or some other type of authentication mechanism. To be effective, an AS must have several important attributes.

RELIABILITY

If the AS is not running, it cannot provide any benefit. Worse yet, if access to all network systems relies on the AS, all access to the network is affected while it is inactive or running incorrectly.

EFFICIENCY AND SECURITY

The AS must be efficient. It must be able to handle large amounts of data and requests for validation, and it must respond quickly. Ideally, a number of administrators in a distributed hierarchy should be able to access the AS to perform tasks. An AS itself must be secure from unauthorized access, and must offer centralized control and audit. If a user definition is disabled or removed at the AS, access to any systems using the AS will not be granted.

Any access, attempted or successful, is audited on the AS level. The degree of required authentication can be defined centrally and easily altered depending on permitted location and time of access. Any problems with user definitions or passwords can be resolved centrally. In other words, the IT department is empowered to deliver the service that it has been asked to give. Once control is given to a centralized system, the exercise of that control can be distributed and structured according to the needs of the organization. The owners of resources can be given appropriate access to the AS to grant access to their resources. Managers can be given appropriate access to the AS to manage their staff's access rights. In addition, because a single user ID/password combination is used to access any system, the critical SSO requirement for end-users and management is met.

SCALABILITY

An AS must be scalable to handle diverse networks. For a small number of PCs on a LAN, the local server on the LAN could provide an ideal AS host. For large networks that involve tens of thousands of PCs, workstations, and mainframe terminals, the sensible solution for a network authentication server is the mainframe or enterprise system. Mainframes have developed over the last 30 years, and they are still the most trusted, reliable, and cost-effective system for network environments. Mainframes offer 99.9% or higher availability, and they are generally accessible from the entire network. They offer processing power and throughput to deal with large numbers of validation requests.

Furthermore, the mainframe runs most mission-critical applications, and to make access to such applications dependent on a less-reliable or -secure system is unthinkable. However, what makes the decision to place an AS on a mainframe system compelling is that huge numbers of users are already registered with mainframe Resource Access Control Facility, CA-ACF2, or CA-TOPSECRET security programs. The cost of redefining all these users to some other central system is prohibitive and unnecessary.

PROTECTING WORKSTATIONS

Many businesses are looking to protect not only hosts and servers from illegal access but, increasingly, their PCs and workstations. The storage and processing capacity of PCs has increased so dramatically that more corporate data is being stored on them, which, in turn, has led to a much greater need for PC-level security.

Protecting large numbers of workstations adds up to complex administration for systems administrators and more complicated access for users. Currently, workstation security vendors are implementing Application Program Interface (APIs) in their products to provide an enterprise log-on to an individual PC. Users sign on to the workstation using the chosen workstation security product by specifying their enterprise user ID and password. This information can be passed to a host AS package and validated along with an optional authentication token. If valid, the user is signed on to both the workstation and an authentication service on the LANs (also the preferred network server), with a single sign-on.

THE MANAGEABLE SINGLE SIGN-ON

Users require a simple way to access many different systems. Client/server applications complicate this situation by having to access other systems to obtain data on a user's behalf—usually without the user being aware of it. From a corporate perspective, users need access that is manageable and cost-effective. By implementing a synchronization backbone and an AS to control access to workstations and network servers, a common enterprise user ID/password combination is implemented across heterogeneous systems.

This single-user ID/password gives a single sign-on to the workstation and server, but it can also give single sign-on to all systems on the network. As the workstation single-user ID/password becomes the same as the one for mainframe security, it can be passed to the application automatically through a host emulator. Whatever user ID/password was used at initial log-on can be retrieved from memory and inserted in the application script.

This user ID/password combination is not stored in a script; rather, it is a symbolic reference to whatever user ID and password were used at the log-on. No other user gaining access to the workstation can use the script to access another system. Instead, no matter which users log on to the workstation, their unique user IDs and passwords are retrieved and passed to the application. Thus, different users can share a workstation without administrative overhead or security risk. Furthermore, to avoid transmitting the password in clear text, the password can be passed encrypted to the application and can be captured and decrypted by an exit within the mainframe security just before validation.

As discussed earlier, virtually all emulators come complete with a powerful scripting language that is capable of extracting the user ID/password combination entered at log-on to insert in the script. Because the AS handles password management functions, the scripting capability is all that most SSO products provide; however, emulators can still be used with the AS to provide an off-the-shelf solution. A few simple scripts common for all users and written using the emulator's built-in script language can implement SSO without additional costs.

For stronger log-on security, the combination of an authentication token (i.e., random one-time password generator) and the encrypted password can be used. An AS provides for the central administration of several popular authentication tokens, any of which can be used to authenticate users. The inclusion of these tokens in the log-on process ensures that the traffic flowing across the network cannot be traced or guessed to gain illegal access.

PASS TICKETS

A simple static encryption technique used to protect the password flowing across the network is normally enough to deter breaches of security and is certainly preferable to passing clear text passwords. However, in certain situations, a more secure form of encryption could be implemented.

The main problem with static encryption is that the encrypted password never changes. If traced, the exact encrypted packet can be re-presented, thus allowing access without revealing the decrypted value. A cyclical encryption technique is easy to implement and is a sufficient method to avoid this problem, because it increments a Data Encryption Standard seed each time access is requested. A better solution would be to implement a more secure form of encryption, such as public or private key encryption, which would not only give secure information, but would clear the identification of the requesting partner's identity.

SECURE PASS TICKETS

Secure pass tickets provide another method for generating one-time passwords and increasing security within distributed networks. However, implementing pass tickets within a Resource Access Control Facility (RACF) environment, for example, raises several issues. Pass tickets rely on the protection of a static key that is held for each application to which access is required. The algorithm that generates the pass ticket is widely available and combines this application key with the user ID requesting access to get the ticket. Access to the key allows a ticket to be generated for any user ID.

Enabling pass ticket support and giving an application key for access by one user ID allows any user ID to access that application. This ability makes it hard to control access to the application and to distribute the authority to do this. This ability also requires that access to Resource Access Control Facility resources for any user ID be trusted to a system off the host, such as a Unix system or even a PC, which may not be acceptable for many corporate security officers.

One way of improving the security of RACF pass tickets while maintaining the benefits is to generate them on the host system only (i.e., through requests to RACF). When access to a host application is required, a request can be made to the AS to generate a pass ticket. Because the AS is resident on the host, it will request a ticket from RACF and give it to the user (previously validated by RACF) for use in logging on to the application.

This process controls the application keys and the generation of pass tickets within RACF. An AS that generates an RACF pass ticket external to RACF is only partially implementing third-party authentication. The ticket is generated by a service on the network, passed by the calling application to the target application, and then checked—not by the original third party, but by RACF. This breaks the three-way link and hence the strength of the strategy. However, by using Resource Access Control Facility as the AS, this scenario is changed to a genuine third-party authentication service. The calling application, the emulator on the workstation, requests a ticket from the AS (which gets it from RACF) and gives it to the host application, which then calls RACF (i.e., the authentication server) to check the ticket.

LOCAL RESOURCE CONTROL

Application access is not the only consideration when addressing authentication services. Users' access to other resources, such as data files or records, must also be considered. Accessing a system is done infrequently enough that the overhead for requesting validation from an AS is negligible. Accessing applications through dynamic menus built from a central repository also reduces the cost of administration. However, because access to data is frequent, the authentication process should be fast. It would not be feasible or desirable, given the current technology, to store the details of which individuals can access which files on a remote system. Therefore, resource control at this level should be implemented locally.

USER GROUPS

Locally implemented access should be administered effectively, especially when dealing with large numbers of users and large amounts of data. For this reason, most corporate IT departments implement a system of user groups or rules. In this manner, users are defined in terms of specific user groups that are, or are not, permitted to gain the required access.

The user groups are most often based on job function, because most people in a similar job function require access to the same resources. For example, a group of sales representatives might all require access to a customer database. Hence, a user group of SALESREP would be set up and given joint access to the database, and then each new sales representative who joined the organization would be joined to the SALESREP user group.

These user groups can be linked across different IT systems, that is, anywhere that access to resources is defined in terms of job function. The owner of a resource on a system can grant access by specific job function, and the resource can then be joined to the appropriate user group. This raises the issue of adding the user ID and joining it to the correct user groups for each IT system. This could be better accomplished just by adding the user to the AS and having the user added automatically to every other system. Such a procedure can be implemented fairly easily by NC-Syncom Command, because it already captures the Resource Access Control Facility administration commands and propagates them to other RACF systems. By extending the product to allow propagation out to other platforms, the effort of adding user IDs to disparate systems is eliminated and benefits realized.

DCE AND KERBEROS

Such new technological developments as the Operations Systems Functions Distributed Computing Environment (DCE) and Kerberos are important. These two technologies, among others, should help forward a secured open systems environment. Data Circuit-terminating Equipment and DCE-enabled applications offer something for solving distributed computing problems. However, for Data Circuit-terminating Equipment to become a standard, the majority of platforms must become DCE-enabled. Even if all the major operating system vendors agree, standardization will take time. DCE services within the operating system must be provided, and use of these services must be permitted within that platform's security system.

As individual segments of the network implement Data Circuit-terminating Equipment in advance of other parts, the need for synchronization between DCE and non-DCE compliant systems becomes even greater.

If a 100% DCE-compliant network becomes available in the next few years, tools will be needed to use the underlying infrastructure and to deliver the benefits expected from it. As DCE becomes more established, many vendors will deliver these tools by incorporating DCE principles in their products, thus providing real benefits for Data Circuit-terminating Equipment and non-DCE environments for the rest of this decade.

Kerberos and other third-party ticketing services, such as Resource Access Control Facility pass tickets, may also become a part of evolving solutions as the commercial benefits of these technologies becomes more apparent.

CENTRALIZED SECURITY ADMINISTRATION AND THE ENTERPRISE AUTHENTICATION SERVER

The AS solution is based on the use of the enterprise or mainframe host system. The various components deliver the benefits of centralized network authentication with the traditional strengths of the enterprise system without incurring large implementation costs or having to develop new administration systems.

USER ID AND PASSWORD RULES

The cornerstone of the enterprise system is the establishment of enterprise standards for user ID and password rules. Since the user IDs and passwords are those from the host security system, a single set of rules should be adopted. User IDs are registered in one place and can be selected for a single enterprise standard, thus uniquely identifying the user. The rules for user-ID and password selection, such as minimum and maximum length, frequency of change, and automatic revoke procedures become common across a diverse network system.

If more than one host security system exists, they can be synchronized together to form a single logical security system. This also allows one system to act as a backup for the other should access to one enterprise system be unavailable. ASs offer LAN gateway integration with the Novell NetWare and IBM LAN Server environments. Thus, LAN users (as well as mainframe users) are validated centrally against the host security package as they log in, as opposed to against repetitive validations against numerous local security databases.

ASs offer a log-on to the workstation with an enterprise user ID and password (and possibly authentication token) that is centrally administered. The user ID and password can then be used to access any servers, hosts, or other systems on the network. This can be achieved via a published API through which security systems across the network can request validation services.

CONCLUSION

There is more to single sign-on than just propagating a user ID and password to systems that need to be accessed. Users signing on to their PCs could be given an individually tailored application menu that is administered through a central control and audit system similar to the AS. Through a GUI such as Microsoft Windows or IBM OS/2, a graphic application menu would be presented following a successful log-on, including icons for all applications the user is allowed to access across the entire distributed network.

If this involved access to a remote system, the credentials used at sign-on could be transparently transmitted to the system using the techniques made available through the use of an authentication server: one user ID, one password, one sign-on, point-and-click access to all authorized applications, enterprisewide, with low administration overhead and high levels of security.

Chapter 37
Managing Heterogeneous Environments

Raj Rajagopal

In a heterogeneous network that includes Windows NT and UNIX, there are products available that let you perform systems administration functions for the complete heterogeneous network from either a Windows NT workstation or a UNIX workstation. Full coverage of these topics is beyond the scope of this book. The book will focus on just the migration and coexistence aspects. The systems administration functions in a heterogeneous environment include:

- Enterprise systems management
- Disk and file backup and restore
- System performance management
- Security management
- Helpdesk software
- Background job scheduling
- Software distribution and asset management
- Output management
- Network management
- Application management

Enterprise systems management provides cohesive, integrated administration of the entire IT infrastructure of an organization, which could include systems, networks, applications, and databases, Internet access, desktops, processors, and PDAs. *Disk and file backup* provides these functions across heterogeneous environments. *System performance management* collects and displays performance data from heterogeneous systems in a consistent manner. *Security management* functions are typically provided by the operating system, and the level of security provided is indicated in a scale. The scale ranges include D (least secure level) to A (most secure level), with intermediate classifications. The level that most

0-8493-9989-0/99/$0.00+$.50

operating system vendors aim for and that is required in many federal computer procurements is C2. Windows NT meets the requirements for the C2 security level and so does Digital UNIX. With an optional product, DEC MLS+, Digital UNIX can meet some security requirements at the B1 level. Digital UNIX, starting with version 4.0, also includes support for Access Control Lists (ACLs). ACLs are standard in Windows NT. UNIX includes some basic *background job scheduling* functions such as *cron* and *at*. Windows NT includes *at*. But many organizations need much more sophisticated job scheduling functions and typically use third-party software. Output management deals with printing, spooling, paging, and other output operations in a heterogeneous environment.

Exhibit 1 lists the different system administration functions to be performed and the various vendor products that are available.

UNIX SHELL AND UTILITIES ON WINDOWS NT

Developers and system administrators in the UNIX environment make extensive use of the UNIX shell — the command prompt environment of UNIX. GUI environments such as the Common Desktop Environment (CDE) have been added to many UNIX systems. But the shell is still very popular. The situation is analogous in the Windows world. DOS is a pure command prompt environment. Initial versions of Windows overlaid a GUI environment on top of DOS. In subsequent versions of Windows, with Windows GUI user acceptance, the user interface has become primarily graphical, although it is still possible to use the command prompt.

Users starting to use Windows NT after using UNIX have the same reaction as the first DOS users who started using Windows. They want to "drop down" into the command prompt environment. You can delete a file, for example, in one of two ways. You can use the DOS *delete* command and key in the file name to be deleted. You can also use the File Manager or Windows Explorer, select the file, and delete the file using a few clicks of the mouse.

UNIX Shell and Windows Command Prompt. The advantage that the command prompt offered then and what the shell offers now is the same—familiarity. UNIX users starting to use Windows NT can use Windows right away if the familiar shell is still available on Windows. This is the main idea behind offering the UNIX shell on Windows NT. There are other advantages of being able to use a UNIX shell on Windows, and these are covered later in this chapter.

Keep in mind, however, that the UNIX shell is much more powerful compared to the functions of the DOS or even Windows NT command prompt. Windows NT has *cmd.exe,* which is a souped-up version of the

Exhibit 1. Systems administration in a heterogeneous environment.

	Enterprise Systems Management	Disk and File Backup and Restore	System Performance Management	Security Management	Help Desk Software	Background Job Scheduling	Software Distribution and Asset Management	Output Management	Network Management	Application Management
Computer Associates	CA-Unicenter TNG		POLYCENTER Performance Manager				POLYCENTER Asset Works		POLYCENTER PathDoctor, Unicenter TNG	
Open Systems Management	COSMOS					COS/Batch	COS/Relay	COS/Report COS/Print		
OpenVision Technology	AXXiON family	AXXiON NetBackup		AXXiON						
PLATINUM Technology	System Management Suite	PLATINUM Tsreorg	ServerVision		PLATINUM Apriori	AutoSys	AutoXfer	AutoDeliver	WireTap, Trans Tracker	DBVision
Tivoli Systems	TME 10						TME 10		TME 10 NetView	TME 10/Plus
Cheyenne Software		ARCserve 6								
Digital Equipment		POLYCENTER Networker	Resource Broker						PATHWORKS, ServerWorks	
Spectra Logic		Alexandria Backup Librarian								
BGS Systems			BEST/1							
BMC Software			Knowledge Modules							PATROL
Candle			Candle Command Center, OMEGAMON							
Compuware			EcoTOOLS, EcoSCOPE							EcoTools

Exhibit 1. Systems administration in a heterogeneous environment. (continued)

	Enterprise Systems Management	Disk and File Backup and Restore	System Performance Management	Security Management	Help Desk Software	Background Job Scheduling	Software Distribution and Asset Management	Output Management	Network Management	Application Management
Datametrics System			ViewPoint							
Axent Technologies				OmniGuard						
Applix					Applix Enterprise					
Silvon Software					Helpline		Insite			
Unison Software						Maestro				
Novadigm							Enterprise Desktop Manager			
DAZEL								DAZEL Output Management System		

command.com of DOS with added commands and additional options to existing commands. UNIX shell functions include:

- The primary difference in power comes from the fact that the shell is more like a programming language than a scripting language, with support for variables, arrays, expressions, procedures, test and branch options, and looping.
- Multi-command buffering to permit you to retrieve prior commands and avoid retyping (DOS permits recall of the last command with the **F3** key, and Windows NT command prompt supports the last few commands with the up arrow) as well as the ability to search prior commands.
- Synchronize the date and time of files on a group of files that need to synchronized — such as the files that make up one version of a product.
- Search all source code files in a directory for specific characters.
- Support for command aliases.
- Sophisticated support for completing partial file names compared to the * and ? options.
- Perform batch processing of commands. This is conceptually the same as the *bat* files in DOS. However, since the commands themselves are more powerful, you can accomplish much more with batch processing compared to *bat* files.
- Schedule tasks on your computer for later processing.

If you are a manager and you are trying to decide if you should invest in a third-party product that provides the UNIX shell on Windows NT, then you have to decide if the cost of the third-party product is worth the advantages listed below:

- Allows your developers and systems administrators to be productive without having to undergo an extensive learning curve
- Existing investment in scripts for application development and systems administration can be protected and reused with very little change

So far, we have been talking about the UNIX shell as if there was just one shell. Actually, there are three primary shells — Bourne, Korn, and C shells. The Korn shell, for the most part, is compatible with the older Bourne shell. The C shell, on the other hand, is not compatible with either Korn or Bourne shells. When you are looking at products that support the UNIX shell on Windows, ensure that the product you select supports the shell(s) you use. The MKS toolkit, for example, supports the Korn shell, while the Hamilton C Shell supports the C shell, and Portage supports both the Korn shell and the C shell.

UNIX shell support in Windows can come from three sources:

- Shareware and freeware sources
- Microsoft, which has developed some UNIX tools
- Third-party sources

As mentioned earlier in the book, the main problem you face with public domain software is one of support. That said, UNIX shell is one area where you get better public domain software compared to other software areas.

Shell Support from Microsoft. Microsoft has some built-in commands that are also used in UNIX. These include TCP/IP commands such as *ping, ftp,* and *rcp*.

Microsoft also includes additional shell commands. These are not built into Windows NT, but they are available in the Windows NT Resource kit. Besides the popular ones such as the *vi* editor, the applications-building utility *make*, the kit also includes *ar, cat, cc, chmod, chown, cp, find, grep, ld, ln, ls, mkdir, mv, rm, rmdir, sh, tape, touch,* and *wc*. The kit doesn't include *diff*, but does include an equivalent utility called *windiff*.

While the list included with the Windows NT Resource kit may be sufficient for some users, it is normally not enough for power UNIX users. UNIX shells are available from third-party sources to provide a more complete UNIX shell environment on top of Windows NT. The third-party shells include:

- MKS Toolkit from Mortice Kern Systems (MKS)
- Hamilton C shell from Hamilton Laboratories
- Portage Base System
- OpenNT from Softway

MKS Toolkit from Mortice Kern Systems (MKS). More details on the MKS Toolkit are available online from MKS at http://www.mks.com.

The MKS Toolkit is more than a shell. It includes the Korn shell, the *vi* text editor, *make* for building applications, the data reporting *awk* language, a *visual diff* utility (a graphical equivalent for the text-based source comparison utility *diff*), and a graphical scheduler to run backup and other unattended jobs.

The MKS Korn shell supports three modes of command line editing:

- Native mode, which emulates the DOS box in Windows
- vi mode to emulate the *vi* editor
- EMACS to emulate the popular EMACS editor

The MKS Toolkit includes online help and an electronic manual. The *tar* format is commonly used on UNIX systems to read and write tapes. Using the MKS Toolkit, you can create a *tar* formatted tape on Windows for use with UNIX systems. The MKS Toolkit is available on Windows 95 and all of Windows NT's supported hardware platforms.

The N*u*TCRACKER product to port applications from UNIX to Windows, from Datafocus, includes the MKS toolkit. N*u*TCRACKER is discussed in Chapter 3.

Hamilton C Shell from Hamilton Laboratories. More details on the Hamilton C Shell are available by e-mail (hamilton@bix.com).

Hamilton C Shell recreates the UNIX shell environment on PCs running Windows 95 or on workstations running OS/2 or Windows NT on all platforms supported by Windows NT (Intel, Alpha, PowerPC [up to Windows NT 3.51], MIPS). The Hamilton C Shell supports the UNIX development shell environment with support for *cat, cp, diff, du, head, mv, rm, tail, touch, tr, wc,* among others. Like the MKS Toolkit, the Hamilton C Shell also supports the *tar* format for generating UNIX-compatible tapes in Windows NT. The Hamilton C Shell supports the Windows NT command line editing keys as in Windows NT and adds functionality by using additional keystroke combinations.

Portage Base. The following is a brief summary of Portage from Consensys Web pages. More details on the Portage Base are available online from Consensys at http://www.consensys.com. (Be careful when you type in Consensys, as there is another company with the name Consensus and the address http://www.consensus.com). Consensys also provides products to port from UNIX to Windows, and these are discussed in Chapter 6.

Let us look at the UNIX shell and utilities function provided by the Portage Base.

The UNIX Shell in Portage. Portage provides both the Korn Shell (*ksh*) and the C Shell (*csh*). Both of these shells run in the console. This means that you can set a very large buffer size, say 200 lines or more, and keep that much interactive history available for browsing. You can launch a *ksh* or *csh* from icons in the Portage program group. You can also simply type *ksh* or *csh* at an NT command prompt. If you want to run multiple shells (maximum of 20 can be active at any one time), the preferred method is probably to use the Portage Windows Interface to start them.

Once you are running *ksh* or *csh*, you are in a UNIX environment. The shell window provides an emulation of a VT100 terminal (a VT100 subset), and your *term* environment variable will be set to vt100. The window also provides a limited *tty* line discipline, and you can use *stty*(1) to view the options in effect or to change a subset of them.

In general, you should be unable to tell the difference between the behavior under one of the Portage UNIX shells and a native SVR4 implementation. A list of the few known differences is provided in the Portage documentation.

If you prefer graphical user interfaces, Portage includes the Portage Windows Interface, which serves a number of important functions:

- It allows you to easily start up and manage multiple UNIX shells.
- It allows you to customize the default settings of your shell windows (e.g., size, colors, etc.).
- It provides a dialog box interface to all Portage UNIX commands.
- It provides easy access to online manual pages for every command.

You can start up the Portage Windows Interface by clicking on its icon in the Portage program group. The program's main feature is a set of 140 buttons providing dialog-box access to UNIX utilities. The Portage SDK has an even larger set of buttons (170) than the Base System. Screen shots are available at http://www.consensys.com.

UNIX Utilities in Portage. All Portage utilities can be run from the NT Command Prompt or console. Since the Command Prompt passes command line arguments to programs unchanged (unlike UNIX shells, which perform wild-card expansion and much more), Portage programs are able to provide an overlapping set of UNIX-like and DOS-like syntax. In particular, from the Windows NT Command Prompt, path names can use either UNIX style / or Windows style \\ notation. Supported functions include:

- Pattern matching is UNIX style, including '*', '?', single quotes, and double quotes
- The Portage environment variables (UNIXROOT, UNIXTMP, SYMLINKS \& CASENAMES) are in effect

Of course, shell-specific features like \$X for environment variables and backquotes for subshells are not available from the Command Prompt.

An example of a valid Command Prompt command line is *ls -lrt /bin/b**.

There are several name conflicts between NT commands and Portage UNIX utilities. The echo command is built into the Command Prompt (as it is in UNIX shells), so it will always use the NT syntax. Other commands like *more* and *mkdir* are not built in, so you will get whichever one is found first by following your PATH environment variable.

When Portage is installed, the *bin* directory is added to the end of your PATH, so by default you will get the NT version of these utilities. You can change the PATH environment variable but that may break existing batch and other Windows NT functions using the Path. The simplest solution is to use one of the UNIX shells, where \$PORTAGE/bin is added to the front of the PATH environment variable by default.

N*u*TCRACKER. More details on N*u*TCRACKER are available from http://www.datafocus.com. As mentioned earlier under MKS Toolkit, N*u*TCRACKER includes the MKS Toolkit under an agreement between Datafocus and Mortice Kern Systems. N*u*TCRACKER also has some additional utilities such as *chmod, whoami, process, sdiff,* etc. The N*u*TCRACKER *Installation and Porting Guide* included in the CD accompanying this book has a complete list of the utilities.

If you are used to using GNU tools, Congruent Corporation provides Toolbuster which provides GNU utilities, compilers, debuggers, editors, etc. for Windows NT.

HETEROGENEOUS NETWORK MANAGEMENT USING SNMP

SNMP stands for Simple Network Management Protocol. It is a standard protocol that is used in many system management software products, including system management software for UNIX systems and heterogeneous systems. Some of the products that use the SNMP protocol include Openview from HP, and TME 10 Netview from Tivoli Systems (part of IBM).

System management software provides centralized and formatted status information about all SNMP supporting devices on the network. The devices that support SNMP could range from simple hardware devices to complete computer systems. The software in these devices that inform the system management software running on servers are called SNMP agents. SNMP agents convey status information to SNMP-based system management servers in one of two ways:

- Send alerts
- Respond to queries

Alerts are for serious errors and are broadcast by the device over the network to get attention. Queries are specific communications between the system management software and the SNMP devices and are typically used to communicate regular status messages.

Most UNIX systems and Windows NT support SNMP.

Installing and Configuring SNMP in Windows NT

SNMP support is implemented as a service (a *service* in Windows NT is the equivalent of a *daemon* in UNIX) in Windows NT, and you install this service the same way as you would any other Windows NT service. (From **Start**, select **Settings**, then choose **Control Panel** and double-click the network icon in the Control Panel. Select the **Services** tab and, from the list of services shown, click SNMP service and click OK.) The SNMP is installed and will be available the next time you restart the machine.

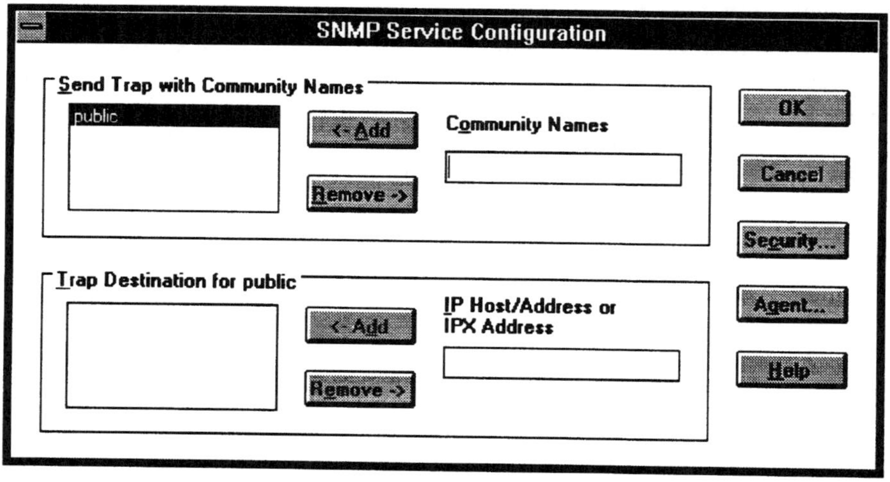

Exhibit 2. SNMP service configuration.

Configuring SNMP involves specifying community names for sending traps and specifying IP addresses. The menu in Windows NT to specify SNMP service configuration information is shown in Exhibit 2.

DIRECTORY SERVICES MANAGER FOR NETWARE

NetWare 2.x/3.x and 4.x servers (those that are managed via the NetWare bindery) have to be managed individually. This includes managing the users in each server as well. Windows NT Server includes global directory services and can help users manage multiple environments. Windows NT server offers users the possibility of single network logon to all services, including applications, and provides administrators with a central point of administration.

With Windows NT Server and DSMN, NetWare customers can centrally manage their mixed Windows NT and NetWare environments with the Windows NT Directory Services. DSMN copies the NetWare user accounts to the Windows NT Directory Service and then propagates any changes back to the NetWare server. This is done without the need to install any software on the NetWare servers.

DSMN simplifies network administration tasks. Administrators can centrally manage their Windows NT Server and NetWare account information while having to maintain only one user account and associated password for each end-user on the network. DSMN includes:

- A point-and-click interface for propagating user and group accounts from NetWare 2.x/3.x (and 4.x in bindery emulation mode) to Windows NT Directory Services.

- Multiple options for setting up initial passwords, selecting which user accounts to propagate each way, handling account deletions, and even doing a "trial run" to test a propagation strategy.
- Windows NT Directory Service manages Windows NT Server from the server console, or from anywhere else on the network (including remotely via dialup) from a Windows NT workstation or, new with version 4.0, Windows 95-based desktop.
- Account database backup and replication to any location on the network.

DSMN simplifies end-user network access. DSMN also simplifies network access for end-users in the following ways:

- New users are up and running quickly because the administrator does the setup in Windows NT Server directory services, and the user account is automatically propagated back to all authorized NetWare servers.
- Each user's account name and password are identical on all NetWare and Windows NT servers, so they use the same name and password regardless of where they log on.
- Using Windows NT server remote access services (RAS), users can log on via dialup with the same account name and password.
- Windows NT Directory Service can authenticate users to applications running on Windows NT server. Thus, with a single logon, users can get access to business applications in addition to Windows NT server file and print services.

DYNAMIC HOST CONFIGURATION PROTOCOL

If you have played around with TCP/IP configuration information such as IP addresses and subnet masks when you set up your Internet service, you have a pretty good idea of the complexity involved in setting up TCP/IP. In a business setting, the administrators used to spend a fair amount of time setting this configuration, primarily because it was necessary to set this up at each client and making changes meant making them at the client level.

Windows NT supports the Dynamic Host Configuration Protocol (DHCP) to reduce the work associated with network configurations, in particular setting IP addresses. DHCP dynamically assigns addresses and ensures that there are no duplicates and thus relieves the major problems with manual configurations. Since it is the DHCP (and not an administrator) that keeps track of addresses, it is easy to reuse addresses and manage the IP address allocation and management centrally.

DHCP lets the administrator specify some parameters for the IP addresses such as "lease durations." When DHCP assigns an IP address to a client, the address is actually assigned temporarily for a finite time called "lease." Lease durations specify how long a computer can use an assigned IP address before having to renew the lease with the DHCP server.

The typical scenario that happens in many businesses that administrators used to dread is when a computer is moved from one subnet to another. Administrators are used to manually assigning a new address and deleting the old one. With DHCP, the IP address is released automatically when the DHCP client is removed from a subnet, and a new address is automatically assigned when the (moved) DHCP client is reconnected on another subnet. There is no manual intervention (from either the user or the administrator) to accomplish the address change. Contrast this with the earlier manual scenario. The dynamic address assignment feature is particularly useful for portable computer users.

How Does DHCP Work?

DHCP is implemented at the client and the server. The DHCP server assigns the addresses while the DHCP client asks for an address. When a DHCP client boots up, the DHCP client broadcasts a discover message. This message is sent to all DHCP servers in the local network as well as other DHCP servers set up to receive the broadcasts. Every DHCP server that receives a *discover* message responds with an *offer* message. The *offer* is sent to the requesting DHCP client (not broadcast). The *offer* contains an IP address and valid configuration information for the client that sent the request. The DHCP client may thus receive multiple responses to its broadcast. The DHCP client must then choose one of the offers. It does this and is said to be in a *choosing state* when it is evaluating the *offers*. Once the DHCP client decides on the offer, it then responds to the offer to complete the address setup.

The selected DHCP server receives the response from the DHCP client to its offer. The DHCP server then sends a DHCP acknowledgment message to the DHCP client. The acknowledgment message contains the address it sent with the offer (in response to the discover message). The acknowledgment message also contains a valid lease for the address and the TCP/IP network configuration parameters for the client. The client receives the acknowledgment and enters a bound state.

The DHCP client can now participate on the TCP/IP network. Since this process occurred some time during the bootup, the client completes the rest of the booting process. If a network connection could not be established (for example, if the computer is not connected to a network or the network card is not installed), the address assignment will not occur and the bootup indicates errors. The address that has been assigned is valid for the lease duration. As mentioned earlier, system administrators decide

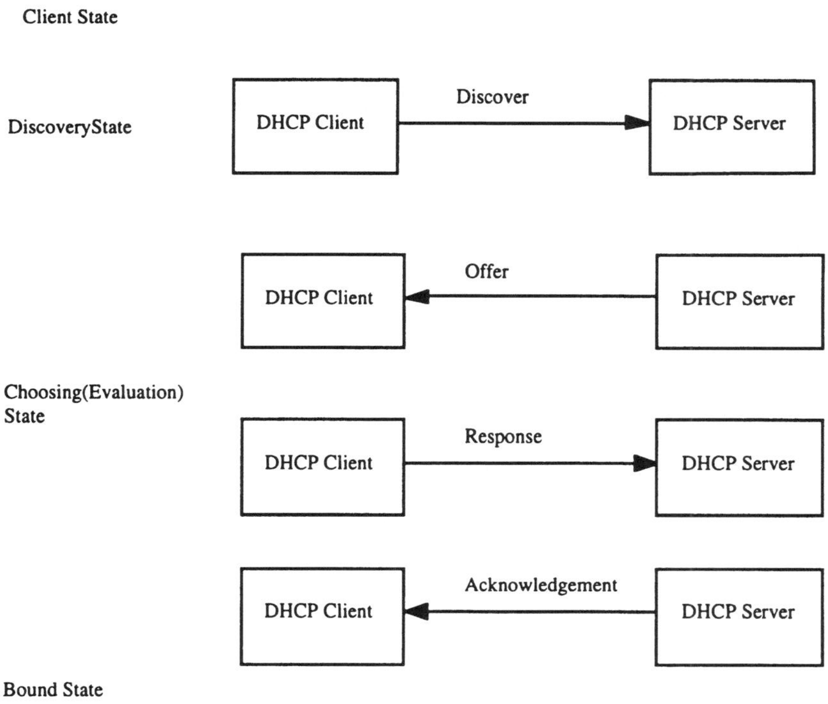

Exhibit 3. DHCP IP address assignment process.

valid lease durations for the installation. The DHCP client attempts to renew the lease when it is about to expire, if an IP address is still required. Typically, it would renew the existing lease. If for any reason, it is unable to renew the lease (the server that assigned the lease is not available, for example), then the DHCP client restarts the discovery process. Exhibit 3 illustrates the DHCP IP address assignment process.

Windows NT Server includes a DHCP Manager. Windows NT system/network administrators use the DHCP manager to define policies for address allocation, leases, etc.

WINDOWS INTERNET NAMING SERVICE (WINS)

WINS solves the problem of locating network resources in a TCP/IP-based Microsoft network. WINS performs this function by configuring and maintaining the computer name and IP-address mapping tables, which can be looked up whenever a name-address mapping is required. WINS performs the mapping updates automatically. Because it maintains the mapping table, WINS can detect, alert, and correct error situations such as duplicate names and addresses. WINS is a complementary service to DHCP and is not a prerequisite. WINS also includes the user interfaces required for administration and configuration of the WINS servers, static name tables, and replication information.

WINS Configuration

We saw earlier how the message exchanges between DHCP clients and servers. Once the DHCP client gets an address with a valid lease, and is in the bound state, the client registers its name with the designated WINS server. The client issues a direct request to the WINS server and sends the *NameRegistrationRequest* with the DHCP client's computer name and leased IP address.

The WINS server uses its mapping table to validate that the requesting computer name is unique on the network. It responds to the client with either a positive or a negative WINS name registration response message. A positive response indicates a successful WINS registration. As part of the registration response, the WINS server includes the Time To Live (TTL) for the name registration. This is roughly equivalent to the lease duration issued by the DHCP server. If the WINS server is unable to complete registration (e.g., if the validation for name uniqueness fails), it sends a negative registration response message. The user is notified of the error.

WINS TTL renewal. Renewal of TTL for a WINS client is, for the most part, simple and automatic. The NetBIOS over TCP/IP (NBT) client process automatically registers the computer name with the WINS-based server whenever the NBT client process is started. The WINS server automatically renews (issues a new TTL whenever NBT registration occurs). There is also a timer service to request an NBT registration in the event that no automatic NBT registration happened in the interim.

Chapter 38
Business Continuity in the Distributed Environment

Steven P. Craig

This chapter describes the process of business recovery planning specifically for local area networks (LANs) and the components that compose the LAN. These procedures can be applied to companies of any size and for a recovery scope ranging from operational to catastrophic events.

INTRODUCTION

Today's organizations, in their efforts to reduce costs, are streamlining layers of management while implementing more-complex matrices of control and reporting. Distributed systems have facilitated the reshaping of these organizations by moving the control of information closer to its source, the end user. In this transition, however, secure management of that information has been placed at risk. Information technology (IT) departments must protect the traditional system environment within the computer room plus develop policies, standards, and guidelines for the security and protection of the company's distributed information base.

Further, the IT staff must communicate these standards to all users to enforce a strong baseline of controls. In these distributed environments, IT personnel are often asked to develop systems recovery plans outside the context of an overall business recovery scheme. Recoverability of systems, however, should be viewed as only one part of business recovery. Information systems, in and of themselves, are not the lifeblood of a company; inventory, assets, processes, and people are all essential factors that must be considered in the business continuation design. The success of business continuity planning rests on a company's ability to integrate systems recovery in the greater overall planning effort.

0-8493-9989-0/99/$0.00+$.50

BUSINESS RECOVERY PLANNING—THE PROCESS

Distinctive areas must be addressed in the formulation of a company's disaster recovery plan, and attention to these areas should follow the steps of the scientific method—a statement of the problem, the development of a hypothesis, and the testing of the hypothesis. Like any scientific process, the development of the disaster recovery plan is iterative. The testing phase of this process is essential because it reveals whether the plan is viable. Moreover, it is imperative that the plan and its assumptions be tested on an ongoing, routine basis. The most important distinction that marks disaster recovery planning is what is at stake—the survival of the business.

The phases of a disaster recovery plan process are

- Awareness and discovery
- Risk assessment
- Mitigation
- Preparation
- Testing
- Response and recovery

Recovery planners should adapt these phases to a company's specific needs and requirements. Some of the phases may be combined, depending, for example, on the size of the company and the extent of exposures to risk. It is crucial, however, that each phase be included in the formation of a recovery plan.

Awareness and Discovery. Awareness begins when a recovery planning team can identify both possible and plausible threats to business operations. The more pressing issue for an organization in terms of business recovery planning is plausible threats, which must be evaluated by recovery planners. Their planning efforts, in turn, will depend on the following criteria:

- The business of the company
- The area of the country in which the company is located
- The company's existing security measures
- The level of adherence to existing policies and procedures
- Management's commitment to existing policies and procedures

Awareness also implies educating all employees about existing risk exposures and briefing them on what measures have been taken to minimize those exposures. Each employee's individual role in complying with these measures should be addressed at this early stage. In terms of systems and information, the awareness phase includes determining what exposures exist that are specific to information systems, what information is vital to the organization, and what information is proprietary and confidential. Answering these questions will help planners determine when an interruption will be catastrophic as opposed to operational.

For example, in an educational environment, a system that is down for two or three days may not be considered catastrophic, whereas in a process control environment (e.g., chemicals or electronics), just a few minutes of downtime may be. Discovery is the process in which planners must determine, based on their awareness of plausible threats, which specific operations would be affected by existing exposures. They must consider what measures are currently in place or could be put in place to minimize or, ideally, remove these exposures.

Risk Assessment. Risk assessment is a decision process that weighs the cost of implementing preventive measures against the risk of loss from not implementing them. There are many qualitative and quantitative approaches to risk analysis. Typically, two major cost factors arise for the systems environment. The first is the loss incurred from a suspension of business operations due to system downtime. The second is the replacement cost of equipment. The potential for significant revenue loss when systems are down for an extended period of time is readily understood in today's business environment, because the majority of businesses rely exclusively on systems for much of their information needs.

However, the cost of replacing systems and information in the event of catastrophic loss is often grossly underrated. Major organizations, when queried on insurance coverage for systems, come up with some surprising answers. Typically, organizations have coverage for mainframes and midrange systems and for the software for these environments. The workstations and the network servers, however, are often deemed not valuable enough to insure. Coverage for the information itself is usually neglected as well, despite the fact that the major replacement cost for a company in crisis is the recreation of its information database.

Notably, the personal computer, regardless of how it is configured or networked, is usually perceived as a standalone unit from the risk assessment point of view. Even companies that have retired their mainframes and embraced an extensive client/server architecture, and that fully comprehend the impact of the loss of its use, erroneously consider only the replacement cost of the unit rather than of the distributed system as the basis of risk.

Risk assessment is the control point of the recovery planning process. The amount of exposure a company believes it has, or is willing to accept, determines how much effort the company will expend on this process. Simply put, a company with no plan is fully exposed to catastrophic loss.

Companies developing plans must approach risk assumption by identifying their worst-case scenario and then deciding how much they will spend to offset that scenario through mitigation, contingency plans, and training. Risk assessment is the phase required to formulate a company's management perspective, which in turn supports the goal of developing and maintaining a companywide contingency plan.

Mitigation. The primary objectives of mitigation are to lessen risk exposures and to minimize possible losses. History provides several lessons in this area. For example, since the underground floods of 1992, companies in Chicago think twice before installing data centers in the basements of buildings. Bracing key computer equipment and office furniture has become popular in California because of potential injuries to personnel and the threat of loss of assets from earthquakes. Forward-thinking companies in the South and southern Atlantic states are installing systems far from the exterior of buildings because of the potential damage from hurricanes.

Although it is a simple exercise to make a backup copy of key data and systems, it is difficult to enforce this activity in a distributed systems environment. As systems have been distributed and the end user empowered, the regimen of daily or periodic backups has been adversely affected. In other words, the end user has been empowered with tools but has not been educated about, or held responsible for, the security measures that are required for those tools. One company, a leader in the optical disk drive market, performs daily backups of its accounting and manufacturing systems to optical disk (using its own product), but never rotates the media and has never considered storing the backup off-site. Any event affecting the hardware (e.g., fire, theft, or earthquake) could therefore destroy the sole backup and the means of business recovery for this premier company. Mitigation efforts must counter such oversights.

Preparation. The preparation phase of the disaster planning process delineates what specific actions must be taken should a disaster occur. Based on an understanding of plausible threats, planners must determine who will take what action if a disaster occurs. Alternates should be identified for key staff members who may have been injured as a result of the event. A location for temporary operations should be established in case the company's building is inaccessible after a disaster, and the equipment, supplies, and company records that will be required at this site should be identified. Preparation may include establishing a hot site for systems and telecommunications. Off-hours or emergency telephone numbers should be kept for all vendors and services providers that may need to be contacted. Moreover, the contingency plans must be clearly documented and communicated to all personnel.

Testing. The testing phase proves the viability of the planning efforts. The recovery planner must determine, during testing, whether there are invalid assumptions and inadequate solutions in the company's plan. It is important to remember that organizations are not static and that an ever-changing business environment requires a reasonable frequency of testing. Recovery planners must repeat this phase of the plan until they are comfortable with the results and sure that the plan will work in a time of crisis.

Response and Recovery. This final phase of the contingency plan is one that organizations hope never to have to employ. Preparing for actual response and recovery includes identifying individuals and training them to take part in emergency response in terms of assessment of damage, cleanup, restoration, alternate site start-up, emergency operations duties, and any other activities that managing the crisis might demand.

Every phase of the planning process, prior to this phase, is based on normalcy. The planning effort is based on what is perceived to be plausible. Responses are developed to cover plausible crises and are done so under rational conditions. However, dealing with a catastrophic crisis is not a normal part of an employee's work day, and the recovery team must be tested under more realistic conditions to gauge how they will perform under stress and where lapses in response might occur. Ideally, recovery planners should stage tests that involve role playing to give their team members a sense of what they may be exposed to in a time of crisis.

DEPARTMENTAL PLANNING

Often, consultants are asked to help a company develop its business resumption plan and to focus only on the systems environment to reduce the overall cost of planning efforts. Often, companies take action on planning as the result of an information systems audit and thus focus solely on systems exposure and audit compliance. These companies erroneously view disaster recovery as an expense rather than as an investment in business continuity. A plan that addresses data integrity and systems survivability is certainly a sound place to begin, but there are many other factors to consider in recovery planning. Depending on the nature of the business, for example, telecommunications availability may be much more important than systems availability. In a manufacturing environment, if the building and equipment are damaged in a disaster, getting the systems up and running may not necessarily be a top priority.

A company's business continuation plan should be a compilation of individual department plans. It is essential that each department identify its processes and prioritize those processes in terms of recovery. Companywide operating and recovery priorities can then be established by the company's management based on the input supplied by the departments.

Information technology, as a service department to all other departments, will be better equipped to plan recovery capacity and required system availability based on this detailed knowledge of departmental recovery priorities.

INFORMATION TECHNOLOGY'S ROLE

Information technology personnel should not be responsible for creating individual department plans, but they should take a leadership role in the plan development. Information technology generally has the best appreciation and understanding of information flow throughout the organization. Its staff, therefore, are in the best position to identify and assess the following areas.

INTERDEPARTMENTAL DEPENDENCIES

It is common for conflicts in priorities to arise between a company's overall recovery plan and its departmental plans. This conflict occurs because departments tend to develop plans on their own without considering other departments. One department may downplay the generation of certain information because that information has little importance to its operations, but the same information might be vitally important to the operations of another department. Information technology departments can usually identify these discrepancies in priorities by carefully reviewing each department's plan.

EXTERNAL DEPENDENCIES

During the discovery process, recovery planners should determine with what outside services end-user departments are linked. End-user departments often think of external services as being outside the scope of their recovery planning efforts, despite the fact that dedicated or unique hardware and software are required to use the outside services.

At a minimum, departmental plans must include the emergency contact numbers for these outside services and any company account codes that permit linkage to the service from a recovery location. Recovery planners should also assess the outside service providers' contingency plans for assisting the company in its recovery efforts.

INTERNAL AND EXTERNAL EXPOSURES

Standalone systems acquired by departments for a special purpose are often not linked to a company's networks. Consequently, they are often overlooked in terms of data security practices. For example, a mortgage company funded all of its loans via wire transfer from one of three standalone systems. This service was one of the key operations of the company. Each system was equipped with a modem and a uniquely serialized encryption card for access to the wire service. However, these systems were not maintained by the information technology department, no data or system backups were maintained by the end-user department, and each system was tied to a distinct phone line. Any mishap involving these three systems could have potentially put this department several days, if not weeks, in arrears in funding its loans.

Under catastrophic conditions, a replacement encryption card and linkage establishment would have taken as much as a month to acquire. As a result of this discovery, the company identified a secondary site and filed a standby encryption card, an associated alternate phone line, and a disaster recovery action plan with the wire service. This one discovery, and its resolution, more than justified the expense of the entire planning effort.

During the discovery process, the recovery planner identified another external exposure for the same company. This exposure related to power and the requirements of the company's uninterruptable power supply (UPS). The line of questioning dealt with the sufficiency of battery backup capacity and whether an external generator should be considered in case of a prolonged power interruption. An assumption had been made by the company that, in the event of an areawide disaster, power would be restored within 24 hours.

The company had eight hours of battery capacity that would suffice for its main operational shift. Although the county's power utility company had a policy of restoring power on a priority basis for the large employers of the county, the company was actually based in a special district and acquired its power from the city, not the county. Therefore, it would have power restored only after all the emergency services and city agencies were restored to full power. Moreover, no one could pinpoint how long this restoration period would be. To mitigate this exposure, the company added an external generator to its UPS system.

APPRISE MANAGEMENT OF RISKS AND MITIGATION COSTS

As an information technology department identifies various risks, it is the department's responsibility to make management aware of them. This responsibility covers all security issues—system survivability issues (i.e., disaster recovery), confidentiality, and system integrity issues.

In today's downsized environments, many information technology departments have to manage increasingly more complex systems with fewer personnel. Because of these organizational challenges, it is more important for the information technology staff involved in the planning process to present management with clear proposals for risk mitigation.

Advocating comprehensive planning and security measures, and following through with management to see that they are implemented, will ensure that a depleted information technology staff is not caught off-guard in the event of disaster.

Policies. To implement a system or data safeguard strategy, planners must first develop a policy, or standard operating procedure, that explains why the safeguard should be established and how it will be implemented. The planners should then get approval for this policy from management. In the process of putting together a disaster recovery plan for a community college's central computing operations, one recovery planner discovered that numerous departments had isolated themselves from the networks supported by the information technology group.

These departments believed that the servers were always crashing, which had been a cause for concern in years past, and they chose to separate themselves from the servers for what they considered to be safer conditions. These departments, which included accounting, processed everything locally on hard drives with no backups whatsoever. Needless to say, a fire or similar disaster in the accounting department would severely disrupt, if not suspend, the college's operations.

The recovery planner addressed this problem with a fundamental method of distributed system security: distribute the responsibility of data integrity along the channels of distributed system capability. A college policy statement on data integrity was developed and issued to this effect. The policy outlined end-user security responsibilities, as well as those of the department administrators.

Establish Recovery Capability. Based on departmental input and a company's established priorities, the information technology department must design an intermediate system configuration that is adequately sized to permit the company's recovery immediately following the disaster. Initially, this configuration, whether it is local, at an alternate company site, or at a hot site, must sustain the highest-priority applications yet be adaptable to addressing other priorities. These added needs will arise depending on how long it takes to reoccupy the company's facilities and fully restore all operations to normal. For example, planners must decide that the key client/server applications are critical to company operations, whereas office automation tools are not.

Restore Full Operational Access. The information technology department's plan should also address the move back from an alternate site and the resources that will be required to restore and resume full operations. Depending on the size of the enterprise and the plausible disaster, this could include a huge number of end-user workstations. At the very least, this step is as complex as a company's move to a new location.

PLANNING FOR THE DISTRIBUTED ENVIRONMENT

First and foremost, planners in a distributed environment must define the scope of their project. Determining the extent of recovery is the first step. For example, will the plan focus on just the servers or on the entire enterprise's systems and data? The scope of recovery, the departmental and company priorities, and recovery plan funding will delimit the planner's options. The following discussion outlines the basics of recovery planning regardless of budget considerations.

PROTECTING THE LAN

Computer rooms are built to provide both special environmental conditions and security control. Environmental conditions include air conditioning, fire-rated walls, dry sprinkler systems, special fire abatement systems (e.g., Halon, FM-200), raised flooring, cable chase-ways, equipment racking, equipment bracing, power conditioning, and continuous power (UPS) systems. Control includes a variety of factors: access, external security, and internal security. All these aspects of protection are built-in benefits of the computer room.

Today, however, company facilities are distributed and open; servers and network equipment can be found on desktops in open areas, on carts with wheels, and in communications closets that are unlocked or have no conditioned power. Just about anything and everything important to the company is on these servers or accessible through them.

Internal Environmental Factors. A computer room is a viable security option, though there are some subtleties to designing one specifically for a client/server environment. If the equipment is to be rack mounted, racking can be suspended from the ceiling, which yields clearance from the floor and avoids possible water damage. Notably, the cooling aspects of a raised floor design, plus its ability to hide a morass of cabling, are no longer needed in a distributed environment.

Conditioned power requirements have inadvertently modified computer room designs as well. If an existing computer room has a shunt trip by the exit but small standalone battery backup units are placed on servers, planners must review the computer room emergency shutdown procedures. The function of the shunt trip was originally to kill all power in the room so that, if operational personnel had to leave in a hurry, they would be able to come back later and reset systems in a controlled sequence.

Now, when there are individual battery backup units that sustain the equipment in the room, the equipment will continue to run after the shunt is thrown. Rewiring the room for all wall circuits to run off the master UPS, in proper sequence with the shunt trip, should resolve this conflict. Room placement within the greater facility is also a consideration. When designing a room from scratch, planners should identify an area with structural integrity, avoid windows, and eliminate overhead plumbing.

Alternate fire suppression systems are still a viable protection strategy for expensive electronics and the operational, on-site tape backups within a room. If these systems are beyond the company's budget, planners might consider multiple computer rooms (companies with a multiple-building campus environment or multiple locations can readily adapt these as a recovery strategy) with sprinklers and some tarpaulins handy to protect the equipment from incidental water damage (e.g., a broken sprinkler pipe). A data safe may also be a worthwhile investment for the backup media maintained on-site. However, if the company uses a safe, its personnel must be trained to keep it closed. In eight out of ten site visits where a data safe is used, the door is kept ajar (purely as a convenience). The safe only protects the company's media when it is sealed. If the standard practice is to keep it closed, personnel will not have to remember to shut it as they evacuate the computer room under the stress of an emergency.

If the company occupies several floors within a building and maintains communication equipment (e.g., servers, hubs, or modems) within closets, the closets should be treated as miniature computer rooms. The doors to the closets should be locked, and the closets should be equipped with power conditioning and adequate ventilation.

Physical Security. The other priority addressed by a properly secured computer room is control: control of access to the equipment, cabling, and backup media. Servers out in the open are prime targets for mishaps ranging from innocent tampering to outright theft. A thief who steals a server gets away not only with an expensive piece of equipment but with a wealth of information that may be prove much more valuable and marketable than the equipment itself.

The college satellite campus discussed earlier had no backup of the information contained within its network. The recovery planner explained to the campus administration, which kept its servers out in the open in its administration office area (a temporary trailer), that a simple theft of the \$2,000 equipment would challenge its ability to continue operations. All student records, transcripts, course catalogs, instructor directories, and financial aid records were maintained on the servers. With no backup to rely on and its primary source of information evaporated, the campus administration would be faced with literally thousands of hours of effort to reconstruct its information base.

Property Management. Knowing what and where the organization's computer assets (i.e., hardware, software, and information) are at any moment is critical to recovery efforts. The information technology department must be aware of not only the assets within the computer room but of every workstation used throughout the organization, whether it is connected to a network (including portables); what its specific configuration is; what software resides on it; and what job function it supports. This knowledge is achievable if all hardware and software acquisitions and installations are run through the IT department, if the company's policies and procedures support information technology's control (i.e., all departments and all personnel willingly adhere to the policies and procedures), and if the department's property management inventory is properly maintained.

Size is also a factor here. If the information technology department manages an organization with a single server and 50 workstations, the task may not be too large; however, if it supports several servers and several hundred workstations, the amount of effort involved is considerable.

Data Integrity. Information, if lost or destroyed, is the one aspect of a company's systems that cannot be replaced simply by ordering another copy or another component. The company may have insurance, hot-site agreements, or quick-replacement arrangements for hardware and global license agreements for software, but its data integrity process is entirely in the hands of its information technology specialists. The information technology specialist and the disaster recovery planner are the individuals who must ensure that the company's information will be recoverable.

Based on the initial risk assessment phase, planners can determine just how extensive the data integrity program should be. The program should include appropriate policies and education addressing frequency of backups, storage locations, retention schedules, and the periodic verification that the backups are being done correctly. If the planning process has just begun, data integrity should be the first area on which planners focus their attention. None of the other strategies they implement will count if no means of recovering vital data exists.

NETWORK RECOVERY STRATEGIES

The information technology specialist's prime objective with respect to systems contingency planning is system survivability. In other words, provisions must be in place, albeit in a limited capacity, that will support the company's system needs for priority processing through the first few hours immediately following a disaster.

Fault Tolerance Versus Redundancy. To a degree, information technology specialists are striving for what is called fault tolerance of the company's critical systems. Fault tolerance means that no single point of failure will stop the system. Fault tolerance is often built in as part of the operational component design of a system. Redundancy, or duplication of key components, is the basis of fault tolerance. When fault tolerance cannot be built in, a quick replacement or repair program should be devised. Moving to an alternate site (i.e., a hot site) is one quick replacement strategy.

Alternate Sites and System Sizing. Once the recovery planner fully understands the company's priorities, the planner can size the amount of system capacity required to support those priorities in the first few hours, days, and weeks following a disaster. When planning for a recovery site or establishing a contract with a hot-site service provider, the information technology specialist must size the immediate recovery capacity. This is extremely important, because most hot-site service providers will not allow a company to modify its requirements once it has declared a disaster.

The good news with respect to distributed systems is that hot-site service providers offer options for recovery. These options often include offering the use of their recovery center, bringing self-contained vans to the company's facility (equipped with the company's own required server configuration), or shipping replacement equipment for anything that has been lost.

Adequate Backups with Secure Off-Site Storage. This process must be based on established company policies that identify vital information and detail how its integrity will be managed. The work flow of the company and the volatility of its information base dictates the frequency of backups. At a minimum, backup should occur daily for servers and weekly or monthly for key files of individual workstations.

Planners must decide when and how often to take backups off-site. Depending on a company's budget, off-site could be the building next door, a bank safety deposit box, the network administrator's house, the branch office across town, or a secure media vault at a storage facility maintained by an off-site media storage company. Once the company meets the objective of separating the backup copy of vital data from its source, it must address the accessibility of the off-site copy.

The security of the company's information is of vital concern. The planner must know where the information is to be kept and about possible exposure risks during transit. Some off-site storage companies intentionally use unmarked, nondescript vehicles to transport a company's backup tapes to and from storage. These companies know that this information is valuable and that its transport and storage place should not be advertised.

Adequate LAN Administration. Keeping track of everything the company owns—its hardware, software, and information bases—is fundamental to a company's recovery effort. The best aid in this area is a solid audit application that is run periodically on all workstations. This procedure assists the information technology specialist in maintaining an accurate inventory across the enterprise and provides a tool for monitoring software acquisitions and hardware configuration modifications. The inventory is extremely beneficial for insurance loss purposes. It also provides the technology specialist with accurate records for license compliance and application revision maintenance.

Personnel. Systems personnel are too often overlooked in systems recovery planning. Are there adequate systems personnel to handle the complexities of response and recovery? What if a key individual is affected by the same catastrophic event that destroys the systems? This event could cause a single point of failure.

An option available to the planner is to propose an emergency outsourcing contract. A qualified systems engineer hired to assist on a key project that never seems to get completed (e.g., the network system documentation) may be a cost-effective security measure. Once that project is completed to satisfaction, the company can consider structuring a contractual arrangement that, for example, retains the engineer for one to three days a month to continue to work on documentation and other special projects, as well as cover for staff vacations and sick days, and guarantees that the engineer will be available on an as-needed basis should the company experience an emergency. The advantage of this concept is that the company maintains effective outsourced personnel who are well-versed in the company's systems if the company needs to rely on them during an emergency.

TESTING

The success of a business recovery plan depends on testing its assumptions and solutions. Testing and training keep the plan up-to-date and maintain the viability of full recovery. Tests can be conducted in a variety of ways, from reading through the plan and thinking through the outcome to full parallel system testing, or setting up operations at a hot site or alternate location and having the users run operations remotely. The full parallel system test generally verifies that the hot-site equipment and remote linkages work, but it does not necessarily test the feasibility of the user departments' plans. Full parallel testing is also generally staged within a limited amount of time, which trains staff to get things done correctly under time constraints.

Advantages of the Distributed Environment for Testing

Because of their size and modularity, distributed client/server systems provide a readily available, modifiable, and affordable system setup for testing. They allow for a testing concept called cycle testing. Cycle testing is similar to cycle counting, a process used in manufacturing whereby inventory is categorized by value and counted several times a year rather than in a one-time physical inventory. With cycle counting, inventory is counted year long, with portions of the inventory being selected to be counted either on a random basis or on a preselected basis. Inventory is further classified into categories so that the more expensive or critical inventory items are counted more frequently and the less expensive items less frequently.

The end result is the same as taking a one-time physical inventory in that, by the end of a calendar year, all the inventory has been counted. The cycle counting method has several advantages:

- Operations do not have to be completely shut down while the inventory is being taken.
- Counts are not taken under time pressure, which results in more accurate counts.
- Errors in inventories are discovered and corrected as part of the continuous process.

The advantages of cycle testing are similar to those of cycle counting. Response and recovery plan tests can be staged with small manageable groups so they are not disruptive to company operations. Tests can be staged by a small team of facilitators and observers on a continual basis. Tests can be staged and debriefings held without time pressure, allowing the participants the time to understand their roles and the planners the time to evaluate team response to the test scenarios and to make necessary corrections to the plan.

Any inconsistencies or omissions in a department's plan can be discovered and resolved immediately among the working participants. Just as more critical inventory items can be accounted for on a more frequent basis, so can the crucial components required for business recovery (i.e., systems and telecommunications). With the widespread use of LANs and client/server systems, information systems departments have the opportunity to work with other departments in testing their plans.

CONCLUSION

Developing a business recovery plan is not a one-time, static task. It is a process that requires the commitment and cooperation of the entire company. To perpetuate the process, business recovery planning must be a company-stipulated policy in addition to being a company-sponsored goal. Organizations must actively maintain and test plans, training their employees to respond in a crisis. The primary objective in developing a business resumption plan is to preserve the survivability of the business.

An organization's business resumption plan is an orchestrated collection of departmental responses and recovery plans. The information technology department is typically in the best position to facilitate other departments' plan development and can be particularly helpful in identifying the organization's interdepartmental information dependencies and external dependencies for information access and exchange.

A few protective security measures should be fundamental to the information technology department's plan, no matter what the scope of plausible disasters. From operational mishaps to areawide disasters, recovery planners should ensure that the information technology department's plan addresses:

- An adequate backup methodology with off-site storage.
- Sufficient physical security mechanisms for the servers and key network components.
- Sufficient logical security measures for the organization's information assets.
- Adequate LAN/WAN administration, including up-to-date inventories of equipment and software.

Finally, in support of an organization's goal to have its business resumption planning process in place to facilitate a quick response to a crisis, the plan must be sufficiently and repeatedly tested, and the key team members sufficiently trained. When testing is routine, it becomes the feedback step that keeps the plan current, the response and recovery strategies properly aligned, and the responsible team members ready to respond. Testing is the key to plan viability and thus to the ultimate survival of the business.

Chapter 39
Controlling a Multivendor Environment

Thomas Fleishman

Acquiring hardware or software systems from more than one vendor can pose significant challenges. It also has its advantages, however, not the least of which are lower cost and better service. The challenges of a multivendor environment can be managed successfully if the data center operations manager approaches them systematically. This chapter discusses these challenges and suggests practical solutions.

PROBLEMS ADDRESSED

One of the more challenging tasks facing the data center operations manager is hardware selection. The data center manager may not always initiate the decision to purchase hardware but is often responsible for selecting, implementing, and operating computing and supporting equipment. Selection can be complicated by third-party vendors that supply components that are compatible with a Central Processing Unit manufacturer's hardware. Further complications have been introduced by the advent of technology, equipment downsizing, cost pressures and the specter of outsourcing, and the maturing of client/server architectures and computing modes.

In today's computing and technical environments, hardware is rapidly becoming a commodity and cost is often the primary factor for acquisition. Because each data center has a unique environment that affects acquisition decisions, either a single-vendor or multivendor approach may be appropriate, although the single vendor environment of the past has all but disappeared, except in very rare cases. The data center manager must recognize, however, that the acquisition of equipment from multiple vendors involves significant administrative and operational challenges. The manager must develop clear policies and procedures within which the

0-8493-9989-0/99/$0.00+$.50

multivendor installation has to function. This chapter addresses some critical issues in multivendor installations.

SELECTION FACTORS

To determine whether acquiring equipment from other than a single mainframe or processor vendor is appropriate, the data center manager should consider the following factors:

- Availability. If a manufacturer does not have a particular component that is required for a specific application, equipment from another vendor may be the only alternative.
- Performance. It is possible that only one vendor's product has the capability to meet specific performance criteria for an installation.
- Reliability. With the proliferation of a broad range of equipment and vendors, the data center manager has a wide spectrum of alternatives. A specified degree of reliability (i.e., a defined mean time between component failures) may necessitate equipment purchase from a given vendor.
- Cost. Equipment from one vendor may cost less than the equivalent components offered by another. Cost is a difficult issue for managers to address because they must determine whether quality will be traded for savings, or if the introduction of yet another vendor warrants the complexities that such a move would initiate. Yet in today's environment, cost is often the primary criteria for the acquisition and the attendant complexities have to be recognized and managed.
- Equipment use and location. The data center manager must consider the environment in which the equipment will be installed. Certain equipment is manufactured to meet more stringent environmental conditions. If such conditions exist, the manager must acquire products that can operate in those conditions. The introduction of client/server computing also necessitates consideration of equipment location and system administration issues since the distribution of computing and related components may mean a less than ideal location for equipment placement; one that may be very different from the ideal environment of the "glass house".
- Ergonomics. Ergonomics is particularly important when workstations and terminals are widely used. The size, screen, keyboard, and other physical attributes of the equipment should be considered in an acquisition decision.

TRADE-OFFS

The data center manager must consider whether equipment from a variety of vendors meets the performance levels established for equipment currently in the data center and assess the risks of installing equipment that does not meet such service levels. For example, replacing disk drives in an online environment entails a significantly higher risk than exchanging tape or cartridge units. The data center manager may not be willing—or even able—to accept the risk of a vendor's equipment not performing at required levels. The cost savings must be significant enough to offset the risks and the potential expense of backup measures that may be necessary, especially as the growth of online systems and the dependence on the availability of automated systems is an increasing reality in the current, very competitive business environment, where an hour of system outage can cost anywhere from several hundred dollars to upwards of $100,000, dependent upon the organization and the application.

Fitting the Current Configuration

Equipment supplies by a new vendor must function in the installation's current configuration. In one data center that acquired a new printer, preinstallation testing showed that the printer could not handle all the special and multipart forms required by users. The printer worked well on some forms but not on others. In other instances, the performance of disk drives was outstanding in installations that had relatively low transaction volumes and data seek activities but substantially below required service levels in very high volume, transaction intensive environments.

Quality of Service

The data center manager must investigate a vendor's ability to provide and sustain acceptable levels of service. Before making such an assessment, the manager should establish internal tracking criteria based on the requirements of the installation. These criteria might include:

- Response time. What is the average time that a vendor requires to respond to a service call? Is the vendor willing to commit to such response contractually? Is the vendor willing to partner with the organization and share in the cost impact of outages caused by the vendor's equipment or poor service?
- Repair. What is the average repair time for a given component?
- Resource availability. Does the vendor provide resources (e.g., technical specialists) in a timely manner?
- Incidence recurrence. If a specific component develops problems, is it fixed on the first service call or is it necessary to recall the customer engineer?
- Dispatch location. Where is the service location from which the repair resource is dispatched? Is the parts depot in the same location?If not, where is it located? How many parts depots does the vendor have?Where is it in proximity to the data center?

- Management attention. In case of serious or recurring problems, does the vendor's management volunteer assistance?
- Escalation procedures. Are clearly established escalation procedures in place in case of extended problem resolution?

Custom Engineering

In a multivendor installation, the level and quality of support from the manufacturer largely determines the success of failure of the installation in terms of equipment performance. The data center manager should initially establish whether the manufacturer can provide:

- On-site support. Will a vendor's customer engineers be on site, or will they be dispatched from a central service depot?
- Continuity. Will the same customer engineers provide support on most occasions, or will they be randomly assigned from a branch or regional pool?
- Experience. Do the supporting customer engineers have proven and demonstrable experience with the type of installation and configuration represented by the organization's data center?
- Customer engineer support organization. Are the customer engineers employees of the equipment manufacturer, or are they employed by a third-party maintenance organization contracted to provide service support? And if it is a third-party service contractor, is their compensation partially based on defined performance levels or do they get compensated strictly on a time and material basis?
- Parts. Are parts locally stored in case of hardware failures that require part exchanges, or will there be potential shipping delays in procuring the necessary items from distant warehouses?

The lack of timely availability of a customer engineer or a critical part can be extremely damaging to an installation's performance. The data center manager should address these issues before the acquisition of equipment. Clearly stated expectations, policies, provisions, and, if possible, contractual guarantees and penalties should be established with the vendor to minimize problems or to allow the organization to speedily withdraw from the agreement without financial consequences.

For example, one vendor acknowledged that the usual repair support that accompanied equipment purchase was minimal and that timely response could not, and would not, be guaranteed. The vendor did, however, offer an alternative maintenance service contract at additional cost, guaranteeing customer engineer arrival at an installation within two hours. In this case, the data center manager was sufficiently impressed with the vendor's equipment to acquire it and pay the higher maintenance charges to obtain guaranteed service.

In another case, the data center manager found a third-party service organization had been contracted to support a hardware configuration for a critical application. Although the vendor agreed to certain service requirements, the organization actually performing the maintenance service was not committed to providing the necessary levels of support. Only after lengthy negotiations and considerable expense was the data center manager able to achieve the service agreements that were required, and he had to do so at significant additional cost.

Financial Status of the Vendor

The data center manager must evaluate the financial condition of all prospective vendors and decide whether they have the proper resources to provide the necessary support and service for the equipment. If the acquisition is sufficiently large in terms of price, or if the equipment being considered is sufficiently strategic, the organization should consider requesting a Dun & Bradstreet analysis of the vendor before concluding any contractual commitments.

Contractual Considerations

The organization might also want to specify certain performance and service criteria for inclusion in the acquisition contract. These criteria can range from service response times to detailed availability targets. Specifically, financial penalties or component replacement may be defined for failure to meet contractual requirements. All contractual demands should be negotiated by legal representatives for the vendor and the organization. The degree of cooperation shown by the vendor during negotiations is an indicator of what the data center manager can expect after the equipment is installed.

MONITORING THE VENDOR

The data center manager must establish objectives for equipment performance and service support before evaluating vendor products. Establishing benchmarks and tracking component performance are two generally accepted methods of evaluation. This is especially critical in today's dynamic computing and business environments, where systems are often supporting mission critical, strategic organizational objectives.

Benchmarks

Before equipment is acquired, the data center staff should become familiar with the vendor's hardware and its specifications to establish performance benchmarks. Benchmarks are important for assessing whether the equipment is meeting its specified capabilities and whether the vendor is complying with the requirements in the installation agreement. The benchmarks should not only address the specific equipment performance, but if possible, such performance should be benchmarked in the environment into which the product will be incorporated, so that the equipment performance benchmark includes interfaces to other equipment residing in the data center and where possible, stress testing of the equipment with the volumes of transactions it will be expected to execute.

Component Performance Tracking

The need to establish an organizational unit responsible for tracking the performance of hardware components is becoming increasingly accepted. Studies conducted in several installations of varying size indicate that component tracking results in a significant payoff. Because a faulty piece of equipment often causes several repetitive and subsequent failures or system degradations, the ability to quickly detect and possibly isolate a faulty device through component failure analysis is a valuable tool for maintaining required customer service.

Component tracking can be used to establish a comparative rating system to help the data center manager determine which vendors provide satisfactory service. Tracking can be performed manually (operations personnel complete incident or trouble reports that are transmitted to an employee who compiles the data and issues a periodic report) or through an automated tracking and reporting system. Because manual tracking is cumbersome, inefficient, and expensive, especially in large data centers, automated tracking and reporting systems are preferable. These packages can be developed or acquired, depending on the capabilities of the staff and the requirements of the particular installation.

As an example, one automated tracking system provides a daily report on all failures (both hardware and software) of each major component in the data center. Each month, the vendor that markets the tracking package provides a comprehensive database compiled from data supplied by all installation's subscribing to the service. The database indicates an installation's performance relative to that of other centers using the same configuration and brand of equipment. For example, if a center has Central Processing Unit A with disk drive B installed and 12 other centers use the same CPU and disk configuration, the monthly report shows a performance ranking for all 13 subscribers. For the data center manager to affectively control a multivendor environment, such a system is mandatory, especially in large, multiple CPU installations.

Communication Among Vendors

To maintain smooth operations in a multivendor environment, the data center manager (or a member of the operations staff) must coordinate communication among vendors. Problems that involve more than one vendor occur frequently because vendors are competing in an active market that does not encourage intercommunications.

Some managers hold weekly meetings of all vendor representatives who have major equipment components in the data center. Even when there are no specific problems, these meetings are valuable in maintaining open channels of communication among the vendors represented in the particular installation.

The issue of communication between vendors, and the management of the process cannot be over emphasized. Even if a data center manager is fortunate enough to have a relatively small number of vendors represented in the shop, this situation will change. The advent of technology is such that vendors who previously were able to lock in a customer with proprietary products can no longer enjoy such luxuries. Open systems make equipment interchangeability not only a reality but a necessity, because open systems are competitive and are becoming commodities that are marketed more on price than on functionality. This marketing strategy is dramatically opposite to what occurs in the proprietary, or closed, system environment.

The advent of open systems brings with it the reality that nearly all shops of any significant size will be multivendor installations and therefore the management of vendors will be a critical skill and success factor for the data center manager.

CASE STUDY

The following case study presents an overview of the problems faced by one data center manager in a multivendor installation.

The manager was under considerable pressure to reduce equipment costs. He assessed the installation and decided that significant cost reduction could be realized by replacing 24 disk spindle that had been acquired from the manufacturer of the Central Processing Unit that was installed at the facility.

The manager contacted several disk drive vendors and leasing companies and, after a period of evaluation, decided to replace the 24 spindles for an approximate annual savings of $73,000. The spindles were acquired on a three-year lease. Shortly after the replacement, it became evident that the acquisition of the new devices was a mistake.

Although the disk manufacturer had an impressive facility and was supplying thousands of units worldwide, the product was relatively new to a large-scale, 24-hour-a-day, high transaction volume, online business environment. Because the support organization was poorly trained, with no prior exposure to the CPU manufacturer's equipment, diagnosing problems was extremely time-consuming, and because CPU-device interfaces were not well understood, communication between the disk and CPU vendors was nearly impossible. No repair personnel were permanently assigned to the data center's account and trouble calls became exasperating as clusters of inexperienced and poorly trained staff tried to resolve problems, while major online systems remained unavailable to users, resulting in losses of thousands of dollars for every minute the systems were down.

After several months, the equipment appeared to stabilize, but the data center began to experience serious channel interface problems. Much of the data center manager's time was spent mediating between the CPU and disk vendors, neither of whom was willing to accept responsibility for the problem. As the interface problems were resolved, the incidence of head crashes increased dramatically. It took approximately four months to trace the problem to some foam-rubber-seal insulation which was disintegrating and contaminating the drives, subsequently causing head crashes.

After assessing the overall situation, the data center manager decided to absorb the penalty in the lease contract and replaced the disks at a cost of $27,000. (The penalty had been agreed to during the contract negotiations as a contingency escape arrangement.)

The disk manufacturer was only partially at fault for marketing a device that was not fully tested and for not planning and staffing a support organization of trained personnel required to service the product. The data center manager was also negligent in failing to perform an indepth evaluation of a new product that was being introduced into a critical business situation. With a project plan outlining specific, clearly defined performance objectives, the manager might have deferred or completely avoided purchasing the product in question. After contacting other installations, the data center manager learned that these problems had also been experienced, in varying degrees, by other users.

SOFTWARE VENDORS

Data center management is also becoming more complex as a result of the increased number of software packages available on the market. A turn-key package may be acquired as an integrated system that requires specific equipment that may or may not be compatible with the existing mainframe configuration; or the software may be acquired to process a specific application (e.g., payroll, general ledger, accounts payable) on the mainframe.

The issues described in connection with hardware vendors remain relevant to a multiple software vendor environment. The data center manager must implement formal procedures and tools to collect performance data on the vendor's products and institute communication processes that allow the multivendor environment to be managed effectively.

This is becoming especially true as smaller minicomputer and microcomputer systems spread throughout user areas, as well as in the data center, as part of the client/server computing evolution. Further complexities are being introduced into the data center by the slowly disappearing delineation between information and communications technologies. These factors, along with the development of complex technologies and products, have led to a situation that essentially precludes the ability to maintain a single-vendor environment. The data center manager must confront the realities of today's information technology industry; the proliferation of software, hardware, and service vendors will not only continue, but inevitably increase.

RECOMMENDED COURSE OF ACTION

The installation of hardware and software from multiple vendors is often justified by cost, performance, and availability. As plug-compatible equipment and purchased software continue to proliferate, the process of managing the multivendor environment becomes more complex and difficult.

The data center manager should approach the multivendor installation by considering the risk/benefit trade-offs in the context of the data center environment. Establishing a project plan that details equipment and software performance and support should be mandatory. If possible, contractual contingency arrangements should be specified and agreed to by all parties concerned before the installation or implementation of the vendor's product.

One way to carry out a multivendor installation plan is to develop a checklist similar to the following:

- Objectives to be achieved through a third-party vendor include:
  - —Performance (e.g., the vendor may be the only source meeting requirements).
  - —Cost (i.e., costs are reduced or benefits per unit cost are enhanced through third-party purchase).
  - —Environment (e.g., there are strict constraints in the operational setting that must be accommodated).
- A review of the performance history of the vendor should include:
  - —Reference checks of current and past customers.
  - —The performance history of the specific product being considered.
- A review of the financial status of the vendor should include:
  - —Financial performance history and trends.
  - —Installation base trends.
  - —Market penetration in comparison with competitors.

  - —Privately owned or publicly financed.
  - —Size in annual revenues and profits.
  - —Debt-to-equity position.
  - —Ability to withstand short-term financial setbacks.
- A review of the installed base of the vendor should cover the following:
  - —The number of customer services.
  - —The location of the customer base.
  - —The rate of new customer acquisition.
  - —The rate of existing customer defection.
- A risk analysis should be carried out that considers:
  - —The impact on the procuring organization if the vendor cannot perform as expected.
  - —Contingency plans for vendor replacement.
  - —Adequate and appropriate contractual protection in case of bankruptcy.
  - —Unchallenged use of the product.
  - —A statement of fair value purchase price for bankruptcy trustee.
- A review of vendor management should include:
  - —Whether the organization is managed by the owner or professionally managed by a nonowner.
  - —Tenure of management.
  - —Management turnover history.
  - —Management remuneration plan (e.g., is a percentage of management's annual compensation incentive based?).

That is a short but representative list of issues to consider in any vendor relationship, particularly in a third-party vendor arrangement.

Chapter 40
The Help Desk in a Distributed Environment

John L. Connor

A help desk is a data center's contact point with its customers. If customers are dissatisfied with the help desk, they are probably also dissatisfied with the data center. This chapter explains why many help desks have not been as successful as their customers would like and discusses ways data center managers can build successful help desks in a distributed client/server environment.

INTRODUCTION

Help desks were originally implemented because there were too many customer calls for the data center to handle. There were too many problems and too little problem-solving time. A help desk consolidated, recorded, and tracked problems. However, help desks were typically set up without goals and objectives and with a minimal investment in training and tools.

This chapter examines what can be done to improve your help desk operations and how traditional technology management—the acquisition by vertical specialization of such tools and product knowledge as MVS, Canadian Independent Computing Services Association, and DB2—fails to satisfy the requirements of a help desk operating in a client/server or distributed environment. The chapter also examines the requirements and tools for a help desk to function successfully in a rapidly changing environment.

THE EVOLUTION OF THE HELP DESK

Historically, data center customers have had their problems solved more by luck and perseverance. Exhibit 1 shows that as newer technologies have emerged the level of problem calls to the data center has

0-8493-9989-0/99/$0.00+$.50

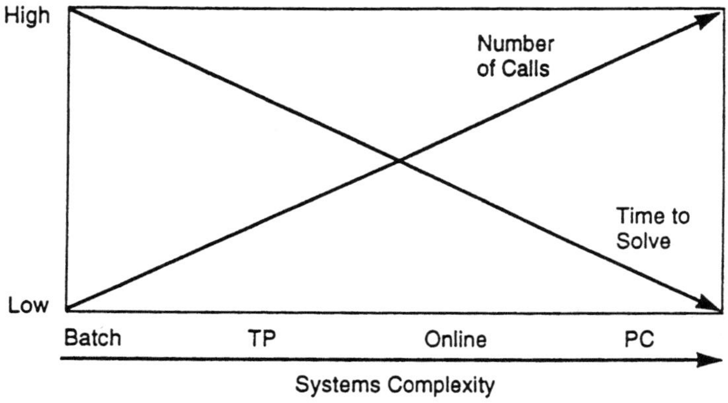

Exhibit 1. Progression of customer calls to the help desk.

increased but the time available for solving these problems has decreased. This situation more than any reason triggered the rise of help desks.

Companies created help desks out of necessity. They found themselves having to support systems and products that were becoming more and more complex and increasingly critical to their survival.

The first step in creating help desks was to have programmers support systems, because they were the only one who understood the systems. The programmers did not have, however, the right people skills and often annoyed customers. They were replaced by professional help desk personnel, who had terrific people skills but were usually clueless about systems. Support became friendly but shallow. A help desk was a place for customer to call to get somebody to call somebody else who could help. This arrangement was not terribly efficient.

Reasons for forming a help desk included:

- Too many customers for the data center to handle.
- Too many problems to be solved.
- Many simple problems to be solved.
- Less time to solve problems.
- Vendors needed central problem management.
- Sharp increase in customer complaints.
- Help desks became a trend.

However, many help desks just happened to be formed because one person or section was delegated to answer calls from customers as the volume grew.

From these murky beginnings, the help desk began to emerge-complete with the poor reputation of many IS departments. As a result of their origins, many help desks were poorly planned and were not as successful as they could have been. Other reason for lack of success included:

- No terms of reference (i.e., goals and objectives).
- No customer consultation.
- Inadequate staff training.
- Poor help desk launch.
- Lack of management support.
- Low investment.
- Poor staffing.
- Low profile factor.
- Lack of tools.

Changing User Requirements

The questions and expectations users have of a help desk have changed dramatically. Users once called a help desk to ask how to do certain function with a product. Now, they want to know how to put a specific item into a specific spreadsheet in a certain document, manipulate it, insert it in a memo, distribute it to five people, get approval, print the document, and distribute it to their customers.

Questions to help desks are getting more complex. What do callers to the help desk ask about? According to a recent survey by the Help Desk Institute, callers to help desks ask about the following:

- Appliances: 36%
- Hardware: 21%
- Data communications: 21%
- Miscellaneous services: 16%
- Voice communications: 3%

The danger is that customers are gradually getting used to and accepting a lower level of support. They have already grown accustomed to having their phone calls answered by a recording. They are getting used to listening to recordings and pressing buttons to navigate through automatic call directors to get to real people who can answer their questions. Is this an efficient way to solve the help desk issues?

The answer is no. There must be a greater emphasis on customer service. Callers should be able to expect help desk staff to solve their problems. However, that means that the people who fill help desk slots must have in-depth knowledge of multiple platforms, software tools, and applications. It is not a matter of technology, it is whether technology if effectively used, and that requires a well-trained staff who can use automated tools to answer their customers' questions.

THE ROLE OF A HELP DESK

Often there are two areas in a IS organization that have responsibility for managing a company's computers. In this chapter they are called:

- The bridge. The replacement for the old-style operations area.
- The help desk or service center. The new proactive, service-oriented replacement for the old-style help desk.

A pitfall in setting up a bridge function is that the expertise of a typical computer department is focused on a number telephones. It is surprising how quickly users learn these strategic telephone numbers and call bridge operators for a considered opinion or advice. Many data centers have effectively implemented integrated, host-based automation, and a single bridge operator may control from one automated console 5 to 20 MVS systems and a multitude of subsystems. Because of this operator's scope of responsibility, these telephone calls can be very distracting. Distractions in the bridge area and their impact on productivity and efficiency are often seriously underestimated.

Because of these distractions, many data centers have set up their help desk facilities along with the bridge area. The actual location is not as important as a help desk's providing an effective level of service, thereby, relieving the bridge of user contact and first level problem diagnosis.

In a fully automated data center, a help desk assumes many functions of operations and operators have become service managers. Therefore, help desk staffers must know the working of the systems they manage. Detailed information on physical links, networks, and installed equipment is important to help desk workers; they need to be fully conversant with the complete operation, in most cases even more so than bridge personnel.

A help desk, like a bridge, relies on concise information being displayed accurately and as required. Without this capability, a help desk will lose credibility with users. But how many installations provide their help desks with this kind of support? Not enough, if the consensus of user opinion on the effectiveness of their IS department is to be believed.

User Attitudes Toward Help Desks

The attitudes of help desk users are likely to differ from the attitudes of help desk staffers, and management should know the feelings of help desk customers. An organization should know the attitude of users to their help desk. A help desk's profile must be generally raised to a higher level if the help desk is to get the support it needs from management and its clients.

In general, a low profile is a direct result of how help desks evolved, which was described in a previous section.

Failure to understand the current level of appreciation jeopardized any attempt to improve a help desk's profile and image. The success of a help desk depends on its staff knowing what its customers want.

A Traditional Help Desk

To define how help desk should now be, it is worthwhile to review how requirements for a help desk were defined a few years ago.

Senior management in a typical organization originally determined that it help desk staff should possess the following:

- Understanding of data processing terminology.
- Perseverance for tracking down responsibilities.
- Ability to troubleshoot problems.
- Understanding of a computer resources team.
- Ability to interact with people.

The basic job responsibilities were defined as following:

- Answering calls for help from users.
- Solving problems when possible.
- Referring calls for further action.
- Logging activities.
- Reporting activities.

On the basis of these job requirements, it seems that what IS organizations wanted as recently as 1989 was to staff their help desks with people who could take calls and look at problems. Problem solving was not high on the list. Companies have been rebuilding elaborate telephone systems, call management systems and problem management tools to accomplish an impossible task: enabling people to support technology they do not understand.

Evolution of Problem Tracking Systems

Originally, help desk staffers would solve problems if they could. Otherwise, they wrote down the pertinent information called the appropriate support person, and passed the information along. Once they passed the information on, there was no record of who called, what the problems was, or who was handling it. Problems with this method include the following.

- No statistics
- Lost information.
- Inability to handle multiple problems from one cause.
- Single problem solved multiple times.

- Poor service management.
- Slow or ineffective call referral.

Thus, problem tracking systems came about. These systems allow a help desk staff person to enter on a screen all pertinent information about a call by just filling in the blanks. The reporting components of these packages can produce a wide variety of statistical information. However, entering information and monitoring results are still manual processes.

HELP DESKS IN A DISTRIBUTED ENVIRONMENT

For years there has been the need for help desks to be proactive. However, this requirement to be proactive has been narrowly defined as reacting to problems in existing systems. To be proactive simply meant to solve problems with the existing technology infrastructure before users had to call the help desk. Is this being proactive? It is improvement, but the focus is still on problem resolution rather than prevention.

To be truly proactive, a help desk must go beyond supporting existing systems and look at the needs of its customers. They must get involved at a much earlier stage and must:

- Assess customer needs.
- Select applications required to satisfy those needs.
- Supervise the installation of new applications.
- Train customers how to use new applications.
- Ensure that the necessary knowledge is delivered effectively to users.
- Resolve problems.

These are not the activities of a typical help desk, which focuses almost exclusively on reactively solving problems. A help desk should perform its traditional role of problem resolution, but its primary role should be that of a customer advocate. Not only should a help desk act as a customer advocate, it should also proactively work to avoid calls from customers. A help desk must solve problems through education, support, and effective knowledge bases to eliminate problems before they happen.

New Role of Help Desks

The roles of a new help desk or service center are still evolving, but will likely include the following:

- Assuring overall productivity of customers.
- Overseeing the Quality Of Service provided to customers.
- Functioning as a customer advocate.
- Maintaining and distributing knowledge bases needed by customers.
- Providing support for existing applications.

A powerful reason for changing a help desk's mission are the changes happening in corporate computing today. The days of monolithic mainframe-based data processing departments are gone, and more important, so is the organizational structure that grew up around it. Today's information systems are evolving into a state of centralized decentralization.

Need for central control. Although networked systems are taking over, companies need a single organization to monitor and access the needs of customers and to act as customers' advocate for providing technology. A help desk staffer's job is more substantive and demanding than ever before, but an effective help desk analyst must understand mainframe hardware and software, operating systems, subsystems, personal computers, and applications, and company practices. Help desks continue to suffer from a poor image, which hampers recruitment efforts.

Also, as the responsibilities of a help desk change in an organization so will its role. More and more, a help desk will report to the president or chief information officer (CIO) rather than to the IS organization.

Tools Required for a Distributed Environment

Today's help desk is the starting point for creating tomorrow's customer-oriented service center. An important question is "How are these new service centers supported through current tools?" Most tools available today are for a reactive help desk. They do not provide the capabilities necessary for proactive support. Many are little more than a place to keep notes about a problem; these products are often called *information management* or *problem entry systems.* They will not suffice for tomorrow's service center.

Most people immediately think of software or hardware when they think of tools for an IS environment. In this case, however, it also means effective people skills. Many individuals in a help desk do not have the basic skills or personal tools to make a service center concept work. However, these skills can be learned. Skills needed for a successful service center include:

- Effective and active listening
- Knowing which types of questions to ask.
- Understanding problem solving by removing assumptions.
- Information gathering.
- Recognizing a problem.
- Knowing and applying problem-solving processes.
- Assessing problems and sorting facts from expectations.
- Decision making(i.e., judgmental versus rational decisions).
- Being able to apply and follow corrective, adaptive, interim, or procedural courses of action.

Centralization and Distribution

A centralized-distributed approach is needed for allocating the tools required for acquiring the skills needed for tomorrow's help desk. Management tasks will be physically distributed but be under central management. Thus, an organization will be able to manage enterprise computing from one central location but still will have distributed agents on local platforms.

For example, a central help desk may be located in headquarters in Dallas and management sites may be located at offices in London, New York, Tokyo, and Chicago. Each management site manages its portion of the enterprise, but they would all be under the direction of the Dallas based headquarters and follow the same standards.

A centralized-distributed help desk system is too complex for the tools of one vender to handle. Previously, a multivendor environment meant one vendor for the tape system, and one vendor for the disk drives. Now more vendors than that are required for the inside of a single PC. Enterprise computing comes in a kit.

Exhibit 2 shows the enterprise kit implemented for a help desk. Various tools are integrated into a central help desk management tool. From one location and one display, all pieces of information needed to manage and solve customers problems are available. When a call comes from a user, a help desk staffer can call up and display the user's configuration from a Configuration Management tool and continue talking to the user. The information collected from the user is entered in the information management system for future reference and problem management.

Choosing Tools

The following steps can help an organization determine which tools are needed for a new help desk. This is an important step in the process of developing a new help desk or service center. It is inadvisable to rush into acquiring technology without proper planning.

- Taking a before picture. Measure the performance of the current help desk operation. This is necessary to calculate the effect of the support technology and help justify expenditures.
- Become an internal salesperson. Management must be convinced of the need and value of the support technology. The cost savings should be calculated and presented.
- Performing a needs analysis. No assumptions should be made about how the current help desk functions. A flow chart must be made to explain every business process and how data is accessed, collected, and passed on at each step. Attention must be paid to steps and data that will not be required once new support technology is implemented.

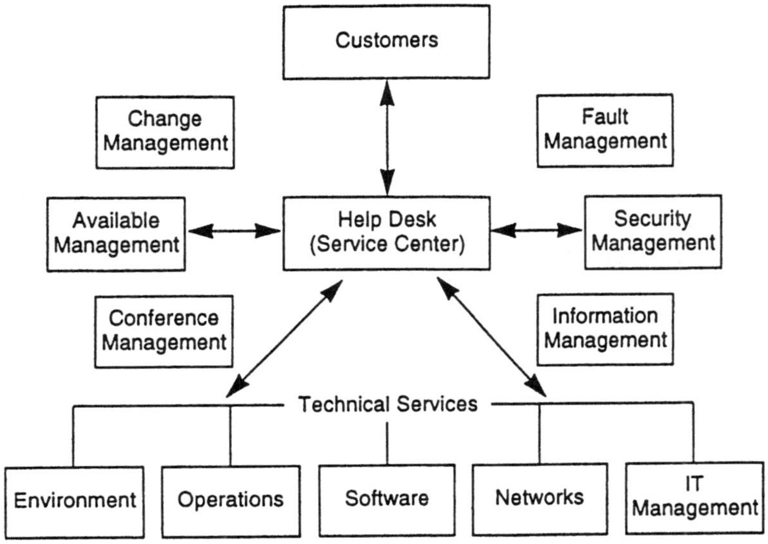

Exhibit 2. The help desk in a distributed environment.

- Having a systemwide strategy. Such a strategy is a comprehensive blueprint and timetable for implementing new technology on different platforms and collecting information. This strategy must consider both the IS and the business plans for the entire company as well as customers' expectations.
- Asking vendors for help. Vendors can be useful in conducting a needs analysis and preparing a systems strategy. Late in the process, specific products can be measured against a Request For Proposal.
- Testing your RFP. Many people just copy down product specifications or features from vendors' marketing literature. A better approach is to ask vendors how their product solves specific problems. Those who draft the request for proposal (RFP) should try to answer the request for proposal (RFP) before they distribute it. This helps ensure that the request for proposal (RFP) actually asks for the information needed. This information is most often used to justify the expenditure of a significant sum of money.

Gathering Requirements Tools

What are the characteristics of the tools needed to renovate a help desk? Key points to investigate are discussed in the following sections.

Designed for automation. Computers can detect and resolve problems much faster than people. Local tools should filter out problems that can be corrected at the local level to reduce network traffic. The tools must be able to pass information back and forth. For example, if a minicomputer system is having a problem, the monitoring tools for that minicomputer passes only the required information to a central facility that help desk personnel monitor.

Designed for end-to-end processes. The help desk staffers need to see what a customer sees and that means enabling them to view information from the customer's terminal or PC. Too often, tools are purchased by vertical specialty (e.g., for MVS, Canadian Independent Computing Services Association, Internet Multicasting Service, database 2, Wide Area Network, LAN, or minicomputer). Tools purchased in this manner do an excellent job of managing the specific vertical specialty, but they only work for a vertical tower. They cannot detect a hardware or minicomputer problem causing a service problem.

Customers' applications do not run in vertical trenches; they run across various platforms. Help desk tools must provide a view consistent with what a customer sees across all platforms. One example why vertical tools do not work any more is found in the operations of a circa-1989 help desk. For example, when a typical customer in 1989 phoned in a response problem, help desk personnel looked at the remote 3274, the modems, the Fractional T1, the 3745, and the host application and quickly found the fault (e.g., a bad modem). This situation has changed. For example, when a customer today calls a help desk about a response problem, help desk personnel may not be able to find a problem and log the call as no trouble found. The problem could not be found because the customer is connected to a LAN, which is connected to a campus Ethernet backbone, which is hooked to a local Asynchronous Transfer Mode switch, which has a gateway on to a WAN system, which is mixed into a T3 circuit across to the 3745and then to the host application.

This example illustrates two important facts. First, the level of expertise needed by help desk staff to solve problems has increased. Second, vertically specialized tools cannot solve such a problem. The solution requires tools that span vertical trenches.

Exploiting the network. There is a wealth of information from the various network managers that are installed in an enterprise IS organization. This information needs to be integrated and correlated with the other service or platform information so that a true picture of the cause of a service problem can be identified.

Shared databases. The various users of help desk tools must be able to share information. A specific local problem may need to be passed to the central help desk if it has not been serviced in the appropriate time frame.

If enterprise problems should be located in one database, why can they not be located in the help desk's management system as well? Technical services or support staff must be notified of problems and locations. Help desk staff needs up to the minute status on the state of a problem.

Capturing data and solving problems as close to the source as possible. An organization must be careful about the amount of service management information it paces on a network. A network can be overloaded. By installing appropriate platform tools, local help desk services can manage their respective platforms and when there is an unsolvable problem, only pertinent information is forwarded to a centralized help facility.

Such an arrangement allows an organization to select the best tools for managing various platforms. As an example, if there is an MVS system, then an MVS automation tool would manage all except the most difficult problems. Perhaps an MVS problem is caused by a minicomputer node failure. The MVS automation tool can never know such information. However, by forwarding the problem from the MVS tool to a central help desk facility, it can be integrated with enterprise information from other tools and be output to a service display showing what the problem is and who is affected by the failure.

Multiple levels of control. With the capability to design a hierarchical structure of workstations for help desk staff, a manager or supervisor can monitor workstations, assign problems to each, and monitor elapsed time to completion. Complex problems can be shared among staff members and workstations.

The Help Desk's View

Exhibit 3 illustrates how automated help desk tools should look to help desk personnel. The exhibit also lists several specific characteristics of a central management tool that integrates all specific platform information from distributed tools, takes automatic action where appropriate, and correlates various sources of information into a coherent display for the help desk staff.

The tool proposed in Exhibit 3 is specifically designed for a multivendor environment. It allows help desk personnel to see the state of the entire enterprise at a single glance on a single workstation display screen. The entire enterprise can be managed from the data center to the networks and distributed systems and client/server applications that span technology platforms.

The enterprise is an easy concept to understand. However, when it comes to implementing systems management tools within the enterprise, issues can be confusing. Management of enterprise systems requires that

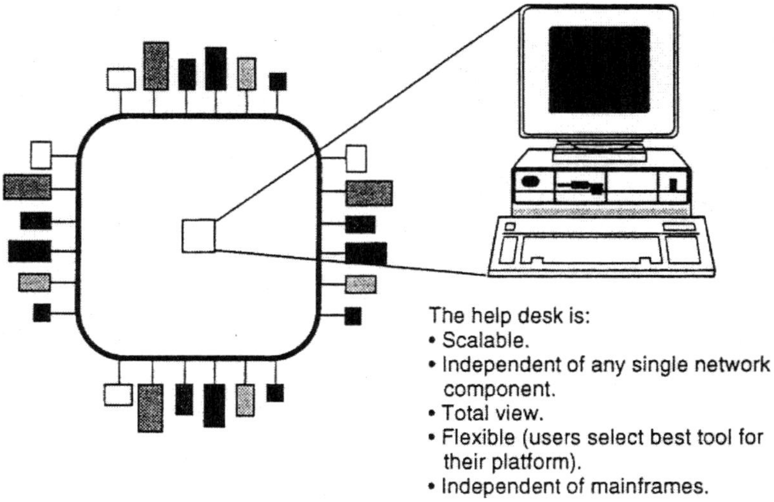

Exhibit 3. Help desk's view of itself in a distributed environment.

data center managers disassociate their thinking from traditional resource management. The tools' real targets are the services provided to customers (i.e., applications, individual sessions, or transactions).

Effective enterprise management systems must span the entire organization. A help desk staffer should be able to see instantly from a single workstation a component failure anywhere in the enterprise. Then, the help desk staffer should be able to select the next level of display for more detailed information and instantly select the appropriate tool to identify, diagnose, repair, reset, or dispatch the problem.

CONCLUSION

A help desk is the interface to the data center that customers see. To a customer, a poor help desk usually means a poor data center. An organization's help desk can always improve. All help desk personnel must understand the strategic importance of their contribution to the success of not only the data center but the entire enterprise.

The success or failure of a help desk ultimately depends on its staff's skills. Therefore, help desk staffers must be experts. Also, an organization should anticipate the transition to enterprise management (i.e., a distributed environment). When building service management tools for a help desk, an organization must design end-to-end solutions. And finally, it must always choose tools that make use of automated processes.

Chapter 41
Job Scheduling in the Open Systems Environment

Randy Keck

Administering and supporting job scheduling has been complicated by the drive toward open systems, which often include client/server architectures. When evaluating job-scheduling software, the data center manager must examine such issues as centralized vs. decentralized computing, high-availability requirements, and mission-critical work loads. Only after the data center manager addresses these issues can an organization be positioned to perform the in-depth software evaluation needed to successfully implement job scheduling within an open systems environment.

INTRODUCTION

Companies that are beginning their investigation into open systems software tools can count on two truths. First, no matter what platforms organizations choose for an open-systems strategy, many of the basic systems software products that are now in place to enable past legacy systems' strategies remain in operation. Job-scheduling products, for example, will still be required to schedule daily, monthly, and quarterly runs within batch window, and organizations will continue to rely on chargeback products to charge out and isolate their costs.

Second, the mode of implementation that systems software has followed in the past will need to change as a direct result of open systems. Client/server architectures, for example, will be needed to provide the flexibility required to align system software requirements with the open systems strategy. In addition, the implementation of systems software will mirror the open-ended computing resources and the administrative and support policies that the software will control. In essence, the very nature of open systems will increase the need for effective connectivity and communications more than ever before. As a result, systems software options

0-8493-9989-0/99/$0.00+$.50

will be required to support the increased demand for both remote execution and the centralized-vs.-decentralized policies that companies will establish to control work load execution.

Job scheduling is a prime example of systems software that will closely follow the path of any open systems strategies. The need to automate the timing, sequence, and selection of work loads during background processing remains one of the top systems software requirements in open systems. However, the approach of open systems requires that job-scheduling policies and implementation schemes be based on the computing environment, along with the mission-critical status of each job. This situation requires every organization to examine such fundamental questions as:

- What are the benefits of a client/server implementation?
- What options are available to meet centralized-vs.-decentralized computing requirements?
- How will the job-scheduling environment be integrated with other systems
- What are the mission-critical availability requirements of each work load?

Only after these issues have been addressed can an organization be positioned to perform the in-depth software evaluation needed to successfully implement job scheduling within an open systems environment.

CLIENT/SERVER: A PREREQUISITE FOR FLEXIBILITY

In terms of job scheduling, a true client/server architecture provides flexible and independent choices for administering, supporting, and executing job-scheduling work loads. This flexibility results in a job-scheduling architecture that can be adapted to virtually every organization's computing framework (See Exhibit 1).

With a true client/server architecture, autonomy can be reached among the points of control on which personnel rely and the points of execution available within an enterprise. This flexibility translates into software that can complement and grow with the behavior of any given environment. The implementation of a client/server architecture must take into consideration the centralized-vs.-decentralized nature of a company's operating environment and the policies that underline its decisions.

CENTRALIZED VS. DECENTRALIZED COMPUTING

Too often, the terms *centralized* and *decentralized* are used without any consideration for the differences between work load execution or for the roles involved in the administration and support of each work load. Decisions about the centralized or decentralized nature of work load

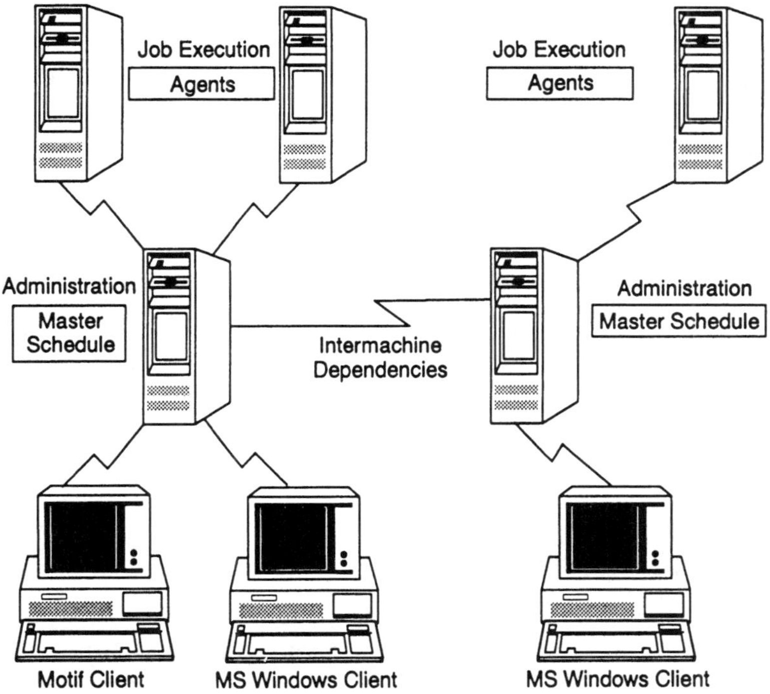

Exhibit 1. The client/server architecture in job-scheduling work loads.

processing should be based on an entirely different set of criteria from decisions about administration and support functions.

Judgments related to the centralized or decentralized nature of work load processing are based on multiple limiting factors, including:

- Network and machine availability
- Platform dependencies
- Application and file location

In the open systems arena, when multiple machines are available to meet the same set of application requirements each job can be centrally administered through a master copy of the schedule, but must be targeted for execution to a remote agent machine based on its platform, application, and file dependency requirements. Actual execution is determined by the availability of the network, machines, and processing loads that are factored into each machine. The degree of remote activity that is associated with a work load should also take into account the mission-critical nature of the application and the level of faults that it must be able to tolerate. Therefore, certain scheduled jobs may need to be run on the same machine as a master schedule to protect against unplanned problems, such as a network failure.

Decisions regarding work load administration are, in contrast to work load processing, based on such criteria as administrative convenience and departmental access to machines. Central access to one master copy of a job schedule, for example, may be considered more convenient than having central access to many schedules located on multiple machines. The inability to tolerate network faults, however, may take precedence over any level of perceived convenience.

Finally, decisions regarding general support closely reflect a company's testing vs. production policies and its software integration requirements. Once an application is in production, for example, a requirement to manage and integrate all systems software through a single network console may dictate the need to support scheduling requirements for the application centrally.

INTEGRATING SYSTEMS SOFTWARE

In nearly every software market niche, product solutions fall into one of two categories. Point solutions traditionally represent products that deliver immediate value by forming best-of-breed solutions for very specific industry needs. Integrated solutions, on the other hand, represent products that generate increased value as they are combined with other products to meet a more generalized market requirement. Point solutions have often remained separate from integrated solutions because each type of solution is often platform dependent, and integration depends on suite-solution purchases from a single vendor. Unfortunately, organizations have been unable to capitalize on the flexibility, timeliness, and best-of-breed characteristics associated with point solutions, while obtaining the look and feel similarity among products that are integrated under one architecture.

Open-Ended Console Management

With the advent of the open systems and PC markets, data center managers are learning that integration can, in fact, be achieved through open-ended frameworks and adherence to *de facto* standards in such areas as networking. In the Unix market, for example, open-ended console management frameworks have been developed by hardware and software vendors to provide an integration scheme that can be shared by any software solution. Such hardware vendors as IBM and Hewlett-Packard have introduced frameworks with NetView and OpenView respectively, whereas such system software vendors as Boole & Babbage have launched integration schemes through such products as Ensign and Command Post. All of these

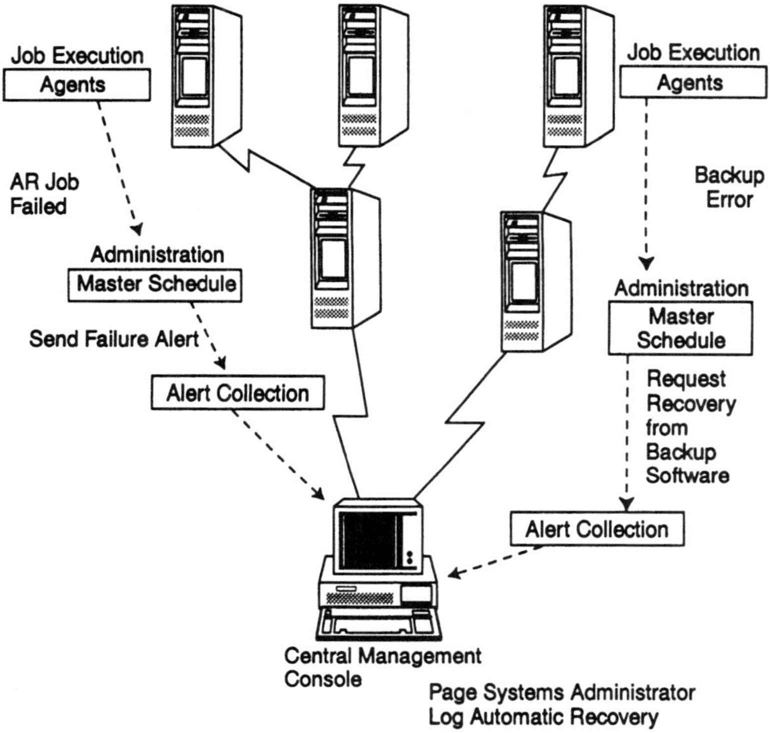

Exhibit 2. Open-ended console management frameworks.

products share the theme of extending a common look and feel to best-of-breed point solutions.

Open-ended console management frameworks not only act as a single point of reference for systems software solutions but also facilitate how the information is routed to end users (see Exhibit 2). Job schedulers, for example, can provide critical job status on an exception basis through alert management schemes. From a networking standpoint, the SNMP protocol has become the *de facto* standard for communicating system and job status information among alert managers and the console management framework. In addition to the SNMP protocol, command pipes often act as the conduit to channel information between different software products.

With the use of sockets, which are standard with Unix-supported boxes, and the TCP/IP networking standard, information can now be channeled across multiple platforms. The degree of integration across an enterprise depends on the value that the company associates with a single point of reference. A single job-scheduling solution that tightly integrates Unix, NT,

Exhibit 3. Job scheduling in open systems environment at a glance.

Job Scheduling Requirement	Client/Server Options
Centralize administration and support of schedules	• Centralize product access and manage alerts through product integration frameworks • Maximize number of remote agents to balance workloads
Decentralize administration and support of schedules	• Maximize number of master schedules • Network master schedules using intermachine dependencies • Limit agents to departmental computing requirements
Integrate system software products	• Select integrated system software frameworks that: a) propose choices for best-of-breed point solutions b) provide centralized access to each solution c) establish alert management through open-ended SNMP and command-level interface
High availability	• Minimize network communication to increase network fault tolerance a) Maximize number of master schedules b) Execute workloads on same machines as master schedules c) Reduce use of agents to less critical jobs
	• Leverage hardware option to increase master fault tolerance a) Locate master schedules on application file servers b) Maximize use of hardware mirroring technology c) Minimize dependencies on single proprietary software mirroring techniques.
	• Establish agent fault tolerance a) Establish multiple remote agents to act as candidates for job execution b) Implement agent code to store and forward messages during recovery of master schedules

and MVS using an open-ended console management framework, for example, is likely to be preferable to three separate job schedulers using the same console management framework (see Exhibit 3). With open systems, the level of integration that is reached can be determined by a company's software requirements, not by the software vendor.

MEETING HIGH-AVAILABILITY REQUIREMENTS

System availability requirements should be measured against the mission-critical nature of each work load and the service-level agreements that have been arranged between operational personnel and the organization's information users. In an open systems environment, the availability of communications to network each of the platforms is a key element to all processing. The number of options available in an open-systems job-scheduling environment to protect communications are numerous. With a client/server architecture, flexibility is the key, and any combination of options can be mixed and matched to meet the different availability requirements of each application and the level of convenience that users demand.

Centralized Administration

Centralized administration through a single master schedule provides the lowest degree of network fault tolerance. In this scenario, the machine on which the master schedule resides acts as a single point of reference for all administration and support activity. Work loads are automatically launched on remote, or agent, servers when job dependency requirements are met. In the event that the network or the machine running the master schedule incurs a fault, the agent ensures that existing jobs run to completion. A store-and-forward mechanism is usually in place to ensure that messages are sent back to the master when control is regained.

Unfortunately, future jobs cannot be launched when communication is broken between the master and its agents. This approach is usually chosen because it conveniently provides a single point of reference for personnel and helps balance work loads across multiple machines. For applications that demand high availability, however, systems managers often seek alternatives that provide a higher degree of tolerance to network faults.

The Role of the Master Schedule

Network fault tolerance can best be obtained by increasing the number of master schedules in the enterprise. Because each master schedule has complete control over its scheduling requirements, a direct correlation exists among the number of master schedules and the degree of availability that can be reached despite network outages. The more master schedules that exist, the less vulnerable each is to network issues. This is especially true when the master schedule and associated jobs are executed on the same machine.

In the event that job dependencies exist among master schedules, the schedules can be networked together to provide intermachine dependencies. Even if as many as 20% of the schedules are networked together, at least 80% of the schedule on each machine continues to operate in the unlikely event of a network outage. A single reference list of all machines containing master schedules can easily be obtained from each workstation client when security clearance is permitted, so machine access is convenient. In addition, because the client/server architecture maintains autonomy between the workstation client and the master schedule, all scheduling functions performed by the master schedule remain independent of networked access by any client workstation. For organizations that are heavily decentralized in their administration roles or that have mission-critical applications demanding high-availability rates, multiple master schedules are often implemented, and jobs are set to execute their work loads on the same machine containing the master schedule.

The degree of fault tolerance that is tied to a master schedule is directly related to the mission-critical nature of its schedule. Takeover schemes are available to minimize unplanned outages of master schedules. The most important element of any takeover plan is to ensure that it mirrors the applications and files. Otherwise, after takeover, an alternate machine may contain the master schedule, but the applications or related files, or both, are unavailable for future scheduling. To properly mirror applications and related data, the job-scheduling software often must remain independent of application and database choices. This means that takeover options should include—and managers should strongly consider—hardware mirroring technology. Not only is this technology more reliable than software choices but the risk of limiting fault tolerance only to certain applications and databases is removed. The concept is to remain open. In addition, if file servers are available, job-scheduling databases can be placed on the appropriate servers to ensure that the application data and the job-scheduling data are always available for processing.

CONCLUSION

Job scheduling in an open systems environment provides many challenges that can be addressed by focusing on the centralized and decentralized needs of the company. As with any form of systems software, however, each decision should be based on the limitations set by a company's computing resources and administrative and support policies. Finally, the very nature of open systems suggests that job-scheduling software should not dictate the enterprise. Instead, the job-scheduling software should provide the flexibility to adapt to the needs of the enterprise.

Chapter 42
Multiple Protocols: The Network Manager's Headache

Joe Pruskowski

Many IS professionals face the task of managing complex networks. This chapter discusses methods of connectivity, including multistacking and the use of software-based gateway technology, in an effort to help managers effectively deal with multiple protocols in the LAN environment.

PROBLEMS ADDRESSED

Rightsizing is a goal of many CIOs today. The basic method to attain true rightsizing is to move information closer to the individual workers within the organization, especially through client/server computing. By their very nature, networks are the logical structure to make this happen.

Many corporations have a mix of both departmental and corporate LAN systems combined with legacy systems, all with disparate methods of communicating in a network. Today's networks are very open, but often very chaotic. Managing such complex networks has become a real challenge for network managers.

For connectivity, IS managers often rely on one of two common methods: stacking multiple protocols, or "multistacking," and using gateway technology. For IS managers facing integration decisions, information on all of the options is critical.

LAN CLIENT SUPPORT

The dominant LAN Network operating system is NetWare, and therefore the standard for LAN protocols is IPX/SPX. Parallel to the LAN, legacy systems are still using their proprietary protocols to support access to mission-critical applications and data. Typically, IBM's System Network Architecture, DEC's Local Area Transport and DECnet, together with a

0-8493-9989-0/99/$0.00+$.50

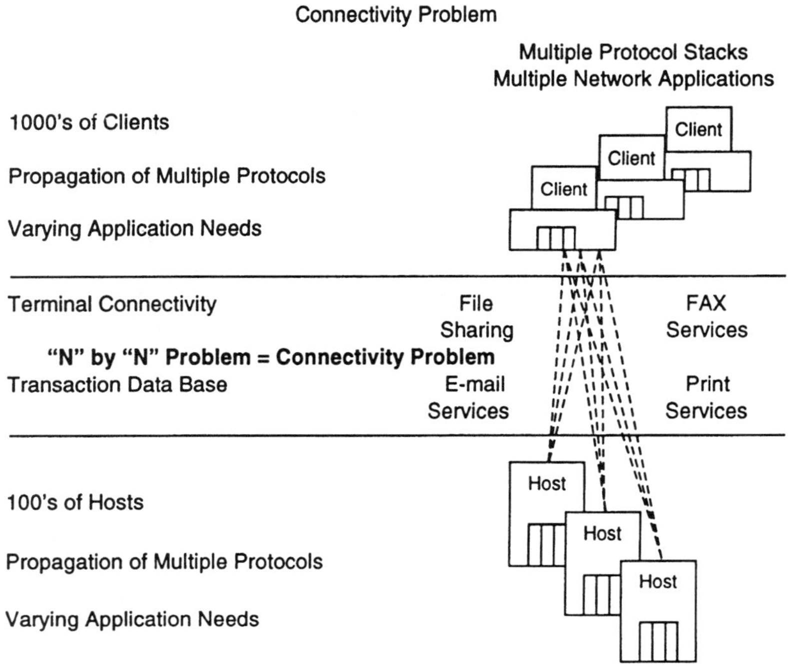

Exhibit 1. Client and host interactions.

variety of applications running on TCP/IP, have become the most prominent protocols running on the host. Exhibit 1 shows the interactions between clients and hosts within the network.

Because the networks in most organizations are made up of a variety of protocols, users in various places on the network cannot access the resources they need. A company attempting to solve this problem must deal with some significant issues:

- Initial setup cost, including purchase and installation cost, for each workstation on the network
- Ongoing administrative support costs, which include the purchase and installation of software upgrades and the maintenance of network address management. Each protocol stack has a different naming scheme. For example, a LAT host name is a simple test string (e.g., SYSTEM1), where a TCP/IP node name is tree-structured dot notation (e.g., SYSTEM1.NORTHWEST.ICXN.COM)
- The limited number of applications supported by any one protocol
- The burden on the infrastructure when there are too many protocols to support efficiently. This burden is realized by the network

hardware, which now must deal with managing multiple protocols. Support personnel must also know how to deal with these protocols.

- The high administrative costs in large, heterogeneous networks. This is a serious problem because the costs continue to climb.

WHAT IS MULTISTACKING?

Multistacking means that every LAN client would have to run all other legacy protocols (e.g., System Network Architecture, Local Area Transport, and DECnet) in addition to its native protocol (e.g., Internetwork Packet eXchange) to gain access to all corporate data. The number of LAN clients that must run multiple protocol stacks in most major corporations is very large—typically measured in the thousands. While in theory multistacking will solve the problem, it comes with an entire set of its own problems, multiplied by the sheer number of LAN clients that are affected.

Some of the major problems that must be dealt with on each DOS/Windows system are:

- Conflicts in memory usage, since many stacks still run in real-mode
- Conflicts in Terminate and Stay Resident(terminate and stay resident) programs
- Conflicts in network address spaces (i.e., differing address schemes)
- Use of network device drivers by multiple protocol stacks, which require complicated setup procedures

CONNECTIVITY ALTERNATIVES TO MULTISTACKING

There are a number of solutions available today that minimize protocol stack propagation, each with its advantages and disadvantages.

Proprietary Vendor-Specific Suites. These are typically sold by the major computer vendors. Examples would be Pathworks from Digital Equipment Corp. and IBM's LAN Server products. These usually provide a high level of functionality, but are mainly account control mechanisms and can be cumbersome to use. In addition, they are usually expensive because license has to be purchased for every user on the network.

Standardization on One Protocol Stack. In an ideal world, this would be Open Systems Interconnection, though TCP/IP seems to be filling this role as a practical solution. However, although TCP/IP is found on the backbones of many corporations, it rarely makes it to the client. TCP/IP can be cumbersome to install on a large number of nodes, but it does provide an excellent "intermediate" protocol. Because TCP/IP can support a wide variety of equipment, there are many parameters that must be set up on each TCP/IP system, not the least of which is the node number, which has to be assigned for each node. This approach can also be expensive, as it is purchased on a per-node basis.

THE SOFTWARE GATEWAY

Another alternative to multistacking is the use of gateway technology. Gateway technology was first introduced as rather expensive hardware. A single vendor had to install and maintain the gateway, typically at a very high cost to the user. New gateway technology is software-only and can be run on virtually any commodity hardware platform. An early example is Novell's NetWare for Systems Application Architecture, which connects LAN clients to IBM mainframes. Another is InterConnections' Leverage Gateway Services, which is based on Novell's NetWare for Local Area Transport technology and connects Digital Equipment Corporation systems with NetWare clients.

The gateway technology emerging today serves as a true gateway—one type of protocol is actually converted to a different type. An example of this would be an inbound terminal session over NetWare Internetwork Packet eXchange that is converted at the gateway to an outbound LAT terminal session. There are several advantages to this new type of gateway:

- It can reside on any Intel 386/486/Pentium hardware platform and provides protocol translation between the LAN client and host environments.
- It is ultimately manageable using the industry-standard Simple Network Management Protocol protocol. The management capabilities are based on the translation tables that are inherent within the gateway. This allows for "logical network management" of network resources, building on the physical management capabilities that are currently being deployed by a wide variety of vendors. Logical network management brings meaningful information to the network manager, such as the number of sessions in use and the number of files transferred.
- Concurrent user licensing is cost-effective. Any supported host can be accessed by the LAN clients. The user company does not have to license each host to allow access from its client systems.
- Concurrent host usage is cost-effective. Any supported host can be accessed by the LAN clients. The user company does not have to license each host to allow access from its client systems.
- The number of protocol stacks on the LAN client and host are greatly reduced.
- There is no need for additional kernel-mode protocol stacks on the host machines.

By applying software gateway technology to the multiple protocol situation, IS professionals have a new set of tools that can help them achieve their goals.

A SAMPLE CASE

The next section examines the system at a major airline reservation center. The center has a large collection of NetWare LANs with thousands of IPX/SPX clients. In addition, there are dozens of hosts that are a combination of Digital Equipment Corporation and Unix systems. These systems are all physically connected, but use very different network protocols to communicate. The LAN clients mainly use Internetwork Packet eXchange, the Unix systems use TCP/IP, while the DEC systems use a combination of Local Area Transport and DECnet.

Personnel at the center take reservations over the phone using a reservation system that runs on Unix and is connected via TCP/IP. From the same desktop system, they also perform outbound telemarketing (e.g., making customers aware of an upcoming new frequent-flyer program) and must access a VAX/VMS system for lead information via the LAT protocol. In terms of connectivity, the company could:

- Install all protocol stacks (i.e., Internetwork Packet eXchange, Transmission Control Protocol, LAT) at each client. Installing all these protocol stacks at each client would add wear and tear on the network management personnel alone. The stacks have to be loaded and configured on each client and, over time, must be maintained. There is also a charge for each stack-per-client.
- Install a TCP/IP stack on all hosts and clients. In most cases, this does not support all of the applications required, so it becomes restrictive and might require at least an IPX stack to be co-resident. Although the network management personnel have fewer stacks to worry about, they still have to configure and manage two stacks at each client.
- Install gateways at the edges of the LAN infrastructure to the host systems. This saves network management personnel wear and tear because the protocol translation gateway is installed at a central point. There are fewer stacks to worry about, and by simply leaving Internetwork Packet eXchange on the LAN clients, the LAN becomes easy to manage on an ongoing basis. Cost is also minimized because money is saved on protocol stacks and their subsequent maintenance.

In the future, more companies will implement strategic protocols such as IPX and TCP/IP across their network backbone while applying software gateway technology to bring legacy systems into the network. Exhibit 2 illustrates the effect of applying gateway technology to simplify the overall network and provide basic functionality for all legacy systems.

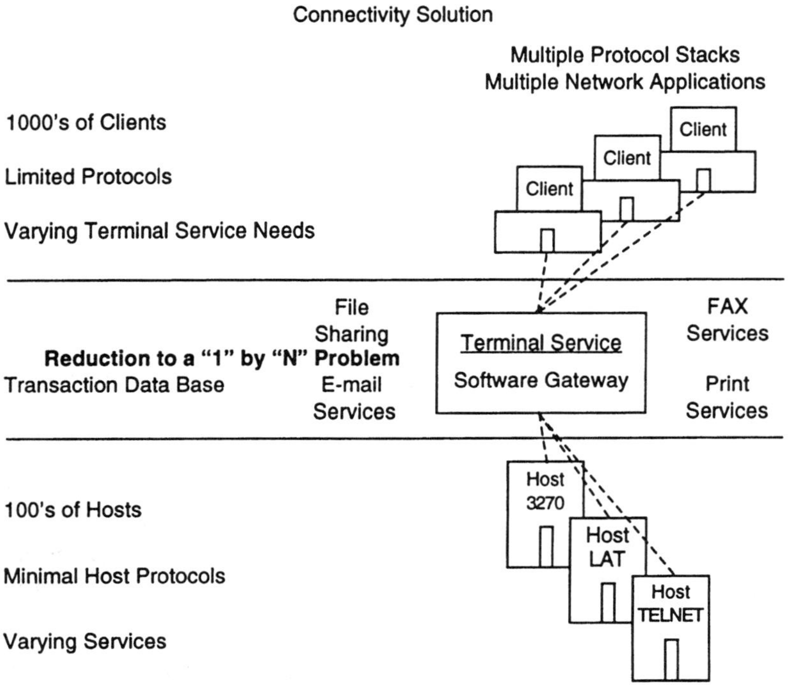

Exhibit 2. Applying gateway technology.

RECOMMENDED COURSE OF ACTION

An optimum plan for managing a multiprotocol environment must achieve certain goals. The minimum set of requirements is:

- Minimize the number of protocol stacks at the client
- Minimize the number of protocol stacks at the host
- Support a variety of critical applications, such as terminal service, file transfer, and printing
- Take a "network-centric" viewpoint
- Provide logical network management of these services

With the emergence of software gateways that run on commodity hardware, it has become cost-effective to provide a high level of connectivity and manageability while allowing network managers to contain their costs.

Chapter 43
Managing Multivendor Networks Using DEC's Polycenter Framework

Nathan J. Muller

Digital Equipment Corp. (DEC) has been working toward the objective of open systems and multivendor integration since 1988, when it articulated its Enterprise Management Architecture (EMA) strategy for managing multivendor environments. EMA is a blueprint for managing open, integrated, heterogeneous, and distributed systems.

EMA distinguishes between the resource being managed and the management software that performs the management function. EMA specifies application programming interfaces that developers use to integrate system and network management in a modular framework. DECmcc used this approach in 1989, however, it addressed only the integration of various network management applications. DECmcc is now known as the Polycenter Framework, and it incorporates components of the Distributed Management Environment (DME) of the Open Software Foundation, or OSF.

Polycenter is the cornerstone for Digital's implementation of EMA, which enables IS managers to spend less time handling crises and more time improving systems, controlling costs, and planning for future resource needs. Polycenter's object-oriented (OO) technology integrates legacy applications and services with new applications and services. OO technology is also intended to facilitate Polycenter's progress toward full compliance with the OSF's DME.

0-8493-9989-0/99/$0.00+$.50

The Polycenter Framework constitutes enabling technology onto which management applications are increasingly layered. The Polycenter Framework provides applications with an infrastructure that enables them to integrate, via a common user interface, shared events or data or use calls within management applications. Management of all resources or objects is then possible.

MANAGEMENT NEEDS

In combination with products from third-party applications developers, Polycenter provides solutions to the most common types of management needs, including:

- **Network management.** Keeping the network available and minimizing the impact of network downtime and its impact on user productivity.
- **Storage management.** Making sure information is protected while being quickly retrievable.
- **Configuration and change management.** Ensuring all components work together successfully by tracking assets and providing appropriate levels of service to users.
- **Fault and problem management.** Keeping systems and applications available so users can perform their work without interruption.
- **Performance and capacity management**. Maintaining systems and network performance to ensure specified response times.
- **Automation.** Automating mundane tasks to avoid end-user frustration and loss of productivity, minimizing chances for human error and optimizing staff time.
- **Security management.** Protecting confidential information and maintaining data integrity and accountability.
- **Accounting and billing management.** Keeping records of system usage and chargebacks for accurate billing and resource planning.

HOW POLYCENTER WORKS

Two important management concepts at work in Polycenter include those of Entity and Director. The Entity refers to a managed object, which can be any resource, such as a bridge/router, terminal server, concentrator, circuit, or LAN. This concept also includes the agent of the object—the software that provides the management capability to the object. The managed object and its agent do not have to be co-resident.

The Polycenter Director is the software that acts as an interface between the user and the managed entities. The framework is designed to accommodate multiple directors, each of which is responsible for monitoring and controlling the entities within its management domain (see Exhibit 1).

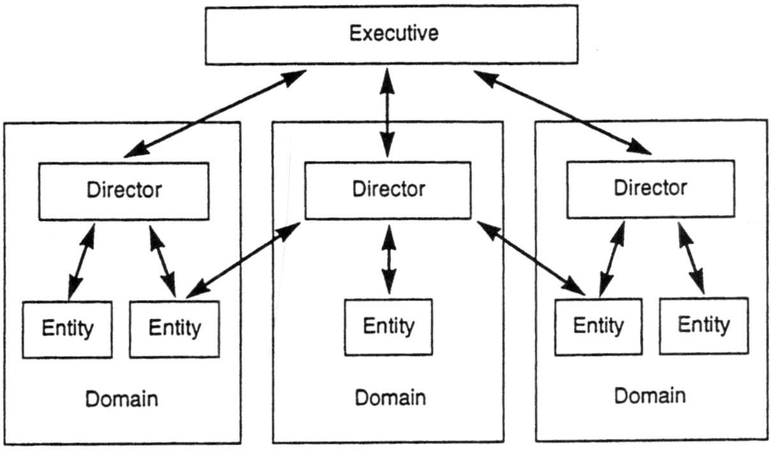

Exhibit 1. Polycenter framework.

The Polycenter framework consists of five interrelated components (Exhibit 2):

- **The Executive.** Coordinates and manages the individual directors.
- **Management Information Repository.** An object-oriented database system built specifically for the Director application, the Management Information Repository contains all the object specifications that drive a particular management system implementation, as well as real-time status and performance information.
- **Presentation Modules.** Provide the means by which operators can interface with the management system.
- **Function Modules.** Provide specific management and control functionality.
- **Access Modules.** Provide the core technology for enterprisewide connectivity and control, regardless of vendor mix.

Presentation Modules

Presentation modules provide a consistent user interface, whether command line, forms, or graphical. Presentation modules include:

- **Command Line.** Provides a terminal-based user interface using command-line I/O techniques that support command-line recall and editing, command abbreviation, online help, symbol substitution, and control sequences. Commands are input through a keyboard and output is to a VT220-compatible terminal, a designated storage device, or a file.

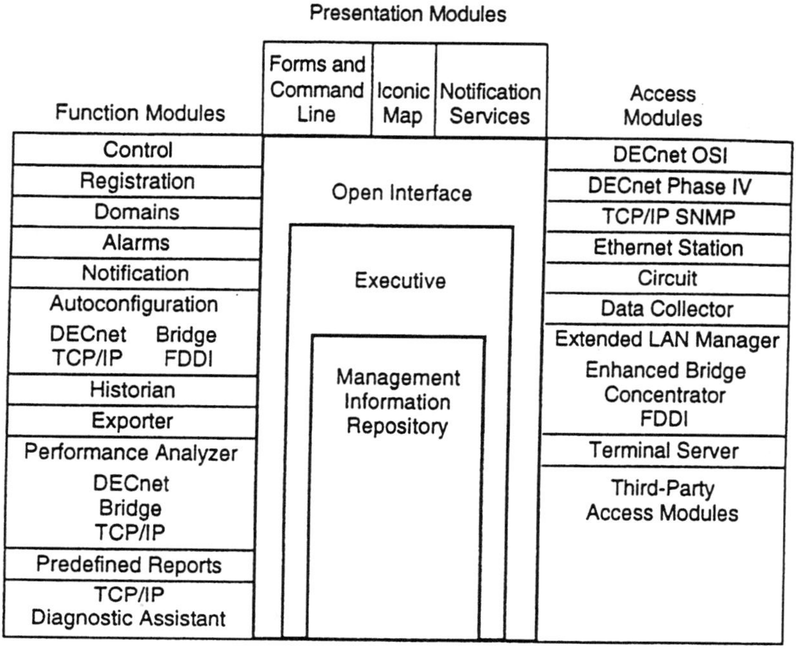

Exhibit 2. Polycenter framework.

- **Forms Interface.** An extension of the command-line interface that provides a screen-based user interface using forms and list I/O techniques. There are two display regions: one for entering data to input fields for issuing commands, the other for viewing the resulting output data.
- **Notification Services.** A facility that enhances the presentation modules by providing a log of system notifications generated inside the Director by managed entities or by applications external to the Director, including those developed by third-party vendors.
- **Iconic Map.** Provides a flexible set of input capabilities, including keyboard, mouse, pull-down menus, and icons. Using information provided by Notification Services, the Iconic Map displays visual color-coded alarm and status indicators and features relationship-driven navigation tools. This presentation module is based on DECwindows.

Function Modules

The function modules extend the functionality of the Director to new and more advanced applications, including the ISO-defined network management functions of configuration, fault, performance, security, and accounting management. Function modules include:

- **Control.** Provides access to the management functions supported by a given device on the network. Device-specific commands are translated into a consistent syntax and can be performed at specified times.
- **Registration.** Registers and maintains the set of known entities within the managed environment, translating easy-to-remember entity names to hexadecimal physical addresses. An entity registered by one Director can be known to all Directors on the network.
- **Domains.** Collects entities into user-defined groups called domains to establish a span of control or specific view of the network. The use of domains allows networks to be divided into logical and more manageable subsets. Domains can overlap with other domains and even include other domains. This arrangement allows network management functions and responsibilities to be distributed among network support staff according to clearly defined domain boundaries.
- **Alarms.** Detect and notify network administrators of alarm conditions in the network emanating from any device that has an appropriate access module. Alarm conditions and their trip thresholds are based on user-defined alarm rules. Alarm rules can be tested on specified entities at specified times (i.e., polled alarms) or executed when the fault occurs (i.e., unsolicited alarms). Upon detection of an alarm, a user-written command procedure is queued for execution.
- **Notification.** Enables the entire range of alerting capabilities to be used by all other management modules. For example, it supports displays of events from the Data Collector access module or a change of an icon color associated with the Alarms module.
- **Autoconfiguration.** Provides automatic discovery, registration, and mapping of TCP/IP nodes, DECnet Phase IV nodes, DEC bridges, and any DEC and non-DEC device that is connected to a fiber-distributed data interface (FDDI) ring.
- **Historian.** Provides an integrated set of facilities for collecting, purging, archiving, and exporting historical management data. This function module periodically collects attribute data and records it in the Management Information Repository. The network administrator can then use various function modules to operate on the collected data. The Historian function module also supports the export of data through the Exporter function module to relational databases outside the Polycenter Framework for off-line analysis and reporting using query languages.
- **Exporter.** Transports real-time data or data collected by the Historian function module to either DEC's relational database or the relational databases of other vendors.
- **Predefined Reports.** Provides sample performance analysis reports, including a template for writing customized reports using a relational database query language.

- **TCP/IP Diagnostic Assistant.** Assists in identifying and resolving common TCP/IP networking problems by using a series of diagnostic actions and test procedures.

Access Modules

Access modules provide a bidirectional control and monitoring pathway to the various manageable entities. They implement the communications protocol that is appropriate for managing a particular entity class. Access modules in Polycenter include:

- **DECnet OSI.** Provides the management pathway to control and monitor DECnet/OSI implementations using Digital's OSI-based Common Management Information Protocol (CMIP).
- **DECnet Phase IV.** Provides the management pathway that is used to control and monitor DECnet Phase IV implementations, including the DECnet side of the DECnet/SNA Gateway and Digital's X.25 router.
- **TCP/IP SNMP.** Implements control and monitoring of TCP/IP network devices that support Simple Network Management Protocol (SNMP). This access module includes full MIB II support and the ability to do onsite enrollment of vendor-specific MIBs.
- **Ethernet.** Provides the management pathway to control and monitor any multivendor device on the Ethernet that conforms to the IEEE 802.3standard. This access module also provides Ethernet control and monitoring functions that can be used by other management modules within the Polycenter Framework.
- **Circuit.** Provides network management control of lines and circuits defined as manageable objects.
- **Data Collector.** Integrates other management information from a variety of management applications and devices. Event or alarm information operating on a VMS or ULTRIX system is sent to a remote agent and then forwarded to Polycenter.
- **Extended LAN Manager.** Manages devices such as bridges and concentrators from Digital and other vendors that are connected to an FDDI ring.
- **Terminal Server.** Provides the management pathway to control and monitor DEC terminal servers.

Other companies can write access modules that plug into the Polycenter Framework. This permits a network manager to monitor and control devices that are linked to the management packages made by those companies.

LEVELS OF INTEGRATION

There are various levels at which developers can make their applications accessible within the Polycenter Framework, including:

- **Visual Integration.** The coexistence of two or more applications on the same display.
- **Launchable Applications.** Programs that can be initiated from the Polycenter Framework menus. This form of integration is used to incorporate public domain software such as the SNMP.
- **Data Collector Access Module.** An input-only mechanism that allows an external application to send events into the Polycenter Framework. The Framework provides all of the sources for sending these events, which the user can then link into other applications.
- **Script Access Module.** An input/output mechanism that allows a script to be run from the graphical user interface. It maps defined commands, such as show memory, into Framework commands to view memory usage on a given system. It can also be used for handling the output of command procedures end users might have.
- **Callable Management Control Center.** Allows applications to be linked with the Framework kernel so its services can be used. In conjunction with the launch function, it allows commands to be made available to the user.
- **Polycenter Framework Access or Function Module Development.** Provides complete integration of an application or set of functions so that the commands are fully integrated into the Framework.

Developer's Toolkit

The Polycenter Framework Developer's Toolkit simplifies the design and implementation of application-specific modules for use with the Framework. The toolkit includes both software and online components, as well as documentation, used in the development of access modules and function modules. The software components include a runtime kernel executive, various service programs, and source code for sample access modules and function modules that are also included in the toolkit.

Common Agent. The Common Agent provides a consistent interface for managing all components and resources of a distributed system. It is a key component of the EMA and is based on the management standards developed by the International Standards Organization and the Internet Engineering Task Force.

The Common Agent provides automated tools so that different system resources can be managed by a variety of applications through standard management protocols. The Common Agent uses open, published application programming interfaces to support multiple management protocols (e.g., SNMP and CMIP), multiple management systems, and multiple managed components (e.g., disks and applications). The Common Agent also supports the management of objects in the OSF DME.

A base kit for the Common Agent acts as a switch, translating information and requests from a remote manager, director, or management application to locally managed resources. It also processes notifications and events occurring from the managed resources or a system (e.g., applications or devices). It allows users to manage more resources remotely yet still use a variety of management applications, frameworks, and protocols.

A separate Common Agent Developer's Toolkit provides component and application developers with automated tools for developing managed object modules, or MOMs. These are management routines that contain information about the objects to be managed, plus access routines that interface to the programming code of each managed object.

CONCLUSION

Only a short time ago network management platforms appeared to be stabilizing, but developments in this area are changing that situation. Digital's Polycenter Framework (formerly known as DECmcc) incorporates components of OSF's DME. In addition, Digital plans to migrate Polycenter users to IBM's RISC-based NetView/6000 management platform, which is based on Hewlett-Packard's OpenView, at present the leading integrated network management solution. The new offering will be known as Polycenter NetView. At the same time, however, IBM has moved away from OpenView to the Tivoli Management Environment (TME) from Tivoli Systems Inc. TME and OpenView use competing object management technologies. It remains to be seen how current users of Digital's Polycenter Framework and IBM's NetView/6000 will respond to the changes.

Chapter 44
Managing Multivendor Networks Using Hewlett-Packard's OpenView

Nathan J. Muller

The task of keeping complex, multiprotocol networks operating smoothly with a minimum of downtime is an ongoing challenge. The process is eased somewhat by management systems, which allow technicians to monitor network performance and remotely diagnose and correct problems associated with each type of device, module, and cable segment.

INTRODUCTION

The diversity of network devices and differences in media and protocols tend to complicate rather than simplify network management, prompting users to seek a unified management solution. Among the most prominent integrated network management solutions are AT&T's Accumaster Integrator, IBM Corp's NetView, Digital Equipment Corp.'s (DEC) Polycenter Framework, and Hewlett-Packard's (HP) OpenView. All of these management systems underwent major shifts in market positioning in recent years, while another important management system, SunNet Manager from SunConnect (a company owned by Sun Microsystems, Inc.), rose to industry prominence.

MARKET ASSESSMENTS

Despite its promise, Accumaster Integrator has not sold well. This has led AT&T to consider abandoning it in favor of NCR's StarSentry and HP's

0-8493-9989-0/99/$0.00+$.50

OpenView. AT&T has announced that it will not upgrade Accumaster Integrator past version 3.0. Doubts among network management customers about the strength of the so-called manager-of-managers strategy for managing multivendor networks are apparently justified.

In OpenView, HP has concentrated on creating a multivendor management platform for Open Systems Interconnection (OSI) and Transmission Control Protocol/Internet Protocol (TCP/IP)-based internets. This plays to the company's strengths in LAN management; HP has been a major player in the LAN protocol analyzer market since the early 1980s, and its expertise in TCP/IP has been used internally since that time.

SunConnect's SunNet Manager has become a leading Unix-based distributed network management system. The system's protocol-independent, distributed-management architecture supports Simple Network Management Protocol (SNMP) and offers a comprehensive set of tools for automated fault isolation and network monitoring. It also automates management functions and includes a broad set of integrated tools. Next to IBM, SunConnect is HP's closest competitor in network management. In terms of installed base, the Yankee Group reports that SunConnect and HP are running neck and neck, with about 3,000 software licenses each.

FOUR MAJOR COMPONENTS OF OPENVIEW

OpenView is widely considered one of the most advanced architectures for integrated network management and is rapidly developing into the *de facto* standard for multivendor network management. It is a distributed, hardware-independent platform that incorporates the best features of existing standards and goes beyond them in the realm of the user interface. The market success of OpenView is demonstrated by the fact that many internetworking vendors offer it as a framework for managing bridges, routers, and hubs. In addition, OpenView also forms the basis of the Open Software Foundation's (OSF) Distributed Management Environment (DME).

There are four major components of HP's OpenView (see Exhibit 1).

- User interface presentation services
- A distributed communications infrastructure
- Data storage management
- Communication protocols

User Interface Presentation Services. HP has placed great emphasis on standardizing the user interface. This is handled by the user interface presentation services component of OpenView. X11 (also known as X Windows) was developed at MIT and is now an American National Standards Institute windowing standard that allows a class of terminals known as X-terminals to integrate various equipment from a variety of vendors with

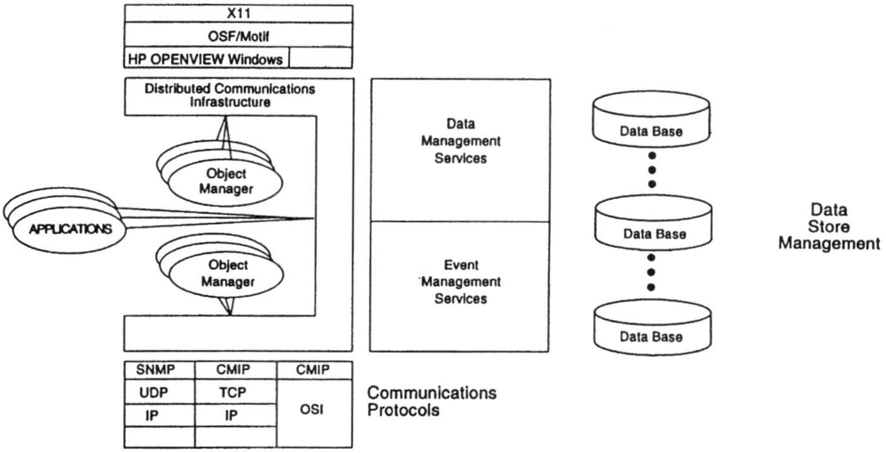

Notes:
SNMP Simple Network Management Protocol
CMIP Common Management Information Protocol
UDP User Datagram Protocol
TCP Transmission Control Protocol
IP Internet Protocol
OSI Open Systems Interconnection

Exhibit 1. The structure of OpenView.

a single window system. In essence, X11 is a software development tool that is used to specify the look and feel of the window system when building graphics-based applications. OSF's Motif provides a windows-based user interface for management applications. OpenView Windows is a Unix-based open graphical user interface (GUI) that other applications can interact with through published applications programming interfaces (APIs).

Distributed Communications Infrastructure. As its name implies, the distributed communications infrastructure makes it possible for management applications to access the services of OpenView across a network, without having to know where the service components are located. The communications infrastructure makes use of the OpenView API to provide access to all management services and protocols, including the Simple Network Management Protocol, OSI's Common Management Information Protocol (CMIP), and CMIP over TCP/IP (CMOT).

Interactions Between Two Management Applications also are Accomplished by Way of the Openview API

- The Event Management Services facility provides a central point to generate, receive, and log network events such as component failures, object state changes, and security violations. This facility routes such events to management applications and historical logs. It also stores events in an event log for future reference or historical analysis of critical parameters, device performance, network traffic, and resource utilization.

- The Data Management Services facility organizes data access to protect the application developer from the need to know the details of data storage, eliminating the need for a data storage subsystem. Instead, data is stored in a common, shared data store. A key feature of Data Management Services is metadata, which is a database representation of all information in the Management Information Base. The metadata compiler integrates information about each new object into the Management Information Base.

Another important feature of OpenView is its object-oriented programmability, which makes it possible to manipulate information about objects. In this scheme, network elements are described as objects, even if they are not managed using the Open Systems Interconnection protocols. Modules, called object managers, translate between the object-oriented procedures within OpenView and whatever mechanisms the real element uses to send and receive management data.

The distributed architecture makes it possible to allocate functions and modules flexibly across multiple management servers. This enables users to implement a scalable management system entirely from powerful yet relatively inexpensive Unix workstations without requiring a single host in the form of a minicomputer or mainframe.

Data Store Management. Data Store Management provides database and event management services. The communications protocols component of OpenView implements OSI and TCP/IP management protocols. Management applications programs access these common services through a set of APIs implemented by the distributed communications infrastructure.

Communications Protocols. HP has developed a distributed, hardware-independent platform that incorporates the best features of existing standards and goes beyond them in the realm of the user interface. HP has concentrated on creating a multivendor management platform for TCP/IP-based and OSI-based internets, providing implementations of SNMP and CMIP over TCP/IP.

RELATED MANAGEMENT PRODUCTS

HP offers a family of network management products capable of managing a variety of networking environments and hardware, including TCP/IP networks; bridges, routers, and hubs; and analog leased lines.

Network Node Manager. HP's OpenView Network Node Manager is an application that simplifies fault, configuration, and performance management functions for multivendor TCP/IP and Simple Network Management Protocol networks. Features include:

- Automatic discovery automatically finds and identifies all the network devices, regardless of vendor, and updates the network map when their status changes.
- Single-view management allows user-developed or third-party applications to be integrated into the system, allowing any network management application to be accessed through the OpenView Network Node Manager at a single management workstation.
- Dynamic data collection and user-defined thresholds allow the OpenView Network Node Manager to make use of Management Information Base data from devices on the network for network planning and troubleshooting. Users can gather historical information about network performance for any management information base element on any SNMP device. Users can also define event thresholds for any management information base object.
- Application builder enables users and developers to create applications to manage SNMP devices without programming to graphically display network device information and to execute programs to handle network events and alarms.

Bridge/Hub Manager. The OpenView Windows Bridge/Hub Manager is actually two separate microcomputer-based products that sit atop OpenView Windows. They provide centralized monitoring and control of HP's Ethernet bridges, and the hubs of HP (i.e., EtherTwist Hub Plus and Fiber-Optic Hub Plus) and other vendors by way of Simple Network Management Protocol. Both products make use of the network map feature of OpenView Windows, in which users can label and identify network devices. Pull-down menus provide a variety of management features, including configuration, monitoring, control, performance management, and problem identification. Specifically, the bridge/hub manager can automatically discover and display network configurations, monitor network traffic conditions, identify and diagnose network problems, enhance security, and increase network reliability by controlling individual links, as well as bridges and hubs.

Users can set the thresholds for network traffic levels and device events. The traffic levels and events can be triggered as alarms that appear at the network management workstation. The data can also be used to monitor network performance and reliability. HP's implementation of the IEEE 802.1 spanning tree algorithm lets users configure redundant links that are activated automatically if a primary link fails.

A graphing facility enables users to graph the level of traffic, number of collisions, number of packets forwarded and filtered, and other network statistics. The data can be exported to such spreadsheet applications as

Lotus 1-2-3 and Microsoft Excel for further manipulation and then exported to other graphic presentation packages where the data can be translated into other, more sophisticated presentation formats (e.g., three-dimensional charts and graphs).

Data Line Monitor. The OpenView Data Line Monitor supervises four-wire, point-to-point, leased analog data lines. This is done with the HP 4948A In-Service Transmission Impairment Measuring Set (ITIMS), which is controlled from an OpenView workstation ITIMS is a network monitoring system that measures performance and aids fault isolation during troubleshooting while the modem network is in full operation. ITIMS is compatible with and can run concurrently with other HP OpenView network management applications.

For routine alarm monitoring, the network administrator can set the data line monitor to automatically test all lines in sequence. For troubleshooting, a single line can be selected and monitored continuously. The system stores descriptions of all lines to be monitored in the OpenView Windows database, including details of the modem type and transmission performance limits. When a problem is detected with a particular line, the color of the line on the network map changes to red and a message is displayed in the OpenView alarm window.

Line Performance is Reported in Two Ways

1. **Routing Monitoring.** Alarm-only mode is used to indicate when the key analog parameters for each line exceed predefined limits.
2. **Selected Monitoring.** For a selected measurement period, the maximum, minimum, and average values of all line characteristics are stored. This mode is used when data is required for line performance benchmarks or trend analysis.

InterConnect Manager. The OpenView InterConnect Manager is an integrated real-time global network management system for networked bridges, hubs, and routers that provides a comprehensive set of configuration, fault, diagnostic, and performance-analysis tools. InterConnect Manager discovers, maps, and manages the devices of HP and other vendors supporting Simple Network Management Protocol and TCP/IP. It also monitors LAN/WAN links that use such protocols as X.25, Xerox Network System, Internetwork Packet eXchange, DECnet IV, and AppleTalk II.

Upon mouse-click command, InterConnect Manager initiates a procedure to discover new devices on the network and then automatically redraws the network map to include the new devices. Any changes in the network configuration are dynamically reported in an event notification facility. The real-time status of the network devices is continually monitored and displayed. Various network statistics are collected and analyzed, including the Management Information Base variables. The user is provided with access to automatically gathered and graphically displayed statistics.

InterConnect Manager's router Configuration Management system is capable of creating and editing router configuration information through the network-management workstation. The new configuration, as well as the operating system software, can be remotely downloaded over the network to the router.

TCP/IP Agent. The OpenView TCP/IP agent provides the means to manage HP 9000minicomputer systems—including the Series 300, 600, and 800computers—through SNMP. The TCP/IP agent responds to requests for information from the network administrator and can automatically send alarms when unusual conditions occur on the agent system. The capability to accept *ad hoc* requests provides the network administrator with faster access for information than would usually be available through the regular cycle of polling agents individually.

OPENVIEW APPLICATIONS

HP offers a suite of knowledge-based network-management applications for OpenView that recommend the actions network administrators can take to control traffic, regulate capacity, and plan for future network growth. The following applications are part of HP's embedded advanced sampling environment (EASE) software package for its EtherTwist family of hubs and bridges:

- **OpenView Traffic Expert.** Collects network performance and traffic information to establish a performance baseline. A report is generated that recommends such actions as moving end nodes or adding filters so network administrators can optimize network performance and avoid conditions that lead to traffic congestion.
- **OpenView History Analyzer.** Compiles historical data that assists in use and future capacity planning. By comparing network statistics to the baseline established by the history analyzer, network administrators can anticipate trends and plan for network additions, changes, and redistribution of network resources.
- **OpenView Resource Manager.** Provides a real-time, simultaneous view of all network segments. By continually tracking network activity, this resource manager can graphically display when network performance is about to exceed preset thresholds.

All three applications support TCP/IP, Internetwork Packet eXchange, DECnet IV, and AppleTalk protocols, and run on Unix-based operating systems.

The full OpenView product family currently runs on Unix-based HP workstations, Solaris-based Sun Microsystems SPARC workstations, IBM RS/600 servers and nodes, and OpenView for Digital Equipment Corporation platforms. To extend the OpenView platform beyond SNMP to the management of HP, IBM, Sun, and DEC worstations, HP offers OperationsCenter (shown in Exhibit 2), a centralized systems-management application that seamlessly integrates the network and systems-management functions across the network. It is a scalable client/server application that uses intelligent agents to monitor and collect status information about network components, applications, and the system. Using filters and thresholds, only requested information is collected from the various management agents and passed on to the OperationsCenter. This cuts down on unnecessary network overhead and minimizes processing at the central management system.

With OperationsCenter, the network manager can program the system to take corrective measures automatically. Other responses include notifying

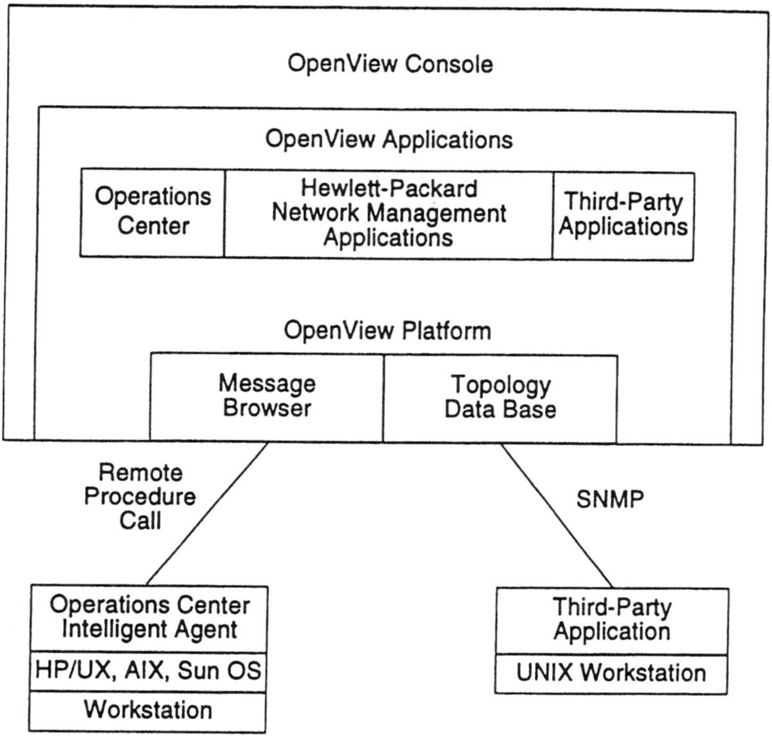

Exhibit 2. The operations center application for OpenView.

the management system operator of an error and requesting authorization to take corrective action, or notifying the operator of the error and waiting for further instructions.

Other OpenView applications that were announced at the same time as OperationsCenter, include:

- **Software Distributor.** Automates software distribution across a distributed network.
- **NetLS.** Manages the distributed licensing of software on Unix networks based on use.
- **Workspace Manager.** Allows the system manager to tailor the status information so only the operator involved with a specific network responsibility will be informed of the appropriate error and status messages.
- **PerfView.** Measures systems performance and capacity, allowing the use of network resources to be monitored.
- **PerfRX.** A performance analysis tool for graphically displaying and analyzing historical trend data. (Runs with the PerfView network management application.)
- **Message Browser.** Responds automatically to alarms filed by intelligent agents or other applications and also prompts an operator, through use of on-screen messages, to take specific actions.

HP also plans to incorporate Network Advisor and LANprobe II into OpenView. Network Advisor is a protocol analyzer that can monitor Ethernet, Token Ring, and FDDI networks, as well as WAN serial connections. It decodes protocols on these networks and connections and employs an integral expert system to advise managers on the causes and solutions of problems to speed troubleshooting. A new OpenView application, Distributed Network Advisor, allows the analyzer to be controlled remotely by Ethernet.

The LANprobe II is a distributed network monitor that allows network managers to supervise large networks. It uses SNMP's Remote MONitoring Management Information Base (RMON management information base) to analyze Ethernet traffic and is used in conjunction with OpenView Probe manager 2.0.

CONCLUSION

HP plans to bring OpenView into full compliance with the Distributed Management Environment (DME) as soon as the Open Software Foundation formalizes the specification. This commitment was demonstrated with HP's release of a network-management application based on portions of DME. HP OpenView Interconnect Lite implements the DME's user interface specification, which provides a consistent approach for interacting with different vendors' management applications.

The program manages interconnected Ethernet and Token Ring LANs from an HP-UX 700 Series workstation or a Sun Operating System workstation. The software discovers, maps, and monitors any LAN device that has an Internet Protocol (IP) address. The application also monitors and controls HP products and provides fault isolation, fault management, and router configuration.

OpenView has proved itself as a worthy network management tool. It provides efficient user interface presentation services, a distributed communications infrastructure, data storage management, and communications protocols. Because of such comprehensive service, OpenView is on its way to becoming the standard for multivendor network management.

Section VI
Communications in a Heterogeneous Environment

Another important facet of heterogeneous computing deals with communications involving heterogeneous systems, protocols, geographic locations, etc. With the advances in telecommunications technology, the number of ways of bringing different departments and locations of an enterprise has increased dramatically along with the amount of information that is shared and used.

Chapter 45 provides an introduction and covers the salient points of an enterprise network.

In distributed computing environments, with so much information traversing wide area internets, it is imperative that the right transmission service be selected to ensure the uninterrupted flow of information among interconnected local area networks (LANs). With the types of applications running over LANs, relatively high bandwidth is required for relatively low-duty cycles. The transmissions onto the wide area networks (WAN) consist of bursts of data set at intermittent intervals.

A variety of carrier-provided services is available to support bursty LAN traffic. Understanding the range of choices and their advantages and disadvantages allows LAN managers to select the best facilities for LAN internetworking—perhaps cost-justifying replacement of existing narrowband networks with new technologies that offer a clear navigation path to broadband networks. Chapter 46 provides an overview of available carrier-provided transmission services and assesses their suitability for supporting LAN traffic.

An enterprise typically is a geographically dispersed, multifaceted organization, an organization comprising many branches, departments, and disciplines (e.g., marketing, manufacturing, finance, administration). In the past, the networking and information technologies deployed in an enterprise were many and disjointed. This leads to incompatibility problems and many enterprises are realizing the need for enterprisewide networking strategy. Chapter 47 discusses the role that network monitoring and analysis take in the administration of networks. It starts by explaining network monitoring and where it fits into the IT management arena before going into the range of functionality that network monitoring brings to the IT manager's arsenal.

In LANs, a common and useful mechanism is broadcast transmission, which is sending a message to all receivers. Such a mechanism is to be avoided in WAN environments due to the large number of receivers involved. A useful mechanism in this case would be multicast networking, which is sending a message to many (but not all) receivers. Chapter 48 covers multicast networking.

A number of options are available when departmental level LANs are interconnected to form a corporate level network. Chapter 49 covers the different internetworking options relating the options to physical and data link layer levels of the OSI model.

Chapter 50 provides a quick overview of valuable information on those critical elements of the network manager's job—network planning, design, and optimization.. Included are descriptions of an effective network-planning effort, modeling and performance issues, and tools for network design and optimization.

As corporate networks become more distributed, the task of managing the networks also grows in complexity. Chapter 51 covers the distributed network management and control aspects.

E-mail has been described as the killer application that will make the Internet and intranets indispensable for both business and personal use. There is evidence that this is coming true. Already there are more than 91 million e-mail users around the world and the number is growing every day. As is to be expected, a number of different e-mail systems from many vendors provide e-mail functions. The basic prerequisite for e-mail is networks. Chapter 52 discusses the different features and services available in e-mail systems and compares the leading e-mail systems on the market.

As mentioned earlier, the explosive growth in e-mail has caused the availability of e-mail products from a number of vendors. Some of the products are host or mainframe based, others are LAN based. In either case, a number of dial-up remote users need access to e-mail. Of course, these products are not completely compatible and there can be problems sending and receiving mail between the different products. Continuing the e-mail focus of heterogeneous communications, Chapter 53 covers migration and coexistence issues that pertain to e-mail and the Internet.

It has been estimated that at least 65% of today's mission-critical applications will be in use for another 10 to 15 years, and this longevity ensures that SNA will be in use for a while. Mission-critical applications were invariably developed to be accessed through 3270 terminals. With more and more 3270s being replaced by PCs, 3270 emulation on LAN-attached workstations (using an SNA LAN gateway) is now becoming the main approach for accessing these applications. This increase in LAN-attached, workstation-based applications has not significantly diminished what constitutes, by far, the bulk of SNA mission-critical application traffic. Chapter 54 covers the management aspects of SNA and LAN internetworks.

Continuing the SNA/LAN integration focus, Chapter 55 discusses several integration methods, but advises careful selection of tools since vendor offerings are still relatively new.

Traditional IBM host networks connect users to mainframes via SNA or bisynchronous multidrop lines. These are usually low-speed analog lines that represent a single point-of-failure between user and host. Next, IBM introduced X.25 as a cost-effective alternative to private lines. Many network planners have chosen not to implement it, however, because of higher user-response times from network overhead delays caused by every node in the X.25 network performing error detection/correction, message sequencing, and flow control. Frame relay, however, performs these functions only at the network access points using an end-to-end protocol; thus, frame relay uses the network more efficiently. Because of the frame-relay benefits, IBM has developed a set of SNA frame-relay products for packet-based WANs. Frame relay is an integral element of the evolution of SNA networks into the future with full support for APPN and ATM and Chapter 56 covers SNA communications over frame relay.

The help desk was created as a central point of contact for users of the data processing services. With the popularity of LANs the help desk started addressing LAN issues as well. At times, a separate network help desk was setup in addition to addressing applications and other data processing issues. As more LANs and WANs connecting heterogeneous environments became part of the overall data processing picture, the role of the network help desk became expanded. Chapter 57 covers the operation of a network help desk in a heterogeneous environment.

Due to the resources and the cost involved with help desks, there have been some attempts at automated help desks. Modeling the thought processes of a team of human experts, a prototype extended network expert operating system (ENEOS) at the Bank of America in San Francisco is helping manage multivendor, multinetwork communications facilities of arbitrary types and topologies. ENEOS's seven knowledge bases, 380 operating rules, 65 LISP procedures, and finite inference frame processor enable it to perform parallel rule processing for the real-time oversight of multinetwork events. Chapter 58 describes ENEOS and its network control implications and details its communications protocols and standards, architecture, and knowledge bases.

Chapter 45

The Essentials of Enterprise Networking

Keith G. Knightson

Enterprise networks and enterprise networking are buzz-phrases on every salesperson's lips, together of course, with "open" and "open systems." Many products are glowingly described with these phrases. Creating an enterprise network, however, requires more than just a knowledge of the buzzwords. This chapter explains the basic subtleties of an enterprise network and the challenges of establishing one.

THE NEXT GENERATION OF ENTERPRISES

An enterprise is nothing more than a fancy name for a given company or organization. It conveys, however, the notion of a geographically dispersed, multifaceted organization, an organization comprising many branches, departments, and disciplines (e.g., marketing, manufacturing finance, administration).

In the past, the networking and information technologies deployed in an enterprise were many and disjointed. In some cases, this was because of local departmental or workgroup autonomy, or simply because of ignorance among different parts of the enterprise as to what information systems were being used, or it was an artifact of historical equipment acquisition procedures.

The allegiance of specific departments to particular vendors was also a factor. When acquisition of capital equipment is performed gradually (rather than implemented all at once, across the board), it is difficult to make sure that all equipment is mutually compatible. Finally, the lack of an enterprisewide view, strategy, or policy with respect to networking and information technology—and the possible convergence solutions—are contributing considerations.

0-8493-9989-0/99/$0.00+$.50

Consolidating the Network

In the same sense that the word "enterprise" conveys the totality of an organization's operations, the phrase "enterprise network" means combining all the networking and information technology and applications within a given enterprise into a single, seamless, consolidated, integrated network. The degree of integration and consolidation may vary; total integration and consolidation may not be always achievable.

For example, an organization may have an SNA network from IBM Corp. and a DECnet from Digital Equipment Corp. In all probability, these two networks have their own communications components; there might be one set of leased lines serving the SNA network and another completely independent set of leased lines serving the DECnet.

It would be useful if all the IBM users could intercommunicate with all DEC users, but a first and evolutionary step might be to have both the SNA network and DECnet share the same leased lines. Now, only one physical network has to be managed instead of two separate ones, and more efficient and cost-effective sharing of the physical communications plant can be achieved.

A second step might be to interconnect the mail systems of the two networks to achieve at least the appearance of a single enterprisewide electronic-mail system.

A third step might be to unify the data and information and its representation as used within the organization. This would enable basic forms of data to be operated on by many applications.

The challenges of building an enterprise network fall into two distinct categories: getting the data (i.e., information) from A to B, and enabling B to understand the data when it receives it from A. These two categories are referred to in this chapter as the "networking challenge" and "beyond the networking challenge." In this context, the network is used as it is in the Open Systems Interconnection (OSI) reference model—that is, layer 3 and below.

THE NETWORKING CHALLENGE

The networking part of the problem has three major components:

- Choosing from and integrating the many network technologies.
- Selecting from the many vendor solutions.
- Moving information from a local to a global environment.

Integrating Network Technologies

The first basic problem with networks is that there are so many of them. In this context, networks are taken to mean the raw network technologies—leased lines (i.e., T_1 and T_3), X.25, ISDN, frame relay, asynchronous transfer mode (ATM), and the many and various LAN access methods.

If all the users in an enterprise are connected to the same network technology, there is no problem. Unfortunately, this is not always the case. Communication between users on dissimilar networks (e.g., two different LANs) is where the problem occurs.

Each network technology has its own characteristics and inherent protocols. From an enterprise viewpoint, this is bad news. For example, users connected to an X.25 network cannot easily be connected to those already connected to a LAN. For example, how would the X.25 user indicate the destination's media access control (MAC) address, and vice versa? X.25 networks understand only X.25 addresses and LANs understand only MAC addresses. The differences between network technologies and native protocols almost invariably prevent their direct interconnection.

Differences in addressing schemes present another difficulty. Addressing considerations alone usually dictate the use of a network interconnection device (NID) at the point at which two network technologies come together.

Exhibit 1 illustrates several network technologies, represented by N_1, N_2, N_3, N_4. Each of these technologies has its own native protocol (i.e., P_1, P_2, P_3, P_4). A way must be found to integrate all these disparate technologies into a single supernetwork, with globally uniform and globally understood characteristics and a single addressing scheme.

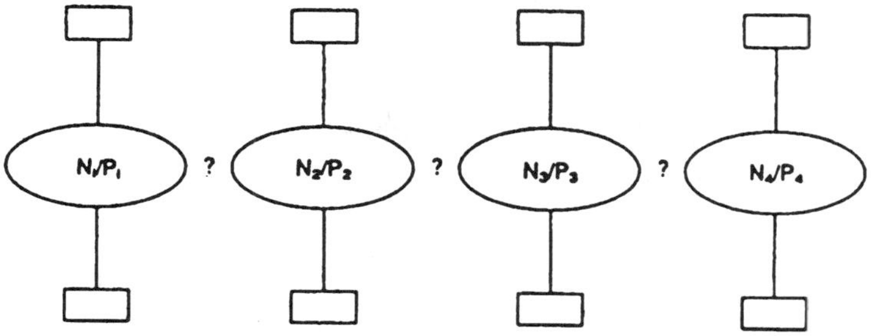

Notes:

- For every (sub)network N_i, there is a network-specific protocol P_i.
- All P_i's are different and thus not directly interconnectable.
- A way to make all the different networks look the same must be found, if the enterprise network is to appear as a single seamless network.

Exhibit 1. The interoperability problem.

This is achieved by operating an integrating, unifying protocol (shown in Exhibit 2 as Px), sometimes known as an Internet protocol, over the top of all the possible basic communications networks. The Internet protocol (IP) of TCP/IP is one such protocol. The connectionless network layer protocol (CNLP) specified in the OSI International Standard 8473 is another. Proprietary systems have their own Internet protocols—for example, Novell uses its Internetwork Packet Exchange (IPX) and Banyan uses Vines.

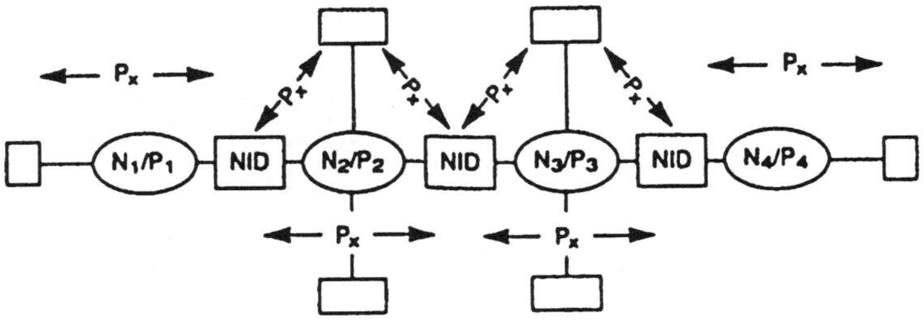

Notes:
NID Network interconnection device
• A neutral protocol P_x is run over the top of every subnetwork.
• Because P_x is now the basis of the enterprise network, the individual networks are called subnetworks.
• P_x operates at the top of the network layer and is usually called an Internet protocol.
• Several Px's exist (i.e., IP, CNLP, IPX).

Exhibit 2. The interoperability solution.

From the architectural standpoint, the technical term for such an Internet protocol is subnetwork independent convergence protocol (SNICP). The protocols used on real-world communications networks (e.g., leased lines, X.25, frame relay, LANs) are known as subnetwork access control protocols (SNACP). The basic internetworking architecture is shown in Exhibit 3.

Unification does not mean simplification. Two protocols operating over a given subnetwork still require two address schemes. Routing tables are then needed in the network interconnection device to map the global enterprise address to the address to be used by the network interconnection device for the next link in the composite path. Exhibit 4 is a simplification of how the two addresses are used. In practice, the "next" address may be more complex, depending on the internetworking protocols under consideration. A network interconnection device of this type is called a router.

Selecting Vendor Solutions

The second basic problem is that each system vendor has a vendor-specific idea of how to build the supernetwork—the type of supernetwork

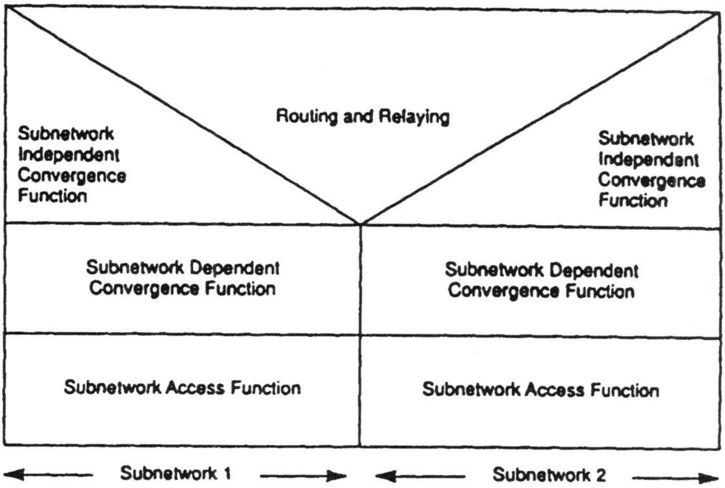

Exhibit 3. Network layer architecture.

protocol, the global addressing scheme, and the internal routing protocols to be used. At worst, this leads to a multiprotocol network, which amounts to several separate internets operating in parallel over the same physical communications plant.

Dealing with Multiple Protocols. An alternative to the multiprotocol network is to choose a single protocol for the entire enterprise supernetwork.

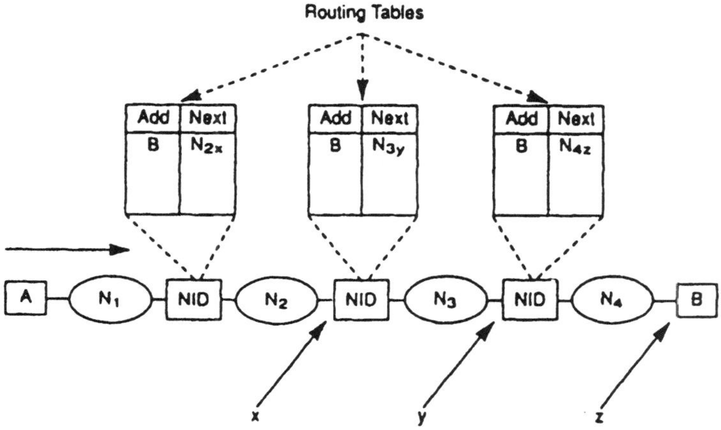

Exhibit 4. Simplified view of addressing.

This inevitably requires finding techniques to accommodate the systems that do not inherently operate this chosen protocol. Techniques include encapsulation (sometimes called tunneling) at the edges of the single-protocol network, or other techniques such as transport service interfaces and application gateways.

However, even with a single protocol, tunneling permits only the coexistence of incompatible systems; there can be little or no interaction between each of **the tunneled applications.** The major advantage of tunneling is that the core of the network is unified, optimizing network management and networking skills. The disadvantage is the effort required to set up the tunneling configurations at the edges.

The best solution is for all vendors to use the same Internet protocol. Increasingly, the protocol of choice for this purpose is TCP/IP. Although not a networking panacea, TCP/IP is the protocol of choice for most networking challenges involving multiple protocols.

Going Global

Many LAN-based systems include internal protocols that advertise the existence of various LAN- based servers. Such a protocol is sometimes known as a service advertising protocol (SAP). Protocol exchanges, frequently broadcast over the LAN, ensure that the availability and addresses of various servers are known throughout the LAN user community. This is useful when the geographic area is confined to a work group or a floor of a building; for example, the knowledge of a set of available printers is useful only in the area that has ready access to one of them. Thus, local messages must be constrained to local environments by putting adequate filtering at the point of access to the wide area portion of the enterprise network. There is no point in telling a user on a LAN in New York that there is a printer available on a LAN in Seattle.

WAN Transit Delays. Another global problem relates to the extra transit delay involved in transport over a WAN, especially for nonroutable protocols. Many protocol stacks used in local environments do not contain a network layer protocol—in other words they have no routing layer. Such protocols cannot be routed directly in a router-based enterprise network. Where it is necessary for such an application to be networked outside a particular local environment, the local protocol stack must be encapsulated within an internetworking protocol. Then it can be launched onto the wide area part of the enterprise network.

Many of the local or nonroutable protocols are designed for very rapid acknowledgment. The transfer of these types of protocols across a wide area may cause problems; applications may prematurely time-out or suffer poor throughput because of lack of a windowing mechanism adequate for the wide area transit delay.

To accommodate such applications, it is necessary to "spoof" the acknowledgments. This means that acknowledgments must be generated by the local encapsulation device. This requires the extra complication of adding a reliable transport protocol on top of the internetworking protocol across the wide area portion of the enterprise network. Once a local acknowledgment has been given, the originator will discard the original so it is no longer available for retransmission. Having given the local acknowledgment, the spoofing device must ensure reliable delivery to the remote end by employing a transport protocol of some sort (e.g., TCP or OSI Transport Class 4). The scheme, shown in Exhibit 5, avoids the end-to-end round trip delay T_r for every packet of data by providing an acknowledgment at time T_1.

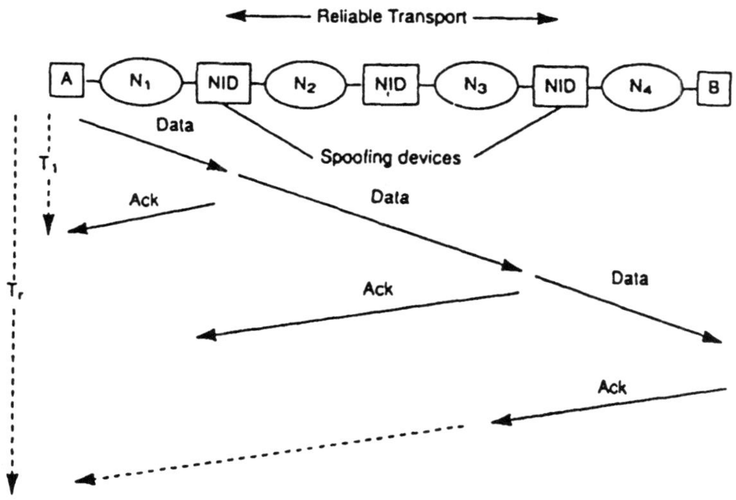

Exhibit 5. Spoofing.

Addressing. Going global also poses some challenges in the area of network layer addressing, particularly with regard to achieving enterprisewide uniqueness and structuring addresses for scalability and ease of routing.

Usually, addresses of stations within a local workgroup are allocated locally. This can present problems when subsequently the local workgroups must be integrated into a single enterprisewide address scheme. If several workgroup addresses—or parts of an address (e.g., an area or server name)—are the same, some changes will have to be made. From an operational perspective, changing addresses is not a trivial matter. It is best to avoid address allocation clashes right from the outset by having an enterprisewide address registration authority set up within the organization.

Some addressing schemes do have some hierarchy associated with them that can be used to avoid address encoding clashes by ensuring that local addresses are only the low-order part of the total address. Even in this case, however, an enterprisewide perspective is necessary to avoid clashes in the high-order part of the address.

Some vendors achieve uniqueness by allocating unique addresses when the equipment is shipped. However, this usually results in a flat, random address space that makes routing considerably more complex because there is no structure in the address to help "scale" the enterprise network from the routing perspective.

If the enterprise is to be permanently connected to the Internet (as opposed to using a dial-up connection), IP addresses must be obtained from an appropriate addressing authority. Until recently, all addresses were dispensed directly from the Internet Network Information Center (InterNIC). More recently, in response to a number of problems associated with addressing practices in the past, IP addresses have begun to take on a more hierarchical form. As such, the enterprise may need to obtain a block of addresses from its Internet Service Provider (ISP), in effect obtaining a subset of the addresses that ISP has obtained from the InterNIC.

This practice ensures that the appropriate hierarchical relationships are maintained, allowing improved routing, and it has the added benefit of more efficiently allocating the available addresses. The primary drawback from the perspective of the enterprise is that addresses obtained in this fashion are no longer considered permanent. That is, if the enterprise changes ISPs, the addresses may also have to be changed.

Hierarchical Schemes. The most widely documented and hierarchically administered address available today is the OSI address space available for OSI Network Service Access Point (NSAP) addresses. A more recently developed scheme is the next generation of IP, now known as IP version 6 (IPv6), described in RFCs 1883-1886. NSAP addresses can consist of up to 40 digits, and IPv6 addresses can be up to 128 bits, either of which allows good scaling potential and simplified routing.

The reason that a hierarchical (i.e., scaled) address scheme is so important has to do with the way that routers operate and the size of the associated routing tables. If addresses were allocated completely randomly but uniquely from a large address space, every router would need a table with every address in it. Not only would the table be extremely large, but the time needed to find an entry could also be a problem. Routing is thus better arranged on the basis of hierarchical distinctions that are implicit in the address scheme.

To service a local workgroup or other limited geographical area, a local router must know only whether the destination address is internal or external. If it is internal, the router knows how to get the message to the destination; if it is external, the router can pass it on to the next-level router. This leads to the concept of areas, groups of areas, domains, and countries being components of a hierarchical address.

When legacy systems must be accommodated with conflicting address schemes and reallocation of addresses is impossible, tunneling may have to be employed merely to avoid interaction between the conflicting addresses. Because conflicting networks are divided into separate virtual private networks, the protocol under consideration cannot be routed natively even if the backbone routers are capable of doing so.

Routing Protocols. To reduce the amount of time devoted to setting up routing tables manually, and to allow dynamic rerouting and a degree of self-healing, routing protocols are often employed to distribute routing information throughout the enterprise network. These protocols are in addition to the internetworking protocol itself but are related to it.

For every internetwork protocol routed in a multiprotocol network, there may be a specific routing protocol (or set of protocols). This also means in general that there will also be a separate routing table for each internetworking protocol. The situation in which several routing protocols are used simultaneously, but independently, is sometimes known as a "ships in the night" situation, because sets of routing information pass each other and are seemingly oblivious to each other even though there is only one physical network.

Some router manufacturers operate a single proprietary routing protocol between their own routers and convert to individual protocols at the edges of the network. There have been some attempts to define a single standard routing protocol based on the International Standards Organization's intermediate system to intermediate system (IS-IS) standard.

In an enterprise network, end systems (e.g., terminals, workstations, mainframes) usually announce their presence and their own addresses to the nearest local router. The local routers record all the local addresses within their area and inform all neighboring higher-level routers of their own area address. In this way, a router at the next and higher level in the hierarchy only needs to know about areas. Recursive application of these principles to a hierarchical configuration can lead to efficient routing by minimizing the amount of routing information to be transmitted and by keeping the size of routing tables small.

As the process of promulgating routing information proceeds across the network, every router in the enterprise network will obtain a table of reachability that it can then use for choosing optimum routes. Route optimality may be based on a number of independent metrics (e.g., transmit delay, throughput, monetary cost). Invariably, a shortest path first (SPF) algorithm is used to determine the optimal route for any particular metric chosen as the basis for routing. Both the Internet and OSI routing protocols use an SPF algorithm.

ROUTERS

Routers are the key interconnection devices in the enterprise network; subsequently, the router market has been one of the key growth areas during this decade. Some router vendors have grown from small $10 million companies to $1 billion companies.

In most cases, routers are purpose-built communications processor platforms with hardware architectures specifically designed for high-speed switching. Several possible pitfalls await the unwary purchaser of routers. Such a purchase involves four important considerations:

- The capacity and architecture, in terms of the number of ports accommodated and throughput achievable.
- Internetwork protocols supported and their associated routing protocols.
- Support of technologies for the connected subnetworks.
- Interoperability between different vendors.

Capacity and Architecture

The number of ports required determines to a large extent the size of the router required, which in turn affects the architecture and throughput of the router. Physical size of circuit boards dictates how many ports can be placed on a single board. The greater the number of ports, the greater the number of boards required and the more critical the architecture.

Routing between ports on the same board is usually faster than routing between ports on different boards, assuming that there are on-board routing functions. Boards are usually interconnected by means of some kind of backplane. Backplane speeds can vary greatly between vendors. Routing functions and tables may be distributed across all boards or may be centralized. The bottom line is that the architecture affects the performance, and performance figures are sometimes slanted toward some particular facet of the architecture. Thus, some routers may be optimal for certain configurations and not so good for others.

Many of the router manufacturers make several sizes of router, which could be referred to as small, medium, and large. All of one vendor's routers may, regardless of size, offer the same functions, but the circuit boards may not be interchangeable between the different models. This can make a big difference when it comes to stocking an inventory of spare parts. There may also be differences in network management capabilities.

When making comparisons, the data communications manager must carefully analyze vendor throughput and transit delay figures. Although worst cases are helpful for the user and network designer, some vendors specify either the best cases or averages. Other metrics involved in measurement may also be different (e.g., packet size assumed, particular internetwork protocol, particular subnetwork).

Other architectural considerations include extensibility and reliability. For example, is hot-swapping of boards possible? If the router must be powered down and reconfigured to change or add new boards, the disruption to a live network can have severe ripple effects elsewhere in the network. Can additional routing horsepower be added easily as loads increase, by simply inserting an additional routing processor?

The question of using standalone or hub-based routers may also be relevant. This is a difficult problem because of the traditional split between the hub and router manufacturers. Hub vendors tend not to be routing specialists, and router vendors tend not to be experts at hub design. Alliances between some vendors have been made, but the difference in form factors (of circuit boards) can result in some baroque architectures and poor performance. Except in the simple, low-end cases, purpose-built standalone routers usually perform better and are more easily integrated with the rest of the network.

Some standalone routers can directly handle the multiplexed input streams from T1 and T3 links, making voice and data integration possible. This is unlikely to be the case for a hub that has been designed mainly for operation in a LAN.

Internetwork Protocols Supported

Most router vendors claim that they support a large number of internetworking protocols. In some cases, however, there may be restrictions on the number of protocols that can be supported simultaneously. There may also be restrictions on the use of multiple protocols over certain network technologies, or hidden subnetwork requirements. An example of the latter might be the need for a separate X.25 permanent virtual circuit (PVC) for every individual protocol, as opposed to operating all the protocols over a single PVC.

Some vendors may also use a proprietary routing protocol scheme for internal routing, only making the standard protocols available at the periphery of the network. This makes it difficult to mix different vendors' router products on the same backbone or within a single routing domain.

Network Technologies Supported

Most manufacturers provide interfaces to a large number of network technologies (e.g., X.25 ISDN, frame relay, T1, T3, Ethernet, Token Ring). The method of support may also vary. For example, in the case of leased circuits, it may or may not be possible to directly connect the carrier's line to the router. Some routers may accept the carrier's framing mechanism directly; others may require an external converter to provide a simple serial interface (e.g., V.35) before connection can be achieved. Buyers should remember that the interaction between these interfaces and the multiple internetwork protocols may not be clearly reported by the vendor.

Interoperability

In the not too distant past, there was little interoperability between routers from different vendors. The reason most often cited was lack of standards for operating multiple protocols over a given subnetwork topology. Fortunately, the Internet community has made substantial progress subsequent to its definition of the Point-to-Point Protocol (PPP), which originally defined encapsulation and discrimination methods for multiprotocol operation over leased circuits. More recently, the utility of PPP has been extended with numerous enhancements. For example, it can now be used over switched services, including dial-up, ISDN, and Frame Relay, and it can be used in a multi-link configuration. It can operate with or without authentication, and with or without compression.

This plethora of options has led to the widespread support for PPP, both in terms of the number of protocols standardized for use with PPP, and in terms of the number of vendors building compatible routers. As such, interoperability among routers of different vendors is much more common than it was just a few years ago.

Network Management

It is extremely unlikely that a common set of management features will apply to all vendors' routers. Thus, if several manufacturers' routers are deployed in a given enterprise network, several management systems probably will be required. In the best case, these systems can be run on the same hardware platform. In the worst case, different hardware platforms may be required.

Filtering

The degree of filtering that can be applied—to prevent local traffic uselessly flooding the enterprise network—may vary with the manufacturer. Various parameters can be used as the basis for filtering—for example, source address, destination address, protocol type, and security codes. The disadvantage of using filtering is the labor involved in setting up the filter tables in all the routers.

BEYOND THE NETWORKING CHALLENGE—THE APPLICATIONS

Gateways, Tunneling, and Transport Service Interfaces. All the considerations discussed so far apply to the internetworking protocols. Multiprotocol networks serve only to share bandwidth; they do not allow applications to interoperate. Where that is necessary, with completely different stacks of protocols, an application gateway must be used. Exhibit 6 shows an OSI-based mail (X.400) application interoperating with a TCP/IP based mail application over an application gateway.

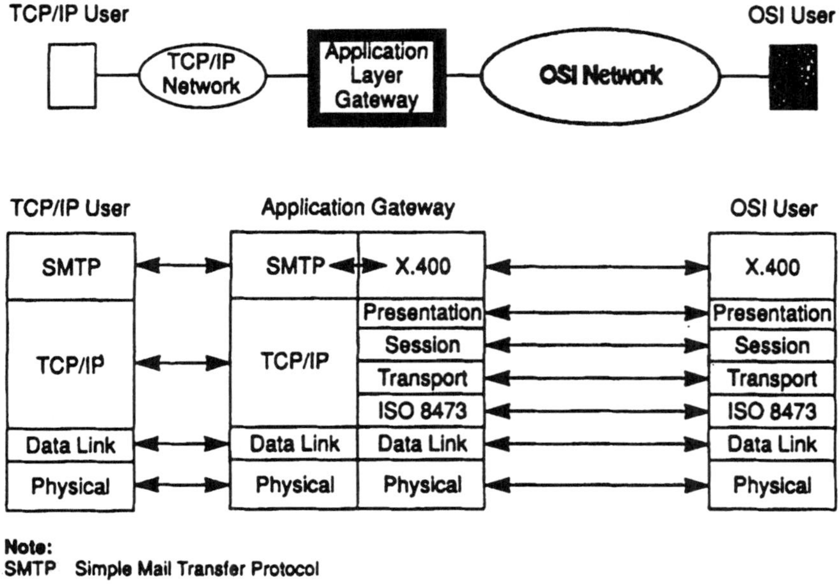

Exhibit 6. Mail application gateway.

Such gateways may be sited either centrally or locally. The use of local gateways makes it possible to deploy an application backbone with a single standard application operating over the wide area portion of the enterprise network (e.g., an X.400 mail backbone). This reduces the number of gateways needed for conversion between all the different applications. Only one conversion is necessary for each application (i.e., to the one used on the backbone). A considerable number of different local systems could interoperate through the "standard" backbone application.

The encapsulation technique already mentioned in the context of IP tunneling allows the applications that can be so configured to operate across the enterprise network. A tunneled SNA application is shown in Exhibit 7.

Another solution that may help in the future is the availability of transport service interfaces for end systems (e.g., workstations, terminals, servers). A transport server interface allows a given application to be operated over any underlying communications protocol stack. In other words, applications and communications stacks can be mixed and matched as necessary. The so-called open operating systems (e.g., POSIX and X/Open) adopt this approach.

The transport layer is a fundamental dividing line in the system architecture. Network-related functions are separate from application-related functions so that applications work with many communications protocols. Exhibit 8 shows an end system containing both an open OSI/TCP/IP stack (shaded) and a proprietary stack (unshaded). Within an end system, protocol stacks can generally be separated into the communications-specific lowerlayer parts and the application-specific upper-layer parts. The two stacks communicate through a transport layer interface (TLI).

SUMMARY

In practice, legacy systems or other requirements result in the existence of a variety of heterogeneous systems. Several techniques can be applied to at least make the heterogeneous systems networkable over a single physical network. Varying degrees of interoperability between them may also be possible.

TCP/IP is the single common protocol that has made the most tremendous advances toward this objective. With the continued progress in developing Internet protocols, coupled with the impending migration to IPv6, the multivendor networking situation will only improve.

Nonetheless, developing an enterprise network architecture continues to pose significant challenges. An overall plan for the network minimizes confusion and puts in place a timed migration strategy toward a completely integrated network. Central control has fallen into disrepute, but

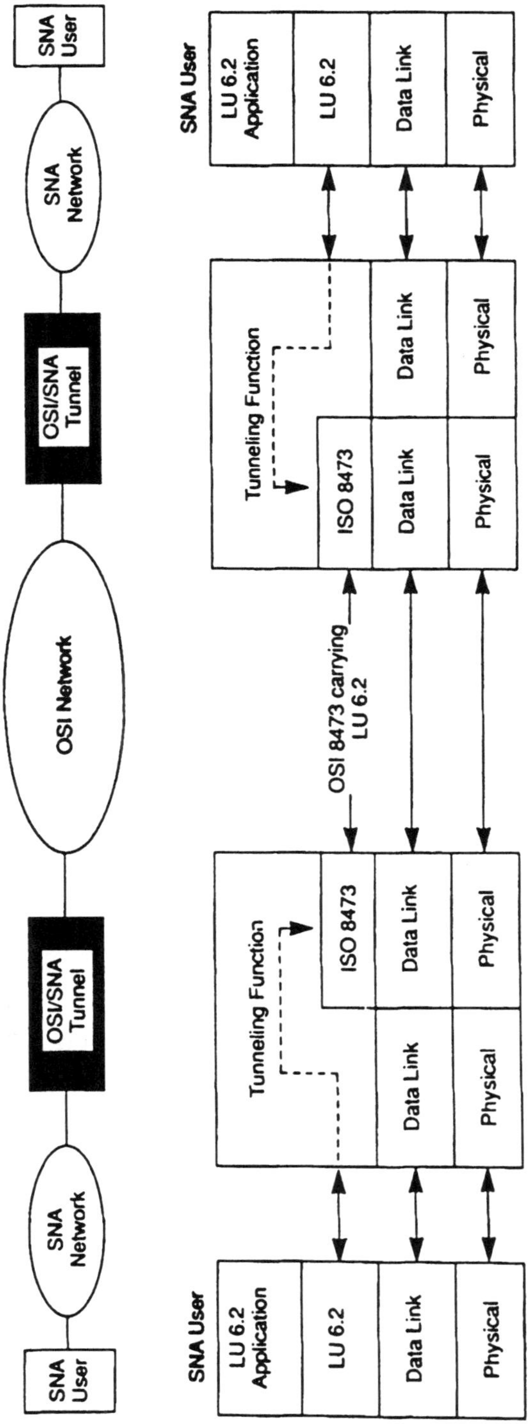

Exhibit 7. Tunneled SNA application.

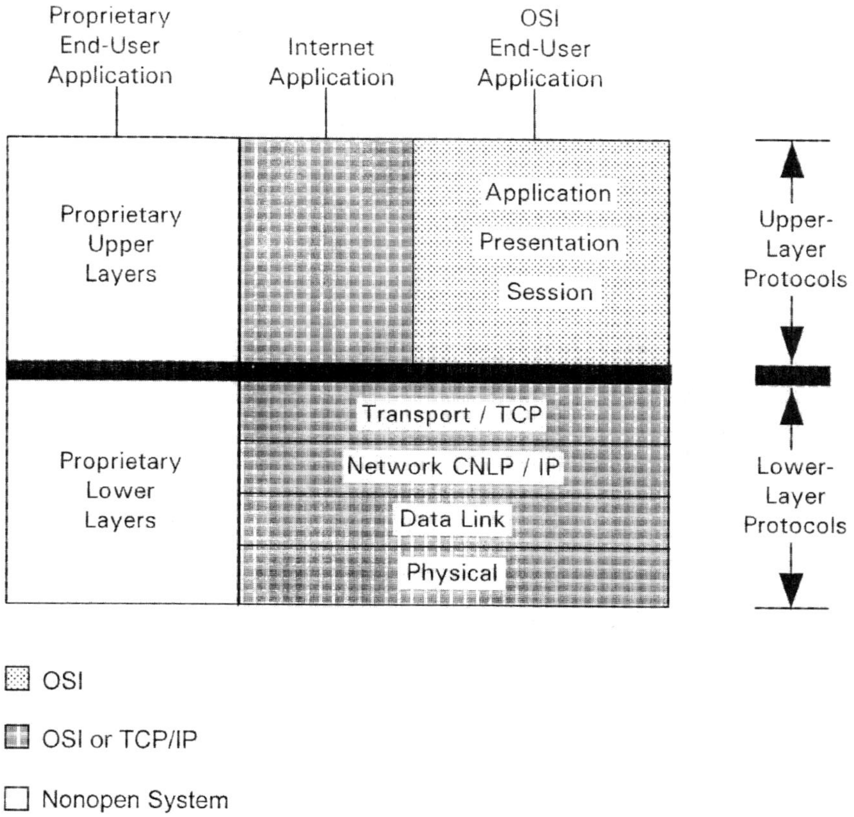

Exhibit 8. Transport layer interface.

without some control over how networking is to be achieved, all the real benefits of an enterprise network will not be realized. Finally, it is probably fair to say that enterprise networking is still something of a black art and is bound to present all data communications managers with some surprises and disappointments.

Chapter 46
High-Speed Services for LAN Interconnection

Nathan J. Muller

In today's distributed computing environments, with so much information traversing wide area internets, it is imperative that the right transmission service be selected to ensure the uninterrupted flow of information between interconnected local area networks (LANs). With the types of applications running over LANs, relatively high bandwidth is required for relatively low-duty cycles. The transmissions onto the wide area networks (WAN) consist of bursts of data set at intermittent intervals.

A variety of carrier-provided services are available to support bursty LAN traffic. Understanding the range of choices and their advantages and disadvantages allows LAN managers to select the best facilities for LAN internetworking, perhaps cost-justifying replacement of existing narrowband networks with new technologies that offer a clear migration path to broadband networks. This chapter provides an overview of available carrier-provided transmission services and assesses their suitability for supporting LAN traffic.

Transmission services are typically categorized as either switched or nonswitched. These, in turn, may be separated into low-speed (narrowband) and high-speed (broadband) services. Exhibit 1 summarizes these options.

NARROWBAND SERVICES

The technologies and transmission media employed to implement switched services determine the speed at which data is routed through the public network. For the purposes of this discussion, narrowband services are those that use data rates of DS-2 (6.312M bps) and below.

0-8493-9989-0/99/$0.00+$.50

Exhibit 1. Summary of carrier-provided communications services.

Nonswitched	Switched
Analog, 4.8K to 19.2K bps	Dialup with modem, 2,4K to 38.4K bps
Digital Data Services, 2.4K to 56K bps	ISDN, 64 K bps to 1.544M bps
Fractional T1, $N \times$ 64K bps	Packet-switched, 2.4K to 56K bps
T1, 1.544M bps	Virtual Private Networks, 2.4K bps to 1.544M bps
Frame Relay, 1.544M to 44.736M bps	Frame Relay, 1.544M to 44.736M bps
Fractional T3, $N \times$ 1.544M bps	SMDS, 1.544M and 44.736M bps
T3, 44.736M bps	Broadband ISDN, 155M and 600M bps
SONET, 51.84M bps to 2.488G bps	
Note: FDDI at 100M bps is not included in this chart because it is a private network solution, not a carrier offering.	

Analog Dialup and Leased Lines

Conventional switches such as AT&T's 5ESS and Northern Telecom's DMS series, which are in widespread use in local central offices, are currently limited to switching in 64K-bps increments. AT&T is upgrading its switches to accommodate higher speeds, but most are suitable now only for voice and low-speed data. The transmission medium is typically copper wire, but because transmission over copper wire may be affected by various impairments, data transmission over modems was for a time limited to 33.6K-bps, or 115.2K-bps when using MNP 5 compression. Modem speeds of 56K-bps became common during 1997.

Because line quality may vary by location and even from one moment to the next, many modem manufactures offer a capability known as automatic downspeeding. When line quality deteriorates, a modem operating at 33.6K-bps could downspeed to 28.8K-bps. At the lower transmission rates, the data is less susceptible to corruption. Correspondingly, a 14.4K-bps modem will downspeed to 9.6K-bps. Sensing better line quality, some modems even return to the higher speed automatically. The advantage of automatic downspeeding is that it keeps channels of communication open; the drawback is that much of the time the modem will transmit at speeds below advertised line rates, which curtails cost savings on line charges and prolongs the payback on the hardware investment. To minimize the effects of line impairments on copper-based voicegrade leased lines, extra-cost line conditioning may be requested from the carrier. But there are no performance guarantees with line conditioning; the carrier promises higher-quality lines on a best-effort basis.

The low speed and uncertain line quality of analog dialup and leased lines renders them suspect for carrying LAN traffic. They may be used as a temporary backup for failed digital lines and only when the volume of LAN traffic is very low. They can also be used to communicate with isolated bridges and other interconnection devices for diagnostic purposes when digital links go down. LAN interconnection requires that higher-quality digital offerings be explored, starting with digital data services (DDS).

DDS

DDS, the first digital service for private-line communications, was introduced by AT&T during the mid-1970s. It offers a range of speeds from 2.4K-bps to 56K-bps. Being a digital service, DDS does not require a modem but a digital termination device called a digital service unit that is required at each end of the circuit. The appeal of DDS for data is the higher quality of digital transmission. Until recently, DDS at 56K-bps was a popular way to connect LANs by remote bridges. However, the 56K-bps line rate is a potential bottleneck to LANs that operate at speeds in the 10M-bps to 100M-bps range.

For this and other reasons, DDS is rapidly being supplanted by newer offerings such as 64K-bps generic digital services and fractional T1. GDS does away with hub architecture—and high cost of DDS—because it can be implemented from any of the local exchange carrier's serving wire centers. The growing popularity of fractional T1, and the fact that AT&T plans to enhance it with management and diagnostic capabilities, has fueled industry speculation that AT&T might be phasing out DDS. Moreover, new 128K-bps digital services are becoming available, implemented by the recently adopted two binary, one quaternary (2B1Q) line code standard.

The 2B1Q line code standard provides 128K-bps of bandwidth over the same pair of wires that now support 56K/64K-bps digital services from the local central office to the customer premises. The standard has been adopted by the American National Standards Institute (ANSI) and major European postal, telephone, and telegraph administrations and others as well, including the European Telephone Standards Institute and the International Telecommunications Union-Telecommunications Standards Sector (ITU-TSS, formerly the CCITT). The 2B1Q scheme is viewed as essential to the success of basic rate ISDN (2B + D).

PACKET-SWITCHED SERVICES

Packet-switching networks thrived during the 1970s and 1980s as a way for asynchronous terminals to access remote computers. The driving force behind the acceptance of packet- switching networks was the ITU-TSS X.25 standards. Packet networks based on the ITU-TSS X.25 standard are generally optimized to run only at 56K-bps, mostly because of the X.25 protocol's overhead burden. This protocol divides the data stream into manageable segments and encapsulates them into envelopes referred to as packets. A single data stream may be segmented into many packets, each containing the address, sequence, and error-control information required to allow a network switch to identify the destination of the packet.

Packet switches can be divided into low, midrange, and high-end categories, depending on the number of ports and the packet throughput. These two measures are interrelated. As the number of switch ports increases, the throughput, or capacity, must also increase or overall performance will degrade. Packet switches designed during the 1970s employed single 8-bit microprocessors, which limited them to a throughput maximum of 100 packets per second (pps), usually measured by a packet size of 128 bytes. During the 1980s, the introduction of more powerful 16-bit and 32-bit microprocessors increased the throughput of packet switches to between 300 and 500 pps.

More elaborate multiprocessor design can increase throughput to 1,000 to 10,000 pps, which is required for support of T1 line rates. To increase throughput beyond this value requires the use of technologies that increase the switch processing speed through either hardware or protocol innovation. Frame relay represents a protocol innovation. Such evolution is worthwhile because public networks offer very powerful network management capabilities.

Packet-switched networks employ in-band management with most of the routing information embedded in the individual packets. For a packet-switched network, a management packet is just another type of packet that is routed along the same routes as data. But reading the packet information presents a considerable software processing burden for the nodes. Circuitswitching devices are faster than packet-switching devices because they are hardware based rather than software intensive. As the core microprocessor technology continues to evolve to deliver higher performance, so do the packet-switched devices.

X.25. Public X.25 packet networks offer users convenience and instant worldwide connectivity. In the private networking environment, some LAN interconnect vendors offer a software interface option that enables a single X.25 connection to support both bridged and routed low-volume traffic, instead of requiring separate connections for bridges and routers.

Frame Relay. For the immediate future, however, frame relay holds the most promise. Although equally applicable to public and private networking, frame relay's advantages are quite compelling in the private networking environment:

- It provides multiplexing with high throughput and can be readily managed.

- It offers an optimized protocol for networking bursts of data—for example, LAN bridging at T1 rates.
- It establishes a standard interface and transport for the many differing data communications requirements of an organization.
- It offers an open architecture for using public-switching services.
- Its implementation is vendor independent.

Frame relay will ultimately provide the benefit of vendor- independent implementation. This is certainly not the case today, because the carriers use either Cisco (formerly StrataCom) or their own proprietary fast packet switches to implement frame relay services. Users must therefore buy frame relay access devices that are certified to work on the selected carrier's frame relay network.

The reasons for using frame relay in the public network are no less compelling:

- It allows user access to public services through ISDN's D, B, and H channels.
- It implements control access through ISDN's D channel at 64K-bps, using Q.931 call-setup procedures.
- It allows existing X.25 packet switches to be upgraded to faster frame relay switches.

Frame relay is discussed in further detail later in this chapter.

Fractional T1

Fractional T1 entails the provision and use of incremental bandwidth between 56K-bps and 768K-bps without having to pay for an entire T1 facility. Instead of paying for a full T1 pipe of 24 DS-0s (at 56K/64K-bps each), fractional T1 allows users to order individual DS-0s or bundles of DS-0s according to the requirements of their applications. Thus, a user may order six contiguous DS-0s, which constitutes a single 384K-bps channel, for the purpose of linking geographically separate LANs over a pair of bridges. This saves the user the expense of a partially filled T1 line while easing the WAN bottleneck between LANs, which was a problem with DDS at 56K-bps.

Because fractional T1 is widely available among interexchange carriers, there is no back-haul problem to contend with, as in DDS. Fractional T1 is an offering of interexchange carriers. To date, among local carriers, only New England Telephone, Ameritech, and PacBell offer tariffed fractional-T1 access (some independent telephone companies offer fractional-T1 access on an individual case basis). For the most part, users must still pay for a full T1 for access, even through they may need only one-quarter of one-half of the bandwidth for LAN traffic.

Apparently, with the falling price of T1, many local telephone companies have come to believe that fractional T1 is unnecessary. For the foreseeable future, this means that the cost savings associated with fractional T1 will accrue only on the long-haul portion of the circuit; the longer the circuit, the greater the cost savings over a full T1.

Integrated Services Digital Network

Primary rate integrated services digital network (ISDN) (23B + D) is another wide area internetworking option. ISDN is a switched digital service that is billed for on a time-and-distance basis, just like an ordinary phone call. However, the 64K-bps B (bearer) channels cannot be strung together the way DS-0s can under fractional T1. Like DDS at 56K-bps, ISDN B channels pose a potential bottleneck for the traffic bursts between LANs.

A number of high-capacity ISDN channels are included with the primary rate interface, two of which are now available from AT&T: the 384K-bps HO channel and the 1.536M-bps H11 channel. These channels are more suited for interconnecting LANs.

Tariffs for ISDN services vary from region to region. Some local telephone companies offer flat-rate service with unlimited local calling, while others charge fees according to a combination of time and distance of use. Interexchange services are time and distance sensitive. Data communications managers should carefully evaluate the available pricing options before determining the suitability of ISDN to a particular situation.

Dedicated T1 Lines

T1 digital lines are an excellent medium for interconnecting LANs from point to point. They offer excellent reliability and availability, in addition to high capacity. An increasing number of bridges and routers offer T1 interfaces. Some T1 vendors have integrated the bridge function into their multiplexers.

The advantage of this hybrid arrangement lies with the nature of the traffic. All of the capacity of the T1 line may not be required for LAN traffic. Therefore, voice and low-speed data from multiple sources can be integrated on the same facility for economical long-haul transport. Each type of traffic can even be separately managed. If line impairments threaten to disrupt high-speed data, these channels can be rerouted to other lines having spare capacity, or to bandwidth- on- demand services like ISDN. Channels carrying voice traffic and low-speed data, which are more tolerant of bit error rates that affect high-speed data channels, can remain where they are.

Another advantage of using T1 multiplexers in conjunction with bridges is that it allows the logical integration of voice and data into a single, centrally managed network. This arrangement becomes all the more important as LANs evolve from workgroup solutions to general-purpose transport vehicles. The higher-order management system of the T1 multiplexer can be used to provide an end-to-end view of the network for performance monitoring, diagnostics, and status reporting. The network elements of both LANs and WANs show up on the same screen of the operator's console to simplify performance monitoring and expedite trouble handling.

Emerging applications are already putting a strain on today's Ethernet and Token Ring LANs, so it should come as no surprise that linking LANs over packet-switched and T1 networks is rapidly becoming inadequate. Other LAN interconnection strategies are called for. Another bandwidth—on-demand service-frame relay—offers an alternative to traditional T1 services. Other alternatives fall into the category of broadband services. There are three transitional service offerings: fractional T3, T3, and switched multimegabit data service (SMDS). They are transitional in the sense that they straddle the narrowband and broadband service categories; that is, they operate in the 1.544M-bps to 45M-bps range and provide the transition to ATM cell switching provided over the emerging synchronous optical network (SONET).

Frame Relay Services

An outgrowth of ISDN, frame relay is a bearer service that has become a high-performance alternative to X.25 packet-switched networks for LAN interconnection. The technical concept behind frame relay is simple: eliminate protocol sensitivity and unnecessary overhead—as well as associated processing at each node—to speed up network throughput. Error correction and flow control already exist at the upper layers of most modem computer communications protocol stacks and thus may be relegated to the edges of the network rather than performed as every node along a path.

Virtually all carriers offer frame relay services, including AT&T, MCI, US Sprint, British Telecom, and Worldcom (formerly WilTel). These networks offer one standard high-speed interface. Initially, frame relay networks will use permanent virtual circuits for connecting a source and destination. The routes are defined in fixed tables located in the network switch, rather than established during a call- setup phase by reading the frame address. Eventually there will be switched frame relay calls, using switched virtual circuits. The pricing strategies for both permanent and switched virtual frame relay differ among the carriers. Although some carriers have published their pricing schedules, flexibility is often achieved through negotiation on an individual basis.

With frame relay, available bandwidth is used in the most efficient manner possible. A frame relay application will momentarily seize the entire amount of available bandwidth to transmit information in bursts. Upon completion of a duty cycle, it relinquishes the bandwidth to other voice and data applications. A management issue with frame relay networks is congestion control. At any given time, several users might want to access the full transmission bandwidth simultaneously. The network must have a means to detect such situations and initiate procedures to prevent an overload condition. Although congestion control is an integral function of X.25 and LANs, the problem is usually more pronounced in frame relay networks. This is because the speed of the access links may be much higher than the frame relay backbone. A LAN operating at 10M-bps, for instance, can easily overwhelm a frame relay link operating at the T1 speed of 1.544M-bps.

Typically, frame relay carriers manage the congestion issue by establishing for each subscriber a committed information rate (CIR), measured in bits per second. By establishing the CIR for a subscriber, the carrier guarantees to route traffic that is submitted at or below that rate. Above that rate, the carrier will accept traffic for transmissions, but will set the discard eligibility (DE) bit on the excess frames, indicating to the network that the frames may be discarded if needed, to alleviate congestion problems. The CIR guarantee is a contractual guarantee, rather than a technical guarantee. It is up to the carrier to ensure that sufficient bandwidth is in place to assure delivery of the aggregate CIR of its subscriber base.

Currently, the alternatives to frame relay include private digital connections, leased lines, dialup modem links, and other packet services. Of these, private digital links are relatively expensive, and the others are often too slow and prone to creating bottlenecks.

Virtual Private Networks

In recent years, virtual private networks (VPNs) have become a workable method for obtaining private network functions. Under the VPN concept, an organization's PBXs are linked together over the public network. The intelligence embedded in the virtual network—at the carriers' serving offices—provides digit translation and other conversion services. The carrier assumes the responsibility for translating digits from a customer-specific numbering plan to and from the carrier's own numbering plan. All routing and any failures are transparent to the customer and consequently to each individual user on the network. PBXs are connected to the carrier's point of presence (POP) through various local access arrangements. The private network exists as a virtual entity on the carrier's backbone network.

Until recently, virtual private networks could handle only voice and low-speed data traffic. New high-speed data capabilities are available that are suited to such applications as LAN interconnection and disaster recovery. Switched 384K-bps and switched 1536-bps are two of the services that are being phased in by AT&T, for example, under its software-defined data network (SDDN). These services offer user the performance of private lines with a bit error rate of 10^{-6}, which equates to 95% error-free seconds on 95% of premises-to-premises calls, 95% error-free seconds on 99% of POP-to-POP calls, and 95% error-free seconds on 98% of premises-to-POP calls.

Fractional T3

As LAN interconnectivity fuels the need for additional bandwidth, an increasing number of users are asking: What is the right solution for connecting LANs at speeds greater than T1 but less than TY Some vendors are trying to capitalize on the appeal of fractional T1 by extending the fractional concept to T3. Although fractional T3 might constitute one solution, it is by no means the most efficient or economical. In fact, it is very unlikely that fractional T3 with the contiguous bandwidth characteristics of fractional T1 will be provided within asynchronous T3 infrastructure.

To obtain an analogous service using DS-3 signaling, which would offer bandwidth in $N \times$ DS-1 increments, the DS-3 signal would have to ensure frame integrity between individual DS-1s. Although this is possible, it is highly inefficient because of the asynchronous multiplexing structure of DS-3.

In constructing the DS-3 frame, DS-1 goes through two stages of multiplexing with bit stuffing and destuffing at each stage. The first stage combines four DS-1s into a DS-2 (6.312M-bps), and the second stage combines seven DS-2s into the DS-3 frame, which equals 28 DS-1s. The DS-1s are not synchronized within DS-3, have differing frame alignment, and do not allow frame integrity that would be required for a fractional T3 offering. Thus, the only practical fractional T3 bandwidth increment afforded by DS-3, other than DS-1, is the 6.312M-bps DS-2 intermediate rate.

The migration to SONET will change this situation and truly open up incremental bandwidth beyond DS-1 (T1). Being a synchronous network, SONET will enforce both byte and frame integrity, which can easily lead to new $N \times$ DS-0 and $N \times$ DS-1 services. It would be far better to look toward fractional SONET services that can be deployed today than toward fractional T3. As SONET evolves it is conceivable that a fractional version of the first level of SONET service (fractional OC-1) could offer services with bandwidths of up to 28 × DS-1 or 672 × DS-0.

SONET is the foundation for broadband ISDN with access lines in the future operating at 155.52M bps (OC-3) or 622.08M bps (C-12). Both ANSI and ITU-TSS standards for broadband ISDN require that the broadband ISDN structure be capable of providing bandwidth in increments of any 64K-bps (DS-0) integer. This sets the stage for fractional services up to 2,016 × DS-0 (C-3) and up to 8,064 × DS-0 (OC-12).

Current discussions of fractional T3 among service providers acknowledge the fact that these are really DS-1 channelized services implemented through M13 multiplexers. AT&T provides this services as an option for its T45 service, which includes an element called M28, an M13 offering. This option is available under AT&T's FCC Number 11 for individual case basis T45.

Another example of this M13-type service is the multiplexing option found in New York Telephone's T3 individual case basis, per FCC Tariff Number 41. The M13 option, however, has a number of drawbacks that prevent it from implementing fractional T3 services that are truly analogous to fractional T1. Among them, M13 cannot be remotely controlled to permit customers to add bandwidth incrementally; this must be done manually by technicians who rearrange patch panels, a process that can take weeks to implement.

One implementation of fractional T3 entails breaking down the local access DS-3 circuit into DS-1 circuits for routing over the service provider's network (POP-to-POP). However, there is confusion about the way to access these T1 channelized services. All T3 channelized T1 services require strict compliance with the M13 format. Some T3 products are not compatible with M13, such as those that adhere to the Syntran structure or use an incompatible proprietary multiplexing scheme for T3. Today, users must choose either M13 or proprietary T3, which are mutually exclusive.

Most service providers do not consider M13-type options to be true implementations of fractional T3. They are looking instead at 1/3 cross-connects and SONET in pursuit of true fractional services above T1. With SONET products currently being deployed and being introduced by more vendors, the next step beyond fractional T1 is not fractional T3, but fractional SONET.

BROADBAND SERVICES

Broadband networks are analogous to multilane highways. Large bandwidth applications require them, but the need may be only temporary and smaller roads may suffice most of the time. The prospect of bandwidth on demand is being viewed with increasing interest among LAN users as well as carriers. An intelligent broadband network that spans public and private domains would be capable of managing multiple high-capacity LAN channels plus video and other bandwidth-intensive applications.

T3 Service

T3 service is offered at the DS-3 rate of 44.736M bps, typically over fiber facilities. The applications touted by T3 advocates include:

- LAN interconnection.
- Multiple T1 line replacement.
- High-speed backbones integrating voice, data, video, and image.

However, T3 requires the use of proprietary optical interfaces and so entails the construction of special individual access lines from the customer premises to the carrier's serving office. Special construction costs at each end differ widely from region to region, from a low of about $8,000 to a high of about $150,000. Because these costs are almost never factored into the crossover comparisons with T1, the true cost of T3 is so high that it is difficult for even the largest companies to justify it.

The majority of T3 devices sold are M13 multiplexers. The M13 is a simple T1 concentrator, which lacks network management capabilities. Although DS-3 is a standard electrical interface that transports DS-1, the optical interface is proprietary. Also, many M13s lack support for such features as binary eight zero substitution (B8ZS), used for clear channel transmission, and extended super frame, used for maintenance, essentially because these formats were developed after the introduction of DS-3/M13. With DS-3, bipolar violations of DS-1 are always lost. Further, DS-3 was rate-adapted long before network management (over T1 networking multiplexers) became widely used. Consequently, DS-3 services generally do not provide the network management features T1 users have come to expect. This situation is changing through the implementation of C-bit parity on T3 facilities. This alternative T3 framing format is roughly equivalent to T1's extended superframe format.

C-bit parity can help ensure reliable service through end-to-end performance monitoring, remote maintenance and control, performance history, error detection, and trouble notification. Most new T3 equipment supports both C-bit parity and M13. Users of M13s must add new interface cards and reconfigure their software to work with the new framing format. AT&T, MCI, and Worldcom are among the carriers that support C-bit parity.

DS-3 is often transmitted over fiber, which requires an interface for electrical-to-optical signal conversion. The lack of optical standards for DS-3 has led to a proliferation of proprietary interfaces, which restrict the ability of users to mix and match different manufacture & equipment end-to-end. T3 services, like AT&T's T45, require the customer to negotiate the type of optical interfaces to be placed in the interexchange carrier's serving offices. In contrast to a ubiquitous service such as DS-1, T45 requires expensive special construction for the local channel, from customer premises equipment to POP.

Ideally, it would be preferable for large organizations to use transmission facilities operating at the 45M-bps rate or higher, rather than to lease multiple T1 lines to obtain the equivalent bandwidth capacity. After all, AT&T's T45 service, which provides about 45M bps of bandwidth between its serving offices, may be cost-justified at five to eight T1 lines, depending on distance.

Because the FCC has ruled against the use of individual case contracts, T3 access connections must be tariffed like any other service. Preliminary tariff filings indicate that it will now take 8 to 15—and perhaps more—T1 lines to cost-justify the move to T3. The individual case contracts require that users commit to the service for three to five years, during which they could lock themselves out of upgrades to SONET.

Users who cannot afford to wait for SONET can opt for T3 now but should not sign long-term contracts with carriers, unless they are prepared to pay hefty penalties to terminate service in favor of SONET.

New York Telephone, for example, charges $12,192 a month for a T3 access line but offers discounts that range from 10% to 30%, depending on the length of service commitment. At a commitment level of 3 years, the user qualifies for a 10% discount; at 5 years, 20%; and at 7 years, 30%. These service discount plans do not protect the user from rate increases; they lock in only the discount percentage. If the user terminates the service before the end of the selected commitment period, New York Telephone charges 50% of the applicable monthly rate for each month the service is disconnected before the end of the discount term.

SONET

SONET access with OC-1 customer premises equipment eliminates the cost of fiber-to-electronics multiplexing from the custom construction costs of T3. This is similar to the migration of T1 multiplexing from within the central office to customer premises equipment on T1 private networks. Incidentally, T1 does not drastically change under SONET standards but remains an entry level to SONET, which is defined identically to today's T1/DS-1, per D4 or extended superframe structures.

SONET is a worldwide standard that includes the fiber-optic interface. SONET transmission begins at a rate of 51.84M bps and reaches 2.488G bps with provision to go to 13G bps. Most SONET standard work has been completed, including standardization of the basic transmission formats and network maintenance and protection, as well as internetworking between different vendors' equipment through midspan meets on the public network.

The enormous amounts of bandwidth available with SONET and its powerful management capabilities will permit carriers to create global intelligent networks that will spawn bandwidth-on-demand services of the kind needed to support new LAN applications, including three-dimensional computeraided design (CAD), CAD conferencing, high-resolution imaging, virtual reality stimulation, and videoconferencing. All of these require the transfer of large blocks of data in bursts.

Such a transport network, which can be used as simply as the current voice telephone network, will emerge from the electro-optical SONET standards that have been winding their way through North American and ITU-TSS standards groups since 1985.

SONET offers advantages over today's WAN solutions that are too competitive to ignore. For example, because T3 is proprietary, it limits product selection and configuration flexibility while increasing dependence on a single vendor. SONET standards change all that, offering seamless interconnectivity among carriers. Under SONET, bandwidth may be managed to the DS-0 level to provide maximum control and support of bandwidth- on-demand services, regardless of carrier. SONET also provides central control of all network elements and permits sophisticated self- diagnostics and fault analysis to be performed in real time, making it possible to identify problems before they disrupt service. Intelligent network elements automatically restore service in the event of failure—a vital capability for large, complex LAN internets.

Eventually, SONET will dominate the transport and switching fabrics of the public network, and will support a wide range of services, including SMDS and broadband ISDN. SONET can even transport the fiber distributed data interface (FDDI) and metropolitan area networks (MANs) to extend the reach of high-speed LANs.

SMDS

SMDS is a public high-speed packet-switched transport service for connecting LANs, host computers, image data bases, and other high-speed applications. SMDS is ideal for bursty data applications, including the interconnection of geographically dispersed LANs, and is capable of supporting such applications as video and imaging.

The Bellcore SMDS standards were finalized in late 1989. To the original standard was added 802.6, a MAN standard approved by the Institute of Electrical and Electronic Engineers (IEEE) after eight years of research and development. The Bellcore standard specifies how customer premises equipment can access an SMDS switch using twisted-pair wiring at the T1 rate or optical fiber at the T3 rate. The IEEE standard incorporates the connectionless data part of the distributed queue dial bus architecture for media access control. This allows up to 16 user devices in a LAN arrangement to share a single access link to an SMDS switch.

SMDS employs a packet-switched, dual counter-rotating ring architecture. The two rings each transmit data in only one direction. If one ring fails, the other handles packet transmission. This protection mechanism safeguards users' data against loss due to a network fault.

Although SMDS shows promise as a LAN interconnection service, it is important to note that current standards have yet to specify network management and billing interfaces. Bellcore is expected to address billing interfaces, and the IEEE 802.6 Committee is expected to broaden its MAN standard to address such areas as network management, high- speed interfaces (e.g., T1, T3, and SONET), and isochronous service. Isochronous service would require that cell-relay switches, which form the switching fabric for SMDS, be expanded to switch voice and video traffic in addition to data.

Broadband ISDN and Asynchronous Transfer Mode

By the time narrowband ISDN emerged from the laboratory during the late 1980s and began to be deployed in the real-time business environment, it was already apparent that ISDN's B (64K-bps) channels would be inadequate to support emerging high-speed data applications. Specifically, users wanted to interconnect LANs and achieve high-resolution images and video—all of which requires considerably more bandwidth. Consequently, ISDN came under increasing attack as being too little, too late.

Standards bodies recognized early on, however, that the requirement for high-capacity channels within the framework of ISDN could be satisfied sometime in the future under a vaguely defined concept called broadband ISDN. Broadband ISDN increases the channel capacity to 600M bps and beyond for high-capacity connectivity and bandwidth on demand. But broadband ISDN requires a transport network of tremendous capacity. With no such network in place at that time, interest in broadband ISDN waned in favor of other broadband technologies and services, such as FDDI and SMDS, which were projected for near-term deployment.

Separately, but at about the same time, SONET was conceived to provide carriers with a standard optical transmission medium for interoffice trunking. Later, in consideration of private network interest in T3 transmission, the SONET concept was extended to include the local loop. More recently, the concept has made its way into the customer premises.

With the advent of SONET, it became apparent that the standardized, high-capacity intelligent transport medium offered by SONET provided the infrastructure that would make broadband ISDN a reality much sooner than originally thought. Thus, originally conceived and developed for different reasons, SONET and broadband ISDN subsequently became interrelated through the work of standards bodies with the idea of creating advanced voice, data, and video networks.

In support of these concepts, the technology now known as Asynchronous Transfer Mode (ATM), based on the use of cell-relay switching, emerged. ATM implements the services of broadband ISDN over SONET-compatible transport media. ATM is being deployed more slowly than some experts predicted, but is making steady inroads nonetheless.

Because the development of ATM and cell relay switching parallels that of the SONET and broadband ISDN standards, many design aspects have been developed to accommodate high capacity services on a worldwide basis. Taking advantage of the widespread availability and capacity of single- mode optical fiber, of which more than 2 million miles have been installed in the US alone, this technology brings the ability to reliably transport enormous quantities of information. ATM services are available at speeds ranging from 45M bps to 622M bps, using cell-switching technology. Not coincidentally, these rates correspond to speeds that have been standardized for SONET fiber-optic systems.

With this much capacity, ATM efficiently carries a multitude of high-speed services that can support such applications as LAN interconnection, videoconferencing, and imaging, as well as bursts of asynchronous data and voice. Although most services will require only a portion of the bandwidth, others may take the entire channel.

Broadband ISDN standards are introducing such maintenance features as trouble indicators, fault locators, and performance monitors. These will interface with any variety of customer equipment—PBX, LAN, T1 multiplexer—and provide transport to the central office where a SONET cross connect or switch will further concentrate or segment the information. The network topology between central offices is most likely to be star or mesh, while the topology between the customer premises and central office could range from star, ring, or point-to-point.

The Internet

Commercialization of the Internet has added new choices for LAN interconnection. From practically any given location, an organization can establish a connection to the Internet using a variety of interconnection speeds and technologies. Numerous Internet service providers (ISPs) offer complete LAN-to-LAN interconnection services as bundled solutions. Yet, even without such services, it is possible to establish LAN-to-LAN connectivity across the Internet.

Typical configuration scenarios involve the establishment of dedicated Internet connections at each location that has a LAN. These connections are made locally using a variety of the services and technologies described in previous sections of this chapter. Low-end configurations are often serviced with 56K-bps digital circuits or with ISDN connections operating at either 64K-bps or 128K-bps. (Note that ISDN connections used in this manner are generally cost-effective only in those areas with unlimited local ISDN calling.) Moderate amounts of traffic are effectively serviced with T1 connections, while high-end users require options such as multiple T1s or even T3 connections. The use of ATM enhances the choices even further. For instance, some ISPs offer 10M-bps service by establishing an ATM point of presence on the customer premises and providing that customer with a 10Base-T connection to the Internet.

Despite the range of high-end solutions available, even the smallest organizations can benefit from use of the Internet to interconnect their sites. For instance, a company with many small offices scattered around the globe can cost-effectively provide interoffice electronic mail with as little as dial-up Internet connections from each site.

Regardless of whether the Internet-based LAN-to-LAN connection is established as part of a bundled ISP service offering or is custom built by the organization, security considerations are of paramount importance. Two aspects of security should be considered in this equation.

First, all traffic traversing the Internet should be considered vulnerable unless steps are taken to encrypt the data. Second, most organizations with dedicated Internet connections implement firewalls to protect their internal networks from unauthorized access. If using the Internet to establish connectivity between protected internal LANs, a careful analysis of the organization's firewall policies and implementation practices is imperative.

Solutions to both these challenges are available, varying widely in cost and complexity, depending on the specific needs of the organization. Thus, it is possible for most organizations to implement adequate safeguards for this type of connection. Despite the added cost of employing such safeguards, use of the Internet in this fashion can be a very attractive, cost-effective alternative.

SUMMARY

With computing resources becoming increasingly distributed over vast distances, the future portends a buildup of LAN traffic between corporate locations. The means to interconnect LANs is provided by myriad current and emerging carrier services that, together, constitute the wide area network. When choosing from among the various transmission services, consideration must be given to the quality and speed of the links for supporting bursty LAN traffic. Choosing a low-speed service limited to 56K/64K-bps may not only create bottlenecks between LANs but entail costly upgrades if the service cannot handle incremental increases in LAN traffic. For this reason, such bandwidth-on-demand services as frame relay, ISDN, and SMDS that run over T1 and T3 links may be more appropriate.

Another factor to consider is whether the organization's needs for LAN interconnection are more effectively met by carrier-provided services via the Internet or by existing private networks. The number of choices and the variety of pricing options are in a constant state of flux, and thus require substantial analysis on the part of the data communications manager. Understanding the available choices and the advantages and disadvantages of each service will enable LAN managers to select the best facilities for LAN internetworking over the wide area network in terms of cost and efficiency as well as reliability and availability.

Chapter 47
Enterprise Network Monitoring and Analysis

Colin Wynd

INTRODUCTION

Growing User Expectations:

Users are starting to expect error-free network connectivity with guaranteed uptime and response time. Users are also expecting that network services are delivered regardless of the underlying technology. Business end-users also expect that data transmission will be secure. This increase in reliance on client/server applications as a fundamental part of conducting business means that end-users need to rely on the network as much as the phone. Thus, whether the IT department is ready or not, the network is expected to be as reliable as the phone system.

The Changing Face of the Business Environment:

Corporations are more geographically dispersed, and entities that once were autonomous are working closely together. The network has become a critical method of communicating between these various groups. Applications are now client/server rather than on a central mainframe, meaning that the network must be operational for the end-users to perform.

As the use of the network increases, more groups can be geographically dispersed. The increased focus on work/life balance has increased the number of work at home participants. The side-effect is that the amount of traffic on the network also increases.

This chapter discusses the role that network monitoring and analysis takes in administrating networks. We start by explaining network monitoring and where it fits into the IT management arena before showing the

0-8493-9989-0/99/$0.00+$.50

range of functionality that network monitoring brings to the IT manager's arsenal.

NETWORK MONITORING AND ANALYSIS DEFINED

Distributed network monitoring is the ability to view a remote network and perform monitoring and analysis on that remote network as if it were local. In the past, portable devices were carried out to remote sites and placed onto the network when problems were occurring on that segment. Having a network monitoring device on a segment only when there are problems means that the segment is not being monitored 99% of the time. Monitoring devices permanently placed on mission-critical segments can constantly monitor traffic. This means that analysis can be performed over and above fault management.

Exhibit 1 shows an example of remote monitoring agents installed on a large enterprise network with a variety of media types such as WANs, switches and media types such as FDDI and ethernet.

The agents or "probes" reside on the remote segments and collect information of the traffic that it sees. The segments can be of any media type from various LAN media types such as ethernet, FDDI, token ring or some WAN protocol such as frame relay. The segments can be geographically dispersed, but in general must be interconnected. The network

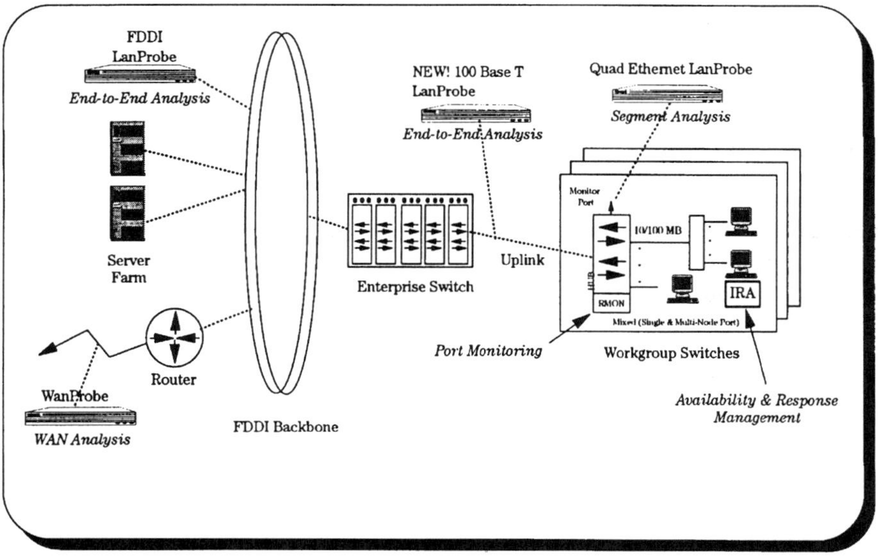

Exhibit 1. Remote monitoring agents installed on a large enterprise network.

management console contains a suite of applications that collect the network information from these remote agents and interprets them using power graphical user interfaces. Interestingly, the network management console communicates with agents using the same network that the agents are monitoring (out-of-band communication between the manager and agents is also possible).

With this configuration network administrators can use monitoring tools to manage the whole network. Some functions that the network administrator can perform are:

Network Performance Management: The ability to continuously monitor certain network statistics to ensure adherence to the service level agreement. Setting network thresholds to identify anomalies and the creation of baselines to aid in determining "normal" network performance.

Network Security Monitoring: Ensuring that only authorized users are accessing the network. This includes both monitoring the effectiveness of firewalls as well as internal security monitoring.

Fault Management And Availability: Being able to troubleshoot network problems in a timely fashion and monitor the availability of servers from end-users perspective.

Capacity Planning: Traffic profile modeling allows the network manager to do a quick "what if" analysis before re-configuring network resources. Having the appropriate data of past network trends determines what changes need to be made in the future to handle the ever growing network growth.

NETWORK MONITORING AND ANALYSIS IN THE IT ENVIRONMENT

The IT management environment covers the whole scope of devices that reside on the network as well as the network itself that enable business end-users to function. We can break this down into four components:

Systems Management is concerned with the performance of the computers on the network, and usually deals with issues like database performance and disk use on file servers.

Element Management is concerned with managing the various networking devices, like bridges, routers, and hubs. Typical management issues deal with configuration tables, throughput, link states, and port partitioning. A device management application usually shows a picture of the device on your screen, complete with installed cards and indicator lights.

Desktop Management is concerned with the end-user workstations and PCs. The management issues are PC config files, disk use, application support, etc.

Network Monitoring And Analysis is primarily concerned with the activity on the wire itself. It is looking at the flow of data across the network in an effort to understand network performance and capacity, and to resolve problems related to networking protocols.

Service level management (SLM) is the strategy of defining, controlling and maintaining the desired levels of IT service for the business end-user. Business end-users define with the IT department the level of service that is needed to support the end-users. The level of service is turned into a set of objectives that the IT department can then monitor.

Network monitoring and analysis allows the IT department to manage one part of the end-to-end management picture. System, Database, Application management issues are not discussed in this chapter.

STANDARDS OVERVIEW

Network monitoring has benefited from several standards. The main standard currently in use for network monitoring is the RMON standard which defines a method of monitoring traffic up to the DataLink layer (layer 2) in the OSI stack. The RMON2 standard which currently has not yet been ratified by the IETF defines how to monitor traffic at the network layer (OSI layer 3) and some portions of the application layer (layer 7).

Simple Network Management Protocol (SNMP)
Simple Network Management Protocol version 2 (SNMPv2)
Remote Monitoring (RMON) standard
Remote Monitoring version 2 (RMON2) standard

Why Perform Network Monitoring?

As part of an IT department's Service Level Agreement (SLA) with its business end-users, IT must maintain a certain level of network service. To be able to do this, the network must be monitored to ensure error-free connectivity, responsiveness and level of throughput. If the network is not monitored then it would be impossible for the IT department to guarantee any level of service.

In today's competitive environment, new client-server applications are quickly appearing in business environments, some examples are the WWW, Lotus Notes, network DOOM. If the network is not being monitored, then the effect of adding one of these network intensive applications is unknown and eventually one will bring the network to its knees. If the environment is being monitored, then network bandwidth can be monitored and traffic trends analyzed to ensure that network bandwidth will always exceed future growth.

The ability to monitor trends changes the IT from being reactive — waiting until something breaks before resolving the problem; to being proactive — resolving potential issues before they break. The IT department should now blend into the background allowing business end-users to focus on their own function.

Who Does Network Monitoring?

Since there are many areas to network monitoring, many people are involved. Here are some generic descriptions:

Network Manager Responsible for long term strategic decisions regarding the network. Involved in looking at new technologies such as 100Base-X or ATM, deciding where and when to modify bandwidth. This person tends to look at network trends, performing forecasting and capacity planning.

Network Engineer Responsible for day-to-day operations of the network. Upgrades network devices, adds capacity. Also acts as a second line of supports for problems that the operations center engineer cannot resolve.

Operations Center Engineer Most large corporations have a centralized monitoring center that are staffed with "level 1" engineers that attempt basic troubleshooting on problems. These engineers monitor for events that are triggered by servers, workstations, or network devices that can alert the operations center on potential problems. These engineers are the first line of support and are constantly in reactive mode.

What Data Is Provided?

Monitoring the network means that information on every single packet on every single segment can be gathered. Network monitoring really means deciding which data is important and should be gathered and which data is redundant. Corporations with a large number of segments need to decide on only a few critical pieces of information otherwise they are inundated with data. The cost of analyzing the network would exceed the actual cost of the network! Some of the most critical measurements that should be gathered are:

1. Utilization: Segment utilization information should be gathered to generate trends for capacity planning purposes; baselining purposes; performance information.

2. Error rates: Total error rate information can give performance indicators; baselining the error rate of the network; correlated with utilization can give indicators of physical layer network problems.
3. Protocol distribution. This can generate trends for changing application mixes; monitoring the usage of new applications and the effect of new applications on the network.
4. Top talkers can also give indications on the performance of the network; performance of machines; load of application and services on the network. Top talkers can also indicate potential new applications that are unknown to the network department (new Internet applications such as PointCast have been discovered using this method).
5. Latency measurements (echo tests) lead to trends in performance.

How Does Network Monitoring Work?

Network monitoring is a large subject and there are many proprietary protocols that are involved. We are only going to cover standards based protocols plus the most widespread proprietary protocols.

The Simple Network Management Protocol (SNMP)

The Simple Network Management Protocol (SNMP) was a draft standard in 1988 and finally ratified in April 1989. SNMP is described by Request For Comments (RFC) 1098. SNMP has three basic components:

Agent A software program that resides in a managed element of the network such as a hub, router or specialized device.
Manager communicates with the agent using the SNMP commands
Management Information Base (MIB) A database that resides with the agent and holds relevant management information.

The diagram in Exhibit 2 shows the relationship between the three components (agent, MIB, and manager).

There are five types of SNMP commands called protocol data units (PDU's):

1. *Get request:* A manager requests (from the agent) the value of a variable stored in the MIB.
2. *Get-Next request:* Used by the manager to request information on multiple variables. Used to reduce network traffic. If one variable is not available, no values are returned. Also used to retrieve unknown rows if available.
3. *Set request:* The manager instructs the agent to set a MIB variable to the desired value.
4. *Get-Response:* Sent by the Agent as a response to a SET or Get-Next command as either an error or identical to the SET to show it was

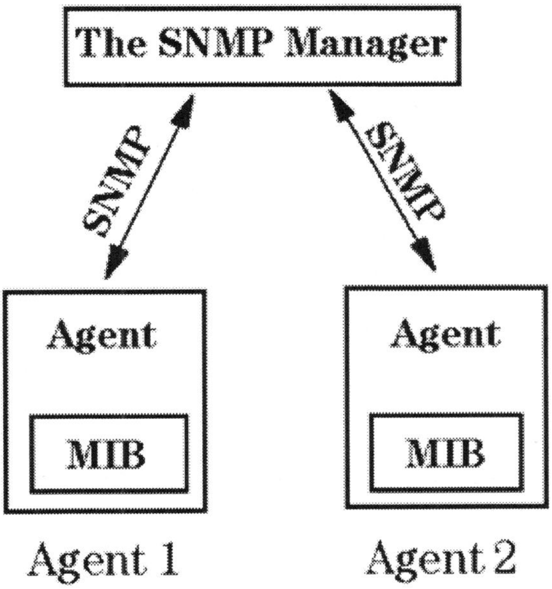

Exhibit 2. Relationship between agent, MIB, and manager.

accepted, or to a Get-Next with the value portions of the request filled in. The Manager checks its list of previously sent requests to locate the one which matches this response and if none found, the response is discarded, otherwise it is handled.

5. *Trap:* One of two unsolicited messages sent from the agent to the manager, often used for event notification.

THE MANAGEMENT INFORMATION BASE TREE

MIBs are hierarchical in nature (Exhibit 3), this allows unique identifiers for each MIB variable (or Object). Some MIBs of interest are:

RFC1213 — MIBII — basic system information and basic level statistics
RFC1757 — RMON (Remote Monitoring)
RFC1513 — RMON (Remote Monitoring) Extension For Token Ring

There are several advantages that network management applications have with SNMP:

- The protocol is easy to implement
- The protocol requires few resources to operate
- The protocol is mature, stable and well understood
- The protocol is widely available (on most computers) and most network devices have some form of agent/MIB embedded within them.

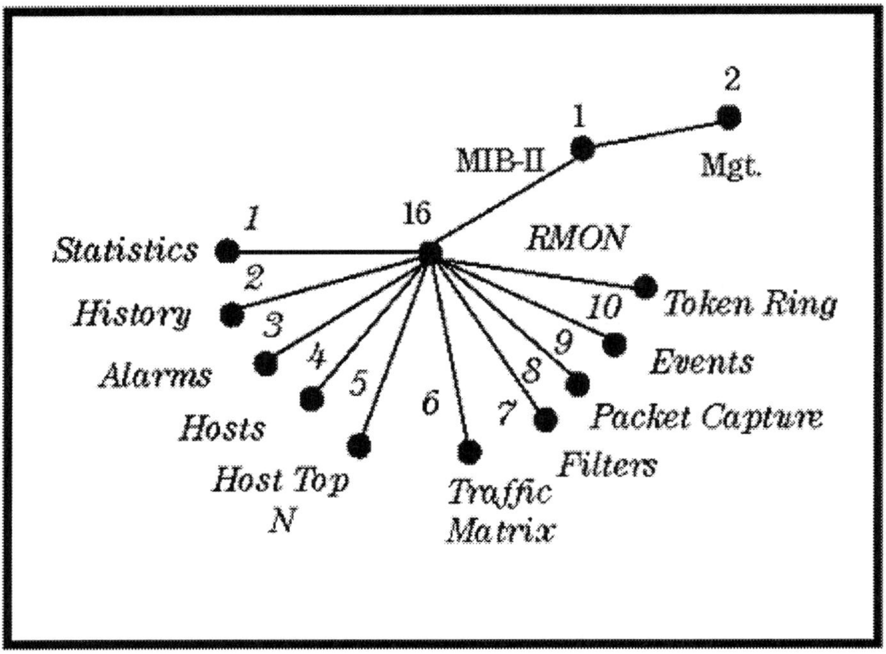

Exhibit 3. The hierarchical nature of MIBs.

However, as networks have grown and the need for network management has become more imperative, several disadvantages with SNMP have become apparent. Some of these disadvantages are:

- Limited security
- Lack of a block transfer
- Polling based protocol
- Trap limitations

SNMPv2

SNMPv2 is a proposed standard that is attempting to address these issues. Some of the proposed extensions to the standard include:

- Manager-to-manager communication capability.
- Additional SNMP commands (PDU's):
  —Get BulkRequest — for getting whole tables
  —InformRequest — A Manager-to-Manager PDU
- Reliable traps

The last area of contention with SNMPv2 is security. Currently there are two proposed drafts that are attempting to address the security issue.

The Remote Monitoring Protocol (RMON)

The RMON standard is a specific standard for performing remote monitoring on networks. The RMON standard is defined by two standards RFC 1757 and RFC 1513. The standard defines a MIB that is broken down into 10 groups, the first 9 define monitoring of ethernet networks and the 10th defines extensions for token ring. There are currently no standards for monitoring FDDI, 100Base-X, or WAN networks. RMON vendors have added their own proprietary extensions for these additional media types. RMON is limited as it only gives visibility up to the DataLink Layer (layer 2) in the OSI stack.

Statistics Group This group contains many segment statistics in 32-bit counters such as packets, dropped packets, broadcasts and multicasts. These are just counters and not studies.

History Group This group contains segment history statistics for various counters such as broadcasts, errors, multicasts, packets, octets. These numbers are for certain time periods. RMON defines two default time periods — five seconds and 1800 seconds.

This means:

Alarms group This covers threshold monitoring and trap generation when that threshold has been reached. Allows alarms to be set of various counters and patch match. Traps can start and stop packet capture.

Host Group Contains host table and traffic statistic counters, plus a time table of discovery.

Host Top N Contains studies for X time and X hosts, listing top talker for the study group.

Traffic Matrix Group Contains matrix of MAC layer (layer 2) conversations. Information such as error, packets, octets sorted by MAC address.

Packet Capture/Filter Group These two groups are used together. Packet capture group contains the packets that have been captured. Multiple instances can be created.

Token Ring Group Contains specific information about token ring such as ring order, ring station table, packet size distribution for history studies.

Remote Monitoring version 2 (RMON2) Protocol

The RMON standard brought many benefits to the network monitoring community, but also left out many features. The RMON2 standard is trying to address this. RMON2 attempts to address these issues by allowing the monitoring of layer 3 (Network Layer) information as well as protocol distribution up to layer 7 (Application Layer).

NETWORK PERFORMANCE MANAGEMENT

Performance management means being able to monitor segment activity as well as intra-segment traffic analysis. Network managers must be able to examine traffic patterns by source, destination, conversations, protocol/application type, and segment statistics such as utilization and error rates. Network managers must define the performance goals and how notification of performance problems should happen and with what tolerances. Some objectives that network managers are faced with are:

- Baselining and network trending: How to determine the true operating envelope for the network by defining certain measurements (such as segment utilization, error rate, network latency) to check your service level objectives and out-of-norm conditions which, if gone unchecked, may have drastic consequences on networked business users productivity.
- Application usage and analysis: Helps managers answer questions such as "What is the overall load of your WWW traffic?", "What times of the day do certain applications load the network?" This allows network managers to discover important performance information (either real-time or historic) that will help define performance service level objectives for applications in the client/server environment.
- Internetwork perspective: Is traffic between remote sites and interconnect devices critical to your business? With Internetwork perspective capabilities you can discover traffic rates between subnets and find out which nodes are using WAN links to communicate. It can also help you define "typical" rates between interconnect devices. Internetwork perspective can show how certain applications use the critical interconnect paths and define "normal" WAN use for applications.
- Data correlation: allows you to select peak network usage points throughout the day and discover which nodes were contributing to the network load at that peak point in time; which nodes they were sending traffic to; and which applications were running between them.

The diagram (Exhibit 4) shows an example of traffic flow between several segments. The thickness of the line (and the color) indicates the volume of traffic. With this information it is easy to identify potential WAN bottlenecks.

The second diagram (Exhibit 5) shows clients and servers correlated with a time graph. Being able to determine how much one particular server affects the network can help in the positioning of that server and again improve performance.

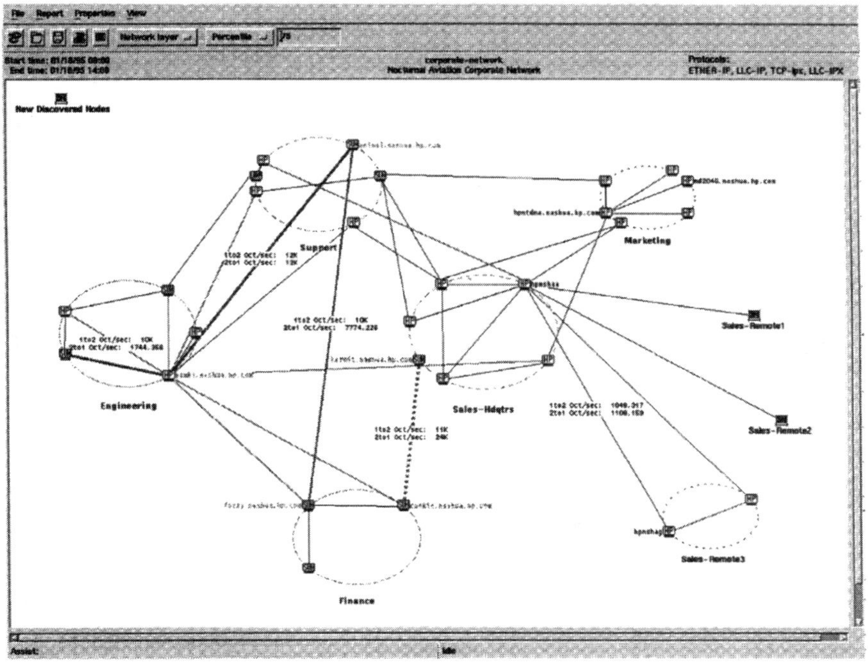

Exhibit 4. Traffic flow between several segments.

NETWORK SECURITY MONITORING

Security management encompasses a broad set of access control policies that span network hosts, network elements, and network access points (firewalls). Consistent policies are the key here; the objective is to support access and connectivity that is appropriate to the business need, while restricting clearly inappropriate network based access. As in other activities, constant monitoring for specific violations is critical, as is a notification mechanism. For certain conditions, immediate, automatic action may be required, (i.e., "Shut down this connection," or "Shut down the firewall"). Monitoring should include both passive and active monitoring (probing).

Access level monitoring ensures that the controls and security that is in place is actually performing to expectations. Monitoring the traffic flow to/flow a firewall for instance ensures that no intruders are accessing internally. Access level monitoring polices the "police" and ensures that nothing has been overlooked by the security.

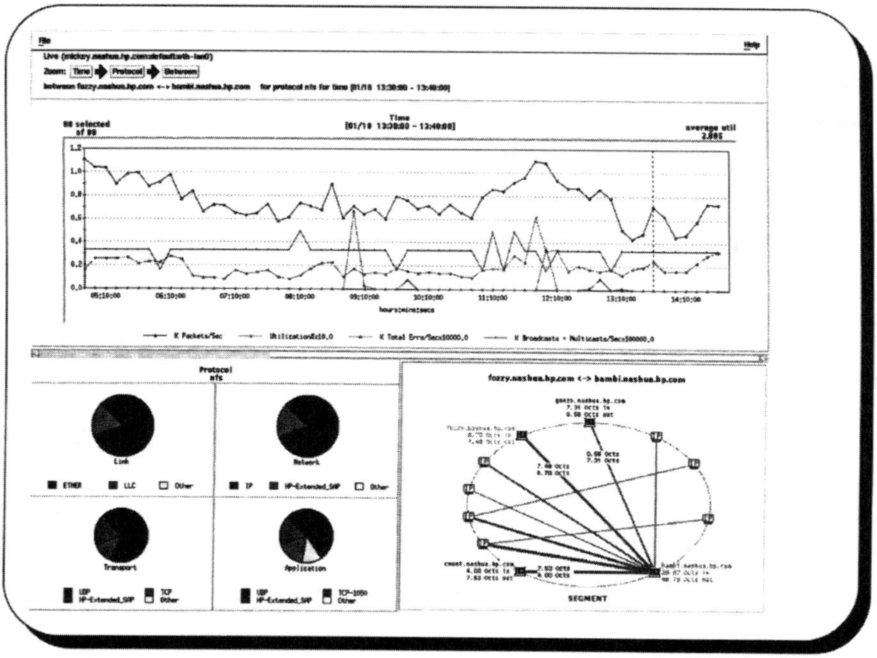

Exhibit 5. Clients and servers correlated with a time graph.

FAULT MANAGEMENT AND AVAILABILITY

Fault management is the continuous monitoring of the network and its elements and the detection of failures within the network environment. When a failure is detected then notification of the failure must occur in a timely fashion. The failure must be qualified with respect to other failures and prioritized.

Fault management systems include software bundles to detect and notify a centralized system of these failures. The centralized system normally includes some form of discover and mapping software that allows the network manager to have a graphical view of the network. These notifications must be correlated so that event storms are eliminated. A trouble ticketing system can also be incorporated so that a document trail is kept of the problem and allows a mechanism to communicate the status of the problem to the end-users.

Another aspect to fault management is availability. This is the monitoring of servers from business end-users perspective to ensure that the machine is available to the end-user. Tracking and notification of any interruption of client/server access is a critical part of the IT department's function.

CAPACITY PLANNING

Network demand is growing at unprecedented rates. New applications such as SAP and the World Wide Web (WWW) are encouraging extensive use of the network. Graphics are now sent regularly over the network (either through a corporation's IntraNet or over the Internet). As network managers increase bandwidth, new applications for the network (such as Voice-over-IP or multimedia) become viable. This causes another spurt of demand for the network.

Capacity planning allows the network manager to look forward by looking at the past and helps the manager to forecast what the demand will be. This means that the IT department can keep one step ahead in demand.

NETWORK REPORTING

Part of the IT department's function is to demonstrate that they are performing their function to the prescribed level. Being able to document that the network is running at the level agreed to in the service level agreement is an important justification tool.

It's critical that any reports are generated automatically otherwise reports will not be generated or the effort to generate them will be too substantial to make it worthwhile.

LIMITATIONS OF NETWORK MONITORING AND ANALYSIS

Monitoring the network with RMON standard means that only DataLink layer (layer 2) information is collected. This is not high enough in the OSI stack to gather information about traffic trends of client-server applications.

The RMON2 standard defines a method of monitoring up to layer 7 at certain times. RMON2 does not define continuous monitoring of all layer 7 traffic, nor does RMON2 define any metrics for performance management.

SUMMARY

Enterprise network monitoring and analysis is a fast changing environment. From the early days, just a few years ago of monitoring the physical layer of the networks to the future of application layer service level management, the whole arena is helping IT management take control of the distributed environment that it spans.

Network monitoring and analysis will always have several aspects that have been described in this chapter, and the tools for implementing service level agreements between business end-users and IT departments are quickly maturing.

However, network monitoring is only part of the total end-to-end solution that must include the whole environment that business end-users operate. This means that systems, databases and application monitoring tools must be deployed in conjunction with the network monitoring tools so that the whole environment can be viewed. Some tools such as HP's PerfView product are just being released that for the first time can integrate seamlessly database, application, network and system information on a single pane of glass for the end-to-end view that is necessary in this complex environment that IT must now work.

REFERENCES

Peter Phaal. *Lan Traffic Management*, Prentice Hall, ISBN: 0-13-124207-5

Dah Ming Chiu and Ram Sudama. *Network Monitoring Explained*, Ellis Horwood, ISBN 0-13-614-710-0

Nathan Muller. *Focus On OpenView*, CBM Books, ISBN 1-878956-48-5

Marshall T. Rose. *The Simple Book*, Prentice Hall, ISBN 0-13-812611-9

Chapter 48
Multicast Network Infrastructures

C. Kenneth Miller

Multicast transmission is the sending of one message to many, but not all, receivers. Multicast network infrastructures are becoming available in all kinds of data networks, including wide area, satellite, and wireless. This new infrastructure is being used for group-oriented data networks.

Broadcast transmission is the sending of one message to all receivers and has been used extensively in LAN environments. Broadcast traffic over wide area networks (WANs), however, should be avoided because it can flood the WAN with unwanted traffic, or broadcast storms.

Multicast provides the mechanism for one-to-many transmission over WANs without creating broadcast storms. Multicast network infrastructures can be created at layer 2 (i.e., the link layer) or at layer 3 (i.e., the network layer). The primary layer 3 multicast transport technique is multicast Internet protocol (IP), which many router vendors support. Layer 3 multicast transport is independent of the underlying network architecture.

Different physical and link layer architectures support multicast and broadcast services. For example, satellite data transmission is a broadcast architecture that easily supports multicast services. Other network infrastructures are multicast LANs, multicast frame relay, and multicast SMDS.

MULTICAST LANS

Every station on the LAN listens to all transmissions. Nodes on a LAN have media access control (MAC) addresses, which are sometimes called physical addresses because they designate a physical node on the network. MAC addresses are global, which means that each one is unique.

MAC addresses come in three varieties: individual (unicast), multicast, and broadcast. Unicast addresses identify end points in point-to-point communications. The MAC broadcast address is the all 1s address. MAC

0-8493-9989-0/99/$0.00+$.50

multicast addresses are primarily used for mapping to upper-layer multicast addresses.

MAC broadcast frames are usually filtered by bridges and routers, confining them to the local LAN and preventing broadcast storms.

MULTICAST FRAME RELAY

Frame relay is a layer 2 protocol designed for use over WANs. Frame relay is a connection-oriented protocol, which means that it emulates actual physical links with permanent virtual circuits (PVCs) and switched virtual circuits (SVCs). PVCs and SVCs represent point-to-point connections with data link connection identifiers (DLCIs) and do not usually have the facility for one-to-many connections. However, the Frame Relay Forum recently released specifications for one-way, two-way, and N-way multicast services over frame relay.

One-Way Multicast. One-way multicast is suitable for electronic distribution of information from an information service provider. (See Exhibit 1.) A multicast server in the network maps the multicast DLCI to the individual DLCIs. Individual DLCIs are also present from the members of the group to the multicast transmitter.

Two-Way Multicast. Two-way multicast enables migration of old IBM synchronous data link control (SDLC) multidrop configurations to a frame relay environment. (See Exhibit 2.)

N-Way Multicast. N-way multicast allows any node to be either a transmitter to the group or a receiver. N-way multicast (see Exhibit 3) was designed for teleconferencing applications.

MULTICAST SWITCHED MULTIMEGABIT DATA SERVICE

Switched multimegabit data service (SMDS) was developed by Bellcore for local exchange carriers to provide high-speed connectivity between LANs in a metropolitan area. SMDS is a subset of the IEEE 802.6 metropolitan area network (MAN) standard and is offered as a service by several carriers.

SMDS uses a connectionless network architecture in which all nodes can communicate to all other nodes on the network, similar to LANs. All packets sent on the network are available for reception by all nodes, which means that SMDS can support multicast, unicast, and broadcast services.

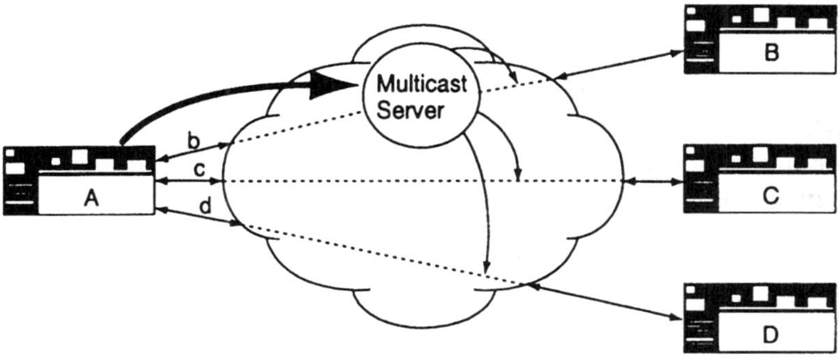

Exhibit 1. One-way multicast.

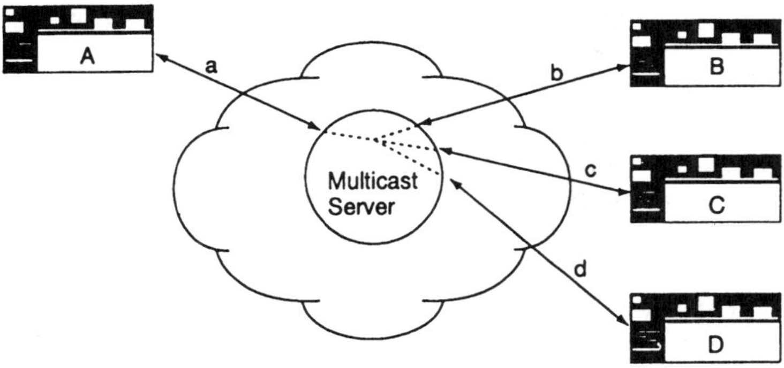

Exhibit 2. Two-way multicast.

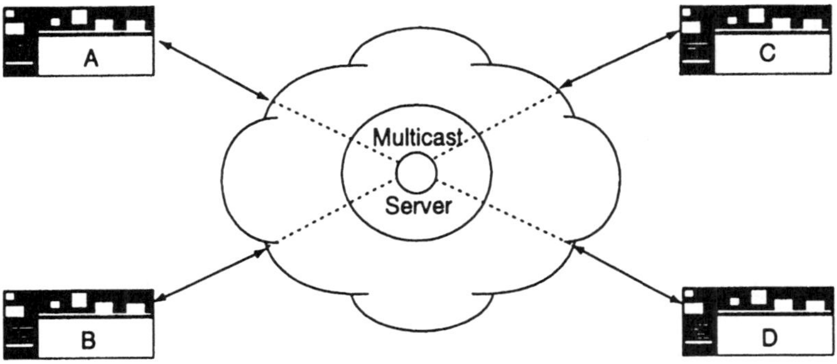

Exhibit 3. N-way multicast.

COMPARING BROADCAST AND MULTICAST IP

IP supports broadcast as well as multicast services. The IP address 255.255.255.255 defines the global broadcast address and is mapped into the MAC global broadcast address on the LAN to which it is attached. The IP global broadcast address is not usually forwarded by routers out of a local network.

A second category of IP broadcast address is the network broadcast address. In this case, the network portion of the Class A, B, or C IP address is sent to the desired network destination; the host portion is the all 1s broadcast address. Network broadcast addresses are forwarded by routers to the designated network, where they are mapped into that network's MAC broadcast address. For example, the Class C IP address 206.42.32.255 is the network broadcast address for network 206.42.32.

Network broadcast addresses can provide so-called directed broadcast services to a particular network or subnetwork over an internetwork.

The IP Multicast Protocol

Multicast IP is a new technology that provides network layer routing of IP Class D group address packets in transmission control protocol and Internet protocol (TCP/IP) networks. Multicast IP operates over any network architecture, and the multicast groups can be set up and torn down within seconds. Multicast IP is destined to be the dominant means for providing multicast services in data networks of all kinds including mixed network environments or internets.

Class D Addressing

Multicast IP uses Class D IP addresses, as shown in Exhibit 4. IP Class A, B, and C addresses are used for point-to-point (unicast) communications

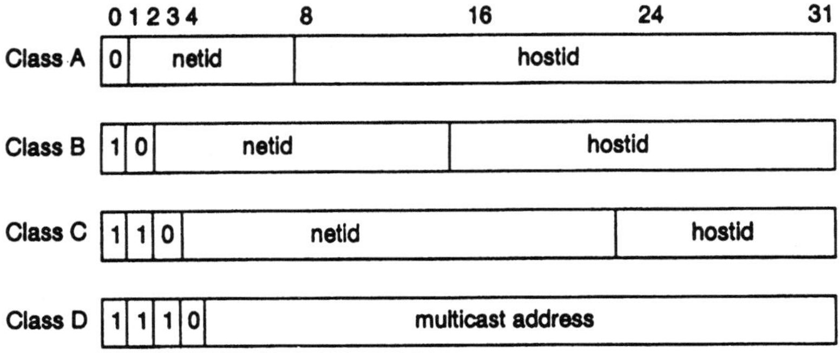

Exhibit 4. IP address types.

and consist of network and host components. Class D addresses, by contrast, have only one component that identifies the multicast group.

Class D addresses occupy the range from 224.0.0.0 to 239.255.255.255 and can be assigned semipermanently or temporarily for the length of time a group is in place. Groups may be set up and torn down in seconds.

Hosts that belong to a group need to support RFC 1112, which is the standard for host extensions for IP multicasting. RFC 1112 specifies the Internet group management protocol (IGMP) that is used by members of a multicast group to inform the nearest router supporting multicast routing of their presence in a particular group. The router is responsible for updating routing tables so that multicast packets with the Class D address associated with that group are forwarded to the subnetwork that includes members of the group.

The IGMP dialog is shown in Exhibit 5. Two messages are provided in the dialog: the IGMP query and the IGMP response. Queries are sent to the all hosts' multicast group address — 224.0.0.1 — and carry an IP time-to-live of 1. Hosts respond to queries with host membership reports for each host group to which they belong.

There are two techniques for reducing the number of concurrent reports and the total number of reports transmitted. A host can start a report delay timer or it can send a report that other members of the same group on the network can overhear.

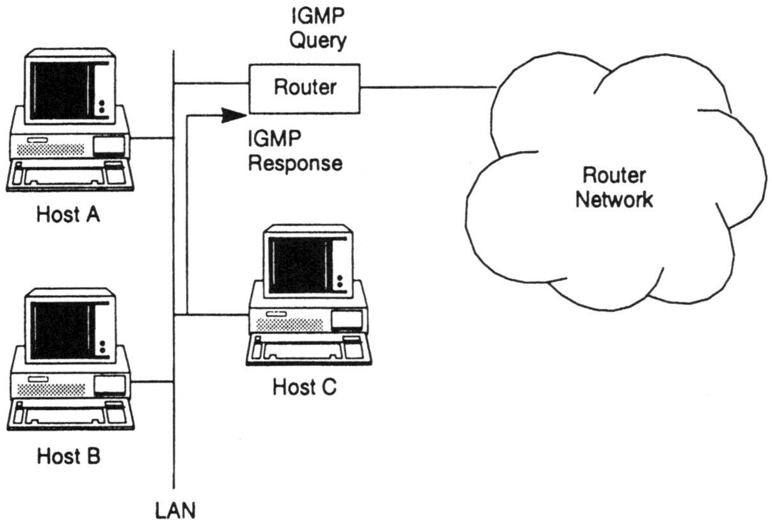

Exhibit 5. IGMP dialog.

Starting a Report Delay Timer. When a host receives a query, it can start a report delay timer rather than sending reports immediately for each of its group members on the network interface of the query. Timers are set to different, randomly chosen values between zero and D seconds. A report is generated for the corresponding host group when a timer expires. Thus, reports occur over a D-second interval rather than concurrently.

Sending a Report that Other Members Overhear. To ensure that other members of the same group overhear the report, it is sent with an IP destination address equal to the host group address being reported and with an IP time-to-live of 1. If a host hears a report for its group on the network, the host stops its own timer and does not generate a report for that group. Thus, usually only one report is generated for each group on the network, by the member host whose delay timer expires first. The multicast routers receive all IP multicast datagrams, therefore they need not be addressed explicitly. The routers need not know which hosts belong to a group, only that at least one host belongs to a group on a particular network.

Multicast routers send queries periodically to refresh their knowledge about memberships on a particular network. Queries are usually sent at intervals of approximately one minute to minimize overhead traffic on the network. However, when a multicast router starts up, it may often issue several closely spaced queries to obtain knowledge of local group membership quickly.

Similarly, when a host joins a new group, it issues a report immediately without waiting for a query in case it is the first member of the group on the network.

New members notify the nearest router of their presence in a group almost instantly, whereas notification of leaving a group depends on query timeout, which can be a minute or more. A new version of IGMP is being proposed that provides for explicit host leave group reports, to speed up the notification to routers of hosts leaving a group.

The Multicast Backbone

The multicast backbone (Mbone) of the Internet is based on multicast IP and covers 3,000 subnetworks. It is predicted that the Internet will be fully multicast IP enabled soon.

The Mbone uses computers to provide the multicast routing capability, and multicast packets are tunneled through unicast links to tie together the islands of multicast networks. It is used mostly by Internet researchers for videoconferencing and dataconferencing.

Two applications used on the Mbone are based on the application level framing (ALF) lightweight session model originated by Internet researchers.

ALF dictates that the best way to meet diverse multicast application requirements is to leave as much flexibility as possible to the application in the application layer. This means that connectivity is viewed as unreliable, using the user datagram protocol (UDP) connectionless transport layer.

Two prominent ALF model applications come from Lawrence B. Livermore Laboratory, which provides the visual/audio tool (VAT) in multimedia videoconferencing. In addition, the Mbone enables a whiteboard application that lets users of a multicast group electronically write on a whiteboard. All members of the group can see what each member has written. Whiteboarding is essentially an electronic dataconference that allows group members to brainstorm visually.

Other videoconferencing tools that provide use over the Mbone are being used in some universities, however, they are not yet commercially available. The Mbone is still in the research stage.

MULTICAST ROUTING PROTOCOLS

Multicast routing protocols are required to perform optimal routing through router networks, just as unicast routing protocols such as IGMP, open shortest path first (OSPF), and routing information protocol (RIP) are needed to perform optimal unicast routing in router networks. Multicast routing protocols should efficiently minimize the necessary traffic for routing multicast data in the network or internetwork.

There are three predominant multicast routing protocols: distance vector multicast routing protocol (DVMRP), multicast open shortest path first (MOSPF), and protocol independent multicast (PIM).

Distance Vector Multicast Routing Protocol (DVMRP)

DVMRP is the oldest multicast routing protocol and uses a technique known as reverse path forwarding. When a router receives a multicast packet (i.e., one with a Class D destination address), it floods the packet out of all paths except the one that leads back to the packet's source, as shown in Exhibit 6. This allows the packet to reach all subnetworks, possibly multiple times. If a router is attached to a set of subnetworks that do not want to receive packets destined to a particular multicast group, the router can send a prune message back up the distribution tree to stop subsequent multicast packets from being forwarded to destinations where there are no members.

DVMRP periodically refloods to reach any new hosts that want to receive a particular group. There is a direct relationship between the time it takes for a new receiver to get the data stream and the frequency of flooding.

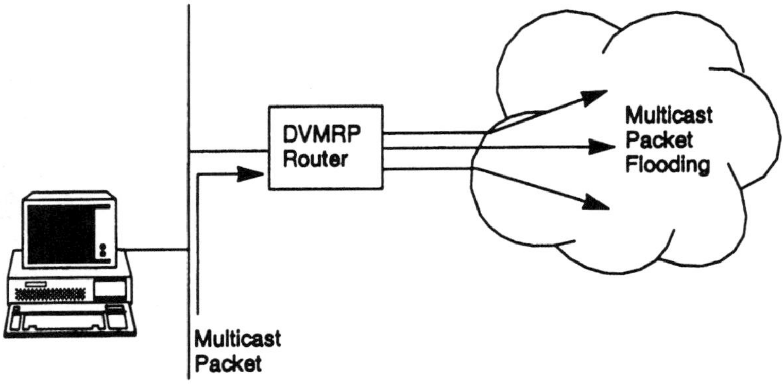

Exhibit 6. DVMRP flooding.

DVMRP implements its own unicast routing protocol to determine which interface leads back to the source of the packets for a particular group. This unicast routing protocol is similar to RIP and is based purely on hop count. As a result, the path that the multicast traffic follows may not be the same as the path the unicast traffic follows.

DVMRP is an inefficient multicast routing protocol because of scaling problems. The periodic flooding with broadcast traffic generates significant overhead in the network, and early versions of the protocol did not implement pruning.

Nevertheless, DVMRP has been used to build the Mbone and has been implemented by some router companies. Bay Networks, Inc. (Santa Clara CA) has chosen DVMRP as its first offering to support multicast routing, and 3COM Corp. (Santa Clara CA) is planning to implement it in the next few months.

Multicast Open Shortest Path First (MOSPF)

MOSFP is an extension of the OSPF unicast routing protocol. OSPF is a link state routing protocol, which means that each router in a network understands all of the available links in the network. Each OSPF router calculates the routes from itself to all possible destinations.

MOSPF includes multicast information in OSPF link state advertisements. MOSPF routers learn which multicast groups are active on which subnetworks.

MOSPF builds a distribution tree for each source/group pair and computes a tree for active sources sending to the group. The tree states are stored, and trees must be recomputed when a link state change occurs or when the timer for the store of the link expires.

The main disadvantage of MOSPF is that it works only in networks supporting OSPF. MOSPF, authored by Proteon, Inc. (Westborough MA) has been implemented in routers available from Proteon and Xyplex, Inc. (Littleton MA).

Protocol Independent Multicast (PIM)

PIM works with all existing unicast routing protocols and supports two types of traffic distribution topologies: dense and sparse. Dense mode is most useful when:

- Senders and receivers are in close proximity to one another.
- There are few senders and many receivers.
- The volume of multicast traffic is high.
- The multicast groups do not change very often.

Dense mode PIM uses reverse path forwarding and is similar to DVMRP. Sparse mode PIM is most useful in network topologies scattered over a large geographic area when:

- There are a only a few receivers in a group.
- Senders and receivers are geographically separated by WAN links.
- The groups change often.

Sparse mode PIM is designed for environments where there are many data streams destined for group members, as shown in Exhibit 7. Each stream goes to a relatively small number of group members. For this topology, reverse path forwarding techniques waste bandwidth.

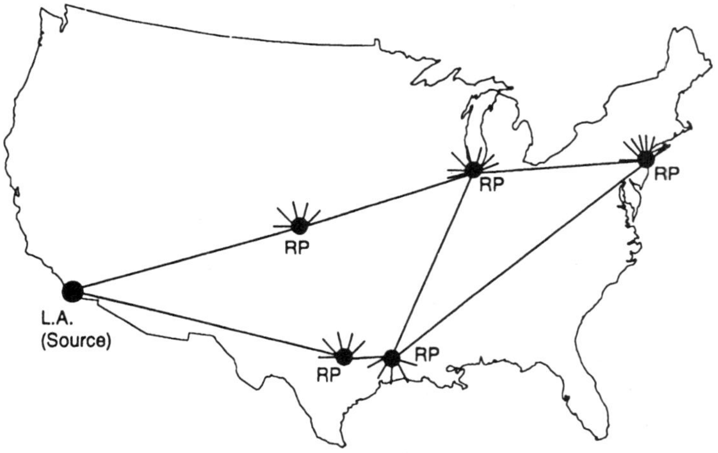

Exhibit 7. Sparse mode topology showing Rendezvous points.

Sparse mode PIM defines a rendezvous point (RP). Receiving members of the group join to a particular RP to create a shared distribution tree. There can be many RPs in a single group. Sources must register with all RPs in a group. Once the data stream begins to flow from sender to RP to receiver, the routers optimizes the path automatically to remove any unnecessary hops. Sparse mode PIM assumes that no hosts want the multicast traffic unless they specifically request it.

PIM simultaneously supports dense and sparse mode for different groups. PIM was authored by Cisco Systems, Inc. (San Jose CA) and researchers from the University of Southern California, Lawrence B. Livermore Laboratory, and Xerox Parc. Work is continuing in the Internet community to improve multicast routing protocols.

APPLICATIONS

Dynamic Groups. Groups defined by Class D addresses can be created and torn down in seconds. (Groups that are easily created and torn down are referred to as dynamic.) Changes to the group can also be performed in seconds, which is useful in many applications.

Videoconferencing. Videoconferencing is a temporary group setup that may exist for the duration of a meeting of any length. It is essentially an electronic meeting.

Dataconferencing. Dataconferencing is the same as videoconferencing without the video. Dataconferencing often involves a whiteboard, such as the program used by the academic community in the Mbone.

Real-Time Distribution of Multimedia Information. There are several new services that provide real-time business news to the desktop. Some of the information provided includes audio, video, and data. Subscribers to these services are constantly entering and leaving the group, therefore the ability to change the size and composition of the group dynamically is very important for this application.

Multicast File Transfer

There are several multicast file transfer applications that involve one-to-many transmission of information in the form of files.

Subscription-based Information Delivery. Subscription-based information delivery is a service that distributes information electronically using a multicast network and a multicast file transfer program. The information might be, for example, news in text and image form or financial trend analysis in audio form.

Information is in the form of files that need guaranteed delivery. Dynamic groups are important in this application because subscribers are constantly changing.

Electronic subscription delivery of information could become a popular service once the Internet is fully multicast enabled. Today, much time is wasted searching for information on the Internet, even with the advent of sophisticated browsing tools. Consumers have newspapers and magazines delivered as print subscriptions; they should be able to receive the equivalent electronically.

Electronic Software Distribution. Software is usually distributed at the time of its release. As the number of hosts on networks grows, software updates become more of a burden, which has led to great interest in the electronic distribution of software using a multicast file transfer program that is guaranteed.

Because distribution of software is not a daily or even a weekly event, it is desirable to terminate the group right after the transfer.

Distributed Publishing. National newspapers and other print publications use regional printing facilities to reduce shipping costs. They send information using a series of point-to-point transfers. Multicast file transfer is a more efficient and less costly solution. In this application, the membership group is relatively static.

Kiosk Applications. Kiosks are being planned to provide a number of new services, most of which need to be updated with information common for all of the kiosks. For example, the US Department of Transportation is sponsoring a project to implement kiosks at various urban and suburban locations. Information about traffic will be periodically downloaded to the kiosks so that travelers can obtain information about traffic patterns. These kiosks would also be used to disperse information of general public interest, such as facts about major sporting events such as the Olympic games.

Kiosks may also be placed in retail stores as a means of showcasing products using multimedia presentations. The latest fashions and sales promotions can be downloaded into the kiosks using multicast networks and a file transfer program.

Data Base Updates. Linked data bases in remote locations can be updated easily using a multicast file transfer program on a multicast network infrastructure.

VENDOR OFFERINGS

There are not many network infrastructures on a wide area basis that support multicast. There are, however, a number of companies providing low-cost videoconferencing products, and many of them support multicast IP or plan to support it. Intel Corp. (Santa Clara CA), Connectix Corp. (San Mateo CA), PictureTel Corp. (Danvers MA), Insoft, Inc. (Mechanicsburg PA), and Xing Technology Corp. (Arroyo Grande CA) all have PC-based videoconferencing products.

Multicast file transfer products are available from StarBurst Communications Corp. (Concord MA) and Legent, a division of Computer Associates International, Inc. (Islandia NY).

SUMMARY

Multicast network technology and the associated applications are poised to dramatically change the use of networked PCs. Videoconferencing and dataconferencing over IP data networks will become common as network speeds increase and multicast IP router networks become pervasive. Multicast file transfer over multicast IP networks makes electronic information delivery on a subscription basis a reality and electronic delivery of information more like the model for printed information delivery.

Multicast file transfer also facilitates software maintenance by providing the ability to easily distribute software updates. Other distributed applications such as groupware and E-mail directory updates can also benefit, proving that multicast technology will be a major component of information distribution in the not-too-distant future.

Chapter 49
Internetworking at the Physical and Data Link Layers

David Koehler

Asembling a departmental LAN has become, thanks to such standards as 10Base-T and robust network operating systems, a matter of assembling the appropriate off-the-shelf hardware and software. The next challenge is connecting individual LANs together in a corporate internet, a job that is not yet as simple as creating the local network.

This chapter focuses on the different internetworking options that are available to the network administrator or manager. Internetworking devices are products that allow processors on remote LAN segments to communicate. Throughout, the term *LAN segment* means a group of processors that communicate using a single LAN protocol, over a shared physical medium, with no modification of the generated bit pattern occurring between the originating and receiving stations. There are four primary internetworking devices: LAN repeaters, WAN transmission units, bridges, and routers. The concept of a layered communication protocol is fundamental to internetworking, and these internetworking devices may be differentiated according to the Open Systems Interconnection (OSI) protocol layer at which the LAN-to-LAN connection is established. However, it should be noted that although the OSI communications stack provides the model for most modern communications protocols, many modern protocols do not follow the exact layer definitions in OSL.

A REVIEW OF OSI

The OSI model comprises seven layers: physical, link, network, transport, session, presentation, and application. Each of the protocol layers has a unique autonomous function and a well-defined interface point to each of the adjacent layers.

0-8493-9989-0/99/$0.00+$.50

The Physical Layer

The lowest layer of the stack is the physical layer. The functions within this layer initialize, maintain, and condition a circuit between the data terminal equipment (DTE) and the data communications equipment (DCE). This level of the protocol can only interpret electrical signals, either binary 1s and 0s in digital signals or continuous voltages in analog signals. Many physical layer standards exist for both point-to-point circuits and the multiple access media that are typical of LANs. Common point-to-point interfaces are EIA-232, V.35, and V.42. A common LAN physical protocol, used for Ethernets, is carrier-sense multiple access with collision detection (CSMA/CD). This protocol is transmitted over the shared Ethernet media using Manchester coding.

The Link Layer

The link layer transfers data across the link and performs bridging in LANs and synchronous data link control (SDLC) transmission over serial lines. The link layer has a defined interface to both the physical layer and the network layer. The well-defined interface between the physical and link layers provides flow control to ensure that the DTE does not become overburdened, and error checking on inbound data. The link layer is also responsible for bit positioning within the data unit. The defined link data unit has a link header (i.e., a prefix) and link trailer (i.e., a suffix) that encapsulates the raw data. It is this defined data unit that is transferred to the network layer.

The Network Layer

The network layer is the place in the protocol model where the concept of the network is introduced. It is also responsible for network addressing and datagram routing between networks; the network layer datagram has a network header for network based addressing. The entire network layer datagram, encapsulated in the link data unit, provides addressing information to the transport layer. Encapsulation is the operation that enables routers to transparently operate between different link layer protocols (e.g., Ethernet and Token Ring).

The Transport Layer

The transport layer is the boundary between the lower and higher network-oriented layers. Higher layer functions are more visible to the end user. The initial few bytes of the network layer datagram are the transport layer header, which contains all the transport layer controls. The transport layer handles end-to-end transport of network layer diagrams traversing an internet, maintaining the flow control and acknowledgement mechanisms. The transport layer also has a well-defined interface to the session layer.

The Session Layer

The session layer is not defined in all communications protocols, but is defined in OSI. A session layer header is passed through the underlying transport layer as data, becoming functional once the transport layer is stripped off. The session layer organizes the exchange of data between workstations, attending to simultaneous transmission, alternate transmission, and resynchronization of user data flow between user applications. An example of a session layer function would be the setup of a terminal or file transfer synchronization process, which is required before a terminal or file transfer application can commence. The session layer has an upper layer interface to the presentation layer that facilitates the transfer of application based data over the established session.

The Presentation Layer

The presentation layer ensures that application-generated data structures are accurately mapped or translated to meet the requirements of the specific applications. A presentation header is incorporated as part of the data unit at the session layer boundary. The presentation layer is concerned with data syntax and the negotiation functions that facilitate peer-to-peer data structure specifications. The presentation layer is responsible for the organization of the data generated through the interface from the application layer.

The Application Layer

The application layer supports end-user applications. It defines the semantics for the representation of user data in graphical user interfaces and supports such process as job management, file transfer, and electronic messaging. This is the protocol layer that affects the end user most directly.

The point of the OSI model is that independent layers (i.e., software modules) communicate through defined interfaces, thereby minimizing the complexity of any single layer. This layered approach to network protocols also simplifies the integration of code enhancements, because the code in all layers except where the change occurs will remain unaffected. Although each layer adds a separate header or trailer, layer encapsulation provides for a well-ordered communication mechanism.

Internetworking devices usually function in the physical, link, and network layers. LAN based repeater and WAN transmission devices (e.g., data service units/channel service units (DSU/CSUs) and modems) operate at the physical layer. Bridges and WAN packet switches function at the link layer. Routers and a portion of the X.25 packet switch function at the network layer.

REPEATERS

LAN repeaters were initially developed to overcome the distance restrictions on single LAN segments. Ethernet has a 500-m length restriction for baseband and a 100-m restriction for a 10Base-T station. Token Ring has a distance limitation of 100 m per ring segment. If internetworking devices did not exist these distance limitations would preclude the use of Ethernet or Token Ring in larger multistory office buildings or factories.

Repeaters are the oldest technology in use today for connecting multiple LAN segments. A repeater is primarily a hardware device, equipped with a microprocessor and some code in ROM. Repeaters were originally packaged as standalone units, but now they are typically integrated into LAN concentrators. The basic function of a LAN repeater is to reproduce the exact bit stream detected on one segment on another LAN segment. One way to describe a repeater's operation is, whatever it gets it throws over the wall.

Repeaters can be local, remote, and multisegment. The local repeater has two LAN ports that connect directly to two LAN segments, which allows processors on either side of the repeater to communicate.

Local Repeaters

Local repeaters (shown in Exhibit 1) used alone are fine for connecting LAN segments on different floors, but not for connecting LAN segments in different buildings. Repeaters can be used in pairs to support remote repeating. Each repeater is connected to its local LAN segment through a transceiver and they are connected to each other through local twisted pair or fiber-optic cable, dial-access phone lines and modems, or leased lines and modems or DSU/CSUs. The local twisted pair or fiber connections are typically used in campus environments to allow LAN-to-LAN communication between different buildings and make use of customer owned cable or fiber.

Wide area public carrier analog or digital services are used to connect LANs that are remote from each other. Analog point-to-point links are established through dial or leased line modems and operate from 2,400 to 56K bps, the speed depending on line type, modulation techniques, and compression algorithms. Digital point-to-point lines use DSU/CSUs and offer data rates of 144K, 1.5M (T1) and 45M (T3)bps.

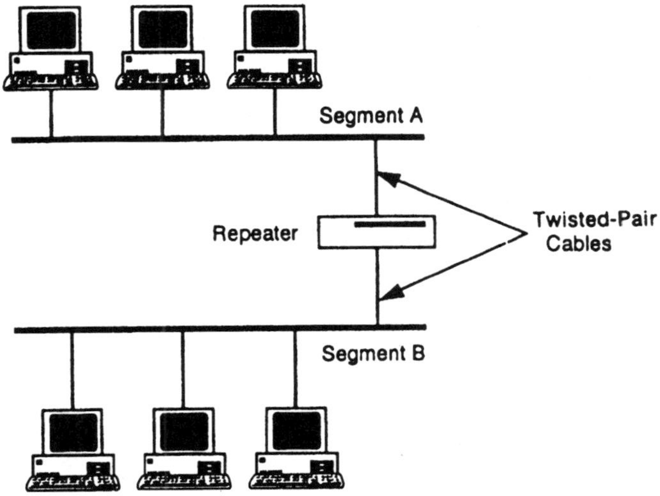

Exhibit 1. Local repeater diagram.

Fractional T1. Fractional T1 options on T1 circuits introduce another option and a source of confusion, because the carrier implies that a digital circuit can be ordered in bandwidth blocks of $N \times$ 56K bps; $N = 5$ would yield a 280K-bps circuit.

To understand how fractional T1 circuits are configured, the anatomy of a digital circuit must e further explained. A carrier circuit is actually comprised of three components,the near end local exchange carrier (LEC) portion, the interexchange carrier (IXC) portion, and the far end LEC portion (as shown in Exhibit 2).

IXCs (e.g., AT&T, MCI, Sprint) offer tariffed fractional T1 services that provide $N \times$ 56K-bps channels between the LECs. However, because the LEC portion of the T1 circuit must be installed on a point-to-point basis between the LEC central office and the customer premise, the T1 circuit cannot be shared or fractionalized. Therefore, a fractional T1 connection is actually allocated as a full T1 on both ends of the LEC portion of the circuit; the fractional T1 bandwidth is restricted to the IXC portion of the circuit.

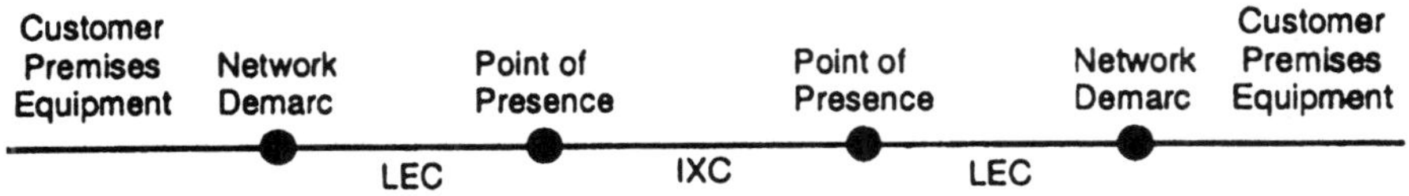

Exhibit 2. The carrier and customer components of a communication circuit.

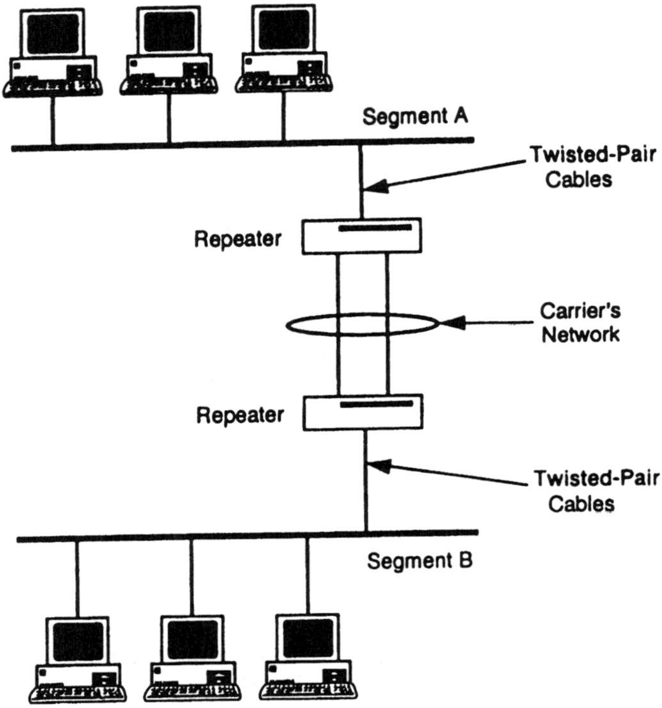

Exhibit 3. Remote repeater diagram.

Remote Repeaters

Remote repeaters (shown in Exhibit 3) can use any of the WAN transmission carrier services for LAN-to-LAN connection. The limitation of the remote repeater technique is the WAN link's speeds: on the order of 9.6K to 1.5M bps, as opposed to 10M bps for a typical LAN. LAN transmission media differ from WAN transmission media, but the repeater still performs the same bit regeneration and signal conditioning.

Multiport Repeaters

The last type of repeater to be discussed is the multiport repeater (shown in Exhibit 4). The multiport repeater is actually a special adaptation of the local repeater, allowing many LAN segments to be connected together through a single device. Multiport repeaters were common in thinnet and thicknet coaxial cable LANs, but have declined in popularity with the advent of 10Base-T concentrators.

All repeaters function at the physical layer. Their primary function is to faithfully reproduce the original bit pattern generated on the original LAN

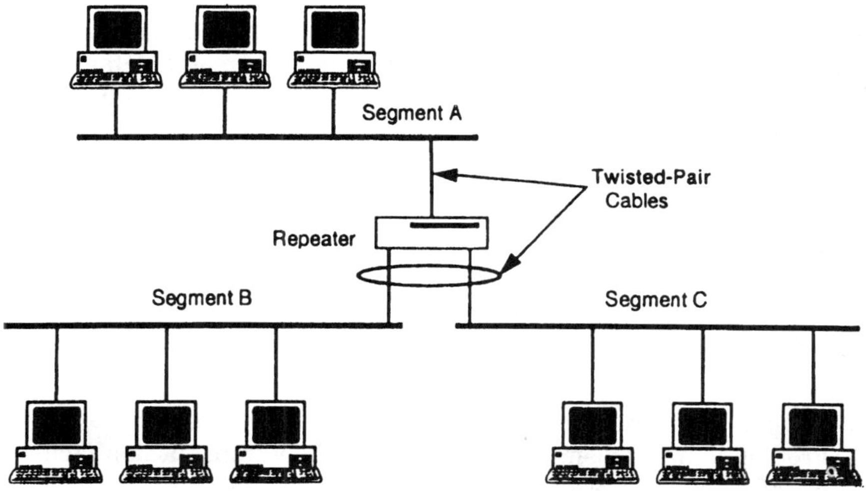

Exhibit 4. Multiport repeater diagram.

segment on all other attached LAN or serial connections. This regeneration function provides electrical isolation between segments and is completely independent of the higher layer protocols. Because repeaters do not have to process higher layer protocol information, data forwarding between segments occurs in real time.

The disadvantages of an internetworking device that processes physical layer bit patterns are that connection between dissimilar LANs (e.g., Token Ring and Ethernet) is not supported, and delay sensitive higher level protocols may experience time-outs. And because repeaters do not process LAN link layer protocols, repeated segments function as one large segment, imposing a limitation on the number of attached devices. But the primary problem is that the round-trip propagation delay of the repeated signal can exceed the link layer IEEE 802.3 and 802.5 specification. The reader should check with the respective concentrator vendor for this specific limitation.

FRAME RELAY SWITCHES

Frame relay is a protocol that was developed to handle LAN-to-LAN traffic more efficiently than point-to-point WAN links. Frame relay is more than a physical layer protocol because it has a partial link layer implementation. When comparing internetworking devices, a frame relay switch has features in common with repeaters and bridges.

The development of frame relay reflects the evolution of customer applications. Traditional mainframe data networks were based on a hierarchical model and constructed on a star topology. The topology was typically defined by point-to-point digital or analog connections set up in a star or tree structure. Fixed bandwidth lines were used because the polling activities of the central processor infrastructure created deterministic traffic. That model, while still useful, is being augmented, and in some instances replaced with a model that includes the distributed processing requirements of LAN-based intelligent workstations.

LAN-based applications and services generate bursty traffic. These traffic bursts are random and can vary from a series of small packets (e.g., a simple remote procedure call) to a series of large file transfers (e.g., a remote load of a network based application). The new requirements for LAN-to-LAN connections can be summarized as follows:

- Provide high WAN transmission speeds, not to transmit large continuous data volumes but to reduce response time.
- Provide a mechanism to better use the WAN transmission facilities when large LAN-based traffic bursts are not occurring.
- Handle the many different protocols (e.g., Transmission Control Protocol/Internet Protocol (TCP/IP), Internetwork Packet Exchange (IPX), Apple Talk, DECnet, and SNA) that require simultaneous WAN transport.

Frame relay operates at the physical and the lower half of the link layers. The original frame relay specification is a derivative of the development work done for the Integrated Services Digital Network (ISDN) and is based on the 1988 International Telephone and Telegraph Consultative Committee (CCITT) I.122 *Framework for Providing Additional Packet Mode Bearer Services* documents. The original standards specify both permanent and switched virtual circuits (PVCs and SVCs) at speeds up to T3 and E3. However, there were some design constraints at the beginning and the pioneering vendors selected a subset of the specifications, consisting of PVCs at rates to T1, for initial product development.

Current frame relay is over PVCs on a frame switching fabric implemented in private networks and by the public digital carrier services. One digital link terminating at the customer premise can carry multiple PVCs. This packet-based multiplexing scheme has the advantage of providing bandwidth to multiple destinations through a single access line. The underlying frame relay specifications allow any of the PVCs to user any percentage of the available bandwidth on the digital access line, depending on the available bandwidth at any given time and the configuration of the PVC.

The frame relay carrier services are defined by several parameters. The data link circuit identifiers (DLCI) are assigned in pairs and uniquely define the PVC. The certified interface rate (CIR) is the guaranteed or minimum bandwidth allocated to any given PVC. Burst mode operation over a frame relay network allows a PVC to support data traffic bursts at rates up to access line speed provided no other PVCs require simultaneous access. Frame relay as a carrier-based service has the following tangible benefits for LAN-to-LAN connection:

- Higher interface speeds, eliminating the bandwidth constraints that exist with such older packet switching protocols as X.25.
- The statistical nature of the frame relay network provides a service with efficient bandwidth use.
- Frame relay networks rely on end-to-end connections, optimizing user response time by not performing error checking on interim hops.

BRIDGES

The fundamental difference between repeaters and bridges is the protocol layer at which they perform internetworking. Bridges operate at the link layer of the protocol stack, and therefore have a very different set of connection attributes. Functionally a bridge can be thought of as a selective repeater, that is, the connected LAN segments logically form one large segment but only traffic destined for a remote segment is forwarded across the bridge.

Bridges do not need to conform to the same configuration rules as repeaters. Bridges and repeaters can be intermixed to meet specific network requirements. A very important advantage the bridge gains over the repeater by operating in the link layer is that the specific CSMA/CD and ring passing functions are restricted to each LAN segment. This difference eliminates the propagation delay restriction incurred in the repeated environment. Also, by operating in the link layer bridges can set up filtering on specific link layer addresses or link layer attributes. Link layer bridging is actually subdivided into two separate sublayers: the logical link controls (LLC) and media access control (MAC).

The LLC functions define access points to higher level services, perform frame sequencing, and issue connection oriented acknowledgments. The MAC layer handles the well-oriented interface to the physical media (i.e., twisted pair or fiber) and provides structured link layer addressing. Before bridges are discussed further the concepts of Ethernet, Token Ring, and Fiber Distributed Data Interface (FDDI) MAC layer protocols are introduced.

Ethernet MAC

The Ethernet frame format and MAC functions were originally developed into a coherent link layer LAN protocol during the late 1970s by Digital Equipment Corp., Intel Corp., and Xerox Corp. Ethernet is a contention access protocol (CSMA/CD), services many processor types (including DOS, Macintosh and UNIX), and assigns use of the medium on a first-come, first-served basis. The Ethernet access mechanism is analogous to a telephone party line, in which multiple phones hare a single telephone line. If someone wants to use the line, the phone is taken off-hook, the caller listens to make sure no one else is using the phone, and either hangs up if someone is already on the line or completes the call if the line is free.

This is the way workstations access an Ethernet. When a workstation initiates a send process, the network interface card first monitors the LAN broadcast medium to determine if it is in use. Once the medium is determined to be clear for transmission then the frame is transmitted onto the physical medium. All stations on the medium (i.e., the LAN segment) hear and ignore the transmission, except the station whose address matches the destination MAC address and the originating station. The originating station receives its transmitted sequence and compares it to the original transmission. If the transmit and receive data match then the data has been successfully transmitted. If the transmit and receive data do not match then it is likely that a collision has occurred and the transmitting station ceases transmission, generates a jam signal to all other stations, and waits a random amount of time before initiating transmission again.

The 64-byte minimum frame size, maximum cable lengths, and maximum propagation delay are critical to the proper operation of the collision detect mechanism. Together these parameters ensure that by the time the last bit of the last byte of information is transmitted, the originating node is guaranteed of detecting a collision between its original transmission and any other workstation transmissions.

Another characteristic that is a result of the shared media is that frame destination addresses fall into three categories, referred to as single-cast, multicast, and broadcast.

Single-cast addressing uses a specific 6-byte destination address for a dedicated machine. In essence, this type of transmission is a point-to-point communication over a broadcast medium.

Multicast addresses look like a standard 6-byte single-cst address but are actually special addresses that can be received by a subset of the stations connected to the LAN segment. Multicast addresses are typically used to support directed software loads.

Broadcast addressing is accomplished by setting a specific destination address (i.e., FF-FF-FF-FF-FF-FF) in the Ethernet frame. Then all stations on the network will receive the transmission. Although broadcasting is an efficient mechanism to get information out to a large number of users, it can consume large amounts of bandwidth as the broadcast frame propagates across the entire network.

The MAC layer frame formats are currently in use, the Ethernet V.2 format and the Institute of Electrical and Electronics Engineers (IEEE) 802.3

	Preamble	Destination	Source	DIX Type Code	Data or Pad	FCS
Octets	8	6	6	2	46 to 1500	4

a. Ethernet

	Preamble	Delimiter	Destination	Source	Length	802.2	Data or Pad	FCS
Octets	8	1	6	6	2	3 to 8	42 to 1497	4

b. 802.3 Frame

Note:
FCS Frame check sequence

Exhibit 5. The Ethernet and IEEE 802.3 frame structures.

format. The differences between the two formats are illustrated in Exhibit 5. First, the 2 byte type field in the Ethernet frame is replaced with the 2 byte length field in the 802.3 frame. The two MAC layer frame header formats are the same length, so the frame types may coexist on the same shared medium. From the network layer up, the two frame types are incompatible, due to different information (length versus type fields) being transferred to the network layer. Another significant difference occurs at the LLC link sublayer. The Ethernet frame has no provisions for an LLC component, the 802 MAC layer protocols include provisioning for an LLC component. Because the frame formats are slightly different, some special care may have to be taken in mixing components if interoperability is to be ensured.

Token Ring MAC

Token Ring is the second most popular MAC layer protocol (Exhibit 6). It is based on a deterministic token passing algorithm and conforms to the IEEE 802.5 specification. The Token Ring protocol is more complex than its 802.3 counterpart. Due to the nature of normal operation, three different frame formats are required.

The starting and ending delimiters are used for error detection and definition of the frame boundaries. The access control field is used to set up a proprietary access and reservation system. A workstation on a LAN segment uses the priority and reservation mechanisms to capture the token as it circulates around the ring. Once the ring is captured, a variable length frame type containing user data, LLC information, and source route information is generated by the workstation. Token Ring is a deterministic

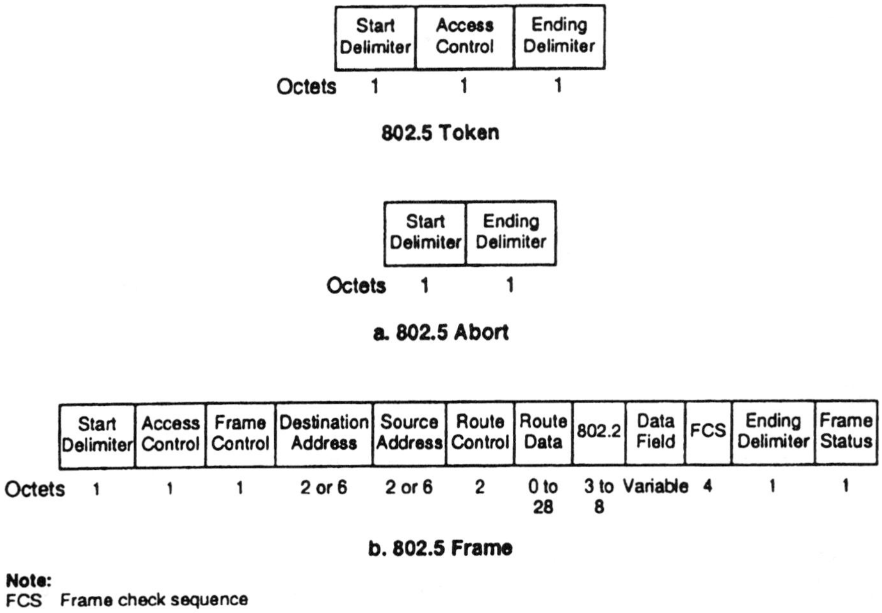

Exhibit 6. IEEE 802.5 frame structures.

protocol that uses a rules-based access mechanism as the core structure of the protocol. The same consideration applies to FDDI.

The first two fields are taken directly from the token and are used for access control as the frame circulates around the ring. The frame control field identified whether a LLC frame transporting user data or a MAC frame carrying ring management data is sent. The source and destination field are similar to the 802.3 frames and contain the respective MAC layer addresses.

The variable length route information field (RIF) composed of route control information and routing data handles the transport of data between LAN segments (through a process called source route bridging). This particular field is discussed in greater detail in the source route bridging section. The information field contains the LLC protocol data unit (the 802.2 sublayer in user frames) and additional ring management information for MAC frames. As with the 802.3 frame, the 802.5 frame makes use of the LLC link sublayer to define source and destination service access pints (SSAP and DSAP) to the network layer protocol.

The 802.2 and subnetwork access protocol (SNAP), illustrated in Exhibit 7, has been defined as an extension to the 802 MAC and 802.2 LLC layers. The reason for the additional link level frame extension is to

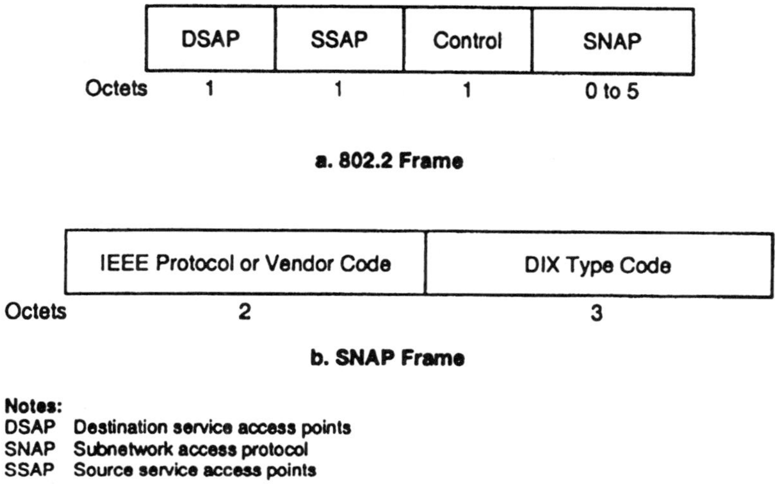

Exhibit 7. IEEE 802.2 and SNAP frame structures.

---

support the encapsulation of IP and address resolution protocol (ARP) datagrams in the 802 frames. The SNAP subheader adds a protocol ID similar in function to the original Ethernet type field and an Ethertype field specifying further framing information. Many of the higher level protocols (e.g., AppleTalk, NetWare, and TCP/IP) either require or can invoke framing options to support the SNAP frame extensions. The SNAP protocol is also compatible with the ANSI FDDI frame format. The 802.2 and SNAP extensions permit the movement of data between different MAC layer protocols (e.g., Ethernet, Token Ring, and FDDI).

FDDI MAC

The FDDI standard American National Standards Institute (ANSI) X3T.9 is a layered protocol that uses a framing format similar to Token Ring. The operation of the FDDI ring differs from Token Ring in that it is based on a dual counterrotating ring that can have a circumference of 200 km while transmitting data at 100M bps. Fault tolerance is a result of the dual-ring architecture. Limits are more typically 100 km and 500 devices, to ensure proper operation in failure mode. Internode distance limits of 2 km for multimode fiber and 10 km for single-mode fiber are also in the specification.

The physical (PHY) layer concerns itself with the actual encoding schemes for data. The physical medium dependent (PDM) layer controls the 1,300-nm light-emitting idodes (LEDs) used to generate light pulses over the optical fiber.

The media access control (MAC) and link level control (LLC) layers handle token passing as well as frame formation and addressing. The LLC protocol used on FDDI networks is based on the 802.2 specification, easing integration with other MAC-level LAN protocols.

The connecting management (CMT) protocol is responsible for establishing connections and defining connect parameters. In fault-recovery mode, the CMT causes the primary and secondary rings to be wrapped into a single ring, thereby bypassing the fault. The FDDI connections controlled by the CMT process must be defined as A, B,S, or M type connections, as follows:

- A: Dual connection, primary ring in and secondary ring out.
- B: Dual connection, primary ring out and secondary ring in.
- M: Single connection, master concentrator.
- S: Single connection, slave end device.

The station management (SMT) protocol keeps track of upstream and downstream neighbors and most FDDI management statistics. In some routers SMT information is integrated into the private extension of the SNMP agent. This facilitates management of an FDDI network with an SNMP management station. On a LAN all SMT versions must be the same to identify the presence of upstream and downstream neighbors.

FDDI is not an IEEE protocol, but the network-dependent frame format is compatible with IEEE interface standards and supports encapsulation of the IEEE 802.2 and SNAP data link layer protocols necessary to support higher-level address resolution. This standards compliant structure ensures full interoperability with 802.3 and 802.5 LANs.

The FDDI standard specifies a fault-tolerant dual ring; the primary ring carries user data at 100M bps, while the secondary ring carries control signals at 100M bps. In the event of component failure, the dual ring self-heals and operates in a single ring configuration until the problem is resolved.

Exhibit 8 shows the normal FDDI operation and recovery sequences on an FDDI ring with dual-attached routers. In this configuration, the primary ring has one inbound and one outbound MAC interface per device through which all data traffic and control information flows. The secondary ring functions as a backup to the primary ring.

When a single failure in the FDDI network occurs (Exhibit 9), nodes that sense an open ring loop the primary path onto the secondary path, thereby automatically restoring data communications. In this case, the control and data traffic share the single restored ring, and all devices with operational FDI connections can communicate.

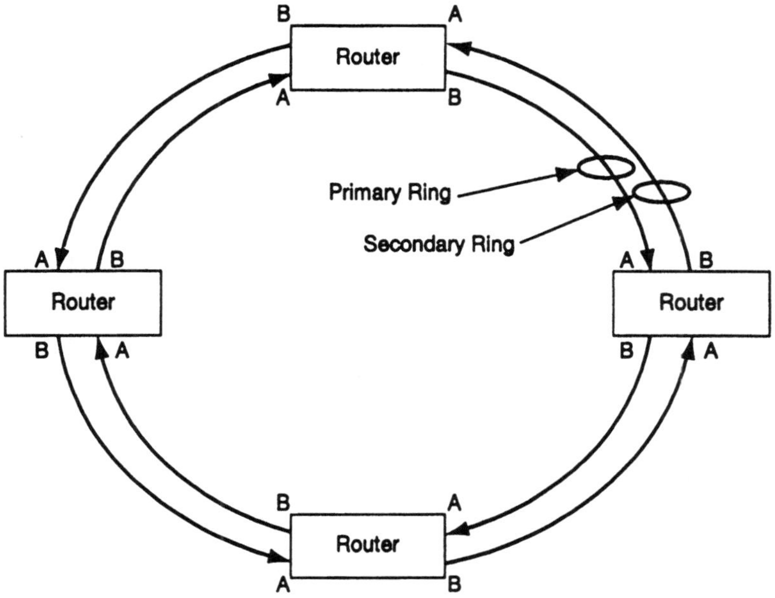

Exhibit 8. Normal dual-attached FDDI operation.

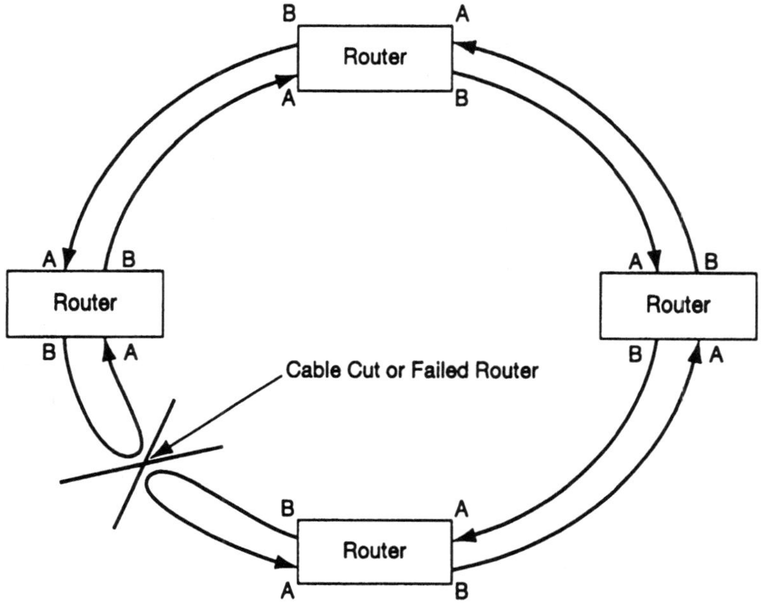

Exhibit 9. Dual-attached FDDI ring single failure recovery.

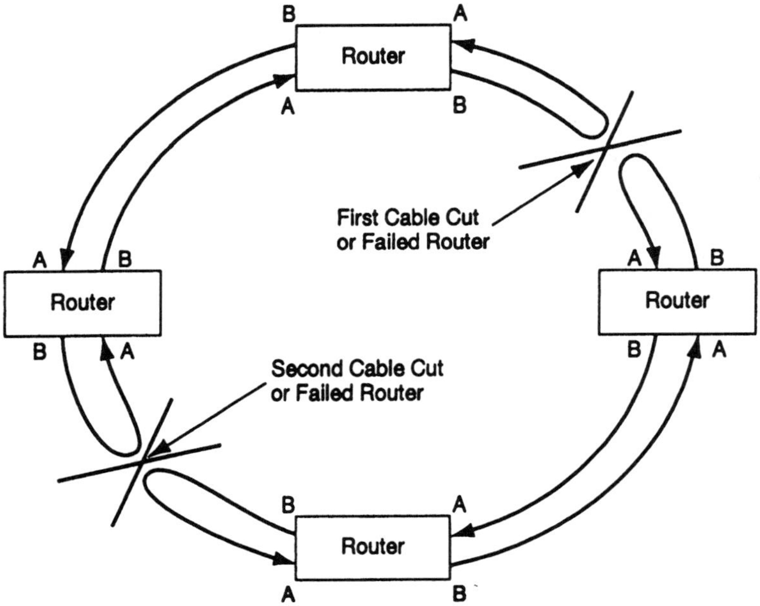

Exhibit 10. Dual-attached FDDI ring dual failure recovery.

The failure of two nodes or fiber links (Exhibit 10) results in partition of the original FDDI network into two counter-rotating rings that support communication on each ring but not between rings. When an FDDI network has multiple simultaneous failures, only local communication is maintained.

The probability of a failure of two nodes or fibers can be substantially reduced with a dual-homed FDDI architecture. A dual-homed architecture, for both the routers and LAN based file servers, is the best possible traffic segmentation. It eliminates single points of failure and is flexible with respect to network expansion. The master hubs are the only dual-attached stations on the FDDI ring. Because the probability of an outage increases with the number of dual-attached devices, the dual-homed LAN maximizes network availability. But the two fiber cables have to be routed separately to ensure that a single cable cut does not segment the network. The A and B interfaces on dual-attached router cards are split between the two master hubs and function as a single attached FDDI device with a single attached host backup connection to the second fiber hub.

The dual master hub configuration also allows FDDI ports to be turned on or shut down by a management station without causing the ring to wrap. Exhibit 11 shows the connection strategy that supports the dual-homed FDDI architecture.

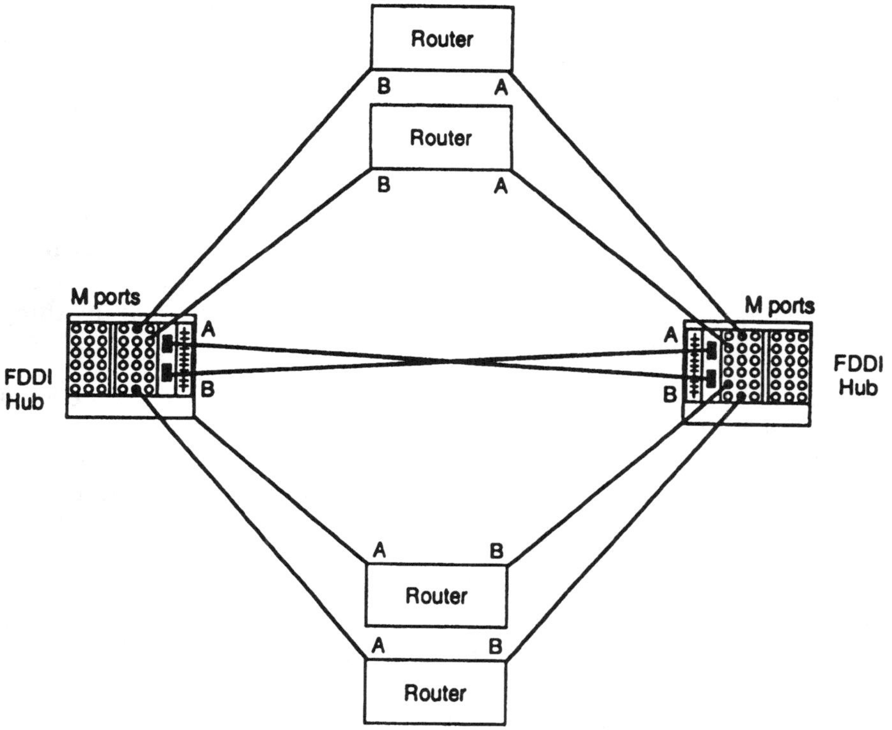

Exhibit 11. Dual-attached, dual-homed FDDI configuration.

BRIDGING

The different link layer protocols make necessary the use of different bridging techniques in homogenous and heterogeneous link layer protocol environments. Transparent bridging and the associated spanning tree algorithm were originally designed to support local and remote bridging between Ethernet segments. Source route bridging was developed by IBM to support local and remote bridging between Token Ring LAN segments. All other bridging types discussed in this chapter have been developed to handle bridging between different link layer LAN implementations. It should be noted that source route bridging has been decertified as a standard and has bee targeted for replacement by source route transparent bridging. However, because of the large installed base of pure source route bridge networks, this technique is described in this chapter.

Bridges, like repeaters, can operate in local and remote modes. Local bridging uses a single bridge, and remote bridging uses bridge pairs. The remainder of this chapter covers bridging concepts as a whole and does not distinguish, in general, between local and remote bridging. Specific points unique to remote or local bridging are highlighted, however, the reader is referred to the repeater section of this chapter for a more detailed discussion of local and remote internetworking functions.

Transparent Bridging

Transparent bridges are so named because their presence and operation is transparent to network hosts. At power-up these bridges learn the topology of the connected segments by examining the source addresses of all incoming frames. This operation leads to the description learning bridge for transparent bridges.

Transparent bridges operate in promiscuous mode to learn the local MAC address of each of the attached hosts. Promiscuous mode operation on each segment allows the bridge to eavesdrop on every frame transmitted. Specifically the bridge builds a bridging table that maintains a correlation between bridge port and LAN MAC addresses. This table supports the forwarding and filtering operation of the bridge. A bridge forwards a frame from one segment to another when the bridge table indicates a correlation between the destination address and a bridge port other than the bridge port over which the frame was received. A bridge filters (i.e., discards) a frame when the bridge table shows a correlation between the destination address and the receiving bridge port. The frame is discarded in this case because the destination address exists on the same segment that the bridge port is connected to.

A question the inquisitive reader may have formulated at this point is, how does the bridge forward frames if it has not yet discovered, by eavesdropping, all the addresses on the attached segments? The answer is fairly straightforward. If a bridge does not have a particular MAC address in its host table, it floods the frame out all bridge ports except the receiving port. Broadcasts and multicasts prompted by higher level protocols are also flooded across a bridged network in this manner. Once the response from the original broadcast is received, the new destination address is added to the bridge table.

A limiting factor of early transparent bridge implementations was that bridge loops, that is, two paths between any two segments, were prohibited. For example, a single host, Cat, is on network segment 1 and another single host, Dog, is on segment 2, and the two segments are joined by two bridges A and B (Exhibit 12). If Cat sends a message to Dog and Dog must respond, the sequence of events is as follows: Cat sends a message out on segment 1 to Dog. Both bridges forward the frames from segment 1 to segment 2. Dog receives both messages (assuming a collision did not occur). Dog's higher-level application discards the duplicate frame. Bridge

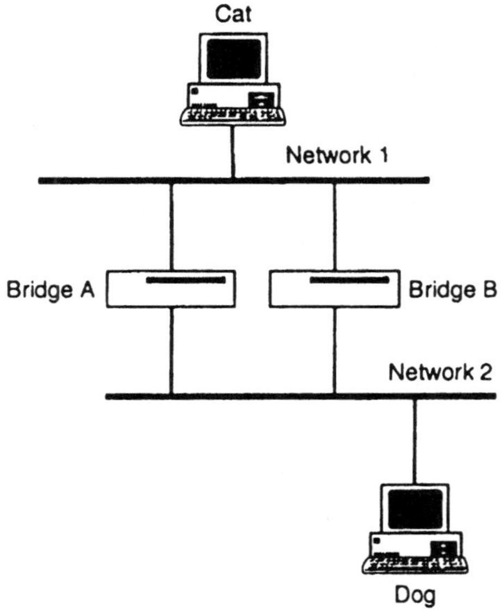

Exhibit 12. Example of a bridge loop.

A receives the original frames forwarded by bridge B and updates its host table to show that host Cat is on segment 2. Bridge B receives the original frames forwarded by bridge A and updates its host table to show that host Cat is on segment 2. Host Dog generates a response for host Cat and transmits onto segment 2. Both bridges discard the frames generated by Dog because both bridge tables show Cat to be on segment 2.

In this example the problem is fairly easy to locate, however, if this was a large corporate internet with 100 bridge links, then this problem would be very difficult to isolate.

A second problem that can arise by configuring bridge loops is broadcast storms. A broadcast storm can be caused by a number of factors, for example, broadcast frame regeneration or forwarding over previously visited interfaces. The latter is the primary issue that affects transparent bridge loops; because in a broadcast frame the destination address is all 1s, the frame will be forwarded around a bridge loop and will never be filtered.

Spanning Tree Algorithm

Digital Equipment Corp. (DEC, Littleton, MA) developed an algorithm known as spanning tree to help address the issue of whether transparent bridging's limitations enable it to have any value outside the simplest configuration. The original spanning tree algorithm developed by DEC was later adopted by the IEEE and modified into what is now known as the 802.1d spanning tree specification.

The spanning tree algorithm functions by designating a loop-free subset of the possible bridged network topology combinations. This is accomplished by allocating each port on each bridge to block and pass frames. A key component of the spanning tree algorithm is that it is dynamic, in that the protocol periodically checks (every 1 to 4 seconds) to see if the bridge topology has changed. If a change is detected the spanning tree algorithm converges on a new nonloop topology. Spanning tree operates on a peer processing premise, in which all bridges cooperate to form the overall bridge topology. In other words, there is no central authority on network topology or administration.

Obviously there must be an underlying set of rules to govern the spanning tree function to ensure the cooperative processing converges to an acceptable bridge topology. Each bridge is assigned an arbitrary number that is concatenated with the bridge MAC layer address. The arbitrary number is used to assign priority to each of the bridges in a given internetwork. The MAC layer address can be used as a tie breaker mechanism, because each MAC address is unique. The lower the assigned number the higher the priority of the bridge. During initial power up of a bridge a bridge protocol data unit (BPDU) is flooded out each network port of the newly activated bridge. This BPDU contains the current spanning tree root, the distance to the root, the bridge address information, and the age of the information in the BPDU. This information is used to select the root of the bridge tree. Once the root is selected the remainder of the tree structure is established. It is advisable to manually control the priority of each bridge so as to configure the bridged internet traffic to flow over a preferred loop free subset.

By using filtering, transparent bridges successfully isolate local segment traffic. This traffic isolation usually improves network response times as perceived by the end user. Because bridges work at the link layer of the OSI model they cannot do any filtering based on higher level protocol traffic parameters (e.g., Novel Inc.'s service advertisement protocol (SAP) or network broadcasts of any type). The extent to which transparent bridges can segment traffic is dependent on the total WAN traffic and the composition of the traffic. Generally, the traffic isolation capability of a bridged internetwork is inversely proportional to the complexity of the WAN topology.

Source Route Bridging

Whereas transparent bridging with the spanning tree algorithm assumes that all bridging intelligence is in the bridge, source route bridging

	Route Control	Ring Number	Bridge Number	- - -	Ring Number	Bridge Number
Bits	8	12	4	- - -	12	4
Octets	1			2 to 28		

Exhibit 13. IEEE 802.5 RIF format.

assumes that most of the intelligence is in the hosts attached to each network. The name source route bridge is derived from the premise that in the route information field (RIF) each source frame contains the entire route to the destination (Exhibit 13). If a given host A wants to send a frame to host B the source route communication process works in the following manner:

- Initially the host looks at cached routes for host B.
- If the host route is not cached, a test frame is sent out to determine if host B is on the local ring.
- If the test frame does not locate host B then an explore frame is flooded out all bridge ports to find the best route to host B.
- As each bridge receives the explorer frame, it appends the RIF field with local ring and bridge number information, and forwards the frame to each output port. (This action is intended to cause the original broadcast to traverse every possible connection path.)
- As each explorer frame reaches the end destination (host B) the content of the RIF field is reserved and sent back to the originating station, host A. (Depending on the complexity of the network, tens or hundreds of inverted RIF field frames are returned, each with a different route specified.)
- Upon receipt of each of the broadcast responses host A chooses one of the routes and inserts the corresponding route information for destination B into its source route cache. Properly configured end stations can store multiple routes.

Source route bridging was developed by IBM and is the predominant bridging protocol for connecting Token Ring LANs. The operational outline described previously shows that the majority of the source route bridge processor load falls on the end workstation. Performance can vary because route decisions are made by individual workstations. Workstation related performance problems are most common in complex network environments or in networks where processor resources (i.e., memory, disk space, I/O, or CPU capacity) are constricted.

The last step of the source route sequence has the originating workstation inserting some number of routes into its route cache. The 802.5 specification does not mandate the criteria for choosing a route, but instead makes several recommendations. Route selection can be based on any one or more of the following metrics:

- The first frame received.
- Minimum hops traversed.
- Largest mean transfer unit path.

The metric used to make the route selection is specific to the vendor's implementation of the source route process. This variability can lead to poor performance if a common metric is not used throughout the network. The heavy load placed on the workstations, combined with hardware limitations, leads to a seven hop limitation, meaning that a real world source route bridge implementation cannot have more than seven bridges cascaded serially. The 802.5 specification allows up to 28 cascaded bridges, but this limit is not achievable.

Another distance related issue with source route bridge implementations is that most implementations are based on the LLC2 specification, which specifies a connection oriented link level protocol with a 2 second timeout. The connection oriented sessions in conjunction with the 2 second timeout can lead to time-out problems in networks that use seven hops. This problem is especially prevalent in networks that communicate over WAN links. The LLC1 link level protocol, which is connectionless and therefore has no timeout function, eliminates this problem in transparent bridging.

Although source route bridging has a number of limiting factors, it also has several advantages over transparent bridging. Source route bridges make use of explicit routes, which means that the routing information is contained in each frame. This mechanism makes problem resolution easier because complete route information is contained in each frame. The explicit route implementation permits parallel routes to exist, which can be used for load sharing or fault tolerance.

Thus far this source route bridge discussion has been limited to bridging between Token Ring LANs. Real world network implementations mix physical and link level protocols. The introduction of distributed applications and integrated business functions requires communication between processors on different LAN types. The advent of new bridges and router/bridges has made possible bridged communications between different LAN media.

Remote Source Route Bridging

Remote source route bridging is the process of bridging Token Ring LANs across non-Token Ring network segments. This is usually done by high-end router/bridges and is accomplished by encapsulating the source route data inside another transport service. MAC layer encapsulation can be used to transport Token Ring traffic over point-to-point serial links.

In this case, the Token Ring frame is placed inside a synchronous data link control (SDLC) frame in order to traverse the serial link. The remote router/bridge strips off the SDLC envelope and delivers the Token Ring frame to the remote LAN segment. Although MAC layer encapsulation is an efficient transport mechanism, the scope of the application is limited to simple serial links. TCP/IP encapsulation of Token Ring frames offers greater implementation flexibility for remote bridging functions. TCP/IP encapsulation can be implemented using IP or TCP encapsulation.

IP is a connectionless network layer protocol and TCP is a connection oriented transport layer protocol. Either encapsulation mechanism allows the Token Ring frames to be routed over diverse media transparently to the original frame structure. The encapsulation mechanism is analogous to a mail delivery service, wherein the mail is delivered to a destination but the contents of the mail are not known by the carrier.

IP encapsulation is used in cases where guaranteed delivery is not as important as fast delivery. TCP encapsulation is used in the cases where the reliability of a connection oriented delivery is paramount. As with any encapsulation technique the encapsulation envelope is added by the bridge/router that receives the original frame, is removed by the bridge/router that delivers the frame to the local LAN segment, and the originating and destination LANs must support the same link layer protocol (i.e., Token Ring or Ethernet).

Translational Bridging

Translational bridging was devised to address the problem of bridging between different LAN protocols. The most common translating bridge combinations are Token Ring to Ethernet and Ethernet to FDDI. Designing fault free translational bridges is far more complicated than the previously discussed encapsulation bridges. Bridging between Token Ring and Ethernet LANs seems fairly innocuous, until the difference in the frame types and operating functions is considered. Although Token Ring and Ethernet use 48-bit addresses, bit order interpretation of the addresses in hardware is inverted. Token Ring interface cards consider the first bit encountered to be the high-order bit, Ethernet interface cards consider the first bit encountered as the low-order bit. As an example, the address 84 (hexadecimal) would appear as 0010 0001 (binary) on Ethernet (with the lease significant bit first) whereas the same address would appear as 1000 0100 (binary) on Token Ring (with the most significant bit first).

This address inversion problem is fairly straightforward to solve for the discrete MAC level addresses. However, a number of higher level protocols user part or all of the MAC layer address as data or to form the higher level address. ARP is part of TCP/IP and performs a mapping function between The MAC and IP addresses. ARP is treated as data by bridges because it is a network layer protocol. Therefore the MAC address embedded in the ARP packet will not be translated, unless nonlink layer processing is performed by the translational bridge. Novell's IPX addresses derive the node portion of the network layer address from the MAC layer address. Because network layer addresses are seen as data by bridges, the node portion of the Novell address is translated, unless special processing outside normal bridge functions is performed.

Token Ring frames contain a number of fields that have no correlation on the Ethernet side. Specifically Token Ring has access control, route control, route data, and delimiter fields. The delimiter fields do not pose a significant problem, however, the RIFs require special handling. By definition the RIFs are supposed to contain the complete explicit route from source to destination. Effectively the translational bridge must provide route spoofing, because the Ethernet side of the route is not discernible. Spoofing is done by stripping and caching the RIF information before reformatting to an Ethernet frame. The appropriate cached RIF value is attached to a frame destined for the attached Token Ring segment.

A problem that has not been uniformly addressed by vendors is the processing of the control fields. Token Ring control fields are used to determine frame priority, frame destination receipt, frames forwarded, frame errors, and maximum transfer units (MTU). These parameters have no parallel functions on the Ethernet side, which requires these values to be set to a default value for frames coming from the Ethernet segment. The default values vary between different vendors and compromise the function of the Token Ring LAN because the default values do not indicate dynamic settings.

Another issue that must be addressed with translational bridging is that Token Ring and Ethernet have different MTU values. Ethernet supports an MTU of approximately 1,500 bytes, whereas Token Ring supports an MTU of up to 8,000 bytes. Token Ring can be configured to support a 1,500 MTU, but large file transfers on the Token Ring side become less efficient.

The last complexity that arises with translational bridging between Token Ring and Ethernet is frame conversion. Both LAN types support 802.2 and SNAP fields, but much of the existing Ethernet base uses the original Ethernet encapsulation with the DEC-Intel-Xerox (DIX) type codes, which have no correlation in Token Ring LANs. A special SNAP code (00-0-F8) is used to handle the DIX code conversions between Token Ring and Ethernet segments. Translational bridging is needed so long as older source route code exists in end stations and source route bridges.

Source Route Transparent Bridging

This chapter began by stating that internetworking is not as simple as implementing 10Base-T. This is a good preliminary warning before the concepts of source route transparent bridging (SRT) are explored. SRT is a draft standard for bridging between different Token Ring and Ethernet environments and is intended to replace the current translational bridging approaches. The motivation for replacing translational bridging is intuitively obvious in light of the discussion in the translational bridging section.

The basic concept of SRT is to extend transparent bridging to Token Ring LANs by having all internetwork traffic forwarded by transparent bridging and the spanning tree algorithm. The SRT operational premise is concise; frames received by an SRT are only forwarded to Ethernet segments if no RIF exists, otherwise forwarding is accomplished by source route bridging (SRB). Specifically the SRT uses the most significant bit of the source address (the ring-in (RII) bit) to determine forwarding status. If the RII bit is 0, then no RIF exists and forwarding is accomplished through transparent bridging.

SRB is installed in SRT bridges to handle legacy Token Ring segments. The SRT has SRB functions but no translating can occur; in other words a Token Ring host cannot communicate with an Ethernet host if the Token Ring host uses SRB. The reason for segmenting the two bridging functions is that the loop and broadcast problems that plagued translational bridges have been eliminated.

It now is evident that the greatest obstacles to migrating to SRT is cost. If Token Ring hosts need to communicate with Ethernet hosts, then all ordinary SRB bridges and host software must be upgraded to support SRT. Once the software and hardware conversion has taken place then the entire bridged internet has the benefit of loop free operation by using spanning tree. Another benefit that SRT offers is that the end node is effectively taken out of the bridging process, thereby reducing bridging complexity and points for failure. SRT should not be considered a bridging panacea. The address bit order embedded MAC layer addressing in ARP and IPX, and MTU problems encountered in translational bridging still remain. But even with the remaining problems SRT offers a viable mechanism to facilitate heterogeneous LAN communications.

SUMMARY

Repeaters and bridges are the means of network interconnection that function at the lowest levels of the OSI hierarchy, which enables them to attain high performance levels but limits their use in multiple access method and multiprotocol internets. Routers are much more flexible, albeit more expensive, internetworking mechanisms.

Chapter 50
Planning, Designing and Optimization of Enterprise Networks

Roshan L. Sharma

INTRODUCTION

Network planning, design and optimization should be an important component of a network management process despite its benign neglect by most network managers. Such a benign neglect resulted from the fact that network design was traditionally accomplished through the use of powerful mainframe computers. Since these computers required the use of large tariff-related databases, a great deal of time was spent in entering input data. A great deal of time was also spent on interpreting the output data that invariably came in the form of a thick stack of computer printouts. Lack of graphics provided no illustration of network topologies. Furthermore, the user was always kept out of the computer room. This made the network design process a mysterious effort scaring even the most experienced network manager. Most of the modern network design tools still employ the old philosophy, which prevents the network managers from deriving the full benefits of new innovations in computer hardware and software.

The VLSI (Very Large Scale Integration) technology has now made the availability of very powerful personal computers, desktop or laptop variety, within reach of every network designer and planner. However, the lack of a user-friendly software for network design and planning had prevented the network managers from making use of the latest desktop hardware. Several new software packages have been created to make use of the new PC hardware platforms. The author has developed one such package called EcoNets as fully described in Reference 1. We will make use of EcoNets later and show how the network planning, design and the optimization process can be simplified to a level unimagined before. In fact,

0-8493-9989-0/99/$0.00+$.50

EcoNets can now be treated as a new type of scientific calculator bringing simplicity and ease of use to every networking specialist.

Any network planning and design effort can be broken into the following distinct tasks.

1. Creating a database for all locations and type of dumb terminals (e.g., telephones), intelligent workstations (WSs), customer premise equipment (CPE such as PABX or data LAN) and communication facilities serving those locations,
2. Modeling all types of end-to-end multihour traffic flows between all locations,
3. Modeling traffic growth during a life cycle of the network system,
4. Defining end-to-end performance requirements for all forms of communications,
5. Designing strategic and tactical network alternatives using available technologies,
6. Selecting the best alternative based on cost, cutover and performance,
7. Testing the performance of a post-cutover network implementation,
8. Updating the analytical tools and getting ready for next design cycle,
9. Documenting the results.

A cursory look at the above tasks will suggest that any network manager must accomplish these tasks in an iterative and a clear fashion. One will need a judicial combination of just plain old perseverance (for Tasks 1 and 9), traffic engineering practices (for Tasks 2 and 3), defining performance requirements (for Task 4), availability of a user- friendly and highly interactive design tools (for Tasks 5 and 8), system engineering skills (for Task 7) and marketing savvy for selling the final solution to the upper management (for Task 6). Such capability requirement for a typical network manager is not that formidable if the right traffic analysis and network design tools are available. We will now describe each of the capabilities that must be controlled by the network manager. The capabilities required for Tasks 6, 7 and 9 are discussed in other appropriate chapters of this book.

THE ENTERPRISE DATABASE (EDB)

The first task is by far the most time-consuming. An enterprise database (EDB) should at least list the exact mailing address, ten-digit telephone numbers, associated Vertical and Horizontal (V&H) coordinates, all CPEs with vendor's name, date of installation, single point-of-contact for maintenance, the utilization level of each CPE, type and number of communication facilities serving each location and associated point-of-presence (POP) central offices of local exchange carriers (LECs) and inter exchange carriers (IECs) with their V&H coordinates. The list can grow into a very large one when the database must also classify the users at each location, with their inter-location communications needs. Despite the difficulty of creating the EDB, many network managers and top company officials have already discovered the importance of such a database. In any case, *the task of network planning, design and optimization is impossible without the availability of such an EDB.*

TRAFFIC ENGINEERING TECHNIQUES AND TOOLS

The next three tasks demand a capability for traffic modeling and traffic analysis. Before we define the traffic engineering efforts, we must first introduce some basic traffic-related concepts.

Basic Traffic Concepts

There are two types of traffic encountered in enterprise networks.

1. Well-behaved voice and video traffic
2. Bursty data traffic

It always is assumed that a connection-oriented voice traffic behaves in a predictable fashion which implies that (1) the call holding times can be expressed by at least first two moments (i.e., an average and a variance) and (2) the finer structure of traffic flows don't require rapid changes in network resource deployment. But a close observation of speech energy over the duration of a talk will show that there are many pauses. Furthermore, two of the four-wire access lines (ALs) and trunks are always idle since only one party can talk at a time. These facts have helped long-distance carriers to send more calls over expensive ocean cables than are possible over available trunks using pure circuit switching by using the time asynchronous speech interpolator (TASI) technology. Such a technology was never cost-effective over cheaper land-based leased line. With the availability of Asynchronous Transfer Mode (ATM) or Broadband ISDN, one will be able to get the same benefit through the use of Variable Bit Rate (VBR) capability. The connection-oriented video traffic should not yield this benefit since intelligent WSs can maintain a full-duplex connection.

The data traffic between two CPEs is always bursty. This is caused by the complex rules of data communication protocols. Very small control messages may be involved in both directions before user- information can flow. Although a full-duplex connection can be maintained, shared transmission lines in a packet switched network can carry variable-length packets from many sources concurrently thus muddying the picture in a hurry. The faster the transmission lines, the burstier the transmission will appear. It becomes clear that a notion of an average message length over a transmission line becomes rather vague.

One can now devise ways to measure traffic intensity considering the above aspects of two major types of traffic encountered in enterprise networks.

Circuit-switched (CS) voice and video traffic intensity is measured in *erlangs* which is equal to the average number of circuits busy during a so-called busy hour (BHR) between two network nodes. We will define such a BHR later. To illustrate, if 15.5 conversations are observed concurrently between two network nodes (e.g., between a PABX and a voice switch or over an access line bundle) during a BHR, then the voice traffic intensity is 15.5 erlangs. The older measure of CS traffic intensity was *hundred call seconds (CCS)*. But such a measure was almost useless since it did not represent any physical truth such as the number of conversations observed.

Packet-switched data traffic intensity can be measured as the traffic rate in bits per second (bps) during a so-called busy hour. Only data rate in bps can describe the bursty nature of data traffic. Experienced network specialists have been using the concept of data erlangs for many years for defining the average data traffic intensity between two network nodes. This is obtained by dividing the observed BHR data rate (R) by the capacity (C) of each separate transmission line. For example, if the BHR data rate between two nodes is 392,000 bps and the capacity of a transmission line is 56000 bps, then the data traffic intensity is 7 erlangs.

Modeling Traffic Flows in an Enterprise Network

Basically there are two kinds of network systems that present unique situations for modeling traffic flows within an enterprise network; (1) a *brand new* network system and (2) an *existing* network system.

Modeling Traffic Flows in a Brand New Enterprise Network. Many network specialists feel helpless in modeling traffic flows for a brand new system. Many approximate methods have been devised over the years for predicting traffic intensities (TIs) between all major CPEs. To illustrate, a voice LAN (or PABX) generates about $0.1{*}N_s$ erlangs of BHR traffic where N_s is the number of active subscribers served by the PABX. Similarly, a data LAN generates about $(2/3)(WSC){*}N_s$ where WSC is the BHR traffic intensity (in bps) generated by each *active* station on the LAN. A breakdown of these traffic expressions into intra-nodal and inter-nodal traffic should be determined by the known pattern observed at each enterprise. Some network designers employ the 70/30 breakdown that implies that 70 percent of the traffic remains within the site (voice/data LAN) and 30 percent of the traffic goes to other CPEs as inter-nodal flows. These TI values can then be entered into an input file that defines each site ID, the related V&H coordinates and the total traffic (in and out) intensity handled by the site. The EcoNets tool calls such a file as the VHD file.

The next task is to model the inter-nodal traffic flows (i.e., exact traffic intensities handled by all the nodes and links in the path of a CPE-CPE connection). These computations are generally performed by the network planning/design software package for each assumed network topology (i.e., number of network switches and the link types employed at each network hierarchy). Some tools employ some critical design parameters to determine the fraction of traffic handled by ALs (connecting CPE and a switch) and trunks (connecting two switches). Eventually, the tool provides the total traffic intensity handled by each resource (node or link) of each network topology considered during a typical busy hour.

Modeling Traffic Flows in an Existing Enterprise Network. One can model exact traffic flows by using the detailed traffic data gathered by intelligent network nodes (e.g., PABX or LAN). The source ID, the destination ID, the call originating time and the call duration for each connection is recorded in a Station Message Data Recording (SMDR) tapes of voice network. Similar data is recorded by the data LAN for the packetized traffic. Simple traffic analysis packages are obtainable for analyzing the exact inter-nodal traffic patterns between all pairs of CPEs. Such data can then be entered in a From-To-Data File (FTF) to define CPE traffic as simple vectors (From-Node ID, To-Node ID, and the BHR traffic intensity) for each CPE-nodal pair. This effort eventually provides actual traffic flows (i.e., the actual traffic intensity handled by all resource, nodes and links) of each network topology studied during a typical BHR.

Modeling Time-Consistent Averages (TCAs) of Traffic Flows. Choosing a busy hour can be a very important task. No network can be economical if one selects the hour with the highest traffic. It may provide the required grade-of-service (GOS) during the busiest hour but at all other hours of the day (especially during the evening and night hours) it becomes an overkill. Nobody can afford such a network. If one selects an hour with the least traffic during the day, the network manager will hear complaints all day long. Therefore, one needs a proven methodology to select the so-called TCA traffic intensity for network design. There are two methodologies — one used in North America and one used by the other countries.

The first methodology requires the selection of a typical month and creating a matrix (30×24) of traffic intensities (TIs) for each network resource for that month. Next, it computes the average traffic intensity for each hour of the day over all 30 days of the month. This process is repeated for each of the 24 hours. The TCA traffic is the maximum value of all 24 TCA values. This value, as it will shown later, determines the size of the resource (number of AL and trunks in the bundle connecting two nodes or the computing power of an intelligent node). Again one needs either the use of a software package for computing TCA traffic intensity (TI) values or a simple approach for approximating the TCA TI values.

The second methodology requires the observation of 36 highest TI values over an entire year and then computing the average of these values to get a TCA value. This must be done for all resources.

Both of these methodologies are known to yield economical networks. It should be emphasized that no single methodology can predict an exact traffic pattern for the future. Traffic values behave like the stock market fluctuations. A single catastrophe, such as an earthquake or a major terrorist-bomb explosion somewhere can also change the traffic patterns drastically. The objective of a good traffic engineering practice is to synthesize a cost-effective enterprise network using a consistent approach.

Modeling Traffic Growths During a Life Cycle of a Network System. In order to estimate the total costs incurred during the life cycle of a network system, one must first model the traffic intensities for each of the life cycle year. Experience shows that the so-called Delphi Approach (based on Socratic approach) works the best. Through interviews of all general managers, one can build good models of traffic growth during every year of the life cycle. There are times when one may find that some division may disappear altogether either through divestiture or pure attrition. The data from all of the interviews must be collected, weighed and processed to create a meaningful model.

PERFORMANCE ISSUES

Before one can define performance requirements for all the communication needs of an enterprise, one must first study the available concepts of performance and then study the exact enterprise needs in each of their business areas.

Concepts of Network System Performance

It is a commonly known fact that most of the existing network systems were implemented without any regard to their performance. As long as they satisfy the basic needs for communications, everyone is happy. No effort is expended in (1) predicting or measuring the actual performance of the system and (2) making any measured system-wide improvements after the system is operational. The lack of any concerted effort in defining and measuring performance of network system may lie in ignorance of concepts related to system performance. One can define the performance of a network system in four ways:

1. Total system costs computed on a monthly basis,
2. System throughputs in terms of all types of transactions handled during a unit time,
3. System-wide quality-of-service (QOS)
4. System-wide grade-of-service (GOS).

Total Monthly Costs. Transmission facilities determine the majority of total monthly cost of MANs and WANs. Since such costs are always paid on a monthly basis (just like our utility bills) to Local Exchange Carrier (LEC), Inter Exchange Carriers (IECs) and Other Common Carriers (OCCs), it simplifies matters a great deal. The other major items are one-time hardware costs and recurring costs of network management and control (NMC). It is a simple matter to convert the one-time hardware costs into equivalent monthly cost considering the life cycle duration (7 or 10 years depending on the enterprise) and cost of loaning money. It is similar to computing the monthly payment for a mortgage. The NMC costs related to spares can be handled just like one-time hardware costs. The remaining NMC costs on a monthly basis can be the same as either the monthly salaries paid to the NMC specialists or the monthly bills paid to an outsourcing company. It is therefore a simple task to compute the total monthly cost of a network system.

System Throughput. System throughput is measured the rate at which the various types of transactions are handled per unit time (usually second or minute). It is equal to the number of call attempts or calls completed per second for a voice network. It is equal to the number of packets handled per second or total bits (in and out) per second handled during a second. The throughput capability of each node is generally defined by the vendor of the equipment. The challenge lies in measuring the system throughput. By enumerating the exact paths of each transaction, one can estimate the system throughput. Consult Reference 1 for additional insight.

System Quality-of-Service (QOS). Performance aspects dealing with transmission quality, perceived voice quality, error-free seconds, data security and network reliability (mean-time-between-system failures) fall into the QOS criterion. Most of these are very hard to compute for the entire system. One can measure these performance aspects for some critical resource to get a feel. See Reference 1 for greater insight.

System Grade-of-Service (GOS). The GOS criterion deals with end-to-end blocking for a voice network and average response time (measured as the elapsed time between the moment send key is pressed and the moment the return reply is discerned by the user) for a data communication. Analytical tools are available (Reference 1) for estimating such GOS parameters for both voice, data and integrated networks.

Defining Performance Goals for an Enterprise

Performance goals of a enterprise network should be developed by the corporate strategic planners. A typical strategic planning cycle lasts several years and it entails the following activities:

1. Continuous evaluation of the needs of the enterprise and its competitors. This activity defines the relationship of system response times to information worker's productivity for each of the transactions.
2. Studying the evolving new technologies, CPEs and networking standards and finding ways to deploy these to achieve cost-effective enterprise networks and/or enhancing the productivity of its workers. This activity provides the cost and performance attributes of new hardware (e.g., ATM switches and LAN switches).

In order to perform its duties successfully, a strategic planning group should be properly structured to act in close cooperation of the corporate Information Technology (IT) department and it should be provided with all the necessary resources and tools. Furthermore, a mechanism should be in place to properly reward all the members of this important group.

All future enterprise networks will have to deal with the ever-increasing demand for (1) voice, video, image and data communications, (2) multiplexing of digitized voice, image and video signals with regular data traffic at all hierarchies of enterprise locations through modern switches (e.g., ATM switches) and (3) unscheduled or varying demands for digital bandwidth at all hours of a day on a dynamic basis.

In order to design such an integrated enterprise network, the strategic planning group needs a user-friendly tool for evaluating alternative solutions very quickly. Such an approach should be an extension of the so-called "back-of-the-envelope" method employed by network managers of yesterday. They were generally concerned with designing only voice networks. The older "back-of-the-envelope" approach is no longer useful due to the complexity of modern integrated, hybrid, multilevel enterprise networks. It has been found that most of the hunches based on the so-called "common sense" are generally wrong when predicting the performance of an integrated network system. A user-friendly tool should help the strategic planning group to get "ball-park" solutions iteratively and interactively in order to fulfill its charter. See Page 120, *An Example of Planning and Design of an Integrated Enterprise Network Using Econets*, for an illustration of a "what if" approach required for rapid planning and designing or obtaining quick conceptual solutions by both the strategic and tactical planning teams.

NETWORK PLANNING AND DESIGN TOOL

Before we review the old and the new network design technologies, it should also be useful to discuss some major network design issues.

Major Network Design Issues

The current published literature dealing with networking is very confusing at best. Most of the published articles are generally characterized by buzz words, a good deal of hype, lots of possible solutions and no single recommendation. Although a part of the problem may lie in the fact that no single approach is ideally suited for all enterprises, no one can defend a lack of clarity that characterizes most published articles. While some articles recommend all virtual lines for enterprise voice networks, other articles emphasize the need for an integrated network management technique. While some articles recommend full freedom in designing departmental LANs and interconnections of these LANs through bridges and routers, other articles show the need for Frame Relay, SMDS and B-ISDN or ATM in order to realize economies-of-scale in integrated enterprise networks. Most of the articles attempt only to expound a new type of switch technology or hardware. They rightfully leave up to the reader to assess the usefulness of the new technology or networking hardware to their enterprise.

Network design process is basically concerned with two issues: (1) topological optimization which determines the way network nodes are connected to one another (including the type of connections) while satisfying a set of critical design and performance constraints and (2) system performance dealing with end-to-end response times, path congestion and availabilities.

Recurring network cost generally is the most important performance criterion and it is mainly determined by its topology. Network topology also determines the remaining performance issues such as response times and availability. Each network design package analyzes these performance issues in only an approximate manner.

Closed-form solutions for end-to-end system performance have been getting harder and harder to obtain ever since the first day a network was installed. Some of the current excitement about the interconnections of data LANs ignores the tribulations involved during the 70's when voice LANs (i.e., PABXs) were being interconnected to create enterprise networks with consistent topologies. Unfortunately, data internetworks encourage point-to-point type connections between LANs. This approach creates an undue network complexity for large networks. This in turn increases costs of NMC. The new ATM technology should eventually reduces this complexity by enforcing a consistent network topology and architecture.

The Old Network Design Technology

The many older network design tools handled only voice or multidrop data networks. Some of the tools that came later handled only interconnections of data LANs to achieve an enterprise data WAN. Furthermore, most of these tools required mainframes. The use of a mainframe introduced an unnecessary curtain between the network designer and the host processor. The network design jobs were entered invariably via the 'batch" approach and the outputs came in the form of large printouts after a good deal of delay. Each change of a design parameter or study of a new technology required a new noninteractive, unfriendly delay. The absence of network-related graphics from outputs caused additional delays in interpreting the significance of results.

The old design technology also required the use of an extensive database of tariffs. These tariffs have been increasing in number and changing quite rapidly since the divestiture in 1984. The complexity of the tariff database was probably the main reason behind the need for mainframes. If such a database is incorporated into a desktop minicomputer or a PC-based workstation, one will experience sizable processing delays. In any case, one will be prevented to get a truly interactive tool.

Since enterprise networks are planned and designed for a future period, this preoccupation with utmost accuracy in tariffs is uncalled for. Furthermore, since network topologies do not change with perturbations in any given tariff (they change only with varying design parameters and technologies), using a simplified set of existing or new tariffs will yield optimized networks in rapid succession even on a user-friendly desktop workstation. These topologies can be studied for a detailed cost analysis at a later period using one of the many available PC-Line Pricer (PCLP) units. This 2-step approach should create a separation between the network design algorithms and the ever-changing tariffs. There should be no need to update the network design package just because a tariff changed slightly.

Network design tools based on the older technology were not only noninteractive, but they also were nonfriendly to use. A lack of a good graphical user interface (GUI) required a lengthy training and a prolonged hands-on design experience before becoming familiar with the tool. A good design package should be an intuitive tool in the hands of an expert network designer and no more. A good hammer and a chisel alone will never guarantee beautiful furniture — one also needs a good carpenter. It should not be hard to understand as to why the vendors of network design tools have always had a hard time in marketing these unfriendly network design tools. Most vendors have gone in and out of business several times under different names.

Some vendors (Reference 2) market software packages based on computer simulation for evaluating system performance. LANs (voice or data) and WANs consisting of interconnected data LANs can be evaluated for performance through computer simulation. A good deal of time must be spent on (1) writing the simulation program based upon the exact network topology and the underlying communication protocols and (2) debugging the software before one can evaluate all of the performance metrics such as throughput and end-to-end response times. Since typical enterprise networks require exorbitant run-times, a simulation tool is no longer an ideal way for synthesizing an optimum network topology. A network topology optimization package based on analytical tools is always the best approach. The resulting topology can be evaluated for studying detailed system response times and availabilities using an expensive simulation tool.

The New Network Design Technology

The new desktop workstation technology now provides several platforms for a user-friendly, interactive tool for optimizing network topology in an iterative fashion while varying the values of critical design parameters rapidly. Some well-known tools for network design also provide special menus for computing end-to-end response times for unusual operational conditions. Some packages even provide special tools for analyzing subsystem security and reliability.

Many new tools based on the graphical-user-interface (GUI) can evaluate any mix of CPEs, transmission facilities and network topologies very rapidly in an intuitive manner. But in no way can this new technology eliminate the need for an expert network designer or an architect. Since the expert designer is always involved with "what-if" type analyses at all times through the graphical-user-interface, the solutions remain always meaningful and topical only if the network design tool provides such solutions rapidly. This approach is becoming an ideal one since the tariffs as we have known are about to disappear. The modern tools allow the entry of approximate tariffs quickly. Next we will describe one network planning and design package called EcoNets. Next we will describe an example illustrating the network planning and design process associated with EcoNets.

Capability Highlights of the EcoNets Network Planning and Design Package

Inputs are in the form of flat, sequential files. Results are provided in the form of (1) graphics illustrating network topology with summary costs of communications facilities and response times (if applicable) and (2) output files containing detailed cost distributions and critical performance data.

The most important input file is called the VHD file listing the site/node ID, Vertical and Horizontal (V&H) coordinates and total busy hour (BHR), time-consistent traffic intensities in bits per second (for data) or millierlangs (for voice) for each location of the enterprise. A from-to-data (FTD) file can also be used to represent exact traffic flows. Another file called the daily traffic profile relates the BHR intensities to the other 24 hours of the day for computing the costs on a daily/monthly basis. For an enterprise with many time zones, several BHR models can be used. The second most important LINK file defines the link-type that serves each location.

The third most important input file called the NLT file defines the link type, capacity (C), allowed maximum data rate (W_m), multiplexing factor (MF defining the equivalent number of voice conversations carried by the link), corresponding tariff number and the multiplying factor for a privately-owned facility (F_{pf}), if applicable. Up to ten link types and corresponding C, W_m, MF, tariff number and F_{pf} can be defined by the NLT file. The Tariff file can define up to 10 manually entered tariffs, each modeled by 17 parameters. Several Link, NLT and Tariff files can be prepared to model many combinations of links and tariffs at all levels of network hierarchy. An input file called the system design file (SDF) defines the design parameters required to model/design the network.

The input file called the FTF defines the BHR From-To traffic for all significant pairs if such data is known. Other input files define the LATA numbers and names associated with each location. Several specialized input files are also employed for modeling/designing ACD networks employing a mix of virtual facilities and leased FX lines.

The File Menu allows the creation and viewing/updating of all input/output files. The Networking Menu allows the modeling/designing of multilevel voice, data and IV/D network using the appropriate star data, directed link and multidrop data network topologies and voice networks based on star topology. One can also model, design and optimize backbone networks on an iterative manner. The Networking Menu also allows the designer to find optimum locations for concentrators/switches by starting with good solutions and improving these through a fast iterative process. By specifying the design parameters, one can model and design traditional data networks based on IBM's SNA (System Network Architecture) traditional packet switched networks based on CCITT's X.25 standard, fast Packet switched networks based on Frame Relay and ATM technology.

By specifying the design parameters, one can model hybrid voice networks using all types of leased and virtual facilities with/without multiplexing. One can also optimize a backbone network topology and model any given topology (for cost and routes). The Analysis Menu allows the designer to model/analyze any point-to-point and several multilink paths for congestion/queuing delays, LAN performance and reliability. An

Analysis Menu item also allows the computation of equivalent monthly cost of hardware and payoff periods for privately owned hardware and transmission facilities.

AN EXAMPLE OF PLANNING AND DESIGN OF AN INTEGRATED ENTERPRISE NETWORK USING ECONETS

An enterprise has 17 sites scattered throughout the United States. Its headquarters are in Las Colinas, Texas. It is engaged in the manufacture, distribution, marketing and maintenance of highly specialized intelligent workstations. Two separate networks serve the enterprise. A voice network connects all its 17 locations (or PABXs) to a voice switch located at Las Colinas with leased voice-grade-lines (VGLs). A separate data network connects workstations located at all of its locations to a Host using the SNA-BSC protocol and 9600 bps lines. The newly appointed network manager wants to study the feasibility of a new network architecture. A consultant is engaged to study the problem.

A database (a subset of the EDB) for network design was created. It is illustrated in Exhibit 1. The seventeen sites, their V&H coordinates and BHR TCA of traffic intensities are shown for both voice (in millierlangs) and data (in bps). Also shown are their names according to a 6-symbol city-state (CCCCST) code. Next a Node-Link-Type (NLT) file is defined for four link types, VGL, 56Kbps line, T1 line and a T3 line. The simplified tariffs are defined for these links types next.

The consultant first modeled the existing voice and data networks. The monthly costs for these two separate networks were computed to be as $60,930 and $10,017 respectively. For a comparison, the EcoNets tool was then employed to study various topologies consisting of 1,2,3,4,5 switches and three links types for voice and only the 9600 bps line for data (higher-speed lines resulted in no improvements).

The results are shown in Exhibit 2. The optimum voice-network topology (Exhibit 3) consisted of two switches (as determined by the EcoNets' center-of-gravity [COG] finding item of Networking Menu) and 56Kbps lines, each of which carries eight digitally-encoded voice conversations. The one-time cost of 17 special hardware boxes that perform voice encoding and multiplexing in the same box did not influence the optimum network topology. The optimum data network topology (Exhibit 4) also consisted of same two switches as for the voice network and 9600bps lines. The cost of these optimum networks was found to be $37,546 and $9,147 respectively. This represented a monthly saving of $23,254 (or about 32.8% of existing costs). No matter which way one looks at this figure, it is a substantial saving.

Exhibit 1. Enterprise database (EDB) 17-node network design (voice/data applications).

Nodal Definition Data						
N#	**-V-**	**-H-**	**Load**	**Lata (BPS/MEs)**	**Link**	**Name**
1	8438	4061	40000	552	0	LCLNTX
2	8436	4034	5000	552	0	DALLTX
3	8296	1094	1300	952	0	SRSTFL
4	8360	906	1300	939	0	FTMYFL
5	6421	8907	1300	674	0	TACMWA
6	6336	8596	1300	676	0	BELVWA
7	4410	1248	1400	128	0	DANVMA
8	6479	2598	1300	466	0	VERSKY
9	9258	7896	1300	730	0	TOAKCA
10	9233	7841	1400	730	0	NORWCA
11	9210	7885	1400	730	0	WLAXCA
12	7292	5925	1400	656	0	DENVCO
13	7731	4025	1300	538	0	TULSOK
14	7235	2069	1300	438	0	NORCGA
15	5972	2555	2500	324	0	COLMOH
16	9228	7920	2500	730	0	STMNCA
17	8173	1147	2500	952	0	TMPAFL
Total BHR Traffic = 68500						

Node-Link Type

Link Type	Link Capacity	MaxLink Rate
1	9,600 bps	6,300 bps
2	56,000	48,000
3	1,544,000	1,440,000

Tariff No. 1

Average Local Loops Charges ($)=294					
Mileage Bands	50	100	500	1000	10000
Fixed Costs ($)	72.98	149.28	229.28	324.24	324.24
Cost Per Mile ($)	2.84	1.31	0.51	0.32	0.32

Tariff No. 2

Average Local Loops Charges ($)=492					
Mileage Bands	50	100	500	1000	10000
Fixed Costs ($)	232	435	571	1081	1081
Cost Per Mile ($)	7.74	3.68	2.32	1.3	1.3

Tariff No. 3

Average Local Loops Charges ($)=2800					
Mileage Bands	50	100	10000	10000	10000
Fixed Costs ($)	1770	1808	2008	2500	2500
Cost Per Mile ($)	10	9.25	7.25	7.25	7.25

Tariff No. 4

Average Local Loops Charges ($)=8000					
Mileage Bands	10000	10000	10000	10000	10000
Fixed Costs ($)	16600	16600	16600	16600	16600
Cost Per Mile ($)	47	47	47	47	47

Daily Traffic Profile

Hour Numbers and Corresponding Fractions of Daily Traffic are as Follows:					
1–0	2–0	3–0	4–0	5–0	6–0
7–0.05	8–0.1	9–0.1	10–0.1	11–0.1	12–0.1
13–0.1	14–0.1	15–0.1	16–0.1	17–0.05	18–0
19–0	20–0	21–0	22–0	23–0	24–0

Additional saving can be achieved by computing the total data rate (in bps) of voice conversations from each site and adding the regular data traffic and constructing a new VHD file. One can achieve an optimum star-data topology consisting of two switches and 56Kbps lines. Its topology is identical to that for the optimum voice network (Exhibit 2) and its monthly cost is about the same as for the optimum voice network. The cost of the separate data network disappears completely. The new monthly saving of $33,392 savings represents 47.1% of the existing costs. These additional savings resulted from the fact that the 56K bps lines used in the integrated

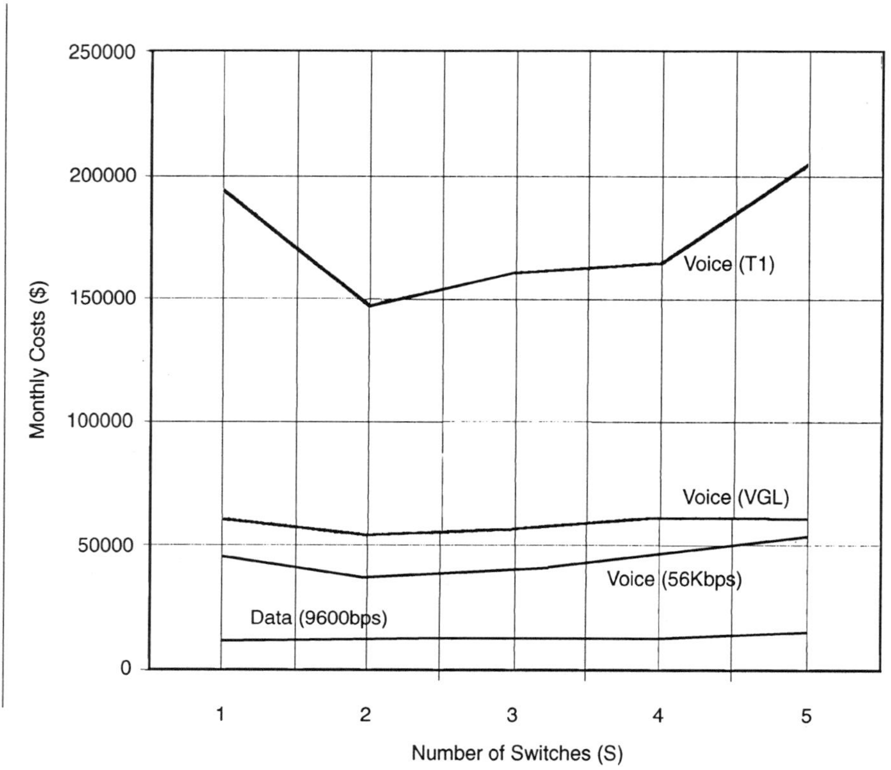

Exhibit 2. Cost vs. number of switches and link types.

voice/data (IVD) network had enough excess capacity to handle the data traffic. Such a phenomenon is similar to the one experienced by network managers working with larger T1 networks of 1980s. Those enterprise voice networks had enough excess capacities (in the T1 trunks) to handle the data traffic. The broadband data networks of the future should have enough excess capacity to handle the voice and image traffic.

The preceding examples illustrate only small enterprise networks. Bigger savings can be expected through optimization of larger enterprise networks. Basically, savings result from two facts: (1) integrated networks make use of excess capacity and (2) aggregation of many separate applications allows the deployment of transmission facilities with higher capacities that generally cost less on a per-transaction basis. Now every network manager has unlimited opportunities to provide a cost effective integrated network to the enterprise. There is no excuse for not attempting to save big bucks for any strategically minded enterprise.

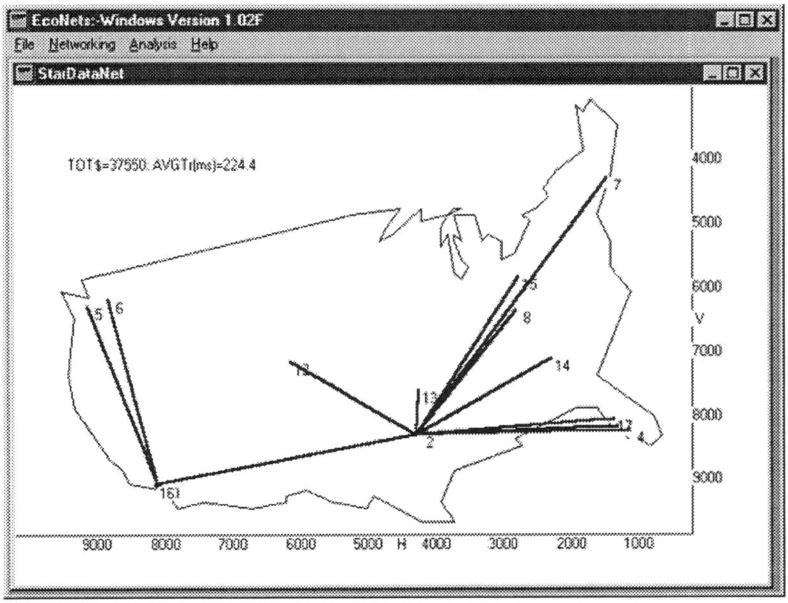

Exhibit 3. Optimum star-data network topology for IVD application.

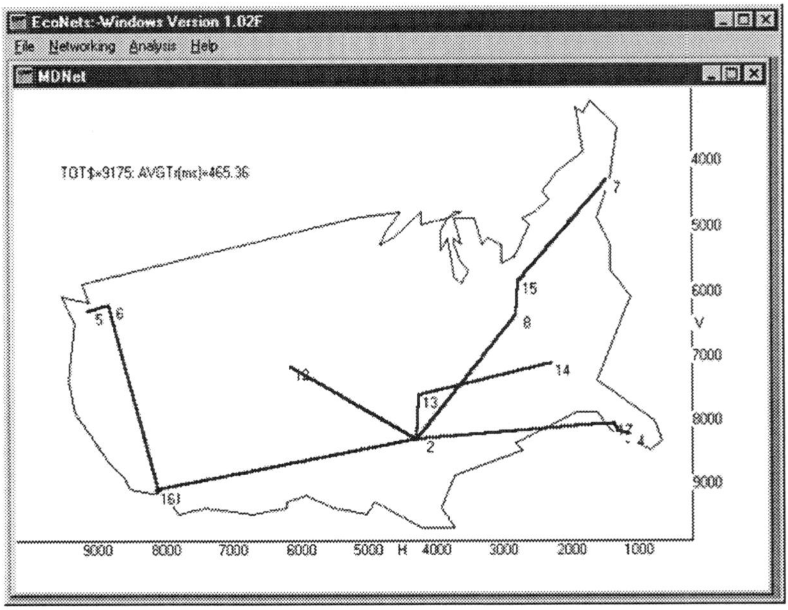

Exhibit 4. Optimum MD-data network topology with two switches.

REFERENCES

1. Sharma, Roshan L. *Introduction to Network Design Using EcoNets Software*, International Thomson Computer Press, Boston, 1997.
2. Fike, J. L and H. D. Jacobsen. *Applying Modeling Techniques in Network Design*, Paper presented at the June 3, 1991 Session M13 at the ICA Conference.
3. Van Norman, H. J. "WAN Design Tools: the New Generation," *Data Communications*, October 1990.
4. Axner, David. "New Tools for Predicting Network Performance," *Business Communications Review*, November 1995.

Chapter 51
Distributed Network Support and Control

Ira Hertzoff

During the 1980s, distributed processing was performed by a client using files and programs stored on a server. Today, distributed processing is split between the server and client to offer desktop power, more efficient network resource use, and better control of network traffic. As these open systems grow in importance, supporting them becomes a networkwide process as opposed to a node-based operation.

Clients on networks using structured query language (SQL) database servers can access a common database. Transparent access to data shared between applications and to databases on multiple servers is provided by widely used front ends (e.g., Lotus 1-2-3, Paradox, and Excel).

In the layered networks of the 1990s, mission-critical data is stored on corporate hosts; local data is stored on multifunctional servers providing back-end SQL database services; and dissimilar clients run multiple front-end applications. Numerous paths into the network permit access to data from both internal and external sources. Distributed networks can be compromised from remote locations and their security seriously jeopardized if a single node is accessible. Distributed network security now depends on how the desktop computer is used and how desktop power is managed. No operation is safe unless all connected operations are secure—protecting only the host is no longer sufficient.

THE NEED FOR PROTECTION

Appropriate procedures and techniques are necessary to protect the network from external or internal manipulation of its programs, data, and resources. An effective program protects a network from physical destruction, unauthorized modification, or disclosure of software and records.

High-technology network penetration is a glamorous subject and certainly a possible threat, but low-tech penetration is much more common and much more dangerous. Intruders who take advantage of procedural

0-8493-9989-0/99/$0.00+$.50

weaknesses represent a greater threat to distributed networks than do industrial spies with, for example, emissions- sensing devices. Protection costs should be balanced against risk reality. The IS manager can offer cost-effective protection against real risks by carefully rating the problems that can occur. If the maximum potential risk is from a disgruntled employee, the IS manager should not specify distributed network security measures to protect against a resourceful and determined adversary (e.g., an unfriendly government).

The Protection Decision

There are three ways to protect a network against risk: self-insurance or risk retention, insurance against economic loss, and installation of security measures.

Insurance. Protection measures should be selected with the assistance of the corporate risk or insurance manager. Large enterprises commonly self-insure for minor risks, obtain outside insurance against larger risks, and use security measures when they are less expensive than insurance. Insurance is a proven method of managing risk and should always be part of a network security plan. A corporation can elect to risk an event and make no insurance or security provisions; if this is a planned rather than accidental decision, it is a valid approach.

SECURITY MEASURES

Distributed networks require three types of protection: disaster recovery, physical security, and data security. Because these areas overlap, a single well-selected security measure can offer protection in more than one. Distributed networks, because their elements are geographically separated, are inherently protected against physical destruction. Distributed networks do not require the complex backup procedures for disasters that single-site operations must have, because the distributed architecture is based on distributed servers and the IS staff is trained to automatically back up files.

Geographically distributed systems pose security risks because if processing does not take place in physically secure computer rooms, desktop computer users can create openings into the network, and software can be introduced into the network from many workstations. Preventing viruses, worms, and the unauthorized copying of software and files requires proper administrative procedures.

The distributed network needs in-depth protection involving multiple layers of defenses. Any single security measure can be improperly installed, be bypassed, or have flaws; the use of multiple security measures protects against weaknesses in any individual measure (see Exhibit 1.)

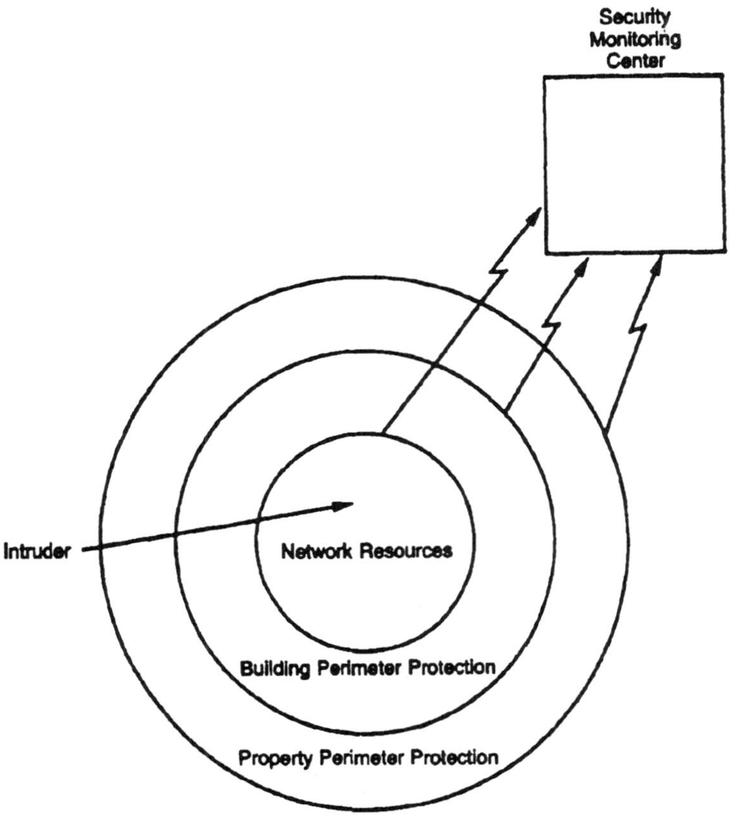

Exhibit 1. Security layers.

Unplanned shutdowns and restarts of any programmable network device must be considered a breach of security and investigated. In particular, operating system restarts should not be allowed or accepted as normal operating practice.

The Auditor's Role. The effectiveness of any security plan must be proved by ongoing reviews conducted by technically competent auditors. To ensure their independence, these auditors must not have any other operating responsibilities. If there is no existing program for conducting audits and training auditors, or if the existing program is inadequate, an effective program should be established.

Multilevel Processing Security. Because various classes of work are usually performed on the same network, processes requiring different levels of security interact. (When all work on a network is at the same security level, processes do not need to be compartmentalized to prevent a user from accessing another user's data.) Security requires that these processes interact only in a known, predictable, and authorized manner.

Secure Processing Over an Insecure Network. The public telephone network and many private communications facilities are inherently insecure. The telephone network is universal (with many points of access and exit) and has well-known security weaknesses. Any secure process that operates over such links must use handshaking techniques to verify that only the desired parties are in communication. Cryptographic techniques applied to the data ensure that data cannot be interpreted if it is intercepted.

Risks of LANs as Gateways to Hosts. When a LAN is used as a front end to a secure mainframe, a serious LAN security breach will compromise the mainframe's security. Such breaches can occur because both secure and insecure operating systems run on the same network and because of the nature of workstation intelligence. A user can program a personal computer to set up a connection through the LAN to secure host databases. Anyone with physical, logical, or remote control access to that personal computer can log into the host as a user. Gateways should be evaluated by how they support network management and security.

LAN Security. Many LAN security systems are inadequate because they were designed for work group automation and are the product of a single-user design mentality. One indication of a poor LAN operating system is the availability of many add-on security products. Access rights tools should be an integral part of the operating system.

The use of LANs as host gateways is economical, but many LAN operating systems expose host passwords by letting them reside in buffers or making them available for decoding by protocol analyzers. In both LAN token-ring and Ethernet networks, each station sees all LAN traffic. A true star topology is therefore superior. Personal computer-based LANs suffer from the weaknesses of their DOS operating system and are prone to virus and worm attacks. Diskless workstations prevent users from loading unauthorized software. Requiring users to load local operating system software from the network reduces the risk of infection.

DISASTER RECOVERY

A network must function under all normal and anticipated abnormal conditions and must be robust enough to survive the unexpected. The IS manager must provide the systems, staff, and procedures necessary to ensure that a disaster—intentional or otherwise—does not cripple the organization. As mission-critical applications become more time-dependent, the acceptable time for restoration of service is decreasing.

Accurate recordkeeping in a configuration control database with connectivity information is fundamental. This type of network management can be the core of a disaster plan generated as the network control staff performs daily operations. Problem management tools can simulate outages, and change control tools can track recovery operations. IS managers responsible for maintaining distributed networks must integrate disaster planning into their daily operations—not as a separate project but as a large problem that requires immediate action and resolution.

Reserve Capacity

To protect data against disaster, the IS manager can, at different locations, place multiple servers with reverse capacities so that each server can absorb additional work loads as necessary. This dual-operating capability should be part of installation planning so that critical applications operate at two or more sites.

Disaster recovery of a distributed network is a network process. Under both normal and abnormal conditions, the network should use its interconnections and facilities to support recovery of failing network elements. SOL databases, mirror-imaged at different points on distributed client-server networks, can be designated to allow automatic recovery.

THE NETWORK AS A BACKUP SYSTEM

With enough network bandwidth, critical files can be stored on several servers. Provisions to switch network control should be made if an event disables the primary control point. In large networks, management domains must be established and plans developed for switching control if a domain management point is unavailable. The swapping of network control should be a normal and periodic procedure familiar to the staff at all sites.

The process of restoring an operation includes recognizing that a disaster has occurred. This function is best handled by the network management center. Incomplete information generated by inadequate tools can delay action until the problem becomes uncontainable. Disaster recovery resources should enhance the network management system rather than create disaster recovery systems that operate in parallel.

Backup Types

Backups are file copies used to protect against errors; they are recycled on a regular schedule. (Archival backups may be retained permanently.) The process of recycling media is called rotation. Backup media can be recycled on a generation basis or on a longer cycle. A distributed network with enough bandwidth can be backed up to a server in a central location. Central backup ensures that remote devices are backed up according to plan and taken off site.

PHYSICAL SECURITY

A network's physical security can be penetrated and seriously compromised in many ways, for example through the destruction of or damage to buildings, cables, switches, power sources, computer hardware, computer files, and programs.

Seals

Security seals are attached to equipment to detect tampering or entry. A damaged seal indicates that a unit has been opened. Managers of large networks should use prenumbered, bar-coded seals. Each seal number should be recorded in a database and assigned to a technician. The number on the seal should be then linked to a specific machine or component.

When a seal is broken during an authorized repair, a new seal should be installed and the number linked to the old seal number, the repair technician, and the actions taken. This approach keeps the configuration database current. It allows the IS manager to positively identify each component, which technician worked on it, and whether it was altered by anyone—authorized or unauthorized—from the state recorded in the configuration database.

Hot Work: Flame, Electrical, and Plumbing Service Control

Effective security practice requires any employee or contractor working on critical systems to obtain proper clearance—a hot work permit or license. The license ensures that responsible managers know when work that can cause a fire or cut power or water is being performed. Permits should be required for all work on communications lines and power sources and for construction that can affect lines. In some cases, a prudent manager may assign a staff member to follow the worker with a fire extinguisher. Avoiding extended downtime makes this precaution a wise investment.

CONTROL OF EXECUTABLE CODE

The IS manager should control the loading onto the network of all executable code to reduce the risk of infection from computer viruses and worms and from unauthorized modification of programs. On a distributed network, all paths that can result in code execution must be blocked, including unintended paths. On a DOS machine, for example, using the Type command on a text file with embedded ANSI.sys commands results in execution of the commands. In this case, a text editor is safer than using Type when checking suspect files. Other unintended paths include service diagnostic disks that can carry viruses and worms from machine to machine; problems can also be caused by a failure to maintain a network operating system software at current revision levels.

Remote Library Control

Effective control practice requires valuable assets to be concentrated and placed in a protected environment. To protect executable code and programs, data center managers must ensure that all network programs are kept in program libraries, which are stored in directories with controlled access.

Authorization to make changes or add programs to the library and the ability to authorize such changes should be assigned to different individuals. Activity journals on each file must be kept to verify accountability. Library data structures should be maintained to improve management insight and control.

ACCESS CONTROL

Access controls limit a particular user's access to specific network resources. One method is to request information that only one person knows (e.g., a password). User IDs, authorization tables, and access rights lists can also be used to control access. Such controls (as audit trails and alarms) are essential to protect against authorized users and should be implemented in the software that controls the program library as well as in the software that prevents unauthorized access to production data. Various access control methods are discussed in the following sections.

Handshaking

Network users should be informed of the last use of their ID and password when they log on the network. They should report any suspicious activity to management or be held responsible for the results of this activity.

Lockwords

Lockwords permit users with knowledge of the file code to access that file without verifying their identity. Multiple resources require multiple lockwords, a problem that, on some LANs, is counteracted by writing batch files to issue lockwords. This practice results in very poor control, and it is difficult to change lockwords. The use of lockword security is unacceptable and is particularly dangerous when LAN gateways to hosts are used.

Passwords

Passwords use access control as their primary security mechanism. Password secrecy is needed to prevent system access, but passwords can be compromised in many ways, the easiest being user carelessness. Procedural controls on the contents of passwords—restrictions on using common words or names—and forcing users to periodically change their passwords are essential. Real-time monitoring of log-ons to discern the use of password detection programs should be continuous, as should logging of unsuccessful attempts into an audit trail.

COMMUNICATIONS SECURITY

Data interception is a concern in organizations with valuable or sensitive data. Data can be intercepted by wiretapping or emission sensing, by unauthorized access to data, and by authorized or unauthorized terminals. Communications security is the key to protecting against data interception. To be effective, communications security must be enforced in five areas: line, transmission, cryptography, emissions, and technical. These areas are discussed in the following sections.

Line Security

Line security involves protecting telephone lines against wiretapping or other types of interception and employs the same techniques used for protecting voice conversations against interception. Often, PBXs and other premises-based equipment are not properly protected. Intruders can enter them in the supervisor mode and, with the right resources, capture and analyze their data stream for user IDs and passwords. The intruders can then use these identifications to gain access to the network.

The IS manager should double-check that PBX security is adequate. Because protocol analyzers and other diagnostic devices can discover passwords and cryptographic keys, their use should be restricted. It is preferable to employ high-level diagnostic programs to identify failing components.

Transmission Security

Transmission security is the protection of network communications against their interception by workstations authorized to access the network but not particular data. It provides protection against the use of authorized devices for unauthorized purposes.

Cryptographic Security

Cryptographic security protects the keys, encryption software, and hardware used for encoding transmissions. The cryptographic system must operate at a level higher than the highest-level information the system protects. Just as a lock does not protect against a stolen key, cryptography does not protect against a lost or intercepted cryptographic key.

Emissions Security

Emissions security protects against the interception of computer emissions (e.g., electrical fluctuations, radiation, or other modulations), by an adversary who can determine what is being processed. This risk is posed primarily by an adversary who is both resourceful and determined (e.g., a foreign government or determined competitor). Emissions-suppressed equipment and cables are available to protect against it.

Optical fiber does not radiate much and is not prone to emission leakage and interception. Light does leak at cable bends, however, and emissions can be read by interception equipment that is very close to the cable. However, the skill required for tapping optical fiber is very high and the risk of discovery is great. Fiber is useful in areas prone to electrical storms because it is nonconductive and can isolate equipment from voltage surges.

Technical Security

Technical security is a broad phrase used to describe protection against noncomputer intrusion devices. Some known devices include:

- Microphones or free-space transmitters (e.g., radio taps)
- Devices built into equipment (e.g., modulators)
- Carrier-current bugging equipment (e.g., power-line modulators)
- Visual or optical surveillance equipment (e.g., video cameras)
- Telephone bugging devices (e.g., infinity transmitters)

DANGERS OF PRIVATE SECURITY

Coordinated networkwide security is necessary to protect against the conversion of corporate resources to private use. It is difficult to determine whether user-developed security measures are adequate or well implemented, and networkwide measures are needed to ensure that the network is not vulnerable to its users.

Control of Client/Server Processes

Host-to-host links over the public network require multilevel security, which must be provided with access control. Network services needing multilevel security are mail, file transfer, and remote log-on. Network applications should be usable without modification.

In UNIX, for example, users should have access to any network application usually provided on the UNIX host. The objective is to create a user-transparent wall around network applications that permits initial setup of the connection to another host but does not allow application-to-host communication until security is ensured for both systems. Users must be allowed to enter passwords, but password interception must be prevented. A verified trusted path mechanism, with network accesses that are audited at the called host, is desirable.

NETWORK MANAGEMENT INTEGRATION

Network management control centers are similar to central station burglar alarm control centers. Alarms in both are forwarded to central monitoring points where computer programs either take action on them or display recommendations for action. Network management control centers monitor line conditions and check for device failures. Message displays indicate if, for example, there is an outage, an intruder is testing passwords, or unauthorized access has been detected.

New Risks

As network management interfaces are standardized according to internationally accepted models, the possibility of an attack on the management system increases. Reconfiguring routers can effectively destroy communications. In assessing the security of the network management system, the IS manager should ask:

- What are its message authentication procedures?
- Should network control messages be encrypted?
- How are trusted users controlled within the system?
- How are external messages from linked networks validated?

Protecting Against Trusted Users. Perhaps the most difficult security problem is caused by authorized users doing unauthorized work. Every authorized user should sign a standard statement indicating that access to the network is granted for approved business purposes only, that they will limit their use to those purposes, and that they will adhere to network security practices.

The audit trail and trend analysis of audit logs are used to detect use changes of authorized users. This is a task for independent, technically competent auditors who should periodically review use patterns. However, this is primarily an after-the-event check. To turn it into a deterrent, these audits must be publicized, along with the corporation's intention to prosecute when users convert network resources to their own use.

The Super-User Problem. Most security systems have a super-user who can start and stop the system. The ID and password of the super-user should be used only when absolutely essential—in other words, the person or persons having super-user authority should also have less powerful rights under a different ID and password. Super-user IDs and passwords should never be used when a less dangerous method of completing a task exists.

Network Administration. The policy of separating IDs for security management from IDs for daily use also applies to network administrators. On LANs, a log-on from a machine with a corrupted hard disk can propagate through the network if the user has management privileges. The risk can be minimized by restricting where and how the management ID is used. It is safest to execute management tasks from a console, not a workstation.

Viruses, Worms, and Contaminated Hard Disks. Conditions that do not seriously affect mainframes (e.g., viruses and worms) are hazardous to distributed networks if proper procedures are not followed. Total protection is impossible, but the risks can be controlled. The key is to control how executable code gets on the network. This can be done by restricting the ports of program entry to the minimum, installing quality-control mechanisms, and educating end users.

Control of unintended portals is more difficult. Software must be kept at current release levels, and new software must be audited before installation. Users with administrative rights must be instructed to protect their boot diskettes and to avoid logging on from unknown machines when using their administrative rights. Then practical, administrative users should work only at their terminals.

CONCLUSION

The prerequisite for distributed network control is a stable, well-managed network. To achieve this, IS managers must ensure comprehensive data security as hardware and software implementation decisions are made and as network processes migrate from host-to-terminal environments to peer-to-peer environments, in which computer resources are often located in open user areas under the control of nontechnical managers.

Chapter 52
Comparing Popular E-mail Systems

Gary Cannon

The commercial e-mail industry continues to grow at an impressive rate. There are almost 91 million e-mail users around the world. This chapter discusses what features and services to look for when shopping for a corporate e-mail system, and compares the leading e-mail systems on the market.

The Internet has grown so rapidly because of users' need to communicate and share information. Although many people were doing just that on commercial networks, the Internet offers more than just e-mail and is less expensive than commercial systems.

The number of e-mail users has grown almost 74% in the past year. More than 47 million people are using LAN e-mail systems, most of which are connected to commercial services. The larger commercial networks cannot accurately estimate how many individual users they support because most users on LANs and larger systems do not have individual accounts on the commercial networks. The majority of users access the commercial systems through corporate gateways.

This number of users continues to grow, and as commercial systems enhance their product and service offerings, there will be continued expansion on the commercial side of the market as well as the Internet.

Many business users rely on e-mail to conduct their day-to-day functions. E-mail ties together many other applications and has contributed significantly to the information explosion.

ELECTRONIC MESSAGING: A HISTORICAL PERSPECTIVE

For years, telex served as the only form of electronic mail and was strictly the domain of government agencies and big business. About 25 years ago, a few operating systems had rudimentary messaging capabilities. IBM Corp.'s Virtual Machine (VM) system could communicate between active terminals, and Digital Equipment Corp.'s Virtual Memory

0-8493-9989-0/99/$0.00+$.50

System (VMS) operating system came up with the basics of what would become VMSmail.

At about the same time, General Electric's Information Services Business Division (ISBD) developed the time-sharing concept with Dartmouth University and introduced an internal system known as Cross File (XFL), which allowed employees to send messages to one another when they were working on projects together. XFL developed into a divisionwide utility and each office had an address. Originally, senders wrote out their message on a piece of paper and handed it to the administrator. Sometime during the day, the message would be entered into the system and the sender could expect a reply in a day or so. Functionally, the system worked fine. Practically, it took a few years before the organization completely accepted the application and integrated it fully into daily operation.

Over the next few years, more users would get addresses and access to the system directly via asynchronous terminals. Message traffic started to increase and ISBD offered the XFL system to other GE divisions.

Electronic mail was referred to as message switching then, which was a regulated application under the law in the U.S. and would remain so until January 1981, when it was deregulated and computer service companies entered the e-mail market. A new commercial application was born and several companies jumped into the market, some as service providers and others as the software developers. E-mail as an industry continued to grow steadily until someone discovered the Internet—now almost everyone has an e-mail address.

PRIMARY ELECTRONIC MESSAGING SYSTEM CATEGORIES

Today there are four primary categories of e-mail systems and users:

1. **Online services.** A relatively small number of services provide e-mail to a large number of users. Examples include CompuServe, America Online, and Prodigy. There are an estimated 12 million users of these services worldwide.
2. **Commercial services.** These are traditional computer service companies with mostly corporate clients providing connectivity between companies. Examples include AT&T, GE Information Services (GEIS), MCI, and Sprint. There are an estimated 1.5 million users of these services worldwide.
3. **Private e-mail.** These e-mail systems are proprietary to companies and large organizations and are maintained and operated by them. Examples include General Motors, Pfizer, and JC Penney. There are an estimated 70 million users of these services worldwide.
4. **The Internet.** An estimated 35 million users worldwide use Internet e-mail.

Features and Functions

When selecting what features an e-mail system should have, the IS department must keep the users in mind. The e-mail system must serve the users. Reliability and maintenance are also critical. There is no 800 number to call if something goes wrong with the LAN server. The LAN is a proprietary system that has to be repaired in-house. As user communities within companies expand, so does the reliability and service problem. As a company grows, so does its local networks, and soon IS and the network staff are maintaining a worldwide collection of them.

Network managers must also be concerned with connectivity. e-mail users, if they do not already, may soon need to communicate with people outside their immediate community. All the popular e-mail systems today have gateways.

X.400 and SMTP

X.400 is the international standard for interconnecting unlike messaging systems. The X.400 recommendations were developed and continue to be upgraded by the Telecommunications Standardization Sector of the International Telecommunications Union, an organization charted by the United Nations that represents most of the countries with modern telephone systems. Almost every e-mail vendor offers X.400 software to connect its system to the commercial world. The software is still expensive, but it is reliable and fast, handles attached files well, and offers excellent security. It does, however, have a slight problem with addressing.

Most e-mail system vendors now offer simple mail transfer protocol (SMTP)gateways with their products to connect to the Internet. SMTP is reliable, almost as fast as X.400, does an acceptable job with binary files, has its own addressing problems, and is inexpensive. There is still the directory problem.

The commercial service world also offers proprietary gateways for many private e-mail systems to their public services, which gives the corporate user a window to the e-mail world. For many private e-mail system clients who do not yet need X.400 software, the commercial services offer a gateway to the X.400 world. All of them also provide gateway services to the Internet.

X.500 Directory Service

All of this connectivity introduces the most serious problem in e-mail today—addressing and directories. Worldwide connectivity does no good if there is no map for getting around.

X.500 is e-mail's atlas. It can interconnect distributed directories, but it is still waiting in the wings. The North American Directory Forum (NADF)has been showing a demo of interconnected X.500 for two years. Commercial service providers are trying to lure corporate clients into using X.500. Some large companies are even experimenting with their own in-house X.500 systems. Because there are still concerns about privacy and security with X.500, many companies are investigating alternatives. This brings additional pressures on the e-mail system vendors to define and offer competent directory services. Companies such as Hitachi are, in addition, introducing directory synchronization products such as SyncWare.

Features and Services Checklists

Following is a checklist of features users should look for when reviewing e-mail products: (several of these services are discussed in the section "e-mail Services"):

- Editing capability
- Distribution lists
- Import/export capability
- File Transfer Body Part (FTBP) or BP-15 (X.400) ability
- A spell checker
- The ability to send forms
- Function keys
- Reply options
- A calendar/scheduler feature
- Directories
- Ad hoc entries
- Fax output
- Fax input
- Message notification
- Delivery options
- Security
- Encryption
- Keyboard combinations
- On-screen help
- Computer-based training (CBT)
- Message storage and archive
- Storage backup
- Communications protocol
- Comm port/comm line backup
- Expansion capabilities

Following is a checklist of services users should look for to ensure sufficient connectivity in an e-mail system:

- SMTP gateway
- X.400 gateway
- Telex
- Fax
- Mail API (MAPI)
- Wireless services
- Pager services

Features for Creating Messages

Fortunately for users, competition in this field is intense and many of the newer e-mail systems have similar features and capabilities. Besides sending and receiving mail, creating messages is the next most important function.

A single function key should initiate this operation and prepare the user to address the message and set options. Most systems set the cursor at the TO: block, and the next keystroke should open the address book and point to the first entry, starting with the letters matching those keyed in.

Identifying the name selection with (in many cases) the return key, the user can set the address book to identify the next entry with further keystrokes. There should be no limit to the number of addresses selected. When the TO: block is filled, then a tab or another keystroke should place the user at the cc: block. This operation is processed in the same way as the TO: block. Many systems also allow for blind copies—these are addressees who receive the message but are not shown in the address block.

Editing Capability

After the addressing tasks are completed, the user can proceed to constructing the message text. The majority of e-mail messages are written on the fly and perhaps include some previously prepared text. Full-page editing features are a must. Cut-and-paste manipulation of the text, along with import of existing files, allows the user to create messages efficiently.

It is extremely convenient to have a spell checker in the e-mail system. If the e-mail system is part of a complete office support system such as MS Office or HP Desk, then the spell checker will be available and probably shared between the individual components. That way the user does not have to keep updating separate new-word dictionary files.

Attaching Files

After users have completed the text of the message, they may want to include some additional files to accompany the message. These can be word processing documents, spreadsheets, drawings, charts, and graphs. Any file that can be stored on the PC, workstation, or mainframe should be able to join the message in transit to its destination. This is a standard capability of most e-mail systems, X.400, and the Internet, although they all handle attached files in different ways. Gateways are improving at allowing attached files to cross these boundaries.

Clicking on the attached file icon or function key should place the user in the directory reserved for attached files. Selecting each with a single keystroke should add the attachments to the file list for this message. Again, there may be no technical limit to the number or size of files, but the speed and reliability of transit may be affected if the files are too large in size.

File Compression

Many organizations struggle with whether to offer file compression. On a commercial service, the cost of the transfer is always important. Equally important is the time of transit. Then the question arises, "Does the receiver on the other end have the same compression algorithm?"

Within the corporate environment, file compression should be easier as long as all employees have moved up to the same version of the software. The cost savings of closing the data center and putting every location on LANs is countered with the problem that most LANs operate independently and with differing versions of the software, making e-mail and file transfers more of a challenge.

Distribution Lists

Associated with addressing are distribution lists. Some systems cannot handle lengthy address lists. This is not necessarily a design flaw; more often, it represents memory limitations of intermediate or receiving systems. A single address entry can add a few hundred bytes to the header; therefore, distribution lists are highly recommended.

Distribution lists can be thought of as header compression techniques. Most commercial services charge for additional message copies, whether they are TOs or cc's. Therefore, the use of distribution lists reduces invoices as well as transit times.

In many systems, distribution lists can only be created by the administrator. Other systems allow users to create and maintain their own distribution lists. In either case, their use is recommended for efficiency. However, many people overuse the distribution list by, for example, sending everyone a message that not necessarily everyone needs to see.

Importing Text

The importing feature can be used during message creation to save portions of messages for future use. IS, for example, can use this feature to explain aspects of messaging to users. An IS staffer can save many previously used answers in files on his or her PC and incorporate them into messages to current queries. This expedites the job of IS and ensures that each user gets a complete and accurate response each time. If a new query comes up, IS can use the export feature to save that response for future use.

When importing text, users may also want to search for a particular string to verify that they brought in the correct file. The ability to search the text of the message being created is a handy feature. For frequent e-mail users, it is almost a necessary tool.

Signature Files

Many users frequently import their signature file, which may consist of, for example, the user's X.400 address, Internet address, and telephone number. Sometimes addresses in the FROM: block of a message get scrambled or expanded by gateways in transit. A signature file contains the correct version of the sender's address. With all the gateways around the world, this is a highly recommended practice.

Forms

Forms are a special type of import. Some e-mail systems allow forms to be generated that are partially filled out by the sender, with the intent that the recipient fill in the rest and return it or pass it on. Forms usually have special fields that are reserved for alpha or numeric import to assist the user in entering required data. The field size can be specified, and on more sophisticated systems, only certain users can enter particular fields. Most systems with forms are restricted to sharing the forms among users of the same system. Going outside that system usually requires that the form be sent as an attached file, if it is possible at all.

E-MAIL SERVICES

Various services such as directories, fax gateways, message notification, security, and connectivity are provided with modern electronic messaging systems.

Directories

Directories are one of the most critical and complex problems facing the messaging industry today. The e-mail population is hovering around 100 million users. This population requires an extensive directory, to say the least.

The X.500 solution, however, has been around for about eight years and acceptance has been very slow. In the short term, most companies are investigating interim solutions.

The bottom line is that the e-mail system should have a flexible directory service that can handle local and remote addresses. Users should be able to enter ad hoc addresses as well as access centrally administered entries from anywhere on the LAN or mainframe e-mail system. When multiple e-mail systems are involved, the gateway system or hub service should contain all entries. Control Data, Soft*Switch, DEC, and Microsoft Exchange all offer this capability. These systems are also X.500 compatible.

SYSTEM DIRECTORIES VS. LOCAL ADDRESS BOOKS

The difference between a system directory and a local address book is that the directory contains all the addresses for an entire system that may include other e-mail systems connected via gateways. The address book is what each user maintains on his or her individual PC or workstation. When users need the address for someone not in their address book, they search the system directory.

The directory should be available to all users and the directories of separate post offices should be able to exchange entries. Directory synchronization packages are also starting to appear on the market. Hitachi's SyncWare interfaces with a variety of e-mail system directories and includes an X.500 gateway. Individual users should also be able to load their address book from the system directory.

One feature very helpful to users is the ability to cut and paste into an address book from text. Frequently users get messages with long cc: lists and would like to be able to copy one or more entries into their address books rather than retype the entry. Sometimes messages come through a number of gateways and the FROM: address is about three times as long as when it started out. If the sender includes his or her original address in the text, the receiver can extract it and simply transfer it to an address book.

Another feature that should be required by network-based directories is the ability to handle queries and updates by mail. This feature allows users with the proper access to send queries to the directory to search for particular entries or names, preferably with a mask character. Updating the directory by mail is also a feature needed by remote administrative users, again with the proper security permissions. This feature is not a requirement obvious to LAN users because everyone is connected and can access the directory. However, when there is a variety of systems and directories interconnected via commercial networks or the Internet, query and update by mail is a time saver.

The directory should have a local find capability that allows the user to search either an address or name for an entry. As directories and address books grow in size and scope, these features will be required by all users.

Eventually, users will be able to query an X.500 directory for any entry they need.

Fax Gateways

Even before the Internet, there was the fax. Fax gateways have existed on commercial e-mail services for more than a decade. PCs have added fax gateways within the past seven or eight years. Recently fax modem prices have fallen, so it is affordable for almost every PC and LAN to send and receive faxes. One major convenience of a fax modem for travelers is that they need not carry a printer on the road with them.

Message Notification

PCs now have literally hundreds of applications for users, and most people only spend a short time each day on e-mail. Therefore, when a message arrives, the user may want to be interrupted and notified. Some systems provide a capability that informs the user of new mail. The form of notification, either a flashing indication in the corner of the screen or a simple beep, should be set by the user. This capability should also include a message when the PC is turned on that there is mail waiting.

Security

As more-critical business information is transported via e-mail, security options have become more important to system implementers. Many of these have been a standard part of electronic data interchange (EDI) for years and are starting to show up in the e-mail side of the industry. As the cost for sending files via e-mail decreases, the need for additional security increases.

Gateways

This may be the most often used capability when selecting e-mail systems. Some companies feel they must decide between either X.400 or the Internet. Most e-mail systems now come standard with a simple mail transport protocol (SMTP) gateway for Internet, and almost every e-mail system on the market has an X.400 gateway.

For an e-mail system or service to survive, it must provide access to the Internet at least via e-mail. The standard that is quoted most often for e-mail access to the Internet is RFC-822, which specifies the rules for SMTP. This is a democratic procedure for posting proposed specifications on the Internet and allowing people to debate the pros and cons of all or part of the specifications. After a proper time period, the request for comment (RFC) committee decides to make the RFC part of the standing rules of the Internet.

X.400 Software

The X.400 standard is administered by committee. The ITU-TSS has standing committees that create and maintain the recommendations for telecommunications. The most familiar of these are the X series, including X.25, X.400, and X.500. Each of these has committees made up of representatives from international telephone companies, U.S. phone companies, and software companies involved in the telecommunications industry. These committees meet periodically to review the status of their efforts and between meetings usually share information via e-mail. When they complete a new version of the recommendations, they gather in a plenary session for approval from the ruling committees and new final versions are published and announced.

The meetings used to occur on a regular four-year cycle, but have recently been changed to an as-needed basis. The recommendations can be purchased from government offices, the UN, or companies associated with the ITUpplementary documents available, such as the implementer's guide. It still helps to have a resident expert when designing and writing an X.400gateway.

Approximately 18 companies around the world actually offer X.400 software. In the U.S., Digital Equipment Corp. and Hewlett-Packard supply X.400 software for their systems. ISOCOR and OSIware (Infonet Software Services) offer X.400systems of a more generic nature to interconnect systems from other vendors. Europe has a number of suppliers of X.400 systems, such as Marben and Net-Tel.

Telex, Fax, and Wireless

Other gateways often required by e-mail systems are telex, fax, and wireless. Telex is still used extensively around the world. All service providers offer a gateway to telex. Some private e-mail systems offer a telex gateway, but this requires a separate service agreement with a telex service provider. This gateway must work both ways, unlike most fax gateways.

ISOCOR offers a fax gateway that permits fax into X.400. The fax user sends a document and, after the connect indication, keys in a code that corresponds to a directory entry in the ISOCOR software. The incoming fax is converted to text and routed to the address in the directory. This is a handy capability for medium- to large-scale service.

With the increase in the use of wireless communications for PCs and the ever-popular pager, many e-mail systems are starting to incorporate gateways for wireless services. This requires a third-party provider, but it does offer the user that last-ditch method for reaching someone away from the office.

Popular Messaging Systems

The following sections focus on the pros and cons of the leading messaging systems on the market today that can be installed in companies.

Lotus cc:Mail

Lotus cc:Mail has dominated LAN-based systems since its introduction a few years ago. cc:Mail provides efficient directory services and most of the features anyone would need. It handles many of the common APIs available and operates on most platforms. Many other e-mail systems imitate cc:Mail, but it has remained the market leader.

IBM Office Vision 400

IBM Office Vision had difficult beginnings. It survived mainly on the strength of IBM in the mainframe market. Distributed Office Support System (DISOSS), which eventually became Office Vision/Multiple Virtual Storage (OV/MVS), is a very large system requiring a well-trained, knowledgeable staff. It is not the most user-friendly system and has the limited 8*8 (DGN.DEN) addressing common to SNA Distribution Services (SNADS)-based systems. PROFS, the precursor of OV/VM, is a much more user-friendly system that can use nickname files, includes a calendar feature, and has a more flexible directory system.

The most popular entry in the Office Vision stable is OV/400. The AS/400platform is quite possibly the biggest seller after the PC. AS/400 is extremely popular in Europe and the U.S. Although OV/400 still uses the SNADS 8*8 addressing, it does have the personal address book feature popular in other systems. OV/400 also has the calendar capability found in OV/VM. Gateways are available for X.400 and the more popular APIs.

DEC All-in-One

Digital Equipment Corp. offers two of the older and most popular e-mail systems today. VMSmail, like Unix Sendmail, is a utility feature in the VMS operating system. It is a command-line-oriented system that is strongly enhanced by the availability of DEC's Message Router system. Even with the overwhelming popularity of full-screen systems, there are still many VMS mail systems active today.

The mainstay for DEC e-mail systems is All-in-One. This is a full-service, full-screen presentation e-mail system. Along with MAILbus, DEC All-in-One supports X.400 and SMTP as well as X.500 directory protocols.

All-in-One can operate on a standalone VAX as well as an entire network of VAXs interconnected via DECnet. With MAILbus, All-in-One interfaces with LANs and other e-mail systems including OV/VM and OV/400 via

SNADS. Many companies with multiple e-mail systems use All-in-One and MAILbus as their central hub system. Distributed directory services (DDS) capability, combined with the X.500 protocols, ensure that this system will be around for a while.

HP Open Desk Manager

HP Open Desk Manager is the premier system for Unix-based e-mail on midrange systems. HP mail is based on SMTP and therefore readily interfaces with the Internet. Hewlett-Packard also offers a full X.400 system, which allows it to communicate with commercial service providers. The flexibility of HP Open Desk Manager includes interfaces to cc:Mail and Microsoft Mail, as well as Wang and Office Vision systems. The directory service is extremely flexible and allows for local and remote entries in various formats. The directory allows the user to search on a number of fields in the database, making this a very useful tool.

Lotus Notes

Compared with the other products, Lotus Notes is a fairly new arrival. However, with the strength of Lotus, now backed by IBM, Notes will most likely be around for a long time.

Notes is a true workgroup system that incorporates the spreadsheet capabilities of Lotus 1-2-3 with a database/foldering capability that has made it instantly popular. Many people wonder how the two products—Lotus cc:Mail and Lotus Notes—will develop. cc:Mail will probably take over as the e-mail engine for Notes eventually.

Microsoft Mail

The dominance of Microsoft in the computer industry has almost guaranteed success for the various e-mail products they offer. The original MSmail for the Macintosh is still popular and one of the most widely used. MSmail for the PC is the old Network Courier, acquired by Microsoft years ago.

Microsoft's new Microsoft Mail Exchange is based on the Windows NT server. It interfaces the older products into the NT systems and includes interfaces to cc:Mail, Lotus Notes, and others. Microsoft Mail uses the X.400 gateway. Other X.400 software vendors also offer gateways for Microsoft Mail. Standard with Microsoft Mail Exchange is the SMTP gateway, which interfaces to the Internet for e-mail. Microsoft is also offering software for direct access to the Internet.

Fisher TAO

Fisher International has been a very strong player in the e-mail market with EMCEE. This is a mainframe-based system that runs on the VMS platform. The newer version, EMCEE/TAO, incorporates paging facilities along with calendar and X.400 gateways. It offers the usual SNADS gateway as well as SMTP and LAN message-handling system (MHS) connectivity. The company plans to add an X.500 capability, which should significantly enhance its market share.

Memo

This mainframe e-mail system was developed by Verimation in Europe for a single client. It became so popular there that the company started marketing Memo in the US. Two years ago, it added X.400, and more recently an SMTP gateway, and the product is still selling. Memo owns a sizeable share of the messaging market, primarily in Europe.

BeyondMail

Banyan Systems' BeyondMail does not command a large portion of the e-mail market, but it is important to mention because it is the guidepost against which e-mail systems should be measured. Since its introduction about five years ago, BeyondMail has had more functions and features than any of its competitors. It easily accesses documents from other applications such as MS Word, WordPerfect, and Lotus 1-2-3. It has a very flexible and powerful directory service based on Novell MHS. It includes an SMTP gateway and runs on Unix, which makes it a natural for linking with the Internet. BeyondMail also runs on Windows, DOS, and Mac platforms. There is also a link to calendar and scheduling systems and a rules-based scripting language that helps the user interface with other applications on the LAN.

QuickMail

CE Software QuickMail is probably the best known of the Macintosh-based e-mail systems. There are more than 2.5 million users. This product is very popular in the advertising and publishing industries. It also runs on Windows and DOS platforms; however, the Mac is where it shines. QuickMail interfaces well with word processing packages on the Mac and is capable of sending attached files, including drawings. There are many gateways to commercial systems and the Internet, making this a popular and versatile system.

GroupWise

Novell is the newest entry into the e-mail market. However, due to the strength of Novell in the industry, GroupWise ranks about third in the LAN market with more than 11% of the mailboxes. GroupWise can link to other systems via MHS and has an SMTP gateway to access e-mail on the Internet.

Several X.400 software vendors offer gateways for GroupWise, making the worldwide reach of this system impressive.

CONCLUSION

This chapter has discussed all of the necessary features to look for in an e-mail package for corporate use. In summary, the leading e-mail packages are described and compared. Most of the different e-mail systems use gateways between each other, so there is little overlap of user populations and almost everyone is able to communicate with each other. Unfortunately, it is still difficult to find someone's address. Among all of the e-mail systems on the market, cc:Mail leads the LAN systems with number of mailboxes installed, and IBM Office Vision is on top of the list of midsize and mainframe systems.

Chapter 53
E-mail and Internet in Heterogeneous Environments

Raj Rajagopal

In earlier chapters we looked at porting applications from one environment to another, developing applications that could run in multiple environments, connecting clients to heterogeneous servers for file and print access, etc. Another function that has become almost as commonplace as the telephone is the e-mail function. E-mail is used for both intra-organization communications and for communications with others who are not part of the organization.

As you would expect, this explosive growth in e-mail has resulted in the availability of e-mail products from a number of vendors. Some of the products are host or mainframe based, while others are LAN based. In either case, you also have a number of dialup remote users who need access to e-mail. As you may also expect, these products are not completely compatible and you may have problems sending and receiving mail between the different products. Continuing our network focus, let us look at migration and coexistence issues that pertain to e-mail and the Internet.

If you are considering migrating from one environment to another (say UNIX to Windows NT), pay special attention to e-mail since the number of users of e-mail is typically more than any production application you may have, most users are not likely to tolerate even a short outage of the e-mail application, and there is no way to shut down inputs to the e-mail system if your e-mail users can receive external e-mail.

HETEROGENEOUS E-MAIL SYSTEMS

There are a number of different e-mail systems. Some of them use proprietary protocols. While most systems easily handle simple inline text, e-mail becomes a problem when you attempt more complicated functions

0-8493-9989-0/99/$0.00+$.50

such as multiple attachments where some of the attachments contain graphics and other multimedia messages. Some of the e-mail systems commonly used include:

- All-in-One from DEC
- PROFS/OfficeVision from IBM
- Notes and cc:Mail from Lotus/IBM
- Microsoft Mail for PC and AppleTalk networks
- Microsoft Exchange Server
- MCI Mail
- AT&T Mail, etc.

Before we look at migration and coexistence issues involving e-mail systems, let us take a look at the components of an e-mail system and how these components are implemented in UNIX mail systems and Windows NT exchange server.

MAIL SYSTEM COMPONENTS*

The components of any mail system include:

- Computer servers acting as "post offices," collecting mail, and providing it to users (storing and forwarding it). Mail servers include support for the following:
  - Message transport protocol specific to mail messaging systems.
  - Server support for user access. In centralized mail systems, this isan engineered integration between mail user agents and the server. In distributed, client/server mail implementations, this is a message access protocol, shared by clients and servers. A protocol is chosen based on desired clients, or client behavior.
  - A method of properly presenting message formats to users (e.g., sending a Microsoft Word document to a UNIX workstation user in a manner the recipient can use as a document).
  - Directory services, which have two basic functions: to store and provide proper mail addresses to all mail users, and to synchronize directories across mail servers for updated, correct addresses.
- The network between servers, including:
  - Physical and logical network (e.g., cable or satellite connections, Internet and/or intranet).
  - Network protocol (e.g., TCP/IP).
- A mail client running on a desktop PC or workstation, or a character-based terminal. The user agent varies based on the user's desktop device and preferences.
- Management utilities, ranging from ad hoc to dedicated management stations.

* Reproduced with permission from Digital Equipment Corporation.

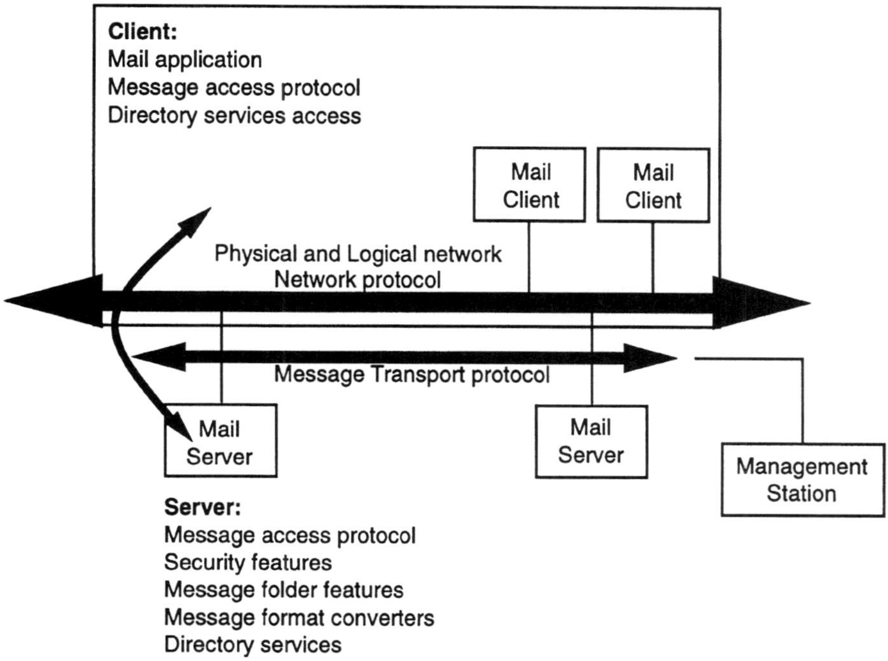

Exhibit 1. Components of an e-mail system.

Exhibit 1 shows the components of a mail system.

Let us look at how these components are implemented in UNIX and Windows NT environments.

E-Mail System Components in UNIX

This section discusses the components of a mail system in a typical UNIX installation.

Mail Server Functions. UNIX mail systems, until recently, have been centralized mail systems, as opposed to logically distributed client/server implementations, even when including UNIX workstations in the environment. For example, when UNIX workstation users write and send mail from their workstations, their mail agent software is working on the central server, providing access to the server's mail application. This centralized characteristic of traditional UNIX mail systems represents the greatest challenge when considering integration with Windows NT, which is a client/server implementation.

The mail server functions in a UNIX system include:

- Message Transport protocol: SMTP (Simple Mail Transport Protocol) is implemented in most vendors' UNIX systems as the Sendmail utility. The Sendmail utility handles more than just the store and forward function between mail servers.
- Server support for user access: In centralized UNIX mail environments (the typical case for both System V and BSD UNIX systems), the mail user's agent software connects to the Sendmail program on the UNIX server, which allows the user to send, receive, and manipulate mail.
- Recent customer demand for client/server implementations of mail systems result in support for an additional access method for UNIX users, a message access protocol called POP3 (Post Office Protocol Version 3). POP3, when supported by both the mail server and client, enables downloading of messages to the client desktop.
- Directory services: Lists of mail users and their proper addresses, as handled by UNIX mail systems, are kept in one of two places:
  - System-wide database of user names, available to Sendmail.
  - User-specific files that define aliases.
- Definitions of nicknames or user names and their mail addresses are available to the user who owns the file.

Network Between Servers. The network between servers includes:

- Physical and logical networks: The UNIX message transport protocol SMTP is now the standard protocol for Internet mail. This development may affect how you choose to implement UNIX and Windows NT integration. For example, if you use Internet mail heavily, your investment in UNIX SMTP-style mail systems transfers directly to this new environment
- Network messaging protocol: These include TCP/IP, and in some Digital installations, DECnet.

Mail Client. The mail client varies, based on the user's desktop device and preferences. UNIX users have several choices of mail user agents. UNIX users with character-based terminals rely on the following command line user agents.

- *binmail*: A command line user agent that ships with most System V and Berkeley-based UNIX systems.
- *mh*: The Rand mail handler (public domain software bundled by some UNIX vendors, including Digital), a command line interface to centralized SMTP mail systems, and using a Sendmail interface.
- *mailx*: A command line user agent that ships with most System V and Berkeley UNIX systems.

UNIX users with graphical workstations or X-terminals have additional options, including:

- *xmh*: This is the Motif-compliant X Windows-based, public domain graphical user agent built on *mh*.
- *dxmail*: This is the X Windows-based graphical user agent, built on mh, that is POP3 aware, meaning it can perform client/server mail functions in cooperation with a POP3 SMTP mail server *dtmail*.
- *dtmail*: This is the graphical user agent that ships with CDE (the Common Desktop Environment). The *dtmail* agent, as shipped by Digital, is POP3 aware, meaning it can perform client/server mail functions in cooperation with a POP3 SMTP mail server.

Additionally, some versions of *dtmail* are MIME capable, meaning those users enjoy automatic format conversion for files sent through the mail system. Digital and Sun Microsystems both ship MIME-aware versions of dtmail.

Traditional UNIX mail systems, centralized with users logging into the server, manage communication from the user to the server via application-to-application communication. Clients use *Sendmail* to log onto the host mail server, communicating directly with the *Sendmail* application on the server, allowing users to read, forward, delete, create, and send messages.

More recent client/server implementations of UNIX mail systems support POP3 in client user agents. Both *dtmail* and *dxmail* are POP3 enabled. Directory services access is provided to mail clients through the mail server and is limited to the use of personal alias files or system-wide Sendmail user databases.

Mail Management Utilities. Management utilities in UNIX mail installations are typically part of the operating system. While some vendors have provided mail management tools, UNIX mail management generally is handled with ad hoc utilities, as opposed to a dedicated mail management station. Useful utilities for system administrators include:

- *sendmail.cf* configuration file: Defines how messages travel throughout an SMTP-based mail system of servers.
- *mailqueue* command: Lists the queue of mail messages being sent, where they are in the network, and why they are where they are.
- *aliases* command: Defines users and their mail addresses at a personal or system-wide level.
- *newaliases* command: Converts alias files from text to binary format for performance improvement in large installations.
- *mailconfig* graphical application: Ships with Digital UNIX to configure mail servers and clients in an SMTP environment. This application

supports multiple network protocols (uucp, DECnet, TCP/IP) and other variances in mail systems.

E-Mail System Components in Windows NT Exchange Server

Mail Server Functions. A mail server consists of a Windows NT system, either Intel- or Alpha-based, running Microsoft Exchange Server software. It includes a message transport protocol. Messages between Exchange Servers travel via Microsoft's RPC (Remote Procedure Call) protocol. RPC is particularly desirable over local area networks, which are typically reliable and fast.

Exchange offers the option of SMTP as a transport protocol, sufficient for participating in a UNIX SMTP mail environment. The Exchange Internet Mail Connector product provides SMTP capability to an Exchange server.

Microsoft implements Mail Application Programming Interface (MAPI) as the message access protocol for Exchange Server, shared by Exchange clients. MAPI is a multifunctional interface for applications that involve mail and messaging, such as Electronic Data Interchange (EDI) applications between different companies.

File Format Conversion. Between Exchange Server and Client, Exchange uses an internal format for converting different file formats between users. When using the X.400 transport, Exchange Server employs a format standard called the File Transfer Body Part to identify different document formats — a Microsoft Word document, for example, contained within a single mail message.

Directory Services and Synchronization. The X.500 International Directory Service Standards were designed to provide a global directory capability for heterogeneous environments. Microsoft based the design and the internal structures of the Exchange Directory on many of the recommendations outlined in the X.500 standards, and has committed to be fully compliant in a future release of Exchange Server. In addition, most of the older mail systems vendors have committed to implement the X.500 directory standard at some time in the future. However, at present, few mail systems are X.500 compliant, so for practical purposes gateways are required among the different mail directories.

The Microsoft Exchange Directory Synchronization Agent (DXA) allows system managers to perform directory synchronization with other mail systems based on Microsoft's MSMail Directory Format. The DXA also uses Microsoft Mail synchronization, rather than directory-to-directory automatic replication and synchronization, which would allow other X.500 directories to communicate directly with the Exchange Directory.

Digital X.500 Directory Synchronizer acts as a partner to the Exchange directory by allowing synchronization among Exchange's directories and other directories that may be used within the enterprise. In effect, the Digital X.500 Directory Synchronizer can filter all directories within an enterprise to ensure that everyone can share directory information, no matter what mail system they use.

Mail Client. For Windows NT users, the mail client varies, based on the user's desktop device and preferences. The mail user agent of choice in an Exchange environment is Exchange Client. Exchange Server also supports clients with MAPI Service Provider Interfaces (SPIs). The message access protocol shared between Exchange Client and Exchange Server is MAPI or POP3. Clients access available directory services via either MAPI or LDAP (Lightweight Directory Access Protocol).

Mail Management. Microsoft Exchange features a dedicated management station for Exchange installations.

HETEROGENEOUS E-MAIL SYSTEM OPTIONS

When a new environment is introduced for one reason, there is a possibility that the environment would be used for other functions available in the environment. For example, an organization may decide to introduce Windows NT to replace an existing application in UNIX, or use Windows NT as a Web server. Subsequently, the organization may look at using Microsoft Exchange for its e-mail needs.

When you have more than one e-mail system in your organization and you are considering the e-mail functions in a new e-mail system, you have the following options:

- Coexist with multiple e-mail systems for the foreseeable future and provide for passing e-mail back and forth between the different systems as needed.
- Migrate from one e-mail system (or multiple e-mail systems) to one e-mail system in a phased manner, coexisting with different systems in the meanwhile.
- Migrate from one e-mail system to another in one step without any coexistence period (also called "hot cutover").

Let us look at the characteristics of each of the options. Let us also look at some tools that will assist you in your e-mail migration and coexistence.

E-Mail Coexistence

In Chapter 1 we compared the advantages and disadvantages of homogeneous and heterogeneous environments. That discussion also applies to e-mail systems. In cases where you have two (or more) large installed bases of users using different e-mail systems, the appropriate option might be to leave the systems as is and not attempt to migrate. This could happen for example when two companies merge or when two or more divisions of a company merge.

While there may be some advantages in reduced maintenance and better compatibility with one e-mail system instead two, the costs and risks involved in migrating the e-mail systems and retraining a large user base are likely to outweigh the potential advantages. But since you are likely to require that the users of the different e-mail systems communicate with each other, you need tools that will facilitate e-mail systems to coexist.

You need tools to pass messages from one e-mail system to another and to permit sharing the user directories between the e-mail systems. If sharing a physical directory is not possible and you are maintaining two or more directories, you should ensure that the directories are consistent between the different systems at all times. If there is no automatic way to ensure consistency, then you may need to come up with manual ways to accomplish this.

You may also have to come up with utilities and procedures when one of the e-mail systems can handle a certain type of attachment that another e-mail system cannot. When you are performing system configuration updates to one or more of the e-mail systems, you have to try to ensure that these changes are not transparent to external users of the e-mail systems.

Phased E-Mail Migration

If the number of users is not large and/or if one or more of the e-mail systems is old and is being considered for replacement, then it may be worthwhile to consolidate e-mail systems and migrate from one e-mail system to another. The longer-term reduced costs of a consolidated e-mail system may outweigh the initial upfront costs of migrating from one e-mail system to another. You have a better return on your IT investment when you have multiple business applications using the same hardware and software environment.

You should ensure that the mail received in one system for a user in another system is transferred seamlessly and without delay. If a user's e-mail ID has to change, you should provide enough lag time to allow for receipt and forward of e-mail at the old address. Migration tools are available to move user and other system setup information from one e-mail system to another.

One of the choices that must be made in migrating to a new e-mail system is whether existing e-mail messages, attachments, etc., should be moved. If existing messages are not moved, then the users must be asked to manually clean up their mail. Migration tools sometimes also migrate individual user's custom setup data besides system setup data.

When you have a large number of e-mail users, you typically will have a number of interconnected post offices. Interconnection ensures that the mail is forwarded to the right post office. Each interconnected post office serves a portion of the user community. One strategy for a phased migration is to migrate one post office at a time. Since the post offices are interconnected, you must update the interconnection information after the migration.

Before you start migrating, ensure that you are not migrating unnecessary data to the new system. For example, there may be outdated data about users no longer on the e-mail system. Check the administrative tools in your current e-mail system that let you identify unnecessary data. One example of such a utility is the PODIAG utility for Microsoft Mail.

One-Step E-Mail Migration

This is an option that is available only in limited circumstances when the number of users using the e-mail system is small and all the users can be migrated at one time, the data to be migrated are small, and the total migration can be done in a short time. When you are planning for any change to your e-mail system, a one-step migration in particular, extensive planning with administrators and users is required.

The plan should also include fall-back procedures in the event that the migration or other changes to the e-mail system runs into problems. As in phased migration, migration tools are available to move user system setup, and user's custom setup information from one e-mail system to another. For example, Microsoft includes a number of migration tools to migrate information from popular e-mail systems to Microsoft Exchange.

One-step migration involves installing and testing the new e-mail system well ahead of the migration date. For example, you can set up the e-mail clients at user workstations. The new e-mail server should be operational and setup data that is not likely to change should be preloaded as much as possible. One-step migrations are also easier to accomplish when the migration is between different versions of the e-mail systems from the same vendor (for example, if you are migrating from Microsoft Mail server to Microsoft Exchange server).

You should arrange for limited testing after the migration from selected user workstations to ensure that the migration was successful. You should also include a list of steps users need to perform (such as setting up the profiles or any custom setups that could not be migrated) before the new e-mail system can be used. One benefit of the one-step method is that, if successful, you are finished, compared to what may be a long, drawn-out process for a phased migration.

E-MAIL CHARACTERISTICS

Before we look at some tools that will help in your migration and/or coexistence of e-mail systems, let us look at some characteristics of e-mail systems. Open Standards are playing an increasing role in e-mail systems. The common standards include X.400, X.500, and the Simple Mail Transfer Protocol (SMTP).

Unlike other business production applications, e-mail systems cannot normally have scheduled downtime when there will be no e-mail activity. e-mail is also a way of spreading viruses (particularly through attachments). e-mail application, more than most other business applications, is required to be accessed remotely by people in the organization who are traveling or working from home.

Besides the mail messages themselves, there are other important functions in an e-mail system, including:

- Public and private address lists
- Handling mail attachments that can have different data types
- Securing e-mail becomes more important as more business transactions are conducted through e-mail
- Privacy issues associated with e-mail, unlike most other business applications

E-MAIL MIGRATION AND COEXISTENCE TOOLS

The following tool functions will assist in your e-mail migration and coexistence:

- Ability to interface with external e-mail systems
- Ability to pass e-mail between the different e-mail systems within an organization
- Ability to keep the different user and other directories in synchronization or migrate directories from one e-mail system to another
- Ensure the security of e-mail messages
- Ability to have a universal mail client

Let us look at some of the tool functions in greater detail.

Interfacing with External E-Mail Systems

Gateways or connectors are used to exchange e-mail between different e-mail systems in an organization as well as exchanging e-mail with users external to the organization. The external users are very likely to use a number of different e-mail systems (the common ones were listed in the beginning of the chapter). Interfacing with external e-mail systems is typically performed using gateways or connectors. Check with your e-mail system provider to see the built-in connectors provided. You can typically develop your own connector if you need to interface with an e-mail system that does not have a built-in connector.

The Microsoft Exchange Server, for example, includes three built-in connectors:

- MSMail connector to interface with the older MS Mail PC or AppleTalk systems
- Internet Mail Connector (IMC) to interface with the Internet for e-mail
- X.400 Connector to interface with systems using the X.400 standard

There are also a number of connectors available from third parties for fax, wireless connections, etc.

Passing E-Mail Between E-Mail Systems

You need to pass e-mail between the different e-mail systems being used in your organization if you decide to have coexisting e-mail systems or if you go for a phased migration. You can pass e-mail messages in one of the following ways:

- Use the Internet
- Use a public X.400 network
- Acquire or develop a custom gateway between the e-mail systems you want to pass e-mail messages between

Use of a custom gateway may be more expensive and may take time to develop. But custom gateways can typically do a better job of seamless passing of messages. Custom gateways also tend to be more secure and reliable.

Check with your e-mail vendor to see if they provide tools to pass e-mail between e-mail systems.

If you are trying to coexist with MSMail and Microsoft Exchange, then the MSMail Connector Interchange (part of the MSMail Connector) will perform format translations between Microsoft Exchange and MSMail and interface with the appropriate message transfer agents (MTAs). The MSMail Connector also includes the MSMail Connector PostOffice, which is a temporary message store that holds messages that are in transition between MSMail and Microsoft Exchange.

If you have Microsoft- and UNIX-based e-mail systems, then you can use the Internet Mail Connector (IMC) shipped with Microsoft Exchange for coexistence. UNIX-based e-mail systems typically use SMTP or POP3

Protocol. POP3 is short for Post Office Protocol 3. IMC supports UUENCODE and MIME for message transfers using SMTP. UUENCODE and MIME are commonly used UNIX encoding schemes. However, binhex (commonly used in Macs) is not supported. MIME mappings to file name extensions are supported, which facilitates automatic handling of mail attachments.

Synchronization of Directories

A common method of addressing e-mail to multiple recipients is through address lists, which are lists of e-mail userids. Often, users served by different e-mail systems within an organization belong to the same address list. In addition, there will be common user lists that should be the same across the different e-mail systems. Thus, the same directory list across different e-mail systems should be synchronized for updates. Common information in e-mail systems is also stored in public folders.

Directory information across e-mail systems can be kept synchronized either manually or automatically (if the e-mail system supports directory synchronization protocol).

Check with your e-mail vendor(s) for directory synchronization tools. Microsoft Exchange, for example, includes a Directory Exchange Agent (DXA) to keep an Exchange directory in synchronization with MSMail directory. The DXA acts as both a server and a requester to the MSMail system.

UNIX-based e-mail systems typically do not support directories or use proprietary directories (particularly for POP3 systems). If you are migrating from a UNIX system that uses a proprietary directory, to Microsoft Exchange, one way to transfer the directory contents would be to export or dump the directory contents and convert the contents into a format suitable for import with the directory import tool provided by Microsoft.

If you want to change naming conventions in your e-mail system, you can alter the exported data prior to import. The exported data is text data and you can use a text editor or write a program to alter the data. Once you have performed the other migration steps to let the user receive e-mail through Exchange, you need to manually erase the import files and user information in the UNIX e-mail system.

If you are migrating from one e-mail system to another, check with your e-mail vendor for directory migration tools. Microsoft supplies a Wizard, MAILMIG.EXE, that handles the migration of MSMail and Lotus' cc:Mail. The Wizard handles migrating mailboxes, messages in the mailboxes, e-mail message attachments, user's custom setup data such as Personal Address Book entries, etc. The Wizard performs the migration in a two-step process. In the first step, it exports the data to three types of files called the packing list, primary intermediate, and secondary intermediate files. The Wizard then imports the extracted data.

By separating the two steps, you can run the steps independently. For some other e-mail systems such as IBM's PROFS or DEC's All-in-One, the Wizard does not perform a complete migration, as it does for cc:Mail. Instead, Microsoft provides *source extractors* that extract the e-mail migration data. You can then manually run the import step using the Wizard. For e-mail systems not supported by Microsoft, you can still migrate by writing your own source extractor. Your source extractor should manually extract the data required for migration and format that data in the format suitable for import by the migration wizard. You may have to manually migrate data in public folders.

Sometimes, the source of your e-mail directory may not be another e-mail directory. You may want to use the list of valid network operating system users. For example, if you are setting up a new e-mail system and want to authorize current network operating system users, you may be able to export the names from the network operating system and import them into your e-mail system. Microsoft includes a directory import feature in the Exchange product that lets network user account information be extracted from a NetWare server or Banyan VINES server (besides Windows NT server).

E-Mail Security

As e-mail is used to conduct regular business information exchange, the need for securing the e-mail messages has become paramount. Newer e-mail systems include features such as encryption and digital signatures to ensure e-mail security.

Universal Mail Client

One way to mitigate e-mail coexistence and migration issues is to have e-mail clients that can interface with a number of different e-mail service providers at the back end. If you are coexisting e-mail systems, the Universal mail client can receive e-mail from a number of different service providers. If you are performing a migration, your users can be accessing e-mail using one provider before migration. After migration, the client can be reconfigured to access another e-mail provider.

For example, the Windows messaging client (formerly called the exchange client) supports what Microsoft calls *Universal Inbox.* This client can be configured to receive e-mail from a number of mail sources such as CompuServe Mail, Microsoft Mail, Exchange server, Internet mail, etc. The connection between the client and the mail source could be a regular office LAN/WAN or a dialup connection (for access from home or while traveling). Windows NT dialup networking support is normally required for dialup connections.

Having looked at some e-mail migration and coexistence tools in general, let us take a look at specific products from Digital for the heterogeneous e-mail environments.

MailWorks and MAILBus 400. MailWorks and MAILBus are two products from Digital for heterogeneous e-mail integration.

Exhibit 2 shows how the products fit in a heterogeneous e-mail solution.

Digital provides MailWorks and MAILBus 400, an X.400 mail backbone that interconnects all clients and servers that support X.400. Microsoft also offers an X.400 connector for integrating Exchange with X.400 backbones. Digital X.500 directory services further integrate the UNIX and Windows NT environments.

MAILBus 400 Software. Digital MAILBus 400 software provides X.400 backbone functionality to UNIX and Windows NT systems. MAILBus 400 automatically recognizes File Transfer Body Parts and presents them to other X.400 servers in the manner expected by those servers. In other words, MAILBus 400 ensures that all components of messages arrive in a form that the end-user can read.

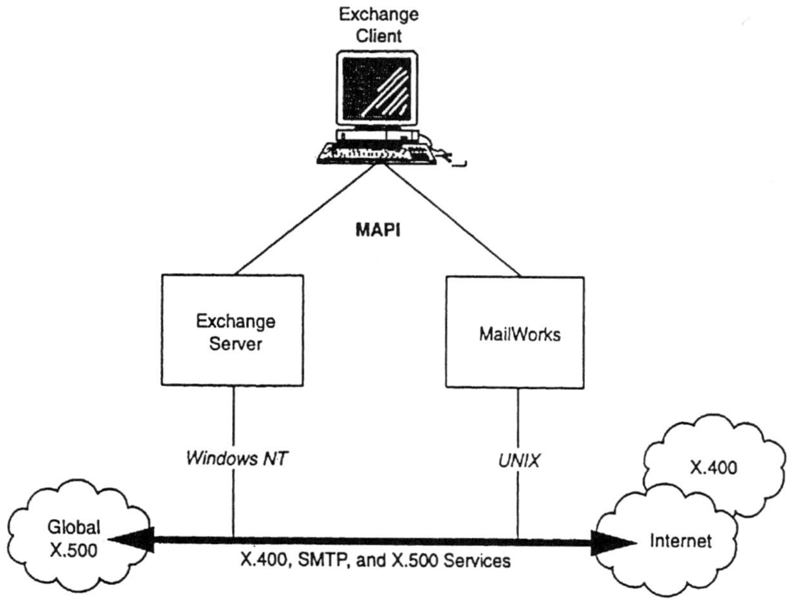

Exhibit 2. E-mail integration products from Digital.

A backbone server can help manage the administration of mail transport agents (MTAs). For example, with the Digital MAILBus 400 backbone services, the administrator notifies the backbone node of a change to the MTA listing, and the backbone node then handles all of the communication among the different systems. Because the backbone server acts as a single repository of current MTA information, replication of that information on each MTA is not necessary. This feature makes it easy to set up and manage a large X.400 installation.

MAILBus 400 uses X.400 as its native backbone transport, but, like Exchange Server, can accommodate SMTP via an SMTP gateway. It thus provides efficient, reliable, high-performance backbone transport and a variety of gateways to foreign mail systems.

Using MAILBus 400, an organization can implement an X.400 backbone with the knowledge that people can exchange messages by using either the X.400 protocol or SMTP, whichever is more appropriate to the application. For example, a company may choose to use X.400 between its Exchange Servers, while transmitting SMTP to the rest of the Internet. Digital has the skill and the capability to help companies decide which of these two backbone technologies is appropriate for them, and to build integration between Exchange Server and other mail systems by using either approach.

PMDF Mailbus 400. For additional X.400 functionality, Digital partners with Innosoft International, Inc. Innosoft's PMDF 400 module provides a direct connection between the Digital Mailbus 400 message transfer agent and the messaging environments that PMDF supports.

Digital X.500 Directory Services. X.500 provides a global address book of names and electronic mail addresses for multivendor messaging systems. X.500 can store employee data (including characteristic attributes) in a single directory. You can use the X.500 Directory Service to create a vendor-independent, enterprise-wide directory service. The product supports the CCITT and ISO X.500 standard for vendor-independent directory service protocols. It is ideally suited for multivendor environments and applications that require distributed access and management.

The X.500 Directory Server software functions as an information store for OSI or TCP/IP networks. Using software clients supplied by Digital (or other X.500 software providers), X.500 Directory Server can access this information regardless of where it resides in the network.

For data consistency, MAILBus 400 stores routing information in the DEC X.500 Directory Service. The directory service provides a shared database of information that requires no manual synchronization. This lowers the cost of ownership by reducing management overhead.

MailWorks for UNIX software lets users access mail addresses from X.500, thus providing access to an enterprise-wide directory of names and electronic mail addresses.

X.500 Directory Service synchronization enables the automated and bidirectional exchange of any electronic directory information, for example, cc:mail and Microsoft Mail, in a multivendor environment.

Administrative and Planning Aspects of E-Mail Migration

Besides the technical aspects of e-mail migration such as the tools and utilities, there are a number of administrative and planning aspects of e-mail migration. These include the following:

- Planning for the migration. This is best accomplished by forming an e-mail migration team with members from the administrator, user groups, and executive oversight.
- User training prior to migration. The training material should include an "equivalent function" list that shows the most commonly used e-mail functions in the current system and how the same functions can be accomplished in the new system. Another tool commonly used and very useful in educating users and reducing user support required is a list of anticipated questions with answers (commonly called FAQs).
- Helpdesk support after the migration. Users tend to have the most number of questions and problems immediately following the migration. A helpdesk should be set up (or an existing one should be beefed up to meet the increased demand).
- E-mail userids and distribution lists should be named as close as possible to the names in the current e-mail system. But if you have been having naming problems, migration of e-mail systems is a good time to adopt a new convention.
- Migration should be attempted in batches and the first few batches should be computer-savvy users. These users are more likely to identify problems and are easier to handle from a helpdesk. Of course, within a set of computer-savvy users, you want to pick the groups that are not facing critical deadlines.
- Every step in the migration plan should anticipate problems and each problem should have solutions to complete the migration and fall-back contingency plans for irrecoverable errors that prevent successful migration.
- In a phased migration, plan to reuse the hardware resources since they are freed up when users are migrated off the e-mail system.

INTERNET FUNCTIONS IN UNIX AND WINDOWS NT

Besides e-mail, which was covered earlier in the chapter, there are other Internet-related functions commonly used. Such functions include FTP,

Exhibit 3. TCP/IP command and utilities in Windows NT.

TCP/IP Command/Utility	Description
arp	Utility to modify IP-to-Ethernet and Token Ring address translation tables to fix routing problems
finger	Displays information about a user on a remote system
ftp	File transfer program to transfer files, commonly used to download files from the Internet
hostname	Displays the current computer's host name
ipconfig	Displays TCP/IP settings in effect
lpq	Displays a remote print queue status (the remote computer should be running the lpd service)
lpr	Print on a computer which has an LPD server running
nbtstat	Displays protocol statistics and connections (uses NetBIOS)
netstat	Displays connections and protocol statistics
ping	Test connection to another TCP/IP node
rcp	Copies files between Windows NT and any computer running the remote shell daemon (RSHD); optionally, you can include subdirectories and files within them
rexec	Transfer a command for execution to another computer (which runs the RSH service)
route	Permits update of network routing tables
telnet	Emulate the local computer to be a terminal for a remote computer. See Chapter 6.
tftp	Transfer files to and from a remote computer (running the tftp service)
tracert	Traces the route to a given destination node

Newsgroups, Telnet, World Wide Web (WWW) and WWW browsers, etc. If you are migrating from one environment to another (e.g., from UNIX to Windows NT), then you need to know what the equivalent functions are in the new environment.

TCP/IP Commands and Utilities

Prior to the advent of Windows NT, most Internet applications were developed in the UNIX environment. UNIX had included the Internet-related communication functions, TCP/IP commands, and utilities support for a long time. Windows NT also includes the same functions, either built-in or through third parties.

Windows NT includes the built-in TCP/IP commands and utilities shown in Exhibit 3.

Windows NT also includes the following built-in Internet Functions at the server level:

- Gopher
- HTTP Support
- WAIS Server/Toolkit

Besides the built-in functions, NT Internet Functions available through third parties include:

- Archie
- Web Browsers such as Netscape and Mosaic (besides Microsoft's own Internet Explorer)

World Wide Web

The point-and-click convenience of the hyperlinks and the World Wide Web have become so popular that the phrase World Wide Web (WWW) is now used synonymously with Internet. The most common software for accessing the WWW is the browser. Since browsers are available for different platforms, if you migrate from one environment to another, you have to get the browser for your environment. Applications written using HTML, CGI, Perl, etc., in one environment (e.g., the UNIX environment) can be ported to another (e.g., the Windows NT environment), and this is addressed in Chapter 3. The user interface of browsers across environments is fairly standard and you can adjust from one to another with relative ease.

Chapter 54

Managing Coexisting SNA and LAN Internetworks

Anura Guruge

The idea of what a network looks like in an IBM-dominated computing environment is in need of a serious update. The all-SNA star network, consisting in the main of 3270 and remote job entry (RJE) terminals multi-dropped off synchronous data link control (SDLC) links to a central S/370 host, is now a relic. New IBM networks consist of microcomputer LANs—both Token Ring and Ethernet—that are appendages of a central, multiprotocol backbone. Systems Network Architecture is just one of the many disparate networking protocols flowing across the backbone. Thanks to the ever-increasing popularity of microcomputers and UNDIX workstations in what are still primarily IBM shops, host- and PC-based applications are now routinely front-ended, complemented, or in some instances totally usurped by LAN-oriented, workstation centric, client/server applications.

This increase in LAN-attached, workstation-based applications has not diminished what constitutes, by far, the bulk of SNA applications: host-based, mission-critical applications. Mission- or business-critical applications are in effect the lifeblood of an enterprise. They provide, support, and sustain the vital operations imperative to the enterprise.

USE OF SNA OVER LANS

At least 65% of today's mission-critical applications will be in use for another 10 to 15 years, and this longevity ensures that SNA will be in use for at least that long. Mission-critical applications were invariably developed to be accessed through 3270 terminals. With more and more 3270s being replaced by PCs, 3270 emulation on LAN attached workstations (using an SNA LAN gateway) is now becoming the main approach for accessing these applications. Access to a host application through

0-8493-9989-0/99/$0.00+$.50

LAN-attached workstations currently accounts for most of the SNA-based traffic that flows across LANs.

Access to a host application is one of four distinct scenarios for the use of SNA over LANs. These four scenarios (illustrated in Exhibit 1) are:

- Access to mission-critical host applications from a LAN- attached workstation or computer system (e.g., AS/400), using SNA logical unit to logical unit (LU-LU) session types 2 and 3 (i.e., 3270 data stream) or LU-LU session type 7 (i.e., 5250 data stream). The host could be an S/3x0 or a minicomputer such as the AS/400 or the S/38. Token Ring is typically the LAN of choice for this type of host access, though it is now possible to access S/3x0 applications using LU-LU session type 2 over other types of networks.
- SNA LU 6.2/APPN-based program-to-program interactions between two LAN-attached systems (e.g., PC to PC, PC to AS/400, AS/400 to AS/400). Many of IBM's contemporary "utility services" for data transfer or remote data access are based on LU 6.2. Hence, the distribution of documents, mail, or files as provided by IBM's office automation packages or remote system access through DSPT can now be realized across LANs.
- Host-to-host SNA paths between IBM 3745 communications controllers, usually over a 16M-bps Token Ring. (For ES/9370s or 43xx hosts with integrated Token Ring adapters, the integrated adapters, rather than 3745s, can be used.) Such LAN connections (subject to their distance limitations) can be cost-effective, high-speed data paths between hosts and attractive alternatives to SDLC link connections or backup paths for channel-to-channel connections between hosts.
- Using an SNA backbone for communications between non-SNA LANs, by encapsulating the LAN traffic within SNA LU 6.2 message units.

A REPERTOIRE OF PROTOCOLS

The popularity of LANs means that enterprises with IBM hosts or minis invariably end up with a repertoire of applications that fall into three main categories: file- or print-server applications, host- and minicomputer-resident traditional applications, and a new generation of client/server, program-to-program applications.

For each of these three applications categories there are native, or preferred, protocols. The protocol set that will typically be used with a given application category can be summarized as follows:

- File/print server. NetBIOS, IPX/SPX, Banyan Vines, TCP/IP, AppleTalk, or XNS.
- Host/mini application access. SNA LU-LU session types 2 (i.e., 3270 data stream) or 7 (i.e., 5250 data stream).

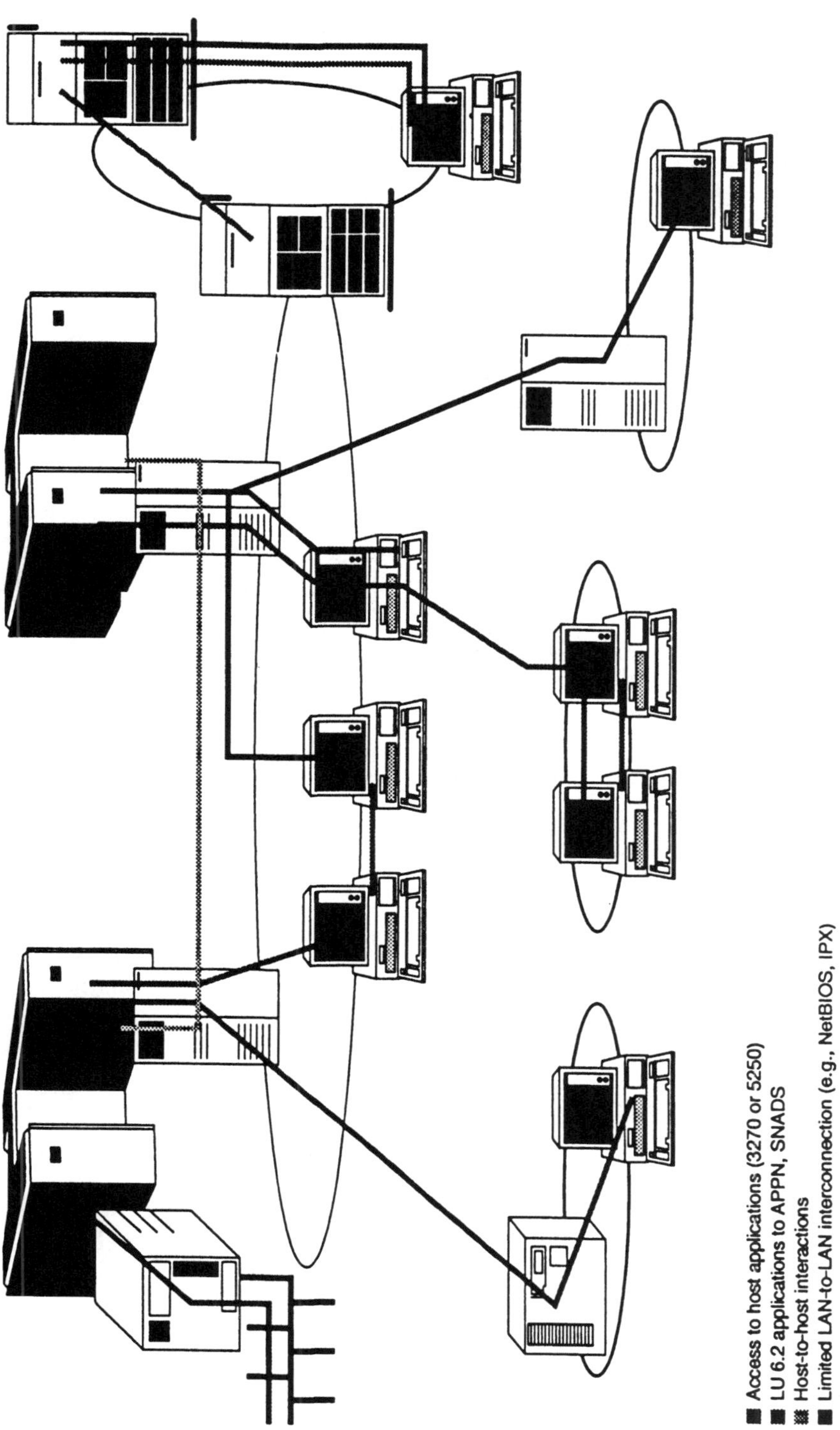

Exhibit 1. SNA over LAN applications.

- Program-to-program communications. SNA LU 6.2 APPN (including SNADS, DIA, DDM, SNA/FS), NetBIOS, TCP/IP, DECnet, IPX/SPX, XNS, or OSI.

The diversity of protocols is not itself a problem because LANs support concurrent multiprotocol data streams. It is not unusual to find SNA, NetBIOS, IPX, and TCP/IP on the same Token Ring LAN.

Networking challenges in the IBM environment are only starting to surface as the scope of LAN-based applications, using the protocol cocktail described, extends beyond LANs that are in close physical proximity to each other to also embrace geographically distant LANs. A workstation on a LAN in Boston requiring access to data on a file server on a LAN in San Francisco or access to an application resident on a host in Chicago is an example.

PARALLEL NETWORKS

Enterprises that now require LAN interconnection between distant locations invariably have an SNA WAN that is hubbed around one or more S/3x0 hosts; this WAN reaches all the remote locations of interest. Companies have sizable investments in these WANs, which also tend to be tried and true; therefore, to minimize costs and to standardize on one set of network management requirements and operational procedures, the natural tendency is to strive for a single WAN backbone that supports SNA and the requisite LAN protocol. This is the problem.

For all their pedigree and sophistication (not to mention cost), SNA WANs in actuality can support only SNA traffic, either LAN or link based. Support for LAN protocols, even the more popular ones such as NetBIOS, IPX/SPX, and TCP/IP, is currently available only on an *ad hoc* basis, using products specifically designed for that purpose. The only potentially general solutions are IBM's frame relay data communications equipment feature for its 3745 communication controller and Computer Communications Inc.'s Eclipse 7020 LAN-over-SNA router.

With these, a user can interconnect LANs across an existing SNA backbone. However, this LAN-over-SNA solution is relatively new to the market, and there is still much doubt as to its feasibility, particularly in terms of throughput and performance. With the exception of these auxiliary, add-on solutions, it is accurate to say that SNA WANs, at present, do not provide a workable cost-effective, high-performance, and general solution for transporting LAN traffic from one location to another.

This frustrating absence of general support for LAN traffic across SNA has forced many enterprises to implement and maintain two parallel WANs: a dedicated 37xx-based SNA WAN for SNA application access and a bridge or bridge/router-based multiprotocol WAN for non-SNA, interLAN traffic, as illustrated in Exhibit 2.

This dual WAN approach obviously works but requires that users install, maintain, and operate two very diverse networks. In some instances, the duplication of the actual long-distance links can be avoided by deploying a multiplexer (e.g., T1) network.

TOWARD A COMMON MULTIPROTOCOL BACKBONE

Bridge and bridge/router vendors have rushed to the rescue of enterprises dreading the thought—and the expense—of parallel networks. The initial, and intuitive, solution was to bridge the SNA LAN traffic while bridging or routing the other LAN protocols as appropriate. This makes it possible (at least in the case of LAN traffic) to have a single universal backbone WAN that interconnects dispersed locations and permits both SNA LAN and non-SNA LAN traffic to be readily transported between various LANs, as illustrated in Exhibit 3.

Two techniques for integrating SNA LAN traffic with non-SNA LAN traffic are predominant: source-route bridging and Internet Protocol (IP) encapsulation. The former may be performed by Token Ring bridges or bridge/routers that include explicit support for encapsulating SNA (and invariably also NetBIOS) traffic.

A third option is proprietary but is still relatively popular: CrossComm's protocol independent routing (PIR) scheme. With the increasing popularity of SNA over Ethernet, transparent bridging—the native bridging technique for Ethernet LANs—will become another option for SNA and LAN traffic integration.

Source-Route Bridging

Source-route bridging (SRB) is the original-and in essence the default—method for interconnecting multiple Token Ring LANs. It permits two or more Token Ring LANs to be uniformly and transparently interconnected, so that they appear to form a single, seamless, consolidated LAN.

SRB may be used to interconnect LANs that are either adjacent to each other (e.g., within the same building) or geographically dispersed. The former scenario, referred to as local bridging, does not involve any WAN connection. The latter, which does require WAN connections, is referred to as remote bridging. A bridge that is performing remote bridging is sometimes called a split bridge by IBM, to indicate that the bridging function has been divided and is being performed at either end of a WAN connection.

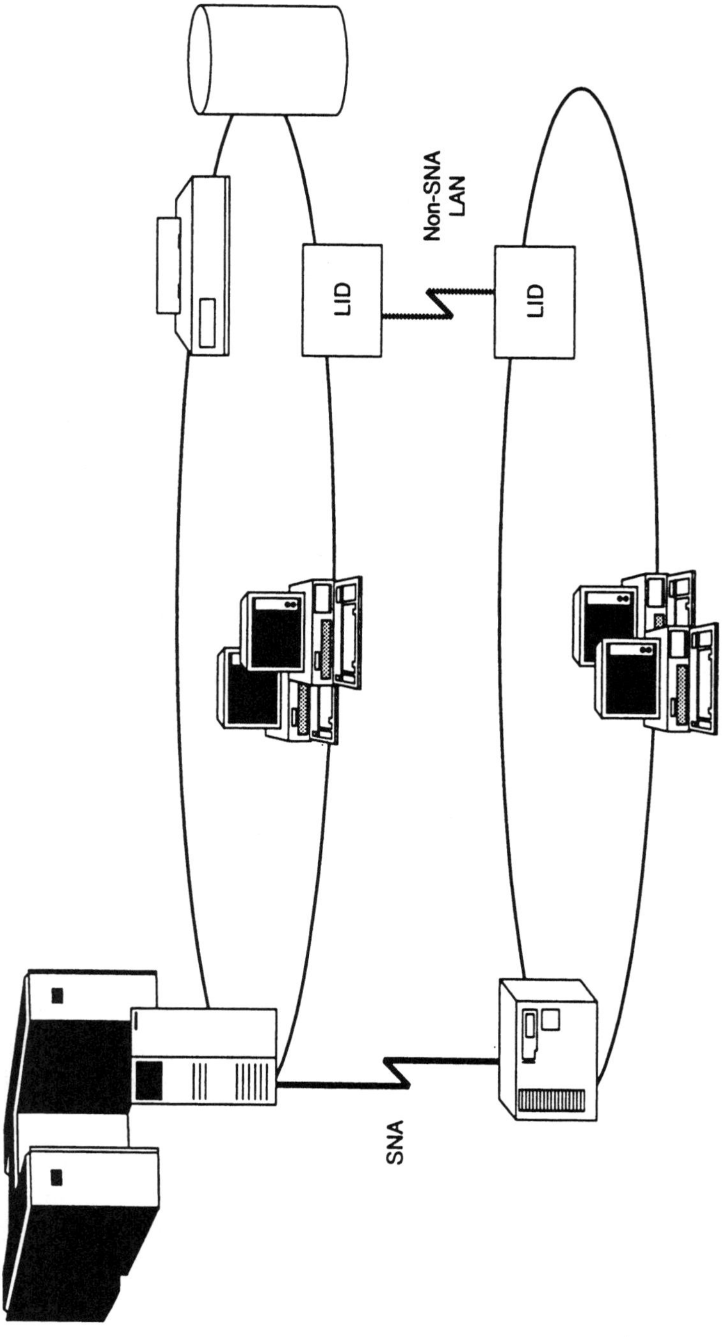

Note:
LID LAN interconnection device (bridge, router, or bridge/router)

Exhibit 2. Parallel backbones for SNA traffic and LAN-to-LAN traffic.

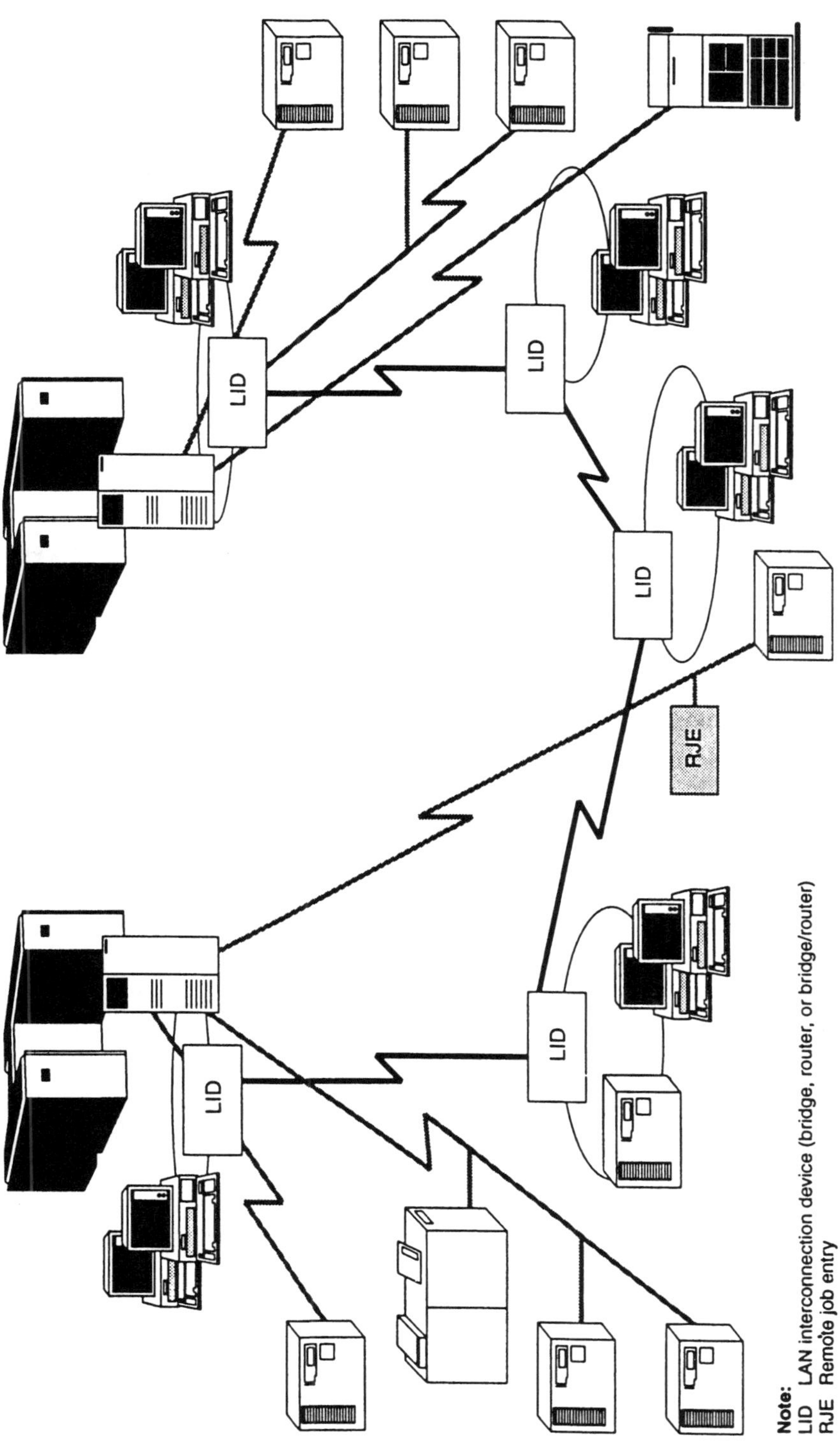

Exhibit 3. Support of all traffic on multiprotocol backbone through bridging and IP-encapsulating SNA.

If the SRB bridge/routers are supporting SNA LAN traffic, these multiple LANs—which behave logically as a single large LAN—are interfaced to the S/3x0 SNA environment through one or more SNA LAN gateways (e.g., a channel-attached 3745, 3174, or 3172). All the attached devices, including the SNA LAN gateway, behave as if they were attached to the same physical LAN. Thus, host system control software (e.g., ACF/VTAM and ACF/NCP) and consequently the host-resident SNA application programs can view, and treat, the various SNA devices on the dispersed LANs as if they were all on one single LAN.

SRB is a straightforward LAN interconnection technique that can accommodate most SNA LAN traffic consolidation. Like all other bridging techniques, SRB is a data link (OSI layer 2) level process. Thus it is independent and transparent to such higher-level (i.e., layer 3 and above) networking protocols as SNA, APPN, NetBIOS, or Novell's IPX/SPX.

How SRB Works

For SRB bridge/routers to be able to provide interconnection between two devices on two different LANs, a path between the two LANs (a chain of intermediate bridges that the data will traverse) has to be established. A dynamic, broadcast search technique is used to establish this path. The technique used is similar to that employed by SNA to locate undefined resources in multihost environments and what is now available in Advanced Peer-to-Peer Networking (APPN) for dynamically locating remote resources.

The SRB broadcast search technique is initiated by the source device, rather than by one of the bridges. It does so by issuing a Token Ring TEST or XID (exchange identification) command. The destination device being sought is identified by its unique layer-2 6-byte media access control (MAC) address. Because the SRB search process is restricted to layer 2, it occurs without any reference to higher-level addresses or names (e.g., SNA/APPN LU names, SNA network or local addresses, or NetBIOS names).

The source device initially issues the TEXT or XID command without any indication that the command should be broadcast outside the local LAN segment to which it is attached. This initial search is known as an on-segment search. If the source receives no response from the destination before the expiration of a prespecified time-out period, it assumes that the destination is on another LAN.

The source device then immediately resorts to an off-segment search by again issuing a TEST or XID command, but this time with a routing information field (RIF) included by the header prefixing the command, and two flags (represented by four bits) set in the header to indicate the presence of the RIF, as well as the need for a broadcast search to be conducted.

The broadcast search flag denotes that the search is to be conducted in one of two ways:

- All-route broadcast.
- Single-route broadcast.

The method is selected by the software on the source device. In general, SNA software requests all-route searches, whereas NetBIOS opts for single-route searches. When an all-route search is specified in a TEST or XID command, each bridge encountering that command makes a copy of it and forwards that copy to every other Token Ring LAN attached to that bridge. With remote bridging, the copy of the TEST or XID command is sent over the WAN connections to the remote bridges.

Traversing All the Routes

When a TEST or XID command is forwarded to another LAN, the bridge updates the accompanying RIF to reflect the identity of the bridge that it has just crossed. The identification is in the form of a 16-bit segment number that consists of a unique number denoting the Token Ring from which the command was copied and a unique number identifying the bridge. Identifying the bridge, in addition to the Token Ring, permits multiple bridges to be used between a pair of Token Rings.

The current Token Ring approach does not permit a RIF to exceed 18 bytes. Hence a routing information field, which must always begin with a 2-byte routing control field, can at most contain only eight segment numbers. Because the first entry in the RIF has to identify the LAN containing the source device, SRB per se permits LAN interconnections over no more than seven intermediary LAN segments. (The routing control field at the start of the RIF, in addition to denoting the type of broadcast search being conducted, has fields to indicate the number of LAN segments currently present in the RIF, the longest information frame that is supported once a session is established, and a flag to indicate whether the command containing the RIF is flowing from the source to the destination, or vice versa).

With all-route searches, the destination device receives as many copies of the TEST or XID command as there are available routes between the source and destination LANs. Each command received reflects in its RIF the exact path that it has traversed, in terms of intermediate LANs and bridges, in the order in which they were crossed. The destination device returns each command it receives, replete with its RIF, back to the source device. The response traverses the same path as that taken by the original command.

As the source device receives the responses from the destination device, it could, theoretically, determine the optimum route by evaluating the route structure found in the RIF of each response. The source may decide that the route containing the least number of intermediary bridges is the optimum path. It could also record the routes specified in the other RIFs to use as potential alternate routes if the initially chosen route fails during the dialogue. Current Token Ring implementations do neither.

Instead, the route traversed by the first received response is assumed to be the best route, given that this route was obviously the fastest for the roundtrip involved in the search process. This, however, may not really be the case. A temporary aberration on what would normally have been the fastest path may have caused a less than optimum path to be selected. The routes specified in the other responses are ignored. The RIF in the first response is then duplicated in the headers of all frames interchanged between the source and destination devices for the duration of that dialogue (e.g., an SNA session). Thus, SRB, just like traditional SNA and even APPN, is an inherently fixed path-routing technique.

The Single-Shot Approach

For a single-route broadcast search, a bridge determines the route over which the TEXT or XID command should be propagated on the basis of a single-route broadcast path maintained by each bridge. This broadcast path is constructed using a spanning tree algorithm. This spanning tree approach, often referred to as transparent spanning tree, is the bridging technique used to interconnect Ethernet LANs. It is also known as transparent bridging.

With single-route searches, the destination device receives only one copy of the TEST or XID command. In marked contrast to the all-route method, the RIF in the command received by the destination contains only a routing control field and does not indicate the route traversed by the command. Just as with an all-route search, the destination device returns the command to the source by toggling the direction flag.

The destination device, however, sets the broadcast flags at the start of the routing control field to denote an all-route search. This causes the response to be returned to the source using all available paths between the destination and source. The route taken in each case is recorded in the RIF as in the case of an all-route search. Thus, in the case of a single-route search, the routing information is collected on the return trip as opposed to the destination-location trip.

The source receives multiple responses and, as with all-route, uses the route taken by the first response received as the optimum path.

SRB's Limitations

The greatest virtue of SRB is that it offers plug-and-play interoperability between devices on different LANs, with minimum predefinition. Usually, just a LAN number and a bridge number are required to set up the bridges.

SRB does, however, suffer from some major limitations. Its fixed-path routing offers no dynamic, alternative rerouting in the event of path failure; it creates overhead traffic during the broadcast searches; and it has an inherent seven-hop limit on intermediate LANs and bridges between the source and destination. Most of the leading bridge/router vendors have devised methods to circumvent these limitations.

To circumvent the seven-hop limitation, most vendors now offer an extended SRB facility, whereby a bridge/router subnetwork from a given vendor, irrespective of the number of SRB bridges/routers and LANs involved, always appears as a single hop to other internetworking devices in the overall network. The technique is totally transparent to other standard SRB bridges/routers, which see just a single RIF LAN segment entry that happens in reality to correspond to a multisegment subnetwork. Most enterprises have not as yet been inconvenienced by the seven-hop ceiling of standard SRB. But extended SRB sidesteps this problem and enterprises can consider larger networks for future use without concern that the seven-hop count will be exceeded.

Broadcast Storms. The additional traffic generated during SRB broadcast searches can be a source of major concern, particularly in remote bridging configurations that use relatively low-speed WAN connections. Bursts of SRB broadcast search traffic that interfere with bona fide data traffic are referred to (somewhat dramatically) as broadcast storms. Such storms have been a perennial source of criticism of SRB, especially from Ethernet users who point out that Ethernet's spanning tree bridging technique does not require a broadcast search.

Broadcast storms can be minimized by the use of SRB proxy responder agents. Such agents provide a local cache directory scheme; the addresses of remote destination devices can be saved following an initial SRB search. Before subsequent broadcast searches are performed, an agent checks its cache directory to see whether it already knows of a route to the destination device being sought. If a route is found in the cache directory, the agent inserts that route in the RIF of the TEST or XID command issued by the source device, then returns the command to the source. This avoids an exhaustive broadcast search.

IP-ENCAPSULATED ROUTING

IP encapsulation is now being aggressively promoted by some vendors, including IBM, as an answer to both SRB's fixed- path routing, as well as the inability of bridge/routers to perform SNA routing. (IP encapsulation of SNA traffic is one of the functions performed by the data link switching feature in IBM's 6611 bridge/router.) A LAN layer-2 logical link control (LLC) frame that contains SNA (or NetBIOS) traffic is inserted in its entirety as a piece of data within an IP data-gram packet and routed across a bridge/ router network as IP traffic.

IP encapsulation does have some irrefutable attractions. It offers dynamic alternative routing in the event of a path failure, policy-based adaptive routing (e.g., fastest or least-cost path for each packet being transmitted), and avoidance of broadcast searches. On the surface, IP encapsulation would appear to be an ideal solution to some of SRB's weaknesses. Unfortunately, this is not exactly the case.

Because IP encapsulated routing is based on Internet Protocol (IP) addresses, destination IP addresses must be allocated to supplement the already existing MAC addresses and, in the case of SNA, network addresses. To be fair, most vendors do not require that destination IP addresses be allocated on a one-to-one basis for each device. Instead, IP addresses can be assigned on the basis of a destination LAN, LAN group, or destination bridge/router. IBM, with DLSw, dynamically correlates the destination MAC address with the IP address of the 6611 serving the LAN containing that device by first conducting an SRB all-route broadcast search. MAC-to-destination 6611 IP address correlations, thus established, are cached for subsequent use. But for each 6611 that is to participate in DLSw, the IP address must be manually defined.

The drawback to IP encapsulated routing is that it reverses the trend toward plug-and-play networking. Enterprise networking is general and SNA in particular have been definition-intensive activities, but the industry as a whole, including IBM, has been making a genuine, concerted effort to introduce simpler plug-and-play configure-on-the-fly networking techniques. IBM has made contemporary SNA, particularly ACF/VTAM Version 3 Release 4, as dynamic as possible. IBM's APPN is the epitome of a modem, dynamic networking scheme. For all its faults, SRB too is close to a plug-and-play technique. IP encapsulation, even with the DLSw enhancements, requires too much manual predefinition to be accepted as a contemporary networking methodology.

EMERGING OPTIONS

Protocol Independent Routing. PIR is an attempt to offer adaptive as well as alternative routing in addition to broadcast search reduction, without the need for manual IP address allocation. It thus provides the dynamic routing advantages of IP encapsulation with the plug-and-play characteristics of SRB. PIR is a compelling solution for midsize networks (those containing as many as 100 LAN segments) in which the bulk of the traffic is SNA or NetBIOS.

Source-Route Transparent Bridging. A feature that is now offered by many bridge/router vendors is source-route transparent (SRT) bridging. SRT permits a bridge to concurrently perform both Token Ring SRB and Ethernet transparent bridging. SRT thus allows the same bridge to support devices on Token Ring LANs using SRB and devices on the same Token Rings, or on Ethernets connected to other ports, that require transparent bridging.

SRT is a scheme for Token Ring and Ethernet coexistence, as opposed to interoperability. Token Ring to Ethernet interoperability, when needed, is provided by source-route translation bridging (SR/TLB) and is available on IBM's 8209 LAN bridge. SR/TLB is not currently available on the IBM 6611, though it is a feature available on some bridge/routers.

BRING IN THE LINKS

Providing support for LAN-based SNA traffic addresses only a part of the overall problem of integrating SNA and LAN traffic. More than half of the current installed base of SNA devices worldwide are connected to SDLC or 3270 binary synchronous communications (BSC) links. Furthermore, for technical, historic, and financial reasons customers are not likely to upgrade or replace these devices to become LAN compatible.

Link-attached devices in use at SNA sites include IBM 3174s, 3274s, 3770s, 8100s, Series/1s, S/36s, S/38s, 3600s, 4700s, 5520s, and minicomputers from Digital Equipment Corp., Wang, Prime, Data General, and others. Thus, to implement a universal, all-inclusive, multiprotocol WAN that supports all types of traffic, bridges or bridge/routers have to support link-based SNA traffic in addition to LAN-based SNA traffic (see Exhibit 4). Leading bridge/router vendors and some bridge vendors now offer at least one method for consolidating SNA/SDLC link traffic with LAN traffic.

The three technologically feasible techniques for integrating SNA link traffic with LAN traffic are:

- Straight synchronous passthrough (which may be supplemented with such value-added features as traffic prioritization).
- Remote polling.
- SDLC to Token Ring LLC transformation.

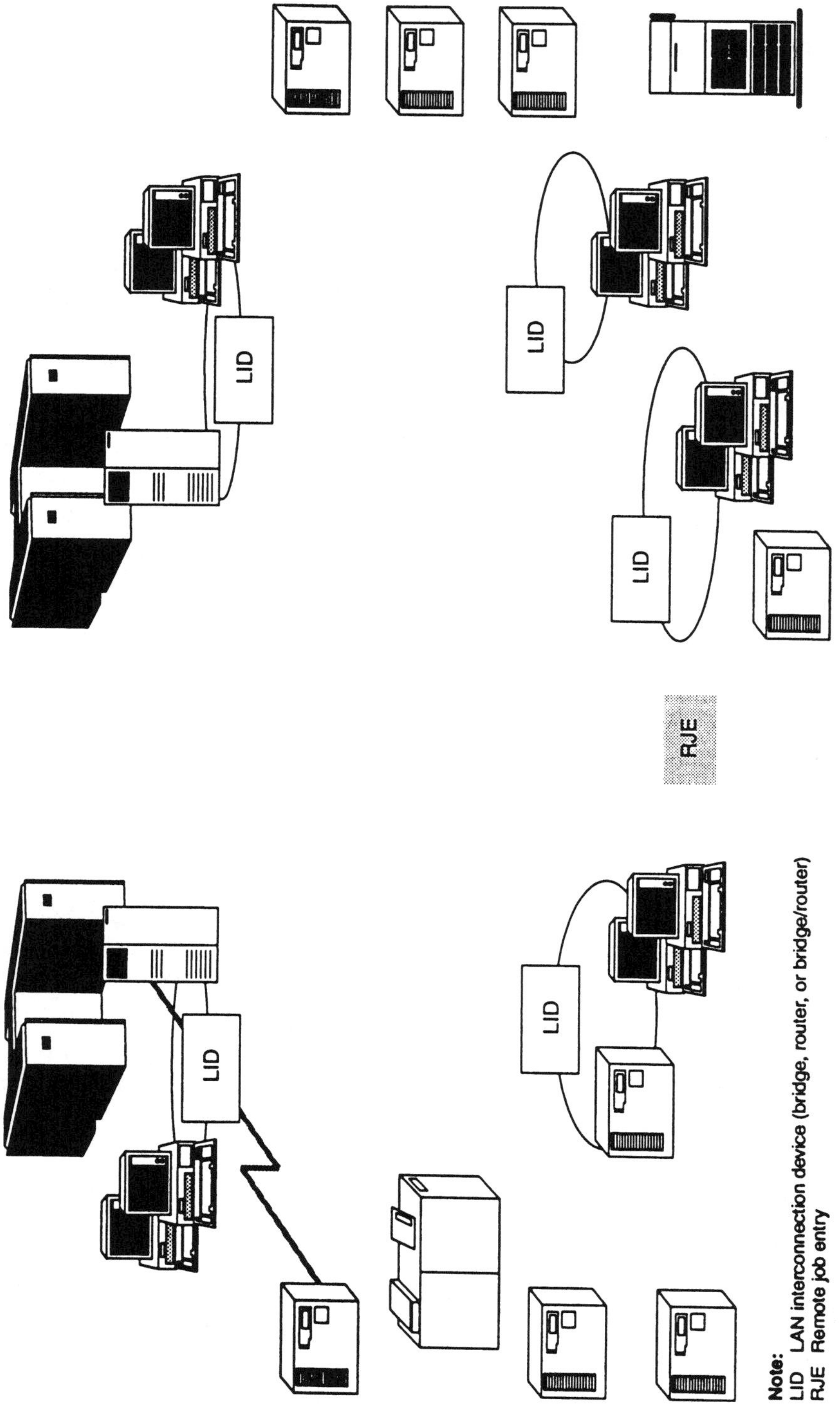

Exhibit 4. Multiprotocol bridge/router-based WAN for SNA, LAN, and link-based traffic.

HANDS-OFF HANDS-ON: SYNCHRONOUS PASSTHROUGH

Synchronous passthrough is the easiest, most intuitive, and least risky technique for using bridge/routers to support SNA/SDLC link traffic. It was the first, and for a while the ubiquitous, solution for SNA link integration. For reasons explained in the next section, it is the least desirable technique. Synchronous passthrough cannot generally be used to support 3270 BSC traffic, although it does support other SDLC-like protocols (e.g., High-level Data Link Control, or HDLC).

With synchronous passthrough, each physical SDLC link from a 37xx port to one or more (i.e., in the case of a multidrop link) remote SNA devices is replaced by a clear-channel, port-to-port connection through the multiprotocol WAN. The 37xx port to which the original SDLC link was attached is now connected to a serial port on an adjacent, upstream, local bridge/ router, possibly with a modem bypass cable or a short-haul modem configuration. The remote devices are attached to a serial port on a downstream, remote bridge/router. The two serial ports on the bridge/routers are then mapped to each other, over a point-to-point route across the multiprotocol WAN, using the bridge/router's configuration utilities.

SDLC traffic arriving at either of the bridge/router serial ports is cleanly transported to the predefined partner port at the other end, This is achieved by an encapsulating technique, whereby every SDLC frame, from the first bit of the start flag to the last bit of the end flag, is included as data within an IP datagram. The bridge/routers do not read the SDLC frame, let alone modify it in any way. What comes in at one serial port goes out unadulterated at the opposite serial port.

In general, synchronous passthrough is a safe bet that permits SNA links to be cut over to a multiprotocol WAN with a minimum of fuss and certainly without the need for either a new ACF/NCP host gen or a software reconfiguration at the device. Most, if not all, of the glitches that were encountered with the first bridge/router implementations as well as such limitations as 1,500-byte frame size have now been rectified.

Because the technique forwards untouched SDLC frames, which in turn may contain complete SNA message units, neither end sees any changes at the SDLC—let alone the SNA—level, with the exception of a possible degradation in link speed. Thus, both sides continue to work as though they were still connected to each other over a physical link, rather than through a complex multiprotocol WAN. This technique insulates customers from compatibility issues that may arise from host software upgrades or new features added to SNA, because whatever works on a leased line should also, in theory, work with synchronous passthrough, except for functions that are extremely time sensitive.

Synchronous passthrough also provides a high degree of compatibility with SNA-based network management systems like NetView, which continue to have total end-to-end SNA control and visibility. There is no mechanism at the moment, however, for SNA to recognize what is happening within the multiprotocol WAN. Thus, the SDLC links invariably appear to be clean links with few or no retransmissions, because retransmissions on the WAN are invisible to the network management system.

Drawbacks of Synchronous Passthrough

The noninterventionist qualities of synchronous passthrough are also its greatest weakness. By keeping all the SDLC frames intact, synchronous passthrough does not in any way reduce the amount of traffic over a given link. If anything, it increases the traffic, because encapsulating SDLC in IP not only makes the transmitted packets longer but adds additional IP control interactions on top of the SDLC interactions. To compensate for this, many vendors now offer some type of data compression capability; some vendors also offer a mechanism to compress the IP header.

For the new WAN link's response time to be comparable to those experienced with the physical link, the bridge/router network has to ensure that each end-to-end connection is allocated bandwidth comparable to that of the original link. Usually this is not an issue. Most SNA links to peripheral devices, as opposed to those between 37xxs, operate at data rates lower than 19.2K bps. In contrast, the trunks in a bridge/router WAN are unlikely to operate at rate slower than 56K bps. However, from the perspective of each SDLC link, the WAN has to be shared with high-speed, high-volume traffic from LANs as well as with traffic from other SDLC links.

Being able to assign a higher transmission priority to link traffic at the expense of LAN traffic is one way to prevent link traffic from being swamped by LAN traffic. CrossComm Corp. (Marlborough MA) and Cisco Systems, Inc. (Menlo Park CA), the leading vendors, are beginning to offer generic traffic prioritization features. These can be exploited to ensure that SNA traffic—link or LAN—gets precedence over other traffic.

The other unfavorable feature of synchronous passthrough is the amount of spurious, nonproductive polling traffic that must be continually transported across the WAN, consuming valuable bandwidth. Any retransmissions sought by either end also must be made end-to-end, again occupying bandwidth.

REMOTE POLLING

Remote polling overcomes the idle-poll and retransmission problems of synchronous passthrough. It can also be used to effectively and efficiently support 3270 BSC traffic. With this technique, only SDLC frames (or 3270

BSC blocks) containing bona fide data—SDLC I-frames (or BSC text blocks), which in turn contain SNA message units—are transmitted across the WAN. Polling and retransmissions are performed and responded to at the periphery of the WAN by special SDLC (or BSC) link-driver modules.

Primary and Secondary Modules. Two types of these modules are available: primary modules, which issue polls, and secondary modules, which respond to polls. The primary modules are deployed in remote, downstream bridge/ routers to which the actual SNA devices are attached, whereas the secondary modules are used in the local, upstream bridge/ routers connected to the 37xx ports.

Just as with synchronous passthrough, there will be predesignated port-to-port mapping, associated with each SNA link, between the router port attached to the 37xx and the corresponding port on the remote router to which the SNA devices are attached. However, in the case of remote polling, a link-address-to-link-address mapping is also required on top of the port-to-port mapping.

Once these mappings have been established, the remote primary module polls the devices attached to its port, using a predefined polling table that specifies the link addresses to be polled plus the order and frequency at which to poll the addresses. As each device becomes active, as indicated by a positive response to a poll, the primary notifies its partner secondary module that the device in question is now active and ready for data exchange, using a bridge/router handshake protocol.

As the primary starts its polling cycle, the local secondary activates its port and waits to receive data from the 37xx port. The 37xx reacts to this by issuing polls. If the secondary receives notification that the subject physical device is active, it responds to the 37xx as if it were the real device.

Once this initial activation sequence is complete, one side starts to receive data frames. It accepts them and forwards them to its partner, which in turn ensures that the frames are delivered to the intended destination device. The relaying of such data frames between the modules is performed on a per-address basis. This process of receiving data frames at one end and forwarding them to the other end for delivery to their rightful destination takes place on a routine basis.

Merits of Remote Polling. Remote polling, also referred to as poll spoofing or local acknowledgment, is invariably considered by customers to be more desirable than synchronous passthrough, as it has the unquestionable merit of reducing the amount of link traffic that must be transported across a backbone. Remote polling also reduces the occurrence of time-outs. Remote polling, just like synchronous passthrough, in no way interferes with the SNA protocols and, as an SNA-transparent scheme, is not affected by modifications made at the SNA level. It also provides Net View with full end-to-end SNA access and visibility but now with slightly more distortion of its perception of the underlying link.

Remote polling has an optional capability whereby link configurations are transformed to achieve cost reductions and even improve polling efficacy. Given that remote polling uses a link-address-to-link-address technique, it is possible to transform and map link addresses of devices on multiple links to addresses on a virtual consolidated link at the 37xx side. For example, the devices on four point-to-point links could be presented to the 37xx through the router backbone, as if they were four devices on a single multipoint link.

SDLC-TO-LLC TRANSFORMATION

This technique is in effect a variation of standard remote polling, exploiting remote polling's inherent physical- to virtual-link transformation capability. In standard remote polling, the same data link control protocol (e.g., SDLC or 3270 BSC) is used both at the host and at the remote device. With SDLC-to-LLC transformation, different data link protocols are used at the two ends: SDLC on the link-attached device and Token Ring logical link control type 2 (LLC-2) at the host. Though typically offered today as an SDLC to Token Ring transformation, this same technique could be used between SDLC and Ethernet and between 3270 BSC and either Token Ring or Ethernet.

The primary reason for SDLC-to-LLC transformation is cost reduction. With SDLC-to-LLC transformation, customers can eliminate serial link ports at the host side, both on 37xx communications controllers and on the bridge/routers adjacent to those controllers.

Instead of transporting link traffic to or from the host through serial ports, LLC transformation converts link traffic to Token Ring LAN traffic and conveys it to or from the host over a standard host (e.g., 3745) Token Ring interface. In other words, SDLC-to-LLC transformation converts SDLC link traffic to Token Ring LAN traffic at the host end so that the hosts can treat the link traffic as Token Ring LAN traffic. The link-specific Token Ring traffic is converted back into link format at the remote end so that it can be transmitted over the actual physical links using SDLC. Customers do not need serial ports for the link traffic and a Token Ring LAN interface for LAN traffic. At the host end, a Token Ring interface works with LAN and link traffic.

SDLC-to-LLC transformation permits SNA customers to support remote link-attached SNA devices using non-3745 SNA gateways (e.g., 3174S or 3172s), which, relative to their SNA gateway functions, support only Token Ring-attached SNA nodes. So in some instances, SDLC-to-LLC transformation permits customers to displace 37xxs that were being used primarily to support link traffic in favor of a lower cost 3174 or 3172 (or similar) SNA gateway. These cost-reduction possibilities are making SDLC-to-LLC transformation the preferred option for link-traffic integration. It is, for example, the only technique for SDLC integration offered on the IBM 6611.

Just as with remote link polling, SDLC-to-LLC transformation does not in any way interfere with or modify I-fields (or 3270 BSC text blocks) that contain actual end-user data. Hence, SDLC-to-LLC transformation, like remote link polling or synchronous passthrough, is transparent to all end-to-end SNA interactions. This noninterventionist approach could, however, cause problems later if a customer uses SDLC-to-LLC transformation to support future—as opposed to existing—SNA devices. Recent SNA network management uses unsolicited SNA generic alerts, which contain self-identifying data in the form of subvectors, with some of these subvectors specifying link characteristics. The problem as it applies to SDLC-to-LLC transformation is that the actual link characteristics reported by the physical device relate to SDLC—whereas, because of LLC transformation, the device appears to the host to be LAN attached.

In this respect, it is worth stressing that all SDLC (or 3270 BSC) link support features offered on bridge/routers should be treated as short-term tactical migration aids, rather than as long-term strategic offerings. They are a cost-effective means for integrating existing link-attached SNA devices into multiprotocol WANs. Network managers should not, however, treat this support as justification for continuing to acquire link- attached SNA devices rather than the equivalent LAN-attachable SNA/APPN devices.

SUMMARY

The technology for implementing a single consolidated WAN backbone that supports SNA, LAN, SNA link, and other LAN traffic is now widely available. SNA LAN traffic can be integrated into the common backbone using one of three techniques described in this chapter: bridging, IP encapsulation, and CrossComm's protocol independent routing. SNA link traffic can be incorporated into a multiprotocol backbone using either synchronous passthrough, remote polling, or SDLC to Token Ring LLC transformation. Of these, the latter technique is the one most frequently used.

Chapter 55
SNA-LAN Integration Strategies

Nathan J. Muller

Use of both SNA networks and LAN internetworks is now so broad-based that for many users, integration is simply the next logical step. This chapter discusses several integration methods, but advises careful selection of tools, since vendor offerings are still relatively new.

INTRODUCTION

Data communications was once a relatively simple task, conducted within the orderly, hierarchical confines of the Systems Network Architecture (SNA) devised by IBM. Increasingly, however, mainframe-based computing has given way to distributed computing over local area networks and LANs interconnected over wide area internetworks. LANs have not entirely replaced SNA systems, though, because both have strengths that most organizations continue to value. Furthermore, many organizations still have big investments in SNA-based systems and application software that cannot be thrown out without causing major disruptions to daily business operations.

The host environment is still valued for mission-critical applications, largely because SNA has proved itself to be a stable and highly reliable architecture. Additional advantages include network accounting, security, network management with NetView, and cost control. Yet, there is still the need to transfer great quantities of information from one location to another over local and WAN in peer-to-peer fashion.

Users value LANs for the connectivity they can provide to a variety of corporate resources and TCP/IP-based WAN for their ability to access remote LANs. Multiprotocol routers make this fairly easy to do over high-speed leased lines and such carrier services as T1, frame relay, and Switched Multimegabit Data Service. To avoid the expense of duplicate networks, users are looking at ways to integrate incompatible SNA and LAN

0-8493-9989-0/99/$0.00+$.50

architectures over the same facilities or services. The consolidation of such diverse resources over a single internetwork offers several benefits:

- It eliminates the need to provision, operate, and maintain duplicate networks (e.g., one for SNA, one for Token Ring, and another for non-IBM environments).
- It allows slow leased-line SNA networks to take advantage of the higher speeds offered by LAN
- It consolidates network traffic and minimizes potential points of failure, saving on network use costs.

More than 50,000 SNA networks and 500,000 cluster controllers are in use. About 10% of the IBM installed base still uses the binary synchronous communications (BSC) protocol. Most users have not yet integrated SNA with multiprotocol routing, but the promises of Synchronous Data Link Control for SNA and LAN integration have many organizations looking at various vendor solutions.

RUNNING SNA OVER LANS OR ETHERNET

There are several approaches to consider. One entails running SNA over LANs for local connectivity. SNA works well when front-end processors connect the host to terminal users over the Token Ring network. The token-passing scheme is deterministic; when time-slice parameters are properly configured, this can prevent terminal-to-host sessions from timing out. However, when traffic must travel between logically adjacent LANs on bridge and router internetworks, there are several problems that must be addressed.

One problem is that most bridge/routers are not able to distinguish between NetBIOS and SNA traffic, giving SNA the priority it needs to avoid session time-outs. Another problem is that even when access priority is available, it is applied only on the first access port into the network and is not continued on intermediate nodes throughout the network. Finally, there is always the possibility that too much traffic may congest the link. Although vendors offer dial capabilities on their bridge/routers to add more bandwidth before internal buffers reach user-defined fills, SNA users are too worried about mission-critical applications and have been reluctant to trust this approach until the technology is more proven.

Running SNA traffic over Ethernet is not advised because Ethernet's access method is a contention-based procedure called carrier-sense multiple access with collision detection (CSMA/CD). This procedure requires that each device on the Ethernet compete for use of the network when it senses that the network is idle. If two or more stations try to access the network at the same time, their data collide, forcing each station to back off and try again at staggered intervals. Thus, Ethernet's method of Media Access Control poses an insurmountable obstacle for SNA traffic.

For wide-area connectivity, a lot of thought has been given to running SNA traffic over TCP/IP-based networks. Generally, TCP/IP is not perceived as being as stable as SNA, largely because TCP/IP is based on a connectionless datagram service linking a relatively large number of routing nodes in a mesh configuration. This results in response times that can vary widely and that can often be slower than SNA users and applications expect. SNA is connection-oriented and assumes a single path between end points. It also has the requirement for a very deterministic response time. Terminal-to-host sessions are lost if terminals do not respond to host polls within a given time, and most multiprotocol routers cannot yet guarantee the type of deterministic response time that SNA requires.

RUNNING LAN TRAFFIC OVER SNA

With these problems in mind, an opposite approach has been developed that involves running LAN and WAN traffic over SNA. This is intended to bring SNA's inherent reliability advantages to the multiprotocol networking environment. However, most circuits used in conjunction with SNA operate at speeds of 19.6K b/s or less. This means that not much LAN traffic can run over the average SNA circuit, even though SNA has flow control to regulate the amount of data hitting the network all at once. Of course, the circuits used for SNA can be upgraded to handle the increased traffic, but this entails expensive upgrades to the front-end processors used to switch those circuits. For example, IBM's 3745 communications controller with a T1 (1.536M b/s) expansion unit can cost between $200,000 and $350,000. A less expensive alternative for running LAN protocols over SNA is to use IBM's Advanced Peer-to-Peer Networking (APPN), which is discussed later in this chapter.

INTEGRATION METHODS

There are several methods used to achieve SNAof the various methods is necessary to any successful LAN.

Emulation

One of the simplest (and oldest) ways for PCs on a LAN to access SNA host applications is through emulation. For a microcomputer to communicate with a mainframe, it must be made to do something it was not designed to—emulate a terminal so that it can be recognized as such by the mainframe. In the IBM environment, 3270 terminal emulation is used to permit synchronous data transfer between the microcomputers and the mainframe. With 3270 terminal emulation, data is exchanged in a format that is readily acceptable to the host.

Terminal emulation is accomplished through a micro-to-mainframe communications package consisting of software and hardware, which usually includes a coaxial cable interface for direct connection to a controller or LAN. Several 3270 terminal emulation products are available, providing 3278 or 3279 terminal emulation and supporting both direct coaxial and modem connections to 3174, 3274, and 3276 controllers without the requirement for additional mainframe software. In addition to allowing the user to save terminal screens, these emulation products allow the user to use hot keys to move between microcomputer and terminal sessions and to switch to file transfer menus and the Disk Operating System command line. With DOS and 3270 profiles, the existing keyboard can function in microcomputer and 3270 terminal configurations. A special program permits the user to modify these profiles or create entirely new ones, which may be enabled or disabled according to the user's needs.

To facilitate dial-up host access, most modems come with software for 3270 emulation. Although emulation products are still popular for accessing legacy data in the hierarchical computing environment, especially for occasional remote dial-up access to the mainframe, there are more efficient and economical interconnection methods available for use in the distributed computing environment that are used in conjunction with bridges, routers, and gateways.

Encapsulation

Encapsulation is the process of putting one type of data frame into another so that it will be recognized by the appropriate receiving device. The process allows different devices that use multiple protocols to share the same network. Encapsulation entails adding information to the beginning and end of the data unit to be transmitted. The added information is used to:

- Synchronize the receiving station with the signal
- Indicate the start and end of the frame
- Identify the addresses of sending and receiving stations
- Detect transmission errors

At the destination device, this envelope is stripped away and the original frame delivered to the appropriate user in the usual manner. There is significant overhead with this solution because one complete protocol runs inside another; however, any increase in transport capacity requirements and associated costs are usually offset by savings from eliminating the separate SNA network.

SDLC is the predominant protocol used between IBM hosts and terminals in an SNA network. Encapsulating an SDLC packet within TCP/IP or another routable protocol alleviates the fixed-path limitation of SNA by

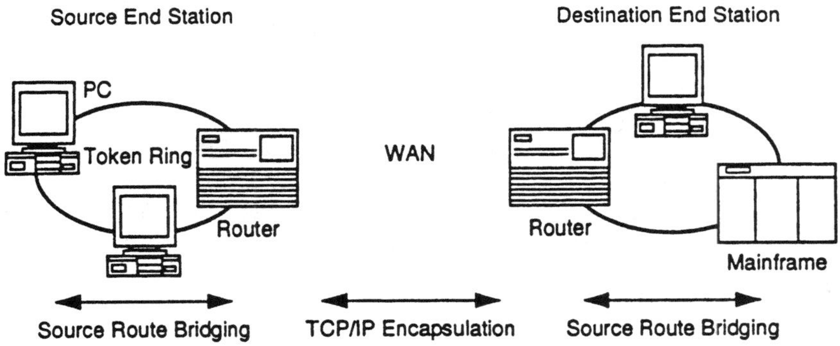

Note:
At the source end station, SNA data is bridged through local source route bridging (SRB) network. The data is encapsulated in TCP/IP packet by an access router and forwarded across the WAN. At the destination end station, the TCP/IP envelope is stripped off at the remote router and the data is delivered in the original SRB format.

Exhibit 1. Encapsulating SNA/SDLC within TCP/IP.

stuffing SDLC data packets into a TCP/IP envelope, which can then be routed across the internetwork (Exhibit 1). This routing method offers the advantages of adaptive and dynamic routing, including best-route selection , load sharing, and the use of redundant links. These are not available under SNA.

SDLC encapsulation within IP solves some problems while creating others. SNA was designed with the assumption that a reliable, connection-oriented data link exists beneath the upper layers of the protocol. The SNA data link control layer provides deterministic delivery of packets. Encapsulating SDLC packets within IP violates SNA's inherent design. In a large IP network with a potentially large end-to-end delay, the nondeterministic nature of IP can become a critical problem.

Under SNA, the primary SDLC station (usually at the host end of the link) and the secondary SDLC station (usually at the establishment or cluster controller end) exchange polls and acknowledgments. The primary station maintains a timer and terminates the session if the secondary station does not respond to polls quickly enough.

One of the problems with IP is that it cannot guarantee delivery of SDLC frames before the timer expires. Another problem is the size of the packets needed to handle simple functions, such as the exchange of frames to keep an SNA session alive when no data is being transmitted. These session keep-alive frames are 2 bytes; if they are encapsulated in a TCP/IP packet with a 20-byte TCP header and a 20-byte IP header, then 42-byte IP packets would continuously traverse the IP network even when the SNA end stations have nothing to send. This puts unnecessary traffic on the network.

One solution to the time-out problem entails the use of routers that answer the polls locally. This local polling termination solution is based on logical link conrol 2 (LLC2), which is a protocol developed by IEEE to facilitate data transmission over Token Ring LANs. Previously, the controllers performed LLC2 polling of remote devices. Now, the LLC2 capability is built into bridges, bridge/routers, and standalone converter units.

With local termination, the router connected to a 37x5 communications controller, for example, acknowledges the polls from the 37x5 controller; the router connected to the 3x74 establishment controller issues polls to the 3x74. Local acknowledgment of the polls obviates the need for acknowledgment data to be sent over wide-area links; it also helps keep SNA sessions active during congestion or after a failure while the router tries to find a new data path. Although this feature works well, it makes network management more difficult, because what was once a single session is now essentially three sessions: SNA LLC2 local acknowledgment from end node to router, a TCP/IP session between routers, and local acknowledgment from remote router to remote end node.

Another solution is to assign priorities to the traffic so that delay-sensitive SNA/SDLC traffic can be sent out by the router before delay-tolerant traffic. Using the router's management system, priority can be assigned according to protocol, port, source or destination address, or any bit pattern defined by a priority control filter. As many as a few dozen filters can be created for each protocol supported on each of the router's synchronous interfaces. For each protocol, some products also allow users to assign priority levels to each application (e.g., urgent, high, normal, and low). Low priority traffic is queued, whereas high priority traffic is forwarded immediately.

Still another priority control mechanism is based on bandwidth reservation. This approach ensures uninterrupted service during peak traffic periods and works by dividing the available bandwidth among the various user protocols, such as TCP/IP, SNA/SDLC, or Internetwork Packet eXchange. Received frames are placed in their respective protocol-related queue and then passed to a serial link queue, from which they are sent out over the serial link. Frames with a protocol assigned a higher percentage of bandwidth are passed to the serial link queue more often than those assigned a lesser amount of bandwidth. During low traffic periods, existing traffic is assigned the unused bandwidth by passing frames of the corresponding protocols more frequently over the serial link.

Encapsulation is one of the most popular solutions for integrating SNA and LAN traffic and for sending both traffic types over the TCP/IP-based

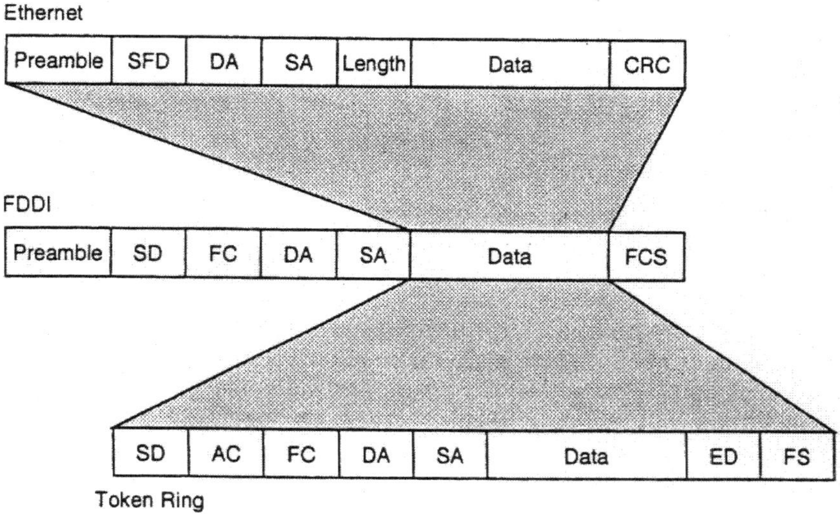

Notes:

AC Access control
CRC Cyclic redundancy check
DA Destination address
ED Ending delimiter
FC Frame control
FS Frame status
SA Source address
SD Starting delimiter

Exhibit 2. Encapsulating Ethernet and Token Ring frames within FDDI.

Internet. It has other uses as well. Encapsulation can be used to integrate IBM and Digital Equipment Corporation host environments over the Internet and to send Ethernet or Token Ring packets over an FDDI backbone (Exhibit 2).

When applied to SNA, the use of encapsulation permits the creation of cohesive, enterprisewide internetworks that have the following advantages:

- They reduce communication costs by combining SDLC serial traffic from SNA devices with LAN traffic.
- They provide an economical migration path for older SNA cluster controllers and front-end processors to Token Ring peer-to-peer networking.
- They improve cluster controller/front-end processor performance by speeding up the communication lines from the slow (4.8K b/s and 9.6K b/s) serial lines employed by SNA to WAN link speeds exceeding 64K b/s.
- They preserve investments in legacy systems, applications, and data.

Frame Relay

One of the newest data transmission technologies is frame relay, a WAN service specifically designed for LAN interconnection. A frame relay access device (FRAD) is used to access the frame relay service. It encapsulates non-frame relay traffic such as SNA into the frame relay format. The FRAD builds a new frame around a received packet. At the remote end, the FRAD performs this process in reverse, taking the original packet out of its envelope before sending it to the appropriate terminal. The FRAD capability is integrated into many bridge/routers.

Translation (also known as protocol conversion) is the conversion of one protocol into another; it is a more processing-intensive task than encapsulation. In the case of frame relay, SDLC traffic is converted into native frame relay packets by a Frame Relay Access Node, eliminating the need for FRADs at all network locations. The SDLC port on the frame relay access node (FRAN) supports such devices as IBM's 3174 cluster controller. The FRAN converts incoming SDLC traffic to the frame relay format and sends it over a frame relay network to a bridge/router or front-end processor. As long as the remote device supports frame relay, no additional FRADs or FRANs are needed. The FRAN even performs local SDLC polling to keep that traffic from entering the frame relay network.

Standalone Converters and Other Solutions

Some internetworking vendors offer economical standalone units that convert SDLC to Token Ring's Logical Link Control protocol. Such devices take SDLC output off a cluster controller, convert it to LLC2, and put it on the Token Ring. Like other LAN traffic, the data can then be fed to the internetwork through a router or bridge. Such products are designed primarily to provide SDLC-to-LLC conversion at remote offices and in workgroup environments.

Some users like the idea of the standalone converter because it is a separate device that can be easily connected or disconnected from the LAN backbone. However, a separate device increases network cost and requires maintenance. Not only can the extra cost and maintenance become an extra burden to network managers, but the device itself constitutes another potential point of failure on the network.

Another solution entails the framing of SNA data within an IP header before it reaches the TCP/IP network. Once the SNA/IP data leaves the controller, it can be routed anywhere in the IP network through all leading routers. When the data is through the network, a mainframe-attached gateway receives the SNA/IP frame, removes the TCP/IP information, and passes the original SNA data to the mainframe through the SNA 3172 channel interface.

Synchronous Passthrough

Synchronous passthrough is a point-to-point SNA/LAN integration method that encapsulates all SDLC frames within an IP frame. The difference between synchronous passthrough and traditional encapsulation is that synchronous passthrough includes SNA's control information, acknowledgments, and polling. The frame is passed over a TCP/IP network between the host front-end processor and downstream SNA devices, such as 3174 cluster controllers, without alteration. Although this method of native mode transport is valued for its simplicity and may make SNA users feel more at ease, it has disadvantages.

The big disadvantage of synchronous passthrough is that it transports general polls and acknowledgments end-to-end across the network. This can increase traffic congestion and the risk of SNA session time-outs from possible extended delays. This congestion can be overcome by adding more bandwidth on the backbone, but this method significantly increases network operating costs. Another disadvantage of synchronous passthrough is that when sessions are dropped, the network management system is not necessarily alerted to the event.

Few SNA users have shown a willingness to move SNA traffic to the Internet, but many router vendors believe that once the level of service can be guaranteed, user acceptance will increase. Accordingly, some vendors have built into their routers the capability to prioritize SNA traffic according to packet type, protocol type, and router port number, ensuring that interactive 3270 terminal traffic on the Internet gets the response time it requires to keep host sessions active.

LU 6.2 Connectivity

Users requiring faster response times than host-based products offer can employ Logical Unit 6.2-based LAN connectivity products. These offer direct connections between LANs , instead of having to go through the front-end processor using SDLC (Exhibit 3). When a front-end processor (FEP) is used, the request is wrapped in an SDLC packet, which is routed through the Front-End Processor. The Front-End Processor offers a high degree of control and security. However, when an LU 6.2 session is used to exchange information between LANs directly, response time is substantially reduced.

Advanced Peer-to-Peer Networking

IBM's solution for SNA is IBM's next-generation SNA technology for linking devices without the use of a mainframe. Specifically, it is IBM's proprietary SNA routing scheme for client/server computing in multiprotocol environments. As such, it is part of IBM's LU 6.2 architecture, also known

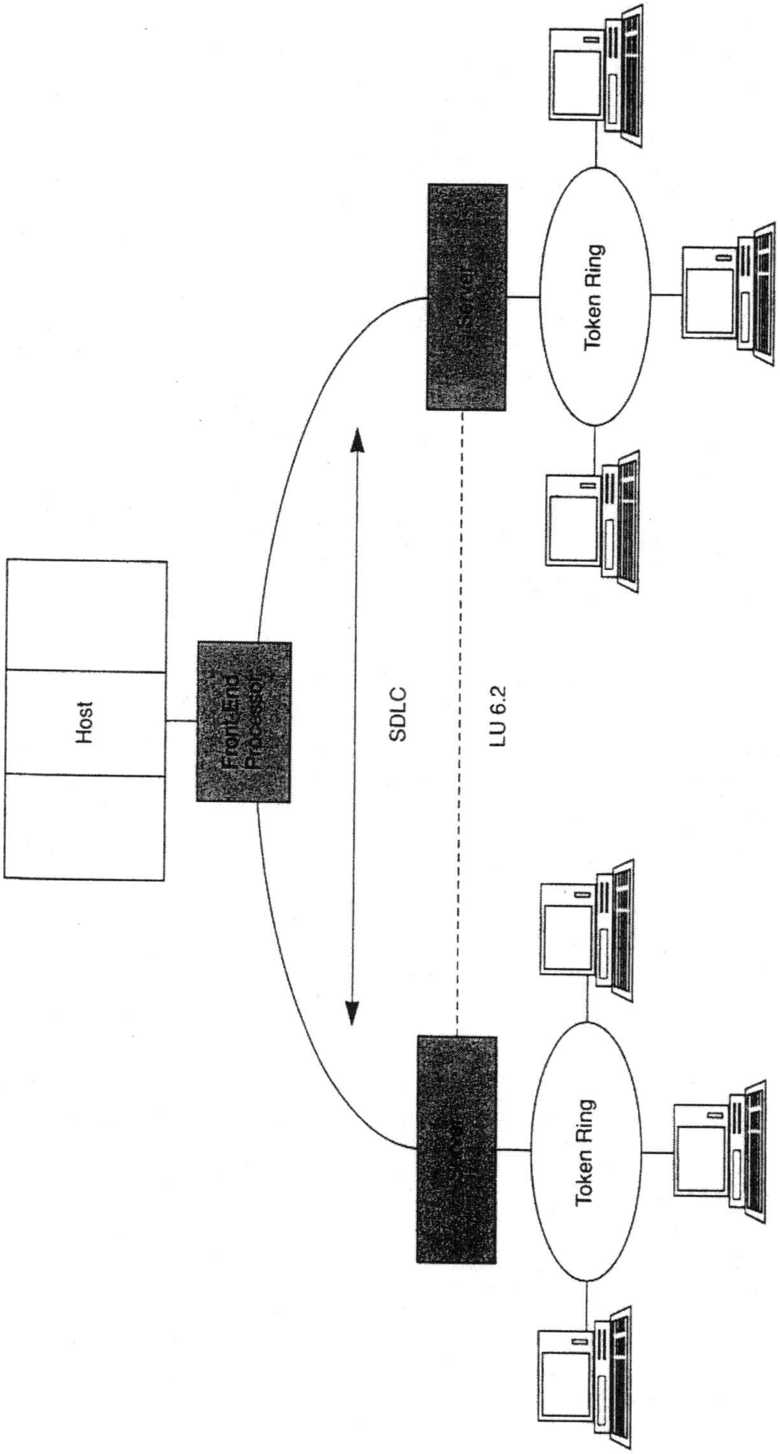

Exhibit 3. LU 6.2-based LAN connectivity.

as Advanced Program-to-Program Communications (APPC), which facilitates communications between programs running on different platforms. The components of the strategy include:

- Integration of WAN (i.e., SNA networks)and LANs across a wide range of protocols
- Development of effective openness, defined as a customer's ability to choose the best product for a given task from several available options
- Recognition that most customer networks have some element of protocol heterogeneity that underscores the need for true openness
- Radical transformation of SNA without disrupting the installed base. Announced and proposed APPN extensions to SNA will help customers leverage existing network investments while providing access to technical advances. In addition, licensing of APPN technology to third-party vendors should contribute to the openness initiative.
- Bandwidth management through APPN and future products that use standards-based carrier services. Value-added capabilities (i.e., priority and route assignment algorithms) will provide higher performance networking at lower costs.
- Establishment of a distributed computing infrastructure that blurs the definitions of networking and computers. Affordable networking services that are easy-to-use, efficient, and reliable will form the basis for increasingly sophisticated distributed computing.

Whereas network processors differ in efficiency, performance, and security, they share enough similarities to make peer-to-peer networking relationships attractive. Before the decade is over, IBM expects applications to run on many platforms across all essential network protocols with support intersecting vendor boundaries. APPN and its extensions are being positioned as integral pieces of a worldwide internetwork that will provide conventional and advanced data services for all classes of network traffic. By effecting peer-to-peer communications among all network devices, APPN helps SNA users connect to LAN networks and more effectively create and use client/server applications. APPN supports multiple protocols, including TCP/IP, and allows applications to be independent of the transport protocols that deliver them by providing a set of common transport semantics.

APPN's other benefits include allowing information routing without a host, tracking network topology, and simplifying network configuration and changes. For users still supporting 3270 applications, APPN can address dependent local unit protocols as well as the newer LU 6.2 sessions, which means that a site's investment in applications relying on older local unit protocols is protected.

The mainframe's participation in APPN is accomplished through IBM's Advanced Communications Function/Virtual Telecommunication Access Method (ACF/VTAM) version 4.1 for MVS/ESA. A longstanding criticism of SNA has been that it requires extensive, repetitive resource definitions. The new version of ACF/VTAM changes the method by which mainframes define routes, device definitions, and message flows for each terminal session, simplifying the definition process and improving efficiency. The plug-and-play changes to Virtual Telecommunications Access Method also make it easier for mainframes to act as peers to the rest of the network and participate in distributed processing.

Included in the APPN architecture are Automatic Network Routing (ANR) and Rapid Transport Protocol (RTP) features. These features route data around network failures and provide performance advantages that close the gap with TCP/IP. ANR provides end-to-end routing over APPN networks, eliminating the intermediate routing functions of early APPN implementations, while RTP provides flow control and error recovery.

APPN has been slow to garner support among potential users, mostly because it is costly to license and complicated to implement. The availability of third-party support may turn Advanced Peer-to-Peer Networking into a successor to SNA and a viable competitor to TCP/IP.

Data Link Switching

IBM's DLSw uses TCP/IP to move SNA and NetBIOS traffic over multiprotocol backbones. The TCP/IP protocol stack provides the dynamic routing and transport functions, whereas the DLSw protocol has features that reduce session time-outs and broadcast overhead. Because it is based on TCP/IP, DLSw can also be used with point-to-point routing and Open Shortest Path First (OSPF) protocols.

DLSw operates at the data link layer, unobtrusive to SNA data, through the connection-oriented protocol function, LLC2 termination. Together, DLSw and LLC2 provide sequential delivery of data, keeping multiprotocol sessions alive and preventing the delays that cause SNA timeouts. In addition to faking the polling requirements of SDLC in a process called "spoofing," DLSw does end-to-end flow control and acknowledges dropped packets.

DLSw is not without its disadvantages, however. For example, DLSw does not allow classes of SNA service to be defined. Such class distinctions are necessary to convey many different types of SNA applications across the network—terminal, printer, and file transfer, for example.

Nevertheless, DLSw is becoming more accepted by the internetworking industry: IBM has implemented DLSw in its 6611 router and about a dozen other vendors have announced their intention to support it in their products. DLSw is currently being studied by the Internet Engineering Task Force for possible submission for standardization by the IEEE.

CONCLUSION

For years, SNA networks and LAN internetworks moved along separate paths. Now the wall between SNA and LAN networks is buckling under the pressure of new user demands. Corporate downsizing and distributed computing are among the trends that are forcing companies to consolidate the two types of networks.

Given the vast installed base of SNA and LAN networks, the movement toward consolidation makes sense. In fact, the case for interconnecting the two types of networks is so compelling that justifying it with cost savings, operational benefits, and simplified administration is often unnecessary.

Despite widespread agreement on the wisdom of joining the two network environments, the products available for executing such plans are still relatively new, and vendor strategies may still need refinement. Users contemplating this type of network consolidation should keep this fact in mind when evaluating and comparing the various approaches and vendor offerings.

Chapter 56
SNA Over Frame Relay

Dick Thunen

Frame relay is replacing expensive leased lines as organizations migrate to packet-based networks. This chapter examines how frame relay has become an integral part of IBM's overall wide-area internetworking strategy for integrating SNA and multiprotocol LANs.

INTRODUCTION

Today most telecommunications carriers provide frame relay services that allow the IBM Systems Network Architecture (SNA) user to reap a number of benefits, including:

- Investment protection in SNA devices
- Lower line costs compared with dedicated links
- Up to 40% increases in network utilization through frame relay's multiprotocol support
- Sustained integrity and control of the SNA network with NetView and Simple Network Management Protocol (SNMP) management
- Integration of SNA and multiprotocol LANs
- High-performance access networking for Advanced Peer-to-Peer Networking (APPN) and a migration path to Asynchronous Transfer Mode backbones.

Traditional IBM host networks connect users to mainframes via SNA or bisynchronous multidrop lines. These are usually low-speed analog lines that represent a single point-of-failure between user and host. Even though these networks subject network managers to the complexities of dealing with a multitude of leased lines, many organizations continue to maintain their IBM host networks because of the mission-critical applications they support.

IBM Corp. introduced X.25 as a cost-effective alternative to private lines. Many network planners have chosen not to implement it, however, because of higher user-response times from network overhead delays

0-8493-9989-0/99/$0.00+$.50

caused by every node in the X.25 network performing error detection/correction, message sequencing, and flow control. Frame relay, however, performs these functions only at the network access points using an end-to-end protocol; thus Frame relay uses the network more efficiently.

IBM has developed a set of SNA Frame relay products for packet-based, Wide Area Network (WANs). Frame relay is an integral element of the evolution of SNA networks into the future with full support for APPN and Asynchronous Transfer Mode.

FRAME RELAY TECHNOLOGY: AN OVERVIEW

Frame relay is a relatively new technology offering virtual private-line replacement. As a network interface, it traces its origins to Integrated Services Digital Network (ISDN).

When ISDN was being developed, two transport services were envisioned: circuit-mode services for voice and transparent data, and packet (i.e., X.25 and Frame relay) mode for data. Frame relay has since evolved into a network interface in its own right, independent of ISDN. It is now specified as a set of American National Standards Institute (ANSI) and International Telecommunications Union (ITU) standards.

The User Perspective

Although services are typically available with transmission rates from 64K bps to T1/E1 (1.53/2.05M bps), Frame relay is defined as an access interface up to T3 or 45M bps. By contrast, the typical Synchronous Data Link Control multidrop line is a 4.8K or 9.6K bps analog line. The transmission of a typical two-page text document on a Frame relay network takes 1/4 second at 64K bps and 1/100 second at 1.53M bps. Transmission of the same two-page text document on an SDLC multidrop line takes 3 1/3 seconds at 4.8K bps and 1 1/6 seconds at 9.6K bps.

To the user, a Frame relay network appears simple and straightforward. Users connect directly to destinations on the far side of the network. Frame relay provides logically defined links—commonly called Data Link Connection Identifier (DLCIs), permanent virtual circuits, or permanent logical links (PLLs)—for a permanent virtual connection.

For example, user A is connected across the Frame relay network through separate permanent virtual circuits to both user B and user C. The permanent virtual circuits are multiplexed across user A's Frame relay interface. Frame relay networks guarantee bandwidth to each permanent virtual circuit, but allow unused bandwidth to be shared by all active users. The guaranteed bandwidth of a permanent virtual circuit is specified as the committed information rate (CIR) of the permanent virtual circuits. A

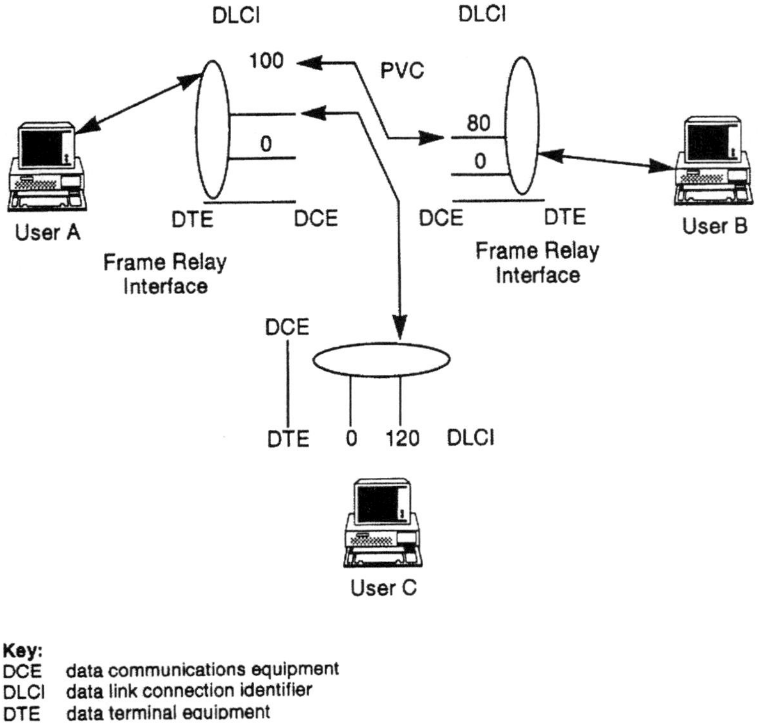

Exhibit 1. Frame relay Permanent Virtual Circuit (PVC).

user's traffic can have transmission data rates in excess of the CIR, referred to as the burst rate of the permanent virtual circuits.

User B appears to user A with Frame relay address data link connection identifiers 100, and user A appears to user B with data link connection identifiers 80. A permanent virtual circuit connects user A's Frame relay interface through the Frame relay network to user B's Frame relay interface. Each user's data link connection identifiers numbers have local significance only. User A has a second Permanent Virtual Circuit with its own data link connection identifiers number connecting to user C. In addition, each user has a Local Management Interface, typically on data link connection identifiers 0 (see Exhibit 1).

The Frame Relay Frame

Each Frame relay access station is responsible for transforming the data into Frame relay packets for transport (i.e., relay) over the network. Each frame contains the following elements:

- ***Flag.*** The flag indicates the start and end of a frame relay packet.
- ***Frame relay header.*** The header contains the destination of the user data packet and management information.
- ***User data.*** The user data contains the data to be transported across the Frame relay network.
- ***Frame check sequence.*** The Frame Check Sequence allows the integrity of the data to be validated.

The Frame relay network receives, transports, and delivers variable-length frames. The Frame relay network consists of a group of interconnected nodes (i.e., switches) that relay the data across the network on the appropriate permanent virtual circuits. A Frame relay switch uses only the data link connection identifiers information contained in the Frame relay header to forward the frame across the network to its destination (see Exhibit 2).

The path through the network is transparent to the user. The data link connection identifier does not include any description of how the connection transverses the network or the routing topology of the network. A frame relay network operates an Open Systems Interconnection (OSI) layer 2 router network. Each Frame Relay Access Node puts the Routing Information (destination Data Link Connection Identifier) in the data link layer (i.e., Frame relay header) of the frame. The Frame relay network uses only this information to relay the frame across the network. (See Exhibit 3.) In other words, the Frame relay network nodes look only at the Frame relay header and the FCS.

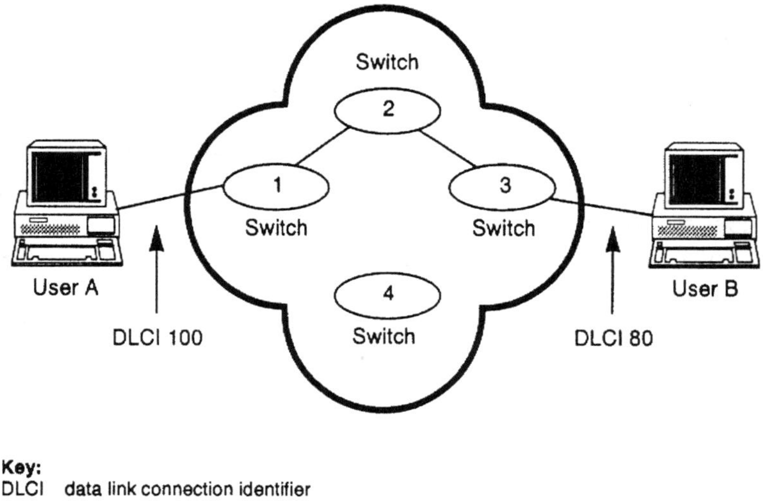

Exhibit 2. Frame relay network showing PVC connecting User A and User B.

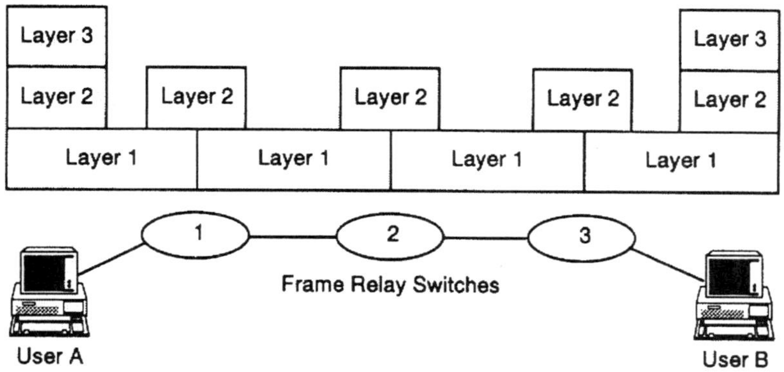

Exhibit 3. Layer 2 router network.

The Frame relay switch, or node, uses the following review process to forward frames across the network:

- The integrity of the frame is checked using the frame check sequence; if an error is indicated, the frame is discarded.
- The destination data link connection identifier address is validated, and if it is invalid, the frame is discarded. The data link connection identifier's destination address is contained in the Frame relay header of the frame.
- All frames that are not discarded as a result of the FCS or Data Link Connection Identifier checks are forwarded. The Frame relay node makes no attempt to correct the frame or to request a retransmission of the frame. This results in an efficient network, but requires that the user end-stations assume responsibility for error recovery, message sequencing, and flow control.
- Thus, Frame relay switches do not look at the user data packets, which makes the network transparent to all protocols operating at levels above OSI level 2.

RFC 1490

Because Frame relay networks do not look at the contents of the user data, any format can be used to packetize the data, such as X.25 or High-level Data Link Control. IBM uses Logical Link Control type 2 (LLC2) as its frame relay SNA data format.

The IBM format is based on ANSI T1.617a Annex F, which covers encapsulating protocol traffic in frame relay. This process has been approved by the Frame relay forum and is included in its Multiprotocol Encapsulation Agreement. IBM's treatment of a Frame relay network is based on standards and promotes interoperability with third-party implementations.

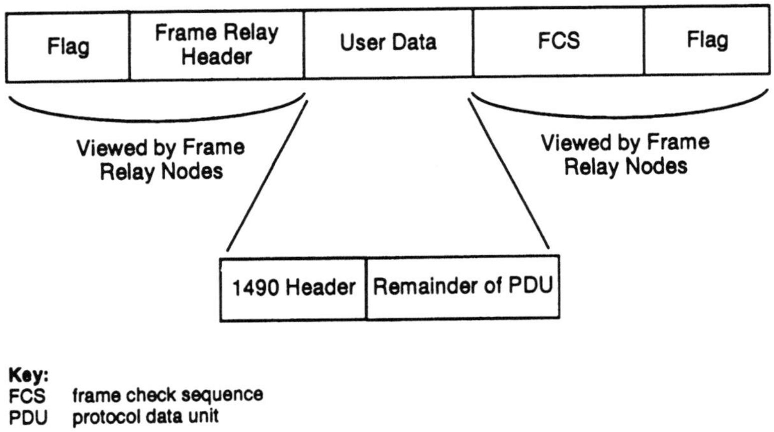

Exhibit 4. RFC 1490 Frame relay Frame format.

IBM uses the LLC2 frame format and protocol for transporting SNA across Token Ring and Ethernet LANs.

For SNA data, the Regional Financial Center 1490 header designates that it is 802.2 (LLC2) data, whether it is SNA subarea, peripheral, or Advanced Peer-to-Peer Networking data, and the LLC2 destination and source addresses. This format, illustrated in Exhibit 4, is also used for NetBIOS data.

Users connected to the network using RFC 1490 Frame relay Data Terminal Equipment have a logical view of the Frame relay network as a virtual LAN. IBM's use of RFC 1490 for its Frame relay equipment provides a familiar metaphor to System Network Architecture users.

Because the Frame relay network does not look at the contents of user data, it allows the multiplexing of multiple protocols across a single Frame relay interface. Frame relay network access nodes are responsible for converting the user data into the appropriate RFC 1490 format for SNA and LAN traffic. In summary, a frame relay WAN:

- Provides packet-mode technology
- Does not utilize store-and-forward
- Relies on intelligent endpoints and high-integrity lines
- Results in low transit delay
- Is transparent above layer 2
- As a result, Frame relay provides a cost-effective alternative to dedicated-line networks.

FRAME RELAY AS A REPLACEMENT FOR SDLC

Frame relay delivers enhanced services compared with alternative SNA WAN techniques such as SDLC. Frame relay:

- Uses the same framing and Cyclic Redundancy Checking bits as SDLC. This means that all front-end processor (FEP) SDLC line interface couplers (LICs), modems, and DSUs/CSUs, can be used with frame relay.
- Usually allows for frames up to 2,106 bytes in a Frame relay network, but IBM's Network Control Program allows for the configuration of up to 8,250-byte frames for use on high-quality, private Frame relay networks. Large packets reduce network overhead and improve network performance.
- Allows network access connections from 56/64K bps to T1/E1 speeds, whereas the typical multidrop connection is 4.8/9.6K bps. User response times are directly improved by efficient network backbone connectivity.
- Is implemented in software (like SDLC), which means that no hardware changes in either the FEP or remote devices are required to move to Frame relay.
- Can be managed by NetView management by network control program (NCP) for both SDLC and Frame relay connections. Therefore, familiar network management tools and practices can be used on the Frame relay network.
- Adds multiple protocol transport. All protocols can be transported across the Frame relay network; SDLC supports only SNA traffic.
- Provides SNA guaranteed bandwidth through the PVC's committed information rate.
- Requires no host application changes to migrate from SDLC to Frame relay.
- Supports point-to-point connections, like SDLC. Frame relay also provides many-to-many connections; SDLC requires a multidrop line to provide one-to-many connections.
- Provides for transparent network routing. SDLC is a single physical path connection.
- Supports burst mode, which lets users exceed their Committed Information Rates of the link.

SNA FRAME RELAY NETWORKS

IBM provides connections for Frame relay networks on all its current networking products, including 3745 communication controller, 3172 interconnect controller, OS/2 RouteXpander/2, 3174 network server, AS/400, and the 6611 network processor. Users can evolve their SNA networks from an SDLC multidrop backbone to a Frame relay WAN. IBM supports all SNA topologies: Intermediate Network Node, Boundary Network Node, SNA

Network Interconnect, and Advanced Peer-to-Peer Networking across a Frame relay network.

IBM's Frame relay products are configured as Frame relay Data Terminal Equipment devices, except the FEP (3745 communication controller), which can also be configured as a Frame relay data communications equipment (DCE) device and can act as a Frame relay switch.

Intermediate Network Node (INN)

IBM's Network Control Program software provides an INN connection—PU4-to-PU4—between front-end processor over a Frame relay network. This support was first announced for network control program (NCP) Version 6, Release 1 (V6R1) in 1992. IBM supports mixed-media, multiple-link transmission groups that can include Frame relay, SDLC, and Token Ring links. Thus, Frame relay can be incorporated with other data link types in a transmission group to give users flexibility in network design.

Because Frame relay is an Open Systems Interconnection level 2 routing protocol, it provides fast INN routing, which is an efficient means of interconnecting multiple FEP. Level 2 Frame relay eliminates SNA processing on intermediate FEP. Furthermore, as each pair of FEPs appears to be directly linked, the intermediate network configuration is transparent to SNA routing algorithms.

SNA Network Interconnect (SNI)

NCP Release 6, Version 1 also introduced SNA over Frame relay for interconnecting multiple SNA networks. Two traditional SNA networks can be connected using a SNI link over Frame relay so the users of one SNA network can access the resources or applications of another across a Frame relay network.

Boundary Network Node (BNN)

NCP Version 7, Release 1 fully expands the role of the network control program (NCP) to that of providing System Network Architecture Boundary Network Node—PU4-to-PU2—connectivity between an network control program (NCP) and an SNA node (PU2/2.1). The FEP can establish an SNA/BNN connection across a Frame relay network with users on a 3174 network processor or users connected through an IBM 6611 network server or RouteXpander/2.

AS/400

IBM's AS/400 supports direct Frame relay connectivity to another AS/400, or through a Frame relay bridge to a 5494 remote controller or PC workstation. SNA nodes connected to an AS/400 across a frame relay network must be SNA Type 2.1 nodes, such as an IBM 5494 remote controller.

APPN

IBM's APPN Network Node products, 6611 IBM Network Processor, AS/400, and OS/2 Communication Manager (RouteXpander/2) can be configured to establish an APPN network across a Frame relay WAN.

APPN end-node applications can thus take advantage of the combined Frame relay and APPN network.

IBM Legacy Devices

Many IBM networks include legacy devices that are incapable of supporting Frame relay network access, such as 3274 controllers, System 3X computers, and 5394 controllers. A Frame relay assembler/disassembler (FRAD) provides connection to a Frame relay network for a non-frame relay capable device.

A FRAD translates the SNA controller's SDLC data stream into Frame relay frames for transport over the network. FRADs based on Regional Financial Center 1490 can interoperate across a Frame relay network with IBM's Frame relay products. Interoperability with IBM requires that the SDLC be converted to LLC2 for encapsulation in Frame relay.

In addition to basic framing functions, a FRAD usually concentrates a number of low- or medium-speed SDLC lines into a single, high-speed Frame relay link. By combining data from multiple, low-speed controllers onto one or more high-speed lines, FRADs reduce overall network costs.

Private Frame Relay Network

NCP Version 6, Release 2 (V6R2) adds Data Circuit-terminating Equipment support to the FEP. The FEP functions as a Frame relay switch (i.e., DCE) for Frame relay data terminal equipment (DTE), such as an OS/2 RouteXpander, so users can create private Frame relay networks based on the IBM FEP. Private Frame relay networks support both SNA and LAN protocols. In summary:

- All current IBM SNA products provide Frame relay network access.
- All SNA topologies are supported across a Frame relay network.
- FRADs can be used to provide high-performance connectivity for Legacy IBM SDLC and Binary Synchronous Communications devices.

IBM MULTIPROTOCOL SUPPORT

IBM's frame relay access products use the Regional Financial Center 1490 standard, which specifies the frame format and characteristics for multiplexing multiple protocols across a Frame relay network on a single Frame relay link.

Treatment of LAN protocols is similar to that described for SNA over Frame relay. The Regional Financial Center 1490 header for LAN protocols indicates whether the packet is being bridged or routed. A bridged frame header includes what media it is originating on—802.3, 802.4, 802.5, FDDI, or 802.6—whether it is being source routed or transparently bridged, and its destination medium access control (MAC) address.

Some routed protocols have an assigned Direct network layer Protocol Identifier, or NLPID, such as IP. For these protocols the NLPID is used to identify the frame. Otherwise, the Subnetwork Access Protocol (SNAP) header for the frame is used to identify frame contents.

RFC 1490 specifies the transport of both bridged and routed LAN protocols across a common Frame relay interface and provides a standard format for the Frame relay packets. RFC 1490 specifies for bridged data the protocol being used—source route or transparent—and thus facilitates multivendor networking based on industry standard implementations. For routed data, however, there is currently no means of specifying the routing protocol being used for a given LAN protocol, so interoperability of routed protocols is more complicated.

All of IBM's Frame relay products provide for multiprotocol support over Frame relay. This support is available over public and private Frame relay networks and includes both the bridging and routing of LAN protocols. The IBM 6611 also allows SNA/SDLC traffic to be transported across a Frame relay WAN.

NETWORK MANAGEMENT

With the addition of frame relay as a packet-mode WAN supported by IBM's Network Control Program software, IBM incorporates support for Frame relay WAN in NetView network management software, including NPM and NTune and NetView/6000, its Simple Network Management Protocol manager. IBM provides a complete picture of the SNA and Frame relay internetwork including both SNA and non-SNA traffic and Data Terminal Equipment devices. Exhibit 5 shows the SNA network management topology.

NetView Management Services

Although simple network management protocol and other open network management standards continue to evolve, NetView remains the only way to provide comprehensive network management, control, and diagnosis of an SNA network. All SNA network nodes are inherently commandable from NetView and report all network management-related

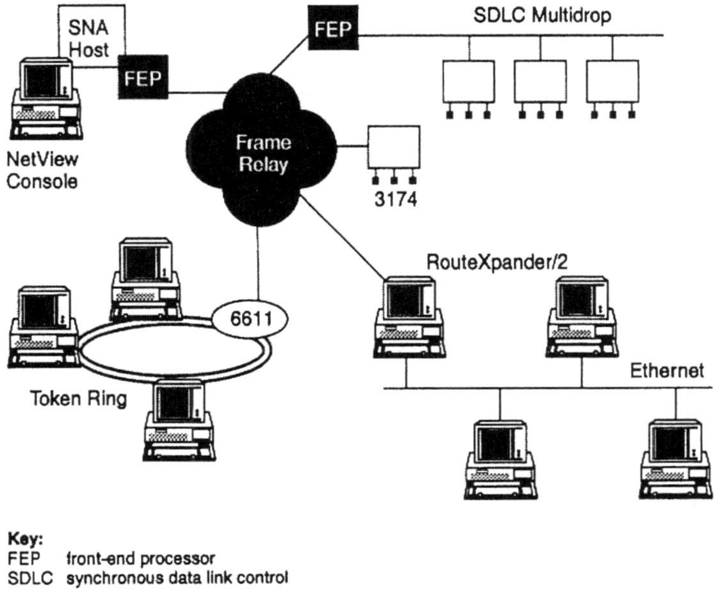

Exhibit 5. SNA network management topology.

activities directly to NetView for processing by one of its function-specific applications.

IBM's NetView support extends NetView management of the SNA network across the Frame relay network to the end user's controller. This support allows complete SNA network visibility and control with no remote-line and physical unit black holes, compatibility with existing NetView tools and applications, and virtually no operator retraining.

Virtual Telecommunications Access Method (VTAM) Network Control Program (NCP)

The Virtual Telecommunications Access Method Dynamic Reconfiguration (DR) facility supports the addition of network control program (NCP) Frame relay Data Link Connection Identifier. Permanent Virtual Circuit can be created or deleted without interrupting the Frame relay network or regenerating network control program (NCP).

Alternative Routing

NCP provides alternative automatic routing by a private Frame relay network if a primary (i.e., public) Frame relay network becomes unavailable.

Local Management Interface (LMI)

A reserved link address (local data link connection identifiers) is used for communication between the FRAD and the Frame relay network. The management interfaces are defined by ANSI T1.617-1991 Annex D and ITT Q.933 Annex A for data link connection identifiers 0. Users are able to specify either the ANSI or ITT Local Management Interface implementation as part of the configuration. This data link connection identifiers is used for communicating network resources (i.e., the list of valid data link connection identifiers), determining the link status of each data link connection identifiers, and determining network status.

The local management interface data link connection identifiers cannot be used for data traffic. A status-inquiry message is used to query the status of the network. The status message is either a keep-alive message or a full-network status report. The status update message reports an unsolicited status change in a network component.

Frame Relay Network Congestion

The Frame relay network provides notification of network congestion to end-user devices. Upon encountering congestion, a Frame relay switch provides forward notification of network congestion along the data route by setting the Forward Explicit Congestion Notification bit in the Frame relay header, as shown in Exhibit 6.

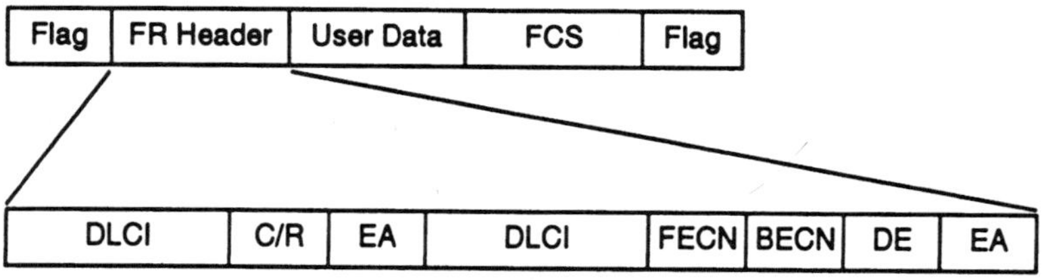

Key:
BECN backward explicit congestion notification
C/R committed information rate
DE discard eligibility
DLCI data link connection identifier
FECN forward explicit congestion notification

Exhibit 6. Frame relay header.

The network also notifies the sending node of congestion along the PVC by setting the Backward Explicit Congestion Notification bit of packets going to the sender along the permanent virtual circuits. The bit is changed from 0 to 1 to indicate the presence of congestion. Network congestion is

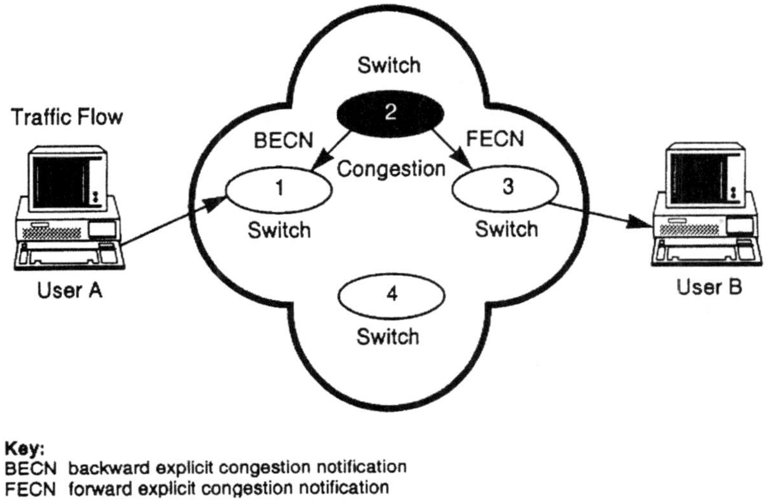

Exhibit 7. Congestion notification.

determined by a switch using the switch's queue length or buffer utilization. (See Exhibit 7.)

It is the function of the Frame Relay Access Node, or data terminal equipment (DTE) device, to respond to the forward explicit congestion notification (FECN) and backward explicit congestion notification (BECN) bits. IBM's Frame relay devices respond by controlling the transmit window size of devices transmitting on the congested Data Link Connection Identifier. When a Frame relay DTE receives notification of network congestion, it reduces its transmit window to 1. Once a network has indicated that it is returning to a normal state, the transmit windows are increased a frame at a time until they return to their normal transmit windows.

Consolidate Link Layer Message (CLLM)

If there are no frames returning to the sender, the end node can determine the presence of congestion over a data link connection identifiers through the CLLM information on the next query. The network is otherwise prohibited from notifying the sender of congestion on the data link connection identifiers.

Discard Eligibility Bit

Frame relay access nodes can mark frames for Discard Eligibility by the network as a means of reducing congestion during moderate traffic congestion periods. When the discard eligibility bit in a frame is set to 1, the user has indicated that the frame can be discarded if it encounters network congestion.

The network sets the discard eligibility bit to 1 on data that follows on a physical link in excess of the Committed Information Rates. Thus, the network can be divided into the following three zones:

- *Guaranteed transmission.* The data flow is less than the CIR
- *Transmit if possible.* The data flow is above the CIR but less than the maximum rate.
- *Discard excess frames.* The data flow is above the maximum rate. The Frame relay network does not notify a user of frames being discarded. It is the responsibility of the FRADs to monitor the integrity of the data flow.

SNMP Management

Proliferation of LAN internetworks often leads to a separate management organization seeking a common management platform for multivendor equipment. Often the solution is simple network management protocol. Most of IBM's Frame relay products can be configured with an Simple Network Management Protocol agent for management by IBM's NetView/6000 simple network management protocol Manager.

Support of concurrent simple network management protocol and NetView enables each functional operations group, System Network Architecture and LAN internetwork, to execute their respective network management and control responsibilities through their management platform of choice.

FRAME RELAY COMPARED WITH ROUTER NETWORKS

IBM's products transmit LAN, System Network Architecture, and Advanced Peer-to-Peer Networking traffic across a frame relay WAN. The following section compares IBM's treatment of a Frame relay WAN and the router approach. The major issues include:

- *Backbone.* A Frame relay network is compared with a meshed-router backbone network.
- *WAN protocol.* IP encapsulation is compared with native-protocol Frame relay transport.
- *SNA support.* Support for all SNA interconnects is compared with data link switching (DLSw).
- *Network management.* Native NetView and Simple Network Management Protocol are compared with Simple Network Management Protocol.

Backbone

The typical router backbone is a mesh of point-to-point links. In these networks, the router backbone is the network. The router is responsible for routing between end-user clients and application servers. Thus, routers are responsible for the definition and maintenance of network topology and the appropriate routing path for applications. Router networks can be referred to as administratively rich.

In a Frame relay backbone, by contrast, the network services are inherent in the Frame relay service. Each Frame relay access device provides application-transparent communication directly with its corresponding node across the network. This simplifies the configuration and administration of Frame relay compared with a router-based network.

WAN Protocol

The router solution to this issue is to encapsulate all traffic in IP packets for transmission over the Frame relay (or other) network in conjunction with a proprietary routing protocol. Thus, the router solution is based on adding IP framing overhead to all data prior to adding Frame relay framing for transmission over the network. Because most router protocols are proprietary and noninteroperable, a single vendor's product must reside on both sides of the network.

SNA Support

The router solution is to use data link switching (DLSw) to terminate SDLC and LLC2 traffic in the router and encapsulate the SNA data in IP using the DLSw routing protocol over the WAN. This provides a single backbone protocol for SNA and non-SNA traffic over the WAN. Once the SNA data is encapsulated in IP, the WAN treats it as any other IP traffic. The router solution requires a second DLSw-compatible router on the destination side of the Frame relay network to remove the SNA data from the IP packet. However, DLSw only covers SNA/BNN PU2 data on SDLC lines and Token Ring LANs and NetBIOS traffic.

IBM uses Regional Financial Center 1490 for the transmission of SNA data over a Frame relay WAN network. RFC 1490 provides for the transport of SNA/BNN PU 2 and type 2.1, but also SNA Intermediate Network, Advanced Peer-to-Peer Networking, and SNA Network Interconnect traffic across a Frame relay network. Therefore, RFC 1490 covers all SNA traffic without encapsulation in IP, and DLSw covers only SNA/BNN PU2 traffic and adds the IP overhead.

Network Management

SNMP is the principal network management tool used with routers, whereas NetView is the network management tool of choice for SNA networks. The simple network management protocol management stations are not usually located in corporate data centers, which necessitates a separate set of Data Link Connection Identifiers for simple network management protocol management to each remote location.

Such a scheme creates a redundant tier of network overhead that reduces bandwidth availability for data, impedes SNA session responsiveness and reliability, obstructs NetView visibility, and complicates network design and problem solving. This results in poor SNA network performance in terms of efficiency and cost.

When SNA is internetworked using routers that do not provide NetView support, a "black hole" is created in the network, preventing the NetView operator from viewing, managing, or monitoring the Frame relay Data Terminal Equipment devices. In particular, routers usually do not support SDLC LL2, LPDA-2, or NPM statistic collection.

IBM provides an integral NetView connection in all its Frame relay products. NetView connections share the same Permanent Virtual Circuit as SNA data, thereby eliminating the need for a separate management network for communication with NetView and its component applications.

CONCLUSION

Frame relay—multiplexing multiple protocols over a common link—is an efficient solution for unifying LAN and SNA networks. Frame relay is the WAN of choice for organizations moving to Advanced Peer-to-Peer Networking. The wide-scale deployment of APPN networks will soon be served by IBM's High-Performance Routing technology to deliver connectionless routing, and Frame relay will be supported by IBM's initial implementations of High Performance Routing (HPR). Exhibit 8 illustrates Frame relay as the unifying network for LAN and SNA.

Current Frame relay network specifications and service-provider implementations are designed for Permanent Virtual Circuit. Permanent virtual circuits provide a direct replacement for leased-line SNA connections, but SNA networks often include switched, dial-up SDLC connections for casual SNA host access. This capability is being added to Frame relay. A number of vendors have initiated standardization of Switched Virtual Circuit (SVC).

Frame relay is also being positioned as the access network for Asynchronous Transfer Mode. A Regional Financial Center that specifies a Frame relay interface to asynchronous transfer mode (ATM) networks is currently being worked through the standards process. This interface,

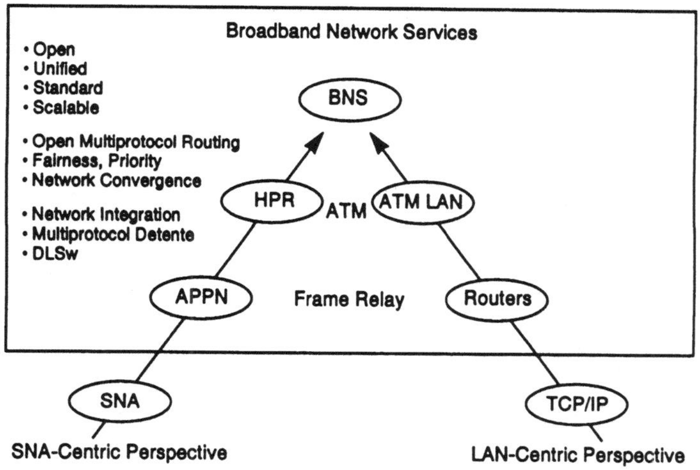

Key:
APPN advanced peer-to-peer networking
ATM asynchronous transfer mode
BNS broadband network services
DLSw data link switching
HPR high performance routing
LAN local area network
SNA systems network architecture
TCP/IP transmission control protocol and Internet protocol

Exhibit 8. Frame relay as the unifying networks for LAN and SNA networks.

referred to as Data eXchange Interface, covers ATM adaptation layer 1 (AAL 1).

Frame relay provides users with short-term payback and long-term preparedness—immediate economic benefits and a migration path to future, High Performance Routing (HPR) and networking.

Chapter 57
Operating a Network Manager's Help Desk in a Heterogeneous Environment

Jeff C. Hafer

Would you consider buying a car if you had no idea whom to call when you had problems? That is the feeling users get in some corporations when they use telecommunications and computers. There are two aspects to maintaining a reliable system. The network (highways and secondary roads) should be monitored and maintained to a satisfactory level without user (driver) involvement. The end user devices and applications (automobiles) require a call from the user to request help from the customer service organization (auto repair shop). Keep this analogy in mind when trying to design and operate a network help desk.

HISTORY OF THE HELP DESK

In many organizations, the help desk was created as a central point of contact for users of the data processing services. These users have accurately been referred to as customers. Users that experienced problems prefer to call a single phone number and have help desk personnel assist in resolving the problem or question. High level technical support could be called when needed. As personal computers, LANs and WANs became part of the data processing picture, the role of help desk became more difficult.

After the divestiture of AT&T, telecommunications functions like PBXs, voice mail, interactive voice response (IVR) and interconnection circuits became the responsibility of the Information Technology group in many companies. Add video conferencing and the diversity of services continues to grow into a complex web. Speaking of the web, the expansive use of the Internet has introduced more variables into the equation.

0-8493-9989-0/99/$0.00+$.50

MISSION OF THE HELP DESK

Before one can set up and operate an effective help desk, it is necessary to determine the mission of the help desk. There is no set formula for every company, network or organization. Some of the basic questions that must be asked are:

- What systems and networks are to be supported by the help desk?
- Will the help desk provide technical support or referral and tracking of problems?
- Is it important for the help desk to provide support 24 hours per day, seven days a week?
- How will second and third level support be obtained (in-house or external)?

If you don't know what you're trying to accomplish, you will never know when you have reached your destination. The best procedures, people and management will not be able to overcome the lack of planning. It has been said that no amount of planning can replace dumb luck. But, a successful help desk operation depends on continuous improvement and it is not possible if there are no goals to work toward or measure against as you move forward.

COST JUSTIFICATION

Building the cost justification for a help function is similar to justifying a set of encyclopedias for your house. It has value, it is expensive, but is it worth the cost? This dilemma is not lost on senior management. Most companies require some form of customer service function, which faces the same difficult task of balancing the cost against the value provided and impact on the business. However, in the case of the help desk, it is the information technology organization that must build the business case.

Since the cost of a quality help desk will be high, it is important to break it down into smaller numbers. What you need to sell to senior management is the product, not the process. In other words, it will be more effective to break down the cost into a per user cost rather than into individual components of the help desk operation. You must estimate the cost of each part of the operation to determine the total cost. Once the total cost is determined, you can divide it by the number of users (customers) that could use the service to create a unit cost value equation. That sounds easy, right? Well, it is not quite that simple.

Suppose the help desk supports telephone systems, voice mail, IVR, video conferencing, host computer operations and client server computer networks. Not all users will use all of these systems. And those that do will not use them to the same degree or place the same value on a 24-hour/day help desk operation. Knowledge of the users and their needs is important when trying to determine the unit cost.

Let's say you estimate the total annual cost of the help desk operation to be $1 million and there are three thousand users in the company. A quick calculation would tell you that the unit cost is approximately $333/user. If the average employee costs the company $45,000 per year with benefits, this would equate to about 15 hours of work. In order for the help desk to be cost justified it would have to save each user 15 hours of work per year. It is highly unlikely that management would believe that to be the case.

WHAT LEVEL OF SUPPORT MANAGEMENT?

A better approach would be to decide what level of support management would consider the bare minimum. It would be easy to get agreement that there must be someone to call when employees experience problems. By determining the cost to provide this minimum level of service, a base line can be established. If management accepts the base line, your role as a network manager is to justify the *additional* expense that would improve the service above the minimum acceptable level.

In this case it may be decided that the minimum level of help function available to users would cost $700,000. The remaining $300,000 would then be the differential that must be justified above the minimum level of acceptable service. By taking this approach, you can state to management that it will cost $700,000 to operate a help desk that can support the users at the minimum level. Additional services could be provided for an additional cost of $300,000 per year. It is important to show what basic and additional services would be provided for each level of service.

Incremental services that would provide value to some companies are listed below. Each company is different. Some may find value in all of these and many more. Others will not benefit from all of them.

- Expanded hours of operation
- Reduced response time for second and third level support by using in-house personnel or provisions in contracts with outside contractors
- Including real-time alarm monitoring for help desk personnel to be more proactive in problem identification
- Obtaining or developing a robust problem tracking system that will allow help desk and technical personnel to monitor outstanding problems and provide status that is available to everyone.
- Increasing the skills of first level support — those that answer the help desk phone — to improve initial support.

If your company uses a charge-back method for services, the level of support can be based on a willingness of the user to pay. Just as bankcards are available in standard, gold and platinum, the level of help desk can be tailored to the needs and desires of the user. In companies where this method is possible, it may be easier to justify the cost to increase coverage hours, tools to improve support and response time to problems.

MANAGING THE HELP DESK PERSONNEL

Depending on the mission of the help desk, the people in the function will have different skills, motivations and compensation. Those factors play a role when determining the best method to manage help desk personnel. Another factor is whether all support is provided from within the organization or if outside groups are used to provide some of this support.

If help desk personnel are company employees, management must ensure that career opportunities are available to those employees. People who answer the phones when customers call must have a combination of technical, communications and interpersonal skills to handle the myriad of questions and complaints that will arise on a daily basis. It is important for these people to see opportunity for growth in the position to keep the level of motivation high. Although no manager appreciates losing good people to another organization, it is important that the employees working in the help desk function understand that it is not a dead-end job.

Operational improvement will occur only if the people responsible for the help desk are given additional responsibilities. Not only will this reduce the amount of second and third level support required, but also the people will see it as an opportunity to expand their individual skills. Those people that do not recognize the value of increased responsibility should be a concern to management.

Frequent team meetings are an excellent method of improving teamwork and broadening the knowledge base of the individuals on the team. This is described in more detail later in the chapter. It is important for managers of this critical function to develop a consistent communications and information exchange among the people – full and part time – that comprise the help desk organization.

PHYSICAL ASPECTS OF THE HELP DESK

Most people think of the help desk as being a customer service area where all the people have similar skill levels and work in the same room. This image was accurate in most organizations up until the early 1990s. In recent years, it has become practical to have help desk personnel logically, rather than physically located together. What this means is that the function performed by these people does not require them to be located in the same room. Technology can make them appear to be in a single location.

It is important that the people who comprise the help desk work together as a team.

In the "good old days," most help desks supported only mainframe applications and HOST-attached hardware. A small staff could be trained in almost all hardware and software used in a company. With the broad scope of technology and applications used in companies, it is impossible to provide reasonable support with a small group of individuals. Unfortunately, it is not economical to assign experts in each area to work full-time on a help desk. An option is to have these subject matter experts assigned to other tasks and still available quickly to support users. A virtual help desk allows this to be possible.

Automatic Call Distribution (ACD) systems provide sharing of calls. The sophistication of today's ACD systems would allow a small group of full time personnel to be located in a common area and people at other locations could be added when needed. With networked ACD, it is possible to have people in other cities included on the help desk team. This has the added advantage of providing extended coverage by staffing in different time zones. The cost of multiple ACD systems, each with networking options, may at first seem cost prohibitive. Do not rule it out on the initial cost without considering the long term benefit and potential cost savings.

Having access to people during normal working hours in multiple time zones could prove very beneficial. For instance, during a particular period normal activity may dictate two full-time people. If problems occur, it may be necessary to add staff quickly for a short period of time. If this occurs outside the normal day shift in one time zone, but during prime time in another, it could make the solution more effective.

TOOLS

Many tools are available to support the help desk. A trip to any vendor exposition that addresses the needs of voice systems, call centers, help desks or computer telephony will provide you with more reading material than anyone would care to carry home. The important thing is to decide what the goals of your help desk should be and determine which tools are most suitable. From there, a quick review of the products should give some idea of what is available at an affordable price.

With the hype surrounding the Internet and Web browsers, many products focus on this area of technology. Like many other quick fixes that telecommunications managers and information technology face, it is important to look past the techno wizardry and consider the business case that would support the investment.

The primary tools that are essential for a successful help desk operation to solve these critical functions are:

- Handle the incoming call effectively
- Provide alarm reporting, if included in the help desk responsibilities
- Allow troubles and questions to be logged and tracked to conclusion
- Provide a means of quickly accessing high level support personnel
- Reporting information that can be used to analyze and improve the help desk operation

As described in the *Physical Aspects of the Help Desk* section, ACD is very effective in handling incoming calls from users. Not only do the users need to have their calls answered quickly, but support personnel must also have access to the people who work on the help desk. Using multiple call groups with different priorities assigned to specific dialed numbers, the ACD can also provide a means of support personnel gaining access to the help desk.

Alarms from systems should report to a centralized location. Depending on the size of the company and degree of technology employed, a network control center (NCC) separate from the help desk could be justified. In some operations, the NCC and help desk could be combined into a single operation. For our purpose, we will assume that separate functions are used. In that case, it is important that help desk personnel have some means of knowing the status of systems for which they provide support to the users. If the alarm and system status information is not readily available, time could easily be wasted searching for a problem that would otherwise be obvious.

There are several reasons to track troubles. One goal of a help desk is to aid in quick resolution to problems. Tracking troubles from the time it is first reported until it is resolved and the user is notified provides a measurement of the effectiveness of the operation. Changes to methods, tools and staffing can be evaluated to determine if the change was worthwhile. Rather than relying on memory, tracking can quickly identify repeat problems and possible solutions.

Many specialized software packages exist to provide tracking and reporting of troubles. These systems look very attractive and some have a price tag that will make new car sticker shock pall, by comparison. Do not automatically assume that the more you pay the better solution you will get. It is true that you may have a more sophisticated system if you are willing to pay more money. It is equally true that it will most likely *require* more input and analysis to provide the value. More importantly, some systems require more time and effort than it is worth for the value desired.

USING A SIMPLE DATABASE

Even a simple database created from a software suite may be suitable for tracking problems. If people that are experienced in creating databases are readily available, this could provide a good start to tracking. After more experience is gained, you could determine if more functionality is cost justified. At that point, an analysis could determine whether to expand the existing database to include new fields, reporting and functionality. If purchasing a system appears to be more desirable, the knowledge gained through a trial would improve the request for proposal.

It would be easier to determine what functions would be necessary, which ones are beneficial and which are unnecessary. The vendors are not in business to convince you to buy the least costly solution. They are trying to convince you to purchase the most sophisticated (read this to mean highest profit) system you can afford. It is your job to evaluate the business case and decide what makes sense and what is unnecessary.

Accessing second level support personnel can be accomplished through a number of methods. The method chosen depends on where these people reside, whether they are dedicated to support functions and whether they are employees or are provided through a service contract. The most effective method of accessing people quickly is by paging. Combining voice mail and paging allows help desk personnel to leave a message describing the problem in a mailbox, which is then programmed to page people.

In order to close the loop, a method should be implemented that will provide feedback to the help desk when the support person has received the page. This can be done with a procedure that requires the person to check in with the help desk. Remember that a separate ACD queue could provide support personnel with a higher priority for calls than users. Some systems could be programmed to provide automatic feedback. For instance, if a message were sent to a mailbox with a receipt requested when the message is read would provide the caller — a help desk person in this case — with positive feedback that the message was heard.

If the mailbox is set to page upon receipt of a message and there is no response, the message will not be read. Therefore, no return receipt will be sent. This method works well to prove a message has been received. Unfortunately, it does not work as well with messages that are not heard. The person on the help desk must keep a ticket open to ensure that all requests for additional support have received attention.

COMMUNICATING WITH USERS

Do not overlook the benefit of providing users with information that can improve system knowledge and reduce the need to call the help desk. In the most basic form, messages should be sent to employees through company publications, broadcast voice mail and email to inform them of pending changes or planned outages. It is also very useful to provide notification when problems occur. This may be more difficult if the means of providing the information (i.e., email) is affected by the problem.

Bulletin boards and Web pages can provide users with a method of obtaining information and answers to frequently asked questions. If users know this information is readily available, it will reduce the number of calls for simple questions. Many questions, such as "How do I print on a printer in a different building?", can be answered with good internal Web pages or bulletin boards, then help desk personnel could spend time dealing with serious problems.

Combining some of the tools can increase the effectiveness immensely. For example, an IVR could be used to front end some of the calls. An experienced caller could select the appropriate choice from a menu and information could be provided without the intervention of a person. This is similar to the online, context-sensitive help available with many computer application programs. For problem resolution or specific help, the caller could select the appropriate choice, which then could page a specified person or group.

Most voice mail systems have the ability for a voice menu that would operate similar to an IVR. If the support person was paged when necessary, the voicemail message could provide information to the person who was paged. This would allow the user to describe a specific problem or ask a question without the interpretation problem that occurs when there is a third person (help desk person) involved.

There is no all-inclusive manual that will provide you with the appropriate tools for your company. Gather several people, including possibly a consultant, who have knowledge of the various tools. Start by defining the major goals for improvement in the help desk operation. Brainstorm some ideas to determine if some tools and combination of tools could potentially bring significant improvement.

Never rule out the systems that are presently in place. As stated above, most telephone systems include basic ACD. The integrated voicemail systems include many features that could be used to improve the operation at little or no incremental cost. In fact, many times the expensive solutions may provide enhancements and options that will seldom be used.

SECURITY

There are two separate aspects to security. Protecting the access provided to help desk personnel from being available to others inside or outside the company. The second issue is that the help desk is the best place to focus users who have problems accessing the network or systems. Some method should be available to restore or change user passwords without compromising the security of the system.

Since help desk personnel may have access to systems beyond what average users are given, it is important to protect the access provided. In the case where all help desk personnel are in a common area this is easy. The area could be secured so that unauthorized personnel could not gain access to the workstations that have open access to systems. If alternate locations are used, the problem would most likely be controlled by procedures and trust in the employees to follow those procedures. Systems that time out would reduce the risk of someone leaving his/her workstation open into the network. While this risk exists for all employees, it is likely that help desk personnel have access to a broader expanse of systems and into a greater depth than all but a few users.

ACCESS TO SECOND LEVEL SUPPORT PERSONNEL

As pointed out earlier, access to second level personnel is necessary to ensure timely response to user problems. If the people staffing the help desk are highly trained and experienced, access to second level people will not occur as frequently as it would if they lack training or experience. Regardless of the frequency of escalating a problem to a second level support person, the response should be quick. By the time a decision has been made to escalate the problem, the user may already be frustrated by the wait for a solution. Do not prolong this waiting period with an ineffective method of contacting these people.

The most effective method of soliciting immediate support is to page the second level support people. In the most basic form, each person could carry a numeric pager and the help desk could dial the pager, leaving a call-back number. Alphanumeric pagers allow the caller to leave a brief message. This can be an effective way to provide information without requiring the person to call back to the help desk. However, the caller must then type a message into a keyboard.

Another method would be to have a voice mail system programmed to page people when messages are left in specific mailboxes. This paging function can be activated for all pages or only those marked urgent. With dedicated mailboxes used exclusively for immediate support requests, the former method is easiest. However, if individual user mailboxes are serving double-duty, it may be more practical to mark the support requests urgent when the message is left. Using a voice mailbox allows help desk personnel to leave messages easily that provide support person with information about the problem and can usually be accomplished quicker than using a keyboard. Another advantage is that information can easily be exchanged among support persons who have a need to communicate quickly while working on problems.

WIRELESS DATA TERMINALS

If detailed messages are regularly required when serious problems arise, wireless data terminals can be used. These devices can provide a means of two-way communication. In addition, some of the devices can be used as an interface device to equipment supported.

Second and third level support personnel do not have to be employees. Contractors can be used, especially at the third level support, to augment in-house staff. While it is not important that users recognize whether employees or contractors are used, a well-run help desk operation should provide seamless connection among all support personnel, the help desk group and users.

If outside contractors are used as part of the support group, make sure that there is a well-defined operating procedure and the contract supports the needs of the company. These arrangements can be very beneficial because they allow a company to have access to highly skilled people on short notice in a situation where there may not be sufficient need for a full-time person with the particular skills. However, the arrangement requires good procedure communications and cooperation among a variety of people in different organizations.

ORGANIZATION, TEAMWORK AND GROWTH OPPORTUNITIES

As stated earlier in this chapter, a successful help desk operation starts by understanding the needs of the company. The role of the help desk must be clearly defined and a mission statement developed. After that is done, it is important to promote an atmosphere of teamwork. The people who work in close proximity must naturally function as a team and be willing to help each other meet the common goals set. While it may be more difficult to do when help desk personnel are located in diverse physical areas — especially if they are in different cities — it is equally important to promote teamwork among all these people.

The teamwork cannot stop with the people who answer the phones, monitor alarms, interface with users and track problem progress. Second and third level support personnel are essential ingredients in successful problem resolution process.

Regular meetings and informal gatherings allow people to exchange ideas that can improve the process and methods used to support users. Informal gatherings generally improve communications and understanding among the people involved. If physical distance makes it impractical to gather these people together, video conferencing can be used. Coffee mugs, tee shirts or other special items that identify these people as part of a single customer support group will promote interaction and teamwork.

Anyone who manages a group of customer support people must accept the need for some variety in the work. It is useful if some degree of job rotation can be used to allow people to learn new skills, maintain enthusiasm and increase the interaction among the people. It is also important for the managers to provide opportunities for people to obtain additional training. People are encouraged to expand their technical and interpersonal skills with an eye toward advancement opportunities. Most people in the information technology field have a desire to learn new skills and move into more challenging positions. Help desk and second level support personnel are no different. Knowing there is an opportunity for advancement can increase the motivation level of at least the better people.

If a help desk manager considers this a job where the greatest challenge is to keep people answering phones and reporting and tracking problems, find someone else to do the job. If the manager sets a personal goal to improve the response with more job knowledge, better team work and development of people that can move upward in the organization, give him/her a bonus.

BRINGING IT ALL TOGETHER

Managing a successful help desk can be measured by the satisfaction of the users. Those users are looking for one place to call to get their problems resolved and questions answered in a timely manner. Proper staffing includes having the correct number of people, appropriate experience and management that will get the most benefit of those people. Proper use of the tools is more important than the selection of the tools. Sophisticated tools can improve the operation, but only if they are understood and used in the best way.

Start with a mission statement and make sure everything fits into that mission. If not, review the mission and conflicting idea. Which is incorrect? Either modify the mission statement or change the planned operation. You don't want to end up at the wrong destination.

Unlike a customer service operation that has the potential to generate revenue through additional sales, the help desk is usually viewed as only a cost of doing business. Always start with the base line cost for the minimum acceptable level of service. Cost for improved service should be built on that base. Make a comparison between the increased cost and added value.

SUMMARY

This will be a challenge, but it can be rewarding. There is a lot of frustration in dealing with problems every day, but there is a great deal of satisfaction in solving them. The bad news is that some users will never be happy. The good news is that most users that call for help are more impressed with a good effort and communications back to him/her than with the measured results. Measured results are necessary for the help desk manager to make sure the operation is always being improved and problem areas are quickly identified and eliminated. Quick response to users will take care of the level of satisfaction. Never forget to give users feedback.

Chapter 58
An Expert Operating System That Manages Multinetwork Communications

Yemmanur Jayachandra
Hal Sanders
Gita Jayachandra

The tide of postdivestiture technology has swept through corporate communications networks, replacing the previously pervasive Bell System's centralized networks with multivendor distributed networks. Managing these networks involves real-time surveillance and control to ensure that all their components operate efficiently and reliably. A system for managing these large, diverse, multivendor networks is long overdue.

Network technology is entering its fifth generation.[1]

The characteristics of each generation are:

- **First**—Shared transmission facility
- **Second**—Switched utility networks of data and voice
- **Third** —Standardized architecture networks, including the Tymnet and Telenet X.25 networks, IBM System Network Architecture (SNA) networks, Northern Telecom SL-1 private automatic branch exchange (PABX), IBM and Rolm computerized PABX, and AT S/85 PABX.
- **Fourth**—Fully interoperable application networks, including the manufacturing automation protocol and technical office protocol (MAP/TOP), IBM System Application Architecture (SAA), OSI file-transfer access management service (FTAM), and CCITT recommendation X.400 message-handling service.

0-8493-9989-0/99/$0.00+$.50

- **Fifth**—New and proposed standards and protocols, including the broadband integrated switched digital network(B-ISDN), synchronous optical network transport (SONET), Bellcore switched multimegabit data service (SMDS), ANSI fiber distributed data interface (FDDI) , and IEEE 802.6 metropolitan area network

During the next decade, all five generations of network technologies will coexist in network environments. Given the current and emerging network technology, the cost of network operations and management for a three-year period could far exceed the capital appropriation cost of the networks themselves, and the qualified MIS professionals to operate them could become increasingly scarce and expensive. The cost of a labor-saving expert system (e.g., ENEOS) for integrated and interoperable multinetwork administration and control could easily be justified.

ENEOS DESIGN

The ENEOS architecture was designed to manage networks of multiple and arbitrary types and topologies and consists of seven knowledge bases, more than 16 units, 200 frames, 380 operating rules, and 65 LISP procedures. It is an easily maintainable expert system capable of autonomously operating various corporate networks and can be easily upgraded to accommodate emerging fifth-generation technologies that contain embedded management channels and protocols.

The ENEOS elements use parallel processing to operate in real time and are partially distributed. A finite inference frame processor engine, the key component of ENEOS, organizes its collection of rules into frames. The finite inference frame processor performs parallel rule processing at high speeds by using frames as case or situation inferences. The use of a frame-based inference engine gives ENEOS the following capabilities and features:

- End-to-end connection management through several heterogeneous networks (e.g., public and private local area, wide area, and metropolitan area networks with multivendor facilities and semi-autonomous operations)
- Self-learning, self-reconfiguring, self-improving, and self-repairing algorithms for fault-tolerant and autonomous operations
- Mechanisms for adapting to internal and external environmental changes or problems by deducing tasks and reorganizing, and for the parallel execution of expert programs for optimal, self-preserving network operations
- Real-time expert system control for trouble-free voice, video, and data communications

- The use of standard, high-level human flexible interface adaptations to accommodate such current and emerging management channels as SONET's embedded operating channel and T1/T3 data channels
- A uniform intelligent user interface that prompts the user for input and suggests actions for optimal network operations

These features enable ENEOS to:

- Provide online network servicing, including in-service tests and controls, ensuring maximum uptime and minimal service outages.
- Measure, with loopback capability, the bitnd the line-signal-to-noise characteristics of any desired line segment
- Use CCITT B-ISDN specifications to control signals and catastrophic degradation.
- Identify the cause of gradual or catastrophic degradation
- Perform self-repair operations by reconfiguring with alternate or backup facilities where available
- Advise the network administrator regarding repair and recovery procedures when manual operations are required

ENEOS can inject various stress and monitoring signals into a pseudochannel (e.g., the embedded operating channel of the SONET, the extended super frame data channel of T1 links, and the management channel of proprietary networks).[2]

ENEOS then uses an expert module to analyze the measured test data, identify the most likely cause of events, and decide to take appropriate actions on the relevant network elements.

An ENEOS network operating environment (see Exhibit 1) involves multiple ENEOSs to ensure reliability and survivability throughout the network; each ENEOS controls its own local network. At any given time, however, only one ENEOS can exercise global control, although all ENEOS elements are physically identical.

An important attribute of ENEOS is its ability to recognize multivendor, multigeneration networks and to adapt its operations to manage them. On a real-time basis, given a global network view, ENEOS can do the following for network management:

- **Configuration**—Reporting network status, including bandwidth management information and autorouting and rerouting
- **Problem-resolution**—Performing comprehensive diagnostics and reporting all problems, noting status and resolution
- **Change**—Executing changes in links, circuits, and nodes and reporting prior and pending moves and changes
- **Performance oversight**—Combining the reporting of alarms with the use of circuit
- **Security**—Keeping out unauthorized users

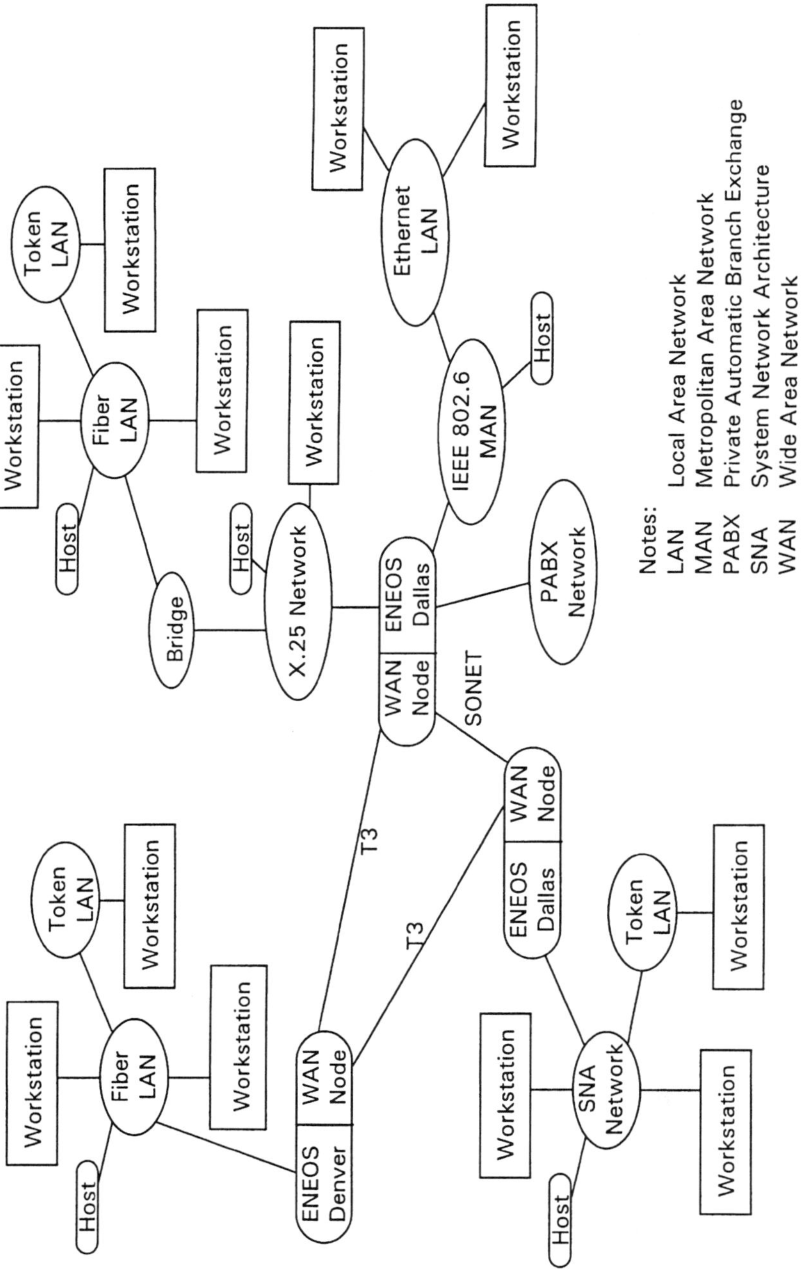

Exhibit 1. ENEOS multinetwork distributed management.

ENEOS can also perform the following offline network management functions:

- Asset management to track network assets inventory (e.g., workstations, file-servers, printers and servers, modems, multiplexers, channel service units, circuits, leased lines, and hosts) and generate inventory reports
- Customized billing and accounting and generation of appropriate reports
- Network administration, expansion and modification, and resource allocation

PROTOCOLS AND STANDARDS

Large business networks consist of elements that range from host computers, workstations, and terminals to front-end communications processors, multiplexers, statistical multiplexers, channel service units, and wideband and narrowband leased lines that use terrestrial fiber-optic cables, copper wires, and microwave statellite transmissions. No single vendor can supply all of these network elements.

There are many popular methods of network control and operation,[3] including subdividing large and complex networks into smaller networks or installing them separately according to geographic region, vendor or equipment type, or application type. Current network-management methods are based on six product categories: modems, LANs, PABXs, and T1/T3 multiplexers, host-based, and public inter- and intra-LATA WAN-based management systems covering the spectrum of all the other management systems (see Exhibit 2).

Exhibit 2. Network management methods organized by product categories.

1. Host-based management			
2. Modem-based management	3. LAN-based management	4. PABX-based management	5. T1/T3 multiplexer based management
6. Public inter- and intra-LATA WAN-based management			
Note: LATA (local and transport area).			

National and international committees are developing standards for network management protocols and messages. Some of the more important of these are the ANSI X3T5 standard for OSI management and the Exchange Carriers Standards Association's T1M1.5 standard for SONET management and maintenance. Important *de facto* standards created by dominant vendors include the IBM NetView and AT&T Unified Network Management System and network management and operation standards. ENEOS incorporates these standards as well as significant enhancements.[4]

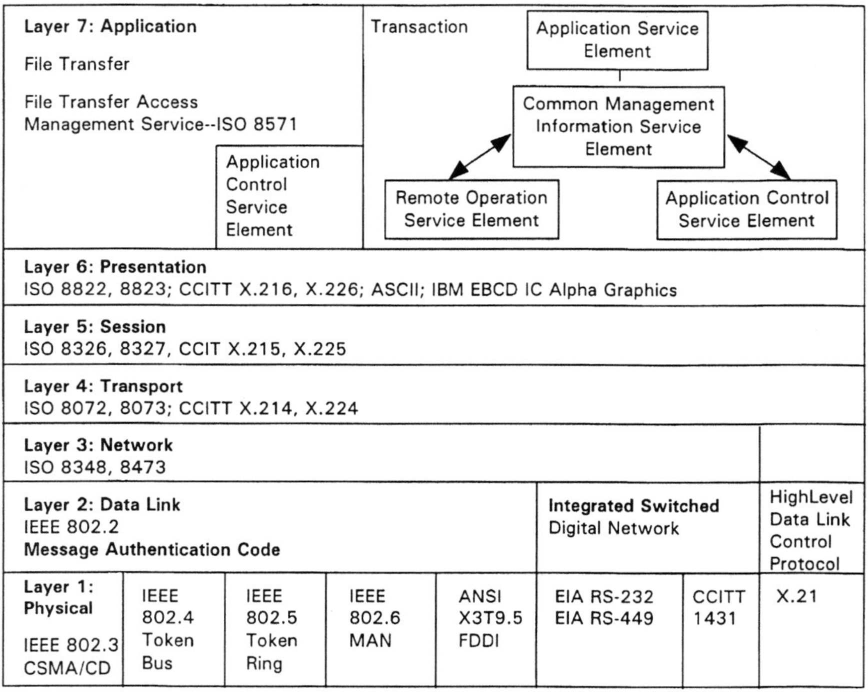

Notes: CSMA/CD: Carrier-SenseMultiple Access/Collision Detect FDDI: Fiber Distributed Data Interface
MAN: Metropolitan Area Network

Exhibit 3. OSI layer services and protocols adopted by ENEOS.

Exhibit 3 lists the OSI network management layers and the protocols that have been adopted in ENEOS.

ENEOS integrates an installed base of subdivided networks into a cooperative network that uses expert system applications, broadening the scope of the emerging OSI network management standards. ENEOS extends its services to multinetworks with three basic modules: the presentation adaptation and learning module, the function adaptation and learning module, and the interface adaptation and learning module (see Exhibit 4).

ARCHITECTURE

ENEOS models the thought processes of a team of human experts when it assesses the current network environment and determines the most reasonable solution to any problem, choosing from a pool of existing possibilities. For ENEOS to support online management with a global network perspective, its architecture had to include stringent real-time capabilities.

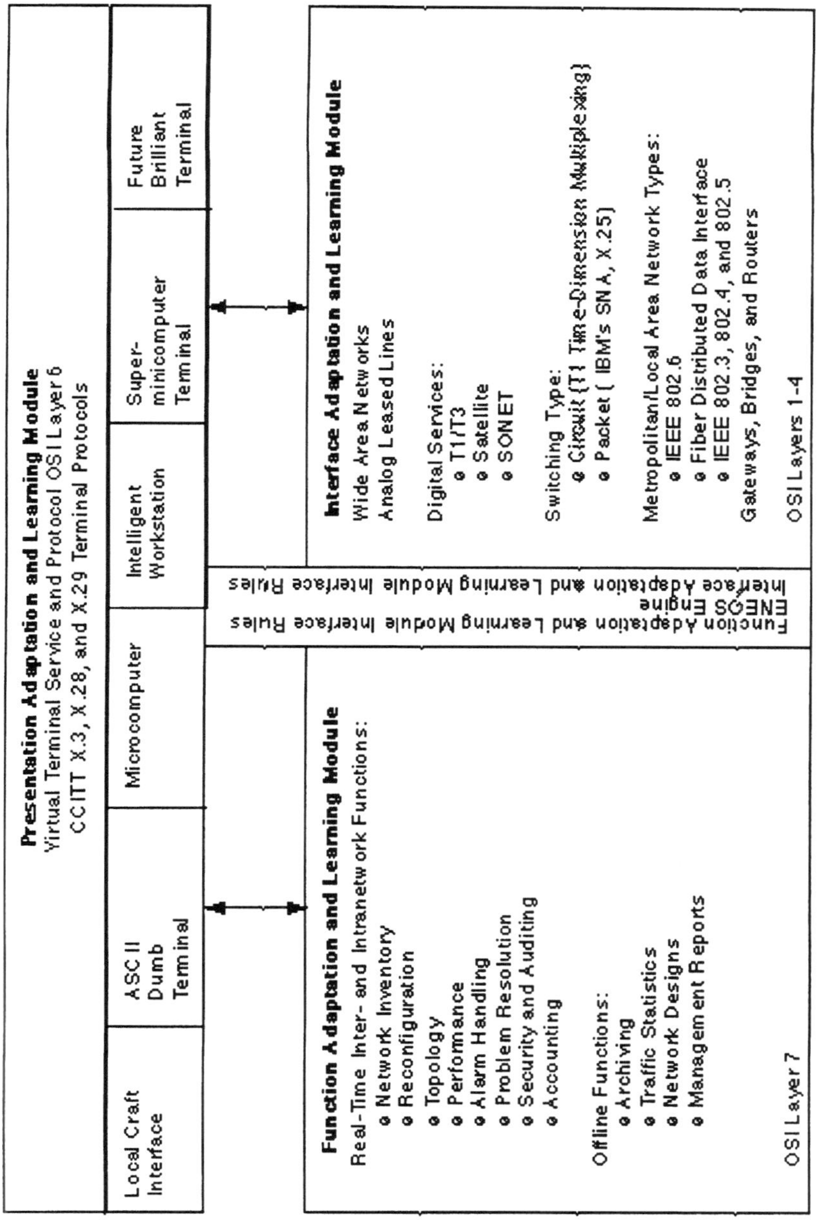

Exhibit 4. ENEOS extended services for multinetwork integrated management.

ENEOS is vulnerable to damage, however, like any network element. To ensure continued operation in the event of damage, the ENEOS architecture allows the cloning and replication of ENEOS functions at alternate ENEOS sites. One ENEOS is elected as a master according to certain election rules; it then controls the global network operations with continuous help from the other ENEOS elements that have local control of their respective domain networks (see Exhibit 1). If the master ENEOS is disabled, a second ENEOS is elected as a master to provide continuous control of global network operations, avoiding communication outages. If a local ENEOS fails, the nearest ENEOS assumes control of the domain. Exhibit 5 shows an architectural functional block diagram for ENEOS.

Multiple networks can be managed through either a centralized system or a distributed system with several linked expert systems.[5]

ENEOS uses a distributed approach because—through smaller mass-produced processors—it provides more computing power than a centralized approach. In a distributed approach, expert system modules can be applied wherever needed throughout the system by working in parallel with local processors, thereby reducing the chances of a failure at a single point.

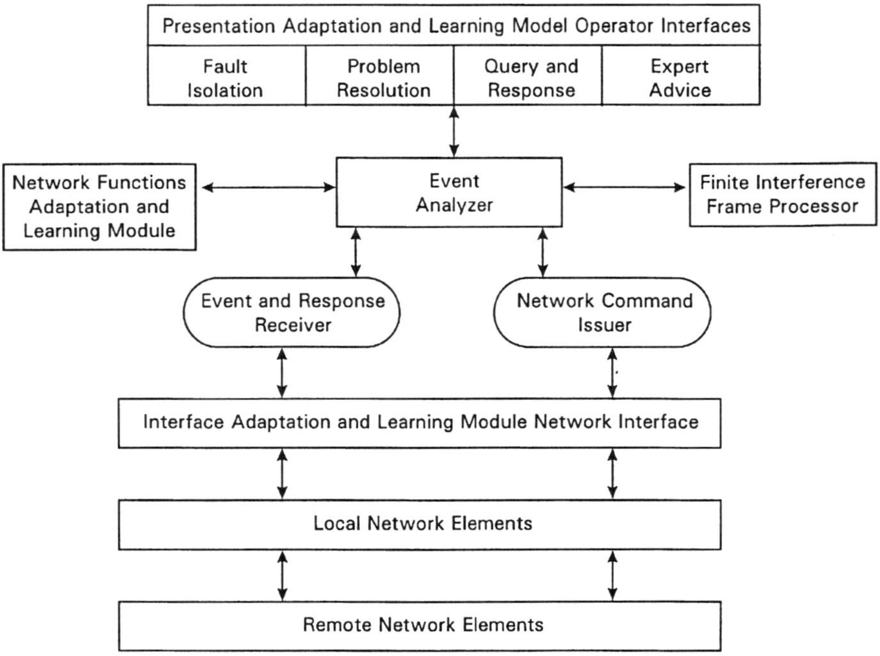

Exhibit 5. ENEOS architectural functional block diagram.

The disadvantages of a distributed processing approach include overhead for cooperative communications among the ENEOS entities, complex election rules for choosing a master ENEOS to control global operations, complex timing and synchronization for coordinating subordinate and master ENEOS entities, and the amount of bandwidth for the management channels. These disadvantages are gradually being eliminated by development of fast processors, inexpensive bandwidth, and sophisticated expert system technologies.

EVENT ANALYZER

As shown in Exhibit 5, the ENEOS event analyzer collects data on events as they are generated by network elements and their components. This analyzer gathers and interprets raw data intelligently, simulating a team of human experts. Its output is either an operational command to a network element, accompanied by an alarm, or simply a status report for the operator. When ENEOS encounters a problem, the system activates audio and visual alarms.

In large networks, event analyzers perform several complex tasks. An abnormal condition triggers many events, each of which provides information that can help identify and resolve the overall problem. A single event is generally not significant, but a group of events taken together can be critical, depending on their patterns.

Correlating events for problem determination and analysis is not a straightforward task; it is affected by time correlation, event attenuation, redundant events, location correlation, partial data, and multiple problems. These factors are explained in the following sections.

Time Correlation. A particular problem may cause other events to occur during a finite time period at unpredictable intervals that range from microseconds to days. Isolating and characterizing a problem that involves a degrading component can take days, and the frequency of events can have a critical bearing on the problem. For example, one frame slip on a T1 line during a day may not be serious, but 10 frame slips an hour can be quite serious.

Event Attenuation. Events generated by some types of problems may not be communicated. Examples are jitter (i.e., short-term variations in signal interval phases commonly caused by nonlinear transmission circuit elements) and wander (i.e., long-term variations in signal phase intervals) in T1 lines due to intermediate repeaters and cross-connect systems that use large buffers. Error-correction codes processed at intermediate network elements can also go unreported.

Redundant Events. Some events occur as a consequence of other events and provide no new information; they may even be reported after the problem has been resolved. This type of event should be masked in the system to avoid distractions while the cause of the problem is being isolated.

Location Correlation. An abnormal problem can have consequences in other network components. In this situation, a problem must be determined from related events that are reported by other properly functioning components.

Partial Data. Problem resolution often proceeds despite incomplete data. Data is gathered incrementally as more events are reported over time. In some cases, event analysis does not always produce a definite conclusion; events can be lost, mutilated, or not reported because of damaged network elements, or false events can be reported as a result of noisy communications. The ENEOS event analyzer generates hypotheses about a given problem, analyzing additional events as they occur and using this information to revise and refine the hypothesis. The inference processor must allow the system to make plausible revisions. Occasionally, the absence of events may be very significant and should also be processed by the inference engine. For example, if events indicating a faulty component or degraded signal stop occurring, any hypothesis regarding a faulty component or degraded signal should be abandoned.

Multiple Problems. A large network usually has some independent problems that are pending resolution. Events generated by these problems are mixed with events caused by the problem. The inference processor should be able to separate such a mixture of events, assigning priorities to the problems according to their severity.

KNOWLEDGE BASES

An expert system's knowledge base contains items called objects. ENEOS's knowledge base contains such objects as corporate networks, gateways, specific network types, sites, nodes , ports, paths, links, intermediate multiplexers, repeaters, front-end controllers, and terminal types. *Ad hoc* collections of objects are created as needed for resolving particular problems. See Exhibit 6 for a condensed taxonomy of ENEOS objects and parameters. Objects and their associated measurements performed or acquired during a problem-resolution session are listed in Exhibit 7.

Network element operators manipulate network objects through a combination of heuristics, test commands, and algorithms, triggering the actions needed for problem resolution. When operations are applied to objects, they may produce children and grandchildren within the hierarchy of objects and sets. Operators' properties characterize their

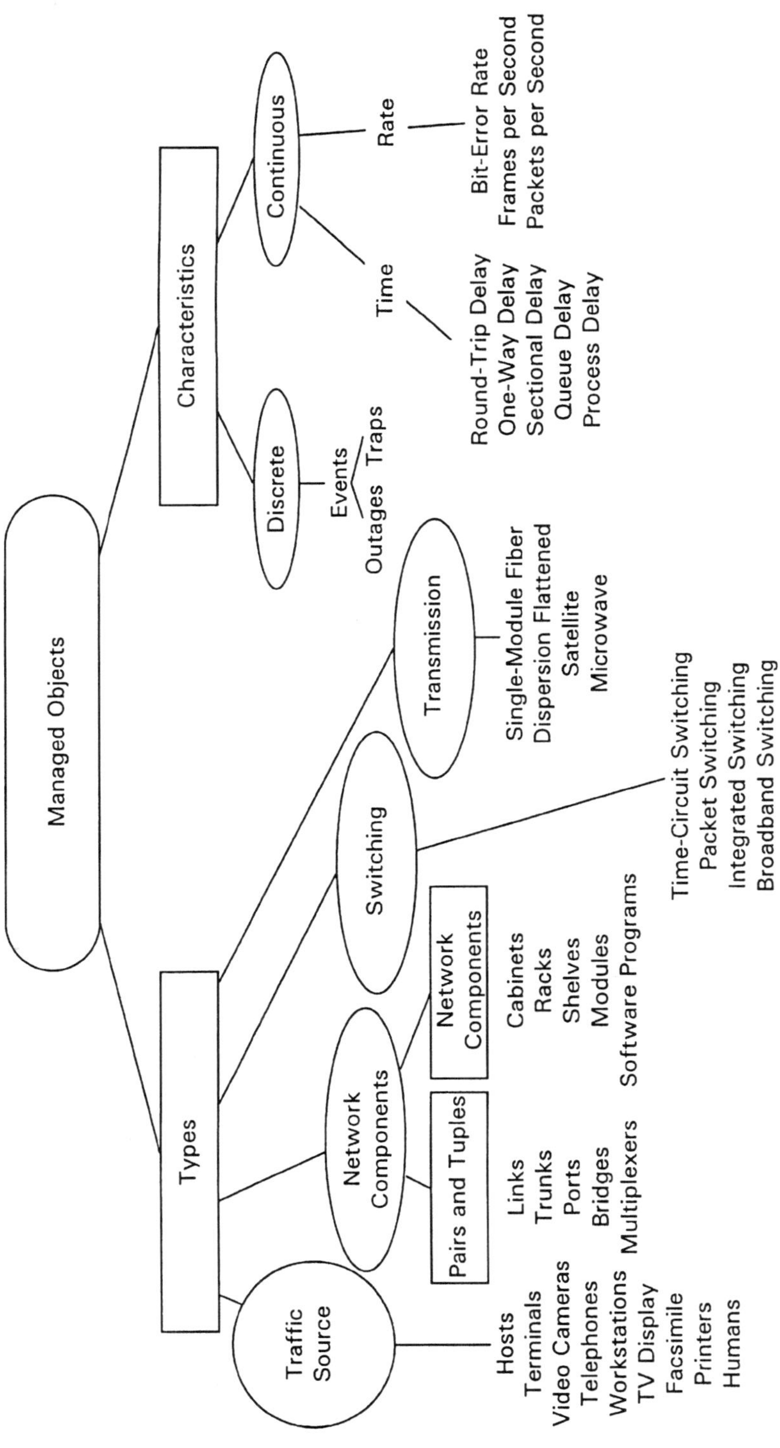

Exhibit 6. Condensed taxonomy of ENEOS objects and parameters.

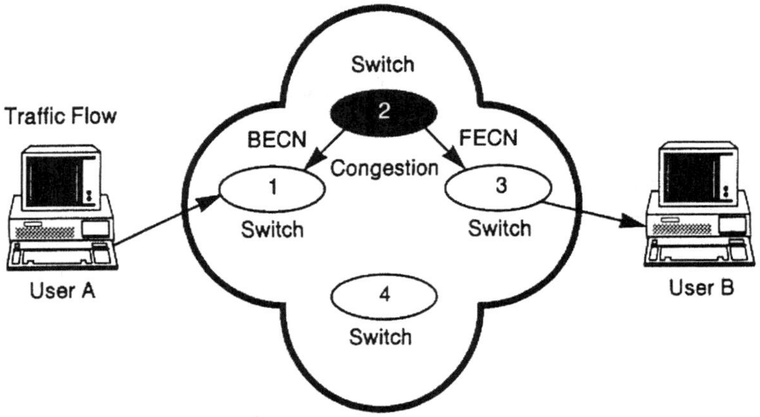

Key:
BECN backward explicit congestion notification
FECN forward explicit congestion notification

Exhibit 7. Typical network element operators.

domains and ranges in the network object taxonomy; they also have procedures that can generate presentation-layer descriptions of icons, tables, charts, and graphic displays. Operators can trigger further actions in network elements that assist in problem resolution (e.g., rerouting traffic through an alternate path to bypass a failed element).

Object-Oriented

Object-oriented knowledge bases, databases, and programming are state-of-the-art AI concepts, offering significant advantages over conventional programming techniques. In ENEOS, objects communicate with one another by sending and receiving messages. An object consists of a collection of information and the protocols needed to manipulate it.

The knowledge base consists of factual, algorithmic, and heuristic knowledge. Examples of factual knowledge in the ENEOS knowledge base are:

- Transmission media, including single-mode dark fiber in dispersion-flattened and polarization-preserving formats and transmitter lasers (e.g., thermoelectric-cooled, distributed feedback, and Faby-Perot lasers)
- Switching and connectivity frames and rules
- Test commands and invocation rules
- Electrical and optical test definitions, including noninvasive optical time domain reflectometry and stress signal tests
- Test thresholds and limits

The declarative knowledge of network elements and communication paths consists of three entities: sets of network element classes, classes of network elements, and instances of network element classes in which each element is represented as a frame.

Frame-based knowledge representation provides a system with deep knowledge because of the complex structures within the frames. Rule-based knowledge systems, however, provide only surface knowledge because of the limited way information can be presented. A typical frame describing an instance of a specific entity contains the following information:

- Element class and hierarchy
- Functional description
- Structural description
- Behavioral description
- Legal operations, including test, preventive, corrective, and adaptive procedures
- Bandwidth resource-management procedures
- Routing algorithms and procedures
- Set of possible instantiations
- Failure rate
- Repair and maintenance procedures

One of ENEOS's most essential tasks is instantiating these types of frames.(See Exhibit 8 for a simple instantiated frame.)

A specific instance of a class of network elements could have two terminals—workstation A and host B—specified in the frames as communicating in connectionless packet mode. By establishing the communications mode between the terminals, ENEOS creates a direct correspondence between the relationships in a given situation, facilitating the natural presentation of global network knowledge.

All knowledge that is to be processed must be represented in frames. Because the operations and manipulations of these frames are expressed as specialized procedures, ENEOS uses factual knowledge of such network elements as the state of communicating terminals, communications protocols, connection mode, links, and time slots in a time multiplexer.

Naming a frame helps control the proper matches of the restricted variables, allowing ENEOS to derive all the test points and test operations for a given problem resolution. In a frame-based procedure, a frame stored in the knowledge base is selected and matched against the collected data to predict the structure of the data.

Using frame-based rather than rule-based processing provides real-time parallel processing capabilities in ENEOS (e.g., how ENEOS relates alarms). A frame is selected with many alarms pointing to other objects and their

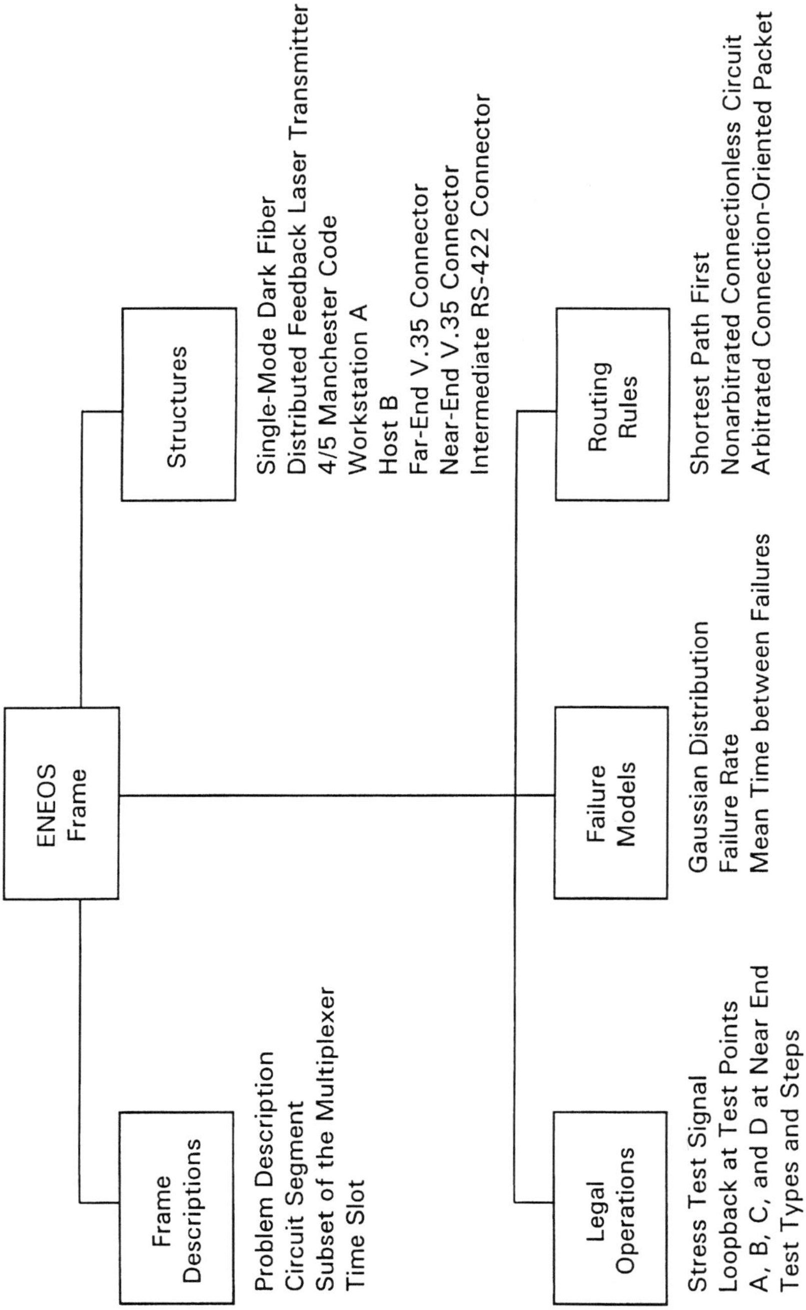

Exhibit 8. An instantiated frame.

relationships. The alarms are classified according to their level in the hierarchy of network components that are sending the alarms; this level number is added to the alarm-signal knowledge base. The frame with the highest alarm level is the master frame, and the matching process is performed according to ENEOS's procedures. Alarm-data collection, processing, and matching must be done in real time for meaningful network-management operations to occur. Coding these procedures, therefore, requires real-time considerations.

FINITE INFERENCE FRAME PROCESSOR

Inference generation in ENEOS is performed in the finite inference frame processor. As noted, this processor is the key component of ENEOS; its functional block diagram is shown in Exhibit 9. The design of all the knowledge bases in the finite inference frame processor is similar to that of the interpreter knowledge base, shown in the central box in Exhibit 9. The

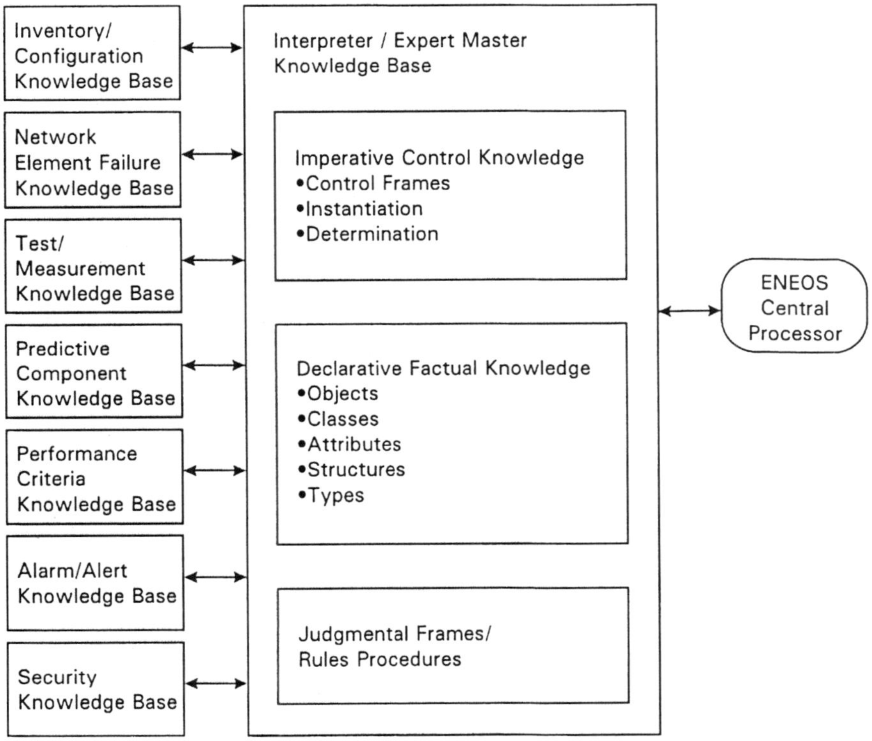

Exhibit 9. A functional block diagram of the ENEOS finite inference frame processor.

design of the knowledge base is an important aspect of the finite inference frame processor.[6]

Knowledge-Base Design

Researchers at Stanford University, pioneers in expert systems technology, have designed several expert systems capable of performing medical diagnostics: EMYCIN, MYCIN, and NEOMYCIN.[7]

The most important design principle of relevance to ENEOS to come from the MYCIN project is that all control knowledge should be represented abstractly and separately from the domain knowledge on which it operates. Control knowledge, like rule-clause ordering, specifies when and how a program should perform such operations as pursuing a goal, acquiring data, focusing on an object, and making an inference.

CONCLUSION

In ENEOS, the knowledge bases and the associated inference engine of the finite inference frame processor have separate components for encoding control knowledge, factual knowledge, and judgmental rules. The inference engine applies the judgmental rules according to the embedded control procedures that define distinct control steps. The control knowledge, coded through an applicative and imperative programming language, defines the control actions that will be executed in a multitask environment. The separate encoding of the control knowledge allows ENEOS to generate inferences that are readily intelligible, explainable, modifiable, and upgradable.

To provide a transparent presentation of both control knowledge and factual knowledge, the knowledge bases in ENEOS are organized in distinct frames that contain an ordered rule structure of separately encoded control blocks. Factual knowledge is coded with network-defined objects, class types, legal-value hierarchies, class instances, and attributes. The imperative control knowledge cooperates with the structures of the declarative factual knowledge to provide built-in control.

Notes

1. R.J. Haas and S.D. Personick, Working with the Industry to Shape Intelligent Network Requirements. *IEEE Transactions in Communications* 26, no 12 (1988); JC. Kohli et al, Emerging Broadband Packet-Switch Technology in Interated Information Networks, *IEEE Transactions in Communications* 2, no.6 (1988).
2. G.W. Cyboron, SONET Data Communication Channels, T1M1 Standards Contribution No T1M1 88-062 (September 9, 1988); J.D. Kuebler and T.H. Grim, Considerations for Operations Network Architecture, T1M1 Standards Contribution No T1M1 88-024 (August 15, 1988).
3. IBM Corp. Netwiew/PC Alert Monitor, IBM Announcement No 286-12 (September 18, 1988); Digital Equipment corp, DNA Network Management, Functional Specification Version

4.3.2, Order No AA-X437A-TK (September 1988); S.M. Klerer, The OSI Management Architecture: An Overview, *IEEE Network Magazine* 2,no 2, (1988).
4. IBM Corp, System Application Architecture—An Overview, Order No GC26-4341 (1988); IBM Corp, Introduction to IBM's Open Network Management, Order No GC30-3431 (1988); Abstract Service Conventions, ISO, DIS 8504/4, CCITT draft recommendation X.3407 (November 1987); Information Processing Systems—Open System Interconnection Management Information Service Definition, ISO, DP 9595/1,2 (August 1987); Second Working Draft of ISO Remote Database Access, ISO, TC/97/SC 21 N-1646 (January 1987).
5. B.M. Thuraisingham and J.A. Larson, AI Applications in Distributed System Design Issues, *IEEE Network Magazine* 2, no 6 (1988); A. Tanenbaum and R. Van Renesse, Distributed Operating System, *ACM Computing Surveys* 17, no 4 (1985), pp 419-470.
6. X. Du and F. Maryanski, Data Reorganization in a Dynamically Reconfigurable Environment, *Proceedings of the International Conference on Distributed Computing Systems* (June 1988); I. Goldstein, FRL—A Frame Representation Language, Memo No 333, MIT Artificial Intelligence Laboratory, 1976; D. McAllester, ONTIC: A Mathematical Representation Language, Technical Report No. 979, MIT Artificial Intelligence Laboratory, 1987; M. Stefik, An Examination of a Frame Structured Representation System, *Proceedings of the Sixth International Joint Conference on Artificial Intelligence*, 1979; M. Minsky, *The Society of the Mind* (New York: Simon & Shuster, 1986).
7. B. Buchanan and E.H. Shortlife, *Rule-Based Expert Programs: The MYCIN Experiments of the Stanford Heuristic Programming Project* (Reading MA: Addison-Wesley, 1984).

Section VII
Security in a Heterogeneous Environment

The following section takes a look at a very important facet of heterogeneous computing that has been getting a lot of focus with the development of the Internet and intranets—security.

Security is implemented at different levels. All operating systems have their own security functions, which are rated. The most common level aimed for at this point is the "C2" level, which is where Windows NT and most Unix operating systems are. Database systems have their own security functions as well, although they may call on the operating system for the implementation of some of their security functions. Other applications, such as e-mail, have their own security functions and they in turn might use the operating system and/or databases for implementing some of their security functions.

Chapter 59 discusses the security features of the Windows NT server. The Windows NT operating system offers substantial security and audit features that have earned it the C2 evaluation for auditing and authentication from the National Computer Security Center (NCSC). This chapter is designed to provide security administrators with a security checklist for going live with Windows NT. Each of the basic security and audit features of the Windows NT operating system is explained, and recommended values for these features are suggested. The security administrator can use these values to create a security baseline when the operating system is initially configured.

Chapter 60 covers Unix security features. Typically, many Unix installations have less-than-optimal security. There are several versions of Unix on the market today with differing security features. However, the Unix operating system's basic security features—including password protection, access permission, user profiles, shell scripts, and file ownership—are implemented in most Unix versions. This chapter covers the basic security features that can be found in most of the currently available versions of the Unix operating system. Several checklists are included at the end of the chapter to assist administrators in ensuring the security of these systems, and Chapter 61 goes on to discuss software tools that are available to detect misuse in Unix systems.

While NetWare 3.X was the leading Network OS of its time, one of the functions it lacked was the ability to manage multiple servers from a single location. In response to this need, Novell released NetWare 4.X. Chapter 62 discusses the differences between NetWare 3.X and NetWare 4.X security, and identifies the enhanced tools that security administrators will have at their disposal for securing the NetWare 4.X environment.

The trade press does not normally mention AS/400 when Unix, NT, and NetWare are covered. This is partially due to the proprietary beginnings of the AS/400, which is considered a legacy system along with the mainframes. However, given the install base of the AS/400 and the fact that many of the operating systems covered in this handbook are candidates to migrate to (from the OS/400), it is worthwhile looking into the security implementation of the AS/400. Chapter 63 covers the security features of the AS/400.

One of the most significant problems in securing distributed systems is authentication. That is, ensuring that the parties to a conversation—possibly separated by a wide area network and traversing untrusted systems and communications paths—are who they claim to be. Kerberos is currently the *de facto* standard for authentication in large, heterogeneous network environments.

Kerberos has been in production for more than six years in one of the world's most challenging open systems environments—Project Athena at MIT. Kerberos is the backbone of network security for Project Athena, where it protects more than 10,000 users accessing thousands of workstations and hundreds of servers. Kerberos protects thousands of sessions and tens of thousands of mail messages per day. As such, Kerberos is arguably the best-tested, most scrutinized authentication protocol in widespread use today. Microsoft is planning to include Kerberos-based security in upcoming releases of Windows NT. Chapter 64 covers implementing Kerberos in distributed systems.

As mentioned earlier, e-mail is already turning out to be the most commonly used computer application—the use of which is growing everyday. Users rely on electronic mail for business or personal communications. However, most of e-mail communications are completely public and can easily be intercepted by electronic eavesdropping. In addition, if the messages are stored in a file, they are subject to perusal months or even years later. There is also the threat of impersonation, meaning that a message may not be from the party it claims to be from. One of the ways to secure e-mail is by using Pretty Good Privacy (PGP). Chapter 65 covers PGP, an e-mail security package that allows users to send messages that are secure from eavesdropping and guaranteed to be authentic.

In an introduction to security on the Internet, Chapter 66 describes the characteristics, applications, and protocols of the network. It also describes and explains the peculiar vulnerabilities that arise from these characteristics and the attacks that exploit them. This chapter offers strategies, tactics, and mechanisms for protecting the traffic on the network. It places special emphasis on firewalls and encryption and strategies for using them.

Applets are small programs that reside on a host computer and are downloaded to a client computer to be executed. While this model makes it very easy to distribute and update software, applets are also one of the newest security concerns of network managers. Chapter 67 describes how applets work, the threats they present, and what security precautions network managers can take to minimize the security exposures they present.

Security in computer systems is implemented at different levels. So far, this section has examined security implementation at the operating system and application levels. Chapter 68 describes how certain features of relational databases can be manipulated to gain unauthorized access to information, then suggests controls that help ensure data security (and, to a lesser degree, data integrity) in an Oracle environment.

Access controls have been built into relational database systems since they first emerged. Over the years, standards have developed and are continuing to evolve. In recent years, products incorporating mandatory controls for multilevel security have also started to appear. Chapter 69 discusses access controls in relational database management systems.

Chapter 59
Windows NT Server Security Features

Carol A. Siegel

The Windows NT operating system offers substantial security and audit features that have earned it the C2 evaluation for auditing and authentication from the National Computer Security Center (NCSC). The features described in this chapter should be implemented according to the policies and standards of the organization. Windows NT uses a client/server architecture in which clients and servers are grouped together to form domains. Each domain contains one or more servers, shares common databases and security policies, and has a unique name. How the domains interact should be determined before the operating system is installed. The trust relationships among these domains must be based on the business needs of the organization in conjunction with its security policies.

CREATING THE SECURITY ACCESS TOKEN

The interactive log-on process is unique to Windows NT and offers certain built-in security controls. To log on, the user must press three keys simultaneously: Ctrl + Alt + Del. By requiring this particular key combination, the operating system terminates any background process, thus preventing any Trojan horse program (e.g., a password grabber) from executing.

After these keys are correctly pressed, a valid user log-on is requested. The user must enter a user name and password. The security subsystem passes this input to the security account manager (SAM), thereby identifying and authenticating the user. SAM compares this information to a security database that contains the individual user profile. After it is authenticated, this profile is downloaded from the server and a security access token is created for that user. This access token is then passed to the Win32 subsystem and the log-on is now complete. The access token is an object that contains such specific information as the user security ID (SID), which uniquely identifies the user, the group security IDs, which are the group SIDs of which a user is a member, and the privileges assigned to

0-8493-9989-0/99/$0.00+$.50

the user. It is this access token that is used to determine whether a user is permitted to access an object.

IMPLEMENTING USER SECURITY

User security is established through the Policies menu in User Manager. The two policies in this menu are account policy and user rights policy. Account policy is a global policy that is applicable to all users in the specified domain (as shown in Exhibit 1).

The account policy comes with certain default settings. Exhibit 2 indicates the default settings and the suggested values.

The user rights policy defines what rights are granted to each system user or group of users. A right is an authorization for a user to perform a certain action on the system. These rights may affect systemwide resources, and they should be assigned with care. Exhibit 3 illustrates how rights are assigned. Exhibit 4 shows the userrights that can be assigned.

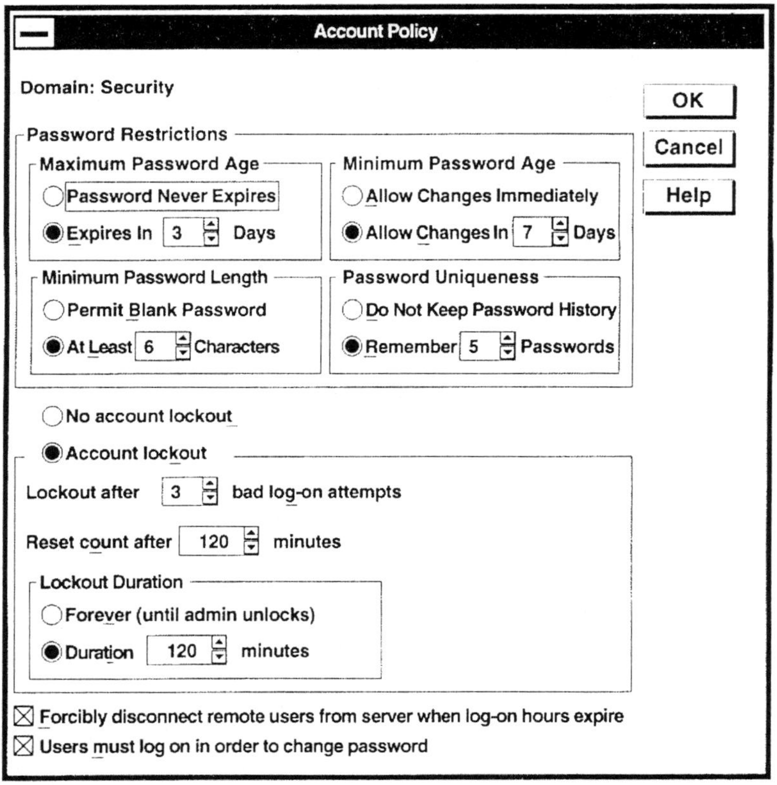

Exhibit 1. Account policy dialog box.

Exhibit 2. Account policy default settings and suggested values.

Account Policy	Default Value	Recommended Value
Passport expires in X days	30 Days	30, 60* Days
Passport change permitted after X days	14 days	7 days
Minimum password length	6 characters	8 characters
Password uniqueness	3 passwords	5 passwords
Account lockout after n bad login attempts	5 attempts	3 attempts
Reset the lockout count after n minutes	20 minutes	120 minutes
Account lockout for n minutes	60 minutes	120 minutes
Disconnect remote users when log-on hours expire	Do not disconnect	Disconnect**
User must log on to change password	Log-on required	Log-on required
Notes: * 30 days for privileged users, 60 days for nonprivileged users. ** Disconnecting will terminate any background processes as well.		

In addition to rights that may be assigned to individual users or groups, each user or group of users can have a profile that may be defined in the User Properties screen, accessible through User Manager for Domains.

Exhibit 5 indicates the default values of the User Properties menu and suggested values. In addition to the User Properties that can be selected, buttons can specify what groups a user belongs to, specific user log-on

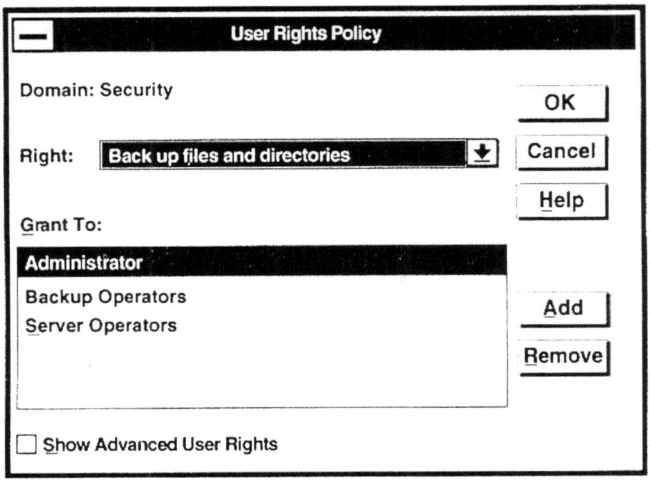

Exhibit 3. User rights policy dialog box.

Exhibit 4. User rights.

Right*	Permits a User:
Access this computer from network	Connect over the network to a computer.
Back up files and directories	Back up files and directories. This right overrides file and directory permissions.
Change the system time.	Set the time of the internal clock.
Force shutdown from a remote system. Not currently implemented.	
Log-on locally	Local log-on
Manage auditing and security log	Specify what types of events and resource access are to be audited; view and clear the security log.
Restore files and directories	Restore files and directories; overrides file and directory permissions
Shut down the system	Shut down Windows NT server.
Take ownership of files or other objects	Assume ownership of files, directories, and other objects in the system.
Note: * There are an additional 18 advanced rights. These are listed in the Windows NT Resource Kit, Microsoft Press.	

Exhibit 5. Default values of the user properties menu.

User Properties	Default Value	Recommended Value
User must change password at next log-on	Selected for new accounts	Select for new accounts or password changes
User cannot change his password	Not selected for all accounts except GUEST accounts	Not selected, except for GUEST account
Password never expires	Not selected	Not selected*
Account disabled	Not selected	Selected for GUEST account. Selected by the security administrator for various reasons
Note: * This may be selected on a case-by-case basis. For example, if a group of accounts were required to change their passwords on a specific day for a legitimate business reason, this feature could be used in conjunction with a manually forced password change by the security administrator for each member of the group.		

scripts, the hours in which the user is permitted to log on, what individual workstations the user is permitted to use, and the expiration date of the account. These features should also be used in conjunction with the overall security policies of the organization.

GROUP SECURITY CONCERNS

Local and global are the two types of groups. Local groups are defined on a node-by-node basis. They can be composed of both user accounts and global groups. In general, they set groupwide access permissions to resources on a local domain. Global groups are defined at the domain level. They set groupwide access permissions across multiple domains. Both local and global groups are created through User Manager for Domains. Individual members can then be added to each group. In addition, built-in local groups (e.g., administrators, users, guests, everyone, backup operators, server operators, account operators, and print operators) come with the operating system. These groups have preassigned rights, built-in abilities and members, but they can be assigned additional members. The rights assigned to these groups are alterable, the built-in abilities are not.

Valid uses for local groups include the following:

- They can be used only in the domain in which they were created.
- They can be used to give access to users for objects in one domain only.
- They can be composed of global groups and individual users.
- They can include users from multiple domains.

Valid uses for global groups include the following:

- They can be used to group individual users of a domain together.
- They can be included in local groups, and by this inclusion they can be assigned rights or permissions to resources.
- They cannot contain local groups.
- They cannot contain other global groups.

In general, local groups should be used as a way of setting groupwide access permissions on resources on the local domain, whereas global groups should be used as a way of setting groupwide access permissions across multiple domains.

DIRECTORY AND FILE PERMISSIONS

File and directory permissions and their ownership determine the manner in which they can be accessed. File permissions are set through File Manager by first selecting a file, then selecting the Permissions command from the Security menu. This will display the name of the file, its owner, and a list of users or groups and their corresponding access to the file. These users or groups can be added or deleted, or their access can be changed. Special access can be granted to files.

Directory permissions are set through File Manager by selecting a directory, and then selecting the Permissions command from the Security menu. Here, users and groups can be granted permissions. Special permissions on directories and some or all files in those directories can also be assigned.

In terms of ownership, the creator of the file or directory is the owner by default. The owner of the file can, however, grant ownership to another user by either changing its permissions or selecting Owner from the Security menu in File Manager and selecting the Take Ownership button. The target user can only take ownership if that ability has been granted. The administrator can, of course, take ownership at any time.

Permissions on shared files or directories can be defined through the Disk menu in File Manager. Through New Share, users or groups can be given access to shared files or directories and their permissions can be specified. However, permissions applied to directories include all subdirectories and their files.

AUDITING FEATURES

Windows NT auditing features can record events to show what users access what object, what type of access is being attempted, and whether the access attempt was successful. Windows NT provides auditing at the system-event level and at the object level. Auditing at the system-event level can be set by selecting Audit Policy under User Manager. Any user holding the Manage Auditing and Security Log right can set auditing at this level.

Selecting User Manager or User Manager for Domains, choosing the Audit command from the Policies menu, and selecting the Audit These Events option turns on auditing. If the Do Not Audit option is highlighted, all auditing is completely turned off. This is the default setting, but it is not recommended in any circumstance. If Do Not Audit is selected, system-level auditing and file and directory auditing are both turned off.

When selecting audit events, all events should be turned on for both successes and failures (or according to company policy). However, the log-on and log-off option may cause a significant number of log entries, depending on the number of user accounts and frequency of log-ons.

Other areas that can be audited are:

- Directories and files
- Registry changes

- Printer use
- User activity for Remote Access Servers
- Clipbook page use

All auditing is turned off by default. Therefore, for directory and file auditing to occur, file and object access must be turned on as part of the Audit Policy screen under User Manager or User Manager for Domains. Then for each directory or file, specific users or groups must be defined.

Security events can be viewed through the Event Viewer by selecting Security from the Log menu. For domains, all auditable events are written to the security log on the domain controller and refer to events that occur on the controller and all servers in the domain.

SECURITY EVENT LOGGING

Windows NT has a security log that records valid and invalid log-on attempts and events related to resource use such as creating, opening, or deleting files or other objects. System administrators or users with the manage auditing and security log right can view the security log events in the Event Viewer by selecting Security from the Log menu. By double clicking on any one event, a more detailed breakdown of that event can be displayed for analysis.

The security log is protected by an audit command language (ACL) that restricts access to all but the administrator. The security log[lang]systemroot[rang][bsol]System32[bsol]config[bsol]secevent.evt must be secured using NT file system so that the ACL can be used. The security log contains a header and version number that is placed at the beginning of each log file. This header can be used to ensure that the file being read or written to is a valid log file. The Event Log service validates an existing file before writing events to it, and it uses the Alert feature to alert the administrator if the file is not a valid event log file. When a log file gets full (e.g., the next record to be overwritten is within the retention period), an Alert is sent to the administrator, and the record is not written to the log. By selecting Log Settings from the Log menu, the system administrator can specify certain Event Log parameters relating to its size and event recording.

SECURITY ALERT MESSAGES

A special feature of the Windows NT operating system is the capability to send an alert message to a designated individual who can report on security-related events (e.g., too many log-on violations) as they occur. Performance Monitor's Alert View can be used together with network alerts to send an alert for any of the counters in Performance Monitor. The user must first specify to whom the alert goes in network alerts then turn on and specify the recipient of the message in Send Network Message in Alert Options. An alert message is sent to the designated receiver, and the results can be viewed in Performance Monitor's Alert View.

Log recording starts at boot time. By default, the maximum log size is 512K bytes per log, but this number can be set in accordance with disk and memory capacities. An administrator cannot, however, set the log for a smaller size than the size of the present log; the log must be cleared first. There are three choices for Event Log Wrapping:

- Overwrite Events as Needed (the default)
- Overwrite Events Older Than X Days
- Do Not Overwrite Events (Clear Log Manually)

It is recommended that your system be benchmarked to determine the optimal maximum log size. This is a balance between storage constraints, the amount of auditing being done, and archiving strategies. The Do Not Overwrite Events (Clear Log Manually) option should be selected so that events are not lost. When the log is full, an alert message is displayed to the system administrator.

PROHIBITED ACCESS MESSAGE CREATION

Through the string editor in the registry, the security administrator can create a message that is displayed to users after the Ctrl + Alt + Del keys are pressed at log-on time. This message appears in a dialog box and requires that the return key be pressed to continue. The text of this message should state the following: "THESE COMPUTER SYSTEMS ARE PRIVATE. UNAUTHORIZED ACCESS IS PROHIBITED. VIOLATORS WILL BE PROSECUTED." To create this message, the registry editor should be accessed and the following subkey selected:

```
HKEY_LOCAL_MACHINE[bsol ]SOFTWARE[bsol ]
  Microsoft[bsol ]WindonwsNT[bsol ]
  CurrentVersion[bsol ]Winlogon
```

To change the caption on the dialog box, double-click on the following:

```
LegalNoticeCaption : REG_SZ :
```

To change the text of the message, double-click on the following:

```
LegalNoticeText : REG_SZ :
```

CONCLUSION

Before the security practitioner goes live with the Windows NT system, certain decisions regarding security should be made. Areas that should be addressed by the practitioner include:

- Account policy
- Password controls
- Account lockout controls
- Log-on restrictions
- User rights policy
- Assignment to users
- Assignment to groups
- Create user properties
- Create user profiles and restrictions
- Groups
- Create overall group architecture
- Create local groups and assign users
- Create global groups and assign users
- Assign global groups to local groups
- Directories and files
- Set permissions on selected directories and files
- Set ownership on selected directories and files
- Create shared directories and files
- Auditing
- Turn on systemwide auditing
- Select items to be audited
- Consider auditing for other areas
- Security event log
- Set log parameters
- Configure alert messages
- Unauthorized access
- Change legal notice caption
- Change legal notice text

Chapter 60
UNIX Security Features

Allen B. Lum

The UNIX operating system was originally developed for use by programmers within an open systems environment. The adoption of UNIX as a common operating system across several different platforms has increased the need for security beyond its original purpose. As a result, many UNIX installations have less-than-optimal security. In addition, there are several versions of UNIX on the market today with differing security features. This chapter discusses basic access controls (e.g., passwords) and directory and file permissions within the UNIX system. The concepts discussed are applicable to all versions of UNIX unless specifically noted otherwise.

UNIX HISTORY

UNIX was developed at AT Bell Laboratories in the late 1960s by Thompson and Ritchie; the name UNIX is a contraction of uni and multics. The original UNIX system software was written in the Assembler language to run on the digital PDP-7 computer. In the early 1970s, UNIX was ported over to the PDP-11 and rewritten in the C programming language. Rewriting UNIX in C enabled the UNIX operating system to be used on other hardware platforms that supported a C compiler.

By this time, Bell Labs had distributed the UNIX operating system free to universities and the federal government. The rapid decrease in the cost of computer hardware—specifically the reduced instruction set computing (RISC) processor, which supports the UNIX operating system—resulted in wide acceptance of UNIX by the business sector.

In 1983, AT announced support of the UNIX operating system under the product name System III. The current version as of this writing is System V Release 4. Other manufacturers have licensed the source code from AT and implemented their own versions with additional features not found in AT's version. Examples of different implementations include SunOS

0-8493-9989-0/99/$0.00+$.50

(Sun Microsystems, Inc., Mountain View, CA) and the ULTRIX systems (Digital Equipment Corp., Maynard, MA).

Until recently, UNIX vendors did not place security features as a top priority because customers had not demanded them. In light of recent network intrusions, however, security needs have come into focus, and vendors are responding accordingly. Each vendor's version of UNIX differs in terms of security features, because the vendors obtain the source code of the UNIX operating system and implement various features depending on their particular target market. It is important to examine the vendor documentation for all possible security features.

Basic UNIX Architecture

The UNIX operating system can be divided into three components. The first is called the UNIX operating system kernel, or simply the kernel. The kernel is the core of the UNIX system and resides in main memory; it must be considered the heart of the UNIX operating system. The second component can be defined as the shell, which serves as the user interface to the kernel, and is typically executed at log-in time. Users communicate to the UNIX kernel by issuing commands through the shell. Common UNIX shells include C and Bourne. The third component consists of utilities that reside on disk and are called into main memory only when requested. Examples of UNIX utilities include sendmail and restore, which send mail and restore backup files respectively.

LOG-IN PROCEDURES

From a security perspective, the log-in procedures provide entry to the UNIX system. When a user logs in to the system, a UNIX program called init automatically starts the getty program, which is executed on each user terminal. The getty program determines the terminal speed and displays the log-in message at the terminal. After the getty program has been executed, the system waits for the entry of the user's log-in ID. The getty program is then replaced by the login program. Before being replaced, getty transmits the characters entered by the user (i.e., the log-in ID) to log in.

When login begins executing, it prompts the user to enter a password. After the password has been entered, login checks the password file (/etc/passwd) and verifies that the password entered is the correct one for that user ID. (The /etc/passwdfile also contains information that defines the user's operating environment.) Start-up files are then executed, as described in the next section.

START-UP FILES

When a user logs in to the UNIX system, several start-up files are executed. These files are used to determine the system and operating

Exhibit 1. Common UNIX start-up files.

File Name	Description
cshrc	Defines such items as paths and directories that are searched when programs are executed. This start-up file is executed each time a shell or subprocess is created. It is used in UNIX systems written in the C language.
Login	Executes specific files that define a user's environment (e.g., a user's terminal characteristics). This command file is executed only after the .cshrc file has been executed.
/etc/prof	Contains commands that are executed at log-in time for each user (e.g., user-defined menus and default file security). This systemwide command fiel is used with UNIX systems that have a Bourne shell. It enables administrators to define security for users (e.g., file protection defaults).
Profile	Contains commands that further define a user's environment and can start user applications. This start-up file is located in the user's home directory and is executed each time a user logs in.
/rsh	Limits a user's capabilities by disallowing the ability to change directories, change the PATH variable, using a command containing a slash, or redirect output.

environment for that particular user. They can define a user's terminal and home directory. Depending on the version of UNIX and the type of shell used, several start-up files can be executed. Exhibit 1 lists the most common shells and associated start-up files.

A user's default start-up shell is specified into the/etc/passwd file, which will be discussed in greater detail later in this chapter. In most UNIX systems, start-up files and their associated shells are as follows:

- C shell (csh)
  - cscrc
  - login
  - logout
- Bourne (sh) and Korn (ksh) shell
  - profile

A different set of start-up files will be executed depending on the user's default shell. If no shell is defined for the user, in most UNIX systems the Bourne shell will be executed. Exhibit 2 illustrates the UNIX log-in process.

There are two schools of thought on the use of the restricted (.rsh) shell. The group that advocates its use claims that the restricted shell offers an excellent security feature as long as the following precautions are taken:

- All users are placed in a menu with appropriate traps so users cannot exit or escape into the UNIX environment.
- The restricted environment requires a password at log-in.

- Users are restricted from access to commands that let them escape to the shell (e.g., the use of the mail utilities or vi editor).

The biggest drawback to use of the .rsh shell is the ability of users to break out of the shell and access a UNIX prompt.

The second group believes that the restricted shell should not be used because of the limitations it places on the user environment. This group suggests alternative procedures that can be set up by the security or systems administrator to perform the same functions as.rsh. These procedures include:

- Using secure C programs to limit the user's ability to perform certain functions.
- Using restricted menus.
- Refusing to give the user access to the shell. The user's menu should be called directly from the log-in routine instead of the shell. The statement calling the menu can be added to the /etc/passwd file.
- Placing users in their own subsystem.

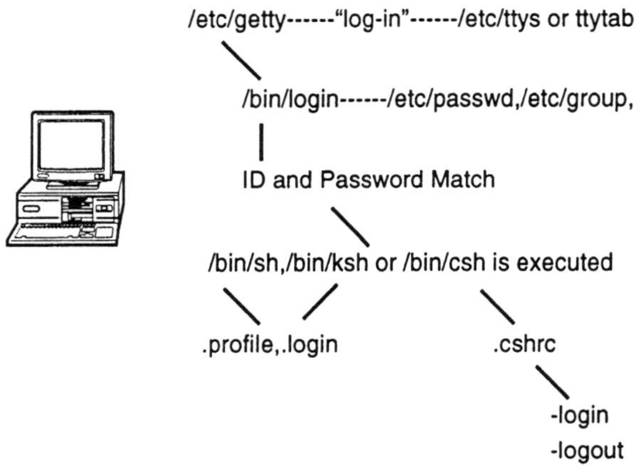

Exhibit 2. UNIX log-in process.

For security to be effective, it is important to restrict the user's ability to update the start-up files, because they control the user's operating environment. Only the systems administrator should have the ability to change or update these files. (The permissions that control user access to files and directories are discussed later.)

Another option that has been used successfully by many companies is to specify an executable program that will be executed instead of a user's shell (i.e., C, Bourne, or K shell) at start-up. This program is typically written in the C language and presents a menulike structure to the user. A user selects an item from the menu, and that item executes an associated program. The advantage of this method is that a user is kept captive to a particular menu.

THE ROOT ACCOUNT

Most UNIX systems have an ID called the root account or root ID, which is used by the system administrator. It is designated with a group ID of 0. The root account has access to all system files and utilities and the ability to change system operating characteristics. As a result, it is important that the passwords to the root account be carefully controlled and frequently changed. The root account passwords should never be given out over the telephone, and they should be distributed only to those persons who need to know them.

The substitute user or superuser (su) command allows someone to log in from another user's directory while that user is still logging in. If the su is used without a user ID, it attempts to log in the user as the root account. In most systems, any attempt to log in as the root account causes an entry to be made in the accounting (sulog) file. (The sulog file is one of several UNIX log files that serve as audit trails for user activities.) Use of the root account for daily activities should be discouraged. Therefore, users should not be allowed to log in to the root account by using the login command; the su command should be used instead, because it monitors all attempts to log in and records them in the system console log.

PASSWORDS

With many computer systems, user IDs and their associated passwords are the first line of defense against unauthorized access. For example, in October 1988, a worm was released into Internet, causing a great deal of damage within the UNIX system. A major component of the Internet worm was its ability to crack user passwords. As described by Rik Farrow:

The worm worked on passwords in three phases. First it tried "easy" guesses—no password, the log-in name, the log-in name twice, the last name, any nickname, and the last name reversed. Each password it [found was] added to the user accounts table (within the worm). The second phase [tried an] internal list [of passwords] that was used to successfully guess passwords on other systems. The words in this list [included] first names, computer terms, locations, and last names all lowercase and correctly spelled. In the third phase, the worm used words in the on-line dictionary, /usr/dict/words.[1]

A little common sense in the selection and use of passwords can go a long way in preventing unauthorized access. As a general rule, passwords should not be easy to guess by anyone. Password standards should be implemented as part of an overall security policy. The following should be used as a guide in the selection of passwords:

- Passwords should have a minimum length of six characters.
- User IDs should not be shared among users.
- Passwords should not be written down. Users should keep their passwords secure.
- People's names and the name of the company should not be used.
- The same password should not be used on different systems.
- Passwords should not be reused. A different password should be established each time passwords are changed.

These are common password standards that should be incorporated into the company's security policy and communicated to all users.

Password Files

The UNIX system stores user passwords in a file called psswd within the /etc directory. Exhibit 3 is an example of a typical entry in the /etc/passwd.

Password files can also be used to restrict users to an authorized set of menus. Most users should not have access to the UNIX operating system environment and related commands. As a security precaution, users should never be placed in the /bin directory (which contains UNIX system commands and programs) or other system directories at start-up time.

```
AUDITOR: VE4$%#$%8902kj3 : 415 : 200 : Allen : /user/allen : /bin/sh :
    1            2          3     4      5          6           7
```

Colons are used to separate the fields. The fields are described as follows:

Field	Description
1	The user's ID name.
2.	The password, in encrypted form.
3	The user ID number. A user ID of 0 allows the user access to the root account.
4	The group ID number.
5	The user's name.
6	The home directory of the user. Users are placed in this directory at log-in time.
7	The program or process that is started at log-in time. For many applications, this process should provide a menu for the user.

Exhibit 3. UNIX directory structure.

Password Encryption

The information in the /etc/passwd file is kept in an encrypted form; passwords cannot be decrypted. All UNIX systems currently on the market use the Data Encryption Standard (DES) to encrypt passwords.

The problem with the /etc/passwd file is that it can be accessed and viewed by all users. Although the passwords themselves are encrypted, hackers can make a copy of the /etc/passwd file and attempt to figure out the passwords. Hackers can make guesses by encrypting the words from a word processing dictionary (or any other dictionary) using the DES and comparing the encrypted results with the entries in the /etc/passwd file. This process can be easily programmed into a workstation.

To prevent unauthorized access to and copying of the /etc/passwd file, numerous vendors have added a shadow password file, called /etc/shadow, which is used in conjunction with the /etc/passwd file. The encrypted passwords are stored in /etc/shadow instead of in the /etc/passwd file. The difference is that only the root account has access to the shadow password file, whereas all users have access to the /etc/passwd file. In addition, the shadow password file contains information not stored in the /etc/passwd file, including password aging information, the minimum number of times a password can be changed, the days since a particular date that the password was changed, the maximum number of days the password is valid, and password expiration dates.

Security Concerns and Risk Assessments

The systems administrator should scan the /etc/passwdfile on a regular basis to look for anything unusual. Sound security practices dictate that:

- **User ID numbers and names should not be duplicated.** If more than than one user has the same ID number or name, individual user accountability is sacrificed.
- **Null passwords should not be allowed.** Null passwords allow users to log in to an ID without a password.
- **User IDs should equal 0 only in special cases.** Any user who has a user ID of 0 obtains root account or superuser privileges. There should be only a limited number of users with root access.
- **Users should not be placed in the system directory(/binor /etc) at start-up time.** Most users should be placed in a user directory (/usr) or subdirectory (e.g.,/usr/allen) and forced to work within a menu that prevents them from gaining access to the UNIX operating system-level commands.

In addition, user groups should be employed to restrict access to projects or sensitive files. All unused accounts or accounts of terminated employees should be deleted.

DIRECTORY AND FILE SECURITY

Each operating system—whether DOS, MVS, or UNIX—has its own unique file and directory structure. In securing the UNIX system, it is important to assign proper protection to files and directories to prevent unauthorized access. The following sections discuss three types of UNIX files—regular files, directory files, and device or special files—as well as symbolic links between files.

Regular Files. Regular files contain data stored in preallocated data blocks. Typical contents include user application and program data as well as executable program images.

Directory Files. Like the regular files, directory files contain data that is stored in preallocated data blocks. Typically, a directory file contains the file names that make up the directory and the numbers that provide reference to devices. The directories are accessed by the reference in a path name. For example, /etc references the /etc directory.

Device Files. Device files contain references to special device routines within the UNIX kernel but do not contain storage data. For example, the routine in the /dev/mem file calls the UNIX operating system to display the computer's memory.

Symbolic Links. Symbolic links are the links between file systems. They provide indirect references from one file to another.

Directory Structure

Like all common operating systems (e.g., DOS for the IBM PC), UNIX has its own defined directory structure. The UNIX directory structure is shaped like an inverted tree, as shown in Exhibit 4. At the top is the root directory; descending from the root are several subdirectories that contain specific UNIX system files. Different versions of UNIX may have subdirectories other than those in Exhibit 4. The files contained in the subdirectories shown in the exhibit are described as follows:

- The /etc directory contains all files related to configuration, installation, and system administration.
- The bin directory contains UNIX system commands and programs.
- The /dev directory contains UNIX files that are used to access all system devices (e.g., disk drives).
- The /stand directory contains standard UNIX programs and files that are required to boot the system. This directory is available only in UNIX System V Release 4.
- The /lib directory contains the UNIX set of programming libraries.

- The /tmp directory contains temporary work and data files that are created by UNIX programs.
- The /usr directory contains user profiles and customized commands.

To ensure security, it is important to restrict users from accessing certain directories. Most users should have only read access to the directories shown in Exhibit 4, with the exception of /usr and /tmp, which may also have write access. Types of access are discussed further in a later section.

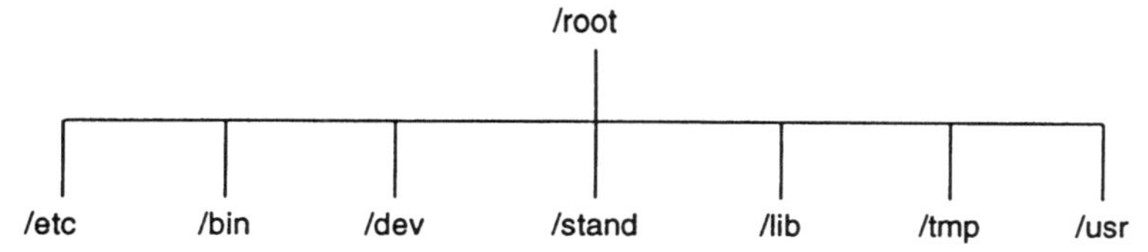

Exhibit 4. UNIX directory structure.

The Root Directory

The root or system directory (/root) contains the UNIX operating system. To prevent unauthorized use of system programs and data, write access to the root directory or subdirectories should be limited to the systems administrator at start-up time.

Security Concerns and Risks Assessments

Most security administrators feel that users should be granted access to only the files and data they need to perform their jobs. System and data files are no exception. The system-defined directories and files must be protected from unauthorized access and use. Should an unauthorized person gain access to system directories, he or she could take control of the system.

Most system files should not be readable or writable by any person except the systems administrator or manager. Permission to write to a system directory might allow an unscrupulous user to place a Trojan horse within the root directory. For example, the ls command, which lists a directory, can be replaced with another ls command that might perform other functions.

DIRECTORY AND FILE ACCESS PROTECTION

Several methods can be used to protect access to UNIX directories and files. Users can be placed into groups that define which files and directories they have access to, or access permissions can be placed on directories and files according to protection masks. In addition, execution behavior bits can be used to assign special privileges. These protection methods are discussed in the following sections.

User Groups

Users can be placed into groups within the UNIX system to restrict access to sensitive information. For example, the accounting department users can be placed into one group that permits them to work only on accounting-related files and data. Anyone not assigned to the accounting user group would be unable to read or modify the accounting group's data. Users are placed into these groups as defined in the group file, which resides in the /etc directory.

The following command will provide a list of the members of the group file:

```
cat/etc/group
```

This command might result in the following output:

```
root::0:root
console::1:root,console
ginn::2:root,bin
sys::3:root,bins,sys
data1::12:allen,john
data2::13:pete,mary
data3::14:allen,mary
```

As in the /etc/passwd file (see Exhibit 3), colons are used to separate information fields. In the /etc/groupfile, the first field is the group name. The second field is the password, which is optional; in this example, passwords were not used. The third field gives the group ID, and the fourth field identifies the members of the group.

The group ID in the /etc/group file corresponds with the group ID contained in the /etc/passwd file. In this example, the root directory is in group 0. The /etc/group file allows users to be members of more than one group; in the example, allen is a member in the data1 and data3 groups. The security administrator must ensure that users are assigned to groups according to their job functions.

Protection Masks

The primary defense against unauthorized access is the use of passwords and the controlled use of start-up profiles (i.e., profile).The secondary defense is the use of permissions. File permissions are associated with reading, writing, and executing files; directory permissions are associated only with reading and writing. Every directory and file has a 10-bit protection mask that defines the privileges associated with it.

The following is an example of a typical protection mask for a file:

```
-rwxrwxr-x
```

The first bit or position in the protection mask defines whether it is for a file or a directory. If the mask is for a file, a hyphen will appear, as in the example. If it is for a directory, a d will appear in this position.

The next nine bits of protection mask can be broken down into three 3-bit groups, as follows:

- **Owner permissions.** The second, third, and fourth bits define what the owner can do to the file or directory.
- **Group permissions.** The fifth, sixth, and seventh bits define what users with the same group ID can do to that file or directory.
- **World or other permissions.** The last three bits define what every authorized user outside the group can do to that file or directory.

For each of these three bit groups, the access permissions are defined as read (r),write (w), and execute (x). Read permission means that the file or directory can be read or copied. Write permission allows a file or directory to be written to or updated. Execute permission indicates that a file can be executed only as a program.

In the example, the owner of the file would have read, write, and execute permissions. Another user in the same group would also have read, write, and execute permissions. All other users on the system, however, would have only read and execute permissions to the file.

In UNIX, the permission rwx can, for each of the permission groups (owner, group, and world), be represented by their octal numbers as follows:

```
x  =  1

w  =  2

r  =  4
```

Thus, a permission for world group that allows read rwx would be 7, the sum of the octal numbers. The permission for world group that allows only execute would be 1. Exhibit 5 shows the correlation between permissions and their octal numbers. The permission mask that would allow full rwx access for the groups would be 777; the permission mask that would allow

Owner			Group			Other		
r	w	x	r	w	x	r	w	x
4			4			4		
	2			2			2	
		1			1			1

Exhibit 5. Numeric Equivalents of Access Permissions.

only rwx access for owner, rx access for the group and no access for the world would be 750.

Read, write, and execute permissions should not be allowed in the world field of the protection masks on application files and data. System programs and utilities should be reviewed to see if world permissions are appropriate. In addition, files and directories should not be readable or writable by all system users unless they contain public data that all users are allowed to see.

UNIX follows a simple set of rules in deciding which category to examine to determine the access permissions for a particular user.[2] If the user is the owner of the file, only the owner permissions should be checked. If the user is not the owner of the file but is a member of the group owning the file, only the group permissions should be checked. If the user is neither the owner nor a member of the group owning the file, only the world permissions field should be checked.

Umask Value

Umask is a value that when subtracted from the default file permission, which is usually 777, defines the default protection of a user's file and directories. The default system file permission is usually defined at the time the UNIX operating system is compiled. The umask value can be defined in system start-up files and in a user's start-up files such as .login or profile, depending on the shell that is used. If, for example, the system default permission were 777 and the user had a umask value of 022, the default file permission would be 755, arrived at as follows:

```
  777  default permission
 -022  umask
  755  default permission
```

Execution Behavior Bits

UNIX has a special setting within the file protection masks that can be defined as execution behavior bits. These bits allow a user to assume the execution privileges of the file owner or group. For example, changing a password requires modification to the /etc/passwdfile, which usually requires root access. Because users occasionally must change their passwords but should not always have root access, the execution behavior bit can be used to grant a user root access or privileges only for execution of the program that changes the password.

The execution behavior bits cause the programs to assume the set user ID or set group ID, discussed in the following sections. There should be no set user ID or set group ID shell scripts on the system. All nonstandard UNIX programs should be checked for set user ID and set group ID programs. Exhibit 6 illustrates the use of execution behavior bits.

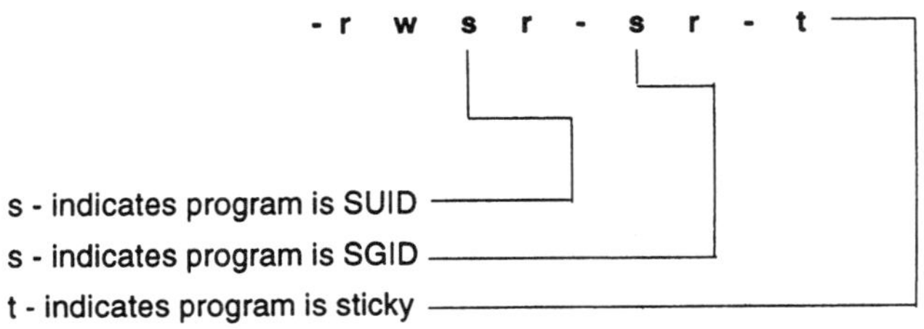

Exhibit 6. The use of execution behavior bits.

The Set User ID. The set user ID bit can be inserted into the owner field of the protection mask to allow the user to assume all privileges of the file owner. To grant set user ID privileges, the letter S is placed in the fourth bit position instead of the letter X.

The Set Group ID. The set group ID behaves the same way as the set user ID, but it allows the user to assume group permissions rather than owner permissions. To grant set group ID privileges, the letter S replaces the letter X in bit position 7 of the group field.

The Sticky Bit. The use of sticky bits causes an executable file to remain in memory after execution, hence the term "sticky bit." This feature improves system performance because once the programs are in memory, they can be started by other users without having the system fetch the programs from disk and load them into main memory.

A sticky bit has a different meaning for directories: in a directory protection mask, the sticky bit prevents a user from moving or deleting files not owned by that user. For example, the world permission for a directory may be set to rwx, which allows all users to delete any file contained in the directory. By setting the sticky bit, however, only the owner and the root user can delete or move the files. The sticky bit is set by replacing the letter X with a T in the world permissions field (i.e., bit 10).

By setting the sticky bit, the security administrator can grant specific privileges to users without compromising overall security. In addition, the use of sticky bits for directories can enhance overall security by controlling the number of users who can delete or move files. The administrator must be careful about which files and directories are set to have a sticky bit.

The octal values of the suid, sgid, and the sticky bit are set in the first position of the 10-bit execution mask as follows:

```
2  =  suid
4  =  sgid
6  =  a  sticky  bit
```

A permission mask (octal value) of 4755 indicates that the file is sgid, a mask of 2777 indicates that the file is suid.

Changing File Permissions

File permissions can be changed by using the chmod command. Only the file owner may use the chmod command. The syntax for this command is:

```
chmod  [ugoa]  +  [rwx]

where:

    u  =  user
    g  =  group
    o  =  other  or  world
    a  =  all  users

[plusmn]  =  the  operation  (i.e.,  add  or  delete  the
             permission)
```

To use this command, the owner selects user, group, or other from the first set of bracketed options, then selects either + or - to add or delete the permission, and finally specifies which permission will be added or deleted by selecting read, write, or execute from the second set of bracketed options. For example, the following chmod command removes the write permission to file data for the other permission field:

```
chmod  o-w  data
```

Another way to use the chmod command is to define the octal value for the file transmissions and then for the file name. For example, the command chmod 777 datafile changes the permission for the datafile to allow read, write, and execute for the owner, group, and world. The command chmod changes the permission to allow read, write, and execute for the owner but only read and execute for the group and the world.

UNIX LOG FILES

UNIX has several files that keep track of various user activities, including the time the user logs in, use of the root account, and the commands executed by each user. A summary of the UNIX log files is presented in Exhibit 7. The UNIX vendor's documentation should be checked to determine how to implement the logging facilities.

Exhibit 7. UNIX log files.

File Name	Description
/usr/adm/lastlog	Records the user's most recent log-in
/etc/sulog	Records each time the root account is used
/etc/utmp	Maintains a record of the time of each user login
/usr/adm/acct	Records every command run by every user

In addition to the log files in Exhibit 7, a general log-in facility called syslog has been implemented for Berkeley's UNIX system. The syslog records messages from the UNIX kernel, user processes, the mail system, the user authorization system(i.e., adding any changes to user IDs), and locally defined events. Several other UNIX vendors have also ported the syslog to their version and implementation of UNIX.

These log files provide an excellent audit trail of user activity. Should any security-related problems occur, these logs should be examined in detail.

UNIX COMMANDS

The UNIX system provides a number of commands that the security administrator or auditor can use to help find security problems.

The Find Command

- Descends the directory tree from the specified pathname
- Locates files that meet the specified conditions

For example, the command find / -perm 007 -print finds all files that are rwx to everyone, the command find $home -print lists files in the home directory, and the command find -name allen -print lists all files of a specified name.

The ls Command

The ls command lists information about a file. For example, the command ls -[options], where options is

- a—lists all files, including hidden files, that begin with a.
- c—lists files by creation time.
- f—indicates file types by / for directory,* for executables, and [commat] for symbolic links.
- i—lists i node for each file.
- t—lists files according to modifications times.
- u—lists files according to access times.

The passwd Command

The passwd command allows the user to create or change a password. Only the owner or privileged user may change a password. For example, the options available to nonprivileged users with the command passwd [options] user are:

- s display pw information:
  —user name
  —password status
  —number of days before password can be changed
  —number of days before password expires
  —number of days before expiration that user is warned

The **options** available to a privileged user with the passwd[options] user command are:

- [ndash]a p used with s to display information for all users
- [ndash]d delete password; user no longer prompted
- [ndash]f force expiration of user password
- [ndash]l lock user's password
- [ndash]n set number of days that must pass before user can change a password

All versions of UNIX include these procedured for the passwd command; the manual should always be checked.

The who Command

The who command displays information about currently logged-on users (e.g., % who).

The pwd Command

The pwd (present working directory) command displays the current working directory. At times, it is very easy to forget where one is in the UNIX directory tree; this command helps users find where they are.

Security Concerns and Risk Assessments

To prevent unauthorized access to programs and data, the security administrator should analyze the permission masks for all key system and data files. On most program and data files and directories, permissions in the world field should be set to r-x to prevent users from having write access.

RECOMMENDED COURSE OF ACTION

The security administrator should examine the overall status of the UNIX system on a regular basis. The Computer Emergency Response Team (CERT) at Carnegie Mellon University recommends the following procedures to help ensure the security of the UNIX system:

- Reviewing log-in and profile scripts. No IFS, path, or shell parameters should need to be assigned.
- Reviewing the various log files on a regular basis.
- Ensuring that there are no temporary or guest accounts on the system.
- Reviewing the file permissions on all start-up files and directories.
- Ensuring that there are no start-up files in public directories (e.g., /tmp).
- Setting a safe path for system directories. For example,/bin and /usr/bin should be set before the user directory is accessed.

Over the past few years, intruders have gained access to UNIX systems by exploiting weak system configurations and setups. CERT has identified several areas that have been used by intruders trying to gain unauthorized access. These areas are discussed in the following sections.

Passwords. As discussed in an earlier section of this chapter, effective password standards provide the first line of defense against intruders. The password file should be scanned for unauthorized user IDs of 0, for accounts without passwords, and for new entries. Vendor-supplied default passwords should be changed when new system software is installed.

The Trivial File Transfer Protocol. The trivial file transfer protocol, which is resident on most UNIX systems, facilitates the movement of files between systems on the network. However, it has been used by intruders to steal password files. To test the system for this vulnerability, the security administrator should log in to the system using the protocol and then enter the following command, which provides access to the password file:

```
get/etc/motd
```

If access to the password file is gained, the trivial file transfer protocol should be disabled. If it is suspected that the password file has already been accessed by an intruder, all passwords on the system should be changed.

Weaknesses in the sendmail Program. The sendmail program allows users to send mail messages to each other. It should be verified that the system has the latest version of sendmail from the vendor. BSD 5.65 (Berkeley System Design, Berkeley CA) helps overcome security weaknesses that intruders have exploited.

Old Versions of the File Transfer Protocol. It should be ensured that the system is running the most recent version of the file transfer protocol (as of this writing, the most recent version is BSD 5.60). The vendor should be asked for information on configuration upgrades.

In addition, the anonymous file transfer protocol (which allows someone to access the system anonymously) should be checked. It is important to follow the instructions provided with the operating system to properly configure the files available through the anonymous file transfer protocol with respect to file permissions, ownership, and groups.

The finger Program. The finger program prints such user information as user ID name, full name, and location and time of log-in. (The network server version is called fingerd.) This program has a security weakness, however, that was exploited by the Internet worm. The systems administrator should ensure that the most recent version of finger or fingerd is being run.

The /etc/hos.equiv and .rhosts Files. These files should be checked for systems outside of the domain. The administrator should verify that all hosts in these files are authorized and that the files do not have write permissions in the world field of their protection masks. Several vendors supply .rhosts files and /etc/hosts.equiv files that have a + within them. The vendor should be asked to explain why the + is there; this element should be removed unless it is necessary.

The cron Process. The UNIX process is included in multiuser environments to run UNIX commands and programs on a regularly scheduled basis. It could be used, however, to execute unauthorized programs. The administrator should examine all files that are run by cron and at (which is used to execute commandes at a later time). Intruders can leave back doors in files run from the cron process, which can let intruders back into the system even after they have been kicked off. In addition, the administrator should verify that all files and programs referenced (directly or indirectly) by the cron process do not have write permissions in the world fields of their protection masks.

The /etc/inetd.conf File. This file should be examined for unauthorized changes or entries. The administrator should look for entries that execute a shell program (signified by /bin/sh). In addition, all programs that are specified in /etc/inetd.conf should be checked to verify that they are correct and have not been replaced by Trojan horses.

Misconfiguration of the uccp Programs. The uccp is a collection of programs that provides basic networking between computers using the UNIX operation systems. If the organization's UNIX system supports uccp, the systems administrator should check the I.cmds file to see if any extra commands have been added. In addition, it should be determined whether it is owned by root rather than uccp and whether it has read permission in the world field of its protection mask. The I.sys file also should not have read or write permissions in its world field.

The usr/lib/aliases File. This file, which shows the mail aliases, should be examined for unauthorized entries. Some files include an alias name uudecode or just decode. If this alias exists in the system and it is not being explicitly used, it should be removed.

Hidden Files. The security administrator should search the system for hidden files (i.e., files that start with a period and are usually not shown when the ls command is executed) with odd names or set user ID capabilities because they can be used to hide information or privileged programs, including /bin/sh. Such names as .. (dot dot space), ..., and .xx have been used, as have ordinary-looking names (e.g., .mail). Places to look include /tmp,/usr/tmp, and hidden directories (frequently within users' home directories).

Unauthorized Versions of Critical System Programs. The integrity of critical system programs (e.g., su, login, and telnet) should be verified. The program that is being run should be compared with a copy that is known to be clean (e.g., the original distribution media).

Inappropriate secure Setting in /etc/ttys and /etc/ttytab. These files show the terminal type; they should be checked for inappropriate settings. In the default setting, one of the terminal types other than the console should be set to secure.

Old Versions of System Software. Older versions of systems often have security vulnerabilities that are well-known to intruders. The best defense against this problem is to upgrade to the latest version.

Identifying Intrusions

CERT recommends the following procedures for determining whether an intruder has gained unauthorized access to the system:

- **The log files should be examined for logins from unusual locations.** This procedure is not foolproof, however; many intruders can remove their log-ins from the accounting files.
- **User directories should be examined for unusual or hidden files.** Many intruders put a hidden directory in a user's account with an unusual name.
- **The system should be examined for any set user ID files.** Intruders often leave set user ID copies of /bin/sh on the system to allow them root access at a later time.
- **The system programs should be examined to make sure they have not been changed.** Intruders have changed UNIX network programs(e.g., /bin/login and telnet). The copies on the system should be compared with a clean copy (e.g., one loaded from the initial installation tapes or disks). Backups should not be trusted, because they could also contain Trojan horses.

Notes

1. R. Farrow, UNIX System Security (Reading MA: Addison-Wesley, 1991) p. 262.
2. Farrow, p. 28.

Chapter 61
Software Tools for Detecting Misuse on Unix Systems

Stephen E. Smaha
Jessica Winslow

Experience has shown that most computer misuse is perpetrated by authorized insiders, and it may be difficult to prevent abuse of assigned privilege. In addition, increased network connectivity over the Internet and other national networks greatly magnifies the risk of penetration by highly skilled outsiders.

In Unix networks especially, it is easy for a user to move from machine to machine, using different user identifiers on each one. Because each machine knows only about the activities it sees, the individual audit trails or security logs are not able to tie together all these activities across machines as belonging to a single user. The sheer volume of network communications traffic and the evanescent nature of network connections make it difficult to ensure accountability without continuous monitoring.

To detect computer and network misuse, it is essential to increase accountability for user activities on computers and networks. Accountability requires reliable and consistent authentication of users plus the trustworthy association of user identities with reports of user activities.

A new generation of misuse detection tools is becoming available that allows systems managers to discover the source, time, and type of misuse shortly after its occurrence. When used in conjunction with improved access controls, better password mechanisms, and encryption of data, these misuse detection tools can provide a higher degree of assurance regarding data confidentiality, integrity, and availability.

This chapter discusses how to select software tools for detecting misuse of Unix computers; advantages and disadvantages of each of the four

0-8493-9989-0/99/$0.00+$.50

types of tools are presented. The chapter describes the important features system managers should look for when selecting a misuse-detection tool and discusses issues that must be addressed in implementing these security software tools.

COMPUTER AND NETWORK SECURITY GOALS

An organization's computer and network security goals can be viewed in terms that are analogous to the law enforcement model of prevention, deterrence, investigation, and interception:

- **Prevention.** Implementation of appropriate measures to increase the difficulty of performing unacceptable activities can prevent criminal behavior.
- **Deterrence.** The credible threat of detection is a major deterrent to criminal behavior.
- **Investigation.** After a crime has been committed, the law enforcement goal is to identify the criminal, collect all relevant evidence, and manage the investigatory process.
- **Interception.** A criminal identified in the act of committing a crime is more likely to be prosecuted and convicted.

The following paragraphs examine if and how security tools satisfy these objectives.

DATA SOURCES FOR MISUSE DETECTION

There are four fundamental data sources used for detecting misuse:

- Audit trails
- Network traffic data
- Specialized network devices
- Keystroke capture

The data available in any particular situation varies substantially among user organizations and Unix platforms. A major technical problem in designing misuse detection tools is the difficulty in integrating more than one type of data into one product because of the vast differences in their source, format, and availability.

Audit Trails

The richest information available is from operating system audit trails, which are designed to provide accountability. Most versions of the Unix operating system are capable of extensive event logging, in addition to the much weaker system accounting files. The old rationalizations for disabling audit mechanisms (e.g., excessive processing and storage overhead) are mostly fictions in this era of cheap processors, large disks, and high-volume tape backups. In addition to audit trail data generated by the operating system, some application programs and database-management systems generate log files with audit trail characteristics.

Network Traffic Data

Network traffic logs, especially from multiple points, are as valuable as audit trails, but they may become incredibly voluminous if they must be stored. Depending on whether only network packet addressing information is captured (i.e., traffic capture) or if everything on the network is captured and stored (i.e., traffic and content capture), a busy network can generate large quantities of data every second, and require far more storage hardware than most sites could afford. However, if network data can be analyzed for important events in real time and does not have to be stored, this is a feasible data source for misuse detection.

It is also tricky to combine network data with host-based information because network events are described in very different terms from host audit trail events. For example, network events usually contain information about hosts (e.g., network addresses), whereas audit events usually describe actions by authenticated users. When logging is done at the network level, network events typically report the source and destination network addresses, protocol and service types, and similar information recorded at the network packet level. At the network level, nothing is known about individual users at a particular host. Host audit events, on the other hand, have access to all the information that the host has about its users. This typically includes user IDs, group memberships, changes in privilege, and where the login originated. Another problem is the reliability of data in network logs, because spoofing a network address is relatively simple.

Specialized Network Devices

Two examples of specialized network devices are firewalls and authentication servers. Network firewalls designed to keep unauthorized external users from penetrating a private network domain may be designed to report unusual traffic or repeated attempts to break into the domain. A central authentication system such as a smart-card system or a Kerberos authentication server can report which users have provided appropriate credentials, as well as failed log-in attempts.

Keystroke Capture

Few environments are able to support full-scale keystroke capture logs for all users. Such logs can make an impressive evidence base for a legal case if the data has been appropriately protected. Aside from the obvious privacy concerns, the biggest problem is the difficulty in performing automated analysis of keystroke logs. We do not yet have analysis engines that can understand both natural language and the contextual meaning of a large number of computer commands. Keystroke information can be ambiguous from a security point of view. For example, most modern operating systems allow simple aliasing of commands, so the command to change a user's privileges could be invoked with an innocuous print command, which would be hard to flag as suspicious without detailed knowledge of the behavior of all the commands.

FOUR TYPES OF SECURITY TOOLS

Four types of security tools are available to address an organization's computer and network security goals. These tools provide the following services:

- Identification and authentication
- Access control
- Static analysis
- Dynamic analysis

Exhibit 1 shows how each type of security tool supports the four security goals. As shown in the exhibit, no individual security tool satisfies all four.

Exhibit 1. Security goals and tools.

Security Goal	Identification and Authentication	Access Control	Static Analysis	Anomaly Detection	Misuse Detection
Prevention	X	X	X		
Deterrence	X	X		X	X
Investigation					X
Interception				X	X

Identification and Authentication

Current Unix operating systems typically provide simple identification and authentication of users with user-generated passwords. Third-party identification and authentication products can improve the quality of passwords by preventing use of easily guessed passwords and by enforcing password aging, for example. Or they might replace the standard password mechanism entirely. Although identification and authentication tools help prevent unauthorized access and could deter misuse by making the log-in process more rigorous, they usually do not provide information for investigating misuse and are not capable of intercepting incidents of misuse.

Available identification and authentication products include password checkers, Kerberos authentication system, and token-based authentication schemes.

Access Control

Unix operating systems check permissions attached to all files and devices and allow access only to authorized user IDs. This prevents unauthorized access as well as deterring attempts to gain access.

Firewalls provide access controls for networks and network hosts. They protect networks from intrusions by providing a single point of entry into the network by means of hardware, software, or a combination of hardware and software controls. File-level access controls are built into Unix.

Access controls might deter unsophisticated intruders after access is denied. However, these controls provide no independent assurance that intruders are not bypassing access controls; they are therefore of limited usefulness for purposes of interception. In addition, access controls do not provide data for investigating misuse, and they require a great deal of planning and ongoing system administration.

There are few add-on file-level access controls for Unix, although Tivoli's Tivoli Management Framework and Computer Associates' CA-Unicenter provide convenient interfaces to existing access control features in Unix. Firewall software products include Raptor Systems' Eagle and Netgate; free software packages are also available on the Internet. Hardware-based firewalls are often based on commercially available routers.

Static Analysis

Static analysis software tools look for vulnerabilities in the security-relevant parts of a computer's file system at a single point in time. These tools ensure that the system's security state and configuration files have not changed in undesirable ways since the prior check. They also verify access controls on system files, check passwords, and conduct limited searches for known viruses or Trojan horse programs.

Static analysis software prevents problems by alerting system managers to weaknesses in system configuration. They are usually simple to operate. Periodic use of static analysis software is recommended to identify changes in security-relevant files.

Nonetheless, there are also limitations to the effectiveness of these tools. First, static analysis tools do not provide accountability—that is, they cannot determine who made the changes or how the changes were made. For example, static analysis tools cannot differentiate between authorized actions of a system manager and unauthorized changes resulting from misuse. These tools also do not deter or intercept misuse, and they usually do not provide evidence for investigating misuse.

Several free products for static analysis are available on the Internet, including:

Purdue University's COPS
Purdue University's Tripwire
Digital Equipment Corp.'s Internet Security Scanner

Commercially available products include:

- Raxco's Security Toolkit
- Los Altos Technologies' Fortres.
- Digital Equipment Corp.'s Polycenter Security Compliance Manager and Polycenter Security Reporting Facility

Dynamic Analysis

In contrast to static analysis tools that look at a snapshot of the system, dynamic analysis tools use an ongoing data source, such as audit trails and network traffic logs, that provides a connection between logged events and user IDs or other authentication information. As a result, these tools provide increased accountability for user actions on computers and networks. Two approaches to dynamic analysis are used to identify security problems: anomaly detection and misuse detection.

Anomaly Detection. Anomaly detection looks for statistically anomalous behavior; it assumes that intrusions and other security problems are rare and that they appear unusual when compared with other user behavior. Anomaly-detection tools are generally used to check events against predetermined thresholds; for example, they might post an alarm when three failed logins have been noted.

The typical way to perform anomaly detection is to compare actual user behavior with a behavioral profile, usually a profile based on historically expected events. Anomaly detection assumes that most people behave in a fairly standard way most of the time. Empirical studies of computer use show that most users employ a very limited set of system commands and applications; as would be expected, programmers and system administrators are major exceptions to this finding.

Anomaly-detection tools can intercept some forms of misuse, particularly masqueraders (i.e., individuals using someone else's login ID and password), by noticing changes in the victim's behavior in real time. Anomaly detection is most effective when applied to homogeneous transactional data, such as records of credit card transactions, securities trading, or telephone calls. It can also provide useful management reports on use of system resources. In general, however, it must be acknowledged that most known attacks are not detected with anomaly-detection techniques.

In addition, not all activities identified as anomalous are necessarily unauthorized or criminal. Users' activities often change, so that profiles of user behavior must constantly change for anomaly-detection techniques to be effective. Without constant updating, anomaly-detection tools tend to generate false alarms.

Anomaly-detection research prototypes have been extremely computationally intensive, using complex statistics. The operating system audit trails required to provide user accountability are not transactional in nature, and have been difficult to process with the statistical techniques used in anomaly-detection tools.

Several research prototypes have been developed using anomaly-detection techniques. There is one commercially available anomaly-detection tool, Digital Equipment Corporation's Polycenter Security Intrusion Detector.

Misuse Detection. Misuse detection looks for patterns of events that are known to reflect misuse of the system (e.g., known attacks and attempts to exploit vulnerabilities) and also for known outcomes of misuse.

Misuse-detection tools are more sophisticated than the other types of security tools, and they meet three of the four security goals. These tools intercept unauthorized activities, investigate suspected problems, and deter misuse by providing accountability checks for user activities. They assume that other control mechanisms attempt to prevent problems, but do not assume that those mechanisms are effective.

There are two steps to misuse detection:

- Defining the sequences of observable events that accompany known bad behavior—these are the signatures of that behavior.
- Detecting instances of those signatures in the available data streams.

The mechanisms for detection can use pattern recognition techniques or expert system rules.

There are a number of advantages and disadvantages to misuse-detection tools. Among the advantages, misuses-detection tools provide user accountability and misuse detection by determining who did what, when, and how it was done. This may reduce organizational liability in the event of lawsuits by providing accountability for user actions. Misuse detection is generally more efficient than anomaly detection because it scans for particular items, while anomaly detection constructs aggregates of items and matches them against statistical profiles.

In addition, misuse-detection techniques generally result in far fewer false alarms than anomaly-detection techniques, because every alarm from a misuse-detection tool is a report of a declared misuse, not just an unusual occurrence. Misuse-detection tools have been successfully tested for their effectiveness using audit trail data of known break-ins. (In a May 1993 challenge to developers of intrusion and misuse-detection software issued by the Federal Bureau of Investigation and the National Security Agency, Haystack Labs' Stalker—the only available commercial product for misuse detection—succeeded in detecting all staged attacks,)

Misuse detection generates reports with evidence that can be used in investigating misuse and prosecuting intruders.

There are disadvantages to these tools as well. Currently available misuse-detection tools are designed to process audit data files and are unable to operate in real time. They do not prevent misuse, and must depend on other mechanisms for preventing intrusions and attacks.

Deployment of misuse-detection tools requires an organizational commitment to collect, store, and manage audit trails that may add administrative and hardware overhead to the cost of the tool. And although the availability of attack and vulnerability information is improving, vendors, government agencies, and computer emergency response teams have strongly resisted disseminating this information for a variety of reasons, including fear of lawsuits and data classification concerns.

SELECTION AND IMPLEMENTATION ISSUES

An organization's needs for misuse detection vary depending on the system configuration and types of data processed and application used. Misuse-detection tools can provide an increased level of assurance of data confidentiality, integrity, and availability.

When acquiring a tool for misuse detection, there are several important features that system managers should consider to ensure that it will work effectively in their environment. In evaluating a misuse-detection tool, system managers should ask the following questions:

- Does the tool work in the typical distributed Unix environment (multiple-segment networks with many attached computers)?
- Does the tool operate automatically after it has been configured?
- Can the tool be easily updated to incorporate new information about attacks and misuses? When a new Unix system vulnerability is discovered and exploited on one computer, a hacker usually attempts the same attack on multiple computers. In addition, as knowledge of these attacks spreads throughout the hacker community, similar attacks begin to propagate across the Internet.

- Does the misuse-detection tool violate user privacy by looking at keystrokes, electronic mail, or user files? These activities alienate users and may be legally problematic, thus making the tool ineffective.
- Can the tool simplify the management of system audit trails? Management of system audit trails includes the collection, storage, and routine disposition of the files for disposal or long-term retention. These management activities can be time consuming, depending on the number of audit trail files generated daily.
- Is the reporting capability of the tool flexible enough to allow connections with such event-notification methods as pagers and network management control centers?

System managers should recognize that misuse-detection tools are a very important part of their overall computer and network security program. But no one element of a security program is sufficient by itself. System managers should continue to rely on external sources of information, including direct observation of human and system behavior. Because misuse-detection tools are extremely powerful, system managers must ensure they are installed properly and used appropriately. The following section addresses these implementation issues.

Using External Sources of Information

Information from such external sources as informants and administrative reports indicating possible computer misuse should prompt system managers to begin investigations For example, a local user or system manager may report that a machine is operating erratically, or may report an apparent attack by an unknown user.

In some cases, reports of misuse may come from a third party that uses more sophisticated detection techniques than are available locally. For example, in cases involving the Internet in which multiple sites are affected by a given incident, a site with sophisticated monitoring tools is most likely to discover the attack; it would then notify other sites involved in the same chain of attacks.

Internal administrative information about employee status can alert system managers to computer misuse. Disgruntled employees can cause substantial damage to computer systems. In addition, malicious employees can inflict damage to computer systems by masquerading as other employees who are absent from work due to illness or vacation. Information from risk analyses, analysis of network topologies and systems configuration, and assessment of vulnerabilities of a site's hardware and software might indicate possible sources of abuse.

Regardless of its source, relevant information always requires further investigation and validation to establish accountability. This investigation depends on details describing who did what and when it was done. Such details can be provided by misuse-detection tools.

Configuring the Detection Tool

Proper configuration and control of the misuse-detection tool is essential. Because of the sensitive information produced, only authorized personnel should be able to access the tool. In addition, the tool should be configured to discover misuse by using all available data. Finally, periodic adjustments to the configuration, such as revising the types of audit trail events collected, can reveal possible deficiencies in the configuration.

Reporting Results

System managers should frequently review reports for evidence of misuse perpetrated by individual users and further investigate the possible misuse by establishing a schedule for detailed review of the identified users' activities on the system. In addition, the system manager can establish an automated schedule for prompt notification of suspicious activities. Timely reporting of the results is essential to prevent the escalation of ongoing misuse and to obtain information needed for a criminal investigation. For maximum effectiveness, these reports and notifications should be limited to authorized personnel. Setting up a hierarchical reporting system can facilitate communication to the proper administrative officials and minimize the impact on human resources.

CONCLUSION

A wide range of computer security tools is available today for the Unix operating system. The choice among tools that provide security goals of identification and authentication, access control, static analysis, or dynamic analysis depends on a particular organization's needs and budgetary restrictions. Examination of each security tool's benefits and drawbacks will provide a clearer view of available options. Exhibit 2 summarizes the features of each type of tool.

Both identification and authentication tools and access controls are more efficient in prevention and deterrence than in investigation and interception of system misuse. Identification and authentication tools prevent unauthorized access (thereby deterring misuse) by making the log-in process more user-specific. Access control tools protect networks by allowing access to the system by one point of entry only. Implementation of either of these requires much planning and system administration.

Static analysis tools alert system managers to vulnerabilities in a computer system at a certain point in time by comparing present results to previous results. While they are helpful in preventing misuse, the efficiency of

Exhibit 2. Features and tools.

Static Feature	Anomaly Analysis	Misuse Detection	Detection
Provides accountability			X
Finds changes to security checks in snapshot look at OS	X		
Looks for known patterns of misuses			X
Detects unusual behavior patterns		X	
High level of reliability in results	X		X
Used on large networks		X	X
Uses audit trail data	X	X	
Handles new users easily			X

these tools for deterrence, investigation, and interception is limited in that they cannot provide accountability for changes within a system.

Dynamic analysis can be divided into two approaches: anomaly detection and misuse detection. Anomaly detection provides interception and deterrence of misuse by comparing actual user behavior with a statistical, behavioral profile. Because activities identified as anomalous may not necessarily be unauthorized, their value in detecting system attacks is limited. Misuse-detection tools seek patterns that can represent attacks on a system and compare data with typical results of misuse. They are also able to provide accountability for user actions. Although these tools can intercept unauthorized activities and investigate possible attacks, they do not operate in real time and therefore are not effective in preventing intrusions.

BIBLIOGRAPHY

Denning, D.E., An Intrusion Detection Model. *Proceedings of the 1986 IEEE Symposium on Security and Privacy,* Oakland CA, May 1986.

Lunt, T., Automated Audit Trail Analysis and Intrusion Detection: A Survey. *Proceedings of the 11th National Computer Security Conference*, Washington DC, October 1988.

Smaha, S.E., Tools For Misuse Detection. *Proceedings of ISSA 93,* Crystal City VA, April 1993.

Snapp, S.R., Bretano, J., et al, DIDS (Distributed Intrusion Detection System). *Proceedings of the 14th National Computer Security Conference,* Washington DC, October 1991.

Stoll, C., *The Cuckoo's Egg.* Simon & Schuster, New York NY, 1989.

Chapter 62
Novell NetWare 4.X Security

Jeffrey L. Ott

The three fundamental components of information security are availability, confidentiality, and integrity.

- **Availability.** The information system (i.e., the LAN, mainframe, mini, or attached network) must be available whenever it is needed.
- **Confidentiality.** The information system and the data on the system must be available only to those who are authorized to use it. This requires the authentication of users who attempt to access the system and other measures, as needed, to limit users' access to only the information that they require for job-related duties.
- **Integrity.** The information system and the data on that system must remain free from unauthorized, intentional (i.e., malicious and preplanned) and unintentional (i.e., accidental) modifications. These threats might come from within the organization or from outside the organization.

Any information security program, application, and implementation must address these three fundamental components.

Network Security Exposures and Risks

Many threats to information systems attack the hardware, software, and information on a system. Network hardware includes all of the physical pieces of the LAN, including the server, cables, wiring, telecom devices, routers, bridges, printers, and peripherals. Network software includes all of the applications, operating systems, and other programs executing on the network. Network information includes all of the information that resides on the LAN, such as application data, configuration parameters, and transmissions.

Threats to a LAN include any intentional or unintentional destruction, modification, or disclosure of information. These threats range from the actions of hackers to industrial espionage and natural disasters. The most

0-8493-9989-0/99/$0.00+$.50

common disruptions of service occur as a result of mistakes made by employees.

Security administrators should begin an analysis of the threats to the software and the information on the LAN by evaluating the physical security of the server. The server should be in a locked room, which will protect the equipment (e.g., the servers, tape backup devices, and media) from theft and from malicious use of the console. The console is the command center of a NetWare LAN; it is from the console that NetWare Loadable Modules (NLMs) are loaded. Anyone with access to the console has the ability to place NLMs—many of which are malicious in nature, such as BURGLAR.NLM and SUPERPWD.NLM—on the system.

The server should be connected to an uninterruptable power supply (UPS). A UPS will provide a window of time in which the system administrator can power down the server during an extended power outage. The UPS also cleans and filters electricity before it reaches the server, thus eliminating power surges, spikes, and brownouts.

Netware Directory Services

NetWare 4.X marks a radical change in NetWare security. The single most important change to NetWare is the introduction of NetWare Directory Services (NDS). NDS replaces the server-based Bindery of NetWare 3.X with a global, hierarchical, loosely consistent and replicated database of all of the network resources and their associated properties. NDS enables NetWare 4.X to be an enterprisewide network operating system, because it allows NDS system administrators to create one flexible hierarchical directory for an entire network, and for an almost unlimited number of network resources. Implementation, administration, and management of NDS should be the first priority of the security administrator handling NetWare 4.X security. Exhibit 1 presents the security-related differences between NetWare 3.X and NetWare 4.X.

An NDS directory is typically illustrated as an upside-down tree, with the roots at the top and the branches and leaves at the bottom. This representation of the NDS architecture should help security administrators to conceptualize the layout of a NetWare 4.X network. Exhibit 2 presents a basic NDS directory tree structure. Security rights in the NDS structure flow down; if a user has access at a higher level in the NDS directory tree, the user will generally have access to branches and leaves beneath the permitted level.

NetWare Directory Services Objects

The NDS database is composed of objects. NDS objects are not physical objects; they are object representations and the object's associated

Exhibit 1. Comparison of NetWare 3.X and 4.X security features.

Feature	NetWare 3.X	NetWare 4.X
Maximum number of user connections per server	250	1000
Object-based naming service	No	Yes
Single login to network	No	Yes
RSA public/private key encryption	No	Yes
Restrict login to specific Macintosh address	No	Yes
NDS event auditing	N/A	Yes
File system auditing	No	Yes
Independent network auditor	No	Yes
Independent network auditor password	No	Yes
Audit user security transactions	No	Yes
Audit supervisor transactions	No	Yes
Audit file-creation statistics	No	Yes
Audit directory creation statistics	No	Yes
Audit volume statistics	No	Yes
Filter transaction logs	No	Yes
Transaction monitoring and auto log updates	No	Yes
Multiple auditors	No	Yes
Remote console session security	No	Yes
Remote console modem callback	No	Yes
Network supervisor	Yes	Yes
Workgroup manager	Yes	Yes
User account manager	Yes	Yes
File server console operator	Yes	Yes
Determine who has console and supervisor privileges	No	Yes
Audit trail name service events	No	Yes
Governmental C-2 level security certification	No	Yes

properties. This allows the physical object (e.g., the user, server, or device) to be physically removed from the server where the NDS resides. This treatment differs from the Bindery treatment of network objects in previous releases of NetWare, in which the Bindery was aware of only those objects that were directly attached to its server. The NDS structure facilitates the management of an enterprisewide network. For example, the administrator does not need to know the address or location of a printer to permit a group of users access to that printer, nor must the administrator create new logon IDs for these users for the printer's server. Instead, the administrator provides access to the requested printer to the group, even if the printer is a continent away.

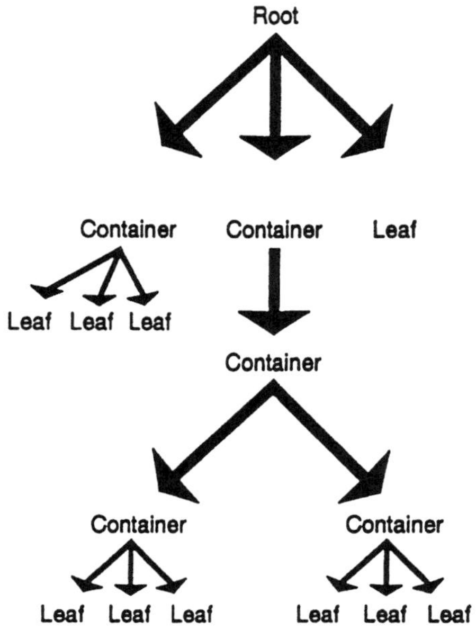

Exhibit 2. NDS directory tree.

Each NDS object has a set of properties, and each object property has associated property values. For example, the user object's associated properties include name, other name, description, location, and telephone number. The data entered for each of those properties are the property values.

There are three basic types of objects in an NDS directory:

- Physical objects (e.g., users, servers, and printers)
- Logical objects (e.g., user groups, queues, and partitions)
- Other objects (managerial objects that help organize the other objects in the NDS directory tree, such as Organization and Organizational Unit objects)

There are also three different classifications of objects:

- Root object
- Container object
- Leaf object

Root Object. When NetWare is installed, the root is placed at the top of the directory tree. The root cannot be renamed or removed, and is always designated with brackets (i.e., [Root]).

Container Objects. When NetWare 4.X is installed, one container object is created. Container objects form the next part of the directory tree after the root. A container holds other objects, which must be other container objects or leaf objects. The container object provides a means to organize a directory logically. Within container objects are two further classifications:

- **Organization.** This organization (O) classification marks the next level following the root. The organization could be divisions or departments within a company, departments in a university, or any other logical grouping. The organization object can contain leaf objects or organizational unit objects.
- **Organizational Unit.** The organizational unit (OU) is a subunit of the organization and is an optional division to help group similar leaf objects. Organizational units can be used to designate, for example, departments within a division or project teams in a department. An organizational unit can contain another OU or leaf objects.

Country and locality are two additional container objects. Although they are used less often, country objects can be used to group multinational companies and locality objects can be used for further classification of large groups.

Leaf Objects. Leaf objects form the end of the directory tree. Leaf objects represent network components and entities and contain no other objects. User IDs, group IDs, and servers are examples of leaf objects. There are 16 different leaf objects definable to NetWare. These are listed in Exhibit 3.

Object Rights and Property Rights

Earlier versions of NetWare provided little control over the security granularity of objects. The supervisor and supervisory equivalent accounts could access everything on the server. Some granularity was provided through the use of the workgroup and account manager IDs; however, this was not adaptable for organizations attempting to decentralize control and security. NetWare 4.X provides flexibility for administering objects across the network by separating the administration of the NDS database from that of the file system rights. This has been accomplished through the addition of object rights and property rights controls in the NDS database.

Object rights govern what a trustee can do to an object, not the actual data stored in that object. The following are the object rights associated with all of the objects in the NDS directory:

Exhibit 3. NDS leaf objects.

User Related Objects	
User	User objects represent actual users who are permitted to log on to the system and use network resources.
Group	Group objects represent a list of users on the network. This permits granting rights based on the needs of a group of users, such as access to network programs and data files.
Profile	Profile objects represent a shared login script. Profile scripts are executed after the container login script and before the user's login script.
Organizational Role	Organizational Role object represents a position or function within an organization. This object can be used in instances where the actual person may change, but responsibilities and duties performed by that person's role do not.
Server-Related Objects	
NetWare Server	NetWare objects represent any server running any version of NetWare. NetWare 4.X servers are automatically added: servers running earlier versions of NetWare must be manually added.
Directory Map	Directory Map objects contain file system path information to facilitate the mapping of the file system. They do not contain an actual file directory structure. Directory Maps are used primarily for log-in scripts.
Volume	Volume objects represent actual physical volumes that are attached to the network.
Printer-Related Objects	
Printer	Printer objects represent physical printing devices that are attached to the network.
Print Queue	Print queue objects represent print queues that are attached to the network.
Print Server	Print server objects represent print queues that are attached to the network.
Informational Objects	
AFP Server	AFP server objects represent NetWare nodes that support the AppleTalk Filing Protocol.
Computer	Computer objects represent nonserver computers or routers that are attached to the network.
Messaging Related Objects	
Distribution List	Distribution list objects contain a list of e-mail recipients.
External Entity	External entities represent a nonnative NDS object that is imported into or registered in NDS. The NetWare MHSTM system uses these objects to represent users from Bindery-based directories to provide an integrated address book for sending mail.
Message Routing Group	Message routing groups represent groups of messaging servers that can transfer messages directly between each other.
Message Server	Message server objects represent messages that reside on a NetWare server.

Exhibit 3. NDS leaf objects. (continued)

Miscellaneous	
Alias	An alias object refers to an object in the network. This object can become a security risk if the alias object refers to an ADMIN ID.
Bindery	Bindery objects are created by NetWare migration utilities to provide for backward compatibility with earlier NetWare versions.
Bindery Queue	Bindery queue objects are created by migration utilities to provide backward compatibility with earlier NetWare versions. These objects represent non-NDS queues, such as Bindery-based printer queues.
Unknown	An Unknown object represents any NDS object that cannot be identified as belonging to any existing object types.

- **Supervisor.** This right designates full access privileges to the object and its properties.
- **Browse.** This right allows the trustee to view the object in the directory tree that contains the NDS database.
- **Create.** This right allows the trustee to create an object in the directory tree below the current one.
- **Delete.** This right allows the trustee to delete an object form the directory tree.
- **Rename.** This right allows the trustee to delete an object's name.

Each object has associated properties. For example, the NDS user object properties include full name, description, e-mail address, home directory, telephone number, and user ID (UID). The property rights flags control who has access to the values associated with the selected property. The following are a selection of property rights:

- **Supervisor (S).** This right grants full privileges to the property.
- **Compare (C).** This right allows a trustee to compare any value to a value of the property. It does not allow the trustee to see the property value, however, and returns only a value of true or false.
- **Read (R).** This right allows a trustee to read the values of the property. The read right automatically includes the compare right.
- **Write (W).** This right allows the trustee to add, change, or remove any value of the property. The write right automatically includes the add-self right.
- **Add/Remove Self (A).** This right allows a trustee to add or remove itself as a value of the property, without affecting any other value. This right is used only in those objects that contain object names as a value, such as group lists or mailing lists.

An administrator can grant all rights to all properties or assign specific rights to individual properties. "Selected rights" properties override any rights granted by "all rights." The proper assignment of property rights can greatly add to the segregation and delegation of duties and responsibilities within an organization. This capability was unavailable in versions of NetWare that preceded 4.X.

Access Control Lists

The Access Control List (ACL) property of NDS directory objects designates which objects have trustee rights, what rights the trustees have, and the Inherited Rights Filter (IRF) for each object. The ACL contains the list of other objects in the NDS directory that have access to an object and its properties. The ACL does not indicate to what the object itself has rights.

Inherited Rights and the Inherited Rights Filter

In the NDS directory tree, object and property rights flow downward from the upper levels of the directory tree and are inherited at the lower levels. This is similar to the flow of directory and file rights in previous versions of NetWare. Only the rights selected with the all properties assignment are inherited; selected rights are not inherited and always take precedence.

A system administrator can block inherited rights with the inherited rights filter (IRF). The IRF stops the flow of rights to the branch or leaf objects from the parent object. It does not grant rights. Specific rights granted at the object level are not affected by the IRF.

Netware 4.X File Security

There are very few differences between NetWare 3.X and 4.X file and directory security. Three notable changes to NetWare 4.X file security are:

- The Inherited Rights Mask (IRM) was replaced with the Inherited Rights Filter (IRF). The IRF behaves in exactly the same manner as the IRM.
- Additional attributes and attribute flags have been added to NetWare 4.X to accommodate data migration and file compression.
- All rights, including the supervisory file right, are granted to users for their home directory during the user-setup process.

Users and other objects must be granted the right to use directories, files, and subdirectories through directory and file rights. Additional protection for directories and files can be achieved through the application of directory and file attribute settings.

Directory and File Rights

Directory rights should be used when rights must be administered to a group of similarly secured files. Instead of granting access to individual files within a directory, the administrator can grant rights at the directory level. Because directory rights flow downward in the directory tree, all files in that directory will inherit the established rights. NetWare file system directory rights are:

- **Supervisor (S).** This right grants the user full privileges to the directory and its files and subdirectories. The supervisory right overrides any restrictions put in place with the IRF. Users with the supervisory right can grant other users supervisory rights to the directory and its files and subdirectories.
- **Read (R).** This right allows the user to open and read a directory.
- **Write (W).** This right allows the user to open and write to files; however, the user cannot display information in the file unless the (R) right is also granted.
- **Create (C).** This right allows the user to create directories and files.
- **Erase (E).** This right allows the user to delete a directory and its files and subdirectories.
- **Modify (M).** This right allows the user to change directory and file attributes. Additionally, the right allows the user to rename the directory and its files and its subdirectories. It does not grant the right to modify file contents.
- **File Scan (F).** This right allows the user to see file names in a directory listing.
- **Access Control (A).** This right allows users to change directory trustee assignments and the directory's IRF. This right also allows the user to modify file trustee rights within the directory. The right allows users to assign any right, except the supervisory right, to any other user.

Rights granted at the directory and subdirectory level flow down and are inherited by all files in that directory. It may sometimes be necessary to assign rights to specific files, thereby overriding rights assigned at the directory level. This is accomplished by assigning file rights. NetWare file rights are basically the same as directory rights, with some minor differences:

- **Supervisor (S).** This right grants the user full privileges to the file, including the ability to assign any right to this file to any other user. The supervisory right also allows the user to modify the file's IRF.
- **Read (R).** This right allows the user to open and read the file.
- **Write (W).** This right allows the user to open and write to the file.
- **Create (C).** This right allows the user to create a file and to salvage a file after it has been deleted.
- **Erase (E).** This right allows the user to delete the file.
- **Modify (M).** This right allows the user to rename the file and to modify the file's attributes. It does not grant the right to modify file contents.

- **File Scan (F).** This right allows the user to see the file name in a directory listing.
- **Access Control (A).** This right allows the user to modify the file trustee assignments and the file's IRF. The right allows users to assign any right, except the supervisory right, to any other user. Just as in NDS object security, file and directory rights can be blocked, but not granted or reassigned, through the use of the IRF.

Directory and File Attributes

NetWare file system provides additional security through the application of directory and file attributes. Attributes control what can be done to a directory or file. Most of these attributes are the same as in earlier versions of NetWare, with the addition of the attributes dealing with compression. Once set, attributes rarely change. Directory attributes and file attributes are listed in Exhibit 4. Attributes that are unique to NetWare 4.X are preceded by an asterisk.

Implementing and Administering Netware Security

Determining the necessary level of NetWare 4.X security depends on many factors. Many organizations attempt to assess how sensitive the programs, data, and files are on the system, and assign security based on these factors alone. However, it is just as important to value the information on the system. Many guidelines and formulas are available for establishing a dollar value for business information. A formal information valuation review should be performed on a regular basis. Available formulas take into account the exclusiveness of the information to the organization, the cost of creation or re-creation, the operational impact if the information is unavailable, and other related factors.

Ideally, LAN security should be implemented when the LAN is installed or when the operating system is converted (e.g., from NetWare 3.X to 4.X).However, this rarely occurs. More often, the security administrator is asked to review a new system the week before it is to be placed into production. This can result in delayed projects and inadequate or incomplete security implementations. However, NetWare 4.X has the flexibility required to meet most organizations' needs.

New Administrative Tools

SYSCON, the DOS-based NetWare system administration utility, is not used in NetWare 4.X. It has been replaced by two different administrative programs. For Windows and OS/2 environments, the program NWADMIN provides a full Windows-based environment for the management of NDS and the file system. NWADMIN supports limited drag and drop: to add users to a group, the system administrator selects can select the users,

Exhibit 4. Directory and file attributes.

Directory Attributes	
Attribute	**Description**
* Don't Compress (Dc)	Prevents compression of files within the directory
Delete Inhibit	Prevents users from erasing directories even when they have been granted the Erase trustee right.
* Don't Migrate (Dm)	Prevents files within the directory from being transferred to secondary storage, such as a tape drive.
Hidden (H)	Prevents a directory from being displayed from DOS DIR scans. NDIR will display the directory if the user has the appropriate File Scan rights.
* Immediate Compress (Ic)	Forces NetWare to compress the files in the directory as soon as possible.
Normal (N)	Flags a directory as Read/Write and nonshareable and removes most other flags.
Purge (P)	Forces NetWare to totally purge all files in the directory after the user deletes them. This attribute prevents files in the directory from being removed by the SALVAGE command.
Rename Inhibit (Ri)	Prevents a user from renaming a directory.
System (Sy)	Prevents directories from being seen by DOS DIR scans and prevents them from being deleted or copied. NDIR will display the directory if the user has the appropriate File Scan rights.
File Attributes	
Attribute	**Description**
Archive Needed (A)	Indicates the file has been modified since the last backup.
Copy Inhibit (Ci)	Prevents the file from being copied (Macintosh files only).
* Don't Compress (Dc)	Prevents compression of the file data, overriding settings for automatic compression.
Delete Inhibit	Prevents users from erasing the file even when they have been granted the Erase trustee right.
* Don't Migrate (Dm)	Prevents the file from being transferred to secondary storage, such as a tape drive.
Execute Only (X)	Prevents the file from being copied, modified or backed up. This attribute is used for .EXE and .COM files and cannot be removed unless the file is deleted.
Hidden (H)	Prevents a file from being displayed from DOS DIR scans. NDIR will display the file if the user has the appropriate File Scan rights.
Index Forces	NetWare to keep the files FAT entries in the server memory for faster file access.
* Immediate Compress (Ic)	Forces NetWare to compress the file as soon as the file is closed.
Normal (N)	Flags a file as Read/Write and nonshareable and removes most other flags.
Purge (P)	Forces NetWare to purge the file immediately after the user deletes. This attribute prevents the file from being recovered by the SALVAGE command.

drag them to the appropriate group, and drop them. Care should be taken when using this utility, because the NWADMIN interface makes it extremely easy to change enterprisewide security through a single drag and drop.

For administrators partial to DOS, there is a DOS-based application, NETADMIN, that is a text-based management tool. It is similar to the SYSCON application, but has been rewritten for NetWare 4.X. Additional DOS-based management tools include FILER and RIGHTS. These tools are designed to help the DOS-based administrator manage NetWare 4.X by using command lines and DOS menus. They do not provide any additional functionality over the Windows-based NWADMIN.

The ADMIN User ID

The ADMIN account of NetWare 4.X has replaced the SUPERVISOR account, which in earlier versions of NetWare controlled and maintained both the file system and network resources, including users.

When NetWare 4.X is installed, two IDs appear: ADMIN and GUEST. The ADMIN account has all of the capabilities of its predecessor. However, with the flexibility of NetWare 4.X's NDS, these capabilities can be distributed to multiple subadministrators throughout the organization. One of the greatest benefits of NetWare 4.X is that it separates file system administration from NDS administration. It is possible to create administrators for different segments of the directory tree. This capability was not included in earlier versions of NetWare, and positions NetWare 4.X for the management of enterprisewide LAN environments.

NetWare Directory Services Security Administration

NetWare Directory Services is delivered with default security settings that provide little security. It may be necessary to implement greater security based on an organization's requirements. If the organization is implementing a decentralized security structure, NDS is designed to create subadministrators for each branch of the directory tree. This is especially useful when organizational units represent different geographical locations. If the sales department is located in Denver and manufacturing is based in Miami, the ADMIN abilities of these two departments can be segregated. Moreover, the overall ADMIN can be prohibited from accessing the individual departments.

Security administrators should focus on containers and groups when implementing NDS security. This approach is more economical than attempting to keep track of individual user rights. For example, if a user needs certain trustee rights to access and run a word processing application on the network, the system administrator should create a group called WP, assign the needed rights to the Group WP, and make the user a member of this group. Because rights flow down the directory, any user in this leaf object WP will inherit the necessary rights.

NDS object rights do not apply to the file system. The one exception to this rule is for the server object. Anyone with supervisory right or write property right to the server ACL will have supervisory right to every volume attached to that server. Therefore, this right should be granted judiciously. As a general rule, supervisory rights should be granted as low in the directory tree as possible.

File System Administration

NetWare files are protected in two ways. First, user access to directories and files must be granted by the administrator. Second, directory and file attributes can be employed to provide additional protection. The handling of rights and the determination of effective rights is the same as in previous releases of NetWare. File system rights can be assigned to containers, groups, organizational roles, users, and the [Public] trustee.

Auditing Netware 4.X Events

NetWare 4.X provides better auditing of network events than did earlier releases. After NDS, the ability to audit network activity is the second greatest security enhancement in NetWare. Auditing system events is critical for establishing effective security on any computer system. Auditing system events aids in identifying security violations, identifying problems in user training, determining if procedures are being followed, and trouble-shooting the network.

NetWare can audit the following types of NDS events:

- Object create and deletes
- Object moves and renamings
- Object security equivalence charges
- User logins and logouts

NetWare can audit the following types of directory and file events:

- Directory and file creation, modification, and deletion
- Directory and file rename, move, and salvage
- Print queue creation, service, and deletion

NetWare can audit the following types of file server events:

- Server outages
- Bindery object creation and deletion in 3.X and 4.X mixed environment
- Volume mounts and dismounts
- Modification of security rights

NetWare 4.X is capable of tracking many different types of events. However, the number of events that are audited on a daily basis should be limited to those events needed for the daily report and security violations related to NDS objects and the file system. Other events can be temporarily audited, as necessary, and then disabled.

In most organizations, an auditor has been assigned the task of occasionally reviewing the activity of the system. Additionally, a security administrator is assigned the responsibility of reviewing daily reports to identify excessive security violations. NetWare 4.X gives these individuals the ability to read and monitor system events, without the ability to change system settings. This is accomplished using the AUDITCON utility.

AUDITCON

The auditor should use AUDITCON to configure and manage the audit subsystem of NetWare 4.X. AUDITCON is password protected; thus, only authorized personnel can run the utility. Once an auditor logs on and changes the password, the auditor is in full control of NetWare auditing and can configure the audit environment, select audit events, create reports, and maintain audit files.

Using AUDITCON, auditors can monitor and track network events, but they cannot open, view, modify, or delete files unless they have been given the appropriate rights by the ADMIN. Additionally, auditors must have browse rights to all of the containers that must be audited.

Audit Reports

AUDITCON allows the auditor to view the audit trail and produce reports, either online or exported to a text file. The audit trail may contain an enormous amount of data, much of which can be confusing if not properly filtered. The auditor should use filters to extract the information required for the report by using existing filters, modifying existing filters, or by creating a new filter. The auditor can filter the audit trail by specifying the following options:

- Report by date and time
- Report by event
- File events
- QMS events
- Server events
- User events

Exclude paths and files. Exclude users. Include paths and files. Include users.

Third-Party Security Audit Tools

Several products are available for the review of NDS and files system security under NetWare 4.X. These products provide a quick and informative look at security on the LAN. They are not active, but report from a snapshot of the security at the time that the product is run. Third-party tools are effective time-savers for performing security reviews of the entire network.

The market leader in this area is the New York-based Intrusion Detection Kane Security Analyzer (KSA). The KSA is a Windows-based application that runs off a workstation attached to the LAN. It reads the NDS and file system databases to produce security reports that are based on standards that the auditor configures. Intrusion Detection, Inc. can be reached at 800-408-6104 or at its web site: http://www.intrusion.com.

Bindview, by The LAN Support Group, is a DOS-based tool that will collect NetWare statistical information and produce security audit reports based on filters and parameters set by the auditor. The LAN Support Group can be reached at 800-749-8439 or at its web site: http://www.bindview.com.

Security Concerns For Netware 4.X

Security implementations must be based on an organization's specific needs and goals. However, there are several areas of concern that should be addressed by any organization that implements NetWare 4.X.

Administration

Under earlier releases of NetWare, one problem faced by many organizations was the widespread use—and abuse—of the supervisor and supervisory equivalent ID. Although this can still be a problem with the use of ADMIN and other IDs with supervisory rights at the root level, security administrators can use NetWare 4.X to limit the abuse of this ID in the following ways:

- Security administrators should grant subadministrators supervisory rights at the container or subcontainer level, but not at the root level. This will allow these subadministrators to perform their duties but will not grant them rights to the entire WAN.
- Security administrators should use IRFs to block higher-level ADMIN IDs from having supervisory rights at container and subcontainer levels. However, it would be best to keep one or two IDs with full access for use in emergencies.
- Security administrators should audit and track all of the activities performed by the ADMIN or ADMIN equivalent IDs.

Users

Security administrators should manage users at the group level. This will simplify administration and management. The security administrator can use the special NDS object, USER_TEMPLATE, to set up each user group in a consistent fashion. A user template can be set up for every container, and the administrator can establish default parameters for user setup, such as log-in time restrictions, password restrictions, group memberships, and print job restrictions.

Alias Objects

Aliases can be a powerful tool for network administrators. An alias takes on the appearance of the original object. For example, if a network administrator needs to establish access to an object for many users, but knows that the object's location will eventually be moved, he or she can set up an alias to the original object and point all of the users to the alias. When the time comes to move the original object, the administrator can do so without interfering with user group. This can be a problem if aliases are created for users with supervisory rights. It is possible for someone to create an alias user ID to the ADMIN ID and thereby gain total access to and control of the system.

Conclusion

NetWare 4.X is Novell's strongest network operating system, and is equipped with features for the implementation and management of a wide area network. Moreover, NetWare 4.X can be configured to meet the security requirements of all but the most restrictive organizations. It provides for secured logins, decentralized and segregated administration of the file system, and the complete auditing of network activities and events by a separate, independent auditor. Security threats to the NetWare 4.X LAN are similar to those that threatened earlier versions of the NOS. What has changed is the capability of NetWare to ward off these threats by providing the administrator with the tools to manage them.

Chapter 63
Implementing AS/400 Security Controls

Wayne O. Evans

Problems Addressed

In an IBM Application System 400 (AS/400) environment, the security manager must establish security controls that adequately protect data without impeding system throughput and ease of use. The security manager and staff must then monitor the system to ensure that all necessary controls have been activated and are functioning as expected.

This chapter presents a program for establishing and maintaining an effective level of control in AS/400 systems, regardless of the type of system configuration employed.

The key control options are discussed and recommendations are presented for setting control parameters that strike the proper balance between information protection and system availability and processing efficiency. Of course, it is not possible to address every possible set of business requirements—some organizations have more-stringent security requirements than others. The chapter assumes a business environment in which there is a relatively even mix of sensitive and nonsensitive business data, and provides guidance as to the appropriate controls for specific security requirements.

The AS/400 provides a wide array of security mechanisms that may seem bewildering to a security specialist who is not familiar with the AS/400 architecture. As with any security implementation, it is important that the security manager first develop a security plan for the design and implementation of controls. This is not just to ensure that a critical control feature has not been overlooked. An effective plan should also guarantee that the costs associated with the proposed security program, including system overhead and the human resources required to manage the

0-8493-9989-0/99/$0.00+$.50

security operation, do not exceed the benefits. (Put differently, the goal should be to provide enough protection so that the cost of stealing the data exceeds its value.) A poorly designed security implementation can often result in excessive controls, which in turn make security management a burden.

This chapter provides a structured plan for establishing the necessary user and group profiles, object authorities, authorization lists, and library controls to minimize the resources needed to manage the security function. Of course, given the often rapid changes in computing environments, any plan designed today will need to be periodically reviewed and updated to satisfy new requirements.

The following section provides an overview of typical AS/400 configurations as well as a description of the basic system architecture. The remaining sections supply details on establishing security controls for each system component.

In October 1995, the AS/400 formally received its first C2 security rating from the United States Department of Defense. This original C2 security rating is for V2R3 of OS/400, Source Entry Utility, Query/400, SAA Structured Query Language/400, and Common Cryptographic Architecture Services/400. The C2 security rating was awarded after a rigorous, multi-year period of evaluation. The AS/400 is the first system to achieve a C2 security rating for a system (hardware and operating system) with an integrated, full-function database.

Object-Based System Architecture

On the AS/400 system, data in the form of either files or programs is stored in storage units referred to as objects. Exhibit 1 illustrates that all objects consist of two basic types of information: common attributes that

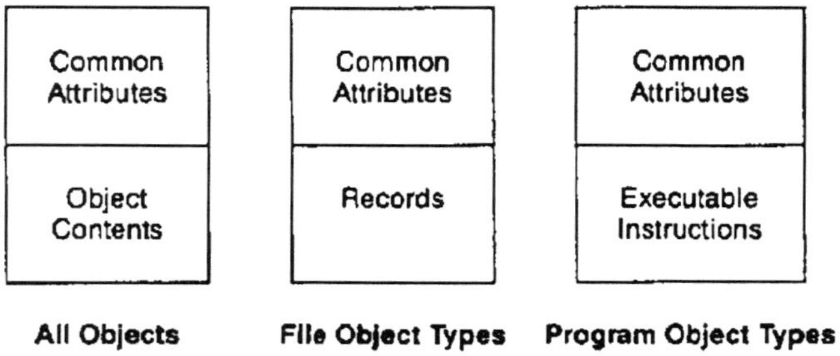

Exhibit 1. AS/400 object structure.

Exhibit 2. Common attributes of objects.

Attribute	Description
Object Name	The user-assigned name used to locate the object. Objects of a different type can have the same name. For example, a file can be named PAYROLL and the program that processes the file can also be named PAYROLL.
Object Library	The user-assigned directory name used to group objects. Objects are located by library and object name. Objects of the same type can have the same name if they exist in different libraries. For example, two files can be named PAYROLL if one is in the PRODUCTION library and the other in the TEXT library. The contents of these two files do not need to be the same. Each job in the system has a library search list called a library list; this is similar to path specifications in other systems. The library search list is used if no library name is specified to locate an object. It should be noted that the library object type is used to store the name of objects and the virtual address used to locate the object.
Object Type	There are more than 80 different object types that are assigned according to the type of object contents (e.g., files, programs, and queues).
Object Owner	The user responsible for authorizing others to use the object. The object owner is usually the person who created the object.
Owner Access to Object	The owner has by default *ALL access to an object, but may revoke some privileges (e.g., to prevent accidental deletion of the object). The owner can always grant authority to the object.
Public Access to Object	By default, users not otherwise authorized to access the object are assigned *PUBLIC access.
Authorized Users	Users specifically authorized to access an object are stored in the user profile for each user rather than in a centralized database. For further information, see the section on user profiles.
Primary Group Profile	A user profile other than the owner, which has access to an object. Only user profiles with a group identification number (gid) may be the primary group for an object.
Primary Group's Access	Primary group authority is stored with the object and may provide better performance than private authority granted to a group profile. Primary group authority is not considered a private authority because the authority is stored with the object and not the user profile.
Authorization List (optional)	Users can also be authorized to access an object using an authorization list. Authorization lists are discussed in detail in the section on object authority.
Object Audit	The auditing of objects can involve no audit, logging of modifications, or logging of all references. The object auditing may specify that auditing be specified in user profile so that the object is audited for individual users.

specify such information as object name, type, and ownership; and object contents that, for example, consist of data records in the case of files and executable instructions in the case of programs. The common attributes are

Objects with similar contents are assigned the same object type—for example, files, programs, and queues. Because security is defined as a common attribute, the same security interface can be used for all objects, regardless of type.

Object implementation provides improved data integrity by preventing invalid operations for a given object type. For example, the call operation is defined as valid for program objects; open, read, and write operations are valid for file objects. Any attempt to call a file or open a program will be rejected. Such strong controls are a significant improvement over systems in which all data is represented as system files. The object typing of AS/400 programs, for example, virtually eliminates the potential for a viral infection of an AS/400 program, because the program object type does not permit one program to modify another.

User Profiles

A user profile is the object used by the system to identify the access and processing capabilities of the user. Profiles are used to identify users in all audit records; therefore, the security administrator should create a user profile for every system user. (Several administrators can be designated to assist with the enrollment and removal of users.)

The user profile contains information for security applications as well as general purposes. The following general information is used to adapt the system to individual users:

- The user assistance level, which specifies the amount of help text that appears on system screens. Levels of *BASIC, *INTERMEDIATE, and *ADVANCED can be specified.
- The current library, which indicates the library name used when new objects are created by the user.
- The previously accessed library and file for each system utility.
- The accounting code used to track the use of system resources for company projects.
- The job description, which establishes the operational environment for the user's processing jobs.

Other general options can be used to control type-ahead capabilities, prompt messages, the level of detail on system screens, and the printing of the user name on output.

The user profile also contains the security-related fields listed in Exhibit 3. In general, these fields control the user's ability to access, add, modify, and delete objects and to use certain system services.

Group Profiles

Group profiles are used to define the authorization for a group of related users in a single profile rather than repeating the same authorization for each user profile. The authorization to objects and the special authority from the group profile are shared by all members of the group. Group profiles are widely used in AS/400 installations because their use simplifies security management and reduces the number of authorizations that must be stored. If the number of stored authorizations is reduced, less time is needed to back up the system.

Assigning users their own profiles is a good security practice. Users can change their password periodically without having to inform others about the change, and, more important, it is possible to identify and monitor individual user activity on the system only when signing on to the system.

Where necessary, a user profile can be established with more or less authority than the groups to which it belongs. In such cases, the object authority granted in the user profile supersedes the authority specified in the associated group profiles. However, any special authority established in the user profile does not supersede the special authority in the group profile. Rather, the special authorities defined in both the user and group profiles are combined additively to determine the effective special authority.

A group profile is not a distinct AS/400 object type. A group profile is simply a special type of user profile. It becomes a group profile when one of the following occurs:

- Another profile designates it as a group profile.
- The user profile is assigned a group identification number (GID).

A designated group profile cannot be a member of another group. Individuals may be members of up to 16 group profiles.

Managing User and Group Profiles

Control Language (CL) commands are used to manage the assignment of user and group profiles as well as object authorities and authorization lists. These commands are described in Appendix A, which appears at the end of this chapter.

The same CL commands used to manage individual user profiles are also used to manage group profiles. The CRTUSRPRF command is used to create the user profile and the group profile. In naming group profiles, it is

Exhibit 3. Security-related fields in the user profile.

Field		Description
USRCLS		The User Class field identifies the role of the user in the system. The choices from highest to lowest level of responsibility are:
	*SECOFR	The security officer has unrestricted access to all objects. Use of this user class should be limited because there is no protection from accidental deletion of objects. The recommended procedure is to provide two user profiles for individuals that are security officers. The nonsecurity officer profile should be used for most system access and the security officer profile should be used only when required.
	*SECADM	The security administrator is authorized to enroll and remove system users. A different security administrator should be assigned to manage the user profiles for each major functional area. The security administrator typically creates and owns the user profiles and, therefore, is authorized to access them. Profiles owned by other administrators cannot be accessed.
	*PGMR	The programmer is authorized to add applications to the system.
	*OPERATOR	The operator is permitted to manage system work and perform backup operations.
	*USER	The user identifies general system users who have no special privileges.
SPCAUT		The Special Authority field identifies additional user privileges. If no privileges are specified explicitly for this field, the system defaults to values based on the selected User Class authorities. (To simplify the enrollment process, it is suggested that only User Class parameters be specified.) The following special authorities can be granted:
	*ALLOBJ	The user has unrestricted access to all system objects (i.e., *All authority).
	*AUDIT	The user is allowed to change the event and object audit related options in system values, objects, and user profiles.
	*SECADM	The user is allowed to enroll and remove users from the system. Users granted both *ALLOBJ and *SECADM privileges are considered to be security officers. These users can change the system values, objects, and network attributes that control system security.
	*SERVICE	The user is allowed to use system service tools. Service tools should by used only by trusted and knowledgeable users, because these tools can be used to circumvent system security controls. For example, improper use of service tools to display or alter an object may result in system failure. A communication line trace might also be used to view line transactions, including the sign-on information of other users.

Exhibit 3. Security-related fields in the user profile. (continued)

Field		Description
	*SPLCTL	The user can access any spool files on the system. *SPLCTL provides the same authority for spool files that *ALLOBJ provides for objects. (Spool files are not defined as external objects.)
	*SAVSYS	The user can save and restore objects that he or she is not normally authorized to use. This privilege is frequently given to individuals responsible for backing up the system.
	*JOBCTL	The user can manage the jobs of other users. This authority is given to system operators.
GRPPRF		The Group Profile field allows users to share the authority of another profile. The section on group profiles describes this option in greater detail.
SUPGRPPRF		The Supplemental Group Profile field specifies up to 15 names of group profiles to be used with this user profile. These profiles, in addition to the profile specified in the GRPPRF parameter, are used to give the user access to objects.
INLMENU or INLPGM		The Initial Menu field or Initial Program field is used to determine the screen a user first sees when signing on. These parameters are frequently used when it is desired to limit users to selecting choices from a menu. Limiting users to menu choices requires a system security level level of 20 or higher.
LMTCPB		The Limit Capability field indicates that users are restricted from entering commands and changing the initial program on the sign-on menu. If users are limited to selecting options from a menu, the system default *NO should be changed to *YES.

recommended that a consistent naming convention be used to distinguish groups so they may be more readily identified on lists of authorized users. For example, the group name might begin with the characters DPT or GRP, signifying that group members belong to a department within the organization.

To create a group profile named DPTSALES, the following command could be used:

```
CRTUSRPRF  USER(DPTSALES)  PASSWORD  (*NONE)

SPCAUT(*JOBCTL)
```

A password of *NONE is recommended to prevent users from signing on under the group profile.

When individual user profiles are created, they can be assigned membership in a group by using the GRPPRF command parameter. For example, to create two users as members of the group profile, DPTSALES, the following CRTUSRPRF commands can be used:

```
CRTUSRPRF  USER(GRANT)  PASSWORD([ndash ][ndash ])
    GRPPRF(DPTSALES)  +
OWNER(*GRPPRF)
CRTUSRPRF  USER(EVANS)  PASSWORD(-[ndash  ])
    GRPPRF(DPTSALES)+
OWNER(*GRPPRF)  SPCAUT(*SAVSYS)
```

Both users Grant and Evans are members of the DPTSALES group and share the object and special authorities defined for this group. However, Evans is also granted *SAVSYS special authority. Because the option OWNER(*GRPPRF) is specified, any objects created by these users will be owned by the DPTSALES group profile. This option is particularly useful in cases where members of a group work on shared projects, because objects created by one group member immediately become available to all members of the group.

Object Authority

An object authority specifies the type of operation that can be performed on a given object. Object authorities are granted to either a user profile or *PUBLIC. Exhibit 4 lists the authorities that can be granted. Because there is no hierarchical relationship among authorities, it is possible, for example, to grant *ADD authority without *READ authority. This arrangement is useful in assigning authority to the message queue of another user; *ADD authority allows messages to be sent to the user, but without *READ authority the user's messages cannot be read by others.

AS/400 also supports a set of object authorities that permit the use of a single term to grant a combination of the individual object authorities listed in Exhibit 4. For example, the *CHANGE authority can be used to grant authorities to display, read, add, update, and delete an object. The combined object authorities, including the *EXCLUDE authority already introduced, are shown in Exhibit 5. Use of these combined terms is recommended.

The CL commands listed under the Object Authority Commands heading in Appendix B are used to create and maintain object authorities. For example, the GRTOBJAUT command is used to grant a user profile authority to an object, while the RVKOBJAUT command revokes such authority. The full command statement must include the object name

Exhibit 4. Object authorities.

Authority	Description
*ADD	Add authority is required to insert new entries into an object.
*AUTLMGT	Authorization List Management authority is required to add or remove users from an authorization list.
*DLT	Delete authority is required to remove existing entries from an object. Delete authority allows only deletion of individual data entries, not the entire object.
*EXCLUDE	Exclude authority prevents access to an object. If a user has no authority to an object, the user may still be able to access the object using the *PUBLIC authority. However, if the user is granted *EXCLUDE authority, all access is denied.
*EXECUTE	Execute authority is required to run a program, service program, or SQL package or locate an object in a library or a directory.
*OBJALTER	Object alter authority is required to add, clear, initialize and reorganize members of the database files; to alter and add attributes of database files; and to add and remove triggers.
*OBJREF	Object reference authority is required to specify a database file as the parent file in a referential constraint.
*OBJEXIST	Object Existence authority is required to delete an object or to save an object to backup media.
*OBJMGT	Object Management authority is required to authorize other users to an object or to move or rename an object.
*OBJOPER	Object Operational authority is required to display the description of an object; it is also required to open a file.
*READ	Read authority is required to retrieve information from an object.
*UPD	Update authority is required to modify existing entries in an object.

and type and the profile name. For example, to give Evans the authority to change the SAMPLE program, the following GRTOBJAUT command can be entered:

```
GRTOBJAUT OBJ(SAMPLE) OBJTYPE(*PGM) USER(EVANS) +
    AUT(*CHANGE)
```

AS/400 Systemwide Security Options

The systems manager specifies system values and network attributes to customize AS/400 to satisfy organizational requirements. Because these options affect system security, only the designated security officer is allowed to modify these values. The authorities of a security officer are assigned in the user profile, as described previously in Exhibit 3.

Exhibit 5. Combined object authorities.

*OBJ OPR	*READ	*EXECUTE	*ADD	*UPD	*OBJ MGT	*OBJ EXIST	*OBJ REFER	*OBJ ALT	*AUTL MGT
*EXCLUDE									
*USE	X	X	X						
*CHANGE	X	X	X	X	X				
*ALL	X	X	X	X	X	X	X	X	X

Security-Related System Options

Security-related system options support the following four types of controls:

- **Sign-On Controls** These controls determine how the system handles attempts to sign on, including limits on reentry of invalid passwords, system action when this limit is exceeded, and restrictions on the devices that the security officer and other privileged users can use to sign on. To discourage users from leaving a workstation unattended without first signing off, controls can be set to limit simultaneous sessions from multiple devices.
- **Password Controls** These controls determine how often passwords must be changed and permit establishing rules for password content to prevent the use of trivial passwords.
- **Active Job Controls** These are the values used when explicit security values have not been specified. For example, a default value can be used to specify the time period for deactivating inactive terminals.
- **Audit Controls** These controls determine the types of events recorded in the system audit log (referred to as an audit journal). Users who have been designated as auditors can change the audit related system values.

A complete listing of system options for sign-on, password, active job, and audit controls is provided in Appendix B, along with recommendations for selecting the values for these options.

The next section describes how to set system values using the QSECURITY system option for sign-on control as an example. The format for entering commands described in this section is similar to that for the other system options listed in Appendix B.

Setting the System Security Level

The QSECURITY system option is used to establish the level of security required by the organization. AS/400 supports four increasing levels of protection. Each higher level requires additional time and resources to manage the security of objects. Therefore, IS and security managers must attempt to establish a level of control that is secure without sacrificing system efficiency. The following values, listed in ascending order of security protection, can be selected for this option:

- No Security (System Value=10). No password is required to sign on, and a user profile is created automatically if none exists. Users can access and delete all objects; accidental deletion of data is not prevented. This level of security is not recommended: it should be considered only for installations in which there are a small number of trusted users and in which physical security measures are adequate.
- Sign-On Security (System Value=20). The user must enter a valid password to sign on, and a user profile must be created. Object-level security is not enforced, although applications can restrict users to a limited selection of menu options. Security management requires only enrolling and removing system users and maintaining menus. This minimal security level is recommended only for installations in which access to data is controlled by menus and in which no access is granted to query and other data utilities.
- Resource Security (System Value=30). This security level enforces user access to objects. Menu security can be used, access to objects can be restricted by library, access to objects can be authorized using user profiles, or public access can be granted. To reduce the time required for security management, objects can be grouped in a library and access to the library can be defined.
- Resource and Integrity Security (System Value=40). New AS/400 systems are shipped with this default setting. In addition to the features of level-30 security, this security level prevents the attempted circumvention of security by programs written in such languages as C and Pascal that employ the full machine interface pointer capability. There are no security management requirements beyond those for level-30 security. This security level is recommended for all installations; however, applications that use internal system interfaces or that access objects directly will not operate at level-40 security.
- Enhanced Integrity for C2 (System Value=50). Systems that require the highest level of security can select level 50. This level is designed to meet the requirements defined by the US Department of Defense for C2 security. It provides enhanced integrity protection in addition to what is provided by security level 40. Security level 50 provides enhanced integrity protection for installations with strict security requirements. Level 50 is not recommended for most installations because the additional checking adds a 5% to 15% in CPU cycles.

CL commands are used to establish and maintain system values. To display the value of a system option, the DSPSYSVAL command is used. For example, to display the current value of the QSECURITY option, the following command would be entered:

```
DSPSYSVAL  QSECURITY
```

The following CHGSYSVAL command changes the value of QSECURITY:

```
CHGSYSVAL  QSECURITY  '40'
```

In addition to these two CL commands, the WRKSYSVAL command can be used to both display and change system values. The WRKSYSVAL command can be used to obtain a full description of system options; the user is prompted for any further action to modify the values of these options.

After a change has been made to a system option, the new value takes effect only after the system has been restarted (i.e., after an initial program load has been performed). This delay is desired, given the significant impact that a change in these values can have on system security.

Defining Security-Related Network Attributes

Network attributes define the system characteristics of the network, including the system name and network security attributes. The attributes JOBACN, DDMACC, and PCSACC have a particular impact on network security. JOBACN specifies how batch jobs from other systems are handled—for example, jobs can be automatically submitted to the job queue for execution or rejected. DDMACC names an exit program that controls the processing of requests to access system files, and PCSACC names an exit program that controls requests from personal computers. Appendix X shows the values for the security network attributes. The work net attribute PCSACC option *REGFAC indicates the system uses a registration facility to determine which exit program (if any) to run. The registration facility can be used to improve system performance by calling only the exits that are required. If an exit program is named in the network attribute the exit program is called for every PC request rather specific request types.

CL commands are used to establish and maintain network attributes. DSPNETA can be entered to display all network attributes; CHGNETA is used to change these attributes. For example, the following CHGNETA command is used to assign the exit program DDMAUDIT in the SECURITY library to the network attribute DDMACC:

```
CHGNETA  DDMACC(SECURITY/DDMAUDIT)
```

Only the security officer is permitted to change the security-related network attributes.

Registration Facility

The registration facility is a service that provides storage and retrieval operations for OS/400 and non-OS/400 exit points and exit programs. An exit point is a specific point in a system function or program where control can be passed to one or more specified exit programs. An exit program is a program to which control is passed from an exit point. The registration facility includes exits for the following security-related functions:

- Client Access (PC Attachment) — Exit programs for file transfer, remote commands, printer, direct access to objects through the integrated file system
- User Profiles — Exit programs for user profile creation, change, deletion and restore
- File Transfer (FTP) — These exit points are used to set up additional security and validation controls for the file transfer protocol (FTP). The FTP client and server request validation exits are for controlling the use of FTP subcommands. The server logon exit point authenticates the user who is trying to log on to the FTP server. Also, you can use the two server exit points to establish an anonymous FTP server site.

Authorization Lists

An authorization list is an object that lists users, their authorities, and the objects to which the members of the list are authorized. When users are added to the list, they become immediately authorized to access all of the objects on the list. Exhibit 6 provides an example of an authorization list. In this example, the users Evans and Grant are listed, as is the GRPSALES group. If Evans and Grant both belong to the GRPSALES group profile, what authorities would they be granted based on the information provided in Exhibit 6? Because access granted to individual user profiles takes precedence over that of group profiles, Evans retains more authority than other members of GRPSALES to the objects secured by the authorization list (i.e., *ALL authority exceeds *CHANGE authority), whereas Grant has less authority (*USE authority is more restricted than *CHANGE authority).

The CL commands used to create and modify the authorization list are provided in Appendix A. The following CRTAUTL command can be used to create the authorization list shown in Exhibit 6:

```
CRTAUTL  AUTL(SALES1)  AUT(*EXCLUDE)
   TEXT('Sales  Department')
```

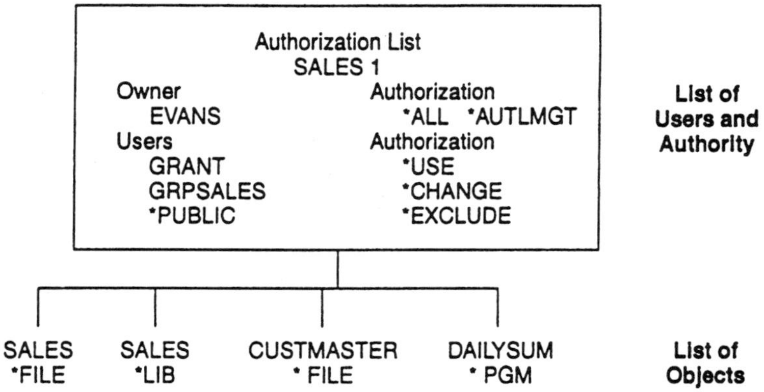

Exhibit 6. Sample authorization list.

These ADDAULTE commands can be entered to add the user Grant and the GRPSALES group to the authorization list with the authorities shown in the exhibit:

```
ADDAUTLE  AUTL(SALES1)  USER(GRANT)  AUT(*USE)

ADDAUTLE  AUTL(SALES1)  USER(GRPSALES)  AUT(*CHANGE)
```

There are several advantages to using an authorization list to secure objects rather than using individual user profiles. First, the same authorization list can be used for multiple objects, which reduces the number of authorities that must be stored. The fewer the number of authorities, the faster it is to back up the system.

Second, the name of the authorization list for an object is automatically recorded when the object is saved. If the object is restored to the same system, the object is reconnected to the authorization list. However, if the object is restored to another system, the authorization list is not automatically attached, because of the possibility that users may be different on the other system. (In the latter event, the security officer must restore the object using the ALLOBJDIF(*YES) parameter of the RSTLIB or RSTOBJ command to allow the authorization list to be attached.)

Third, the security of a file cannot be changed when a file is open by any job. Often, an installation has some critical files open for extended periods; the security officer at such an installation needs to find a time when no one is on the system. This is inconvenient and often requires changes at late hours. If an authorization list is used to secure the file, the users on the authorization list can be changed while a file is open. This practice allows the security officer to make security changes in a timely manner.

Last, objects attached to a library are secured by an authorization list, as specified by the library attribute. This feature eliminates the requirement of having the security administrator authorize all newly created objects.

Adoption of Authority by Programs

A program can be assigned an attribute that permits users of the program to gain the authority of the program owner while running the program. This feature eliminates the need to specifically authorize users to the objects references by the program. The internal program logic may, of course, enforce limits on the operations the user can perform. For example, the program can restrict the processing of transactions that exceed $1,000.

Program adoption of authority can simplify security management. However, programs that adopt the owner's authority must be carefully designed to eliminate potential security exposures. Access to such relatively unrestricted functions as command entry and query facilities should be avoided. (For example, if the adopting program were to present the user with a command line, the user would be able to access any object to which the program owner was authorized.) Adopting programs should also provide sufficient controls over the job's library search list to prevent the addition of a library containing a program or command designed to circumvent security. The design of programs called by the adopting program also must be examined, because the adopted authority is shared by all called programs.

The following CRTCLPGM command can be used to create the CL program SAMPLE that adopts the owner's authority:

```
CRTCLPGM  PGM(SAMPLE)  USRPRF(*OWNER)
```

The USRPF(*OWNER) parameter specifies that the program is to adopt the owner's authority. The DSPPGMAD command is used to list all programs that adopt the aithority of the user specified with the command. The ouptut from this command can be stored in a database file for audit purposes.

The default for programs is to use adopted authority from previous programs in the stack. Programs can be changed with the Change Program (CHGPGM) command or Change Service Program (CHGSRVPGM) command to set the USEADPAUT parameter to *NO, which will prevent the use of previously adopted authority. A system value Use Adopted Authority (QUSEADPAUT) can name an authorization list. When the system value names an authorization list, only the users have *USE authority and can create programs that use previously adopted authority.

Authority Search Order

As demonstrated by the preceding discussion, AS/400 supports a variety of mechanisms for assigning authority. During processing, the system follows a prescribed order of search among these authorization mechanisms to determine if an operation is permitted. The search stops at the first authority found. The search path and logic are shown in Exhibit 7.

As shown in the exhibit, several factors define the precedence of authorization:

- Access specified in the individual user profile overrides that in the group profile.
- Access granted to a profile overrides that in the authorization list.
- Public access is used if no other authorizations are found.

Establishing a Security Strategy

As discussed, AS/400 provides various mechanisms for securing data and applications. Access can be restricted through use of menus, library security, and object security. Each of these methods of protection provides different levels of security; in most installations, no single method is sufficient to cover all security requirements. Therefore, in defining a security strategy, a combined approach that uses all of these methods is recommended. The following sections briefly review the set-up requirements for using the menu, library, and object security methods and then discuss how these methods can be used in combination to provide optimum protection for all system users.

Menu Security

Menu security offers a very simple security strategy. Upon signing on to the system, users are restricted to selecting processing options from a menu. The menu can be designed to provide only those options required for performance of job duties—for example, predefined queries or file transfer requests. Users do not need to be authorized to access individual objects.

Menu security can be used in systems in which the QSECURITY system option is set to a value of 20 or higher. The user profile options INLPGM and INLMENU are used to define the screen the user first sees when signing on. The user profile option LMTCPB should be set to *YES to prevent the user from changing the initial menu and program on the sign-on screen.

The protection offered by menu security is limited. Menu security does not prevent a PC user from accessing data by file transfer, remote commands or the integrated file system. Library or object security should be used in addition to menu security to properly protect information.

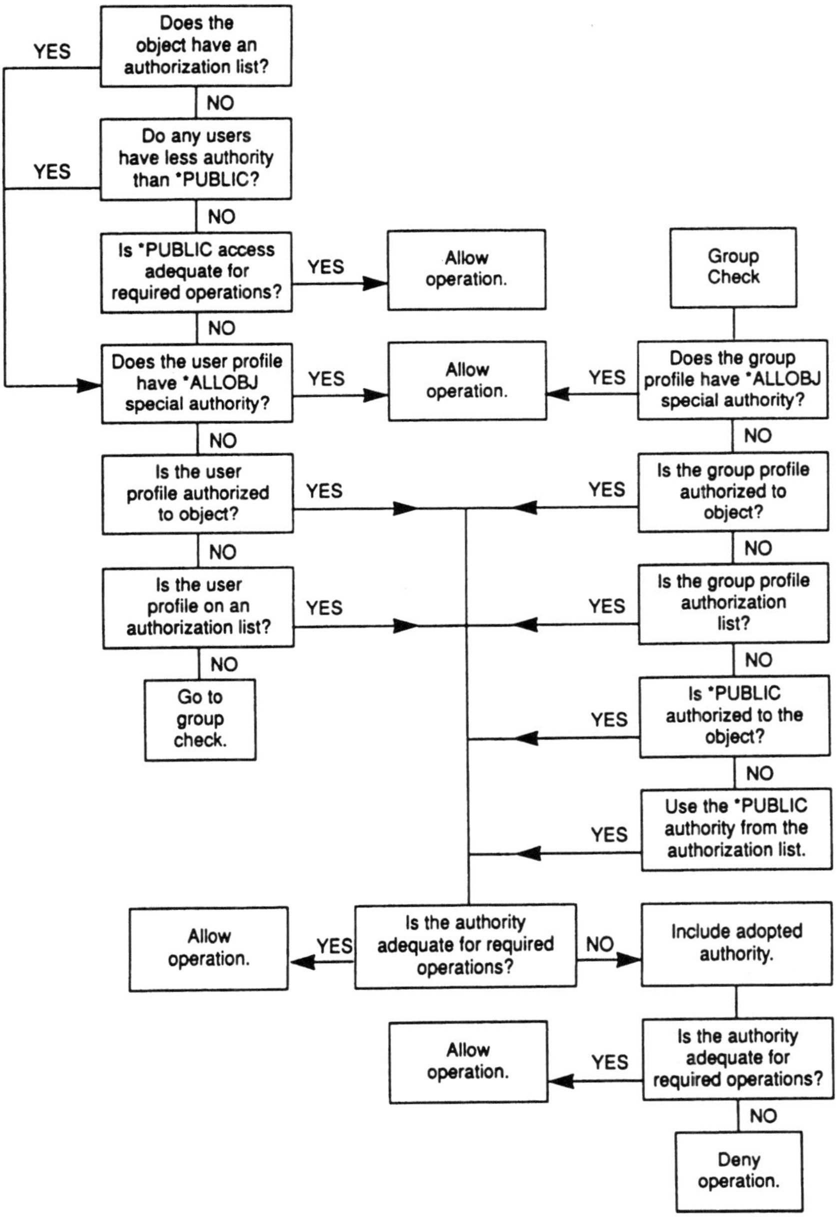

Exhibit 7. Authority search order.

Library Security

Library security protects objects by grouping them into a library and restricting access to the library. Only users authorized to the library can access objects in it. The objects themselves are assigned *PUBLIC access authority. To implement library security, the QSECURITY system option must be set to a value of either 30, 40, or 50.

Object Security

Object security refers to the granting of access to individual objects. To gain access to the object, users must be authorized to both the object and the library in which it resides. Although object security provides the highest degree of separation of users according to access authority, its management can be excessively time-consuming unless group profiles and authorization lists are used. This type of security is recommended only for such objects as payroll files and other sensitive information that requires the highest level of protection.

An Integrated Approach to Security

Because access requirements differ among different types of system users, the organization's security needs are generally best served by using a combination of security approaches. The following recommendations are based on an analysis of the security requirements of different groups of system users.

General system users should be restricted to using menus to perform such predefined sets of tasks as file transfers. More-skilled users, however, often require the use of system utilities to perform such functions as database queries of the downloading and uploading of files. Allowing these users direct access to system functions can help eliminate a backlog of processing requests to the centralized IS department. However, menu security measures are inadequate because query and other system facilities permit unrestricted access to all objects. To control access to objects, library security and, where necessary, object security must be employed. Skilled users should be given *USE authority to files in order to restrict them to printing the results of the query rather than storing the results in a file. The user profile option LMTCPB should be set to *YES to prevent the user from entering system commands.

Programmers can be restricted from changing objects in the production environment through the use of library security techniques. Programmers should be given individual libraries for application development. The development process should be controlled using change management facilities. Release of completed applications to the production environment should be similarly controlled, and both the source and the executable programs should be stored.

It should be noted that because system commands are objects, it is possible to restrict access to these commands to selected users. For example, to prevent users from using the TFRSECJOB system command to transfer processing to a secondary job, the following CL command can be executed to revoke *PUBLIC access:

```
GRTOBJAUT  OBJ(TFRSECJOB)  OBJTYPE(*CMD)
    USER(*PUBLIC)  +  AUT(*EXCLUDE)
```

The user Grant can be given limited access to the TFRSECJOB command, as follows:

```
GRTOBJAUT  OBJ(TFRSECJOB)  OBJTYPE(*CMD)
    USER(GRANT)  +  AUT(*USE)
```

AS/400 Audit Support

The security manager and EDP auditor are usually most interested in answers to these two questions:

- What are the current settings of the AS/400 security parameters?
- What security-related events have occurred over a period of time?

The most recent releases of the OS/400 operating system have offered significant improvements in the mechanisms provided to answer these questions.

Audit Reports

The CL display commands contained in Appendix A can be used to list security-related information. (The display commands are denoted by the DSP prefix.) When used with the OUTFILE options, these commands retrieve information to a database file. Database query utilities can then be used to produce reports containing such information as:

- All objects authorized to a user profile
- All user profiles authorized to an object
- User profiles that have a high level of access (e.g., *ALLOBJ authority)
- Objects secured by an authorization list
- User profiles that belong to a group

To reduce the volume of data that must be reviewed at any one time, the results from previous periods should be saved. These results can then be compared with the results of current analysis in order to identify differences.

Audit Journals

A journal is an object that is used to record data in such a way that it cannot be modified. An audit journal is used to store such security-related events as access failures as well as most types of successful access operations, including the creation and deletion of objects and security-related changes to object authorizations. The security officer uses the QAUDLVL system option to specify the types of events to be recorded. The values permitted for this option are shown under the Event Audit Options heading in Appendix D.

Data contained in the audit journal can be retrieved to a database file. Database query utilities can then be used to summarize this information for analysis and reporting.

The audit features have been extended to meet the C2 audit requirements. All security-related changes can be audited. Audit can be selected for all or individual users, and the actions of users or reference to objects can be audited. However, excessive auditing can affect system performance.

Recommended Course of Action

The first step in securing the AS/400 system is to identify critical data files and applications and establish the appropriate level of access control over them. At most AS/400 installations, system security should be set at level 30 to 40 to ensure adequate protection of resources. To optimize system performance, *PUBLIC authority should be used when possible; otherwise, objects with similar security requirements should be grouped in a library to which access is restricted. To simplify the enrollment and removal of users, individual user profiles should reference group profiles whenever possible.

Certain controls common to most system installations should also be considered. Password expiration and validation system values should be implemented to enforce the periodic changing of passwords and to prevent the use of trivial passwords. A timeout period should be set for inactive terminals and vendor-supplied passwords should be changed to prevent easy access to the system by hackers. In particular, passwords to the following vendor-supplied profiles should be changed: QSECOFR, QSRV, QSRVBAS, QPGMR, QSYSOPR, and QUSER.

For most organizations, an integrated strategy using menu, library, and object control mechanisms can provide an efficient and cost-effective solution to their security requirements. This strategy should be augmented by a security awareness program that stresses the role of system users in protecting information assets. Any implementation of new or modified security controls should be explained in a positive manner so that users accept the need for such changes and appreciate the importance of secure access to company information.

Chapter 64

Implementing Kerberos in Distributed Systems

Ray Kaplan
Joe Kovara
Glen Zorn

One of the most significant problems in securing distributed systems is authentication. This is, ensuring that the parties to a conversation — possibly separated by a wide area network and traversing untrusted systems and communications paths — are who they claim to be. Kerberos is currently the de facto standard for authentication in large, heterogenous network environments.

Kerberos has been in production for more than six years in one of the world's most challenging open systems environments — Project Athena at MIT.[1] Kerberos is the backbone of network security for Project Athena, where it protects more than 10,000 users accessing thousands of workstations and hundreds of servers. Kerberos protects thousands of sessions and tens of thousands of mail messages per day. As such, Kerberos is arguably the best-tested, most scrutinized authentication protocol in widespread use today.

HISTORY OF DEVELOPMENT

Many of the ideas for Kerberos originated in a discussion of how to use encryption for authentication in large networks that was published in 1978 by Roger Needham and Michael Schroeder.[2] Other early ideas can be attributed to continuing work by the security community, such as Dorothy Denning and Giovanni Sacco's work on the use of time stamps in key distribution protocols.[3] Kerberos was designed and implemented in the mid-1980s as part of MIT's Project Athena. The original design and implementation of the first four versions of Kerberos were done by MIT Project Athena members Steve Miller (Digital Equipment Corp.) and Clifford

0-8493-9989-0/99/$0.00+$.50

Neuman, along with Jerome Salzer (Project Athena technical director) and Jeff Schiller (MIT campus network manager).

Kerberos versions 1 through 3 were internal development versions and, since its public release in 1989, version 4 of Kerberos has seen wide use in the Internet community. In 1990, John Kohl (Digital Equipment Corp.) and Clifford Neuman (University of Washington at that time and now with the Information Sciences Institute at the University of Southern California) presented a design for version 5 of the protocol based on input from many of those familiar with the limitations of version 4. Currently, Kerberos versions 4 and 5 are available from several sources, including both freely distributed versions (subject to export restrictions) and fully supported commercial versions.

FUNCTIONAL OVERVIEW

Kerberos is an authentication protocol that has been built into a system that provides networkwide security services. Kerberos can solve many of the security problems of large, heterogeneous networks, including mutual authentication between clients and servers. The basic idea behind Kerberos is that a trusted third party (the Kerberos security server) provides a means by which constituents of the network (principals) can trust each other. These principals may be any hardware or software that communicates across the network. In addition to authentication, Kerberos offers both privacy and integrity for network messages.

There is considerable detail in describing how Kerberos works, and the actual exchanges that take place over the network are a bit complicated. However, the basic idea is quite straightforward and follows this five-step process:

1. On behalf of a user (or surrogate, such as a program), a Kerberos client program in the user's workstation asserts the user's identity to the Kerberos server and verifies it locally on the workstation.
2. Kerberos client software on the workstation asks the Kerberos security server for the credentials necessary to use the service that the user requested.
3. The Kerberos security server sends the user's credentials for the requested service to the Kerberos client where they are cached.
4. A client application on the workstation picks up the user's credentials from the workstation's credential cache for that user and presents them to the application server that it wants to use.
5. The application server authenticates the client application to the service that the user requested and the server delivers the requested services.

Exhibit 1 illustrates how this works.

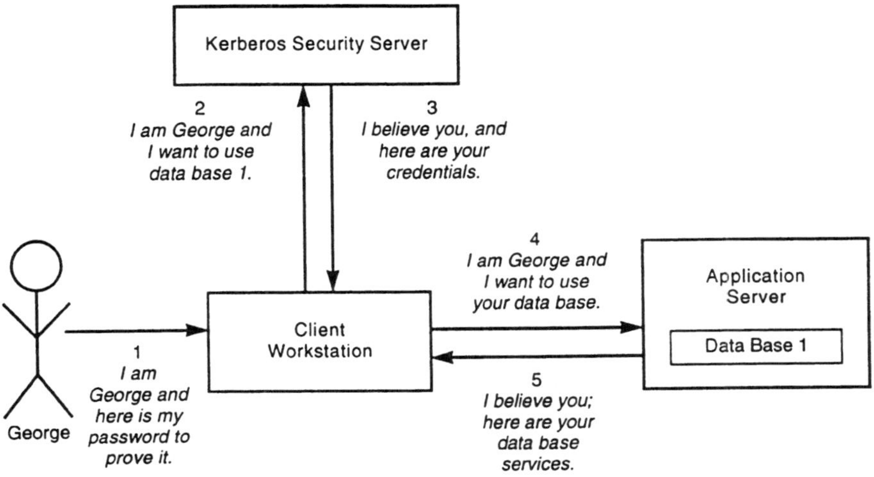

Exhibit 1. Kerberos authentication process.

SCOPE OF SECURITY SERVICES

In his treatise on distributed systems security, Morrie Gasser[4] categorizes the security services that a distributed system can provide for its users and applications as: secure channels, authentication, confidentiality, integrity, access control, non-repudiation, and availability.

Secure Channels. A secure channel provides integrity and confidentiality services to communicating principals. Kerberos offers these services.

Integrity. An integrity service allows principals to determine if the message stream between them has been modified in an unauthorized manner. The Kerberos safe message includes a checksum that is used as an integrity check. Each principal in the Kerberos safe message exchange separately derives this checksum from the message using one of several available algorithms. The algorithms include a one-way message digest hash that has cryptographic strength. The nature of such a checksum is that it cannot be adjusted to conceal a change to the message.

Confidentiality. A confidentiality service is designed to counter passive wire-tapping by restricting the availability of message traffic to an authorized set of principals. The traffic itself and both source and destination addresses of the traffic are of interest. Obviously, the traffic itself can contain confidential information. In particular, Kerberos is specifically designed to minimize the transmission of passwords over the network and encrypt passwords under those few conditions when they are transmitted over the network. Kerberos also provides encryption of an application's message data if the application desires it.

Network addresses and traffic volume may be used to infer information. Consider that an increase in the traffic between two business partners may predict a merger. The Kerberos private message provides protection for message traffic between principals using the bulk data encryption technology such as the Data Encryption Standard (DES). Kerberos does not provide a defense against traffic analysis.

Authentication. An authentication service permits one principal to determine that the identity of another principal is genuine as represented. It is often important for both sides of an exchange to mutually authenticate. Kerberos currently uses a trusted third party (the Kerberos authentication server) to mediate the exchange of shared secrets between principals in order to authenticate principals to one another.

Access Control. An access control service protects information from disclosure or modification in an unauthorized manner by controlling which principals are granted access. Kerberos does not directly offer this service, although the protocol provides for the inclusion and protection of access control information in messages for use by applications and operating systems.

Nonrepudiation. Nonrepudiation services offer proof to the sender that information was delivered and proof to the recipient as to the origin of the information. Typically, such proof is used by an arbitrator to settle a repudiation-based dispute. For instance, in the case of E-mail between two people or electronic funds transfer between two business entities, a court of law would be the arbitrator that adjudicates repudiation-based disputes that arise. Kerberos offers the basic authentication and integrity services from which a nonrepudiation service could be built. Kerberos does not offer the arbitration services that are required for the complete implementation of such a service.

Availability. Availability services provide an expected level of performance and availability such as error-free bandwidth. Perhaps the best example of an availability problem is a denial of service attack. Consider someone simply disconnecting the cable that connects a network segment to its router. Kerberos does not offer any services to deal with this set of problems.

Summing up, Kerberos is an authentication protocol that has been extended to offer privacy and integrity of network messages. It does not offer protection against traffic analysis or availability services. Since it does offer authentication services, it can serve as a platform on which to build access control and non-repudiation.

APPLYING KERBEROS

The best way to think about Kerberos is as a suite of security services. An individual or program that wants to use Kerberos services must make explicit calls in order to obtain those services. A typical scenario is a user sitting at a workstation who wants to use an application that requires the user to first authenticate himself or herself to the application using Kerberos before the application will respond. First, the user runs a Kerberos utility on the workstation called kinit. Kinit obtains the user's Kerberos credentials from the Kerberos Authentication Server (AS) and caches them on the user's workstation. The user's credentials are now available for any application that demands them.

Here is how this looks for version 4 of Kerberos from MIT under UNIX:

```
% kinit
Zippy Corporation (node 1.zippy.com)
Kerberos initialization
kerberos name: george
Password: a-good-password
%
```

For a commercial implementation of version 5 of Kerberos under UNIX, this might look like:

```
% kinit
Password for george@zippy.com: a-good-password
%
```

Under VMS, the same operation for version 4 of Kerberos might look like:

```
$ KINIT
Kerberos initialization for "george"
kerberos name: george
Password: a-good-password
$
```

There are several players in a Kerberos authentication scheme: principals, an AS, and a ticket granting service (TGS). Principals are entities that use Kerberos security services. Principals can be human users or programs — typically users who are logged in at their workstations or the server-based applications that they want to use across the network. The functions of the AS and TGS are usually run on the same machine. This combination of services has come to be called a key distribution center (KDC). (This nomenclature is unfortunate; in cryptographic parlance, a KDC is a center established for the purpose of providing keys to the parties that wish to communicate.) The Kerberos KDC provides a means for authentication between principals.

The details of the Kerberos authentication exchange are simple, robust, and elegant — although not necessarily intuitive. The Kerberos principal asserts its identity by sending a clear text string to the AS. The AS provides Kerberos with credentials for that principal in answer to that request. However, before sending these credentials to the requesting principal, the AS encrypts them with a secret that is shared between the principal and Kerberos. This shared secret is the principal's Kerberos password, which is held in encrypted form in the key distribution center's data base. Once on the principal's workstation, these credentials are decrypted with a password that the user provides to the Kerberos client. If the principal can decrypt these credentials provided by the AS, the principal can use them. If the principal cannot decrypt these credentials provided by the AS, the principal cannot successfully use them. Thus, the initial authentication of a principal happens on the client workstation — not on the Kerberos security server.

This design has two very important features. First, because the principal asserts its identity using a clear test string and the AS encrypts the principal's credentials before it sends them back to the principal, authentication requires that no passwords ever be sent over the network — in clear text or encrypted. A wiretapper looking at the Kerberos initialization transaction would only see two messages, both of which are useless to the attacker:

- A clear text string going from the principal to the KDC, saying "Hello, my name is George."
- An incomprehensible (encrypted) text string from the KDC to the principal.

The ticket that the AS sends in response to the client's assertion of identity does not contain the client's encrypted password, but the ticket itself is encrypted with it. Therefore, the client workstation can decrypt it using the password that the user types. Consequently, the user's password only resides on the workstation for the very short period that it takes to decrypt the initial credentials.

Second, because the Kerberos client uses a password that it obtains from the user on his or her own workstation to decrypt the credentials from the AS, another user at another workstation cannot impersonate the legitimate one. Credentials are useless unless they can be decrypted, and the only way to decrypt them is to know the principal's password.

Kerberos credentials are authenticators called tickets. The authenticator that is exchanged between the principal and the AS in the Kerberos initialization sequence is called a ticket granting ticket (TGT). The TGT is so named because it is used to obtain tickets for various services the principal may wish to access. The TGT simply provides proof in subsequent requests for services without the user having to reauthenticate (e.g., type in the password again). This initial Kerberos exchange is summarized in Exhibit 2.

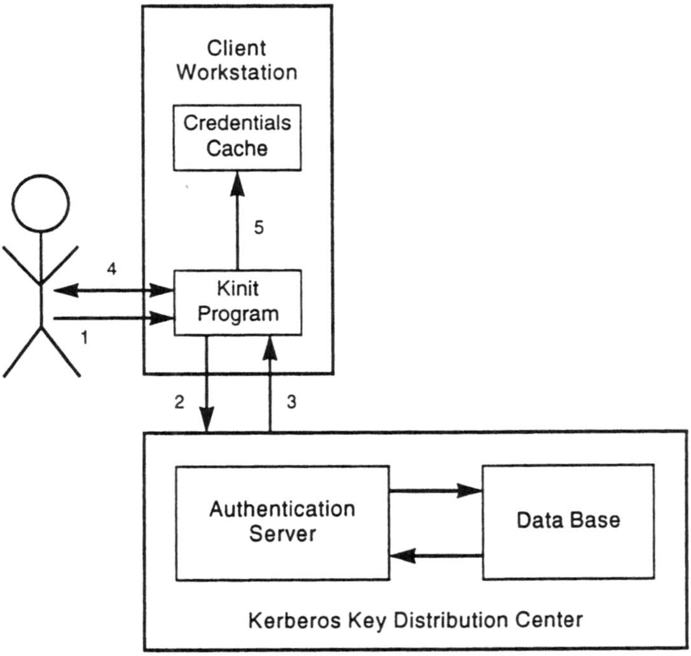

Step	Description
1	The client workstation user initializes the Kerberos environment by running a program, or a program does it on his or her behalf.
2	The kinit program asserts its identity to the authentication server (AS) by sending the client principal name to the AS.
3	The AS credentials contain the names of the client, a time stamp, and a session key that will be used by both the principal and the key distribution center for subsequent communications. This authenticator is encrypted by the AS before it is sent to the principal. It is called a ticket granting ticket (TGT).
4	The kinit program prompts the user for his or her password.
5	If kinit can decrypt the TGT using this password, the TGT is saved in the principal's credentials cache.

Exhibit 2. The initial Kerberos exchange.

At the conclusion of this initial exchange, the client workstation holds a TGT for the client principal. From this point on, these Kerberos credentials are cached on the user's workstation. TGTs are used to obtain additional credentials specifically for each server application that the client principal wants to use. These service-specific credentials are called application service tickets, and they are obtained from the aforementioned Kerberos TGS.

Finally, these application service tickets are used by the client principal to authenticate itself to a server principal when it wants to use the Kerberos-authenticated service that a particular server principal is offering. Once activated, the client program transparently handles all other transactions with Kerberos and the application server.

Client principals authenticate themselves to their servers with service tickets that they obtain from the Kerberos TGS on behalf of their user, based on the TGT that was obtained by the user when they initialized Kerberos. This process is summarized in Exhibit 3.

Except for having to run kinit to obtain the initial TGT, enter the Kerberos password, and start the desired application client, Kerberos is transparent from the user's point of view. It is possible to embed the functions of kinit (getting the TGT from Kerberos) in the workstation's login sequence such that everything except the entry of the user's password is transparent. In fact, a smart card or authentication token can be integrated with both Kerberos and the client workstation. In such a scenario, all users have to do is insert their tokens into their workstations. The tight integration of these pieces would allow the authentication sequence and the desired application to be activated automatically. Coupled with good security management of the workstation and the KDC, these basic features provide simple and robust security.

Client principals — be they the client side of applications or such native operating system utilities as UNIX login or telnet — must explicitly call for Kerberos services. In the public domain versions of Kerberos, applications use Kerberos services by calling Kerberos library functions. Some commercial implementations of Kerberos version 5 incorporate the generic security services applications programming interface (GSSAPI) as its standard application programming interface. Digital Equipment Corp. put forth this interface as a standard for security services. The GSSAPI is being considered by the Common Authentication Technology Working Group of the Internet Engineering Task Force as a standard for the Internet community. As outlined in the example of how the Kerberos protocol works, a client would use a sequence of GSSAPI calls to authenticate itself to an application server. Such a sequence of calls using the GSSAPI might look like this:

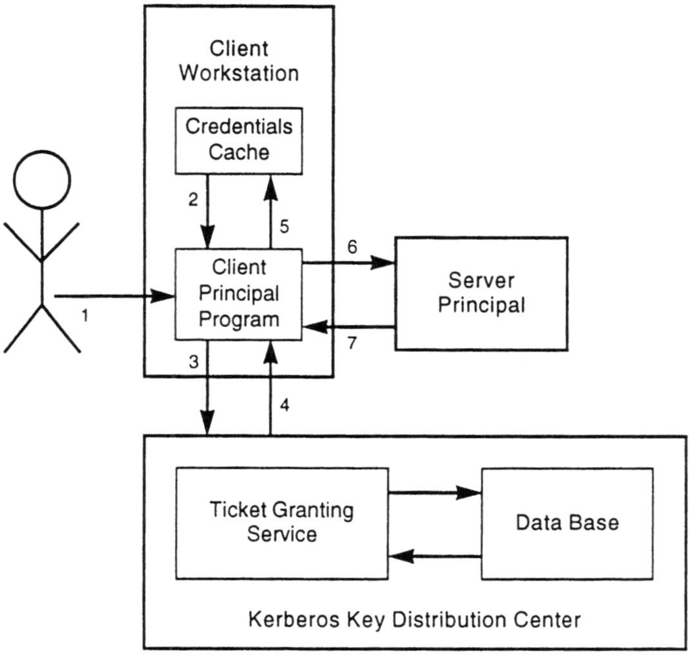

Step	Description
1	The user runs a kerberized client application.
2	The kerberized client application takes the client principal's ticket granting ticket (TGT) from the credentials cache.
3	The kerberized client application sends the client principal's TGT and its request for a specific applications service ticket to the Kerberos ticket granting service (TGS).
4	The TGS returns the application service ticket for the requested ticket to the client principal program.
5	The client principal program stores the application service ticket in the client's credentials cache with other service tickets that the client principal acquires from time to time.
6	The client principal program authenticates itself to the application server by presenting the application service ticket.
7	Optionally, the client principal program may require the server to authenticate itself. The combination of steps 6 and 7 is the mutual authentication service.

Exhibit 3. Obtaining an application service ticket from Kerberos.

gss_acquire_cred

Obtain Kerberos credentials (i.e., a token, called a ticket).

gss_init_sec_context

Initialize the client's security context loop here, wait for success; then pass the Kerberos token (ticket) to the named server and start to consume application services.

When incorporated into an existing production environment, Kerberos is not transparent. Each client or application server that wants to use Kerberos services must have calls to those services included in its code. As with any other security-related coding, this "kerberization" must be done based on sound applications design and discipline to ensure that it is done properly.

Currently, a few operating system vendors include Kerberos in the software that they ship. Third-party Kerberos suppliers provide Kerberos libraries and modify or rewrite standard operating system utilities to "kerberize" them. The convention in such operating systems as UNIX is that kerberized programs simply replace standard utilities, and users see no difference in the commands that they type. In some implementations for such operating systems as VMS, the standard commands are modified to include instructions that specify Kerberos (e.g., telnet/authorization = Kerberos). In other Kerberos implementations, the standard operating system utilities are actually replaced with appropriately named kerberized counterparts such as ktelnet. Finally, in such operating system implementations as Kerberos for Microsoft Windows, Macintosh, and Next's NextStep, programs may actually have their own graphical user interfaces, just as would any other program in that environment. In these cases, a user just clicks on the appropriate icon.

For example, in a typical kerberized Windows environment, a user would simply click on the desired application icon to activate it after the user's Kerberos password had been entered. From there on, the application program handles the authentication in cooperation with Kerberos behind the scenes. An environment in which users only need to enter their passwords once has fostered the idea that Kerberos is a single-sign-on system. However, Kerberos can only provide this seemless access to kerberized applications. If workstation users must use many different nonkerberized applications that require them to log on with individual passwords, the addition of Kerberos to their workstation environment alone will not change things. Again, each application must be kerberized.

TECHNICAL ISSUES

The success of a Kerberos implementation depends on how carefully it is designed and how completely it is planned. Lack of these two critical elements is the major reason that the implementation of any security scheme fails. A detailed consideration of the authentication mechanism itself (e.g., what it is, how it works, how to use it, how to apply it, and its weaknesses) is important. A number of details may need to be addressed. These include: the topology of the network; the placement of authentication in the protocol stack; the use and availability of network services (such as time and naming); and the relative security of the basic network infrastructure. Understanding these details is a prerequisite to proper operation, performance, and administration of Kerberos.

Protocol Placement

In Exhibit 4, network segments A (which connects the primary KDC management capability to the KDC), and B (which connects other mission critical applications) may be more critical than network segments D and E (which connect relatively less important applications). Therefore, network segments A and B need to be carefully engineered, perhaps more so than network segments D and E. (As a reminder, Kerberos is an application level protocol. While most Kerberos implementations use TCP/IP, Kerberos itself is an authentication protocol that is independent of the underlying transport protocol.)

Using the Kerberos authentication protocol across a security firewall may make the firewall's design, implementation, and operation more complicated. Many such firewalls use filtering or proxy agents that operate at the application layer in the protocol stack. Because the security firewall exists to protect the rest of the network from network segments D and E (including systems C and D, and whatever else they are connected to), the security firewall needs to understand how to deal with Kerberos traffic. Of course, the firewall may also need to deal with application server traffic from system D if its application is in use elsewhere in the network.

Time Services and Network Naming

Although Kerberos was designed to bring authentication to a network that generally lacks security-related services, the degree to which Kerberos can be trusted largely depends on how carefully it is implemented and the robustness of its supporting network services.

Kerberos requires trusted, loosely synchronized clocks in the network. Dorothy Denning and Giovanni Sacco's work on the use of time stamps in key distribution protocols shows that enforcing limited lifetimes for authentication credentials based on time stamps can minimize the threat of replaced credentials. This can only be guaranteed through the use of trusted, or authenticated, network time services.

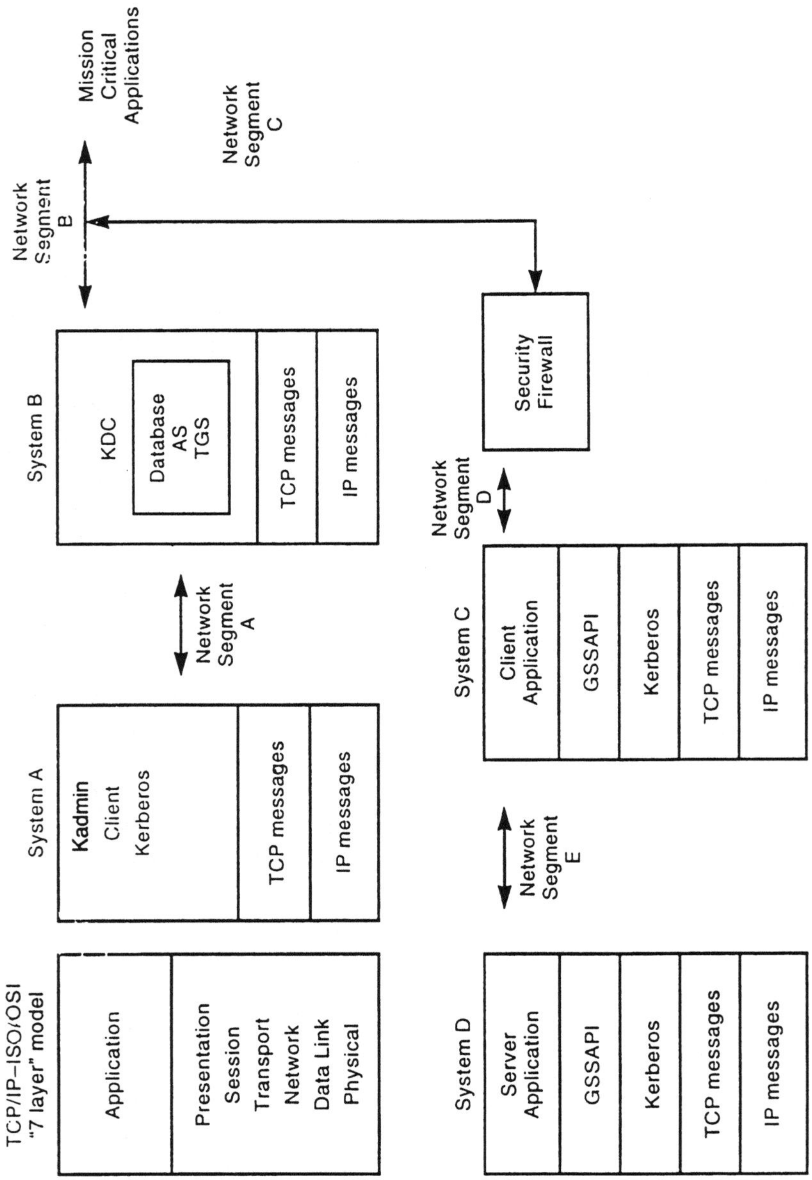

Exhibit 4. Network topology and authentication protocol.

Kerberos authenticates to the names of its principals. Principals must have a secure way to determine the names of other principals that they are willing to communicate with. However, IP network addresses and network name services (e.g., TCP/IP Domain Name Service, DNS) can be spoofed. There are several ways to ensure that principal names can be trusted. For example, a principal name might be placed in an access control list of an application server. Alternatively, local knowledge of a designated application server might be hard coded into an application client. Finally, use of a name service can provide some measure of assurance, because answers from the name server must be authentic.

Within the limits of the encryption and key exchange protocol technology that Kerberos uses, its authentication is held together by trust. The KDC and principals must trust one another to be who they represent themselves to be. This keystone is held in place by trusted time services and robust means for principals to identify one another. Kerberos provides a mechanism for securely authenticating principals. However, in the real world, it is also necessary to secure the information about which principal one is willing to talk to.

The KDC, Application Servers, and Their Clients

As explained earlier in this chapter, the KDC, kerberized application servers, and their clients must be protected so that their operation cannot be unduly influenced. The KDC must be physically secure and must not allow any non-Kerberos network activity. For example, allowing the KDC to run a network protocol that is a known security risk (e.g., UNIX Trivial File Transfer Protocol (TFTP) or UNIX sendmail mailer) is an invitation to disaster. In general, the only application that should run on the KDC (and its slave servers) is Kerberos.

Both servers and clients must be protected from compromise. Although they are less critical than the KDC and its slaves, if a server or a client is compromised, their roles in the Kerberos authentication process can no longer be trusted. Although it may seem odd that the principals that Kerberos is authenticating need to be protected, consider that all security is built on a foundation of basics such as good control over both physical and logical access to the computing environment. If physical and logical access to Kerberos principals is not properly managed, client and server identities can be spoofed. Additionally, if users do not properly manage their Kerberos passwords (or it is not properly managed for them with a smart card or token device), their identity can be spoofed.

Kerberos Administration

Kerberos administration must be coordinated with other administrative tasks. For example, many organizations maintain their user community controls in a data base that is updated periodically, with changes propagated to individual systems and applications (e.g., individual LA authorization data bases). When an employee leaves the company, among the access privileges needing to be revoked is that user's Kerberos access. It should also be recognized that in preparing for the initial implementation of Kerberos, new passwords must be distributed to a large number of users — not a trivial task.

Kerberos Performance and Network Topology

Kerberos overhead is small, and generally a small amount of additional overhead on signon is considered acceptable. Individual transactions can be authenticated quickly, because Kerberos uses a fast message digest hash for an integrity check and DES for privacy. After the initial Kerberos ticket granting ticket (TGT) is processed, all such operations take place in memory (of both the client and server principals) so there is little additional overhead involved. However, the specific requirements for each implementation should be carefully evaluated.

Special requirements for Kerberos performance and availability can be met by deploying secondary (slave) KDCs to network segments where they can be accessed directly, and where they can be available during periods when the main KDC is unavailable. Updates are made to the main KDC's data base, and the data base is then replicated periodically to the read-only, slave KDCs.

In order to ensure that an organization does not end up with a plethora of different authentication techniques, any new mechanism must be compatible with existing and planned efforts. Compatibility must exist among applications, internal organizational standards, standards in the organization's industry and, of course, international standards in the network and computer industry. Adopting authentication as a part of an overall strategy for security provides a solid foundation. However, the decision should be guided by emerging standards for such services.

The GSSAPI, the emerging standard for Internet security services, is a logical choice as an insulator between the suppliers of security services (such as Kerberos authentication) and security service consumers (such as application programs). Because it is an application program interface, the GSSAPI does not provide interoperability between different security mechanisms in and of itself. Interoperability requires a common mechanism between cooperating players using the mechanism. Widespread interoperability among disparate authentication mechanisms requires that they all communicate with one another. The GSSAPI can hide the complications of this interoperability from the programs that use it to access security services.

What the GSSAPI does provide is insulation from change — it is possible to replace the underlying authentication mechanisms easily and without changes to applications written to use the GSSAPI. A decision to adopt the GSSAPI, with Kerberos as its mechanism, allows weaker, more problematic authentication mechanisms in existing applications to be economically replaced. That is, the initial investment in recoding programs to use the GSSAPI would not be wasted because the underlying authentication mechanism can be changed at will without having to recode the entire application each time security technology advances.

Because current Kerberos implementations support only TCP/IP, shops that run DECnet or SNA may not be able to use Kerberos to authenticate in these environments. In the same vein, Kerberos support for older operating systems may be needed. These environments require special treatment to move Kerberos into them. In the worst case, such environments cannot be changed directly. For example, an older application that is not easily modified to add Kerberos can be frontended with a mechanism that isolates it and provides the desired Kerberos services.

Kerberizing Applications, Their Servers, and Clients

In order to add Kerberos-based authentication to an application, it must be broken down into a client part and a server part (if it is not already so divided). This is done in order to separate the parts of the application that participate in Kerberos authentication — the client part is authenticated to the server part (or possibly mutual authentication is performed). This division is necessary even if the application does not have a true client/server architecture. For those client-server applications, the division usually follows the application's existing client-server structure. The fundamental questions are:

- What client-server structure most accurately represents the components of the application?
- How is the client-server structure to be imposed on the application?

These are very broad questions with implications for an application's utility and security. Implementation of the answers also has a major effect on the cost of kerberizing an application.

Although it may ultimately be desirable to reimplement all applications as kerberized client-server, this is not always feasible. An example is a terminal-based application on a timesharing system. Such applications implicitly assume that the transmission path between the terminal and the host is secure. But this may not hold true when terminals and hosts are separated by a network. The client-server answer to this problem is typically to eliminate the terminal and replace it with a client (running a GUI-based front end), and replace the host application with a back-end server.

Kerberizing both client and server parts of the application then make the application's security independent of the intervening network. Suffice it to say that each client/server architecture and each class of network device must be kerberized in a way that takes into consideration its idiosyncrasies.

COST FACTORS

The design, planning, and implementations for widespread authentication is expensive. Planning for authentication may raise basic security-related questions that will also need to be addressed.

Software Costs

The least expensive approach is to use the public domain version of Kerberos. However, this alternative leaves the user with no support and all the idiosyncrasies of this version. (It is possible to purchase support for the public domain version.) It should be noted that many organizations do not allow the widespread deployment of public domain software.

Commercial versions of Kerberos are available with service and support. The vendors can provide trained security professionals and can offer a variety of security services to assist organizations secure their systems.

Cost of Securing the KDC

An additional cost that is often overlooked is the cost of securing the KDC and the slave KDC servers required for redundancy. The KDC requires special treatment, and the network's topology may require more than one slave. Separate machines and physical housings for these KDCs are often required. Fortunately both primary and secondary KDCs can run on small machines. For example, MIT's Project Athena runs 3 DEC station model 2100s as KDCs (one primary and two secondary) for over 1300 workstations and more than 100 servers. These systems are small, easy to operate, and relatively inexpensive. (Each is configured with 12 MB of memory and 332 MB of disk space.)

Personnel Costs

Merely installing the KDCs is not sufficient; people must be properly trained in the administration and operation of these systems. In addition, a complete Kerberos implementation team must be organized and trained.

VULNERABILITIES

As does any authentication scheme, Kerberos has certain weaknesses. The problem for Kerberos implementors is to learn how to deal with these weaknesses.

The Kerberos design assumes that server principals are kept in moderately secure areas, that the key distribution center is in a secure area, and that the key distribution center runs only trusted software. Remember that Kerberos comes out of MIT's Project Athena. At MIT, care is taken to ensure that a minimum amount of trust is placed in client workstations. This includes provisions for trusted booting from trusted servers and no system or applications software on the workstations' local disks. In an ideal environment, local disks are wiped clean between boots to ensure that the after-effects of infected software do not remain to haunt users.

Still, a question remains: Has the workstation been compromised in a way that would allow an attacker to set aside these protections, install a covert channel, and collect a user's Kerberos password as it was typed on the workstation? Although such an attack is not simple, it is possible. Accordingly, workstations in such environments should be kept under the lock and key of controlled physical access and inspected periodically to ensure that they have not been tampered with.

Moving from a closely controlled environment to one in which workstations boot and run from local disks, several new concerns arise. Besides having to carefully control physical access to such workstations, the security of these machines must be managed very carefully to ensure that local software has not been compromised. This is usually done by means of regular technical inspections, backed up by more rigorous periodic assessments.

For instance, in a workstation environment that uses UNIX systems, each workstation might be inspected nightly by automated tools that report their findings to a central security management facility. The hope is that these inspections will detect any security problems so that they can be expediently resolved. Authentication schemes such as Kerberos cannot solve fundamental problems such as dishonest employees, people that pick bad passwords, or lack of adequate network or host security management.

Finally, because the Kerberos key distribution center contains all of the shared secrets as well as provides security services, it must be very carefully protected and managed. Although client workstations may be in relatively public areas and run software that is not entirely trusted, the KDC must be trustworthy. This means that the access to the KDC must be carefully controlled and monitored.

The KDC should support no applications, users, or protocols other than Kerberos. (That is, everything except Kerberos has been removed from this machine.) Ideally, this system will not support remote network access except by means of the Kerberos services it offers. If the KDC itself is to be remotely administered, the necessary operations must be accomplished over a special, secure channel that cannot be compromised. (Of course, kadmin — the Kerberos administrative tool — operates using Kerberos private messages.)

If the KDC is compromised, its shared secrets are at risk and it security services cannot be trusted. However, such an attack is far from easy. Kerberos uses the DES for encryption operations; the entire KDC data base is encrypted using the master key. To successfully attack the KDC, an intruder would need to access the KDC or otherwise obtain a copy of the KDC's data base. For example, a wiretapper could grab a copy of the KDC's data base as it is being propagated to a Kerberos slave KDC server. Because this transfer is done using Kerberos private messages under a randomly generated key that only the KDC and the slave KDC server share expressly for this transaction, such a wiretapper would first have to break that encryption to get at the message traffic that contained the data base being propagated. The intruder would then need to mount a successful cryptanalysis attack against the master key to obtain the data base.

Although contemporary experience with DES shows that successful attacks are possible, they are far too expensive and computationally intensive for anyone but such organizations as the National Security Agency (NSA) to attempt. Perfecting a mechanism to protect Kerberos from such a cryptanalytic attack is impractical for any but the most sophisticated and best funded government intelligence organizations.

The Kerberos protocol does not restrict the type of encryption that is used, and it may include any number of different encryption methods. In fact, design efforts are underway to include public key-based encryption in Kerberos. In any case, a public key-based Kerberos would be subject to the same type of attacks as the current, DES-based implementation.

FUTURE DEVELOPMENTS

As it matures, Kerberos is being incorporated into everything from the most mundane network application software to such specialized network hardware as access control devices for PCs and routers, terminal servers, and modems. It is also coming to be incorporated into some of the most advanced network applications. As operating system functions become distributed, effective authentication and security services have become even more critical. As a consequence of widespread attacks on TCP/IP's highly distributed Network File System, for example, authentication for it has become mandatory (even though it is not widely used). Kerberos has increasing appeal to the implementors and integrators of distributed systems because it is well tested and readily available.

The continuing search for distributed system security solutions has revealed many alternatives to Kerberos, including systems based on RSA Data Security's Public Key Cryptography Standards (PKCS) and those based on the Open System Foundation's (OSF) Distributed Management Environment (DME) and its associated Distributed Computing Environment (DCE). Implementations based on PKCS do not yet offer interoperability between their respective environments, let alone with other authentication schemes. A consortium of European companies (including Bull, ICL, and Seimans Nixdorf) is working on a standard called Secure European System for Applications in a Multivendor Environment (SESAME). SESAME is still in the standards development stage.

The obvious questions that arise when considering a network security system are:

- When will it be widely available?
- What will it cost to implement?
- Will it be interoperable?
- Will it stand the test of time?

While the authors cannot answer these questions for other network security systems, they believe that Kerberos has already answered these questions in the affirmative. There have been no known successful attacks against Kerberos, and production experience shows that the methods for protecting Kerberos described in this chapter are both feasible and effective. In short, Kerberos has become a de facto network standard; it is well understood, well tested, and implementations are available from a variety of sources on a wide range of platforms.

Notes

1. Project Athena is a model of "next-generation distributed computing" in the academic environment. It began in 1983 as an eight-year project with DEC and IBM as its major industrial sponsors. Their pioneering model is based on client-server technology and it includes such innovations as authentication based on Kerberos and X Windows. An excellent reference — George Champine, *MIT Project Athena, A Model for Distributed Campus Computing,* Digital Press, 1991.
2. Needham, R.M. and Schroeder, M., Using encryption for authentication in large networks of computers, *Communications of the ACM* 21 (December 1978), pp. 993–999.
3. Denning, D.E. and Sacco, G.M., "Timestamps in key distribution protocols, *Communications of the ACM* 24 (August 1981), pp. 533–536.
4. Gasser, M., Security in distributed systems, in *Recent Developments in Telecommunications,* North-Holland, Amsterdam, The Netherlands; Elsevier Science Publishers, 1992, pp. 145–228.

Chapter 65
E-mail Security Using Pretty Good Privacy

William Stallings

Users who rely on electronic mail for business or personal communications should beware. Messages sent over a network are subject to eavesdropping. If the messages are stored in a file, they are subject to perusal months or even years later. There is also the threat of impersonation and that a message may not be from the party it claims to be from.

Protection is available in the form of Pretty Good Privacy (PGP), an e-mail security package developed by Phil Zimmermann that combines confidentiality and digital signature capabilities to provide a powerful, virtually unbreakable, and easy-to-use package.

PGP DEFINED

The most notable features of this e-mail security program are that it:

- Enables people to send e-mail messages that are secure from eavesdropping. Only the intended recipient can read a PGP message.
- Enables people to send e-mail messages that are guaranteed authentic. The recipient is ensured that the PGP message was created by the person who claims to have created it and that no one has altered the message since it was created.
- Is available as freeware on the Internet, many electronic bulletin boards, and most commercial services such as CompuServe.
- Is available in versions for DOS, Macintosh, UNIX, Amiga, OS/2, VMS, and other operating systems.
- Works with any e-mail package to create secure E-mail messages.

0-8493-9989-0/99/$0.00+$.50

E-MAIL RISKS

PGP provides protection from the threat of eavesdropping. A message sent over the Internet can pass through a handful of mail forwarders and dozens of packet-switching nodes. A systems administrator or someone who has gained privileged access to any of these transfer points is in a position to read those messages.

Although e-mail users may feel they have nothing to hide, they may someday want to correspond with their lawyers or accountants using the Internet, or they may work for companies that want to send proprietary information over the Internet. Many people already use the Internet for sending highly personal or sensitive messages.

There is also a civil liberties issue to be concerned about. The police, intelligence, and other security forces of the government can easily monitor digital and computerized e-mail messages, looking for key words, names, and patterns of exchanges. Any user could be innocently caught up in such a net.

Authenticity of messages poses another potential risk. It is not difficult to spoof the network into sending a message with an incorrect return address, enabling impersonation. It is also relatively easy to trap a message along its path, alter the contents, and then send it on its way.

For example, if a user is on a shared system, such as a UNIX system that hooks into the Internet, then the impersonator could be someone with "superuser" privileges on the system. Such a person could divert all incoming and outgoing traffic from an unsuspecting mailbox to a special file. The impersonator could also have access to a router, mail bridge, or other type of gateway through which all traffic between the user and a correspondent must pass. Such impersonators could use their privileged status on the gateway to intercept mail and to create and send mail with a fraudulent return address.

PGP'S HISTORY: PRIVACY

PGP is a legitimate tool that can be used for legitimate reasons by ordinary citizens, although some users consider it slightly suspect.

Phil Zimmermann began working on PGP in the 1980s and released the first version in 1991. One of the key motivating factors for PGP's development was an effort by the FBI to secure passage of a law that would ban certain forms of security algorithms and force computer manufacturers to implement security features for e-mail that could be bypassed by government agencies. Zimmerman saw this as a threat to privacy and freedom. Thus, PGP was conceived as a package that could be used by the average person on a small system to provide e-mail privacy and authenticity. Zimmerman accomplished this by:

- Selecting the best available security algorithms as building blocks.
- Integrating these algorithms into a general-purpose application that is independent of the operating system and processor and that is based on a small set of easy-to-use commands.
- Making the package and its documentation, including the source code, free and widely available.

Because PGP uses encryption algorithms, it was subject to export controls. An encryption algorithm lets users scramble a message in such a way that allows only the intended recipient to unscramble it.

Encryption algorithms are classified by the US government as armaments and fall under the International Trafficking in Armaments Regulations (ITAR). ITAR requires that users get an export license from the State Department to export armaments. In practice, the State Department will not grant any such license for strong encryption algorithms, and PGP uses two of the strongest.

This problem does not need to concern the average user because there is no law against using PGP in the US. There is also no law outside the US to prevent use of a product that was illegally exported from the US. Furthermore, some of the more recent versions of PGP actually originated outside the US, eliminating the problem altogether.

A second problem has to do with patents. One of the two encryption algorithms in PGP is known as Rivest-Shamir-Adleman (RSA). Anyone using PGP inside the US was, for a time, potentially subject to a lawsuit for RSA patent infringement.

A new release of PGP, known as version 2.6, which was developed at MIT with the supervision of Phil Zimmermann, has patent approval from the RSA patent holders. Like the original PGP, this version has also made its way onto bulletin boards and Internet sites outside the US. In addition, a compatible non-US version 2.6 was created outside the US. As long as a user chooses any of the flavors of version 2.6, there is no infringment on any patents.

CONVENTIONAL ENCRYPTION

PGP exploits two powerful security functions: conventional encryption and public-key encryption. Conventional encryption is the classic approach to secret codes that dates back to the time of ancient Rome and even earlier. A conventional encryption scheme (see Exhibit 1) includes the following five ingredients:

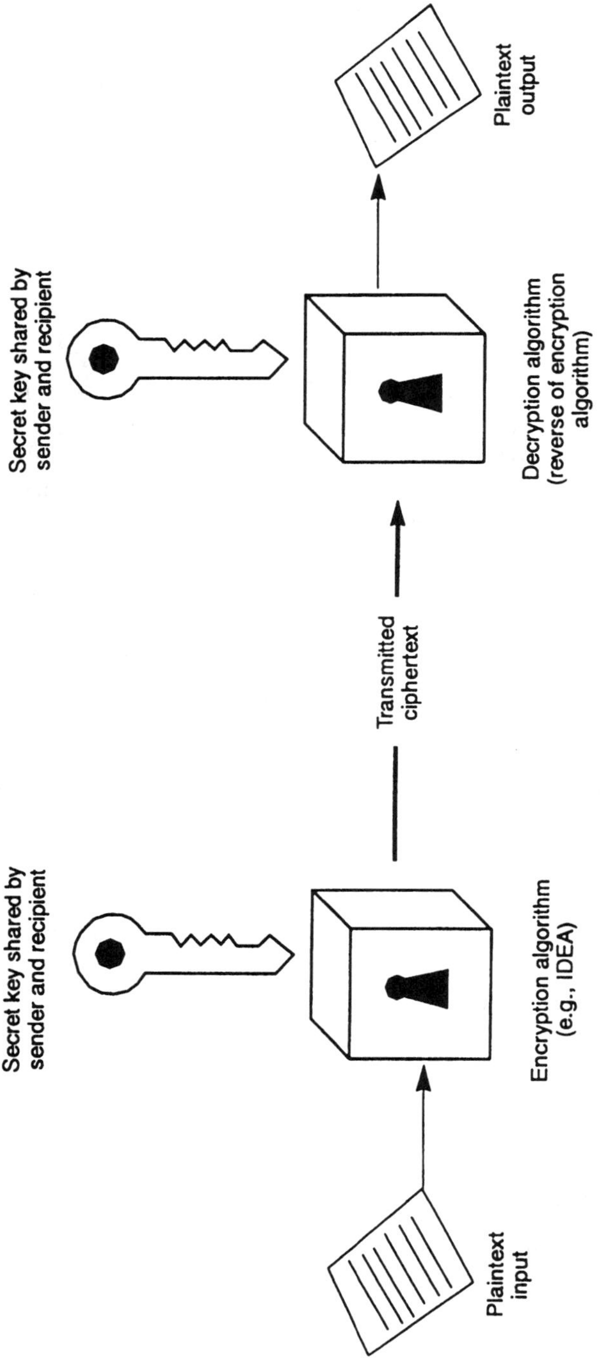

Exhibit 1. Conventional encryption.

- *Plaintext.* This is the readable message or data that is fed into the algorithm as input.
- *Encryption algorithm.* The encryption algorithm performs various substitutions and transformations on the plaintext.
- *Secret key.* The secret key is also input to the algorithm. The exact substitutions and transformations performed by the algorithm depend on the key.
- *Ciphertext.* This is the scrambled message produced as output. It depends on the plaintext and the secret key.
- *Decryption algorithm.* This is essentially the encryption algorithm run in reverse. It takes the ciphertext and the same secret key and produces the original plaintext.

The Caesar cipher, used by Julius Caesar, is a simple example of encryption. The Caesar cipher replaces each letter of the alphabet with the letter standing three places further down the alphabet, for example:

plain: meet me after the toga party

cipher: phhw ph diwhu wkh wrjd sduwb

The alphabet is wrapped around so that the letter following Z is A. The decryption algorithm simply takes the ciphertext and replaces each letter with the letter standing three places earlier on in the alphabet. A general Caesar cipher involves a shift of k letters, where k ranges from 1 through 25. In this case, k is the secret key to the algorithm.

The Caesar cipher is not very secure. Anyone who wanted to decipher the code could simply try every possible shift from 1 to 25. PGP uses a much stronger algorithm known as the International Data Encryption Algorithm, or IDEA.

The International Data Encryption Algorithm

IDEA is a block-oriented conventional encryption algorithm developed in 1990 by Xuejia Lai and James Massey of the Swiss Federal Institute of Technology. The overall scheme for IDEA encryption is illustrated in Exhibit 2. IDEA uses a 128-bit key to encrypt data in blocks of 64 bits.

The IDEA algorithm consists of eight rounds, or iterations, followed by a final transformation function. The algorithm breaks the input into four 16-bit subblocks. Each of the iteration rounds takes four 16-bit subblocks as input and produces four 16-bit output blocks. The final transformation also produces four 16-bit blocks, which are concatenated to form the 64-bit ciphertext. Each of the iterations also uses six 16-bit subkeys, whereas the final transformation uses four subkeys, for a total of 52 subkeys. The

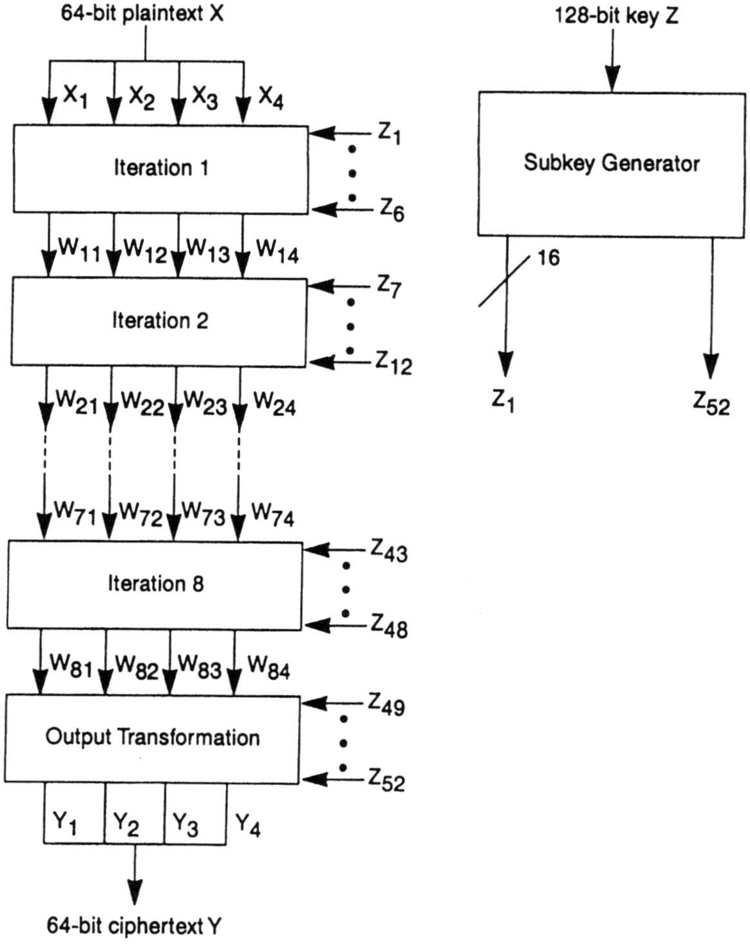

Exhibit 2. Overall IDEA structure.

---

right-hand portion of the exhibit indicates that these 52 subkeys are all generated from the original 128-bit key.

Each iteration of IDEA uses three different mathematical operations. Each operation is performed on two 16-bit inputs to produce a single 16-bit output. The operations are:

- Bit-by-bit exclusive-OR, denoted as $\oplus$.
- Addition of integers modulo 2^{16} (modulo 65536), with input and output treated as unsigned 16-bit integers. This operation is denoted as $\boxplus$.

- Multiplication of integers modulo $2^{16} + 1$ (modulo 65537), with input and output treated as unsigned 16-bit integers, except that a block of all zeros is treated as representing 2^{16}. This operation is denoted as θ.

For example,

$$0000000000000000 \; \theta \; 1000000000000000 = 1000000000000001$$

because

$$2^{16} \times 2^{15} \bmod (2^{16} + 1) = 2^{15} + 1$$

These three operations are incompatible because no pair of the three operations satisfies a distributive law. For example:

$$a \boxplus (b \theta c) \neq (a \boxplus b) \, \theta \, (a \boxplus c)$$

They are also incompatible because no pair of the three operations satisfies an associative law. For example,

$$a \boxplus (b \oplus c) \neq (a \boxplus b) \oplus c$$

the use of these three separate operations in combination provides for a complex transformation of the input, making cryptanalysis very difficult.

Exhibit 3 illustrates the algorithm for a single iteration. In fact, this exhibit shows the first iteration. Subsequent iterations have the same structure, but with different subkey and plaintext-derived input. The iteration begins with a transformation that combines the four input subblocks with four subkeys, using the addition and multiplication operations. This transformation is highlighted as the upper shaded rectangle. The four output blocks of this transformation are then combined using the XOR operation to form two 16-bit blocks that are input to the lower shaded rectangle, which also takes two subkeys as input and combines these inputs to produce two 16-bit outputs.

Finally, the four output blocks from the upper transformation are combined with the two output blocks of the MA structure using XOR to produce the four output blocks for this iteration. The two outputs that are partially generated by the second and third inputs (X_2 and X_3) are interchanged to produce the second and third outputs (W_{12} and W_{13}), thus increasing the mixing of the bits being processed and making the algorithm more resistant to cryptanalysis.

The ninth stage of the algorithm, labeled the output transformation stage in Exhibit 2, has the same structure as the upper shaded portion of the preceding iterations (see Exhibit 3). The only difference is that the second and third inputs are interchanged before being applied to the operational units. This has the effect of undoing the interchange at the end of the eighth iteration. This extra interchange is done so that decryption

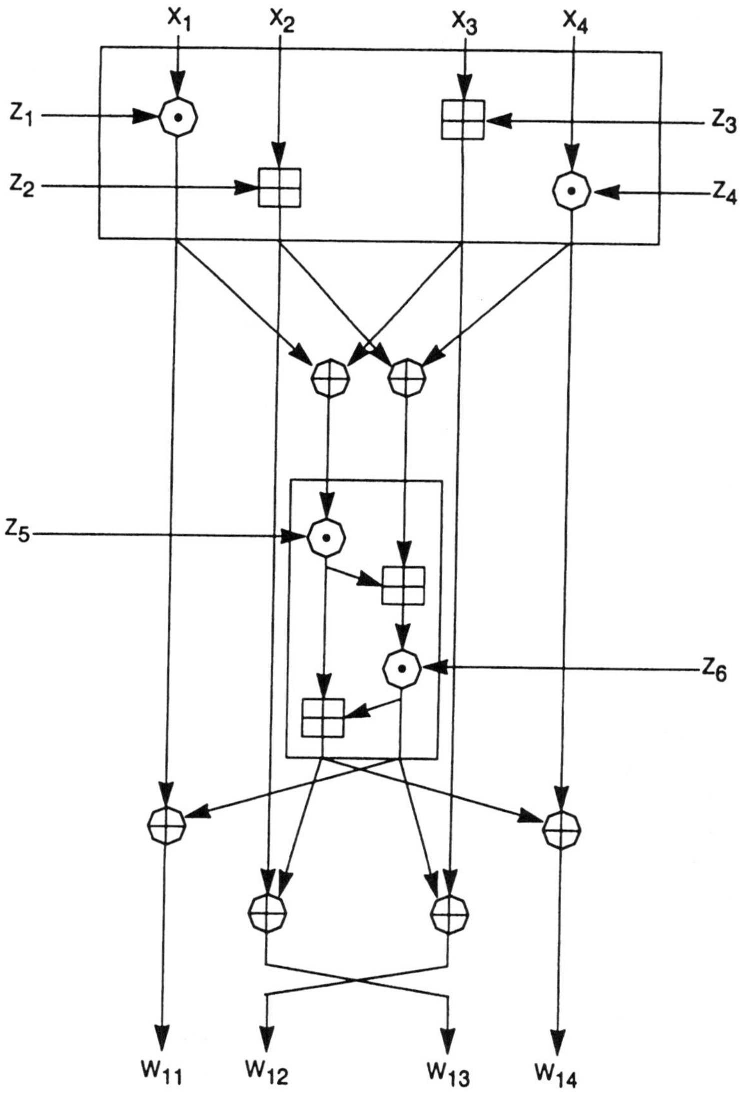

Exhibit 3. Single iteration of IDEA (first iteration).

has the same structure as encryption. This ninth stage requires only four subkey inputs, compared to six subkey inputs for each of the first eight stages. The subkeys for each iteration are generated by a series of shifts on the original 128-bit key.

IDEA has advantages over older convetional encryption techniques. The key length of 128 bits makes it resistant to brute-force key search attacks.

IDEA is also very resistant to cryptanalysis and was designed to facilitate both software and hardware implementations.

PUBLIC-KEY ENCRYPTION

One essential characteristic of IDEA and all conventional encryption algorithms is the need for the two parties to share a secret key that is not known to anyone else. This is a tremendous limitation, especially for an E-mail application.

If PGP depended solely on the use of IDEA, before a user could correspond with anyone, that user would somehow have to arrange to share a secret 128-bit number with the message recipient. If there is no way to communicate securely, it becomes difficult to send the key.

A new approach to encryption known as public-key encryption offers a solution to this problem. With this method, developed in 1976 by Whitfield Diffie, there is no need to convey a secret key. Instead, each person has a private key and a matching public key. Encryption is done with one of these two keys and decryption uses the other. The private key is kept secret, known only to its holder. The matching public key is just that—public. The private key holder can broadcast the matching public key.

Public-key encryption can be used to ensure privacy in much the same way as IDEA (see Exhibit 4). Users put plaintext and the intended recipient's public key in the encryption algorithm. The algorithm uses the plaintext and the public key to produce ciphertext. At the receiving end, the decryption algorithm, which is the reverse of the encryption algorithm, is used. In this case, the input is the ciphertext and the receiver's private key. This message is secure from eavesdropping because only the receiver has the private key necessary for decryption. Anyone who has a copy of the recipient's public key can create a message that can be read only by this recipient.

Authentication can also be performed by putting plaintext and the sender's private key in the encryption algorithm. The algorithm uses the plaintext and the private key to produce ciphertext. At the receiving end, the decryption algorithm, which is the reverse of the encryption algorithm, is used. In this case, the input is the ciphertext and the sender's public key.

This message is guaranteed to be authentic because only the sender has the private key necessary for encryption. Anyone who has a copy of the sender's public key can read the message and verify that it must have come from the alleged sender.

The public-key scheme used for PGP is the RSA algorithm. RSA takes variable-length keys. Typically, the key size for both the private and public keys is 512 bits.

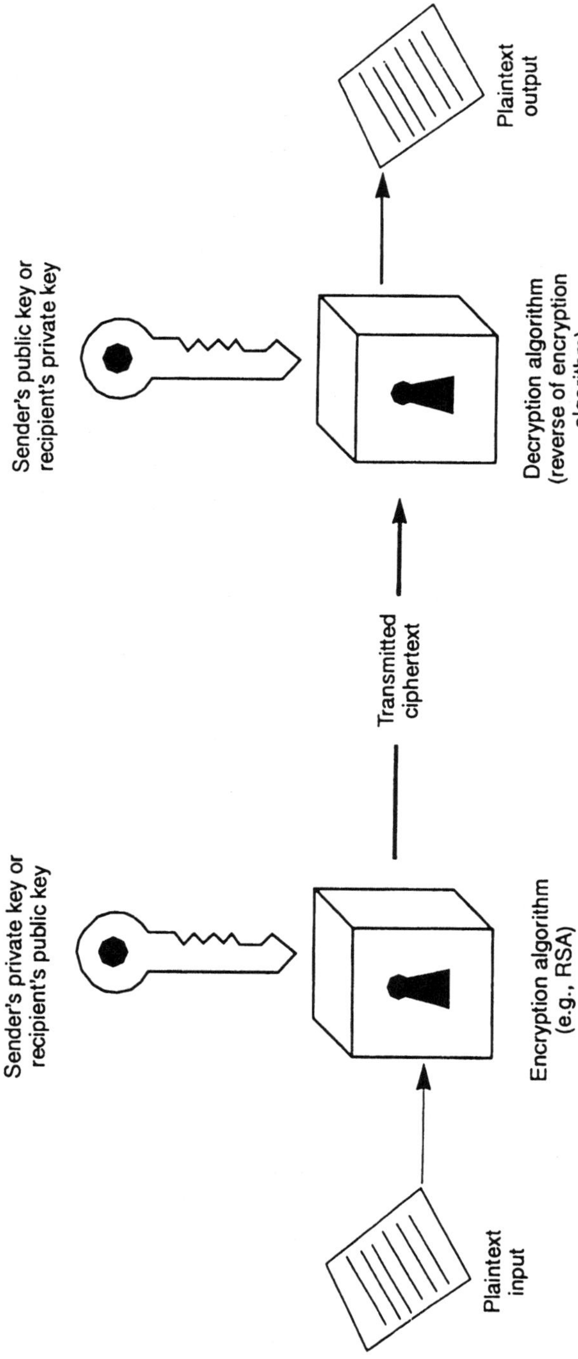

Exhibit 4. Public-key encryption.

The RSA Algorithm

One of the first public-key schemes was developed in 1977 by Ron Rivest, Adi Shamir, and Len Adleman at MIT and first published in 1978. Named for its creators, the RSA scheme has since reigned as the only widely accepted and implemented approach to public-key encryption. RSA is a block cipher in which the plaintext and ciphertext are integers between 0 and $n - 1$ for some n.

Encryption and decryption take the following form for some plaintext block M and ciphertext block C:

$$C = M^e \bmod n$$

$$M = C^d \bmod n = (M^e)^d \bmod n = M^{ed} \bmod n$$

Both sender and receiver must know the value of n. The sender knows the value of e, and only the receiver knows the value of d. Thus, this is a public-key encryption algorithm with a public key of KU = $\{e, n\}$ and a private key of KR = $\{d, n\}$. For this algorithm to be satisfactory for public-key encryption, the following requirements must be met:

- It should be possible to find values of e, d, n such that $M^{ed} = M \bmod n$ for all $M < n$.
- It should be relatively easy to calculate M^e and C^d for all values of $M < n$.
- It should be infeasible to determine d given e and n.

Exhibit 5 summarizes the RSA algorithm. To understand the algorithm, users should begin by selecting two prime numbers, p and q, and calculating their product n, which is the modulus for encryption and decryption. Next, the quantity (n), which is referred to as the Euler quotient of n, which is the number of positive integers less than n and relatively prime to n should be determined. Then an integer d, that is relatively prime to (n), (i.e., the greatest common divisor of d and (n) is 1) should be selected. Finally, e should be calculated as the multiplicative inverse of d, modulo (n). It can be shown that d and e have the desired properties.

The private key consists of $\{d, n\}$ and the public key consists of $\{e, n\}$. Suppose that user A has published its public key and that user B wishes to send the message M to A. Then, B calculates $C = M^e \pmod{n}$ and transmits C. On receipt of this ciphertext, user A decrypts by calculating $M = C^d \pmod{n}$.

An example is shown in Exhibit 6. For this example, the keys are generated as follows:

- Two prime numbers, $p = 7$ and $q = 17$, are selected.
- Calculate $n = pq = 7 \times 17 = 119$.

Key Generation	
Select p, q	p and q both prime
Calculate $n = p \times q$	
Calculate $\phi(n) = (p-1)(q-1)$	
Select integer e	$\gcd(\phi(n), e) = 1;\ 1 < e < \phi(n)$
Calculate d	$d = e^{-1} \bmod \phi(n)$
Public key	$KU = \{e,n\}$
Private key	$KR = \{d,n\}$

Encryption
Plaintext: $M < n$
Ciphertext: $C = M^e \pmod{n}$

Decryption
Ciphertext: C
Plaintext: $M = C^d \pmod{n}$

Exhibit 5. The RSA algorithm.

- Calculate $(n) = (p-1)(q-1) = 96$.
- Select e such that e is relatively prime to $(n) = 96$ and less than (n); in this case, $e = 5$.
- Determine d such that $de = 1 \bmod 96$ and $d < 96$. The correct value is $d = 77$, because $77 \times 5 = 385 = 4 \times 96 + 1$.

The resulting keys are public key KU = {5, 119} and private key KR = {77, 119}.

The example shows the use of these keys for a plaintext input of M = 19. For encryption, 19 is raised to the fifth power, yielding 2,476,099. Upon division by 119, the remainder is determined to be 66. Therefore, 19^5 66 mod 119, and the ciphertext is 66. For decryption, it is determined that 66^{77} 19 mod 119.

How Hard Is It to Break the Code? There are two possible approaches to defeating the RSA algorithm. The first is the brute-force approach: trying all possible private keys. Thus the larger the number of bits in e and d, the more secure the algorithm. However, because the calculations involved, both in key generation and in encryption/decryption, are complex. The larger the size of the key, the slower the system will run.

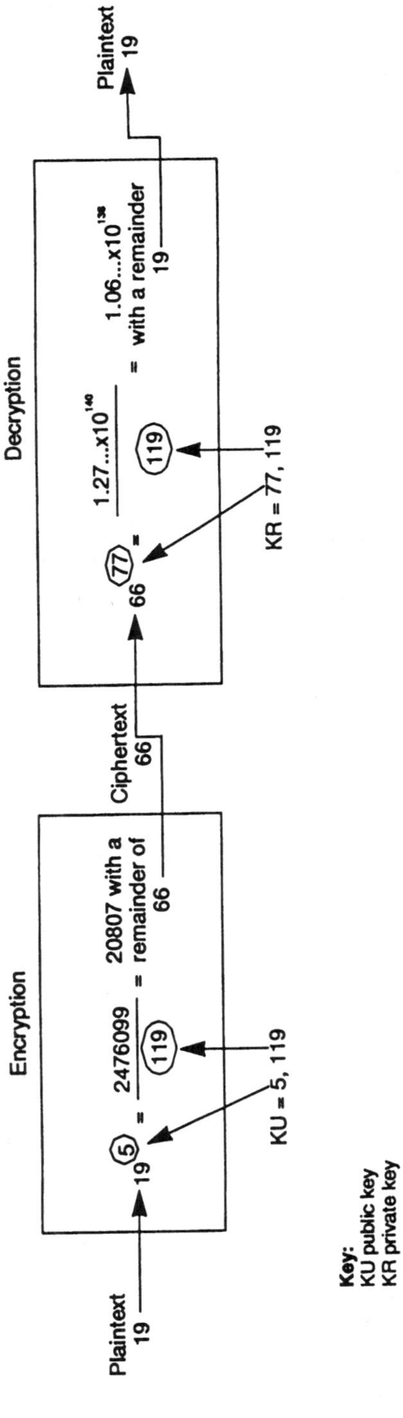

Exhibit 6. Example of RSA algorithm.

Most discussions of the cryptanalysis of RSA have focused on the task of factoring *p* into its two prime factors. Until recently, this was considered infeasible for numbers in the range of 100 decimal digits, which is about 300 or more bits. To demonstrate the strength of RSA, its three developers issued a challenge to decrypt a message that was encrypted using a 129-decimal-digit number as their public modulus. The authors predicted that it would take 40 quadrillion years with current technology to crack the code. Recently, the code was cracked by a worldwide team cooperating over the Internet and using more than 1,600 computers after only eight months of work. This result does not invalidate the use of RSA; it simply means that larger key sizes must be used. Currently, a 1,024-bit key size (about 300 decimal digits), is considered strong enough for virtually all applications.

HOW PGP WORKS

Digital Signature

It may seem that RSA is all that is needed for a secure e-mail facility. Everyone who wants to use PGP can create a matching pair of keys (PGP will do the necessary calculation) and then distribute the public key. To send a message, it must first be encrypted with the private key to guarantee its authenticity. Next, the result of step one must be encrypted with the recipient's public key to guarantee that no one else can read the message.

This scheme is technically valid but impractical. The problem is that RSA, and all other public-key schemes, are very slow. To double-encrypt messages of arbitrary length is far too time-consuming. Users could experience delays of minutes or even hours waiting for their PCs to do the number-crunching.

Instead, PGP exploits the strengths of conventional and public-key encryption. When a message is sent, it goes through two security-related stages of processing: digital signature and encryption.

The digital signature is one of the most clever innovations to come out of the work on public-key encryption. To use digital signature, users take the message that they want to send and map it into a fixed-length code of 128 bits. The algorithm for doing this is called MD5 (message digest version 5). The 128-bit message digest is unique for this message. It would be virtually impossible for someone to alter this message or substitute another message and still come up with the same digest.

PGP then encrypts the digest using RSA and the sender's private key. The result is the digital signature, which is attached to the message. Anyone who gets this message can re-compute the message digest and then decrypt the signature using RSA and the sender's public key. If the message digest in the signature matches the message digest that was calculated, then the signature is valid. Because this operation only involves encrypting and decrypting a 128-bit block, it takes little time.

For the encryption stage, PGP randomly generates a 128-bit secret key and uses IDEA to encrypt the message plus the attached signature. The recipient can discover the secret key by using RSA. PGP takes the secret key as input to RSA, using the receiver's public key, and produces an encrypted secret key that is attached to the message. On the receiving end, PGP uses the receiver's private key to recover the secret key and then uses the secret key and IDEA to recover the plaintext message plus signature.

Getting Public Keys

Public-key encryption techniques make use of two keys for each user: a private key that is known only to one user, and a corresponding public key that is made known to all users. With these two keys, it is possible to create digital signatures that guarantee the authenticity of a message and to support the encryption of a message in such a way that only the intended recipient can read it.

There is, however, a common misconception that each user simply keeps his or her private key private and publishes the corresponding public key. Unfortunately, this is not a simple solution. An impostor can generate a public- and private-key pair and disseminate the public key as if it were someone else's. For example, suppose that user A wishes to send a secure message to user B. Meanwhile, user C has generated a public- and private-key pair, attached user B's name and an E-mail address that user C can access, and published this key widely. User A has picked this key up, uses the key to prepare her message for user B, and uses the attached E-mail address to send the message. Result: user C receives and can decrypt the message; user B either never receives the message or could not read it without holding the required private key.

One way around this problem is to insist on the secure exchange of public keys. For example, if user B and user A know each other personally and live near each other, they could physically exchange keys on diskettes. But for PGP to be useful as a general-purpose e-mail security utility, it must be possible for people in widely distributed sites to exchange keys with others that they have never met and may not even know.

Public-Key Certificates and Distributed Security

The basic tool that permits widespread use of PGP is the public-key certificate. The essential elements of a public-key certificate are:

- The public key itself.
- A user ID consisting of the name and e-mail address of the owner of the key.
- One or more digital signatures for the public key and user ID.

The signer testifies that the user ID associated with this public key is valid. The digital signature is formed using the private key of the signer. Anyone in possession of the corresponding public key can verify that the signature is valid. If any change is made, either to the public key or the user ID, the signature will no longer compute as valid.

Public-key certificates are used in several security applications that require public-key cryptography. In fact, it is the public-key certificate that makes distributed security applications using public keys practical.

One approach that might be taken to use public-key certificates is to create a central certifying authority. This is the approach recommended for use with the privacy-enhanced mail (PEM) scheme. Each user must register with the central authority and engage in a secure exchange that includes independent techniques for verifying user identity. Once the central authority is convinced of the identity of a key holder, it signs that key. If everyone who uses this scheme trusts the central authority, then a key signed by the authority is automatically accepted as valid.

There is nothing inherent in the PGP formats or protocols to prevent the use of a centralized certifying authority. However, PGP is intended as an e-mail security scheme for the masses. It can be used in a variety of informal and formal environments. Accordingly, PGP is designed to support a so-called web of trust, in which individuals sign each other's keys and create an interconnected community of public-key users.

If user B has physically passed his public key to user A, then user A knows that this key belongs to user B and signs it. User A keeps a copy of the signed key and also returns a copy to user B. Later, user B wishes to communicate with user D and sends this person the public key, with user A's signature attached. User D is in possession of user A's public key and also trusts user A to certify the keys of others. User D verifies user A's signature on user B's key and accepts user B's key as valid.

COMPUTING TRUST

Although PGP does not include any specification for establishing certifying authorities or for establishing trust, it does provide a convenient means of using trust, associating trust with public keys, and exploiting trust information.

Each user can collect a number of signed keys and store them in a PGP file known as a public-key ring. Associated with each entry is a key legitimacy field that indicates the extent to which PGP will trust that this is a valid public key for this user; the higher the level of trust, the stronger is the binding of this user ID to this key. This field is computed by PGP. Also associated with the entry are zero or more signatures that the key ring owner has collected that sign this certificate. In turn, each signature has associated with it a signature trust field that indicates the degree to which this PGP user trusts the signer to certify public keys. The key legitimacy field is derived from the collection of signature trust fields in the entry. Finally, each entry defines a public key associated with a particular owner, and an owner trust field is included that indicates the degree to which this public key is trusted to sign other public-key certificates; this level of trust is assigned by the user. The signature trust fields can be thought of as cached copies of the owner trust field from another entry.

Trust Processing

If user A inserts a new public key on the public-key ring, PGP must assign a value to the trust flag that is associated with the owner of this public key. If the owner is in fact A, and this public key also appears in the private-key ring, then a value of ultimate trust is automatically assigned to the trust field. Otherwise, PGP asks user A for an assessment of the trust to be assigned to the owner of this key, and user A must enter the desired level. The user can specify that this owner is unknown, untrusted, marginally trusted, or completely trusted.

When the new public key is entered, one or more signatures may be attached to it. More signatures may be added later on. When a signature is inserted into the entry, PGP searches the public-key ring to see if the author of this signature is among the known public-key owners. If so, the OWNERTRUST value for this owner is assigned to the SIGTRUST field for this signature. If not, an unknown user value is assigned.

The value of the key legitimacy field is calculated on the basis of the signature trust fields present in this entry. If at least one signature has a signature trust value of ultimate, then the key legitimacy value is set to complete. Otherwise, PGP computes a weighted sum of the trust values. A weight of $1/X$ is given to signatures that are always trusted and $1/Y$ to signatures that are usually trusted, where X and Y are user-configurable parameters. When the total of weights of the introducers of a key/user ID combination reaches 1, the binding is considered to be trustworthy, and the key legitimacy value is set to complete. Thus, in the absence of ultimate trust, at least X signatures that are always trusted or Y signatures that are usually trusted or some combination, is needed.

Signature Trust and Key Legitimacy

Periodically, PGP processes the public-key ring to achieve consistency. In essence, this is a top-down process. For each OWNERTRUST field, PGP scans the ring for all signatures authored by that owner and updates the SIGTRUST field to equal the OWNERTRUST field. This process starts with keys for which there is ultimate trust. Then, all KEYLEGIT fields are computed on the basis of the attached signatures.

Exhibit 7 provides an example of the way in which signature trust and key legitimacy are related. The exhibit shows the structure of a public-key ring. The user has acquired a number of public keys, some directly from their owners and some from a third party such as a key server.

The node labeled "You" refers to the entry in the public-key ring corresponding to this user. This key is valid and the OWNERTRUST value is ultimate trust. Each other node in the key ring has an OWNERTRUST value of undefined unless some other value is assigned by the user. In this example, the user has specified that it always trusts users D, E, F, and L to sign other keys. This user also partially trusts users A and B to sign other keys.

The shading, or lack thereof, of the nodes in Exhibit 7 indicates the level of trust assigned by this user. The tree structure indicates which keys have been signed by which other users. If a key is signed by a user whose key is also in this key ring, the arrow joins the signed key to the signer. If the key is signed by a user whose key is not present in this key ring, the arrow joins the signed key to a question mark, indicating that the signer is unknown to the user.

Exhibit 7 illustrates that all keys whose owners are fully or partially trusted by the user have been signed by this user, with the exception of node L. Such a user signature is not always necessary, as the presence of node L indicates, but in practice most users are likely to sign the keys for most owners that they trust. So, for example, even though E's key is already signed by trusted introducer F, the user chose to sign E's key directly.

It can be assumed that two partially trusted signatures are sufficient to certify a key. Hence, the key for user H is deemed valid by PGP because it is signed by A and B, both of whom are partially trusted.

A key may be determined to be valid because it is signed by one fully trusted or two partially trusted signers, but its user may not be trusted to sign other keys. For example, N's key is valid because it is signed by E, whom this user trusts, but N is not trusted to sign other keys because this user has not assigned N that trust value. Therefore, although R's key is signed by N, PGP does not consider R's key valid. This situation makes perfect sense. If a user wants to send a secret message to an individual, it is not necessary that the user trust that individual in any respect. It is only necessary to ensure use of the correct public key for that individual.

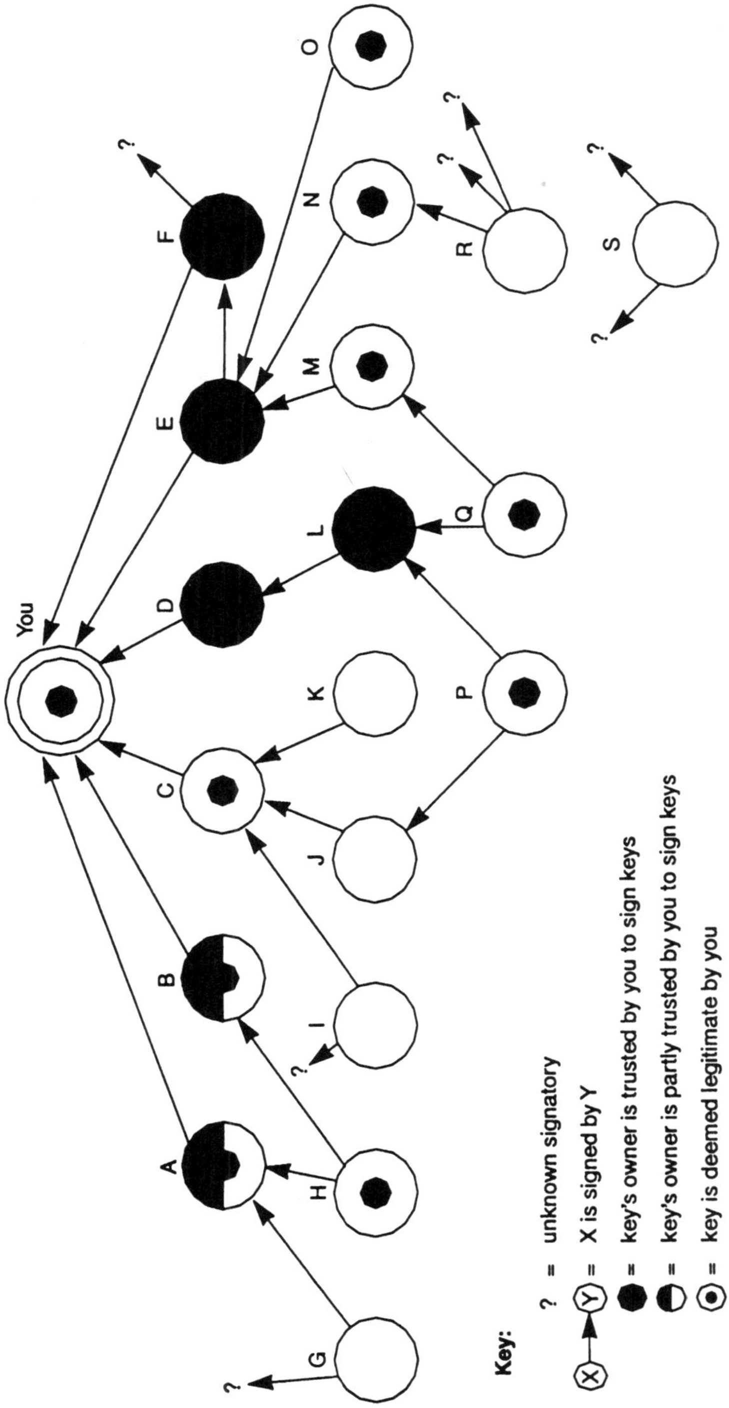

Exhibit 7. PGP trust model example.

Exhibit 7 also shows a detached orphan node S, with two unknown signatures. Such a key may have been acquired from a key server. PGP cannot assume that this key is valid simply because it came from a reputable server. The user must declare the key valid by signing it or by telling PGP that it is willing to fully trust one of the key's signers.

It is the PGP web of trust that makes it practical as a universal e-mail security utility. Any group, however informal and however dispersed, can build up the web of trust needed for secure communications.

SUMMARY

PGP is already widely used. PGP has become essential to those struggling for freedom in former Communist countries. Ordinary people throughout the world are active participants in the alt.security.PGP USENET newsgroup. Because PGP fills a widespread need, and because there is no reasonable alternative, its future is secure. One of the best lists of locations for obtaining PGP, with the file name getpgp.asc, is maintained at two file transfer protocol sites on the Internet: ftp.csn.net/mpj and ftp.netcom. com/pub/mp/mpj.

Chapter 66
An Introduction to Internet Security and Firewall Policies

William Hugh Murray

The Internet can be defined and described, in part, in terms of its characteristics. Although it is possible for a network to have some of these characteristics without having them all, they are related in subtle ways.

Public and Open

Perhaps one of the most important characteristics of the Internet, at least from a security point of view, is that it is essentially public and open. It is public in the sense that, like the phone system, anyone can use it. It may be necessary to go to a pay phone, a kiosk, or the public library, but anyone can use it. Libraries have been known to hand out user IDs with the same frequency as library cards. No requirements exist to be able to use the Internet. In addition, as in broadcast TV, radio, or magazine advertising, most of the traffic is public. Its value increases with the number of people who see it. Although it has not always been so, most of the servers and services available on the Internet do not know or care who their users are. No user identification or authentication is required. The servers may count the accesses and they might like to know the demographics of those who visit, but otherwise, the greater the number of visits, the more successful the site is considered.

Similar to its being public, the Internet is open. Like the postal system, where for the price of a postage stamp, anyone can send a message, for the price of an accommodation address, anyone can receive a message. Although there may be an agreement to pay, no other permission is required and, as a rule, payment in advance is not required. The Internet is also open in the sense that with a minimum of notice to or cooperation of others a connection can be made. A node at the edge of a network can be added easily and unilaterally, creating a new connection between

0-8493-9989-0/99/$0.00+$.50

networks. Therefore, it is difficult, in fact nearly impossible, to know what the network looks like.

Although only a small percentage of the traffic on the Internet is sensitive to disclosure and most applications and services are free, almost all traffic is sensitive to contamination and most services are sensitive to interference. Moreover, although many who offer public information on the Internet want many people to see it, they want it delivered intact; they do not want it modified, they do not want it broken, and they do not want to be responsible for errors or omissions. The public and open nature of the Internet makes this quite difficult to achieve. It also makes it difficult to achieve confidentiality and accountability for that traffic and those applications that require them.

Inclusive Network of Networks

By definition, an internetwork is a network that connects networks. Therefore, the Internet is a network of networks. It is one collection of all networks, and the economic advantage of a connection is so great as to be irresistible. Moreover, although isolated networks may exist in the short term, in the long term, the internetwork will be one. Isolated networks that persist will be sparse, small, and so temporary as to be insignificant.

Mesh Topology

The Internet has a mesh topology, which means that, except at the edges, most nodes are connected to two or more other nodes. In addition, there are multiple paths between any two points on the network, because the topology maximizes the potential that a message will get through and maximizes the total message-carrying potential (i.e., bandwidth) of the network. On the other hand, at least by default, users do not know what path their traffic will follow or what nodes and links their messages will traverse.

Flat

Ideally, the Internet is flat, as opposed to hierarchical. Information flows directly from the origin to the destination rather than in to a central switching point, and then back out to the destination. Therefore, the cost to send a message between any two points on the network is the same as between any other two points. The time required for a message to move between any two points is roughly the same as for any other two points chosen at random. Finally, the bandwidth between any two points is roughly the same as for any other two points.

As expected, messages flow more quickly between nodes that are close together. However, it is possible for part of a message to circle the globe, even when addressed to a nearby node. So, at least on average, across all randomly chosen pairs of nodes, the Internet is flat.

Broadcast

A node that desires to send a message to another node broadcasts that message to the remainder of the network. Depending on the routing algorithm used, the originating node may prefer nodes that it thinks are in the direction of the destination. However, it is possible for a message to traverse the globe even when addressed to a nearby node. Other nodes that receive the message look at the destination address in the message and forward it in the general direction of that destination. This is similar to a point-to-point network in which the path between two points is determined in advance and dedicated, at least for the instant, to carrying that message. Although every packet does not pass every node and it is possible for users to influence the path that their traffic follows, few users have the necessary special knowledge to take advantage of this capability. They do not know how to exercise the control or to distinguish one path from another. Such control, if used, would limit the paths and bandwidth available to the traffic and be achieved at the cost of a reduction in the chances that the traffic would get through quickly.

Different Types of Internet Connections

Three kinds of connections are available on the Internet.

Packet-Switched. Related to the idea of broadcast is that of packet-switched. A message is broken into packets, each packet is labeled as to origin and destination and then broadcast onto the network. Other nodes forward the packet in the general direction of the destination. It is possible that adjacent packets in a message will follow different paths to the destination. This is the opposite of circuit-switched networks, such as the voice network, in which a circuit or path is determined in advance and all parts of the message follow the same path. In a packet-switched network, an intervening node may see only a part of a message. On the other hand, it increases the number of nodes that may see a part of it.

Peer-Connected. Nodes on the Internet are "peer connected." No node dominates or controls another. Thus, by default, all nodes behave as if they trust all other nodes as they do themselves. The implication is that the level of trust is equal to that of the least-trusted node.

Any-to-Any Connection. Like the postal system, and except as otherwise restricted, any device connected to the Internet can send a message to any other device. There is no requirement for an answer but, at a minimum, the destination device must recognize the message and make a decision about it. For example, at MIT the soft-drink vending machines are connected to the Internet. If the addresses are known, they may be queried from anywhere in the world.

Increasing Interoperability

If connectivity is the ability to send a message to any node, interoperability is the ability to get a meaningful answer back. Already, the Internet is better at answering questions than most individuals are at asking. The Internet can provide a report of freeway traffic in Los Angeles, hotel availability in London, or the schedule of every opera house in the world for the next two years. It can also locate all the bed-and-breakfast lodgings in most places in the world, and get an index to the treasures of the Vatican Library or of the British Museum. Individuals can locate and download graphics, moving images, and general and specialized software. A query on "Mona Lisa" returns references to both 1,000 different prints of Da Vinci's La Gioconda and a sound clip of the Nat King Cole song. If the necessary software is unavailable to interoperate with another system at a particular layer, software can be downloaded at another.

As protocols and interfaces become more standard, they become more useful. As the use of a standard increases, so does the propensity to comply with it. The less standard an interface, the more it must include information about its intended or productive use.

No Central Authority

Although there are authorities such as the Internet Activities Board (IAB) and the Internet Engineering Task Force (IETF), which make architectural and design decisions for the Internet, no one is obliged to follow them. The individual networks are independently owned and operated. There is no central authority that is responsible for the operation of the entire network. Because the network is global, it is not even subject to the authority of any single nation state.

Internet Protocols

The Internet can also be defined and described in terms of the communication protocols it employs. One, somewhat pure, definition is that the Internet is that collection of interconnected networks that employ the transmission control protocol/Internet protocol (TCP/IP) suite of protocols. A more practical definition is that the Internet is that set plus those networks connected to it by appropriate gateways. (For purposes of this definition, a gateway is a node that translates traffic from one protocol to another.)

The Internet Protocol

The fundamental protocol of the Internet is IP, the Internet protocol. IP is the network layer protocol for the TCP/IP Protocol Suite. It is fundamental in the sense that all other protocols are built on it. It is connectionless, best-effort, packet-switched, and unchecked. "Best effort" means that the network will do its best to deliver the packet, but there are no guarantees. "Unchecked" means that there is no redundancy in the protocol to enable either the sender or the receiver to know whether the packet was received correctly. There is no acknowledgment of the receipt of the message. The receiver cannot be sure that the message comes from where the origin address of the packet says that it comes from.

IP is to the Internet as the post card is to the postal system, limited in capacity, function, and intent. However, just as a message of any length can be sent by using multiple post cards, or by using one post card to acknowledge or to check on another, IP packets can be composed in such a way as to compensate for all of these limitations. These compositions make up the higher-level protocols.

The Transmission Control Protocol

The Transmission Control Protocol (TCP), is the standard Internet protocol (IP) for the transfer layer. It defines how IP packets are sent back and forth between a sender and a receiver to provide many of the things that IP does not. However, even TCP does not provide security nor the reliability of origin and destination. Both the sender and the receiver know that they are talking to someone who is orderly and well behaved, but they do not know for sure that it is their intended party, and they do not know if anyone might be listening in.

The Oldest and Most Widely Used Protocols

The following are among the oldest and most widely used protocols on the Internet:

- **Telnet.** This was originally intended for connecting host-dependent terminals to remote systems or applications. Today, it is used by terminal emulator programs on workstations.
- **File Transfer Protocol.** FTP is used to move files from one system to another.
- **Simple Mail Transfer Protocol.** SMTP is used for e-mail.

The applications of these protocols are discussed in subsequent sections.

Other Common Protocols

In addition to those protocols previously discussed are the following:

- **Serial Line Internet Protocol.** The serial line Internet protocol (SLIP) is used to exchange IP traffic with a device, usually a workstation, that is running the proper protocols but without a separate address. It is used to connect workstations to hosts or to Internet service providers through the dial-switched network. It is analogous to an extension cord or a remote.
- **Point-to-Point Protocol.** The point-to-point protocol (PPP) is similar to SLIP, but is associated with leased lines. It is usually used to connect a single system to a boundary or "edge" node.
- **Network Time Protocol.** The network time protocol (NTP) is used to set and synchronize the system clocks of Internet nodes. It is able to synchronize all systems in a network to within milliseconds of each other, i.e., to within the accuracy and precision of the system clocks themselves.
- **Secure Protocols.** Recently, secure versions of these protocols have been specified, and reference implementations of these protocols are available for Unix systems. Additional implementations should be available in 1996.

Internet Applications

Recall the analogy that describing the Internet can be likened to five blind men trying to describe an elephant. For most, the Internet elephant looks like its applications. The Internet is open as to its applications. No real limit to the number of applications exists, and new ones are added every day. However, some applications are sufficiently significant that a description of those applications describes how the net looks to most users.

E-mail

The most widely used application on the Internet is e-mail. Recent statistics suggest between 50 and 100 million users, and 1 billion users are estimated as early as 2000. E-mail rivals television, copiers, and facsimile machines in its rate of growth. Moreover, as was the case with copiers and facsimiles, it is becoming difficult to remember how business was conducted before e-mail.

Internet e-mail uses the simple mail transfer protocol (SMTP), and the multipurpose Internet mail exchange (MIME) protocol. MIME runs on top of SMTP to permit the exchange of files, programs, sounds, images, and moving images. E-mail is the most interconnected and interoperable application. Even those networks that have resisted connection to the Internet at other levels are connected at the e-mail layer.

In addition, e-mail is the most ubiquitous application in the Internet; it interoperates with many of the others. Several servers on the Internet accept mail messages, convert them into requests for other services, convert the answers to those mail messages, and send them back to the requestor. Thus, a user who has access to e-mail functionality has access to all of the information on the network (i.e., Internet).

Logging on to a Remote System

One of the earliest and most obvious of Internet applications was to create a session between a terminal on one system and an application on a remote system. This kind of application uses a client process on the origin system, the telnet client. It is initiated by entering the command, telnet, on the originating system. The parameters of the command specify the target system and any nondefault characteristics of the connection request. The request is responded to by the Telnet server, a started process (a daemon in Unix parlance) on the target system. The protocol is also called Telnet. The user on the origin system sees a prompt from the answering server process, for example, the operating system or an application, on the target system. The user is usually expected to log on, that is, send a user identifier (i.e., user ID) and authenticating data (i.e., a password) to the target system. However, for the target system, the user identifier and password are optional.

File Transfer

The FTP is used to exchange file system objects between systems. It is symmetric, and works in either direction. Either system may initiate a transfer in either direction. The FTP process (daemon in Unix parlance) must have access to the file system. That is, in systems with closed file systems, the process or the user on whose behalf it is operating must possess the necessary access rights (e.g., read, write, or create) to the file object or directory on which it wants to operate.

A convention called "anonymous FTP" permits the protocol to be used for public applications. The user can log on to the system with a user ID of anonymous, which requires no password. By convention, users are requested to put their origin system and user ID in the password field. However, the value in this field is not checked or validated in any way; a blank will work as well as the truth.

Vulnerabilities on the Internet

The vulnerabilities on the Internet are closely related to its characteristics, its protocols, its uses, and its history. In addition, because the

Internet is a broadcast network, messages are vulnerable to disclosure, replay, and interference.

The large number of components on the Internet make it vulnerable to flaws in the implementation of those components. Because there may be many instances of a flaw, elimination of them is extremely difficult. A recent example of such a flaw was an instance of incomplete parameter checking in the Unix system logging routine, syslog. This error permitted a very long log entry to exceed the space provided for it, overlay program space, and get itself executed.

Many components in systems peer-connected to the Internet contain "escape" mechanisms. These are invoked by an otherwise unlikely character sequence to cause what follows this escape sequence to be handled, not by the component itself, but by the environment in which it runs, often with the privilege of the "escaped from" component. A famous escape mechanism, exploited by the infamous "All Souls" worm, was the debug feature of the sendmail mail handler. This option was invoked by an escape sequence in a message that caused what followed it to be passed through to Unix to be executed as a command. The worm used this feature, among others, to copy and execute itself.

Because nodes are peer connected and trust each other, compromise of one may result in compromise of many, perhaps all. In a peer-connected network, the level of trust in the network is equal to that of the least trusted node or link.

Many of the vulnerabilities described in the preceding paragraphs are features rather than flaws. In other words, they are desired and valued by some users and managers. Because of their value, their total elimination is unlikely.

Every node on the Internet has a system manager or privileged user. This user is not subject to any controls intended to ensure that users and their systems are orderly and well-behaved. In single-user systems, the only user is a peer of the privileged user in the multi-user system. That user is assumed to have the same motivation, training, and supervision as the manager of a multi-user system. The vast number of such users ensures that at least some of them will be disorderly and unreliable. Because they are all peers and because the systems are peer connected, it makes little difference which of them are trustworthy.

The Internet is so large and complex that no one, not the designers, not the implementers, not the operators, and not the users, fully apprehends it, much less comprehends it. All are the blind men. Nonetheless, its immense scope and size make it unlikely that it will ever be perfect. Attackers look on it as a "target rich" environment. Although most nodes on the network are implemented, configured, and operated so as to resist attack, the great number of them ensures that there will always be some that are vulnerable.

Finally, two of the vulnerabilities on the Internet, insecure links and insecure nodes, are fundamental. In other words, they are inherent to the Internet's nature, use, intent, or at least its history. Contrary to popular belief, they are not the result of errors, flaws, or failures on the part of the designers, implementers, or operators of the network. Rather, these insecure links and nodes are the result of attempts to have the greatest chance of getting a message from point A to point B in the least amount of time. They are never going to go away; it is not simply a matter of time. Indeed, at least for the next five years, they are likely to get worse. That is, vulnerabilities will increase faster than the ability to fix them. Moreover, the number of insecure links and nodes in the network are both growing at a much faster rate than the number of secure ones. This vulnerability is certain and extremely resistant to change.

Attacks on the Internet

The conditions for a successful attack include necessary access, special knowledge, work, and time. Because of its nature, all of these things are somewhat more available on the Internet than on other networks. Because the Internet is open, almost anyone can gain access. Most of the special knowledge in the world is recorded, encapsulated, and available on the Internet, mostly for the taking; although every now and then permission is required. Even much of the necessary work to launch a successful attack has been encapsulated in computer programs. Thus, they can be perpetrated by those who lack skill and special knowledge and who are not prepared to do the work themselves.

Eavesdropping

As packets move through the net, they can be observed by privileged users of the nodes or by using special equipment to listen in on the links. These attacks are easily automated.

Packet and Password Grabbers

A packet grabber is an automated eavesdropping attack, a program that copies packets as they move through an intermediate node (i.e., a node between the origin and destination). A password grabber is a special case of a packet grabber that identifies and stores for later use user IDs and passwords as they pass through an intermediate node. Because, at least as a general rule, unprivileged processes cannot look at traffic in transit, password grabbers must be installed by privileged users. However, recent experience suggests that they are often placed in penetrated systems. Writing password grabbers requires special knowledge and work. However, so many copies of those programs now exist that the attack can be used even by those who are without the knowledge and not prepared to do the work. The Internet has so many password grabbers that passwords in the clear are not sufficiently reliable for commercial or other sensitive applications, and the problem moves from the category of an attack to that of a pervasive problem.

Address Spoofing

The origin address on the IP packet is not reliable. The sending system can set this address to any value that it wishes. Nonetheless, by convention and for convenience, many systems rely on this address to determine where a packet came from and to decide how to treat it. Packets carrying the origin address of recognized systems may be treated as though they had originated on a trusted system. Again, with sufficient work and knowledge, it is possible to write a program to exploit this trust. Toolkits for building this kind of attack have been written and distributed within the hacker community.

Trojan Horses

A Trojan Horse attack is in one in which a hostile entity, for example, armed warriors, is concealed inside a benign or trusted one, for example a gift horse, to get it through a protective barrier or perimeter, in the original case, the walls of the city of Troy. In computer science, it usually refers to a malicious program included in another program or even in data. Although most systems are vulnerable to this kind of attack to some degree or another, and it has always been a concern, until the proliferation of desktop computers and viruses, it was not a problem.

As previously discussed, both node-to-node connectivity and trust and open file systems make the Internet particularly vulnerable. Trojan Horses can and do travel over any of the popular protocols and in any of the popular object types. For example, they can travel in files over FTP, as documents over MIME, or in arbitrary objects called by HTML scripts fetched from World Wide Web (WWW) servers by browsers. Although some browsers and interpreters (e.g., HotJava) are designed to resist such attacks, most are not. Even in situations in which the browser or interpreter is resistant, it is always possible to dupe some users in a large population.

Trojan Horses are easily executed because they have attractive names or descriptions or the names of frequently used programs. They may require a minimum of user cooperation. For example, the PRANK (virus) was implemented as a MS Word macro and could spread in any Word document. Simply asking Word to open an infected document would contaminate that copy of Word and any document that it subsequently opened. If an infected document were attached to an e-mail message, an act as simple as double clicking the icon for the document would be sufficient to execute the macro. Because such a macro can contain and call an arbitrary program, there is no limit to the sophistication of the program or the contamination it can cause.

Trojan Horse attacks are of special concern on the Internet because they compromise trust of end-point nodes, of the net, and of applications on the net.

Browsing

Browsing is going through the network to look at available, public, accidentally, and erroneously available data in search of something of value. Specifically, in an attack sense, this search method looks for special data that will reduce the cost of an attack against other nodes. For example, many systems implement or provide directory services. These directory services return the names of enrolled users, i.e., user identifiers. The information returned by these public services is used by the attacker to identify targets and thereby reduce the cost of attack. Attackers also use browsing to identify and download attack programs.

Exhaustion

When confronted with good security and when all other attacks fail, an attacker can always fall back on trying all possible combinations of data (e.g., user identifiers and passwords) until he or she finds one that gets through. Traditional systems resisted such attacks by disconnecting disorderly devices (i.e., devices that failed to successfully log on). Because the Internet is a broadcast network, there is no connection to break. A system must look at every packet addressed to it and make a determination as to what to do with it. It is possible to spread the attack over time or across addresses so as to disguise the attack as errors or noise.

Denial of Service

Denial-of-service attacks are those that cause failures by overloading or consuming all available resources. On the Internet, this class of attack includes "spamming" or overloading a target with unwanted traffic. Although the target is not damaged in any permanent way, it may be unable to provide critical services to those intended to use it.

Defending Against Attacks on the Internet

A vast number of options exist that the implementers, operators, and users of the net can do to limit these vulnerabilities and the attacks against them. However, in considering them, keep in mind that these vulnerabilities are fundamental to the nature of the Internet. The only way to eliminate all of the risk is to either eliminate the Internet or alter it so fundamentally that it will lose its identity. Clearly, neither of these options are viable. Rather, the defenses should be balanced against the vulnerablities so as to preserve essential trust. Discussions of some broad categories of defense mechanisms follow in the subsequent section.

Isolation and Compartmentation

Of course, the most obvious defense against network attacks is simply not to attach, to connect, or to participate in a network. Not only is this defense effective, it is also demonstrable to the satisfaction of third parties. However, the value of the security obtained rarely compensates for the lost value of connecting or participating in a network. Moreover, it has often been said that sensitive defense systems are safe because they are not connected to public networks.

Because the value of connecting to a network is high and because the cost of that connection is low, isolation is difficult to maintain. Even a very small system or a single desktop workstation can form a connection between networks.

Policies

In the presence of known connections, people can provide protection. They can recognize attacks and take timely and appropriate action. However, for this to be effective, it must be planned and pervasive. If management wishes to rely on individuals, it must tell them in advance what action to take. A policy is an expression of management's intention. It should contain a recapitulation of the user behavior that management relies on. It should also clearly delineate the responsibilities of employees and managers. Finally, it should specifically address the responsibility to report anomalies.

Bastions

Bastions are "projecting" fortifications. They are strong systems that can be seen from the outside (i.e., the public network), but which are designed to resist attack (e.g., by recognizing only a very limited repertoire of application-specific commands). Bastions normally hide the generality and flexibility of their operating systems from the network. A full-function gateway system that can be seen from the public network is called a bastion host. Such a gateway must be able to protect itself from its traffic. Finally, because most protective mechanisms can be bypassed or circumvented, all applications and services that can be seen from the network should be able to resist their traffic.

Filters

Filters are processes that pass some traffic while rejecting some other traffic. The intent is to pass safe traffic and to resist attack traffic. Filters may operate on headers or content. Many filters operate on the basis of the origin address in the header. They pass traffic that appears to have originated on recognized or trusted systems. They may also operate on a combination of origin, protocol, and destination. For example, they may pass mail traffic from unknown origins to the mail port on the post office machine and reject outside traffic addressed to the Telnet port on the same machine. Filters are important. For further information, see the subsequent section.

Wrappers

Wrappers are proxy programs or processes. They can be viewed as traffic-filtering programs. They are designed to protect the target from unintended traffic, known attacks, or to compensate for known weaknesses. They often assume the name of the process that they are intended to protect (i.e., common functions or known targets). For example, suppose that a privileged program is known to have a flaw or an escape mechanism that can be exploited by a packet or a message. A wrapper can be given the name of that program, placed ahead of it in the search order, and used to protect against messages of the dangerous form. After eliminating all messages of the dangerous form, the remainder are passed to the "wrapped" program as normal.

Using wrappers is a preferable alternative and it presents a lower risk to cure a vulnerability than patching or replacing the vulnerable program. They have been employed to great advantage in Unix systems, in which it is often easier to use the wrapper than to find out whether the particular version of Unix or one of its subsystems that is being used has a particular problem. The most famous wrappers are a collection known as COPS. These are used to protect Unix systems from a set of known attacks and vulnerabilities.

Filters: the Most Popular Defense

Filters are the most popular defense to ward off network attacks. The intent is to pass normal traffic while rejecting all attack traffic. Of course, the difficulty is in being able to recognize the difference between the two. Filters are normally based on the origin, the destination, and the kind of traffic. Traffic is permitted to flow from trusted or known sources to safe or intended destinations. Of course, most destinations will ignore traffic that is not addressed to them but will certainly listen to attack traffic that is addressed to them. Filtering on destination address can protect the system from seeing attack traffic at the expense of protecting it from all traffic.

Filters Implemented by Using Routers

In part, because networks are usually connected to each other through routers, routers are a favorite place to filter traffic. The same logic that is used by the router to decide where to send traffic can be used to reject traffic (i.e., to decide to send it to the "bit bucket." For example, only those packets that appear to have originated on systems whose addresses are recognized (i.e., on a list of known systems) will be accepted.

Packets by Address: IP Address and Port

A filter must have criteria by which to decide which traffic to pass and which to reject. The criteria must appear in the packet. The most frequently used criteria are the IP origin and destination addresses. Typically, this is expressed as an address pair. In other words, traffic appearing to originate at *A* and addressed to *B* can pass this router. Although it could say all traffic originating at *A* can pass or all traffic intended for *B* can pass, this is significantly less rigorous or secure.

The origin and destination are usually expressed as IP addresses and may be further qualified by port. That is, traffic originating on the mail port of *A* can pass to the mail port on *B*, but to no other port.

Protocols

The protocol is also visible in the packet and is useful for routing and security purposes. For example, the filter can pass traffic in the SMTP protocol to pass to the mail server, while not allowing other IP traffic addressed to the same service to pass. Because the intent of the traffic is more obvious in the higher-level protocols, filtering by protocol can be very effective and useful.

Firewalls

It is beyond the scope of this chapter to provide instruction on how to build or even to operate a firewall. Within the allotted space, it is difficult to simply convey an understanding of their nature and use. A basic definition and discussion follows.

The *American Heritage Dictionary* defines a firewall as "a fireproof wall used as a barrier to prevent the spread of a fire." By analogy, a network firewall is a traffic-proof barrier used to prevent the spread of disorderly or malicious traffic. More specifically, a firewall is a special collection of hardware and software that connects two networks and that is used to protect each of the assumptions as to which side of the firewall a fire will start on.

Like most analogies, this one is instructive even at the extremes where it begins to break down. In the analogy, a firewall is assumed to resist fire equally in both directions. It is symmetric; it does not have to treat fire on one side of the wall differently from fire on the other. It must resist fire, but it must pass people. However, it is easy to distinguish people from fire, and all people and all fire, on either side of the wall, are treated the same. The task of the network firewall is to distinguish between threatening and non-threatening traffic and to do so differently depending on which side the traffic originates. In the presence of fire, a firewall need not pass people; resisting fire is more important than passing people. However, the network firewall will rarely be permitted to reject all traffic in the name of rejecting all attack traffic. It will usually be required to pass legitimate traffic, even in the presence of known attack traffic.

Moreover, a firewall is not is a box; it is not a product that can be purchased off the shelf. At time of this writing, more than 40 vendors offer products that are described, at least in part, as firewalls. Although similarities among them exist, there are also fundamental differences in their approaches. Even given a complete understanding of company requirements and security policy, gaining sufficient knowledge about tens of products to decide which one is most appropriate is a major challenge.

Firewall Policy Positions

Four fundamental policy positions are available to network operators. The firewall policy will be the result of these postures and of the applications on the network.

Paranoid. The first of these positions is called paranoid. It is motivated by extreme caution and probably fear, and characterized by the absence of a connection to the Internet.

Prudent. The second position is called prudent or restrictive. It too is motivated by caution, but also by a recognition of the value of connection to the Internet. It is characterized by the fact that everything that is not explicitly allowed is implicitly forbidden. For example, a private Internet user would have to be explicitly authorized to Telnet to a system on the public Internet.

Permissive. The permissive posture is the opposite of the restrictive policy. Under this policy, everything that is not explicitly forbidden is implicitly allowed. Obviously, it is the intent of this policy to forbid the necessary conditions for all known attacks. This policy is intended to provide a level of protection with a minimum of interference with applications. This is the policy most likely to be applied when applying a firewall to an existing connection. It is particularly useful if little is known about the applications and if there is a strong desire not to interfere with or break those applications. It is the policy most likely to be recommended by Internet service providers who are motivated to maximize the value of the connection.

Promiscuous. The promiscuous policy is that anything goes. Under this policy, there are multiple connections and any legitimate packet can flow from any source to any destination.

Choosing a Firewall Policy

Why anyone would want to be in postures one or four? Remarkably, position one is the default position for business. Most businesses have not yet connected to the Internet. Position four is the default policy for the Internet; all connections and traffic are tolerated in the name of maximizing the bandwidth and the potential for getting messages through.

If an Internet service provider is asked for guidance on a firewall policy, it will likely recommend that the position should be on the promiscuous side of permissive. The service provider will supply a list of restrictions to address all of the attacks that it knows about. However, this permits exposure to a large set of fundamental vulnerabilities. This is, in part, because the Internet service provider believes in the value of the net and does not wish to deny its clients any benefits without necessity.

This author recommends a position on the paranoid side of prudent or restrictive. In other words, permit only that traffic that is associated with a particular value for which the net is being used. The flow of all other traffic should be resisted.

A Conservative Firewall Policy

A conservative firewall policy is intended to position an institution or network on the paranoid side of restrictive. The intent is to protect not only against known and expected attacks, but also against those that have not been invented yet. It is driven by fundamental vulnerabilities, rather than by known threats and attacks. It attempts to take only those risks that are necessary to accommodate the intended applications.

In addition, no information about the private network should be available on the public net. Private net addresses should never appear on the public net; they should be replaced or aliased to an address that the firewall owns. Addresses on packets and messages should be re-encoded at the firewall. Similarly, users' internal e-mail addresses should not appear on the public net. These private addresses should be replaced with the name of the site or enterprise at the firewall on the way out and replaced on the way in.

Protocols should not traverse the firewall. Traffic should be decoded and re-encoded at the firewall. For example, an SMTP carrying a message should be decoded into a message and then re-encoded into another SMTP for transmission at the firewall.

Reusable passwords should not traverse the firewall in either direction. Incoming passwords may be replays and are not reliable evidence of the identity of the user. Outgoing passwords may be similar to those used by users on the inside, and their use across the firewall could compromise internal systems. A preference for Secure Telnet or FTP should be made. These protocols provide end-to-encryption for all traffic, including the password. Alternatively, one-time passwords (e.g., SecureID or s-key) could be used. Although these do not protect all traffic, they protect against replays.

Proxies should represent the public net to the private net. For example, when a user of the private net wishes to access a World Wide Web (WWW) server on the public net, he or she should be transparently routed through the WWW proxy on the firewall. This proxy should hide the user's address from the public net, and protects both nets and the user. The user cannot misrepresent his or her address to the public net, and a process on the public net can directly attack only the proxy, not the user.

Only a limited set of limited applications should be permitted. Under this policy, such a limited application as e-mail is permitted, and such a very general application as Telnet is discouraged. Telnet is very general, flexible, and its intent is not obvious. It is vulnerable as a target and useful for attack.

Only those public applications that are intended for use on the public net should be placed on the public net. The public should not be permitted to traverse a firewall simply for the purpose of gaining access to public applications.

Applications on the public net should be implemented on dedicated and isolated servers. The server should be dedicated to a single use; it should not rely on the operating system to protect the application. Public servers should not know about the private net. Any connection to the private net should be to an application and over a trusted path. Privileged access to such servers should require strong authentication.

The public should not be granted read and write access to the same resource. For example, if the public can read a web page, they should not be able to write to it. The ability to write to it would permit them to alter or contaminate the data in a manner that could prove embarrassing. If a directory is provided to which the public can send files, they should not be able to read from that directory. If they can both read and write to the directory, they may use it simply as storage in lieu of their own. They may also use it to store contraband data that they would not want on their own systems and that might also prove embarrassing.

Encryption

Encryption is the application and use of secret, as opposed to public, codes. It is a powerful defense that can deal with many of the problems related to vulnerable links and even some of those related to insecure nodes. It is inexpensive and effective. In addition, multiple implementations are available. However, it is limited in the open node problems that it can deal with and may require some management infrastructure. Exhibit 1 displays some of the encryption choices available for selected applications on the Internet.

Exhibit 1. Encryption on the internet.

Application	Encryption
E-mail	PGP, SecureXchange, PEM, S-MIME
File	PGP, RSA Secure, Entrust
Application	DES, IDEA, stelnet, sftp
Client/Server	Secure Socket Layer (SSL)
Gateway-to-gateway	Digital, IBM, TIS
World Wide Web	s-http
Secure IP	S/WAN

Encryption is used for two fundamental purposes on the net. The first is to preserve necessary confidentiality on the net, which is the traditional use of cryptography. The second is to enable some confidence about who one is talking to. In other words, if conversation is in a language that can only be spoken by one other, the correct parties are speaking to one another.

Encryption can also be used to resist password grabbers and other eavesdropping attacks.

Using the Internet in a Relatively Safe Environment

The following are recommendations for using the Internet in a relatively safe way. Although few will follow all of these recommendations, there is risk involved in any deviation from the recommendations. Moreover, although complete adherence to these recommendations will not eliminate all vulnerabilities, it will address many of them. Finally, although complete adherence will not eliminate all risks, following these recommendations provides a reasonable balance between risk and other values.

- **Do not rely on the secrecy or authenticity of any information traversing the internet in public codes.** Names and addresses, credit card numbers, passwords, and other data received from the public net may be replays rather than originals. Amounts and account numbers may have been tampered with.
- **Choose a single point of connection to the Internet.** Although the Internet is inherently mesh connected, and more than one connection may be necessary to avoid single points of failure, the more connections, the more points of attack and the more difficult it is to maintain consistent controls. The fewer the number or points of connection, the fewer the potential points of attack and the easier to maintain control.
- **Connect to the Internet only with equipment dedicated to that purpose.** When computers were expensive, it was economic to put as many applications as possible on the costly hardware. Communication software was added to connect existing multi-use, multi-user systems to the net. Attacks exploited this gratuitous generality. Because of less-expensive hardware, hardware connected to the net should be dedicated to that use. All other applications should be run on other systems.
- **Choose application-only connections.** Many of the compromises of the Internet have resulted from the fact that the components were connected at the system layer and that attacks have succeeded in escaping the application to the more general and flexible system layer. If an attack encounters the e-mail service, it should see nothing else. If it escapes the e-mail application, it should see nothing. Under no circumstances should it see the prompt of an operating system that knows about any other system. In other words, the operating system should be hidden from the public net.
- **Limit the use of Telnet.** Telnet, particularly to the operating system, is a very general and flexible capability. It can be used for attack and is vulnerable to attacks. Most of its functions and capabilities can be accomplished with safer alternatives.
- **Use end-to-end encryption for commercial applications on the net.** Although most of the applications and traffic on the public net are public, commercial and other private applications on the public net must be conducted in secret codes.
- **Require strong authentication.** Users of private applications on the public net or of the public net for commercial applications must use strong authentication. Two independent kinds of evidence should be employed to determine the identity of a user, and the authentication data must be protected from capture and replay.

- **Log, monitor, and meter events and traffic.** Given enough time, almost any attack can succeed. It is important to be able to recognize attack traffic and correct for it early. Attacks can usually be recognized by a change, often a sudden increase, from normal traffic patterns. It is useful to know what normal traffic looks like to be able to recognize variances on a timely basis, and to communicate the condition of those variances to managers who can take timely corrective action.

Conclusion

For similar reasons, the Internet is as ubiquitous as the telephone. It gives users such an economic advantage over nonusers so that the nonusers are forced to become users. Pundits are fond of saying that no one is making money on the Internet. This position is fatuous and suggests that tens of thousands of enterprises are behaving irrationally. What is meant is that no one is conducting commerce on the Internet, at least not in the sense that they are selling, distributing, billing, and being paid over the Internet. Of course, many firms are doing one or more of these. Many others are making money, mostly by reducing costs. Many companies are using the Internet because it is the most efficient way to support customers.

The Internet holds out the promise to empower, enrich, and perhaps even ennoble. A minimum level of public trust and confidence must be maintained if that promise is to become a reality. That trust is both fragile and irreparable.

Because fundamental vulnerabilities on the network exist and because all possible attacks cannot be anticipated, a conservative policy and a responsive posture are required.

Chapter 67
Applets and Network Security

Al Berg

The World Wide Web is the place that users are most likely to encounter applets today. Java (and to a lesser degree, JavaScript) have become webmasters' tools of choice to add interesting effects to their Web sites or to deliver applications to end users. Most of the scrolling banners and other special effects found on today's Web pages depend on applets to work. Some Web pages use applets for more substantial applications. For example, MapQuest (http://www.mapquest.com) uses Java and ActiveX to deliver an interactive street atlas of the entire US. *Wired* magazine offers a Java-based chat site that, when accessed over the Web, allows users to download an applet that lets them participate in real-time conferencing.

The Security Issue

Every silver lining has a cloud, and applets are no exception. Applets can present a real security hazard for users and network managers. When Web pages use applets, the commands that tell the client's browser to download and execute the applets are embedded in the pages themselves. Users have no way of knowing whether the next page they download will contain an applet, and, most of the time, they do not care. The Internet offers an almost limitless source of applets for users to run, but no one knows who wrote them, whether they were written with malicious intent, or whether they contain bugs that might cause them to crash a user's computer.

Applets and computer viruses have a lot in common. Both applets and viruses are self-replicating code that executes on the user's computer without the user's consent. Some security experts have gone so far as to say that the corporate network manager should prohibit users from running applets at all. However, applets are becoming an increasingly common part of how users interact with the Internet and corporate intranets, so learning to live safely with applets is important for network managers.

0-8493-9989-0/99/$0.00+$.50

What Are the Risks?

According to Princeton University's Safe Internet Programming (SIP) research team, there have been no publicly reported, confirmed cases of security breaches involving Java, though there have been some suspicious events that may have involved Java security problems. The lack of reported cases is no guarantee that there have not been breaches that either were not discovered or were not reported. But it does indicate that breaches are rare.

As Web surfing increasingly becomes a way to spend money, and applets become the vehicle for shopping, attacks on applets will become more and more profitable, increasing the risk. Sun, Netscape, and Microsoft all designed their applet languages with security in mind.

Java: Secure Applets

Java programs are developed in a language similar to C++ and stored as source code on a server. When a client, such as a Web browser, requests a page that references a Java program, the source code is retrieved from the server and sent to the browser, where an integrated interpreter translates the source code statements into machine-independent bytecodes, which are executed by a virtual machine implemented in software on the client. This virtual machine is designed to be incapable of operations that might be detrimental to security, thus providing a secure sandbox in which programs can execute without fear of crashing the client system. Java applets loaded over a network are not allowed to:

- Read from files on the client system
- Write to files on the client system
- Make any network connections, except to the server from which they were downloaded
- Start any client-based programs
- Define native method calls, which would allow an applet to directly access the underlying computer

Java was designed to make applets inherently secure. Following are some of the underlying language security features offered by Java:

- All of an applet's array references are checked to make sure that programs will not crash because of a reference to an element that does not exist.
- Complex and troublesome pointer variables (found in some vendors' products) that provide direct access to memory locations in the computer do not exist in Java, removing another cause of crashes and potentially malicious code.

- Variables can be declared as unchangeable at runtime to prevent important program parameters from being modified accidentally or intentionally.

Java: Holes and Bugs

Although Sun has made every effort to make the Java virtual machine unable to run code that will negatively impact the underlying computer, researchers have already found bugs and design flaws that could open the door to malicious applets.

The fact that Sun has licensed Java to various browser vendors adds another level of complexity to the security picture. Not only can security be compromised by a flaw in the Java specification, but the vendor's implementation of the specification may contain its own flaws and bugs.

Denial-of-Service Threats

Denial-of-service attacks involve causing the client's Web browser to run with degraded performance or crash. Java does not protect the client system from these types of attacks, which can be accomplished simply by putting the client system into a loop to consume processor cycles, creating new process threads until system memory is consumed, or placing locks on critical processes needed by the browser.

Because denial-of-service attacks can be programmed to occur after a time delay, it may be difficult for a user to determine which page the offending applet was downloaded from. If an attacker is subtle and sends an applet that degrades system performance, users may not know that their computer is under attack, leading to time-consuming and expensive troubleshooting of a nonexistent hardware or software problem.

Java applets are not supposed to be able to establish network connections to machines other than the server they were loaded from. However, there are applets that exploit bugs and design flaws that allow it to establish a back-door communications link to a third machine (other than the client or server). This link could be used to send information that may be of interest to a hacker. Because many ready-to-use Java applets are available for download from the Internet, it would be possible for an attacker to write a useful applet, upload it to a site where webmasters would download it, and then sit back and wait for information sent by the applet to reach their systems.

What Kind of Information Can the Applet Send Back?

Due to another implementation problem found in August 1996 by the SIP research team at Princeton University, the possibilities are endless. A flaw found in Netscape Navigator 3.0 beta 5 and earlier versions, and Microsoft

Internet Explorer 3.0 beta 2 and earlier versions, allows applets to gain full read and write access to the files on a Web surfer's machine. This bug means that the attacker can get copies of any files on the machine or replace existing data or program files with hacked versions.

Giving Java applets the ability to connect to an arbitrary host on the network or Internet opens the door to another type of attack. A malicious applet, downloaded to and running on a client inside of a firewalled system, could establish a connection to another host behind the firewall and access files and programs. Because the attacking host is actually inside the secured system, the firewall will not know that the access is actually originating from outside the network.

Another bug found in August 1996 by the Princeton team affects only Microsoft Internet Explorer version 3.0 and allows applets (which are not supposed to be allowed to start processes on the client machine) to execute any DOS command on the client. This allows the applet to delete or change files or programs or insert new or hacked program code such as viruses or backdoors. Microsoft has issued a patch (available on its Web site at http://www.microsoft.com/ie) to Internet Explorer that corrects the problem.

Princeton's SIP team also found a hole that would allow a malicious application to execute arbitrary strings of machine code, even though the Java virtual machine is only supposed to be able to execute the limited set of Java bytecodes. The problem was fixed in Netscape Navigator 3.0 beta 6 and Microsoft Internet Explorer 3.0 beta 2.

JavaScript: A Different Grind

Netscape's JavaScript scripting language may be named Java, but it is distinct from Sun's applet platform. JavaScript is Netscape Navigator's built-in scripting language that allows webmasters to do cross-platform development of applets that control browser events, objects such as tables and forms, and various activities that happen when users click on an object with a mouse.

Like Java, JavaScript runs applications in a virtual machine to prevent them from performing functions that would be detrimental to the operation of the client workstations. Also like Java, there are several flaws in the implementation of the security features of JavaScript. Some of the flaws found in JavaScript include the ability for malicious applets to:

- Obtain users' e-mail addresses from their browser configuration
- Track the pages that a user visits and mail the results back to the script author
- Access the client's file system, reading and writing files

A list of JavaScript bugs and fixes can be found on John LoVerso's Web page at the Open Software Foundation (http://www.osf.org/[sim]loverso/javascript/).

ActiveX: Microsoft's Vision for Distributed Component Computing

Microsoft's entry in the applet development tool wars, ActiveX, is very different from Java and presents its own set of security challenges. ActiveX is made up of server and client components, including:

- Controls, which are applets that can be embedded in Web pages and executed at the client. Controls can be written in a number of languages, including Visual Basic and Visual C++.
- Documents that provide access to non-HTML content, such as word processing documents or spreadsheets, from a Web browser.
- The Java virtual machine, which allows standard Java applets to run at the client.
- Scripting, which allows the Web developer to control the integration of controls and Java applets on a Web page.
- The server framework, which provides a number of server-side functions such as database access and data security.

Java applets running in an ActiveX environment (e.g., Microsoft's Internet Explorer Web browser) use the same security features and have the same security issues associated with JavaScript. Microsoft offers a Java development environment (i.e., Visual J++) as well as other sandbox languages (i.e., VBScript, based on Visual Basic and JScript, Microsoft's implementation of Netscape's JavaScript) for the development of applications that are limited as to the functions they can perform.

When developers take advantage of ActiveX's ability to integrate programs written in Visual Basic or C++, the virtual machine model of Java no longer applies. In these cases, compiled binaries are transferred from the server to the Web client for execution. These compiled binaries have full access to the underlying computing platform, so there is no reason that the application could not read and write files on the client system, send information from the client to the server (or another machine), or perform a destructive act such as erasing a disk or leaving a virus behind.

Using Authenticode for Accountability

Microsoft's approach to security for non-Java ActiveX applications is based on the concept of accountability knowing with certainty the identity of the person or company that wrote a piece of software and that the software was not tampered with by a third party. Microsoft sees the issues related to downloading applets from the Web as similar to those involved in purchasing software; users need to know where the software is coming from and that it is intact. Accountability also means that writers of malicious code could be tracked down and would have to face consequences for their actions.

The mechanism that Microsoft offers to implement this accountability is called Authenticode. Authenticode uses a digital signature attached to each piece of software downloaded from the Internet. The signature is a cryptographic code attached by the software developer to an applet. Developers must enter a private key (known only to them) to sign their application, assuring their identity. The signature also includes an encrypted checksum of the application itself, which allows the client to determine if the applet has changed since the developer released it.

ActiveX: The Downside

This approach provides developers and users with access to feature-rich applications, but at a price. If an application destroys information on a user's computer, accountability will not help recover their data or repair damage done to their business. Once the culprit has been found, bringing him or her to justice may be difficult because new computer crimes are developing faster than methods for prosecuting them.

Microsoft acknowledges that Authenticode does not guarantee that end users will never download malicious code to their PCs and that it is but a first step in the protection of information assets.

Further information on ActiveX can be found on Microsoft's Web site (http://www.microsoft.com/activex) and at the ActiveX Web site run by CNet Technology Corp. (http://www.activex.com).

An Ounce of Prevention

So far, this chapter has discussed problems posed by applets. Following are some steps that can be taken to lessen the exposure faced by users.

Make Sure the Basics Are Covered

Users need to back up their data and programs consistently, and sensitive data should be stored on secure machines. The surest way to avoid applet security problems is to disable support for applet execution at the browser. If the code cannot execute, it cannot do damage.

Of course, the main downside of this approach is that the users will lose the benefits of being able to run applets. Because the ability to run applets is part of the client browser, turning off applets is usually accomplished at the desktop and a knowledgeable user could simply turn applet support back on. Firewall vendors are starting to provide support for filtering out applets, completely or selectively, before they enter the local network.

Users Should Run the Latest Available Versions of their Web Browsers

Each new version corrects not only functional and feature issues, but security flaws. If an organization is planning to use applets on its Web pages, it is preferable to either write them internally or obtain them from trusted sources. If applets will be downloaded from unknown sources, a technical person with a good understanding of the applet language should review the code to be sure that it does only what it claims to. Mark LaDue, a researcher at Georgia Tech, has a Web page (available at http://www.math.gatech.edu/[sim]mladue/HostileApplets.html) containing a number of hostile applets available for download and testing. Seeing some real applications may help users recognize new problem applets that might be encountered.

Conclusion

IS personnel should monitor the Princeton University SIP group's home page (located at http://www.cs.princeton.edu/sip) for the latest information on security flaws and fixes (under News). It is also a good idea to keep an eye on browser vendors' home pages for news of new versions.

Applets offer users and network managers a whole new paradigm for delivering applications to the desktop. Although, like any new technology, applets present a new set of challenges and concerns, their benefits can be enjoyed while their risks can be managed.

Chapter 68
Oracle Database Security

Mary Ann Davidson

Basic requirements for system security are evaluation of the data at risk, assessment of the vulnerabilities of the data, and evaluation of the methods that can be used to reduce the threat to data to an acceptable level of risk. This process results in a written security policy (i.e., the set of laws, rules, and practices that regulate how an organization manages, protects, and distributes sensitive information).

A security policy needs to address the following aspects of data security:

- **Confidentiality.** Users see and modify only data that they are authorized to see.
- **Integrity.** Data is modified only in appropriate and meaningful ways.
- **Availability.** A given resource will be usable during a given time period.

Each organization may weigh these requirements differently. A military or government organization conducting covert operations might weigh confidentiality of data more highly than integrity of data, whereas a financial institution processing large financial transactions might weigh integrity of data more highly than confidentiality. These different requirements for security result in different security policies for each organization.

A security policy may contain a variety of measures designed to address perceived threats, including:

- Personnel measures (e.g., background checks and vetting)
- Procedural measures (e.g., shredding sensitivity printouts and performing routine backups)
- Physical measures (e.g., securing microcomputers, removing disk drives, and locking rooms) containing computers)
- Technical measures (e.g., authentication of users by the system and encrypting data)

0-8493-9989-0/99/$0.00+$.50

These measures must work together in a cohesive manner to provide adequate system security. For example, locking computers in a separate room may prevent physical theft, but will not prevent the theft of data that can occur if there are inadequate access controls for the data itself.

This chapter deals primarily with the confidentiality aspects of database security (and, to a lesser degree, the integrity of data) and the technical measures used to ensure them in Oracle Corp.'s database servers: Oracle7 and Trusted Oracle7. However, it should be emphasized that many of the security exposures and controls discussed here are relevant to any relational database environment.

Limiting Access to Data

Most database servers provide the ability to limit user access to data by means of access controls. Discretionary access control allows users to grant access to portions of data they control to other users. For example, Jane can grant Scott the ability to select data from table EMP, which she owns. Discretionary access control is an important security mechanism in controlling initial access to information; however, it has important limitations in controlling further dissemination of information. For example, Jane may not want Elena to have access to EMP data, yet Scott can circumvent this by copying data from EMP into a table called MY_EMP, then granting access to MY_EMP to Elena.

Mandatory access control addresses the limitations of discretionary access control by controlling access to data based on its sensitivity as indicated by a label and the clearance of the user trying to access the data. Users can access data only if their clearance meets or exceeds that of the data they are trying to access. Mandatory access control, in which separation of sensitive data and access to that data is always automatically enforced, is the key component of multilevel secure systems.

Discretionary Access Control

A basic concern in database security is ensuring that users access only the data that they need to access, and that they modify data only in accordance with an organization's business rules. For example, a human resources database contains a variety of information about employees, some of which (e.g., salaries) is quite sensitive. An organization might limit access to the human resources database to human resources employees and department heads (department heads being limited to viewing information on employees in their respective departments only). An organization might also allow updates to salaries only within proscribed limits during normal business hours.

Privileges. A privilege is an authorization to perform a particular database operation; without privileges, a user cannot access any information in the database. A basic security policy is to grant users only those privileges they need to perform their jobs, a principle known as least privilege. A system privilege is an authorization for users to perform specific operations (such as CREATE TABLE). An object privilege is the ability to perform an operation on a specific database object (such as UPDATE (table) EMPLOYEES).

Most commercial databases segment system privileges in some manner, some by providing predefined roles (e.g., a security administrator role) consisting of a group of privileges. The drawback to using predefined roles is that the group of privileges provided off the shelf may still be greater than those the user needs. Oracle7provides more than 70 different system privileges, helping to ensure least privilege. Oracle7 also implements security by default; users have no privileges in a database unless they are specifically granted privileges.

In Oracle7, the creator of an object by default has all privileges(INSERT, UPDATE, DELETE, SELECT) on that object. Object privileges can be granted, at the owner's discretion, to any other user (or role). For example, Jane, the creator of table EMP, can grant Scott the ability to query the EMP table:

```
GRANT  SELECT  ON  emp  TO  scott
```

With this privilege, Scott can query the EMP table but cannot query any other tables in the database nor update the EMP table.

By providing these two types of very granular privileges, Oracle7 allows implementation of separation of function and control of user access to information at a very fine level, ensuring that database users are only authorized to perform those specific operations required by their job functions.

Configurable Roles. Configurable roles also simplify privilege administration. In Oracle7, roles are user-defined collections of privileges that can be granted to and revoked from users and from other roles. For example, a database administrator can create a PAYROLL_CLERK role, grant it all privileges necessary for payroll clerks to perform their jobs, then grant this single role to all payroll clerks. To later grant or revoke a privilege to all payroll clerks requires only that the additional privilege be granted or revoked to the PAYROLL_CLERK role. Roles can also be assigned to other roles, such as a PAYROLL_CLERK role assigned to a MANAGER role. In Oracle7, a role can be defined to prompt the user for a password when that role is invoked, providing another layer of security for the system. Because of the useful administrative and security aspects of the roles facility, Oracle submitted this technology to ANSI/ISO X3H2 SQL standards committee in 1989, and it was accepted into the SQL3 specifications.

Roles can also be used to restrict the set of privileges accessible to a user at any time. For example, default roles can be enabled for a user whenever he connects to the database, although other roles can only be enabled specifically by a user. A role can be disabled to prevent a user from using privileges when it is no longer appropriate (e.g., when changing jobs). In addition, a role can be dropped completely from the database, making it no longer available to any user. A role can be enabled within an application to restrict users from exercising the privileges of the role outside of a specific application function. For example, the PAYROLL_CLERK role can be enabled automatically at the beginning of the payroll application, then automatically disabled when a payroll clerk exits from the application, ensuring the privileges of the role are not used in any way other than what is allowed by the business rules defined within the payroll application.

Database Views. Database views (content- or context-dependent subsets of one or more tables) can also be used to limit access to information. For example, a view can be defined that allows a manager to view only the information in the EMP table that is relevant to employees in his or her own department:

```
CREATE VIEW emp_salaries AS
    SELECT empno, salary FROM salaries
    WHERE mgrname=user;
```

Similarly, a view can be defined that allows payroll clerks to update payroll information on certain days of the month only. This flexibility allows organizations to restrict the data that users can see or modify to only that data that they need to access, at only the appropriate access times.

Stored Procedures

Stored procedures offer another way to limit user privileges, the data that can be accessed, and the set of related operations that can be performed within the database. In Oracle7, a user can define a procedure so that it performs a specific business function and then grant another user the ability to execute that procedure without granting him any access to the objects and operations that the stored procedure uses. This prevents users from exercising privileges to perform operations outside of the context of the predefined authorized procedure.

For example, the following INCREASE_PAY stored procedure allows managers to increase their employees' salaries. By executing this stored procedure, managers are allowed to increase employees' salaries by no more than 15%:

```
CREATE PROCEDURE increase_pay (employee_no in
    number, increase_amount in number)
    AS BEGIN
        IF increase_amount <=.15
        THEN
            UPDATE emp_salaries
            SET salary=salary*(1+increase_amount)
            WHERE empno=employee_no;
    ELSE
        NULL;
        END IF;
    END;
```

Although managers with UPDATE privileges on the EMP_SALARIES view can perform this transaction, the stored procedure enforces business rules within the database by restricting managers from giving their employees increases that violate these rules.

Although users explicitly execute stored procedures, triggers are automatically executed within the DBMS based on prespecified events. In Oracle7, a trigger can be defined to execute either before or after an insert, update, or delete operation on a specific table, so that when the operation is performed on that table the trigger automatically executes. The security benefits of triggers are similar to those of stored procedures: more granular access controls and consistent rule enforcement.

Mandatory Access Control

Discretionary access control, with its ability to limit access to data, provides excellent security for most organizations. However, some organizations that process secret or sensitive information must further mediate access to data according to its sensitivity. For these organizations, Oracle provides Trusted Oracle7, a multilevel secure database.

Operating System Labels. In a multilevel secure system, all data in the system (including operating system and database) is labeled with its sensitivity. Labels are always associated with the information in an object, and they cannot be changed at the discretion of a user. A multilevel secure system also stores a clearance for each user. This clearance denotes the range of labels that a user is authorized to access. The system ensures that users are prevented from accessing information beyond their clearance level.

Trusted Oracle7 uses the same labels as those that the underlying secure operating system supports, including sensitivity labels, information labels, and integrity labels. Use of operating system labels helps ensure a consistent mandatory access control policy between Trusted Oracle7 and the underlying secure operating system as well as ease of label administration.

Tag Mappings. Trusted Oracle7 minimizes the overhead of multilevel security in several ways. For example, rather than storing the entire operating system label in the ROWLABEL column, Trusted Oracle7 stores a variable-length tag that maps to a valid operating system label, thus reducing label storage. The label/tag mappings are cached in memory, as are label dominance relationships, to ensure high performance.

Mandatory Access Control Privileges. Trusted Oracle7 enforces the mandatory access control policy implemented by the underlying secure operating system (see Exhibit 1). On most multilevel secure systems, this mandatory access control policy specifies that users can read, write, and modify (i.e., SELECT, INSERT, UPDATE, and DELETE) information that exactly matches their sensitivity label, and can only read (i.e., SELECT) information at lower (dominated) levels.

Trusted Oracle7 provides three mandatory access control privileges—READUP, WRITEUP, and WRITEDOWN—in addition to the granular system privileges provided in Oracle7. These mandatory access control privileges allow authorized users (for example, security officers) to

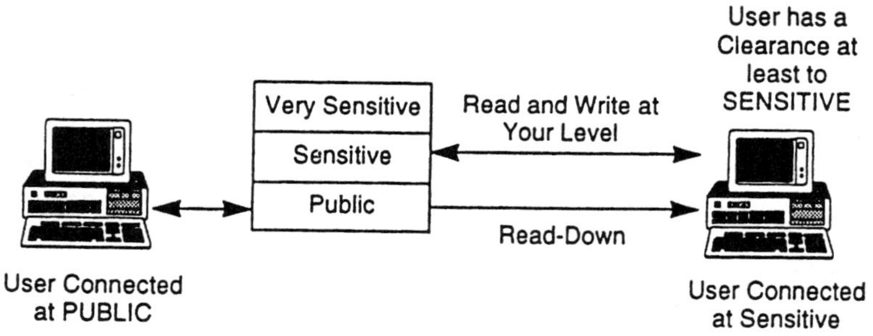

Exhibit 1. Mandatory access control policy enforcement.

reclassify (i.e., upgrade or downgrade) database information as appropriate, without (as with some multilevel secure systems) requiring them to export rows to an operating system file, disconnect from the database, log out, log in at a different sensitivity label with OS relabel privileges, reconnect to the database, and import the rows at the new label. Mandatory access control privileges are also necessary for performing such various administrative tasks as full database export and import.

In Trusted Oracle7, mandatory access control privileges are always tied to the corresponding operating system privileges, preventing users from performing privileged operations within the database for which they may not be authorized in the operating system. This allows enforcement of a cohesive, integrated security policy that includes all system components.

Integrity versus Confidentiality. There is an inherent tradeoff in multilevel secure systems between integrity and confidentiality, as illustrated in Exhibit 2. An unclassified user attempts to insert a record into the FLIGHTS table using a primary key (100) that is already used by a secret record. If insertion is allowed, the integrity of the table is compromised; if the record is rejected, the unclassified user learns that a record at a higher level exists, compromising confidentiality. Many databases always enforce confidentiality over integrity by requiring the insertion of the duplicate record (i.e., polyinstantiation). Trusted Oracle7 allows the database designer to enforce either integrity or confidentiality (or both) on a constraint-by-constraint basis, providing better support for each organization's unique requirements. All events in which confidentiality can be compromised through exposure of a covert channel can be audited, further enhancing security.

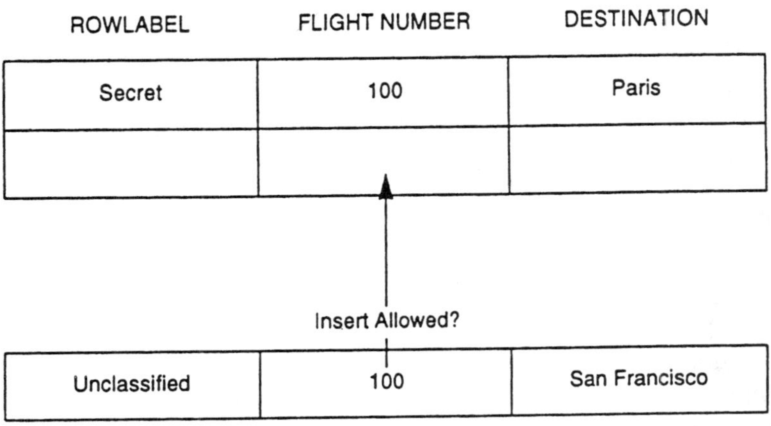

Exhibit 2. Integrity vs. confidentiality.

Auditing of Database Activity

A critical aspect of any security policy is maintaining a record of system activity to ensure that users are held accountable for their actions. Many databases (and operating systems) provide basic auditing abilities. The usefulness of auditing in an operational environment depends on several factors. First, the information gathered must be easily retrieved and analyzed to be useful. Second, the information retrieved must be limited to that information in which an organization is interested. Third, auditing must not adversely impact the performance of operations being audited.

The Oracle7 audit facility allows auditing of database activity by operation, by use of system privilege, by object, or by user. For example, auditing can be as general as all user connections to the database, or as specific as a particular user creating a table. The granularity and scope of these audit options allows monitoring of specific database activity without the performance overhead that more general auditing entails. Audit trail records are stored in an Oracle table, making the information available for viewing through *ad hoc* queries or any appropriate application or tool.

Triggers can be used to provide customized auditing of particular transactions or data. For example, a trigger can be defined on the EMP table to generate an audit record whenever an employee's salary is increased by more than 10%. This record can include selected information (e.g., before and after values of SALARY).

Oracle7 also provides the option of sending audit records to the database audit trail or the operating system's audit trail when the operating system is capable of receiving them. This option combined with the selection of audit options and the ability to customize auditing with triggers or stored procedures provides administrators with the ability to implement a custom auditing scheme for their organization's operations.

Database Encryption

Although multilevel secure systems address the limitations of discretionary access control quite well, there are still organizations that feel a need to safeguard data in the database by using encryption.

Full Database Encryption

Why might an organization consider encrypting an entire database? One reason is to limit the readability of the database files in the operating system. Clearly, access to database files in the operating system should be limited through groups or rights identifiers. However, an organization may also wish to make these files unreadable to a person who otherwise has legitimate access to the database files, but has no database privileges, such as a system administrator.

Encryption of an entire database is problematic. In an operational environment, encryption must not prevent users from accessing an object they are otherwise privileged to access, or their ability to perform their jobs can be impaired. For example, a user who has SELECT privilege on EMP should not be limited by the encryption mechanism from seeing all the data he or she is otherwise cleared to see. Provided that discretionary access control (and mandatory access control in a multilevel secure system) is well implemented, there is little additional security provided within the database itself from full database encryption. Any user who is privileged to access data within the database has neither more nor less privilege as a result of encryption.

Prudent security practice requires that an encryption key be changed periodically, which results in an obvious drawback to full database encryption; changing the key requires that the entire database be decrypted and reencrypted using the new key. This process is time-consuming and must generally be performed when the data is not being accessed.

If data within database tables is encrypted to provide additional security for database files, the indexes that access those tables must also be encrypted, because they may also contain sensitive data. The result of encrypting all data and all associated indexes is a drain on performance. For example, a user querying the EMP table must wait while the indexes are decrypted, the data in table EMP is decrypted, and the query is satisfied. The results of other operations that affect such data as UPDATEs or INSERTs must also be encrypted. Consequently, most organizations would find any additional security provided by full database encryption in an operational environment to be a poor tradeoff for the performance degradation that they would experience.

Although full database encryption is problematic, there may be a benefit to encryption of data stored off-line, such as backups or archived data. (Of course, the first line of data protection is to secure archived data in a facility to which access is controlled—a physical measure.) Because data is not being accessed online, performance need not be a concern. Commercial databases do not, as a rule, provide this service, but there are several vendors who can provide offline encryption services.

Partial Database Encryption

As discussed earlier, a system administrator or database administrator typically has the most privileges in a system and must also generally be cleared to the highest level. Therefore, in addition to using discretionary access control and mandatory access control, an organization may wish to encrypt certain sensitive data and only provide the ability to decrypt and read the data to selected individuals. For example, a FLIGHTS table might contain information about cargo that no one except an intelligence officer needs to see. This data could be encrypted, with only the intelligence officer having access to the decryption key. As in the case of full database encryption, the encryption should not limit access by users who are otherwise cleared to see the data.

Commercially available databases do not generally provide this functionality; however, there are a number of strong encryption algorithms that can be licensed from vendors such as RSA Data Security. These encryption algorithms can be incorporated into an application so that only selected users can view and modify the encrypted data. (Note that certain encryption technologies are subject to export controls; this is one reason that database vendors do not provide this facility within the database. Oracle Corp. does provide network encryption support, as discussed in the following section.)

Vulnerabilities of Distributed System

Although the mechanisms described above address basic database security issues, distributed systems have additional vulnerabilities due to the nature of decentralized operations.

- Network snooping, which could threaten the confidentiality of passwords and data passing over a network
- Data modification or replay of transactions, which could threaten the integrity of data passing over a network
- Establishing user identity across a network in a reliable fashion

Network Snooping. Network snooping occurs when someone is able to read data as it is being passed over a network. Physically shielding all connection lines in a network from electronic or mechanical taps may be either physically impossible (as in WANs) or economically prohibitive. The interception of passwords, sensitive data, or both is a threat to the confidentiality of data as it passes over a network.

Data Modification. Modification of data occurs when an intruder or unauthorized user is able to read data in transmission and modify it. For example, a transaction passing from the personnel system to the payroll system to issue an employee bonus in the amount of $1,000 could be intercepted and modified to $5,000 before issuance. Replay of transactions occurs when a transaction is intercepted in route to its destination and replayed so that it occurs multiple times. For example, a transaction to increase an expense report in the amount of $100 could be intercepted between an expense report module and a disbursement system, and replayed so that the $100 increase occurs 10 times.

Establishing User Identity. Establishment of user identity is of concern over a network; can it be verified that user A connecting to server B from client C really is user A? This threat is best addressed by network authentication services, which is not treated in this chapter.

Although these are not the only threats to the confidentiality and integrity of data passing over a network, they are representative of the major vulnerabilities of distributed systems. Organizations that have heterogeneous distributed systems cannot rely solely on the security mechanisms of their operating systems, databases, and applications. They must identify and address the vulnerabilities inherent within the network to ensure the security of their systems.

Confidentiality of Passwords

In distributed systems, there are a number ways in which passwords are vulnerable to compromise. One such vulnerability is that of a password passing from a client to a server. If the password is passed in plain text (e.g., unencrypted), any eavesdropper snooping for data on the network can read the password. This is potentially more damaging than reading the data itself, because access to a password also gives the snooper access to the privileges of the user whose password is intercepted, and the interceptor can then see and modify data that the user can see and modify. In addition, the compromised password results in a loss of accountability, because it is then impossible to tell whether actions are being executed by the user or the malicious interceptor.

Password replay is also a threat to password confidentiality. If an encrypted password is passed over the network in precisely the same encrypted form each time a user attempts connection, then a malicious interceptor need only supply the username and encrypted password to masquerade as the user.

Password Encryption

Most distributed systems cannot easily shield their networks from all attempts to intercept passwords; password encryption is a basic precaution against a compromised password. Many systems encrypt passwords that are stored in the database itself (or in an operating system file) so they cannot be read and used by those who otherwise have access to those files. It is an extra measure of security to encrypt the password as it is passed from the client to the server for authentication.

Oracle's solution to this password vulnerability is the Oracle Password Protocol, which is available in Release 7.1 of Oracle7 and Trusted Oracle7. The Oracle Password Protocol improves the security of password communication by using a session key valid for a single database connection attempt. The key is used to encrypt the password before passing it over the network. Each connection attempt uses a separate key for encryption, making the encryption more difficult to decipher (and minimizing the risk from encrypted password replay). The Oracle Password Protocol is used to encrypt passwords in all connection attempts, whether a local connection, server to server, or client to server.

As shown in Exhibit 3, the Oracle Password Protocol relies on a shared secret between the client and the server—the encrypted password of the user. First, a user enters his username and password, and the Oracle Client sends just the user ID across the network to the Oracle Server (see step 1 in Exhibit 3). The server generates a random number that is used as the session key. The server locates the user's encrypted password stored in the database and uses the encrypted password as the key with which it encrypts the session key. The server then sends the encrypted session key to the client (step 2). The client encrypts the password the user has entered and uses it to decrypt the session key. The client then encrypts the entered password using the session key and sends it to the server (step 3). The server decrypts the password using the session key, then re-encrypts it using the DES-based encryption algorithm used to create the stored, encrypted password. The Oracle Server compares the entered password with the password stored in the database. If they match, the server allows access.

Integrity and Confidentiality of Data Passing Over the Network

Unless an organization can physically shield all connection lines in a network (which may not be physically or economically feasible), there is an

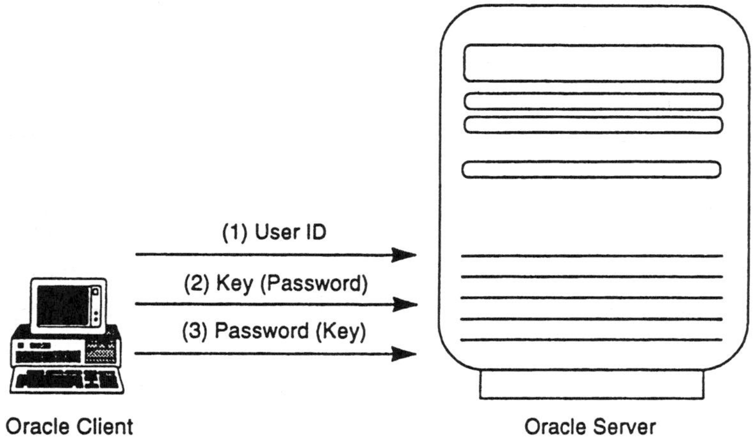

Exhibit 3. Oracle password protocol.

inherent risk to data passing over networks. A sniffer may be able to read the data as it passes over the network, compromising confidentiality, or even modify the data in an undetected manner, threatening integrity. Several mechanisms can be employed to safeguard the confidentiality and integrity of data passing over a network.

Checksums

One means of ensuring that data passing over a network has not been tampered with is the use of cryptographic checksums. A checksum is a mechanism that computes a value for a message packet based on the data it contains and passes it along with the data to authenticate that the data has not been tampered with. The recipient of the data recomputes the checksum and compares it with the checksum passed with the data; if they match, it is likely the data was not tampered with during transmission. The important property of a checksum is that a malicious interceptor would have to perform much more computing to alter the message in such a way as to yield the same checksum as the original message.

Oracle Corporation's Secure Network Services for SQL*Net provides both security of data transmission and protection against replay of transactions. To detect modification or replay of data during transmission, Secure Network Services can optionally generate a cryptographically secure message digest using RSA Data Security's MD5 algorithm and include it with each packet sent across the network. On reception at the destination, an integrity check is performed on each packet. This makes it virtually impossible for an intruder to alter data or commands without detection, and ensures that any attempt to do so is immediately reported to the user and written to the system log files.

Network Encryption

Checksums can only ensure that data is not tampered with during transmission; network encryption can ensure both integrity and confidentiality of data during transmission. Current implementations of network encryption may be quite expensive and nonportable, relying on hardware to encrypt data on network lines after the lines leave the machine but before they leave a secure site to enter a network. In addition, hardware-based encryption is not practical for all networks, such as LANs with many workstations, requiring an encryption unit for each node.

Secure Network Services for SQL*Net provides network data encryption using the RSA Data Security's RC4 encryption algorithm. For each SQL*Net session, Secure Network Services generates a random 40-bit key, and uses it to encrypt network traffic, including all data values, SQL statements, and stored procedure calls and results. The use of the encryption module can be initiated or required by either the client, the server, or both to guarantee data protection. The encryption is done at high speed, and performance impact (which varies depending on the platform) is minimal, given the increased level of security provided. In the future, Secure Network Services will support both 56-bit key and 40-bit key DES-based encryption algorithms.

Conclusion

Such relational databases as Oracle7 can provide a number of mechanisms to ensure confidentiality of data. In addition, the advent of such multilevel secure databases as Trusted Oracle7 provides enhanced data separation through the use of mandatory access controls. With the increase in distributed operations, host-based database security must be augmented by network security controls to provide authentication and encryption services.

Chapter 69
Relational Database Access Controls Using SQL

Ravi S. Sandhu

This chapter discusses access controls in relational database management systems. Access controls have been built into relational systems since they first emerged. Over the years, standards have developed and are continuing to evolve. In recent years, products incorporating mandatory controls for multilevel security have also started to appear.

The chapter begins with a review of the relational data model and SQL language. Traditional discretionary access controls provided in various dialects of SQL are then discussed. Limitations of these controls and the need for mandatory access controls are illustrated, and three architectures for building multilevel databases are presented. The chapter concludes with a brief discussion of role-based access control as an emerging technique for providing better control than do traditional discretionary access controls, without the extreme rigidity of traditional mandatory access controls.

RELATIONAL DATABASES

A relational database stores data in relations that are expected to satisfy some simple mathematical properties. Roughly speaking, a relation can be thought of as a table. The columns of the table are called attributes, and the rows are called tuples. There is no significance to the order of the columns or rows; however, duplicate rows with identical values for all columns are not allowed.

Relation schemes must be distinguished from relation instances. The relation scheme gives the names of attributes as well as their permissible values. The set of permissible values for an attribute is said to be the

0-8493-9989-0/99/$0.00+$.50

attribute's domain. The relation instance gives the tuples of the relation at a given instant.

For example, the following is a relation scheme for the EMPLOYEE relation:

EMPLOYEE (NAME, DEPT, RANK, OFFICE, SALARY, SUPERVISOR)

The domain of the NAME, DEPT, RANK, OFFICE, and SUPERVISOR attributes are character strings, and the domain of the SALARY attribute is integers. A particular instance of the EMPLOYEE relation, reflecting the employees who are currently employed, is as follows:

NAME	DEPT	RANK	OFFICE	SALARY	SUPERVISOR
Rao	Electrical Engineering	Professor	KH252	50,000	Jones
Kaplan	Computer Science	Researcher	ST125	35,000	Brown
Brown	Computer Science	Professor	ST257	55,000	Black
Jones	Electrical Engineering	Chair	KH143	45,000	Black
Black	Administration	Dean	ST101	60,000	NULL

The relation instance of EMPLOYEE changes with the arrival of new employees, changes to data for existing employees, and with their departure. The relation scheme, however, remains fixed. The NULL value in place of Black's supervisor signifies that Black's supervisor has not been defined.

Primary Key

A candidate key for a relation is a minimal set of attributes on which all other attributes depend functionally. In other words, two tuples may not have the same values of the candidate key in a relation instance. A candidate key is minimal — no attribute can be discarded without destroying this property. A candidate key always exists, because, in the extreme case, it consists of all the attributes.

In general, there can be more than one candidate key for a relation. If, for example in the EMPLOYEE previously described, duplicate names can never occur, NAME is a candidate key. If there are no shared offices, OFFICE is another candidate key. In the particular relation instance above there are no duplicate salary values. This, however, does not mean that salary is a candidate key. Identification of the candidate key is a property of the relation scheme and applies to every possible instance, not merely to the one that happens to exist at a given moment. SALARY would qualify as a candidate key only in the unlikely event that the organization forbids duplicate salaries.

The primary key of a relation is one of its candidate keys that has been designated as such. In the previous example, NAME is probably more appropriate than OFFICE as the primary key. Realistically, a truly unique identifier, such as social security number or employee identity number, rather than NAME should be used as the primary key.

Entity and Referential Integrity

The primary key uniquely identifies a specific tuple from a relation instance. It also links relations together. The relational model incorporates two application-independent integrity rules called entity integrity and referential integrity to ensure these purposes are properly served.

Entity integrity simply requires that no tuple in a relation instance can have NULL (i.e., undefined) values for any of the primary key attributes. This property guarantees that the value of the primary key can uniquely identify each tuple.

Referential integrity involves references from one relation to another. This property can be understood in context of the EMPLOYEE relation by assuming that there is a second relation with the scheme:

DEPARTMENT (DEPT, LOCATION, PHONE NUMBER)

DEPT is the primary key of DEPARTMENT. The DEPT attribute of the EMPLOYEE relation is said to be a foreign key from the EMPLOYEE relation to the DEPARTMENT relation. In general, a foreign key is an attribute, or set of attributes, in one relation R_1, whose values must match those of the primary key of a tuple in some other relation R_2. R_1 and R_2 need not be distinct. In fact, because supervisors are employees, the SUPERVISOR attribute in EMPLOYEE is a foreign key with $R_1 = R_2 =$ EMPLOYEE.

Referential integrity stipulates that if a foreign key *FK* of relation R_1 is the primary key *PK* of R_2, then for every tuple in R_1 the value of *FK* must either be NULL or equal to the value of *PK* of a tuple in R_2. Referential integrity requires the following in the EMPLOYEE example:

- Because of the DEPT foreign key, there should be tuples for the Electrical Engineering, Computer Science and Administration departments in the DEPARTMENT relation.
- Because of the SUPERVISOR foreign key, there should be tuples for Jones, Brown and Black in the EMPLOYEE relation.

The purpose of referential integrity is to prevent employees from being assigned to departments or supervisors who do not exist in the database, though it is all right for employee Black to have a NULL supervisor or for an employee to have a NULL department.

SQL

Every database management system (DBMS) needs a language for defining, storing, retrieving, and manipulating data. SQL is the de facto standard in relational DBMSs. SQL emerged from several projects at the IBM San Jose (now called Almaden) Research Center in the mid-1970s. Its official name now is Database Language SQL.

An official standard for SQL has been approved by the American National Standards Institute (ANSI) and accepted by the International Standards Organization (ISO) and the National Institute of Standards and Technology as a Federal Information Processing Standard. The standard has evolved and continues to do so. The base standard is generally known as SQL'89 and refers to the 1989 ANSI standard. SQL'92 is an enhancement of SQL'89 and refers to the 1992 ANSI standard. A third version SQL, commonly known as SQL3, is being developed under the ANSI and ISO aegis.

Although most relational DBMSs support some dialect of SQL, SQL compliance does not guarantee portability of a database from one DBMS to another. This is true because DBMS vendors typically include enhancements not required by the SQL standard but not prohibited by it either. Most products are also not completely compliant with the standard.

The following sections provide a brief explanation of SQL. Unless otherwise noted, the version discussed is SQL'89.

The CREATE Statement

The relation scheme for the EMPLOYEE example, is defined in SQL by the following command:

CREATE	TABLE	EMPLOYEE	
	(NAME	CHARACTER	NOT NULL,
	DEPT	CHARACTER,	
	RANK	CHARACTER,	
	OFFICE	CHARACTER,	
	SALARY	INTEGER,	
	SUPERVISOR	CHARACTER,	
	PRIMARY KEY	(NAME),	
	FOREIGN KEY	(DEPT)	REFERENCES DEPARTMENT,
	FOREIGN KEY	(SUPERVISOR)	REFERENCES EMPLOYEE)

This statement creates a table called EMPLOYEE with six columns. The NAME, DEPT, RANK, OFFICE, and SUPERVISOR columns have character strings (of unspecified length) as values, whereas the SALARY column has integer values. NAME is the primary key. DEPT is a foreign key that references the primary key of table DEPARTMENT. SUPERVISOR is a foreign key that references the primary key (i.e., NAME) of the EMPLOYEE table itself.

INSERT and DELETE Statements

The EMPLOYEE table is initially empty. Tuples are inserted into it by means of the SQL INSERT statement. For example, the last tuple of the relation instance previously discussed is inserted by the following statement:

INSERT	
INTO	EMPLOYEE(NAME, DEPT, RANK, OFFICE, SALARY, SUPERVISOR)
VALUES	VALUES('Black', 'Administration', 'Dean', 'ST101', 60000, NULL)

The remaining tuples can be similarly inserted. Insertion of the tuples for Brown and Jones must respectively precede insertion of the tuples for Kaplan and Rao, so as to maintain referential integrity. Alternatively, these tuples can be inserted in any order with NULL managers that are later updated to their actual values. There is a DELETE statement to delete tuples from a relation.

The SELECT Statement

Retrieval of data is effected in SQL by the SELECT statement. For example, the NAME, SALARY, and SUPERVISOR data for employees in the computer science department is extracted as follows:

SELECT	NAME, SALARY, SUPERVISOR
FROM	EMPLOYEE
WHERE	DEPT = 'Computer Science'

This query applied to instance of EMPLOYEE previously given returns the following data:

NAME	SALARY	SUPERVISOR
Kaplan	35,000	Brown
Brown	55,000	Black

The WHERE clause in a SELECT statement is optional. SQL also allows the retrieved records to be grouped together for statistical computations by means of built-in statistical functions. For example, the following query gives the average salary for employees in each department:

SELECT	DEPT, AVG(SALARY)
FROM	EMPLOYEE
GROUP BY	DEPT

Data from two or more relations can be retrieved and linked together in a SELECT statement. For example, the location of employees can be retrieved by linking the data in EMPLOYEE with that in DEPARTMENT, as follows:

SELECT	NAME, LOCATION
FROM	EMPLOYEE, DEPARTMENT
WHERE	EMPLOYEE.DEPT = DEPARTMENT.DEPT

This query attempts to match every tuple in EMPLOYEE with every tuple in DEPARTMENT but selects only those pairs for which the DEPT attribute in the EMPLOYEE tuple matches the DEPT attribute in the DEPARTMENT tuple. Because DEPT is a common attribute to both relations, every use of it is explicitly identified as occurring with respect to one of the two relations. Queries involving two relations in this manner are known as joins.

The UPDATE Statement

Finally, the UPDATE statement allows one or more attributes of existing tuples in a relation to be modified. For example, the following statement gives all employees in the Computer Science department a raise of $1000:

UPDATE	EMPLOYEE
SET	SALARY = SALARY + 1000
WHERE	DEPT = 'Computer Science'

This statement selects those tuples in EMPLOYEE that have the value of Computer Science for the DEPT attribute. It then increases the value of the SALARY attribute for all these tuples by $1000 each.

BASE RELATIONS AND VIEWS

The concept of a view has an important security application in relational systems. A view is a virtual relation derived by an SQL definition from base relations and other views. The database stores the view definitions and materializes the view as needed. In contrast, a base relation is actually stored in the database.

For example, the EMPLOYEE relation previously discussed is a base relation. The following SQL statement defines a view called COMPUTER_CI_DEPT:

CREATE	VIEW COMPUTER_SCI_DEPT	
AS	SELECT	NAME, SALARY, SUPERVISOR
	FROM	EMPLOYEE
	WHERE	DEPT = 'Computer Science'

This defines the virtual relation as follows:

NAME	SALARY	SUPERVISOR
Kaplan	35,000	Brown
Brown	55,000	Black

A user who has permission to access COMPUTER_SCI_DEPT is thereby restricted to retrieving information about employees in the computer science department. The dynamic aspect of views can be illustrated by an example in which a new employee, Turing, is inserted in base relation EMPLOYEE, modifying it as follows:

NAME	DEPT	RANK	OFFICE	SALARY	SUPERVISOR
Rao	Electrical Engineering	Professor	KH252	50,000	Jones
Kaplan	Computer Science	Researcher	ST125	35,000	Brown
Brown	Computer Science	Professor	ST257	55,000	Black
Jones	Electrical Engineering	Chairman	KH143	45,000	Black
Black	Administration	Dean	ST101	60,000	NULL
Turing	Computer Science	Genius	ST444	95,000	Black

The view COMPUTER_SCI_DEPT is automatically modified to include Turing, as follows:

NAME	SALARY	SUPERVISOR
Kaplan	35,000	Brown
Brown	55,000	Black
Turing	95,000	Black

In general, views can be defined in terms of other base relations and views.

Views can also provide statistical information. For example, the following view gives the average salary for each department:

CREATE	VIEW	AVSAL(DEPT,AVG)
AS	SELECT	DEPT,AVG(SALARY)
	FROM	EMPLOYEE
	GROUP BY	DEPT

For retrieval purposes, there is no distinction between views and base relations. Views, therefore, provide a very powerful mechanism for controlling what information can be retrieved. When updates are considered, views and base relations must be treated quite differently. In general, users cannot directly update views, particularly when they are constructed from the joining of two or more relations. Instead, the base relations must be updated, with views thus being updated indirectly. This fact limits the usefulness of views for authorizing update operations.

DISCRETIONARY ACCESS CONTROLS

This section describes the discretionary access control (DAC) facilities included in the SQL standard, though the standard is incomplete and does not address several important issues. Some of these deficiencies are being addressed in the evolving standard. Different vendors have also provided more comprehensive facilities than the standard calls for.

SQL Privileges

The creator of a relation in an SQL database is its owner and can grant other users access to that relation. The access privileges or modes recognized in SQL correspond directly to the CREATE, INSERT, SELECT, DELETE, and UPDATE SQL statements discussed previously. In addition, a REFERENCES privilege controls the establishment of foreign keys to a relation.

The CREATE Statement

SQL does not require explicit permission for a user to create a relation, unless the relation is defined to have a foreign key to another relation. In this case, the user must have the REFERENCES privilege for appropriate columns of the referenced relation. To create a view, a user must have the SELECT privilege on every relation mentioned in definition of the view. If a user has INSERT, DELETE, or UPDATE privileges on these relations, corresponding privileges will be obtained on the view (if it is updatable).

The GRANT Statement

The owner of a relation can grant one or more access privileges to another user. This can be done with or without the GRANT OPTION. If the owner grants SELECT with the GRANT OPTION, the user receiving this grant can further grant SELECT to other users. The latter GRANT can be done with or without the GRANT OPTION at the granting user's discretion.

The general format of a grant operation in SQL is as follows:

GRANT	privileges
[ON	relation]
TO	users
[WITH	GRANT OPTION]

The GRANT command applies to base relations as well as to views. The brackets on the ON and WITH clauses denotes that these are optional and may not be present in every GRANT command. It is not possible to grant a user the grant option on a privilege, without allowing the grant option itself to be further granted.

INSERT, DELETE, and SELECT privileges apply to the entire relation as a unit. Because INSERT and DELETE are operations on entire rows, this is appropriate. SELECT, however, implies the ability to select on all columns. Selection on a subset of the columns can be achieved by defining a suitable view and granting SELECT on the view. This method is somewhat awkward, and there have been proposals to allow SELECT to be granted on a subset of the columns of a relation. In general, the UPDATE privilege applies to a subset of the columns. For example, a user can be granted the authority to update the OFFICE but not the SALARY of an EMPLOYEE. SQL'92 extends the INSERT privilege to apply to a subset of the columns. Thus, a clerical user, for example, can insert a tuple for a new employee with the NAME, DEPARTMENT, and RANK data. The OFFICE, SALARY, and SUPERVISOR data can then be updated in this tuple by a suitably authorized supervisory user.

SQL'89 has several omissions in its access control facilities. These omissions have been addressed by different vendors in different ways. The following section identifies the major omissions and illustrates how they have been addressed in products and in the evolving standard.

The REVOKE Statement

One major shortcoming of SQL'89 is the lack of a REVOKE statement to take away a privilege granted by a GRANT. IBM's DB2 product provides a REVOKE statement for this purpose.

It is often necessary that revocation cascade. In a cascading revoke, not only is the privilege revoked, so too are all GRANTs based on the revoked privilege. For example, if user Tom grants Dick SELECT on relation R with the GRANT OPTION, Dick subsequently grants Harry SELECT on R, and Tom revokes SELECT on R from Dick, the SELECT on R privilege is taken away not only from Dick but also from Harry. The precise mechanics of a cascading revoke is somewhat complicated. If Dick had received the SELECT on R privilege (with GRANT OPTION) not only from Tom but also from Jane before Dick granted SELECT to Harry, Tom's revocation of the

SELECT from R privilege from Dick would not cause either Dick or Tom to lose this privilege. This is because the GRANT from Jane remains valid.

Cascading revocation is not always desirable. A user's privileges to a given table are often revoked because the user's job functions and responsibilities have changed. For example, if Mary, the head of a department moves on to a different assignment, her privileges to her former department's data should be revoked. However, a cascading revoke could cause lots of employees of that department to lose their privileges. These privileges must then be regranted to keep the department functioning.

SQL'92 allows a revocation to be cascading or not cascading, as specified by the revoker. This is a partial solution to the more general problem of how to reassign responsibility for managing access to data from one user to another as their job assignments change.

Other Privileges

Another major shortcoming of SQL'89 is the lack of control over who can create relations. In SQL'89, every user is authorized to create relations. The Oracle DBMS requires possession of a RESOURCE privilege to create new relations. SQL'89 does not include a privilege to DROP a relation. Such a privilege is included in DB2.

SQL'89 does not address the issue of how new users are enrolled in a database. Several DBMS products take the approach that a database is originally created to have a single user, usually called the DBA (database administrator). The DBA essentially has all privileges with respect to this database and is responsible for enrolling users and creating relations. Some systems recognize a special privilege (called DBA in Oracle and DBADM in DB2) that can be granted to other users at the original DBA's discretion and allows these users effectively to act as the DBA.

LIMITATIONS OF DISCRETIONARY CONTROLS

The standard access controls of SQL are said to be discretionary because the granting of access is under user control. Discretionary controls have a fundamental weakness, however. Even when access to a relation is strictly controlled, a user with SELECT access can create a copy of the relation, thereby circumventing these controls. Furthermore, even if users can be trusted not to engage deliberately in such mischief, programs infected with Trojan horses can have the same disastrous effect.

For example, in the following GRANT operation:

```
TOM: GRANT SELECT ON EMPLOYEE TO DICK
```

Tom has not conferred the GRANT option on Dick. Tom's intention is that Dick should not be allowed to further grant SELECT access on EMPLOYEE to other users. However, this intent is easily subverted as follows. Dick creates a new relation, COPY-OF-EMPLOYEE, into which he copies all the rows of EMPLOYEE. As the creator of COPY-OF-EMPLOYEE, Dick can grant any privileges for it to any user. Dick can therefore grant Harry access to COPY-OF-EMPLOYEE as follows:

```
DICK: GRANT SELECT ON COPY-OF-EMPLOYEE TO HARRY
```

At this point, Harry has access to all the information in the original EMPLOYEE relation. For all practical purposes, Harry has SELECT access to EMPLOYEE, so long as Dick keeps COPY-OF-EMPLOYEE reasonably up to date with respect to EMPLOYEE.

The problem, however, is actually worse than this scenario indicates. It portrays Dick as a cooperative participant in this process. For example, it might be assumed that Dick is a trusted confidant of Tom and would not deliberately subvert Tom's intentions regarding the EMPLOYEE relation. But if Dick were to use a text editor supplied by Harry, which Harry had programmed to create the COPY-OF-EMPLOYEE relation and execute the preceding GRANT operation, the situation might be different. Such software is said to be a Trojan horse because in addition to the normal functions expected by its user it also engages in surreptitious actions to subvert security. Thus, a Trojan horse executed by Tom could actually grant Harry the privilege to SELECT on EMPLOYEE.

Organizations trying to avoid such scenarios can require that all software they run on relational databases be free of Trojan horses, but this is generally not considered a practical option. The solution is to impose mandatory controls that cannot be violated, even by Trojan horses.

MANDATORY ACCESS CONTROLS

Mandatory access controls (MACs) are based on security labels associated with each data item and each user. A label on a data item is called a security classification; a label on a user is called security clearance. In a computer system, every program run by a user inherits the user's security clearance.

In general, security labels form a lattice structure. This discussion assumes the simplest situation, in which there are only two labels — S for secret and U for unclassified. It is forbidden for S information to flow into U data items. Two mandatory access controls rules achieve this objective:

1. *Simple security property.* A U-user cannot read S-data.
2. *Star property.* A S-user cannot write U-data.

Some important points should be clearly understood in this context. First, the rules assume that a human being with S clearance can log in to the system as a S-user or a U-user. Otherwise, the star property prevents top executives from writing publicly readable data. Second, these rules prevent only the overt reading and writing of data. Trojan horses can still leak secret data by using devious means of communication called covert channels. Finally, mandatory access controls in relational databases usually enforce a strong star property:

- *Strong star property.* A S-user cannot write U-data, and a U-user cannot write S-data.

The strong star property limits users to writing at their own level, for reasons of integrity. The (weak) star property allows a U-user to write S-data. This can result in overwriting, and therefore destruction, of S-data by U-users. The remainder of this chapter will assume the strong star property.

Labeling Granularity

Security labels can be assigned to data at different levels of granularity in relational databases. Assigning labels to entire relations can be useful but is generally inconvenient. For example, if some salaries are secret but others are not, these salaries must be placed in different relations. Assigning labels to an entire column of a relation is similarly inconvenient in the general case.

The finest granularity of labeling is at the level of individual attributes of each tuple or row or at the level of individual element-level labeling. This offers considerable flexibility. Most of the products emerging offer labeling at the level of a tuple. Although not so flexible as element-level labeling, this approach is definitely more convenient than using relation- or column-level labels. Products in the short term can be expected to offer tuple-level labeling.

MULTILEVEL DATABASE ARCHITECTURES

In a multilevel system, users and data with different security labels coexist. Multilevel systems are said to be trusted because they keep data with different labels separated and ensure the enforcement of the simple security and strong star properties. Over the past fifteen years or so, considerable research and development has been devoted to the construction of multilevel databases. Three viable architectures are emerging:

1. Integrated data architecture (also known as the trusted subject architecture).
2. Fragmented data architecture (also known as the kernelized architecture).
3. Replicated data architecture (also known as the distributed architecture).

The newly emerging relational database products are basically integrated data architectures. This approach requires considerable modification of existing relational DBMSs and can be supported by DBMS vendors because they own the source code for their DBMSs and can modify it in new products.

Fragmented and replicated architectures have been demonstrated in laboratory projects. They promise greater assurance of security than does the integrated data architecture. Moreover, they can be constructed by using commercial off-the-shelf DBMSs as components. Therefore, non-DBMS vendors can build these products by integrating off-the-shelf trusted operating systems and non-trusted DBMSs.

Integrated Data Architecture

The integrated data architecture is illustrated in Exhibit 1. The bottom of the Exhibit shows three kinds of data coexisting in the disk storage of the illustrated systems:

1. *U-non-DBMS-data.* Unclassified data files are managed directly by the trusted operating system.
2. *S-non-DBMS-data.* Secret data files are managed directly by the trusted operating system.
3. *U+S-DBMS-data.* Unclassified and secret data are stored in files managed cooperatively by the trusted operating system and the trusted DBMS.

At the top of the diagram on the left hand side a U-user and S-user interact directly with the trusted operating system. The trusted operating system allows these users to access only non-DBMS data in this manner. As according to the simple security and strong star properties, the U-user is allowed to read and write U-non-DBMS data, while the S-user is allowed to read U-non-DBMS data and read and write S-non-DBMS data. DBMS data must be accessed via the DBMS.

The right hand side of the diagram shows a U-user and S-user interacting with the trusted DBMS. The trusted DBMS enforces the simple security and strong star properties with respect to the DBMS data. The trusted DBMS relies on the trusted operating system to ensure that DBMS data cannot be accessed without intervention by the trusted DBMS.

Fragmented Data Architecture

The fragmented data architecture is shown in Exhibit 2. In this architecture, only the operating system is multilevel and trusted. The DBMS is untrusted and interacts with users at a single level. The bottom of the exhibit shows two kinds of data coexisting in the disk storage of the system:

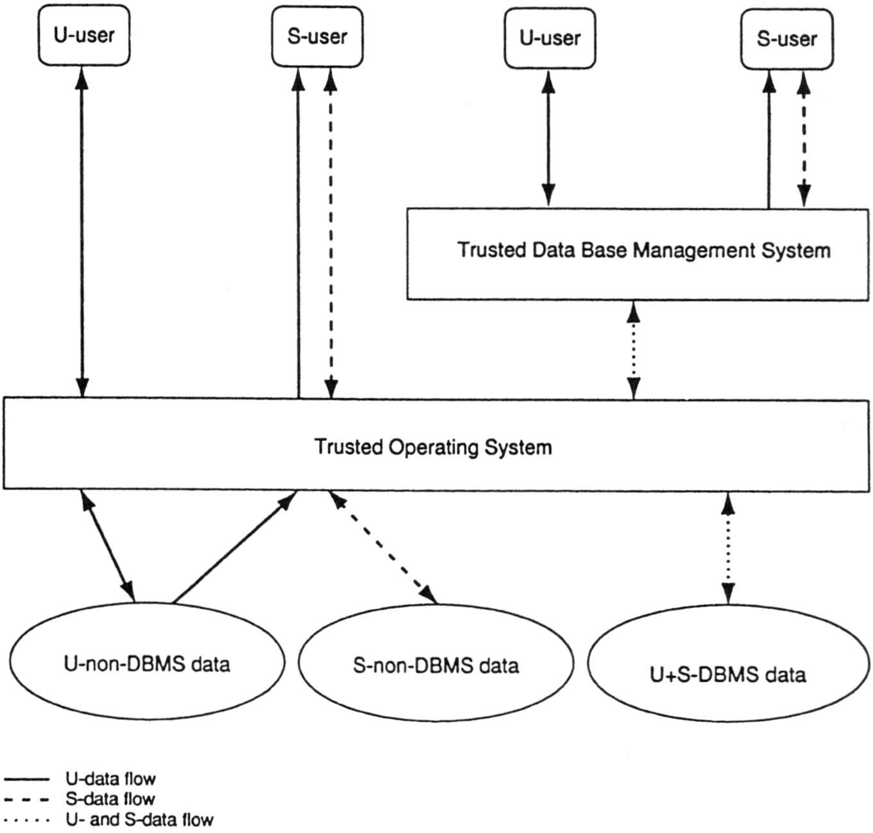

Exhibit 1. Integrated data architecture.

1. *U-data.* Unclassified data files are managed directly by the trusted operating system.
2. *S-data.* Secret data files are managed directly by the trusted operating system.

The trusted operating system does not distinguish between DBMS and non-DBMS data in this architecture. It supports two copies of the DBMS, one that can interact only with U-users and another that can interact only with S-users. These two copies run the same code but with different security labels. The U-DBMS is restricted by the trusted operating system to reading and writing U-data. The S-DBMS, on other hand, can read and write S-data as well as read (but not write) U-data.

This architecture has great promise, but its viability depends on the availability of usable good-performance trusted operating systems. So far,

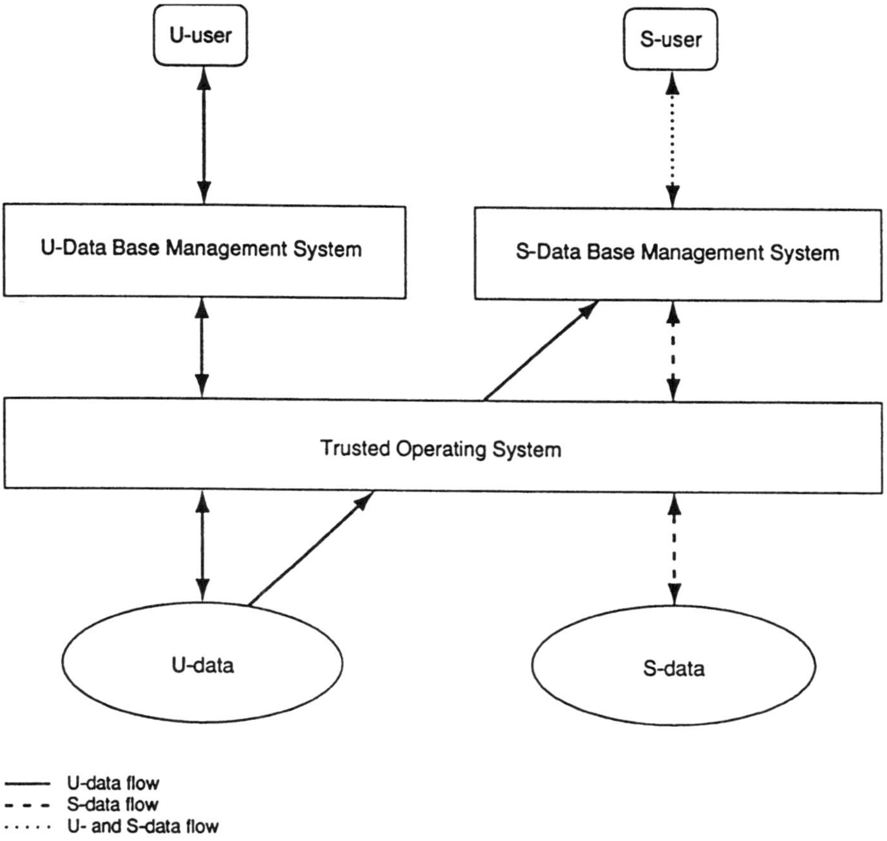

Exhibit 2. Fragmented data architecture.

there are few trusted operating systems, and these lack many of the facilities that users expect modern operating systems to provide. Development of trusted operating systems continues to be active, but progress has been slow. Emergency of strong products in this arena could make the fragmented data architecture attractive in the future.

Replicated Data Architecture

The replicated data architecture is shown in Exhibit 3. This architecture requires physical separation on backend database servers to separate U- and S-users of the database. The bottom half of the diagram shows two physically separated computers, each running a DBMS. The computer on the left hand side manages U-data, whereas the computer on the right hand side manages a mix of U- and S-data. The U-data on the left hand side is replicated on the right hand side.

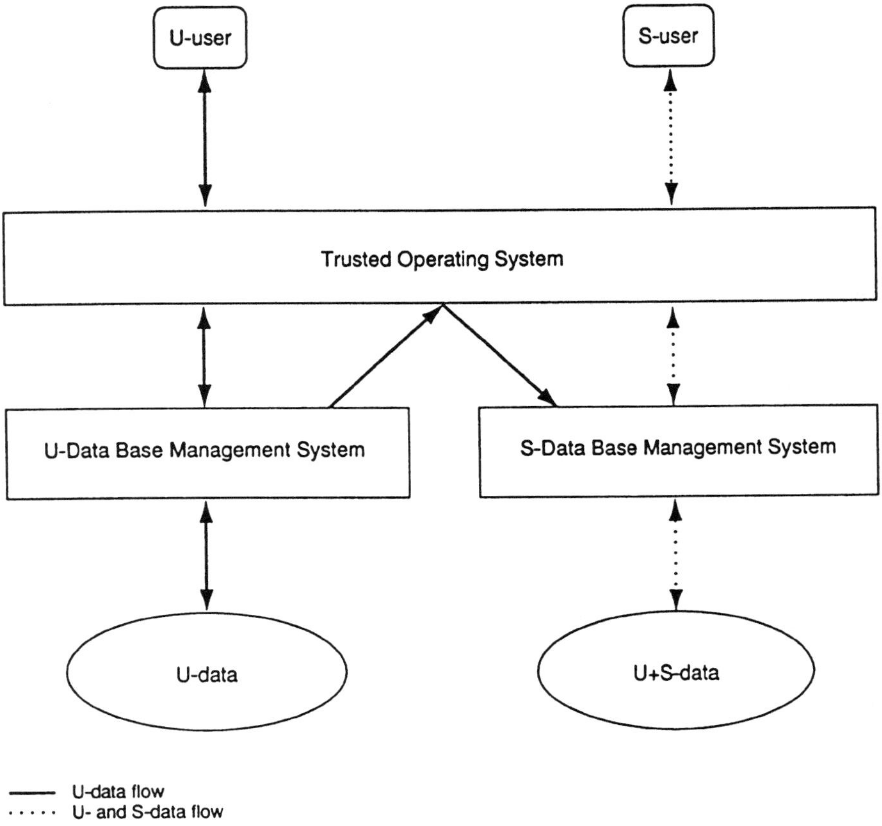

Exhibit 3. Replicated data architecture.

The trusted operating system serves as a front end. It has two objectives. First, it must ensure that a U-user can directly access only the U-backend (left hand side) and that a S-user can directly access only the S-backend (right hand side). Second, the trusted operating system is the sole means for communication from the U-backend to the S-backend. This communication is necessary for updates to the U-data to be propagated to the U-data stored in the S-backend. Providing correct and secure propagation of these updates has been a major obstacle for this architecture, but recent research has provided solutions to this problem. The replicated architecture is viable for a small number of security labels, perhaps a few dozen, but it does not scale gracefully to hundreds or thousands of labels.

ROLE-BASED ACCESS CONTROLS

Traditional DACs are proving to be inadequate for the security needs of many organizations. At the same time, MACs based on security labels are inappropriate for many situations. In recent years, the notion of role-based access control (RBAC) has emerged as a candidate for filling the gap between traditional DAC and MAC.

One of weaknesses of DAC in SQL is that it does not facilitate the management of access rights. Each user must be explicitly granted every privilege necessary to accomplish his or her tasks. Often groups of users need similar or identical privileges. All supervisors in a department might require identical privileges; similarly, all clerks might require identical privileges, different from those of the supervisors. RBAC allows the creation of roles for supervisors and clerks. Privileges appropriate to these roles are explicitly assigned to the role, and individual users are enrolled in appropriate roles from where they inherit these privileges. This arrangement separates two concerns: (1) what privileges should a role get and (2) which user should be authorized to each role. RBAC eases the task of reassigning users from one role to another or altering the privileges for an existing role.

Current efforts at evolving SQL, commonly called SQL3, have included proposals for RBAC based on vendor implementations, such as in Oracle. In the future, consensus on a standard approach to RBAC in relational databases should emerge. However, this is a relatively new area, and a number of questions remain to be addressed before consensus on standards is obtained.

SUMMARY

Access controls have been an integral part of relational database management systems from their introduction. There are, however, major weaknesses in the traditional discretionary access controls built into the standards and products. SQL'89 is incomplete and omits revocation of privileges and control over creation of new relations and views. SQL'92 fixes some of these shortcomings. In the meantime such vendors as Oracle have developed RBAC; other vendors, such as Informix, have started delivering products incorporating mandatory access controls for multilevel security. There is a recognition that SQL needs to evolve to take some of these developments into consideration. If it does, stronger and better access controls can be expected in future products.

Section VIII
Distributed Heterogeneous Systems

A special class of heterogeneous systems is those that not only have products from a number of vendors, but where these products are also geographically distributed. Although distributed systems have been around since the mainframe days with SNA connecting distributed computers, the advent of client/server and intranets and the Internet have brought distributed processing into the main stream of computing.

Continuing our coverage of distributed databases from Section III, Chapter 70 discusses distributed database management systems (DDBMSs) that function in a homogeneous environment, distributed processing in client/server architectures, and some of the issues involved in handling heterogeneous, autonomous, and federated environments.

Distributed data management promotes the sharing and integration of data between corporate departments and systems and the access to that data in heterogeneous systems environments—an arrangement that reflects corporate structure and business requirements. Chapter 71 explores some of the business drivers that influence the design of distributed database technology, and identifies and discusses the 13 functional requirements—or rules—that are the foundation of DDBMSs.

Although distributed networks improve productivity by making applications, processing power, and mass storage readily available to a large user population, networks also make those resources more vulnerable to abuse and misuse. The situation is especially pronounced in connection with electronic data interchange, electronic funds transfer, and electronic mail services, in which unauthorized use, information theft, and malicious file damage can result in substantial financial losses. Chapter 72 describes security issues and options for distributed environments.

Distributed computing takes advantage of high-powered client machines by offloading some of the processing required to these machines. Distributed computing thus brings the computing and data closer to the user. But this also makes it more difficult for the IS departments, which are traditionally responsible for managing the IT for an organization, to manage the distributed computing environment. Chapter 73 covers the management of distributed computing.

Chapter 70

Developments and Challenges in Distributed Data Communications Management Systems

Bhavani Thuraisingham

Although many definitions of a DDBMS have been given, there is no standard definition. This chapter uses the definition of a DDBMS given by Ceri and Pelagatti:[1]

> "A distributed database is a collection of data that is distributed over different computers of a computer network. Each site of the network has autonomous processing capability and can perform local applications. Each site also participates in the execution of at least one global application, which requires accessing data at several sites using a communications subsystem. A distributed database management system supports the creation and maintenance of a distributed database."

Exhibit 1 illustrates a DDBMS. In this system, the nodes are connected through a communications subsystem. This subsystem could be a LAN or a long-haul network. Each node has its own local database management system (DBMS), which is capable of handling local applications. In addition, each node is also involved in at least one global application.

The features of a typical DDBS include the following:[1]

- **Hierarchical control.** Local database administrators are responsible for a set of local databases. A global database administrator has the

0-8493-9989-0/99/$0.00+$.50

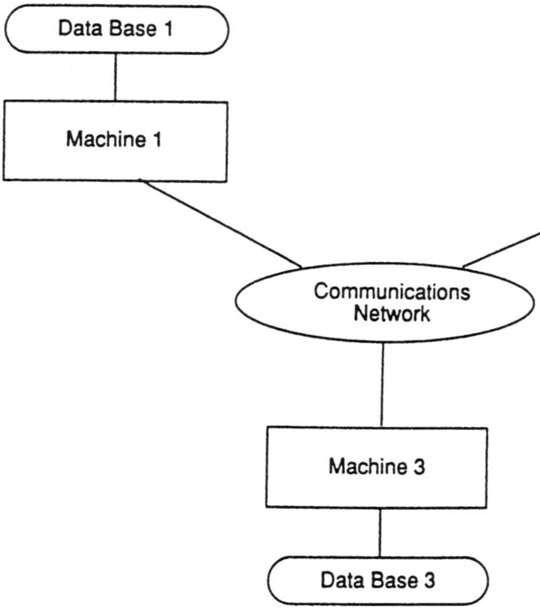

Exhibit 1. A DDBMS in a distributed architecture.

responsibility for the entire database as well as for the local administrators.

- **Data independence.** The physical representation of the database is transparent to the user. In addition, the data distribution is transparent to the user.
- **Redundancy.** To ensure availability of data, multiple copies of the data are maintained.
- **Efficient access.** To ensure efficient access, requests are optimized at two levels. Global optimization determines which data is to be accessed and where the data is located. Local query optimization determines how to perform the local database accesses.
- **Transaction management.** A DDBMS should have the capability of distributed transaction management. Consistency of the data has to be ensured when concurrent transactions execute.
- **Privacy and security.** Data should be accessed or modified only by authorized individuals.

Exhibit 2 illustrates a system architecture for a DDBMS. The distributed execution monitor is responsible for global optimization and generating the execution strategies at the global level. The functions include distributed query processing, distributed transaction management, and

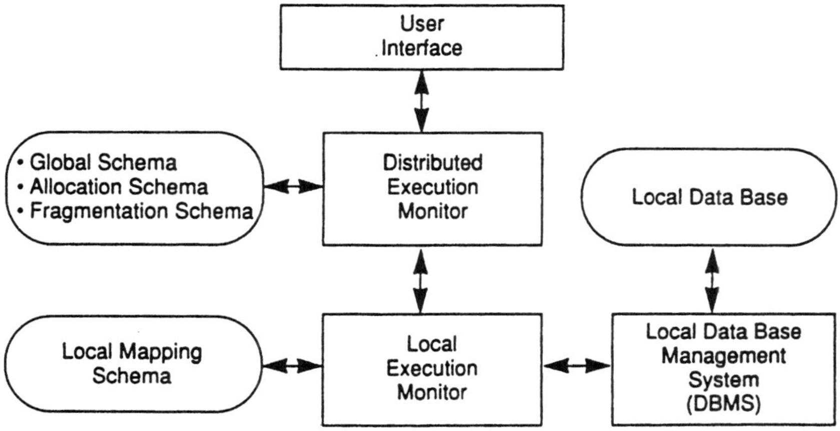

Exhibit 2. The system architecture of a DDBMS.

distributed Metadata management. The local execution monitor is responsible for local optimization and processing and interfaces to the local database management system. The various schemas shown in Exhibit 2 as well as query processing, transaction management, and Metadata management are discussed in subsequent sections of this chapter.

Distributed Database Design

The design of a distributed database involves the creation of schemas for the database's global, fragmentation, allocation, local mapping, and physical attributes, as follows:[1]

- **Designing the global schema.** The entire distributed database is regarded as a single database, and it is designed at the conceptual and logical levels. Different data models can be used to represent the data at the conceptual and logical levels. Here a homogeneous environment is assumed, so the conceptual and logical levels coincide. The relational data model is used at both levels.
- **Designing the fragmentation schema.** Each database relation could be fragmented into several components. The fragmentation schema includes a description of the various components of a relation.
- **Designing the allocation schema.** The distributed database is scattered across several nodes. The allocation schema describes where the relations and fragments of relations are stored.
- **Designing the local mapping schema.** This consists of mappings between the global representational model and the local representational model.

- **Designing the physical schema.** This refers to creating the internal schema of the local databases.

The designs of the conceptual schema and the physical schema are similar for both centralized and distributed systems, so there is no need to discuss them further. Local mapping schemas are necessary only if the global representational model is different from the local representational models. In this case, a homogeneous environment in which the global as well as the local models are relational is assumed. Subsequent sections discuss fragmentation and allocation schemas.

Fragmentation Schema

The database relations could be partitioned into one or more fragments. The Metadata that describes the fragments is the fragmentation schema. There are three types of data fragmentation:

Horizontal fragmentation. The global relation is partitioned into horizontal subsets. The criteria for partitioning depend on the value of some attribute. Exhibit 3 uses samples from a personnel database to illustrate three horizontal partitions of a relation, depending on the values of the city attribute. The first partition consists of all tuple with city NY. The second partition consists of all tuples with city LA. The third partition consists of all tuples with city MPLS.

Vertical Fragmentation

The global relation is partitioned vertically—that is, the attributes of the relation are grouped. The tuples identifier belongs to each group of attributes. Exhibit 4 shows the vertical fragmentation of the relation Electro-Magnetic Pulse. Group 1 consists of social security number (SS#) and name attributes. Group 2 consists of social security number, salary, and city attributes.

Mixed fragmentation. There are two ways to obtain mixed fragmentation. Either a relation is horizontally fragmented first and each horizontal

SS#	Name	Salary	City
S1	N1	70K	NY
S2	N2	80K	NY
S3	N3	75K	NY

SS#	Name	Salary	City
S4	N4	85K	LA
S5	N5	80K	LA

SS#	Name	Salary	City
S6	N6	50K	MPLS

Exhibit 3. Horizontal fragmentation.

SS#	Name
S1	N1
S2	N2
S3	N3
S4	N4
S5	N5
S6	N6

SS#	Salary	City
S1	70K	NY
S2	80K	NY
S3	75K	NY
S4	85K	LA
S5	80K	LA
S6	50K	MPLS

Exhibit 4. Vertical fragmentation.

partition is vertically fragmented, or a relation is vertically fragmented first and each vertical partition is horizontally fragmented.

Allocation Schema

The allocation schema describes the allocation of fragments to nodes. Fragment allocation depends on whether the database is nonredundant or redundant. Determining a nonredundant allocation is less complex. A best-fit approach can be used to determine where the fragment should be stored.

When fragments are replicated, additional complexity is introduced. Two of the methods used for allocating replicated fragments are:

- For each site, it is determined whether the benefit of allocating a fragment is less than the cost. If it is, the fragment is allocated.
- First, the solution to the allocation problem of a nonredundant database is determined. Then replication of fragments is progressively introduced, starting from the most beneficial site. The process is stopped when it is determined that no additional replication is beneficial.

One copy of the fragment is usually designated as its primary copy; the other copies are its secondary copies.

Query Processing

There are two aspects to query processing in a DDBMS: query transformation and query optimization.

Query Transformation

The query transformation process transforms a global query into equivalent fragment queries. This process is performed according to transformation rules and does not depend on the allocation of the fragments. Rules used in the transformation process in centralized systems include the factoring of common subexpressions and pushing selections and projections down in the query tree as much as possible. If selections and projections are performed before the joins, the cost of the joins can be reduced by a considerable amount. Additional rules for query transformation have been formulated for distributed databases to take into account the horizontal and vertical fragmentation. These rules are described in detail by Ceri and Pelagatti.[1]

An example of query transformation follows. The horizontal fragmentation of the relation EMP is shown in Exhibit 3. If a query to retrieve all the tuples in the relation EMP is requested, the query is transformed into the following fragment queries:

- Select all tuples from fragment 1 (i.e., city NY).
- Select all tuples from fragment 2 (i.e., city LA).
- Select all tuples from fragment 3 (i.e., city MPLS).
- Form the union of all the results.

Query Optimization

Whereas query transformation focuses on modifying a query at the logical level, the query optimization process optimizes the query with respect to the cost of executing the query. That is, the alternative execution strategies produced by the query transform must be examined by the query optimizer in terms of the cost of executing them. The cost is usually determined by the number of tuples that are transmitted and the number of join or semijoin operations that must be performed.

The following problems are associated with query optimization:[1]

- **Determining the physical copies of the fragments on which to execute the query.** This process is known as materialization.
- **Selecting the order of execution of operations.** The query transformation process gives a partial order among the operations, but the query optimizer must decide the order of operation when two operators are at the same level in the query tree.
- **Selecting the method for executing each operation.** This is especially important in the case of join and semijoin operations. The optimizer must determine which fragments must be transmitted from one site to another.

Transaction Management

Transaction management in a DDBMS involves the handling of distributed transactions. A distributed transaction is one that executes at multiple sites. The portion of the transaction that executes at a particular site is a subtransaction associated with that site.

Two types of log files are maintained at each node; one is the local log file, which records the subtransaction execution, and the other is the global file, which records the actions of the coordinator of all of the subtransactions. When a transaction commits, either all of the local subtransactions must commit or none should commit, in which case the transaction aborts. The technique used to ensure this requirement is the two-phase commit protocol.

If transactions are executed serially, there will be a performance bottleneck. Therefore, transactions usually execute concurrently. As a result, it must be ensured that the multiple transactions maintain the consistency of the distributed database. Concurrency control techniques ensure the consistency of the distributed database when transactions execute concurrently. There are additional problems in a DDBMS because of the replication of files. It has to be ensured that all of the copies of a file are consistent. The techniques of locking, time-stamping, and validation have been proposed for concurrency control in a DDBMS.

An additional problem of transaction management in a distributed environment is ensuring the consistency of the data in the presence of network partitions. Network partitions occur when certain nodes or links fail.

The various concurrency control techniques used in a DDBMS are described first, then recovery and reliability issues are discussed.

Concurrency Control

In order to ensure consistency, the transaction has to be serializable.

Serializability: A schedule is a sequence of operations performed by multiple transactions. Two schedules are equivalent if their outcomes are the same. A serial schedule is one in which no two transactions execute concurrently. An objective in transaction management is to ensure that any schedule is equivalent to a serial schedule. Such a schedule is called a serializable schedule. Various conditions for testing the serializability of a schedule have been formulated.

Three popular concurrency control techniques that ensure the serializability of schedules are locking, time-stamping, and validation.

Two-phase locking is used to provide concurrency control (i.e., a transaction acquires all necessary locks first before any are released). Two types of locks can be obtained: shared locks and exclusive locks. A shared lock for a data item is requested by a transaction for the read operation. The request is granted if no other transaction has a write lock for the same data item. An exclusive lock is requested by a transaction for the write operation. The request is granted when no other transaction has either a shared lock or an exclusive lock for the same data item.

In a distributed environment, if multiple copies of the data exist, it may be necessary to obtain locks on more than one copy. Three schemes to obtain locks are:

- Exclusive locks are obtained for all copies of the data item. Shared locks are obtained for only one copy.
- Both shared and exclusive locks are obtained for a majority of copies of the data item.
- Only the primary copy of the data item is locked.

Locking can cause deadlocks, which are detected by using a graph called a distributed wait-for graph. The purpose of the algorithm is to detect cycles in the graph.

In the time-stamp technique, each transaction is assigned a time stamp when it begins execution. Similarly, a data item is also assigned a read stamp and a write stamp, which are the time stamps of the most recent transaction that read or updated that data item. When a transaction requests to read or write a data item, certain checks are made between the time stamp of the transaction and the read and write stamps of the data item. If the checks are satisfied, a transaction continues; otherwise, the transaction aborts and restarts with a new time stamp.

There are some additional considerations. The time stamps assigned to the transactions are global time stamps. Because it is difficult to keep the system clocks at each node synchronized, other techniques to assign global time stamps have been devised.

In the validation technique (also called optimistic concurrency control technique), each local transaction is validated first. During this validation, certain checks are performed. If the subtransaction does not pass the validation test, the subtransaction is aborted. This in turn will cause the global transaction to be aborted. A subtransaction that passes the validation test enters a global validation phase. If it fails the global validation, it is aborted. Otherwise, a message is sent to the coordinator that it has passed the global validation. If all the subtransactions pass the global validation, the transaction is committed.

Recovery

A popular recovery technique for distributed transaction is the two-phase commit protocol. In this protocol, one site (usually the site of origin) acts as the coordinator, and other sites at which the transaction executes act as participants. The coordinator and the participants maintain log records and write all their actions on the records. First, the coordinator sends a message to the participants to prepare to commit. Each participant sends a message to the coordinator as to whether it is ready to commit. If all the participants have answered positively, the coordinator sends a commit message to all participants. Otherwise, the coordinator sends an abort message to the participants. If a participant receives a commit message, the subtransaction at that site is committed. If an abort message is received, the subtransaction is aborted.

The two-phase commit protocol has been extended (e.g., to three-phase commit) to accommodate various types of failures (e.g., site failures and network partitions).

Metadata Management

Metadata includes all of the schema information and the constraint information. Schema information, which is also called the data dictionary, is maintained at two levels. One is the global data dictionary and the other is the local data dictionary. The local data dictionary is the dictionary associated with the local DBM S. Only the global data dictionary is discussed here.

The global data dictionary includes information on the global schema, the fragmentation schema, the allocation schema, and the local mapping schema. These schemas are used for the various DDBMS functions(e.g., query processing and transaction management). The constraints handled are the integrity constraints and the security constraints. In addition to the schema and constraint information, the Metadatabase may also contain database statistics. The statistics include profiles of the database.

Metadata management issues common to centralized and distributed systems are maintaining the consistency of the constraints and representing and storing Metadata.

Consistency issues are only now receiving some attention; for example, logic programming techniques are being investigated for consistency checking of integrity constraints. Metadata representation and storage have received considerable attention. Many of the relational database systems use the relational model to represent the Metadata also. Furthermore, the same storage structures and index strategies are used for the data and the Metadata. A major issue in Metadata management in a DDBMS is the distribution of Metadata.

Allocating Metadata

There are three ways to distribute Metadata: centralization, full replication, and distribution.

Centralized Metadata. All the Metadata is stored in one location only. This approach has a limitation, because if the site that stores the Metadata fails, the Metadata cannot be accessed by the other sites.

Fully replicated Metadata. All the Metadata is replicated at each node. The advantage of this approach is the availability; the disadvantage is that the Metadata has to be kept consistent.

Distributed Metadata. The Metadata is distributed (not replicated). That is, the Metadata is fragmented and each node stores zero or more fragments. Usually, the Metadata associated with the local data is stored at that site. Since there is no replication, no two fragments have any Metadata in common.

A combination of the three approaches can also be used. For example, part of the Metadata (e.g., that which is frequently used) could be stored at each site. The rest could be distributed or stored at one site only. Another approach is to maintain a cache at each site to store the frequently used Metadata.

Information about the allocation of the Metadata is usually stored in a directory. That is, the directory is the meta-metadatabase. The directory itself could be centralized, replicated, or even distributed. If the dictionary is not replicated, another directory is needed that specifies where the directory is stored. This way, a hierarchy of directories can be constructed. At some point in the hierarchy, the corresponding directory will be sufficiently small that it can be replicated at each node.

Client/Server Architectures

Most vendors are migrating to the client/server architecture. In such an architecture, the DBMS consists of two components: one at the client and one at the server. The application development environment resides at the client, whereas the server is responsible for data management. The client and the server can reside in a single machine or at different machines connected over a network.

Although the client and the server are usually developed by the same vendor, the ultimate goal is for different clients (developed by different vendors) to communicate with different servers. For example, the client of vendor A should be able to communicate with the server of vendor B. The multiple client/server architecture is illustrated in Exhibit 5. To facilitate communication among multiple clients and servers, the ISO/IEC and is developing a standard called RDA.[2] This draft standard calls for a generic interface for communication between a client and a server. Exhibit 6 shows a possible way of mapping the components of the system architecture onto the client/server architecture. The distributed execution monitor is part of

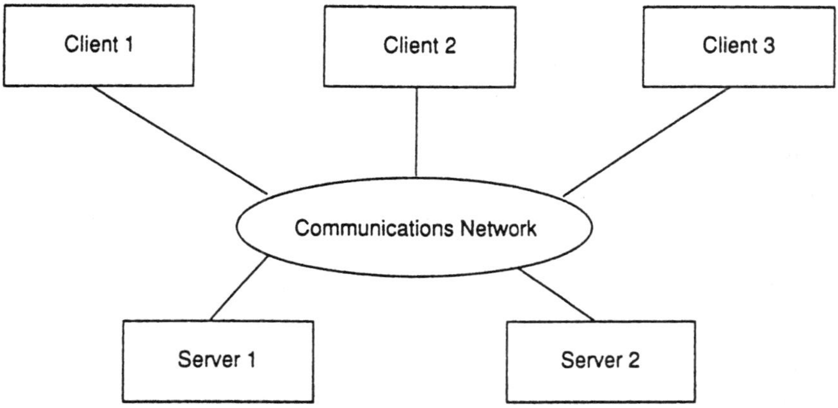

Exhibit 5. Architecture with multiple clients and multiple servers.

the client, and the local execution monitor is part of the server. The two monitors could possibly communicate using the RDA protocol. A more detailed investigation of the communications issues must be carried out.

One of the main goals for the migration to a client/server architecture is to accommodate heterogeneity. Interoperability between different DBMSs is becoming increasingly important. Some of the difficulties involved in interconnecting different DBMSs are discussed in the next section.

Interoperability Issues

Although research on interconnecting different DBMSs has been under way for more than a decade, many of the difficult problems have not been handled until recently. This section discusses heterogeneity and autonomy.

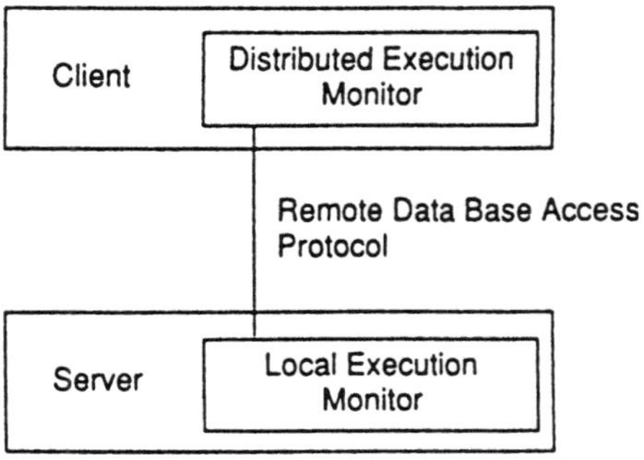

Exhibit 6. Mapping the DDBMS components to the client/server architecture.

Heterogeneity

In the discussion of query processing, transaction management, and Metadata management for a homogeneous environment, it has so far been assumed that the local DBMS are relational and that they use the same algorithms. In a heterogeneous environment, the DBMSs are not the same. One DBMS could be relational and another could be object-oriented. Even DBMSs based on the relational model could use different query language and algorithms. Interconnecting different DBMSs is difficult. This section discusses the issues involved in interconnecting heterogeneous components identified by Scheuermann et al.[3]

Schema (or Data Model) Heterogeneity. Not all the databases in a heterogeneous architecture are represented by the same data model. Therefore, the different conceptual schema must be integrated. To do this, translators that transform the constructs of one data model into those of another are being developed.

The object-oriented approach is also being investigated for handling schema heterogeneity. The idea here is for the users to have a generic view of the entire system. Translators are then necessary to translate the constructs between the generic representation and an individual representation.

Transaction Processing Heterogeneity

Different DBMSs may use different algorithms for transaction processing. Work is being directed toward integrating the various transaction-processing mechanisms. Techniques that integrate locking, time-stamping, and validation mechanisms are being developed. It has been suggested that, in a heterogeneous environment, strict serializability may have to be sacrificed for a weaker form of serializability.

Query Processing Heterogeneity

Different DBMSs use different query processing and optimization strategies. One of the research areas here is to develop a global cost model for distributed query optimization.

Query Language Heterogeneity

Different DBMSs use different query languages. Even if the DBMSs are based on the relational model, one could use SQL and the other relational calculus. Standardization efforts are under way to develop a uniform interface language.

Constraint Heterogeneity

Different DBMSs enforce different and often inconsistent integrity constraints. In a personnel database, one DBMS could enforce a constraint that all employees must work at least 40 hours, whereas another DBMS might not enforce such a constraint.

Semantic Heterogeneity

Data may be interpreted differently at different components. For example, the entity address could mean just the country at one component while another component could interpret it to be the number, street name, city name, and country. It has been recognized that semantic heterogeneity is very difficult to handle.

Research is being conducted on providing solutions to the interoperability of heterogeneous database systems. The problems become even more complex if there are several types of heterogeneity to be handled. For example, the various systems could use not only different data models but also different algorithms. Any solution to the problem in the near term should be customized—that is, the customer's requirements should be identified and solutions should satisfy these requirements.

Autonomy

Although the different DBMSs in the network should cooperate so that users of one DBMS could access remote data, it is also desirable that the local DBMSs have some degree of autonomy. Cooperation and autonomy have conflicting goals. In most cases, the database administrators of the DBMSs have to negotiate with one another to cooperate while maintaining some degree of autonomy. Sheth and Larson have identified various types of autonomy.[4] These include:

- **Design autonomy.** Total design autonomy would imply that for each component a different design can be chosen. For example, the data to be managed, the policies to be enforced, the query processing and transaction management algorithms used, and the semantic interpretation of data could all be unique to that component.
- **Communication autonomy.** Total communication autonomy implies that a component will determine who it wishes to communicate with.
- **Execution autonomy.** Total execution autonomy implies that the local operations of a component are not affected by the global users in any way.
- **Association autonomy.** Total association autonomy implies that a component can decide what information to share with the others and when to share it.

Autonomy is becoming especially important for a federated environment. A federated database system (FDS) has been defined to be a collection of cooperating database systems that are possibly autonomous and heterogeneous.[4] The intent is for a database system to continue its local operation and at the same time determine for itself when to participate in a federation. The database systems participating in the federation could be homogeneous, in which case they are all designed and operate identically, or they could be heterogeneous with respect to several aspects (e.g., data models, designs, semantics, constraints). While heterogeneity brings about complexities not present in a homogeneous environment, autonomy, which enables a database system to make its own decisions about when to join or leave a federation, makes the task of developing an FDS even more difficult. Recently, several research-and-development activities on FDSs have been reported. Although some promising results have been obtained, several tasks, such as multiuser updates have yet to be carried out successfully. It has been more or less agreed that the solutions to interconnecting multiple database systems are still in the future.

Conclusion

Research in DDBMS has been active for the past several years. As a result, many prototypes are now available, and the principles of homogeneous DDBMSs are well understood. Vendors are providing data distribution tools using client/server architectures, and standardization efforts are also under way. Current research is focusing mainly on handling heterogeneous and autonomous environments. This is because as DBMSs are put into use more widely, interoperability of these DBMSs within heterogeneous and autonomous environments is necessary, creating difficulties that are not present in a homogeneous environment.

The steps to achieving interoperability are by no means straightforward. Therefore, research should proceed in two directions. One is to provide solutions to interconnecting heterogeneous database systems to satisfy a customer's needs. A series of prototypes, increasing in complexity, should be developed to test the policy and algorithms before developing an operational system. The other is to explore the principles of interconnecting DBMSs in heterogeneous and autonomous environments as well as to develop appropriate standards. Such a two-way approach would not only satisfy the immediate needs of customers but provide the direction for developing useful DDBMSs in the future.

Notes

1. S. Ceri and G. Pelagatti, *Distributed Databases, Principles and Syst ems* (New York: McGraw-Hill, 1984).
2. "Remote Database Access, " ISO/IEC DIS 9579-1 and ISO/IEC DIS 9579-2 (1993).
3. P. Scheuermann et al., "Report on the Workshop on Heterogeneous Database Systems," *ACM SIG MOD Record* 22, no. 3 (1990).
4. A. Sheth and J. Larson, "Federated Database Systems for Managing Distributed, Heterogeneous, and Autonomous Databases," *ACM Computing Surveys* 22, no. 3 (1990).

Chapter 71

Distributed Processing for Distributed Databases

Michael D. Krasowski

Legacy data is stored in DBMSs but is not easily shared, and legacy databases are usually built without consideration for the company's future business requirements. They are generally developed as point solutions that consist of specific hardware, operating systems, and DBMS software (e.g., engineering applications independent of business applications).

Traditionally, MIS departments relied on a single vendor. Now, many applications need multivendor solutions, and many installations include multiple hardware vendors, operating systems, and DBMSs. Although the distribution of data is acceptable, the inability to share it is unacceptable. Distributed database technology allows data to be shared and gives autonomy to the users who most need the data.

Incremental Growth

Although large mainframes can cost $150,000 to$175,000 per MIPS, quite powerful workstations are available for $5,000 per MIPS, or less than 5% of the cost per mainframe MIPS. Although workstation performance cannot be equated simply with that of mainframes, workstations present an opportunity for work groups to manage their own data.

Adding computing resources has generally involved upgrading to a large mainframe or adding a new mainframe and spreading the costs to all users of the service. Most in-house chargeback algorithms, however, do not fairly distribute the costs of the service to the departments that most use it. Incremental additions to the workstation hardware environment support

0-8493-9989-0/99/$0.00+$.50

not only a flexible IA environment but the financial philosophy that users should be directly responsible for the costs they incur in managing their data. Centralized, monolithic databases on expensive mainframes inhibit incremental growth; distributed database technology permits incremental hardware growth at reasonable cost.

Reliability and Availability

Performance can be improved by using DDBMSs because data can be stored locally on the workstation or server on a local-area network (LAN) without compromising the ability to share data. Workstations attached to LANs that manage data through a DBMS are called database servers. Terminals or workstations must communicate with the mainframe through wide-area networks (WANs) or broader backbone networks, limiting the effects of slower response times and higher communications costs.

Distributed database technology allows data to be replicated in an orderly way. Users can then access copies of data in the event of CPU failure, network failure, or virtually any other system problem. Distributed database technology improves performance because the data is closer to the work group, which does not depend on a single, central site.

The Rules of Distribution

A DDBMS should support 12 functional requirements (i.e., rules) and a zero rule. These rules are a subset of the system's total requirements; MIS managers must still quantify the importance of distributed technology to their companies. Distributed databases do not necessarily imply distributed processing, although DDBMSs may support distributed processing.

Each DDBMS-connected computer is an autonomous DBMS, and its users can access any data in the network as if it were stored at their site, although the data is physically stored in distinct DBMSs at various sites (see Exhibit 1). The 13 rules are discussed in the following sections; the examples cited are based on the relational model. (Rules 1 through 12, which are subsidiary rules that refine the functional capabilities required by rule 9, affect each other and should not be viewed as having equal importance; some may be more or less important than others, depending on an individual company's IA.)

Rule 0. Rule 0 is a system as it appears to the user.

Rule 1: Local Autonomy. Local data is locally owned, managed, and controlled; each site in the network is autonomous. Local operations remain local, and the fact that the site is participating in a DDBMS should not affect the applications that ran successfully before this participation was implemented. This rule helps preserve the investment in legacy systems and

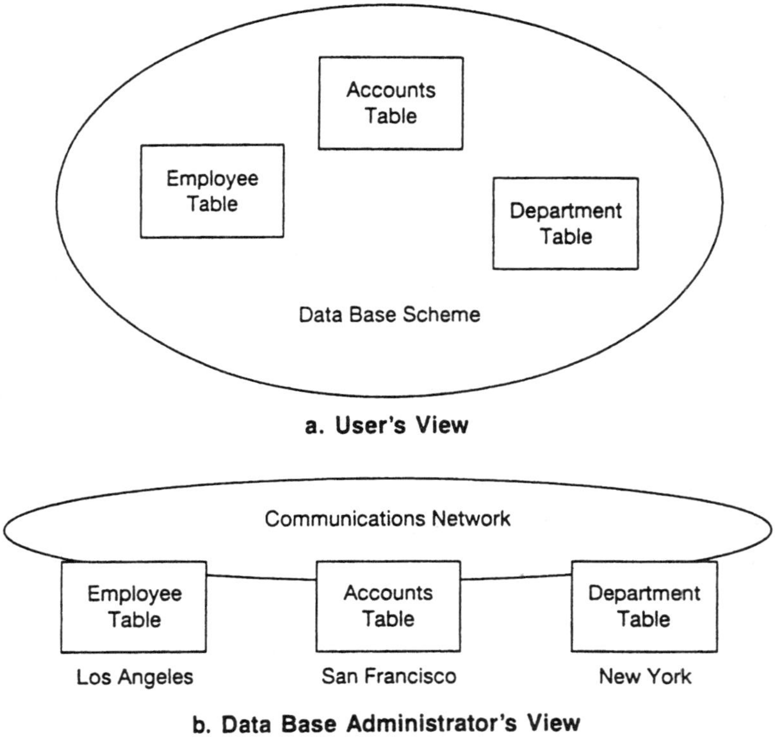

Exhibit 1. DDBMS model.

data while allowing interconnection with other systems and incremental capacity growth at each site.

Rule 2: Independence from Central Site. Implied by Rule 1, this rule helps avoid bottlenecks and weaknesses at central sites. If all users rely on a central site that fails, all users are affected. Therefore, no single site should have the central dictionary, central query processing, central concurrency control, central recovery control, nor should it store all the data. Other sites that participate in the DDBMS may have copies of the data needed (see Rule 6).

Rule 3: Continuous Operation. The DDBMS should operate continuously and should not have any planned shutdowns. It should also allow for the addition or removal of sites from the distributed database network without affecting service at other sites or of existing applications. Relations (i.e., tables), pieces of relations (i.e., fragments), or copies of relations (i.e., replicas) should be capable of being created or removed without disrupting processing at other sites. If a new release of the DDBMS software is installed at one or more sites (but not at all sites), there should be no disruption of service.

Rule 4: Location Independence. Users of distributed databases should never have to know where data is physically located. The data they are using may be at their local site, at remote sites, or both. Applications logic can be simplified in that the programmer does not have to specify at which site the data is located, reducing application code. This information should be kept in a catalog or data dictionary to be referenced by the programs. The data or tables should be movable, however, from one location or site to another (i.e., data migration) for performance reasons without any effect on application logic.

The data dictionary of the DDBMS must be able to map local names (e.g., EMPNUM) to global names (e.g., EMPLOYEE-NUM at New York but created at Los Angeles). If the EMPNUM table is moved, the data dictionary must be updated to reflect the new location; the data dictionary subsystem itself must be distributed and consistent at all sites, and the global name must never change.

Rule 5: Fragmentation Independence. Because a table or relation in a DDBMS environment is a single, logical object, it may be necessary for performance reasons to organize a table into multiple, physical subtables. Although the fragments are totally unknown to the user, the database administrator must be aware of the fragments, define them, and allocate them to the appropriate node. The following is an example of an SQL fragment definition in which customer accounts must be physically split for each branch:

```
CREATE TABLE ACCOUNTS

ACCOUNTS#, BRANCH, CUSTOMER, BALANCE, TYPE)

CREATE FRAGMENT SF1

AS SELECT ACCOUNT#, BRANCH, CUSTOMER, BALANCE, TYPE

FROM ACCOUNTS WHERE BRANCH-SF

CREATE FRAGMENT LA1

AS SELECT ACCOUNT#, BRANCH, CUSTOMER, BALANCE, TYPE

FROM ACCOUNTS

WHERE BRANCH-LA
```

The database administrator must also be able to define the location of the fragment or table to the global catalog; that portion of the global catalog is often called the file or table allocation catalog—for example:

```
LOCATE  FRAGMENT  LA1  AT  CPU12

LOCATE  FRAGMENT  SF1  AT  CPU65
```

Users see only the table ACCOUNTS and should not have access to any fragment name or knowledge about the physical location of the fragments. Database administrators have access to and control of the fragment and allocation portion of the catalog.

The DDBMS software can reconstruct the fragments by using the relational operators UNION and JOIN. The example in Exhibit 2 is called a horizontal fragment because it was split on a tuple (i.e., row) boundary. Fragments SF1 and LA1 can be recombined by using the UNION operator: SF1 LA1 is equivalent to ACCOUNTS. A table split on an attribute (i.e., column) boundary is called a vertical fragment and can be recombined by using the JOIN operator.

Vendor support of fragments involves many difficult implementation issues. For example, if a user updates the table ACCOUNTS, updating one or both of the fragments may be necessary. In addition, updating a table (actually a fragment) would cause the record (or tuple) to migrate to the appropriate site to conform with the fragment definition in the catalog (e.g., account record ACCOUNT#=123 is located in the fragment SF1 because ACCOUNTS BRANCH=SF; if the branch is changed to LA for account record 123, the DDBMS would migrate that record to fragment LA1).

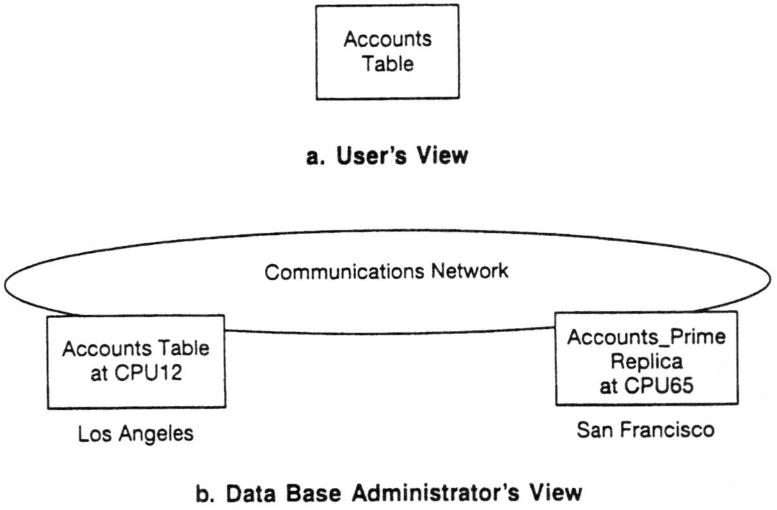

Exhibit 2. Replicas.

Fragments behave like relational VIEWs. Updateable VIEWs are either not supported by some vendors or supported only on views of a single table. If vendors do not solve the updateable view issue, they cannot solve this problem.

Rule 6: Replication Independence. A relation or fragment can be represented by more than one distinct, physically stored replica or copy at more than one site. Replicas are totally unknown to the user (except for the database administrator) and serve two purposes:

- Performance — If a query can be serviced locally (using a replica and avoiding the network overhead), performance over a nonlocal query can be improved. The term query refers not only to requests to read data but also to insert, delete, and update operations. These operations may be initiated interactively or embedded in an application.
- Availability of data — If the site where the data resides does not respond to the query, the DDBMS can search for the closest replica and retrieve the data (see Exhibit 2). The following is an example of an SQL replica definition in which customer accounts must be physically replicated at other branches:

```
CREATE TABLE ACCOUNTS

(ACCOUNT#, BRANCH, CUSTOMER, BALANCE, TYPE)

CREATE REPLICA ACCOUNTS_PRIME

FROM ACCOUNTS
```

The database administration must also be able to define the location of the replica to the global catalog through the table allocation catalog—for example:

```
LOCATE ACCOUNTS AT CPU12

LOCATE REPLICA ACCOUNTS_PRIME AT CPU65
```

Because replicas are live copies, when an update is performed on the primary copy of the table, all replicas must also be updated; this process is called update propagation. Management of update propagation is tricky, depending on the algorithm for handling the propagation of the updates. Each copy must reflect the update. As the number of replicas increases, although read-only access times decrease, update response times increase (because there are more replicas to keep in synch).

Other schemes or partial solutions include deriving read-only copies, called snapshots, which resolve the update propagation issue but introduce another problem: retention of data that no longer supports business requirements. (Surprisingly, users can live with this data, especially when it is consolidation or summary data.) Snapshots are like views, except that they are stored in the database. The following is an example of an SQL snapshot definition in which a replica of the ACCOUNTS table must be refreshed or updated every day:

```
CREATE SNAPSHOT ACCOUNTS_PRIME
AS SELECT*
FROM ACCOUNTS
REFRESH EVERY DAY
LOCATE SNAPSHOT ACCOUNTS_PRIME AT CPU65
```

Rule 7: Distributed Query Processing. Distributed query processing is a query (e.g., read or update) that can span more than one site and is more complex than it appears. A request should support multisite views and integrity constraints, which can be foreign keys across nodes, primary keys across nodes in the case of fragments, or a logic constraint on a query. For example, certain employee information in a particular department is located at a different site from the employee and department tables, but multisite views and integrity constraints still appear to the user as a single-site database.

Due to such complexities and others (e.g., cardinality, including the table's number of tuples or records, machine capacity of each site, and network speeds and disk space constraints), a query optimizer should be an integral part of any DDBMS. Query optimization becomes much more complicated in a distributed environment, however, where queries can involve the services of several local servers. The optimizer must determine which requests to send to which site, how best to combine the results, and how to analyze communications speeds and the amount of traffic on the data lines. For example, when a distributed database is first activated, it polls the participating local databases and updates its system catalog or dictionary with current information about those local databases. The optimizer's output is the query execution plan used by the coordinator node; the optimizer organizes the query into subqueries, sends the subqueries to appropriate nodes, receives and consolidates the results, and presents the resultant data to the process that initiated the query.

Because the optimization process can involve system overhead at one or more sites, the ability to compile queries before they are used can be desirable. Over time, the execution plan derived from a combined query becomes less efficient as the dynamics of the database change.

Rule 8: Distributed Transaction Management. This rule covers two important areas of transaction management: recovery and concurrency. A transaction is an all-or-nothing proposition; either all activities required to complete the transaction are completed or none can be completed. A single transaction can involve many sites and many updates at each site.

Recovery is the process of correcting errors caused by failure and restoring the database to a consistent (i.e., correct) state. In a distributed DBMS environment, there is a greater possibility for failure, yet the effect of a failure is less than in a centralized DBMS environment because data may still be available locally or at other remote sites that have not failed. If a transaction performs some, but not all, updates and then fails, those updates (called uncommitted updates) must be rolled back to their state prior to the update.

If there is failure and the transaction completes successfully, the uncommitted updates must be committed, or made permanent; rolling back uncommitted updates is the recovery-control process. A method or protocol is required to ensure that the transaction is either committed at all sites or rolled back at all sites. The two-phase commit protocol is the most common method for ensuring reasonable consistency.

The two-phase commit protocol requires that one site manage the committing or the rolling back of the transaction; the site that initiated the transaction is generally responsible for managing this process and is called the coordinator. If one site is selected to manage every transaction and if that site fails, none of the transactions in any of the sites can be initiated or completed. This loss of autonomy violates the spirit of local autonomy (Rule 2). The sites that help complete the transaction are called participants. Because transactions could come from any site and could be required to execute at any site, each site must be able to act as coordinator and participant.

Concurrency control helps ensure that two processes do not operate on the same data simultaneously. Three forms of inconsistency can result:

- Lost updates — Updates are lost through improper backups or undoing a transaction.
- Dirty reads — Data is read before a transaction is committed.
- Nonrepeatable reads — The system reads data before and after an update.

To prevent these anomalies, systems use locking. For example, if two transactions from two coordinators (e.g., from sites B and C) are pending at site A, site A is responsible for locking out one transaction while allowing the other transaction access to the data.

There are many varieties of locking schemes and different levels of granularity (e.g., table, tuple, or field). In distributed database environments, each local site is responsible for managing the locking of its data. Because each site is a different system, site A may not know that it is waiting for a lock to release at site B, and site B is waiting for site A to release a lock, a condition called global deadlock. The easiest and most common deadlock detection scheme is the time-out. With time-out, after a predetermined period of time, the DDBMS assumes that a global deadlock has occurred and the coordinator begins rolling back the transaction.

Rule 9: Hardware Independence. A DDBMS has achieved hardware independence when the same DDBMS software can operate on multiple hardware platforms. The fact that one vendor's product can run on 50 platforms and another on only five does not mean that the 50-platform product is better. If the information architecture specifies three hardware platforms, the vendor that supports those platforms has achieved hardware independence.

Rule 10: Operating System Independence. Operating system independence closely resembles hardware independence (Rule 9) and requires no further explanation.

Rule 11: Network Independence. A DDBMS that can be supported on different hardware and operating systems must support a variety of communications protocols. From the viewpoint of the DDBMS, the hardware, the operating system, and the communications network can all be considered providers of reliable services.

Rule 12: DBMS Independence. DBMS independence is the next logical sequence of data independence following rules 9, 10, and 11. Different (i.e., heterogeneous) DBMSs can participate in a distributed database environment. What appears to users as a single logical database may be several physical databases, each supported by different DBMS software. For example, users of DBMS software product X want to access data at another site that uses DBMS software product Y. A common interface is required to allow each vendor's DBMS product to participate in a multivendor distributed database environment by handling all the functional requirements of the rules. No common interface currently exists, however, although there are provisions, called gateways, for retrieval and update between relational DBMSs as well as between nonrelational DBMSs, which use very complicated gateways.

A gateway is an interface between DDBMS products from different vendors (see Exhibit 3). If DDBMS product X must interface with three other DBMS products, it must supply three gateways. Gateways work in one direction only, however, so if DDBMS product X has a gateway to DBMS Y, X's users can access data in Y, but not the other way around—unless a gateway that interfaces with X is provided by product Y. The number of gateways proliferates quickly for vendors willing to participate in

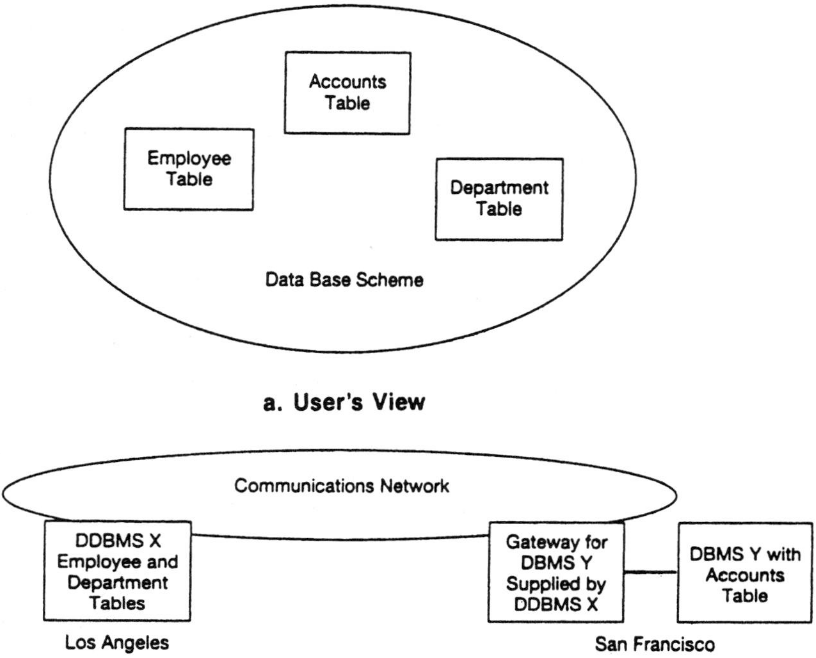

a. User's View

b. Data Base Administrator's View

Exhibit 3. Gateways.

heterogeneous DDBMS environments. A common distributed database interface is needed to address all the issues, including recovery, two-phase commit, locking protocols, and internal data representation translation.

Conclusion

Although DDBMS technology is immature, and DDBMS vendors implement only some of the functional requirements identified in the rules described in this chapter, the vendors' strengths are primarily read-only access and limited update in a heterogeneous hardware, software, and network environment that includes gateways. As DDBMSs evolve, however, sharing and integration capabilities should improve.

Distributed database technology should also enable companies to protect investments in their current DBMSs while allowing new database developments in which incremental costs are added more closely to the users of the data. Adding distributed database technology to the information architecture should support the integration of some legacy data as well as the business requirements that drive the distribution of data throughout the company and around the world.

Chapter 72
Securing Distributed Data Networks

Nathan J. Muller

Access controls are needed to prevent unauthorized local access to the network and to control remote access through dial-up ports. The three minimum levels of user access usually assigned are: public, private, and shared access. Public access allows all users to have read-only access to file information. Private access gives specific users read-and-write file access, whereas shared access allows all users to read and write to files.

Perhaps the most difficult application to secure is the shared database environment offered by LANs. When a company offers network access to one or more databases, it must restrict and control all user query operations. Each database should have a protective key, or series of steps, known only to those individuals entitled to access the data. To ensure that intruders cannot duplicate the data from the system files, users should first have to sign on with passwords and then prove that they are entitled to the data requested. Passwords should have a minimum of six or seven characters; passwords with fewer characters are too easily broken by brute-force guessing.

Plaintext passwords are especially vulnerable on LANs because each guess increases the chance of unauthorized entry by a factor of 1 x n, where n equals the number of passwords on the LAN. A user ID should be suspended after a certain number of passwords have been entered to reduce the chance of a trial-and-error procedure's being used to successfully access the operating system. In addition, to help track any inconsistencies, the IS security function should obtain a daily printout of the keys and passwords used.

Password Protection

To maintain confidentiality, passwords should be difficult to guess or discover with random keyboard combinations. The most effective password is one that is long and obscure yet easily remembered by the

0-8493-9989-0/99/$0.00+$.50

workstation user. Changing passwords frequently and using a multilevel password-protection scheme can also help ensure confidentiality.

There are two systems of password protection that organizations can employ to maintain security: hierarchical and specific. With hierarchical passwords, users employ a defined password to gain access to a designated security level, as well as all lower levels. With specific passwords, however, users can access only the intended level. Although specific-level passwords offer greater security, they require that a senior, trusted employee have multiple passwords to access the many databases and associated levels used daily. Password levels, especially specific levels, also make the task of network management more complex.

LAN administrators (who may be from the IS group or a functional department) must select and implement a particular password security method; they must also ensure that the connected workstations play an active role in supporting password use. For example, when a user enters the password, the monitor should automatically blank out all key entries to minimize the risk of exposing the password to casual observers. The LAN administrator can also install password routines that do not display any information on the screen or that sound an audible alarm and lock the keyboard after a specified number of failed entry attempts. In addition, the LAN administrator should survey the password master file, keep the file on disk, change any infrequently used passwords, and review risks periodically whenever a breach of security is suspected.

Distributed Authentication and Authorization

As with traditional mainframe and minicomputer systems, the security features of the operating system are crucial to network security. LAN software usually offers log-on security, which requires a user to enter a password to access the system. Most passwords identify the user and associate the user with a specific workstation and perhaps a designated shift, work group, or department. Passwords provide a minimum level of security and do not require special equipment, such as keys or card readers.

Reliance on passwords has drawbacks, however. Chief among them is that users do not always maintain password confidentiality—nor does the network itself. The danger of focusing only on passwords is that after any intruders get through this security shield, they have free rein and may be able to access any resource on the network, including connections to EDI gateways and other electronic messaging systems that provide access to the stored files of the organization's creditors and trading partners.

Authentication services provide an effective way to implement password protection in the distributed environment. As an alternative to requiring every computer to store and manage the passwords of all users, an authentication service stores a unique number (or key) that corresponds to each user's password. The authentication server knows all of the passwords on the network and checks them on behalf of the clients. When a user wants to access a network resource, the authentication service checks the submitted password against the key assigned to that user. If the password and the key match, the authentication service verifies to the network resource that users are who they claim to be.

Authentication services can also be configured to perform a variety of useful access functions. Not only can they verify the separate identities of two users, they can set up a verified channel over which the two users can exchange messages, requests, or data.

Related to authentication services are authorization services. Once unique identities and a means of verifying them have been established, distributed security requires a mechanism that allows legitimate users to gain access to the services they need but shuts out others. Access control lists (ACLs), widely used in standalone systems, are the basis for distributed authorization services. When a user accesses a resource, the authorization service checks that person's identity against the resource's ACL to determine the user's clearance to perform an operation or to access privileges, and either clears the access request or rejects it.

There are two levels of authorization: discretionary control and mandatory control. Discretionary access control allows privilege levels to be defined (if desired) for users in the environment. Mandatory access control requires that privileges be defined for every user and resource in the environment. Mandatory access controls add an implementation cost and can be complicated to administer; however, they may actually be more cost-effective than enforcing and managing such controls manually or through centralized procedures.

Key and Card Systems

The simplest key systems require users to insert a key in a lock to turn on the computer. Some vendors market external hard disks, keyboards, and modem switches incorporating key locks. With lock-and-key systems, however, intruders can pick the lock or duplicate the keys. To help minimize this threat, security personnel should keep keys in a secure cabinet where the keys can be checked out and their use can be monitored.

LAN administrators can also employ a magnetic card-reading system to control access to workstations. Card systems offer more flexibility than simple key systems in that they allow users to access data from any available workstation simply by inserting a card into a reader attached to the workstation; most banking ATMs use this type of security, combined with access codes and personal identification numbers (PINs). The card key system allows access-level definition for each user rather than for each workstation.

These cards are more difficult to duplicate than metal keys. Whereas lost keys can be copied and returned without ever being reported as missing, the loss of a magnetic card is generally reported promptly. If users plan to take cards out of the building, the cards should not contain a company logo, street address, or anything that could identify the company. A simple printed statement to mail the card to a post office box is sufficient. The LAN administrator should reserve a post office box for this purpose, listing it under a fictitious company to maintain complete security.

Although cards with magnetic stripes are the most popular, other types—bar-code, plastic, and proximity cards—are also available. Some companies favor plastic cards with magnetics embedded in the core for employee entrance control as well as workstation control. Although cards encoded with bar codes for optical readers may be chosen, they are relatively easy to duplicate. Proximity cards, which can be read by radio frequency at distances ranging from a few inches to 10 feet, may be unsuitable for offices in which the workstations may be close together.

LAN administrators should not issue the same card for both workstation identification and access to other areas of the company. The workstation deserves a higher level of security and closer control of card distribution than company-access cards. The IS department can also choose smart cards as possible security alternatives. These devices, which contain embedded microprocessors, accommodate a range of security tasks, including performing online encryption, recording a time-on/time-off log, and providing password identification. Such devices offer a viable security option for both local and remote access control. The major drawback of both key and card systems is that access control can (willingly or unwillingly) transfer to someone other than the authorized user.

SECURING DISTRIBUTED DEVICES AND FILES

In addition to controlling access to databases, LAN managers should evaluate all shared resources that can be accessed through the network (e.g., applications, directories, or corporate files) and should implement some type of access restriction for each. Other security measures that can be employed, often in combination, include:

- Diskette and drive controls.
- Data encryption.
- Callback systems.
- Network operating systems with built-in security features.

Diskette and Drive Controls

LAN security is weakest at the point of entry. Removable disks are vulnerable to physical theft, unauthorized access, false data, and viruses. To avoid theft and unauthorized copying of removable diskettes, data cartridges, and hard drives, these items should be stored in a locked cabinet; critical diskettes (e.g., backup copies of sensitive files) can be stored in the corporate safe. Users should create several backup copies of sensitive files weekly or daily to provide a reliable source of archived data for restoral in the event of a system failure.

Backup copies of data help to prevent the spread of computer worms and viruses. If an infected diskette should contaminate network resources, multiple backup copies made before the virus infection occurred are available to restore the affected files, application programs, databases, and operating systems.

A removable hard disk is ideal for transferring large files between machines, for archiving and backup tasks, and for use as a secondary storage device. Some removable drives are entirely-self-contained; others use removable cartridges that contain only the disk itself. Removable cartridges are best for applications in which security and long-term portability are the most important considerations.

Disk-locking programs are available to prevent program diskettes from operating properly if copied or used with an unauthorized host computer. LAN administrators can protect data diskettes and files with passwords or modify them so that they allow access to data only when used with a specific program disk.

Eliminating access to removable diskettes provides the highest level of protection against data theft. A bar placed over the diskette drive can prevent intruders from removing diskettes or completely removing the drive from the computer. Keyboard locks are another option to prevent access to the hard disk.

Another method of securing diskette copying activities is to employ diskless workstations. A diskless workstation allows users to store all information on the network server or local hard disk, thereby eliminating the need for diskettes. These workstations offer several potential benefits from a security standpoint. They eliminate the possibility of diskette theft, unauthorized copying, or concealing information downloaded from the host computer. The absence of diskette drives also lessens the risk of introducing a virus into the network through infected input diskettes.

The environment in which diskless workstations operate presents another security benefit. Networks composed of these workstations rely on a centralized storage medium, such as a network file server, to boot an operating system and launch applications, download information, and generate hard copy on network printers. The diskless workstation usually houses local RAM storage and a microprocessor chip (e.g., an Intel 80386) that processes the information after it has been downloaded from the server. In this configuration, the diskless workstation assumes a dual role. First, it retains the information processing capability of a typical microcomputer. Second, it assumes a role in the network configuration that is similar to that of a host-dependent dumb terminal, relying on the file server to store, distribute, and print information.

For many organizations, diskless workstations may be impractical. If they are selected, however, the secure placement of printers, terminals, and file servers, as well as the placement of users with access to those resources, must be examined. This security procedure ensures that a user assigned to a diskless workstation cannot copy or print information stored on a standard LAN workstation with a nearby printer.

In the final analysis, the type of disk storage facility required depends on the duties of each workstation user. Therefore, a variety of safeguards should be in place to accommodate the differing needs of users.

Data Encryption

Data encryption, also known as cryptography, is a method of scrambling information to disguise its original meaning. The concept of cryptography is simple: two communicating devices are programmed to use the same scheme to code and decode messages. Encryption provides the only practical means of protecting information transmitted over dispersed communications networks. Because intruders cannot read encrypted data, the information is not vulnerable to passive or active attack.

When implemented along with error detection and correction, encryption offers a highly effective and inexpensive way to secure communications links. For example, file encryption with decryption at the user workstation adds security to both the file server and the transmission medium. The data is secure from other workstations, illegal taps, and interception of spurious electromagnetic radiation.

Because common carriers use a variety of media that radiate signals—including unshielded copper lines, microwaves, and satellites—data encryption should be implemented whenever sensitive data is transmitted through the public data network, as in EDI and EFT, for example. Although either the hardware or software can perform encryption, hardware-based encryption provides more speed and security, because an intruder who is skilled in programming will not usually be able to interfere with the encryption hardware. Online encryption requires the installation of encryption and decryption units at both ends of the communications link.

Cryptographic methods involve the use of an encryption key, a string of characters used in conjunction with an algorithm to scramble and unscramble messages. For example, if intruders know the algorithm, they will be unable to decode the scrambled information unless they also know the specific encryption key. The more characters the key contains, the more difficulty an intruder encounters when attempting to breach security. The strength of a crypotographic system lies in the quality and secrecy of the keys selected.

Another encryption method, public key systems, offers a relatively high degree of security. Public key encryption techniques use a two-part key structure to eliminate the problem of sharing a single encryptiony permits users to encode data files with a public key that is associated with a specific user. The public key can encrypt but not decrypt a file. A private key, associated with each set of public keys, enables users to decrypt files. The key used to decrypt a file is associated with, and available to, only a single user; this minimizes the likelihood that a key will be copied or discovered by unauthorized users. Furthermore, because the decryption key is valid for only one user, it cannot be used to decrypt files intended for a different user. There is no need to keep the public keys secret or to risk compromising private keys by transmitting them between various users.

Presently, encryption methods offer the only practical means for protecting information transmitted through complex communications networks using telephone lines, microwaves, or satellites. Users must select an encryption system that ensures a sufficiently complex encryption algorithm to present an effective obstacle to would-be intruders. The encryption method selected must be weighed against the need for data security as well as the cost factors, including the cost of decreased data throughput and overall system performance. Moreover, encryption is not a panacea. It adds overhead, especially when implemented by software. Data can still be lost if the encryption key is forgotten or the data file is maliciously or accidentally deleted.

Callback Systems

Callback security systems, which are commonly used with password and ID security schemes, control remote dial-up access to hosts and LAN servers through modems. These systems usually employ an interactive process between a sending and receiving modem. The answering modem requests the caller's identification, disconnects the call, verifies the caller's identification against the user directory, and then calls back the authorized modem at the number matching the caller's identification.

Callback security ensures that data communication occurs only between authorized devices. The degree of security that callback modems provide is questionable because of the widespread use of such telephone functions as call forwarding. It is also possible for a knowledgeable intruder to stay online and intercept the return call from the answering modem. In addition, callback security may be inappropriate for some networks, because it assumes that users always call from the same telephone number. Traveling employees and users who must connect to the LAN through a switchboard cannot use this technique.

Neither passwords nor callback modems provide complete security for remote communications. The difficulties inherent in remote authentication make a combined security method imperative. Two identification methods (e.g., callback modems combined with data encryption) may be more effective than a single method.

Another approach combines password security with the callback feature. With this technique, the password is verified and the inbound call is disconnected. The security system then calls the remote user at a predetermined telephone number to enter the pass-data mode. If a hacker breaks the password, the security system will call back a secure location, thereby denying the hacker access. This system is effective but very slow and is limited to a finite number of stored telephone numbers.

These approaches rely on establishing links to a central site device, such as a front-end processor or communications controller. In all cases, security is implemented through the use of ASCII passwords or DTMF tones after the modem handshake. Security procedures can be implemented before the modem handshaking sequence, rather than after it, to effectively eliminate the access opportunity from potential intruders. In addition to saving time, this method uses a precision high-speed analog security sequence that cannot be detectable even by advanced line monitoring equipment.

NETWORK OPERATING SYSTEMS SECURITY

Security is to a large extent dependent on the LAN operating system. Network operating system developers have tried to build in features, such as log-on passwords and access rights, that make it possible to exert some control over these problems, but LANs still have holes. Some third-party developers have created monitoring and security programs, but these also have limitations.

Most network operating systems simply divide the server's memory into sections, called volumes, allowing the LAN manager to assign different levels of user access to particular parts of the same resource. Some network operating systems (e.g., Novell's NetWare) offer several additional levels of security. For example, access to a directory is determined by a combination of user and directory access rights. Other features include audit trails that record which users log on to the network and the programs and resources they access.

Auditing systems can detect intruders impersonating authorized users and assist in network recovery in the event of an attack. Networks that do not have adequate built-in network operating system security can be enhanced with encryption or access-control software. Some third-party software products offer enhanced auditing features designed to make security administration easier. Using the software's auditing capabilities, network managers can quickly compile a list of users as well as the network access rights each has been given—a task that can otherwise take hours.

Accountability

Auditing services give users the means to enforce accountability in a distributed environment or to do a back-track analysis to discover the source of a security breach or a database integrity compromise. There are two factors to consider when deciding to implement distributed auditing services: the cost of auditing and the administrative interface to distributed auditing.

Auditing services in a distributed system usually record more information than standalone auditing systems. In a distributed environment, it is often useful to record authentication and authorization information along with data describing significant activities. The result is larger logs and a greater cost in terms of system overhead—from 10% to 12%, depending on how logs are implemented and tuned on individual servers.

It is not difficult to log information about system activities in a distributed environment. What is difficult is coordinating the auditing services and using the collected information. To date, no vendor provides a solution that makes it possible to manage multiple distributed auditing services from a central location.

Virus Protection

Among the dangers of inadequate network security are the alteration and destruction of valuable records and whole databases by worms and viruses introduced into the network through unauthorized programs brought into the workplace by unknowing users. Worms and viruses are usually differentiated according to their degree of transferability. A virus, for example, limits its damage to the LAN workstation through which it entered and is transported by external action, such as by sharing diskettes. Worms are self-replicating and move by their own initiative to different network nodes.

Virus protection is a necessity because computer viruses can have a multiplier effect on sensitive network resources. If a standalone microcomputer becomes infected, there is little chance that the virus will spread to other machines, unless diskettes are shared. If a mainframe is infected, the damage can be more severe, but there still is only one system to restore.

When a virus invades a LAN, however, the damage can be far-reaching. Diskettes used to boot servers are a prime source of LAN infections. Because workstations communicate with the network file server to obtain shared programs and data files, a virus can spread rapidly to every computer that accesses the server.

To protect against a catastrophic virus attack, network managers should implement internal barriers between connecting systems. These barriers (e.g., different encryption codes for separate programs or network devices) cannot completely insulate a network from a virus attack; however, they restrict damage to only that area of the network where the virus has entered. If a LAN subsystem is only a pass-through from a data source to a major interior system, a virus can be detected and blocked from entering the interior system. The technique involves making hash totals at the input and output of the subsystem and matching them. If a virus has intervened, the totals will not match and the data should be blocked from passage. Networks that can be accessed by dial-up lines should have a barrier (e.g., an encryption change) at the second entry port or interface in a multisystem network.

Borrowed or secondhand programs represent the most frequent source of virus infection. Companies should consult a reputable dealer and make sure that the vendor's seal is intact on the package before purchasing or using any diskette software. Companies that purchase secondhand software should verify that the supplier has tested the software for viruses; they should then retest the software (using one or more of the many virus-detection packages available) before loading it onto the network. When the programs are loaded onto the network, companies should monitor the size of directory files for any unexplainable changes and maintain archived versions and hard copies of the files for purposes of comparison.

Some antivirus data security software packages identify only changes being made to files; others identify and remove viruses and repair the damage the viruses inflict. Boot-sector viruses locate themselves on the first sector of a floppy disk, whereas file viruses invade executable files. Antivirus software can identify and eliminate viruses before the damage occurs. Some packages disinfect files, boot sectors, and memory without harming the infected portions of the system. As yet, no product can guarantee complete protection against a virus attack, and new types of viruses are constantly being discovered.

THE NETWORK SECURITY PLAN

With security issues becoming increasingly important among businesses of all types and sizes, it is wise to have a security plan in place. The plan's extensiveness is directly proportional to the network's complexity. At a minimum, the plan should address the following:

- Access levels and definitions
- Rules for access (e.g., password policy and volume access)
- Work groups and how they fit into the network's access rules
- Physical installation and access guidelines, including approved add-in security protection
- Accountability guidelines
- Internetwork connections and access requirements
- Levels of administration and accountability
- Periodic software upgrade, auditing, and installation policies

The security plan should have the power of a corporate policy, signed and authorized by management's highest level. Department heads should administer the plan. Every user should be required to read and sign off on the plan. Security plans should be reviewed and revised at least annually, perhaps more frequently if employee turnover is a problem.

The ideal network security plan must protect against the theft, alteration, and interception of network information. It should also deter theft or vandalism of equipment, the duplication or resale of programs, and unauthorized use of computer time by wiretapping or unauthorized dial-up. Companies should first implement procedures to deter unauthorized users who may be tempted to breach the system. When properly implemented, such deterrents bolster confidence in the integrity of the organization and its information assets, assuring management, staff, customers, and trading partners that the system is safe and dependable.

When deterrence fails and an intruder attempts to breach the system, the preventive techniques described in this chapter can guard against further damage. Companies should choose one or more security methods that offer password control, data encryption, alarms to notify network managers of a security breach, and audit trails to locate the source of the breach. Companies should design a security plan that can expand to accommodate network growth and take into account the increasing sensitivity of data applications.

CONCLUSION

In the past, most companies were concerned more with the nuts-and-bolts aspects of interactive communication and resource sharing than with security issues. Consequently, the design of most network operating systems reflected these priorities. With the increase in virus and worm attacks, however, many organizations want their network operating systems to incorporate protective measures that both provide and restrict access to information. Vendors are beginning to upgrade existing operating systems with advanced network security features.

When the distributed networking environment is examined, layer upon layer of risk can be found, especially with the implementation of EDI and EFT systems that convey sensitive financial transactions. Absolute protection of network resources from intruders may be too expensive and impose too much overhead to be practical. It is therefore essential to weigh the risks against the costs when deciding what security measures to implement.

Chapter 73
Managing Distributed Computing

Richard Ross

Many of the top concerns of managers in 1S departments relate directly to the issues of distributing information technology to end users. The explosive rate at which information technology has found its way into the front office, combined with the lack of control by the IS organization (ostensibly the group chartered with managing the corporation's IT investment), has left many IS managers at a loss as to how they should best respond. The following issues are of special concern:

- Where should increasingly scarce people and monetary resources be invested?
- What skills will be required to implement and support the new environment?
- How fast should the transition from a centralized computing environment to a distributed computing environment occur?
- What will be the long-term impact of actions taken today to meet short-term needs?
- What will be the overall ability of the central IS group to deliver new standards of service created by changing user expectations in a distributed computing environment?

In large companies during the past decade, the rule of thumb for technology investment has been that the opportunity cost to the business unit of not being able to respond to market needs will always outweigh the savings accruing from constraining technology deployment. This has resulted in a plethora of diverse and incompatible systems, often supported by independent IS organizations.

In turn, these developments have brought to light another, even greater risk—that the opportunity cost to the corporation of not being able to act as a single entity will always outweigh the benefit of local flexibility.

0-8493-9989-0/99/$0.00+$.50

For example, a global retailer faces conflicts if it has sales and marketing organizations in many countries. To meet local market needs, each country has its own management structure with independent manufacturing distribution, and systems organizations. The result might be that the company's supply chain becomes clogged—raw materials sit in warehouses in one country while factories in another go idle; finished goods pile up in one country while store shelves are empty in others; costs rise as the number of basic patterns proliferate. Perhaps most important, the incompatibility of the systems may prevent management from gaining an understanding of the problem and from being able to pull it all together at the points of maximum leverage while leaving the marketing and sales functions a degree of freedom.

Another example comes from a financial service firm. The rush to place technology into the hands of traders has resulted in a total inability to effectively manage risk across the firm or to perform single-point client service or multiproduct portfolio management.

WANTED—A NEW FRAMEWORK FOR MANAGING

A distributed computing environment cannot be managed according to the lessons learned during the last 20 years of centralized computing. The distributed computing environment is largely a result of the loss of control by the central IS group because of its inability to deliver appropriate levels of service to the business units. Arguments about the ever-declining cost of desktop technology are well and good, but the fact of the matter is that managing and digesting technology is not the job function of users. If central IS could have met their needs, it is possible users would have been more inclined to forgo managing their own systems.

It is not just the technology that is at fault. Centralized computing skills themselves are not fully applicable to a distributed computing environment. The underlying factors governing risk, cost, and quality of service have changed. IS departments need a new framework, one that helps them to balance the opportunity cost to the business unit against that to the company while optimizing overall service delivery.

DEFINING THE PROBLEM: A MODEL FOR DCE SERVICE DELIVERY

To help IS managers get a grip on the problem, this chapter proposes a model of service delivery for the distributed computing environment (DCE). This model focuses on three factors that have the most important influence on service as well as on the needs of the business units versus the corporation—risk, cost, and quality (see Exhibit 1). Each factor is analyzed to understand its cause and then to determine how best to reduce it (in the case of risk and cost) or increase it (as in quality).

Service Delivery

	Contributing Factor	How It Contributes
Risk	Development methodologies	Description and rationalization of logic and points of integration
	Training	Ability to design low-risk systems
	Piloting	Testing of integration
	Quality assurance procedures	Enforcement of testing
	Use of standards	Standard integration points
	Size of system	Number of integration points
	Operating environment	Number of integration points
	Degree of automation	Dependence on human factors
	Requirements planning	Highlighting likely areas of risk
	Disaster recovery planning	Highlighting likely areas of risk
	Integration of help desk	Ability to view total operational environment
	Number of systems	Number of integration points, amount of required knowledge
	Number of architectures	Number of integration points
	Volume of processing	Number of actions the system must perform in a given period of time
	Dependence on network	Number of linkages between user and data or application
	Rate of change in business	Rate of change of systems
	Security	Introduction of unplanned conditions into system
	Scalability	Number of integration points, number of architectures
	Training	Ability of staff to react
Cost	Number of personnel	Overall staff costs
	Training of personnel	Price per person
	Degree of automation of operational environment	Required personnel number
	Standards use	Number of activities, required personnel number, economies
	Number of architectures	Number of integration points
	Pace of change within business	Pace of systems change
	Service levels required	Personnel number, equipment levels
	Degree of integration of applications	Integration points
	Scalability of architecture	Number of architectures, integration points
	Degree of centralization	Degree of standardization
	Degree of user freedom	Number of activities, required personnel number
	Performance monitoring	Proactive service
	Number of business units supported	Staff numbers
Quality	Standardization of environment	Acceptance by users
	Number of personnel	Attention to users
	Training of personnel	Ability to respond
	Degree of user freedom	Flexibility
	Applicability of service delivered to business	Responsiveness
	Business process redesign	Appropriateness of application
	Clearinghouse	Reduction in business unit overhead

Exhibit 1. A model of service delivery.

Risk

Risk in any systems architecture is due primarily to the number of independent elements in the architecture (see Exhibit 2). Each element carries its own risk, say for failure, and this is compounded by the risk associated with the interface between each element.

This is the reason that a distributed computing environment will have a greater operational risk than a centralized one—there are more independent elements in a DCE. However, because each element tends to be smaller and simpler to construct, a DCE tends to have a much lower project risk than a centralized environment.

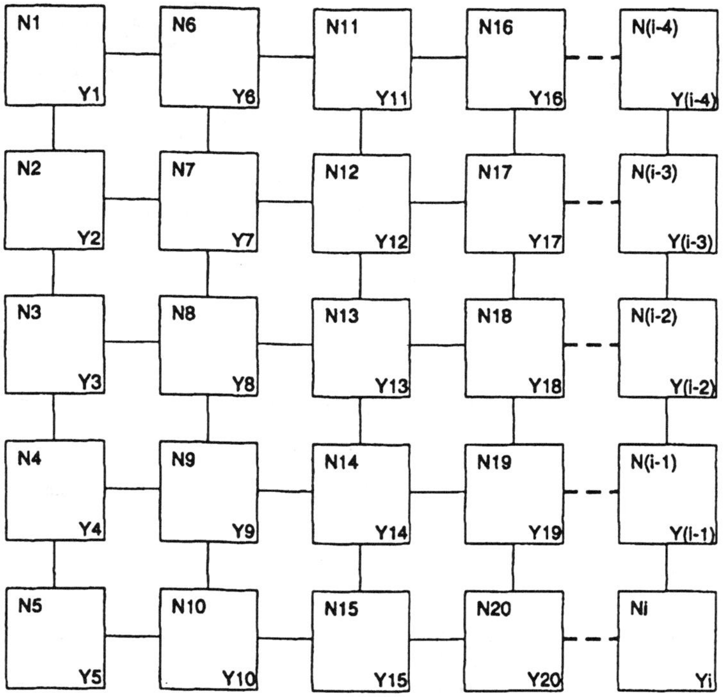

N = Component number

Y = Component risk

Given fully independent components, total network risk is equivalent to the sum of the individual component risks, 1 to I. Thus, the way to minimize risk is either to minimize I (i.e., to have a centralized computing environment) or to minimize Y for each component by standardizing on components with minimum risk profiles.

Exhibit 2. Optimization of risk in a network.

Thus, one point to consider in rightsizing should be how soon a system is needed. For example, a Wall Street system that is needed right away and has a useful competitive life of only a few years would be best built in a distributed computing environment to ensure that it gets online quickly. Conversely, a manufacturing system that is not needed right away but will remain in service for years is probably better suited for centralization.

One other difference between a distributed environment and a centralized environment is the impact of a particular risk. Even though a DCE is much more likely to have a system component failure, each component controls such a small portion of the overall system that the potential impact of any one failure is greatly reduced. This is important to take into account when performing disaster planning for the new environment.

Cost

Cost is largely a function of staff levels (see Exhibit 3). As the need for service increases, the number of staff members invariably increases as well. People are flexible and can provide a level of service far beyond that of automation. Particularly in a dynamic environment, in which the needs for response are ill-defined and can change from moment to moment, people are the only solution.

Unfortunately, staff is usually viewed as a variable cost, to be cut when the need for budget reductions arises. This results in a decrease in service delivered that is often disproportionately larger than the savings incurred through staff reductions.

Perceived Quality

Quality is a subjective judgment, impossible to quantify but the factor most directly related to the user's perception of service where information technology is concerned. In essence, the perception of quality is proportional to the user's response to three questions:

- Can I accomplish this task?
- Am I able to try new things to get the job done?
- Am I being paid the attention I deserve?

Except for the sheer ability to get the job done, the perception of quality is not necessarily a factor of how much technology a user is provided with. Instead, quality is largely a function of the degree of freedom users have to try new things and whether they are being listened to. This may mean that for many organizations, a simpler environment—one in which the user has fewer technological options but has ready access to human beings—will be more satisfying.

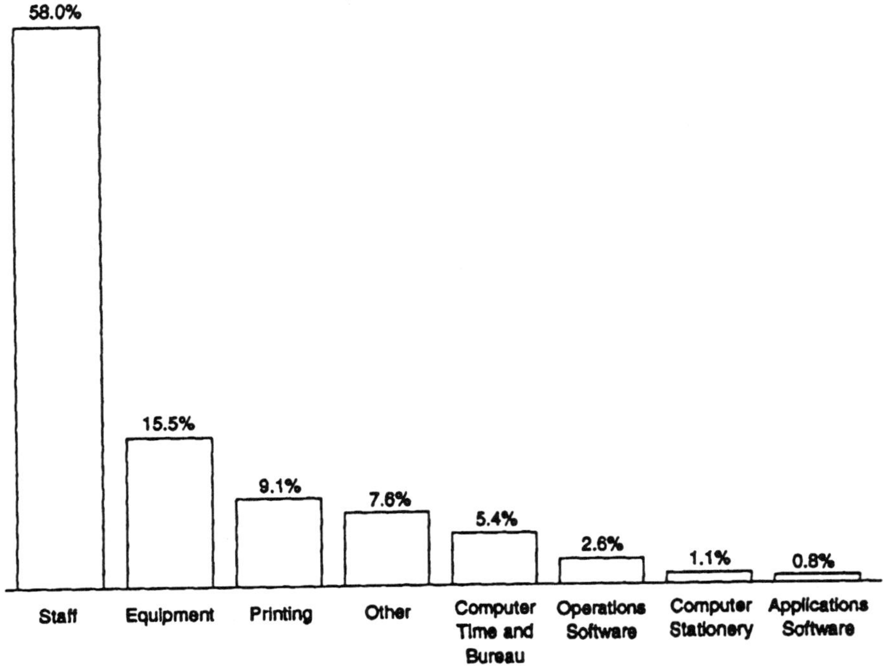

Note:
*Average of organizations studied; total IS costs
SOURCE: Decision Strategies Group

Exhibit 3. Cost profile of the IS function.

This view is in direct contrast with the approach many companies have taken of delivering more capabilities to the users in an effort to increase their perception of service delivered. One of the most important factors in the perceived quality of service delivery is the ability of the support technology to work unnoticed. Because of the similarities between this need and the way in which the US telephone network operates (a customer picks up the phone and the service is invariably there), the term dialtone is used to describe such a background level of operation.

"Dialtone" IS Service. One problem with highly functional IS environments is that users must think about them to use them. This is not the case with the telephone system, which operates so dependably that people and businesses have integrated it into their routine working practices and use it without much conscious effort. The phone companies maintain this level of usefulness by clearly separating additional features from basic service and letting the customer add each new feature as the customer desires.

Contrast this with the typical business system that represents an attempt to deliver a package of functions on day one and to continually increase its delivered functionality. The impact on users is that they are forced to continually adapt to changes, are not allowed to merge the use of the system into the background, and must continually stop delivering on their jobs just to cope with the technology. This coping might be as simple as looking something up in a manual or changing a printer cartridge, or it may mean not working at all while the system is rebooted.

COMPLEXITY: THE BARRIER TO SERVICE DELIVERY

In general, the basic driver to each of the three service factors is complexity. Complexity increases risk by increasing the number of interfaces between system elements as well as the number of elements themselves. It increases cost by increasing the need for staff as the only way to deal with ill-defined environments. Finally, it affects quality by making it harder to provide those services that users base their perception of quality on (i.e., dialtone and personal attention), in response to which even more staff are added.

This is the paradoxical environment in which IS operates. To improve the quality of service, they find themselves increasing the risk and cost of the operation. Improved application delivery cycles result in more systems to manage. End-user development tools and business unit-led development increases the number of architectures and data formats. Increasing access to corporate data through networks increases the number of interfaces.

Conversely, trying to improve the risk and cost aspects, typically through standardization of the environment, usually results in decreased levels of service delivered because of the constraints placed on the user freedom. This paradox did not exist in the good old days of centralized computing, when the IS organization dictated the service level.

FIVE PIECES OF ADVICE FOR MANAGING DISTRIBUTED COMPUTING

The measure of success in a distributed computing environment is therefore the ability to deliver service through optimizing for the factors of risk, cost, and quality while meeting the needs of both the business units and the corporation. It sounds like a tall order but it is not impossible. There are five key practices involved in corporate information processing

- Manage tightly, but control loosely.
- Organize to provide service on three levels.
- Choose one standard—even a single bad one is better than none or many good ones.

- Integrate data at the front end—do not homogenize on the back end.
- Minimize the use of predetermined architectures.

Manage Tightly, Control Loosely

A distributed computing environment should be flexible and allow users to be independent, but at the same time should be based on a solid foundation of rules and training and backed up with timely and appropriate levels of support.

In the distributed computing environment, users must react with the best of their abilities to events moment by moment. IS can support users in a way that allows them to react appropriately, or can make them stop and call for a different type of service while the customers get more and more frustrated.

BPR and Metrics. Two tools that are key to enabling distributed management are business process redesign (BPR) and metrics. BPR gets the business system working first, highlights the critical areas requiring support, builds consensus between the users and the IS organization as to the required level of support, and reduces the sheer number of variables that must be managed at any one time. In essence, applying BPR first allows a company to step back and get used to the new environment.

Without a good set of metrics, there is no way to tell how effective IS management has been or where effort needs to be applied moment to moment. The metrics required to manage a distributed computing environment are different from those IS is used to. With central computing, IS basically accepted that it would be unable to determine the actual support delivered to any one business. Because centralized computing environments are so large and take so long to implement, their costs and performance are spread over many functions. For this reason, indirect measurements were adopted when speaking of central systems, measures such as availability and throughput.

But these indirect measurements do not tell the real story of how much benefit a business might derive from its investment in a system. With distributed computing, it is possible to allocate expenses and effort not only to a given business unit but to an individual business function as well. IS must take advantage of this capability by moving away from the old measurements of computing performance and refocusing on business metrics, such as return on investment.

In essence, managing a distributed computing environment means balancing the need of the business units to operate independently while protecting corporate synergy. Metrics can help do this by providing a clear basis for discussion. Appropriately applied standards can help, too. For example, studies show that in a large system, as much as 90% of the code can be reused. This means that a business unit could reduce its coding effort by some theoretical amount up to that 90%—a forceful incentive to comply with such standards as code libraries and object-oriented programming.

Pricing. For those users who remain recalcitrant in the face of productivity gains, there remains the use of pricing to influence behavior. But using pricing to justify the existence of an internal supplier is useless. Instead, pricing should be used as a tool to encourage users to indulge in behavior that supports the strategic direction of the company.

For example, an organization used to allow any word processing package that the users desired. It then reduced the number of packages it would support to two, but still allowed the use of any package. This resulted in an incurred cost to the IS organization due to help desk calls and training problems. The organization eventually settled on one package as a standard, gave it free to all users, and eliminated support for any other package. The acceptance of this standard package by users was high, reducing help calls and the need for human intervention. Moreover, the company was able to negotiate an 80% discount over the street price from the vendor, further reducing the cost.

This was clearly a benefit to everyone concerned, even if it did not add up from a transfer pricing point of view. That is, individual business units may have suffered from a constrained choice of word processor or may have had to pay more, even with the discount, but overall the corporation did better than it otherwise would have. In addition to achieving a significant cost savings, the company was able to drastically reduce the complexity of its office automation environment, thus allowing it to deliver better levels of service.

Organize to Provide Service on Three Levels

The historical IS shop exists as a single organization to provide service to all users. Very large or progressive companies have developed a two-dimensional delivery system: part of the organization delivers businessfocused service (particularly applications development), and the rest acts as a generic utility.

Distributed computing environments require a three-dimensional service delivery organization. These services are:

- Dialtone, or overseeing the technology infrastructure
- Business-focused or value-added services, or ensuring that the available technology resources are delivered and used in a way that maximizes the benefit to the business unit

- Services that maximize leverage between each business unit and the corporation

Dialtone IS services lend themselves to automation and outsourcing. They are complex, to a degree that cannot be well managed or maintained by human activity alone. They must be stable, as this is the need of users of these services. In addition, they are nonstrategic to the business and lend themselves to economies of scale and hence are susceptible to outsourcing (see Exhibits 4 and 5).

Value-added services should occur at the operations as well as at the development level. For example, business unit managers are responsible for overseeing the development of applications and really understanding the business. This concept should be extended to operational areas, such

Common Operational Problem	Responsiveness to Automation
Equipment hangs	●
Network contention	◑
Software upgrades	●
Equipment upgrades	○
Disaster recovery	●
Backups	●
Quality assurance of new applications	●
Equipment faults (e.g., print cartridge replacement, disk crash)	○
Operator error (e.g., forgotten password, kick out plug)	○
Operator error (e.g., not understanding how to work application)	●

Responsiveness
High ●
Medium ◑
Low ○

SOURCE: Interviews and Decision Strategies Group analysis

Exhibit 4. Responsiveness of operations to automation.

Dialtone Function	Applicability
Equipment maintenance	●
Trouble calls	●
Help desk	●
Installations	●
Moves and changes	●
Billing	◑
Accounting	◑
Service level contracting	○
Procurement	○
Management	○

Applicability
High ●
Medium ◑
Low ○

SOURCE: Interviews and Decision Strategies Group analysis

Exhibit 5. Applicability of outsourcing to Dialtone.

---

as training, maintenance, and the help desk. When these resources are placed in the business unit, they will be better positioned to work with the users to support their business instead of making the users take time out to deal with the technology.

People do not learn in batch. They learn incrementally and retain information pertinent to the job at hand. This is why users need someone to show them what they need to accomplish the job at hand. Help desks should be distributed to the business units so that the staff can interact with the users and solve problems proactively, before performance is compromised, and accumulate better information to feed back to the central operation.

The third level of service—providing maximum leverage between the business unit and the corporation—is perhaps the most difficult to maintain and represents the greatest change in the way IS does business today. Currently, the staff members in charge of the activities that leverage across all business units are the most removed from those businesses. Functions such as strategic planning, test beds, low-level coding, and code library development tend to be staffed by technically excellent people with little or no business knowledge. IS managers must turn this situation around and recruit senior staff with knowledge of the business functions, business process redesign, and corporate planning. These skills are needed to take the best of each business unit, combine it into a central core, and deliver it back to the businesses.

Choose One Standard

If the key to managing a distributed computing environment is to reduce complexity, then implementing a standard is the thing to do. Moreover, the benefits to be achieved from even a bad standard, if it helps to reduce complexity, will outweigh the risks incurred from possibly picking the wrong standard.

The message is clear: there is more to be gained from taking inappropriate action now than from waiting to take perfect action later.

It should be clear that information technology is moving more and more toward commodity status. The differences between one platform and another will disappear over time. Even if IS picks a truly bad standard, it will likely merge with the winner in the next few years, with little loss of investment. More important, the users are able to get on with their work. In addition, it is easier to move from one standard to the eventual winner than from many.

Even if a company picks the winner, there is no guarantee that it will not suffer a discontinuity. IBM Corp. made its customers migrate from the 360 to 370 architecture. Microsoft Corp. is moving from DOS to Windows to Windows NT. UNIX is still trying to decide which version it wants to be. The only thing certain about information technology is the pace of change, so there is little use in waiting for things to quiet down before making a move.

Integrate Data at the Front End

At the very core of a company's survival is the ability to access data as needed. Companies have been trying for decades to find some way to create a single data model that standardizes the way it stores data and thus allows for access by any system.

The truth of the matter is that for any sufficiently large company (i.e., one with more than one product in one market), data standardization is unrealistic. Different market centers track the same data in different ways. Different systems require different data formats. New technologies require data to be stated in new ways. To try to standardize the storage of data means ignoring these facts of life to an unreasonable extent.

To try to produce a single model of all corporate data is impossible and meaningless. The models invariably grow to be so large that they cannot be implemented. They impose a degree of integration on the data that current systems technology cannot support, rendering the largest relational data base inoperative. And they are static, becoming obsolete shortly after implementation, necessitating constant reworking. Moreover, monolithic data models represent unacceptable project risk.

The standardization approach also ignores the fact that businesses have 20 to 30 years' worth of data already. Are they to go back and recreate all this to satisfy future needs? Probably not. Such a project would immobilize the business and the creation of future systems for years to come.

Systems designed to integrate and reconcile data from multiple sources, presenting a single image to the front end, intrinsically support the client/server model of distributed computing and build flexibility into future applications. They allow data to be stored in many forms, each optimized for the application at hand. More important, they allow a company to access its data on an as- needed basis. These integration systems are an important component to successfully managing future growth.

Less Architecture Is More

To overdesign a systems architecture is to overly constrain the organization. Most architecture arises as a function of rightsizing of applications on the basis of where the data must be stored and used. Understanding this helps the IS manager size the network and associated support infrastructure.

The management of risk and impact also drives architecture by forcing redundancy of systems and, in some cases, mandating the placement of data repositories regardless of user preferences. Assessing project versus operational risk helps to determine whether a system is built for central or distributed use.

Economics. This view is one in which the business needs drive the shape of the architecture. It results in a dynamic interconnection of systems that respond flexibly to business needs. Under a centralized computing environment, it was impractical to employ such an approach. It took so long and cost so much to implement a system that investment had to come before business need. This necessitated preplanning of an architecture as an investment guide.

The economics of distributed computing are different. Systems cost much less and can be quickly implemented. This means that their use can be responsive to business needs instead of anticipative. It also results in a greater net present value, for even though their operational costs might be

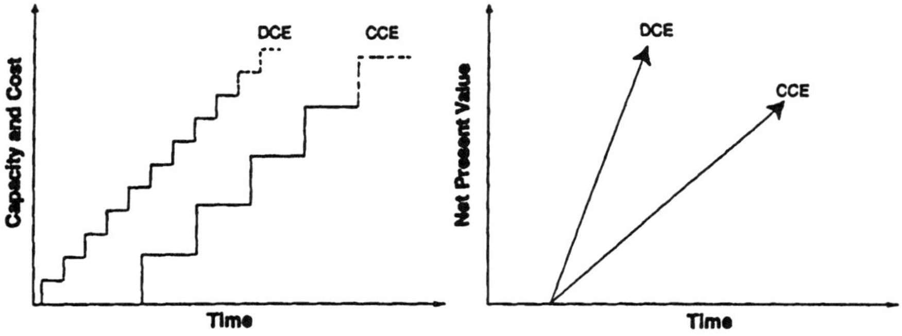

Distributed computing environment (DCE) has a higher net present value because its capacity can be used sooner relative to its marginal costs when compared with the centralized computing environment (CCE).

SOURCE: Decision Strategies Group

Exhibit 6. Net present value of distributed versus centralized computing.

higher, distributed computing environments are more immediately useful for a given level of investment (see Exhibit 6).

SUMMARY

This framework for managing the new computing environment relates directly to the business. If managers of IS functions are able to master it, they can enhance their opportunities to become members of the corporate business management team instead of simply suppliers of computing services.

Success in a distributed computing environment requires a serious culture shift for IS managers. They must loosen up their management styles, learning to decentralize daily control of operations. They must provide direction to staff members so that they can recognize synergies among business units. Some jobs that were viewed as low-level support activities (e.g., value-added services such as help desk and printer maintenance) must be recognized as key to user productivity and distributed. Others, viewed as senior technical positions (e.g., dialtone functions such as network management and installations), might best be outsourced, freeing scarce IS resources.

Most important, IS must understand the shift in power away from themselves and toward users. The IS organization is no longer the main provider of services; it now must find a role for itself as a manager of synergy, becoming a facilitator to the business units as they learn to manage their own newfound capabilities.

Section IX
Implementing Heterogeneous Systems

Section IX covers actual implementation of heterogeneous systems. It includes case studies and how-to information about implementing heterogeneous systems.

Organizations implementing migration and coexistence solutions across heterogeneous environments should consider a number of different factors that can be broadly grouped as follows:

- Industrywide factors
- Enterprise-specific factors
- Solution-specific factors

Chapter 74 covers these factors in detail and summarizes the advantages and disadvantages of the different approaches.

Many factors, particularly lower cost and the ability to meet requirements, influence the final decision in acquiring computer systems. This acquisition approach invariably leads to the establishment of a multivendor systems environment. While this approach lowers the overall cost, managers must recognize that the decision to install equipment from multiple vendors involves additional administrative responsibilities (e.g., special policies and procedures). Chapter 75 addresses the critical acquisition issues in multivendor installations.

Besides cost and the ability to meet requirements, other factors that must be considered are vendor support services (both before and after installation), hardware maintenance contracts, software maintenance practices, and training programs. These factors affect the upfront acquisition as well as ongoing maintenance and are critical to the system's success. Chapter 76 covers these additional factors.

Merging two Wide Area Network (WANs) is a process comprising several steps that, when carefully planned, can ensure a successful implementation.

In the case of the Resolution Trust Corporation (RTC) and the Federal Deposit Insurance Corporation (FDIC), considerations included Network Operating System compatibility, enhancing e-mail and directory services, applications support, server and workstation memory and processor upgrades, applications support, and routing software upgrades. Chapter 77 covers a case study that details the methodologies that brought together two WANs with more than 17,000 end users.

Chapter 78 is a case study of a corporation relocating a portion of its support staff to a remote location. The problem solved is how to give that staff network data access without providing network servers and additional staff at the new location. The company's corporate locations interconnect through a Banyan WAN for access to business software, national databases, and e-mail. Each location contains a network service area for user support and connects to other locations, including the Virginia headquarter offices.

Chapter 79 is a case study of a frame relay implementation in a large manufacturing company with headquarters in the southeast. This company has an agency distribution system of 36 warehouses and five central distribution centers in the U.S. and Canada. The company also has 11 manufacturing facilities in the U.S. and Canada. The company's networking environment consists of IBM's OS/2 LAN Server, with MSDOS, Windows, and OS/2 on the requesting stations. The mainframe is an IBM 3090/400 connected to 3000 or more combined mainframe and LAN requesters.

Many organizations are hoping to reap the benefits of object-oriented (OO) systems development such as greatly improved software quality, reusable objects, and a means of creating truly distributed software across heterogeneous environments. However, virtually no organization is starting development without legacy systems. Besides the existing legacy code base, all organizations embracing object technology also worry about the existing software development skill base. The biggest people-related question many IS organizations face is whether it is possible to retrain software developers to use object technology. Chapter 80 addresses this question.

Chapter 74
Solution Selection Factors and Guidelines

Raj Rajagopal

Organizations evaluating migration and coexistence solutions across heterogeneous environments should consider a number of different factors. The factors can be broadly grouped as follows:

- Industry-wide factors
- Enterprise-specific factors
- Solution-specific factors

Let us look at each of the factors in detail.

Industry Factors

Microsoft Windows is established on the desktop. The familiarity of the interface, coupled with the likelihood of the Windows interface being present predominantly in the increasing home computer market, assures that the bulk of new shrink-wrapped applications will be Windows based. New enterprise applications are being developed predominantly as distributed client/server applications, while legacy applications are somewhat slowly removed from the mainframe. There are many mission-critical applications on UNIX, and UNIX is still a proven and good candidate for expanding current enterprise applications as well as new ones. Windows NT seems to be gaining market share at the expense of NetWare and to some extent UNIX. Given the above, organizations with legacy and other non-Windows-based applications are looking at Windows-based solutions not only for the desktop, but for enterprise applications as well. An organization has to decide how these and other factors (not directly related to UNIX/Windows NT migration coexistence and not covered in the book) apply to their situation.

0-8493-9989-0/99/$0.00+$.50

Enterprise Factors

The factors listed below differ between enterprises and would influence the selection of migration/coexistence solutions.

- The existing UNIX install base, including in-house developed and commercial off-the-shelf (COTS) packages. If the install base is small, the organization may prefer to use a porting tool and attempt to move toward a homogeneous environment. If the install base is large, the organization may prefer to leave the current application environment as is and add Windows using a solution like Windows in an X-terminal.
- Investment, skills, and availability of current in-house information systems staff. The skills to be considered include both system development and system administration skills. An existing homogeneous UNIX skill base may prompt an organization to build Windows skills prior to adopting Windows in the organization for mission-critical work.
- The need for office automation tools for different classes of users may prompt an organization to provide Windows applications for office users, and UNIX and Windows applications to others.
- Protection of existing legacy applications investment should be considered.
- Cost/benefit trade-offs between savings from a homogeneous environment and cost of moving applications and retraining must be considered.

Often, strategy decisions regarding migration and coexistence are made at the enterprise level. The primary factors leading to migration or coexistence choices are the same as that of homogeneous and heterogeneous environments. The following summarizes the advantages and disadvantages of migration and coexistence approaches.

Migration. Advantages include:

- Improved productivity through interface consistency
- Reduced system administration costs
- Reduced network administration costs
- Easier exchange of documents and data within the organization
- Possible to include all the functionality of the new environment
- Possible to achieve better performance

Disadvantages include:

- Costs of moving to a homogeneous environment
- Cost of maintaining a homogeneous environment
- Possibility of lock-in to one or more vendors
- Extensive retraining of users using different systems

Coexistence. Advantages include:

- You can pick the most cost-effective solution at any given point.
- The natural evolution is toward coexistence in heterogeneous environments.
- There are no additional costs involved in trying to move to another environment.
- In many cases, it is faster to make an application available to heterogeneous clients than porting.
- Up-front costs tend to be smaller than porting.

Disadvantages include:

- Interface inconsistency problems
- Need to perform system administration for multiple environments
- Need to connect and bridge different types of networks
- Exchange of documents and data is difficult and often requires format translations and loss of data fidelity
- Long-term costs of maintaining multiple environments may be more than the upfront cost of migrating and the lower cost of maintaining a nearly homogeneous environment
- Application performance for heterogeneous clients may not be the same as that of the clients the application was designed for

Build vs. Buy. Another enterprise-level factor that applies across migration and coexistence solutions is the build vs. buy decision. This, of course, is applicable to more than just migration and coexistence solutions. Some of the solutions we have discussed in the book, such as manual porting between environments and using tools based on advanced object technologies, require a skill level that may not be available internally to many organizations.

There are many firms that provide migration and coexistence services. These services include planning, evaluation, and implementation. Some of the companies that provide these services include DEC, Tandem, etc.

Solution-Specific Factors

There is a set of factors that applies to all migration/coexistence solutions, such as EUI differences, workstation resources, and standards. There are also factors that are unique to a given migration/coexistence solution. Let us look at both sets of factors in this section.

EUI Differences. It is virtually impossible that every mouse click, every keyboard stroke or combination, every function key, etc., will produce identical responses between the native Windows interface and a simulated one. The Graphical User Interface (GUI) approach in the UNIX environment, while trying to give a "comparable look-and-feel" to Windows, attempts to provide functionality superior to Windows. The differences in the way the interfaces behave could be annoying to the user if it becomes necessary to routinely switch back and forth between UNIX and Windows applications.

Workstation Resources. If both UNIX and Windows applications exist on the desktop, the resources required at the workstation (e.g., memory, disk space, etc.) increase compared to having applications of only one type. This factor may particularly trouble laptop users and those applications that require significant processing at the workstation, i.e., "fat" clients.

Standards. Many organizations, particularly in the government or under contract with it, want systems that are compliant with open system standards. The different flavors not withstanding, UNIX is more open than NT, although there are aspects of NT that are open. The WIN32 is a published API, and NT runs on multiple processor families, including Intel, PowerPC, and Alpha. However, Microsoft still controls the API and the only practical support for the API comes from Microsoft's operating systems. In fact, some of the migration/coexistence solution vendors have agreements with Microsoft that provide them access, among other things, to Microsoft source code. There have been some recent efforts to standardize the WIN32 API, the results of which remain to be seen. In the UNIX world, one can think of POSIX applications without having a specific vendor in mind. Organizations are taking a serious look at NT and the possibility that the desktop success of Windows will spill over to servers with NT and they want to be prepared. Although Windows NT is POSIX compliant, the POSIX subsystem is implemented as a separate subsystem within NT and is not really suited for developing POSIX applications. For example, the POSIX subsystem in NT lacks GUI support (includes only character support), and it is unlikely that future versions of NT will be UNIX 95 (and follow on) compliant.

Factors Related to X-Servers

X-servers let a Windows machine access UNIX applications. The factors relating to X-servers that you should consider include:

- No modifications are required in the UNIX applications.
- X-server is a Windows application and behaves like any other Windows application and includes features such as cut-and-paste, etc.
- The setup involves installing the X-server software and establishing connectivity to the UNIX server. As such, it is typically faster than other means of making UNIX applications available on Windows NT, such as porting.

Factors Related to Porting

Porting source code is applicable only if you have the source. This rules out most COTS products and old applications for which you no longer have all the sources.

Manual Porting. The biggest advantage of manual porting is that once you have accomplished the port, you no longer need the source in the environment you are porting from. The biggest downside is that it takes time and effort to accomplish manual porting. Manual porting is appropriate under the following conditions:

- Your application is small enough that manual porting can be accomplished within a reasonable time and with reasonable effort.
- Manual porting makes better business sense than other ways of making the application available in the ported to environment, such as tool-based porting or emulation.
- Your application has a long enough life expectancy that it is likely to be used as is without requiring replacement or a rewrite in the near future. If the application is close to its life expectancy, you may be better off rewriting or replacing the application.
- Once you manually port the application, you can realize significant savings in the porting-from environment through reduced usage (or no usage) of that environment.
- You have access to in-depth programming skills in both environments. If you do not have the skills internally, you may need help from third parties. For example, if you are porting a UNIX application to Windows NT, you need programming skills in both UNIX and Windows NT.

Tool-Based Porting. Your business application may have been developed from scratch, purchased as a package, or purchased as a package and modifications made to fit your environment. If you bought a package, then you need to check with the package vendor to see if they offer a version that runs in the environment you are interested in. You should also check if the vendor offers porting assistance, in particular for the custom modifications you may have. An in-house application would be an appropriate porting candidate under the following conditions:

- The application has a long useful expected life.
- The current development and maintenance programmer skill base dealing with the application would require a big learning curve for a new environment.
- The benefits of making the application work in the new environment outweigh leaving the application as is or rewriting it.

- The application size is large enough to gain some benefits when ported, but not so large that it would make porting a long, error-prone, and risky process.

There are some business benefits that can be derived by porting:

- The biggest benefit of porting is that it permits a stepping-stone approach to a potentially complex migration from one environment to another.
- Porting permits your system administrators and their custom utilities to immediately transition and be productive in the new environment.
- Porting permits you to continue to use your development and maintenance skills while you transition to the new environment.
- Depending on your applications, you may be able to get the applications working in the new environment with little effort.
- Your end-users can start using your existing applications in the new environment without having to relearn the applications.
- You can take advantage of unique features available in the new environment as a post porting step, but this may introduce divergence in the source between your sources in the old and new environments.
- If you need to run your applications in multiple environments, then porting is one way to keep a common source across environments.
- Keeping a common source is much more cost effective for development and maintenance than individual source libraries for different environments.

The disadvantages of porting are:

- You still need to keep and maintain the original source. Tool-based porting does not mean one-way migration.
- There may be annoying differences in end-user interfaces. For example, certain Windows GUI elements such as pop-up menus and window repainting operate differently from X/Motif widgets. The reverse is true as well. Some UNIX features may not be supported in Windows NT. For a user who has both a native application and a ported application, it may be annoying to go back and forth between applications where the end-user interface is not consistent. You may feel this annoyance if you run an old DOS application under Windows and you are unable to use your mouse.

If as a manager you are wondering how serious a porting problem you have, then check your code against for the following list of things that makes it easy to port:

- Code in which end-user interface handling and business logic handling are isolated
- Code in which vendor extensions to standards are isolated

- Code in which dependencies on a specific operating system are isolated (particularly true for UNIX with its many flavors)
- Overall program fiow is separated into logical, modular blocks

Most of the porting today is between UNIX and Windows NT, although there are some others such as OS/2 to Windows NT. Factors for and against UNIX are given below.

UNIX is preferred by some customers for the following reasons:

- Proven in mission-critical applications
- Proven high-end availability
- Proven scalability
- Proven performance
- Proven integrity
- User familiarity with current UNIX production applications

Some factors for not considering UNIX include:

- UNIX, though it is supposed to be open, may still require considerable effort to move from one vendor to another.
- UNIX workstations are typically more expensive than PCs, and UNIX versions of software are also typically more expensive than a Windows version of the same or equivalent software.
- Users might prefer Windows-based Office products and prefer to have one simple consistent desktop.

If the customer has a Windows NT application (that was bought or developed as a test application) and would like to deploy it as a production application with other production applications on UNIX, then porting from Windows NT to UNIX is an option. Depending on factors such as the size of the application and the available skill set, this option may be preferable to rewriting the application in UNIX.

Factors Related to Cross-Platform Development

If you are developing applications and want to able to run your application without being tied to a specific environment, then cross-platform development is a solution. You cannot take an existing application and run it through any cross-platform development tool to achieve the ability to execute across platforms. You need a porting tool to do that. But for new applications, you can use 4 GL or object-oriented frameworks to enable you to execute across platforms. If you are using a third-party API or tool for cross-platform development, keep in mind that you may become dependent on the vendor for your applications. Also, watch out for royalty fees (for these and other migration and coexistence solutions), and factor the fees into your overall evaluation.

Factors Related to Emulators. The biggest advantage of emulators is that they enable applications to execute in another environment without the need for having the source (such as shrink-wrapped applications). The biggest drawback it that emulation invariably has a performance penalty (which may or may not be acceptable or may be expensive to fix). Emulation also has the user interface consistency problem mentioned earlier in this chapter.

SOLUTION SELECTION GUIDELINES

We looked at a number of different solutions for migration and coexistence between heterogeneous systems. Before we look at some guidelines in using the solutions, let us look at an administrative or procedural solution that is sometimes overlooked.

You should include procedural solutions for review when you are evaluating migration and coexistence solutions. For example, consider the need to make Windows-based desktop office products available to a predominantly production UNIX-application user set with only occasional need for Windows applications. A procedural solution would be to set up a stand-alone Windows system or a pool of Windows systems for common use rather than enabling Windows applications on the desktop of each production user. Organizations that have tried this approach sometimes note a loss of productivity when people have to interrupt their work and train of thought and physically move to another location and return to their regular desk to continue their work.

Alternatively, you can also consider providing two machines. While this may save the trouble of people having to move from their seats, there are footprint problems to be considered. In many instances, the desktops do not have enough space to accommodate two machines. In addition, the use of two machines also increases power consumption and the need for maintenance. The primary advantage of the administrative approach is that you do not have to invest in a migration and coexistence solution. This approach works best when the users spend a very small fraction of their time in one environment compared to their work time in the production environments.

If applications are working well and the only issue is connectivity between different types of servers for file services, print services, etc., client interoperability tools would help. Exhibit 1 lists the application guidelines and applicable solutions.

Consideration of the above factors and guidelines should help customers narrow their migration/coexistence solution choices and make a more informed selection of their migration/coexistence solutions.

Exhibit 1. Applications guidelines and applicable solutions.

Application Guideline	Applicable Solutions
Application source not available (e.g., shrink wrapped applications or old applications)	Porting solutions that need source code cannot be used
Performance	Native applications, in general, tend to have better performance than emulated solutions due to the absence of extra steps at run time
Supported applications	Although most solutions try to ensure support for the most popular Windows applications, some DOS applications and applications using certain Windows modes and device drivers do not work with some solutions.
Application data interchange	Windows applications running in another environment normally have DDE and OLE support, although the same may not be true for interchange between Windows and UNIX applications on the same desktop (clipboard interchange may still be possible)
Application location	In some solutions, it is executed on a server like NT and accessed by clients on a network; in others, the application gets executed at the client. In the former case, costs associated with installing and maintaining a server need to be included in the overall solution cost
Networking support	Varies between solutions, although most try to provide TCP/IP and NetWare support

Heterogeneous System Administration Considerations

When you have multiple environments, you can make it easy for the end-user if the system and network administrators of the different environments collaborate to ensure consistency. The following are some areas for consistency:

- Ensure that the password conventions (length, allowed characters, expiration duration, etc.) are the same between the different environments as much as possible. (This is in case you are unable to establish a common logon across environments.)
- Establish common group names across the different environments.
- Establish a common response center/helpdesk. If users can report by e-mail, try to have one e-mail ID for system and network support regardless of the user's environment. The same should also be true for help hotlines and help through intranet Web addresses, etc.
- Provide cross-permissions between administrators. There will always be an instance when an administrator of one environment is available

to handle a user's problem and knows what to do, but is unable to help because the administrator does not have the right access.
- Provide cross-training for a minimal set of administration activities across environments for the administrators.

Selecting and implementing a migration and coexistence solution is a choice that organizations must make based on their circumstances and requirements. The good news is that there are a variety of approaches and products supporting these approaches for you to choose from. Each organization has to look at each of the factors mentioned, evaluate how these factors apply to their situation, and select an approach that is consistent with short- and long-term goals of the organization. This book lists the factors that should be considered. It also lists the different approaches that can be taken.

Once an approach is selected, a detailed requirements list should be prepared and the different products that support the approach should be evaluated against the requirements. This book includes brief descriptions of many of the products and also includes supplemental information in the CD as well as online and other contact information for the product vendors.

Chapter 75
Acquiring Systems for Multivendor Environments

Thomas Fleishman

IS and communications systems managers may not always initiate the decision to purchase hardware or software packages, but they are often responsible for selecting, implementing, and operating the associated peripherals and such supporting equipment as communications systems. Selection is often complicated, however, by third-party vendors whose products are not compatible with the CPU manufacturer's hardware.

Many factors, particularly lower cost, influence the decision to establish a multivendor systems environment; the price of equipment from third-party vendors is generally competitive and equipment performance is at least equivalent to, if not better than, that of the hardware available from the CPU manufacturer.

Managers must recognize that the decision to install equipment from multiple vendors involves additional administrative responsibilities (e.g., special policies and procedures). This chapter addresses the critical issues in multivendor installations.

SELECTION FACTORS

To determine whether the acquisition of equipment from a vendor other than the mainframe vendor is appropriate, managers should weigh the following technical and financial factors:

- *Availability.* If a CPU supplier does not have a particular component required for a specific application, equipment from another vendor may be the only alternative.
- *Performance.* Only one vendor's product may be capable of meeting specific performance criteria for an installation.

0-8493-9989-0/99/$0.00+$.50

- *Reliability.* With the proliferation of both equipment and vendors, managers have many alternatives. A specified degree of reliability (i.e., a defined mean time between component failures) may dictate equipment purchased from a different vendor.
- *Cost.* Equipment from one vendor may cost less than the equivalent components offered by another. Cost is the most difficult issue to address because quality may be sacrificed for savings.
- *Equipment use and location.* Managers must consider the environment in which the components will be installed. Certain equipment is manufactured to meet more stringent environmental conditions; if such conditions exist, the manager must acquire products that can operate in those conditions.
- *Ergonomics.* Ergonomics is particularly important when terminals and microcomputers are widely used. The size, screen, keyboard, and other physical attributes of the equipment should all be weighed in the acquisition decision.

TRADE-OFFS

Managers must consider whether equipment from a third-party vendor meets the performance levels established for equipment currently in the department and assess the risks of installing equipment that does not meet this level. For example, replacing disk drives in an online environment entails a significantly higher risk than exchanging tape or cartridge units. Managers may not be willing—or even able—to accept the risk of a new vendor's equipment not performing at required levels. The cost savings must be enough to offset the risks and the potential expense of remedial backup measures.

Fitting the Current Configuration

Equipment supplied by a new vendor must function in the installation's current configuration. For example, in one department that acquired a new line printer, preinstallation testing showed that the printer could not handle all the special and multipart forms required by users. The printer worked well on some forms but not on others. In other instances, the performance of disk drives was outstanding in installations that had minimal pack-mounting requirements, but fell below acceptable levels in operations that required a great deal of pack mounting and demounting.

Quality of Service

Managers must also investigate a vendor's ability to provide and sustain acceptable levels of service. Before making such an assessment, the manager should establish internal tracking criteria based on the requirements of the installation. These criteria might include:

- *Response time.* What is the average time that a vendor requires to respond to a service call? Is the vendor willing to commit to such response through a contract?
- *Repair time.* What is the average repair time for a given component?
- *Resource availability.* Does the vendor provide resources (e.g., technical specialists) in a timely manner?
- *Incidence recurrence.* If a specific component develops problems, is it fixed on the first service call or is it necessary to recall the customer engineer?
- *Dispatch location.* Where is the service location from which the repair resource is dispatched? Is the parts depot in the same location? If not, where is it located?
- *Management attention.* In cases of serious or recurring problems, does the vendor's management get involved?
- *Escalation procedures.* Are established escalation procedures in place in case of extended problem resolution?

Customer Engineering

In a multivendor installation, the level and quality of support from the manufacturer largely determines the success or failure of the installation in terms of equipment performance. Managers should initially establish whether the manufacturer can provide:

- *On-site support.* Would a vendor's customer engineers be on site or dispatched from a central service depot?
- *Continuity.* Would the same customer engineers provide support on every occasion or would customer engineers be randomly assigned from a branch or regional pool?
- *Experience.* Are the supporting customer engineers experienced with the type of installation and configuration in the manager's department?
- *Customer engineer support organization.* Are the customer engineers employed by the equipment manufacturer or employed by a third-party maintenance organization contracted to provide service support?
- *Parts.* Are parts stored locally in case of hardware failures that require part exchanges? Or could there be major shipping delays in procuring the necessary items from distant warehouses?

Managers must address these issues before acquiring third-party equipment. Clearly stated expectations, policies, provisions, and if possible, contractual guarantees should be established with the vendor to minimize problems or to allow the organization to withdraw from the acquisition agreement without financial penalties.

For example, one vendor acknowledged that the usual repair support provided for purchased equipment was minimal and that timely response could not and would not be guaranteed. The vendor did, however, offer an alternative maintenance service contract at additional cost, guaranteeing the arrival of customer engineers at an installation within four hours. In this case, the manager was sufficiently impressed by the vendor's equipment to buy it and pay the higher maintenance charges to obtain guaranteed service.

In another case, the manager found that a third-party service organization had been contracted to support a piece of hardware. Although the vendor agreed to certain service requirements, the service organization actually performing the maintenance service was not committed to providing the necessary support. Only after lengthy negotiations and considerable expense was the manager able to obtain the appropriate service agreements.

Vendor's Financial Conditions

Managers must evaluate the financial condition of prospective vendors, deciding whether a vendor has the resources to provide support and service for the life of its equipment. If the acquisition is sufficiently large in terms of price or the equipment being considered is sufficiently strategic, the organization should consider reviewing a Dun & Bradstreet analysis of the vendor before entering any contractual commitments.

Contractual Criteria

The contracting organization might want to specify certain performance and service criteria in the acquisition contract (e.g., service response time and availability schedule). Financial penalties or component replacement may be defined for failure to meet contractual requirements. All contractual demands should be negotiated by legal representatives for the vendor and the organization. The degree of cooperation shown by the vendor during negotiations usually indicates what the manager can expect after equipment installation.

AN EYE ON THE VENDOR

Managers must establish objectives for equipment performance and service support before evaluating a vendor's products. Establishing benchmarks and tracking component performance are two generally accepted methods of evaluation.

Benchmarks

Before equipment is acquired, the systems department staff should become familiar with the vendor's hardware and its specifications to establish performance benchmarks. Benchmarks can help determine whether the equipment meets its advertised capabilities and whether the vendor complies with the requirements in the installation agreement.

Performance Tracking

An organizational unit must be established to track the performance of hardware components. This unit can establish a comparative rating system to help the manager determine which vendors provide satisfactory service. Tracking can be performed manually (e.g., for operations personnel file incident or trouble reports, which are transmitted to an employee who compiles the data and issues periodic reports) or through an automated tracking and reporting system. Because manual tracking is cumbersome, inefficient, and expensive, especially in large departments, automated tracking and reporting systems are preferred. These packages can be developed or acquired, depending on the capabilities of the staff and the requirements of a particular installation.

Studies conducted in large installations indicate that component tracking can deliver a significant payoff. Besides being a straightforward way to rank vendors, component tracking is a proven operations aid. Because a faulty disk, tape drive, or channel may cause failures in other components or systems degradations, the ability to quickly detect a faulty device is a valuable aid in maintaining appropriate service levels.

The following scenario illustrates the usefulness of component tracking. An automated tracking system provides a daily report of all failures (i.e., hardware and software) of each component in an IS department. The vendor of the tracking package provides a monthly comprehensive data base compiled from data collected from all installations that subscribe to the service. The data base indicates an installation's performance relative to the other organizations using the same configuration and brand of equipment. For example, if an organization has a CPU A with disk drive B installed, and 12 other organizations use the same CPU and disk configuration, the monthly report shows a performance ranking for all 13 subscribers. For managers with multivendor environments, such systems are almost mandatory, especially in large, multiple CPU installations.

Vendors' Mutual Interest

Problems that involve more than one vendor often occur because vendors compete in markets that discourage communications between vendors. To maintain smooth operations in a multivendor environment, managers or members of their operations staff must coordinate communication between vendors. This communication can be encouraged through frequent meetings that include representatives from all vendors. Even when there are no specific problems, these meetings help open channels of communication between the vendors whose products are installed in a particular department.

CASE STUDY: RECOGNIZING RESPONSIBILITY

Under pressure to reduce equipment costs, a manager decided to reduce costs by replacing 24 disk spindles acquired from the manufacturer of the facility's CPU. The manager contacted several disk drive vendors and leasing companies, and after a period of evaluation, chose to replace the 24 spindles, saving, in theory, approximately $73,000. The spindles were acquired on a three-year lease. Shortly after the replacement, it became evident that the acquisition of the new devices was a mistake.

Although the disk manufacturer had an impressive facility and was supplying thousands of units worldwide, the product was relatively new in large-scale, 24-hour-a-day, online business environments. Because the support organization was poorly trained, with no prior exposure to the CPU manufacturer's equipment, diagnosing problems was extremely time-consuming. In addition, CPU-device interfaces were not well understood, therefore, communication between the disk and CPU vendors was nearly impossible. No repair personnel were permanently assigned to the data center's account and trouble calls became exasperating as clusters of inexperienced and poorly trained staff tried to resolve problems, while major online systems remained unavailable to users, resulting in losses of thousands of dollars for every minute the systems were down.

After several months, the equipment appeared to stabilize, but the department began to experience serious channel interface problems. Much of the manager's time was spent mediating between the CPU and disk vendors, neither of whom was willing to accept responsibility for the problem.

As the interface problems were resolved, the incidence of head crashes increased dramatically. It took approximately four months to trace the problem to the foam-rubber-seal stripping insulating the spindle door. The frequent mounting and demounting of packs hastened the deterioration and disintegration of the stripping, eventually contaminating the packs and causing head crashes. After analyzing this situation, the manager decided to absorb the penalty in the lease contract and replaced the disks at a cost of $27,000. (The penalty had been agreed to during the contract negotiations as a contingency escape arrangement.)

The disk manufacturer was only partly at fault for marketing a device that was not fully tested and for not planning and staffing a support organization of trained personnel for servicing the product. The manager was negligent in failing to perform an in-depth evaluation of a new product that was being introduced into a critical business environment. With a project plan outlining specific, defined performance objectives, the manager might have deferred or completely avoided the product in question. After contacting other installations, the IS manager learned that other users had experienced similar problems.

SOFTWARE VENDORS

IS and communications systems management is complicated by the increasing number of commercial software packages. A turnkey package may be acquired as an integrated system that requires specific equipment that may not be compatible with the existing mainframe configuration; or the software may be acquired to process a specific application (e.g., payroll, general ledger, accounts payable) on the mainframe.

As they do for third-party hardware purchases, managers must implement formal procedures and tools to collect performance data on the vendor's products and institute communications processes that allow the multivendor environment to be managed effectively.

This is becoming especially true as smaller minicomputer- and microcomputer-based systems spread throughout user areas as well as in the IS department. Further complexities are being introduced by the disappearing delineation between information and communications technologies. These factors, along with the development of complex technologies and products, essentially preclude the ability to maintain a single-vendor environment. IS and communications systems managers must confront the realities of today's information technology industry: the proliferation of software, hardware, and service vendors is likely to increase.

SUMMARY

Managers should approach the multivendor installation by considering the risk/benefit trade-offs in the context of their IS or communications environments. Establishing a project plan that details equipment and software performance and support should be mandatory. If possible, contractual contingency arrangements should be specified and agreed to by all parties before the installation or implementation of a vendor's product.

To carry out a multivendor installation plan, IS and communications systems managers should:

- Identify objectives to be achieved through a third-party vendor, emphasizing
  - Performance (e.g., the vendor may be the only source to meet requirements).
  - Cost (i.e., costs are reduced or benefits per unit cost are enhanced through third-party purchase).
  - Environment (e.g., strict operational constraints that must be accommodated).

- Review the performance history of the vendor, emphasizing
  - Reference checks of current and past customers
  - The performance history of the product being considered
- Review the vendor's financial condition, emphasizing
  - Financial performance history and trends
  - Installation base trends
  - Market penetration in comparison with competitors
  - Whether it is privately owned or publicly financed
  - Annual revenues and profits
  - Debt-to-equity position
  - Ability to withstand short-term financial setbacks
- Review the vendor's installed base, emphasizing:
  - The number of customers serviced
  - The location of the customer base
  - The rate of new customer acquisition
  - The rate of existing customer defection
- Perform a risk analysis that considers:
  - The effects on the procuring organization if the vendor fails to perform as expected
  - Contingency plans for vendor replacement
  - Adequate, appropriate contractual protection in case of bankruptcy
  - Unchallenged use of the product
  - A statement of fair value purchase price for bankruptcy trustee
- Review vendor management, emphasizing
  - Whether the organization is managed by the owner or professional management
  - Tenure of management
  - Management turnover history
  - Management remuneration plan (e.g., is a percentage of management's annual compensation incentive based?)

Chapter 76
Evaluating Vendor Support Policies

James A. Papola

The primary criteria for selecting communications equipment are usually current and future user requirements and the performance characteristics of the hardware and software. However, vendor support services (both before and after installation), hardware maintenance contracts, software maintenance practices, and training programs may be just as critical to the system's success. Buying a system on the basis of hardware and software performance alone, without considering the support services the vendor offers, can be precarious. Vendors often market products and services separately, so asking vendors to submit a quotation schedule with their bids will help to clarify the actual support services they offer.

DEVISING A QUOTATION SCHEDULE

For managers to evaluate vendor policies effectively, they need information that is current, objective, and in a quantified form. The sample quotation schedule in Exhibit 1 can be used to structure the information-gathering process. The communications systems manager should first review the quotation schedule to become familiar with the specific information used to compare vendor policies and then choose those areas most pertinent to the desired project or application. Potential vendors should then be asked to respond to each item in writing. Questions can be added to the quotation schedule if the acquisition has specific requirements, but the quotation schedule should remain clear and to the point. The communications systems manager must ensure that the items are worded to elicit brief, quantifiable responses from the vendor.

The vendor must address all the items on the quotation schedule. The vendor may use specifications and other printed material as long as exact references are noted in the quotation schedules. If one vendor asks for a clarification of a point, the manager must provide that clarification to all bidders.

0-8493-9989-0/99/$0.00+$.50

Instructions

All bidders must supply a completed quotation schedule with submitted bids. All items must be completed where appropriate. The quotation schedule from the successful bidder will become part of the contract with that vendor. All submissions must be valid for at least 60 days.

Hardware Pricing

1. Purchase price of recommended system: ________
2. Lease or rent plans (operating lease):
   - Month to month ____/mo.
   - 12-month term ____/mo.
   - 24-month term ____/mo.
   - 36-month term ____/mo.
   - Other ____/mo.
3. Lease plans (finance and full payment lease):
   - 12-month term ____/mo.
   - 24-month term ____/mo.
   - 36-month term ____/mo.
   - Other ____/mo.
4. Discounts:
   - Are quantity discounts available? If yes, explain (include quantities).

     ____

     ____
   - Are there discounts on dollar volume? If yes, explain (include thresholds).

     ____

     ____
5. Installation costs: ________
6. Installation time: ________
7. Shipping costs: ________
8. Delivery time: ________

Hardware Installation

Attach a copy of installation specifications, including environmental and power requirements. Be sure that specifications include clearance dimensions.

9. Will shippers deliver to dock or installation site?

   ____

   ____
10. Is installation by user possible? If yes, is there any impact on warranty?

    ____

    ____
11. Is factory acceptance testing available?

    ____

    ____
12. Is site acceptance testing available?

    ____

    ____
13. Duration of performance test period:

    ____

    ____

Exhibit 1. Sample quotation schedule.

Hardware Warranty

14. Duration of warranty period: ______
15. Start of warranty period: ______
16. Is warranty affected by user installation? If yes, explain.

____

____

17. Working hours for warranty service: ______
18. Extra charges for warranty service:
    - Outside regular business hours ______
    - Travel expenses ______
    - No defect found ______
19. Guaranteed response time for warranty service: ______
20. Is response time upgradable for extra fee? If yes, what is the cost?

____

____

21. If system is purchased, who owns replaced parts or components?

____

____

Hardware Maintenance

22. Types of maintenance service available:
    - On call 8 hours ____/mo.
    - On call 16 hours ____/mo.
    - On call 24 hours ____/mo.
    - Per call or incident ____/hr.
23. Extra charge for:
    - Weekend service ______
    - Outside regular business hours ______
    - Travel ______
    - Overtime work that began during regular business hours ______
24. Guaranteed response time: ______
25. Cost of improved response time: ______
26. Cost of improved system uptime: ______
27. Is equipment refurbishment included in maintenance?

____

____

Software Licensing

Please provide the following information for each proposed software item, both system and application.

28. Owner of software: ______
29. Types of license available:
    - Renewable Cost/yr ______
    - Perpetual or fully paid Cost ______
    - Other Cost ______
30. Software is licensed to:
    - CPU ______
    - System ______
    - Site ______

Exhibit 1. (continued)

- User ______
- Other (specify) ______

31. License extends to:
    - Object code ______
    - Source code ______
    - Quantity discount ______
    - Secondary license ______
    - Upgrades ______
    - Backup copy for disaster recovery ______
32. Distribution method (e.g., tape, disk): ______

Software Installation

33. Installation cost: ______
34. Performed by:
    - Salesperson ______
    - Customer engineer ______
    - Systems engineer ______
    - User ______
    - Other (specify) ______
35. Warranty:
    - Duration of warranty period ______
    - Start of warranty ______
    - Acceptance testing (vendor or user)

    ____

    ____

Software Maintenance

36. Maintenance cost: ______
37. Maintenance includes:
    - Debug ______
    - Fixes ______
    - Enhancements ______
38. Average response time to trouble reports: ______
39. Method of reporting trouble:
    - Phone ______
    - Mail ______
40. Method of forwarding repair information:
    - Phone ______
    - Mail ______
    - New copy ______
    - Online ______
41. Repairs performed by:
    - Vendor representative ______
    - User ______
42. Discounts for new or enhanced release: ______
43. New releases installed by:
    - Vendor representative ______
    - User ______
44. Discounts for second license: ______

Exhibit 1. (continued)

Availability of Source Code Escrow Agreement

45. Under what conditions is source released from escrow?

____

____

46. Ownership of user-development enhancements:
    - User ______
    - Owner ______
    - Joint ______
47. Number of copies of software documentation distributed with license: ______
48. Cost of additional copies: ______
49. Is software license transferable if hardware is sold?

____

____

Exhibit 1. (continued)

All potential vendors must be advised that the quotation schedule for their system will be included in the contract with that vendor. By taking this step, the manager can eliminate much vendor sales hype.

Another dilemma that may face the communications systems manager is the fact that equipment, software, and services can be acquired from a wide variety of sources. These sources include: direct from the manufacturer, a third-party distributor, electronic specialty stores, and office supply retailers. Depending on what is being acquired, any one of these sources is acceptable, but the level of support that may be required should always be considered.

Hardware and Software Comparison Categories

Each category in the quotation schedule is briefly described in the following sections. The categories cover most of the necessary evaluation criteria. Not all categories may be needed, because an application or user may require only certain types of support. The manager may also need to add questions to evaluate a support area in more detail, or more specific equipment, such as LANs or multimedia networks.

Hardware Pricing. Policies regarding a manufacturer's pricing structure are one of the primary considerations to be made before purchasing any computer system. This section asks vendors to supply information pertaining to sales posture, available discounts, trade-in allowances, original equipment manufacturer equipment resale, available lease programs, sales, shipping charges, and delivery schedules. Although this is an important category, pricing and sales policies should never be the only criteria when a purchase is contemplated.

Hardware Installation. After a hardware configuration is chosen, attention must be paid to the concomitant installation planning and the amount of support the vendor can actually provide. Installation specifications for facility and site preparation, physical planning, and system checkout are all extremely important. A competent, cooperative, and thorough vendor can usually make all the difference between a relatively trouble-free installation and an installation beset with delays and aggravation.

Hardware Warranty. Another important consideration is the extent and breadth of the hardware warranty. The warranty's duration, services included, charges for nonwarranted items, and field service and repair personnel response times are all extremely important determinants of the quality and usefulness of the warranty.

Hardware Maintenance. After the warranty period expires, contract and per-call maintenance must be carefully considered to plan for most contingencies. The communications systems manager should understand the standard and expedited services available as well as the services that affect different price structures. The availability of maintenance of foreign peripherals and the costs of maintenance training may also need to be evaluated.

Another critical element in maintenance is the size of the IS shop. In some cases, it might be advisable to have only one or two technicians specifically responsible for a particular account.

Software Licensing. Software support is important in terms of the cost of license fees and the extent of the license. The form of the software, the updates, and the availability and cost of new versions are critical in choosing a vendor, unless independent software will be developed or purchased. The communications manager must remember that he or she is purchasing a nonexclusive "license to use" the software, nothing more. The same software is also being used by many others, including possibly a competitor.

Initial Software Installation. The vendor's professional services are extremely critical to the smooth start-up of a system. Especially important is the length of the warranty period, the status of the software delivered, and the personnel responsible for the installation.

Software Maintenance. After the system is installed, the types and levels of maintenance must be ascertained, including the time frame of maintenance and software fixes, the updates, the cost, and other important software maintenance factors.

Software Documentation. Software documentation is extremely important to ensure the effective use of the hardware installation. The availability and cost of the vendor's offerings in software documentation should be carefully evaluated.

Internet Access Providers. Internet access providers (IAP) are popping up all over the world. Most are acceptable, but care must be taken in selection for specific types of use. For example, an IAP whose busiest times are between 8:00 a.m. and 4:00 p.m. may not be able to provide a suitable response time to some business applications.

SUMMARY

The quotation schedule provided in this chapter is only a guideline; a more detailed schedule can be developed as a proposed system becomes more specific. Including the quotation schedule in the final contract will eliminate interpretation hassles after the sale. Furthermore, every point covered in the quotation schedule, and ultimately in the contract, can be negotiated.

The single most important element in evaluating vendors is planning. Allow enough time for vendors to respond to the quotation schedule and to quantify and evaluate their responses. Taking the time to completely understand the vendor's position on key points will give the manager the necessary leverage in negotiations.

Chapter 77
WAN Network Integration: A Case Study

Charles Breakfield

The original project was created to merge the Banyan WAN at the FDIC and the RTC. The RTC's corporate charter expired on December 31, 1995, and its assets were to be integrated into the FDIC's operations.

The RTC's origins—and its reason for being—date back almost 10 years. When banks and savings and loans (S&Ls) became insolvent in the late 1980s, they called on the Federal Deposit Insurance Corporation (FDIC) and the Federal Savings and Loan Insurance Corporation (FSLIC) to prop them up. The task was so overwhelming that Congress was petitioned to assist. As a result, the RTC was created, designed to handle the disposition of the assets and liabilities of the failed banks and S&Ls until 1995. When the RTC's corporate charter expired, all activities and assets rolled over to the FDIC. Its systems were developed independently of the FDIC's but with this inevitability in mind.

The FDIC had no plans to keep RTC employees after December 31, so FDIC personnel would assume all existing RTC computer network activity. This would be practical only if both organizations were similar in design and layout. Therefore, the project, which began in August 1993 and took 10 months to complete, was implemented to make the RTC's wide-area networks (WANs) compatible with the FDIC's.

The Challenges and Benefits of Implementation

The RTC's Banyan WAN encompassed the 7,000 employees and contractors located in California, Colorado, Texas, Kansas, Georgia, New York, Virginia, and Washington DC. The WANs needed to be connected to the FDIC's WANs, which encompassed 10,000 employees who are similarly located. All the RTC Banyan servers targeted for upgrade were production

0-8493-9989-0/99/$0.00+$.50

servers being used 8 to 12 hours a day, six days a week. Server upgrades had to be coordinated so the end users were not disrupted during the day and so there would be a fallback position if a server upgrade failed.

Several other areas for upgrades were also targeted. An operating system upgrade was required as part of the integration proposal. The FDIC's 337 Banyan servers, from Banyan Systems Inc., are running on one NOS, Vines 5.52(5); the 329 RTC Banyan servers were running on Vines 4.11(5), two revisions old. This network operating systems upgrade was required to bring the RTC up to the same level the FDIC was running before merging the two organizations. Also, Banyan no longer wanted to provide fixes (i.e., software patches that solved "bugs" or problems) or enhancements for an older version of Vines, so the RTC had to upgrade its network to continue to receive operating system support.

As part of the operating system upgrade, a server hardware upgrade also was necessary, to support the enhanced version of software. Additionally, the Cisco routers in the Resolution Trust Corporation network needed to be upgraded.

The Business Opportunity

As part of the implementation, new functionality offered by the newest revision of Vines version 5.52 would allow the corporation to use the new features to operate the business better. The enhanced functionality of the new e-mail under Banyan Vines 5.52(5) was one of the main reasons for the upgrade, because the RTC's most important application was the e-mail system, and the most heavily used applications were the e-mail and the directory services, Streettalk Directory Assistance (STDA). The full listing of the combined organizations (a total of 17,000 users) under STDA would provide access to all end users by all end users. Additional network management tools and diagnostic tools were included as part of the new network. Better performance tuning and use of resources would also be easier to accomplish under Vines 5.52(5).

Technical Benefits

The technical benefits of the Vines 5.52(5) operating system were:

- The new file format, S10, under Vines 5.52(5) allowed up to 4GBs of inodes per file system, up from the old file format, S5, under Vines 4.11(5), which allowed 64K bytes of inodes. Each file or directory was represented by one inode. More files or directories per volume were required by the RTC.
- The Access Rights List functionality was greatly enhanced under 5.52(5). Access control could then be given all the way down to the file level within directories or within subdirectories to a user or a group

of users. Security issues could be tailored to the file level, which was not possible before.

- Greater network management was offered through the network management statistics on memory usage, server processes, hard drive activity, and CPU usage. The improved tools promised better server monitoring and network management.
- Valuable to the RTC were the tape backup and restore processes built into the operating system. Under Vines 5.52(5), the operator can back up and restore not just file services, but also specific directories and files with much greater ease.
- New printer functionality was also gained by migrating to Vines 5.52(5). Multiple print queues were serviced by one printer, and print queues were set up to print to other printers if a printer was overloaded. Print jobs were redirected by queue operators or done automatically.
- A less obvious benefit, but still an important feature, was the new routing matrix algorithm that was implemented into Streettalk. The overhaul to the routing matrix in Banyan Streettalk all but eliminated the sporadic occurrence of network "broadcast storms," which were an inherent problem.
- New functionality was offered under Banyan Vines STDA. User IDs could be defined to include additional attributes on each user put into the system. The security could be set so no one could look at the associated attributes in the AVD file that holds them. The information contained in the AVD file could be masked and display only the users under STDA that the personnel department and the end user wanted displayed for e-mail purposes.

Priorities

The majority of the mainframe applications used by the RTC and FDIC were located at the Virginia location in Rosslyn VA and required 3270 emulation for host access. The RTC network was independent from the FDIC network, to begin with, but there were certain priorities to consider to bring them together.

As these are government institutions dealing with assets of failed banks, network security was a priority. The original decision to go with Banyan was based in part on its WAN capabilities and the tight security design of the user log-in process. Each time a user logged in, his or her unique network ID was time- and date-stamped to prevent unauthorized access by a computer hacker. The flexibility to log in anywhere in the network and still maintain a high level of security was key to the way the RTC did business.

A requirement of the new version of the NOS was that it support all existing off-the-shelf software. All standard applications, word processing, spreadsheets, databases, and e-mail were provided on the local Banyan servers. The current suite of standard software packages that the RTC supported included WordPerfect 5.1, Lotus 2.4, and Paradox 3.5. All workstations ran either DOS 5.0, which was preferable, or DOS 3.3 with 386 Max version 5.0 as the memory manager. Saber, a software package, was used for the menuing front-end for all users to access all applications. All the applications were to be compatible with the Vines 5.52(5) upgrade.

Elements Targeted for Change

All applications in use at the RTC when the project began needed testing in a lab environment before delivery into the production environment. Preliminary testing showed complete compatibility across all applications with the Vines 5.52(5) upgrade.

The workstations in the field were configured with only 2MBs of random-access memory (RAM). RAM requirements of the new operating system shell, as well as the applications to be run for daily applications, had to fit into the 2MBs of memory. There were no plans or budget to upgrade RAM in field workstations.

Each of the two styles of Banyan server (the RTC's and the FDIC's) required identical configuration in naming conventions of groups, file services, print services, 3270 services, e-mail naming standards, amount of disk space, memory configurations, server names, NIC settings, and cabling specifications for connectivity.

Several Banyan servers also required hardware upgrades before the new operating system could be installed. Banyan server hardware upgrades included faster processors (i.e., Intel 486 chips), larger server hard drives, and faster NIC cards, when feasible.

The Cisco routers used to connect each office to the WAN also required an upgrade, as they supported only Vines 4.11(5) IP protocol stack. The revision of the routing software in the Cisco routers was 9.x, and the RTC needed a 10.x revision.

Upgrade Costs

An upgrade server key option had to be purchased for each RTC server—a $5,000 option for each server. Since RTC servers needing the upgrade numbered 329, the cost totaled $1,645,000.

Each corporate network server required one 1.3GB hard drive per server before the upgrade could take place. Each CNS server also required a drive 0 larger than the existing 80MB drive. The upgrade process required that each CNS have a 330MB drive in slot 0, a 330MB in slot 1, and the 1.3GB drive in slot 3. The larger drive 0 would accommodate the new operating system requirements. The actual number of CNS Banyan servers was not known but was estimated at 40% of the total 329 Banyan servers, or a total of 132 Corporate Network Server servers to be upgraded. Each 3GB upgrade drive was valued at $5,400, for a total of $712,800 to upgrade all CNS servers. The Compaq SystemPro accounted for the balance of the RTC 329 servers, or about 197 servers. Of the 197 SystemPros, roughly 50% needed hard drive upgrades, roughly 30% needed CPU upgrades, and approximately 40% needed to upgrade to 32-bit NIC cards (either Token Ring or Ethernet). Hard drive upgrades (and controllers) cost approximately $4,500 each, for a total of $445,500. CPU upgrades and system PROMS cost approximately $1,900 for each of 59 servers, or $47,400.

The hardware upgrades for the servers were required only for drive 0 of the CNS. The hardware upgrades for the other servers were done in conjunction with the Vines 5.52(5) upgrade for two reasons. First, the hardware upgrades had already been planned and budgeted for before the Vines upgrade. The existing server hardware was two to four years old at the time of the project and required upgrading because hardware failures were occurring more frequently. Second, because the servers needed to be rebuilt from scratch, it made economic sense to do the hardware upgrades just before laying down the operating system and files. This would save overtime costs that would be incurred if the servers were refurbished after upgrading the operating system.

Router Upgrades

The last items to be upgraded in the network were the Cisco AGS and AGS+ routers, which were scheduled for upgrade after the servers were completed. The Ciscos were running the 9.4.0 software version, which did not fully support Vines 5.52(5). Full functionality for Vines 5.52(5) was promised if RTC upgraded the hardware and software. Additional memory was required to run the software update 10.0.4. The total number of Cisco routers that needed an upgrade was 30. (Some of the 3000 series did not need the hardware upgrades but did need the software.) The hardware upgrades were approximately $1,500 each, and the software upgrades were $3,000 each, for a total of $45,000 and $90,000, respectively.

Man Hours

Each production server upgraded from Vines 4.11(5) to Vines 5.52(5) needed two RTC network engineers, each working four to six hours (five hours, average) of overtime per server if the following methodology were used. If a figure of $17 per hour for labor costs is used, each server would cost approximately $170 to upgrade. If the 329 servers were upgraded at that price, the labor cost to upgrade all the servers was $55,930. The total costs are summarized in Exhibit 1.

Exhibit 1. Total estimated RTC upgrade costs, per component.

Banyan Server Upgrades	$1,645,000
CNS Server Upgrades	$712,800
SystemPro CPU Upgrades	$112,100
SystemPro Hard Drive Upgrades	$445,500
SystemPro NIC Card Upgrades	$47,400
Cisco Hardware Upgrades	$45,000
Cisco Software Upgrades	$90,000
Upgrade Labor Costs (OT only)	$55,000
Total (Estimated)	**$3,153,730**

Upgrade Modeling and Refinement

All the first-line network engineers were trained on the Vines 5.52(5) operating system first and then were involved in testing specific aspects of the operating system at each site. The results were communicated via Lotus notes, video conferences, and face-to-face roundtable meetings.

The upgrade methodology was tested, refined, and then taught to the staff members who would actually be doing the upgrades. The modeling and refinement activity was particularly valuable in that it gave the staff time to practice before operating on live servers and corporate data. These practice sessions were the greatest insurance policy available in this process. In fact, the real success for the project began in these early planning sessions.

Each type of production server, Compaq SystemPro and Banyan CNS, needed upgrading to Vines 5.52(5). Every server required the internal hard drives to be reformatted to take advantage of the S10 file format before having the data restored from tape. Within the restore-from-tape process, all the files needed the ARLs converted to the new 5.52(5) format.

The overall upgrade approach to both servers was the same: to build a like server, either a SystemPro or CNS, offline to replace the production server. By starting on Monday morning, an identical Banyan server could be built, tested, and ready for live data to be restored beginning at 5:00 p.m. on Friday. Typically, a server was fully tested and ready for the final data files by Wednesday night or Thursday morning. The offline servers were built during regular business hours, so overtime was needed only on Friday night, for the last stage of the conversion process.

The SystemPros were upgraded with Intel 486 processor boards, new ROM chips, and new 510MB hard drive array pairs and SCSI II controller cards. The upgrade process was greatly hindered by these extra variables, because of a 50% failure rate with the Seagate 510 drive array pairs. Not all

SystemPro hard drives were upgraded, and the existing Conner 210 drive array pairs and SCSI I controller cards were reused. In each configuration, the Compaq SystemPro was left to run the comprehensive drive array and to run controller card diagnostic tests for 24 to 48 hours before being formatted with the S10 file format under Banyan Vines 5.52(5). Although this was a time-consuming action, the servers that made it into production were very reliable.

Additionally, any Token Ring or Ethernet NIC that were not 32-bit Enhanced Industry Standard Architecture (EISA) were replaced with 32-bit EISA boards for improved performance.

The Banyan CNS servers, for the most part, had a like configuration. Each was a 386-class machine with an 80MB drive as drive 0, a 330MB drive for drive 1, and a 330MB drive for drive 2. The new 5.52(5) operating system would just fit on drive 0, but that left no room for file swap space, for growth in the internal routing table, or for e-mail service. The upgrade position was to remove the 80MB drive and replace it with the 300MB drive in slot 3. A 1.3GB was purchased for each CNS for installation as the third drive. All applications, all noncore Banyan services, and all data are placed on this drive. All core Banyan services were installed by default onto the first drive, and the 330MBs provided ample room. For the most part, the second drive (a 330MB hard drive) was left for growth but was largely unused. No CNS servers were scheduled for upgrades with 486 processors.

The Process

The beginning process was the same for each style of server. Diagnostics were run on each; each drive was formatted multiple times (time permitting);and the Banyan Vines operating system was loaded. At this point, the Banyan server key on the production server was carefully removed and placed on the offline server. The offline server was brought up and given the same name as the production server. The identity of the new 5.52(5) server was critical and required the server key to build its internal routing tables. It was essential that the two servers not be connected to the network at the same time.

Once the new server had been brought up and named properly, it needed to be patched with a total of 10 Banyan patches (i.e., fixes, to be installed for full functionality) before anything could be done. The order of patch installation was important, and several versions were tried and discarded before the list was stable. However, some patches were more trouble than the problems they fixed—even having to be replaced only hours after they had been applied. Patches were installed after the data was loaded and converted as well as before. Both methodologies worked.

The offline Vines 5.52(5) server targeted to replace the production server then had all the same services created using the same naming convention for file restoration and conversion. It is important to note that if a file service was not within the naming standards, the name was converted.

Print and file services. All print services were rebuilt, as opposed to restored. The new print services at the FDIC were different enough to warrant setting up the RTC services from scratch. The Banyan operating system also would not permit moving and converting the print services. Print services were created on the target server during the week.

All file services were created on the target server to match the production server, and each service containing data was moved individually and converted. The applications file service was restored from the standard application tape that was created at the beginning of the upgrade process. Because this was a static file system, meaning that usually no changes to the applications occurred, this service could also be restored. After the first server was converted, a Vines 5.52(5) tape backup of the applications was created and then used for restoring target servers for upgrades. This process saved time converting ARLs. The ARLs, however, still needed to be reworked to be server specific—so the restore was not as trouble free as it sounds.

Any other service on the production server, such as asynchronous dial-in, 3270 SNA service, server-to-server, and WAN links, were also created and set up on the target server before Friday evening. Any lists created on the production server needed to be printed out and rebuilt by hand before the target server was brought online. The list itself was added to the server before the data files were restored and converted. Names could be added to the list only after the server was brought online.

The Group Moves

The only activities that could not be done before Friday afternoon were the group moves, and the transfer of the e-mail, data files and updates to the Adminlist for the target server. Promptly at 5:00 p.m. on Friday, the groups were moved from the production server to tape and then restored to the target server. The group moves were done before the file services, because in the process of the file conversion, the ARLs were updated to the new Vines 5.52(5). The file services (i.e., the actual data) were backed up to tape and then restored to the target server. ARLs and the group and user IDs were matched. If the groups with their users had not been there before moving the files, it would have been necessary to go back in and edit the ARLs on the target server.

Moving E-Mail and STDA

The e-mail service was moved from the production server to the target server via tape backup. This process was straightforward and reliable. The STDA was recreated on the target server once the target server was moved to production status and cabled to the WANs and the old server was removed. Again, the proper sequence was removed and the new target server moved into place. The STDA service could not be moved with reliable results, so Banyan recommended that it be recreated; however, it could not be created before the server was placed on the WANs. The target server needed the connection to the WANs so it could rebuild the internal STDA database from upstream neighbors. The creation and forced rebuild on Friday night gave three days for the rebuild process to operate before Monday morning. Sometimes, though, three days is not enough time for STDA to rebuild properly, and the database had to be killed and recreated before it will work properly.

Moving the ARLs

The ARLs were one of the last major areas left to update once the target server became the production server. The administrators were usually part of another group that were kept on a different server. Sometimes the Adminlist could not be updated with the names of administrators until the new production server could "see" the target server. At those times, two different methods to force the update process on the new production server were used. A dummy group was created on the new server, which forced a detail broadcast to the WANs that updated all the surrounding servers, and, as a result, all WANs began to "see" the new server. When the server could "see" and "be seen," the dummy group was deleted.

The other method was to use a Banyan utility that would "goose" Streettalk and force the surrounding servers to exchange routing information and update their respective routing tables. The STSYNC utility is effective in getting servers to synchronize with each other. The last upgrade detail was updating the boot disks for the users. This process typically required that someone physically visit each workstation that was physically attached to the upgraded server and run the NEWREV PROGRAM, which copied down the new boot files to the workstation. This process was quickly automated by the staff members so when a user of a group that resided on a newly upgraded server logged in, a batch file ran that copied the necessary files to their workstation and then required them to reboot. This process saved an enormous amount of time. Because entire groups with the associated users were being moved, no password changes for the end users were required. This helped make the conversion more transparent to the end user.

Some Glitches

Final issues for the conversion were to double-check the ARL of the root in each file service, as they did not convert reliably and had to be modified by hand. Oddly enough, the remaining ARLs in the rest of the directory tree were usually correct and did not need modifying. Some tailoring of the ARLs did occur after the fact, to comply with the new RTC standards that were published before the upgrade was started.

One ARL problem encountered was with lists on the server that were used in the ARLs of files and directories. If the ARLs were being changed or updated with the Banyan Vines utility Netpro, the workstation would receive an out-of-memory error and terminate. The reason for this was that Netpro could not update ARLs with a list that was not there, so it buffered the transaction and went on to the next ARL update, and so on, until the workstation ran out of memory. The lesson learned here was to make sure that all lists were at least placed on the server, empty or not, so the ARL conversion would operate properly.

In the particular upgrade scenario for the site, two and sometimes three server conversions a week could proceed with the equipment on hand. As servers were replaced with new production servers running Vines 5.52(5), the 4.11(5) servers coming offline became the new target machines in the upgrade process for the following week. The assorted 20 Banyan servers took 10 weeks to convert from Vines 4.11(5) to Vines 5.52(5). All staff members worked in teams that rotated each week, so no network administrator was needed for consecutive weekend work, and no mental "burnout" that would have resulted from such a demanding schedule occurred.

As in all well-thought-out plans, there is always an overlooked X variable that comes back to foil complete upgrade success. As all sites reached the final stages of the server upgrade process, a problem surfaced that no one had anticipated: Paradox 3.5 would not support more than 25 concurrent users on a Banyan Vines 5.52(5) platform.

Lab applications testing did not explore the Paradox application to this extent. Both Banyan and Borland were contacted about fixes or workarounds. Banyan declined to assist Resolution Trust Corporation in this problem, saying it was an application problem. After many phone conversations with Borland, their technicians did concede that it was a problem with Paradox 3.5. But because Borland was no longer supporting that product version, the technicians suggested that RTC upgrade to Paradox 4.0 to solve the problem.

There was no money budgeted, however, for upgrading approximately 329 servers with only 2MBs of RAM to the 4MBs of RAM that Paradox 4.0 required to operate. Therefore, Borland's solution was cost prohibitive.

Ultimately, the solution was somewhat unsatisfactory but effective. Each site left one Banyan Vines server at 4.11(5) that contained the Paradox NET and SOM files. These files allowed Paradox 3.5 to run normally for all the end users who were attached to Vines 5.52(5) servers. Fortunately, Banyan supports mixed versions of its Vines operating systems, so long as they are within one version of each other (e.g., 4.X and 5.X systems can be mixed and still talk to each other).

The Final Integration

The last stage was opening the main Cisco router, which was connected to the RTC and FDIC networks, to full Banyan Vines traffic from both sides. As part of the initial procedure, certain action items were completed before the wave of router table updates went surging through the respective networks.

First, all RTC Vines servers had their communication buffers set to at least 400,000 before the cut over. All CNS servers had to have a primary drive that was larger than 80MBs (300 MB were preferred). All network servers were scanned to ensure that no duplicate server names (or server key numbers) were in the two systems. All end users were prohibited from logging on and using the network beginning at 5:00 p.m. that Friday. The STDA directory services on each server were stopped on Friday morning and were not allowed to rebuild again until Sunday night. Finally, no production servers were trying to get their Streettalk updates across a WAN link that was slower than 56K bytes per second. The STDA was also stopped to prevent any unnecessary WAN traffic while Streettalk was trying to update the internal routing tables of all the production servers.

Full server backups were completed and verified before the process began, to provide an absolute fallback position in the unlikely event that each organization had to return to a preintegration status. The actual process of the integration was that the servers in each network needed to have their internal routing tables updated to know about the additional 300-plus servers on the other network. Since Vines does this dynamically, the staff's primary job was to monitor the health of each server and in fact, the whole RTC network while the update process unfolded. Once the main Cisco router was allowed to pass Streettalk traffic and updates both ways, it became much like an information tidal wave slamming into each site. At 9:00 p.m. Friday night, the information updates were rolling toward the location, and server memory utilization stats were watched to see if any server started swapping information from memory to disk, a sure sign that the server was in danger of being swamped.

By 10:00 p.m., the Streettalk routing updates were in full swing, and the available server memory was dropping to levels too low for comfort. Staff stopped all unnecessary file server processes in an effort to free up and make available more server memory for the routing table updates. By 11:00 p.m., the servers in the network had stabilized, and available server memory began to climb, a sign that the critical time had passed and that the network was stabilizing.

At 9:00 a.m. Saturday morning, the staff returned to restart all the services that had been stopped the night before and began testing the services to which the end users would need access on Monday morning—with the exception of STDA. Once all services were tested, and no lingering problems existed, the staff began to deal with the STDA issue.

It was decided to permit the regularly scheduled rebuilds to go as planned, but the FDIC would not be included in the rebuilds for another 10 days. This would allow Streettalk time to "settle" before subjecting it to another data "blitz" from an STDA that would have added another 10,000 names to the existing 7,000-name database. The final integration of the two STDAs proved to be modest and concluded the entire data integration process rather quietly.

Conclusion

In retrospect, this network integration might have been overplanned, considering how smoothly it went; however, the Vines 5.52(5) server upgrades that blindsided the team on the Paradox issue were underplanned. Data center operations managers looking at integrating similar or even dissimilar networks save time and aggravation if they include field personnel who will be participating in the upgrade/integration process. Bringing in the senior network personnel, training them, and including them in the integration process made all the difference in the merger of the FDIC and RTC Banyan WAN. People scheduled to do the work who "buy in" to the project help breed enthusiasm and interest in the success of the project and provide unexpected benefits.

For example, field personnel identified many incidental problems that no one at corporate headquarters had even considered. The success of the overall project was ensured by the corporate people involving the field network engineers. Every effort should be made to get the hardware and software vendors involved at the beginning of the project to assist and comment during the planning stage. Banyan Systems placed one of its certified Banyan engineers on site at headquarters to help with the integration process. Additionally, Compaq sent its engineers out to RTC sites to help resolve the SystemPro hardware problems that were first encountered when the new drives were installed before the operating system upgrades. Each vendor that was contacted and included in the upgrade planning before implementation improved the chances for success with either technical advice or on-site involvement. Resolution Trust Corporation suppliers also contributed in the upgrade process when involved.

Finally, communication among all the players in an upgrade of this size is critical. Information is useless unless it is in the hands of the right people at the right time. Using Banyan e-mail, Lotus Notes, and televideo conferencing, headquarters staff and field engineers were able to communicate critical pieces of information to the proper people in a timely manner. As a result, the upgrade and integration success was accomplished with existing personnel who were also responsible for the day-to-day operations of the existing user community.

Chapter 78
Remote LAN/WAN Connections: A Case Study

Charles Breakfield
Roxanne Burkey

The organization discussed in this chapter is a national corporation headquartered in Virginia. Currently, the company's corporate locations interconnect through a Banyan Wide Area Network (WAN) for access to business software, national databases, and e-mail. Each location contains a network service area for user support and connects to other locations, including the Virginia headquarters.

Space reconfiguration at a corporate location in Texas prompted a move of approximately 125 support staff to the fourth and sixth floors of an adjacent building, approximately 100 feet away from the primary building. The Banyan WAN resided on the seventh floor of the primary building, and the main support areas for data access were to remain there.

The relocating staff, however, required network data access from two of the existing servers on the seventh floor to perform their work, but providing network servers and the associated support staff to the new location was not an option. Exhibit 1 illustrates the wiring layout of the primary building.

An additional consideration was that the organization was consolidating business activities. Broader plans for the year were to consolidate network operations to enable an overall reduction in support staff. Therefore, any system changes made for this relocation of the 125 support staff had to:

- Be limited in cost
- Use existing materials
- Require no additional staffing
- Adhere to the existing network standards
- Contain limited leasing and licensing agreements

0-8493-9989-0/99/$0.00+$.50

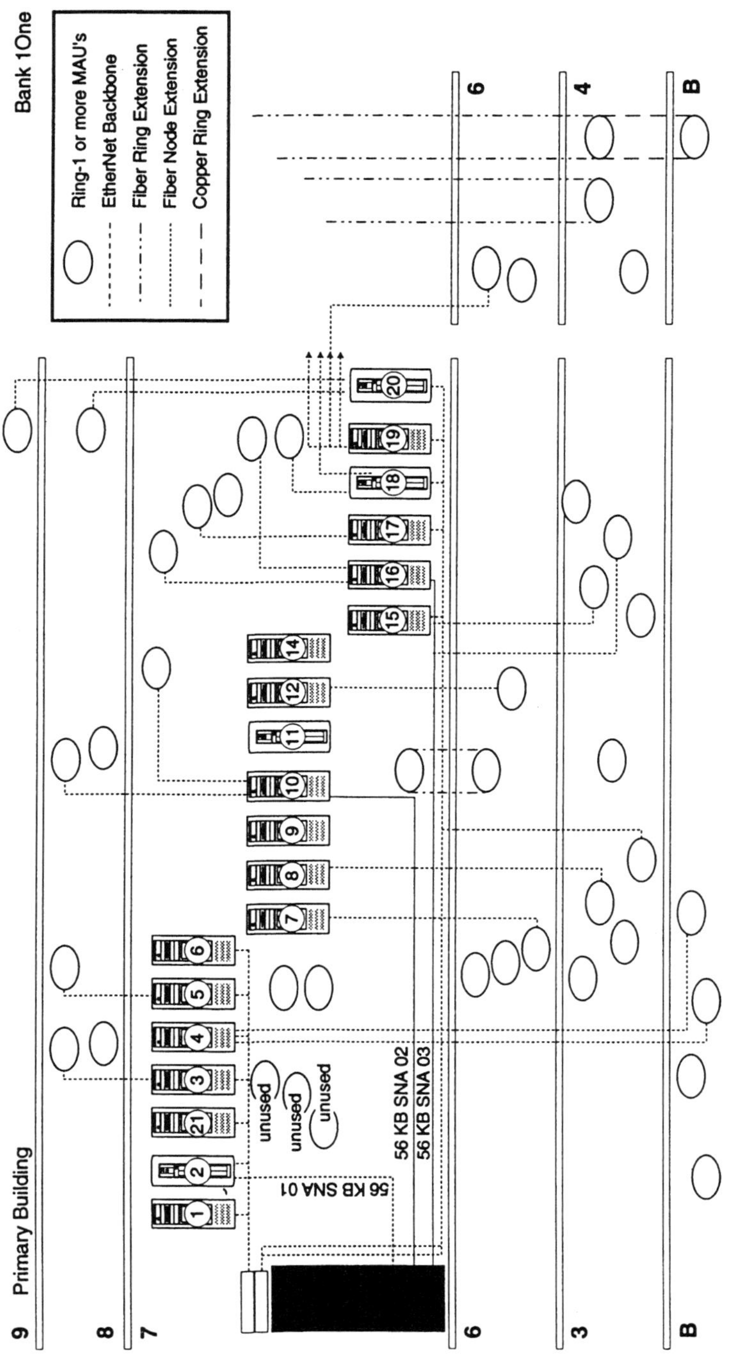

Exhibit 1. FSC server wiring layout.

A feasibility study determined the technology needed for data connection from the fourth and sixth floors of the adjacent building to the seventh-floor server room of the primary building.

This chapter describes the three connectivities (i.e., fiber optics, infrared, and microwave) considered in the feasibility study, the advantages and disadvantages of each, the estimated time to complete installation, and the draft estimated costs. The chapter also puts all these factors in the context of the company's business operations.

Finally, the chapter also supplies a proposed plan for the solution's implementation and installation. The recommended course of action is based on the technology feasibility, time frames, costs, and flexibility for known future organizational changes.

Establishing A Baseline

A feasibility study certified the data connection method among the existing services and the remote new services and outlined the most viable option for connectivity within the confines determined by upper management. The study began with an itemization of existing resources and criteria for deciding on technology options.

Existing Resources

Staff members familiar with the existing Banyan network conducted the study over a nine-week period. Detailed reviews of the existing and planned systems included a review of the wiring configuration for the new space, data specifications, building requirements, and existing AT&T services to determine the project requirements.

The staff investigated the possibility that appropriate technology might already be in use elsewhere in the company, as well. They conducted a nationwide, corporatewide investigation of the options available for data connectivity requirements. A step was also completed to locate in-house support staff with experience with similar installations, problems that might come up with a specific technology, and available materials.

Defining the Options

The criteria for evaluating the options were determined based on the initial request and follow-up discussions with staff. The criteria, in order of importance, included the operational time frames, connection reliability, technical support provisions, and cost.

The physical hardwire and wireless connection possibilities were reviewed based on the criteria, and three viable options were selected to undergo in-depth analysis. After the technology investigation was complete, a review with building management was conducted to ensure acceptance of the recommendation.

Defining the Existing Resources

The existing Banyan WANs were located on the seventh floor of the primary building. Staff was in place at the primary location to support the requirements of Banyan WAN users at the primary building and of users selected for the move to the adjacent building.

The adjacent building's floor configuration included free-standing cubicle work areas and walled offices with free-standing desks. Each workstation required power to support the electrical equipment, an RJ-45 data jack for the phone connection, and an IBM data connection to support the existing Token Ring topology.

Wiring closets were installed on each floor at the remote location; the closets had three wire racks as well as punch blocks. The wire racks contained the data cables terminated into patch panels and mounted in the top third of the wire racks. The power drops for the walled offices included voice, data, and power connections. Power poles fed voice, data, and power connections for each cubicle. Each workstation contained Type 2 cable, Type 1 data cable for the Token Ring connection, and 4-pair wire for the voice connection.

Defining the Business Objective

Banyan support service for the remote location was possible by means of one of the following:

- Hiring additional staff for Banyan server support
- Moving existing support staff to the new location
- Providing remote support by the existing staff running back and forth between the buildings
- Establishing a remote connection into the existing server configuration while maintaining current staffing levels

The option that best suited the company's long-term needs was establishing a new connection into the existing configuration at the primary site, without adding support staff. The project then was to provide a data interface between the two buildings.

The requirements for data access included a network connection from the three wire racks in the fourth-floor wire closet and three wire racks in the sixth-floor wire closet of the adjacent building to the wire racks located in the seventh-floor server room of the primary building. The final link between the selected technology and the target servers would require connection to a Token Ring Type 1 drop cable. The cost considerations had to include any adapters or converters needed for linking the existing system to the recommended technology.

There were, in this case, possible limitations on the use of physical hardwiring networking items; the building management might determine certain equipment to be dangerous to the property, building staff, or other tenants. Because physical wiring above ground was not allowed, the access had to take place below ground under the parking garage or via equipment to be located on the roof.

Connectivity Options

The method selected had to provide reliable connectivity for data while remaining cost-effective. To meet this requirement, both physical and wireless connectivity options were explored. Several potential methods were reviewed, three of which were selected for final consideration.

Physical Connections

Physical wiring of a WAN is the single largest cost factor of materials and installation labor.

Twisted-Pair Cable. Cable standards include either twisted-pair or coaxial cable. Hardware connection performance for a Token Ring network environment is measured by the rate at which it can move data. Twisted-pair cable can reliably move data at the rate of 10M bits per second and coaxial cable can reliably move data at 16M bits.

Fiber Optic Connectivity. Fiber optic connection is considered by many today as the premier connection for voice and data. It provides a reliable connection and allows for an increase in system throughput.

Wireless Connections

Today, wireless network connection is concentrated in three areas, including spread spectrum UHF, infrared, and microwave radio technologies.

Spread Spectrum UHF. This is designed to appear as background noise in most radio-frequency transmitters and receivers. Consequently, data is very secure; only an authorized user is able to access the data. Data is not susceptible to interference from other signals or electronic devices; however, transmission speed is limited and best suited for a small LAN environment.

Infrared. Infrared is the type of signal used over most fiber optic links but without the fiber media. These devices can achieve speeds of 16M bits. Products available include those specifically designed for a Token Ring environment with multiple-access units. This technology is effective in environments with an unobstructed line of site.

Microwave. Microwave technology offers speed for transmission to 6.7M bits at a range of 130 feet and supports Ethernet. This technology has the benefit of providing ownership of materials, allowing lower costs on future relocations.

Eliminating Inappropriate Connectivity Technologies

Two of the technologies described in the previous sections were eliminated from any in-depth consideration. Twisted-pair cables were dismissed as an option because the preliminary review indicated a lack of reliability at this project's distance—100 feet. Twisted-pair cables also have limitations in handling the anticipated data traffic.

Spread-spectrum UHF was also eliminated. Even though it is a secure connectivity option, it is limited in speed and best suited for small LANs. Consideration of this application to future, smaller-scale projects was recommended.

The three options given serious consideration are discussed in the following sections. Exhibit 2 and Exhibit 3 summarize the advantages and disadvantages of each technology.

Exhibit 2. Advantages of fiber optic, microwave, and infrared technologies.

Option 1: Fiber Optic	Option 2: Microwave	Option 3: Infrared
Impervious to electrical noise and interference typically present in all office environments	Low signal attenuation	Freedom from government regulation, no licensing or usage fees
Systems using fiber are immune to RFI	Portability of equipment, owned by the organization	Portability of equipment, owned by the organization
Fiber optic poses no risk of carrying lightning charges to computer equipment	Cost-effective for line-of-sight connection and when frequency bank congestion is low, this is cost-effective	Ease of interconnecting additional locations
Fiber is conducive to a Token Ring environment	Conducive to a Token Ring environment	Immunity to radio interference
Rapid installation	Reasonable installation time	Reasonable installation time
High data security	Signal scrambling is available to increase data security through some vendors	Security of the data
Upwardly scalable		

Exhibit 3. Disadvantages of fiber optic, microwave, and infrared technologies

Option 1: Fiber Optic	Option 2: Microwave	Option 3: Infrared
Additional repeaters are needed to boost the signals for long distances	The capacity of 6.7M bits is less than the 16M-bit needed at its peak times	Atmospheric conditions affect reliable data transmission
Fiber cable runs cannot be subjected to sharp turns	Outside installation support required and no existing training available	High up-front equipment investment and installation support
Cable terminations and splices must be specially prepared	Signal or transmission unreliability during excessive rains	Potential safety issue for retina damage caused by looking directly into the beam
The materials belong to the property		Potential delay of licensing from the FCC, possible installation delay

The First Option: Fiber Optics

Fiber optics is a communications media linking two electronic circuits by a strand of glass. It is lightweight and small, making it more attractive for projects in which space is at a premium. A graded index fiber performs best, because of its ability to carry multiple signals, with the least amount of signal loss due to dispersion. Wide bandwidth, low signal loss, and electromagnetic immunity are the three most outstanding features of fiber optics.

Fiber Optic Data Transmission

Fiber optic systems transmit data as a series of light pulses, generated either by light-emitting diodes (LED) or lasers. The Bit Error Rate (BER) for fiber optic cabling is as much as 10,000 times lower than standard electrical media. The connections are further simplified by the absence of ground loops, crosstalk, ringing, and echoing.

Light propagation through fiber depends principally on three factors, including the composition, size, and light injected into the fiber. Transmitting sources commonly use LED in place of laser. With a longer lifetime than a laser light, LED is easier to use and maintain. An LED source has a higher and broader output pattern but is not capable of single-mode compatibility. The transmitter output power is coupled with the diameter of fiber, so that power increases with core diameter.

Detectors perform the opposite function from the source by converting optical energy to electrical energy. The photo diode produces current in response to incident light. Detectors are typically packaged in the same receptacles as sources. Receiver sensitivity specifies the weakest optical signal it will receive. This is affected by the amount of noise, or signal clarity, during signal receipt as measured by bit error rates or the signal-to-noise ratio (SNR).

Fiber Optic Cabling

Fiber optic cable is available in either single mode or multimode. Single mode has an aperture of about nine microns, has a low attenuation rate, and is ideally suited for long-distance networks. Multimode is available at apertures from 50 to 100 microns and has a higher attenuation rate, because signals enter at an angle and bounce off the fiber walls as they travel. This allows for use of multiple paths, making it best suited for short-distance applications. Fiber cable comes in simplex (containing one fiber), duplex(containing a sending and receiving fiber), or hybrid, in which duplex is combined with twisted-pair.

A network requires only two strands of fiber; however, a multiple-strand cable is often used for backup reliability for transmission. The fiber diameter used for this type of connection is 62.5 em and has a standard cladding diameter of 125 em. This combination offers high speed, low attenuation (3.75 dB/km), and a high bandwidth of 1000 MHz/km at 1300nm.

Fiber optic cabling is versatile, with the ability to serve as a backbone, front end, and back end of LAN networks. Both Ethernet and Token Ring network configurations are adaptable to fiber optic cabling in place of standard copper wiring. The cost of this media typically makes it best suited to campus, building, and data center network environments. Exhibit 4 displays the potential connection configuration considered for this project.

Advantages

Fiber optic connections offer a wide variety of advantages over other hardwire and wireless options. Fiber:

- Transmits data as a series of light pulses, making it impervious to electrical noise and interference typically present in all office environments
- Is immune to radio-frequency interference (RFI)
- Does not conduct electricity, thus protecting computer equipment from lightning charges
- Is a highly secure data transmission medium, because it does not radiate energy, and tapping data from it is extremely difficult
- Is conducive to an Ethernet or Token Ring environment, as with most hardware installations
- Is upwardly scalable

In addition, the installation of fiber is rapid.

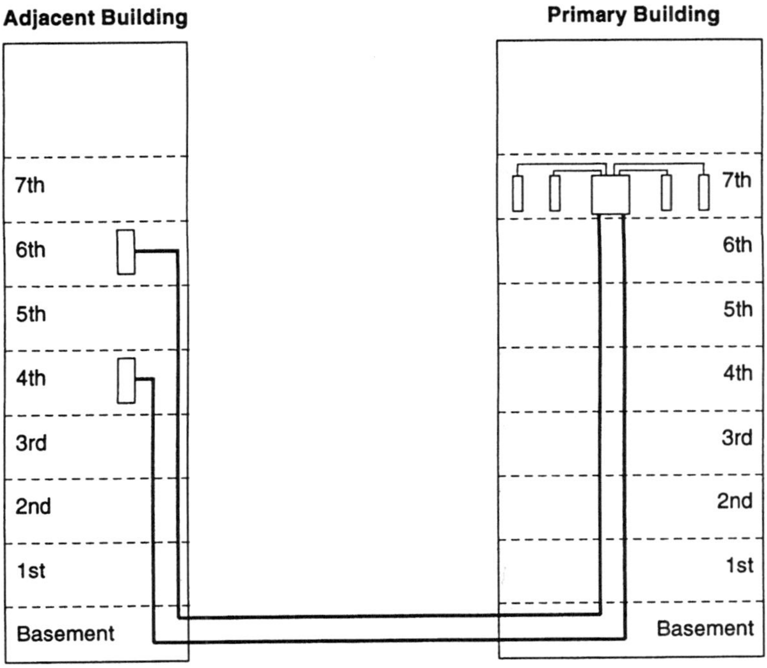

Exhibit 4. Fiber-optic cable run.

Disadvantages

The disadvantages of this technology include:

- Additional repeaters are needed to boost the signals over long distances, which incurs costs.
- Fiber cable runs cannot be subjected to sharp turns.
- Cable terminations and splices must be specially prepared.
- Materials cannot be removed once they are installed.

Costs

The basic cost to set up the fiber optic option for the remote location would be as shown in Exhibit 5.

The Second Option: Microwave

A microwave radio system can transmit voice, data, and video and uses direction radio broadcast transmission methods, operating in the 2 gHz to 40 gHz frequency bands, as displayed in Exhibit 6.

A line-of-sight relationship is required between transmitting and receiving antennas, which must resist winds reaching 70 miles per hour. The

Exhibit 5. Cost of fiber optics.

Materials Description	Unit Price	Quantity	Total Price
15-foot Patch Cables	$45	10	$450
Fiber Breakout Box	$150	4	$600
Eight-strand Fiber Cable			
62.5/125 m per Foot	$2	1,500	$3,000
DB-9 Type 1 Cable	$50	4	$200
Additional Wire Racks			
for the Seventh Floor			$250
Fiber Optic Repeaters	$1,400	8	$11,200
Outside installation	$30	32	$960
Total Fiber Optic Installation			**$16,660**

transmission is primarily stable, though certain conditions, such as excessively hard or prolonged rain, can reduce reliability of data transmission.

There are two types of microwave systems available, the short-haul and long-haul. The short-haul system is for transmissions up to and including 250 miles. This method is typically used by universities, businesses with multiple locations, hotel chains, and hospitals. The long-haul system is designed for transmissions greater than 250 miles. This method is typically used by common carrier (i.e., AT&T, GTE, and Sprint), utility companies, oil companies, broadcast companies, and paid television.

The increased number of satellites available for transmitting signals is reducing the overall ongoing costs of microwave systems. For international businesses, satellite transmission is an alternative to poor voice and data communications in some countries' public communications systems, particularly those classified as third-world. The wireless aspect of the system provides portability for companies that change locations frequently or those planning future location changes.

Licensing Requirements

Microwave technology requires licensing, based on the frequency bandwidth. Licenses are issued by the Federal Communications Commission (FCC) and take from two weeks to several months to obtain, depending on the request load. Licensing is granted for one year, with annual renewal options.

Antennas must comply with FCC standards for acceptable performance. The connections must also comply with Underwriter Laboratories (UL) standards.

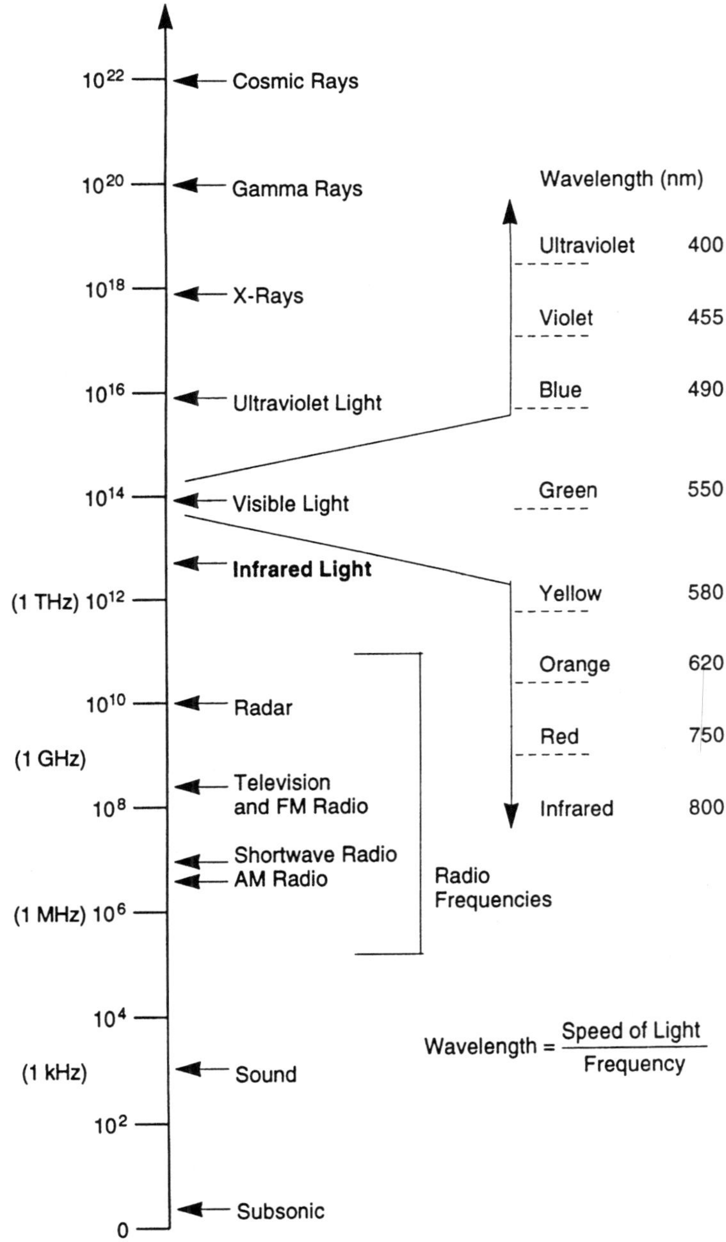

Exhibit 6. Electromagnetic spectrum.

Advantages

The advantages for this system include:

- Low signal attenuation
- Equipment portability
- Cost-effectiveness when there is a line-of-sight connection and frequency bank congestions are low
- Signal scrambling for increased data security

Disadvantages

Microwave's disadvantages include:

- The bandwidth is limited to a 6.7M-bit capacity, with an estimated 16M-bit peak-time potential.
- Outside installation support is required.
- Signals are unreliable during excessive rains.
- There is a potential delay in receiving licensing from the FCC, which could prevent meeting the installation schedule.

Costs

The basic cost to set up the microwave radio system for the corporate remote location would be as shown in Exhibit 7.

Exhibit 7. Cost of radio system.

Materials Description	Unit Price	Quantity	Total Price
Microwave Radio System	$10,000	1	$10,000
Microwave Interface Unit for Networks	$3,000	2	$6,000
Antennas	$2,100	2	$4,200
Subcontracted Installation	$2,200	1	$2,200
Licensing Fee One Year (Requires Annual Renewal)	$520	1	$520
Total Microwave Radio Installation			**$20,950**

To minimize downtime, there was an optional system maintenance contract available that included immediate replacement of faulty equipment for $250 per month. This annualized to $3,000. Staff training would also be required to provide system maintenance. Backup equipment would increase overall costs by 50%.

The Third Option: Infrared

A Free-Space Infrared Local Area Network (FIRLAN) system is based on infrared (IR) technology and can be used to build or replace a traditional

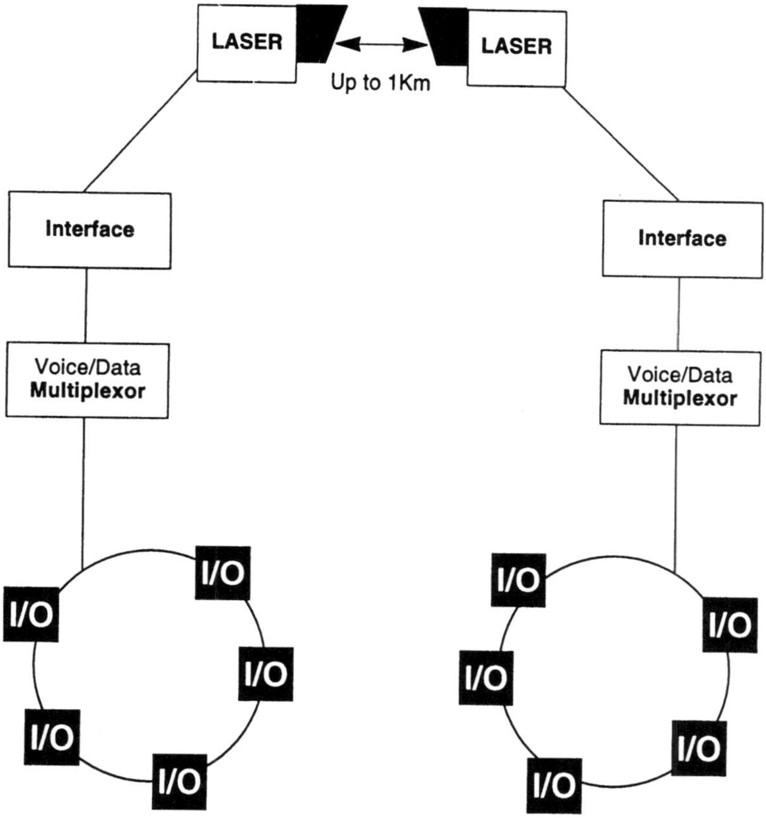

Exhibit 8. The typical T1 connection setup.

hardwire network. The FIRLAN provides point-to-point or point-to-multipoints transmission of Ethernet signals between segments or stations, as well as T1 line signal transmission, as shown in Exhibit 8.

IR technology replaces cables with wireless optical links using line-of-sight IR transmission. Some systems use lasers as a basis for optical transmission. This is superior to standard IR transmission devices, especially under high ambient lighting and poor weather conditions.

It is recommended with IR systems that the installer have an IR viewer for alignment accuracy. The units are mounted on the corner, at the windows, or on the roof of the building to which they are attached and preferably are mounted to masonry construction. The supporting structure for the viewers cannot be wood or sheet metal.

IR systems offer industry-standard LAN and WAN interfaces, enabling the use of standard Network Interface Card and network software. FIRLAN

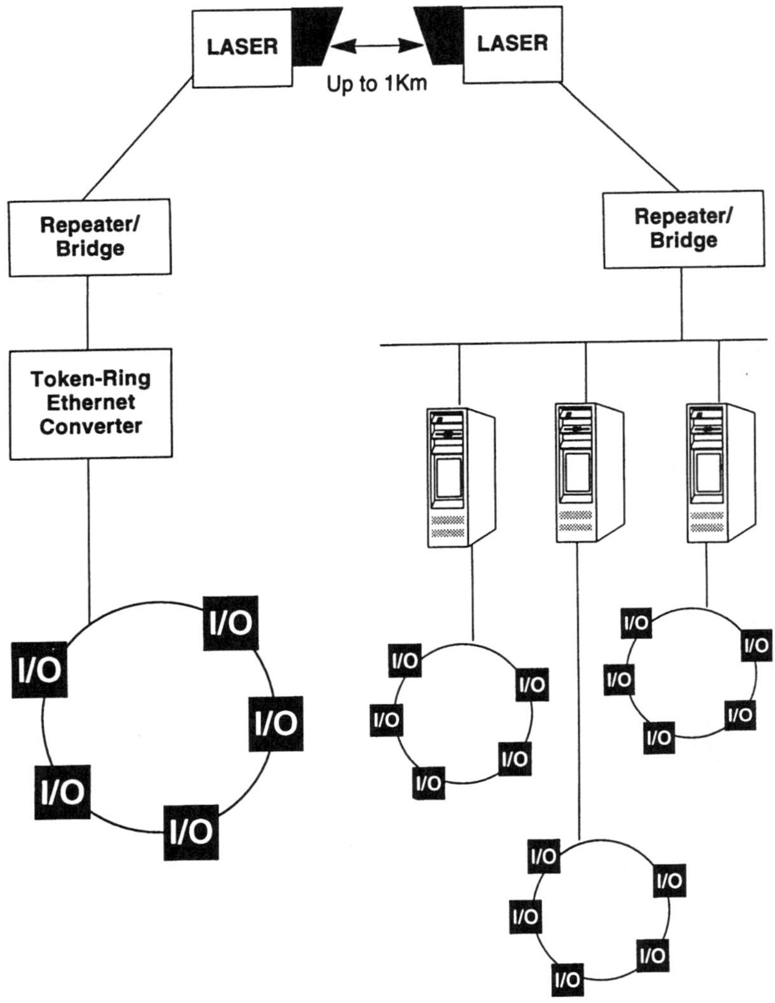

Exhibit 9. The typical Ethernet setup.

provides seamless Ethernet integration, setting the required bit rate at 10M bits, and defines the physical interfaces and operating characteristics for the hardware, as shown in Exhibit 9.

Conditions Affecting Effectiveness. The three most significant atmospheric conditions that affect laser transmission include absorption, scattering, and shimmering. All three conditions can reduce the amount of light energy received by the receiver. The phenomena affect the laser transmission to varying degrees.

Absorption along the transmission path is caused mainly by the water vapor and carbon dioxide content in the air, which in turn depend on the humidity and altitude. The gases that form in the atmosphere have many resonant bands(i.e., transmission "windows") that allow specific frequencies of light to pass. These windows occur at various wavelengths, including the visible range. If a system uses a near IR wavelength of light (820 wavelength, or 820 nm) for laser transmission, however, absorption is not a great concern.

Scattering has a greater effect than absorption, because a smaller percentage of the transmission beam reaches the receiver. The atmospheric scattering of light is a function of light's wavelength and the number and size of scattering particles in the path.

Specific conditions that cause scattering problems include the following:

- **Fog.** The worst condition, fog, produces a scattering effect in all directions. This is attributed to water drops with a radius less than a few microns. Smog has a similar effect.
- **Snow.** Its effect varies depending on its water content. A very wet snow is closer to rain, which has less effect on visibility than fog. An extremely dry snow, on the other hand, is closer to fog and has a similar effect. The severity of the problem is in direct correlation to the radius of the particles; therefore, snow's scattering effect varies.
- **Rain.** Rain-related attenuation is one hundred times less than that of fog. Although the liquid water content of a typical heavy shower is 10 times that of a typical dense fog, the raindrop radius is about 1,000 times larger than that of a fog droplet. This causes less scattering effect.

There is a way to minimize the effects of scattering. A product designed with a fade margin of 17 dB, for a 1,000-meter link would activate an automatic turn off when visibility drops below 800 meters.

Shimmer, also known as mirage or atmospheric turbulence, is the visual distortion of images in heat situations and imposes a low-frequency (normally below 200 Hz) variation on the amount of light detected by the receiver. This low-frequency variation can result in excessive data error rates or video distortion on a laser communication system.

The shimmer effect is a combination of time of day, terrain, cloud cover, wind, and height of the optical path above the source of shimmer. Localized differences in the air's index of refraction cause fluctuations in the received signal level by directing some of the light out of its intended path. Beam fluctuations may degrade system performance by producing short-term signal amplitudes. Signal fades below the threshold result in error bursts. Selection of an optical path several meters above heat sources, however, greatly reduces shimmer effects.

In addition to the atmospheric conditions mentioned, direct sunlight into the front of the transmission or receiving unit affects performance. Sunlight can saturate the receiver photo diode, resulting in outages that can last for several minutes, depending on the time of year and the angle of the sun. In addition, direct sunlight can saturate the feedback diode in the laser, resulting in transmitter shut off.

Licensing Requirements

There are no licensing requirements. However, the Center for Devices and Radiological Health (CDRH) of the US Food and Drug Administration is the agency responsible for reviewing IR technology. The technology complies with the federal regulations covered by 21 CFR 1010 and 21 CFR 1040 (HHS Publication FDA 88-8035).

Advantages

FIRLAN advantages include:

- Freedom from government regulation through licensing
- Equipment ownership when a company changes locations
- Connectivity ease when locations need to be added
- Immunity to radio interference
- Data security

Disadvantages

Specific FIRLAN disadvantages include:

- The effect of atmospheric conditions on reliable data transmission, which may prohibit its use in some locales
- High up-front equipment investment and installation support
- Potential safety issue of retina damage caused by looking directly into the beam

Cost

The basic cost to set up the system is as shown in Exhibit 10.

The Final Analysis

Several new factors became apparent during the research process. These became part of the decision-making process: the availability of fiber repeaters with no other designated use; discovery of an existing infrared installation at a company location on the East Coast; and building management, fearing harm to its employees, resisting the use of infrared lasers.

Exhibit 10. Cost of infrared.

Materials Description	Unit Price	Quantity	Total Price
Ethernet Link IEEE 802.3M bits to10M bits. Includes Two Laser Sets with AUI Connection	$15,000	1	$15,000
Mounting Cost	$600	2	$1,200
Bridge Ethernet to Token Ring	$2,000	2	$4,000
Converter	$2,000	1	$2,000
Total for Basic System Setup			**$22,200**

Optional Items	Cost	Description
Spare system	$9,250	Backup Set
Replace Service Contract	$1,300	Annual Contract for Unit Replacement Within 24 Hours
On-site Survey and Installation Charge	$4,000	To Ensure All Required Equipment Is Available for Installation
Installation and Maintenance Training Cost	$1,200	Training for actual Installation
Suggested Options		
On-site Survey and Installation	$4,000	To Ensure the Installation IsWell Planned
Installation andMaintenance	$2,400	Sending Two People for Installation Training and Maintenance Training
Total Costs:	**$6,400**	

To complete the analysis, these items were included in the final recommendation. The analysis of the technology benefits is provided to gain insight from the available technology and present the applicable situation scenarios for each option. (Exhibits 2 and 3are grid comparisons of these technologies.)

Weighing the Factors

The comparison of the technologies alleviates concerns for data security, as all three methods provide for secure data. Both of the wireless technologies, however, offer a lower data reliability factor on a daily basis. The weather in the region of the remote corporate location is subject to dramatic shifts, which are detrimental to the wireless technologies. Obviously, electrical outages could affect the users in the same way for physical wire options; these outages would also affect any work they might conduct.

All three technologies are available to install within the time frames required, with the possible exception of the FCC licensing required for the microwave option. Certainly, the licensing for the microwave option could have a serious impact on the ability of the staff to work on the scheduled date. This is a high consideration from a work-due-date standpoint and the organization's potential liability for missed due dates.

It would be advantageous to own the equipment as offered by either the microwave or infrared options for net costs, given the organization's business goals to downsize in the near future. The high up-front costs for the technologies were also noted. This investment in materials would have to be to the long-term advantage of the organization.

Cost Comparisons

Costs are certainly a consideration, but they are not always the prime consideration. The following cost comparisons are based on the pure costs of the three systems for network data connectivity. Items to be considered in the final cost estimates include estimates for equipment required for connectivity, purchased equipment depreciation, and use of any existing equipment.

Total cost of fiber optics	$19,600
Total cost of microwave	$20,950
Total cost of infrared	$28,600

The depreciation on the purchased equipment averages approximately 50%, based on the schedule of depreciation that was current at the time of decision making. This would reduce the cost of the microwave by $10,475 and infrared options by $14,300. A significant savings in using fiber optics would come through permission to use the existing company fiber optic repeaters for the remote location installation. This would reduce those costs by $11,200. Factoring in these considerations yields the following numbers:

Total cost of fiber optics	$8,400
Total cost of microwave	$10,475
Total cost of infrared	$14,300

From a cost-comparison aspect, fiber optics would be the most cost-effective method of installation.

Recommendations

To recap, the considerations for the recommended solution must address the following issues in order of importance. The solution must:

- Be fully functional in time to coincide with the contractor's relocation to the company's new space in the adjacent building
- Provide reliable connectivity and an acceptable response time similar to that which is currently available

- Be supportable by the existing technical staff
- Come in line with the costs of the other solutions

Each of the technologies was reviewed based on the above criteria. The recommendation discussed in this chapter was based on this specific situation and may not meet criteria for other situations. The technical notes following the recommendation provides highlights for future technology reviews.

The Decision on Microwave Technology

Given the required installation time for this project, the microwave solution was eliminated, because it requires a licensing lead time before equipment is operational. Bandwidth throughput of the microwave solution was also a point of concern, because the cabling installation at the remote-location workstations called for 16M bit Token Ring, and total peak throughput of the microwave solution is only 6.7M bits. Also, existing data traffic at peak usage would reach bandwidth saturation points. The microwave technology solution, therefore, fails the first two points of the selection criteria.

The Decision on Infrared Technology

Several factors in the final review of the infrared laser link requirements eliminated this solution. Network uptime would be compromised by the lasers' being mounted on the roof from east to west because of the building management's requirement for worker safety. In spite of staff in other locations being available to lend support, the local staff lacking experience in the necessary skill set to maintain or repair the laser units was a concern. In addition, the need to purchase a backup unit to have an on-site spare would make the solution cost prohibitive. The infrared solution failed to satisfy the last three points of the selection criteria.

The Decision on Fiber Optics

A fiber optic installation could be completed within the stated time frame, and the use of Token Ring fiber optic repeaters would maintain high levels of data throughput to reduce the threat of bandwidth saturation. The existing staff had some expertise in fiber optic repeaters and fiber optic cable installation, which would reduce maintenance response times. Further, if any new technology that provides greater bandwidth were to appear on the horizon, it would be best served through the fiber optic installation. Lastly, the cost was not prohibitive. Therefore, this technology provided the response best suited to the selection criteria and is the most viable solution.

As a final note, the microwave and infrared solutions required total backup units to be quickly recoverable. The cost for backup units would increase the overall cost of these options by approximately 30%. The fiber optic recommendation, on the other hand, contained a backup system with the extra strands included in the cable runs. Short of someone cutting the entire cable, these strands would be available if a failure were to occur. The switch to the available strands could be completed quickly, increasing the overall reliability of this connectivity solution.

Implementation and Installation Planning

As with most projects, the final installation phase was the most critical. The situation under discussion required precise timing for user access to the Banyan network on a specific day. The implementation and installation phase for this project centered around connectivity on December 15, 1994, the scheduled date for the staff's move to the adjacent building. The build-out schedule for the space showed that the equipment installation was finished on December 12, 1994. To complete the connection for network access between the two buildings, the following process was recommended. It allowed for potential delays and provides some recovery time. The process involved:

- Issuing a final Request For Proposal by November 22, 1994, on the selected option with a maximum two-day response time. At least three vendors were to be considered.
- Issuing a purchase order by November 28, 1994, to cover the materials cost and installation fees.
- Receiving and inventorying materials by December 9, 1994.
- Installing materials on December 12 and 13, 1994. Testing connections and workstation access as each floor was completed.
- Testing all connections on December 14, 1994.
- Going fully functional on the morning of December 15, 1994.The staff was prepared to troubleshoot all problems encountered as the user community attached to the Banyan network.

Action Plan

Network expansion, in any form, requires a baseline knowledge of the systems used, the organization and business direction, the liabilities a business may face with each major process change, and the effects of any downtime. Information systems are the lifeline of most businesses today, and these systems must exhibit enough flexibility to change as quickly as business directions change.

Technology is changing so dramatically that many system needs are available if the time and effort are applied to research what is available and to understand how to make it work for a given application. This effort is best served with staff experienced with the business, systems, and available technology.

Each of the technologies reviewed in this chapter is applicable to certain situations; therefore, the criteria requirements for each situation must be carefully weighed against the direction of the business organization. The proper knowledge base determines the correct direction for this type of connection or for any system expansion plans. Full analysis and good planning on the front end increase the project success rate.

Chapter 79
Frame Relay in an IBM Environment

Glenn R. Brown

The typical wide area network (WAN) design for most IBM computing environments is spoke-and-hub. Usually, a mainframe is located at a central point through which all data from every remote site must pass. This topology is illustrated in Exhibit 1. If a site in northern California must communicate with a site in southern California, the data is sent from northern California to the mainframe at corporate headquarters on the east coast and then to southern California. Both time and money are wasted, as the sites are bearing the cost of sending the data on the long trip through the hub. If the spoke-and-hub network connects Token Ring LANs , the seven-hop count limit must be considered; it may be exceeded if widely distributed LANs have to communicate with each other through the central point.

An alternative to the spoke-and-hub, a meshed or webbed network, provides multiple paths to sites but can also be needlessly expensive because of the costs of the many lines. Transparent source route bridges can link nodes on a meshed network so that the seven-hop Token Ring limit is avoided, but the higher line costs remain. If the nonroutable NETBios protocol is used, the overhead involved can mean an 8% to 25% loss of available bandwidth.

The central point in a spoke-and-hub network is a potential operational problem. As a single source of failure, a relatively minor accident (e.g., a cut cable) can bring down the network. For the company described in this case study, lost business might cost $250,000 to $500,000 per hour, and a cable cut can take four or more hours to repair.

Background

A large manufacturing company with headquarters in the southeast has an agency distribution system of 36 warehouses and five central distribution centers in the U.S. and Canada. The company also has 11 man-

0-8493-9989-0/99/$0.00+$.50

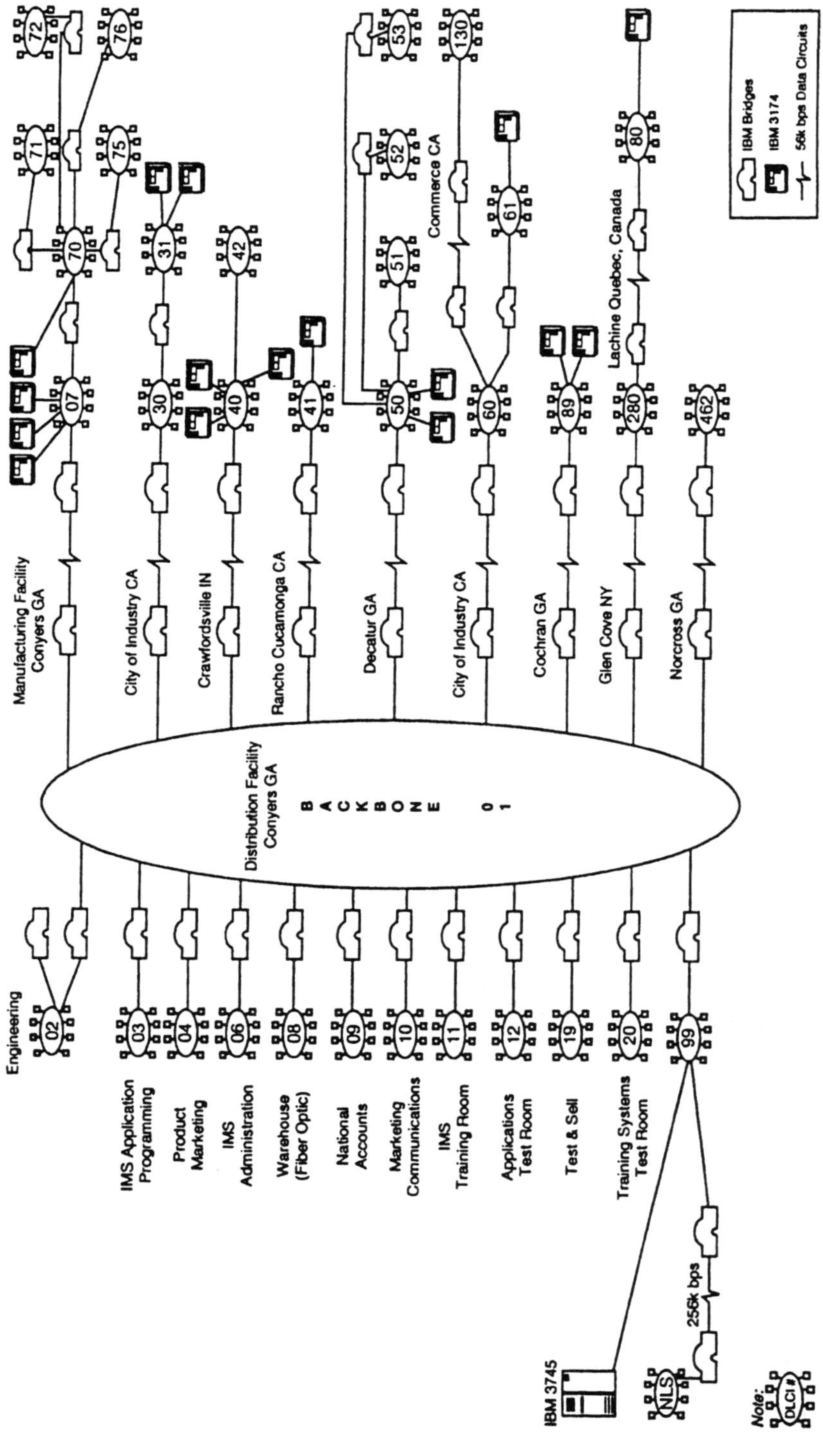

Exhibit 1. Spoke-and-hub WAN-LAN.

ufacturing facilities in the U.S. and Canada, with yearly revenues of approximately $700 million.

The company's networking environment consists of IBM's OS/2 LAN Server, with MSDOS, Windows, and OS/2 on the requesting stations. The mainframe is an IBM 3090/400 connected to 3000 or more combined mainframe and LAN requesters.

All remote sites must communicate to the central site as well as with each other for manufacturing schedules, distribution requests, inventory tracking, mainframe reports, e-mail, word processing, spreadsheet information, computer-aided design drawings, and database information. The central site is headquarters for general ledger, payroll, and human resources data processing.

Current Network Costs

The network comprises 12 56K-bps leased digital circuits, which cost, altogether, $286,000 per year. Two additional voicegrade phone circuits with 14.4K-bps modems cost $16,800 per year. To web or mesh into the network three additional sites, with each site having one or two permanent circuits to other sites, would cost an additional $248,014 per year. Management refused to approve this approach to expanding the network.

Once the decision was made to redesign the network, the following requirements were established:

- At the minimum, the same level of service must be provided, even if no cost reduction is possible.
- Faster service for site-to-site communications must be provided.
- Modification of the existing IBM 3174 controllers and the IBM 3745 front-end processor (FEP) must be avoided.
- Redundancy and backup circuits must be provided.

The Network Redesign

First, the bridges in the spoke-and-hub network were changed for bridge routers, in order to route NETBios and SNA traffic by encapsulation in Internet Protocol (IP) packets. The spoke-and-hub solution was replaced with a frame relay network. Data link connection identifier (DLCI) is a frame relay value that identifies a logical connection. Each site has a DLCI, allowing the definition of multiple virtual circuit with specified Committed Information Rates (CIRs), over a single actual local exchange loop circuit. This eliminates the need to obtain (and pay for) multiple circuits. Using the DLCI, multiple Permanent Virtual Circuit (PVC) was defined within a single circuit, as shown in Exhibit 2.

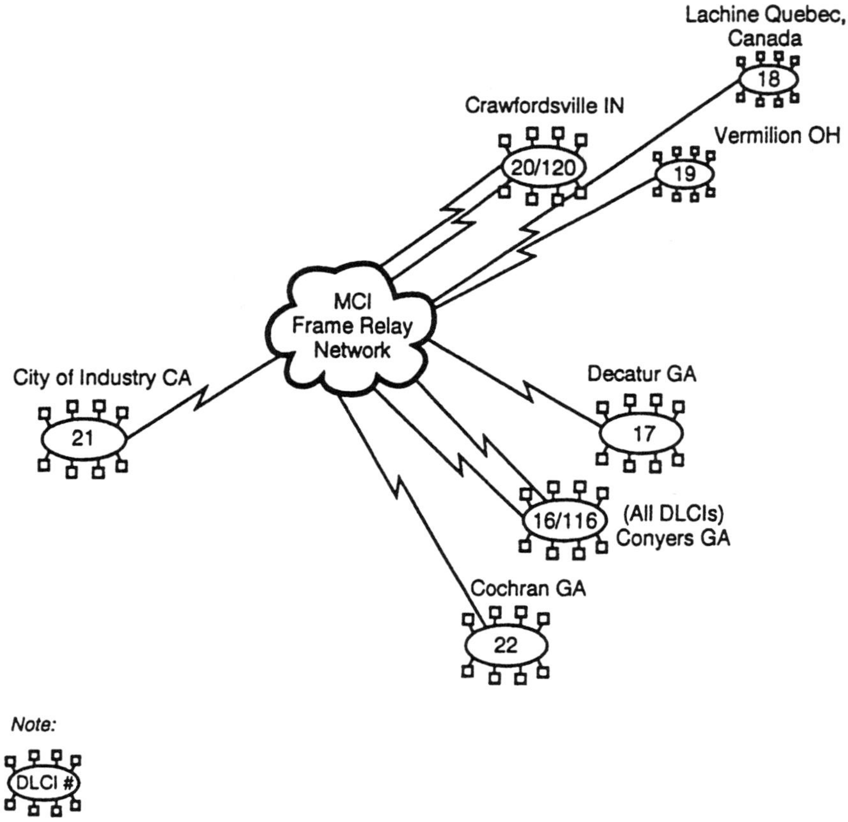

Exhibit 2. Frame relay DLCI network.

Challenges

It was necessary to ensure that the frame relay service carried the current NETBios and SNA traffic, that it did eliminate the central site as a single point of failure, and that the bridge routers operate in a NETBios and SNA environment. For SNA traffic, the central site remains a potential single point of failure even with frame relay, but LAN-to-LAN traffic is not disrupted if the central site is lost.

Local acknowledgment or spoofing was a requirement to help reduce the traffic load on all circuits. Mainframe traffic acknowledgments would be kept local and microcomputer traffic would be routed intelligently through IP.

Challenges for Equipment Providers

Customer premise equipment from Wellfleet Communications (Billerica MA), CrossComm Corp. (Marlboro MA), and Cisco Systems (Menlo Park CA) was tested. The frame relay providers tested were WilTel (Tulsa OK), AT&T (Bridgewater NJ), and MCI (Dallas TX).

The largest challenge for the vendors was routing the nonroutable NETBios and SNA protocols while maintaining communications to the mainframe from the Token Ring interface coupler (TIC)-attached controllers. Another requirement was the attachment of an SDLC controller to the WAN through an LLC2 (logical link control type 2.A) conversion, which converts the SDLC to a Token Ring or NETBios transmission.

Of the equipment vendors, only Cisco was able to do this. One vendor's equipment would not operate with a TIC-attached IBM 3174 controller, and the other vendor's equipment could not keep the IBM 3174 controllers in session for more than a few hours. IBM has since introduced the 6611 multiprotocol router, but this was not available at the time of this evaluation.

Services from all three frame relay carriers worked with few problems. Cost became the deciding factor, and MCI was selected.

Test Phases

A frame relay connection between two nearby sites was tested to determine the effects of frame relay on remote NETBios and SNA traffic, as illustrated in Exhibit 3. Crucial performance characteristics that required testing were speed degradation, reliability of TIC-attached IBM 3174 controllers, and reliability of local acknowledgment.

Next in the testing phase was to bring up additional sites and determine the gains in transfer time on the fully meshed frame relay network. Three sites—Georgia, Indiana, and California—were upgraded. California can communicate directly to Indiana and Georgia; Indiana can communicate directly to Georgia and California; and Georgia can communicate directly to Indiana and California. The file transfer time savings should average around 30%.

Reliability in the Canadian circuits had to be tested. All U.S. carriers must be compatible with Canadian Bell, however, response times and problem resolution were unknowns. Carriers are currently establishing alliances with Canadian Bell, so U.S. equipment can be placed in the Canadian Bell regions, thereby reducing circuit mileage costs.

Next in the test phase was to check the conversion of SDLC to LLC2 for non-TIC-attached IBM 3174 controllers. The test results showed that:

- Pin 11 of the cable on an RS-232 connection to the SDLC IBM 3174 controller should be removed. Pin 11 is needed only for IBM testing when

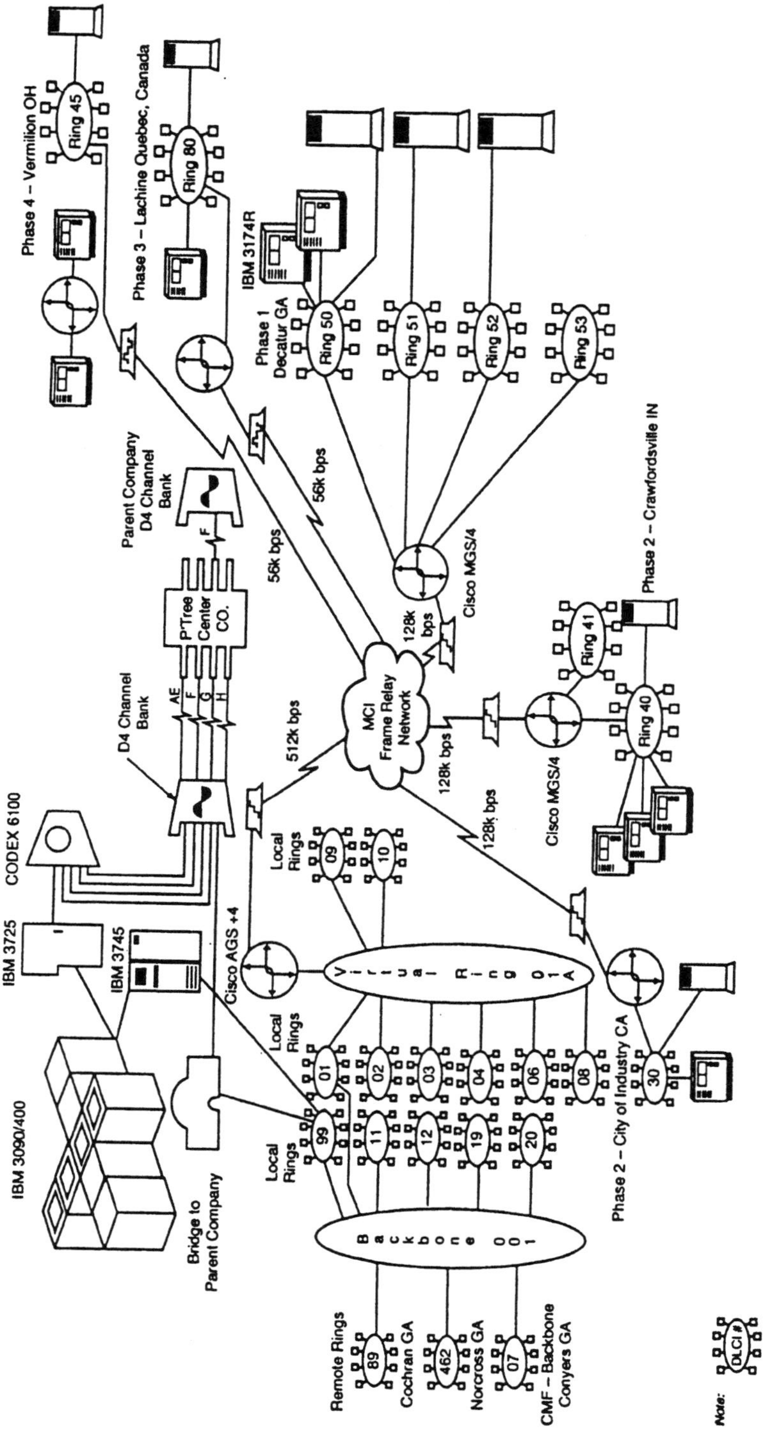

Exhibit 3. Frame relay test phases.

connected to a digital sharing device (DSD) and is not needed in a Cisco router configuration.

- Each controller required its own RS-232 Data Circuit-terminating equipment serial port, which meant that all sites having non-TIC-attached controllers required four port serial cards instead of two.
- Users reported quicker response time on their terminal sessions using frame relay than on the shared 19.2K-bps dedicated circuit previously used.

Redundancy

A carrier's frame relay network is self-healing. If a carrier switch goes down, the carrier can temporarily reroute the traffic from the disabled switch to another switch to keep a network functional.

Backup of the connection to the frame relay point-of-presence is usually done through a dial-up device, but this did not provide adequate bandwidth. The solution was to obtain two local circuits, routed over different paths, and divide the load between them. If one circuit goes down, the entire load is shifted to the remaining path. A DLCI network does not automatically provide this type of backup, so it must be addressed by the network's designers. This is illustrated in Exhibit 4.

Frame Relay Benefits

For five sites, voice and data communications were combined on a T1 link to the point of presence (POP). The elimination of the separate local data circuits saved approximately $12,000 per month. Voice and data communications were combined using a drop-and-insert Channel Service Unit, which provides 20 voice circuits for four sites, and 16 voice circuits for the host site. Data and voice are separated by the local provider, with the data then being forwarded to the MCI frame relay POP. The drop-and-insert CSU provides the alternating mark inversion signaling for the Northern Telecom voice switches.

Frame relay provides the ability to overcommit the circuit. The Committed Information Rates can be significantly higher than the actual available bandwidth, allowing communication to several sites simultaneously through one circuit.

Costs for the original SNA spoke-and-hub network exceeded $300,000 per year. Costs to fully mesh the network would have run over $500,000. Costs for the frame relay network, however, are only slightly more than $200,000 per year.

Frame relay offers low-cost connectivity to additional sites (at $75 to $150 for each additional PVC) and entails less overhead than an X.25 network.

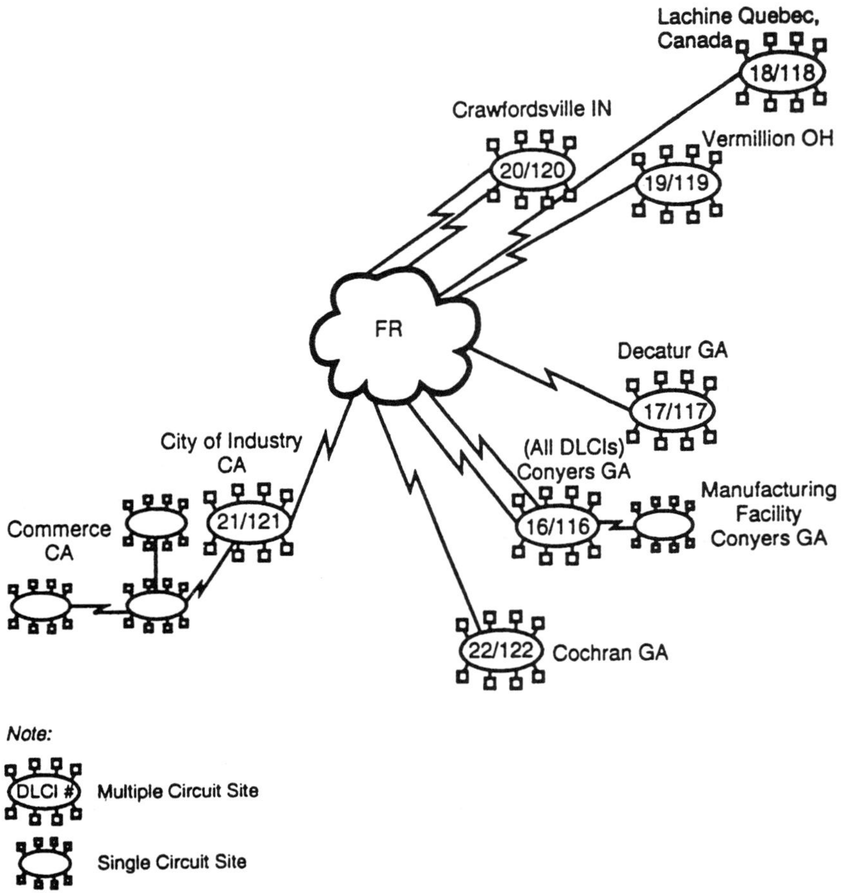

Exhibit 4. Frame relay backup DLCI network.

Current Network Structure

The structure of the new frame relay network is illustrated in Exhibit 5.

Action Plan

The frame relay network described in this chapter markedly reduced delay time as perceived by network users, reduced network costs, improved network reliability, and lessened the cost and difficulty of network expansion.

Cost and user's networking requirements are driving the industry toward the implementation of high-speed frame relay, or hyper-frame relay, which offers CIR of either 4M- or 16M-bps for LAN interconnection.

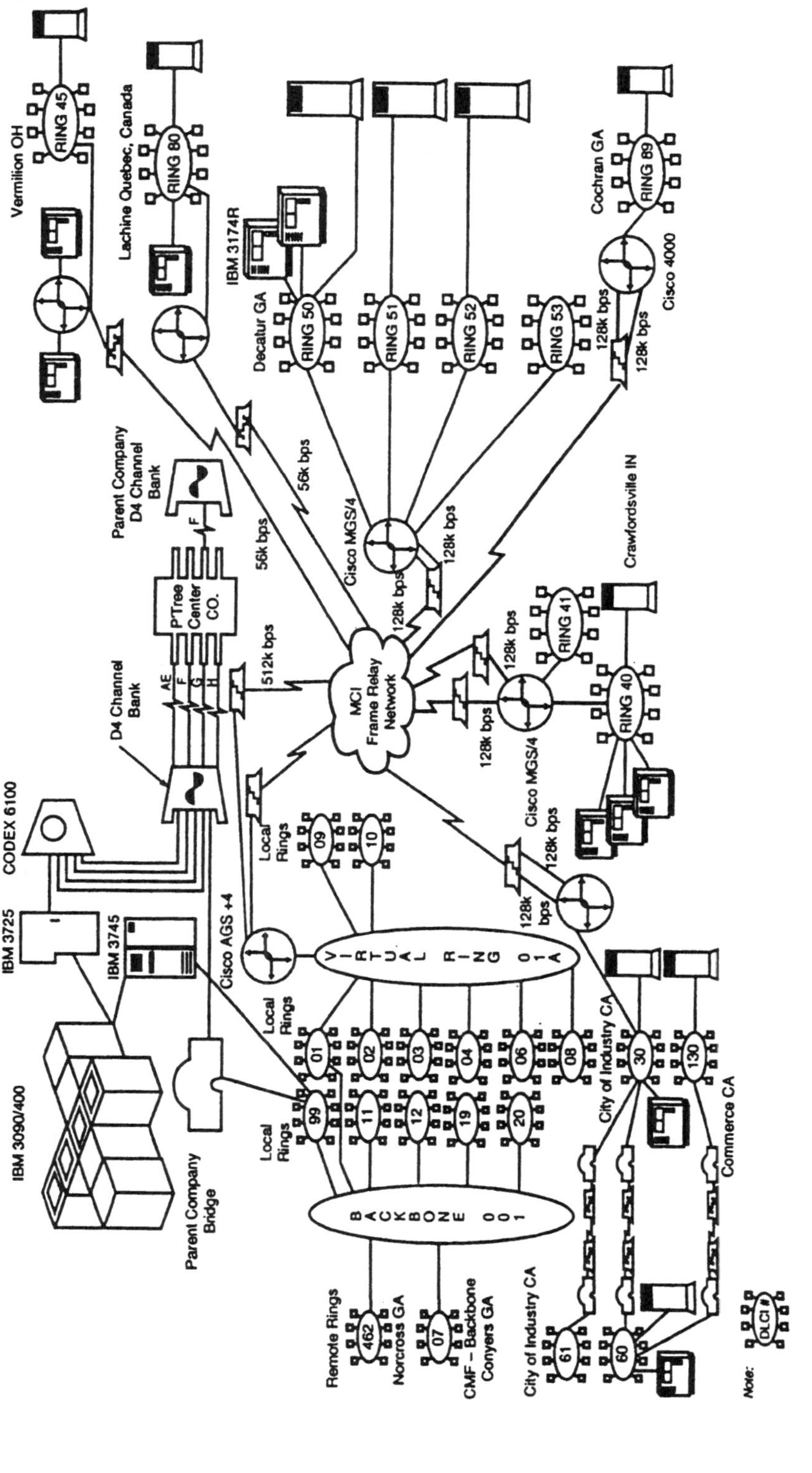

Exhibit 5. Redesigned backbone network.

Chapter 80
Turning Host Developers into Object Technicians

Steven Rabin

The benefits of object-oriented (OO) systems development include greatly improved software quality, reusable objects, and a means of creating truly distributed software across heterogeneous environments. The most sophisticated IS organizations and their tools are, however, no substitute for enlightened developers, organizationwide, as OO techniques change the way systems development is done.

The use of OO concepts and techniques must be carefully planned and introduced into the development environment. All too often, top management has unreasonable expectations, while developers are unsure how to design, much less develop, in this new environment. Rather than improving software quality, this situation has the opposite effect of producing inferior code and problem-plagued objects. Integrating objects into the development mix must be done transitionally. It is an evolutionary rather than revolutionary process.

This article explores the three fundamental aspects of a successful implementation of OO technology as part of a distributed systems strategy. These are:

- Preparing people for a new way of developing systems
- Integrating new tools into the IS development hierarchy
- Revising the IS organization's methodology to create quality reusable objects

Development methods must be reviewed so that changes can be accomplished with as little negative impact on current productivity as is reasonable. It is therefore important to approach the transition of development methods in such a way as to effectively get people involved and motivated.

0-8493-9989-0/99/$0.00+$.50

Readiness to Move to OO

Businesses are actively pursuing ways to move applications that have traditionally run in a closed mainframe environment to distributed environments. At the same time, analysts are examining and reengineering the business processes that have been encapsulated in these existing applications. Astute IS organizations are using this time to consider the advantages of object orientation.

OO may be the wave of the future, but COBOL has been the language of choice for more than 30 years. Business logic is encapsulated in the millions of lines of COBOL code that exists today. If a company is looking for an opportunity to reengineer business processes and associated code, it should also be examining the use of OO as a possible vehicle for all or some of this reengineering.

OO transition issues affect programmers, applications designers, quality assurance personnel, and development management. Developers face an uncertain future as they move away from the professional skills they have acquired over their careers. The skills required to design and develop a 3270-based, action-oriented host system using proprietary architectures and host system services (e.g., VTAM, SNA, CICS) do not easily transfer into this new environment. A variety of questions must be answered in order to determine what is required and the best way to proceed. IS management should ask:

- Is a replacement strategy realistic?
- What are the ways to conserve (or optimize) the current investment in resources (both code and skill sets)?
- How can object systems be integrated into existing systems?
- What are the tools and skill sets required to move to this new environment?

The remainder of this chapter addresses these questions from the management and developer's point of view.

Part of a Distributed Systems Strategy

A good way to begin is to consider the future of object technologies and development tools. Bold claims about object-oriented tools abound, all of which potentially lead to unrealistic expectations; nonetheless, many IS shops are already (or will soon be) in the process of adopting this technology for the development of their next-generation applications (see Exhibit 1). By 1998, robust distributed client/server OO tools and system services will be available. By the year 2000, more than 80% of development organizations are expected to be using object technologies as the basis for their distributed development strategies.

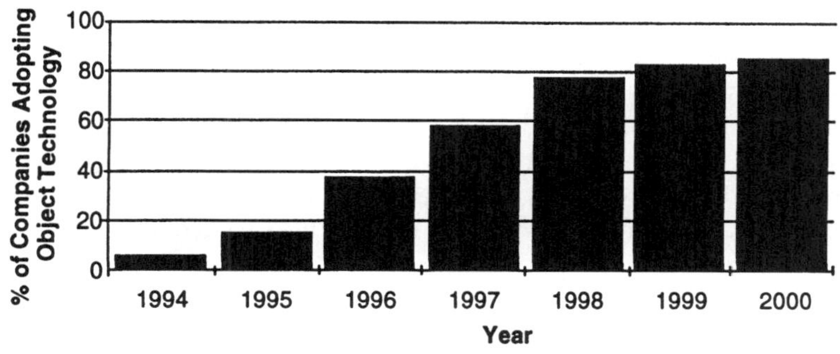

Exhibit 1. Future of object technology.

Design Considerations

Cross-platform OO tools are one of the key ingredients required for the success and implementation of this technology. They must be able to handle mission-critical applications and provide the key system services required for enterprise applications, including data management, transaction management, and messaging in a high-volume application processing environment.

Object projects are different from traditional development projects for a number of reasons. Analysis and design procedures are different; so are the methodologies and tools used. The code structure/syntax is new also. There is C++ instead of C, and OOCOBOL instead of COBOL, for example. Development and run-time facilities also must change to exploit the use of objects across the enterprise. The composition and role of the development team change as well. Finally, new means of testing and maintaining object-based systems need to be implemented.

Development Cycle Changes

The conventional development cycle incorporates rigid development phases. These phases usually have specific start and stop points that are difficult to alter. Systems design is performed in one of the initial phases, so any subsequent changes to the design cause confusion, delays, and misplaced logic. This is certainly true when no design/development tool is being used and in many cases is true even when an integrated CASE (ICASE) tool is used. This approach to development is best characterized as a big bang approach. After months or years of development, the application is implemented in one big push; out with the old and in with the new.

Rapid Prototyping

OO development is much more of an evolutionary process. Rapid application prototyping is one method often used. This allows for a series of ever-improving prototypes to be developed until the application is ready for delivery. The initial prototype has basic functionality. This prototype is improved and enhanced until it is close to the deliverable. Finally, the application is delivered even though it continues to evolve through maintenance.

The reason this approach works well is that the prototype is developed using component objects. These objects define basic business functions and are incorporated into the prototype as required. Individual objects are easily modified and enhanced as the application is readied for delivery. Even after implementation, system modification is best characterized as further refinement of the prototype (excluding programming bugs).

Rapid application prototyping offers a variety of benefits to developers. Simple objects that are easy to understand can be created first, then used as a learning tool in initial prototypes. Even if some of these early objects need to be thrown away and re-created, they serve a valuable purpose, from both the training and application points of view. The idea of working with simple objects (maybe as part of the desktop presentation) is a reasonable way to introduce developers to the technology.

Incorporating OO Methods and CASE

Current design practices incorporate some relatively old practices, such as structured analysis and design, as well as newer facilities like ICASE, Use Case, and entity-relationship modeling. The further advanced an organization is with regard to applications design methods, the easier the transition is to OO design.

There are several techniques being used in conjunction with OO applications development. The point of this article is not to review or compare each of them, but to emphasize that one of them must be selected and incorporated into the environment.

It is difficult, if not impossible, to move people to OO without the use of a design facility specifically geared to OO development. One technique is not necessarily better suited to the task than any of the others. Selection must be based solely on its applicability to the organization and its current methodology. A sampling of the methods to study includes:

- OO recursive design
- Object modeling technique
- OO software construction
- OO software engineering

Much has been written, both good and bad, about the use of CASE tools. In the mid-1980s there was as much hype about the benefits of CASE as there is today about OO. Although all of the promises did not meet user expectations, CASE still offers value to the art of software development and design. The same is true of OO development. Exhibit 2 offers a framework that can serve as the basis of transforming applications development.

So many organizations use some form of CASE tool that it is important to consider them in the light of this discussion. Host developers accustomed to using CASE facilities are faced with several significant differences when reviewing OO CASE tools for OO analysis and design. First and most important is that OO tools incorporate real-world modeling as the basis of the method. Once defined, these models are converted into objects. The better these objects simulate the business environment, the easier it is to create specific instances through the use of an objects method. These objects are finally encapsulated with their data and thus have the potential of being logically distributed across the enterprise.

OO Concepts for the Host Developer

For the people who actually create, enhance, and maintain code, one of the major challenges is understanding how object technology translates to the developer's specific environment (i.e., language, tools, and services). Developers must first master the basics. These fundamental aspects of OO technology must be internalized, activated, and then applied. Once basic OO terms are understood from both the conceptual and practical points of view a developer is well on the way to mastering OO technology.

Keep in mind that the use of OO terms in actual practice is not a simple thing. The industry often speaks in terms of the paradigm shift when moving to OO development. This paradigm shift is reflected in the understanding and use of concepts such as objects, classes, instances, messages, methods, encapsulation, abstraction, polymorphism, inheritance, persistence, binding, and typing.

If developers already grasp these concepts and are able to appropriately use them in the design/development of the application, they understand object technology. More often, however, significant training and education plans need to be included in the transition strategy for developers. Although this article is not intended to explain all of the fundamental concepts and terminology of OO, it is important to see how the key OO terms can be related to the world of the host developer. The ability to compare and describe new technology in light of older, more familiar technology is an excellent way to begin the transition process. Devising some means of bridging a developer's current knowledge to new technology can reduce any anxiety associated with the introduction of OO methods.

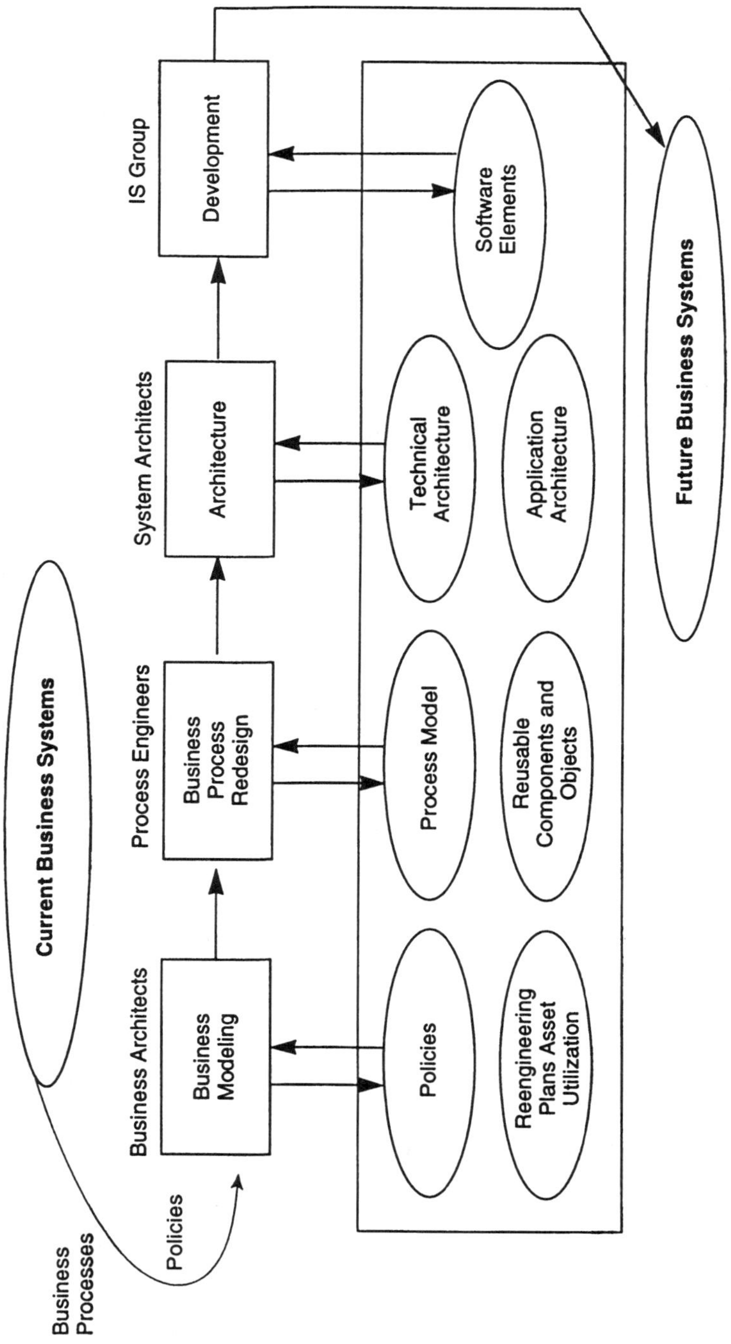

Exhibit 2. Transformation framework.

New Terms, Familiar Concepts

Objects are described in a variety ways. Steve Jobs, of NeXT Computers, defines an object as a chunk of "intelligence that knows how to act in a given situation"—a reasonable definition, but not one that helps a programmer learn how to use and create an object.

Somewhat more familiar to the developer is this definition: An object is a "program" made up of methods (or subroutines) that simulate the activities of the object. Objects always capture or simulate the activities of real-world events; each method represents one specific state of the object.

Messages

Objects communicate via messages. There is little physical difference between messages sent between objects and calls between programs. The difference lies in the fact that calls between programs are static based on the linkage between subprograms. Accessing another object's methods is dynamic because the called object is able to inherit the characteristics (and data) of the calling object.

Instances and Persistence

The idea of object instances and persistence are also terms that can be related to things the host developer is familiar with. Instances are nothing more than the specific occurrence of an object, similar to a row of data in a relational table or the execution of a specific program. Persistence refers to the storing of objects in a database or file. One of the foundations of business data processing is that information can subsequently be retrieved in the same way (or state) in which it was stored.

New Terms and Concepts to Learn

Terms such as messages, instances, and persistence are simply new names for relatively old concepts. Object technology is obviously a lot more than these few simple terms, however. In fact, the following two concepts are much more difficult for the host developer to grasp because there is no corresponding notion in legacy systems.

Encapsulation

The concept of encapsulation is a basic underlying principle of OO. It states the requirement that an object's data and processes are bound and distributed together. This directly contradicts the idea of data independence, which is one of the principles of traditional computing.

One of the goals of mainframe development has always been to get as many programs as possible to share as many subroutines as possible. A corresponding goal is getting as many programs/subroutines as possible to share the same data. Encapsulation represents a direct departure from this philosophy. Object development attempts to ensure that every object is shielded and protected from all of the other objects it comes in contact with. Each object owns its own data, methods, and protocols. Any other object requiring access to those items must "ask" the owning object to pass them over. Objects inherit data/methods from objects (especially related objects of the same class, as in object class libraries) they come in contact with.

Polymorphism

The concept of polymorphism is the process of making the same name do different things depending on the object that inherits it. In traditional development environments, variable names are, for the most part, meaningless. Although they may have meaning to the developer, they have little if any meaning to the operating environment. A field named NET-AMOUNT-DUE would provide the same results as one entitled SDFDSF-ZFSZFD-ND as long as they were defined similarly (i.e., numeric vs. alphanumeric).

Under polymorphism, not only do the names of things have meaning, but the same names can exhibit or trigger different behaviors based on the object receiving them. A simple example is the idea of a currency-conversion object. This object behaves differently when confronted with francs than with dollars.

One problem often encountered by developers new to OO is the creation of "dead objects." These objects look exactly like other objects but when faced with changing circumstances, they cannot adapt. These objects are not able to exhibit different behavior. They consume resources in the system but never provide adequate results.

Although encapsulation and polymorphism may be difficult for the host developer to grasp, they are the key reasons OO offers such promise for the development of distributed applications. Encapsulation and polymorphism can be incredibly helpful and efficient in those situations where the developer of an object does not wish to be concerned about the details of how or where things get done.

Language Issues

Sometimes knowing one thing makes learning a new thing easier. In this case, the transfer of learning is positive. In the programming arena, however, it is often the case that being experienced in one paradigm gets in the way of learning a new one, resulting in a negative transfer of learning. This shouldn't come as a surprise to many readers. Conventional programming has been mainly focused on functional decomposition and structured programming. These are disciplines that work in a variety of development environments but are quite different from the OO way of approaching problems.

Unlearning a paradigm (especially one that works) is usually difficult. This problem is compounded when a new programming language must be learned as well. Take the case of COBOL programmers wanting to migrate to the emerging world of objects. If a new language must be learned in addition to the new way of approaching a problem, it can be overwhelming. It is hard enough developing an application in a new environment let alone in a new environment with radically different rules and a new language.

For the developer to be able to work in an OO environment, languages and tools need be considered. The use of C++ is one choice but not necessarily the best one for host developers who usually have a wealth of experience using COBOL. In addition, there is nothing intrinsically better about using C++ than any other language, COBOL included. Excellent OO programs can be written in C++ or OOCOBOL just as easily as terrible programs can be developed in these languages.

Flavors of Languages

OO languages are available in three flavors:

- **Enhanced languages.** These are third-generation languages that have been modified to include the constructs necessary to develop OO programs. C++, OOCOBOL, and Visual Basic fall into this category.
- **Native languages.** Specifically designed to develop OO programs, these languages are often scripted and tied to specific tools. Eiffel, Actor, and Smalltalk fall into this category.
- **Visual languages.** These high-level languages are tied to specific development environments. PARTS and Visual Age are members of this group.

Regardless of the language and tools selected, it is important to consider the entire gamut of OO development and where each piece fits (see Exhibit 3).

Smalltalk is becoming popular in the business community because it is a high-level language that enforces, as a pure OO language, rules of encapsulation. Smalltalk is considered by many to be especially applicable for business applications because of its ease of learning, its mature class library, and its enforcement of OO discipline. In addition, Smalltalk has a fairly rich infrastructure in terms of its development tools and interfaces to other subsystems, such as OO databases and other languages and system services (i.e., CICS). A committee is currently defining the language for ANSI certification.

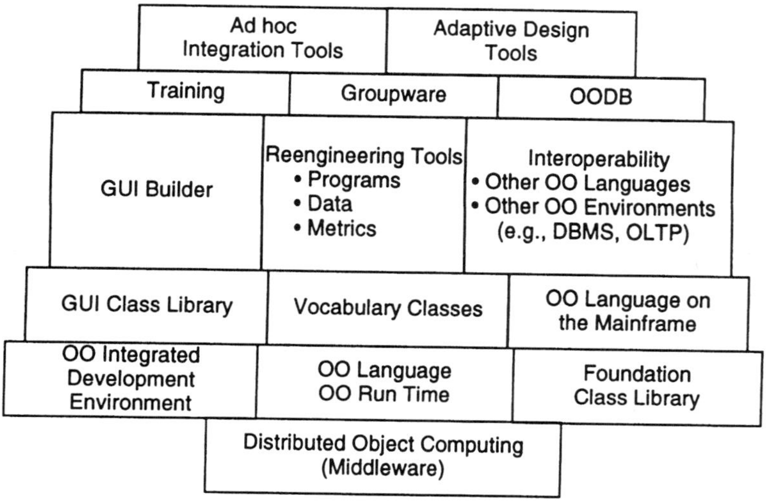

Exhibit 3. The big picture of OO.

Although there are advantages and disadvantages to each OO language, some are better adapted to helping developers move to this new environment. OOCOBOL is already familiar to developers and allows organizations to use their existing assets. These assets are both the developers' expertise and knowledge and the millions of lines of existing business application code. Although much of this code requires reengineering, it contains the operational logic and business rules of the organization.

OOCOBOL is an extension of the existing COBOL standard and so is familiar to most developers. While the issues of development environments and object libraries still hold, the experience in using OOCOBOL for people with a COBOL background (which includes most host developers) often produces much less of an obstacle in making the transition to problem solving using the OO approach.

For example, one way to engage COBOL programmers is to ask them to think of ways in which they can extend the range of data types found in standard ANSI 85 COBOL. COBOL has a built-in set of classes (e.g., COMPUTATIONAL, PACKED DECIMAL). They have polymorphic methods called ADD and SUBTRACT. In fact, these data types can be extended. The result is usually a rather artificial arrangement using copybooks, shared between client programs and separately compiled, that implement the interface to the data type.

Because copybooks can be nested, one can even contrive a semblance of inheritance. The "methods" in the separately compiled programs are reached through an EVALUATE statement that examines a parameter of the called procedure indicating which service is being requested. The main drawback of this approach is that so much of the detail of the encapsulated data (and even the code used to select the "methods") is exposed to the client programs.

It is a bit of a stretch to describe the current COBOL language in terms of OO. The value of the above example is to describe scenarios familiar to host programmers. This approach not only teaches the principles of OO in a familiar setting for the COBOL programmer, but it also convinces the programmer—as opposed to the manager or executive—that OO makes the programmer's and maintenance programmer's jobs easier. This is the key to promoting OO within the applications development department.

Leveraging Existing Assets

The many COBOL programmers working today have encoded the business processes of the companies in COBOL programs over a long period of time. It is important to leverage these assets when reengineering business processes into the new world of OO. Making the transition to OO from COBOL is therefore a key issue for IS management.

The idea of migrating applications developers and code to leverage existing assets to the maximum extent is a sensible, practical, and cost-efficient approach. It involves a concentrated code analysis process to understand the current state of the code and how it can best be used. Once the analysis phase is complete, the serious work of redevelopment engineering can proceed.

The heart of the redevelopment process is the transformation methodology that combines top-down (business vision) and bottom-up (technical vision) approaches. The result is the overall organization's transformation policy: a strategic statement or contract defining what the system will be and what it will take to get there.

Once the plan is formalized and in place, the business of redeveloping the system can begin in earnest. The analysis of the existing system now helps identify overlapping functions—that is, the functions the target system and current system have in common. A variety of projects have shown that as much as 60% of an existing system's code can be reused in the new system.

Because these functions could be used repeatedly during the development process, reusable code in the form of objects is suggested. In addition to determining functional code that already exists, all other functions should be identified and catalogued. These catalogued functions are natural candidates for objects and an excellent way to get developers to understand how to identify and create objects.

Functions, processes, and the application code compose only half of the equation. Data relationships and requirements must also be examined. Overlapping data—common data between the current and target system—needs to be analyzed and catalogued. A data repository can track the data requirements of the system and ensure that data is not duplicated. The idea of encapsulation must be used to help define how the data is used, how it is modified, who uses it, and in what instances. In this way, the developer learns about the data requirements of the application at the detailed function or object level.

These techniques do not by themselves create an OO application. COBOL expertise does not equal OOCOBOL expertise. It does, however, suggest an approach to get host developers started thinking in the right direction. Once the application is defined at the object and nonobject levels, the user interface can be considered.

Starting OO Development

GUI Builders. There are many tools and facilities available for creating sophisticated OO GUI interfaces. These interfaces need to be highly intuitive and often contain common components across screen sets. Common components or screen objects are relatively easy to build and have value because they can be easily reused.

Starting OO development at the user interface portion of applications not only makes sense, it is something that can be accomplished through the use of a variety of OO GUI tools. Implementations of Smalltalk all exploit the window-icon-mouse-pointer approach and, more important, take advantage of the transfer of learning that comes about through the use of protocols such as IBM's Common User Access specification. Another example is the Dialog presentation development system from MicroFocus that directly interfaces to COBOL programs. That the user interface can be created at the same time the fundamental principles of OO are being learned is a double advantage.

Business Processes

It must be pointed out that the common belief that sexy user interfaces are what OO is all about is misleading. Business processes are equally amenable to object-oriented techniques.

Many of the problems of creating, extending, and maintaining business applications stem from the amount of translation that occurs between the problem being addressed and its computational solution. A simple request from the shop floor to the warehouse becomes a transaction involving terminals, files, and synchronization points in the non-OO world. Using OO, this is simply a message that is sent from the shop floor object to the warehouse object. The complexities involving this activity are hidden within the implementation of each object.

Done properly, the objects in the original problem specification and the objects in the computational solution are directly related, making for easier understanding and hence maintenance. In other words, the business definition of the problem is also the computational solution to the problem. This is, however, different from the way most organizations and certainly host developers design and develop applications.

Team Development

OO development teams create different aspects of the application. A framework team develops the reusable objects while an application team develops or assembles the application. This means that the application team owns the application but the framework teams owns the components of that application. This is different from traditional code ownership and requires flexibility and communication among the different teams.

Data Acquisition

The next issue of concern is the aspect of data acquisition and persistence. How does the application store the data and what is the bridge between the non-OO aspects of the code possibly using a relational data base management system and the OO aspects of the code that possibly uses an object-oriented database? This dual database strategy must tie relational legacy data with objects—that is, data residing on the host using DB2, for example, must interface with objects residing on distributed servers using Object Store, for example. The migration process thus involves not only developers, but technologies that must be carefully considered.

The least confrontational solution is to use SQL as a common access mechanism. Not only do host developers know SQL, but it is able (or almost able) to bridge the gap between these environments. SQL2 is the current ANSI standard that most developers are familiar with. It is being successfully used with the current implementation of relational databases on a variety of platforms. Of particular importance is its support of referential integrity and stored procedures.

The definition work on SQL3 is currently in progress. It will replace the current ANSI standard SQL and provide support for objects, including object identification, classes, methods, and inheritance. Once completed, SQL (or what some are now calling OQL) will be able to provide distributed access to objects similar to its ability to provide distributed access to data.

Eventually, all aspects of object management will be handled via standard SQL calls. As the SQL language adds capabilities and new syntax, it will be able to accommodate new object environments, including OMG's CORBA, IBM's SOM, and Microsoft's OLE, thus allowing for the transition of SQL to incorporate objects along with a long-term blueprint for full OO systems. Developers can adapt the data acquisition portion of application code by taking advantage of new features as required. This represents an evolutionary, not revolutionary, path to object technologies.

OO Client/Server Integration

The integration of OO technology with the demands of distributed client/server applications is another significant issue. OO must be able to integrate with existing technology, both legacy and distributed models.

Current and Future Generations of Systems

First-generation client/server systems now under development are rather modest in their design owing to the absence of sophisticated tools (both development and system services) and the lack of expertise in this relatively new technology. The next generation of client/server applications will be more robust, providing transparency of data, transparency of process location, and the ability to access local, relational, and nonrelational data. The third generation of client/server solutions will incorporate most of the features organizations have been looking for in distributed solutions. In this case, systems include distributed client platforms, reliance on middleware, heterogeneous data sources, mixed access technologies, high transaction volumes, and mission-critical integrity.

OO features will be incorporated throughout each generation of client/server system. As distributed technologies and associated tools mature, so will the use of OO, though its use will vary depending on the expertise of the organization. First-generation applications are allowing developers to experiment with OO but, for the most part, not export them to the production solution. The time is nonetheless well spent by developers, who are learning the basic concepts of OO while attempting to develop component pieces for use in actual applications. Second and third generations of client/server applications will use OO in ever-increasing amounts. By necessity, the third generation of these systems will require OO to efficiently provide the required solution.

The use of Smalltalk, OOCOBOL, and other tools offer developers a means to satisfy the requirements of each generation of client/server applications. For example, Smalltalk may be initially used to develop the desktop-presentation portions of the application. As the requirements of the application increase in complexity, reusable Smalltalk application objects can be developed for distribution across the enterprise (Smalltalk can be

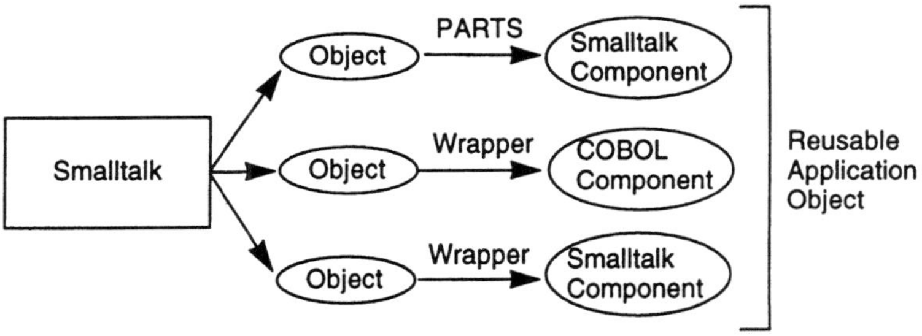

Exhibit 4. Smalltalk application assembly.

integrated with standard language calls)—for example, a COBOL program calling a Smalltalk object or a Smalltalk object calling a COBOL (or OOCOBOL) routine.

The functional requirements of the third generation of client/server applications require OO databases, object request brokers, and object request servers. The object request broker acts as sophisticated middleware transparently transporting objects across the enterprise. A combination of Smalltalk and language objects will all be serviced in this scenario (see Exhibit 4). From the developer's point of view, the use of Smalltalk and OOCOBOL objects means that the work done early in the transitional phase can be used in later stages to a large extent.

Anticipating the Costs of the Transition

In the early stages of transition to OO techniques, it is reasonable to expect an average of three redesigns before a set of objects are suitable for use in production. The organization must be willing to invest in these "lost objects" and consider it a part of the expense of training. One study found that more than 13 reuses are required to cover the cost of developing a reusable component. This situation is in part due to the current state of the technology, especially tools, but a portion of the problem must also be attributed to the design methodologies currently being practiced (thus the criticality of moving to one of the OO design methods). As development organizations gain experience and their inventory of available objects increases, this number will go down.

Key decisions must also be made about the applications' operating environment before any code is developed. Are the facilities of a relational data base management system to be used, an online transaction processing system, or a combination of the two? Is the data base relational or OO? If OLTP is required, how can that be effectively interfaced to the OO portions of the system? Because both technologies may be required, how are they to be integrated and what communication methods handle the distributed object management? The realities of the current state of OO middleware is important to understand if the application is to be architected with a combination of technologies.

LANs, multiuser environments, GUI interfaces, and distributed processing facilities must also be modeled in order to determine where each piece fits and the tools available to integrate the application into a seamless unit. For example, PM, Windows, and Motif each specify a different GUI interface. Each GUI has specific requirements (to go along with individual APIs) and requires careful consideration (regardless of the tool being used to create the interface). The next generation of operating systems and interfaces should also be looked at.

Building reusable components and then distributing those components is critical to the success of the distributed client/server application—that is, different objects executing on the platform best suited to provide the solution. A common example is a system that has been distributed with front-end processing occurring on distributed clients with data acquisition elements residing on a host or hosts (including distributed servers). Managing these diverse resources in an effective and optimal manner is key to the success of any mission-critical application.

Conclusion

Migrating a development organization to object-oriented methods is a long-term investment decision involving all aspects of the development environment and affecting the way the organization will conduct business. The transition process is not limited to but certainly includes the actual developers who may have little understanding of OO concepts. System architects, designers, analysts, and programmers must all understand the basic paradigm shift that moving to an OO environment entails.

While object-oriented technology brings certain benefits to the table, it also raises many concerns. How much training is required and what is the expense? What will it take to actually move current application methods to OO and what is the cost of this conversion? Other concerns include the maturity of the technology and related tools, lack of standards, and execution speed.

Integrating OO technology into the current production mix will require tools that are open and do not include proprietary technology. Finally, the enterprise model for the organization's next-generation applications must be supported. This requirement includes robust performance, data integrity, and the services provided by a transaction processing monitor.

Although these concerns are real and need careful consideration, OO technology offers the only realistic solution to the promise of truly distributed client/server applications. Faster development, higher-quality code, reduced costs, and easier maintenance have been promised by each new development technology. In each case, improvements have been made, but none compare with the results experienced by early OO adopters. Increased scalability through the use of objects as building blocks allows heterogeneous environments to be transparently supported.

As development organizations move to OO environments, they are facing and resolving problems related to interfacing objects to current technology, training and design methodology issues, and the basic conflict developers face when moving away from data independence principles to encapsulation.

The biggest investment the organization will be required to make is in training. The second biggest investment is ignoring the cost of training. Many organizations that make the mistake of selecting tools (both development and system services) before or in conjunction with formalized training find themselves lost in the technology and select tools that don't match the way the organization will ultimately develop objects and applications. The richness and stability of the selected environment is critical along with its potential for growth and its ability to interact with both object and nonobject environments.

Regardless of the development methodology, language, and tools eventually selected, it is important to spend as much time as required to consider this move and how to effectively transition the organization and its developers to this new world.

Section X
Auditing Systems

Organizations continue to rely more and more on computer technology. Although the initial use of computers involved only a conversion from manual to automatic transaction processing to increase productivity and decrease cost, the current use of computers is changing the way business operates. The computer is such an integral part of day-to-day operations in most organizations, that when the computer is not functioning (i.e., down), the business cannot perform its routine transactions. Organizations are mixing hardware platforms from different vendors with a combination of commercially available software and in-house-developed software. As a result of these changes, business risk increases.

With the increased reliance on computers to perform daily transactions and with the higher risks associated with new technology, management needs adequate assurance that the controls governing its computer operations are adequate. Management looks toward the audit function to provide this assurance. EDP auditing is needed to evaluate the adequacy of automated information systems to meet processing needs, to evaluate the adequacy of internal controls, and to ensure that assets controlled by those systems are adequately safeguarded. However, because of the rapidly changing technology and the new risks associated with that technology, specialists are needed to perform these control assessments.

Windows NT offers numerous control capabilities that are typically optional and, therefore, must be reviewed to ensure that they are effectively implemented. In addition, Windows NT introduces improvements in security capabilities. However, there remain potential weaknesses that must be addressed when reviewing Windows NT systems. Chapter 81 discusses an approach for auditing Windows NT applications, including procedures and menu screens to review when a Windows NT application is encountered. The audit approach focuses on understanding the environment, evaluating the risks and the controls, and making audit recommendations.

Many Unix environments have been created with open connectivity in mind. Because of this, access to system resources by local users and by users from other systems tends to be quite open. Access from other systems requires extensive analysis. In addition, a large number of Unix versions, each with its own idiosyncrasies, exist. Unix is also a multiuser operating system, and a Unix audit is likely to involve numerous machines, as would be found in an audit of a microcomputer environment. Auditing a Unix environment will likely combine these challenges. Chapters 82 and 83 provide some specific items to review during parts of such an audit.

Chapter 81
Auditing Windows NT LANs

Paul Cullen

Like any LAN, Windows NT processing controls should be based on standards developed by user and data processing managements. These standards should define the practices and controls adopted by management to ensure that processing is performed with a prudent level of risk. Standards should be developed in the areas of data security, systems development, program change control, problem management, and disaster recovery planning. Windows NT has made improvements in the areas of logical security and system recovery by providing controls similar to those in mainframe environments. However, the auditor should be aware of security weaknesses that exist in the NT LAN environment. These weaknesses are discussed later in this chapter. In addition, the auditor should develop a picture of the audit environment, including an understanding of the business functions, information flows, and data storage to assess the effect of control weaknesses accurately.

Evaluating the Risk

Like the processing on any platform, Windows NT controls should be implemented based on the risk inherent in the application. Risk should be assessed in the areas of information confidentiality, loss of data and software, and processing integrity. Users typically confuse applications with the software used to run the application. For example, a typical error is the assumption that Microsoft EXCEL spreadsheet software is an application that could easily be replaced. This assumption does not consider the consequences of errors in the spreadsheets or the effort required to reconstruct a spreadsheet if it is lost. In addition, users frequently assume that mainframe and minicomputer applications are high risk and that applications running on Windows NT LANs are low risk. This paradigm is changing with the growth of client/server processing as LAN applications have been developed for financial reporting, processing payroll, and handling customer transactions. Auditors should verify that Windows NT

0-8493-9989-0/99/$0.00+$.50

Exhibit 1. A simplified risk analysis.

Risks	Related Controls
Inappropriate disclosure of information security	Physical security
	Windows NT LAN logical security
Loss of data or software	Contingency plan, uninterruptible power supply
Processing errors	Edits checks, test plans
Processing interruptions	Problem management, capacity planning

application risks have been accurately assessed and that controls are in place to address the risks. Exhibit 1 is a simplified risk analysis table that shows risks and related controls.

Audit Procedures

The following are suggested procedures that can be incorporated into an audit program to ensure that risks are properly assessed and that controls are in place to address those risks.

Obtain an Overview of the NT LAN. As a first step, the auditor should obtain an overview of the Windows NT LAN, including how it is used and managed. This step begins with identifying the LAN administrator and his or her designated backup. This person is responsible for resolving LAN problems, adding new users to the LAN, making changes to LAN software, and backing up programs and data to ensure that the applications can be recovered in the event of a disaster. The LAN administrator should not have conflicting responsibilities such as performing the duties of a controller who has full control of accounting information.

Determine What Applications Run on the LAN. The next steps cover the review of what applications run on the LAN. At this step, the auditor documents the applications and evaluates the risks and exposures associated with those applications. The risks inherent in LAN applications determine the required controls and resulting audit procedures required to verify the adequacy and effectiveness of those controls.

Review the Network Systems Manuals. The auditor should review the network systems manuals to determine the systems' capabilities. This review provides a basis for possible recommendations to management. In addition, the auditor should review the use of LAN monitoring equipment and its capabilities and the Windows NT LAN performance statistics, which are discussed later in this chapter. Many types of equipment are available to monitor LAN traffic for fine-tuning operations and diagnosing problems.

However, these seemingly useful products add risk, because they also can view and capture sensitive data being transmitted across the network. Although these products are necessary tools to be used in LAN administration, their use should be limited to authorized individuals.

Identify Gateways. Gateways are used to connect networks running on different architectures. They are commonly used to connect LANs to mainframe computers. PCs on the LAN can then act like "smart terminals" by allowing users to have mainframe sessions. Some gateway products can capture data flowing from the PC to the mainframe, so there is the potential for sensitive information, such as passwords and other confidential data, to be captured. Gateways should be physically secure and restricted only to authorized individuals.

Perform an Inventory of Shareware Software. The auditor should determine if public domain or "shareware" software is being used. This software may not be properly licensed, and the company could be infringing on a copyright by using it. In addition, public domain software is arguably more likely to contain computer viruses that could infect and destroy data on an individual PC or on an entire LAN.

Review Fixed Assets Purchasing and Maintenance Procedures. The auditor should identify and review the inventory or fixed assets process for controlling the purchases and maintenance of hardware and software. Windows NT LAN equipment consists of expensive and typically marketable fixed assets. These types of fixed assets must be controlled to prevent abuse, loss, or theft. The review of inventory should include the tracing of equipment (i.e., hardware) and software to inventory records and license agreements to verify their accuracy and to verify that license agreements and copyrights are not being violated.

Data Security

An important area in performing an audit of Windows NT LAN is to determine that the LAN applications and data are adequately secure. As an initial step, the layout of the LAN should be documented and physical security over the Windows NT LAN should be evaluated to determine logical controls required to compensate for weaknesses in physical security.

Access Controls

Access to a Windows NT LAN is based on a user ID and password. Passwords can be set as mandatory by the LAN administrator. LAN administrators add users and define capabilities by using the User Profile Management Service's menu. Users are assigned to groups and then are given access to resources, such as directories, either by user ID or group

ID. Windows NT has a guest group and account. The guest account does not have access rights on NT Servers.

Dial-up access capabilities should also be controlled. Many companies believe that LAN operating system security alone is not adequate to control dial-up access that can allow access to anyone with a PC, modem, and communications software. PC products are available that allow a user to dial into a LAN workstation from any location and to control the workstation, which removes the ability to rely on physical security. Additional security features, such as callback or encryption modems, should be considered to improve dial-up access security. In addition, Windows NT has a feature called Remote Access Services that allows a remote workstation to access the server via a modem and dial-up access line. The Remote Access Services feature can provide additional controls, such as callback and password encryption.

The auditor must also understand the access controls available within the LAN operating system. This understanding typically begins with a review of the LAN administrator's manual for the PC operating system.

Security or access to the LAN can be cumbersome if a separate logon is required for the PC, the network operating system (i.e., multiple servers), the application, and the mainframe interface. Vendors are beginning to work together to interface logons to provide integrated PC, LAN, and mainframe security solutions. This trend will likely continue and become more refined as processing is distributed in the End User Computing (EUC) environment.

The auditor must also identify on what platform processing is performed and where data is stored. Application software and data can be stored on the PC workstation, on the LAN server, or on the mainframe. Further, the application software can provide some internal security. This situation creates the need for up to four data security checkpoints: the workstation, the LAN operating system, the application, and the mainframe. The auditor must assess the strengths and weaknesses of each of these platforms to ensure that the applications programs and data are adequately secure based on their risk assessment and corporate standards.

When auditing security administration, the auditor should review security administration processes for adding new users, assigning and modifying access capabilities, and removing access when it is no longer needed. In addition, security violations and audit trails of security administration activity should also be reviewed. These steps are the same for Windows NT LAN-based systems as they are for applications being processed on other platforms.

Data Security Testing

The purpose of data security testing is to verify that access capabilities are authorized and appropriate based on the user's job function. The auditor's initial step is to review the log-on password protection. Passwords can be scripted inbat files that execute when the workstation is started (i.e., turned on or powered up). Then, everyone who has access to that workstation can access the LAN. Windows NT also functions as a workstation or a server by allowing other workstations to access its disk drives and printers. Logical access controls over each Windows NT workstation through the network must be assessed. If access is allowed only to a dedicated server, the auditor should only identify the servers and review network logical access controls over those servers. Security can also be implemented by workgroup or domain. A domain is a number of servers that are grouped together to administer security by recognizing the same user accounts. Domains can also be connected through a device called a trust relationship. Some software packages allow systems (or security) administrators the ability to access and control a user's workstation, typically for problem resolution. The use of these packages and controls that prevent inappropriate access must be evaluated for their adequacy and effectiveness.

The last steps for the auditor in reviewing data security are to review the system security parameters and access capabilities and verify that they are appropriate based on job function. The auditor should review user IDs and group IDs and the accompanied resources that they have access to by tracing them to the proper authorization and by verifying their appropriateness. LAN administrator authority should be limited, because he or she could allow access to all system resources. It is possible for LAN administrator IDs to take ownership of directories, even though this action is logged.

User IDs and Passwords

Security for Windows NT is controlled by user IDs with LAN administrator authority. There is no user ID with audit authority. Therefore, the auditor must work with a LAN administrator ID to review access controls. To view security documentation on Windows NT, the auditor must select Administrative Tools from the Program Manager to view the user and group IDs. Exhibit 2 shows the Administrative Tools screen with the User Management icon highlighted. Exhibit 3 shows the screen that pops into view after the User Management icon has been selected. At this screen, the auditor can view the users on the system and trace them to organization charts to verify that they are valid.

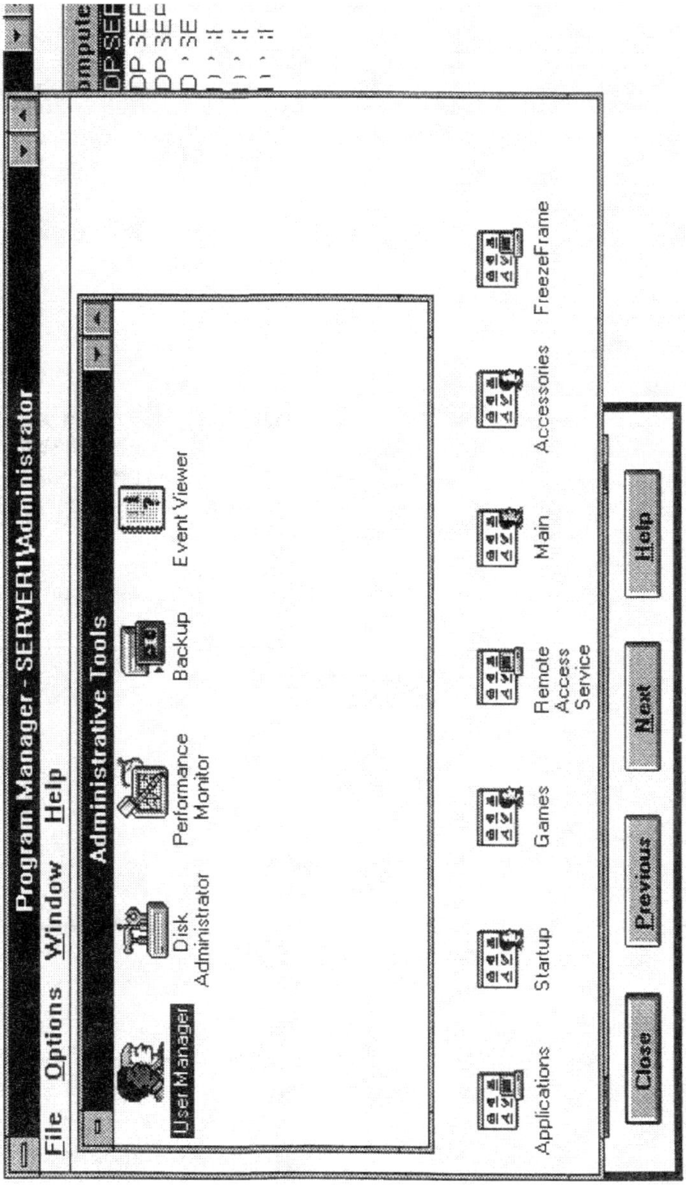

Exhibit 2. The administrative tools screen.

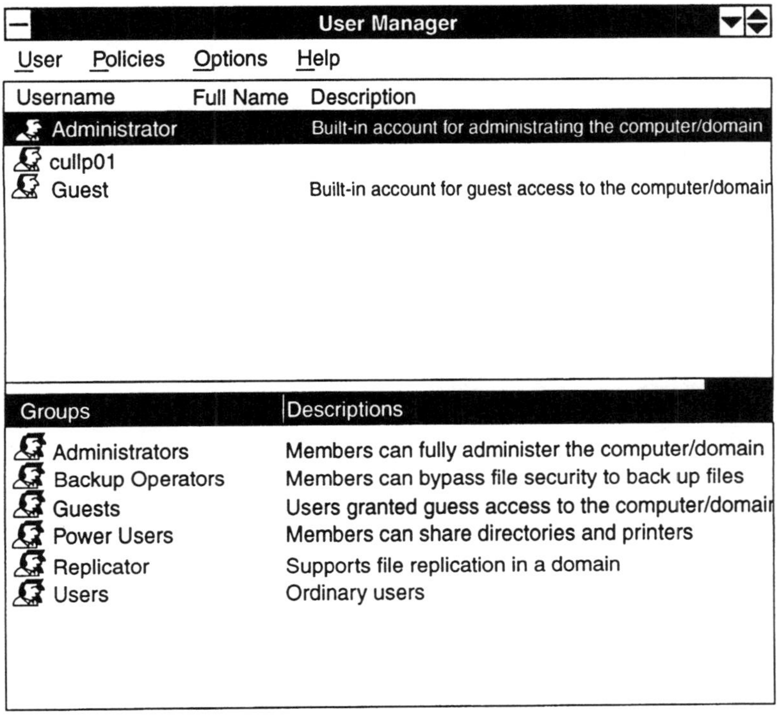

Exhibit 3. After selecting the user management icon.

Setting User IDs and Passwords. Windows NT also allows the user ID and password requirements to be set at the system level. This security features enables the auditor to verify that the system complies with the corporate information security standards. Exhibit 4 shows the screen labeled Account Policy that permits the following actions:

- Force a password change (every 90 days)
- Allow password changes every 10 days to prevent users from reusing passwords
- Set a minimum password length (six characters)
- Keep a password history to prevent users from reusing passwords
- Lock out an account after invalid log-on attempts to prevent password guessing

Setting User Hours and Assigning User Rights. The LAN administrator can also control the hours that a user ID can log on. User IDs can also be assigned various rights as shown in Exhibit 5. These are the various user ID rights:

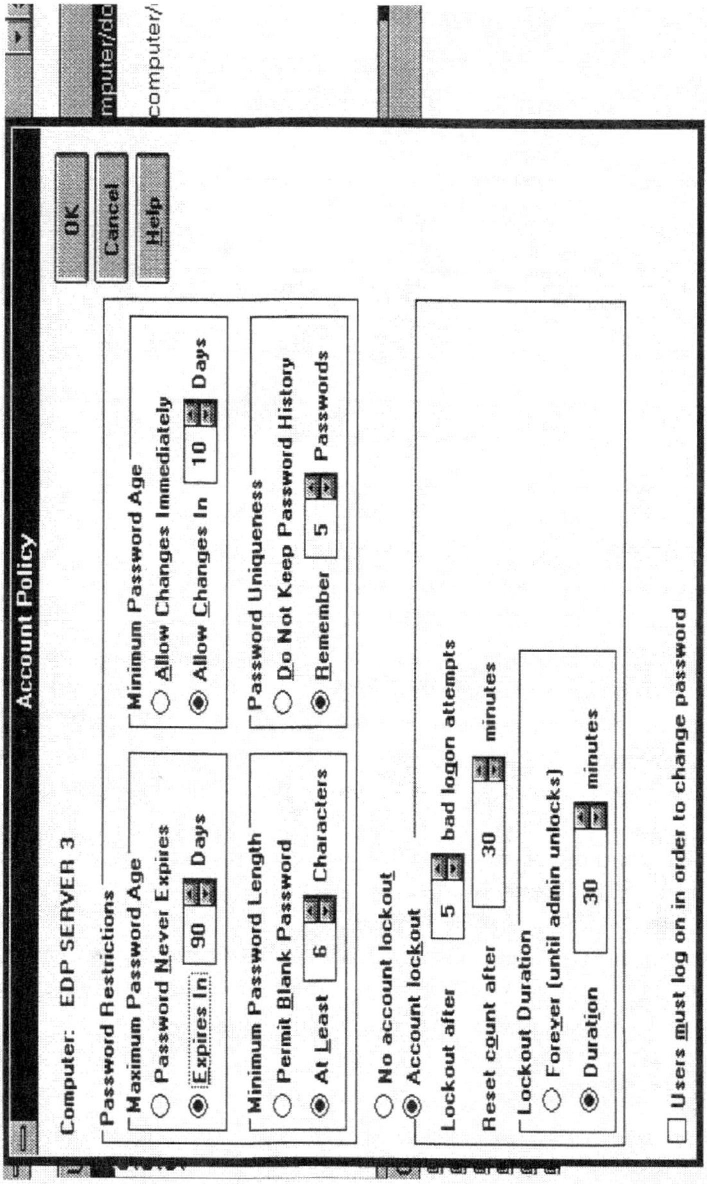

Exhibit 4. Setting User IDs and password requirements.

- Access the computer from the network.
- Back up files and directories by superseding file and directory permissions.
- Change the system time.
- Force shutdown from a remote system.
- Load and unload device drivers.
- Log-on locally by using the computer's keyboard.
- Manage auditing and security log by specifying what types of events are audited.
- Restore files and directories by superseding file and directory permissions.
- Shut down the system.
- Take ownership of files or other objects.

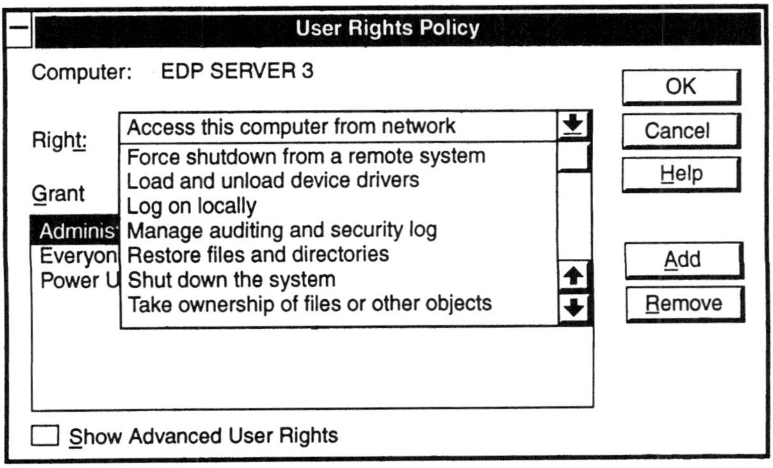

Exhibit 5. Assigning user rights.

Setting User Descriptions and Passwords. Exhibit 6 shows the User Properties Menu that allows a LAN administrator to enter a user description and password. In addition, the LAN administrator can perform these functions:

- Enter a user's password
- Force the user to change the password at logon
- Set a password expiration interval
- Disable the user ID
- Lock or unlock the user ID

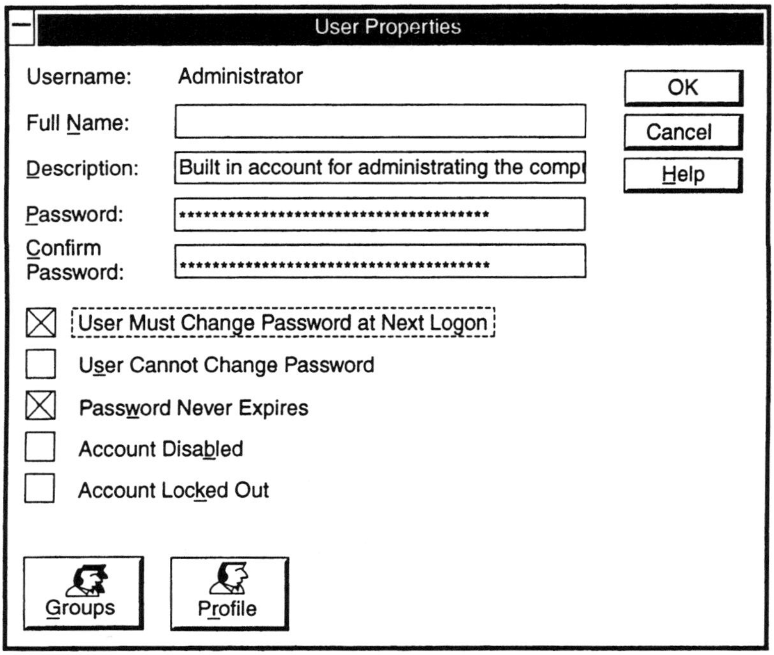

Exhibit 6. User properties menu.

Restricting Access to Directories and Files. Windows NT restricts access to directories and files based on user and group IDs. Exhibit 7 shows the screen labeled Directory Permissions. The screen allows the LAN administrator to assign access to the root directory and its accompanying capabilities. These are: RWXDPO, which mean read, write, execute, delete, change permissions, and take ownership. In addition, Windows NT has a full control option that allows all access to the owner and systems administrators.

This method of security allows management to restrict access based on the job functions of a user or group of users. The disk drive must be formatted using the New Technology File System (NTFS) for this level of security. The auditor should verify that access to system resources, such as directories and files, are appropriate based on the user and group authorities assigned to the individuals.

Windows NT Auditing Features

Windows NT also provides an audit access to resources feature. This can be activated at the system level, as well as the file or directory level.

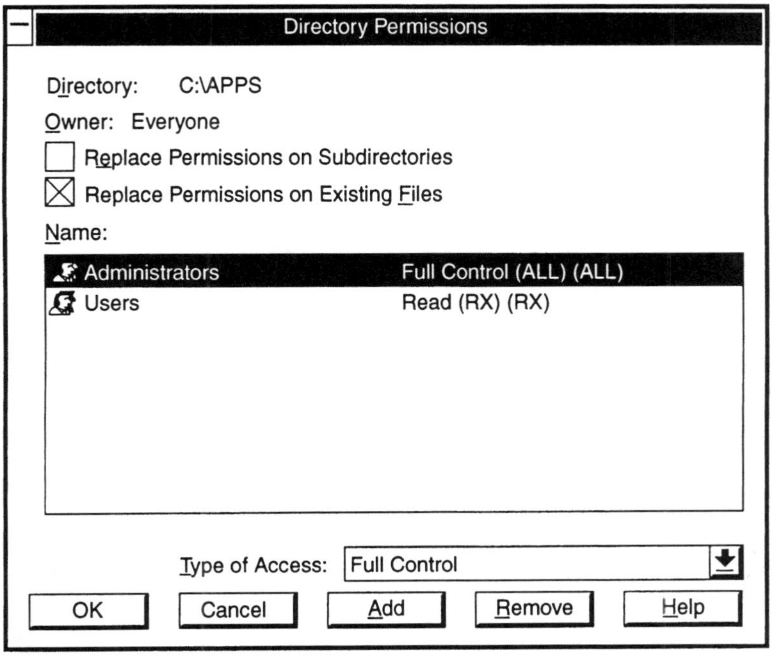

Exhibit 7. Directory permissions.

Exhibit 8 shows the events that can be audited including columns for successful attempts and denied-access attempts (i.e., failures):

- Logons or logoffs
- File or object access
- Use of user rights
- User and group management
- Security policy changes
- System restart and shutdown
- Process tracking

Auditing is an optional feature, and the preceding parameters should be set to record security-related events. Exhibit 9 shows the Windows NT Event Viewer that allows the LAN administrator to view security-related events. This log includes the date, time, source, event category, event type, user ID, and computer name. The auditor can select events for more details as shown in Exhibit 10.

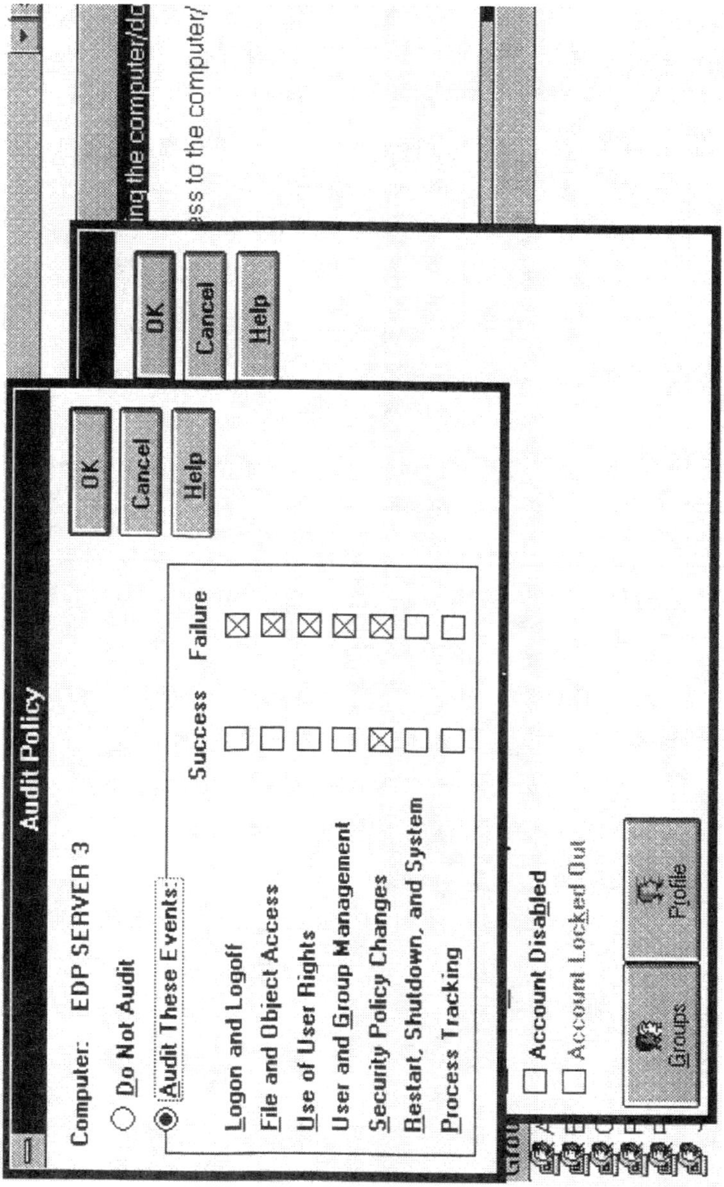

Exhibit 8. Events that can be audited.

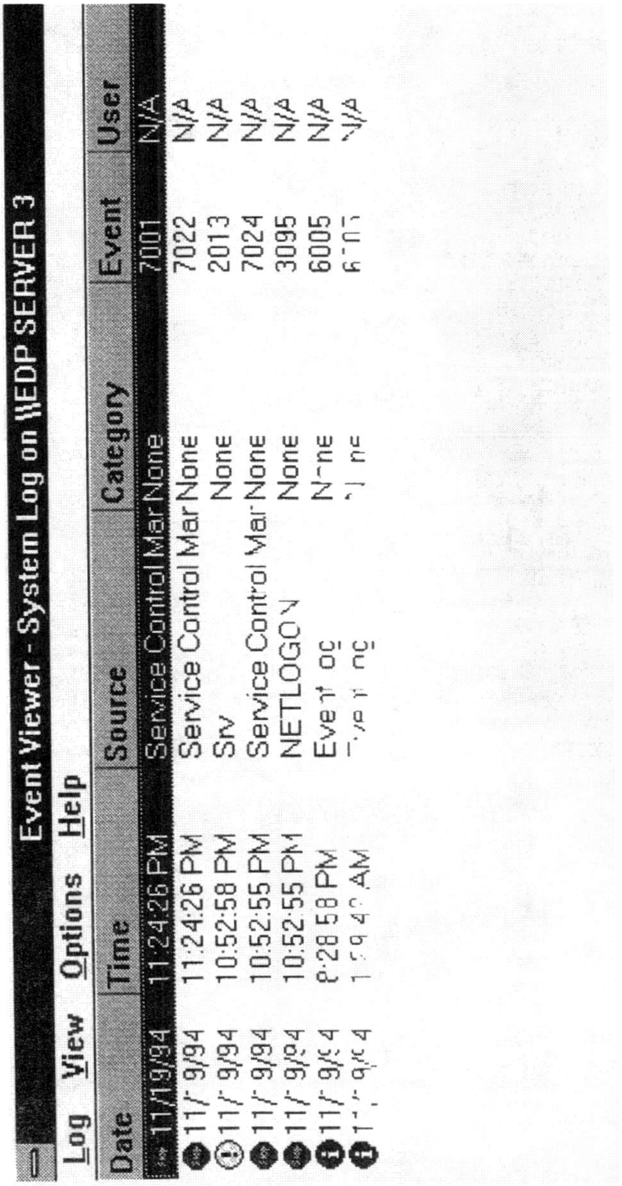

Exhibit 9. Event viewer.

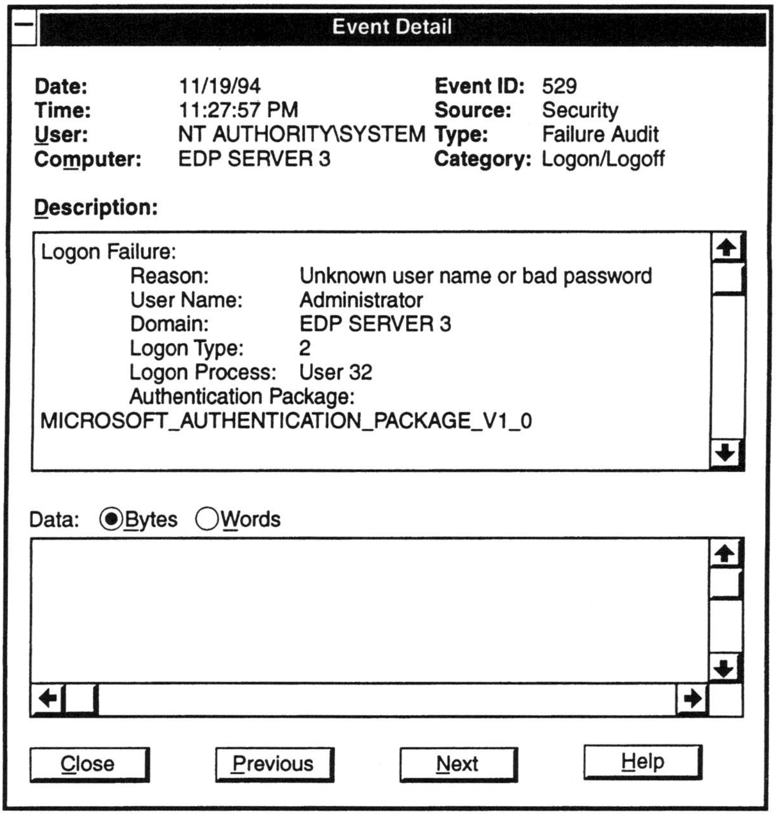

Exhibit 10. Event detail for security-related incidents.

Other LAN Administrator Features

In addition, Windows NT provides these services to be used by the LAN administrator:

- The alerter that sends messages to specified users regarding security, user, server, and printer problems
- The clipbook server that allows pages to be seen remotely
- The computer browser that maintains an up-to-date list of computers
- The directory replicator that duplicates directories and files across computers
- The event log that logs system security and application events
- The messages option that allows messages to be sent and logged
- The net logon that verifies the username and password supplied by each person who logged on to the network or gained access to the server

- The net pop up that displays a messages box
- The replicator that duplicates a master set of directories and files
- The server that allows the sharing of printers and files
- The uninterruptible power supply (UPS) that is used to keep a computer running in the event of a power failure
- The workstation option that provides network connections and communications

Performance Monitoring and Capacity Planning

Windows NT has improved capacity and performance statistics reporting in addition to error logging. This feature can show the capacity of the computer as well as indications of performance problems. Windows NT can track utilization in terms of the percentage of processor time and user time.

Problem Management

The purpose of problem management is to determine that the Windows NT system problems are being recorded, analyzed, and resolved. Windows NT has logging capabilities for operating system and hardware errors. However, application software and user errors are not logged. Therefore, LAN administrators should keep a manual log or database of all problems including user, application, operating system, and hardware errors. This log should contain the date the problem occurred, problem description, length of downtime, priority of resolution, actions taken to resolve the problem, and date the problem was resolved. The problem log should be analyzed on a periodic basis to find weaknesses in testing, hardware reliability, and user training requirements.

Another concern for auditors is whether problems are resolved within the appropriate time frames. For critical time frame applications, companies may need to contract for LAN equipment support within specified time frames and have backup equipment to ensure that the network is performing according to business needs. In addition, a complete problem log can show problem trends with hardware, operating system software, application software, and communication software. The Event Viewer Screen as shown in Exhibit 9 under the Administrative Services menu option shows the system error log. A LAN administrator can select a specific error to see an explanation of what happened. Exhibit 11 shows an Event Detail screen for the specific event selected. As previously mentioned, these options can also be used to identify breaches in security.

Program Change Control Management

The audit of program change control management is to determine that system changes are authorized, tested, documented, communicated, and controlled. A process should also be in place to ensure that production

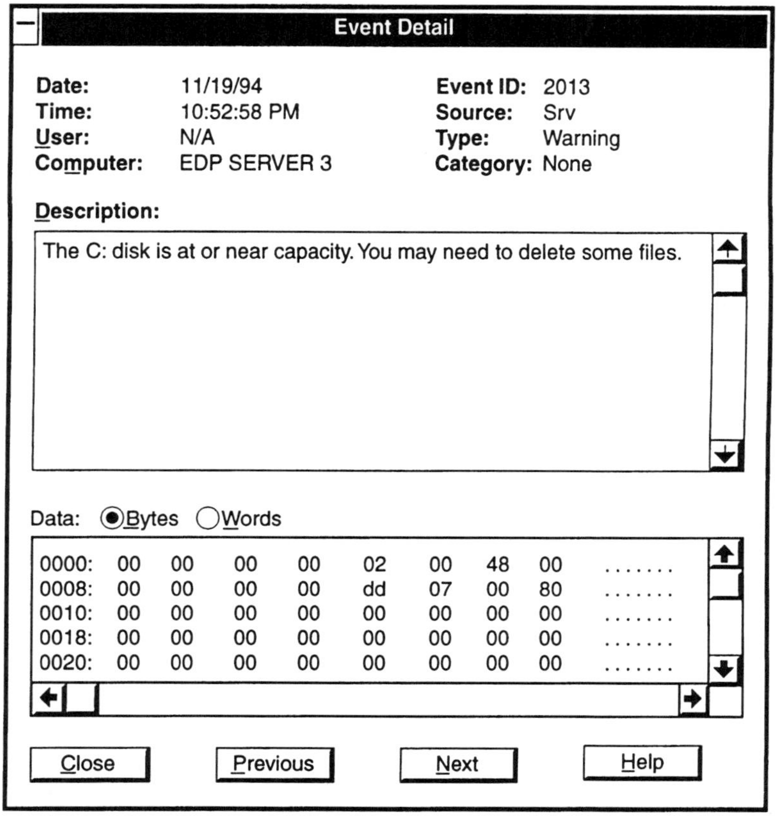

Exhibit 11. Event detail for specific error incidents.

---

source and executable code are synchronized and secure to prevent inappropriate program alteration and to be able to reconstruct the system files. Although PC-based change management software is available, Windows NT LANs typically do not have the change management facilities that are found in mainframe systems. Therefore, LAN administrators manually control production code on restricted subdirectories on the LAN servers. Once a change has been tested and approved, an independent party should move the code to a restricted library on the servers or distribute the software to workstations. This process ensures the integrity of the software version that is running in production and that unauthorized changes are not introduced into the system.

Windows NT LAN software also frequently is developed by commercial software vendors. Because users are not involved in program development, they do not feel the need to test the software. However, user acceptance testing should be performed before each software release is propagated to ensure that the system is performing according to user expectations and to prevent the corruption of user files. The auditor should review the process for unit, system, and user acceptance testing. There should be evidence showing that users have signed off and approved the change and that the systems documentation was updated if appropriate.

Disaster Recovery and Contingency Preparedness

Disaster recovery planning is basically no different for Windows NT LAN systems than for any other system. The business unit must identify the risk of the applications and the time frame required for recovery. Based on this assessment, a disaster recovery plan should be developed identifying who will be responsible for recovering the system, where recovery will be performed, and what equipment is required for recovery, including any communications equipment. Backups of workstation and server programs and data are frequently kept in the form of backup tapes. A common approach is for users to back up workstation data to the server and then back up the server to tape. The backup tapes should be kept in a secure off-site location, and the frequency of the backups should be assessed based on how often the data is updated and the amount of effort required to reconstruct the files. The security of the off-site location is critical, because the logical security provided by the LAN operating system does not protect data on backup tapes. Windows NT has an uninterruptible power supply (UPS) service that works with special UPS hardware. This shuts down the computer in an orderly manner while the UPS is supplying power. In addition, Windows NT has a replicator service that automatically copies files or directories as well as supports mirrored disk drives.

The disaster recovery plan should be tested periodically to ensure that it is sufficient to recover all critical functions. This test should include recovery from the backup tapes to verify that the backup process is effective.

Systems Development and Project Management

The audit or review of systems development and project management is basically the same for Windows NT LAN systems as for other systems and is closely related to the program change control review previously discussed. Windows NT LAN software development is often done by groups of small databases available from commercially (i.e., off-the-shelf) purchased packages or by contract programmers. This area may not have its own development staff. However, a development methodology, project management, and user involvement or training should be employed for Windows NT LAN systems development in the same manner as with the development of any other systems.

Technology strategic planning should also be performed to ensure that the LAN system and applications are compatible with the corporation's wide area networks and technology strategic plans. The strategic plan should be based on the business unit's plans. In addition, the operating system and hardware should provide for the future migration to other kinds of platforms.

The auditor should review the systems development methodology for inclusion of critical elements. Other concerns regarding the development of Windows NT LAN systems include a cost benefit analysis to ensure that the payback from the system justifies its cost, that there was competitive bidding to ensure that the prices paid for the hardware and software are reasonable, and that the purchases are properly approved by an appropriate level of management. Finally, if software is developed by vendors or contract programmers, copyrights and software ownership must be clearly defined by the contract or agreement.

Processing Integrity

Processing integrity for Windows NT-based systems has some unique control concerns in addition to the basic input, processing, and output controls that apply to all application systems. Audit retrieval software should be considered for reviewing this system as is the case with a review of any other computer system.

Users typically install applications on a Windows NT platform because it is a low-cost alternative to mainframe development. Hardware and software should be benchmark-tested before it is propagated to ensure that it has enough capacity.

Another concern for Windows NT-based systems is control over concurrent updates, which is the ability to control two people updating the same file or record at the same time. This ability can be controlled by the LAN operating system or by the application software. LAN servers typically fail in one of two ways. First, they can be too restrictive by preventing two or more people from accessing the same disk drive or subdirectory at the same time. This restriction can obviously be inefficient when the desire is to share data. The second way LANs can fail is by letting two or more individuals into the same file or even into the same record but not preventing the loss of one person's update or the corruption of a file.

LAN applications are typically used to process data that is distributed by downloading it from a mainframe or minicomputer environment. Processes should be developed to ensure that the distributed databases are current and that users are all working from the same data.

Recommended Course of Action

High-risk applications are being developed on Windows NT LAN platforms. Management must assess the risk of these applications and implement appropriate controls. Auditors must verify that this assessment is performed and that adequate and effective controls are established based on the application risk. Although the steps required for assessing Windows NT controls are basically the same as for assessing controls on most other platforms, they should be tailored to match the unique characteristics of the NT LAN platform. However, some of the weaknesses inherent in Windows NT include:

- LAN administrators have unlimited access on the server. However, their activity is logged.
- Windows NT systems can be formatted using the DOS File Allocation Table (FAT) file structure. If this is the case, the computer could be booted using a DOS diskette, bypassing Windows NT security. In addition, if the FAT file structure is used, file and directory security is disabled.
- The Windows NT LAN system has logging capabilities. However, reporting capabilities need improvement. The entire log file must be manually searched to find specific entries.

In summary, Windows NT LANs can provide for adequate controls to run critical or sensitive business applications. However, the auditor must review how Windows NT is implemented to ensure that the applications are adequately controlled.

Chapter 82
Auditing Unix: General, Log-In, and Superuser Security

Dan Schultes

The following guidelines may provide additional insight before the audit. They are written under the assumption that the scope of the audit is a large number of Unix systems, all of which can't be fully reviewed in a limited timeframe. These guidelines are meant to assist in determining the systems to review. Many of these guidelines are also practical for non-Unix audits.

Defining and Assessing Control Risks. Through conversations with sysadmins and local management, data repositories and other key systems should be identified. A limited number of file servers hold the largest amount of data. A schematic should be obtained, if possible. Other systems may be especially critical to the area, such as a master Network Information Service (NIS) server (formerly know as yellow pages) or a system that contains critical operational or financial information. NIS allows sharing of common configuration files, such as /etc/passwd across Unix systems, thus streamlining administration of user IDs and eliminating the necessity of users synchronizing their passwords across systems. Generally, a sysadmin will administer all systems similarly. As a result, a sampling of the most critical systems, with instruction to incorporate recommendations across the entire environment, is an efficient approach to these audits.

Identifying Connectivity. An understanding of connectivity will allow a more complete understanding of the risk associated with the systems. Connectivity to the outside world, literally to thousands of people looking for new systems and companies to electronically compromise, dramatically increases the potential for a security exposure. An attacker can use a wide assortment of tools and knowledge, easily obtainable on the Internet, to attempt to compromise the connected Unix environment. The following questions should be answered:

0-8493-9989-0/99/$0.00+$.50

- Do the systems connect to systems outside of the company? If so, are the connections to vendors or to others on the Internet? If the connection is to vendors, how secure are the vendor systems?
- Are there modems attached to any of these machines that allow inbound connections? What type of inbound connections are allowed?
- What is the extent of perceived connectivity to other Unix systems within the company?
- What is the extent of their connectivity to other platforms (e.g., the production MVS environment, Novell servers, VAX systems, VM)? What type of information (e.g., log-in passwords) is being sent between the platforms?

Identifying Applications, the Job Functions that Use the Applications, and the Directories on which the Applications Reside. This will help the reader identify the directories encountered, as well as provide an understanding of the business use of the systems.

Identifying Management Concerns. Identifying concerns of local or other management will help define the audit scope.

Distributing a List of Tasks to the Sysadmin to Expedite the Audit.

The list should be distributed as soon as the systems to be reviewed have been selected. It may take the sysadmin a few days to fulfill this request, because commands differ slightly between the various Unix versions and because the sysadmin undoubtedly has other pressing responsibilities. Systems should be selected on the basis of previous discussions to determine criticality and risk, various security administration methods, a cross section of clients and servers, and different Unix versions. The list of tasks includes a request to set up a user ID for auditing, running commands to print specific configuration files, and locating various individual configuration files. The list of tasks shown in Exhibit 1 should be completed for each selected system. When all tasks are completed, the auditor should have a printout, a login for auditor, and five files created in the default directory for auditor.

Audit Program

A Unix audit program is divided into the following sections:

- General security
- Log-in security
- Superuser security
- File security
- Remote system security
- Unix-to-Unix copy protocol (UUCP) security
- Backup, disaster recovery, and change control

Exhibit 1. Sysadmin tasks to expedite the audit.

1. Please print the contents of the following files, noting the system name on each printout (note that since Unix file names vary based on release and version, many of these files will not be found on the systems being reviewed).

   /usr/lib/uucp/L.sys/usr/lib/uucp/USERFILE/usr/lib/uucp/Systems
   /usr/lib/uucp/Permissions /usr/lib/uucp/L.cmds
   /usr/lib/uucp/remote.unknown /usr/adm/sulog/var/adm/sulog
   /etc/security/sulog /usr/spool/.Admin/Foreign/etc/passwd
   /etc/group /etc/shadow /etc/.profile/etc/environment
   /etc/hosts.equiv /usr/etc/inetd.conf /etc/inetd.conf /etc/exports
   /etc/security/passwd.adjunct /etc/ttytab /etc/passwd.bak
   /etc/group.bak /etc/security/passwd /etc/security/group etc/security/login.cfg /etc/security/mkuser.default/etc/security/limits
   /etc/security/user
   /.pofile/.login/.cshrc/.rhosts
   /usr/lib/cron/at.allow /usr/lib/cron/at.deny
   /usr/lib/cron/cron.allow /usr/lib/cron/cron.deny
   /usr/spool/cron/at.allow /usr/spool/cron/at.deny
   /usr/spool/cron/cron.allow /usr/spool/cron/cron.deny

   If using NIS, then print:

   /yp/passwd/yp/hosts.byname /yp/group
   /yp/netgroup

2. Please setup a user ID, auditor, for our use on the audit.

3. Please note the following two items for the remaining commands:

   a. /...home/auditor refers to the home directory setup for the auditor.

   b. system_name refers to the nickname of the system on which the command is executed.

4. Print the permissions (ls -laR/) for each file server and place in auditor's home directory:
   ls -laR />/...home/auditor/system_name.permiss

5. Please list the names and permissions to all users' .rhosts:
   find /...home/*-name .rhosts -print -exec cat{}\;>/...home/auditor/system_name.rhosts

6. For setuid and setgid analysis, please list all root-owned setuid and setuid programs and the permissions to them:
   find / -perm -4000 -o -perm -2000 -user root -exec ls -la{}\;>
   /...home/auditor/system_name.setuids

7. Find all vi startup files and permissions to them:
   find / -name.exrc -exec ls -la{}\;>
   /...home/auditor/system_name.vi.startup

8. Find all .cshrc, .login, .profile, .sunview,. mailrc, and .netrc files and show permissions to them:
   find /...home\(-name .cshrc -o -name .login -o -name .profile -o -name .netrc -o -name .sunview -o -name .mailrc\) -exec ls -la {}\;>/...home/auditor/system_name.
   login.files

This chapter will cover the areas of general security, log-in security, and superuser security.

General Security

The objective of this section is to obtain information to analyze overall system controls in the audited Unix environment. The procedures are as follows:

1. The security policy pertaining to the Unix environment should be obtained. The following concerns should be adequately addressed in the policy:
   - User log-in:
     - —Log-ins without passwords should not be allowed.
     - —Passwords that cannot easily be guessed should be required.
     - —Password aging should be required.
     - —An account should be disabled after a limited number of failed log-in attempts.
     - —User IDs should not be shared.
     - —Log-in shells should be terminated after a period of inactivity.
   - Sysadmin:
     - —The use of the root log-in should be restricted.
     - —Other users' programs should not be run as root or under the sysadmin's personal user ID.
     - —A default path should be provided that searches system directories first.
   - File permissions:
     - —User home directories, log-in scripts, and start-up files should have write permission enabled only for that user.
     - —User network files (.rhosts and .netrc) should have read and write permission disabled for group and other.
     - —System directories and executable files within them should have write permission disabled for group and other.
   - Network:
     - —Trusted-host access should not be allowed from systems that are not secure.
     - —File systems that are NFS-mounted from other hosts should be checked for setuid or setgid programs.
     - —The use of tftp should be restricted, and when it is used, only single-directory access should be allowed.
     - —File systems with root authority should not be exported.
   - Monitoring:
     - —The existence of, changes to, and changes in permissions of root-owned setuid and setgid programs should be monitored.

- — The su log should be monitored for su (switch user) attempts to root .
- — Failed log-in attempts should be monitored.
- — The location of .exrc files (editor initialization files) should be monitored; they should not exist in public directories.
- — Network files should be monitored to ensure access is not given to untrusted hosts.
- — Changes in permissions to, and sizes of, executable programs owned by the system should be monitored.
- — UUCP activity should be monitored.

If a sysadmin asks for assistance in establishing a baseline monitoring system, good references are COPS and TRIPWIRE. Both are free products that provide extensive baseline monitoring and other Unix security checks. They can be obtained on the Internet as follows in Exhibit 2:

```
COPS from ftp.uu.net: /pub/security/cops_104.tar.Z

TRIPWIRE from ftp.cs.purdue.edu: /pub/spaf.COAST/
     Tripwire
```

1. Physical security should be documented and evaluated in the following manner:
   - — Are the machines in a physically secured location or secured against single-user root access? The RS/6000 will not boot in single-user mode if the key lock has been placed in the secure position. Workstations using the Sun operating system can require the use of the root password for single-user mode (described in the superuser security section in part two of this series of chapters).
   - — Are important diskettes available near work areas? As in microcomputer audit, data and software should be properly secured.
2. Connectivity should be discussed with the sysadmin. Existence of modems, connections to local area networks (LANs), the Internet, other companies, and other systems within the company should be documented. It should also be documented whether access is through UUCP, TCP/IP, or other methods.

Log-In Security

To understand log-in security, the auditor must understand the configuration of the Unix password file.

Unix uses the /etc/passwd file to define all users to the system. An example account entry within /etc/passwd is used to explain a user definition:

```
dan:BhN6vlm9lo9pW:108:101:Dan  Schultes:
   /usr/home/dan:/bin/sh
```

The seven fields in /etc/passwd are separated by colons. Using the example /etc/passwd entry, the fields are described as follows:

1. **dan.** This is the user name; it is used as part of log-in authentication.
2. **BhN6vlm9lo9pW.** This is the encrypted password. The field is 13 characters long. The first two characters are the salt, and they are calculated at the time the system encrypts the password , on the basis of the system time and the process ID of the passwd command. The last 11 characters are the result of the encryption. If this field is blank, a password is not required for the user name. In systems that use a shadow password file, the encrypted password will be replaced by a single character, such as an *x* or an exclamation point. The shadow password file would then contain the encrypted passwords.
3. **108.** This is the user ID number (uid).The uid uniquely identifies every user and is used to authenticate access, identify processes, and identify file ownership. A uid of 0 designates the user has superuser access.
4. **101.** This is the group ID (gid). The gid is used to combine user IDs into groups of users with similar access requirements.
5. **Dan Schultes.** This is the comment field. Most sysadmins will list the user's real name in this field. The comment field is interrogated by the finger command on some systems. It is also used by cracker programs and attackers to gain clues to user passwords.
6. **/usr/home/dan.** This is the home directory. The log-in program will attempt to change directory to this directory when the user logs into the system.
7. **/bin/sh.** This is the log-in shell. As its last act, the log-in program executes the program found in this field. The log-in shell can be replaced with another program that restricts certain users' activities.

The objective of this section is to determine that login security is appropriate. The following procedures should be executed:

- Access to the Unix system should be obtained. The procedures used to define a user should be documented. Procedures should be evaluated, including use of default passwords , sharing of uids. Good control in defining a user would include:
  - Defining the user ID with a password that is difficult to guess.
  - Defining an appropriate home directory; if home directories are shared, determining if that is appropriate.
  - Use of password aging to cause th new user to change passwords immediately upon initial log-in and on a periodic basis thereafter. Password aging, depending on the version of Unix, can be defined in

/etc/passwd/etc/shadow /etc/default/passwd/etc/security/login.cfg.
- Setting the user's group to a group of users with the same security requirements.

- Additional log-in control should be documented and evaluated. It should be determined whether the following are provided:
  - Logging and monitoring of invalid log-in attempts.
  - Revoking of user IDs after a limited number of invalid log-in attempts
  - Terminating log-in shells after a period of inactivity.
  - Ensuring passwords are not easy to guess (it should be determined whether the script that changes passwords follows certain editing criteria or that password-cracker programs are used to identify weak passwords).
  - Termination of inactive user IDs.

A copy of the password file should be obtained as requested above or by using the cat/etc/passwdcommand. If NIS is used:

— Additional log-in user IDs should be obtained as requested previously, by using ypcat command, or by logging into the NIS master server and using the cat/var/yp/src/passwd command.

— It should be ensured that NIS is not shared across networks. Otherwise, host names or user names within the network can be determined from external networks.

— It should be determined if sysadmin uses a shadow file. It is much more secure to use a shadow file because it prevents someone from running a cracker program against a password file containing encrypted passwords , searching for Joe accounts (accounts of individuals who do not have a password), and searching the password file for clues to users' passwords (names are generally displayed in the comment field of /etc/passwd).

— Adequacy of passwords should be evaluated. Using /etc/passwd, it should be determined if all user IDs have a password assigned to them or are disabled from log-in . Determine if any user IDs share the same uid. Attempts to guess passwords of 3or 4 user IDs should be made. The Internet worm tried logins without passwords and passwords of the log-in name, the log-in name twice, the last name and the last name. It also used comments in /etc/passwd,the last name reversed, an online dictionary, and a 432-word internal list. Non-login user IDs (such as daemon, bin, sys, adm, uucp, nuucp, sync, install, and listen) can have plain-text passwords that when decrypted would be nonsensical. A comprehensive test would be to use the Crack program. (The Crack program can be obtained through anonymous ftp from INFO.CERT.ORG.) Commonly, over 20%of passwords are crackable.

A + user ID at the bottom of /etc/passwd means that NIS also administers passwords for this system. The /etc/passwd entry should not be +::0:0:::because if the NIS server fails, some installations would allow user ID +to log into the system as root without any password .

Superuser Security

The objective of superuser security is to determine if access to superuser authority is appropriately secured. The superuser is the main security flaw in the Unix environment because the superuser can do virtually anything to the system. This explains why most attackers who break into Unix systems attempt to become superusers.

The procedures for ensuring superuser security are as follows:

- Documenting and evaluating individuals functioning as sysadmins. It should be determined what users have been given superuser authority in /etc/passwd. User IDs with superuser authority are designated with a uid of 0.It should be determined whether all user IDs with superuser authority are necessary.
- Documenting and evaluating when and how sysadmins use their superuser authority. In addition, determining if superusers execute programs for others while logged in with superuser authority. Various security literature suggests:
- Judicious use of setuid programs in lieu of giving out the root password to a large number of people is preferred.
- A user ID without superuser authority should be used when the function the user is doing does not require superuser authority. Consider the following: a superuser account is left logged on at an unattended terminal; a user sits down at the superuser's terminal; in just 10 seconds the follow-on user might enter the following commands:
  — cp /bin/sh /usr/lib/.mysh (Make a copy of the shell in a public directory.)
  — chown root /usr/lib/.mysh (Make root the owner of the copied shell.)
  — chmod 4755 /usr/lib/.mysh (Make the copied shell a root-owned setuid program and world executable, defined in step 5 below.)
- The sysadmins use of the su command to root should be documented and evaluated. This is accomplished by using the su command with no parameters. The su command (switch user) allows someone to obtain the access privileges of another. The system verifies the switch by requiring the user to enter the password of the target user ID. The following points should be kept in mind:
- Using the su utility should not place the current directory at the beginning of the path. Instead, the resulting search path should include the current directory at the end of the search path or not at all. Proper set-

ting of the resulting path is essential to ensure that the subsequent execution of programs, which will execute with root privileges, are the actual system commands and not copies of system commands that have been modified to provide someone an opportunity to execute with root privileges. For example, adding the three commands noted in the previous step to a copy of a system command in a public directory could allow the perpetrator to gain superuser authority.

- Execute the su command as /bin/su-. This ensures that the root's profile is executed and the system's su is executed, and not a copy of the su command(possibly malicious) planted in another directory. Many sysadmins will simply use su. To maintain a secure system, the sysadmins will want to ensure that the appropriate command is executed (as the sysadmins will provide root's password to the system for verification) and that the root's profile is executed, therefore setting a secure path for subsequent commands under root authority.
- All su attempts should be logged and monitored. This will let sysadmins know which user IDs know the root password and which user IDs have attempted to become a root. An audit may reveal that the sysadmin is not sure of everyone who knows the root password .

For workstations using the Sun operating system, it should be verified that the use of the root password for single-user mode is required by the absence of the secure keyword in the /dev/console entry in /etc/ttytab. Otherwise, a user can boot single-user root by depressing the *stop* and *A* keys, followed by entering the b-s command, without the use of a password. Security to root-owned setuid and setgid files should be documented and evaluated. Setuid and setgid programs allow an executable program to run with the effective file-accessing power of the program's owner (setuid) or group (setgid) rather than that of the user. In the case of root -owned setuid programs, the person executing the program has root authority for the duration of the program. Root-owned setuid programs are necessary for such tasks as changing passwords , because the passwd command requires write access to the /etc/passwd file, which normal users should not have. Setuid and setgid programs should be writable only by their setuid and possibly setgid. Update access to root-owned setgid programs would allow someone to insert commands that would be executed under root's authority, for example, creating a root-owned shell or modification of the program such that someone could use a parameter at any later date to assume root authority. There should be no root-owned setgid programs in any user directory (otherwise the user would be able to update the setgid program, because the user probably owns the personal directory). The setgid should be confident of all root-owned setgid programs. Monitoring of changes to these programs is essential for a secure system. Control over system startup (/etc/rc) and system shutdown (/etc/shutdown), including access to the commands, should be documented and evaluated. Because startup and shutdown will be executed under root's authority, update access to these files would allow someone to insert commands that will be executed with root's authority.

Conclusion

This chapter, the first part of two, offers the auditor particular Unix audit methodologies for ensuring general security, log-in security, and superuser security.

The following chapter provides the auditor with an examination of file security, remote system security, UUCP, and backup, disaster recovery, and change control. Continuing attempts to crack passwords and compromise Unix systems provide auditors with reason to frequently review their organizations' Unix environments.

Chapter 83
Auditing UNIX: Security Issues, Change Control, and Disaster Recovery

Dan Schultes

The connectivity provided between most UNIX systems requires special attention to protect against inappropriate remote system access and UNIX-to-UNIX copy protocol access. Attempts to crack passwords and continual discoveries of new ways to compromise UNIX systems are constant reminders of the time and energy many are willing to expend to gain access to UNIX systems. Security to UNIX systems is also affected by the dramatic increase in their numbers at most corporations and the corresponding push for sysadmins to manage larger numbers of processors. This added responsibility may result in a large decline in the amount of time sysadmins allocate to system security. This provides tremendous reason for auditors to review their companies' UNIX environments.

AUDIT PROGRAM

A UNIX audit program is divided into the following sections:

- General security
- Log-in security
- Superuser security
- File security
- Remote system security
- UNIX-to-UNIX copy protocol (UUCP) security
- Backup, disaster recovery, and change control

This chapter will cover the areas of file security, remote system security, UUCP, and backup, disaster recovery, and change control.

0-8493-9989-0/99/$0.00+$.50

FILE SECURITY

In the area of file permissions, the lsss to files within a directory. An example of the output from the lsis shown in Exhibit 1.

Exhibit 1. Output from the ls-la command.

$ ls -la		
total 120		
drwxr-xr-x	3	dan user66 512 Nov 21 09:01 .
drwxr-xr-x	34	bin bin 6656 Jan 12 10:18 ..
- rwx- - - - - -	1	dan user66 238 Jun 14 1994 .profile
- rwxrwx- - -	1	dan user66 481 Jul 11 1994 checkdir
- rwxr-xr-x	1	dan user66 481 Jul 11 1994 checkdir2
drwxr-xr-x	9	dan user66 512 Nov 21 09:03 crack

Fields for the fifth line of the example are defined in Exhibit 2.

Exhibit 2. Fields for fifth line in Exhibit 1.

Field Contents	Meaning
-	File type.
rwxrwx- - -	File permissions.
1	Number of hard links.
dan	Name of the file's owner.
user66	Name of the owner's group.
481	File size.
Jul 11 1994	File modification time.
checkdir	File name.

The file types discussed are shown in Exhibit 3.

Exhibit 3. File types.

Contents	Meaning
-	The file is a regular file.
d	The file is a directory.
l	The file is a symbolic link (BSD only).
b	The file is a block device (disk or tape).

In the example, .profile, checkdir, and checkdir2 are regular files and crack is a directory within the listed directory.

The next nine characters, taken in groups of three, indicate the permissions available to that file. The first three characters list the owner's access to the file, the second three characters list the group's access to the file, and the last three characters list others' (everyone else on the system) access to the file. Each character triplet defines read, write, and execute authority for owner, group, and other, respectively. Five kinds of permissions are available for owner, group, and other, as shown in Exhibit 4.

Exhibit 4. Kinds of permissions available.

Symbol	Access	Meaning
r	read	User can open a file and read its contents.
X	write	User can overwrite the file or modify its contents.
X	execute	This is applicable only for executable files. If a user has execute access to a file, he or she can execute the file by entering its path name.
-	none	Designates that the authority (whether it be read, write, or execute) is not permitted for the owner, group, or others.
S	setuid or setgid	If s is listed in the owner's execute permission field, this is a setuid program. If s is listed in the group's execute permission field, this is a setgid program. Setuid programs are discussed in step 5 of the superuser security section in the first part of this series.
T	sticky bit	Indicates that the program stays in memory after execution, similar to a terminate and stay resident program in DOS.

In the example above, read, write, and execute access is permitted to .profile only for the owner of the file (dan), as the - symbol indicates that read, write, and execute access is denied to the group and others. Read, write, and execute access is permitted to checkdir for both the owner and group (user66). Read, write, and execute access is permitted for checkdir2 for the owner, while read and execute access is permitted for the group and others (the - indicates that write access is not permitted to the group or others).File permissions do not apply to symbolic links. Access to these files is dependent on permissions on the file, not the link's permissions.

File permissions can also be expressed in a four-digit octal format. An active read bit is worth 4 points, an active write bit is worth 2 points, and an active execute bit is worth 1 point. Exhibit 5 links file permissions to their octal representation.

Three examples surrounding octal values follow:

- A file permission of rwxrwx— - would have an octal representation of 770.

- A file permission of rwxrwxr—x would have an octal representation of 775.
- A file permission of rwsrwx— - (which designates the program as a setuid program, value of 4000, plus read, write, and execute available for the owner, value of 0700, plus read, write, and execute available for the group, value of 0070) would have an octal representation of 4770.

The objective of file security is to document and evaluate the security provided for files. The procedures are discussed in the following sections.

Exhibit 5. Octal representations of file permissions.

Octal number	Permission
0004	Others can read.
0002	Theirs can write.
0001	Others can execute.
0040	Group can read.
0020	Group can write.
0010	Group can execute.
0400	Owner can read.
0200	Owner can write.
0100	Owner can execute.
4000	Setuid program.
2000	Setgid program.
1000	Sticky bit.

File Definition

By using /etc/group and /etc/passwd, it should be determined whether groups have been appropriately defined. Access is many times granted to groups, so members of a group should have similar data access requirements. The /etc/group file maps group IDs appearing in the /etc/passwd file to group names, and also permits users to be members of multiple groups. The /etc/group file lists every group on the system and its corresponding group identification number (gid). The following sample /etc/passwd file is used to illustrate /etc/passwd contents:

```
wheel:*:0:root,pam

accounting:*:101:brian,tim,robert

planning:*:102:

marketing:*:103:allison,cara,sarah
```

Four groups (wheel, accounting, planning, and marketing) are defined to the system. Fields in the first line of the sample /etc/group are defined as follows:

- accounting. Group name. For BSD systems, the wheel group designates a special group that contains a list of the only user names that can su to become the superuser.
- *. The group's password. An asterisk means that there is no password. A password can be set for System V systems, which would allow a user to use the newgroup command to change to that group. This approach invites lax security through sharing of passwords, and unexpired passwords.
- 101. The group's gid.
- brian, tim, robert. The list of the users who are in the accounting group.

Members of a group include group members defined in /etc/group as well as uid group assignments made in /etc/passwd. For example, Brian is in the accounting group (based on /etc/group definitions) in addition to the planning group (based on his entry in /etc/passwd).

System Files

Security given to system files should be analyzed. Subsequent audits of UNIX environments can be enhanced by creating scripts to check system file permissions. A sysadmin should be asked to help create a script or teach the fundamentals of the ôvi' editor (ôvi' is not intuitive). Most of these scripts will simply contain lstored on an account that will be available at the time of future UNIX audits. As might be expected, the scripts will expand as more files are recognized as possible security concerns. System file access should be checked as follows:

- **/usr/adm/sulog, /var/adm/sulog, or/etc/security/sulog should have a permissions mode of 600 and be owned by root.** These files show successful and unsuccessful attempts using the su command. Write access to them could hide attempts at determining root's password.
- **/usr/lib/uucp/L.sys or/usr/lib/uucp/Systems should be readable and writable only by root.** They contain telephone numbers and passwords for other systems contacted using UUCP. UUCP provides for the transmission of both ASCII and binary files between different systems. Its use is less prevalent today because of the proliferation of TCP/IP.
- **/.profile, /etc/hosts.equiv, /etc/shadow,/etc/passed.adjunct, and /etc/urb should be readable and writable only by root.** These files contain root's profile(executed at root log in or when using the su command to become root), systems trusted by the system being

reviewed, and shadow password files. If the shadow password file is used, it should be ensured that the backup password and group files created when the shadow file is created can not be accessed inappropriately (/etc/passwd.bak and/etc/group.bak).

- **Such AIX files in /etc/security as passwd, group, login.cfg, mkuser. default, user, and limits should be readable and writable only by root.** These are system configuration files that can only assist someone in attacking the system.
- **/usr/spool/crontabs/root, /usr/spool/cron/at.allow, at.deny, cron. allow, and cron.deny should be writable only by root (on some systems, these files would be in/usr/lib/crontabs and/usr/lib/cron/ cron, respectively).** Cron is a scheduling mechanism that allows programs to be executed on a systematic basis. The at command is used for running a command a single time at a later date. The first file defines commands that will run on a systematic basis under the authority of root. Write access to this file would allow running jobs under the authority of root. The other files define user IDs allowed to use cron.
- **/etc/.profile, /etc/inetd.conf, and/etc/hosts should be writable only by root.** /etc/.profile defines the default user profile./etc/inetd.conf defines what programs should be run when incoming network connections are caught by the inetddaemon. An attacker with write access to /etc/inetd could change an entry to start up a shell or other program on receipt of a message. For example, an attacker could change the following entry:
- daytime stream tcp nowait root internal daytime stream tcp nowait root /bin/ksh ksh -i This would allow an attacker to connect to the daytime port and receive a root shell at any time superuser access is desired to the system. /etc/hosts defines names of other systems, most likely those to which users on the host system connect frequently and that may trust the host system, again giving an attacker additional targets.
- /usr/lib/uucp/Permissions,usr/lib/uucp/L.cmds, andusr/lib/uucp/ USERFILE should be readable and writable only by root and the UUCP administrative user ID. These files allow for UUCP file transfer and remote command execution.
- The ed and vi commands (editors) should not be root-owned setuid commands as they are subject to the ! command (allows a user to escape to the shell to execute a command, in this case with superuser access). The sysadmin will indicate their location.
- No .exrc files should be in public directories because .exrc files are executed when the ex and vi editors are started. An attacker could place the following in every directory that allows them write access:

```
cat [rang ] .exrc! (cp /bin/sh /tmp/.secret;
chmod 4755 /tmp/.secret& control-D to end file
```

If the superuser ever starts either the ex or vi editors in those directories, the superuser would have inadvertently created a setuid shell, which the attacker can use at a later date to become superuser.

Besides checking files specifically noted above, file permissions to programs in the system directories should be checked. Proper protection of these files will prevent someone from maliciously overstoring a system command with a modified form of the command, thereby making a Trojan horse. The following should be checked:

- No executable programs should be owned by root and public-writable. Otherwise, an attacker could update the file so that when the program is executed, the program becomes or creates a setuid program (using the chmod command). This could result in the creation of a setuid program with superuser authority if root is the executor of the program.
- **All entries in /dev (or /dev/dsk and /dev/rdsk in later releases) pertaining to disks (e.g., dsk0, dsk1, rdsk0, rdsk1), memory (/dev/mem), and the kernel (/dev/kmem) should be readable and writable only by root.** A few entries (e.g., /dev/null,/dev/tty, and /dev/console should be world-writable. To determine file systems (defined in /dev) associated with local directories, the df command should be issued.
- **Password files and system commands in /etc,/etc/security, or /usr/etc should be writable only by root (/etc/passwd is password file; /etc/group defines groups and users associated with each group; system start-up file is /etc/rc for BSD or /etc/inittab for System V; system shut-down file is /etc/shutdown; /etc/sendmail is the UNIX mail program).** Write access to the passwd file could allow someone to add users or change uids (e.g., change a user ID to 0), thus making that user a superuser. The startup and shutdown files will execute under the authority of root, so modifications to these files should be prevented.
- **System commands and all binary programs in / (root directory), /bin, /usr/bin, /usr/lbin, /usr/lib, /lib, /usr/ucb, /usr/5bin, /etc/uucp, /usr/lib/uucp, /usr/spool/uucp, /UNIX, /usr/spool/cron/crontabs, /usr/spool/cron/atjobs, /usr/spool/cron, /usr/lib/cron/crontabs, /usr/lib/cron/atjobs, and /usr/lib/cron should be writable only by root.** Overstoring system commands would allow introduction of Trojan horses. Overstoring cron files could allow changes to the job execution schedule as well as provide an opportunity to run a job under the authority of another user.

Profiles

A copy of the systemwide profiles (/etc/profile and /etc/environment), which initialize the UNIX environment, should be obtained. In addition, a copy of a normal user profile setup (.profile for Bourne shell use, .cshrc for starting C shell, and .login for C shell log in) should be obtained. User profile setups execute subsequent to systemwide profiles. It should be evaluated whether the scripts do the following:

- **Set a correct path.** Current directory, designated by a colon in some versions and a period in other versions, should be at the end of the path to prevent inadvertently executing a nonsystem command with the same name as a system command. The nonsystem command may have been placed in a public directory for malicious purposes. The following path places the current directory at the beginning of the path, which is not desired: PATH=:/bin:/usr/bin:/usr/bin/lbin. The following path correctly places the execution of the current directory at the end of the path:

```
PATH=/bin:/usr/bin:/usr/bin/lbin:.
```

- **Set a restrictive umask.** The umask, short for user mask, removes certain permissions from all newly created files. The umask command takes a number as an argument to mask the associated access permissions for that file. The umask is expressed in octal. Octal is explained at the beginning of the section on file security. For example, a umask of 002 will deny others write permission on newly created files and a umask of 077 will deny the group and others all permissions (read, write, and execute). The umask command without arguments will list the current value of umask for the user ID issuing the command.
- **Display last log-in time.** On login, the system will tell the user the last time the account was used.

System Directory Access

Access to system directories should be determined. Permissions to a directory (e.g. dir1) should be listed as follows:

- lsverstore any file from the directory, regardless of the access to the individual files. This is usually a surprise to most sysadmins. Removing (rm), changing a file's name (mv), and creating new files (e.g., cp, command [rang] file) all change the contents of a directory. Only when a file is being opened do the individual file's permissions come into play. Therefore, rm and mv don't require file access, only directory access. Removing or renaming a file requires execute and write permissions on the directory the file is in, because both the rm and mv commands reference the file by name (directory execute permission) and modify the directory (write). As an example, if the /etc directory has write and execute access available to others, anyone could remove the /etc/passwd file as follows: rm/etc/passwd. The system's response, if read access to/etc/passwd is available to all users, would be: rm: passwd: 444 mode ?(444 is the octal access permission allowing owner, group and others read access). A response of y will remove the file, as the above message is simply a warning.

Another example describes how to overstore /etc/passwd to make a new superuser: cp/etc/passwd /home/dan/passwd (copy password file to home directory). The file should be edited as needed, i.e., changing the entry for dan to: dan::0:0:Super Dan:/:/bin/sh. In the command mv /home/dan/passwd/etc/passwd (move the modified password file), the system's response, if read access is available to all users, would be: mv: passwd: 444 mode ?. A response of y will overstore the passwdfile as, again, the previous message is simply a warning. su dan can be used to obtain superuser authority. More recent UNIX versions prevent removing or overstoring files in this manner if the sticky bit is set on the directory.

As with system files previously discussed, a script should be kept to check file permissions to the following system directories. The script should contain entries with ls -ldcommands followed by the applicable directory name (e.g., ls-ld /bin). As previously discussed, these scripts should be stored where they can be used on subsequent audits and change as needed. Write access to system directories (/bin, /usr/bin, /lib, /dev, /etc, /usr, /usr/lib, /usr/ucb, /usr/lib/uucp, /,/usr/etc, /etc/uucp, /UNIX, /usr/lbin, /dev/dsk, /dev/rdsk, /usr/spool/cron, /usr/spool/cron/crontabs, /usr/spool/cron/atjobs, and /etc/security) should be limited to root./usr/lib/uucp and/usr/spool/uucp directories must be owned and writable only by the owner (uucp).

Access to User Data

Access to user data should be analyzed. The default location of user data should be determined. This might be in individual home directories or in public directories. It should be determined whether users have any sensitive information on their systems and its location. In addition, file permissions should be analyzed for user data.

Security given to user profiles (.profile for Bourne or Korn shells), trusted host files (.rhosts), user startup files for various programs (.exrc, .netrc, .cshrc, and .login), and other log-in scripts (.mailrc and .sunview) should be analyzed. These files should be readable and writable only by the owner of the directory. In addition, directory access to HOME directories should be analyzed. Only the directory owner should have write execute access.

REMOTE SYSTEM SECURITY

If one system trusts another system (host), then any user who has the same user name on both systems can log in from the trusted system to the target computer without password authentication. Trusted users are similar to trusted hosts, except they refer to individual users, not hosts. Trusted hosts and users obtain access through remote UNIX commands (e.g., rlogin, rsh, rcp). Trusted hosts and trusted users have been responsible for many security breaches and have allowed them to propagate quickly, as was the case in the Internet worm. After a security breach has been made, an attacker may check for trusted hosts and users and assume that the trusted hosts and users also trust the local system.

Trust is transitive. If system A trusts system B, and system B trusts system C, then system A trusts system C, even if not explicitly defined. To illustrate, a user on system C can rlogin to system B and then rlogin to system A (because now the user is operating from system B). There is no way to prevent a user from system C from entering system A through system B. Security on a trusted system must be equivalent to security on the system that trusts it. A security breach on a trusted system means a security breach can occur on all systems trusting the compromised system.

The objective of remote system security is to determine that security is appropriately provided to protect the system from unauthorized access through remote systems. The procedures are covered in the following sections:

Trusted Environments

Any UNIX environments that have been defined as trusted to the system should be documented and evaluated. Trusted hosts and users are defined in three ways:

- /etc/hosts.equiv provides a hostwide definition of trusted hosts and permits all users working on a listed host to assume the authority of like-named user IDs on the host system, without password authentication. The remote user ID must also appear in the local host's /etc/passwd file, or a log-in name and password would still be required. A wild card of a plus sign (+) in /etc/hosts.equiv, which is how many Sun systems are delivered, means all hosts are trusted and this a major security exposure. Remote root access cannot be obtained through /etc/hosts.equiv and is defined in the following section.
- During the remote access process, if the/etc/hosts.equiv file does not allow remote access for the remote system, the system will check the home directory of the user logging in for a .rhosts file. If the file exists and contains the name of the remote host, the remote user will not be

prompted for a password. This gives individual users the opportunity to trust specific users from remote systems. It is a good idea to prevent or limit the use of individual .rhosts files. A sysadmin should be in a better position to analyze the security on a remote system to determine if trusting the system is appropriate. For AIX, remote access is defined for an individual in /etc/security/user.

- Only the /.rhosts file (.rhosts file in the root directory) is searched when determining trusted root access. The /.rhosts file is used to allow a superuser on a remote host to become superuser on the local host without ever entering a password. This is convenient but not secure. Trusting of root from remote systems is frequently found, especially in areas where a sysadmin administers a large number of systems. The ease of masquerading as a different host makes the use of /.rhosts unsafe.

For illustration purposes, it can be assumed that a sysadmin administers a number of UNIX hosts and has used the /.rhosts files to allow trusted root access. Security breaches could occur as follows:

- A user (attacker) is superuser on a system.
- Attacker changes the Internet protocol (IP) address associated with the attacker's system in the etc/hosts file to the IP address of a system they believe to be trusted by many systems (such as the IP address of the machine in the office of the sysadmin noted above).
- The attacker could then effectively masquerade as the sysadmin's system and gain superuser authority to those systems that allow trusted root access from the sysadmin's local machine, all without supplying a password. It should be noted that the attack described here would need to originate from a system on the same subnetwork as the target system. In addition, to avoid confusion surrounding data packet delivery, the sysadmin's machine would need to be shut off.

Wizard Password

The /etc/sendmail.cf file should be checked for a possible wizard password. It was used in spreading the Internet Worm. The OW parameter should be missing or set to * (ôOW*'), which prevents the use of the wizard password. An encrypted password immediately after OW means that a password is available to exploit the mail hole.

Debug Feature

The debug, kill, orwiz features of sendmail should be checked to see if they are available. Debug was also used in spreading the Internet Worm. This can be checked by performing the following:

- Entering telnet system_name 25 (in which system_name is the system name of the system being reviewed) to connect to the sendmailport, which is usually 25.
- Entering each of the following parameters, one at a time: debug, kill, and wiz.
- If sendmail responds to the debug, kill, or wiz commands with any of the following messages:200 Debug set, 200 Mother is dead, 500 Can't kill Mom, Please pass, oh mighty wizard, 500 You are no wizard!, or any message other than 500 Command unrecognized, the sendmail program is unsafe.

Anonymous ftp

The use of anonymous ftp, which allows people on the network who do not have an account on the host system to retrieve or deposit files into a special directory, should be analyzed. Anonymous ftp is defined through the ftp user ID in /etc/passwd. A sysadmin will copy portions of certain directories and the passwd file to the ftp home directory to provide minimal functionality for anonymous users. When properly set up, the ftp's home directory (defined in /etc/passwd) becomes anonymousftp's root directory so that anonymous users cannot break out into higher directories, thus restricting the access of anonymous ftp users. Security should be checked by performing the following:

- Logging in to system by using anonymous as the user ID and using any password.
- Ensuring that someone cannot break out into higher directories using cd.
- Ensuring that no one has write access to any ftp directories or files within those directories, except for the pub directory where the shared files will be stored.
- Ensuring that the copied password file only contains the ftp entry. Otherwise an attacker would have knowledge of many log-in account names. If encrypted passwords remain in the copied password file and are not replaced with asterisks, the attacker would almost certainly be able to gain access to the system through password cracking.

Dates of Programs

The creation date of the finger program should be determined.

If it predates November 1988 it is susceptible to the Internet Worm.

At one time, the standard UNIX mail utility would execute a system-level program while reading mail if the line begins with an exclamation point. By using this, someone could send mail to superusers and have them unwittingly execute a system command by opening their mail. This should be tested by performing the following:

- Entering mail user ID using the reader's own user ID
- Entering this is a test
- Entering !ls
- Entering end of test
- Entering a period or cntl-d to end the message
- Receiving mail and seeing if ls

If a system still uses a version of sendmail that allows execution of commands in this manner, the sysadmin should replace sendmail with a newer version. Alternatively, the sysadmin could install a script that filters exclamation points from incoming mail.

/etc/inetd.conf Command

The command /etc/inetd.conf should be checked. The auditor should ensure that no network programs start a shell program (e.g., /bin/csh). An example of this is shown in step 2 of the file security section.

It should be determined whether tftp is available by looking for the tftp entry in /etc/inetd.conf. Users accessing a system through tftp will not be members of any group or be assigned any uid. Their access to all files is the access allowed for others. If used, tftp access should be limited to a single directory through the tftp entry in /etc/inetd.conf. If tftp is available, it should be determined whether tftp access is limited to a single directory from remote systems by performing the following:

- Logging in to another system, systema
- Entering tftp systemb, in which systemb is the system being reviewed
- Entering get /etc/passwd/home/dan/passwd.systemb
- If password file is copied, tftp represents an exposure

Embedded Script Execution

The auditor should ensure that actions have been taken to prevent a script embedded in the sendmail reply to field from being executed when mail is sent to a nonexistent user ID and is subsequently opened by the postmaster (who may have superuser authority). The configuration file (/etc/sendmail.cf) must be modified such that the Mprog line should read: Mprog, p=/bin/false (rather than p=/bin/sh).

Remote Mounting

The auditor should evaluate the extent to which the system has made its file systems available for remote mounting. Exporting file systems gives other systems the ability to access exported files without user authentication by the host system. Exporting of file systems is defined through /etc/exports. File systems can be exported with certain restrictions, including read only, only to specified systems, to certain systems with root authority, or to all systems. The simplest /etc/exports file contains a list, one per line, of all file systems that can be mounted remotely. The problem is that the simplest form of /etc/exports places no restrictions on which systems can mount the host's file systems.

UNIX-TO-UNIX COPY PROTOCOL SECURITY

UNIX-to-UNIX copy protocol is a collection of programs that have provided simple networking for UNIX computers since 1977. UUCP is used for sending mail to users on remote systems, transferring files between UNIX systems, and executing commands on remote systems. UUCP has been popular in the UNIX world because it comes with most versions of UNIX, requires no special hardware (it runs over standard RS-232serial cables and over standard modems), and stores all messages and commands for batch execution at night, thereby lowering networking costs.

The objective of UUCP security is to document and evaluate the use of UUCP and determine if outside users have been appropriately restricted. UUCP is used much less frequently than it was in the past, because of the proliferation of TCP/IP for network connectivity. Important aspects of UUCP are summarized in the following list. The auditor should:

- Determine if system uses the Version 2 UUCP or the more secure HoneyDanBer UUCP; Version 2 UUCP uses /usr/lib/uucp/L.sys and USERFILE while HoneyDanBer uses /usr/lib/uucp/ systems and permissions as control files.
- Determine if the outside users have been appropriately restricted through their user ID definition. Using the /etc/passwd file, the auditor should determine if outside users:
  - —Each have a different log-in user ID and password
  - —Have been placed in a single group that is used for nothing else
  - —Do not have the standard shell; they should be set up with the uucico shell, which implements all the security restrictions of the UUCP system
  - —Have a home directory of /usr/spool/uucppublic or /usr/spool/uucp
  - —Cannot use user IDs uucp and nuucp, which is accomplished by disabling these user IDs
  - —Do not share same uid and gid of user IDs uucp and nuucp

Check commands that can be executed remotely. Check if callback is used, which is preferred. Check UUCP logs for activity.

BACKUP, DISASTER RECOVERY, AND CHANGE CONTROL

Backup, disaster recovery, and change control have two objectives: to determine if adequate procedures have been established to permit the recovery of the system in the event of a disaster or other interrupts, and to determine if change control procedures are in place to prevent unauthorized changes to system and application programs. The auditor should perform a review of backup, disaster recovery, and change control procedures. This review is very similar to reviews of these areas for other operating systems. Various UNIX literature suggests restoration of a corrupted UNIX system from installation tapes, then applying local customization. This would prevent the reapplication of viruses, worms, and Trojan horses.

CONCLUSION

As shown throughout this chapter, security breaches to a UNIX environment can occur in a variety of ways. Security to other operating systems generally revolves around adequate protection to system software and configuration files, as well as proper log-in controls. Weaknesses surrounding these areas will compromise the operating system to one degree or another. Because of the design of the superuser within UNIX systems, the ability to apply changes to many of these files in the UNIX environment as well as to setuid and setgid programs unique to UNIX can cause an attacker to become superuser, thereby giving them total access. The possibility of someone becoming superuser and the diligence required to prevent such an occurrence will keep the most proficient sysadmin busy.

It is essential to establish a rapport with the UNIX sysadmin and security personnel to accomplish successful audits of UNIX environments. Sharing knowledge surrounding securing of these systems is essential to providing a useable, yet secure and controlled environment. Many books can provide a basis for operating on a UNIX platform. A good example is *Learning the UNIX Operating System*, published by O'Reilly & Associates, Inc. (1994). As with any other operating system, familiarity facilitates the audit of that environment. Another means of providing familiarity is to obtain an account on a UNIX system. This access can be accomplished through the use of a token ring or Ethernet card and a TCP/IP product on a microcomputer. From the auditor's personal workstation, a TCP/IP function, telnet, can be used to log in to various UNIX systems.

Appendix A
Additional Information

Migration/coexistence products and vendor contact information.

Product(s)	Product Vendor
Access NFS for Windows NT RhaPC-d	Intergraph Corporation One Madison Industrial Park Huntsville, AL 35894-0014 (800) 291-9909 (205) 730-2000 e-mail: nfs_info@ingr.com http://www.intergraph.com
Allegris	Intersolv http://www.intersolv.com
Amadeus	Amadeus Software Research amadeus-info@amadeus.com
ApplixBuilder, ApplixWare	Applix, Inc. http://www.applix.com
BEA Jolt BEA TUXEDO	BEA Systems http://www.beasys.com
Best/1	BGS Systems http://www.bgs.com best1@bgs.com
Chameleon NFS32	NetManage, Inc. 10725 N. De Anza Blvd. Cupertino, CA 95014 (408) 973-7171 Fax: (408) 257-6405 http://www.netmanage.com
DCE Services for Windows NT	Digital Equipment Corporation http://www.digital.com
DISCOVER	Software Emancipation http://www.setech.com
eXalt-X	Intergraph http://www.intergraph.com

(continues)

Migration/coexistence products and vendor contact information. (continued)

Product(s)	Product Vendor
eXceed for Windows NT eXceed for Windows NT SDK NFS Maestro for Windows NT	Hummingbird Communications, Ltd. 1 Sparks Avenue North York, Ontario M2H 2W1 Canada (416) 496-2200 Fax: (416) 496-2207 +41 22 733 18 58 e-mail: sales@hummingbird.com http://www.hummingbird.com
eXcursion	Digital Equipment Corporation http://www.digital.com
Explora	National Computing Devices http://www.ncd.com
Foundation Design/1	Andersen Consulting http://www.andersenconsulting.com
HP 500 Applications Server	Hewlett-Packard http://www.hp.com
InterDrive	FIP Software http://www.ftp.com
MainWin Studio	MainSoft Corporation 1270 Oakmead Pkwy., Suite 310 Sunnyvale, CA 94086 (800) 624-6946; (408) 774-3400 e-mail: info@mainsoft.com http://www.mainsoft.com
MKS Toolkit for Windows NT	Mortice Kem Systems, Inc. 185 Columbia Street, West Waterloo, Ontario Canada N2L 5Z5 (800) 265-2797; (519) 884-2251 +44 171 624 0100 Fax: (519) 884-8861 e-mail: sales@mks.com http://www.mks.com
NTerprise	Exodus Technologies http://www.exodustech.com
NTRIGUE (for Windows NT)	Insignia Solutions, Inc. 2200 Lawson Lane Santa Clara, CA 95054 (408) 327-6000 Fax: (408) 327-6105 +44 131 458 6849 Fax: +44 131 451 6981 e-mail: info@isltd.insignia.com http://www.insignia.com

Migration/coexistence products and vendor contact information. (continued)

Product(s)	Product Vendor
N*u*TCRACKER, N*u*TCRACKER X-Server	DataFocus, Inc. 12450 Fair Lake Circle, Suite 400 Fairfax, VA 22033-3831 (800) 637-8034; (703) 631-6770 Fax: (703) 818-1532 e-mail: nutcracker@datafocus.com http://www.datafocus.com
OmniGuard	Axent Technologies http://www.axent.com
Omni SQL Gateway	Sybase http://www.sybase.com
OpenNT	Softway Systems, Inc. 185 Berry Street, Suite 5514 San Francisco, CA 94107 (415) 896-0708; Fax: (415) 896-0709 (800) 438-8649 e-mail: OPENNT@softway.com http://www.softway.com/opennt/
PATHWORKS	Digital Equipment Corporation http://www.digital.com/info/pathworks
PC-DCE	Gradient Technologies http://www.gradient.com
PC-Xware for Windows 3.1, Windows NT, and Windows 95, WinCenter Pro	Network Computing Devices, Inc. 350 North Bernardo Avenue Mountain View, CA 94043 (800) 600-5099 (415) 694-0650 e-mail: info@ncd.com (WinCenter Pro) e-mail: info@pcx.ncd.com (PC-Xware) http://www.ncd.com
Portage	Consensys Computers, Inc. 35 Riviera Drive, Unit 9 Markham, ON, Canada L3R 8N4 (800) 388-1896; (905) 940-2900 Fax: (905) 940-2903 e-mail: sales@consensys.com http://www.consensys.com
Reflection X for Windows NT, Reflection Z (VT420) for Windows NT	Walker, Richer and Quinn (WRQ), Inc. 1500 Dexter Ave. N., PO Box 31876 Seattle, WA 98103-1876 (800) 926-3896; (206) 217-7100 +31 70 375 1100 e-mail: sales@wrq.com http://www.wrq.com
Street Talk	Banyan Systems http://www.banyan.com

(continues)

Migration/coexistence products and vendor contact information. (continued)

Product(s)	Product Vendor
Systems Toolkit	Object Space http://www.objectspace.com
SNA Client for UNIX	Parker Software http://www.parkersoftware.com
SoftWindows	Insignia Solutions http://www.insignia.com
UnixWare NetWare Services	Santa Cruz Operations http-//www.sco.com
ViewPoint	Boundless Technologies http://www.boundless.com
VisiODBC Driver Sets, SDK	Visigenic http://www.visigenic.com
WABI	Sun Microsystems http://www.sun.com
Willows Toolkit	Willows Software http://www.willows.com
Wind/U	Bristol Technology, Inc. 241 Ethan Allen Hwy. Ridgefield, CT 06877 (203) 438-6969; Fax: (203) 438-5013 e-mail: info@bristol.com http://www.bristol.com
WinDD	Tektronix http://www.tek.com
WinTED	TriTeal http://triteal.com
WinTerm	Wyse Technology http://www.wyse.com
XoftWare for Windows NT	NetManage http://www.netmanage.com
XVision	Santa Cruz Operations http://www.sco.com
XVT Development Solution for C++, C, Windows NT (DSC++)	XVT Software, Inc. 9900 Pearl East Circle Boulder, CO 80301 (800) 678-7988; (303) 443-0969 http://www.xvt.com/xvt
zApp	Rogue Wave Software http://www.roguewave.com

NEWSGROUPS

Newsgroups where the subject matter of this book are discussed from time to time include:

- comp.os.netware.connectivity
- comp.os.netware.misc
- comp.os.ms-windows.nt
- comp.os.ms-windows.nt.admin.misc
- comp.os.ms-windows.nt.admin.networking
- comp.os.ms-windows.nt.misc
- comp.os.ms-windows.programmerwin32
- comp.windows.ms.programmerwin32
- comp.os.ms-windows.nt.setup
- comp.os.ms-windows.nt.software.backoffice
- comp.os.ms-windows.nt.software.compatibility
- comp.unix.admin
- comp.unix.questions
- comp.unix.osfosfl
- comp.unix.osfmisc

ONLINE SERVICES FORUMS AND SOFTWARE

	Microsoft Forums
CompuServe Forums	go winnt — Windows NT forums
	go msl — Microsoft software library
	go mskb — Microsoft Knowledge Base
	go WIN32 — 32-bit developer's forum
	go microsoft — General Microsoft forum
	DIGITAL Forums
CompuServe Software	go decpci (Topic #15 is WIN NT/ALPHA DEV)
	MSWIN32 (files include iftpd.zip and mftpd.zip)
America Online	goto microsoft
Microsoft Network	GO WORD: MSNTS

WHITE PAPERS

A number of companies have produced white papers on different aspects of Windows NT, UNIX, and NetWare migration and coexistence.

The following white papers are available from Microsoft. You can download them from ftp://ftp.microsoft.com/bussys/winnt/winnt-docs/papers.

File Name	Description
DSMNGD.EXE	Microsoft Directory Service Manager for NetWare
FPNW_REV.EXE	Microsoft File and Print Services for NetWare
NT4UNIX.EXE	Microsoft Windows NT from a Unix Point of View
Nwipnts.exe	Microsoft Windows NT Server 3.5: Integration of Windows NT Server DHCP and WINS into a Novell NetWare IP Environment
UNIXINT.EXE	Windows-family Integration with UNIX Systems
WISE.EXE	Windows Interface Source Environment (WISE) Integrating Windows solutions with UNIX and Macintosh systems in the Enterprise
DCE.EXE	The Microsoft Strategy for Distributed Computing and DCE Services
DHCPWINS.EXE	Microsoft Windows NT Server 3.5: Dynamic Host Configuration Protocol and Windows Internet Naming Service
DNSWREXE	DNS and Microsoft Windows NT 4.0
DS_STRAT.EXE	Microsoft Directory Services Strategy
SERVMAC.EXE	Microsoft Windows NT Server 3.5 1: Services for the Macintosh
TCPIPIMP.EXE	Microsoft Windows NT 3.5/3.5 1: TCP/IP Implementation
TCPIPIMP2.DOC	Microsoft Windows NT 3.5/3.51/4.0: TCP/IP Implementation TCP/IP Protocol Stack and Services, Version 2.0

All .exe documents found in this directory are self-extracting zipped doc files created in Microsoft Word for Windows 6.0.

If you do not have Microsoft Word or a compatible word processor you can use the free Microsoft Word Viewer on Windows platforms to view and print this document.

You will find the free word viewer at ftp.microsoft.com/softlib/mslfiles/wordvu.exe. And for Windows 95, at ftp.microsoft.com/softlib/mslfiles/wd95view.exe

Digital — White papers covering Windows NT and UNIX are available from Digital at http://www.windowsNT.digital.com and http.\\www.unix.digital.com. White papers are also available from many of the other vendors mentioned in this book at their Web addresses.

COURSES

Porting NetView Applications from UNIX to Microsoft Windows NT offered by Digital Equipment Corporation.

Porting Applications from UNIX to Microsoft Windows NT, offered by Digital Equipment Corporation. Provides a technical overview of the issues involved in porting from UNIX to Windows NT systems. Course number: EY-P868EQPLO-W3.

JMH Associates

Windows NT and Win32 Programming for UNIX Programmers, covers programming in the Win32 environment for programmers who are familiar with UNIX programming. Contact jmhart@world.std.com.

Solomon Software Technologies

Windows NTfor UNIX Programmers, provides in-depth coverage of the Windows NT system and products, with some detailed treatment of implementation and design issues. For information, contact 71561.3603@ compuserv.com.

Demopoulos Associates

Windows NT and DIGITAL UNIX: A Technical Comparison, covers the architectural and functional similarities and differences of the two operating systems. Contact ted@osf.org.

FTP SITES

FTP Site	Files Available
ftp.microsoft.com	Microsoft support files, patches, drivers, for Windows NT, Windows 95, etc.
rhino.microsoft.com	Windows NT TCP/IP applications, information
ftp.cica.indiana.edu	Windows NT shareware and freeware
sunsite.unc.edu	Shareware and freeware, including Windows
ftp.uu.net	Code samples and development information Microsoft information in /vendor/microsoft
ftp.iastate.edu	Utilities-Check /pub/nt[cpu-type]/ for ftpdserv.zip and others

BOOKS

Windows NT 4 Advanced Programming by Raj Rajagopal and Subodh Monica, Osborne/McGraw-Hill. Provides programming concepts and examples for a number of Windows Technologies, including OLE2, ActiveX, Advanced GUI, OpenGL, TAPI, ODBC, DAO, Internet programming, WinSock 2, GDL etc.

Windows NT Answer Book by Jim Groves. Microsoft Press. ISBN 1-55615-562-X. Contains the most commonly asked questions with answers.

Inside Windows NT by Helen Custer. Microsoft Press. ISBN 1-55615-481-X. Covers the internal architecture and implementation of Windows NT.

Migrating to Windows NT by Randall C. Kennedy. Brady Publishing. ISBN 1-56686-103-9. Primarily discusses migration from DOS and Windows and covers how Windows NT emulates those environments.

Distributing Applications Across DCE and Windows NT. O'Reilly & Associates, Inc. Explains how to use the Microsoft DCE-compatible RPC and DCE implementations based on the OSF DCE to build DCE-based applications.

The Windows NT Resource Kit in three volumes from Microsoft Press:
- *Windows NT Resource Guide.* ISBN 1-55615-598-0.
- *Windows NT Messages.* ISBN 1-55615-600-6.
- *Optimizing Windows NT.* ISBN 1-55615-619-7.

Cross-Platform Development Using Visual C++ by Chane Cullens and Ken Blackwell. M&T Books. ISBN 1-55851-428-7. Describes how to use Visual C++ to create applications for Windows, Windows NT, UNIX, and Macintosh platforms.

Win32 System Services: The Heart of Windows NT by Marshall Brain. Prentice Hall. ISBN 0-13097825-6. Describes the Win32 APIs and provides examples.

Application Programming for Windows NT by William H.Murray. Osborne McGraw-Hill. ISBN 0078819334.

Windows NT 4 Programming from the Ground Up by Herbert Schildt, Osborne/McGraw-Hill. Introductory programming book for Windows NT.

RPC for NT by Guy Eddon. R&D Publications, distributed by Prentice Hall. ISBN 0131002236.

Networking Windows NT 3.51 by John D. Ruley. Wiley. ISBN 047112705 1.

ORGANIZATIONS

Organizations involved with topics covered in this book include:

Organization	Web Address
USENIX - Technical and Professional Association	http:Hwww.usenix.org
UNIFORUM	http://www.uniforum.org
Open Group	http://www.og.org
Object Management Group	http://www.omg.org
Open Software Foundation	http://www.osf.org
UNICODE	http://www.unicode.org

Appendix B
Glossary

A

access right The permission granted to a process to manipulate a particular object in a particular way (e.g., by calling a service). Different object types support different access rights.

application programming interface (API) A set of routines that an application program uses to request and carry out lower-level services performed by the operating system.

asynchronous I/O A method many of the processes in Windows NT use to optimize their performance. When an application initiates an I/O operation, the I/O Manager accepts the request but does not block the application's execution while the I/O operation is being performed. Instead, the application is allowed to continue doing work. Most I/O devices are very slow in comparison with a computer's processor, so an application can do a lot of work while waiting for an I/O operation to complete. See also *synchronous I/O.*

audit policy Defines the type of security events that are logged for a domain or for an individual computer; determines what Windows NT will do when the security log becomes full.

auditing The ability to detect and record security-related events, particularly any attempts to create, access, or delete objects. Windows NT uses *Security IDs (SIDs)* to record which process performed the action.

authentication A security step performed by the Remote Access Server (RAS), before logon validation, to verify that the user had permission for remote access. See also *validation.*

B

batch program An ASCII file (unformatted text file) that contains one or more commands in the command language for Windows NT. A batch program's filename has a .BAT or .CMD extension. When you type the filename at the command prompt, the commands are processed sequentially.

C

character based A mode of operation in which all information is displayed as text characters. This is the mode in which MS-DOS-based and OS/2 version 1.2 applications are displayed under Windows NT. Also called character mode, alphanumeric mode, or text mode.

client A computer that accesses shared network resources provided by another computer (called a server). For the X Window System of UNIX the client/server relationship is reversed. Under the X Window System, this client definition becomes the server definition. See also *server.*

computer name A unique name of up to 15 uppercase characters that identifies a computer to the network. The name cannot be the same as any other computer or domain name in the network, and it cannot contain spaces.

D

Data Link Control (DLC) A protocol interface device driver in Windows NT, traditionally used to provide connectivity to IBM mainframes and also used to provide connectivity to local area network printers directly attached to the network.

default profile See *system default profile, user default profile.*

demand paging Refers to a method by which data is moved in pages from physical memory to a temporary paging file on disk. As the data is needed by a process, it is paged back into physical memory.

device A generic term for a computer subsystem such as a printer, serial port, or disk drive. A device frequently requires its own controlling software called a *device driver.*

device driver A software component that allows the computer to transmit and receive information to and from a specific device. For example, a printer driver translates computer data into a form understood by a particular printer. Although a device may be installed on your system, Windows NT cannot recognize the device until you have installed and configured the appropriate driver.

directory services The defining element of distributed computing, and, ultimately, a logical name space capable of including all system resources regardless of type. The goal is a blending in which the directory and the network become synonymous.

disk caching A method used by a file system to improve performance. Instead of reading and writing directly to the disk, frequently used files are temporarily stored in a cache in memory, and reads and writes to those files are performed in memory. Reading and writing to memory is much faster than reading and writing to disk.

distributed application An application that has two parts — a front-end to run on the client computer and a back-end to run on the server. In distributed computing, the goal is to divide the computing task into two sections. The front-end requires minimal resources and runs on the client's workstation. The back-end requires large amounts of data, number crunching, or specialized hardware and runs on the server. Recently, there has been much discussion in the industry about a three-tier model for distributed computing. That model separates the business logic contained in both sides of the two-tier model into a third, distinct layer. The business logic layer sits between the front-end user interface layer and the back-end database layer. It typically resides on a server platform that may or may not be the same as the one the database is on. The three-tier model arose as a solution to the limits faced by software developers trying to express complex business logic with the two-tier model.

DLC See *Data Link Control.*

DLL See *dynamic-link library.*

domain For Windows NT Server, a networked set of workstations and servers that share a Security Accounts Manager (SAM) database and that can be administered as a group. A user with an account in a particular network domain can log onto and access his or her account from any system in the domain. See also *SAM database.*

domain controller For a Windows NT Server domain, the server that authenticates domain logons and maintains the security policy and the master database for a domain. Both servers and domain controllers are capable of validating a user's logon; however, password changes must be made by contacting the domain controller. See also *server.*

domain database See *SAM database.*

domain name The name by which a Windows NT domain is known to the network.

Domain Name System (DNS) A hierarchical name service for TCP/IP hosts (sometimes referred to as the BIND service in BSD Unix). The network administrator configures the DNS with a list of *hostnames* and IP addresses, allowing users of workstations configured to query the DNS to specify the remote systems by *hostnames* rather than IP addresses. DNS domains should not be confused with Windows NT *domains*.

dynamic-link library (DLL) An *application programming interface (API)* routine that user-mode applications access through ordinary procedure calls. The code for the API routine is not included in the user's executable image. Instead, the operating system automatically modifies the executable image to point to DLL procedures at run time.

E

environment subsystems User-mode protected servers that run and support programs from different operating systems environments. Examples of these subsystems are the Win32 subsystem, the POSIX subsystem, and the OS/2 subsystem. See also *integral subsystem.*

environment variable A string consisting of environment information, such as a drive, path, or filename, associated with a symbolic name that can be used by Windows NT. You use the System option in Control Panel or the **set** command to define environment variables.

event Any significant occurrence in the system or in an application that requires users to be notified or an entry to be added to a log.

Event Log service Records events in the system, security, and application logs.

Executive module The Kernel-mode module that provides basic operating system services to the environment subsystems. It includes several components; each manages a particular set of system services. One component, the Security Reference Monitor, works together with the protected subsystems to provide a pervasive security model for the system.

extensibility Indicates the modular design of Windows NT, which provides for the flexibility of adding future modules at several levels within the operating system.

F

FAT file system A file system based on a file allocation table maintained by the operating system to keep track of the status of various segments of disk space used for file storage.

fault tolerance The ability of a computer and an operating system to respond gracefully to catastrophic events such as power outage or hardware failure. Usually, fault tolerance implies the ability to either continue the system's operation without loss of data or to shut the system down and restart it, recovering all processing that was in progress when the fault occurred.

file sharing The ability for Windows NT Workstation or Windows NT Server to share parts (or all) of its local file system(s) with remote computers.

file system In an operating system, the overall structure in which files are named, stored, and organized.

FTP service File transfer protocol service, which offers file transfer services to remote systems supporting this protocol. FTP supports a host of commands allowing bidirectional transfer of binary and ASCII files between systems.

Fully Qualified Domain Name (FQDN) In TCP/IP, *hostnames* with their *domain names* appended to them. For example, a host with hostname *tsunami* and domain name *microsoft.com* had an FQDN of *tsunami.microsoft.com*.

G

global account For Windows NT Server, a normal user account in a user's home domain. If there are multiple domains in the network, it is best if each user in the network has only one user account, in only one domain, and each user's access to other domains is accomplished through the establishment of domain trust relationships.

group In User Manager, an account containing other accounts called members. The permissions and rights granted to a group are also provided to its members, making groups a convenient way to grant common capabilities to collections of user accounts.

H

Hardware Abstraction Layer (HAL) Virtualizes hardware interfaces, making the hardware dependencies transparent to the rest of the operating system. This allows Windows NT to be portable from one hardware platform to another.

home directory A directory that is accessible to the user and contains files and programs for that user. A home directory can be assigned to an individual user or can be shared by many users.

host table The HOSTS or LMHOSTS file that contains lists of known IP addresses.

hostname A TCP/IP command that returns the local workstation's *host-name* used for authentication by TCP/IP utilities. This value is the workstation's *computer name* by default, but it can be changed.

I

integral subsystem A subsystem such as the Security subsystem that affects the entire Windows NT operating system. See also *environment subsystems*.

interprocess communication (IPC) The exchange of data between one thread or process and another, either within the same computer or across a network. Common IPC mechanisms include pipes, named pipes, semaphores, shared memory, queues, signals, mailboxes, and sockets.

K

kernel The portion of Windows NT that manages the processor.

Kernel module The core of the layered architecture of Windows NT that manages the most basic operations of Windows NT. The Kernel is responsible for thread dispatching, multiprocessor synchronization, hardware exception handling, and the implementation of low-level, hardware-dependent functions.

L

LLC Logical link control, in the Data Link layer of the networking model.

local printer A printer that is directly connected to one of the ports on your computer.

local procedure call (LPC) An optimized message-passing facility that allows one thread or process to communicate with another thread or process on the same computer. The Windows NT-protected subsystems use LPC to communicate with each other and with their client processes. LPC is a variation of the remote procedure call (RPC) facility, optimized for local use. Compare with *remote procedure call.*

locale The national and cultural environment in which a system or program is running. The locale determines the language used for messages and menus, the sorting order of strings, the keyboard layout, and date and time formatting conventions.

logon authentication Refers to the validation of a user, either locally or in a domain. At logon time, the user specifies his or her name, password, and the intended logon *domain*. The workstation then contacts the *domain controllers* for the domain, which verify the user's logon credentials.

LPC See *local procedure call.*

M

MAC Media access control, in the Data Link layer of the networking model.

mandatory user profile For Windows NT Server, a user profile created by an administrator and assigned to one or more users. A mandatory user profile cannot be changed by the user and remains the same from one logon session to the next. See also *personal user profile, user profile.*

MS-DOS-based application An application designed to run with MS-DOS, which therefore may not be able to take full advantage of all of the features of Windows NT.

N

named pipe An interprocess communication mechanism that allows one process to send data to another local or remote process. Windows NT named pipes are not the same as UNIX named pipes.

NBF transport protocol NetBEUI Frame protocol. A descendant of the NetBEUI protocol, which is a Transport layer protocol, not the programming interface NetBIOS.

NDIS See *Network driver interface specification.*

NetBEUI transport NetBIOS (Network Basic Input/Output System) Extended User Interface. The primary local area network transport protocol in Windows NT.

NetBIOS interface A programming interface that allows I/O requests to be sent to and received from a remote computer. It hides networking hardware for applications.

network device driver Software that coordinates communication between the network adapter card and the computer's hardware and other software, controlling the physical function of the network adapter cards.

network driver interface specification (NDIS) An interface in Windows NT for network card drivers that provides transport independence, because all transport drivers call the NDIS interface to access network cards.

NTFS (Windows NT file system) An advanced file system designed specifically for use with the Windows NT operating system. NTFS supports file system recovery and extremely large storage media, in addition to other advantages. It also supports object-oriented applications by treating all files as objects with user-defined and system-defined attributes.

O

object type Includes a system-defined data type, a list of operations that can be performed upon it (such as wait, create, or cancel), and a set of object attributes. Object Manager is the part of the Windows NT Executive that provides uniform rules for retention, naming, and security of objects.

OLE A way to transfer and share information between applications.

P

packet A unit of information transmitted as a whole from one device to another on a network.

page A fixed-size block in memory.

partition A portion of a physical disk that functions as though it were a physically separate unit.

permission A rule associated with an object (usually a directory, file, or printer) in order to regulate which users can have access to the object and in what manner. See also *right.*

personal user profile For Windows NT Server, a user profile created by an administrator and assigned to one user. A personal user profile retains changes the user makes to the per-user settings of Windows NT and reimplements the newest settings each time that the user logs on at any Windows NT workstation. See also *mandatory user profile, user profile.*

port A connection or socket used to connect a device to a computer, such as a printer, monitor, or modem. Information is sent from the computer to the device through a cable.

portability Windows NT runs on both CISC and RISC processors. CISC includes computers running Intel 80386 or higher processors. RISC includes computers with MIPS R4000 or Digital Alpha AXP processors.

print device Refers to the actual hardware device that produces printed output.

print processor A dynamic link library that interprets data types. It receives information from the spooler and sends the interpreted information to the graphics engine.

printer In Windows NT, refers to the software interface between the application and the print device.

protocol A set of rules and conventions by which two computers pass messages across a network. Networking software usually implements multiple levels of protocols layered one on top of another.

provider The component that allows a computer running Windows NT to communicate with the network. Windows NT includes a provider for the Windows NT-based network; other providers are supplied by the alternate networks' vendors.

R

redirector Networking software that accepts I/O requests for remote files, named pipes, or mailslots and then sends (*redirects*) them to a network service on another computer. Redirectors are implemented as file system drivers in Windows NT

remote administration Administration of one computer by an administrator located at another computer and connected to the first computer across the network.

remote procedure call (RPC) A message-passing facility that allows a distributed application to call services available on various computers in a network. Used during remote administration of computers. RPC provides a procedural view, rather than a transport-centered view, of networked operations. Compare with *local procedure call.*

resource Any part of a computer system or a network, such as a disk drive, or memory, that can be allotted to a program or a process while it is running.

right Authorizes a user to perform certain actions on the system. Rights apply to the system as a whole and are different from *permissions*, which apply to specific objects. (Sometimes called a *privilege*.)

RISC-based computer A computer based on a RISC (reduced instruction set) microprocessor, such as a Digital Alpha AXP, MIPS R4000, or IBM/Motorola PowerPC. Compare with *x86-based computer.*

router TCP/IP gateways — computers with two or more network adapters that are running some type of IP routing software: each adapter is connected to a different physical network.

RPC See *remote procedure call.*

S

SAM See *Security Accounts Manager.*

SAM database The database of security information that includes user account names and passwords and the settings of the security policies.

scalability Scalability depends on the overall architecture of the entire application server. The three critical components of a scalable system are: operating system, application software, and hardware. No one element by itself is sufficient to guarantee scalability. High-performance server hardware is designed to scale to multiple processors, providing specific functionality to ease disk and memory bottlenecks. Applications and operating systems, in turn, must be able to take advantage of multiple CPUs. All three components are equally important.

Schedule service Supports and is required for use of the **at** command, which can schedule commands and programs to run on a computer at a specified date and time.

Security Accounts Manager (SAM) A Windows NT protected subsystem that maintains the SAM database and provides an API for accessing the database.

security ID (SID) A unique name that identifies a logged-on user to the security system of Windows NT. A security ID can identify either an individual user or a group of users.

server A LAN-based computer running administrative software that controls access to all or part of the network and its resources. A computer acting as a server makes resources available to computers acting as workstations on the network. For the X Window System of UNIX, the client/server relationship is reversed. Under the X Window System, this server definition becomes the client definition. See also *client.*

Server service A service in Windows NT that supplies an API for managing the Windows NT-based network software. Provides RPC support, and file, print, and named pipe sharing.

service A process that performs a specific system function and often provides an API for other processes to call. Services in Windows NT are RPC enabled, meaning that their API routines can be called from remote computers.

session A connection that two applications on different computers establish, use, and end. The session layer performs name recognition and the functions needed to allow two applications to communicate over the network.

socket Provides an end point to a connection; two sockets form a complete path. A socket works as a bidirectional pipe for incoming and outgoing data between networked computers. The Windows Sockets API is a networking API tailored for use by Windows-based applications.

standards Windows NT provides support for many standards, some of which are: AppleTalk, Apple File Protocol, C2, Connection-oriented Transport Protocol (Class 4), Connectionless Network Protocol (CLNP), Domain Name Service (DNS), Dynamic Host Configuration Protocol (DHCP), Ethernet, Fiber Distributed Data Interface (FDDI), FIPS 151-2, Frame Relay, IEEE 802.x, IEEE 1003.1, IPX/SPX, Integrated Services Digital Network (ISDN), ISO 8073, ISO 8473, ISO 8208, ISO 8314, ISO 8802, ISO 9660, ISO 9945-1, ISO 10646, ITU FAX Standards, ITU Modem Standards, NetWare Core Protocol (NCP), OpenGLTM, OSI, POSIX, Point-to-Point Protocol (PPP), Personal Computer Memory Card International (PCMCIA), Serial Line Interface Protocol (SLIP), Simple Network Management Protocol (SNMP), Token Ring, TCP/IP, Unicode, and X.25.

synchronous I/O The simplest way to perform I/O, by synchronizing the execution of applications with completion of the I/O operations that they request. When an application performs an I/O operation, the application's processing is blocked. When the I/O operation is complete, the application is allowed to continue processing. See also *asynchronous I/O.*

system default profile For Windows NT Server, the user profile that is loaded when Windows NT is running and no user is logged on. When the Welcome dialog box is visible, the system default profile is loaded. See also *user default profile, user profile.*

T

TDI See *Transport Driver Interface.*

Telnet service The service that provides basic terminal emulation to remote systems supporting the Telnet protocol over TCP/IP.

text file A file containing only letters, numbers, and symbols. A text file contains no formatting information, except possibly linefeeds and carriage returns. Text files are also known as flat files and ASCII files.

thread An executable entity that belongs to a single process, comprising a program counter, a usermode stack, a kernel-mode stack, and a set of register values. All threads in a process have equal access to the processor's address space, object handles, and other resources. In Windows NT, threads are implemented as objects.

Transport Driver Interface (TDI) In the networking model, a common interface for network components that communicate at the session layer.

transport protocol Defines how data should be presented to the next receiving layer in the networking model and packages the data accordingly. It passes data to the network adapter card driver through the *NDIS Interface*, and to the *redirector* through the *Transport Driver Interface.*

trust relationship Trust relationships are links between domains that enable pass-through authentication, in which a user has only one user account in one domain, yet can access the entire network. A trusting domain honors the logon authentications of a trusted domain.

U

Unicode A fixed-width, 16-bit character encoding standard capable of representing all of the world's scripts.

user account Consists of all the information that defines a user to Windows NT. This includes the username and password required for the user to log on, the groups in which the user account has membership, and the rights and permissions the user has for using the system and accessing its resources. See also *group.*

user default profile For Windows NT Server, the user profile that is loaded by a server when a user's assigned profile cannot be accessed for any reason, when a user without an assigned profile logs on to the computer for the first time, or when a user logs on the Guest account. See also *system default profile, user profile.*

user mode A nonprivileged processor mode in which application code runs.

user profile Configuration information retained on a user-by-user basis. The information includes all the per-user settings of Windows NT, such as the desktop arrangement, personal program groups and the program items in those groups, screen colors, screen savers, network connections, printer connections, mouse settings, window size and position, and more. When a user logs on, the user's profile is loaded, and the user's environment in Windows NT is configured according to that profile.

user right See *right.*

username A unique name identifying a user account to Windows NT. An account's username cannot be identical to any other group name or username of its own domain or workstation. See also user account.

V

validation Authorization check of a user's logon information. When a user logs on to an account on a Windows NT Workstation computer, the authentication is performed by that workstation. When a user logs on to an account on a Windows NT Server domain, that authentication may be performed by any server of that domain. See also *trust relationship.*

virtual DOS machine (VDM) A Windows NT protected subsystem that supplies a complete environment for MS-DOS and a console in which to run applications for MS-DOS or 16-bit Windows. A VDM is a Win32 application that establishes a complete virtual x86 (that is, 80386 or higher) computer running MS-DOS. Any number of VDMs can run simultaneously.

virtual memory Space on a hard disk that Windows NT uses as if it were actually memory. Windows NT does this through the use of paging files. The benefit of using virtual memory is that you can run more applications at one time than your system's physical memory would otherwise allow. The drawbacks are the disk space required for the virtual-memory paging file and the decreased execution speed when swapping is required.

volume A partition or collection of partitions that have been formatted for use by a file system.

W

Win32 API A 32-bit application programming interface for Windows NT. It updates earlier versions of the Windows API with sophisticated operating system capabilities, security, and API routines for displaying text-based applications in a window.

Windows on Win32 (WOW) A Windows NT protected subsystem that runs within a VDM process. It provides an environment for 16-bit Windows capable of running any number of applications for 16-bit Windows under Windows NT.

Windows Sockets An IPC mechanism based on the WinSock specification and compatible with the Berkeley Sockets IPC under UNIX. The WinSock specification allows hardware and software vendors to design systems and applications that can access virtually any type of underlying network, including TCP/IP, IPX/SPX, OSI, ATM networks, wireless networks, and telephone networks.

workstation In general, a powerful computer having considerable calculating and graphics capability. For Windows NT, computers running the Windows NT Workstation operating system are called workstations, as distinguished from computers running Windows NT Server, which are called servers. See also *server, domain controller.*

Workstation service A service for Windows NT that supplies user-mode API routines to manage the Windows NT redirector. Provides network connections and communications.

WOW The subsystem for running Windows for MS-DOS under Windows NT; sometimes also called Win16 or Win32.

X

x86-based computer A computer using a microprocessor equivalent to an Intel 80386 or higher chip. Compare with a *RISC-based computer.*

Index

A

Access NFS, 25-12
Account Lockout, 4-10
Accumaster Integrator, 44-1
ActiveX, 19-4, 67-5, 67-6
Allegris, 9-11, 9-12
  constructor, 9-13
  datadesigner, 9-14
  object repository, 9-13
America Online, 52-2
AppleTalk, 54-2
Applets, 15-2, 16-6, 19-3, 19-4
  secure, 67-2
  viruses *vs.*, 67-1
Application development, 9-1. *See also* Portable object-oriented frameworks.
  client, 19-4
  cost issues, 19-5
  cross-platform, 9-2
    using graphical user interfaces, 9-6
    using Java, 9-15
    using proprietary APIs, 9-3, 9-4
  distributed, 9-16
    database access, 9-22
    defined, 12-2
    interoperability, 12-6
    message-oriented, 9-21
    middleware products, 9-21, 12-1
    object-oriented design, 9-24
    platform-independent code, 11-8
    scope and goals, 11-4
  with 4GL tools, 9-9
  Java, 15-3
  portable object-oriented frameworks for, 9-10
  with WIN32 API, 9-7
  with WISE, 9-7
Application gateways, 19-8
Application management, 21-2
  applications orientation in, 21-6, 21-7
  approaches, 21-3
    instrumentation, 21-3
    modeling, 21-4
  criteria, 21-6
  heterogeneous environment, 37-1, 37-3
  paradigm, 21-2
  vendor-supplied, 21-5, 21-7, 21-8
Application Programming Interfaces, 5-3
  emulated, 9-5
  layered, 9-4
    plus extensions, 9-5, 9-6
    supporting least common subset, 9-4, 9-5
  proprietary, 9-4
Application stack, 21-7
APPN Network Node products, 56-9
Artisoft Lantastic, 1-9
AS/400, 56-8
  adoption of authority by programs, 63-15
  authority search order, 63-16, 63-17
  authorization lists, 63-13, 63-14
  defining security-related network attributes, 63-12
  establishing a security strategy, 63-16
  group profiles, 63-4
  object attributes, 63-3
  object authority, 63-8, 63-9
  object-based system architecture, 63-2
  profile management, 63-5
  registration facility, 63-13
  security
    audit support, 63-19, 63-20
    integrated approach, 63-18
    library, 63-18
    menu, 63-16
    object, 63-18

options, 63-9
active job controls, 63-10
audit controls, 63-10
password controls, 63-10
QSECURITY, 63-10
sign-on controls, 63-10
recommended course of action, 63-19, 63-20
user profiles, 63-4
security-related fields, 63-6
Association implementation, 8-21
Asymmetric Multiprocessing, 5-5
Asynchronous Transfer Mode (ATM), 18-8, 18-9, 18-10, 18-11
ATM. *See* Asynchronous Transfer Mode (ATM).
Auditing
defining and assessing control risks, 82-1
guidelines, 82-1
identifying applications, 82-2
identifying connectivity, 82-1
identifying management concerns, 82-2
procedures, 81-2
sysadmin tasks to expedite, 82-3
Authentication server, 36-5, 61-3, 72-2
characteristics
efficiency and security, 36-5
reliability, 36-5
scalability, 36-6
emulators and, 36-7
local resource control, 36-9
pass ticket generation, 36-8
password management function, 36-7
user group identification, 36-9
workstation protection, 36-6
Authenticode, 67-5
Autonomy, 27-2, 27-3, 70-13
association, 28-8, 70-13
communication, 70-13
control, 28-8
design, 28-7, 70-13
execution, 28-8, 70-13
local, 71-2
types, 28-7, 70-13

B

Backbone, 18-9
campus/metropolitan area, 18-10, 18-11
frame relay, 56-14, 56-15
LAN, 18-9
multicast LANs, 48-6
protocol, common, 54-5, 54-7
resigned, 79-9
router collapsed, 18-10
Background job scheduling, 37-1, 37-2, 37-3
Back-up system, 35-11, 37-1, 37-3, 51-5
Bandwidth, managing, 19-10, 19-11
Banyan Vines, 54-2
technical benefits, 77-2
Banyan's products, 33-25, 33-26, 54-2
BEA Jolt, 9-34
BestWeb Pro, 24-4
BeyondMail, 52-13
Bindery, 33-4
Bluebird client systems, 17-6
Borland C++, 7-5, 7-10
Bridges, 15-7, 30-9, 49-9
Bridging, 18-5, 49-17
remote source route, 49-22
source-route, 49-20, 54-5. *See also* Source-route bridging.
source-route transparent, 49-25, 54-13
spanning tree algorithm, 49-19
translational, 49-23
transparent, 49-18
BW-Connect NFS, 10-3

C

C data types, 5-28
Cache manager, 5-7
Callback systems, 72-7
Case study
gateway technology, 30-9
multiple protocols, 42-5
multivendor environment, 39-7, 75-6
network design, 50-13
Chameleon 32 NFS, 10-3
Chameleon product set, 10-27
Checksums, 68-13
Circuit-level gateways, 19-8
Client Services for NetWare, 33-3
configuring NetWare connection, 33-5
installing software and setting up accounts, 33-5
setting your options, 33-8
Client/server computing, 11-7, 20-9, 20-12, 26-4
architecture, 26-5, 70-10, 70-11
job scheduling, 41-2, 41-3
Code development, 11-7
Command and control systems, 20-5, 20-7
components, 20-8, 20-9
data interpretation tools, 20-8

database infrastructure, 20-8
display interface, 20-8
Command Lines and Text, 5-18
Common Object Request Broker Architecture (CORBA). *See* CORBA.
Communication(s)
back-flow, 30-7
facilities, 11-9
global, 45-6
infrastructure, 30-5, 44-2
interprocessing methodologies, 2-4
multivendor environment, 39-6
protocols, 44-2, 44-4
security, 51-8
UNIX *vs.* Windows NT, 35-8
Compiler, 5-24, 5-27
CompuServe, 52-2
Conceptual schema heterogeneity, 26-2, 26-6, 28-7
data specification, 28-7
database tools, 28-7
domain mismatch, 28-7
naming mismatch, 28-7
schematic discrepancy, 28-7
update, 28-7
Concurrency, 8-24
Constructor calls, 5-26
Conventional encryption, 65-3, 65-4
IDEA, 65-5
ingredients, 65-3, 65-4
ciphertext, 65-5
decryption algorithm, 65-5
encryption algorithm, 65-5
plaintext, 65-5
secret key, 65-5
CORBA, 15-7, 26-1
advantages, 26-4
components, 26-2
interface definition language, 26-3, 26-4
object model, 26-2
object request broker, 26-3
Corvus OMNInet, 1-2
Cross compiler support, 5-37
Cross-platform applications, 74-7
using proprietary APIs, 9-3
advantages, 9-3
disadvantages, 9-4

D

Daemons, 5-8
Data conversion, 32-1
Data encryption, 72-6
Data link switching, 55-12
Data requirements, 11-8
Data types, 22-2, 22-3
user-defined, 22-3
Database
creation, 50-2
distributed, 23-1, 23-3, 70-1. *See also* Distributed Computing Environment (DCE).
allocating metadata, 70-9, 70-10
allocation schema, 70-3, 70-5
architecture, 70-3
autonomy, 70-13
components, 23-3, 23-4
data independence, 70-2
design, 70-3
distributed processing, 71-1
efficient access, 70-2
execution manager, 23-9
features, 23-2, 70-1
fragmentation schema, 70-3
gateways, 23-7
global schema, 70-3
hierarchical control, 70-1
horizontal fragmentation, 70-4
incremental growth, 71-1
local mapping schema, 70-3
location and replication, 23-2
metadata management, 70-9
mixed fragmentation, 70-4
multisite update capability, 23-3
physical schema, 70-4
privacy and security, 70-2
query optimization, 70-6
query processing, 70-5
query transformation, 70-5
redundancy, 70-2
reliability and availability, 71-2
request optimizer, 23-4, 23-5, 23-6
rules, 71-2
continuous operation, 71-3
DBMS independence, 71-9
distributed query processing, 71-7
distributed transaction management, 71-7
fragmentation independence, 71-4
hardware independence, 71-9
independence from central site, 71-3
local autonomy, 71-2

location independence, 71-4
network independence, 71-9
operating system independence, 71-9
replication independence, 71-6
technology, 23-2
transaction management, 70-2
concurrency control, 70-7
recovery, 70-8
transparency, 23-3
two-phase commit protocol, 23-9
vertical fragmentation, 70-4
export, 28-5
federated, 27-2
defined, 28-2
features, 27-2
heterogeneous, 9-32. *See also* Heterogeneity.
integrating, 26-4
response delivery, 26-6, 26-7
import, 28-5
local, 28-5
manipulation, 22-13
relational, 22-1. *See also* Relational database.
reserve capacity, 251-5
sharing, 28-11
update operations, 22-13
Database access
common user, 2-6
distributed, 9-22, 27-1
heterogeneous, 9-32
Electronic Data Access, 9-32
Empress, 9-32
HyperStar Fast Path Server, 9-33
Omni SQL Gateway, 9-33
Database gateway(s), 29-1, 42-5. *See also* Gateway technology.
add-on software, 29-8
capacity planning issues, 29-2
amount of data passing through server, 29-4
concurrent user connections, 29-2
network protocols, 29-4
online teleprocessing volume, 29-3
remote procedure calls, 29-3
SQL access, 29-2
disaster recovery, 29-7
security, 29-5
set-up, 29-1
technical support, 29-6
usage considerations, 29-7
Database integrity, 22-2
DB2 and, 22-4
entity, 22-2
Ingres constraints, 22-5
Oracle constraints, 22-6
protection, 38-11
referential, 22-2, 22-4
rules and, 22-9
semantic, 22-2
Sybase constraints, 22-8
triggers, 22-9
Database sharing, 28-11
DataDirect, 6-25
DB2, 22-4. *See also* Relational database.
aplication tools, 22-23
evaluation, 22-27
integrated searches, 31-8
join function, 22-18
programming language support, 22-21
rules, 22-4, 22-9
text extender, 31-9
update restrictions, 22-15
DCE, Distributed Computing Environment (DCE)
DEC All-in-One, 52-11
DECnet OSI, 43-6
DECnet Phase IV, 43-6
Desktop(s)
accessing UNIX applications from, 10-17
application, 18-2
ATM to, 18-8
changing, network and, 18-2
enterprise. *See* Enterprise desktops.
operating system, 2-1
requirements, 2-12
Device drivers, 5-7
DHCP management. *See* Dynamic Host Configuration Protocol (DHCP).
Digital Equipment Corp.
Enterprise Management Architecture, 43-1
polycenter framework, 43-1. *See also* Polycenter.
Disaster recovery, 29-7, 38-2, 51-4, 81-17
control, 83-15
strategies, 38-11
adequate backups with secure off-site storage, 38-12
adequate LAN personnel, 38-13
alternate sites and system sizing, 38-12
fault tolerance *vs.* redundancy, 38-12
personnel, 38-13

DISCOVER, 6-30
application sets, 6-31
Disk and file backup, 37-1, 37-3
Distance Vector Multicast Routing Protocol (DVMRP), 48-7
Distributed Computing Environment (DCE), 9-16. *See also* Heterogeneous environment; Multiple database(s).
access control, 51-7, 81-3
application development, 9-16
database access, 9-22
extending existing strategy, 11-6
message-oriented, 9-21
middleware products, 9-21, 12-1
object-oriented design, 9-24
platform-independent code, 11-8
redevelopment strategy, 11-5
scope and goals, 11-4
tools, 11-9
application management, 21-2
approaches, 21-3
paradigm, 21-2
vendor-supplied, 21-5, 21-7, 21-8
authentication server, 36-5. *See also* Authentication server.
business issues, 12-2
integration, 12-3
business recovery planning, 38-2
client/server development, 11-7, 80-14
code development, 11-7
communication facilities, 11-9
complexity, 73-7
control of executable code, 51-6
costs, 73-5
data modification, 68-10
data requirements, 11-8
database. *See* Database, distributed.
"dialtone" IS service, 73-6
disaster recovery, 29-7, 38-2, 51-4. *See also* Disaster recovery.
diverse interfaces, 11-9
help desk, 40-1, 40-9. *See also* Help desk.
centralization, 40-7, 40-8
new role, 40-6
skills for, 40-7
tools, 40-7, 40-8, 40-9
view, 40-11, 40-12
integrity and confidentiality of data, 68-12
interoperability, 12-4, 70-11. *See also* Interoperability.
applications, 12-6
database, 12-5
GUI/MUI, 12-6
network, 12-4
object/software component, 12-5
platform, 12-5
workgroup/workflow/e-mail, 12-6
Kerberos in, 36-10, 64-1. *See also* Kerberos.
management, 73-1, 73-7
architecture selection, 73-13
choosing standard, 73-12
model of service delivery, 73-3
organization for, 73-9
problems, 73-2
middleware products, 9-21
network snooping, 68-10
object-oriented applications, 9-24
password synchronization, 36-4
passwords, 68-11. *See also* Password(s).
perceived quality, 73-5
planning, 38-9
problems, 36-3
protection. *See* Security.
recovery planning, 38-2
awareness and discovery, 38-2
mitigation, 38-4
policies, 38-8
preparation, 38-4
response and recovery, 38-5
restoration of full access, 38-8
risk assessment, 38-3
risks and mitigation costs, 38-7
testing, 38-5, 38-13
redevelopment strategy, 11-5
remote library control, 51-7
risks, 73-4
runtime services, 9-18
security, 51-2. *See also* Security.
systems administration, 38-1
departmental planning, 38-5
recovery planning, 38-2
UNIX, 9-17
vulnerabilities, 68-10
Windows NT, 9-17, 9-18
Domain Name Service, 5-15
DOS
compatibility, 2-4
networking capability, 2-14
system requirements, 2-12
third-party software market, 2-12
DSC++, 9-10
Dumb terminals, 15-9

Dynamic Host Configuration Protocol (DHCP), 4-2, 37-11
mechanism of operation, 37-12, 37-13
Dynamic publishing, 24-5
formulating query, 24-5
Java applets, 24-5, 24-6
security mechanisms, 24-7

E

EcoNets, 50-1, 50-11
Electronic Data Access, 9-32
e-mail, 12-6, 21-9
characteristics, 53-10
coexistence, 53-7
tools, 53-10
commercial services, 52-2
directories, 52-7, 53-12
synchronization, 53-12
features and functions, 53-10
attaching files, 52-5
creating messages, 52-5
distribution lists, 52-6
editing capabilities, 52-5
file compression, 52-6
forms, 52-7
importing text, 52-6
signature files, 52-7
heterogeneous environment, 53-1, 53-7, 53-14
historical perspective, 52-1
Internet, 52-2
migration
administrative and planning, 53-16
one-step, 53-9
phased, 53-8
tools, 53-10
online services, 52-2
private, 52-2
problems, 52-3
products, 53-14
MAILBus 400, 53-14
MailWorks, 53-14
PMDF Mailbus 400, 53-15
X.500 directory services, 53-15
risks, 65-2
security, 53-13, 65-1. *See also* Pretty Good Privacy.
services, 52-7
systems, 52-2
BeyondMail, 52-13
coexistence, 53-7
components, 53-2
UNIX, 53-3
Windows NT server, 53-6
criteria for selection, 52-4
DEC All-in-One, 52-11
features and functions, 52-3, 52-4
Fisher TAO, 52-12
GroupWise, 52-13
heterogeneous, 53-1, 53-7
HP Open Desk Manager, 52-12
IBM Office Vision 400, 52-2
interfacing with external, 53-10
Lotus cc:Mail, 52-11
Lotus Notes, 52-12
Memo, 52-13
Microsoft Mail, 52-12
options, 53-7, 53-8, 53-9
QuickMail, 52-13
selection, 52-4
UNIX, 35-10
Windows NT, 35-10
Empress Heterogeneous Database Server, 9-32
Emulators, 4-3, 10-29
application, 17-6
authentication server and, 36-7
built-in, 17-9
hardware-based, 17-7, 17-14
public domain, 17-14
software-based, 17-7
SoftWindows, 17-7
terminal, 4-3, 17-6, 17-14
WABI, 17-9
WISE, 9-8
Encapsulation, 8-24, 14-7, 80-7
Encryption, 72-6
conventional, 65-3. *See also* Conventional encryption.
data, 72-6
Internet, 66-18
Java, 16-4
network, 68-13
Oracle, 68-8
partial database, 68-9
password, 60-7, 68-11
PGP, 65-3
public-key, 65-9, 65-10
RSA algorithm, 65-11, 65-12, 65-13
End-user support, 1-8
ENEOS, 58-2, 58-4
architecture, 58-6
change, 58-3
configuration, 58-3
design, 58-16

event analyzer, 58-9
features, 58-3
finite inference frame processor, 58-15
knowledge bases, 58-10, 58-12
performance oversight, 58-3
problem-resolution, 58-3
protocols and standards, 58-5
security, 58-3
Enterprise, 45-1
defined, 45-1
Enterprise desktops, 17-1
business requirements, 17-2
network, 17-3. *See also* Network computers.
technical requirements, 17-1
Enterprise Management Architecture, 43-1
Enterprise server
basics, 20-8
mainframe as, 20-1
upgrading considerations, 20-10
data center operations, 20-13
integrating PC/LAN clusters, 20-13
migrating to core DBMS, 20-11
network infrastructure, 20-13
tools for new applications, 20-11
Enterprise systems management, 37-1, 37-3
Ergonomics, 39-2, 75-2
Error handling, 5-36
Ethernet, 18-3, 43-6
bridging, 18-5
3Com, 1-2
encapsulation, 55-7
MAC layer frame formats, 49-10
100M-bps, 18-8
shared, 18-3
switched, 18-7
EtherShare, 1-2
eXalt-X, 10-27
eXceed, 10-23
Windows NT, 10-23
eXceed XDK, 6-17
eXcursion, 6-17
Executing Object Code, 5-9
eXpertise, 10-28
Explora, 17-4
Explorer, 33-12
Export database, 28-5

F

Fax gateway, 52-9, 52-10
FDDI, 49-13, 49-15
Federated database system, 27-2
autonomy, 27-2, 27-3, 70-13
association, 28-8, 70-13
communication, 70-13
control, 28-8
design, 28-7, 70-13
execution, 28-8, 70-13
types, 28-7, 70-13
characteristics, 28-6
construction, 27-4
distributed DBMS in, 27-7, 27-8
ODBC drivers in, 27-4, 27-5
Web publishing tools in, 27-6
defined, 27-1, 28-2
export schema, 27-2, 27-3
features, 27-2
functional requirements, 28-8
data importation, 28-10
information discovery, 28-9, 28-13, 28-14
information exportation, 28-8, 28-12
information importation, 28-9, 28-15
information querying, 28-11, 28-18
schema importation, 28-9
transaction processing, 28-11, 28-18
heterogeneities, 28-6
conceptual schema, 28-7
database model, 28-6
local transparency, 27-2
reference architecture, 28-4
information sharing techniques, 28-4
replication transparency, 27-2
transparency, 27-2, 27-3
unified schema, 27-2, 27-3
update heterogeneity, 28-16
user access, 27-2
Fiber optic connectivity, 78-5
advantages, 78-6, 78-8
cabling, 78-8
costs, 78-9, 78-10
data transmission, 78-7
disadvantages, 78-7, 78-9
File access, 10-3
File Transfer Protocol, 25-15, 66-5
Firewall(s), 19-8, 61-3, 66-14
application gateways, 19-8
circuit-level gateways, 19-8
functions, 19-9
packet filtering, 19-8
policy, 66-16
conservative, 66-16
positions, 66-15
paranoid, 66-15
permissive, 66-15

promiscuous, 66-16
prudent, 66-15
selection, 66-16
types, 19-8
FIRLAN. *See* Infrared technology.
First-in-first-out management, 5-6
Fisher TAO, 52-12
Fragmentation
horizontal, 70-4
independence, 71-4
mixed, 70-4
schema, 70-3
vertical, 70-4
Frame relay, 46-4, 46-7, 48-2, 49-7, 55-8, 56-17
access station, 56-3
flag, 56-4
frame check sequence, 56-4
frame relay header, 56-4
user data, 56-4
alternative routing, 56-11
backbone, 56-14, 56-15
benefits, 79-7
header, 56-12
in IBM environment, 79-1
IBM multiprotocol support, 56-9
networks, 56-7, 79-4
alternative routing, 56-11
APPN, 56-9
AS/400, 56-8
backup DLCI, 79-8
boundary network node, 56-8
congestion notification, 56-12, 56-13
consolidate link layer message, 56-13
discard eligibility bit, 56-13
intermediate network node, 56-8
legacy devices, 56-9
local management interface, 56-12
management, 56-10, 56-14
NetView, 56-10
private relay, 56-9
SNA network interconnect, 56-8
SNMP management, 56-14
VTAM, 56-11
N-way multicast, 48-2
one-way multicast, 48-2
Permanent Virtual Circuit, 56-3
redundancy, 79-7
as replacement for SDLC, 56-7
RFC 1490, 56-5, 56-6
SNA support, 56-8, 56-14, 56-15
test phases, 79-5, 79-6
two-way multicast, 48-2
user perspective, 56-2
vs. other router networks, 56-14
WAN protocol, 56-14, 56-15

G

Gateway G-Net card, 1-2
Gateway Service for NetWare, 33-15, 33-16, 33-17, 33-18
configuring, 33-23
Gateway technology, 19-8, 29-1, 30-9, 52-9. *See also* Database gateway(s).
case study, 30-9
mail application, 45-13
4GL tools, 9-9, 9-10
G-NEt, 1-1
Graphical user interfaces, 2-13
cross-platform, 9-6
interfaces between applications and, 7-13
interoperability, 12-6
portability overview, 7-12
porting, 7-1
separating application from, 7-11
GroupBox, 14-6
GroupWise, 52-13

H

Hamilton C Shell, 37-7
Handshaking, 51-7
Hard disk contamination, 51-11
Hardware, component tracking, 39-6
Hardware abstraction layer, 5-3
Help desk, 40-1
centralization, 40-7, 40-8
changing user requirements, 40-3
communication with users, 57-7
cost justification, 57-2
database for tracking problems, 57-7
evolution, 40-1
history, 57-1
mission, 57-2
personnel management, 57-4
physical aspects, 57-4
progression of customer calls, 40-2
rationale, 40-2
responsibilites, 40-5
role, 40-4, 40-6, 57-10
security, 57-7
software, 37-1, 37-3
staff, 40-5
support management, 57-3, 57-9
tools, 57-5
tracking systems, 40-5

traditional, 40-5
user attitudes toward, 40-4
wireless data terminals, 57-10
Heterogeneity, 9-32, 26-1
constraint, 26-2, 70-12
database model, 28-6
federated database system, 28-6
handling, 26-5, 26-8
integrating, 26-4
query language, 26-2, 70-12
query processing, 26-2, 70-12
schema, 26-1, 26-2, 26-6, 28-7, 70-12
semantic, 26-2, 26-6, 28-7, 70-12
transaction processing, 26-2, 70-12
types of, 26-5, 28-6
update, 28-16
Heterogenous environment, 37-1. *See also* Distributed Computing Environment (DCE).
administration considerations, 74-9
e-mail systems, 53-1. *See also* e-mail.
factors in solution selection
build *vs.* buy, 74-3
cross-platform development, 74-7
enterprise, 74-2
guidelines, 74-8
industry, 74-1
porting, 74-4
solution-specific, 74-3
standards, 74-4
workstation resources, 74-4
X-servers, 74-4
help desk. *See* Help desk.
management using SNMP, 37-9, 37-10
solution selection, 74-1
system administration functions, 37-1
application management, 37-1, 37-3
asset management, 37-1, 37-3
background job scheduling, 37-1, 37-3
disk and file backup, 37-1, 37-3
enterprise system management, 37-1, 37-3
help desk software, 37-1, 37-3
network management, 37-1, 37-3
output management, 37-1, 37-3
performance management, 37-1, 37-3
security, 37-1, 37-3
software distribution, 37-1, 37-3
HOSTS file, 5-15
HP 500 Windows application server, 10-15
HP Open Desk Manager, 52-12
HTML. *See* Hypertext markup language (HTML).
HyperStar Fast Path Server, 9-33
Hypertext markup language (HTML), 24-1, 24-3

I

IBM Office Vision 400, 52-2
ICA client approach, 10-9
IDEA. *See* International Data Encryption Algorithm (IDEA).
Import database, 28-5
Information discovery, 28-9, 28-13, 28-14
Information exportation, 28-8, 28-12
Information importation, 28-9, 28-15
instance, 28-16
schema, 28-15
Information sharing techniques, 28-4
Information system(s), 20-4
command and control, 20-5, 20-7
infrastructure, 20-3
integrated product/service delivery, 20-5
precision, 20-4
resources, 20-2
server-based strategy, 20-2, 20-4
strategic, 20-5
strategy cost, 20-5
yield management, 20-6, 20-7
Infrared technology, 78-5, 78-12
advantages, 78-16
conditions affecting effectiveness, 78-14, 78-15
cost, 78-16, 78-17
disadvantages, 78-16
licensing requirements, 78-16
Ingres, 22-5
application tools, 22-23
database manipulation, 22-16
evaluation, 22-27
join function, 22-19
programming language support, 22-21
triggers, 22-10
Inheritance
implementation, 8-12, 14-8
approaches, 8-13
method 1, 8-13
method 2, 8-14
method 3, 8-17
Powerbuilder, 14-8
Visual Basic, 14-8
Inline functions, 5-26
InterDrive NT, 25-14

International Data Encryption Algorithm (IDEA), 65-5
overall structure, 65-6
single iteration, 65-8
Internet, 46-15
address spoofing, 66-10
applications, 66-6
e-mail, 66-6. *See also* e-mail.
file transfer, 66-7
logging on to remote system, 66-6
attacks, 66-9, 66-12
defenses, 66-12, 66-13
bastions, 66-12
broadcast, 66-3
browsing, 66-11
central authority, 66-4
characteristics, 66-1
flatness, 66-2
mesh topology, 66-2
network of networks, 66-2
public nature, 66-2
commercialization, 46-15
connections, 66-3
any-to-any, 66-3
packet-switched, 66-3
peer-connected, 66-3
denial of service, 66-11, 67-3
eavesdropping, 66-9
e-mail, 52-2
encryption, 66-18
filters, 66-13, 66-14
functions, 53-16
interface applications, 9-34
interoperability, 66-4
Mbone, 48-6
packet and password grabbers, 66-9
policies, 66-12
protocols, 66-4
fundamental, 66-5
network time, 66-6
oldest and most widely used, 66-5
point-to-point, 66-6
secure, 66-6
serial line, 66-6
standard, 66-5
recommendations for safe use, 66-19
risks, 67-2
safe use, 66-18, 66-19
security, 66-1
Trojan Horse attack, 66-10
vulnerabilities on, 66-8
wrappers, 66-13
Internet access providers, 76-7
Internet Engineering Task Force, 16-6
Internet group management protocol, 48-5
Internet Name Service, 4-3, 5-14
Internet platform, 2-11
Internetwork Packet Exchange/Sequenced Packet Exchange, 16-6
Interoperability, 12-4, 45-3
applications, 12-6
database, 12-5
graphical user interface, 12-6
GUI/MUI, 12-6
heterogeneity issues, 26-1, 70-12. *See also* Heterogeneity.
constraint, 26-2
query language, 26-2
query processing, 26-2
schema, 26-1
semantic, 26-2, 26-6
transaction processing, 26-2
middleware solutions, 12-7
network, 12-4
object/software component, 12-5
platform, 12-5
router, 45-12
solution, 45-4
workgroup/workflow/e-mail, 12-6
Interprocessing communication methodologies, 2-4
Intranet(s), 19-1
cost issues, 19-5
"fat" *vs.* "thin" client, 19-2
IP administration, 19-10
JAVA-enabled browsers, 19-3, 19-4
managing bandwidth, 19-10
operating system, 19-7
performance, 19-5
server management, 19-9
switching, 19-6
IntranetWare, 19-7
IPX/SPX, 33-22, 34-2, 54-2

J

Java, 9-15, 19-3, 19-4
ActiveX and, 19-4
advantages, 16-3
applets, 15-2, 16-6, 19-3, 19-4, 67-2
user interface controls, 24-6
application development, 15-3
codes, 16-6
costs, 15-4
effectiveness and efficiency, 15-3

program and programmer portability, 15-4
program support and maintenance, 15-5
speed, 15-3
technical training, 15-5
bridges to ODBC and CORBA, 15-7
cost savings, 16-3
database and, 15-6
encryption and signatures, 16-4
holes and bugs, 67-3
influence, 16-2
interpretive languages *vs.*, 16-5
native applications, 15-8
for non-programmers, 15-6
operating system and, 15-7
performance, 16-3
platform independence, 16-5
portability, 16-3
rapid development, 16-3
reliability, 16-3, 16-4
rules enforcement, 16-4
scripting languages, 19-4
security, 15-8, 16-3, 16-4
shortcomings, 15-10
strong memory protection, 16-4
JavaScript, 67-4
Job scheduling, 35-13
background, 37-1, 37-2, 37-3
centralized administration, 41-7
client/server, 41-2, 41-3
role of master schedule, 41-7
Joins, 22-18, 22-27

K

Kerberos, 36-10
administration, 64-13
applying, 64-5
authentication process, 64-2, 64-3, 64-15
costs, 64-16
defined, 64-2
five-step operation, 64-2
functional overview, 64-2
future developments, 64-18
history, 64-1
implementation, 64-5, 64-10
protocol placement, 64-11
time services and network naming, 64-11
initial exchange, 64-7
KDC, 64-7, 64-13, 64-17
obtaining application service ticket, 64-9
performance and network topology, 64-14
security services, 64-3
access control, 64-4
authentication, 64-4
availability, 64-4
confidentiality, 64-3
integrity, 64-3
nonrepudiation, 64-4
secure channels, 64-3
Kiosk applications, 48-11

L

LAN. *See* Local Area Network (LAN).
LAN segment, 49-1
Legacy data conversion, 32-1
application modification and, 32-9, 32-10
cost-benefit analysis, 32-5
phases, 32-1, 32-2
analysis and planning, 32-1, 32-4, 32-5
fine-tuning, 32-1, 32-11
migration, 32-1, 32-5, 32-6, 32-7, 32-8, 74-2
rationale, 32-3
test suites following, 32-11
Line Print Requester, 25-18
Linear memory addressing, 5-6
Local address books, network directories *vs.*, 52-8
Local area network interconnection, 46-1, 54-4, 54-6
broadband ISDN and asynchronous transfer mode, 46-14
broadband services, 46-10
dedicated T1 lines, 46-6
frame relay, 46-4, 46-7
high-speed services, 46-1
narrowband, 46-1
packet-switched, 46-3
integrated services digital network, 46-6
Internet, 46-15
narrowband services, 46-1
analog dialup and leased lines, 46-2
DDS, 46-2
packet-switched services, 46-3
fractional T1, 46-5, 49-5
fractional T3, 46-9
frame relay, 46-4
X.25, 46-4
SMDS, 46-13
SONET, 46-12

T3 service, 46-11
virtual private networks, 46-8
Local area network (LAN). *See also* Network operating system(s).
backbone, 18-6, 79-9
bridges, 49-9
bridging, 18-4, 49-17
spanning tree algorithm, 49-19
transparent, 49-18
client support, 42-1
DOS, 2-2
implementation, 2-2
frame relay switches, 49-7
as gateways to hosts, 51-4
global communication, 45-6
addressing, 45-7, 45-8
routing protocols, 45-9
interconnection. *See* Local area network interconnection.
multicast. *See* Multicast LANs.
multiple protocols, 42-1
case study, 42-5
multistacking, 42-3
protection, 38-9
data integrity, 38-11
internal environment, 38-9
physical security, 38-10, 51-6
property management, 38-11
repeaters, 49-4
local, 49-4
multiport, 49-6
remote, 49-6
routing, 18-5
security, 51-4. *See also* Security.
segment, 18-4, 49-1
shared, 18-2
single sign-on, 36-2, 36-7
SNA and, 54-1, 54-3
switching, 18-6
vendors, 1-1
virtual, 19-6
Local database, 28-5
Lockwords, 51-7
Lotus cc:Mail, 52-11
Lotus Notes, 52-12
LU 6.2 connectivity, 55-9, 55-10

M

Mac client support, 17-9, 17-10, 17-11
MAILBus 400 software, 53-14
MAILWorks, 53-14
Mainframe computer, 20-8
as enterprise server, 20-1, 20-10
upgrading considerations, 20-10
data center operations, 20-13
integrating PC/LAN clusters, 20-13
migrating to core DBMS, 20-11
network infrastructure, 20-13
tools for new applications, 20-11
Mainframe interface(s), 9-24, 20-1
Microsoft BackOffice, 9-24
Microsoft SNA server, 9-26, 9-27, 9-28
Microsoft SQL server, 9-29
Microsoft Transaction Server, 9-30
Novell NetWare for SAA, 9-31
SNA Client, 9-28, 9-29
SNA gateways, 9-25, 9-27, 9-28
UNIX, 9-24
Windows NT, 9-24
MainWin, 6-20, 6-21
Management Information Base Tree, 47-7
Memo, e-mail system, 52-13
Memory-mapped files, 5-15
Metadata management, 70-9
Method resolution implementation, 8-18
Micro Focus Operating Systems Extensions, 11-10
Microsoft, 1-7
authenticode, 67-5
built-in UNIX commands, 37-6
NetWare administration functions, 33-18
Microsoft Access, 7-9, 7-10
Microsoft BackOffice, 9-24
Microsoft Mail, 52-12
Microsoft SNA server, 9-26, 9-27, 9-28
Microsoft SQL server, 9-29
Microsoft Transaction Server, 9-30
Microsoft Windows Interface Source Environment, 9-7. *See also* WISE.
Microsoft WISE, 9-7. *See also* WISE.
Microwave radio system, 78-6, 78-9
advantages, 78-12
costs, 78-12
disadvantages, 78-12
licensing requirements, 78-10
Middleware, 9-21, 12-1, 30-9
interoperability problems, 12-7
message-oriented, 12-8
trends in development, 12-10
types, 12-7
Migration tool, 4-6, 33-23
Misuse detection, 61-2, 61-7
data sources, 61-2
audit trails, 61-2
authentication server, 61-3

firewalls, 61-3
keystroke capture, 61-3
network traffic data, 61-3
limitations, 61-8
reporting results, 61-10
steps, 61-7
tools, 61-8
configration, 61-10
selection, 61-8
MKS Toolkit, 37-6
Mobile federation, 28-2
characteristics, 28-2, 28-6
heterogeneities, 28-6
reference architecture, 28-4
working scenario, 28-3
MS-DOS, 2-2. *See also* DOS.
problems and limitations, 2-3
from UNIX, 25-21
MsNet, 1-7
Multiattribute utility analysis
importance weights, 22-28, 22-29, 22-30
overall utility scores, 22-29, 22-30
scoring, 22-26, 22-27
utility functions, 22-28
Multicast LANs, 48-1
applications, 48-10
dataconferencing, 48-10
dynamic groups, 48-10
real-time distribution of multimedia information, 48-10
videoconferencing, 48-10
backbone, 48-6
class D addressing, 48-4
file transfer, 48-10
database updates, 48-11
distributed publishing, 48-11
electronic software distribution, 48-11
kiosk applications, 48-11
subscription-based information delivery, 48-10
frame relay, 48-2
Internet group management protocol, 48-5
IP address, 48-4
IP protocol, 48-4
routers, 48-5
routing protocols, 48-7
DVMRP, 48-7
MOSPF, 48-8
PIM, 48-9
switched multimegabit data service, 48-2
vendor offerings, 48-12
Multicast Open Shortest Path First (MOSPF), 48-8
MultiLine edit, 14-6
Multimedia user interface, 12-6
Multiple database(s), 30-1. *See also* Distributed Computing Environment (DCE).
alternatives, 30-4
communication infrastructure, 30-5
design decisions, 30-6
communications back-flow, 30-7
data architecture, 30-6
data item map, 30-7
database linkage, 30-6
positive feedback mechanism, 30-7
preventing feedback loops, 30-8
recovery, 30-8
split transactions, 30-8
update paths, 30-7
functional bridge
components, 30-9
constructing, 30-9
gateways, 30-9
middleware, 30-9
solution, 30-4
transaction carriers, 30-9
transactions, 30-9
triggers, 30-10
goal, 30-2
managerial challenge, 30-2
master database determination, 30-5
criteria, 30-6
physically separate but conceptually linked, 30-3
rationale, 30-2
user's perspective, 30-3
Multiple protocols, 42-1, 45-5, 45-13
Multistacking, 42-3
alternatives, 42-3
connectivity, 42-3
proprietary vendor-specific suites, 42-3
standardization on one protocol stack, 42-3
gateway technology, 42-4
Multiuser security, 2-8, 2-9
Multivendor environment, 39-1. *See also* Vendor(s).
acquiring systems, 75-1
customer engineering, 75-3
fitting current configuration, 75-2
quality of service, 75-2
selection factors, 75-1
availability, 75-1

equipment location and use, 75-2
ergonomics, 75-2
reliability, 75-2
trade-offs, 75-2
case study, 39-7, 75-6
communication, 39-6
component performance tracking, 39-6
installation plan, 39-9
OpenView management. *See also* OpenView.
polycenter framework, 43-1. *See also* Polycenter Framework.
problems, 39-1
vendors' mutual interest, 75-5

N

NetBEUI, 33-22
NetBIOS, 2-4, 54-2
NetView, 44-1, 56-10
NetWare, 9-31. *See also* Novell NetWare.
NetWare directory services, 62-2
access control lists, 62-8
manager, 37-10
object rights and property rights, 62-5
objects, 62-2, 62-4
container, 62-5
leaf, 62-5, 62-6, 62-7
root, 62-4
security administration, 62-12
Netware Lite, 1-9
NetWare Name Service, 33-5
NetWare Print services, 33-12
NetWare server, 33-9
connecting to, 34-8
locating and logging, 33-9, 33-10
logging off, 33-11
Novell *vs.* Microsoft built-in, 33-15
Netware S-NET, 1-1
Network adapter card, 34-2
configurations, 34-2
step-by-step setup, 34-4, 34-5
Network computers, 17-3
Bluebird client systems, 17-6
DEC personal workstations, 17-4
Explora, 17-4
ViewPoint, 17-5
WinTerm, 17-3
Network design, 50-9. *See also* Network planning.
case study, 50-13
EcoNets capabilities, 50-11
major issues, 50-9
Network directories, 25-16
features, 52-9
fax gateway, 52-9
gateways, 52-9, 52-10
message notification, 52-9
security, 52-9
local address books *vs.*, 52-8
mapping network drives, 25-16
replication, 25-17, 25-18, 25-19
drive mapping *vs.*, 25-17
monitoring, 25-17
Network encryption, 68-13
Network engineer, 47-5
Network File System, 4-4
Network interface cards, 1-2
Network interoperability, 12-4, 45-2
Network management, 37-1, 37-3. *See also* Network operating system(s).
challenge, 45-2
ENEOS architecture, 58-2, 58-3, 58-4
heterogeneous environment, 37-1, 37-3
integrating technologies, 45-2
multiple protocols, 45-5
polycenter, 43-2
vendor solutions, 45-4
Network manager, 47-5
Network monitoring, 47-1
agents, 47-2
capacity planning, 47-3, 47-13
data provided, 47-5
defined, 47-2
fault management and availability, 47-3, 47-12
limitations, 47-13
performance management, 47-3, 47-10
personnel, 47-5
protocols, 47-5
rationale, 47-1, 47-4
security, 47-3, 47-11. *See also* Kerberos.
standards overview, 47-4
Network Neighborhood, 33-10
Network operating system(s), 1-1
as back-up system, 51-5
built-in file server access, 25-6
pathworks, 25-6
client/server *vs.* peer-to-peer, 1-9
directories. *See* Network directories.
monitoring. *See* Network monitoring.
peer-to-peer, 1-9, 55-9
peer-to-peer *vs.* client/server, 1-9
recovery strategies, 38-11
adequate backups, 38-12
adequate LAN personnel, 38-13

alternate sites and system sizing, 38-12
fault tolerance *vs.* redundancy, 38-12
personnel, 38-13
security, 72-8. *See also* Security.
accountability, 72-9
plan, 72-11
virus protection, 72-9
software drivers, 1-9
Network planning, 50-2. *See also* Network design.
case study, 50-13
performance, 50-6. *See also* Performance.
tasks, 50-2
database creation, 50-2
defining end-to-end performance requirements, 50-2
designing network alternatives, 50-2
documenting results, 50-2
modeling end-to-end multihour traffic flows, 50-2
modeling traffic growth, 50-2
selecting best alternative based on cost, cutover and performance, 50-2
testing performance of post-cutover implementation, 50-2
updating analytical tools and preparation for next design cycle, 50-2
traffic flow, 50-3
Network redesign, 79-3
Network reporting, 47-13
Network snooping, 68-10
Network technology, 58-1, 58-2
Networked Dynamic Data Exchange, 2-4
NFS, 25-9
architecture, 25-10
common products, 25-11
components, 25-10
daemons, 25-11
Maestro, 25-12
Novell NetWare, 9-31
ADMIN user ID, 62-12
administration functions from Microsoft, 33-18
advantages, 3-6
AUDITCON, 62-14
auditing events, 62-13
bindery, 33-4
Client Service, 4-5
directory and file attributes, 62-11
directory services, 37-10. *See also* NetWare directory services.
dominance, 1-4
File and Print Services, 4-5, 33-18
file system administration, 62-13
file system directory rights *vs.* file rights, 62-9
Gateway Service, 4-5, 33-15, 33-16, 33-17, 33-18, 33-23
login scripts, 5-8
migration and coexistence options, 33-1
migration tool, 4-6
name service, 33-5
new applications, 9-1
OS/2 *vs.*, 1-6
porting, 5-9
security, 33-4, 62-1. *See also* Security.
concerns, 62-15, 62-16
file, 62-8
implementing and administering, 62-10
Windows access, 33-2, 33-17
3.X *vs.* 4.X, 62-3
NT Command Prompt, 6-10
NTerprise, 10-16
NTRIGUE, 10-10
features, 10-11
web browser, 10-12
N*u*TCRACKER, 6-6, 6-7, 37-9
server, 10-24
UNIX functionality supported by, 6-8
NWADMIN, 33-21, 33-24
menu options, 33-21
NWLink, 4-6
NWLink IPX/SPX, 34-2
installation, 34-3, 34-7

O

Object Linking and Embedding (OLE), 2-4, 13-1
Digital/Microsoft agreement, 13-3
network portal model, 13-3
V2 interfaces, 13-5
Object model for graphics editor, 8-4, 8-13, 8-21
ObjectBroker, 2-4, 13-1
Object-Oriented design
benefits, 80-1
big picture, 80-10
business processes, 80-12
CASE and, 80-4
client/server integration, 80-14
considerations, 80-3
costs, 80-15
data acquisition, 80-13

defined, 8-1
development, 80-12
cycle changes, 80-3
teams, 80-13
distributed application, 9-24
encapsulation, 80-7
enhanced languages, 80-9
for host developer, 80-5
implementation, 8-3
implementation strategy, 80-1
instances and persistence, 80-7
language issues, 80-8
leverage existing assets, 80-11
native languages, 80-9
new terms, 80-7
as part of distributed system strategy, 80-2
polymorphism, 80-8
rapid prototyping, 80-4
transformation framework, 80-6
Visual Basic and, 8-1
visual languages, 80-9
Object-relational database
for advertising, 31-3
business applications, 31-2
fashion industry, 31-2
insurance industry, 31-3
for claims processing and rate setting, 31-4
database extenders, 31-7, 31-8
features, 31-5
support for large objects, 31-6
triggers and constraints, 31-7
user-defined functions, 31-6
user-defined types, 31-5
hallmark, 31-2
infrastructure, 31-5
integrated searches, 31-8
for interactive shopping, 31-3
key to, 31-7
for product distribution, 31-2
ODBC drivers, 27-4, 27-5
OLE. *See* Object Linking and Embedding.
Omni SQL Gateway, 9-33
OMNInet, 1-1
Open Software Foundation, 9-16
Open Systems Interconnection model, 49-1
layers, 49-1
application, 49-3
link, 49-2
network, 49-2
physical, 49-2
presentation, 49-3
session, 49-3
transport, 49-2
Open-ended console management frameworks, 41-4, 41-5
OpenNT, 6-13
product family, 6-14
X Server, 10-28
OpenView, 44-1
applications, 44-7
Message Browser, 44-9
NetLS, 44-9
OperationsCenter, 44-8
PerfRX, 44-9
PerfVIew, 44-9
Software Distributor, 44-9
Workspace Manager, 44-9
bridge/hub manager, 44-5
communications protocol, 44-4
components, 44-2
communication protocols, 44-2
data storage management, 44-2
distributed communications infrastructure, 44-2
user interface presentation services, 44-2
data line monitor, 44-6
data store management, 44-4
interactions between two management applications, 44-3
interConnect manager, 44-6
line performance reporting, 44-6
network node manager, 44-4
object-oriented programmability, 44-4
structure, 44-3
TCP/IP agent, 44-7
OpenView History Analyzer, 44-7
OpenView Resource Manager, 44-7
OpenView Traffic Expert, 44-7
Operations center engineer, 47-5
Oracle, 22-6
application tools, 22-24
checksums, 68-13
database manipulation, 22-16
evaluation, 22-27
join function, 22-20
password protocol, 68-12
programming language support, 22-22
security, 68-1. *See also* Security.
auditing, 68-8
configurable roles, 68-3
data access, 68-2
database views, 68-4

discretionary access control, 68-2, 69-10
encryption, 68-8
integrity *vs.* confidentiality, 68-7
mandatory access control, 68-5, 68-6
operating system labels, 68-5
privileges, 68-3
stored procedures, 68-4
tag mappings, 68-6
triggers, 22-10
Oracle Rdb Distributed Product Suite, 9-22
OS/2, 1-4
application to Windows NT, 6-29
common user access and, 2-6
DOS compatibility, 2-6
graphical user interface, 2-13
limitations, 2-6
multiuser capabilities, 2-6
multiuser security and administration, 2-8
Netware *vs.*, 1-6
networking capability, 2-14
operating system development support, 2-14
preemptive and deterministic multitasking, 2-5
software support, 2-5
system requirements, 2-12
TCP/IP support, 2-8
user-driven priority schemes, 2-4
virtues, 2-5
OS/2 version 2.0, 1-5
OS/2 Warp, 2-5, 2-13
OSF/Motif, 7-6, 7-10
Outer joins, 22-18, 22-27
Output management, 37-1, 37-3

P

Packet eXchange, 4-8
Packet filtering, 19-8
Parallel networks, 54-4
Pass tickets, 36-8
Password(s), 51-8, 81-5
changing administrator, 35-4
confidentiality, 68-11
encryption, 60-7, 68-11
files, 60-6
management function, 36-7
protection, 72-1
security concerns, 60-7
synchronization, 36-4
UNIX, 60-5
wizard, 83-11
PC-DCE, 9-20, 9-21
PC-Interface, 10-3
PCnet, 1-2
PC-NFS, 10-3
Performance, 50-6
concepts, 50-6
defining, 50-6
monthly costs in, 50-7
system grade-of-service in, 50-7
system quality-of-service in, 50-7
system throughput in, 50-7
Framework management, 43-2
goals, 50-8
intranet, 19-5
Java, 16-3
line reporting, 44-6
management, 37-1, 37-3, 47-3, 47-10
multivendor environment, 39-6
network monitoring, 47-3, 47-10
Windows NT Server, 3-3, 4-8
Platform-independent code, 11-8
PMDF Mailbus 400, 53-15
Pointer calculation, 5-28
Point-to-Point Protocol, 4-7
Polycenter Framework
access modules, 43-3, 43-6
circuit, 43-6
data collector, 43-6
DECnet OSI, 43-6
DECnet Phase IV, 43-6
Ethernet, 43-6
extended LAN manager, 43-6
TCP/IP SNMP, 43-6
terminal server, 43-6
accounting and billing management, 43-2
automation, 43-2
components, 43-3
access modules, 43-3
executive, 43-3
function modules, 43-3, 43-4
management information repository, 43-3
presentation modules, 43-3
configuration and change management, 43-2
fault and problem management, 43-2
function modules, 43-3, 43-4, 43-5
alarms, 43-5
autoconfiguration, 43-5
control, 43-5
domains, 43-5

exporter, 43-5
historian, 43-5
notification, 43-5
predefined reports, 43-5
registration, 43-5
TCP/IP diagnostic assistant, 43-5
levels of integration, 43-6
accessor function module development, 43-7
callable management control center, 43-7
data collector access module, 43-7
launchable application, 43-7
strip access module, 43-7
visual integration, 43-7
network management, 43-2
operation, 43-2
presentation modules, 43-3
command line, 43-3
forms interface, 43-4
iconic map, 43-4
notification services, 43-4
security management, 43-2
solutions to management needs, 43-2
storage management, 43-2
toolkit, 43-7
Common Agent, 43-7, 43-8
Polymorphism, 14-9
Portable object-oriented frameworks, 9-10
Allegris, 9-11, 9-12
constructor, 9-13
datadesigner, 9-14
object repository, 9-13
DSC++, 9-10
Systems Toolkit, 9-15
zApp Developer's Suite 3, 9-14
Portable source code. *See* Source code.
Portage, 6-9
Portage Base, 6-10, 37-7, 37-8
Portage SDK, 6-12
Porting
Borland C++, 7-5, 7-10
C programs, 6-5
checklist for changes, 5-22
considerations, 6-1
business, 6-2
technical, 6-3
database applications, 6-22
defined, 5-9
disadvantages, 74-6
distributed applications, 6-27
effort needed, 7-10
3GL/4GL applications, 6-27
graphical user interfaces, 7-1
Borland C++, 7-5, 7-10
Microsoft Access, 7-9, 7-10
OSF/Motif, 7-6, 7-10
TCL/TK, 7-6, 7-10
Visual Basic, 7-8, 7-10
Visual C++, 7-3
X-Windows, 7-6, 7-10
international applications, 6-28
manual, 5-9, 74-5
Microsoft Access, 7-9, 7-10
OS/2 application to Windows NT, 6-29
OSF/Motif, 7-6, 7-10
products, 6-6, 6-18
scripts, 6-6
steps, 6-4
TCL/TK, 7-6, 7-10
Think C, 7-2
tool-based, 74-5
transaction-processing applications, 6-26
from UNIX to Windows, 6-6
Visual Basic, 7-8, 7-10
Visual C++, 7-3
web applications, 6-27
from Windows to UNIX, 6-17
X-Windows, 7-6, 7-10
POSIX, 5-23
Powerbuilder, 14-3
classes, 14-5
elements, 14-3
application, 14-3
controls, 14-4
editor, 14-4
libraries, 14-4
painters, 14-3
PowerBar, 14-4
scripts, 14-4
windows, 14-3
encapsulation, 14-7
inheritance, 14-8, 14-9
object-oriented features, 14-10
objects, 14-6
command, 14-6
GroupBox, 14-6
MultiLine edit, 14-6
picture box, 14-6
RadioButton, 14-6
SingleLine edit, 14-6
StaticLine edit, 14-6
windows, 14-6
software quality assessment, 14-11
Visual Basic *vs.*, 14-10, 14-11
Visual C++ *vs.*, 14-10, 14-11

Pragmas, 5-26
Presentation Managers, 2-13
Pretty Good Privacy, 65-1
  digital signature, 65-14
  encryption use, 65-3
  getting public keys, 65-15
  history, 65-2
  operation, 65-14
  public-key certificates, 65-15
  signature trust and key legitimacy, 65-17
  trust model, 65-19
  trust processing, 65-15
Prodigy, 52-2
ProNet, 1-1
Proprietary vendor-specific suites, 42-3
Protection, 38-9. *See also* Security.
  data integrity, 38-11
  internal environment, 38-9
  password, 72-1
  physical security, 38-10, 51-6
  property management, 38-11
  against trusted users, 51-10
Proteon Token Ring, 1-2
Protocol(s), 29-4. *See also specific protocol* e.g., Simple Network Management Protocol (SNMP).
  common backbone, 54-5, 54-7
  file/print server, 54-2
  host/mini application access, 54-2
  multiple, 42-1, 45-5, 45-13
  repertoire, 54-2
  routing, 45-9
  trivial file transfer, 25-4, 25-7
  two-phase commit, 23-9
  Windows NT, 33-22, 34-1
Protocol Independent Multicast (PIM), 16-8, 16-9, 48-9
PSERVER, 33-24
Publishing
  dynamic, 24-5
    formulating query, 24-5
    Java applets, 24-5, 24-6
    security mechanisms, 24-7
  static, 24-2, 24-4
  with World Wide Web, 24-5, 24-6, 27-6

Q

QSECURITY, 63-10
Query processing, 26-2, 70-5, 70-12, 71-7
QuickMail, 52-13

R

RadioButton, 14-6
Recovery. *See also* Disaster recovery.
Redundancy, 38-12, 70-2
Reflection, 25-14
Reflection X product, 10-24, 10-25
Relational database, 69-1
  access control
    discretionary, 69-10
    mandatory, 68-5, 68-6, 69-11
    role-based, 69-16
  application tools, 22-22
  benefits, 32-3, 32-11
  defined, 69-1
  design issues, 32-3
  entity integrity, 22-2, 69-3
  evaluation, 22-26, 22-27
  extended data types, 22-2
  integrity, 22-2, 22-4, 69-3
  joins and, 22-18
  labeling granularity, 69-12
  multiattribute utility analysis, 22-26, 22-27
  multilevel database architectures, 69-12
    fragmented, 69-13, 69-14
    integrated, 69-13, 69-14
    replicated, 69-15, 69-16
  object, 31-1
    for advertising, 31-3
    business applications, 31-2
      fashion industry, 31-2
      insurance industry, 31-3
    for claims processing and rate setting, 31-4
    database extenders, 31-7, 31-8
    features, 31-5, 31-6, 31-7
    hallmark, 31-2
    infrastructure, 31-5
    integrated searches, 31-8
    for interactive shopping, 31-3
    for product distribution, 31-2
  primary key, 69-2
  referential integrity, 22-2, 22-4, 69-3
  semantic integrity, 22-2
  SQL, 69-4
  success, SQL and, 22-1
Remote Access Server, 4-7
Remote copy program, 25-3
Remote LAN/WAN connections, 78-1
  action plan, 78-20
    defining business objective, 78-4
    defining existing resources, 78-4
    defining options, 78-3

feasibility study, 78-3
implementation and installation, 78-20
recommendations, 78-18
connectivity options, 78-5
comparisons, 78-6, 78-7, 78-17
cost comparisons, 78-18
evaluation, 78-6
fiber optic, 78-5, 78-6, 78-7, 78-8, 78-9, 78-10
infrared, 78-5, 78-12, 78-14, 78-15, 78-16, 78-17
microwave, 78-6, 78-9, 78-10, 78-12
physical connections, 78-5
fiber optic connectivity, 78-5
twisted-pair cable, 78-5
wireless connections, 78-5
infrared, 78-5
microwave, 78-6
spread spectrum UHF, 78-5
Remote Monitoring Protocol, 47-4
alarms group, 47-9
history group, 47-9
host group, 47-9
host top N, 47-9
Packet Capture/Filter Group, 47-9
statistics group, 47-4
Token Ring Group, 47-9
Traffic Matrix Group, 47-9
Remote Monitoring Protocol version 2, 47-4, 47-9
Remote polling, 54-16
merits, 54-17
modules, 54-17
Remote Procedure Calls, 4-3, 29-2, 29-3
Replication, 23-2, 25-17, 25-18, 25-19
drive mapping *vs.*, 25-17
independence, 71-6
monitoring, 25-17
transparency, 27-2
Resolution Trust Corporation, 77-1
RhaPC-d, 6-27
Risk analysis, 38-3, 81-1, 81-2
Router(s), 18-10
considerations, 45-10
capacity and architecture, 45-10, 45-11
filtering, 45-13
internetwork protocols supported, 45-11
interoperability, 45-12
network management, 45-12
network technologies supported, 45-12
filter implementation, 66-15
multicast, 48-5
Routing, 18-5
configurations, 18-6
IP encapsulation, 54-12
protocol independent, 54-12
protocols, 45-9

S

SCO UnixWare NetWare services, 33-24
Secure pass tickets, 36-8
Security, 33-4, 37-1, 37-3. *See also* Kerberos; Novell NetWare, security; UNIX, security; Windows NT Server, security.
access control, 51-7, 81-3
anomaly detection, 61-6
AS/400 controls, 63-1. *See also* AS/400, security options.
auditor's role, 51-3
callback systems, 72-7
communication, 51-8
control of executable code, 51-6
crytographic, 51-8
data testing, 81-5
database gateway, 29-5
deterrence, 61-2
discretionary access control, 68-2, 69-10
diskette and drive controls, 72-5
e-mail, 53-13
emissions, 51-9
ENEOS, 58-3
goals, 61-2
help desk, 57-7
interception, 61-2
investigation, 61-2
issues, 59-9, 62-1, 68-1
Java, 15-8, 16-3, 16-4
key and card systems, 72-3
LAN, 51-4
layers, 51-3
line, 51-8
management, 37-1
mandatory access control, 68-5, 68-6, 69-11
measures, 51-2
mechanisms, 24-7
Microsoft, 67-5
multilevel processing security, 51-3
multiuser, 2-8, 2-9
NetWare, 33-4
new challenges, 51-10
Novell NetWare, 62-1
physical, 38-10, 51-6

Polycenter Framework, 43-2
prevention, 61-2
private, 51-9
processing over insecure network, 51-3
remote library control, 51-7
risks, 62-1
super-user device, 51-11
technical, 51-9
tools, 61-4
access control, 61-5
dynamic analysis, 61-5
identification and authentication, 61-4
static analysis, 61-5
transmission, 51-8
UNIX, 4-10, 5-8
Windows NT, 3-3, 3-4, 4-10, 5-8
Semantic heterogeneity, 26-2, 26-6, 28-7
Serial-line IP, 4-7
Server(s). *See also specific servers,* e.g., NetWare server.
authentication, 36-5. *See also* Authentication server.
basics, 20-8
mainframe as, 20-1
upgrading considerations, 20-10
data center operations, 20-13
integrating PC/LAN clusters, 20-13
migrating to core DBMS, 20-11
network infrastructure, 20-13
tools for new applications, 20-11
Simple Mail Transfer Protocol (SMTP), 52-3, 66-5
Simple Network Management Protocol (SNMP), 4-2, 37-9, 37-10, 43-6, 47-4
advantages, 47-7
commands, 47-6
components, 47-6
version 2, 47-4, 47-8
Single sign-on, 36-2, 36-7
SingleLine edit, 14-6
Sitka 10net, 1-9
Smalltalk, 80-9
SMDS, 46-13
SMTP. *See* Simple Mail Transfer Protocol (SMTP).
SNA, 55-1
LAN traffic through, 55-2. *See also* SNA-LAN integration.
over Ethernet, 55-2
SNA Client, 9-28, 9-29
SNA gateways, 9-25, 9-27, 9-28, 54-1
SNA LU-LU session types, 54-2
SNA-LAN integration, 54-1, 54-3
links, 54-13, 54-14
methods, 55-3
data link switching, 55-12
emulation, 55-3
encapsulation, 55-4, 55-5
frame relay, 55-8, 56-1, 56-17. *See also* Frame relay.
LU 6.2 connectivity, 55-9
peer-to-peer networking, advanced, 55-9
standalone converters, 55-8
synchronous passthrough, 55-9
remote polling, 54-16, 54-17
SDLC-to-LLC transformation, 54-18
synchronous passthrough, 54-15
drawbacks, 54-16
SNMP. *See* Simple Network Management Protocol (SNMP).
Software
distribution, 37-1, 37-3
drivers, 1-9
electronic distribution, 48-11
integrating, 41-4
object-oriented *vs.* component-based, 14-1
open-ended console management, 41-4, 41-5
third-party market, 2-12
vendors, 39-8
SoftWindows, 17-7
application support, 17-8
features, 17-8
network support, 17-8
peripherals support, 17-8
SONET, 46-12
Source code, 5-9
portable, 5-4
writing, 5-24
access to base class private members, 5-24
anonymous unions, 5-26
C data types, 5-28
class definitions, 5-24
compiler differences, 5-24
compiler warnings, 5-27
constructor calls, 5-26
inline functions, 5-26
interchanging types, 5-25
new and delete functions, 5-26
pointer calculation, 5-28
pragmas, 5-26
type casting, 5-25

using conditional compilation, 5-27
variable declarations, 5-25
Source-route bridging, 54-5, 55-5
all-route searches, 54-9
broadcast storms, 54-11
limitations, 54-11
mechanism of operation, 54-8
single-shot approach, 54-10
Spanning tree algorithm, 49-19
SQL. *See* Structured query language (SQL).
Static publishing, 24-2, 24-4
StaticLine edit, 14-6
StreetTalk, 33-25
Structured query language (SQL), 22-1, 31-1
base realations and views, 69-6
CREATE statement, 69-4, 69-8
embedded, 22-21, 22-27
GRANT statement, 69-8
INSERT and DELETE statement, 69-5
privileges, 69-8
REVOKE statement, 69-9
SELECT statement, 69-5
UPDATE statement, 69-6
SunNet Manager, 44-1, 44-2
Sun's Network File System, 4-4
Sybase, 22-8
application tools, 22-25
database manipulation, 22-17
evaluation, 22-27
join function, 22-20
programming language support, 22-22
triggers and rules, 22-10
Symmetric Multiprocessing, 5-5
Synchronous passthrough, 54-15, 55-9
drawbacks, 54-16
Systems management, 37-1, 37-3
performance, 37-1, 37-3
Systems Network Architecture. *See* SNA *terms.*
Systems Toolkit, 9-15

T

TCL/TK
porting, 7-6, 7-10
program structure, 7-6, 7-10
TCP/IP, 33-22, 54-2
commands and utilities, 53-17
OpenView, 44-7
TCP/IP SNMP, 43-6
Telex, 52-10
Telnet, 10-17, 25-2, 66-5
Text extender, 31-9
Thin-client, 17-3
Think C, 7-2, 7-10
Third-party software market, 2-12
Token Ring, 1-2, 1-3, 18-3, 49-11, 54-5
encapsulation, 55-7
shared, 18-4
Tops, 1-9
Traffic flow, 50-3
circuit-switched, 50-4
concepts, 50-3
data, 50-3
modeling
existing network, 50-4, 50-5
during life cycle of system, 50-5
new network, 50-4
time-consistent averages, 50-5
packet-switched, 50-4
time-consistent averages, 50-5
voice and video, 50-3
Transaction processing, 6-26, 26-2, 28-11, 28-18
Transport layer interface, 45-16
Triggers, 22-9, 22-10, 30-10, 31-7
Trivial file transfer protocol, 25-4, 25-7
Tunneled applications, 45-6, 45-15
Type casting, 5-25

U

UNICODE, 6-28
Universal mail client, 52-13
UNIX, 5-36
access from Windows desktops, 10-17
X-server in, 10-21
administration functions, 35-1
administrator logon, 35-2
anonymous ftp, 83-12
application programming interfaces, 5-8
architecture, 60-2
audit program, 82-2
file security, 83-2
general security, 82-4
log-in security, 82-5, 82-6, 82-7
remote system security, 83-10
superuser security, 82-8
automatic job scheduling, 35-13
backup/recovery, 35-11, 83-15
changing administrator password, 35-4
changing administrator privileges, 35-3

commands, 60-15
ls, 60-16
passwd, 60-16
pwd, 60-17
who, 60-16
cross compiler support, 5-37
cross-platform applications, 9-2
daemons, 35-13
DCE, 9-17
debug feature, 83-11
demand paging, 5-6
development support, 2-14
directory structure, 60-8
DOS compatibility, 2-10
e-mail, 35-10
components, 53-3
mail client, 53-4
mail management utilities, 53-5
mail server functions, 53-3
environment and utilities, 6-9
error handling, 5-36
file definition, 83-4
history, 2-9, 60-1
implementation, 2-10
input/output management, 5-7
Internet functions, 53-16
Internet platform, 2-11
interoperability with Windows NT 4.0, 4-1
LAN manager, 4-4
limitations, 2-10, 2-12
Line Print Requester, 25-18
linear memory addressing, 5-6
load balancing, 35-13
log files, 60-15
log-in procedures, 5-8, 60-2, 60-4
mainframe interface, 9-24
misuse detection, 61-1, 61-7. *See also* Misuse detection.
MS-DOS access from, 25-21
multiuser security, 2-9
NetWare and, 33-24
new applications, 9-1
with 4GL tools, 9-9
with WIN32 API, 9-7
operating system, 5-1
passwords, 60-5
encryption, 60-7
files, 60-6
security concerns, 60-7
porting, 5-9, 5-10
printing, 25-20
requirements, 2-12
root account, 60-5
root directory, 60-9
security, 4-10, 5-8
areas to address, 60-17
directory and file, 60-8, 60-9
changing file permissions, 60-14
execution behavior bits, 60-12, 60-13
protection masks, 60-10
unmask value, 60-12
user groups, 60-10
identifying intrusions, 60-20
password, 60-6
remote system, 83-10
system files, 83-5
user profiles, 83-9
security policy, 82-4
SNA Client, 9-28, 9-29
start-up files, 60-2
systemwide profiles, 83-8
terminate process/task, 35-13
transferring files to Windows NT, 6-5
user interface, 10-2
user-driven priority schemes, 2-4
Windows compatibility, 2-10
Windows libraries, 4-5
Windows NT server access from, 10-21, 25-15
Windows NT *vs.*, 4-10, 5-2
administrative functions, 35-1
application message queues, 5-35
architectural differences, 5-12, 5-35
backup/recovery, 35-11
bits and bytes differences, 5-13
changing administrator password, 35-4
changing administrator privileges, 35-3
communication services, 35-8
compress/uncompress/expand commands, 35-12
debugging tools, 5-36
disk administration, 35-5
distributed computing differences, 5-14
file input/output differences, 5-16
file names, 35-6
file services, 35-5
file system differences, 5-15
graphical user interface, 5-18
handle differences, 5-14
logging error level, 35-18
logon/logoff procedures, 35-2
logs, 35-16
memory-management differences, 5-15
multiuser *vs.* single-user differences, 5-21

name resolution differences, 5-14
network supports differences, 5-20
preemptive multitasking, 5-35
print services, 35-8
process/task management, 35-13
security model differences, 5-19
shared memory model, 5-35
sharing files, 35-6
shutting down system, 35-4
signal differences, 5-13
storage and order alignment, 5-35
style differences, 5-22
user management, 35-13
user-interface differences, 5-17
UNIX shells, 6-11, 37-5
functions, 37-5
Hamilton C Shell, 37-7
Microsoft, 37-6
MKS Toolkit, 37-6
N*ut*CRACKER, 37-9
Portage Base, 37-7, 37-8
Windows, 37-5
UNIX-to-UNIX copy protocol, 83-14
User IDs, 62-12, 81-5

V

Vendor(s)
application management, 21-5, 21-7, 21-8
availability, 39-2
benchmarks for evaluation, 39-5, 75-4
contractual considerations, 39-5
cost, 39-2
custom engineering, 39-4
equipment use and location, 39-2
ergonomics, 39-2
evaluation factors, 75-2
continuity, 75-3
contractual criteria, 75-4
customer engineer support organization, 75-3
dispatch location, 75-3
experience, 75-3
financial condition of vendor, 75-3
incidence recurrence, 75-3
management attention, 75-3
onsite support, 75-3
parts availability, 75-3
repair time, 75-3
resource availability, 75-3
response time, 75-3
financial status, 39-5, 75-4
LAN, 1-1
monitoring, 39-5
multiple. *See* Multivendor environment.
network adapter card specific for, 34-5
performance tracking, 75-5
policies, 76-1
problems, 39-1
quality of service, 39-3, 75-2
quotation schedule considerations, 76-2, 76-3, 76-4, 76-5
hardware installation, 76-6
hardware maintenance, 76-6
hardware pricing, 76-5
hardware warranty, 76-6
initial software installation, 76-6
software documentation, 76-6
software licensing, 76-6
software maintenance, 76-6
reliability, 39-2
selection factors, 39-2
software, 39-8, 75-7
Videoconferencing, 48-7
ViewPoint, 17-5
VINES, 33-25
Virtual local area network (VLAN), 19-6
Virtual Telecommunications Access Method Network Control Program, 56-11
Virtual-memory management, 5-6
Virus(es), 51-11
applets *vs.*, 67-1
protection, 72-9
Visichannel architecture, 6-24
Visigenic database connectivity software, 6-23
VisiODBC DriverSets, 6-23
Visual Basic
application structure, 7-9
association implementation, 8-21
classes, 8-5, 14-5
concurrency and, 8-24
development environment, 14-3
editor, 14-3
forms, 14-3
modules, 14-3
projects, 14-3
standard and custom controls, 14-3
subroutines, 14-3
toolbars, 14-3
editor, 14-3
encapsulation, 8-24, 14-7
forms, 14-3

inheritance, 14-8
comparisons, 14-9
implementation, 8-12
method 1, 8-13
method 2, 8-14
method 3, 8-17
method resolution implementation, 8-18
method 1, 8-18
method 2, 8-19
method 3, 8-19
modules, 14-3
object allocation, 8-8
method 1, 8-10
method 2, 8-10
object-oriented features, 8-1, 14-10
objects, 14-6, 14-7
combo boxes, 14-6
forms, 14-6
labels, 14-6
list boxes, 14-6
text boxes, 14-6
passing arguments to methods, 8-7
porting, 7-8, 7-10
Powerbuilder *vs.*, 14-10, 14-11
projects, 14-3
software quality assessment, 14-11
standard and custom controls, 14-3
subroutines, 14-3
toolbars, 14-3
Visual C++ *vs.*, 14-10, 14-11
Visual Basic 3.0, 14-2
Visual C++
classes, 14-5
elements, 14-4
App studio, 14-4
App Wizards, 14-4
class wizards, 14-4
Microsoft foundation class library, 14-4
projects, 14-4
Workbench, 14-4
encapsulation, 14-7
inheritance, 14-9
object-oriented features, 14-7, 14-10
porting, 7-3
Powerbuilder *vs.*, 14-10, 14-11
software quality assessment, 14-11
Visual Basic *vs.*, 14-10, 14-11

W

WABI. *See* Windows Application Binary Interface (WABI).
WAN network integration, 77-1
ARLs move, 77-9
e-mail and STDA moves, 77-9
final integration, 77-11
group moves, 77-8
man hours, 77-5
print and file services, 77-8
process, 77-7
router upgrades, 77-5
spoke-and-hub, 79-2
upgrade costs, 77-4
upgrade modeling and refinement, 77-6
WAN transit delays, 45-6
Web.Data, 24-4
Willows Toolkit, 6-22
WIN32 API, 9-7
WinCenter, 10-12
WinCenter Connect, 10-14
WinCenter for Workgroups, 10-14
WinCenter Graphics Accelerator, 10-14
WinCenter Pro, 10-13
WinDD, 10-7, 10-8, 10-9
Windows
Client Services for NetWare, 33-3
NetWare printer, 33-12
locating, 33-13
print queue, 33-14
third-party software markets, 2-12
X-station access, 10-4
advantages, 10-5
disadvantages, 10-6
Windows 3.0, 1-2, 1-4, 2-4
Windows 3.1, 2-12
Windows 95, 33-4
Windows Application Binary Interface (WABI), 17-9
Windows applications, 9-1
accessing, 10-9
ICA client approach, 10-9
Windows X support, 10-9
X-station, 10-2
Windows Binary Application Interface, 10-3
Windows for Workgroups, 2-3
networking capability, 2-14
networking with, 2-4
Windows for Workgroups 3.11, 4-9
Windows Internet Name Service, 4-3, 5-14
Windows Internet Naming Service (WINS), 37-13
configuration, 37-14

Windows NT, 2-7, 81-15
486 emulator for RISC systems, 17-9
adding network software, 34-6
administering Mac clients from, 17-12, 17-13
administration functions, 35-1
administrator logon, 35-2
application programming interfaces, 5-8
applications development, 4-11
auditing events, 81-12
auditing features, 81-10
automatic job scheduling, 35-13
changing administrator password, 35-4
changing administrator privileges, 35-3
cross-platform applications, 9-2
daemons, 35-13
DCE, 9-17, 9-18
application developer's kit, 9-19
runtime services, 9-18
security server, 9-19
demand paging, 5-6
DFS, 9-20
DHCP management, 4-2, 37-11
ease of use, 4-10
e-mail, 35-10
event viewer, 81-13
eXceed, 10-23, 10-24
formatting, 81-19
graphical user interface, 2-13
implementation, 3-7
input/output management, 5-7
Internet functions, 53-16
Internet Name Service, 4-3
LAN software, 81-14, 81-16
disaster recovery and contingency preparedness, 81-17
processing integrity, 81-18
systems development and project management, 81-17
linear memory addressing, 5-6
load balancing, 35-13
login scripts, 5-8
logs, 35-17
mainframe interface, 9-24
migration and coexistence options, 33-1
migration tool from NetWare to, 33-23
NetWare access, 33-3, 33-9
management utility from Novell, 33-21
with Network Neighborhood, 33-10
printer services, 33-12
protocol support and administration, 33-21
user administration using server applet, 33-20
using Explorer, 33-12
using find, 33-10
network adapter card, 34-2
network support, 3-5, 3-6
networking capability, 2-14
operating system
components, 5-3
executive, 5-3
kernel, 5-3
memory management, 5-5
process management, 5-4
processor support, 5-5
protected subsystems, 5-3, 5-4
development support, 2-14
features, 5-1, 5-2
OS/2 application to, 6-29
PC-DCE, 9-20
performance monitoring and capacity planning, 81-15
porting, 5-9
POSIX support, 5-23
printers, access from Mac client, 17-12
printing to UNIX, 25-18
problem management, 81-15
program change control management, 81-15
protocols, 33-22, 34-1
reliability, 4-11
requirements, 2-12
security, 3-3, 3-4, 4-10, 5-8, 81-5
services, 5-8
SNMP support, 4-2, 37-9, 37-10
TCP/IP configuration, 35-9
TCP/IP support, 4-2
TCP/IP utilities, 4-2
Telnet, 10-17, 10-18, 10-19
Telnet and third-party terminal emulators, 4-3
terminate process/task, 35-13
transferring files from UNIX to, 6-5
UNIX commands, 37-6
UNIX interoperability, 4-1
UNIX server access from, 25-1
file transfer protocol, 25-2, 25-3
remote copy program, 25-3
Telnet, 25-2
trivial file transfer protocol, 25-4
using serial link, 25-5
UNIX *vs.*, 4-10, 5-2
administrative functions, 35-1
application message queues, 5-35

architectural differences, 5-12, 5-35
backup/recovery, 35-11
bits and bytes differences, 5-13
changing administrator password, 35-4
changing administrator privileges, 35-3
communication services, 35-8
compress/uncompress/expand commands, 35-12
debugging tools, 5-36
disk administration, 35-5
distributed computing differences, 5-14
file input/output differences, 5-16
file names, 35-6
file services, 35-5
file system differences, 5-15
handle differences, 5-14
logging error level, 35-19
logon/logoff procedures, 35-2
memory-management differences, 5-15
multiuser *vs.* single-user differences, 5-21
name resolution differences, 5-14
network commands, 35-19
network support differences, 5-20
preemptive multitasking, 5-35
print services, 35-8
process/task management, 35-13
security model differences, 5-19
shared memory model, 5-35
sharing files, 35-6
shutting down system, 35-4
signal differences, 5-13
storage order and alignment, 5-35
style differences, 5-22
user management, 35-13
user-interface differences, 5-17
user interface, 10-2
user management, 35-13, 81-7, 81-8, 81-9
X servers, 4-3
Windows NT 4.0, 3-1. *See also* Windows NT.
Windows NT Resource kit, 37-6
Windows NT Server, 3-1
application portability, 4-4
DCE-compatible RPC, 4-3
directory services, 4-8
e-mail systems components, 53-6
directory services and synchronization, 53-6
file format conversion, 53-6
mail client, 53-7
mail management, 53-7
mail server functions, 53-6
FTP for, 4-4
Mac client support, 17-9, 17-10, 17-11
performance, 4-8
performance monitoring capability, 3-3
remote access, 4-7
scalability, 3-2
security, 59-1
alert messages, 59-7
auditing features, 59-6
creating access token, 59-1
directory and file permissions, 59-5
event logging, 59-7, 81-13
group, 59-5
implementing user, 59-2
issues, 59-9
prohibited access message creation, 59-8
standards-based distributed processing support, 4-3
standards-based file systems and data sharing, 4-4
system requirements, 3-2
Windows NT Server 3.5, 4-9
Windows NT Workstation, 3-1
performance monitoring capability, 3-3
system requirements, 3-2
Windows Open Services Architecture, 4-4
Windows sockets, 4-3
Windows X support, 10-9
Wind/U, 6-18, 6-19
WinTED, 10-16
WinTerm, 17-3
WISE, 9-7
emulators, 9-8
WISE SDKs, 9-7, 9-8
Workgroup/workflow/e-mail interoperability, 12-6
World Wide Web, 24-1, 53-18
common gateway interface, 24-2
database publishing using, 24-5
formulating query, 24-5
Java applets, 24-5, 24-6
HTML documents, 24-1
security mechanisms, 24-7
uniform resource locators, 24-2
Worms, 51-11
WS_CLIPSIBLING, 5-19

X

X400, 52-3, 52-10
X.500 Directory Services, 52-3, 52-9, 53-6, 53-15
X.25 packet networks, 46-4
X server, 4-3, 10-16, 10-21, 10-28
  advantages, 10-22
  disadvantages, 10-22
  operation, 10-22
  products, 10-23
XNS, 54-2
X-Station, 10-2, 10-3, 10-4
  advantages, 10-5
  common products, 10-7
  disadvantages, 10-6
XVision, 10-26
XVision Eclipse, 10-26
X-Windows, 7-6, 7-10

Y

Yield management systems, 20-6, 20-7

Z

zApp Developer's Suite 3, 9-14